The Course of My Life

THE COURSE OF MY LIFE

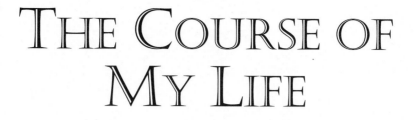

My Autobiography

EDWARD HEATH

Hodder & Stoughton

Copyright © 1998 by Dumpton Gap Company

First published in 1998 by Hodder and Stoughton
A division of Hodder Headline PLC

The right of Edward Heath to be identified as the Author of the Work has been
asserted by him in accordance with the Copyright, Designs and Patents Act
1988.

10 9 8 7 6 5 4 3 2 1

British Library Cataloguing in Publication Data
A CIP catalogue record for this title is available from the British Library.

ISBN: 0 340 70852 2

Designed by Behram Kapadia
Typeset in Monotype Bembo by
Rowland Phototypesetting Ltd.
Bury St Edmunds, Suffolk
Printed and bound in Great Britain by
Clays Ltd., St Ives plc

Hodder and Stoughton
A division of Hodder Headline PLC
338 Euston Road
London NW1 3BH

Contents

List of Illustrations		vii
Acknowledgements		ix
Preface		xi
1.	A KENTISH BOYHOOD *Early Years 1916–1935*	1
2.	FROM BROADSTAIRS TO BALLIOL *Oxford 1935–1937*	23
3.	THE APPROACHING STORM *Oxford 1937–1939*	46
4.	FIGHTING FOR FREEDOM *The War Years 1939–1945*	72
5.	WINNING THE PEACE *Civvy Street 1946–1950*	107
6.	'WELCOME TO WESTMINSTER' *Early Years in the House 1950–1956*	139
7.	STEADYING THE SHIP *Government Posts 1956–1960*	163
8.	'CRIS DE PERROQUET' *The First European Negotiations 1960–1963*	201
9.	CLIMBING THE LADDER *Front Bench Duties 1960–1965*	241
10.	MOULDING THE PARTY *Leader of the Opposition 1965–1968*	270
11.	'TO GOVERN IS TO SERVE' *Return to Power 1969–1970*	297

12. Trying to Turn the Corner   325
    Economic and Industrial Affairs 1970–1972

13. Fanfare for Europe   354
    Britain Joins the Six 1963–1974

14. Tripartism on Trial   396
    Economic and Industrial Affairs 1972–1973

15. The Broken Emerald   420
    Northern Ireland 1970–1974

16. The Home Front   446
    Domestic Policy and Domestic Life 1970–1974

17. The World Stage   468
    Foreign Policy (Non-Europe) 1970–1974

18. Tough Going   500
    1974–1975

19. A Fresh Lease of Life   539
    1975–1979

20. The Dogma that Barked on the Right   574
    Domestic Politics 1979–1997

21. North–South and East–West   601
    International Affairs 1975–

22. The Dragon Awakes   629
    China 1974–1997

23. Missions of Mercy   650
    Iraq and the Gulf 1990–1997

24. Beyond Westminster   671
    1979–1997

25. Ever Closer Union   693
    Britain and Europe 1975–1997

    Coda   727

    List of Abbreviations   737
    Index   740

List of Illustrations

My parents on their wedding day, 1912

Aged three, my thoughts had already turned to travel

An early photo with my mother and John, *c.* 1922

The family

With John *c.* 1928

My parents and ERG

My first trip in an aeroplane, 1931

Treading the boards at Chatham House, *c.* 1934

Obviously feeling on top of the world, *c.* 1934

A piece of paper that changed my life. I carried it everywhere with me for years afterwards in my wallet

Punting at Oxford with Donovan Martin, a Balliol contemporary

My own photographs of the Nuremberg Rally, one with Hitler in his car

A gutted Synagogue in Southern Germany, 1937

With the Wincklers

With the Spanish Minister of Education, Barcelona, 1938

Lindsay's campaign was one of the most thrilling political experiences of my Oxford days

Homeward bound . . . the lights of New York disappear in the dusk, 11 January 1939

Back in Oxford for the Beneš debate, February 1940

My photograph of the old bridge at Wesel and the bailey, destroyed by the retreating Germans, 1944

The church at Wesel, 1945

Hamburg, 1945

War's end, with Colonel Slater

The triumphant football team at 86 HAC

Back home at last, marching to the left of the front rank

Campaigning in Bexley, 1950

Bexley 1950

With the painter Augustus John and his wife

At No. 10 in 1958 with Sir Freddie Bishop, Harold Macmillan, John Wyndham (Lord Egremont), Philip de Zulueta and Anthony Barber

Two of my greatest political influences, Anthony Eden and Winston Churchill, return to No. 10 for President Eisenhower's visit, 1959

Another great influence. With Harold Macmillan at Chelwood Gate, April 1959

Explaining the functions of the Government Chief Whip's Office to Nikita Khrushchev

Visiting the 'Wall of Infamy' Berlin 1963; with Sir Frank Roberts, the British Ambassador to West Germany (*Bundesbildstelle Bonn*)

Looking in on Igor Stravinsky and Pierre Monteux – 50th anniversary of the 'Rite of Spring'. Royal Albert Hall, 1963

Conducting carols in Broadstairs

With Her Majesty the Queen Mother, Sir Arthur Bliss, Sir Robert Mayer and Sir Malcolm Sargent

'I've got a lovely bunch of coconuts'

With my god-daughter Siân Gibson-Watt (*Camera Press London*)

Tickling the ivories at Albany

With Lyndon Johnson, the President of the United States, who replaced Kennedy in such tragic circumstances

'Harold You're Cheating Again!'

Right foot forward. With Robert Allan, a war hero and later Anthony Eden's Parliamentary Private Secretary, and his family

Talks with the German Chancellor, Willy Brandt, London, March 1970

'To Govern is to Serve': Outside No. 10 Downing Street, June 1970 (*PA News*)

The government front bench, June 1970

With Her Majesty the Queen and the Nixons at Chequers, October 1970

Inspecting British troops in Germany, April 1971

Relaxing with Prince Charles, Balmoral, September 1971

Short tacking in the second short race, Admiral's Cup 1971

Outside Chequers with Brian Faulkner, Prime Minister of Northern Ireland, and Jack Lynch, Taoiseach of the Republic, 27 September 1971

President Nixon shows the strain of office. Lord Martonmere, the Governor of Bermuda, prepares to take away his support

Leaving *HMS Glamorgan* with President Nixon and Tim Kitson

The proudest moment of my life. Signing the Treaty of Accession, Brussels, 24 January 1972

'Suit alors!' President Pompidou arrives at Northolt, March 1972

With Brian Trubshaw after my first flight in Concorde, May 1972

Playing the renaissance organ in Frederiksborg, Denmark, in June 1972

Back in Northern Ireland, November 1972

With Leopold Stokowski at the Royal Abert Hall, February 1973

With Chairman Mao in 1974

With Dmitri Shostakovich and Victor Hochhauser outside No. 10

With Anthony Eden and Harold Macmillan at the Savoy Hotel,
    December 1973
Sailing at Burnham, 1974
Morning Cloud is holding *Toujaine*, steered by Sir Maurice Laing
The Great Debate – Oxford, 3 June 1975
The 'Yes' campaign comes to Bexley – Young Conservatives at Crook
    Log, Bexleyheath, Spring 1975
Three advertisements which demonstrate that the political objectives of
    the European Community were never concealed from the people of
    the United Kingdom
One of the last photographs of me with my father, 1976
Rehearsing Mozart with Clifford Curzon, 1976
'The Great Book-Signing Tour' 1976
One of my earlier meetings with Deng Xiaoping
'Thou unnecessary letter!' – but more of a dis-appointment than a real
    disappointment . . .
Campaigning with my lifelong friend Madron Seligman in Chichester,
    1979
Recuperating in Torquay, 1981
At home in Wilton Street (*Observer*)
Harold Macmillan's 90th birthday party at Wilton Street, with Alec
    Home (*Daily Express*)
'You've never had wine so good.' (*Daily Express*)
Two views of my relationship with Mrs Thatcher during the latter
    stages of her premiership
With Fidel Castro in Havana, September 1984
Private Eye captioned this photograph 'All the old jokes together again'
Another furry farewell
Meeting Saddam Hussein in Baghdad, negotiating for the release of
    British hostages, 1990
'I'm back!' Eightieth birthday celebrations at No. 10, July 1996 (*PA News*)
Slava Rostropovich seems pleased to see me back at No. 10 (*Daily
    Telegraph*)
With the Majors, Sara Morrison and the Priors (*Daily Telegraph*)
With Yasser Arafat at Wilton Street, 1997
With Joe Cooper at Arundells
In my garden. The spire of Salisbury Cathedral is visible
With Zhu Rongji, Premier of the People's Republic in China, 1998
With Alastair Stewart and the Lady Mayor of Bexley after my 1997
    carol concert
On the doorstep of Arundells

Acknowledgements

This book covers the events and experiences of a long life, and has been many years in gestation. There are many people to thank for the help and support they have given me in its preparation.

I should like to thank those whom I engaged at various times specifically to undertake the research which a book of this kind entails and to support me in the early stages of drafting a text: in chronological order, the Hon. Michael Trend MP, Charles de Lisle, Dr Richard Weight, Dr Mark Garnett and Joanna Boyes.

They and I have been assisted at one time or another by Rosie Anderson, Dan Bates, Caroline Bowis, Richard Bull, Richard Burn, Patrick Guthrie, Jane Harris, Jonathan Hollowell, Penny Langran, Dan Leader, Gilly Mathieson, Sarah Nicholls, Morag Pearce, Corinne Pluchino, Henrietta Rolston, Stas Rzeznik, Jeff Stacey and Moira Stephens.

A Member of Parliament is in the fortunate position of being able to call on the services of the staff of the House of Commons Library. They are uniformly and invariably helpful and courteous. I am particularly grateful to them. The staff at a variety of other distinguished institutions have been no less helpful and assiduous: The Bodleian Library, Oxford; Chatham House School, Ramsgate; The Churchill Archives Centre, Churchill College, Cambridge; The Conservative and Unionist Party; the *Daily Telegraph*; The Public Record Office; and Trinity College, Cambridge.

A special debt of gratitude is due to my agent, Michael Sissons, and his colleagues at Peters Fraser & Dunlop, who have helped to steer the book – and me – through the complications of proceeding from the writing to the publication of the finished work. I should like to thank no less warmly Martin Neild, Roland Philipps and Angela Herlihy of Hodder & Stoughton, and their colleagues, both for their practical assistance and for their unvarying support, encouragement and patience. In particular, I should like to thank Peter James, who read, and suggested improvements to, the final draft with excellent judgement and a wholly admirable attention to detail.

There have been many other people who have contributed to making this book what it is in various different ways: for instance, by allowing us to call upon their memories to check on particular periods and episodes, by agreeing to read and suggest comments and improvements to my account of events in which they were involved or of which they have special knowledge, and by providing assistance beyond the call of duty in helping to locate papers which we needed to consult. I am especially grateful to Robin Ackerley, Lord Aldington, Lady Armstrong, Sir Christopher Audland, The Countess of Avon (for access to the Avon Papers), Lord Baker of Dorking, Lord Barber, Peter Batey, Mr and Mrs Andrew Battarbee, Professor Vernon Bogdanor, Joe Boyle, Lord Bridges, Mrs Joy Bryer, Lord Butler, Lord Carr of Hadley, Lord Carrington, the late Colonel George Chadd, Kenneth Clarke, Nicholas Clegg, Michael Cockerell, John Collins, Sir Julian Critchley, Nicholas Edgar, Sir Robert Fellowes, Barry Fowler, Edward Greenfield, Sir Peter Gregson, Lord Healey, Mrs Muriel Heath, Mrs Diana Helmicki, Michael Heseltine, Lord Howe of Aberavon, Sue Hudson, Lord Hunt of Wirral, Lord Hurd of Westwell, Mark Kelly, Sir Anthony Kershaw, Sir Timothy Kitson, Roger Lavelle, Sir Robin McLaren, Mr and Mrs Noel McManus, Sir David Madel MP, Sir Donald Maitland, Mrs Norma Major, The Hon. Mrs Sara Morrison, Sir Michael Palliser, Lord Prior, Lord Pym, Christopher Roberts, Lord Roll of Ipsden, Howard Ruse, Anthony Sampson, Julian Sandys (for access to Lord Duncan-Sandys' papers), Dr Anthony Seldon, Madron Seligman, Sabih Shukri, Richard Simmonds, Lady Soames, Mr Jeffery Speed, Mrs Julia Staddon, The Earl of Stockton (for access to the Macmillan Archive), Nick Stuart, Robert Vaudry, Lord Walker of Worcester, Lyn Wagstaff, the late Sir Brian Warren, Mrs Julia White, Viscount Whitelaw, Sir Richard Wilson and Mrs Rosemary Wolff.

Despite the length of this list, there are no doubt other people whose contributions deserve to be acknowledged but who are not named. That would be omission by inadvertence, not by design; they can be sure that I am no less grateful to them than to those I have named.

There are three people of whom I can truthfully say that without their unwearying and unstinted support this book would not now be being published. Michael McManus and Anthony Staddon, from my private office, have over the last nine months put aside most of their normal duties in order to concentrate on the preparation of the book for publication: an exhausting and seemingly endless process of drafting, re-drafting, checking, collating, editing and proof-reading. Robert Armstrong has supported me in my discussions with my agent and with my publishers. He has allowed me to draw on his memories of the times when he worked as my Principal Private Secretary at No. 10, and has brought his eagle eye and his skill in drafting to bear on the process of checking, editing and proof-reading the text. My gratitude to all three of them is heartfelt and profound.

All these people have helped to make the book better and more accurate than it might otherwise have been. I alone am responsible for any remaining faults and errors.

Edward Heath
April 1998

Preface

I t has become customary or, as some would say, inevitable for former Prime Ministers sooner or later to produce their memoirs. In my case it is nearly twenty-five years since I left office and these accounts are therefore later rather than sooner. This has the advantage that, instead of being still mixed up with the heat and strife of the daily operations at 10 Downing Street and in the House of Commons, I have had the time and opportunity to reflect, in the light of subsequent history, on the events with which I was directly concerned. It is true that this approach has had the disadvantage of providing ample opportunities for hostile critics to distort and to confuse both the policies of 1970–4 and their results, preying in particular upon the ignorance of those under twenty-five today, who were not even born at that time. On the other hand, it enables me to show that, over a wide field, the Conservative government of 1970–4 has now been fully justified.

During the period after the Conservative Party had resumed power in 1979, I commented freely at that time in the House of Commons and in public speeches on the continuous change being made in the party's policies, from those which had previously been formed from the backbone of its 'One Nation' philosophy. To have produced a major political autobiography, however, might have caused what many people, including those who agreed with me, would have regarded as a total and unnecessary division inside our ranks. No one expects any government under our system to last for eighteen years, but I have now taken the opportunity of describing frankly both my actions during this time and the philosophy which led to them.

Many people have told me that they have heard, rightly or wrongly, of my period of government in the early 1970s – a total of only three and three-quarter years, let us not forget – but that they know almost nothing of my life and experiences before that – and of what brought about my premiership, the policies I have pursued, and the philosophy I have propounded. It is for this reason that I am devoting a considerable proportion of this autobiography to my early life leading up to the Second World War, the war itself, business and politics when peace was restored, as well as to the development of our national life up until the present day. In this I have been helped by the fact that I have kept all the documents I have received, and those with which I have been associated, since the age of thirteen. I have also included my outside interests in music and sport, in particular ocean racing, as well as my travels in every continent – indeed over almost the whole world. All have made an impact on the other aspects of my life. So let me start from the beginning and carry it as far as I can. I hope it will help to explain almost everything, including the mistakes I have made and the successes I have achieved.

Chapter 1

A Kentish Boyhood
Early Years 1916–1935

Legend has it that my father's family can be traced back to King Richard atte Hethe of Aveton Giffard in Devon in 1332. More detail can be found from the time of William Heath, who lived at the same location in the early sixteenth century. He died in 1546. The line is then continuous from Richard Heath, who died in 1583, and his wife Agnes. His direct descendant John Heath, born in 1734, was a tailor at Blackawton. His son Richard Heath, born in 1763, was a fisherman at Cockington; and it was his son, also Richard, born there in 1797, who abandoned the west country and moved to Ramsgate in Kent, where he became a coastguard. From that time onwards the Heaths stayed in east Kent. My great-grandfather, George Heath, was first a merchant seaman, then served in the Trinity House Life Service and became a pier man.

It was not until I was seven years old that I was properly introduced to the house where I had been born, in St Peter's-in-Thanet. This parish is part of Broadstairs, a small holiday resort on the Kent coast just by the North Foreland, which is so well known to every mariner and inshore sailor for its very powerful lighthouse on the English Channel. Looking out from the cliffs on a clear day, it is possible to see straight across to Calais and a stretch of the French coast. After their marriage in 1913 my parents had moved to 1 Holmwood Villas on Albion Road in St Peter's, a small semi-detached villa with trams running past the front door. We had the ground floor – a small bedroom, sitting room and kitchen. I was born there during an air-raid on the night of Sunday 9 July 1916. When I was six months old we moved to Crayford, some eighteen miles south-east of London, where my father went to be employed at the Vickers aircraft factory. My life was to come full circle in 1950 when I was elected Member of Parliament for the constituency of Bexley, next door to Crayford.

My father's parents lived at 1 Approach Road, Broadstairs – a corner house that I well remember from early childhood, because we used to spend every Christmas Day there. Stephen Richard Heath, my grandfather, started work as a dairyman but then became a porter at Broadstairs station on the old London and South-Eastern Railway. He was slight in build and jovial by nature, always cracking jokes with the passengers. My grandmother, Julia Louisa Hobday, a Ramsgate girl born in 1863 who had married him in 1886, was an exceptionally warm-hearted woman. She always looked after our welfare and worked constantly to keep my grandfather under some kind of control, especially after the many occasions on which he became rather too jovial. Whatever the circumstances of the previous night, she always got him off early to the station the next morning. Although he was slightly inclined to drink too much, my grandfather always took good care of his family. He lived until he was seventy-seven, and my grandmother lived well into her eighties. They spent their last years in a small terraced house only a few yards from where we were living in Broadstairs, and their back garden almost met ours.

My mother was a Pantony, and the youngest of four children. For as far back as we can trace they have been a Kentish family, living by the early years of this century in St Peter's. In fact, as they were from south of the Medway, they were 'men and maidens of Kent' rather than 'Kentish men and women'. There are still Pantonys to be found in that part of the world and in Maidstone, the county town. My mother's family was also quite small, especially once my uncle Edward, after whom I was named, had died from a heart attack while cycling through St Peter's shortly after he returned from the First World War. My grandmother died soon afterwards. I never knew her, but her photograph shows her to be a stoutly built, well-dressed and impressive woman. I can well understand how she overawed my grandfather. He was slight and gently bent by the time I used to meet him walking back from work in the late afternoons. He was a gardener at one of the big houses in the village of Reading Street, a couple of miles from St Peter's, and was devoted to that garden, which he showed off to us with pride. He lived with the eldest of his four children, my uncle Bill, and Bill's wife Gladys, in a small terraced house in the village. Uncle Bill was later to become groundsman at Chatham House Grammar School at Ramsgate, at which I was to gain a scholarship.

Towards the end of his life my grandfather was frequently incapacitated. Among his close family only Uncle Bill had the house room to accommodate him, and the rest of the family was appalled when he bundled the old man out of his house during his last illness and into what was then still termed the 'Workhouse' at Minster to die. We appreciated that my grandfather's fragile state of health had made life difficult for Uncle Bill and his family, but he was never really forgiven by any of us for this callous treatment. My father, who had no time for the Pantonys, disliked Bill with particular intensity.

I was over seventy before I learned from Uncle Bill's widow Gladys that my mother's parents had never been married to each other. My parents spared me that knowledge. My mother's elder sister Emily, who died in 1984 at the age of ninety-nine, lived on the Isle of Wight – which, in the 1920s and 1930s, seemed to me a remote and far-off place. She ran a general newsagent's store with her husband, another Uncle Bill, and I often visited them both from the age of fourteen. Standing on a wall by their shop I watched the Schneider Trophy race for seaplanes, which the British won against the Italians in 1931, with a plane that later became the basis for the Spitfire. Uncle Bill died on the island at the age of 103, and I frequently visited him during his last years. Their great-grandson Stephen Wickens is one of my godchildren.

My father was brought up in Broadstairs, and had in his youth been apprenticed as a carpenter. He was an excellent craftsman, and his work was greatly admired by all who saw it. The earliest examples which I can remember were the money boxes – mine of mahogany, my brother's of oak – which he made in order that we might be able to collect our small savings in them. Each was inscribed with our name. They stood one on each end of the mantelpiece and were brought down regularly, so that we could put part of our pocket money into them. Every week we dropped in a few pence and at an appropriate time, such as a birthday or a feast day, we were allowed to take out some coins for the celebration. I still have my beautiful mahogany money box in my study.

My father was a quiet and unassuming man. He always gave his two sons a lot of leeway, so that we could find our own feet in the world. Above all, I think that we learned from him the importance of initiative and ambition, self-determination and independence of spirit. He was splendidly cosmopolitan in his way: he enjoyed meeting all kinds of people, and encouraged his sons to do the same. He was also secretary of the local branch of a friendly society, 'The Ancient Order of Foresters'. He made sure that we had the opportunity to cultivate the various interesting and notable people whom he met through his work, particularly during the 1930s.

My mother was a wonderful woman, and she looked after all of us extraordinarily well. She had been a lady's maid, and had travelled to Switzerland in her work. In the 1960s, I drove my father and his then wife to Interlaken, where she had stayed. I once spent a few days as a youngster in the rather grand house of Mrs Taylor, the lady who had employed her, when I went to London for a Prom concert. This certainly gave me an early insight into a very different sort of lifestyle from that of our own family. My mother and father never had holidays, but always made sure that my brother and I did. She probably exhausted herself in the process, but she always did everything she could to ensure that her two sons should suffer no disadvantages at any stage of our careers, and she imbued both of us with a very strong sense of right and wrong. She taught us from the earliest age about how to behave, and what was the correct approach to people. She set great store by a tidy and clean appearance, and demanded the highest standards of politeness from us. My mother also had a strong religious sense and, although she was generally too busy to worship regularly herself during our time in Thanet, she ensured that I went to church without fail.

My lasting memory of my mother is of her beauty and calmness. These were qualities apparent to everyone who met her. At home we adored her for these traits, and also because she was always so supportive of us. As my father was constantly working so hard, both during the day with his building and at night with his heavy paperwork, a large part of our family life depended upon her. She never failed us. One quality, perhaps above all others, which made a permanent impact upon me was her fairness to everyone. Our family always respected her for it and I have tried to emulate my mother's example. It also gave her genuine pleasure to invite friends and neighbours into the house, which enabled both my brother and me to widen our contacts and broaden our knowledge of the world. Since there was never any alcohol in the house, it was always a question of an invitation to tea or coffee. That also explained why I never touched alcohol myself until I was out of my teens.

When I was four years old my brother John was born. As I was first taken to see him in my mother's bedroom I looked at his bubbling mouth and pointed to it excitedly, calling out 'Bubbles, bubbles!' From that moment onwards he was known in the family as 'Bubbles'. I suspect that as he grew up he rather disliked this, but in the family he never grumbled about it. From the beginning both of my parents were determined that the two of us should be treated in the same way. There would be no favouritism for one or the other. When John's first marriage came to an end, his ex-wife produced a book in which she claimed that my parents had been guilty of excessive favouritism towards me. This book was denounced by the whole family. Although John's interests and mine did certainly diverge in various ways, this was never a cause of friction between us. Indeed, in many respects it had a creative effect upon both of us. I followed the sports in which he participated; and he closely followed, and supported, my musical activities. We were both in Coleman's House at school and, when I became a prefect and then house captain, far from trying to take advantage of my position, or causing trouble for me, he was always a quiet and reliable supporter.

Neither of us wanted to go into private business, much to my father's disappointment, and John's concern was with administration. It was in local government that he made his career. He was an excellent technician, as was shown by his work in the Royal Electrical and Mechanical Engineers during the Second World War. He was also a warm-hearted, understanding brother who frequently telephoned me to congratulate me on some individual success in politics, or to try to cheer me up when I was caught up in the vicissitudes of my chosen profession. He and his wife usually attended my eve-of-poll meetings in Bexley, and they always made a particular point of telephoning me on election morning and election night. Nobody gave me greater comfort in the wake of any attack on me in the press.

In Crayford we lived in a small, semi-detached council house – one sitting room and a kitchen down and two bedrooms up – at 106 Green Walk. My own memories of this time are generally no more than fragments. At the Vickers plant, my father worked factory hours, so we used to see a great deal of him. He was a keen gardener and grew vegetables in the garden behind our house. In fact, apart from a tiny lawn, the whole space was used for growing our own supplies. I was never allowed to forget an eruption of mine one spring day, when I systematically tore all the plants from the ground, collected them in a heap and trampled on them. Although my father rebuked me for this act of wanton vandalism, there was never any question of physical punishment for my brother or myself. Later on I became an assiduous gardener myself, cultivating sweet peas in a greenhouse during the winter, and a range of cacti. Sadly I had to abandon this pursuit when I went up to Oxford, and resumed it only when I moved to Salisbury some fifty years later – although nowadays I do not get my hands quite so dirty.

One of the features of life that I remember clearly from those early days in Crayford was being taken by our next-door neighbours, Mr and Mrs Butler, a devoutly religious couple, to the Christadelphian Chapel each Sunday. Neither of my parents had any Christadelphian connection, but as they were both so busy they were delighted to let our neighbours take me to that service. The Christadelphians, a group who reject the Trinity and concentrate their teaching instead upon the Second Coming, left no particular theological mark of their faith upon me, but the general impact of their orderly, well-mannered approach to life and the background of their vigorous hymn singing have long remained. The Butlers were good people and attended their chapel every Sunday, as well as on occasional weekday evenings. They did so because they believed that it was right and that, in taking me with them, they were carrying out their natural obligations to their neighbours.

*   *   *

Just after I turned five, I started to attend the small church school some fifteen or twenty minutes away from our house. Jim Bennett, our next-door neighbour, who was the same age as I was, started at the same time and together each day we made our way to and from the school, occasionally having scrapes with other boys *en route*. Together we made a formidable pair and usually managed to survive these encounters unscathed. The school was a temporary-looking building with a corrugated-iron roof, painted in a dull shade of reddish-brown. The discipline was sound, and the teaching must have been too, because when I transferred to another school after we moved back to St Peter's I never had any difficulties in coping with the curriculum. Jim and I stayed in touch for many years afterwards. There were really no sporting activities at school but we kept fit with our strenuous walking, particularly when we were occasionally taken over to Dartford Heath near by.

Our time at Crayford was a happy one, though there were comparatively few outside activities. My mother was too busy looking after my young brother. Every Friday evening my father went to the local club to play billiards. For the rest of the time he concentrated on his ardent gardening. Occasionally, we would go to the ramshackle local cinema in Crayford down near the river, but in general there was neither the time nor the money for social activities. At Christmas we used to travel down by train and bus to stay with a friend of my parents, known to us all as Aunt Gladys, at her home in a village close to Tunbridge Wells. We looked forward immensely to these occasions, and she maintained the connection for many years afterwards by coming to stay with us at Broadstairs.

Both sides of my family felt that their roots were in Broadstairs, and our move to Crayford had been made out of wartime necessity rather than preference. By the summer of 1923 my mother and father felt a yearning to return to their original hometown and so, after seven years, waving cheerfully, we went back. Broadstairs was quite celebrated at the time, because of an enduring connection with Charles Dickens. Buildings throughout the town proclaimed on plaques their own links, often spurious, with the great man. As the visitor came around from Bleak House, renamed from Fort House after *David Copperfield* was written there, he or she came upon the Royal Albion Hotel, which still has its marble sign boasting that Dickens had worked on *Nicholas Nickleby* there and, after that, another house alongside the Promenade, where Dickens was alleged to have continued with his literary labours. But the attraction that still makes me chuckle was a charming white house just off the Promenade, which had a small plaque over the door announcing to any prying tourist that 'Charles Dickens did not live here'.

My family moved into a rented house rather larger than the one in which I was born and about half a mile further up the road towards St Peter's village. It was on two floors, but my brother and I still shared a bedroom. For us its main attraction was that it had a long garden at the back, covered in fruit trees and running right down to the railway cutting at the bottom. It became a sports ground, or rather perhaps a hunting ground, for the two of us and for our schoolfriends. My father started work as a carpenter with a small local firm of building contractors, Snowdons, at Kingsgate, a village about five miles up the coast. He cycled to and fro each day. Kingsgate was not one of the old villages of east Kent: it had been created virtually from scratch in the inter-war years, on three long straight avenues going down to the high cliffs above the sea. Although Snowdons did build a few houses, their main activity was taking care of a sizeable number of splendid residences in Kingsgate where the wealthy came intermittently for their seaside holidays. In due course my father was made a foreman and there was great excitement some years later when he was able to buy a Velocette two-stroke motor cycle. This provided a pillion for me or my brother, and my father later taught me how to ride it.

Meanwhile, I went off to the Church of England primary school, about a mile from our home, and 100 yards from the village church. A grey flint building, the school had only two classrooms, each taking a class of well over thirty, and a total staff of three. The headmaster, Mr Taylor, a broad-chested and somewhat burly figure with tortoiseshell spectacles, set the formal tone when he presided over prayers each morning. He was also one of the churchwardens and we envied the handsome house in which he lived up the narrow lane opposite. James Bird, his deputy, taught me for the three years I was at the school. His son William, younger than myself, turned out to be one of the best treble soloists of his generation. Both in our church choir and in his performances at the carol concerts in Broadstairs, his rendition of 'O for the Wings of a Dove' made a worthy comparison with the famous recording of Ernest Lush.

The headmaster and his deputy were both devoted and traditional professionals, concerned only with turning out products who by their learning and general behaviour would be a credit to the church and its school. They knew that not only the vicar and clergy, who paid regular visits, but also the leading parishioners who supported the school, were constantly watching the results of their efforts. The teaching was solid, the discipline was unobtrusively effective and without corporal punishment, and we won our full share of places to the nearby Chatham House Grammar School at Ramsgate.

I began to learn the piano soon after we returned to St Peter's. A cousin of my mother's, always known as Aunt Edith, was an excellent pianist and when she discovered my interest in music she used to invite me over to her home at Cliftonville for tea so that I could listen to her play. I realised later that Sinding's 'The Rustle of Spring', Durand's 'The First Waltz' and Grieg's 'Wedding Day at Troldhaugen' were not really part of the mainstream classical repertoire. But then neither were the ballads that the Heath side of the family used to sing gathered around the piano at my grandmother's – 'Love's Old Sweet Song', 'The Lost Chord' or 'When You Come to the End of a Perfect Day'.

But all of that was put right by my piano teacher, Grace Locke, the daughter of the keeper of the flower shop opposite the church. This was just around the corner from Mr Creasey's, the pork butcher, who provided the pigs' brains, pigs' livers, pigs' chitterlings, pigs' trotters and other delectable pieces of pig that my mother cooked for us, and also the unskinned pork sausage meat which we invariably had for breakfast on Sunday morning. Further down the street on the opposite side to the school was Mr Warren, the beef butcher, a far more expensive purveyor of meat. We had a custom in our family that my brother and I could always choose the main meal on our respective birthdays. Invariably I asked for pigs' liver from Mr Creasey, while my brother preferred lambs' kidneys from Mr Warren.

Having decided that I should learn the piano from Miss Locke, my parents set out to buy me an instrument. One Saturday afternoon we went over by tram to Cliftonville to investigate at Messrs Thornton Bobby, where various instruments were demonstrated to us. My parents finally decided on an upright piano of the firm's own make. The cost was £42, which my parents paid by twenty-four monthly instalments of £2 each. This represented a massive investment in my future for which I have always been immensely grateful. A little later my parents bought a violin for my brother, in order that he might have an opportunity similar to mine. For a while he practised hard on it and sometimes we played together. But he did not really discover his own love of music until some time after he had given up the instrument, which he did fairly rapidly. He then developed a great love of opera and classical music, indulged in many visits to both and built up a fine collection of recorded music. The Thornton Bobby piano proved to be a hard-wearing instrument which lasted me at Broadstairs for the next forty years. On this began the arduous and seemingly never-ending practising of scales and arpeggios, and the gradual build-up of the classical repertoire with which young musicians inevitably start. Miss Locke did not believe in her pupils spending time taking musical examinations; she did, however, insist upon our working our way through all the pieces which were set by the examination boards.

My musical development was further enhanced when, shortly after taking up the piano, I joined the choir of St Peter's parish church as a treble. This well-balanced choir consisted of some twenty-four boys and a dozen men. Long established and with a good reputation, it sang many different kinds of music, but its real foundations were understandably in the musical traditions of the Anglican Church. We boys had rehearsals on a Tuesday evening, and the musical incentive to attend was enhanced by the payment of a penny halfpenny each for every rehearsal. The full choir rehearsals were on Friday evenings. On Sundays we were paid twopence a time. On festive occasions we sang Stainer's *Crucifixion*, Spohr's *Last Judgement*, Handel's *Messiah*, Haydn's *Creation* and the setting of the *St Luke Passion* which was at that time still attributed to J. S. Bach. On a normal Sunday we made do with a single anthem.

I remained a chorister until my voice broke when I was fourteen, and one of my greatest delights was to be the treble soloist in Wesley's anthem 'Blessed Be the God and Father of Mankind', which, properly sung, still gives me immense joy. But the most rewarding occasion of all was when we sang at a society wedding one Saturday afternoon, were invited to the reception afterwards and each got paid the princely sum of two shillings and sixpence. It was in this church that I heard some of the most prominent preachers of our time, including the Rev. Studdert Kennedy, popularly known as 'Woodbine Willie' for his work as a chaplain in the First World War, and Canon Dick Sheppard, the well-known pacifist, famous for his broadcasts as vicar of St-Martin-in-the-Fields and then as dean of Canterbury. It was here that, at the age of fourteen, I was confirmed.

No doubt helped by the self-confidence I gained from performing in public from an early age, I was never afflicted by a fear of examinations. I was not yet ten years old when I sat for the scholarship examination at Chatham House Grammar School, on 1 May 1926. All the candidates whose papers were of a sufficiently high standard were later interviewed individually by the headmaster, H. C. Norman. The intellectual test had already been dealt with, and this was more of an opportunity for him to assess the character of a boy. I must admit, therefore, that I was puzzled by his questions, because the answers to them all seemed to me to be so obvious. However, he appeared to be completely satisfied by my replies. Later I came to respect him and to appreciate his wisdom, for my parents were informed on 11 June that I had won a scholarship to cover the fees of the school, which were four guineas a term. My parents made a separate application to the Kent Education Committee for help with travel expenses and the cost of the lunchtime meals at school, and we were granted an additional 18s 9d per term, a substantial help in those days. Actually I found the school meals so off-putting that, with my parents' support, I quickly sought permission to go out to a local café for lunch.

Shortly afterwards, I was given a terrier, who was named ERG after my own initials. He was a well-trained and good-natured dog, so there are no tales of unexplained disappearances or of postmen grievously bitten. We could see the new recreation ground on the other side of the railway at the bottom of our garden where youngsters would play soccer throughout the winter, but my father dissuaded me from joining in any of these junior games because he was afraid that I might get injured, which would interfere with my piano playing or my academic routines. Instead I took to playing tennis with my friends in the garden of the nearby Vicarage. But soccer had been my father's main sporting activity in his younger days and I was rather hurt. I did play the odd game of rugby at Chatham House, but obeyed the soccer interdiction. This, however, did not prevent my taking a keen interest in professional football later on in life.

I have long been a supporter of Arsenal FC and I am delighted that, in their most recent squad selections, they have been putting my own principles of wide international co-operation into practice particularly in their excellent 1997–8 campaign. In my army days, George Swindin, the Arsenal goalkeeper, became my regimental PT instructor. I was Prime Minister when the tremendous Arsenal team of 1970–1 did the double – winning both the league championship and the FA Cup – although, unlike Harold Wilson five years earlier, when England won the World Cup, I saw no justification for claiming the credit. Sadly, I could not be at Wembley in May 1971 to see Arsenal defeat Liverpool by two goals to one in the FA Cup Final, because I was committed to sailing with *Morning Cloud* in the Seine Bay Race. My father and stepmother did go, however, and they both thoroughly enjoyed a thrilling game, as well as the generous hospitality of the Football Association. My brother had a natural talent for games, which I did not – so, when the time came, he followed my father's example and became a vigorous and successful sportsman at both of his schools. His soccer playing was stopped only by his service in the war.

In the summer of 1926 my father decided to move into Broadstairs. He had always wanted to own his own house and he found one which pleased him at the top of King Edward Avenue on a hill looking down to the sea. Number 4, known as Helmdon, was a semi-detached house which he checked professionally and found to be in first-rate condition. Its only drawback was a very small back garden. He became involved in a heavy mortgage, with which he and my mother struggled for many years, in the end successfully. They provided boarding accommodation for seaside visitors during most of the summer months. The house had three bedrooms together with two rooms and a kitchen and scullery downstairs. It was large enough to take two sets of visitors who could use two bedrooms and the downstairs front room, provided that my brother and I used the small bedroom at the back of the house and my father and mother slept on a let-down couch in one of the downstairs rooms, which also served as my father's office.

This new way of life meant intensive hard work, especially for my mother, but my parents set great store on owning their own house. It was disconcerting for us to have two other families in the house, changing over every fortnight from May to October, but it meant that we met a lot of people from different parts of the country. Some of them came regularly year after year, and became firm friends of our family. My brother and I could show them the town, help them with their shopping and enjoy ourselves on the beach with them. I also began to take part in sand-design competitions organised by the *Daily Mail*. Whenever I won, the supplement to our pocket money was most welcome.

Sometimes we also persuaded my father to take a break from his labours on a Sunday evening, and we would go down to the promenade to listen to a band, usually military. We would stroll along and listen to the music, go down to the harbour and then stand and listen to the musicians again. In the summer we used to go down to Joss Bay, a glorious sandy stretch alongside the North Foreland lighthouse, and less crowded than the main bay in Broadstairs itself. There we used to picnic at lunchtime, swim and sunbathe, and then return in time for my father's evening meal. It was a long walk there and back but there was something idyllic about those inter-war years in Broadstairs. Like so many seaside resorts, Thanet has fallen on harder times in recent years. Many more people take their holidays abroad, and the local economy has failed to replace jobs lost through the decline of the light industries which used to flourish in the area.

Another early musical experience for me was 'Our Carol Party' in Broadstairs. Our Carol Party had been started in 1923 by Kathleen Harding, who looked after a disabled lady in the town by the name of Miss Bright-man, the daughter of a Broadstairs doctor. For the first few years, the carollers sang at the private schools and at the larger houses in the town every festive season. They always had an overriding commitment to per-forming their carols authentically and to the highest musical standards, thereby giving the local population an opportunity to appreciate how splendid many of these tunes can be when they are performed in a serious fashion. They also collected money for local charities, in particular the homes for convalescent children. After my family moved to Broadstairs proper in 1926, I was invited to be the treble soloist for that year's perform-ance of 'Good King Wenceslas' by Our Carol Party, and collected the donations afterwards.

Some of the carols we performed were unfamiliar to me, and to most of our listeners: we had some German carols and some French carols; we always tried to use obscure harmonisations of the better-known tunes; and we sang lesser-known English songs collected from the countryside. Everything was performed *a cappella*, and with great control and discipline. Always we were told to concentrate on the beauty of the sound. Rehearsals began in October and our first 'public' performances took place at the beginning of December. Half of the money raised went towards holiday funds for the sick children, and the other half was used to buy presents for them. In my early years with Our Carol Party, I was judged to be roughly of an age with the recipients, and was therefore commissioned to choose the presents for them. At that age buying one present is exciting enough, but being invited to buy over a hundred is a dream come true. After lunch on Christmas Day, we piled into cars and delivered the gifts to the delighted children. For nearly fifteen years, I spent the afternoon of every Christmas Day in this way.

In the mid-1930s, Kathleen Harding moved away to the south coast, and I was asked to take over Our Carol Party. Shortly afterwards, in Oxford in December 1935, I encountered a town carol concert for the first time and, in the autumn of 1936, I proposed something similar to the chairman of the Broadstairs and St Peter's Urban District Council. The town clerk agreed to this, and Our Carol Party blossomed into a full-scale annual town carol concert, with a choir of around sixty people and an orchestra. The chairman and members of the council came *en bloc* to the first town carol concert, and sat in the front row. Without giving them prior warning, I followed a tradition of the Oxford concerts by asking them to sing one of the verses of 'God Rest Ye Merry, Gentlemen' alone. This was not a success, and I did not try the trick again, although the Broadstairs carol concerts continued, with the exception of 1939–45, for four decades.

Perhaps our closest family friends at this time were the Ravens. Martin and Hugh Raven, two brothers, were both doctors and pillars of the local community. They both lived by the sea, on opposite sides of the harbour, and they shared an enthusiasm for music, amateur stage productions and cultural life generally. I knew Hugh Raven's two daughters especially well, not least because they sang in Our Carol Party, together with their brother Tom. I also have vivid memories of singing madrigals with them around the dining table at their home. Margaret, one of the sisters, went out to Rhodesia many years ago and we still write to each other from time to time. My closest friend, however, was her sister Kathleen, or Kay. She was a delightful girl and we shared many interests, including tennis and swimming as well as music. Knowing each other in so many different ways, we corresponded frequently throughout the war, when I was moving around the country with the Royal Artillery Regiment and she was in the WAAF. After I returned home in 1946, we still remained separated because we were working in different parts of the country. One day she suddenly let me know that she was marrying someone else. I was saddened by this. I had been under such pressure, re-adapting myself to civil life and earning a living, that maybe I had taken too much for granted. I subsequently learned that Kay had a happy life with her children, but we never met again.

From autumn 1926, Chatham House Grammar School became the centre of my life for nine years. My brother moved into Holy Trinity Church School, near the pier in Broadstairs, and joined me at Chatham House four years later. He did not win a scholarship, so my parents paid his fees and his travelling expenses to ensure that we were both treated in the same way. Chatham House had originally been a private school, established in the same buildings and grounds in 1797, but had been taken over by the local education authority in 1911. It housed some 450 boys, along with a staff of thirty. The girls' grammar school was at Clarendon House, half a mile away on the other side of the town. We all used to travel together in the trams, and the two schools combined for social activities, as well as for music and drama.

My studies at Chatham House required me to work assiduously at school, and also brought with them a great deal of homework each night and at weekends. I was usually the youngest in the class, and sometimes found myself more than a year younger than the average. I seem to have coped well enough with this, according to my termly reports. My parents spent an evening each term at the school being told by the masters how I was doing and what the problems were. The crisis arose when, at the age of thirteen, I was lined up to sit the School Certificate Examinations. At the meeting the term before they were due, my parents were advised that I should delay the examination for a year. On returning home they reported this to me but I begged them not to agree to such a suggestion. It would be different if I had to delay going into the sixth form after the examination, but it would be unbearable if I was not allowed to take it at all. They persuaded the staff to agree. I succeeded in securing the School Certificate, but not the Matriculation, which was required if I was to go on to the next stage of university examination. That I did the following year.

If I displayed any particular academic aptitude in my early years at Chatham House, it was probably for mathematics and science. I spent much time on languages, although little emphasis was placed on German, which I regretted in later years. Spanish, however, was the favourite subject of the second master, Dr E. Alec Woolf, and he persuaded many to take it up with the promise that Argentina in general, and Buenos Aires in particular, was going to provide the greatest opportunities in the world for our generation. His was an enthusiasm which I did not share, and those who did master Spanish and went out to work in Latin America never discovered the advantages they expected. Looking back on it, however, I realise that it was being well taught in Latin that stood me in the best stead throughout my later activities. The structure it imposes on the mind in youth can in turn impose a firm intellectual discipline in later life, improving the clarity of both thoughts and words. It was this discipline, I believe, learned through my early studies of Latin, that gave me the foundations for making effective speeches without notes.

In the spring of 1931, Dr Woolf made the arrangements for a school trip of fourteen pupils to Paris. He also taught at St Lawrence College, Ramsgate, a public school, and although all the others in the group came from there he invited me to join in. My parents readily agreed to my travelling and generously paid the cost. The result was my first flight in an aeroplane, which in those days was an unusual treat, still wholly unfamiliar to most people. We flew from Croydon Airport and spent eight days in Paris, which gave me my first experience of the world beyond the south-east of England.

We were all absolutely fascinated, and our appreciation of the city was enhanced by the amount of free time we had each day when we could do what we liked. We stayed in a small boarding house, but the real fun came when we were allowed to choose individually for ourselves the restaurant in which to have our midday meal. There was, of course, a marvellous variety, and we must have read nearly every outdoor menu board in Paris. We went to see the obvious places of interest – Notre Dame, the Louvre and the Arc de Triomphe – and spent hours walking up the Champs Elysées looking at the magnificent shops and going into the motor showrooms to collect catalogues, some of which I still have.

The highlight of all this was going to L'Opéra Comique to see *Carmen*, my first visit to an opera house. I have seen so many performances of *Carmen* that nothing from this particular production really sticks in the memory. What has always remained vividly with me, however, was watching a delightful, fair-haired young lady in the box beneath ours struggling to replace her shoulder straps as they repeatedly slipped down in a most revealing fashion throughout the performance. Later one night some of us were bold enough to slip into the Folies Bergères, something which, I think, I may have neglected to mention when I recounted the events of the trip to my parents. I suppose that fourteen was a little young for Paris, but I have loved the place ever since.

After matriculating I had to decide whether to concentrate on the sciences or the arts. Given my previous results, there was apparently much to be said for going for the sciences, but I chose the arts, with which I could combine economic theory and history – subjects which particularly interested me. I was always especially concerned to consolidate my performance in economics and, in the autumn of 1931, I began cycling the ten miles to Birchington every Wednesday night to attend the economic history lectures provided there by the Workers' Educational Association. The Master of Balliol College, Oxford, A. D. Lindsay, was at that time a vice-president of this organisation, which existed 'to stimulate and to satisfy the demand of workers for education, and to work for a national system of education which shall provide for all children, adolescents and adults full opportunities for complete individual and social development'. The Association relied almost entirely on voluntary subscriptions, and I found its branch at Birchington admirable. Whether I had chosen to enter a profession, commerce or politics, I would have derived a sound intellectual basis for my adult life from my subjects at Chatham House, the WEA and my private reading of English and French literature.

At Chatham House I took part in more and more extra-mural activities. In sports I concentrated on cross-country running through the winter, for which I certainly had the stamina, and on swimming and tennis in the summer. I could not afford even the smallest boat and, although I was envious of the dinghies in the harbour at Broadstairs, it was not until more than forty years had passed that I seriously took up sailing. I was never any good at cricket, but for three years before I left school I was scorer for the First XI. This was such a strong team that once every summer term the Kent county side came over for a one-day match. This was how I met A. P. F. Chapman, Frank Woolley, 'Tich' Freeman, Leslie Ames and others of that generation. They were as gentlemanly off the pitch as they were skilful and sporting on it. I followed the Kent team's activities closely and, during the Canterbury cricket week, I used to cycle some seventeen and a half miles each way every day for the games. I have now been a member of Kent County Cricket Club for over fifty years and of the MCC for some thirty.

I wish that I had been able to spend more time at school on drawing, painting and developing my appreciation of the visual arts. This might have been more use to me than the hours spent on carpentry and metalwork which were part of the curriculum, but at which I was no good whatever, despite my family background. Instead I concentrated far more on the performing arts. On the stage I appeared in a variety of plays, and annually in the school nativity play, eventually ending up as the central angel presiding over all the junior angels. What I enjoyed more than anything was playing the lead in a comedy called *It Pays to Advertise*.

I also recall performing the role of Titinius in Act IV of *Julius Caesar*. My only line was 'Good-night, Lord Brutus,' shared with the character of Messala, but I heard tell of some bloody deeds, and learned some important political lessons, on that stage. The comedies usually put on at Easter were lively and full of opportunities to show off. Before every performance we threw ourselves with great gusto into a tremendous schedule of rehearsals, all of them outside school hours. That was how I learned to concentrate on rehearsals at least as much as on the performances themselves.

Music also occupied much of my time. The school orchestra was large and well trained, producing performances of a consistently high standard. It was conducted by the short but effective figure of 'Tufty' Goodram, who was the senior English master at the school, and masters as well as pupils played in it. Many of its members became professional musicians, including Leslie Woodage and William Overton, two trumpeters who developed their craft in the Salvation Army and went on to make their careers in the BBC Symphony Orchestra. I sometimes accompanied the orchestral musicians on the piano and occasionally conducted them. By this time I was also including musical theory in my sixth-form subjects, and passed the Elements of Music examination, as an additional subject, at the University of London in June 1932. A school prize for piano playing was established at around this time and I became the first winner, playing pieces by Bach, Mozart and Chopin.

My principal activity, however, was in the Literary and Debating Society, which was the province of Mr Wilsher, the school geography master, and was strongly supported by the fifth and sixth forms. Debates started with either one or two of us on each side. We were given complete freedom of choice in framing the motions for debate. I recall proposing such motions as 'Sweepstakes should be abolished' and 'Sunday cinemas should be abolished': those were innocent times indeed. A number of masters used to drop in to listen but they generally played no part. This rule was broken, however, when the Society decided in March 1933 to copy the Oxford Union Debating Society and consider the motion that 'This House will under no circumstances fight for King and Country'. The fact that it had been carried by 275 votes to 153 at Oxford a month earlier had aroused much controversy and was reported back to Hitler by the German ambassador in London, as a supposed indication of Britain's unwillingness to fight for its own interests.

In what has always been considered to have been one of the best debates in the school's history, I opposed the motion in the debate on 30 March. Members of staff, as well as several Chatham House Old Boys, joined with sixty or so current members of the school in taking part. The debate raged fast and furiously, and, when tempers were beginning to mount after an hour and a half, the chairman had to postpone further discussion until the following Monday. Although the weekend gave us some time to cool off, the vote was finally taken amid a great deal of shouting and the motion was defeated by forty-five votes to thirteen. On a subsequent occasion I proposed that capital punishment should be abolished, another hotly contested debate and a proposal with which I was later to become much involved as Chief Whip and as leader of the Conservative Party. At school I was defeated by one vote.

I also took part in some debating outside school. I was invited, thanks to the influence of a distinguished solicitor and neighbour of my family, Fitzroy Weigall, to be one of several speakers to address the Broadstairs Literary and Debating Society on 24 October 1933 on the theme 'Things I hate'. This was a popular theme at the time; and, I suppose, the 1930s equivalent of the *Room 101* television show. I addressed this topic once again a year later, at Chatham House. At this time I was also given the opportunity of attending the men's Sunday afternoon discussion meetings at St Peter's Church Hall which, though they were not party political, were always dealing with the main issues of the day, both national and international. These debates and discussions must have brought home to my family and friends how marked my interest in political questions was becoming. On 26 March 1934, I represented the Chatham House Debating Society at the Isle of Thanet Debating Society, moving that 'This House deplores the whither-ance of Britain'. There was a strong adumbration of my subsequent political preoccupations in what I said then: 'the history of post-war Europe is the story of how countries are trying to meet new circumstances, to build up a new Europe on the still smouldering ashes of the old'. Despite the ferocity of some of my early debating rhetoric, my fascination with politics was founded far more on the intellectual and political arguments than on any enthusiasm for becoming an adolescent demagogue. Indeed, I did not need a stage and an audience to start debating. During the school holidays, I particularly enjoyed sitting outside an ice-cream parlour in Broadstairs talking earnestly with my friends about the major issues of the day. I suppose I just liked arguing.

The climax of these activities was the mock general election on 31 January 1935. We held lunchtime meetings in the open air, speaking on orange boxes. The final performances and the votes were held in the gymnasium, which was also the main school hall. I stood as the national government candidate and, without telling anyone, wrote to the local Conservative Member for the Isle of Thanet, Captain H. H. Balfour, asking him if he would send me a letter of support which I could read out at the final meeting. He did so in his own hand and, at the conclusion of my final speech, to the complete astonishment of everyone present from the headmaster downwards, I was able to announce the support of the local Member of Parliament and read out his letter. I was thereupon elected with a majority of 150 votes over my nearest rival.

I suppose that I was already incurably addicted to politics by my teenage years. Young people have always been unwilling to accept the world as they find it and, in my experience, they generally want to change things in some way or other. Personally, I have always believed that anyone who wants to see a better world – with greater prosperity for all, fewer injustices and more opportunities – cannot afford to sit around being an armchair critic. If you want something done, then you have to be a doer; and I resolved, early on, to be a doer. I was also increasingly influenced by the recession, followed by depression, that cast a shadow over my later childhood. As I learned later, Thanet did not suffer the same terrible poverty during those years as did the north of England, Wales and Scotland, but I was still haunted by the daily spectacle of witnessing so many people enduring hardships, hopelessness and loss of dignity. No amount of economic studies could help me to make sense of a system which was depriving people of the opportunity to make a contribution to society. I resolved to do everything within my power to spare future generations similar horrors.

I had become a prefect in September 1933, then house captain and finally deputy school captain. The prefects were expected to take part in running school activities and in maintaining order and discipline, occasionally by means of corporal punishment: for this purpose, only the use of a gym shoe was permitted. Perhaps my greatest satisfaction before I left Chatham House came in 1934, when I shared with my close colleague Jim Hobbs, the school captain, the most senior prize of all, the Leslie and Douglas Prize for Character. Jim lived half a dozen doors away from us, down the hill. He was a gifted scientist, and went up to Trinity a year before I went to Balliol, the next-door college. He went on to become a senior figure at Tate & Lyle, and ultimately retired to Canterbury where he was tragically killed in a car accident. Other close friends at that time were Wallace Fairweather, who still lives at Westgate and is the father of one of my goddaughters, Pamela; and Teddy Denman, a lifelong friend who sadly died in 1991, the father of Pempy, another goddaughter. Teddy looked after many of my interests, including some business affairs in the City of London and sailing matters in the Royal Temple Yacht Club.

Although I would never underestimate the debt I owe to Chatham House, it was at this stage in my life that I began to learn more and more outside the confines of the classroom. In particular, the world of the arts was opened up for me by Sir Alec Martin. He and his family owned one of the large houses at Kingsgate for which my father was responsible when their owners were away. They generally visited it at Easter and in the summer holiday and, when he was there, Sir Alec would invite me to supper on Sundays with a group of artists and supporters of the arts. He was chairman of Christie's, the auctioneers, a firm which he had joined at the age of fourteen, and a skilled raconteur. He told a wealth of anecdotes about everyone, from the richest collectors in their stately homes to the most temperamental of artists, such as Augustus John, Walter Sickert and Jacob Epstein. 'Come along and sit and listen,' he would say to me. 'Don't say anything. You don't understand our business. You are a musician – but in time you will learn.' That I certainly did, and when I worked in London after the war I used to have a sandwich lunch and then either seek out an art gallery or drop in on Sir Alec at Christie's.

I particularly cherish one piece of advice that he gave me, when I had seen a picture and wanted to know whether it was worth the price a gallery was asking for it. 'That is not the way to go about it,' he said. 'You must first ask yourself whether you really like the picture. It may take you a little time to decide that, but if the answer is yes, you must then ask yourself whether you could live with it. If you can satisfy yourself on that count, ask yourself whether you can afford to buy it, and if the answer to that is yes, come and tell me. I will then look at it with you, tell you whether it is genuine and, if so, what price it is worth.' I could not have had sounder advice.

On another occasion he told me that he had recently visited a very distinguished customer near Gloucester, and on his way back had remembered that a lady living near by had written to him asking him to value a picture which she possessed. As he drove further and further into the city, with the houses getting older and smaller, he thought that he must have made a mistake. But, arriving finally at the address in his notebook, he knocked on the door and an elderly lady appeared. She invited him to have a cup of tea in the front room. He looked around while he was waiting for it and could see nothing of real interest. Over tea, she offered to bring him the picture. He looked at it in astonishment because it was by Matisse – his *Femme nue drapée*. 'And where did this come from?' he asked. 'I was walking along Bond Street when I saw it in a gallery window,' she replied. 'It became my heart's desire. I had to save up and borrow enough money for the £200 which was being asked for it. And how much do you think it is worth now?' she asked. 'At least £7,500 at auction, but probably much more.' 'How splendid,' she replied, 'I would like you to offer it first to the Tate Gallery.' So he had left with it under his arm. 'There it is against the wall,' he said to me, pointing to it, 'turn it around . . . I have offered it to the Tate, but they aren't prepared to pay for it.'

However, that was all sorted out in the end, and it can now be seen in the gallery.

After two years' study in the sixth form I was awarded intermediate degrees in economics and commerce by London University. The latter included accountancy, which greatly pleased my father, because he always wished me to become a chartered accountant; and my 'uncle' in Margate, although an 'incorporated' and not a 'chartered' accountant, was willing to help. My own overwhelming enthusiasm at the age of eighteen, however, was for getting to a university, and the next problem was how to gain admission to one – and then to find some way of financing my time there through a scholarship, loans and help from outsiders. I knew that my family would never be able to provide the money to fund me for three years.

After my treble voice had declined into an initially not entirely controllable bass-baritone in my fifteenth year, I had started to learn the organ under the parish organist at St Peter's, Alfred Tatham, who lived at Dumpton with his delightful wife. He had previously been the organist at Romsey Abbey, and was a most capable and self-confident person, the very antithesis of the struggling musician. By this time, he was responsible for music at a number of the private preparatory schools with which Broadstairs and St Peter's abounded, including St Peter's Court, at one time attended by two sons of King George V (Prince Henry and Prince George), Hildersham House, Stone House, Selwyn House, Port Regis and Wellesley House. Mr Tatham gave me the firmest foundation in organ music by insisting that I should master the works of Johann Sebastian Bach, before moving on to the Mendelssohn sonatas, the French composers and the contemporary British ones.

Thanks to this excellent grounding, I felt confident enough to start my campaign to enter the world of higher education with an attempt to gain the organ scholarship at St Catharine's College, Cambridge in 1934. I was unsuccessful but consoled myself with the thought that Cambridge had never really been my first choice and I was, in any case, rather young for it. I then went for the prestigious scholarship at Keble College, Oxford, which was renowned for the major positions occupied by its organ scholars after leaving college. The outgoing organ scholar was Joseph Cooper. Joe was already well known far beyond the confines of his College for his brilliant playing, so much so that in the end he was reputed to have lost the confidence of the Senior Common Room. He was adept at improvising the voluntary as everyone left chapel and, when at his last service he played 'Today I feel so happy' and hotted it up, his contemporaries cheered. His swan-song did not, however, prove so popular with the college establishment. We later became close friends. His real wish was to become a concert pianist, for which he spent some time at the Vienna Conservatoire. The interruption in his studies for war service put paid to that, and he ultimately became best known as the presenter of *Face the Music* on BBC Television. He much wanted me to appear on the programme as a guest of honour, but the BBC forbade it on the ground that I was not a professional musician. I suggested that he should inform them that I had been paid $5,000 for conducting half of a programme with the Cleveland Symphony Orchestra during their summer series; if that was not professional, I would like to know what was. It made no difference, and I never appeared.

I was interviewed for Keble by Dr Thomas Armstrong, himself a former Keble organ scholar and later organist at Christ Church, the Oxford cathedral. His son Robert was to be my principal private secretary at No. 10. Dr Armstrong was most interested and patient, but I was not well enough accustomed to the exercises which he asked me to do in plain chant. I was sad to lose out on this opportunity, but I realised afterwards that it was for the best because I was then able to compete for entry into Balliol College, which was what I really wanted. I had never visited Balliol until I went there to sit the scholarship examination, but the College already had an unrivalled reputation for producing many of the leading figures in British public life. The organ scholarship was not then available and I sought entry instead on the basis of a Modern Greats scholarship involving philosophy, politics and economics. I did not win one of the two scholarships, but I was awarded entry. The philosophy tutor wrote that 'Heath's work in Economics was on the border line of being Exhibition standard ... it looks as though, if he waited until he was a year older, he might very well get an Exhibition'. An Exhibition is an award slightly below the standard of a Scholarship. I did not want to wait for another year, however, so I settled for entry in autumn 1935, as a commoner.

Meanwhile my father had become foreman of his firm of builders and, when the owner died in the early 1930s, he took it over. Throughout, both my father and mother were working intolerably hard and my father devoted more and more of his time at home at night to his office work, dealing with estimates and accounts. He stayed up late and I well remember being woken up by my mother shouting downstairs to him from her bedroom, 'Do come up to bed, dear, you will be worn out.' It meant that neither of them could have proper holidays. However, in due course my father was able to buy a small Hillman Minx car which I drove with him and the family along the coast road to Birchington and back on my seventeenth birthday: an indulgence made possible only because, in those days, driving licences were not required.

As I prepared for Oxford I realised that an inevitable change in my way of life lay ahead. I was to keep a room at home in Broadstairs until the end of the 1960s, and remain in close touch with school contemporaries, teachers and friends in the area for even longer. I already sensed back in 1935, however, that, once I had gone up to Oxford, I should see less of my family and life would never be the same again.

Chapter 2

FROM BROADSTAIRS TO BALLIOL

Oxford 1935–1937

On a sunny autumn day in October 1935 I loaded my baggage into my father's Hillman Minx and set off with my parents on the four-hour drive from Broadstairs to Oxford. It was the first time they had been anywhere near the city and I could see how impressed they were by its historic grandeur. On our arrival at Balliol they found a more modern nineteenth-century building which was far less attractive than Magdalen, University College, The Queen's and others which they had seen while driving through the city. We were greeted at the porter's lodge and guided through the front quad to my room on Staircase 10. As we made our way there, we saw for the first time part of the original buildings in the libraries and the old Senior Common Room. The original chapel had been replaced with new buildings some sixty years earlier – and it was in its replacement that I was to spend so much of my time at Oxford.

I was the first member of my family ever to go to a university and my parents were, naturally, delighted. But I already suspected that they were also apprehensive about the financial difficulties that they were facing. They had also wondered, they told me some time later, whether our humble background would put me at a permanent disadvantage compared with many of my contemporaries. I was aware of this risk, but such was my sense of exhilaration at going up to Oxford for the first time that I cannot claim to have been deeply unsettled by such thoughts.

For me, as for many freshmen, this was my first experience of living away from home, so we shared a somewhat emotional farewell before my parents drove off back to Broadstairs. Once they had gone, I soon gave way totally to my rising excitement, as I sensed how all the yearning and hard work of the last few years was now reaching its culmination. This was the beginning of an entirely new life. Balliol had some 280 members, mostly undergraduates, and my life in college began with getting to know my contemporaries at the freshmen's dinner on the evening of Wednesday

9 October. Then I gradually met others of more senior rank, which was a mind-opening experience. I soon found that Balliol had the most cosmopolitan collection of undergraduates of any college, with a large number of scholars from Africa and India, as well as from Australia, Germany and the United States. One such overseas Balliol student, albeit after my time, was Seretse Khama, who became President of Botswana; I was later to defy the Conservative Whips in 1950 by voting against a proposal from the Labour Commonwealth Secretary Patrick Gordon Walker to ban Seretse from his native country in an attempt to suppress the nationalist movement there.

By presenting its undergraduates with such an extensive circle of potential friends and acquaintances, the College provided a breadth of human experience, and understanding, that I had never previously experienced. The College was also rightly renowned for its emphasis on public service, tolerance and intellectual integrity. This was deeply ingrained both in the social life of the College and in the tutorial system. At Balliol, the sons of wealthy parents, such as Hugh Fraser, the son of Lord Lovat, mingled with those of us living on scholarships or loans: the public school and grammar school products were all mixed in together.

With his aristocratic Scottish family background, Hugh was a buoyant character who always seemed to be enjoying life. His lively sense of humour constantly caused him to break into laughter in the quad and, although he played a limited part in University Conservative Party politics in those days, his political views and ambitions used to infiltrate his speeches in the Oxford Union. Having been brought up in a small coastal town, and having never travelled further north than London, nor west of Southampton, I had a lot of adjusting to do. I had rarely encountered public schoolboys before, other than those from St Lawrence College at Ramsgate, close to Chatham House, and I was a little apprehensive about the prospect of suddenly being surrounded by them. In those days, overcoming class differences was not easy.

In another college, I might have faced deep class prejudice. But at Balliol what little snobbery there was tended to be intellectual rather than social and, to my delight as well as surprise, I soon found myself mixing easily with freshmen from almost every conceivable background. I also learned an early lesson in intellectual rigour when, over dinner in hall, I put forward a proposition on nineteenth-century politics. I felt that I had done so convincingly, if a little dogmatically. 'I can't sit and listen to nonsense like this,' said my colleague opposite, Rodney Hilton from Manchester Grammar School. 'Let me put you right.' He did so with great force, both in argument and in volume. He later got a first in history, and spent the rest of his life as a professor and writer. He did me an immense favour by forcing me to rethink all my views before propounding them – and making me prepare my lines of argument rather more thoroughly in time for my first tutorials.

Two Balliol contemporaries who became particular friends were George Hood from Newcastle Royal Grammar School, who was later ordained and spent much of his life as a missionary in the Far East, and Freddie Temple, Rugby-educated and the nephew of a future Archbishop of Canterbury, William Temple. Freddie sat opposite me at the freshmen's dinner, and we hit it off immediately. Another freshman I got to know was Nigel Nicolson, a likeable Old Etonian and subsequently a controversial Tory MP, who gave us a glimpse of a very different world. He came from Sissinghurst in Kent, where his parents, the authors Harold Nicolson and Vita Sackville-West, behaved and entertained in their celebrated and exotic fashion. Such a lifestyle must have seemed even more bizarre to another of my friends, A. R. W. Bavin, who came from a poor family in the East End of London, as I saw for myself when I stayed with them one night during vacation. The senior scholar in our year, Robert was one of the few from humbler backgrounds who did at times seem to find the Balliol hothouse overwhelming. He never developed much social self-confidence, and sadly did not achieve the prominence in the civil service which his superb brain, and his double first, led everyone to expect. He made the best Senior Scholar's speech that I ever heard at a St Catherine's Day dinner at Balliol, an event which is held annually to commemorate the patron saint of the College.

I found it tremendously bracing to spend each day mixing with such a varied and talented group of people, and student life at Balliol certainly presented all of us with as many opportunities for socialising as anyone could wish for: at meals three times a day; during an undergraduate discussion over a drink in someone's rooms; at the fortnightly concerts in hall on Sundays; or in connection with sporting activities – which were in my case rather limited. This all taught me how to hold my own in company at all levels, and also provided me with some very close lifelong friends. I soon laid to rest any concerns on my parents' part that I might feel isolated or socially out of place there.

As I settled down into college, attending tutorials and lectures and busily playing a part in various organisations, I always had hanging over me the problem of how to pay for my university career. On my admission to Balliol the Kent Education Committee, responsible for the area in which my family lived and for my former grammar school, granted me a loan of £120 a year, which was to be repaid as soon as I left Oxford. A prominent City solicitor, Royalton Kisch, whose house my father looked after while he was away, kindly made me an additional loan of £40 a year, for which he later refused repayment. But I still had to lean on my family for about £20 a term, a heavy burden on them. I was able to help a little myself during my vacation by coaching the son of a prominent resident at Dumpton Gap, Mr Suenson-Taylor, through his public school entry examination, but the troubling question was for how long my parents could continue their support. If my father's business had hit a bad patch, there was every possibility that my Oxford career, and with it my growing aspirations for the future, might have been curtailed. During that first term, this fear never left me. It was aggravated by the further anxiety about whether I would be able to get a suitable job afterwards to enable me to repay the Education Committee loan.

On arrival at Balliol, I learned that the organ scholar was retiring at the end of the academic year, and that a contest would be held in December to select his successor. This gave me hope, for the organ scholarship would bring in another £80 per year. Balliol had a very high reputation for its music, established largely by Benjamin Jowett as Master in the late nineteenth century. In addition to the organ scholarship, there was also the Nettleship scholarship for composition, of which the distinguished musician, critic and writer Sir Donald Tovey, later Professor of Music at Edinburgh University, had been the first holder. Both scholarships required the holder to read for a major degree, in addition to anything else for which they might sit in the way of music. On my arrival the composition scholarship was held by George Malcolm, already a brilliant pianist who later gained world fame also as a conductor and organist, but perhaps most of all as a player on the harpsichord. George was two years my senior but he was always most supportive towards me. Although our interests and enthusiasms converged, however, most of my activities were occupying the day time, while he was always attracted to the in-college late-night life. Sadly, for a variety of reasons, George never enjoyed the acclaim which his talents ought to have attracted.

In preparation for the organ scholarship, I took lessons twice a week at St Aldate's church and practised every day on our own organ in the College chapel. This was a rather old-fashioned, two-manual instrument with a limited number of stops and a straight pedal board. For the contest I concentrated on pieces by Bach, Mendelssohn and Vaughan Williams. The adjudicator was Dr Ernest Walker, a well-known composer in his day who had long been associated with the College. I told him what I had prepared, and he invited me to play the Bach 'St Anne' Fugue, three movements from Mendelssohn's Sonata No. 2 and, to finish, the 'Rhosymedre' Prelude by Vaughan Williams. I did not encounter any of the other contestants and got no indication from Ernest Walker of the result. That night, however, I returned to my room to find a short note waiting for me from the tutor for admissions, Roy Ridley. 'Dear Heath,' it read, 'I am so glad to be able to let you know at once that we elected you tonight to the Organ Scholarship.' My relief was immense and, as I received it for three years, I was able altogether to spend four years at Balliol, rather than the usual three for someone studying Modern Greats. This was a real privilege, and I was determined to make the most of it, both by keeping up my academic work rate and by taking full advantage of the many other opportunities of student life.

At the time I went up, Balliol's already formidable reputation was being further enhanced by the then Master, A. D. Lindsay. 'Sandy' Lindsay had previously been Professor of Moral Philosophy at Glasgow University, a chair once held by Adam Smith. There the comparison ended, for Lindsay was a socialist whose Christian faith was an integral part of his political philosophy. In 1926, two years after he became Master, he had caused an uproar, both among the College parents and more widely in the University, by supporting the General Strike; and, in 1931, he had entertained Mahatma Gandhi for a fortnight in the Master's Lodge during the Indian leader's visit to Britain.

In college, we were all automatically made members of the Junior Common Room, and were charged ten shillings a term for it. The first meeting I attended, which was packed, took place on the second Sunday after my arrival and the president, David Wallace, announced that we had been invited to contribute to a fund for sending food and medicine to those affected by the Japanese invasion of Manchuria. The problem was how to pay for it. Should ten pounds, for example, be taken from JCR funds, in which case the organisers might think that there had been no personal interest shown by the Balliol undergraduates? The alternative was to take a voluntary collection there on the spot, but this might not amount to very much. As the meeting was fairly evenly divided between these two options, the president needed all his diplomatic skill to handle it. In order to suggest that our corporate concern had been backed up by many acts of individual support, which had ensured a generous collection, he proposed that the committee should send a donation of twelve pounds, thirteen shillings and eight pence from the JCR's funds. This odd sum would amount to a convincing demonstration of both our corporate generosity and the individual personal interest of everyone present!

That night the president of the Junior Common Room also announced that the bursar, a retired colonel, wished to speak to us. The broad-chested, imposing frame of Colonel Duke strode through the meeting and, standing in front of the fireplace, he declared: 'The smoke from the chimneys of that bloody Trinity next door is ruining the food in the Senior Common

Room kitchen.' For those unfamiliar with inter-college politics in Oxford, to each other the two colleges were always 'bloody Balliol' and 'bloody Trinity'. 'That mustn't be allowed to go on,' he finished and strode out of the room.

Late that night a small party (of whom I was not one) left college, having obtained permission to get back in late after hours, and went up to a building site in north Oxford where they secured some ladders, together with sacks of sand and cement. Back in college they put the ladders against the wall and climbed up to the roof over the Trinity kitchen. There they mixed the cement and the sand and, having dampened them appropriately, pushed the mixture down the Trinity kitchen chimney. Leaving the product to harden, they took the ladders back to the site and returned to college. The operation was successful. When the Trinity chefs lit their kitchen fires the next morning, the smoke at first went up the chimney and then poured back again into the kitchen, bringing with it soot and age-old dirt of every kind. The Trinity breakfast for everyone was ruined, but the Balliol dons had theirs unspoilt. Such co-operation between junior and senior members seems to me the hallmark of a great and happy college.

Outside the College I joined various University organisations, starting with the political and the musical. As both my political thinking and my commitment to political life hardened, I had naturally faced a choice between the competing parties. Without question, the key for me was freedom of the individual. Politicians and philosophers may squabble about the true nature of freedom, and many will always subvert its slogans and concepts to suit their own ends. But true freedoms – freedom of thought and expression, freedom from the knock on the door in the dead of night, freedom from nuisance and harassment, freedom to develop and to live a fulfilling life – these were the freedoms which inspired me and so many of my generation in the 1930s. These are values which, by their nature, are often taken for granted in good times. But, for Europeans in the 1930s, they seemed to be values which could shortly be eclipsed for ever.

The Liberals remained committed to an open society, and to freedom in both the social and economic spheres, a potent combination, but it was already clear to me that they were a spent force in British politics and that nothing practical could be achieved by supporting them. I never considered joining the Labour Party as an alternative – because, in those days before the advent of the 'spin-doctor', everyone could see socialism for what it was: a doctrine of control, centralisation and public ownership. Nonetheless, out of curiosity, I did attend the TUC conference at Margate in September 1935, shortly before going up to Oxford, the first such conference I had attended. It was intriguing to see for myself the heart and soul of the party. I remember thinking how elderly the delegates looked, as outdated as the ideas they were propagating.

The conference itself was a dramatic one, which set the scene for the Labour Party conference a few weeks later, at which George Lansbury, the party's pacifist leader, parted company with Labour's own policy of sanctions against Italy and with its policy on rearmament. It was Ernest Bevin, supported by resolutions taken by the TUC at Margate, who caught the mood of the country; and shortly afterwards Lansbury was forced to step down in favour of Clement Attlee. I was pleased that the trade unions were finally committing themselves to tackling fascism, but was still convinced that socialism smacked too much of state control. I concluded that a moderate form of Conservatism offered the best foundation for a free society, and that the best course for me was to campaign for that brand of thinking, within the Conservative Party. But I continued to believe in fairness and deplored the snobbishness of many Conservatives, as well as the envy and hatred of the party which were the consequence of it.

Although Baldwin was a moderate Conservative who genuinely wanted to unite the country, he and the party were too stuck in the old class system for my liking. For me, as for most of my political colleagues, it was the emerging new Conservatism, inspired by Winston Churchill, Anthony Eden and Harold Macmillan, which offered the best hope for building a modern, truly meritocratic Britain. For me, then as now, these were the true Conservatives: compassionate men who believed in opportunity, and a decent standard of living, for all. Indeed, it was probably Churchill who later was to set out the values of One Nation Conservatism most clearly, when he explained in a post-war speech that 'We are for the ladder . . . Let all try their best to climb . . . but what happens if anyone slips off the ladder? Our reply is "We shall have a good net and the finest social ambulance service in the world."'

Naturally, therefore, I made first for the Oxford University Conservative Association (OUCA), which I joined almost immediately. As soon as I contacted OUCA, I was made the Balliol OUCA secretary, in time even to authorise my own membership card. After discovering that it was quite normal to belong to any or all political societies at the same time, I joined the undergraduate Liberal and Labour groups, too, so that I could also hear their main speakers. It was at a Labour meeting that I had the chance to hear Major Attlee, the party's new leader.

Most exciting of all was becoming a member of the Oxford Union Society, whose debating activities have produced so many of our foremost politicians in what is now over a century and three-quarters of its existence. I eagerly attended the first meeting of term, a debate on home affairs. This debate remains for ever in my memory because it was wound up by Sir John Simon, then Home Secretary. He held us spellbound for half an hour dealing systematically with every point which had been raised by the other speakers, entirely without a note. I had never witnessed such a performance before and, although I had always hitherto written out in full my speeches at school or for other audiences, I made a quiet but firm resolve that this was the model I should set out to emulate.

Attendance on Thursday night each week at the Union debate immediately became imperative. However, whereas many freshmen at once made their maiden speeches on the floor of the house, I did not feel confident enough to do so in my first term. I was doubtful whether I was sufficiently acclimatised to the Union style to be able to influence those present, and I had no desire whatever to make a speech just for the sake of doing so.

Towards the end of my first term I wrote to my old headmaster at Chatham House, H. C. Norman. Summarising my early endeavours, I told him: 'Settling down and work . . . have left no time for doing great things, and I am now very sceptical of biographies in which it is related how great men "hit" Oxford in their first week.' 'The College is delightful,' I went on, adding that I had joined the Union, where I had 'spent the term sitting at the feet of the great men of the day, so that next term I may speak a bit better.' All these external activities, however, had to be fitted in around a busy term's work, for there were 'Mods' – first-year examinations – to take before Easter. Perhaps my strongest impression of all from those early days at Oxford was the excitement of being left to organise and discipline myself; and of being treated, for the first time, as a grown-up, and accepted as a serious adult by the dons.

There was also the inspiring experience of getting to know the Master. In our first year we had to go and see Lindsay, in pairs, each with a weekly essay. These sessions were initially approached with trepidation. The essay had to be on a topic, maybe an issue of morality, quite separate from the subject studied for our degree courses, and Lindsay was an exacting listener. In fact, he would generally pull everyone's essays to pieces. The challenge was finding the will and strength of argument to fight back and win through. Everything had to be intellectually rigorous, properly thought through and emotionally genuine. It was not long before I appreciated that, although he was socially reserved, Lindsay was a generous-spirited man, who also possessed a broad and piercing intellect. He was open-minded and so opened our minds too: he was marvellously gifted at encouraging lively debate.

He regarded participation in discussion not only as the best way of finding the right course of action, but also as the prerogative of the individual in a free society. In his view, it was both the right and the responsibility of intelligent people to debate the issues of the day. I am sure that he was correct to argue that a climate of constructive and open debate is the best possible buttress for a free society, for, so long as debate and good humour flourished in our land, repression of the kind which was spreading across mainland Europe in the 1930s was always going to be unthinkable. Although Lindsay's own principles were strongly social democratic, he was completely non-dogmatic and non-doctrinaire both in argument and in deed. He believed that democracy alone, and the freedom of expression it underpinned, could give each individual the chance to live his or her own full life. Lindsay had more influence on me at Oxford than anyone else. Ironically, by hastening my intellectual development, this great socialist probably strengthened my innate Conservatism: and the more I exposed my instinctive political views to intellectual questioning, the more solid and rigorous their foundations became.

It was little wonder that, after their first year, most Balliol men missed those weekly encounters with Lindsay. So, when I was elected president of the Junior Common Room in my final year, I suggested that it would be useful if he opened the Master's Lodge one evening each week for a discussion with him. He readily agreed. Anybody from the College could go, and we would sit around every Wednesday evening, many on the floor, while he would lean on the mantelpiece. We plied him with our views and argued fiercely about every issue of the day: philosophical, literary, political or religious.

The College tutors formed a remarkable group of men. I spent my first two terms preparing for my Mods, for which a considerable amount of time was spent on the history of both the Middle Ages and modern times. Tutorials with these dons were astonishingly frank and informal. Even though the masters of Chatham House had spent an immense amount of time with us out of school hours, I had never enjoyed the kind of free, open and relaxed relationship with them that I now enjoyed with the Balliol dons. This was brought home vividly to me in an early tutorial with the medieval historian Vivian Galbraith, later to become a professor, first at Edinburgh and subsequently back at Oxford. After listening to me reading an essay on 'The Power of the Crown in the Fourteenth Century' in which I argued that the Privy Seal was increasingly used to control the sovereign, he exploded: 'You have got the whole thing arse about face! You see,' he went on, 'the King used the Privy Seal to keep control of his own Council, not the reverse.' From then on no idea was too outrageous for examination, and I revelled in the arguments which tutorials encouraged.

Humphrey Sumner, who later became Warden of All Souls, was the senior tutor for modern history, which in those days was largely nineteenth century – and he was almost the exact opposite of Vivian Galbraith. His smooth, polished manner and his grasp of every minute detail was displayed to the full in his masterpiece *Russia and the Balkans*, published during my time at Balliol, in 1937. He always tried to jolly us gently along, and his enthusiasm for his subject was infectious. Moving later on to the real meat of the degree, I was tutored in philosophy by Charles Morris, later to become a notable headmaster of King Edward's School in Birmingham; and by John Fulton, who taught political theory and history with an exceptional grasp of the practical, as well as philosophical, problems involved. He later became the Principal of University College, Swansea, then Vice-Chancellor of Sussex University. He was also chairman of the Royal Commission which reported on the organisation and procedures of the civil service in 1968. My economics tutor was Maurice Allen. He possessed a brilliant intellect, but the facility with which he himself mastered the most complicated and abstruse concepts sometimes made it a little difficult for him to understand the problems that the rest of us might encounter when we tried to take them on board. Going to the International Monetary Fund and then into the Bank of England as an economist after the Second World War, he chose to give up academic life, stayed at the Bank and became one of its directors. Being near at hand in the City, and at home at Sandwich, he remained a close friend until his death.

This free-thinking atmosphere, combined with the turbulent political situation of the time, helped me to develop my beliefs. After the failure of the second Labour administration in 1931, a national government had been formed to combat the depression. It was made up largely of Conservatives with support from a section of the Liberal Party and a small number of Labour people and was led, by the time I reached Oxford in 1935, by Stanley Baldwin. Baldwin's leadership was calm and moderate, appealing to all classes and offering hope for the future to a people desperate for peace and prosperity. Despite the national government's popularity, the majority of socialists opposed it and, with just over fifty Members in the House of Commons until the election on 14 November 1935, the Labour Party in those years was very much in the wilderness. Meanwhile, across mainland Europe fascism was on the rise: Mussolini had been in power for thirteen years, Hitler for two; and even in Britain we had Oswald Mosley's Blackshirts fighting their running battles on the streets of the East End of London with their communist counterparts.

My beliefs at this stage were shaped both by my own ever-widening experiences of the world and by the many books which I read while at Oxford. I consumed Pelican paperbacks on politics, philosophy and economics with particular zeal. Written mostly by stalwarts of the left such as G. D. H. Cole, Harold Laski and R. H. Tawney, these popular sixpenny editions, with their distinctive blue covers, were the bibles of left-wing young men in the 1930s. On the whole, although I found them stimulating, they only confirmed me in my antipathy towards socialism. I also remember being very impressed indeed by George Bernard Shaw's fable *The Adventures of the Black Girl in her Search for God*. In this short work, Shaw set out the development of man's idea of God. The book was condemned by many of the clerical authorities of the time, but I recall that it sold some 200,000 copies within a year of publication. I was later to meet Shaw at Lady Astor's house in St James's Square at an evening party. I had met her when she had spoken at one of my Union debates. Shaw was well into his eighties and just sat quietly as people were introduced to him. The light was only shining dimly by then, and I had the impression that the famous writer was all too aware of the limitations that his advanced age imposed upon him.

More than anything else, however, it was two books which came to prominence during my time at Oxford that convinced me, once and for all, that neither socialism nor the pure free market could provide the answer to the problems which beset us. The first was John Maynard Keynes's *General Theory of Employment, Interest and Money*, published in 1936. Inspired by a world depression which had been caused by laisser-faire policies, it put forward a wholly new view of economics, which Keynes and his followers used to demonstrate that full and stable levels of employment could be maintained if governments intervened counter-cyclically in the economy. Although his ideas were not put into practice in Britain until after the Second World War, they provided some intellectual basis for Roosevelt's 'New Deal', which was already successfully pulling America out of depression. It was the Keynesians, and Keynes's Cambridge protégé John Hicks in particular, who proved that the New Deal could work as well in principle as it did in practice.

The second work which made a big impact on me was Harold Macmillan's *The Middle Way*, published in 1938. This was, in Macmillan's words, 'a plea for planned capitalism', arguing that a degree of economic planning could make commerce and industry more efficient and generate the resources which would help protect the needy in society, without any threat to individual liberty. Indeed, it was only this form of mixed economy that could sustain the political freedoms that we cherished. These works provided the philosophical basis for the One Nation Group which I helped to found as a young MP after the war.

My Christian faith also provided foundations for my political beliefs. In this, I was influenced by the teaching of William Temple. Temple's impact on my generation was immense. He believed that a fairer society could be built only on moral foundations, with all individuals recognising their duty to help others. Like Lindsay, he was a socialist and, in his wish to redress the balance of power between those who own and those who produce, he sometimes failed to see that some would seek through socialist measures not justice, but power for its own sake. He was, however, the first Anglican leader for decades to set out the Church's teachings in modern terms. He propounded a view of morality which was not preoccupied with sexuality, but which was relevant to the myriad problems besetting the individual in the personal, professional and social spheres. On mainland Europe, the related but more conservative doctrines of Christian Democracy had, regrettably, been submerged by fascism and nationalism. But many of us were already intrigued and rather attracted by the apparent kinship of Christian Democratic thinking with our own moderate Conservatism, which we similarly predicated upon the view that the individual can be truly fulfilled only as part of a social unit.

During my second term at Oxford, I felt confident enough to make my maiden speech at the Union and, in February 1936, I put in my name to speak against the motion 'That England is fast following in the footsteps of Imperial Rome, with no clear role in the world and little influence left'. Maiden speeches are always supposed to be terrifying occasions, but it did not strike me that way after so much debating at school. At that time, I was accustomed to writing my speeches out in extended note form, and did so on this occasion. I condemned the prevalent view that we were a declining power, particularly in face of German and Italian military growth. We succeeded in defeating the motion, by a margin of 83–77. My speech was warmly received and written congratulations were soon being passed along to me. The University magazine, *Isis*, described it as an 'an extremely forcible and able maiden speech'. A few weeks later I was on my feet again, opposing the motion that 'the present system of education is unsuited to a democratic state'. Defending the right of more affluent parents to choose their children's education, I argued that 'equality of education means equality of wealth, and equality of wealth means communism'.

I also wasted no time in auditioning for the Oxford Bach Choir, which I joined as a first bass; we rehearsed on Monday evenings. It was originally intended that our first work of 1936 should be Vaughan Williams's *A Sea Symphony*, but this was pre-empted by our Memorial Concert for King George V, who died on 20 January; we sang the Brahms *Requiem* in his memory. We had only ten days in which to prepare it, but Sir Hugh Allen, the former director of the Royal College of Music and Professor of Music at Oxford, was brought back to conduct it and immediately got down to business. The rehearsals, three nights a week, went on past the usual hour and a half, and until ten o'clock at night. At the first rehearsal, Sir Hugh suddenly realised that some of the sopranos and altos from North Oxford were sneaking away down the side of the sloped seats of the science laboratory lecture hall where we rehearsed, in order to catch their last buses home. He stopped, threw down his baton, flung his arms high and, looking up at Cyril Bailey, the senior Balliol don and oldest member of the choir, shouted at the top of his voice. 'My God, Cyril, it's the same women creeping out early now as thirty years ago!' The performance was both historic and musically accomplished.

In due course we caught up with Vaughan Williams's *A Sea Symphony*, a work which has always kept its hold on me, from its brilliant opening trumpet call summoning the sea, followed by the choir crashing in with great waves, up to the pianissimo chords at the end of the last movement: 'O my brave soul! O farther sail!' It is said that the first performance of the work, which took place at the Leeds Festival in October 1910 under Vaughan Williams's own baton, had, to put it kindly, received mixed reviews. But, after hearing Sir Hugh Allen perform in with the Oxford Bach Choir on an earlier occasion, Vaughan Williams wrote words on his score to the effect 'I thought I had written an unsingable work, but tonight you have sung it magnificently.'

We also performed Haydn's *The Seasons*, but the overwhelming impact on me was made by Beethoven's *Missa Solemnis*, which we sang in Oxford Town Hall. One of Beethoven's greatest works, it has played its part at intervals throughout my life in performances by some of the world's most renowned conductors, including Toscanini, Solti, von Karajan, Giulini and Haitink. As I have written elsewhere, I have found music to be a joy for life, and devotional music of this calibre often gives me the most intense joy of all. Perhaps this is because, in common with many of my contemporaries in this country, I first experienced great music through performing it in the English choral tradition. I owe so much to the Oxford Bach Choir above all others for some truly life-enhancing experiences, which profoundly deepened my appreciation of several works. Nothing can get you inside a work, and the mind of its composer, quite like studying and then performing it.

Music was not, however, my only form of relaxation. I discovered the delights of punting with friends along the River Cherwell. Otherwise I did nothing more strenuous than dancing, and playing tennis; lawn tennis in the summer and table tennis in the winter. As the university magazine *Isis* later put it, I held the table tennis bat 'as if it were a soup spoon', a technique which dazzled some opponents. I returned to my family home in Broadstairs for the long summer vacation of 1936 a contented young man. For all the excitement and stimuli of Oxford life, I had missed my parents and my brother John.

I never went home during term time, since I had no car – for in those far-off days only a few chic Londoners had them. That summer, I reverted to a familiar routine of swimming, sunbathing, walking along the cliffs with my dog Erg, playing tennis with old friends such as the Ravens and cycling around southern England. I also worked on my Oxford books, and caught up with old Chatham House friends and masters. I continued to live frugally, drinking little alcohol and never smoking. As a result, my total expenditure while up at Oxford, including clothes, travel and holidays, averaged just £220 a year. Of course, a summer in Broadstairs did not feel quite the same now that my horizons had broadened. Our family life was just as close and pleasant as it had ever been, but, after the heady experience of Oxford, it was to be predicted that the long days in Broadstairs would eventually pall a little for me. So I resolved that, during the next summer vacation, I would use some of my savings to make my first trip abroad since the visit to Paris in 1931.

Returning to Balliol in October 1936, I took up my duties as organ scholar, and also became secretary of the Balliol College Musical Society, which had been established in October 1885 by John Farmer, who had been brought from Harrow by Benjamin Jowett in that year to become the first director of music at Balliol. Farmer had studied at the conservatories of Leipzig and Coburg and collected the Harrow School Songs. The Musical Society was renowned throughout Oxford for the top-class soloists and chamber musicians who played to it on alternate Sunday evenings. At that time, free tickets were available to any member of the University and there was always a full house. Helped by this new position, I got to know Ernest Walker, who had awarded me my organ scholarship, and he would recount to me how well he had known Brahms and showed me some of his original manuscripts.

The most significant event of my time in charge of the Balliol Music Society was the 1,000th concert in 1937, part of which I conducted. We decided on principle that everyone taking part had to have some connection with Balliol, and were able to include two splendid compositions by Balliol men: Ernest Walker's *Four Songs Op. 10* for mixed-voice choir, with piano accompaniment played by George Malcolm; and Donald Tovey's *Balliol Dances* for two pianos. The Balliol Choral Society – consisting of men from Balliol and Trinity, plus sopranos and altos from Somerville and Lady Margaret Hall – sang the choral works. Even those members of the Balliol choir who came from other colleges satisfied the 'Balliol test', but our problems of qualification began when we decided to open the concert with *Zadok the Priest* for choir and orchestra by Handel – and later when

Ernest Walker and Victor Hely-Hutchinson played the Bach Double Concerto in C Major. We were a proud college, and the Balliol credentials of Bach and Handel had to be demonstrated. This was all settled when Cyril Bailey, senior tutor and one of the stalwarts of Oxford music, announced that the College had declared both Bach and Handel honorary fellows for the evening.

As the College organ scholar, I was now required to be in chapel at eight o'clock every weekday morning, to play the organ at daily service, as well as every Sunday evening, during my remaining three years. I learned from the Master that the interior of the chapel was to be refurbished, which would involve several months' work. It had long been known that the Visitor to the College, Lord Blanesburgh of Alloa, had arranged for the necessary funds for the chapel renovation to be provided for in his will. Lindsay had now succeeded in persuading him of the pleasure it would give to Balliol if the work could be carried out in the peer's lifetime, in order that due honour might be done him for this gift. The new panelling was to be carved from a special walnut which was already prepared and stored in Wales. I pointed out to the Master that in this context the existing aged organ case of oak would not blend harmoniously with the new panelling. Might it not therefore be possible to have a new case built in the same walnut, and perhaps persuade the Visitor to provide a new organ as well? I was delighted when I was told that he had agreed to do this. A new three-manual Harrison was built, the first to be installed since the Coronation organ of 1936 in Westminster Abbey. While this was being done, I accompanied services on a Steinway grand piano. The new organ and stalls were dedicated on Friday 6 May 1938 by two Balliol archbishops, Cosmo Lang of Canterbury and William Temple of York. I played for the service, and the recital afterwards was given by William Harris, the organist of St George's Chapel, Windsor Castle.

Some of my own most rewarding musical activities during these years came about through my work with the Balliol Players. They were a group some twelve or fifteen strong who toured Berkshire, Oxfordshire and the west country at the end of each summer term with a Greek play, mostly staged in the open air. For two years they invited me to write the music for them and to produce it on the tour: I wrote the music for a production of Aristophanes' *The Frogs* in 1937 and, together with Walt Rostow, later a foreign affairs adviser to President Lyndon Johnson, for a production of the same author's *Acharnians* in 1938. This was how I first got to know that part of England and had the opportunity to play the organ in Bath Abbey. One Sunday afternoon at Corfe Castle in Dorset, the town produced its local brass band, the Wareham Silver Band. Coming down from our preparations for the performance at the castle on the hill I was then invited to conduct it, my first experience of such a band. Some fifty years later I returned to brass-band music, conducting the Black Dyke Mills Band, for many years the foremost such band in England, in a recording, now transferred to compact disc, which included a new work, 'Morning Cloud', composed by Robert Farnon in honour of my ocean racing yachts of that name.

Politics, however, remained my central interest. As the College OUCA representative responsible for recruiting new members, I had to visit every member of each new intake in the hope of persuading them to sign up. Becoming known in this way provided a strong base of personal support for my subsequent elections as president of the Junior Common Room, chairman of OUCA and president of the Union. It later transpired that I was the only person to have held all three offices while an undergraduate. Winston Churchill came to Oxford in October 1936 to support his close friend and scientific adviser Professor Frederick Lindemann, who was standing as the Conservative candidate in a by-election for the University seat. Then in his 'wilderness years', Churchill addressed a packed meeting at the Union. This required him to break a pledge he had made never to return to Oxford, in the wake of a rancorous dispute between the Oxford Union Society and his son Randolph.

After the notorious 'King and Country' debate in 1933, Randolph had campaigned to have the page in the Union minute book recording that evening of shame expunged from the record. He wrote to life members of the Society and proposed that a special adjournment motion should be introduced to bring this about. When this motion was voted upon, it was heavily defeated, very largely because Randolph was so loathed in the University. But that was not the end of his humiliation, for he eventually ended up in the hands of the police, after a posse of Union members had chased him around Oxford with the intention of debagging him, and found himself fined two pounds for parking illegally.

In his speech to us upon his return to Oxford in 1936, Winston Churchill stressed the urgent need for Britain to rearm. When he added that the University required a definite and Conservative set of principles, rather than a wishy-washy set of opinions, he was applauded enthusiastically. Afterwards Lindemann took Churchill and three others, including me, back to his rooms in Christ Church for a nightcap. There we sat on the floor by the fire listening to the great man expounding his views on political affairs over a series of whiskies. It was the first time I had met Churchill, and I was struck not only by the force and clarity of his arguments, but by his sheer presence. He also reinforced my determination to help articulate and later implement a new brand of Conservatism. Around two in the morning he patted the side of his chair and declared, 'It is time I went off to that ducal palace.' So off he went to stay at his birthplace at Blenheim with his cousin, the Duke of Marlborough, leaving us to talk our way back into college long after the gates were locked, and then explain ourselves to the dean the next day.

Soon after Churchill's visit, the abdication of his friend King Edward VIII burst upon the country. In the JCR at Balliol we had read an early indication of the King's relationship with the American divorcee Wallis Simpson in a four-page weekly rag, the *Week*, edited by Claud Cockburn, which did not receive any publicity in the national media. But we had not expected so explosive a conclusion. We were in sympathy with the King's widely publicised remark on his visit to Wales, that 'Something must be done' about the ravages of unemployment. But compared with the Spanish Civil War which had started a few months previously, and the increasingly obvious threat presented by the Hitler regime, the abdication seemed to most of us undergraduates to pose no particular problem – and was certainly not as gripping as royal events in modern times.

Meanwhile I was continuing to feature regularly in the Union, injecting a little humour into speeches which, I hope, generally bore the Balliol hallmarks: thorough research and clear arguments. After four speeches during the summer term, I was delighted to find myself invited in October 1936 to make my maiden 'paper' speech. This entitled me to one of the opening speeches, a mention on the fly poster and the prestige of speaking from the despatch box rather than the floor. Opening the debate, I argued strongly against the return to Germany by the allies of its former colonies. This was no straightforward task, for at the time there was a growing feeling that the only way to deal with Hitler and his regime was to placate the German people by restoring to them some of their Great War losses. However, as I put it: 'Paying Danegeld never did pay and never will.' The motion was defeated by 191 to 94, marking another stage in the strong movement of Union opinion against Germany. It was the first public demonstration of my belief that the Nazi regime was a menace, and one to which we should in no circumstances give way. When I sat down I received scribbled notes of congratulation from Shebbeare, the then Labour president of the Union; from Anderson, chairman of the University Conservatives; and from Walton, the Liberal chairman. At the end of the debate I was invited up to the Committee Room for drinks with them all.

As my confidence grew, and my own face, name and political opinions became more familiar around the University, I decided to stand, in June 1937, for the presidency of OUCA. My understanding of the threat posed by the dictators probably helped me to defeat John Stokes, an agreeable man but a Franco supporter, who later became a decidedly right-wing Tory MP. In addition, I was elected president of the Federation of University

Conservative Associations. As both offices lasted for a year, I had the chance to begin influencing the direction of University politics. My principal task, though, was to revive OUCA after a period in which it had foundered and rather lost direction. It was extremely important that we should meet the challenge of the left, which was still claiming the allegiance of the majority of politically active undergraduates.

In May 1937, the Coronation of King George VI took place and, shortly afterwards, Stanley Baldwin retired. He had dominated British politics for fifteen years and, of the few Prime Ministers who have been fortunate enough to bow out at a time of their own choosing, none has done so at more fitting a moment. Having led the national government to re-election on the back of his personal popularity, an improving economy and Labour disarray, he fully deserved his dignified departure. Baldwin had also handled the abdication of King Edward VIII with rare skill and wanted to see some glory restored publicly to the monarchy when the new King was crowned at Westminster Abbey. Although George VI was a delicate, highly strung man with none of the immediate charisma of his elder brother, he was both dedicated and dependable and, above all, did not share his brother's fascination with Hitler and the Nazis.

In the summer of 1937 my parents arranged an exchange programme for me with a German student whose home was in Düsseldorf. He came over to England for two weeks in July already speaking good English and proved to be excellent company. I took him round to meet my friends and he was especially at home on the nearby farm in Joss Bay where my Scottish friends the Lyons family lived. Shortly after his return to Düsseldorf I joined him there, having saved some money and, again, with help from my parents. Düsseldorf proved to be a glorious city, the musical home of Mendelssohn and Schumann in the last century, both of whom had worked in its opera house. A lot of its social life was to be found along the banks of the canal through the centre of the city, where all day long we could join groups sitting under the sunshades with a drink on the table, busily engaged in arguing about the political situation, though without personal reference to the Nazi rulers. We then went down to join his parents at Bad Homburg, a luxurious spa just outside Frankfurt, whose like I had not encountered before.

After this exchange, I decided to travel alone down to southern Germany with the idea of spending some six weeks in a quiet spot, both improving my German and getting some work done on the subjects for my degree. I set off for Munich as my first stop-over. There I stayed in a small hostelry near the centre of the city, and visited historic buildings. I spent the evenings in beer cellars, where I took part in student sing-songs. Unfortunately, my rendition of 'Drink to Me Only with Thine Eyes' ran aground after a couple of lines. I was acutely aware in Bavaria of the preponderance of Nazi uniforms and memorials, and quickly came to realise that Hitler's power was far more ingrained than many people back in Britain had so far come to appreciate. Alongside these horrors, however, cultural life in Bavaria was still flourishing. I remember in particular an open-air chamber music concert in the Residenz in Munich with performances of Mozart's 'Eine kleine Nachtmusik' and of Beethoven's Wind Sextet. The small opera house was enchanting but it was out of season for performances.

In the daytime I made a point of visiting the three art galleries. The Alte Pinakothek was overwhelming, with its glorious array of masterpieces by so many artists – quite unlike what I was to see a year later in Madrid, where one of the most striking aspects was the concentration of works by a few of the great masters. There were, however, only a handful of people in this gallery. Then I went off to the Neue Pinakothek, which contained only contemporary works – although I can remember none of any consequence. Those there were obviously politically selected and very ordinary, as were the two other people in the gallery! I then set off for the exhibition of 'Entartete Kunst', contemporary works forbidden by the Nazis for individual ownership, and displayed there to demonstrate the moral turpitude and collapse of those outside the regime's control. On my arrival I was astonished to find a queue four people deep and nearly half a mile long, slowly winding its way into the gallery. I strolled down it to take my turn and, once inside, I found that the queue remained just as solid, moving slowly and attentively around this display of current works, yet showing no emotional reactions to it whatever. What conclusions could I draw from this? Presumably, it would have been inadvisable – politically incorrect – to show any outward signs of appreciation.

I left Munich for Königsee, a small village not far from Berchtesgaden where I found a boarding house on a hill overlooking the picturesque lake. It appeared to me to be quiet and peaceful, a haven where I could return to my studies in peace, with swimming to refresh me whenever I wished. The lake proved, however, to be far too cold for bathing, and the clouds passing at rooftop level prevented me from opening any of the windows. I decided to move inland to a town, Bad Reichenhall, where, with the help of a Lutheran minister whose brass plate I found on the wall of his home, I was taken up to a charming house in the village of Bayrisch Gmain, a few hundred yards from the Austrian border.

I then became the paying guest of Professor Winckler. He and his wife had retired there after he had ceased to be a professor of languages at Berlin University. I could not have been more fortunate. His was the old style – for he was dignified and restrained in his manner, broad-minded and liberal in his outlook, and as well informed as was possible on international affairs. His wife was a very practical hostess. The fact that I did not master the German language there was no fault of theirs. But not everything was sedate and civilised in Bad Reichenhall. Each morning and afternoon, I was aware of local schoolchildren being marched to and fro between school and home singing Nazi songs.

Together the Wincklers and I spent a lot of time climbing in the nearby mountains. In the evenings, I crossed over to Austria. Salzburg lay near by. There I gained my first experience of the Salzburg Festival, where I saw a puppet show and heard the Mozart *Requiem* in the cathedral on 29 August, although I could not afford a ticket to hear Arturo Toscanini conducting the Vienna Philharmonic Orchestra in Mozart and Brahms. Since then Salzburg has become my natural festival home, in particular for the Easter Festival started by Herbert von Karajan after the war, but also very often for some of the summer performances. It is one of the joys of musical life to go to Salzburg, safe in the knowledge not only that the Festival will offer some of the finest musical treats to be found anywhere, but also that each year one will be able to share these experiences with so many European friends of long standing. Sadly, the number of British visitors there seems to grow fewer and fewer each year.

Just as I was about to leave my host and his wife in Bayrisch Gmain, I received a personal invitation, forwarded from the German embassy in London, to attend the forthcoming Nazi Party Rally, in Nuremberg between 6 and 13 September. I was to be a guest of the committee for foreign visitors to the party congress, who would provide me with accommodation, breakfast, tickets of admission for the important functions, and excursions. I was puzzled as to how this came about, for I had no connections with either the German embassy in London or the Nazi Party authorities in Germany. I then discovered that it had been arranged through our neighbour on the opposite side of the avenue in Broadstairs, Fitzroy Weigall, whose son Tony, although a boarder at Harrow while I was at Chatham House, became a close friend. He was at Oxford ahead of me and was then ordained. The Weigalls were a well-known Kentish family and it was Tony's uncle, prominent in Kentish cricketing circles, who had heard that I was in Germany. He knew of my political interests, and thought that it would be useful for me to go to the Nuremberg Rally to find out what the Nazi leaders were really like. I accepted the invitation, and all the necessary arrangements were duly made for me. I stayed in a hotel in Bamberg, a delightful historic city, with a magnificent and architecturally noteworthy cathedral, having an elevated choir and sanctuary at the east end and an elevated congregational platform at the west.

The group of guests from outside Germany was quite small and I quickly got to know two very well indeed: John Baker-White, the Member of Parliament for Canterbury, a prominent publicist for the Conservative Party; and Duncan Carmichael, deputy chairman of the United Dominions Trust and a canny Scot. Every day we were driven by coach into Nuremberg for the Rallies. These were all of a formidable size, and provided on different days for the military, the reservists, the agricultural workers and the young. When the stadium was packed and appropriately hysterical, Hitler would be driven along the road standing up in his car taking the salute, surrounded by his guards, until he stopped and mounted his box. From here he would take the salute of the whole stadium. Our own seats were almost alongside that box.

Outside the stadium, we could move quickly into the streets and watch the military march past the hotel where the leaders were staying, and were often to be seen on the balcony. All of this was impeccably well organised and immensely impressive. It made me recognise for the first time what a fearsome threat Hitler and his forces would be. The political Rally proper was held in the superb city hall, which could accommodate several thousand Nazis. The atmosphere was heated up by a symphony orchestra playing Wagner, and it became more intense as the leaders filed on to the platform. Then came the great fanfare on the arrival of Hitler himself. I was sitting on the inside of the walkway leading up to the platform. It was so narrow that I wondered how Hitler was going to move up it flanked by his guards. In fact, he walked up alone with guards behind him, his shoulder brushing mine as he went past. The crowd cheered continuously until he sat down, and then he listened intently to the speeches of his colleagues, which were mainly attacks on socialism and the supposed role of the Jews in promoting Bolshevism. Hitler reserved his own speech for the great parade outside.

When I saw him close by me, I realised at once that he had not come to office as a result of his physical dominance. His physique was actually extremely modest. It was through the power of his speech-making, and his ability to strike all the right chords with the German people, that this man was bringing Europe to the brink of oblivion. Although his speeches were in many ways disorganised and often rambled on, he knew all the right buttons to press with his audience – an audience who felt that they had suffered at the hands both of those who drafted the Versailles Treaty and of their own nation's weak leaders during the 1920s and early 1930s. In a dreadful way, Hitler's rhetoric gave the Germans the leadership and sense of nationhood that they sought. He made them feel good again about being German.

On the evening of the city hall rally, I was invited to an SS cocktail party which turned out to be a comparatively small affair, consisting mainly of regional functionaries from the Nazi Party and foreign visitors. At this party were all the senior leaders except Hitler himself. Each shook me by the hand and talked for a few minutes, always about my impressions of the rally. Göring was far more bulky and genial than I had imagined, but Goebbels was the reverse – small, pale and, in that setting, rather insignificant-looking. I shall never forget how drooping and sloppy Himmler's hand was when he offered it to me. I later often wondered how such a physically unimpressive man could have harboured such evil and proved so effective as a political figure. This thought came back to me while I stood outside my tent in a field alongside the Rhine one morning in May 1945, listening to a radio report that the captured Himmler had succeeded in committing suicide.

It was a remarkable experience for a young undergraduate to find himself present, albeit as an observer, with those who represented both the heart and the head of the Nazi movement. It is impossible to recapture in words the overwhelming physical impact of these occasions. Although we never felt ourselves to be in danger of attack, the violent and nationalistic nature of the sentiments which whipped up this fervour clearly spelled serious trouble for Europe, and everybody present at those rallies could recognise with perfect clarity the expansionist nature of Nazi intentions. I never for a moment thought either that we could change these dominating attitudes or that we could do any form of a deal with those who held them. When I returned home, I was certainly horrified by the events I had watched, but at the same time I had at least rid myself entirely of any illusions about what my generation would have to face. I was utterly convinced now that a conflict was inevitable, and that it was one for which we must prepare immediately if we were to save Europe from the evil domination of National Socialism. This experience subsequently dominated my political life, my service in the army and then my post-war attitude to international affairs. It also reminds me that it is both ludicrous and offensive to draw any parallels between, on the one hand, the empire that Hitler and his acolytes were trying to build and, on the other, the united, democratic and free Europe that the present German government supports.

Back home, the foreign situation continued to dominate my thoughts. Chamberlain, after a long wait, succeeded Baldwin and, for a time, Anthony Eden, the Foreign Secretary, hoped that the new Prime Minister would launch a fresh initiative abroad. It was not to be. The vigour which Chamberlain brought to No. 10 went largely into moving along the path of appeasement, and I began to think how totally out of touch with the modern world he looked, in his wing collar and formal attire. Although I later watched Macmillan cultivate the image of an Edwardian gentleman, he did it with style, panache and humour. Chamberlain, on the other hand, resembled nothing more than a small-time businessman. I had seen him in action in Margate in October 1936, deputising for Baldwin at my first Tory Party conference. Britain was coming out of depression, and as Chancellor it was up to him to convey the good news. Watching from the balcony, I found him infinitely boring. Indeed, very little was going on at the highest level of the Conservative Party at that time which could inspire a politically active young man, and there seemed to be no grounds for great optimism about what the future held for the party, for the country or for our continent of Europe.

Chapter 3

The Approaching Storm
Oxford, 1937–1939

By the time I returned to Balliol in early October 1937 to begin my third year, I felt fully established at the College, and had an expanding circle of friends. It became commonplace for a group of them to congregate in my rooms – the organ scholar always had room No. 1 on Staircase 1, close to chapel and to the College's front entrance – shortly after ten in the evening, where over coffee, plum-cake and biscuits we would argue about every conceivable subject. In addition to those already mentioned, such as Freddie Temple, George Hood and Robert Bavin, we were now joined by some of the members of the Balliol intake of 1937: in particular Ashley Raeburn, a refugee from Nazi Germany who afterwards became a civil servant at the Treasury and then went on to work in Shell, and Tim Bligh, a science scholar who had been at Winchester and went on to become principal private secretary to Harold Macmillan at No. 10. Tragically, he died early in life.

Freddie Temple joined fiercely in our arguments about personal and political morality and, on one occasion, wrote to his uncle, William, then Archbishop of York, to obtain his views on our unresolved doubts. Freddie went on to become a bishop himself, as did Stephen Verney, another lively member of our group. Both were pacifists. In 1937 Julian Amery came up to Balliol, where his father Leo had been a brilliant undergraduate (then a leading politician in Conservative governments), and joined with others such as Hugh Fraser in another group for political activities. Julian found his father's act somewhat difficult to follow, although he always made his mark in College discussions. I was delighted when he persuaded his father to speak in the Union at a debate on conscription in the spring of 1939.

The man who was, and has remained, my closest friend from within that circle was Madron Seligman. Madron was a mild-mannered Harrovian from a wealthy London family who also came up to Balliol in 1937, halfway through my time there. He is a descendant of the American composer

Edward MacDowell and was a particularly fine sportsman, excelling at cricket, rugby and skiing. In skiing he represented the University, gaining a Blue. Although my sporting ability was limited, we shared many other interests, including music and politics. I remember with particular vividness driving down to London on the morning of Whit Sunday in that glorious early summer of 1939 with Madron and two girlfriends. We picnicked on the way, and then went to the Queen's Hall to hear an unforgettable performance of Beethoven's *Missa Solemnis*, with the BBC Symphony Orchestra and the BBC Choral Society conducted by Toscanini. Both of those girls tragically lost their lives during the war.

Outside this circle, I also got to know Denis Healey, who came up to Balliol a year after me, and who went on to become a Labour Chancellor of the Exchequer and deputy leader of his party. Denis was an earnest Marxist in the late 1930s, and swiftly became a leading figure on the Oxford left. He was noted in college, above all, for his brilliant academic mind – culminating in a double first in Mods and Greats. He was also recognised as a powerful advocate for undergraduate interests and, when I was elected president of the Junior Common Room, he was elected secretary. We had no difficulty working closely together.

In my final year at Balliol, we were joined by Roy Jenkins, another grammar schoolboy with leftish views. Politically, Roy was already very much a man of the mainstream. His speeches in the Union were quiet, earnest and intellectually persuasive. His father was at that time parliamentary private secretary to Clement Attlee, leader of the Labour Party in opposition, and he frequently came to Oxford to take Roy out to lunch. He showed me great personal kindness in inviting me to join them on several occasions, sometimes together with Anthony Crosland, who was based next door to us at Trinity College. Crosland, with whom Jenkins had already struck up a friendship which lasted throughout their parliamentary lives, was at that time more concerned with the League of Nations and Liberal Party activities. He was never really prominent in the Oxford Union until after the war, and then he became its president. His early death in 1977 was a great blow to the Labour Party, which lost both an excellent administrator and an effective political thinker. Almost sixty years after we had met at Oxford, both Roy Jenkins and Denis Healey honoured me with touching speeches at my eightieth birthday celebrations in London (see p. 690–2).

My first Oxford Union debate of real importance was in October 1937. Dr Hugh Dalton, the Chairman of the Labour Party and a formidable public figure, came to Oxford to trumpet the party's new manifesto. We all knew that Dalton would undoubtedly set out a forceful case for the Labour programme, published at the recent conference in Edinburgh, which committed the party for the first time to the nationalisation of everything from steel to the Bank of England. Although I felt that the then national government lacked imagination and compassion when it came to dealing with poverty, I was certain that wholesale nationalisation was not the answer to our country's ills. I relished the prospect of confronting one of its chief architects in a Union debate. The question for debate was 'That this House approves the Labour Party programme', and in opposing this I was supported by Philip Noakes, the undergraduate secretary of the Cambridge Union.

It is remarkable, looking back now, how many of the problems ventilated that night are still on the political agenda. After an opening dig at Hugh Dalton, in which I said he was 'known for his intimate understanding of the working class, gathered, if I may coin a phrase, on the playing fields of Eton', I divided the Labour programme into two sections: measures of socialisation and measures of social reform. Having pointed out the losses experienced by nationalised industries in other countries and condemned the vagueness of Labour's industrial proposals, I then questioned how such an ambitious social programme could be funded. I concluded by listing the achievements of the national government in reducing unemployment, supporting new factories and new industries, together with trading estates, and giving help to local authorities for facilities to improve public health. To these I added my own proposals, especially for dealing with unemployment, such as the provision of factories at special rents, contributions to street works and drainage, targeted financial help for special areas and the setting up of a commission on the location of industry. Britain pioneered the development of policies to deal with the problems of declining regions. The coalition government introduced Special Areas Acts in 1934 and 1937, under which government assistance was provided in the north-east, central Scotland, South Wales and west Cumberland. Some twenty-five years later, my own opportunity would come to help take regional development further. The Labour Party programme was rejected at the Union that night by 162 votes to 125 – a dramatic and thrilling result, for it was the first time in many years that the left had been defeated at the Union.

Hugh Dalton was so furious that, when he was invited to the customary drinks party after the debate, he curtly refused and stalked out. The president, Alan Fyfe, a Conservative product of Glasgow University and then a Balliol man, was delighted. A most impressive and quick-witted speaker, he had achieved the highest office in the Union very speedily and this was now crowned with the first defeat of a Labour plenipotentiary for nearly ten years. Alan was to die, of wounds sustained in Normandy, in 1944. As a result of this debate I was elected to the office of secretary of the Union at the end of the term, comfortably defeating Ashley Bramall –

subsequently my first parliamentary opponent in Bexley – and, at the end of the following term, I was elected librarian, the office next to president.

Meanwhile, many leading Conservatives came to speak to OUCA at my invitation. Nancy Astor, the first woman MP to take her seat in the House of Commons, came shortly after the Dalton debate and sent me an encouraging letter afterwards. 'I really thought it was a very good and keen meeting and a progressive one too,' she wrote. 'I was very glad of this, as I sometimes think people do not realise what a lot of progressive and reforming zeal there is within the ranks of the supporters of the present Government.'

A few days later, I set out to define this in a speech to the OUCA. Warming up the audience with a pop at our opponents – 'one cannot but think that socialists suffer from premature senility in youth and arrested development in old age' – I called on members to spread the word about the Tory revival in Oxford. 'Some of us,' I said, 'feel that perhaps University politics receive more than their due of publicity . . . but what is certain is that the quite erroneous impression all over the country, over the continent and over the Dominions, that Oxford consists of a lot of rather unbalanced political maniacs of the left, must be removed.' I reminded the OUCA members that, as so many young people elsewhere were being 'swept away' by ideologies such as communism or fascism and increasingly talked of them as the 'only ideals which exist in the world', it fell to us to reaffirm that Conservatism 'far from being a matter of making us "yes men" to those above, in authority, is for us a vital, moving, constructive force in which we find our highest ideals'.

Within months, however, my loyalty to Chamberlain's national government was severely tested. In February 1938, Anthony Eden resigned as Foreign Secretary, in the wake of a series of disagreements with Chamberlain, sustained attempts by colleagues at mediation between the two of them and much soul-searching. The reaction to Eden's departure only underlined the depth of parliamentary and public support for his staunch anti-appeasement policies. He was cheered in Downing Street before his resignation had become public knowledge; and Sir John Simon, by now Chancellor of the Exchequer, thought the crisis so great that it might bring down the government. For some time Eden had been the leading critic of appeasement, having opposed Chamberlain's decision not to intervene in the Spanish Civil War in September 1936. He was also bitterly opposed to Chamberlain's attempt to do a deal with Mussolini after Italy's invasion of Abyssinia. But he resigned not over Abyssinia, as many people nowadays seem to think, but over Spain. I heard the news of Eden's resignation in the rooms of one of my few Balliol friends to possess a wireless, the sociable and perceptive Philip Kaiser, who later became an ambassador for his native

United States of America. The news left me speechless, and I returned to my room utterly despondent. With Eden, whom we so admired and revered, now gone, who would stand up to the dictators and prevent Europe being dragged into war?

After Anthony Eden's dramatic announcement, I immediately called a special meeting of OUCA members to decide our collective attitude towards his resignation. After a long and fiery Sunday afternoon discussion, the majority came down firmly in support of Eden and against Chamberlain. For this reason I invited Eden to be the guest of honour at our annual OUCA dinner on 14 November 1938, the other named guest being Sir Thomas Inskip, whom Chamberlain had made Minister of Defence. Everyone came to the dinner with high expectations that, in this, his first major speech outside Parliament since leaving the Cabinet, Eden would vigorously condemn Chamberlain's foreign policy and announce his own intention of leading the party. But no such oration emerged. Sitting next to me, he took his menu, got out his pencil and scribbled a few anodyne notes for a speech on the back. Despite my attempts to egg him on, his remarks were of a most general and cautious kind. He made a few complimentary comments about us and that was just about that. There was no damnation of Chamberlain, nor even of Hitler. We all dispersed at the end, disappointed men.

I first met Harold Macmillan when he came up for a college reunion, or 'Gaudy', at Balliol in 1938. As the organ scholar, I played at the service in chapel and was then invited to dine with the 'years' represented there, after which we all adjourned to the Junior Common Room. I joined Macmillan there, and witnessed a scene which was to become very familiar over coming decades: Macmillan holding forth to a small group, expounding politics with both wit and passion, listening to other people's arguments, unless they bored him, and finally, at a late hour, departing for bed. It was Macmillan at his best, and I was confirmed in my belief that his views, set out that year in his book *The Middle Way*, represented a sound set of answers to our economic and social problems, avoiding the evils of both an unregulated capitalist system and a dirigiste socialist approach.

Meeting such figures and hearing their views first-hand gave me a privileged sense of involvement, at the age of only twenty-one, with the momentous issues of the day. This was underlined when Winston Churchill asked a small group of us from Oxford, including Julian Amery, to meet him in the River Room at the Savoy Hotel in London in March 1938. Initially the lunch had to be postponed because of the annexation of Austria by Germany, on which Churchill had decided to speak in the House of

Commons, but he was true to his word and the lunch took place shortly afterwards. Champagne, his favourite daytime drink, was ordered and, to our delight, Churchill stayed well into the afternoon answering our anxious questions. We had been deeply shocked when Hitler went in to Austria and immediately grasped his true intentions; Churchill shared our fears and encouraged us to make a lot of noise in Oxford about what was really going on.

I gleaned further insights into the minds of other senior politicians during a memorable discussion at the Commons. For reasons which we never fully understood, Julian Amery, Hugh Fraser and I, all Balliol men, Conservatives and active in the Union, were invited to dine privately at the House of Commons by the Cabinet Minister Lord Winterton. On arrival at the House we found that both Sir John Simon, who was still Chancellor of the Exchequer, and David Margesson, then Chief Whip, were also present. After a fascinating discussion over dinner, the Chief Whip said to Simon, 'Now, John, these three young men are all interested in coming into politics. Tell them when they should become Members of Parliament.' A lengthy pause followed with Sir John deep in thought. Finally, he said, 'My advice would be for them to come in when they are thirty-three.' We were all duly impressed, so much so that we dared not ask him for any explanation. It was only many years later, when reading Simon's memoirs, that I discovered that this was the age at which he himself had entered Parliament, in 1906. As it turned out, Hugh Fraser jumped the gun, entering the House when he was twenty-seven. Julian Amery and I went into the House together in 1950, when he was thirty-one and I was thirty-three, precisely in line with Sir John's advice.

Having been elected librarian of the Union for the Trinity Term of 1938, I was now in a position to stand for the presidency. Beforehand there was a slight interlude. On 19 May 1938, I spoke in the Eights Week Debate, the Union's tongue-in-cheek counterpoint to the rowing contests taking place that week on the river and proposed the motion 'That this House deplores the decline of frivolity'. I found the lead-up to it a worrying process, since I had no pretensions to being a comedian. But although – to everyone's surprise, including my own – my adopted style of speech went down rather well, we were defeated by 113 to 154. I am still quite proud of the ditty I composed for the occasion:

> The flaw in our present-day polity
> Is its lack of a light-hearted quality
>   So the watchword today
>   I think I may say
> Should be Liberty, Fraternity, Frivolity.

But I did not feel very frivolous at the end of the term when I was standing for the presidency of the Union, and was opposed in the Presidential Debate on 2 June 1938 by my Australian rival Alan Wood. He was the Union treasurer and a Liberal and, more damagingly for me, he was also a Balliol man and senior to me in years. He proposed 'That this House would welcome the replacement of the National Government by a Popular Front Government'. The strongest defence of Chamberlain I could manage was to say that, while his foreign policy had divided the country and might possibly end in war, he just might be right in believing that his attempts to preserve an 'honourable peace' stood as much chance as a tougher approach. Alan Wood carried the motion by 154 votes to 113, and the presidency by 197 to 165. He was later wounded on military service, crossing the Rhine towards the end of the war which we had both sought to avert. This was always going to be a difficult election for me to contest, because the Labour Party had no candidate, and its supporters therefore naturally fell behind the Liberal. The Conservative vote was never going to be sufficient to overcome this combination, and I could not even count on the complete Balliol vote, which was normally powerful enough to carry any College candidate, for this was inevitably divided between myself and my rival. I could not disguise the fact that I was intensely disappointed, but I then set about carrying on the battle in the autumn term of 1938, by now into my fourth year and all too aware of how difficult it could be to keep at the forefront of Union affairs when no longer in office.

In the summer of 1938, together with three other Oxford undergraduates, I received an invitation from the Republican government of Spain, which had then been involved for nearly two years in its civil war, to spend two or three weeks in Catalonia, the last great province remaining under its control. I was invited in my capacity as chairman of the Federation of University Conservative Associations. My colleagues were Richard Symonds, a socialist from Corpus Christi who joined the United Nations secretariat after the Second World War; Derek Tasker, a Liberal from Exeter College who was later ordained and became the Canon Treasurer of Southwark Cathedral; and George Stent, a South African from Magdalen, who was probably the furthest to the left of us all in his political views. For all of us, it was to be our first taste of war.

We were to witness a conflict which aroused, in our generation, passions every bit as fierce as those stirred up by the war in Vietnam thirty years later. The struggle between the Republicans and General Franco's fascists had gained particular international significance because of the intervention of Germany and Italy on Franco's side, and the refusal of the Chamberlain government to do more than isolate Spain. Moreover, many of our contemporaries had gone off to Spain to fight, the majority on the Republican side, and many had lost their lives. My sympathies were firmly with the elected government of the Spanish Republic simply because it was not a dictatorship, although it was somewhat to the left and was supported by the Soviet Union.

The base for our visit was Barcelona, and we travelled there via Calais, Paris and Perpignan. At one point, our night train came to a juddering halt. Opening the window, we discovered that a wheel had come off, but not from our carriage. We arrived late at Perpignan, our destination in France. After a superb lunch in a restaurant overlooking the main square of the town, we were then driven at breakneck speed along the coast, a lot of it at quite a height, on the winding mountain roads down to Barcelona. We found the capital city of Catalonia in darkness – it was never lit up for fear of air-raids – and settled in to a comfortable hotel. Instructions in our rooms told us to go down to the basement in the event of an air-raid alarm. It was just as well that we did not heed those instructions, opting instead for the excitement of watching the bombers flying past. During one raid, a bomb went straight down the hotel lift shaft, skittling to the bottom and killing all those who had rushed down to the basement shelter.

Our visit had been planned so that we could study the government's different activities, particularly in the social services, meet the political leaders and visit some of Spain's historic treasures. The Republican forces had, by this time, been forced back across the River Ebro and into Catalonia, while some of their troops were still besieged in Madrid. We visited the British contingent of the International Brigade at the front. This gave me my first opportunity of meeting Jack Jones, who was to be the leader of the Transport and General Workers' Union, with whom I would have to deal as Prime Minister, and who, following his retirement, became a redoubtable campaigner on behalf of pensioners. When the survivors of the Brigade returned to London after the final capitulation of the Spanish government to Franco, I joined colleagues from across the political spectrum at Victoria station to welcome them home.

We did try at one stage to fly to Madrid, leaving at midnight so that we had a chance of avoiding Franco's fighters. But, as we approached the capital, the anti-aircraft fire was so concentrated that our pilot refused to attempt a landing and we returned to Barcelona. A few days later, we set out to drive south from Barcelona to Tarragona and, when we were nearly halfway there, a single aeroplane flying low along the road spotted our procession of cars and machine-gunned us. His aim was poor and we were able to stop the cars, dive into the ditch alongside the road and crawl along it away from our vehicles. Having failed with three further attempts to kill us all, the aircraft flew off. We got back into the cars, but abandoned the attempt to reach our destination. Our Spanish leader then declared that the safest course would be to turn down to the coast and get back to Barcelona that way. Thus it was that I discovered Sitges, at that time a small historic village with a castle and church together on the seafront, to which had been added a row of modern houses, with one hotel at the end. I returned there in the summer of 1950, for the second half of a holiday in Southern Europe, my first return to Spain. It was still delightful then, but when I went back there at the end of the 1950s it had been devastated by tourists and plastered with unsightly advertisements, not a few of them being for British-style 'Fish and Chips'. I have always believed in fostering the unity of European culture, but this was not exactly what I had in mind.

Our Spanish hosts were especially anxious to show us how much they were doing for education, not only for students but also for servicemen during intervals in their active service. The cultural activities included a performance of Brahms's Symphony No. 1 in Barcelona on 10 July, whose passion made up for any rough edges, and a performance of *Carmen* in the opera house which we saw on the following Sunday evening. The opera appeared to be very normal until the shot rang out in the last act. Panic ensued among the war-weary audience. People jumped out of their seats, until they were reassured by the management that the gunshot was no more than a theatrical effect, and did not herald the arrival of General Franco. We spent a day at the monastery at Montserrat, into whose cellars many of the treasures from the Prado in Madrid and other galleries had been moved for safety. There I saw some of the greatest works of Velasquez, El Greco and Goya which in later years I have seen back in their proper homes. The monastery, where I was entertained again in the 1980s, is now the centre of a massive tourist industry.

The political situation, however, was the main purpose of our visit and we were reminded of this at the dinner given for us late at night by the Prime Minister, Dr Juan Negrín, in his home in the hills overlooking the city. This was also attended by other senior ministers including Alvarez del Vayo, the Foreign Minister, with whom we had already had a two-hour talk on international affairs three days earlier. I marvel now at how cool and collected they all were, with Madrid isolated, General Franco's forces about to cross the river, their people ravaged by shortages of food and grievous defeat facing them within, at the most, a few months.

Dr Negrín was a distinguished scientist as well as a competent organiser, who recognised only too clearly the terrifying scale of what he and his allies were up against. He also foresaw that this civil war could well prove to be the precursor of a wholesale European conflict between the forces of fascism and the free democracies. He characterised the situation in 1938, with appeasement still predominating, as a 'clash between cowardly prudence and rash audacity'. He had already prophesied what would happen to Austria and Czechoslovakia, and no stronger or better-informed voice was raised at that time against further appeasement of the Axis powers. Negrín was a man of integrity and inner strength. When he had first been required to sign a death sentence passed by a military tribunal, a shadow had passed over his face and he had reflected that 'We must sanction all death sentences that may be necessary so that Spain may live.' He had also made successful use of a three-month indisposition to master Hungarian, a complicated and impenetrable tongue unrelated to other Southern or Central European languages. The equally impressive del Vayo, previously a foreign correspondent and then an ambassador, also warned us with the greatest intensity that, unless the international community rallied soon to the Spanish Republican cause, the effects of his people's struggle would ultimately extend far beyond Spain.

For this was no ordinary civil war. It was a struggle between fascism, supported by Italy and Nazi Germany, on one side and communism, supported by the Soviet Union, on the other. The outcome would determine who was to have control over the Straits of Gibraltar and the western Mediterranean. Moreover, the Germans were providing Franco with armaments and hardware of every kind. They were patently using this civil war as an opportunity of testing their latest weapons of destruction against both a military enemy and civilian targets. In their brutal eyes, Spain was providing a convenient testing bed for the hardware of the Nazi war machine. It was beyond the comprehension of our hosts that the French and the British could ignore this. They believed that Eden was right in his analysis, but he had resigned, while Chamberlain did not realise what was going on. To their minds Churchill was the only politician who could bring all this home to the European peoples. The post-dinner discussion, which went on until three o'clock in the morning, made clear to me, more than anything else at that time, the turbulent political future my generation faced – and with it the ever growing likelihood of a new European war.

Everyone we met seemed to be inspired by Dolores Ibarruri – La Pasionaria – the renowned and courageous communist whose emotional oratory did so much to maintain the morale of those on the Republican side. She was a miner's daughter, born in 1895, and did everything during the Civil War from running a crèche for the children of fighters to manning machine-gun posts. Although she was a devout Marxist, La Pasionaria reached across political boundaries by turning the Civil War into a crusade for the independence of her country. It was moving after Franco's death, over forty years later, to see this aged but still distinguished and defiant lady return to a free democratic Spain under the renewed monarchy. I was again reminded of my Spanish visit at a party in New York in the 1970s, when a young man approached me saying, 'My father often told me how he met you, talked to you and warned you about the forthcoming conflict just before the outbreak of the Second World War.' 'How interesting,' I replied, 'and may I ask you what is your name, and what do you do?' 'I am a banker on Wall Street,' he replied, 'and my name is del Vayo . . . When Franco captured Catalonia my father escaped to France, and when there was no longer any hope for an independent Spain he came to live in the United States.'

It was almost time to go home when I recorded my impressions of Republican Spain, in the form of my first ever radio transmission, authorised for broadcast from Barcelona on 17 July 1938. I explained:

I did not quite know what I was going to find, as this was our first experience of actual warfare . . . I imagined we might come to a wrecked city and find a terror-stricken people, haggard and worn . . . with rioting and looting and feelings running high . . . What we did find surprised us all . . . Everything is perfectly normal, life is going on almost as usual . . . people thronging the streets, sitting in cafés, laughing and talking with far from long faces . . . the liberty of the individual has impressed me greatly . . . There are no secret courts here . . . During the raids the same calmness and normal behaviour continues . . . people go quietly to a shelter, there is no sign of panic . . . But they realise what it all means, as people who have never seen them never can realise . . . the destruction of defenceless men, women, and children, bombed in unprotected villages, is most ghastly . . . I have seen the planes 200 feet above my head, heard the bombs, and the village I had passed through five minutes before was in ruins . . . Yet still the morale of the people is untouched.

The news from Spain which we had been receiving back home had not prepared me for what we encountered. In the event, I left Spain with a very strong feeling that support for Franco was chiefly to be found among the wealthy and the landowners. Their fear seemed to be that, if they did not submit themselves to a right-wing dictatorship, a communist revolution would be the inevitable alternative. My group was far from convinced: we saw for ourselves that the Republican government was introducing progressive social reforms and encouraging a bracing, democratic atmosphere among its people. Most of the men we met were not extremists, by any token, rather they were practical, hard-nosed individuals. All of us were hardened in our resolve to put their case as forcefully as we could back in the United Kingdom.

It was not until 1964, after I had opened the British Trade Fair in Barcelona as Secretary of State for Industry, Trade and Regional Development, that I flew over to Madrid for a meeting with General Franco at his home in the Pardo Palace. I had hesitated before accepting an invitation from the Spanish ambassador for such a meeting, because I guessed that General Franco knew of my visit to Spain during the Civil War, the broadcast I had made from Barcelona and the articles I had later written. I was assured, indeed, that he knew all about my Civil War activities and had expressly indicated that he wished to meet me. He greeted me in his study where his desk and the shelves all round were piled high with files awaiting his attention. He was much smaller than I had realised and had a rather withered appearance. The shakiness of his left arm seemed to indicate the onset of some disease. However, he embarked on a long and lucid discussion, largely about the power of the Soviet Union and the threat of communism. He occasionally mentioned my earlier visit to Spain during the Civil War, but now seemed to regard it as of little consequence. His other main interest was how I saw the future development of Europe, and he greatly regretted that Britain's entry into the European Community had been vetoed by General de Gaulle. Perhaps he foresaw even then that his country would one day rejoin the free world, and itself become a member of the Community.

When I left Franco, I was glad to have had the experience of such a meeting, but never expected him to preside over the Spanish for another twelve years. By the time of his death, their businessmen had built up a robust economy founded upon thriving industries, many of which deservedly enjoyed an excellent international reputation. As a result, there was a smooth handover to a constitutional monarchy, greatly aided by the remarkable qualities of the new King himself, Juan Carlos, and combined with the rapid development of a free and democratic system of government.

After I returned from Spain, I spent my summer holiday of 1938 at home in Broadstairs – swimming, sunbathing and working on my academic studies. But, much as I enjoyed this, world events were far from quiet. Neville Chamberlain, the Prime Minister, flew three times to Germany to seek an agreement with Hitler on the Sudeten question, which Hitler was stoking up so as to have an excuse for invading Czechoslovakia. On 30 September 1938, a settlement was announced which provided for the transfer of the Sudeten areas of Czechoslovakia to Germany. Poland and Hungary also made territorial gains at Czechoslovakia's expense. On his return Chamberlain was received by cheering crowds joyfully expressing their relief. After his arrival at Downing Street, he gave way to the shouts of the crowd and addressed them from an upstairs window. There he waved what became a famous piece of paper and proclaimed, 'Peace in our time.' When I discussed this many years later with Alec Douglas-Home, as Lord Dunglass Chamberlain's parliamentary private secretary at the time, he told me that, on the plane coming back from Munich, he had warned the Prime Minister against making any such statement, either at the airport or at Downing Street, and Chamberlain had sworn that he would resist any temptation to do so. In all the bustle, however, Alec lost contact with Chamberlain at No. 10. The Prime Minister, overwhelmed by the reception, made the public statement that he had promised not to make. He quickly realised the blunder he had made, and it bedevilled the rest of his life.

Those of us who had supported Eden were certain that Hitler would not keep to the Munich Agreement and that Chamberlain had embarked on an immensely dangerous course which would end in failure, with a European war and all its consequences. These fears were expressed most eloquently by Churchill, in the Commons debate on the agreement held on 5 October. Exposing with devastating acuity the weaknesses of Munich, which he described as a 'disaster of the first magnitude', he called for 'a supreme recovery of moral health and martial vigour'. He was right: we had to prepare for war. At Oxford, Munich had to be the subject of the Union's first debate of term and, on Thursday 13 October 1938, I proposed the motion 'That this House deplores the Government's policy of Peace without Honour'. The motion was opposed by Jerry Kerruish, another former president of OUCA, and I was supported by Christopher Mayhew, an ex-president of the Union who was to become a Labour minister in Attlee's government, but who later found socialism unsustainable and forsook Labour for the Liberal Party.

The debate was a stormy one. Deriding the Munich Agreement as 'the peace which passeth all understanding', I attacked Chamberlain for a 'policy which brought us to the brink of war, that pulled us out at such a terrible cost and that points at we know not what future tragedies'. I also accused Chamberlain of 'turning all four cheeks to Hitler at once', a comment which earned me some criticism. There was immense interest in the debate and we won by 320 votes to 266, with Roy Jenkins numbered among our many supporters on the Labour side.

The consequences of Munich for everyone at Oxford extended far beyond the Union chamber. The sudden death in August of the Deputy Speaker of the House of Commons and sitting Member for the City of Oxford, Captain Robert Bourne, necessitated a by-election. This was announced for Thursday 27 October 1938. This campaign, too, was inevitably fought on the question of Munich. I put forward my name to the Oxford Conservative Association as a possible candidate for the seat, pointing out that I was by now well known in Oxford political circles. When asked what particular qualifications I had for the post, I replied that I was opposed to the Munich Agreement and was therefore convinced that, at the very least, I would be a superior Foreign Secretary to Lord Halifax! After all, he had inadvisably involved himself with the Nazi hierarchy and the 'peace with honour' agreement. The Conservatives, however, chose Quintin Hogg, a barrister and fellow of All Souls, later Lord Hailsham.

Pressure then grew for the nomination of a single candidate by all the remaining parties, who would be united in fighting the election on an anti-Munich platform. Local Labour figures, including Richard Crossman and Frank Pakenham – later Lord Longford – began to urge Sandy Lindsay to stand as an Independent Progressive candidate, provided that the Labour and Liberal candidates stood down in his favour. The majority of OUCA members were opposed to the Munich Agreement, as I was, and I became the leader of the anti-Munich element from the association. We too wanted Lindsay to stand against Hogg. The Labour candidate, Patrick Gordon Walker, later to be a prominent member of post-war Labour governments, and the Liberal candidate, Ivor Davies, were already in place. Gordon Walker in particular was very reluctant to withdraw. But they were both subjected to intense local and national pressure and agreed to stand down in Lindsay's favour. Although Lindsay was a well-known socialist, his was an extraordinary decision, for no sitting master of an Oxford or Cambridge college had ever stood for Parliament. Furthermore, he had only just stepped down as Vice-Chancellor of the University. But much of the establishment was firmly behind him, as he discovered for himself when he took extensive soundings, both within and beyond Balliol.

The vital collective decision to back a single candidate for the by-election, and Lindsay's own agreement to stand, took place on the afternoon of Sunday 16 October. That evening, after all of this had been arranged, Lindsay asked if he could have a word with me in my capacity as president of the Junior Common Room. He wanted me to call a meeting after dinner that evening, at which he would say a few words. The JCR was packed, and Lindsay swept in with his gown wrapped around him, to proclaim: 'I have to tell you that I have this afternoon, rightly or wrongly, agreed to stand as an Independent Progressive candidate in the Oxford by-election. All I want to say to you is this. Whatever I may have to do, ignore it. Don't take any part in it yourselves. Stick to the College.' He then swept out. Most of us did stick to work at the College but many found time to fit in some street canvassing, attendance at open-air meetings and one or two other incidental affairs relating to the by-election.

Harold Macmillan, then the Conservative MP for Stockton, wrote to

Lindsay informing him that 'if I were a voter in the Oxford constituency I should unhesitatingly vote and work for your return to Parliament at this election ... the times are too grave and the issue is too vital for progressive Conservative opinion to allow itself to be influenced by Party loyalties or to tolerate the present uncertainty regarding the principles governing our foreign policy'. He could not have echoed my own feelings more accurately, or more potently. On one occasion, Macmillan came to Oxford himself to join in the campaign. He was delighted to see that, across every large poster advertising the official Conservative Party candidate, Quintin Hogg, we had pasted the injunction 'Love me, love my Hogg'.

Perhaps the most agreeable aspect of a generally good-humoured campaign was that the rival Conservative teams used to lunch each day in the University Carlton Club, all the pro-Hoggs at one long table and the pro-Lindsays at another. Despite the dauntingly high stakes, the relationship between the two camps could hardly have been more jovial. Meanwhile, support for Lindsay's stand came from all over the country. I recall him receiving many letters from unemployed Welsh miners whom he had taught in his Workers' Education Authority days. Randolph Churchill also helped us to campaign and, on one occasion, held out the receiver during a telephone call with his father so that everyone in the room could hear Winston's voice thundering: 'Lindsay must get in!' In his election address, dated 18 October 1938, Lindsay summed up our feelings. Although he praised Chamberlain for his determination, he was scathing on the subject of Munich and appeasement:

> Along with men and women of all parties I deplored the irresolution and tardiness of a Government which never made clear to Germany where this country was prepared to take a stand ... I look with the deepest misgiving at the prospect before us ... all of us passionately desire a lasting peace ... but we want a sense of security, a life worth living for ourselves and our children: not a breathing space to prepare for the next war.

What made the biggest impact on me was Lindsay's eve-of-poll meeting in Oxford Town Hall, which was so packed that I only just managed to get a seat in the side gallery. After an introductory speaker, the quiet, reserved figure of Lindsay entered the hall and moved up to the stage to the cheers of a now standing crowd. There he put his case in the simplest terms, but at the highest level, for making a stand against the tyrannical dictatorship in Europe, our own continent. We were all deeply moved, many to tears. That speech must have influenced so many of my Oxford generation and, indeed, people right across the whole country when it was widely reported, following the result of the by-election. This was one of the most thrilling political experiences of my Oxford days. The by-election saw a reduction from 6,645 to 3,434 in the Conservative Member's majority, a significant fall in those days, especially in the light of the importance attached to the by-election by the Chamberlain government. This result made its impact both on the government and on the House of Commons. It demonstrated quite clearly how a substantial part of the country felt, and made it clear to the nation's leaders that a similar policy would not be acceptable again.

For the Presidential Debate in the Union on 17 November 1938 we recognised that Munich was still everyone's major concern, but moved on to a broader canvas. In contrast with the previous Presidential Debate, six months earlier, I was now able to express my true feelings about the Chamberlain government, moving 'That this House has no confidence in the National Government as at present constituted'. One factor in the debate was more familiar, however: I found myself, for the second time in just over a month, in opposition to my colleague from Magdalen, Jerry Kerruish. My parents drove up from Broadstairs and were delighted with all the fuss made of them at the dinner before the debate. Accusing Chamberlain of failing to capitalise on a spiritual awakening in Britain, I concluded: 'What this country needs is a government which will call on the people of every type and class, and will not be afraid to tell the people what they aren't afraid to know; a government which will build up the defences of this country, make it strong again and show to the world that it still believes in individual liberty and the decencies of life; a government in which the people can have confidence, behind whose leaders it can unite; and a government which will be worthy of their greatness.'

We won the debate; and the following day, in a record poll, I was elected president of the Union for the Hilary Term with 280 votes to Jerry's 155. Hugh Fraser was elected treasurer and Frank Giles, later a distinguished diplomat, was elected secretary. Both were Balliol men, and subsequently helped to sustain a long series of Balliol presidents. This clean sweep was also the first time in many years that socialists had been completely unrepresented among the officers of the Union. Despite our major contests, Jerry Kerruish and I always remained on excellent terms and he came at the end of his life, after retiring as a cleric, to live just a hundred yards from me in the Cathedral Close at Salisbury.

As a consequence of this victory, I found myself featured in the national press for the first time. In those days it was still unusual for a Union president to come from my sort of background, and the *Sunday Express* ran a feature with the headline 'Jobbing Builder's Son Is an Oxford Star'.

The paper's intentions may have been good but my family took exception to the description, and the new headmaster of Chatham House, the Rev. B. V. F. Brackenbury, wrote to the *Express* to protest that my father was, in fact, a respected local businessman. The paper had also named me as 'Richard Heath'. The whole incident was an early lesson in the ways of the media.

Having now achieved my ambition of being elected president of the Union, I set about putting my ideas for its future into practice. My main purpose was to raise the status of the Union both inside and outside the University. It had still not entirely recovered from the blows inflicted upon it by the 'King and Country' motion, passed two Oxford generations earlier, and the effects of this decline in esteem were felt in a number of respects: in falling membership, in a reduction in contributions from benefactors, with the consequent effects on our financial position, and also in the reluctance of many distinguished figures from different walks of our national life to take part in debates.

I decided that, although there might be a case for my spending a number of weeks concentrating on trying to persuade visitors to speak at the Union in the weekly debate, the most urgent action required was in the field of membership and financial support. To this end, and with the agreement of the senior treasurer, I took the step, unusual in those days, of commissioning a firm of London business consultants, Harold Whitehead and Staff, to report on 'The office routine and staff duties of the Oxford Union Society', with a view to improving the management of the whole establishment. They worked speedily and reported before the end of December 1938. Their examination of the general administration of the Society was reassuring in that they found few wasteful procedures and no evidence of financial improprieties. Indeed there was a marked tribute to the integrity and capabilities of Mr Bird, the steward. However, they emphasised the need to pay off the heavy bank overdraft and mortgage liabilities, so eliminating the annual interest charges.

Ultimately, the Union had to increase its membership, and to do that it had to make itself more attractive. This would naturally require immediate capital expenditure on alterations and additions to premises and furnishings. After the report had advocated more effective means for canvassing undergraduates, and a revision of subscription rates or their means of payment, which did not appeal greatly to us, its most pointed suggestion was that credit facilities be offered, 'within carefully restricted limits', for meals and refreshments. It was the implementation of the latter which was to produce considerable success in my term as president. Being able to enjoy excellent food and wine outside one's college on credit proved to be an immense attraction, and a rapid consequence was a substantial increase in membership. A marked disadvantage, however, was that it later proved impossible to ensure that all the members met their bills. However, the internal administration of the whole of the Union was completely modernised, the hours worked by the staff were made more reasonable and the buildings were brought up to date. My first forward-looking operation was successful and proved to be lasting.

The climax of all this was an end-of-term party on a scale we had never before experienced. All the great rooms were cleared, and music, entertainment and dancing were provided, with everyone in black tie. The food and drinks were excellent. The Union was packed with many senior members of the University and their wives. It was the first time such an event had ever been held in the Union, and I was delighted that it was such an uproarious success. The term ended, as even the *Isis* magazine admitted, 'in a blaze of glory'. An additional reward arrived in January 1939, when I was named the 950th 'Isis Idol'. The 'Idol' was a typical Oxford institution, making tongue-in-cheek pin-ups of the University's leading men and women. In the characteristic argot of the journal, I was described thus: 'Teddy Heath was born in the summer of 1916, some two months before the Tank . . . lacking the thickness of skin of this early rival, he soon outstripped it in charm of manner, and has since proved its equal in ability to surmount obstacles.' *Isis* also observed that its Idol's election to the Union presidency had been due 'not to his politics, but to his ability and character, and he has already shown the power of handling meetings . . . he takes his office and the Union very seriously, and is full of hopes and plans for the good of every side of the Society's activity'.

For the debates in my term, I wanted to broaden the range of subjects as well as improve the quality of the speakers. I decided to begin by introducing a theological motion, the first ever. The Union's standing orders specifically excluded any debate of a religious nature, but by wording the motion in the terms 'That a return to religion is the only solution to our present discontents', we avoided any controversy about individual beliefs. Nobody challenged me about its inclusion in the programme. The proposer was the dean of St Paul's, W. R. Matthews. I asked George Bernard Shaw to oppose the motion, but, regrettably, the great playwright declined my invitation. He replied, 'the invitation is very tempting; but octogenarians must resist such temptations on pain of making pitiable exhibitions of themselves . . . twenty years ago I should have moved as an amendment "that as it costs less to feed, clothe, lodge and amuse a higher mathematician and his family than a steel smelter, the resolution is as irrelevant politically as it is paradoxical theologically".' This was written very clearly in his own hand on the other side of his customary reply card, on which a message was printed stating that 'Mr Bernard Shaw is obliged by advancing years to discontinue his personal activities on the platform . . . and he begs his correspondents to excuse him accordingly.' The left-wing poet Stephen Spender was a capable substitute and, to my surprise, the motion was carried comfortably, by 276 votes to 94.

Our mid-term debate was really arranged to suit Hugh Fraser, who would be running for the presidency later in the term. He proposed on 16 February 1939 'That the future of the working classes lies with Progressive Conservatism', and his friend Lady Astor came to support him. On the telephone she told me firmly that she wanted me to get 'a really hot Commie' for her to oppose. I did approach the communist leader Harry Pollitt, but without success, and she was not amused when she found that I had been able to secure only John Parker MP, the secretary of the New Fabian Research Bureau, whom she regarded as a wet socialist. The motion was defeated by five votes, this narrow result showing that the battle between right and left in Oxford was still unresolved, despite the defeat of Hugh Dalton eighteen months earlier.

The Presidential Debate in March 1939 reflected the growing belief that, with Hitler having now broken the Munich Agreement and invaded Czechoslovakia, war was near at hand. Churchill was the obvious choice to move the motion 'That this House would welcome the immediate introduction of a scheme of compulsory national service'. I therefore wrote to Churchill in the following terms:

> The present generation of Oxford men has never had the opportunity of hearing you at Oxford, and if you would return to repeat your triumphs of the past – which to us are mighty legends told us by life-members – I can assure you that the Union hall could not contain all those who would come to hear you. Professor Lindemann will vouch for me as an excellent rebel Tory, which explains why I am so anxious that you should come.

Churchill did indeed consult Lindemann, but still he declined. He did, however, reply generously and emphasise 'how much I would like to come and support you in your period of office'. Nonetheless, he regretted that his workload was too heavy. I was naturally disappointed, but Leo Amery made a fine substitute. Amery was one of the leading Conservative critics of Chamberlain, and his famous cry 'In the name of God, go!' in the Commons in 1940 was to help topple Chamberlain and pave the way for Churchill's triumphant entry into No. 10. At dinner before the debate, Amery was scathing about the Cabinet. 'I have no time', he told me, 'for governments in which members of the Cabinet go around calling each other by their Christian names. They have no independence. I would rather they did not speak to each other outside the Cabinet Room if it meant they would stand up for what they believe in once they are inside it.' Amery was opposed on that occasion by Vernon Bartlett, the diplomatic correspondent of the *News Chronicle*, who had recently been elected as an Independent MP in a surprising by-election victory. The motion was defeated by 192 votes to 173, but the next day Hugh Fraser was duly elected president for the Trinity Term.

I wanted my term to end on a glamorous and light-hearted note in the debating chamber on the final Thursday of term, 9 March 1939, and I invited the actor Charles Laughton to speak. He sent an amusing reply:

> May I thank you for your most flattering invitation to speak before the Oxford Union on March 9th? My instinct is to accept blindly and face the difficulties later. I have never taken part in a debate, in fact my only experience of public speaking is from various stages of cinemas in English and American provincial towns – buttering up the inhabitants and congratulating them upon their new Town Hall, Bathing Pool, Lord Mayor or what have you.
>
> If you could give me some kind of information upon how long one is expected to speak and in what form, I can at any rate say whether I think I am capable of having a crack at it.
>
> I suggest the motion might be something to do with my job. Is one allowed to draw comparisons between the Publicity Department of the German Reich and the Publicity Department of Fox-20th Century? – I always thought that Goebbels handled the Czech business on very similar lines to the way Darryl Zanuck handled Shirley Temple – or to deplore the fact that whereas every messenger boy in England answers you by saying 'OK toots', no messenger boy in America answers you by saying 'Strike me up a gum tree not 'arf it ain't'. In other words, should this country adopt the publicity methods of Dr Goebbels and/ or the methods of the Fox-20th Century Film Corporation (which are the same thing) to save our Empire and/or our film trade (which may or may not be the same thing) or perish?

The motion was drafted according to the jocular and witty tone apparent in the celebrated actor's letter: 'That this House prefers the Poet to the Pub'. Unfortunately, Laughton cried off at the last moment, and his place winding up the paper speeches was taken by the writer Peter Fleming. Laughton explained, in the terse vernacular of a hasty telegram,

> Expected to have finished shooting our film yesterday but unfortunately camera man ill, one of our scenes went wrong and it is absolutely impossible for me to get to Oxford on Thursday. Very much regret

letting you down this last moment. Would not do so if there were any way out.

On the whole, however, I had an upbeat ending to my term as president of the Union. The organisational reforms to which I aspired had been brought about; the number of members had increased, making our financial backing far more sound; and the distinguished speakers had helped to raise the level of debates, both serious and frivolous. I also enjoyed various opportunities to speak to eminent audiences beyond Oxford and the Union. The occasion I remember best was being invited to speak in the Great Hall of the Bank of England, after a splendid dinner. I was offered complete freedom in choosing a subject, with one proviso: I was not to mention either God or the Bank of England. I had always understood that the two amounted to much the same thing.

There was a general feeling in Balliol at this time that we ought to raise funds to help the unemployed. We decided that the fairest and most telling way would be to provide a simple dinner in hall for which everyone would be charged the full amount, regardless of whether or not they ate it. I discussed this with Colonel Duke, the College bursar, who was most helpful. He undertook to provide a two-course meal of steak-and-kidney pudding and vegetables, followed by cheese and biscuits, for one shilling and threepence per head, while charging the customary two shillings and ninepence. Thus, one and sixpence per head could be paid into any funds we chose for the unemployed. All this was on condition that all the members of the College agreed to be charged on their normal accounts. I accepted this. The arrangement was advertised on the notice board in the Junior Common Room and the hall was full. All went well until the Master, who had already banned Lobster Newburg from high table in order to show solidarity with the less well-off, led in the members of the Senior Common Room and their guests to high table, where they found to their amazement that they too were all being served with steak-and-kidney pudding and cheese and biscuits. I had forgotten to warn them that, on this occasion, they too would be required to show solidarity, by consuming the same fare as members of the JCR.

As my final year at Oxford continued, I had to decide what my future career was going to be and how I was going to embark upon it. My father's desire for me to become an accountant had still not caught my imagination: as I told him, I had no desire to 'spend my life looking at other people's figures'. Industry was another possibility mentioned by the family but rejected, at least at that stage, by me. At one point my mother was keen that I should become a clergyman. It was certainly an exciting time for the Church of England. However, despite a deeply held faith and a considerable interest in ecclesiastical affairs, I did not feel a true calling, nor would such a career have provided me with the opportunity I sought to shape the affairs of my country.

The most promising avenue seemed to be the law. In the previous autumn I had been awarded the Gerald Moody scholarship at Gray's Inn, worth £100 a year, so that I could be called to the Bar. My application for the scholarship had been arranged by Trevor Watson, a member of the General Council of the Bar, whose impressive modern house in Kingsgate, Tigh Na Mara, was one of those looked after by my father. He had promised that, if I was successful in my Bar exams, he would take me into his chambers. He also distinguished himself in 1939 by talking my father into contesting a council seat in the local elections of April that year, as an independent candidate. I came down especially from Oxford to address an election meeting for my father at Bohemia, the hall I knew so well from my town carol concerts. The lawyer was to take the chair at this meeting, and turned up in a somewhat stimulated state. I would not suggest that Watson was singlehandedly responsible for my father's defeat at the polls, but his performance that night did not secure much support.

So the law, then, was one career open to me. But my old schoolfriend 'Tick' – A. C. Tickner – wrote to say that, although I had done well for a Chatham House boy, he was ultimately disappointed in me because 'the Bar seems rather too conventional a finish for you'. I had my doubts too, but it promised to be a lucrative career, and one which could lead on quite naturally to politics. So I paid my admission fee to Gray's Inn – £58 13s – and began to make regular journeys from Oxford to London to attend the required number of dinners there with barristers, other scholars and students. These were all very pleasant occasions, with everyone sitting at long tables and eating in messes of four each, with a four-course dinner and two bottles of wine between us, all for the sum of three shillings and sixpence each. After dinner I would go down to the House of Commons to listen to whatever debate was going on, leaving to catch the midnight train back to Oxford.

Despite the conviviality of these occasions, I was still reluctant at this stage to turn my back irrevocably upon the option of a life in music, as so much of my time had already been devoted to my musical pursuits. I appreciate now that, had I chosen to do this while still at school, I might have followed a different academic course, perhaps preparing myself for the Royal College of Music, of which I later became a governor for ten years, or the Royal Academy of Music, and spending all of my spare time attending concerts, studying scores and participating in every kind of musical activity. Many prominent musicians, however, have emerged directly from our universities, and perhaps there was still a chance of doing so myself after Balliol. When I came to consider my options towards the end of my time at Oxford, I went to see Sir Hugh Allen, the Heather Professor of Music, who was well known to have the widest influence in musical institutions all over the world. I had sung under his baton in the Oxford Bach Choir and he had been to my concerts in college. I explained the problem to him, and he then analysed my options very clearly. 'You can get yourself called to the Bar, make a lot of money, go into politics and probably become Prime Minister,' he began. 'That's one course. Alternatively, you can decide to go for music. If so, I'll get you into the Royal College, but don't set out to be a music teacher or an organist. I have seen you at work and you must set out to become a conductor and to get right to the top. I believe you can do it, but if so you must be prepared to be just as big a shit as Malcolm Sargent.'

With my Union presidency over by Easter 1939, I now had to concentrate on the forthcoming examinations for my degree in philosophy, politics and economics, which were only a matter of weeks away. After the results had been announced at the end of July, Charles Morris, the senior tutor at Balliol, wrote to me:

> You seem to have got a very nice Second in the Schools, and I daresay that all things considered you are quite satisfied. It all seems very satisfactory.
>
> I enclose a copy of your marks as I expect you would like to see them. I hope you are having a good holiday.

'All things considered' is, perhaps, the operative phrase. I was disappointed at not getting a first, and felt that I ought to have got one. But considering all my other activities in politics, in the Union, in the College and with music, he was probably right that 'a very nice Second . . . all seems very satisfactory'.

After finishing my last term at Oxford in July 1939, I had a few weeks left before taking up my scholarship at Gray's Inn and beginning to work for the Bar examinations. My thoughts immediately turned again to travelling. Madron Seligman wanted to go to Spain, now ruled by General Franco, but I was denied a visa on account of my visit to the old regime the previous summer, so we decided instead to make for what appeared to be the biggest trouble spot in Northern Europe, the Baltic port of Danzig – latterly Gdansk – which was at the centre of Hitler's dispute with Poland. The city stood at the head of the 'Polish Corridor', a narrow strip of land dividing Eastern and Western Prussia which had been established under the Treaty of Versailles to break up German influence in the region, and to provide Poland with access to the sea. Danzig was now an autonomous 'free city' under the League of Nations, but everybody knew that Hitler wanted to reincorporate it into the Fatherland.

We crossed the Channel and travelled by train to Brussels, from which, after a brief stop, we crossed the frontier into Germany. The atmosphere was very tense, and both Madron and I were acutely aware of how the attitude towards the British had changed among the German population. We came to the conclusion that there was, somehow, both an intensified dislike towards us and a marked increase in respect. Even those to whom I had an introduction would discuss politics with us only when walking in the open air in the park. When we arrived in Berlin, we looked at the grotesque new Chancellery and then went for a full briefing from Anthony Mann, the *Daily Telegraph* correspondent there, whom I knew from Balliol days. We found him in a thoroughly depressed mood, and he told us that he had heard that the Nuremberg Rallies due the following month had been extended by two days. He did not like the sound of that, and believed that these rallies would mark the beginning of real trouble for Europe. We spent the rest of that day, Friday 11 August 1939, taking in as many of the sights as we could, including the imposing yet terrifying sight of Hitler's celebrated Olympic Stadium, several times the size of Wembley. Anthony Mann was subsequently arrested in Copenhagen in 1940 by German occupation forces and spent the rest of the war interned in Denmark.

Anthony Mann's warnings had filled us thoroughly with foreboding by the time we caught the 2319 night train from Berlin to Danzig. This was packed full of drunken Austrians who had been commandeered by the Nazi regime for compulsory labour at the other end. We desperately but unsuccessfully tried to get some sleep by clambering into the luggage racks, but were never left in peace. One man threatened to shoot Madron's nose off and another threw his baggage on top of him when he was in the rack. Some of the drunkards were so far gone that the ticket collector had to bang their heads together to rouse them when we reached our destination the following morning.

Not surprisingly, we were both tired out when we reached Danzig, and immediately sought beds in the usual ports of call – the YMCA and comparatively inexpensive boarding houses – only to find that they too were all packed with forced labour. The only bed-and-breakfast place we could find with a room to spare was run by a fierce, argumentative Nazi woman and her family: like many people in the city, they wanted a Nazi takeover. They still treated us well, however, and charged a low rate for the room. We visited the local spa and then had a fruitless conversation with an officious and unwelcoming junior official at the British consulate. We bought him lunch, but gleaned virtually nothing from him, beyond the blindingly obvious fact that the situation was growing perilous, and we ought to clear off as soon as possible. We had seen for ourselves how much military dockside activity there was, and we were told by the press attaché at the Polish high commission that there was at least a full division of German troops in Danzig by this stage, with more men and equipment arriving all the time. This view seemed to be confirmed by what was going on around the docks.

In Danzig we attended a symphony concert in Zopot, the city's watering resort, looked at the historic buildings and paid a visit to the new port of Gdynia. Then we decided to go by boat up-river to Warsaw, at that time still a lovely, sophisticated city and one very much under French influence. Its softness of style, welcoming atmosphere and easy pace of living were reminiscent of Paris. We reported to the British embassy, where the ambassador and his staff were horrified to see us, as was the consul-general who, having held his post for more than twenty-five years, was avowedly the best informed Briton in Poland, as well as the owner of the finest set of Meissen porcelain in that country. With the exception of Robert Hankey, later a distinguished diplomat, everybody advised us to get out of Poland as soon as possible. However, we went to the Europejski Hotel for mid-morning coffee, because we had been told that the diplomats, the politicians, the businessmen and the press invariably gathered there each morning to exchange the latest information. Having heard their foreboding forecast, we decided to start on the long hitch-hike back home. As the Polish traffic, including troops, was all moving towards the German frontier, we were successful at first, but then encountered difficulties in the train crossing the border, especially when we were found to be already holding German marks.

Once we had resolved that issue, we started looking for a lift to Dresden. This proved difficult. Much of the traffic was military, German civilian drivers were none too keen to give foreign students a lift and we had some long walks on hot days with bulky rucksacks on our backs. We saw massive German forces in tanks and trucks moving towards the Polish border, a far more threatening sight than the comparatively impotent-looking Polish troops crawling with a sense of resignation rather than fervour to the opposite side of the same frontier.

When we reached Dresden, we went to the city art gallery and saw Raphael's *Madonna di San Sisto*. Madron and I looked at that beautiful work for an hour or more, as we talked about the world outside falling apart. In Dresden we also had a meal with my old friend Professor Winckler and his wife. They too were fearful that Europe was on the point of war. After lunch, the Professor accompanied us to the top of the hill outside the city. We stopped to say goodbye, and watched him go back before starting on the downward slope. He did not wave to us, and never turned around. I thought, 'We shall never see each other again.' That proved to be true, although we did exchange letters after the war.

Madron and I then went on hitch-hiking and reached Leipzig, rather ominously in the middle of an air-raid practice, where the newspaper posters were all proclaiming the success of the Ribbentrop–Molotov meeting, at which it appeared that agreement had been reached on a Nazi–Soviet pact. We knew then that we had to get out, and quickly. There was no train leaving the city that night, but we managed to find a couple of bedrooms in a house near to the station, where we got an early train the next morning to Kehl. The journey to the French border was most unpleasant. As soon as we started speaking English, the others in our compartment – mostly Nazi-indoctrinated girls – showed open hostility. We sought refuge in the corridor and counted ourselves lucky that we avoided being beaten up or handed over to officialdom. As if we did not already have enough problems, Madron then insisted upon pulling out his penny whistle, playing once again the same old tunes I had heard incessantly for the past three weeks – all slightly out of tune. I had come to dislike these dirges intensely, and had already lost my temper with him after his umpteenth rendition of 'Colonel Bogey' on the platform of Leipzig station. Now, as we tried to escape Germany on this ghastly train, out came the wretched penny whistle again. It drove me up the wall. We had another flaming row, but at least I won on this occasion and we had some peace afterwards.

Once we reached the border, we walked across the bridge over the river to safety in France. After a quick lunch and a tram ride we started our hitch-hike again. We were saved by a French army captain reporting for service to Paris. Having driven all the way from Nice he was exhausted, and readily agreed to take us on board provided we drove him. Madron took the wheel, while the officer slept in the back. Late that night, we arrived to find a blacked-out Paris, dropped off the car and spent the night in a small hotel. The next day, we reported to the British embassy. 'Unless you get out now,' was the simple advice, 'you will never get out at all.' Madron took a train to Brittany, where his family had a holiday home, while I jumped on another, bound for Calais. So full was the cross-Channel boat that, as it pulled away from the quay, it seemed about to capsize, taking all those waving goodbye down with it. My parents met me at Dover a week before Poland was invaded. It had not been possible for me to get in touch with them while we were away. They must have had some anxious moments, but they never mentioned them, and never complained. We had cut things pretty fine.

Chapter 4

FIGHTING FOR FREEDOM

The War Years 1939–1945

My parents had both heaved an understandable sigh of relief when I telephoned them from the dockside at Dover, and they came at once to collect me by car. I then spent a week, culminating in a particularly tense thirty-six hours, waiting to see whether our government would carry out its commitments to Poland. The indecision and procrastination on Saturday 2 September almost drove me to despair, as it seemed that we might again default on our obligations. Then, at 11.15 on the morning of Sunday 3 September, Neville Chamberlain made the announcement: Britain was at war with Germany. I felt an unexpected sense of relief. All around people started digging trenches and building shelters. There was almost panic soon afterwards when the air-raid sirens in Broadstairs suddenly sounded, but the first of their many wails proved to be a false alarm.

The declaration of war settled the immediate question of which career I should choose. I immediately offered myself to the University Recruitment Board in Oxford and I was called for an interview there on 9 September 1939. After that, I was allocated to the Royal Artillery, but told that I would probably not be required for several months. This left open the possibility of continuing with arrangements made in the spring of 1939 for me to go on a debating tour of American universities.

There was a long-established tradition for two debaters from British universities to make such a visit each year. The tourists of previous years had included Richard Acland, who was later to found the Common Wealth Party, Michael Foot and Stafford Cripps. In 1938, Christopher Mayhew, a future parliamentary colleague, had been one of the two debaters. On this occasion, Hugh Fraser and I had been chosen, but Hugh had been in training as a territorial with his family regiment when war was declared and he had immediately been embodied into active service. The steward of the Oxford Union was informed on 24 September that 'the War Office are not in favour of releasing Mr Fraser to undertake the tour proposed', and it was therefore decided that Peter Street, a former treasurer of the Oxford Union and a Liberal, would accompany me instead. The question then was whether a tour of this kind in the United States at such a sensitive time was still appropriate. The Foreign Office decided that it was. Before we left on the tour they briefed us thoroughly and emphasised that under no circumstances were we to give any appearance of interfering in the internal affairs of the United States. Nor were we at any time to discuss the war. There seemed to be no chance whatsoever of getting away with that, but the Foreign Office official concerned told us very firmly that to do so would create a diplomatic incident, and that we would immediately be sent back home in disgrace. He should go down in posterity as the original author of the line 'Don't mention the war.'

We left for the United States with mixed feelings. Apart from the blackout and the rationing, life at home was continuing much as usual. Poland's resistance had been brutally suppressed and its territory divided between the Germans and the Russians. This period came to be known as the 'phoney war'. We were aware that, in these circumstances, there was a lot to be said for us doing something positive in America. On the other hand, the war might suddenly burst into life and we would be away from it, probably faced with great difficulty in returning by sea. However, as the authorities wanted us to carry out the tour, we just had to get on with it. When we arrived at Southampton, I was handed a telegram of encouragement from Madron Seligman. 'Like Churchill's speech, your work worth battalion field kitchens and brace captive balloons,' it read. 'Good luck!'

I had been looking forward immensely to seeing the United States for the first time. Naturally I was attracted by its variety and its glamour, but the trip would also give me the opportunity of assessing for myself the Americans' attitude to European affairs and, perhaps, of explaining to my own generation there why we felt so strongly about the situation in Europe. American opinion on the war was still ambivalent at that time. In the months leading up to the invasion of Poland and Chamberlain's declaration of war, opinion polls there had detected both a growing hostility to Germany and a strong view that, should war be declared, the USA should supply Britain and France with food, raw materials and even weapons. So far as it went, this was encouraging. But a sizeable majority remained opposed to the US entering any conflict. I was determined to return home with a firm grasp of how we could harden the broad support for our cause into eventual support for a full-scale US military intervention.

The liner *United States* had few passengers aboard when it left Southampton on 28 October 1939. This meant that, although we were travelling third class, the rest of the rooms were thrown open to us. The menu and service on board did not seem to have been affected by the war; nor did thoughts of being attacked by German naval vessels cross our minds. I spent some time preparing speeches for the tour. It was customary for the British team to draw up twelve resolutions, and send them out six months or so ahead of the tour, so that individual American universities could each make their choice. We had to prepare a speech on each motion, which could be used several times if necessary. None of the suggested motions was very profound and they included propositions such as 'England has lost her former greatness' and 'America needs Roosevelt for a third term'. We were to be told which had been chosen by our hosts on arrival at each university.

The New York City skyline, as we came up the Hudson River on a bright November morning, surpassed our wildest expectations. On the river, too, the activity was intense as we nosed into our berth. Those next few days, as we quickly got to know American habits, still live vividly in my memory: breakfast in a drugstore; salad lunches; and huge steaks in the evening. Those to whom we had personal introductions could not have been more hospitable, and I went with a delightful American girl called Emily Cross to hear the New York Philharmonic Orchestra in Carnegie Hall. It was conducted by John Barbirolli, who had recently succeeded Toscanini as the orchestra's permanent conductor. The programme included Elgar's Introduction and Allegro for Strings, one of Barbirolli's specialities. All of this seemed to underline the cultural kinship between the Americans and ourselves. Emily joined me afterwards for supper in the restaurant at the top of the newly built Rockefeller Centre. As we sat there, I could not help contrasting the blazing lights of New York with the blacked-out streets at home. This seemed to be a friendly city bubbling with vitality, and quite irresistible to a young man such as myself. I next saw that girl waiting outside the Members' Lobby of the House of Commons soon after I was elected to Parliament in 1950. Meanwhile, she had become the wife (in 1940) of one of my colleagues there, John Vaughan-Morgan, the MP for Reigate.

Already Peter and I had eagerly devoured the contents of a special tourist guide to the city, and I shall always regret never seeing the celebrated 'tiglon' of Central Park Zoo, a creature alleged to be the result of a union between a Siberian tiger and an African lion – 'no friendly puss, this big fellow shuns and is shunned by, 1,125 other Zoo inmates'. I felt on top of the world in New York, never tired and never wanting to sleep. That city still has the same special quality for me, although its life has become even faster and it is seldom that you see one New Yorker stop in the street and speak to another.

On our arrival the organisers told us that our first major debate would be at the University of Pittsburgh, in a modern skyscraper modestly named the Cathedral of Learning, which boasted an auditorium seating several hundred people. Every ticket had been taken and our debate was to be broadcast on radio across the whole of the Eastern states. But they had publicised the debate on a motion which was not one of the original twelve put forward by us. They had considered these to be too anodyne and obscure, and had announced that we would propose the motion 'That the United States should immediately enter the war on the side of the allies', to be opposed by the Pittsburgh team. This was a real bombshell. All the warnings from the Foreign Office flashed into our minds: 'inter-ference in American internal affairs'; 'diplomatic incident'; 'return home at once'. We firmly but politely regretted that we could not debate such a motion, and explained why. In that case, they replied, the Pittsburgh debate would not take place and, as this was the only subject which interested most of the other universities too, the entire tour would have to be cancelled. We asked for time to consider this dilemma.

Back in the quiet of the hotel, not only the warnings from the Foreign Office, but also the constructive advice, came back to mind. We had been told that, in the last resort, we should not hesitate to telephone the British ambassador in Washington. We turned up the appropriate telephone number and rang the embassy. I asked to speak to Lord Lothian and, much to my surprise, was put straight through to him. He already knew of our visit and, having explained our problem to him, I suggested rather sadly that perhaps we had better pack our bags and catch the same boat home. 'No,' he said, 'I don't think you ought to be quite as hasty as that. Let me turn it over in my mind for a moment or two and see whether there isn't some way round this problem. After all, you've come a long way and there's some useful work to be done here. It's a pity to waste it all just because of this.' I waited while the ambassador pondered. Finally he pro-nounced his decision. 'Yes. I think I've got the answer. It's quite obvious that the war is the one thing in which the students here are interested and so are you. In any case they'll never stop talking to you about it when you aren't debating, so you may as well deal with it when you are. You should tell them that you will accept this debate, but only on condition that one of you speaks for and the other against. Then nobody can say that you are trying to bring the Americans into the war.'

We decided to put this judgement of Solomon into practice at most of our engagements, and released a formal statement of our intentions. In this, we explained that questions about America – relating either to its internal affairs or its role in world affairs – were 'of course matters entirely for American decision and we feel it presumptuous for us in the present circumstances to debate them'. We went on, however, to explain that 'we are willing to do so provided that you will take responsibility for the subject of debate should any further difficulty arise'. We also explained that we would, wherever possible, like to divide on each motion. This notice was given advance publicity at each of our tour stops, and proved to be generally acceptable. Peter and I changed places for alternate debates, just to ensure that we had each mastered both sides of the case. It also proved to our American friends that it really was the debate that interested us. Lord Lothian had proved to be both helpful and wise. He had never been a particular favourite of my generation, because of his connection with the Cliveden set, named after the Astors' country seat in Berkshire where they met. They were associated in our minds with appeasement – but, on this occasion, Lothian certainly solved our problem for us. When we arrived for the debate in Washington, he invited us to the embassy and greeted us in his study with the words, 'Well, you haven't succeeded in creating a diplomatic incident yet.' There I saw Lutyens' great house on Massachusetts Avenue, where thirty years later I was to entertain the President of the United States, Richard Nixon, to lunch on one of his rare visits to a foreign embassy in his homeland.

Pittsburgh was a typical industrial city of the rust-belt, and the red glow of the blast furnaces and the munitions factories lit up the sky at night. 'The war's made us busy,' we were firmly told, 'but there's no boom.' The Cathedral of Learning had sixty grand pillars as its major architectural feature, and I was proudly informed that each one had cost $10,000. Fortunately, I soon discovered that not all Americans were quite so boastful. Our time there proved to be more or less typical of our university visits: breakfast with other students, usually including the rival debating team followed by a look around the campus and university buildings, lunch with members of the faculty and the debate in the evening, very often broadcast. There was a reception afterwards, usually several hundred strong, and the whole day would be interspersed with radio and press interviews, an exchange of information with the local British consul and meetings with any British residents in the area. All in all, we worked pretty hard. At the end of most debates, hosts wanted to go on arguing into the early hours. It was all right for them: they had time to recover the following day. We usually had to leave early for our next university engagement.

The evening in Pittsburgh, the first on which we put the ambassador's advice into practice, went well enough from our point of view, as we both found ourselves listening intently for the first time to the highly formal debating technique of the American teams. Each speech started with a proposition or, in opposition, a counter-proposition, which was followed by a list of the detailed arguments in favour, after which they would deal one by one with the arguments against. The speech ended with another formal summary of the debater's position. On a number of occasions a panel of judges awarded points on the basis of the success with which this formula was implemented. The Oxford Union has never indulged in such formalities, and we were quite incapable of complying with them. We soon decided never to make a speech which attempted to gain any points. We resolved to stick to our own style and endeavour to illuminate the argument, while also entertaining the audience. This generally left our opponents nonplussed, for they knew no way of countering it.

On the whole, the audience seemed to appreciate our performances. They were rather a straitlaced lot, but they appeared to enjoy such an informal exposition. One charming girl came up to us after that debate and said, 'You've broken every rule in the book tonight, but it was far more fun. I'm going to do the same.' The more senior figures we encountered were less enthusiastic about our approach, however, and I am sure that any departure from the standard American debating formula would have been quickly stamped upon once we had gone.

Pittsburgh over, we went to Chattanooga – by the proverbial choo-choo, of course – and thence on to a tour of the Southern states. Leaving early in the morning, we went by road to Charleston. This was the first of our many excursions on a Greyhound bus, that famed American institution. Our worst journey was from Charleston to Greensboro by an early-morning train, then by Greyhound to Bristol, Virginia, involving five changes before arriving there at 8.30 p.m. During these travels we would talk to our neighbours about their own part of the country, their problems and their views of Britain and the war. Some of them were going on travelling overnight. Racial discrimination was strictly enforced and coloured people were kept at the back of the coaches. The economic situation was also less rosy down in the South. 'The war has taken away our best markets,' we were told. 'England can only buy war materials now. The North-East may be prosperous, but we have to suffer.'

But this tour of the South still holds many magical memories for me. The lovely undulating red-brick wall at the University of Virginia in Charlottesville; the share-croppers' huts on pitifully impoverished land and a near-hysterical crowd dancing to Negro jazz on a hot humid evening outside Alabama; turkey and cranberry sauce for a Thanksgiving Day dinner in Atlanta; the warm orange groves in Florida; and an alligator farm near Daytona Beach – all are still vivid in my mind. In Florida, I remember my surprise upon seeing a young black boy sitting on an alligator's back and tickling its jaws. In that wonderful Southern drawl, he assured me that I need not concern myself for his safety: 'Ah's safe on dis ole alligator,' he explained calmly. 'In de winter 'is nervous system am run down.' I also recall my visit to George Washington's home at Mount Vernon and, most impressive of all, the Lincoln Memorial in America's capital city. The living conditions for many people, white and black, seemed to us intolerable, especially in the Southern states. Yet, although the South was so much less prosperous than the North, the warm-hearted hospitality there created a charm which was somewhat lacking in the fiercely competitive industrial North. We also found that people in the Southern states were more interested in the human, rather than the diplomatic, side of the war and were less critical of British policy.

Returning to New York after a brief debating encounter in Philadelphia, we started on the second part of the tour which led us to the North and the West, first to Syracuse, and then to Dartmouth, way up in the hills in New Hampshire, a richly forested, quiet and unspoilt spot. Dartmouth is a private and, by American standards, small college and, I thought, in many ways the most attractive of all those we saw. Their hospitality was obviously very agreeable too. According to my notes, I began by praising Dartmouth as 'a place where men are men and rum is rum – and it's not often you find the two apart'. We then set off on our own for a private tour of three of the Ivy League universities, Harvard, Yale and Princeton, private because they would not pay a share of the tour to the organisers and were never included in it. These three, richly endowed, each with its own treasures, were in complete contrast with everything we had seen so far, and reminiscent of our Oxford colleges. Everywhere we were asked to take messages back to people's relatives in Britain, and we grew ever more aware that these ties between our two countries were to be found everywhere, and could not easily be broken. This seemed to provide substantial grounds for optimism. In Philadelphia, one man spent a great deal of effort putting us right. When we thanked him, he replied, 'Not at all, you're English and you know where our sympathies lie.' We heard similar sentiments expressed time and time again, most surprisingly by a group of Irishmen in Boston. The Irish Republic was neutral during the Second World War, but people were saying in 1939 that Ireland 'had not yet decided which side to be neutral against'.

I wanted to do one more thing before going back to New York, where I had arranged to spend Christmas with a Balliol contemporary and Yale history graduate, Daniel McNamee, and his family at their home up on the Hudson River. This was to see Chicago, the centre of American isolationism, for myself. During our tour we had lived on a daily subsistence allowance, economising and staying with friends wherever possible, in order to save up enough to make at least one substantial journey independently of our hosts. So, the week before Christmas, we took a train to Chicago. Since there was no debating there, we could explore the city, look over it from the tops of skyscrapers, drive along Lakeside, go down to the stockyards and spend some time in the shops. The 'windy city' made a double impression upon me: its sense of individualism and independence created a feeling of intense power; yet I could sense too a continuing struggle between different groups in the city for control of that power. Chicago was certainly exciting, but it lacked the champagne quality of New York. The great lake and the houses close by it were beautiful, but parts of the urban environment were appallingly dilapidated.

Moving on after Christmas with the McNamees, and now operating separately from Peter Street, I greeted 1940 at a New Year's Ball in Cleveland with another Oxford friend, Frank Taplin. He had been noted at Queen's for the witty and topical lyrics which he sang to his own accompaniment. Gene Krupa, one of America's greatest ever drummers, and his band, then at the top of their form, whipped up the dancers into a frenzy and made the evening a wild success. In the next few days I saw a lot of Cleveland; it is a city that I came to like and to which I have frequently returned. Frank is still a close friend.

After that, I spent a weekend up in Connecticut as a guest of 'old' Tom Watson, in his spacious residence. He was world-famous as the founder of IBM, which he had built up into a dominant position in the world of electrical machinery. I had met him before on a number of occasions when he and his wife visited Oxford with their daughter so that she could see Jack Irwin, originally a Princeton man, but then a colleague and friend at Balliol. Later they were to marry, and he made his career as a lawyer in New York before becoming a member of the Nixon Administration at the State Department. On the Monday, Tom Watson took us both down to his plant at Poughkeepsie. It was an exhilarating experience which made a lasting impression on me. The whole plant was spotless wherever we went, and all the workers were in immaculate overalls. After completing the tour, Tom Watson took us into lunch: not into some small private room reserved for the chairman and his colleagues, but into a large, high-roofed, glass-sided hall at which small groups of workers were enjoying their meals, busily engaged in light-hearted chatter. Seeing a vacant table, our host tipped the chairs against it, and we went to help ourselves to our food. This was an eye-opener.

There was no question of having differing levels according to status in the firm, nor was there any question of starting off with sawdust on the floor and, if fortunate with promotion, ending up with linoleum and a table cloth – or, if appointed a wealthy director, having it laid with silver and glassware. This was a democratically organised body in which everyone's social status was the same, whatever their working position within the firm. After lunch I was shown Tom Watson's own office. His desk was entirely free of paper. There was only one item which caught the eye. In the middle stood a plaque on which was engraved the one word, 'Think'. Returning to our car we passed the golf course, where many of the firm's employees were already actively engaged. 'That's provided for them by the firm,' said Tom Watson. 'But how on earth can they be playing now?' I asked. 'Oh, they are from the first shift. They have had their lunch, and a lot of them like to spend part of the afternoon on the golf course,' replied my host proudly. No wonder IBM had such a high reputation and was an immense success.

After those memorable visits early in January 1940, I left for New York and soon sailed for home on the Cunard White Star *Georgic*. This was a gloomy voyage: there were only around fifty people on board, and we had to provide our own entertainment. This time the thought of a submarine attack was never far from our minds. Perhaps it was our imagination, but the liner seemed to steam off course and certainly took far longer than usual to complete the voyage. On a bleak Sunday morning in mid-January, we steamed up the Mersey and into Liverpool docks. The clouds were low, it was drizzling with rain and there was hardly a soul around. I felt acutely aware that this was a country at war. Having got my baggage out through customs, I found a train bound for London. It was bitterly cold and the compartments were unheated. There was no food available. The train trundled slowly south, seemingly stopping at every station and gradually filling up. The journey to London lasted for many hours and, after humping my baggage across from Euston to Victoria, I arrived late that night at my home at Broadstairs. I had no idea what the future held and there were still no instructions from the Royal Artillery. All I knew was that my present travels were over; and what travels my wartime service would bring I could not know.

It certainly gave me intense pleasure to be back with my parents again for a few months at the beginning of 1940, but we were all naturally worried about my brother John. He had been a territorial in the East Kent Infantry Regiment, the Buffs, and was called up immediately upon the outbreak of war. He had then crossed the Channel with them in the early months of the war. Our parents were now awaiting news. So far as we knew he was safe and in good health, but this was a dismal situation, made worse by the grim winter weather. It was not until 20 February 1940 that I was called to the Oxford University Joint Recruiting Board, headed by none other than Sandy Lindsay. The Board recommended, three days later, that I should be trained for a commission in the Royal Artillery, adding the simple but encouraging comment 'Good'. But I still had to go on waiting until August of that same year before I was finally called up, although I did have one false alarm when I was summoned to go to Canterbury to join the Buffs myself. Then, two days before I was due to report, I received another notice saying that 'owing to unforeseen circumstances', presumably meaning that someone had blundered, my calling-up notice had been cancelled. There was therefore little to do except watch events and maintain a continuous correspondence with former colleagues in the same position. I did at one stage suggest to Penguin Books that they might wish to commission a work from me about my experiences in the United States, but they politely refused.

I got the chance, however, of having one piece of contentious writing published while waiting for my call-up. In March 1940, Lord De La Warr, President of the Board of Education, used a radio broadcast to set out his objective of 'the restoration of full-time education for every child of every age-group in every type of area'. The *Spectator* commented that 'soon, there will be due for consideration the whole question of the public schools and other secondary schools and their relation to all children of the nation, not excluding those beginning in the elementary schools'. This was followed on 5 April 1940 by an article from Mark Bonham Carter, entitled 'The Public Schoolboy's View', in which he suggested that perhaps 25 per cent of places in public schools should be taken by children on state-financed scholarships – akin to what became the Assisted Places Scheme. He recognised that such a proposal would be met with hostility by many of the public schools, but emphasised that he did not wish to change many of their ideals: 'the ideal of the gentleman, so long as it remains a moral and not a social distinction, is a good one, and the attempt to instil a sense of responsibility into the consciousness of the young, if not altogether successful, is certainly not unworthy'. He also stressed that there should not be any financial inequality between the scholars and their fee-paying companions, and that they should all live under exactly the same conditions.

I answered this in the *Spectator* a fortnight later, my 'Secondary Schoolboy's View' contributing a different perspective to the debate. Many of the public schools were known to be in financial difficulties at this time, and I was convinced that this was the main motivation behind the proposals for state bursaries to such schools: 'when economies and a simpler mode of life prove insufficient it seems resort must be had to the Government for financial aid through a system of State scholars'. Meanwhile, nobody spared a thought for the youngsters who would have to be the first to endure this experiment in social engineering, nor for the effects on the schools from which they would make an exodus. After all, these youngsters were the leaders in embryo of their houses, in work and in sport, in music and debate, and their loss would lower the standards of their schools all round.

I had not been through a process of transfer from the maintained system to a more privileged one at the age of thirteen myself, but I had seen snobbery and inequality aplenty between students at Oxford. Although my own college proved to be largely free from such unpleasantnesses, I knew that many students in other colleges were scarred by it. 'To have to answer that one's father is a bus driver, or a carpenter, perhaps,' I wrote,

> to know that one's parents cannot afford to travel to school functions, or to see them there, unhappy and ill at ease, and feel oneself shudder at a rough accent or a 'we was'; to be asked to stay with a school friend and to have to refuse for fear of asking him back to a humble villa; to have no answer to others' stories of travel in the holidays; worst of all, to see one's parents, who have made such sacrifices, grieve because they know one cannot have all the things one's associates have; that is what it will mean for a State scholar.

I was genuinely fearful that such an experiment would merely substitute for one system of apartheid another, more painful one. 'At Oxford,' I continued, 'I've seen public and secondary schoolboys together; and, even in that home of tolerance, there is the unhappiness which I am sure would exist, many times multiplied, were this scheme to be adopted in our schools. Our legislators will ignore it at their peril.'

The search for genuine equality of opportunity in education is quixotic, of course, and the same debate continues today. Certainly, most independent schools are now very forward-looking, and have generally rid themselves of both corporal punishment and the distasteful elements of class arrogance which used to mark them out. They are also, I feel, far more likely these days to integrate their activities with those of their local communities. It remains true that their alumni have a degree of self-confidence which is less commonly inculcated in the maintained sector. I still believe, however, that a policy of extracting the highest fliers from the state sector in significant numbers would have an unacceptably debilitating impact on those who remained.

Madron Seligman had become president of the Oxford Union and had succeeded in persuading Edvard Beneš, the exiled Czech President, to speak there in a debate on the motion 'This House has no faith in liberal Western democracy as a basis of government', to which Madron also invited me. Beneš made a passionate speech in support of democracy, which I seconded, and secured the support of the whole house. The debate was also attended by the Czech ambassador in London, Jan Masaryk, the son of his country's founder – later to die in mysterious circumstances just after the communist takeover in post-war Prague. This debate took my mind back vividly to the days of Munich and 'Peace in our time', when we had all argued so vehemently in that same chamber about whether Chamberlain's actions would inevitably lead to the occupation of Czechoslovakia. Although some familiar faces were still present for the Beneš debate, we all knew that others were now already serving in His Majesty's Forces, which made the impact of this later occasion even more shattering.

Then there came what many had expected and we had all feared: the German invasion of the Low Countries and France. Neville Chamberlain resigned as Prime Minister and Churchill took his place, even though he had been First Lord of the Admiralty at the time of the Norwegian fiasco, one of the few substantial engagements thus far in the European war. I was hugely relieved, for it had been well known that the Foreign Secretary, Lord Halifax, had been Chamberlain's chosen successor. I was convinced that it would be a massive blunder to appoint a Prime Minister from the House of Lords, especially at a time of war, when the greatest possible popular support was needed; and, in any case, I felt that Halifax had not distinguished himself during the period of appeasement. Indeed, Chamberlain had used Halifax to manipulate Eden out of the Foreign Office, when he encouraged him, without reference to Eden, to accept an invitation to go hunting with Göring in Germany only a few months before Munich. When the crunch came, however, it may well have been Halifax himself, backed by the then Chief Whip, David Margesson, who insisted on Churchill's appointment. Margesson was never mentioned as having been present at the meeting which settled this issue at No. 10, but it is customary for the Chief Whip's presence never to be noted in the minutes. The feeling on the government backbenches at that time certainly mirrored feeling in the country, and the general view was that only Churchill had the necessary resolve to deal with the growing crisis.

Churchill immediately formed his government and, despite all their differences and their long-established mutual antagonism, Churchill included Chamberlain in his War Cabinet and allowed him to remain the leader of the Conservative Party. It was long the custom that former leaders wishing to remain in politics should be immediately offered a top position. Lloyd George invited Balfour into his government in 1916 and, as I mentioned, Churchill kept Chamberlain on the front bench in 1940. I invited Sir Alec Douglas-Home to take the Foreign and Commonwealth Office brief in my Shadow Cabinet when I became leader of the Conservative

Party in 1965, and then to be Foreign Secretary when I became Prime Minister in 1970. That tradition was later abandoned.

One of Winston Churchill's top priorities was to strengthen French opposition to the enemy. In 1930, he had supported a plan for European Union suggested by the then Prime Minister of France, Aristide Briand, but the idea had been dropped by the League of Nations Assembly. He now revived that idea as a matter of the greatest urgency, making several visits to France between late May 1940 and the middle of the following month, as the German army was advancing. His strategy culminated in the 'Declaration of Union', written on 16 June 1940, which read as follows:

At this most fateful moment in the history of the modern world the Governments of the United Kingdom and the French Republic make this declaration of indissoluble union and unyielding resolution in their common defence of justice and freedom against subjection to a system which reduces mankind to a life of robots and slaves.

The two Governments declare that France and Great Britain shall no longer be two nations, but one Franco-British Union.

The constitution of the Union will provide for joint organs of defence, foreign, financial, and economic policies.

Every citizen of France will enjoy immediately citizenship of Great Britain; every British subject will become a citizen of France.

Both countries will share responsibility for the repair of the devastation of war, wherever it occurs in their territories, and the resources of both shall be equally, and as one, applied to that purpose.

During the war there shall be a single War Cabinet, and all the forces of Britain and France, whether on land, sea, or in the air, will be placed under its direction. It will govern from wherever it best can. The two Parliaments will be formally associated. The nations of the British Empire are already forming new armies. France will keep her available forces in the field, on the sea, and in the air. The Union appeals to the United States to fortify the economic resources of the Allies, and to bring her powerful material aid to the common cause.

The Union will concentrate its whole energy against the power of the enemy, no matter where the battle may be.

And thus we shall conquer.

The Cabinet Secretary, Edward Bridges, whose son Tom later became one of my private secretaries at No. 10, had produced a first draft of the Declaration on the morning of 16 June. Churchill then revised it repeatedly during the afternoon with Cabinet colleagues, from whom the final draft received unanimous agreement. When General de Gaulle, Jean Monnet and René Pleven (the Declaration's instigator) saw its final form, they were all highly excited and relieved, and hoped that it would give the French government, and its military commanders, the assurance it needed to carry on the war in North Africa. This was also the view of the French Prime Minister, Paul Reynaud, when he received the text in Bordeaux that same day. Although he twice read the Declaration through to his colleagues, and wholeheartedly supported it himself, it did nothing to improve their demoralised and defeatist condition. Marshal Pétain and General Weygand, in advocating capitulation to Germany, apparently had no problem in carrying the day and overruling Reynaud, who was forced to resign as Prime Minister. How different the course of the war might have been, and the state of Europe after it, if this Declaration of Union had become a reality.

Though the Declaration was intended as a dramatic statement of Anglo-French unity, it rested on a popular sentiment which had been growing through the late 1930s in support of closer association between Britain and France. Many people recognised that the two nations shared a considerable community of interests that should be given formal expression. The failure of this Declaration symbolised the capitulation of France, and soon British forces were being driven back to the coast at Dunkirk. Among them was my brother John. The small boats from our corner of the Channel coast, in particular Ramsgate and Margate, went across as part of the flotilla that helped with the evacuation. The *Perseverance*, a small motor pleasure boat, together with a few other motor boats handled by their individual owners, also went across from Broadstairs and joined the fleet. Fortunately the weather held up throughout the entire evacuation. The thought of what would happen if it broke into gales and rough seas was too horrifying to contemplate. On landing, the troops were whisked off to depots inland, so unfortunately John did not enjoy an opportunity to come home before being transported to the Buffs' depot in Canterbury. In fact, I was to meet him only once during the conflict, on the European mainland after D-Day.

A few weeks after Dunkirk, the bombing of our corner of Kent from across the Channel began to become serious. Thanet was repeatedly hit by quick 'in and out' raids, almost at sea level. As we heard the whine of the bombs we had to make a mad dash for our Anderson air-raid shelters. Although the bombing raids at that time did comparatively little damage, many people had already left the town to go inland, a route which my father was to follow later in the summer. His business as a builder collapsed and he obtained employment with the City of London Corporation. He and my mother went to live in Sutton, Surrey, where I visited them whenever I was on leave from the army, and where they stayed until after the end of the war.

Now the real war was on. We British were isolated. During this time,

I kept in close contact with friends and contemporaries from Oxford days, including Ashley Raeburn. In a letter to another colleague from Balliol who had already been called up, I wrote: 'This rock on which Hitler will break himself is the rock on which Europe will have to be rebuilt afterwards, and this time we shall not throw away that chance. We shall do it alone, and we alone, it will be said, were the only ones who could do it. We shall have finally justified ourselves.'

When my own call-up came in early August, I was ordered to report to the Royal Artillery Training Headquarters, near Storrington in Sussex, and some fifteen miles from Worthing on the south coast. It was a very pleasant place indeed, with the camp nestling in a beautiful corner of the South Downs. The weather was splendid all the summer and, in the early evening after our day's work was done, we could get away from it all by climbing to the top of the Downs, taking a look at the distant sea and clambering down by another route. At weekends, when not on duty, we visited the other villages near by.

The first three days at the camp were spent in familiarising ourselves with our new environment: the large living hut, which accommodated around twenty of us; the dining room; the other messes in which we might have to serve; and, of course, the guard rooms in which we would each do our periods of duty. We were issued with our clothes and general equipment, and on the third day we had our vaccinations. My father had always barred me from being vaccinated because he was convinced that this procedure was unjustifiably dangerous. But the Medical Officer insisted. I began to believe that my father had been right all along when, about four or five days after the vaccination, my left arm began to swell considerably, then to stiffen and finally to turn black. I reported to a doctor the next morning, and he immediately rushed me into the camp hospital. By this time I was beginning to feel deadly ill and swallowed whatever I was given. My official documents had been taken away from me, but, waking up in a hot sweat in the middle of the night, I rang for the ward orderly and demanded back my AB47 pay book. 'You don't need that now,' he said, 'because you will be paid automatically all the time you are in hospital.' 'I don't want it for that,' I replied, 'the last two pages are blank and I want them to make my will.' With a strange look in his eyes, he complied. I filled it in, but it was never used, for a week or so later I had fully recovered.

Once I got back to the normal routine, I soon began to know the rest of the hut. In my days at Balliol, I had grown used to having people around me with whom I had at least something in common. This was quite different, for these men came from every sort of home and family, background and job. But the spirit was excellent, and the men gladly and openly described and discussed all aspects of their lives, including their sexual activities. When we were paraded for an address by the Medical Officer, one felt there was little new information that he had to offer them. The relationship between the members of the hut was understanding and tolerant. There was little attempt to score points, although the opportunities within such a socially disparate crowd were obvious and manifold. Although I was well used to a communal life, the Gunners camp was very different from Oxford: here we did not enjoy the freedoms which were encouraged in the atmosphere of individual self-development which I knew from Balliol days.

I soon found a soulmate in my fellow recruit Robert Irving, who proved to be an excellent all-round musician as well as a fine pianist. Three years older than me, Robert had been a scholar at Winchester College, and later taught music there. After the war he was, briefly, associate conductor of the BBC Scottish Orchestra, and then became, for nine years, conductor of the orchestra at the Sadler's Wells (later the Royal) Ballet Company. It was in the United States, however, that he really made his name. He was for some thirty years musical director of the New York City Ballet, and I heard him conduct there in the early 1980s. Together in those wartime days, we frequently used to walk into the village of Storrington for a drink at the local hostelry, the White Hart, where, to my astonishment, we discovered Sir Arnold Bax, the then undervalued and now almost entirely forgotten British composer, occupying a corner seat which he had evidently made his own. We both cherished his wealth of anecdotes about music and musicians. Bax had retreated there from London in the company of Harriet Cohen, the renowned concert pianist. On Sunday afternoons we listened to chamber music together in the house of a friendly neighbour who possessed a Bechstein grand piano.

When the Battle of Britain began in the middle of August 1940, we were in the front line. We watched day after day as the planes fought overhead. As many of them crashed, we went off to find them, and to provide any help we could for survivors, whether they were British or German. At night, the searchlight batteries stationed alongside the camp were operating through the darkness, and we would often get called out again for the same purpose. All too often there was little that could be done. After three months I was recommended for a commission, went to Reading to be interviewed and was approved. In consequence, I went off in the autumn of 1940 to the Officer Cadet Training Unit (OCTU), at Shrivenham in Wiltshire. My musical activities with Robert Irving were broken off because he failed to pass the interview, left the Gunners and was transferred at his own request to the Royal Air Force, where he became a tail gunner in a bomber. However, on arrival at the OCTU, I could catch up with an earlier musical acquaintance, Joseph Cooper, the one-time organ scholar at Keble College, Oxford, whom I had attempted to succeed in that position. He was busily engaged, as usual, in organising musical and theatrical entertainments of every kind.

At Shrivenham, my training was concentrated on the practical skills of gunnery. I was trained in ground and anti-aircraft gunnery – the 3.7-inch AA guns that we were to use in the European campaign were suitable for both purposes. The OCTU was well organised and concentrated intensively on its work, but there was occasionally time to explore the Wiltshire Downs and often, at weekends, I would enjoy a meal at the Bell in Faringdon, a delightful country pub. Shrivenham was also made more bearable for me by its proximity to Oxford. On a few free weekends, I was able to cadge a lift to Oxford and look at the bookshops, have dinner with some of the dons still left there, stay in college for the night, go to a chapel service and get back to camp on Sunday evening. It was, however, a different Oxford from the one I had known, and those stationed there for wartime purposes were naturally absorbed in their immediate tasks. It all became rather remote and Oxford's attraction to me died a natural death. It was some considerable time after the end of the war before I re-established a close connection with it.

I was commissioned in the Royal Artillery in March 1941, and posted to 107 Heavy Anti-Aircraft Regiment, Royal Artillery, which had been formed on 4 September 1940, at its headquarters at Chester. This was my first direct experience of the north of England. After a preliminary interview with the Commanding Officer and the Adjutant, I was sent for an interview, together with another newly commissioned second lieutenant, to one of the Regiment's four batteries – 335 Battery at Warrington. After talking to each of us individually, the Battery Commander, Major George Chadd, asked me to come back. 'I have decided to take you,' he said. 'The other one didn't even salute!' He subsequently asked me to form a Battery Concert and Dance Band, to help lift the morale of the troops. Our resources were inevitably limited, but a trumpet, a saxophone, a piano and drums gave us everything we needed to get going, and we were later joined by two vocalists. Our band was soon in demand across Merseyside, and our own arrangement of 'Tiger Rag', with which we ended our programme, became quite celebrated. One Sunday afternoon, the band was booked to play at a Troops' Tea Dance in Chester. No transport was available, nor was it permitted for such frivolous excursions. So Captain Williams, our Regimental Medical Officer, told me that I could borrow his ambulance as nobody ever seemed to question where that went. Before reaching Chester we were held up at a canal bridge, and so we took the opportunity of having an impromptu rehearsal, practising our signature tune 'When You're Smiling, the Whole World Smiles with You' in the back of the vehicle. Unfortunately, the Commanding Officer's staff car drew up behind us at that point, and, recognising his own regimental ambulance, Colonel Barrow instructed his driver to investigate this noise. When the ambulance doors opened, we were caught red-handed. All of a sudden, the whole world did not seem to be smiling quite so broadly.

As my first battery commander, George Chadd made an instant impression on me. He had been a territorial officer in Norfolk, and a cross-section of the senior NCOs in our battery had served with him in the TA. In his instructions he was always clear, accurate and precise. At the same time, he maintained a genuine and active interest in everything that was going on in the battery and a robust good humour towards everyone. George and I were subsequently to enjoy a lifelong friendship, ending only with his death, in his ninetieth year, in 1997. I was best man at his wedding, and even had to deputise on the organ when the church organist was rushed off to hospital for an appendix operation the night before the service. I was also godfather to George's eldest son, Christopher, who, tragically, was drowned when sailing on my racing yacht *Morning Cloud 3*, after it sank in a gale off the Sussex coast (see p. 527).

Stationed with the guns and troops at Moore, just outside Warrington, I quickly realised the difference between the theory of the drills I had so far been taught and the hard practical experience of being available at any moment of the day or night, to deal with marauding bombers. Being at Warrington for this period enabled me to arrive at a considered view of the prevailing social and environmental conditions in the north of England. I was astonished, indeed horrified, to see this creation of the Industrial Revolution – the rows of tiny houses back to back, the cobbled streets, the litter and the dirt, as well as the decaying remnants of industrial activity. I realised then how much needed to be done in this town alone to bring it up to the levels which would be regarded as acceptable in the south.

After taking up my post at Warrington, it was not long before I was sent off to Ty Croes on Anglesey, a rural island off the North Wales coast, for a three-week advanced gunnery course. This process of itinerant gunnery instruction continued, on and off, until my regiment went to mainland Europe in 1944. Although visits to Europe were out of the question for the time being, I was certainly getting to know more and more of my own country. I learned a great deal from the training on Anglesey – and it was necessary to do so, especially as most of the others there had enjoyed considerably more practical experience on gun-sites than I had. However, I did not particularly distinguish myself in the eyes of the authorities. At the first lecture, a Brigadier outlined a tactical situation, in which we and the guns were placed on one side of a large ravine, with the enemy on the other side. 'What would you do now?' he demanded and, looking slowly around the room, pointed a heavy finger at me. Drawing on my OCTU briefings I replied very smartly, 'Sir, I would sit down and make an appreciation of the situation.' Whereupon he looked furiously at me and then exploded: 'Don't be such a bloody fool, giving me that sort of nonsense. I asked what would you *do . . . do . . . do.*' He then turned his fire on to my neighbour.

On my return to Battery Headquarters I was posted on to command 'D' Troop at 'V' Site – known as Vic Site – near Alvanley, north-east of Chester and south of Liverpool, the city it had been stationed to protect. I was greatly helped in this posting by the excellence of my number two, Sandy Pearce, who arrived soon afterwards. Sandy had been in the leather business before the war, but like so many others had quickly adjusted to army life. He later spent his career in South Africa, but now lives just outside Cambridge. I soon realised how valuable the three months I had spent at the Storrington Camp were going to prove. They had enabled me to familiarize myself with the outlook and habits of the men who now made up the gun crews which I had to command. I better understood their ways of thinking, how to meet their needs and how to secure their loyalty. These lessons were first put to a practical test when the continuous large-scale bombing of Liverpool took place in May 1941.

Outside London this was the heaviest bombardment of any British city, going on all night, every night, for around a fortnight. The gun crews had to sleep during the day, whenever they could get a break from the constant work of maintaining the guns and collecting more ammunition for repulsing the next attack – and we all had, of course, to be ready at every moment of the day and night to help drive away the enemy. This posting lasted for around six months, and our only real break from the gunfire and constant vigilance was the occasional trip into Chester, which escaped the bombing virtually unscathed, or Liverpool, where we would have a drink in the one hotel in the centre of the city which was still standing – the Adelphi, now judged worthy of its own television show. We were all haunted by the sight of this historic city at the end of that intensive bombardment. Despite the relentlessness of their attacks, however, the Luftwaffe never succeeded in preventing the working of the port.

At Vic Site, the senior NCOs and many of the Gunners were from the Norfolk Territorial regiment which had originally been the foundation of our wartime unit. One of the sergeants once reported to me, in a typically robust and matter-of-fact way, that an accident had occurred to one of the men in his gun-pit. I asked him to fill in the usual form, giving a full account of what had occurred. He sat down and wrote out, 'The gun crew had been carrying out normal gun practice. I ordered the crew to swing the gun round as speedily as it could to face an imaginary on-coming plane. To my surprise, the gun suddenly jerked to a stop. On going to investigate, I found the head of Gunner Ettridge jammed between the gun barrel and the wall of the gun-pit. I therefore reversed the gun in order to extract the head of Gunner Ettridge which has now been removed to hospital.' I never did find out what the hospital could do to put poor Gunner Ettridge back together again.

On 17 March 1942, I became Adjutant of the regiment and went still further north, to the new Regimental Headquarters at Preston, where I spent my time dealing with four batteries spread from Blackburn to Blackpool. The Lancastrians were always welcoming, but the troops found the atmosphere altogether less agreeable when we spent the three months of March, April and May 1942 in Erdington, a suburb of Birmingham. The factory workers there were earning a great deal of money, and spent it copiously in the pubs. I was particularly astonished and appalled, perhaps naively, to discover that the women there drank glasses of port and lemon. Birmingham seemed to enjoy a charmed life while we were there, with hardly a single air attack, but it was the differences in living conditions and social activities which made their impact on the Gunners.

During 1942, I was also sent to Manorbier in South-West Wales, close to Tenby, for a course in advanced gunnery. I booked into what I had been told was the one decent hotel in the town, the Imperial. There I found all of the brigadiers who were also attending the course, and travelled with them in a bus to the camp on the first morning of training. Upon arrival, I was told that I had been expected at the camp the night before, where all my fellow students were – and that there was still a billet for me there. I did not much fancy that, however, and decided to stay on at the hotel, along with the brigadiers, and commute with them each day. It was in this camp that I met a senior gunnery instructor, Captain Michael Fraser, who was subsequently to become a close friend. When I entered Parliament, he was at the Conservative Research Department and, later, I appointed him Deputy Chairman of the party. Michael Fraser's spruce appearance and tremendous physical as well as mental energy made an immediate impact. He was always precise, both in his instructions and in his explanations of them. I came to respect Michael's judgement immensely, as many others in the Conservative Party subsequently came to do after the war when he made such a success of his backstage political life. At the beginning of 1943, we headed southwards to Buckinghamshire and carried out exercises around towns such as Amersham and Beaconsfield. After these postings we went on to spend several weeks in Chichester, which was always so vulnerable to attacks from across the Channel. It was here that I had my first experience of appearing at a court martial, in the case of one of my battery commanders, who had been found in the early hours of the morning lying drunk in a ditch.

With the exception of the dance band which I set up when in the north-west, the war years were very thin for me musically. We spent so much time travelling around that I had no opportunity to keep my own volumes of music with me for study, and there were also few signs of concert life in most of the places that we visited. I think all that I managed in the north-west was to hear the London Philharmonic Orchestra playing works by Brahms and Beethoven in Preston early in 1942, conducted by Edric Cundell, and I was always desperately jealous of those who could go to hear Myra Hess's famous lunchtime recitals in the National Gallery in London. On a brief stopover in the capital, however, I did manage to hear Clifford Curzon play Brahms's D Minor Piano Concerto at the Stoll Theatre, Kingsway in late March 1943. In later years I got to know Curzon well, and admired both his pianistic skill and his delightful, modest personality. He played Mozart's C Minor Piano Concerto with me when I conducted the London Symphony Orchestra in 1976 to celebrate the publication of my book *Music: A Joy for Life*.

The one really major musical event of the war years which I did succeed in attending was the première of Ralph Vaughan Williams' Symphony No. 5 in D. Concerts were still held in the Royal Albert Hall despite the Blitz and I was one of the comparatively small number of people who made it to that historic promenade performance, by the London Philharmonic Orchestra on 24 June 1943. Vaughan Williams was by then over seventy, and the simplicity of his conducting was perfectly in keeping with the nobility of his latest symphony. An air-raid warning had sounded before the concert began, but that was ignored. Listening to a musical utterance of such beauty and power put all of that out of our minds. As the last movement shifted into the great chorale 'Lasst uns erfreuen', everyone in the hall felt deeply moved to have been present for this latest blossoming of Vaughan Williams' genius, in a work which was in such contrast to the savagery of his preceding symphony. There were few moments of spiritual illumination in those dark days, but that extraordinary, rather dishevelled figure on the podium had provided one of them.

It was during a stint at Redesdale in the north-east, just a fortnight later, that I thought the end had come for me. I had endured bouts of severe gastric pain for some months, but limited my treatment to digestive tablets. I was in charge of regimental gunnery practice on the morning of 7 July 1943 when I began to suffer a really acute attack of pains in my abdomen. The Medical Officer, who was in attendance in case of accidents, saw me in agony and immediately decided that action must be taken, for the problem had gone on long enough. I had no strength to resist when he insisted upon taking me in his car to the Royal Victoria Infirmary in Newcastle to get my problem seen to. As we drove in his car into the centre of the city, every pothole we hit caused me agony. I felt like death, and was already enduring the worst journey of my life when the most appalling storm broke upon us, with lightning, thunder and blinding rain. I really did begin to think that the end was nigh – and all in true Wagnerian style.

Seeing a man trying to shelter under a tree, we stopped and the Medical Officer asked him for directions. He replied, 'Oh, the Infirmary's quite close: take the next on your right, then it's immediately on your right.' Leaving him to contend with the elements, we drove on. We followed his directions, went through some austere-looking grey gates and pulled up before a broad, dark building. The MO got out and rang a heavy bell. At first there was only an ominous silence, so he tried again, twice. Finally we heard the door being unbolted, and a wizened man appeared, like some grim Dickensian vision. 'Is this the Royal Victoria Infirmary?' asked the MO. 'No,' replied the cheerless figure, 'it's the mortuary. The hospital is next door.' I have never been a superstitious man, but I did begin to fall a little into the grip of pessimism at this point. We drove straight on to the hospital next door where I was whisked into a private room. Once I had settled in there, I wrote a letter to my parents and brother, in case I did not survive whatever lay ahead. Although excerpts from this letter make it all too apparent how wretched I was feeling, they also accurately reflect my feelings towards my family:

It would be extraordinary if anything happened this way in a war, instead of on the battlefield or in a blitz. But it's the risk of living and life wouldn't be possible without it.

Please do not grieve for me. Our life together has always been a happy one, and I have made full and good use of the life I have been given. My regret is that it will not be possible to look after you in later years after all you have done for Bubbles [my brother, John] and myself. It is very little that we have so far been able to repay. I am sure I can leave you both safely in Bubbles' hands.

It is not possible to thank you for all you have done, for your love, for my schooling, my career, and for the sacrifices which you have all the time made. Everything I have done I have owed largely to my early training and the standards you taught me.

Fortunately, this sombre letter did not have to be delivered, for I was operated on successfully the next morning. I was told that the appendix which the surgeons removed was the grisliest they had ever seen, being thoroughly gangrenous, and that they had it pickled and put it on exhibition. After the operation, I went to Penshurst, in Kent, for a month's recuperation and while there read Thomas Mann's brilliant parable of a family's rise and fall, *Buddenbrooks*. By the time I returned to active service, at nearby Ashford, it was clear that I would soon be resuming my travels in mainland Europe.

We stayed several months during the latter part of 1943 in the south, training at Blandford and on Salisbury Plain. In December we moved on to Northampton and then, at the very end of the month, my entire regiment was posted again to the north-east. The army decreed that we should do this over Christmas, and we had to endure two days on the road, spending the night of 23 December in Doncaster and reaching Catterick staging camp late on Christmas Eve. As an alleged special dispensation, we were told that we could spend Christmas Day at the camp. This turned out to be less of a privilege than it was implied to be. On arrival at the camp, already tired and dispirited, we found it deserted, and the regiment had to provide for itself. I could not conceive of a more depressing transit camp than Catterick, and this was, without doubt, the worst Christmas I have ever experienced.

We were thankful to get up to Otterburn on Boxing Day, where we were to spend most of our time on the ranges, with the occasional break at Newcastle at the weekend. When I became the Secretary of State for Industry, Trade and Regional Development in 1963, I already knew the north-east and its principal city Newcastle well, thanks to this posting. By then, the main theatre had again fallen into disrepair. In the war years, it was alleged to have become a brothel. I organised its restoration and was present at its opening as an opera house – only for it to burn down a year later. Our preparations in early 1944 then took us to Whitby, further down on the east coast, for coastal gunnery practice. Almost deserted as they were, the harbour and old town were undeniably attractive, but my favourite spot was a tiny village along the coast, Sandsend, with its excellent pub. I have always wanted to go back there, but never did in case I should find the place a disappointment upon my return. It is often said that the best cure for nostalgia is to return to the site of any past happiness which prompts it, and twice I have tested this. Returning to Alvanley, I found just an ordinary field, surrounded by a broken-down hedge, with nothing to evoke the extraordinary, bustling time I remembered, when a whole troop of Gunners was engaged single-mindedly in the defence of a great city. Of those in the village to whom I spoke, few remembered those days. Many years later I recrossed the bridge at Nijmegen to visit the farmhouse that we had used as our headquarters there. I found that the farm had a new owner and, once again, nothing remained to show that we had ever been there. This has cured me of ever wanting to see the sites of my wartime memories again.

The allied invasion of France took place on 6 June 1944. What time remained before crossing the Channel our regiment completed in the southern counties of England and, on 23 June, we were told to proceed to Middleton, near Bognor, to carry out the waterproofing of our guns. This took us six days and we then moved our guns to the London docks at the beginning of July. At 0830 hours on Monday 3 July, we finally began to board our ship at the Royal Albert Docks at Tilbury. During the day, we embarked the men and packed them into the hold, in preparation for our voyage across the English Channel. We spent that night lying off Southend and a flotilla of other landing craft assembled around us during Tuesday 4 July, a gloriously sunny day which the men spent sunbathing, reading or playing cards. The senior officers were briefed that afternoon on what lay ahead, and we sailed off by night down the Thames, in complete darkness. On Wednesday 5 July we passed through the Straits of Dover, sailed along the south coast past the Isle of Wight, and then crossed the Channel. The record shows that we came opposite the Normandy beaches, at last, at about 1700 hours that day. What an amazing and inspiring sight it made, as hundreds of other ships came into view while we were going ashore at Arromanches.

We disembarked without hindrance, brought our artillery on to French soil on 6 July and, on the following day, left the assembly area and moved on to the small village of Thaon. After a short stay there we established our headquarters and base on the hill just outside Ouistreham, while the batteries carved niches for themselves in the trees further downhill. They were deployed in support of the 6th Airborne Division, who had made the first landing and in a brilliant operation had captured the Pegasus bridge across the River Orne. My own first command post, dug into the ground with tree trunks over the top, was in an orchard on a slope overlooking the battle area to the east. Our guns had a range of over sixteen miles, sufficient for reaching the Germans, who were deployed a considerable distance on the other side. The Germans quickly retaliated to the pounding we were giving them, and we soon suffered our first casualties.

Getting into action in France rapidly dispelled the frustration I had so often felt at home. We were no longer just defending ourselves against the German planes, we were now part of the counter-attacking allied forces, bent on driving the German army out of France and the other occupied territories. The people of Normandy, and so much of the rest of France that I loved, were suffering terrible hardships through these battles, and we were all determined to bring the whole business to a close as quickly as possible. The debris of war that we had seen as we landed on the Normandy shore, littered with wrecked equipment, damaged boats and discarded clothing, hardened our resolve. We were now taking positive action to kick the Nazi war machine out of Western Europe. I was back once again on my European travels, and the nine months of campaigning which followed were among the most demanding in my life.

Whenever I was not preoccupied as Adjutant in the command post, there was always administration to be dealt with: the fact that we were carrying out mobile operations in an overseas theatre of war in no way seemed to diminish the amount of information required on seemingly innumerable forms by those sitting in the War Office back home. Away from gunnery duties, I spent my time communicating with the Regimental Quartermaster at rear headquarters, Major William Harrington RA, a regular soldier, about supplies. No regiment could have been better served throughout the whole war than we were by Harry. He had everything under control and met all our needs fully and promptly – wherever we were. I lost a good friend when he was drowned some years later in the Dead Sea, being unable to right himself after turning over on to his stomach while bathing.

I also had to ensure that the soldiers' mail gave away no military information of any importance, as well as briefing the rest of the regiment about the campaign. In this I was invariably helped by my Intelligence Officer, Stephen Wilde, a director of a steel firm from Sheffield who always had every necessary piece of information at his fingertips. There was virtually no relaxation to be found for the men in the nearby village, except to have an occasional drink of the local brew of Calvados, a firewater of the most powerful kind which quickly wreaked havoc on those accustomed only to beer. Each officer was rationed to one bottle of whisky per month, and we tried to make it last by diluting it with lemon squash. There was a little reminder of home when I heard at the beginning of August that my BA and MA had been conferred upon me in Oxford, in my absence.

Our first major operation was the bombardment of Caen, beginning at dawn on 9 July, my twenty-eighth brithday, after heavy air attacks on the city the night before. In this, we were taking part in the largest bombardment the world had yet seen. It continued for several hours, after which we moved down into the town to find that everything was destroyed and the roads were covered with the rubble of the fallen buildings. The Sappers were doing their utmost to level things out so that we could advance more easily and keep up the pressure on the retreating Germans. It was a painful business to have taken part in the destruction of one of France's oldest and most renowned towns, but we could reassure ourselves that it was part of the beginning of the end of the war.

The town of Falaise was taken by the allies during the third week of August, and our next major battleground was the operation to close the 'Falaise Gap'. As we pressed on through the Gap, we saw the remains of shelled vehicles, the bodies left behind in ditches by the retreating Germans and the stinking carcasses of animals in the fields – the full carnage of war on a scale we had not previously encountered. I realised then that this horrifying battleground would be repeated on many occasions, as we advanced across country. The speedier and the more successful we were, the deeper would be the piles of bloodied bodies of men and animals through which we would pass.

American troops first crossed the Seine at Mantes on 20 August and, on the following day, our forces finally closed the Gap, taking 50,000 German prisoners of war in the process. The allies then began to sweep across France, which would lead us through Belgium and, ultimately, into Germany. We joined a long column moving north-east first to the Seine, then through Amiens on 1 September and Arras on the 2nd and thence on to the Belgian frontier, where we were greeted with wild delight. In every village on the way to Tournai, flowers were thrown on to our trucks, flags were thrust into our hands, we were loaded with fruit and people leaped on to the gun carriages shouting with joy. By now the German army had been divided, with those to the west being trapped between the main road north of Antwerp, which we held, and the Channel coast.

Although we were still alert to the possibility of further attacks from the Germans, our greatest fear on this trek was that we would arrive to find that the bridges on the way to Antwerp had been blown up. In fact, the resistance movement had already prepared for our arrival with skill and courage by removing the German charges from under the pillars of the bridges, and we were able to get straight over them without any trouble. Late at night on Monday 4 September 1944, we arrived at Wilryck on the outskirts of Antwerp, where we stayed until the 22nd. Our recce units were among the first in the docks at Antwerp, where they took over two barge-loads of supplies. One provided enough camouflage clothing, anoraks and padded trousers to keep the whole regiment warm throughout the winter. The other contained, among other things, some excellent liqueurs which were appropriately distributed and made life much more palatable for everyone. We subsequently discovered that one regiment in Brussels had captured all the reserves of champagne and listed a special 'champagne point', where their supply vehicles could collect the quantities of fine wine left behind by the Germans, as well as essential supplies such as petrol, oil and lubricants. Although they were no doubt celebrating in what was considered to be a superior fashion, I thought on balance that our winter clothing and liqueurs represented the better capture.

As we fought across France, we had little chance of getting to know the people, but as we took full control of Antwerp in those September days our experience was quite different. We were greeted as the liberators of Wilryck, where a square was subsequently named after Colonel Slater, the Commanding Officer of the regiment, and lasting friendships, often leading to marriage, were made. On the thirtieth anniversary of our entry into the city, many members of the regiment returned there at the invitation of the mayor to take part in the celebrations. We also experienced Antwerp, a city of distinction whose broad, tree-lined avenues and imposing merchants' houses still spoke of the wealth of a historic trading port. The mayor of Antwerp, M. Heuseman, who had been a prominent and celebrated Belgian politician before the war, came back to claim his own. He entertained us well and exuded optimism and enthusiasm when we discussed the political prospects for his country.

After we took Antwerp, our guns were constantly in action, controlled from an observation post at the top of the main hotel in the city, and I spent the greater part of my time in the command post at the side of the road. I also had my only experience of a former concentration camp at this point. On 18 September 1944 I visited the old fort of Breendonck, near Willebroeck, which had been used by the Germans for the internment and murder of thousands of prisoners, mainly Belgians. Although the site had been partially cleared by the time I saw it, and all the inmates were long gone, it was a terrible, haunting place. I saw a gas chamber, a torture chamber and the open courtyard, where prisoners had been bludgeoned to death. Hooks in the ceiling, strategically placed electric sockets and runnels under the torture tables provided testimony to the atrocities that had taken place there. The atmosphere of horror was still stifling; and everyone who visited that place left it with a strengthened resolve to take this conflict quickly to the heart of Germany and to bring all of these unspeakable outrages to an end, once and for all, in the name of humanity.

One night a sergeant from the guard came into the command post to say that he had taken charge of a man who claimed to be an officer of the Welsh Guards and wanted to be directed to the line of route of the Guards' armoured division. He was in civilian clothes and carried no identity papers. It all seemed very bizarre. I told him to bring the man in so that I could hear his story myself. He looked plausible, but I was not confident of his tale. He told me that he had been wounded and sent home to England to recover. Bored and frustrated with the delay in rejoining his regiment, he had made his own way back. Having crossed the Channel he found an abandoned car. In it he had driven across France and Belgium, cadging supplies of fuel on his way – and now he wanted some help. He had no proof to give me either of his story or of his identity. A thought occurred to me. 'Do you know Philip Toynbee?' I asked him. 'Yes,' he replied. 'Well,' I said, 'Philip Toynbee was at Oxford with me and I know he is in the Welsh Guards. Give me an accurate account of Philip Toynbee's life and habits and I will arrange for you to be taken over to your regiment.' The description he set out tallied with my own experience of the one person we both knew, a former communist president of the Oxford Union, and I sent him on his way with a guide. It was a risk but it was worth taking. I next met that man on the beach of a small hotel in which we were both staying, in the south of Spain in 1961. His name was Richard Powell, and, by that time, he had become director-general of the Institute of Directors.

We then got orders to leave Antwerp and to move up into Holland. On 17 September, US airborne troops landed at Eindhoven and Nijmegen; and British troops also parachuted into Arnhem, on the Rhine. Initially, on 23 September, we moved to the harbour area at Veerle and then, on the following day, we continued east and up to Eindhoven to support the allied efforts there. Never have I seen such congestion as there was on the roads around Eindhoven on that black, filthy night. We managed to get through the town, set up a headquarters and began to deploy our guns. It was so difficult for the troop commanders to get their bearings that, when dawn broke, two of the troops found that, instead of being on opposite sides of the town as they should have been, they were in adjacent fields. Things did not seem to be going too well. On the road outside our command post General Montgomery had a meeting with General Horrocks, who was commanding XXX Corps, and his staff, to get a grip on the whole situation.

We were ordered to push straight on from Eindhoven, because the Arnhem offensive, in the face of fierce German opposition, had turned into a bloody setback for our troops. We became part of the air defence for the British forces trying to relieve their surrounded comrades in Arnhem, who were now fighting desperately for their lives. Having got the regiment over the bridge at Nijmegen on 27 September, we deployed our headquarters alongside that of the Irish Guards and spread out the batteries to support the Dorsets, who had managed to get halfway along the road to Arnhem. Crossing the bridge in a jeep had been a question of fine timing, as it was being shelled. Coming down the slope from the town we had to put our foot hard down, and hit the temporary Bailey bridge with sufficient momentum to get across the bridge in between shells. It was remarkable how seldom they ever landed on the bridge.

After this action we had a brief lull, during late October and early November 1944, and took the opportunity to organise some entertainment for ourselves in Nijmegen. We also ate well, because our regimental sergeant-major believed in supplementing our rations by living off the countryside. He once returned from one of his expeditions to Elst, the furthermost point our troops occupied along the road to Arnhem, with the splendid carcass of a freshly slain pig. He explained that, if it had been left alone grazing, it would not have been looked after properly.

There has long been much discussion and speculation about what the course of the war would have been if the para attack on Arnhem had succeeded and the allied forces had been able to continue their movement all the way up to Berlin. It was all brought home vividly to me on the last night before the summer recess of the House of Commons in July 1958. On hearing the business for that day announced in the House of Commons, Sir Winston Churchill leaned over and asked if it meant that there would be two three-line whips that evening. I pointed out that, in fact, there would be three. 'In that case,' he replied, 'it would appear to be a rare but appropriate occasion to dine at the Chief Whip's table.' Delighted, I told him that I would invite Harold Macmillan as well.

In the course of dinner they got on to the subject of Arnhem and Churchill started to deploy the condiments, knives and forks and spoons around the table as he went back over the disastrous events of that fateful battle. The argument continued vigorously until the division bell called us to vote and, once again, the argument was never settled. This dinner was not entirely wasted, however. When Churchill and I had returned to the dinner table, he murmured quietly to me, as he sipped his cognac, 'My dear, I must give you one of my pictures.' He was as good as his word, and that picture has hung in my home ever since. It was followed later by a second.

In the winter of 1944–5, we moved towards Germany as part of the offensive in the Reichswald. We were then deployed along the Maas opposite Roermond, as a holding operation. When the Ardennes offensive by the German army began on 16 December, we were used at Heide, to tie down the German forces on the other side of the river. We spent a gloomy Christmas alongside the Maas and were told to celebrate on Christmas Eve, as the enemy would be sure to attack us on Christmas Day. Even though nothing of the sort happened, we did not feel much like celebrating anything. The final, desperate attempt by the remnants of the German army to turn the tide in their favour culminated in their defeat a month later at the end of the Battle of the Bulge, on 28 January 1945. On 8 February, the allied forces launched Operation Veritable, to capture the land between the Rivers Rhine and Maas, and we played our part in supporting the allied offensive as it gradually moved up to the Rhine, which American troops first crossed in early March.

There was an interesting political interlude for me at this point. During a quiet period before the allies started their final advance into Germany, I was able to seize a forty-eight-hour leave in England which I spent with my parents at their wartime home in Sutton. The train back from London to Harwich left shortly before midnight and, while I was waiting, I decided to look in at the station tearoom. I was rather taken aback to find sitting there Roy Jenkins' father Arthur, who had entertained me on his visits to Oxford before the war. 'What on earth are you doing here at this time of night?' I asked him. He replied that he was waiting for Mr Attlee, then the Deputy Prime Minister. 'After his late-night meetings with Churchill,' he explained, 'he likes to get away from it all and we have a quiet drink together in some unusual place.' Shortly afterwards, Attlee arrived and sat down with us, quietly smoking his pipe. 'This,' said Jenkins, 'is young Heath, who was at Oxford with Roy.' 'Oh,' said Attlee. 'He's now commanding a battery of guns near the Rhine,' continued Jenkins. 'Oh,' said Attlee again. 'From what he's been saying he's obviously still interested in politics.' 'Oh,' said Attlee, for the third time. 'I think he'll make a damn good politician,' said Jenkins, ploughing on. 'I think we ought to try to grab him as one of our candidates.' 'Oh,' said Attlee. At this point the notice for my train came up, and I bade them both good night. This was the nearest I ever came to becoming a Labour candidate.

My regiment crossed the Rhine at the beginning of April, and we entered German territory for the first time during the night of the 5th at Marienbaum, north-west of Essen. I celebrated VE Day on 8 May with my battery, in the region of Kleve. The war had ended, but our work was far from over. We then started a battlefield-clearance operation of the area west of the Rhine and, at the end of May, we moved up to Hanover, as part of the occupying forces there. We took over a modern sanatorium, which was empty and denuded of all its staff. At long last, members of the battery could enjoy every comfort. The sanatorium's grounds provided us with all the sporting facilities we needed and we were in fine trim. This was just as well, for we were given the task of running a large prisoner-of-war camp near by. We quickly got the two German Divisions for which we were responsible organised into clearing up the damaged city. On my first recce I took the German generals around it in my jeep so that they could see how much needed doing. At the end of the tour I said to them, 'This is going to be a long job. It could take up to a quarter of a century to clear up this town.' 'If you British will only let us get on with the job,' one replied, 'we'll have this city in good shape in ten years.' They did.

When my Brigade Commander set me the task of organising the reconstruction of the city, he told me that we must set out our priorities. This we could do alternately. 'What is your first priority?' I asked him. 'To get the racecourse rebuilt, so that my armoured regiments can get back to horses,' he replied. 'What is yours?' he then asked. I announced at once, 'To rebuild the opera house at Herrenhausen on the edge of the city. My men must have culture.' Both projects were rapidly completed, and much relieved the daily monotony of the troops' lives. I was glad to be able to see Mozart's *Così fan tutte* as that house's first post-war production. I had decided early on not to stand at the general election of 1945, because I did not feel that I could abandon my colleagues in the regiment at such a time. As it turned out, of course, that election was a historic débâcle for my party, which further strengthened my conviction that I had taken the correct decision in not standing.

In those summer months of 1945, I was therefore able to explore much of the north German plain. Hamburg, although also badly damaged, still had its attractive lake in the centre of the city, and it was possible to stay in the Atlantic Hotel, which had somehow remained intact. Near by, Lüneburg Heath had already passed into history as the place where the European war had ended. To the south were the Harz mountains, whose charming villages were also quite unspoilt, and we could drive to them on a free day. There was much to be done, some of it enjoyable, some productive, but our activities consisted mostly of repetitive chores. In September 1945, I was posted as second-in-command of the 86th Regiment of the Honourable Artillery Company, then stationed just outside Brussels, a regiment which I was later to command for some months in Germany. This began my association with the oldest regiment in the British army, founded by Henry VIII under a royal charter in 1537.

The responsibilities of the men for guard duty and maintaining public order were certainly time-consuming and exhausting, but we still faced the challenge of finding ways to sustain their interest and their morale, especially in the light of Field Marshal Montgomery's non-fraternisation instructions. The difficulties in carrying these out became more and more obvious and, later on, the considerable number of Anglo-German marriages spoke for itself. Then a football tournament was organised for the British Army on the Rhine (BAOR), and I formed an HAC regimental soccer team to compete in it. This was composed of professionals, some of whom came from distinguished clubs including Tottenham Hotspur, Celtic and Hull, together with the manager of Brighton and Hove Albion. I was able to provide the team with its own living quarters in a capacious house, with grounds large enough to provide a football pitch. Its members were freed from the normal dreary duties and obligations of their colleagues, but I insisted that these benefits would be maintained only so long as they kept on winning their matches. This incentive proved effective. Special arrangements were always made for off-duty forces to be transported to wherever the team was playing in order to support it. We had some exciting matches and, as the team consistently won, the morale of both team and regiment rose steadily. We finished off winning the BAOR Championship.

The memory of one unpleasant experience I had during this time, in September 1945, has always remained with me. I was ordered to take command of a firing squad which had to carry out a sentence of execution. The soldier to be shot was of Polish extraction. He had been found guilty by a court martial of crimes of aggravated rape and murder, the penalty for which was death. There was no doubt about the soldier's guilt, or about the correctness of the sentence under martial law as it then existed. I must confess, however, that I still found it difficult to sleep that night having to report to Hanover prison at 0755 knowing that there was no choice but to carry out the execution in accordance with the sentence of the court, and I was acutely conscious of the heavy responsibility of giving the command to fire.

When the squad marched out, the condemned man, in open-necked shirt and slacks, had already been blindfolded and bound to a short post. It was then a question of timing, calling the men ready to fire, giving them the opportunity of sighting their weapons, but not delaying overlong because that might unsettle their aim. They all knew that one rifle had a blank shot in it, and each of them could always believe it was theirs. I then gave the order to fire. The body slumped to the ground, it was checked by another officer and I marched off the squad. Looking back on it, I believe this made a mark on my mind which later crystallised the view to which I have adhered for nearly four decades of my political career, as to the justification for abolishing the death penalty in peacetime.

There was one more drama to unfold for me before I left Germany to be demobilised. On 12 February 1946 I drove from Osnabrück, through Kassel and on to Frankfurt, where I spent the night. The centre of this historic city was in ruins: the celebrated square, where *Everyman* had been performed each summer was completely wrecked, and the red-brick cathedral, which I had seen on my first visit to Germany in 1937, now had only part of its walls and roof left. The next day I made for Würzburg and then directly on to Nuremberg, which I also found partially destroyed. Being staged there was the greatest drama of all in even that town's long history, the Trial of the Major Nazi War Criminals. Eight rooms in the Grand Hotel had been allocated to British service and civilian personnel who were in Nuremberg to view the trial, and I checked in there. No charge was made for accommodation, and many of my comrades took advantage of the same cathartic experience that I went through between 11 and 13 February 1946. For all of us, this was the final vindication of our long years of war and I was particularly glad of the opportunity to get a glimpse of that sombre final act, for it took place on the same stage where, eight years before, I myself had witnessed the hideous prelude.

As I walked along the badly damaged city wall to the Court House, my mind went back to that autumn of 1937. Along this street had marched the seemingly endless Nazi columns. There on the balcony of the Deutscher Hof Hotel, Hitler had taken the salute from the fanatical, admiring crowd; beside him had stood Hess and Ribbentrop. There in the Grand Hotel, Streicher the Jew-baiter and some of the lesser fry used to live. Near by Goebbels had held his press conferences, and here at the city gates Göring had reviewed his Luftwaffe: Göring in his Mercedes, fat, smiling and bemedalled; Göring always popular, waving his plump hand to the cheering people. Gone, now, were the crowds and the bright red banners flaunting their swastikas over the streets; they were but empty vanity. A slight fall of snow was gently covering the rubble and debris of the city, hiding its shame. Hitler, Himmler and Goebbels were dead by their own hand; and the others were in the dock in the Court House – where I was soon to see them.

From my comfortable seat in the visitors' gallery, the court presented a strange scene of varied colour, bright lights and subdued noise and bustle. The judges sat on their raised dais, and beneath them were the recorders and stenographers and the banks of prosecuting counsel, defending counsel and interpreters. A mass of press representatives filled the space available to them. Distinctive and familiar uniforms mingled with the dark clothes of the lawyers; and the rustle of stenographers and pressmen moving in and out mixed with the quiet chanting of the interpreters into their micro-phones. This is pure theatre, I thought: it cannot be what we understand by justice. Then I put on my headphone, and at once all of the superfluous noise vanished. Now I heard only the firm, authoritative voice of the British judge, Lord Justice Lawrence, and realised that this was indeed the voice of justice. The theatrical trappings below were just the incidentals of modern life serving the film-men up in the gallery and the pressmen on the floor.

I looked towards the dock. In two rows of ten they sat: Göring, reduced to wearing a plain, ill-fitting grey uniform – no medals now – alert and attentive, vigorously nodding his head in agreement or shaking it in denial; Hess, with his pale pinched face; von Ribbentrop, always busy writing notes; Keitel and Jodl, the soldiers, staring silently and sullenly ahead;

Schacht, the businessman, whose relationship with the Nazis had been more turbulent, and who had distaste etched into his face at having to sit in public with such unpleasant people; von Papen and von Neurath, politicians both but still the diplomats, polished and immaculate. These all stood out. But how unimpressive were Seyss-Inquart, who had betrayed Austria and ruled occupied Holland; Rosenberg and Fritsche, the propagandists; and von Schirach, formerly a fanatical and dangerous young zealot, but now a visibly broken man. For a time, the whole free world had quaked before these men. Ultimately, however, they had brought not glory, but ruin and misery, to their own land and its people. We had lived in their shadow for a decade, but now history was free to deliver a final verdict upon them.

When the court adjourned for a quarter of an hour, I saw the Nazi leaders arguing heatedly among themselves about the evidence they had heard: evidence which had been gathered from every corner of Europe, from the Chancelleries and concentration camps, from the occupied countries and from Germany itself, of how the Nazis plunged the world into war, led Germany to its undoing and brought themselves, at last, into the dock in that Court House in Nuremberg.

While I was in court, Field Marshal von Paulus, who had commanded the German Sixth Army at Stalingrad, was produced by the Russians as a witness for the prosecution. Tall and, by now, slightly stooping, he told in a quiet voice the story of the attack on Russia; of how it had been planned, the orders given for the treatment of the Russian people and, finally, of the defeat and capture of his army. He was examined by members of all the prosecuting teams. I felt particularly proud of the skill with which the British team, led by David Maxwell Fyfe, later Lord Kilmuir, did its job, and we all watched the faces in the dock as the hideous tale unfolded. I thought of all the plans of aggression and domination that had been revealed; of the horrors of the concentration camps – of the shrunken heads of strangled Poles and the tattooed human skins on lampshades that I had seen among the exhibits in a room outside – and forced labour; of the thousands of displaced people from every European country who were still scattered across the continent searching desperately for a home; and of those makeshift graves that we had left behind us as we moved up from Normandy to the Baltic. My mind went further back, to the evening of 3 September 1939, when Neville Chamberlain had broadcast to the nation and warned, 'It is the evil things that we shall be fighting against – brute force, bad faith, injustice, oppression and persecution – and against them I am certain that right will prevail.'

As I left the court I knew that the shadow of those evil things had been lifted, and their perpetrators now faced justice. But at what a cost. Europe had once more torn itself apart. This must never be allowed to happen again. My generation did not have the option of living in the past; we had to work for the future. We were surrounded by destruction, homelessness, hunger and despair. Only by working together right across our continent had we any hope of creating a society which would uphold the true values of European civilisation. Reconciliation and reconstruction must be our tasks. I did not realise then that this would be my preoccupation for the next fifty years.

Chapter 5

WINNING THE PEACE
Civvy Street 1946–1950

We were all relieved when VJ Day came, for we knew that our forces in the Far East would no longer have to fight on in that bloodiest of theatres, against the most implacable of enemies. But those of us serving in Germany also knew that we continued to face a prolonged wait in the shattered heart of Europe, helping to keep order. When the 86th Regiment was demobilised in the spring of 1946, I still had a few weeks' service to complete. I spent the time at southern German universities, including Göttingen and Heidelberg. This gave me the opportunity to refresh some of my musical skills. It was only on 5 June 1946, almost exactly two years after D-Day, that I was to return to England. On that beautiful summer's day, I reflected on the incredible range of events we had experienced – and thought, not least, of those of our colleagues who were not spared to return home.

My return to Broadstairs was a quiet one. I was met at the station by John, who claimed I had put on so much weight that he almost failed to recognise me. I could understand why. It was the consequence of good living during my last few months in Germany. I immediately embarked on an intensive programme of walking and cycling around Thanet as well as swimming in Broadstairs Bay. The euphoria of VE Day had long since subsided and there was no red, white and blue bunting in the town to welcome me back to Helmdon, the home to which my family had now returned. But it was a happy reunion. We all caught up with each other's news. My father had been busily re-establishing his building business at Kingsgate in preparation for what he was sure would be a post-war building boom. His optimism was not misplaced, for within a year the business had grown to twice its pre-war size, so there was no longer a question of taking in boarding visitors in summer. That night my brother and I had separate rooms. I subsequently turned the larger one into a work room as well as a bedroom. Meanwhile, John had, to my parents' disappointment, decided not to join the family business – and started work in a local radio shop instead.

In the weeks that followed, I thought hard about my future. The landslide Labour victory of 1945, in which they won 393 seats compared with the Conservatives' 213, had obviously made it more difficult for me to have any chance of going into active politics, and I faced the immediate problem of establishing a permanent income. Shortly after my return home, I wrote to my German friend Professor Winckler, who had, thankfully, survived the war and set out for him my view on how this incredible result had come about. One reason, I said, was that 'people felt that, after a world war, they wanted leaders who were going to build a new world quickly and not spend time finding excuses why they should not build one ... the average man who had been fully employed during the war thought of the unemployment he suffered before the war and decided he would not have the Tories again.' I felt bitterly sorry that Churchill had been thrown out of office, but the Conservative cause had not been helped when he claimed, during his first party broadcast of the 1945 campaign, that 'No socialist government conducting the entire life and industry of the country could afford to allow free, sharp or violently worded expressions of discontent ... they would have to fall back on some form of Gestapo.' It later emerged that this objectionable phrase had been instigated by Lord Beaverbrook. The Conservatives who remained in the House of Commons after 1945 were a combination of the survivors of the 1930s and the new generation, who had served in the war. Among the latter were Antony Head, later Minister of Defence at the time of Suez; Toby Low, later Lord Aldington, who was to become one of my closest friends and a sound adviser; and Lord John Hope, who had fought with great distinction at Narvik, Salerno and Anzio and later helped me in my search for a parliamentary constituency to contest.

Churchill and Eden, as expected, emerged as the leading figures in the denuded parliamentary party. In November 1945, the 1922 Committee of Conservative backbenchers had told them in no uncertain terms that they wanted to see action from their leaders. But, shortly afterwards, Churchill went to the United States on a tour and Eden was left in charge. Although Churchill had relied upon several senior Labour figures in his War Cabinet, and co-operated closely in the military sphere with the USSR in order to defeat Germany, his rhetoric against socialists of every description once the war was over quickly became somewhat strident. After going into opposition, Churchill virtually dedicated his life to countering the growing threat from the East, through transatlantic co-operation and a united Europe.

Once the Labour government had taken over, however, it set about establishing the welfare state rather than exterminating its opponents. So the Conservative Party, whose policies had seemed so far behind the times in 1945, had the opportunity to regroup and deal with vital questions of both policy and organisation. Rab Butler was charged with reformulating policy, and Lord Woolton with recreating the organisation. The challenges we faced were similar to those which confronted the Conservative Party in the wake of the 1997 defeat at the hands of Tony Blair. The major difference is that Churchill and Eden were up against a radical left-wing Labour Party, so that the moderate centre ground was more or less there for the taking. After the 1997 election, we had a tougher fight on our hands because that ground, our natural position, was already being occupied by our opponents. Nonetheless, in the 1990s as in the 1940s, it is the only ground upon which elections can be won.

The biggest political question in my mind was which road the Conservative Party would choose for the future. It was only if the party decided to acclimatise itself to the new Britain of the late 1940s that I could foresee a political career for myself. But, in the meantime, I had to find a job which would give me enough money to live on, which would enhance my prospects of finding a winnable seat in Parliament and upon which I could fall back should I hit a bad spot in politics. I could still have taken up the scholarship to read law at Gray's Inn which I had won in 1938 – and, while looking for a job in 1946, I did indeed spend several months reading hard for the first set of Bar exams – but I found the law rather dry and it would have taken me six years to earn even a modest salary. As I was already almost thirty years old, I decided that this was too long to wait and set about exploring other options. Moreover, Trevor Watson, the distinguished QC who had previously backed me and had planned to take me into his chambers dealing with patent affairs, had died during the war at the age of fifty-six. Sandy Lindsay, still Master of Balliol, tried to fix me up with a job in Oxford, as a personal assistant to Arthur Ellis, the Regius Professor of Medicine. But the Professor decided, with a true instinct, that I was not for him. I had met Duncan Carmichael, deputy chairman of the United Dominions Trust, during the Nuremberg Rally in 1937 (see p. 43), and I contacted him for advice, writing, 'I feel now I want to get cracking ... my qualifications are only potentialities but I think the fact that I got a Second in Modern Greats at Balliol, that I was President of the Union and held the rank of Lt Col, when CO of my regiment, shows a certain potential. At the moment the problem is to canalize it.'

I first tried to canalize my potential by getting into business, and my opening attempt to do so was with ICI. They wished me to join them, but said that it would be quite impossible for me to combine political activity with being a member of their staff. What was more, if I left them to go into the House of Commons, they could not accept me back if I were to lose my seat afterwards. I then had a series of interviews with Unilever, the large Anglo-Dutch concern. They said they would much like me to join the firm and made no mention of any political disqualification. Twenty-five years later, I was invited to a party in my honour by Lord Cole, the outgoing chairman of that company, whom I was subsequently to appoint as chairman of Rolls-Royce. After dinner, he presented me with a copy of a preliminary character assessment of me made by an interviewer from his company in 1946. The flattering conclusion read: 'Heath is one of those rare men who is extremely competent intellectually yet a normal, pleasant, honest person ... I found him very likeable and he seems a sensible, tolerant man with a good sense of humour, good manners and address.' According to the firm's records, I told them that I had reconciled myself 'without any regrets ... to abandon[ing] the possibility of a political career'. I certainly had no recollection of that. What I do well recall was that I asked the chairman and the two directors flanking him at the final interview whether I could hope to be on the board by the time I was forty. They said in astonishment that they had never been asked such a question before and, although they thought it might be possible, they could not guarantee it. In the end, I decided to decline their offer of a management traineeship.

I then heard from Sir Giles Guthrie, formerly a brilliant pilot who had won the London to Cape Town Race and then had a tremendous record in the Second World War. He wanted me to join the North Central Wagon & Finance Company of Rotherham, in which he had a large investment, as its deputy chairman, with a view to my becoming its chairman in three years' time, when the occupant was due to retire. This was very tempting, until I enquired of him where I would be operating. He replied, 'Rotherham, our headquarters.' The thought of spending the next part of my life, or possibly all of it, cut off from my family, from many of my friends and, above all, from the centre of national politics, did not appeal to me. So I declined the invitation. In retrospect, this might have been a miscalculation, as I now realise that it would have been possible to establish myself financially through a few years of that activity and then to move back, with various directorships, into the political arena. But the experience was not wasted, for my path and that of Sir Giles were to cross again.

I was reminded of this venture some years later, when David Eccles told me how he had gone to Hyde Park Gate seeking clearance from Winston Churchill, then Leader of the Opposition, for a speech he was about to make. Churchill asked him where he was proposing to make it, to which David replied, 'Rotherham.' 'Ah,' said Churchill, 'I once had to change trains in that town and during the interval I decided to make use of the facilities provided on the station platform. When I closed the door I saw scribbled on it "They must have rum bums in Rotherham, or these seats would bother 'em"! Go away and be sure you make a good speech,' the great man concluded, with that mischievous smile of his.

Having failed to find a satisfactory passport to the upper echelons of business, I turned instead to the civil service, and sat the relevant exams in the summer of 1946. I also had to be tested by what was known as the house-party technique. I was summoned to a large house at Egham in Surrey, where my competitors and I were put through a series of exercises designed to establish whether we had the makings of good Whitehall men. The main exercises involved discussion groups, in which we had to study a brief and present it to the group, while assessors sat by to see if we had mastered the all-important art of the committee. This was rounded off by an individual psychological test. I survived it all, and passed out top of the list, with my old friend from Oxford days, Ashley Raeburn, five points behind me in second place. Although I did not choose to pursue a lifelong career in the civil service, I could at least always say quietly to myself in later years, when officials became difficult, 'I could have been in your place if I had wanted to be.'

When it came to considering the civil service, a great deal depended on where I was posted. On my application form, I had indicated a preference for the Treasury, where I thought my knowledge of finance from my Oxford degree, and my experience of the world, would stand me in good stead. In the interviews, a considerable effort had been made to entice me into the Foreign Office, because of my travels before the war and my service in Europe from 1944. That would have involved being posted abroad, which, I was convinced, would firmly and finally have made it impossible for me to launch a political career at any time. Twenty years later Douglas Hurd proved me to have been wrong. Unlike Douglas, however, I turned down the Foreign Office and was then sent instead to the fledgling Ministry of Civil Aviation. This was a bitter disappointment for me because it had none of the status or influence of the Treasury.

On 4 December 1946, I began my new job in the Ministry's Long-Range Planning Department at Ariel House in Aldwych, as an assistant principal on a salary of £416 a year, plus £90 'consolidated bonus', and took a small bedsit in nearby Holborn. There were six or so similar occupants in the house, with a lounge in which we could gather in the evenings. I found it difficult to manage the transition from colonel of my regiment, with all its appurtenances, to being a junior official in a bedsit. I had told Carmichael that 'if it is impossible to combine politics and earning my living [in industry], I shall have to give up all ideas of politics . . . make for the civil service and lead a leisured, respectable and penurious life!' Although my rather humble bedroom at Holborn might have appeared to confirm my penury, my time at the Ministry of Civil Aviation was anything but leisurely. This new Division was headed by the immensely capable and energetic Peter Masefield, and our brief was to recreate the British civil aircraft industry which, unlike its American counterpart, had disappeared upon the outbreak of war. After several months in Broadstairs, it was good to be doing something useful again, but I quickly became frustrated by the time-consuming red-tape of Whitehall bureaucracy, and the freezing winter of 1946–7 added to my gloom. It was one of the worst on record and it was compounded by a fuel crisis caused by the incompetence of the Labour government, which had been so busy nationalising coal the previous year that it had failed to get enough of it stockpiled.

My work at the department was incredibly wide-ranging. Peter Masefield was particularly keen that a small British light aircraft should be produced, for use as individual transport by tourists, businessmen or farmers throughout the world. This would have given us an enormous market, but although the designs were approved they never came to fruition. There was no demand for such a vehicle in Britain because everyone concerned seemed to be too short-sighted to see the potential advantages for producing rapid communications, both within these islands and between us and the European mainland. The obstacles which arose, as if by magic, to the use of airfields for these purposes were also extremely daunting. The result is that, in comparison with similarly industrialised countries on both sides of the Atlantic, our use of small aircraft has been limited ever since.

Masefield and the Long-Range Planning Department were also deeply involved in the decisions being taken on passenger aircraft for the national airways, which were still using out-of-date military machines which had been converted for passenger routes. I learned first-hand about the dangers inherent in too much direct state intervention. If the department attempted to back a 'winner', it would, as often as not, find itself propping up a loser. One case in point was the high-winged 'Elizabethan' passenger monoplane, sponsored by the government. Only twenty-four of these were sold, whereas de Havilland's similar, privately financed plane sold over 440. Subsequently, British airlines became obsessed with the purchase of American civil aircraft, which offered the considerable convenience of a world-wide system for providing spares. This line of thinking caused problems later in the 1960s over the VC10, which had been designed solely with Commonwealth routes in mind, when the British airlines decided that it was not what they had wanted after all. Yet this was a superb and highly economic aircraft, also one of the quietest of its type.

I sat on numerous committees, including one overseeing the building and development of the new airport at Heathrow. Every time I arrive at Heathrow I shudder to think that I was in any way, however slightly, involved in the creation of that monstrosity. The finest airport in the world from the point of view of aircraft control, it is probably also the worst in the developed countries from every other point of view. I recall how we used to sit around a large table, listening to the departmental under-secretary responsible leading an animated discussion about the corridor width in feet and inches that would be necessary to make things comfortable for passengers who wanted to move from place to place. Having worked that out to the nearest inch, we were then forced back to the drawing board later on, to see how much space we could actually afford for passengers to move about in. I recall that, during the initial planning, the designers had also neglected to provide any parking spaces at the new airport.

A major part of my responsibilities was to ensure that plans for new aircraft tallied with the landing and take-off facilities at both existing and future airports. We soon came upon a major problem with the first generation of jet aircraft under construction by the de Havilland Aircraft Company at Hatfield. The prototype DH104, later known as the Comet, was due to fly in around three years' time and was intended to carry passengers on BOAC's transatlantic stopping services and Empire air routes. When we assessed the design 'footprint' loads of a fully loaded DH104 against the forecast bearing strengths of the runway surfaces at most of the proposed destinations, we discovered that the plane faced serious problems in Ireland, Iceland and Newfoundland, throughout the Middle East and in Africa, from Nairobi southwards.

When Peter Masefield telephoned Geoffrey de Havilland at Hatfield to warn him about this, his immediate response was that something should be done about the quality of the offending airstrips. But we knew that this was not an option, and set about finding a new way of spreading the considerable load of this new plane. I was sent up to Hatfield with a proposal that each main leg of the plane's undercarriage should incorporate a four-wheel 'bogie', together with a twin-wheel nose leg. I overcame the initial scepticism of the de Havilland design team and they came to Ariel House shortly afterwards with a new design which was curiously reminiscent of what we had proposed. The first two Comets flew with the original wheel layout, but the production aircraft from April 1952 incorporated what Peter Masefield came to call the 'Heath modification'. In the end, 125 Comets were built and 47 were exported.

Living in London for the first time was revealing. In Holborn, theatreland was on my doorstep. Among the plays I enjoyed at this time, I particularly recall a splendid production of Noël Coward's *Present Laughter*.

After a few months, however, I exchanged my place in Holborn for another in the more attractive surroundings of Courtfield Gardens in South Kensington. This was handy for shopping at Harrods, in Knightsbridge, which I had first visited as a serving officer in 1942, when I opened an account. A glance at my engagements diary for 1947 reveals a busy social life. I have always valued keeping in touch with old friends, exchanging views on the issues of the day and hearing from the inside what is going on in different walks of life. During my time at the Ministry, I used to enjoy regular lunches near by – often at Simpson's-in-the-Strand – with Oxford friends, fellow civil servants and political activists. Occasionally my mother would be up in town and we would have tea together at the Criterion, in Piccadilly. After six years in uniform, I found that a desk job took a good deal of getting used to and made strenuous efforts to keep myself in good physical shape. I played squash regularly and returned to golf, playing with friends back in Broadstairs.

I did not go home every weekend – the train fares were too expensive – so it tended to be one in three or four. But in the summer of 1947 I had a three-week holiday in Broadstairs, which gave me an opportunity to catch up with my parents and brother. The late 1940s still retain a slightly unreal aura, I think, for most of the people who lived through them. I read voraciously, taking *The Times*, the *Daily Telegraph* and the *Daily Worker* every day, as well as the weekly *Spectator*, which I found quite sensible and literate in those days! I also studied Hansard and followed the parliamentary debates. Labour was driving through its radical policy agenda and, for a year or two, the Attlee government maintained its popularity – despite the vicissitudes of life for most of the population.

I was delighted when Field Marshal Viscount Alanbrooke, the British Chief of the General Staff for so much of the Second World War and Colonel Commandant of the Honourable Artillery Company, contacted me in February 1947, asking me to re-form a Territorial regiment of the HAC. The 2nd Regiment HAC (HAA), a heavy anti-aircraft regiment, was formed on 1 May 1947. Initially, recruiting was a struggle. I sent letters to the men I had commanded, enclosing a picture of us all together in Germany. Although I received a flood of replies, the response to my call-up was disappointing. Some former soldiers were emigrating to escape the gloom of Austerity Britain; many more were just settling down into married life and did not have the time to become involved.

But the Cold War was rapidly setting in and Churchill had recently warned, in his celebrated Fulton speech, of the 'Iron Curtain' which was descending across Europe. The Berlin Airlift of June 1948 dramatically highlighted the seriousness of this growing crisis, with the result that a good number of my old colleagues did eventually begin to come forward to rejoin the regiment in preparation for what seemed like a possible world war. As I wrote in a letter to Joe Forrest, a wartime colleague who was still out in Germany working as a reporter, in August 1948, people were almost fatalistic, and 'quite determined that if war comes we shall have to show these tiresome people that they can't behave like this. What an amazing blessing it is that the British always assume they will win wars! It would be awfully difficult for politicians if they didn't.'

The tense international situation gave an extra sense of purpose to my work, as CO of the regiment, in organising our activities. Every Tuesday evening was drill night and part of my civil service leave was devoted to our fortnight-long annual training camp out in the countryside – 'one mad rush of manoeuvres from 7am until 2am', as I told Joe in that letter – but the dinner which rounded off camp was an event to savour. Time-consuming though my regimental commitments were, they were also thoroughly enjoyable. One characteristic of the HAC was that, when the parades and drills were concluded, there was no difference of rank between any of the members. This could sometimes mean that a junior member of a firm was commanding on parade one of his daytime business seniors. This worked satisfactorily, but a problem arose when men who had finished their national service, whether commanding or in the ranks, were posted to the HAC for their part-time activities. We knew that most of them would not wish to become actual paid-up members of the HAC. Should they then be treated as if they were? All three commanding officers were of one mind on this question. They insisted to the elected Court responsible for the Company as a whole that they should be treated like all other members of the regiment. I am glad to say that this view was fully accepted. As a commanding officer, I never had a single example of a national service man's behaviour falling below the standard set by the rest of the regiment. Willie Whitelaw once said that what separates the new generation in British politics from ours is the fact that they never experienced the comradeship of serving together in the armed forces. How true that is.

Being in London, I joined the Coningsby Club, a Tory dining club which recruited some of the brightest graduates from Oxford and Cambridge. There I often met Michael Fraser, whom I had got to know as a fellow officer, and we were able to take part in a general discussion of the political scene. Michael was an intelligent and thoughtful man, but also a very practical one. He was fun to be with because he had an enormous zest for life which included a passion for music. At times, he could also be extremely funny. We had kept in touch during the war and, since being demobilised, he had put his excellent brain to use in the Conservative Research Department which was then being run by Rab Butler. Under Butler, the CRD was fast becoming a powerhouse of progressive Conservatism, charged with providing the new ideas which the party needed to challenge Labour in the post-war era. The 'Backroom Boys', as they were known, also included Enoch Powell and Iain Macleod, who later became my Chancellor of the Exchequer, before his tragically early death. I have to say I was somewhat envious of Michael Fraser because the CRD was evidently the place to be for ambitious young men who wanted to transform Conservatism. He did try to get me a job there but, in August 1947, wrote to let me know that there were simply no vacancies. Nonetheless, I knew that I could not stay in the civil service for much longer. I made up my mind to contest a parliamentary seat at the next general election, and such political activity was explicitly precluded by my contract with the Ministry of Aviation.

I therefore made contact again with Marjorie Maxse, a vice-chairman of the party whom I had known before the war. She got me the toehold in politics for which I longed, by adding my name to the list of prospective candidates held at Central Office. In March 1947, I was invited for my first interview, at Ashford, a safe Conservative seat in my own county of Kent, only an hour's drive from my home at Broadstairs. The interview was held in a country house with the selection committee seated in a half-circle around a blazing log fire. The atmosphere was very agreeable and we soon got down to business. I sat to the chairman's right and was told at once by him not to bother with making a speech. They already knew, and agreed with, my views. The point of the meeting was to enable them to ask questions, which they proceeded to do.

One of the first came from the wife of the retiring Member, who said that her husband, who had held the seat since 1943, had answered every letter that he received from any constituent in his own hand. 'Are you,' she enquired, 'prepared to do the same?' Knowing that I would not be able to compete with such a demand, I was forced to reply that my writing was, unfortunately, so hard to decipher that I was sure that the constituents would prefer my replies to their letters to be typed by a secretary. Fortunately, she seemed content with this. There was no further incident, until the chairman said that everything was very satisfactory and he thought it was high time that we adjourned for a buffet supper.

A fortnight later I was invited to a meeting on the Saturday morning, with just the chairman and senior officers, who explained that the potential candidates had now been reduced to two and they had some further questions they wished to put to me. The chairman told me that they wanted someone who would remain solely a constituency member and that I would be expected to refuse any offer of a post in a future Churchill government. I replied that, although an offer such as this seemed highly unlikely, if Mr Churchill invited me to serve in his government, it would be difficult for me to refuse. The chairman then asked if I would give up my command of the 2nd Regiment of the HAC if I was selected – a question which surprised me because the Conservative Party had always emphasised the importance of voluntary service. I told him that I would not be willing to do that: I had responsibilities to the men in the regiment and to the country. At this, all the officers appeared saddened and the chairman said that if I could not undertake to leave the Territorial Army and refuse an appointment in Mr Churchill's government, then they much regretted that they could not recommend me to the selection committee as their candidate, much as they would like to do so.

Before leaving, I asked the chairman what lay behind these two extra-ordinary requests. He replied, 'Our present Member of Parliament has devoted all his time to the constituency and we want his successor to do the same . . . I am sorry about that.' I, too, was saddened, but said that I quite understood. They then recommended William Deedes, at that time a journalist on the *Daily Telegraph*. Some fifteen years later, he was to become responsible for public relations in Macmillan's Cabinet. He has since commented that I was rejected in this semi-rural constituency because I appeared there on a Saturday morning wearing a dark-blue suit and stiff white collar. I am flattered that he does not believe that he outdid me on merit, but the truth is that I did not at that time possess either a dark-blue suit or a stiff white collar.

The next interview I had was for the Rochester and Chatham constitu-ency. In sharp contrast to Ashford, the chairman of the selection committee told me bluntly, 'We want someone who will become a Cabinet minister.' This seemed much more fertile ground for an ambitious young man and I was rather encouraged. I was allowed only a moment of optimism before being flattened. 'But I am afraid,' continued the chairman, 'that we do not think that you will ever hold office of any kind.' So that was that. Then, in August 1947, I went for an interview at the safe seat of Sevenoaks, a constituency that I would dearly have liked to represent. The retiring Member of Parliament, Colonel Ponsonby, knew me well and told me that he very much wanted me to be successful. Unfortunately, I arrived late at the final interview, on 12 September, in the wake of a long session at the Ministry poring over aircraft plans. I had no time to get my thoughts in order and made a thoroughly bad speech. They chose John Rodgers, who quickly became a friend after we both entered the House in 1950, and he was to represent the constituency for nearly thirty years. I was not downcast by this and felt sure that there was a constituency waiting for me, if only I had the patience to endure a few more such sessions.

One weekend, while in camp with my regiment in late August 1947,

I received a telegram inviting me for a preliminary interview at Bexley, on Saturday 6 September. Bexley is situated on the edge of London, in the north-west corner of Kent and close to Crayford, where my family had lived during the First World War. Surrounded by a large industrial area, but itself almost entirely residential, the historic village of Old Bexley had mushroomed after electrification of the railway line in the 1930s. Its semi-detached houses were mostly bought by aspirant people, many of whom worked in offices in central London or had skilled jobs in industry. In the 1930s Bexley, then part of the Dartford seat, had been held by Frank Clarke, a prominent coal merchant on Thameside and a Conservative. But in the landslide of 1945 the new seat of Bexley was won by Mrs Jennie Adamson of the Labour Party, with a majority of 11,763. She was a member of Labour's national executive and had been the MP for Dartford between 1938 and 1945, before the boundary changes which created the seat of Bexley. Within less than a year, she had resigned the seat upon being appointed deputy chairman of the Assistance Board.

At the resultant by-election, held on 22 July 1946, the seat was held for Labour by a contemporary of mine from Oxford days, Ashley Bramall. I wrote to him when he won the seat, congratulating him on his victory and encouraging him to speak in the House about the state of Germany. He wrote back almost immediately, assuring me that he had already made his maiden speech on that very subject. Bramall was elected in 1946 with a greatly reduced majority of only 1,851 – the fall in Labour support being, no doubt, at least partially attributable to the introduction of bread rationing by the Labour government the day before. So this was now an eminently winnable seat. It would also be an extremely convenient one for me. It lay on the main road from London to Broadstairs and was only a few miles from my new base in Swanley village where I had, fortuitously, just started lodging with the father of my Balliol friend Tim Bligh, now in the Treasury. The Priory was a spacious house with a housekeeper, and Sir Edward Bligh's charge was lower than my rent in London. Sir Edward was a formal and slightly austere man, who was head of the Welfare Department at the London County Council (LCC). He could hardly have been more hospitable. When I became Minister of Labour in 1959, he wrote me a warm letter of congratulation and told me that he still referred to my erstwhile room as the 'Colonel's Room'. He also reminded me about a 'shelf which collapsed on to your bed because of its load of blue books and political literature, a symbol (the literature, not the collapse) of your enthralment to your visions of the public good'.

I was first summoned to a meeting before the selection committee in Bexley on the afternoon of Saturday 6 September. I arrived at the association's headquarters in Bexleyheath, to find that it consisted of a cellar under a small house. Everyone was closely packed together. Their rugged chairman, Edward Dines, presided. It appeared that there were some four-teen candidates being interviewed altogether, and Dines wanted them to pick 'an educated local boy made good who could understand the lives and aspirations of ordinary people'. I made a short speech, then answered their questions. The interview appeared to go well, and I was invited to a further meeting on the evening of Thursday 18 September. On that occasion I was the second of three possible candidates to be considered, and I was later called back to be told that I had been chosen to be recommended to a full meeting of the Association at the Bexleyheath Conservative Club on 7 November, when I should be formally adopted. This was exciting. Dines then proposed that I should follow him in his car to the real home of Conservatism in Bexley. Not knowing what this meant I got into my car and meekly followed him as we drove down to the old village and, having parked our cars, went into the King's Head for a drink. We were greeted by the splendid landlady, who always sat on a high stool at the back of the bar, occasionally pointing her finger silently and sternly at anyone who got out of hand. It has remained the favourite hostelry for me and my constituency team ever since. During the general election campaign of April 1997, I believe that my team and I succeeded in visiting almost every hostelry in the constituency – starting, as ever, with the King's Head, and also ending up there. For all my years as a member for Bexley this has certainly been my 'spiritual' home.

A few days after my selection, I had a meeting with the agent, A. G. Mulholland, to discuss the way forward. He had a nasty surprise for me. In a move quite out of keeping with the party's new thinking, and indeed against its rules, he asked me for a substantial personal contribution to the association's funds. He then invited me to sign a document promising a donation of £100 a year – a sum which the Bexley officers realised was well beyond me, for my wartime savings had gone into paying off my student loan, and there had been little opportunity to save since. I refused to sign the agreement, in which stand I was supported by Edward Dines, who knew that I would instead do my utmost to help the association to raise money from our supporters, both inside and outside the constituency. It was my first insight into Mulholland's character.

At my adoption meeting at the Conservative Club on 7 November, every seat was taken, with people around the walls. The *Bexleyheath Observer* reported that 'the attendance was the largest at a political meeting in the borough for a long time'. My parents were there to see me become a prospective parliamentary candidate. Proceedings began with a lusty ren-dition of 'Land of Hope and Glory'. Then I spoke, telling the party faithful, in what turned out to be an understatement, that I hoped to serve them 'for a long time', following which the chairman invited questions. There was a long pause and he asked again whether anyone wished to ask me anything. He once more repeated his request, saying, 'Surely somebody must want to ask a question.' I thought to myself, 'You damn fool, why can't we get away without any questions?' But he had provoked a clerical gentleman standing against the wall, who asked whether I would move into the constituency. Having anticipated this question, I had done some telephone research with council officials on the availability of accommodation in the borough. I replied that, since being recommended by the selection committee, I had carefully studied the housing position in the Borough of Bexley and discovered that, not only were many houses being occupied by two families as a result of evacuees moved into them from the areas of London bombed during the war, but there was also a waiting list for council housing consisting of more than 11,000 people. It would therefore be particularly unfair if I were to try to claim a privileged right to a house in Bexley, just because I was a parliamentary candidate. What was more, Bexley was more or less directly between London, where I worked and lived during the week, and my home at Broadstairs. So I had no need of new accommodation. This was greeted with loud applause and has exonerated me ever since from living in the borough – and from all those difficult questions about which local butcher, grocer or milkman should get my business.

My selection as a parliamentary candidate was not the only notable event in my life that autumn. A week after the Bexley interview, my brother married Marian Easton, a local girl, at our parish church of St Peter's-in-Thanet. My parents were happy with the match and I was John's best man, though I barely knew his bride, for I had not been living at home during their courtship. The marriage was not successful and, after some years, John gave her an excuse for divorce.

Having been adopted as a parliamentary candidate, I was required, under civil service rules, to resign immediately from the Ministry. I had informed Peter Masefield on 3 November that I expected to be adopted on 7 November, and I was asked to extend my service slightly beyond that date, to 22 November. I agreed to this, and made a point of expressing to Peter 'my appreciation of the interesting and pleasant work which I have enjoyed in your Division during the past year'. It is hard to imagine how things might have turned out differently, but I suppose that, had I gone to the Treasury as I had originally intended, I might well have found a comfortable niche for myself and stayed there for the rest of my career. Despite the frustrations at Civil Aviation, I left with considerable respect for the integrity and professionalism of the civil service, together with an intimate understanding of how government machinery works – an understanding which subsequently stood me in good stead. Peter Masefield went on to hold a series of distinguished appointments, including chief executive of British European Airways, and later chairman of the British Airports Authority. He wrote me a particularly warm letter when I received the Garter in 1992.

Meanwhile, I had to find another job. I sought, once again, the aid of John Cartland, head of the Oxford University Appointments Board, later tragically murdered in the South of France, to find me something which could be combined with politics. He suggested journalism, and found that there was a vacancy at the *Church Times*, a family-owned weekly with an Anglo-Catholic approach to ecclesiastical matters. The paper was seeking a 'sound and informed High Churchman with considerable journalistic experience' to be its first news editor. I was not a High Anglican, nor did I have much experience of journalism. Furthermore, although I cared deeply about Church affairs, my strictly theological knowledge was limited. What I knew of religious matters was drawn largely from my long-standing connections with St Peter's-in-Thanet and Balliol chapel, and from late-night talks about such questions with Freddie Temple at Balliol. I wrote to Cartland warning that 'I might not quite fit in there,' but when I attended an interview on 2 February 1948 with the paper's editor, Humphry Beevor, he thought otherwise. The salary of £650 a year was attractive compared with the civil service, so I accepted his offer and began to work at the paper's offices, near Kingsway in central London, in February 1948. I learned immediately afterwards that the selection committee at Bexley had let it be known the previous autumn that they would not consider a journalist as their candidate. Fortunately I managed to convince them that I was entering my new profession at the respectable end of the journalistic spectrum.

My duties on the *Church Times* as news editor included supervising two news reporters, sub-editing their copy and selecting and editing contributions from cathedral clergy and other parish and diocesan correspondents up and down the country. I also undertook reporting assignments in the evenings. The paper went to press on Wednesday nights. Then we worked late, and I was responsible for overseeing the make-up of pages in the print room. As a newcomer, I made the odd bloomer. Editing a report of an annual festival of 'UMCA', I changed the initials to YMCA – Young Men's Christian Association – throughout the copy. It was unfortunate that, at the time, I had no acquaintance with UMCA, the Universities' Mission to Central Africa. The horror in the editor's room was unlimited when my ignorance became known – as was the ribaldry in the news room.

Meanwhile, I was continuing to nurse the constituency of Bexley.

Victory for the Tories at the next general election depended on how constructive the party was prepared to be at a national level. Lord Woolton was by now enjoying his first successes in reviving the party organisation. Unlike Labour's, it had been allowed to run down during the war, and this had been one of the reasons for our defeat in 1945. Building up the local organisation was also the major task confronting me in Bexley. I made many speeches locally, which were always carried in detail by the local press of that time. Throughout my time at Chatham House School and Oxford, I had had many opportunities to hone my speaking skills and my political arguments. I had given a few lectures on current affairs during my army days, but my selection at Bexley gave me an incentive to blow away any cobwebs at high speed. I spoke there on both foreign and domestic affairs, dealing among other things with the future of Germany, the situation arising from the Russian occupation of Czechoslovakia and the need for a general economic regeneration of Western Europe.

As early as May 1948, I made a speech warning against the apparent complacency of the Labour government. Its policy was to pretend that, thanks to the Marshall Aid given by the United States, we could just 'carry on as usual – everything will be all right'. I also criticised Labour's refusal to send British representatives to the Hague European Congress, which had been attended by most Western European nations. 'The reason', I told party workers, 'is that the government is anxious that a Western Union should be founded on purely socialist principles . . . that is a very short-sighted policy, because everywhere in Europe today we are seeing a swing away from the left towards the right.' Looking back, one can discern other factors which consciously or unconsciously affected both the Labour government's decision and public opinion in Britain. Not least was the very powerful psychological factor that we British thought of ourselves as intrinsically superior, because we were the victors in the Second World War and we were dealing with the vanquished. On that basis there was no reason why the British needed to take part in any of these proposed activities.

Writing an anonymous editorial in the *Church Times* on 26 November 1948, I commented that 'The average citizen of Great Britain still regards union in Europe as a distant ideal but not a practical proposition. On the continent, however, the man-in-the-street realizes the weakness of his nation in isolation.' With the first glimmering of interest in a European Community, the change from Empire to Commonwealth and the rapid growth of the two superpowers, I was already beginning to sense that Britain needed to come to terms with its limitations, and what role it might carve out for itself in this new situation. My pre-war and wartime experience had by now convinced me that our future must lie inside a

European Community, as part of an organisation which would be strong enough to deal on an equal footing with the emerging superpowers.

On domestic matters, I dealt most scathingly of all with Labour's proposals for future nationalisation, in particular steel, to which I devoted considerable study, including visits to a number of steel mills in Sheffield. I attacked the government for pursuing policies which had led to a dramatic devaluation of the pound. I also talked about the role of the state in modern society. To these were added such individual matters as the need to free the airlines to face greater competition; and the dawning opportunity for Britain to become the world's supplier of small private aircraft. In dealing with both of these subjects, I could draw upon my experiences in the Ministry of Civil Aviation. At the end of 1948, I told the Bexley Conservative Ladies' Luncheon Club, 'I fear there is a feeling that hard work is Victorian and out of date, but we as a country must realise there is no short cut.' I believe that people were, by this time, starting to recognise that fact, and were becoming disenchanted with the failure of the Attlee government to match up to the high expectations which its own leaders had generated in the country during the 1945 general election campaign.

Meanwhile, my position on the *Church Times* was beginning to prove rather frustrating. I did not feel that I was learning very much and, in such a small organisation, the prospects of promotion were limited. Although I got on well enough with the other journalists and the trade unionists in the print room, I found it difficult – as we all did – to see eye to eye with Beevor, a tall, dark, bearded figure who always remained extremely remote. His editorial stance was Anglo-Catholic and his politics were firmly on the left. He wrote well, usually limiting his contribution to the leading article each week, but he never interfered with anything which I had written myself or which I had edited.

After my first year on the *Church Times*, my father wrote to say, 'I'm sorry to know that you are not happy, or making any headway in the right direction in your job . . . it is no use looking on the black side, so keep trying . . . something is going to turn up for you.' By this time my work on the paper included an increasing number of reporting engagements to which I was often only alerted at short notice. The main problem was combining such unpredictable working commitments with my task of nursing a marginal constituency. Although my weekly surgery was held on a Saturday, I could never guarantee my attendance at a variety of party meetings and at the numerous social events which I was expected to attend on weekday evenings. As the general election drew nearer at the end of the Labour government's first five years, the hierarchy of the paper also felt things were getting more and more difficult. Their fear was that, as it became more widely known that the news editor was a Conservative candidate, some of their readers might become upset and their circulation would suffer. As a result, in March 1949, the chairman and the editor invited me to discuss the situation with them. After pointing out their anxieties they suggested that it would be more appropriate for all of us if we were to arrange a timely parting. They did not press this with any degree of urgency but I accepted that it was the best solution, and agreed to leave the paper in the autumn. Beevor wrote me a warm letter of valediction, and even wished me well with my political career.

I then moved to banking in the City of London. This was made possible by Sir Giles Guthrie, whom I had first met three years before (see p. 110). Guthrie invited me to become a trainee banker in Brown Shipley, a merchant bank, where I began work in October 1949. Brown Shipley had been founded in Liverpool in 1810, and in 1848 had saved Barings Bank from collapse – an act which proved to be beyond the wit of man almost a century and a half later. There was only one way of learning about banking, I was told, and that was to serve for a time in each and every department in the bank. Those who had undergone the same training process that I was being put through included Montagu Norman, who went on to become Governor of the Bank of England for twenty-four years, and Oliver Lyttelton, who was in Churchill's wartime Cabinet and had become Shadow Chancellor of the Exchequer. I was well taken care of there.

On my first day the manager showed me around every department, instilling in me as we went along the enlightened principles on which the firm operated. It was the bank's philosophy that, if a client was encountering a difficult period through no fault of his own, such as international economic circumstances, our responsibility was to help nurse the company back to prosperity, not to wash our hands of it and force it into bankruptcy. The opportunity for short-term gain was in any case limited because, in those days, there was not the same degree of financial speculation in the City. We were also operating with fixed exchange rates, which gave very little opportunity for making – or losing – money on the foreign exchanges. The only occasion upon which Brown Shipley appeared to have lost a large amount of money was on my very first day. At the end of my tour of the bank, I was taken to the vaults to be shown the gold bars in store, only to find that they had vanished. On going back to the manager's office we discovered from his deputy that the bars had been moved to safekeeping in a security store close to the Mansion House without the manager being informed. We both went to look for ourselves to make sure that it was so. It was.

Brown Shipley's philosophy was underpinned by a high degree of personal contact with the client. At that time, much of the bank's financing was concerned with timber and wool, which often took me up to Bradford and other towns in the north to assess whether our clients were managing their affairs effectively. I had been posted to the north during the war, but these trips gave me my first opportunity to familiarise myself with that part of the world in peacetime. I found the people there to be tough and resilient, qualities which they needed as they worked hard together to overcome the economic problems of post-war Britain. Harold Wilson, who was then President of the Board of Trade, had lit what he alleged to be a 'Bonfire of Controls' in 1948. This was certainly welcomed by our clients, but it was too little, too late. My experiences in Yorkshire convinced me that a unique opportunity had been missed in the immediate aftermath of war, while our competitors steamed on ahead of us. Post-war history shows, I think, that the correct formula for those times was carefully targeted government support for nascent or recovering industries – along with a concerted crackdown on pettifogging regulations. The Labour government got all this the wrong way around. After training, I was to work in the bank full-time. In the event, mindful of my slender income, I even continued to work there after I was elected to the House of Commons, spending the mornings in the bank and, after lunch, going to Parliament.

I had to take a large cut in income to move to Brown Shipley, where my salary was only a token £200 a year. But it was well worth it because, despite the frequent trips to the north, my hours were far more regular than they had been at the *Church Times* and, consequently, I was able to spend more time in Bexley. This was a relief, because it was an increasingly exciting time in politics. The fuel shortage of 1947 had led to a full-scale economic crisis, culminating in the devaluation of sterling by the Labour Chancellor, Stafford Cripps, in September 1949. Then, in the wake of the devaluation, Attlee announced a crisis Austerity Plan. From then on, we felt sure that we had Labour on the run.

Over the next year I resolved to meet as many as possible of Bexley's 60,000 electors. On weekday evenings, and regularly on Saturday afternoons, I would lead a canvassing group around the constituency. We also strengthened the Bexley association, increasing its membership from 800 in 1946 to 3,500 in 1947 and 6,000 by the end of 1948. What became a thriving branch of the Young Conservatives was created and we established a Businessmen's Luncheon Club, in parallel with that of the ladies. The more I saw of the constituency and its people, the more I felt at home.

I set out to win the intellectual argument by challenging the sitting Labour Member of Parliament for Bexley to public debates on the major issues of the day. The intellectual battle had to be fought on two fronts.

First, there was the negative and largely unrewarding one of countering the Labour Party version of history between the two world wars. Here my record at Oxford, of being progressive in social and economic policy and opposed to appeasement, stood me in good stead. Ashley Bramall, having been at Oxford with me, was unable to dispute any of this. The second was to put forward my proposals, and those of the Conservative Party as they emerged, for dealing with the economic and social problems of the post-war world. In particular, I pressed the government to free the economy from its restrictive bonds, repudiating further nationalisation, restoring the great public industries to private ownership and meeting the needs of the homeless. There were, of course, plenty of targets for attack as well, in particular the sterling crisis and the devaluation of the pound by Sir Stafford Cripps, the failure of energy supplies under Emmanuel Shinwell, and the consequent increase in unemployment.

As well as local party workers, I enlisted the help of many friends from Broadstairs, Oxford and the HAC. But the most dedicated were a boisterous group of local Young Conservatives. Their sense of fun was not always appreciated by Bramall. At one debate between us early in 1950, one of the Young Conservatives came in after Bramall rose to his feet, wandered nonchalantly up the hall to the front row, where an empty seat was always to be found, took a small packet out of his pocket and then slowly unfolded a copy of *The Times*, which he settled down to read. Bramall had to speak over him. On another occasion, two rows of YCs came in, sat down, produced bags of walnuts and proceeded to crunch the shells loudly under their heels each time Bramall made a point. It completely unsettled him, and the debate was mine. In those days all such meetings were packed out, and the questions flowed continuously. I concentrated on our own policies and always tried to avoid the subject of the Labour candidate. The crowds were serious and good-tempered and there was little heckling.

In retrospect, the road to Westminster was not so much a Long March as an Interminable Dinner-Dance. I joined most of the sporting, cultural, business and purely social organisations in Bexley, attending just about every function held there between 1947 and 1950, including the Commercial Travellers' Dance in Welling, the Bexley, Dartford and Erith Dental Group Dinner, the Constitutional Club Whist Drive, the Angling Society Dinner and many other enticing events which challenged my digestion, my dancing skills and my memory for names and faces. I made more speeches, presented more prizes and danced more waltzes than I had ever done in my life.

It was during this time that I first met Margaret Roberts, as Baroness Thatcher then was. She was a formidable research chemist in her early twenties, and had been selected to fight the neighbouring constituency of

Dartford. We did not see a lot of each other but we each spoke at one of the other's meetings during the 1950 general election campaign. She had a considerable fight on her hands because the sitting Labour Member of Parliament, Norman Dodds, lived in the constituency, was extremely active there as well as in the House of Commons and was immensely popular. Although Dartford boasted a high Labour majority, this was not typical of my corner of Kent and south-east London, where several marginal Labour seats had been targeted by Conservative Central Office as possible gains at the next election. The others were Woolwich West, which was to be contested by William Steward, a businessman, gentleman farmer and local LCC councillor; and my neighbouring seat of Chislehurst, which was to be contested by Patricia Hornsby-Smith. Central Office were keen for the constituencies to co-operate, so Pat and I campaigned together a good deal, attending each other's constituency meetings and organising joint fund-raising events.

However, all the get-togethers in the world could not win us the election. Ideas were what mattered. The party rightly condemned Labour's obsession with nationalisation. By the time I confronted Hugh Dalton at the Oxford Union in 1937, I was convinced that it was not a panacea for all Britain's ills, and his spell as Chancellor of the Exchequer from 1945–7 had not changed my views. I could understand the thinking behind the nationalisation of the Bank of England in 1946, which would certainly help governments to take a firmer grip on the economy. I also perfectly well understood the nationalisation of the coal industry, where some of the worst abuses of capitalism had occurred over the years, abuses which, together with the overvalued pound, had led to the General Strike of 1926. But the nationalisation of steel and road haulage was manifestly unnecessary. So too were the many restrictions that Labour had placed on business, which remained in place despite Wilson's 'Bonfire of Controls', and I told my electors so. Yet there were too few issues after the war with regard to which Conservatives could easily stand up and say 'this is our policy', and by 1947 the young in the party were growing impatient. The stalwarts of the parliamentary party were preoccupied with fighting a guerrilla war against the Labour government's legislation in the House of Commons, a hopeless task given the size of Attlee's majority.

In fairness, the Conservative Party had not been wholly blind during the days of the coalition government to the challenges that it would face after the war. A Post-War Problems Committee, headed by Rab Butler and David Maxwell-Fyfe, had been set up in 1941 and was sporadically active until the end of the conflict. But this had largely been window-dressing, and the party leadership greatly underestimated both the extent to which the party machine had disintegrated and the degree to which people's post-war perceptions of the Conservative Party would be coloured by pre-war events. They also understandably overestimated the extent to which the gratitude and loyalty of the people towards Winston Churchill would be expressed in the form of peacetime votes. In the aftermath of the 1945 general election defeat, Churchill made it plain, early on, that he intended to confine his positive political statements to expositions on foreign affairs, in which he began to set out his vision for the increasingly interdependent world in which we found ourselves.

With regard to domestic policy, he generally confined himself to attacks on any act of what he termed 'positive folly' on the part of the Attlee government. But others were arguing that, in Rab Butler's words, the Conservative Party needed to 'convince a broad spectrum of the electorate, whose minds were scarred by inter-war memories and myths, that we had an alternative policy to socialism which was viable, efficient and humane, which would release and reward enterprise and initiative but without abandoning social justice or reverting to mass unemployment'. By the time of the 1946 party conference at Blackpool, the mood of the party was clear. The delegates overwhelmingly supported calls for a fresh, positive restatement of Conservative principles, and they wanted this published and propagated as soon as possible.

Rab Butler was charged with taking this process forward, and he became the true architect of modern 'One Nation' Conservatism. On social affairs, Winston remained a liberal at heart, and it did not take long for Lord Woolton to persuade him that the party had to move on in that sphere. With Woolton's active support, Rab had already breathed new life into the moribund Conservative Research Department (CRD) and set up the Conservative Political Centre (CPC) as an educational wing of the central party machine. Despite Churchill's reservations, but with Eden's strong support, an Industrial Policy Committee was then set up in 1946, including five Shadow Cabinet members and a handful of backbenchers. Under Rab's chairmanship, they were charged with producing a new statement of Conservative industrial policy. Members of the committee took soundings in the party across the country as the final draft was prepared, and the Industrial Charter was produced in May 1947. It represented a dramatic break with the past – so great a break, indeed, that Churchill and even Eden, allegedly in the case of Eden only under instruction from Churchill – rather distanced themselves from any specific policy commitments that it was felt to imply.

The Charter fixed the course of Conservative policy towards industrial relations for the next thirty years. It set out basic employment rights for workers, accepted that the unions were an important part of society and stated plainly that a Conservative government would work with them for the good of the nation. This all reassured the unions that our intentions were honourable, and paved the way for the excellent relations which Conservative Ministers of Labour, including myself, were able to enjoy with them during the 1950s. It is easy, with hindsight, to say that this was a mistake which stored up trouble for the future. But there is no necessary reason why trade unions should go beyond their proper sphere. The present generation all too easily forget that, after the war, there was a general feeling that workers had played their part with honour and courage both on the battlefield and in the factories. Their leaders were also, on the whole, in the habit of negotiating responsibly in those days. They still cherished their industrial role. Of the vaulting and damaging political ambitions of later union leaders there was hardly a sign. Nobody particularly wished to damn them at that stage by bringing in legislation to curb union powers. Moreover, there seemed to be no need for it, because there was a potent spirit of national co-operation in Britain which lasted for some time after the war.

This was all in accord with the long-cherished foundation stone of Conservative principles, that our task was, in Disraeli's words, the 'elevation of the condition of the people'. Rab subsequently described the Industrial Charter as a 'painless but permanent face-lift' for the Conservative Party, and came to regard it as the party's first step to political recovery for the party. He was right, because it foreshadowed a complete package of sensible, moderate and attractive policies: the mixed economy; greater opportunities for enterprise; and a new accent on industrial partnership. This was music to my ears, as it was to those of many of my contemporaries. Other similar policy documents soon followed, including an Agricultural Charter, an Imperial Policy and policy documents for both Scotland and Wales. As a result, the Conservative Party began, deservedly, to get rid of its reactionary label and prepare itself for post-war government.

For an active political debater, however, it was still disappointing that there was so little opportunity at that time for discussion within the party itself. At the party conference at Llandudno in the autumn of 1948, I spoke about the party's publicity. I praised the progress which had already been made since 1945 in improving the way in which we put our case, but asked that three improvements should be considered: to give us more publicity suitable for use in the workshop, in the factory and among trade unionists; to give us pamphlets at lower prices; and to concentrate resources far more within the marginal seats. All of these propositions have become more familiar with the passage of time. I received a congratulatory word from Lord Woolton, the Chairman of the party, from the platform. But I took no part in the ghastly party conference at Olympia in the autumn of 1949, known to be the last before the forthcoming general election and therefore held in London for publicity purposes, a miscalculation never since repeated.

At the Central Council meeting in London in March 1949 I seconded a slightly impatient motion put forward by Ian Harvey, later Member of Parliament for Harrow, 'That this Council believes that the policy of the Conservative Party with regard to all major issues now facing the nation must be clearly stated without any further delay. It contends that this policy, much of which is already foreshadowed in the Charters issued by the Party, must be clearly formulated in terms which can be readily understood and assimilated by the whole electorate.' In my speech I urged party leaders to formulate 'a crystallisation and restatement of our policy . . . in the plain, direct language of the ordinary man and woman'. This was not well received by the platform, who resented being told by young upstarts to place their house in order. Although the party hierarchy might have considered my views to be somewhat rebellious, that reaction only illustrated how out of touch they were with the large section of their party who were yearning for some solid fare to put before potential supporters. Butler replied to the debate, assuring us that work was being carried out on the programme, that we must not become impatient and that, in any case, it was too soon to publish any programme of the detailed kind that we were demanding. Behind the scenes, however, he was now almost ready to give us precisely what we wanted.

At one of the annual meetings of candidates from all over the country, Churchill addressed us after dinner. It was then already apparent how much he was ageing, and the chairman refused to allow any questions to him after his speech, for fear that he would not have a grasp of the detailed points which bright young candidates might wish to raise. I recall two particular occasions from other such conferences which I attended. Someone once asked Harold Macmillan, after he had treated us to a characteristically brilliant performance, whether our more radically minded candidates would really be allowed to speak their minds during the next campaign. He replied charmingly and, for most people, disarmingly, 'Truth is many sided.' With this remark from a fellow Balliol man, I felt somewhat disillusioned, but I learned to live with Harold's deceptively laid-back attitude.

The other especially memorable event was a speech made by Iain Macleod, then dealing with the reform of the social services in the CRD. This was the first time that anyone had put forward a comprehensive Conservative approach for dramatically improving the targeting of social services. He received a tremendous response. At last, we hungry candidates had been given some solid material on what was bound to be one of the most controversial matters at the election. Conservatives in the House of Commons had generally opposed Attlee's improvements in the social services with such vehemence that the party was considered to be totally against them, despite our own substantial achievements in this field earlier in the century. This had been costing us dear in the constituencies, and we were all immensely grateful for Iain's exposition, which showed us how we might solve our problems. I seized upon it in my own election address and early in the new parliament Iain Macleod became a member of the One Nation Group, which I helped to found. When we came to power in October 1951, social services reform provided one of the main planks of Butler's first budget and contributed immensely both to its acceptance by the public and to its success over time.

In July 1949, the party produced a document entitled *The Right Road for Britain*, which brought together policies in many areas, going far beyond the charters. This was just what I had wanted, and it was enthusiastically endorsed by the party conference that year, becoming the basis for the 1950 general election manifesto, which was entitled *This Is The Road*. There were a number of right-wing malcontents who were opposed to the changes and viewed Rab as the enemy within. It rapidly became clear, however, that the new course was, substantially, winning back the crucial middle ground, and with it an all-important section of the electorate. Of course, right-wing Conservatives today argue that the change in our fortunes came about naturally, because the British people were fed up with socialism. This is simply not so. Certainly, they were disillusioned with rationing and the host of other controls which Attlee's government had inflicted on them. But while, as I put it in one speech at this time, it fell to the Conservative Party to dispel the pernicious myth that the state could be regarded as a 'cushion' to lie on, it was also clear that an overwhelming majority of voters did not want to do away with the welfare state. The British people felt that they had earned the right to live in a more compassionate and socially-minded land, by their exertions and sacrifices during the war. Had the Conservative Party refused to accept this simple truth, it would have remained in opposition for many more years. This only added to the jealousy towards Rab, however, which simmered away on the backbenches for some time and, sadly for him, grievously damaged his chances in 1957 of becoming Prime Minister.

Meanwhile, back in Bexley, my agent, Mr Mulholland, was about to carry the spirit of austerity a bit far for my tastes. 'Mr Heath,' he told me one day, 'the sports car has to go.' I had just assured an open meeting that 'whatever the situation before the war, we have moved with the times . . . we do not pander to the wealthy,' and Mr Mulholland felt that the many Bexley people who were struggling to make ends meet would not be persuaded that the Tory Party was changing for the better if I pulled up outside future events in a gleaming dark-green MG. In vain did I argue that, having taken a large salary cut in order to give the constituency my full attention, I was not exactly a rich man. Besides, I loved tearing around in a very fast and rather fashionable British car. But I recognised that Mulholland was right, and the following Sunday traded in my MG after two years, for a respectable Vauxhall saloon.

If Mulholland was right about the car, he was not getting much else right. In the summer of 1949, he made a clumsy attempt to dispose of the senior officers of the association and replace them with his own stooges. Shortly after my adoption as candidate, I had realised that all was not well with the association. Within only a few days, the agent had set alarm bells ringing for me by making it absolutely plain that he considered that the responsibility of running everything belonged to him, not to the officers – and certainly not to me. I was not at all sure what he meant by this, but I did not much like the sound of it. My suspicions were soon reinforced by private information about what Mulholland was up to behind my back. My informants were the Young Conservatives who sat on the management committee and who had been working closely with me in canvassing the constituency. They warned me that the agent wished to get rid of the chairman, the treasurer and other senior officers of the association, in order to replace them with his own nominees. His plan was brought into play in early August 1949.

Knowing that most people would be away on holiday, he called a special meeting of the general committee at forty-eight hours' notice, to be held not in its customary meeting place at the association HQ in the centre of the borough, but in a club at the extreme end of the constituency, which was more difficult for many people to reach. The YCs feared the worst and begged me to intervene. My own notice of the meeting, marked 'For Information of the Candidate', arrived on the very morning of the meeting. I immediately telephoned Marjorie Maxse at Central Office, who agreed to see me at once. I explained the situation to her and she sent for the deputy area agent, the area agent being on holiday, and asked him to bring over his copy of the rules of our association. I had already pointed out that seven days' notice was necessary for a special general meeting and that this had not been given. On arrival, the deputy area agent agreed that the meeting was unconstitutional. After we had discussed it for a few minutes, a plan was worked out. I was to request the association's president, Martin Holt, to take the chair at the meeting.

He was a most distinguished man, scion of an important banking family and an Olympic fencing champion, who had, until the Second World War, lived in one of the two great houses in Bexley, Mount Maskell. He had told me at my adoption meeting, 'I regard my main responsibility as president to be on hand when you need me.' Now I did need him and told him so. He fell readily in with the plan. I called at his home in west London and drove him to the meeting. He walked in just before it was due to start and, to the astonishment of all present, to the particular annoyance of the lady who had already been told by the agent to sit in the chair as she was to become chairman and to the intense fury of the agent, announced that he would preside at the meeting. The president was followed by the deputy area agent. He explained that, although he had not been invited, he was entitled to be present under the rules, and sat down alongside the president. I then entered and joined them. With one blow of his gavel, the president called for order and asked the agent to read out the notice calling the meeting. After Mulholland had read this out, the president turned to the deputy area agent and asked, 'Is that in accordance with the rules?' The deputy area agent, rising to his feet, replied, 'No, sir,' and proceeded to read out from the rule book the requirement of seven days' notice. The president then gave one further blow with his gavel and announced to a now stunned committee, 'This meeting has not been properly constituted and therefore does not exist. We will all now depart.' He rose to his feet and left. Then a noisy squabble broke out and very quickly the full facts of what was afoot were dragged out before the members of an angry, shouting and, in some cases, frustrated committee. This was the plight of those who had been promised key positions by Mulholland. Back at Central Office, Miss Maxse noted 'an intolerable agent . . . Best thing that could happen for Bexley is to sack Mulholland'.

This was my first and only crisis in Bexley. Here I was, faced with the possibility of a general election campaign beginning at any time. The association was torn apart; the agent had been exposed trying to rig the association; the chairman and treasurer, hearing of the meeting organised in their absence, resigned; and I was left without two of my three senior officers. At another, and this time properly notified, meeting two weeks later, some excellent interim appointments were made, with everybody recognising the dangers which faced us. When these new officers investigated the state of our affairs, they found that there were no longer any funds within the association. Even worse, the Fighting Fund, which had already grown to over half of our expected election expenses and consisted almost entirely of money which I had personally raised, had also disappeared. Shortly afterwards, Mulholland resigned and vanished. We subsequently discovered that he had served a prison sentence only three years earlier. I had to set about raising the Fighting Fund all over again in only a few months. Fortunately the president promised to contribute pound for pound against everything that I raised.

After we had endured a few weeks without an agent, Marjorie Maxse found me an outstanding replacement in Reginald Pye. Born in India, he had been a rubber-planter in Sumatra, before settling in Kent as a stamp-dealer. Later he had become fully qualified as a party agent. After being interviewed in Bexley, and appointed, he came to the constituency shortly before Christmas 1949. It was the start of a happy partnership. Reg Pye was a straightforward man who worked tirelessly for me for over a quarter of a century. We fought seven campaigns together, in the process turning Bexley into a safe seat, and his cool-headed optimism prevented my spirits from flagging on the many occasions when it seemed as though the rough and tumble of politics might overwhelm us. When Clement Attlee called a general election for 23 February 1950, it came as a surprise for it ran against many an accepted election nostrum. February is normally an unpleasant time of year, when voters are still suffering the hardships of winter; and large parts of the country may be snowbound, with a sub-sequent fall in the turnout of voters. However, all the work that we had put in since I had been selected meant that we would be well prepared for the battle, whenever it came.

At my first talk with Mulholland after my adoption I had asked him which was the worst locality from our point of view. 'Little Moscow,' he replied, referring to a collection of temporary huts put up during the First World War to house munition workers from the Woolwich Arsenal a few miles away. The huts of this shanty town had not only survived for nearly forty years, but were still packed with the poorest people in the constituency. 'You can't go there,' I was told, 'it's too dangerous for a Conservative.' Horrified that these people were considered electoral untouchables, I said, 'Get me a couple of dozen Young Conservatives and we'll cover the whole area this coming Saturday.' Off we went and, to everyone's surprise, we received a warm welcome. The inhabitants of 'Little Moscow' always began by saying 'My God, we've never had a Tory here in our lives!' before engaging me in good-humoured political argument. I always suspected that many of them had never been canvassed by any other party either. Labour was already in the habit of taking support from such areas for granted. At the end of the day, we were all worn out. But we were satisfied that we had taken our cause to the heart of the Labour area and, when the evening came, we rewarded ourselves with a few beers nearby. The counter-attack against Labour had begun.

At the beginning of the election campaign, our party workers – can-vassers, stewards, organisers and leaflet distributors – spent three evenings together discussing the policies we were putting forward and the answers to any possible questions that might be asked. The new agent had arranged for me to address eighteen meetings, three each on the last six evenings of the campaign, which represented a fairly strong dose of the candidate for an area only three miles square in size. He also planned for me to canvass each morning from ten until one, each afternoon from half-past two to half-past five and, until the evening meetings began, from seven to ten. I asked him when I was going to have time to prepare the eighteen different speeches that I would need for the meetings. 'Make the same speech at each of them,' he replied. 'They are all in different places and they will all be attended by different people.' This was certainly labour-saving, and proved to be politically effective. We had three suitable places for larger meetings. The most important was on the open ground in front of the Clock Tower in the centre of Bexleyheath, which was much sought after by campaigners. Here the local Jehovah's Witnesses proved to be important, if unexpected, allies. According to the precepts of their faith, they are barred from taking part in politics. What they did, however, was to assure me privately that they would occupy the Clock Tower for their own meeting early every Saturday morning, duly hand it over to me when I arrived, and then take charge again when I left – thus making it available to me, whenever it suited me, throughout the whole day.

At all the evening meetings the feelings in the packed audiences were intense. I arrived at one, the last in the evening, at a school in Welling to find an orgy of rowdy exchanges, with many of the people present, including the chairman, on their feet. No one took any notice of me as I crept along the wall to the table at the top where I sat down. Even then I had to tug at the chairman's coat to attract his attention. Holding up his notes in an attempt to gain silence, he proclaimed: 'The candidate's arrived. Let us hear what he has to say.' As an uneasy quiet descended upon the meeting, he declared: 'I will tell you about him.' He then attempted to impress my local credentials upon the audience. 'He was born in Kent,' he began. This provoked no response from the onlookers. He went on rather more loudly: 'He was educated in Kent.' Still there was no response. Finally, he concluded: 'And he lives in Kent.' To this, a man at the back shouted: 'And for all I bloody well care, he can die in Kent!'

The other memorable incident at one of my meetings arose from the fact that all the meetings were well organised and stewarded by Young Conservatives, who did the same task each evening and who, by the last eve-of-poll meeting, had heard the same series of points made a considerable number of times. By tradition, this final meeting is always held in the old village of Bexley at the Freemantle Hall which, according to its trust deed, can be used only by Conservatives. It is always packed full, with standing room only along the sides and at the back, and people crammed in the doorway. My father and mother came up for this, as did my brother and his wife. On this occasion, I had reached an important part of my speech about how things had changed in the housing market over the past twenty years. I told how I had visited over 25,000 homes during the course of the campaign – and some of them still had the original 'For Sale' notices painted prominently on the end walls. 'What price did they ask?' I demanded, expecting the usual dumb silence in response. To my astonishment, however, there came a shout of 'Three hundred and seventy-five pounds!' from my trusty YCs, massed at the back of the hall. 'And what was the deposit?' I asked. 'Five pounds!' came the reply. 'And who paid it?' I asked, warming to this unexpected exchange. 'The builder!' they shouted. They knew my scripts as well as I did. The air was full of excitement and afterwards, by tradition, we retired to the King's Head next-door, our morale high, talking only of victory the next day.

During the 1950 campaign, I not only returned to Little Moscow, but covered more than nine-tenths of the constituency on foot, meeting many thousands of voters in the process. An election address went to every household in the constituency, in which I pledged myself to reductions in taxation, full employment, further developments in social policy – and 'closer association with Western Europe and America, which Mr Churchill has done so much to foster'. The questions on the doorstep hardly varied. Would we Conservatives take Britain back to the mass unemployment of pre-war days? Were we really going to cut back on the social services, and would we abolish the National Health Service? Wouldn't the poorer sections of the community suffer badly if rationing was abolished? Wasn't Mr Churchill really only interested in having another war? On doorstep after doorstep and in numerous speeches, I reassured people that none of these anxieties was justified.

I spent all the campaign living in the Black Prince Hotel in Old Bexley. On polling day, I rose early in order to be at one of the polling stations when it opened at 7 a.m. It was dark and bitterly cold, but people were already calling in to vote on their way to work. I then set off on a tour of the other stations. By mid-morning, I had got round them all and felt that my prospects seemed good. I was cheered by a telegram of good wishes from Margaret Roberts, proclaiming 'I hope you Gallup to the top of the poll.' I made an afternoon tour and remained pretty confident that I would be returned, with a majority of between four and five thousand. But I had not allowed for the social and economic make-up of the constituency. On my third tour, in the evening, I was horrified to find hordes of obvious Labour supporters pouring into the polling stations on their way home from work. In some streets the trade union activists resembled a gang of socialist Pied Pipers, as they mustered their members and shepherded them in to cast their votes, no doubt mostly for Labour. I realised then that the great majority of Conservative voters had been out early, and began to revise my expectations downwards. But there was little that we could do about it at that stage. At party headquarters, our canvassers and car drivers were massing with nothing left to do. We now knew that every Conservative voter and every doubtful voter had been chased up, and I grew very worried.

That evening I went to the count about an hour after it started, and the tension was already palpable. I paced around anxiously, watching the piles of votes for Bramall and me grow higher and higher, without either of us taking any obvious lead. There was an added touch of drama when the town clerk, an imposing begowned and bewigged figure with spectacles perched on the end of his nose, suddenly collapsed from the strain of being the returning officer in so tight a contest. After receiving first aid from the mayor, he recovered in time to complete the count and summoned the candidates. He pointed to me first and Ashley Bramall went pale. A quick glance over his shoulder told me that Bramall and I both had between twenty-five and twenty-six thousand votes, and I learned that I was leading by 166. The Liberal, a charming lady called Miss Hart who claimed to be a direct descendant of Sir Humphry Davy, inventor of the eponymous safety lamp, went up at this point to see that she had managed just over 4,000 votes. Jumping excitedly up and down she exclaimed: 'Oh, look how close it is! What shall we do, what shall we do?' To which the town clerk in a stentorian voice replied: 'Whatever we do, madam, I do not think it will concern you.' I next saw her nearly fifty years later, when I spoke at a literary dinner at the Hurlingham Club in Fulham in May 1997.

Bramall was now white with anger. The communist candidate – Mr Job, a local electrician – had polled 481 votes, and Bramall turned on him, accusing him of losing the election for Labour. I took Job on one side and said to him, 'Don't be discouraged by what he said, just keep on persevering.' (He did run again, in 1955, but was unable to fight subsequent elections, because a Conservative government appointed him a member of the Central Electricity Generating Board.) My Labour opponent immediately demanded a recount. I asked my agent to have our people man all the doors, to ensure that no one was escaping with bundles of my votes in their pockets. Bramall's people had been irritable throughout the count, and I did not trust them. Having got so far I had no intention of allowing victory to slip through my fingers. On the second count my majority dropped to 133. Bramall demanded another recount. I was alarmed: another four like that one, I said to myself, and I would have no majority left. It was now 1.45 a.m. and, at this point, the town clerk told Ashley Bramall: 'If you want another recount, you must pay for it yourself!' This Bramall said he could not do. It was agreed that the counters would just flick through the counterfoils once more, at no cost to any of the parliamentary hopefuls. This produced no change in the figures, and I was declared duly elected.

Although I would experience far grander moments of victory in years to come, this was one of the happiest moments of my life. Cheers went round the hall as the YCs hoisted me on to their shoulders and carried me off through the streets, back to our headquarters. There, surrounded by the blue and white remains of our campaign material, we toasted our victory, drinking the health of everyone from Churchill himself to our agent, Reg Pye. At 4 a.m., Pat Hornsby-Smith rang to say she had scraped in by 167 votes at Chislehurst. William Steward made it in Woolwich West by a majority of 139. The three of us had been elected with a combined majority of under 500 votes. Among my fellow Conservative candidates in neighbouring seats, only Margaret Roberts failed to be elected.

A little the worse for wear, we set off to celebrate at a grand house near the Sevenoaks Road, with my Vauxhall leading a convoy of vehicles. The celebrations there continued until well after dawn. The loudest toast of all that night was for Mr Job. Thanks to him I had, at the age of thirty-three, become a Member of Parliament. I also owed an immense debt to Reg Pye: not only had he run the campaign and the polling-day activities with immense efficiency, but he had also been instrumental in garnering for me an overwhelming majority among the 752 postal votes which were cast at the election. It was estimated that the Conservative Party owed ten of its seats at that general election to the introduction of postal votes, and four to the intervention of communist candidates. In two Conservative seats both the estimated Conservative surplus among postal voters and the communist vote were substantially in excess of the winning candidate's majority. Bexley was one, and Shipley the other. It had been a very narrow squeak. The following day we discovered that the socialists had held on to power nationally, but with their majority now reduced to single figures. We were naturally disappointed, but felt sure that one further push would soon see Churchill back in Downing Street, and so it proved. It made an exhilarating prospect for a newly-elected Member.

Chapter 6

'WELCOME TO WESTMINSTER'
Early Years in the House 1950–1956

At the entrance to the House of Commons, I was stopped by the police constable on duty.

'A new member, sir?' he enquired politely.

'Yes,' I replied.

'Your name and constituency, sir?'

I told him.

'Ah yes,' he said, in a way which led one to feel that he was already well acquainted with those details and almost tempted me to cross-question him on my majority and the names of my defeated opponents. 'Welcome to Westminster,' he concluded. This was certainly a pleasant start.

When Parliament assembled after the 1950 general election, the House of Commons was an exciting place. The Labour government had been returned with an overall majority of only seven, and there had been a large intake of young Conservative Members, mostly in their thirties, who would go on to play an increasingly important role in Conservative governments until the middle of the 1970s. Alongside myself among the freshman back-benchers were Reginald Maudling, Iain Macleod, Robert Carr, Angus Maude and Enoch Powell. Our front bench was dominated by Winston Churchill, as indeed was the House of Commons itself, on the occasion of the great setpieces. As a result of his declining energies, however, much of the day-to-day work of managing the House fell to Anthony Eden. Financial affairs were handled by Oliver Lyttelton, a delightful man whose political judgement many of us distrusted, for he seemed either not to understand or not to appreciate the Keynesian approach to economic questions. Home affairs fell to Oliver Stanley, by far the wittiest speaker on our side of the House.

All the Labour stalwarts were still there: Attlee, whose interventions were few and far between, but effective in their simple directness; Bevin, immense in presence but already an ailing figure as Foreign Secretary;

Herbert Morrison, who guided government business with skill and good humour; and Stafford Cripps, the lean, pale and austere Chancellor of the Exchequer. Aneurin Bevan, then Minister of Health, was both the butt and the scourge of our benches. He was the man all Tories loved to hate, never ceasing to provoke and infuriate us. It was only when, under instructions from the Whips, we refused to be roused and listened to him in complete silence as he wound up a major debate, that we realised how much he depended upon our show of anger to get his own party's adrenalin running. In those days, the House of Commons still met in the chamber of the House of Lords, where it had been based since the Commons was bombed in 1941. As we assembled there, it reminded me more than anything of the debating chamber of the Oxford Union. Nothing could be more natural. I felt as if I was coming back home. Yet it was a telling reminder of how much still needed to be done to reconstruct Britain.

The One Nation Group was formed after a debate on housing in the spring of 1950. Duncan Sandys made a long, rambling and faltering speech, which drove those sitting behind him to despair. He had been out of the House for five years and, to our increasing discomfiture, was thoroughly trounced in the debate by Nye Bevan, who followed him. After the opening speeches, three of us – Angus Maude, Gilbert Longden and myself – got into a huddle in the Smoking Room, where we were later joined by Cub Alport.

It was apparent to us all that many of the party's old guard were out of touch with the new intake and, unless someone pressed hard, we might be in Opposition for a long time. We wanted to work it out over dinner, but there was no room in the Members' Dining Room. Fortunately, despite having no guests, we were allowed to take a table in the Guests' Dining Room downstairs. The only answer, we concluded, was to form a group to work out policies on those areas where we were seen to be weakest, to mobilise party and then public opinion and, ultimately, to force the Shadow Cabinet and the party in Parliament to accept them for the next manifesto. We discussed who should be invited to join us and added the names of Robert Carr, Richard Fort, Enoch Powell and John Rodgers. Finally, we decided to invite Iain Macleod. There was some doubt about him to begin with, because we were suspicious that he might remain under the influence of the party machine, with which he was closely involved, as part of the Conservative Research Department. However, knowing that he was sympathetic to our ideas, we decided to take the risk, and Iain proved to be an asset to our work.

Nine, we figured, would be quite enough to cover not only housing, which had stimulated our project, but also the rest of the social services, including education, health, the disabled, pensions and insurance and their financing. Each member of the group took responsibility for producing one chapter. This would be discussed by the group as a whole, and each author would then produce his revised edition. I agreed to write the chapter on the financing of the social services, their present position and future outlook. This was to be put at the end of the publication, summarising how we could finance the proposals in the preceding chapters. We met regularly, on two afternoons a week, discussing and amending our respective papers and sometimes rewriting them. Our object was to produce a coherent policy for the social services, setting our priorities for the next Conservative government and demonstrating financially how they could be implemented.

We resolved to publish our plans before the next party conference, in October. The various chapters were put into one volume by Maude and Macleod during the summer vacation, and the work was ready for publication in September 1950. After a great deal of discussion about its title, we decided upon *One Nation*, drawn from Disraeli who, in his notable book *Sybil*, warned that his country was dividing into 'two nations between whom there is no intercourse and no sympathy . . . the Privileged and the People'. The booklet made an immediate impact and became the basis for the social policy of the Conservative Party over the next quarter of a century. To this day, it is still the banner under which the traditional Conservative rallies. We had become the One Nation Group.

It was natural that, with such a large intake of Conservative Members, there should be a flood of maiden speeches from the backbenches. I decided that there was no real hurry and there was no pressure from my constituents for me to leap to my feet. The Labour government was not going to last five years, but it was certainly not going to face another election within a few weeks. Besides, I very much wanted to make an impact with my own debut by saying something substantial on a major theme that was close to my heart. In the early days of a parliament there is always a temptation for Members to repeat large sections of their election campaign speeches, which sound out of date and infinitely boring.

I eagerly attended the first meeting of the 1922 Committee in the new parliament, which Churchill came to address. After welcoming the new Members, he went on to say that the Labour government would obviously not last its full term and that we should work as closely as possible with the Liberals, to ensure that Labour was properly defeated at the next election. There had, in fact, already been two cases of a mutual agreement between the parties not to put up candidates against each other. This was all helped by Churchill's close friendship with Lady Violet Bonham Carter, who was still a powerful influence in the Liberal Party. This approach made obvious sense as a practical means of getting rid of the Labour government, but to our astonishment Churchill was bitterly attacked by Derek Walker-Smith and then by John Boyd-Carpenter. To many of the younger MPs, they both seemed to be outdated products of a largely irrelevant Toryism. It seemed that they had little consideration for the views of their leaders, nor any grasp of the political methods by which we could achieve power. Churchill was obviously affected by their outburst. At one moment he wiped away a tear which was beginning to run down his face and, after a brief half-hearted reply, he left. The baying of the 1922 Committee on that day was a revealing experience of the Tory Party at its ugliest, which I was to experience again on a number of occasions.

I took the opportunity of the Whitsun recess in 1950 to go back to West Germany. It was the first time I had returned to the continent since leaving the army in 1946. My first port of call was Bonn, the capital, then I went back to Düsseldorf and stayed at the one new hotel which had been built, the Breidenbacher Hof. I was staggered by what I saw there. When I had last driven through that city, on the way to Brussels on a forty-eight-hour leave in 1945, it had been so devastated that I could not recognise it as the same place I had first visited in 1937. Now, the entire city had been rebuilt from its state of utter destruction, shops were flourishing and once again there were the open-air cafés along the canal, thronged with young people drinking beer and gossiping together. It was as though the war had never taken place.

On the first night I dined with Sefton Delmer of the *Daily Express*, one of the world's foremost foreign correspondents at that time. He explained the rapid pace of change which was already taking place in West Germany. I was immensely impressed: German power was rising from the ashes and it was obvious that this would soon become a strong and thriving nation once again. I realised that, in order to prevent a repetition of the events that had led to two world wars, something had to be done quickly to tie West Germany into a binding arrangement with other European nations. In Bonn, I had met both Christian and Social Democrat members of the Bundestag, and talked with them about their views on European developments. Both they and my German friends were buzzing with excitement about what was already being called the 'Schuman Plan'. A few months earlier, Robert Schuman, the French Foreign Minister, had asked Jean Monnet for a package of proposals on European unity which he could give to Konrad Adenauer, the Chancellor of West Germany.

Monnet was a leading French businessman who had spent most of the war in Washington working for the British Supply Council. He had also been one of the prime movers behind the abortive attempt to unite England

and France as a single country, in June 1940 (see page 84). At the end of the war, Monnet returned to Paris and devised a plan to put the coal and steel industries of France and Germany, and of any other country in Western Europe which cared to join them, into a joint organisation. This was to be a supranational authority. It would control completely the two materials essential for manufacturing weapons of war, preventing signatory countries from ever again embarking on the manufacture of armaments unbeknown to their neighbours. Those critics in the United Kingdom who declare that there must be no supranational or political element in the European Union fail to recognise that this has been present right from the very beginning. It was this plan which Monnet had taken to Georges Bidault, the French Prime Minister, in the spring of 1950. What happened after that was described to me by Jean Monnet himself.

When Schuman asked him to put forward some thoughts on European unity, Monnet informed him that he had already developed a plan, but had given it to Bidault. He enquired after his plan, and was told that it was now to be found in the Prime Minister's desk, in the third drawer down. After Schuman had finally received it, he told Monnet that it was just what he had been looking for, though he recognised at once that this represented only a first step along a lengthy road, remarking that 'Europe will not be built all at once or as a single whole; it will be built by concrete achievements which first create *de facto* solidarity.' This showed remarkable foresight about how the Community would develop. Schuman then presented the plan to Chancellor Adenauer, and both governments announced their acceptance of it at the same time, and it became known as the Schuman Plan. Had the French Prime Minister not left it in the third drawer of his desk it might well have been christened the Bidault Plan.

In the British zone of West Germany, our priorities had been to arrest and intern some 50,000 known Nazi leaders, to feed the people and to rebuild democracy. In November 1945, a TUC delegation travelled to the Ruhr to advise on the establishment of free trade unions, which we actively encouraged, and responsible political parties were re-formed. Our economic priority was 'the establishment of a balanced self-supporting economy devoted mainly to agriculture and peaceful domestic industries'; and the British occupying forces were immediately forced to introduce rationing on the citizens at a level barely above subsistence. In July 1945, they were allowed 1,000 calories a day. In October this was raised, but only to 1,550 calories. The situation had to be stabilised as quickly as possible, if Germany was to be democratically rebuilt in a form which would sustain peace in Europe for future generations.

Within a couple of years, a combination of German hard work and outside help had begun to rebuild both the economy and the level of morale. I have kept a report of a speech that I made in Welling, in my constituency, back in 1948 which captures my thoughts at the time: 'At the moment, the Germans are looking back on the inter-war years as a period of good time, and that is bad from our point of view, because we wish to encourage a democratic movement. We must therefore show the Germans that democracy works – that it produces food and homes, or else they will say that, as a system, it is of no use.' When I re-read those words today, I cannot but reflect upon how far the Germans have come. Euro-sceptics today invoke the fears of the German problem but totally fail to understand it. They are so blinded by their distrust and fear of Germany that they fail to grasp the simple fact that the *raison d'être* of the European Union is political, to integrate Germany into Europe, using its powerful geopolitical position for the benefit of our continent as a whole.

The House of Commons debated the Schuman Plan on 26 and 27 June 1950, and I decided that this would be the ideal opportunity to make my maiden speech. I wanted to be as thoroughly prepared as possible and sent a telegram to Kenneth Hunt, an old army colleague now based at Essen, asking him for German reactions to the Schuman proposals. He confirmed what I had suspected, that it was possible to distinguish two definite strands of German opinion. On the political front, there was unreserved approval for the Plan, but on the economic front there was far more caution, especially among representatives from the German steel industry. He concluded his letter by saying:

> It seems to me that the simplest way of putting it is that two pretty smart customers are out to get the best of the bargain and that the implications and outcome of their dealings are going to be so far-reaching that we ought to be in on it from the outset. The German and French interests when they get down to detailed discussion will be so conflicting that by acting as a referee in the middle Britain might well regain the leading position and win back the prestige in Europe which has been so easily frittered away.

Anthony Eden, though never a fervent European, proposed the positive motion that day, and warned that 'should the Schuman Plan break down . . . we should see a return to the narrowest forms of European nationalism with far-reaching repercussions'. He was strongly opposed by Stafford Cripps. When I spoke some two and a half hours into the debate on the first day, I was rather shocked when Cripps just leaned back and laughed at my suggestion that the government should take part in the discussions. In my criticism of the government, I made clear the growing sentiment on the Tory benches that we were now the pro-European party:

The Chancellor of the Exchequer spoke looking at the worst point of view the whole time. He spoke of the high authority, suggesting that we should have no say in arranging the power of the high authority. Surely that would not be the case. He said we should be taking a risk with the whole of our economy. We on this side of the House feel that, by standing aside from the discussions, we may be taking a very great risk with our economy in the coming years – a very great risk indeed. He said it would also be a great risk if we went in and then withdrew. We regard it as a greater risk to stand aside altogether at this stage.

Foreshadowing my later views about the basis on which Britain should enter the European Community, I set out my impression of the thinking of the Germans at that time:

> I found that their attitude was governed entirely by political consider-ations. I believe there is a genuine desire on their part to reach agreement with France and with the other countries of Western Europe. I believe that in that desire the German government are genuine and I believe, too, that the German government would be prepared to make economic sacrifices in order to achieve those political results which they desire. I am convinced that, when the negotiations take place between the coun-tries about the economic details, the German government will be pre-pared to make sacrifices . . . I believe that these discussions would give us a chance of leading Germany into the way we want her to go.

I concluded my remarks with the following plea: 'It was said long ago in the House that magnanimity in politics is not seldom the truest wisdom. I appeal tonight to the government to follow that dictum, and to go into the Schuman Plan to develop Europe and to coordinate it in the way suggested.'

To my immense pleasure, Eden passed me a note of warm congratu-lations afterwards. Macmillan would go on to write in his memoirs that I 'had impressed the whole House'. Unfortunately, this debate turned out to be the only opportunity I would have to speak in the House on European unity until I was appointed Lord Privy Seal in 1960. Between 1951 and 1959 I was in the Whips' Office and, by convention, government Whips cannot speak in the House of Commons. Then, in 1959, I became Minister for Labour – and Ministers do not trespass outside their areas of responsibil-ity, either at Westminster or on party platforms.

A constant theme in Sir Winston Churchill's speeches after the war was his enthusiasm for getting France and Germany locked into a political union in Europe. The best-known of his speeches on that theme was made in the City Hall Square in Zurich, on 19 September 1946. When I became Prime Minister, I found that Chequers, the Prime Minister's country home, possessed no painting by Churchill. He had given two to me personally which I treasure, but I also thought it would be very appropriate if one were to be hung on the wall of the White Parlour. I approached Lady Churchill, who then presented me with a portrait of the Lake of Geneva painted by her late husband when he was staying there in the summer of 1946. In 1971, Duncan Sandys, Churchill's son-in-law, told me how Churchill's family had noticed during that holiday that, evening by evening, he seemed to become increasingly cantankerous. Finally, Duncan had asked him why he was so grumpy. He replied that he was due to make a speech in Zurich. 'On what subject?' Sandys had asked. 'A comparison between the British parliamentary system and the Swiss cantonal system of government,' replied Churchill. 'But,' said Sandys, 'you know nothing about it.' 'That', retorted the great man, 'is why I am so irritable.' Sandys then suggested that he should give up that idea and make a speech on the question they had been discussing every night after dinner, namely the future of Europe. That was the origin of the Zurich speech.

In the early 1960s, the BBC approached me and asked whether I would like to hear a tape of that speech. I gathered the British negotiating delegations from London and Brussels together around me in my room at the Foreign Office, and played the tape. I shall never forget the impact on us all. Churchill began with a vivid description of the appalling state of Germany, and then said:

> All the while there is a remedy which, if it were generally and spontaneously adopted, would as if by a miracle transform the whole scene, and would in a few years make all Europe, or the greater part of it, as free and as happy as Switzerland is today. What is this sovereign remedy? It is to re-create the European family, or as much of it as we can, and provide it with a structure under which it can dwell in peace, in safety and in freedom. We must build a kind of United States of Europe.

Then he came to his specific proposal. This, we must remember, was in September 1946: 'I am now going to say something that will astonish you. The first step in the re-creation of the European family must be a partnership between France and Germany . . . The structure of the United States of Europe, if well and truly built, will be such as to make the material strength of a single state less important.'

He was very wise to use the words '*a kind of* United States of Europe', to indicate that we should not seek to copy the United States of America. We should, rather, find our own way of living together in peace, as the states of that union had done in the eighteenth century. Our own system

My parents on their wedding day, 1912

Aged three, my thoughts had already turned to travel

An early photo with my mother and brother John (left), c. 1922

The family

With John (on the right) *c.* 1928

My parents and my dog, ERG

My first trip in an aeroplane, 1931 – fourteen was a little young for Paris, but I have loved the place ever since

Treading the boards at Chatham House, 1934

Obviously feeling on top of the world, 1934

BALLIOL COLLEGE,
OXFORD.

Dear Heath

I am so glad to be able to let you know at once that we elected you to night to the Organ Scholarship.

yours

A piece of paper that changed my life. I carried it everywhere with me for years afterwards in my wallet

Punting at Oxford with Donovan Martin, a Balliol contemporary

My own photographs of the Nuremberg Rally, one with Hitler in his car. The scale of the Nazi threat to Europe was brutally apparent

A gutted Synagogue in Southern Germany, 1937

With the Wincklers in Bayrisch Gmain, Bavaria, 1937

With the Spanish Minister of Education, Barcelona, 1938

Lindsay's campaign was one of the most thrilling political experiences of my Oxford days

Homeward bound ... the lights of New York disappear in the dusk, 11 January 1939

The Beneš debate at the Oxford Union, 1940. The ex-President of Czechoslovakia is speaking. I am sitting behind him to his left; Madron Seligman is in the chair with Anthony Crosland to his left, and Roy Jenkins is in the Secretary's chair

War's end

My photograph of
the old bridge at
Wesel and the bailey,
destroyed by the
retreating Germans,
1945

The church at Wesel,
1945

Hamburg, 1945

should be constructed in our way, in the light of our history, and to suit our purposes. It was a magnificent, epoch-making speech and it inspired the Hague Conference in 1948, officially boycotted by the Labour Party, which worked out a programme for bringing about the friendship and unity which Churchill had advocated.

On one occasion, the great Hungarian-born conductor and pianist Sir Georg Solti was dining with me and saw the picture. 'I too was in the square on that day,' he told me, 'a poor musical student, attracted by the crowd who saw and heard Churchill make that resounding call, not to arms, but to a new, peaceful Europe.' On 19 February 1962, Churchill asked me to address his constituency association on this very subject. I readily agreed and was overjoyed when he gave me permission to play the record of his Zurich speech of 1946. It was a marvellous meeting, and the audience of well over 300 people gave warm support to the European ideals we both shared.

It was in the debate in 1950 in which I made my maiden speech that Winston Churchill himself first made it absolutely clear that he too would lend his weight to British participation in moves towards European unity, declaring that: 'We are prepared to consider and, if convinced, to accept the abrogation of national sovereignty, provided that we are satisfied with the conditions and the safeguards . . . national sovereignty is not inviolable, and it may be resolutely diminished for the sake of all the men in all the lands finding their way home together.' This shows conclusively that, for all of his practical reservations during the late 1940s and early 1950s, Churchill was never *in principle* against our membership of the European Community. He was later to confirm this in a celebrated letter to his constituency chairman in August 1961, in which he insisted: 'I think that the Government are right to apply to join the European Economic Community.' In fact, we took the first steps towards participation in a united Europe under his 1951–5 government, by signing an association agreement with the European Coal and Steel Community (ECSC) in 1954.

In the immediate aftermath of war, it was simply a question of priorities: and the priority was bringing the French and Germans together. At that time, furthermore, Britain was still discharging its responsibilities as a world power. For many people, this image of Britain would persist until the Suez operation in 1956. Up to that time, public opinion in Britain was probably still too fragile to countenance political overtures towards mainland Europe. The country was entirely engrossed in overcoming the immediate material effects of the war, dealing with the continuing problems of rationing and seeking suitable jobs for those who had served in the forces. It also took a decade or so for people to realise that the Commonwealth was never going to provide an adequate basis for British influence; and that neither the United States nor the European Community was very susceptible to being swayed by the British from outside. By the 1960s the United States had nearly twenty years' experience of global leadership and the European Community, under the strong influence of de Gaulle and Adenauer, was performing better economically than the UK.

While Churchill was making these momentous speeches about political union in Europe, the Labour government was expending its energies in its programmes of nationalisation. The Prime Minister, Clement Attlee, did not make a significant contribution to European affairs. He was well aware of the pervasive anxiety in Britain that, once the defeated countries had regained their economic strength, they might come to challenge our own dominance. The Labour government's fears strengthened with the proposal to form the ECSC. Ministers thought that it would be based on a coalition of non-socialist parties in a capitalist Europe. They were also reluctant to cede control over industries that they had only just nationalised. After consulting with Jean Monnet on possible terms of participation, the Attlee government decided not to join in the conference that drafted the ECSC treaty. This was a very short-sighted – and, for the United Kingdom, an immensely damaging – decision. It was quite simply an abrogation of leadership.

Looking back, it is interesting to see how much of the agreement centred on the different interpretations of the words 'en principe', which appeared in all discussion documents. For the six participating countries ('The Six'), this clearly meant that they agreed *in principle* with the objective of the discussions, but if these should prove to be unacceptable when put into practical terms they would not be bound by them. The British interpretation was that, if we accepted the principle, then we were bound by the outcome, whatever the consequences. This difference in philosophical approach still haunts us quite unnecessarily. At that time this argument was used by all those who, for one reason for another, wanted to prevent the development of European unity. It cost us not just our membership of the ECSC, but also membership of the European Economic Community (EEC), which set out the rules for 'an ever closer union', and EURATOM, which was established to co-ordinate the creation of an atomic industry in Europe. Whenever I spoke with mainland Europeans during the late 1940s and the 1950s, they were totally dismayed by the continuing British failure to take the lead in Europe. We became the despair of our many friends, and we managed to patronise the French to such an extent that they became almost entirely hostile. In 1960, I asked Jean Monnet, during lunch at his apartment overlooking the Arc de Triomphe, whether he had not been bitterly disappointed by the attitude of the British. 'No,' he replied rather wearily, 'just somewhat depressed. But I always told myself that when the British realised the whole thing was a success they would ask to join. And', he added, looking me straight in the face, 'here you are.'

When the House rose for the summer of 1950, I took a short holiday with John Rodgers, the Member for Sevenoaks. We drove across France, and down to a small hotel set in the cliffs in a piece of unspoilt coast west of Cannes. The days were spent diving off the rocks into the Mediterranean, sunbathing and picnicking with girlfriends of his near by. In the evenings, we went into Cannes, where John was adept at finding small but excellent restaurants off the beaten track. This enjoyable break was made notable by a phone call from Churchill's close friend and ally, Brendan Bracken, the Irish-born adventurer who had made such a significant contribution to the British war effort, as Minister of Information. Bracken had spoken for me in my constituency during the election and, having heard I was in the South of France, had rung to say that he was staying with Lord Beaverbrook at his villa, La Capponcina at Cap d'Ail, two miles west of Monte Carlo – and Lord Beaverbrook wanted to invite us both over to lunch on Sunday. I accepted with alacrity. On a glorious morning, we drove along crowded roads to the villa. After drinks on the terrace we went inside, and Bracken said, 'Max, I'm sure these young men would like some wine,' whereupon Beaverbrook pressed a button on the table and his butler duly appeared. 'Wine,' said the great press magnate. The butler returned with a small bright-red penny notebook on a silver tray. Beaverbrook opened it and ran his finger down several pages of wines. After protracted study he looked up, turned back to the first page and said, 'A bottle of rosé.' Then he took a pencil off the silver tray and amended the number of bottles of rosé on his list by one. This, I said to myself, may not be how tycoons make their fortunes, but it is certainly how they hang on to them.

After lunch, we set off for Monte Carlo. As we got into the car, the Sunday newspapers arrived. Beaverbrook immediately picked out the *Sunday Express* and threw the others on to the floor. Having commented upon it page by page, he smacked it with the back of his hand and exclaimed, 'That is a great paper, and a clean paper! Any parents can have it in their home without worrying what their children are going to read in it. That is a paper to be proud of.' Ten years later, I was staying in the same hotel when I got a similar call from Lord Thomson, the Canadian owner of *The Times*, the *Sunday Times* and Scottish Television. He too invited me over to lunch at his villa – the Villa d'Ecosses. After lunch the Sunday papers arrived. He picked out the *Sunday Times* and tossed the rest away. Licking his thumb and forefinger, he turned over the pages as he counted the columns. Finally, he turned to me and said, 'Eighty-four columns of advertising – now that's a fine paper.'

Earlier in the summer of 1950, I had revolted against the party whip for the first time. The Labour government had got itself entangled over the succession to the leadership in Botswana and had prohibited Seretse Khama from returning to his own country, fearing that he might stir up nationalist unrest in the region. The Conservative Opposition forced a debate on the question, to which Patrick Gordon Walker, the Commonwealth Secretary, made a lame reply. In the early hours of the morning, Quintin Hogg made a powerful speech in support of Seretse Khama and then forced a vote at around 1 a.m. Our Whips decided to vote with the government, but some thirty of us followed Quintin Hogg into the lobby. As I was moving along the bench, Henry Studholme, the MP for Tavistock, one of our Whips and normally the nicest of men, angrily shouted at me to follow them and not the rebels. I refused. It gave me considerable satisfaction that I had stood by my own convictions. Seretse Khama's case seemed to me to be a just one. Furthermore, he was a Balliol man.

After business one night in February 1951, to my surprise, I was approached by Brigadier Harry Mackeson, the Deputy Chief Whip, and asked whether I would accept an invitation from the Chief Whip to join his office. Although I was pleased to be asked, I had to consider two things before accepting. First, I was sure that we would soon be back in government and knew that, as a government Whip, I should not be able to speak on the floor of the House. I was also uncomfortably conscious that the Whips' Office was not known as a springboard for political careers and, coming so soon after my maiden speech, the Trappist vow that I might have to take could foreclose my prospects altogether. Secondly, I would have to resign from the One Nation Group. We had decided at our formation that, if one of us was invited to become a member of the front bench, then he must leave the group. One Nation was beginning to have some influence and I might be surrendering an opportunity to be at the forefront of an important reforming movement.

I had to take some advice. The only senior person of experience whom I knew personally was Lord Swinton, a member of the pre-war Cabinet, whom I had met at the Conservative College which occupied part of his home in Yorkshire. I explained the position and Swinton said firmly, 'You should take it, my boy. You cannot tell where it will lead but it is the first step on the ladder. The rest is then up to you.' I decided that Swinton was right and I would take my chances. As for my constituents, they were pleased that their Member would be the first of the 1950 intake to receive any sort of promotion.

That same afternoon I accepted the offer and Mackeson took me to see the Chief Whip, Patrick Buchan-Hepburn, who told me that he would put out a press statement. It appeared that the vacancy had arisen because Colonel Walter Bromley-Davenport, a boisterous character, had told one of our Members not to leave the House because he was unpaired. The Member refused, whereupon the Whip gave him a hefty kick which brought him to the ground. The Member complained to the Chief Whip, who decided that Bromley-Davenport would have to go. Hence the rather unusual notice which appeared in *The Times* the next day, to the effect that Colonel Walter Bromley-Davenport, the Member of Parliament for Knutsford (majority 16,913), was leaving the Whips' Office in order to give more time to his constituency; and his place would be taken by Mr Edward Heath, the Member for Bexley (majority 133). Buchan-Hepburn took me to see Churchill shortly afterwards. He was just leaving the Smoking Room as we arrived and I walked a short way along the corridor with him. He patted my shoulder and said, 'It will mean much hard work and it will be unremunerated, but so long as I am your leader it will never remain unthanked.' All three claims proved to be absolutely true. After a decent interval, Bromley-Davenport joined, rather appropriately, the British Boxing Board of Control.

In the House we watched the rapid disintegration of Attlee's second Labour government. After the resignation of Cripps, to the surprise and annoyance of some of his senior colleagues, Attlee appointed Hugh Gaitskell Chancellor of the Exchequer. His budget in the spring of 1951 led to the resignation of Aneurin Bevan, Harold Wilson and John Freeman over the question of social security benefits. Gaitskell attempted to introduce a two-tier system which dramatically divided his party. In the prolonged debates on the Finance Bill that summer, the Labour Party tore itself apart. Everyone on our benches was excited, because we sensed that the government was in its death throes. As a Junior Whip, it was my task to stand at the door of the division lobby while the government supporters were counted. As they wearily limped through for the final division, at the end of a continuous thirty-two-hour session, I heard the sound of voices welling up from among the Labour ranks. It was the miners leading the singing of the hymn closest to their hearts, 'Guide Me, O Thou Great Redeemer', to the familiar tune 'Cwm Rhondda'. The MPs from the South Wales valleys, who had already struggled through so many difficult times in Welsh history, were once again raising their voices and carrying their colleagues with them. It was an unforgettable moment.

Meanwhile, Ernest Bevin had retired from the Foreign Office when it became clear that his heart would not carry that burly body much longer. For the last foreign affairs debate in which he appeared, he arrived late, walking very slowly into the chamber. Churchill had opened the debate and when he saw Bevin he paused. From where I was sitting, I could see tears welling up in Churchill's eyes as he recognised what a strain it was on Bevin to be present. He immediately thanked him for coming. Bevin was replaced by Herbert Morrison, who had been deeply immersed in the organisation of the 1951 Festival of Britain and found it impossible to disentangle himself from it. He was clearly not up to the job of running the Foreign Office.

Nonetheless, it still took many of us by surprise when, on 19 September, Attlee announced that there would be a general election on 25 October. At the time I was in North America. Brown Shipley had arranged for me to go to New York during the recess so that I could gain further experience at Brown Brothers Harriman, our opposite number on Wall Street. I had then gone up to visit the Canadian Parliament; and it was in Ottawa that I heard the news. It so happened that the NATO conference of Foreign and Defence Ministers was being held in the city at the same time. On the morning of 19 September, I had just got into the lift of the hotel on my way to the office when Eddie Shackleton, the Labour MP for Preston, ran along the corridor and held open the door as it was about to close. He was rapidly followed by Herbert Morrison, whose parliamentary private secretary he had been for the past six months. Recognising me, Eddie said, 'Have you heard? Attlee has just called a general election!' 'And the bloody fool didn't ask me first,' added Morrison tartly. I hastily returned to New York and got a berth on the *Queen Mary*, sailing the next day. Going up on deck as she was manoeuvring out of dock I found Manny Shinwell, who was then Minister of Defence, leaning on the rail looking at the skyscrapers. We chatted for a while before he turned to me and said, 'Well, young man, your people are going to win this election. Not by very many perhaps, but they will manage it this time.' I believed we would win too.

My political optimism, however, was completely overshadowed by news of my mother's illness. She had been taken ill just before I left England. My father telephoned me at my London flat to tell me that she had been operated on for cancer in Ramsgate General Hospital. I had rushed down to see her and was appalled by her condition. I had wanted to put off my visit to America, but my father had strongly urged me to go. They were optimistic that she would improve by the time I got back. But, when I reached England, I found that her health had taken a serious turn for the worse. She had been moved back home and was obviously dying. I fought the election campaign in Bexley with this shadow hanging over me. Instead of staying in the constituency, I drove home to the coast every night and then back to Bexley again the following morning to continue canvassing. Each evening I played the piano in the sitting room under her bedroom, all the pieces I knew she loved most, among them the songs my father always sang – and simple pieces such as Ketèlbey's 'In a Monastery Garden', Grieg's 'Wedding Day at Troldhaugen', 'Love's Old Sweet Song' and 'When You Come to the End of a Perfect Day'. My mother died in the early hours of 15 October 1951. It was a devastating blow for me, the first I had sustained in my family life and one that I hardly knew how to handle. My father always believed that the diagnosis should have been made much earlier, and that her life might then have been saved. Ashley Bramall, once again standing for Labour in Bexley, proposed to me that, on the day of her funeral in our parish church, St Peter's-in-Thanet, there should be no political activities of any kind. It was a magnanimous gesture which I greatly appreciated. I received messages of condolence from many friends and colleagues, including one from Margaret Roberts, who wrote a most generous letter, saying 'I am so glad your mother saw your initial success and the way in which you followed it up with a steady ascent to great things.'

I canvassed each day from ten in the morning until ten at night, though I made fewer speeches than in the 1950 campaign. The national campaign was dominated by two fears. The first was the influence of the *Daily Mirror's* campaign against Churchill and our party as warmongers. The second was the danger that the public would react against our proposals to remove food subsidies, on the ground that this would increase the cost of living. Despite the scaremongering of the Labour press, it was clear, on the doorsteps and in the meeting halls, that opinion was swinging behind us. My task was made easier because many constituents had by now got to know me well and by the fact that the Liberal candidate had disappeared – although, to my regret, the communist candidate had also dropped out. My majority went up from 133 to 1,639 and a Conservative government was returned with an overall majority of sixteen.

The victory was a remarkable achievement for Churchill at the age of seventy-six. However, by immediately creating himself Minister of Defence as well as Prime Minister, he indicated that his mind was still in the pattern of his triumphant war years rather than being attuned to the requirements of post-war society. Anthony Eden naturally became Foreign Secretary, R. A. Butler was made Chancellor of the Exchequer, as a recognition of all he had done in the field of policy-making while we were in opposition and Oliver Lyttelton, who had handled financial affairs in a rather insensitive way, was given the Colonial Office. I expected to remain an unpaid Junior Whip, but Patrick Buchan-Hepburn nominated me for promotion as one of the Lords Commissioners of the Treasury. This had nothing to do with the Treasury, but enabled me to be paid. I had severed my connection with Brown Shipley, so this was a considerable help. The government had much to deal with, above all an appalling economic situation, to which task was added a very heavy legislative programme to denationalise steel and transport and to reform the social services. The government also had to cope with the crises in Korea and Iran.

As the weeks and months passed in the new parliament, dissatisfaction grew on the backbenches, mainly because of impatience at the lack of progress in implementing the proposals in our election manifesto. It also became obvious that for a Prime Minister to be directly responsible for defence was too great a burden. Field Marshal Lord Alexander of Tunis was appointed to take over. Although Alexander was greatly respected for his wartime service, his appointment only emphasised the weakness of the Cabinet, which already contained overlords, such as Lord Cherwell (formerly Professor Lindemann), who had no parliamentary experience.

I came under immense pressure when I was made pairing Whip, responsible for the arrangement of 'pairs' between members of the government and senior members of the Opposition when they needed to absent themselves from a division, and for approving the arrangements made by MPs for themselves. I also always had to ensure that there would be more than 100 Members present to support a motion to bring to an end any debate. This meant coming to the House at ten o'clock every morning, working with the head of the Whips' Messengers Office, Mr King, on the day's pairs, and then dealing with requests throughout the rest of the day while the House was sitting. I came up the steps to the Whips' Office on the morning of 6 February 1952 to be greeted by one of the messengers with the words 'King's dead.' 'Good Lord,' I said, 'how on earth are we going to get through today's pairing without him?' 'No, no,' the messenger stammered, 'I said the King has died.' The death of King George VI was a very sad event for a nation which had grown to respect him enormously during the war years. It was also, in a meaningful sense, the end of an era.

We often had to track down members at their home in the early hours of the morning, an operation which required tremendous tact. 'Of course not,' said one rather sleepy wife when I asked if her missing husband was with her, 'he's at the House of Commons if you want him.' Although embarrassing, such chance events helped us to keep an eye on Members with long-term matrimonial problems which, in turn, often enabled us to avoid scandal. Naturally, we were able to demand a high degree of loyalty from colleagues in return for our concern, interest and discretion. My hard work paid off for, in April 1952, I was appointed Joint Deputy Chief Whip and then Deputy Chief Whip. I gave up my pairing responsibilities and had to handle some difficult situations with the Prime Minister. One evening we were rather thin on the ground. All the Whips were summoned and began ringing round their members. On checking the numbers, I discovered that we were still short. Churchill was dining at the Savoy and I was faced with the choice of bringing him back to the House or running the risk of defeat. We knew that it took seven minutes by car for him to return, and understood that the Opposition intended to divide the House at nine o'clock. I finally passed a message to the Savoy, and Churchill promptly appeared at the appointed hour in his dinner jacket. Most unusually for him, he then sat on the front bench wearing it. The Opposition decided to have a bit of fun at his expense and I sat beside him in agony for the next twenty minutes as they prolonged the debate until we voted. Our majority was three. Afterwards, I went down with Churchill to his car and apologised for interrupting his dinner and for the low majority. He was as magnanimous as ever. 'Never mind, you mustn't worry,' he muttered as he got into his car, 'but one is always enough.'

When we took office again, Churchill had laid down that not more than four members must travel together in the same aeroplane because of the danger of an accident causing by-elections. 'You must not,' he said, 'put all your baskets in one egg!' Moreover, any group must contain an equal number of Conservatives and Labour. However hard we tried, it was obviously impractical to arrange this for air flights all over the world. On one occasion, I discovered quite by accident that a parliamentary delegation of eight members was going to Finland. For the first half of the journey they intended to comply with the rule by travelling in two different aircraft, but on the second part they would all be in the same one. I reported this to the Chief Whip. 'You had better go and tell the Prime Minister yourself,' he replied. I found Churchill sitting in the middle of his long table in the Prime Minister's room in the House of Commons. He looked up and I began to explain the situation to him. 'Eight Members of Parliament', I began, 'are going to Helsinki.' 'Must they go to Helsinki?' he enquired. I described that it was an official delegation, and the President of Finland would be meeting them. There was silence. I continued by saying that they were going via Copenhagen, which I pronounced, with memories of Danny Kaye in my mind, 'Kubenhaagen'. He looked at me and said fiercely, 'These words are meant to be pronounced by Englishmen in an English way, and in future you will say "Copenhagen". Good-day.' I left hurriedly, and he never knew that eight Members of Parliament were travelling in the same aeroplane.

My Territorial Army commitments continued for a time after my election to Parliament – and my second speech in the House of Commons, on 8 March 1951, was in support of a Conservative amendment to the Labour government's Army Estimates for 1951–2, which called attention to the serious shortage of volunteers for the TA. I was particularly concerned that, although the volunteer should not expect to profit from belonging to the TA, he was very likely, at that time, to find himself seriously out of pocket as a consequence of signing up. Apart from the weekly drill nights, the regiment came together for two weeks each year at a shooting camp, sometimes on the Norfolk coast and otherwise on the coast of West Wales. Everyone was intensely proud of the Honourable Artillery Company, with its special dark-blue berets, its own spearhead badge and its unique customs, both on and off parade. In addition, the regiment had its own hut at Bisley where we could spend the weekend rifle shooting – and there was always a good party on the Saturday evening.

I gave up the command of 2nd Regiment HAC in 1951, after four years. Lord Alanbrooke had written to me on 27 February, offering me the appointment of Master Gunner within the Tower of London, a ceremonial appointment always held by a former commanding officer of the Honourable Artillery Company. I had already agreed informally that I would accept this appointment and, from August 1951, I took command at the firing of the salute from the Tower for special events, such as royal birthdays. During my three years as Master Gunner we also had the Coronation of Her Majesty Queen Elizabeth II to celebrate.

On one occasion, a much dreaded disaster befell us, when three of the four guns that we were using all jammed up, in rapid succession. The ammunition, which had been collected from the army store in Kensington Gardens, had been issued unchecked and no one was aware of how damp it was. The correct drill when a round fails to fire is to leave it for at least ten minutes. In desperation, with only one gun still firing, the troop commander opened the breach of a jammed gun, seized the round and, with dramatic force, hurled it over the ramparts and into the Thames – an action, unfortunately, caught by the press photographers present. Even this heroic act did not save the day, however. Two rounds before the conclusion we were left with no guns firing. It was humiliating. The question was inevitably asked as to what punitive action would be taken against the young troop commander. I decided that he should be treated clemently. He had risked injury to himself out of loyalty to the Crown, and his aim had been so good that there was no risk either to the River Thames or to anyone on it, but we certainly took more care in future. I asked Lord Alanbrooke if I should report the incident to the War Office. 'Certainly not,' he replied. 'Let them find out for themselves if they want to.' So far as I know, they did not.

As I was getting to know Churchill rather well by this time, I invited him to be the guest of honour at the St George's Day dinner at the home of the HAC, Armoury House, Finsbury, on Thursday 23 April 1953. In this he had been preceded by Anthony Eden who had accepted my invitation for an HAC Dinner before his illness. Eden had been in sparkling form and I shall never forget the look on the faces of the regimental guard of honour lining the stairs up to the dinner as he passed by them. Each of them grinned as they got a glimpse of their hero.

It was unfortunate that, during the week of Churchill's dinner, we were dealing with the final stages of the controversial Transport Denationalisation Bill. The House of Lords sent the Bill back with many amendments, and the Opposition was determined to take advantage of this. On Wednesday 22 April, we sat all day and much of the night but made little progress, so the Chief Whip and I decided to send for Churchill. Just before one o'clock in the morning, he came into the chamber and, after waiting for one speech to finish, rose to his feet and emphasised his determination to get the Bill through the House, 'before the week is out'. Our side vociferously cheered the opening of his announcement, but slipped further down the backs of their seats into ominous silence as they realised the implications of what the Prime Minister had said. He was prepared for the House to continue sitting through Thursday night, Friday night and all day on Saturday. Churchill sat down, turned to me and asked, with an impish smile, 'Do you think I went a little far?'

At ten o'clock on the Thursday morning, Churchill telephoned me himself and said that, because of the undertakings he had given the House, he regretted that he could not be the guest of honour at the HAC dinner that evening. I was dismayed, and begged him not to take such a decision. After all, the dinner would be over by 10.30 p.m. and he would not be needed to dress the House down again before one or two o'clock on the Friday morning. He told me to come and see him in his room after Questions. To my immense relief, he now said that he would come, and asked at what time I needed him. I replied that we should leave No. 10 at 7.00 p.m., arrive at the Regimental HQ at 7.15 p.m., meet Lord Alanbrooke and the other wartime Chiefs of Staff for some sherry and then go in to dinner at 7.30 p.m. 'I cannot possibly do that,' he replied. 'Tell Lord Alanbrooke to start dinner promptly, then come for me at No. 10 at 7.30 p.m. We will arrive at your regiment at 7.45 and go straight into dinner.' Seeing my worried face, he added, 'You know, my dear, you often get a better reception if you arrive a little late.' How right he was.

When we arrived, the doors of the Great Hall were flung open. Everyone seated at dinner immediately rose to their feet and cheered him loudly all the way round to his place. His speech that evening was an immense success but to my ear it had a slightly familiar ring. As a boy at school, I had listened on the radio to a speech he had made at a St George's Day dinner in 1933. It was a powerful plea to support the League of Nations.

Twenty years on, he delivered the same speech, substituting the United Nations for the League of Nations. Nonetheless, he remained acutely aware of the contemporary situation. As we drove back together through the City to the House of Commons, we watched the bombsites go past and Churchill was saddened by the pervasive derelict areas which were still untouched.

In July 1953, the country was told that Churchill's doctors had advised him that he should rest for at least a month. Patrick Buchan-Hepburn told me privately that Churchill had, in fact, suffered a stroke. The rest of the Whips' Office knew nothing and it was a well-guarded secret outside. Eden was already ill and Butler presided over Cabinet meetings, although Churchill remained nominally in charge. That year, the party conference was being held in Margate, some three miles from my home at Broadstairs. It was customary to invite the local MP to move the vote of thanks to the leader of the party at the end of his concluding speech. There was some hostility towards the Member for Thanet, however, so I was summoned back from a visit to the USA and asked to step in. It was an opportunity for me to make my mark, and I took it. After paying tribute to the great man, I reaffirmed the principles of Tory democracy which had inspired him in his youth. 'It is still the challenge to our generation,' I told Conference, 'to go forth and to convert our democracy to the principles of Toryism, so that we can purge ourselves of the weakening influence of socialism.'

Churchill's speech was the first he had made since his illness. Although few people realised just how ill he had been, the whole world was waiting to see what sort of performance he would put up. None of us on the platform knew whether he would pull through or not. All went well until Churchill finished a page, turned it over and began with the next page. Unfortunately, his secretary had inserted a corrected page but left the old one in. He began to recite the same piece. The Chief Whip and I looked at each other and shuddered. This must be the end of the road, I thought. But Churchill stopped and, looking up, said, 'I seem to have heard this somewhere before . . . I think we should move on a little.' He turned over the page and continued. We breathed a sigh of relief.

The new parliamentary session was comparatively calm. We had got through the more controversial legislation, the economy was steadily improving, which was rightly attributed to Rab Butler's budgets, and we had removed restrictions of almost every kind, except for those on some foodstuffs. The most controversial issue was Churchill's retention of the premiership. By 1953, Eden was intensely restless and frustrated at not having succeeded him, and Patrick Buchan-Hepburn spent much time placating him. When Churchill finally relinquished the premiership, on 5 April 1955, the event lacked some of its potential impact because of a newspaper strike. This prevented any press coverage of the resignation, and delayed an immediate expression of appreciation of his life's work. Churchill moved from his seat at the despatch box to the corner seat below the gangway, a position I myself have occupied since I ceased to be leader of the Conservative Party in 1975. It was quite clear that he was determined to stay in the House of Commons for as long as possible.

While Prime Minister, Churchill was equipped with a hearing aid, but at his first appearance in his new seat I noticed that he was turning the knob vigorously to and fro but apparently hearing nothing. At the end of Questions I moved down and asked him if anything was wrong. He told me that he had the same equipment as when he was Prime Minister but now he was unable to hear anything that was being said in the chamber. There was no fault in the machine, because he could hear me talking to him perfectly well. I promised to do what I could about it. I sought out the parliamentary engineers who said that, when Churchill was Prime Minister, they had fitted an amplifier in the back of his seat which had been tuned to his hearing aid. They had also thrown a general magnetic field over his area which his machine would pick up. They had simply forgotten to move it over to his new place. I sent him a message that everything was in hand and waited for his next appearance at Question Time. He sat down and I watched while he adjusted the knob on his hearing aid and then saw his eyes light up as the sound came through. He turned to me and nodded vigorously. Later in the afternoon I went along to the Smoking Room for a cup of tea. There he was in his usual chair with a glass in front of him explaining to the group around him the problem he had experienced, adding with pride and a smile, 'You see, it's all because I am at the centre of a large magnetic field.'

Churchill's successor as Prime Minister, Anthony Eden, used to ring me as his Chief Whip at home early in the morning and at all hours of the day and night elsewhere, very often because of some rumour that had come to his notice or of some petty item that he had read in the press. I never tried to argue with him about any of these things. My task was to soothe him, and to keep everything as quiet as possible, for as long as possible. This I could usually do by diverting his attention to something else more agreeable. Much has been made of Eden's displays of irritation. These were usually concerned with the media or with individuals who had failed to deliver the desired results. I never once saw them occur in the House of Commons, either when he was handling parliamentary business in opposition or when he was answering questions or making speeches as Foreign Secretary or Prime Minister. He normally preferred to deliver a written speech but, on the few occasions when he chose to wind up from rough notes, he could deliver a persuasive performance which would hold the House from beginning to end, and his rapid and witty repartee delighted his fellow MPs.

Anthony Eden's knowledge of art was prodigious and his collection of pictures, mostly of the Impressionists and Post-Impressionists, was very fine indeed. He was one of the first to recognise the importance of Cézanne, which he did in a lecture he gave while still at Oxford. In this field I heard him explode on one occasion. Lunching with him at Pewsey, his lovely country house in the shadow of the Downs, a young American art connoisseur from one of that country's major museums started questioning Anthony about his views on art. The young man was, apparently, an expert on the Renaissance and said to his host, 'I assume that you have considerable experience of Renaissance pictures.' 'No,' said Anthony, 'I am afraid I only know about the Impressionists and those who followed them.' 'Oh,' said the young man, with obvious distaste. 'Of course, you do realise the Impressionists only painted as they did because they were all short-sighted. They could not see what they were painting properly, and those were the results.' This was more than Anthony could bear. He blew up and gave a thunderous exposition about the art forms of the Impressionists which left the young man dazed for the rest of the meal.

Eden's assumption of the premiership was commonly looked forward to as the beginning of a splendid new era. Not only had he been at Churchill's right hand during the war, he had also been the virtual leader of the Conservative Party during the years of opposition and – except during his illness in 1953, when Butler briefly took over – since we had returned to power. He had achieved considerable success in foreign affairs, particularly in the creation of the Western European Union, a military alliance based on the Brussels Treaty of 1948 which was expanded in 1954 to take in Germany and Italy, and in the settlement in Vietnam. Furthermore, the country had a young Queen, people were still talking of the 'New Elizabethan Age', the economy was expanding and Rab Butler's promise to double the standard of living in twenty-five years appeared to be no idle boast or economic fantasy, but a realistic possibility. This felt like time for a fresh start.

It was not surprising, therefore, that Eden decided to have an election straight away. The government had been in office for three and a half years, but required a larger majority to implement its plans in full – and Eden himself wanted a personal vote of confidence from the electorate. After a short and very limited budget, Parliament was dissolved on 6 May 1955 and a general election took place on 26 May. My Labour opponent at this election was a sixty-year-old novelist, playwright and film producer called Rubeigh James Minney who had once edited the *War Weekly* and the *Strand* magazine. As I had with Ashley Bramall, I willingly shared a public platform with him for a debate.

This election campaign was the smoothest, the least nerve-racking and the most agreeable of all the fourteen that I have fought. In the constituency I could feel the tide rolling us along. Everyone was confident that we would do well and I knew that my majority would be increased. I therefore had no hesitation in accepting invitations to campaign in Eden's own constituency of Warwick and Leamington, which he himself was forced to neglect because of his national obligations, and also in Harold Macmillan's at Bromley, near my own. He was taking part in the international negotiations in Vienna over the future of Austria. The government was returned with an overall majority of fifty-nine, and life in the Whips' Office became considerably easier. However, as the risk of being caught out and beaten by the Opposition lessened, so cohesion within the party became harder to maintain. Meanwhile, the economy was becoming overheated and the pressure grew on Butler to introduce a deflationary autumn budget. Many on the backbenches were opposed to raising taxation or reducing expenditure so soon after winning an election when the campaign had been based on the increasing prosperity of the country. The party was torn, as it has been many times since the war, between policies which were good for the economy and those which were good for our short-term ratings in the country.

Rab Butler, weakened by the long illness and death of his wife Sydney in the autumn of 1954, was greatly worried about the situation. To my surprise, because I was still only Deputy Chief Whip, he took me on one side at the party conference in October and asked me what he should do. I told him I thought he should do what was right economically. In the end, we got the worst of both worlds. When the House returned he produced a budget which had been so whittled down by the Cabinet that it was ineffective so far as the economy was concerned and puzzling to many backbenchers, as well as to the man on the street. It was difficult to understand how the Chancellor could deal with rising prices and inflation by putting up indirect taxation – and making pots and pans more expensive. The Finance Bill was largely handled in the House of Commons by Sir Edward Boyle. He was, as always, charming, but on this occasion failed to carry much conviction.

The government rapidly began to lose support, demands grew for a reshuffle and the Prime Minister himself came under fire, so he decided to reconstruct his government after the House rose for the Christmas recess. Patrick Buchan-Hepburn resigned as Chief Whip and told me that Eden wanted me to take over from him. As a result, I was brought into the discussions on the shape of the new government, the last of which was held on the Sunday morning before Christmas around Eden's bedside in his flat at No. 10. Macmillan was moved from the Foreign Office, a position he had held for only nine months, to become Chancellor of the Exchequer. Butler was made Lord Privy Seal and Leader of the House of Commons, which meant that we would work closely together over the next four years. Selwyn Lloyd gave up Defence and became Foreign Secretary. It was generally deduced from this that Eden wanted to become his own Foreign Secretary, and he certainly found Selwyn Lloyd much easier to work with than Macmillan. Patrick Buchan-Hepburn accepted the Ministry of Works, not least in the belief that this would give him scope and influence for his artistic interests, for he was a good painter.

The last appointment to be made was that of Minister of Supply. I put forward the name of Aubrey Jones and, after long discussions, this was accepted. I remember this vividly, because that Sunday afternoon I was due to conduct the annual town carol concert at my hometown of Broadstairs (see p. 12). As I listened to the toing and froing of the argument over Aubrey Jones, I became more and more anxious about whether I was ever going to get to Broadstairs. Finally, at twenty-past one, it was all settled and I was able to take my rather hasty leave, with apologies, driving myself at full speed to Broadstairs. I arrived there just eight minutes before the concert was due to begin. This mad dash came to seem like the perfect forerunner of the turbulent times ahead.

Chapter 7

STEADYING THE SHIP

1956–1960

T he job of the Chief Whip is, above all, to hold the parliamentary party together. There are many different approaches to this, depending upon the prevailing circumstances and the nature of the individual concerned. It is essential to have an immensely strong personal bond of trust with the leader of the party, and I was very fortunate indeed to work in this capacity with two men whom I had always respected, Anthony Eden and Harold Macmillan. But a particularly unhappy episode, perhaps the unhappiest of Britain's entire post-war history, tested my loyalty to breaking point, and I was forced to take the hardest decision of all. In doing so, I subjugated my own views and doubts to the overriding need to hold the Conservative Party together at a time of crisis – not for my benefit alone, nor even for that of the party but, I profoundly believe, for the long-term benefit of the country.

When I accepted this position, I was fully aware that few Chief Whips had gone on to hold a Cabinet post, and none had ever reached the summit. This did not, however, mean that I had given up all personal ambition. I felt from the start that if I could fill the post effectively, it would stand me in good stead for the future. Having had four years already in the Whips' Office, I was quite clear about what I wanted to achieve as Chief Whip. I was determined to get away from the generally held view, constantly and graphically described in the press, that the Whips were a gang of ignorant bullies, forcing Members of Parliament to vote in certain ways, all too often against their wishes. This was generally an unfair charge, but I wanted to transform communications between Whips and back-benchers by encouraging much closer, friendlier and more personal contacts between each Whip and the Members for whom he was responsible. To help bring this about, I introduced a system of immediate reporting of all forms of intelligence on writing pads back in the office. One copy of each note would be placed at once on the responsible Whip's desk, a second would be kept by the Whip who had gained the information and a third was left for everyone in the office to read. It quickly became the established habit that the first thing for each Whip to do upon returning to the office was to look for these reports on the views of our Members on the major topics of the day. This enabled us all at our daily meeting, between lunch and Question Time, to decide what I should report to the Prime Minister and his colleagues, and how we should handle the Members whose views were recorded. This rapid reporting of colleagues' views enabled Ministers to respond more speedily to the concerns of colleagues and, in turn, produced a much friendlier atmosphere and a more effective means of influencing Ministers.

I had an excellent Deputy Chief Whip, Martin Redmayne, to whom I delegated the task of looking after the daily machinery in the House of Commons, in particular in the chamber itself. It was his responsibility to ensure that voting procedures were properly followed, that the system of pairing each of our Members who wished to be absent with a similar Opposition Member was being fully observed, and that our voting results were always in a majority.

I tried to explain my functions as Chief Whip to Bulganin and Khrushchev when they visited London at Anthony Eden's invitation in April 1956. I met the two of them at a small reception given by the then Speaker in the Speaker's House at the Commons. Anthony introduced me to the Soviet leaders. 'This,' he explained, 'is the Chief Whip.' This was duly translated by the interpreter. Both of the guests looked very puzzled. 'I will explain to you what he does,' Eden continued. 'His job is to persuade members of our party to support its leaders with their votes in the House of Commons.' At this, the pair looked even more nonplussed. 'How do you mean, persuade them to support you?' asked Khrushchev. 'Surely you just tell them to do so?' 'Under our system,' said the Prime Minister, with a smile, 'we have to persuade our people – and that's his job.' 'What a funny system,' grunted Khrushchev, turning his back and looking for someone else to talk to.

The Suez crisis began with the nationalisation of the Suez Canal by Egypt's militant nationalist leader, President Gamal Abdel Nasser, on 26 July 1956. In August 1954, I had extended a trip to the Commonwealth Parliamentary Association Conference to go from Cairo to the Cape. The humid conditions in Cairo were hardly conducive for sightseeing, although I certainly made the most of my stay. I saw the Nile, the impressive Mosque of Sultan Hasan and the highlight of my tour, Tutankhamen's tomb, but my visit was also a political education. King Farouk had been displaced from his throne two years earlier, and the future of Britain's Suez Canal base under the draft Anglo-Egyptian agreement was the subject of fierce debate. I seized this opportunity both to visit our base on the Canal and to meet the new leaders of Egypt.

The British Ambassador invited Colonel Nasser, then thirty-six years old and shortly to become president of his country, to a dinner at our Embassy along with other Egyptian luminaries. It was a marvellous evening and, much to the relief of our host, our visitors appeared most friendly and relaxed. In the early hours of the morning Nasser and I went to sit in the garden for a private discussion. He spoke to me of the difficulty of establishing a democracy. He wanted Egypt to move towards the democratic systems of the West, and asked for my experiences of the British parliamentary system. I am sure that his intentions were sincere, although perhaps at that stage he underestimated the task ahead. I left Cairo for Nairobi fully convinced that it would be impossible for Britain to retain its position in the Canal zone under the agreement we had signed without the general consent of the Egyptians.

Nasser's action in 1956 was sparked by the United States' announcement that it was no longer going to help finance his pet scheme, the Aswan Dam, because of his friendly relationship with the Soviet Union and his recognition of communist China. Nasser was playing off the superpowers against each other, in order to get as much money out of each of them as he could. But it was the height of the Cold War and, so far as the Pentagon was concerned, a country was either for the West or against us. Although the Soviet Union stepped in to provide the whole loan, Nasser saw a chance to flex his muscles in the Middle East by retaliating against the Western imperial powers.

I heard about Nasser's seizure of the Canal late at night just after the House of Commons had risen. Our business for the day was apparently complete, and I was returning from a farewell drink with a few colleagues in the Smoking Room. As I walked across the dimly lit lobby, I saw Julian Amery and a couple of other Members huddled together by the door into the chamber. One of them called out, 'Have you heard the news? Nasser has taken over the Canal.' I returned to my office and telephoned No. 10 to find out what was happening. The Prime Minister was entertaining the Iraqi Prime Minister, Nuri es-Said, but had gathered together the members of the Cabinet at the dinner to discuss the situation. He had also called an emergency Cabinet meeting for the next morning.

At that meeting, it became clear that we were hopelessly ill prepared for any firm and immediate action in the Middle East, despite the fact that we had only recently left the area. Lord Mountbatten, Chief of the Defence Staff, stated that there were no plans to deal with this eventuality at the Canal. We all sat in silence for a few moments before the meeting broke up. The Chiefs of Staff went on talking about an invasion plan and the rest of us followed the Prime Minister into the Chamber to hear his first public statement on the crisis.

There had not been time for Members to change their plans and come to the House of Commons on a Friday so it was to only a moderately sized gathering that Eden made a calm, firm and effective speech which seemed to satisfy all our Members. For the Opposition, Hugh Gaitskell responded with his full support, asking only that the problem should be handled through the United Nations, to which Eden gave a non-committal response. Eden seemed to think that all was well. Yet, as I watched the Labour Members, I noticed Manny Shinwell, sitting two rows behind Gaitskell, shaking his head. Other members of the Opposition were singularly quiet. As I walked back with Eden to his room, I told him that the agreement he had apparently secured in the House that morning was not going to last when things got more difficult. Gaitskell was too new in office to deliver it, even if he wanted to. Moreover, he was no Attlee. When opinion in his party changed, I was sure that he would go with it. This subsequently proved to be the case.

After his announcement to the House, Eden resumed the Cabinet meeting so that Ministers could raise points of departmental interest. As they finished and began to get up from their seats, Lord Mountbatten said, 'Prime Minister, there is one other important question on which I would like an answer. Princess Margaret is due to visit East Africa and, of course, the navy plans to take her through the Suez Canal. Would it be right for us to do so now that Nasser occupies the Canal or shall we take her round the Cape? If there is no time, then perhaps she ought to fly out.' The Prime Minister drily replied, 'You had better ask Princess Margaret.' She very sensibly kept well clear of the Canal.

I kept in close daily touch with the Prime Minister throughout August. Towards the end of the month, the Whips were deluged with messages from Members. The party was remaining steady, but cracks were beginning to appear. Some were calling for speedier action, while others were worried that a peaceful solution was not being found and that the pressures were inexorably building up for the use of force. After the last Cabinet meeting in August, when Eden and I were alone together, I told him frankly about the approaching dangers. The Opposition were moving further and further from him and, the more time passed, the harder it would be to secure any effective action.

When the House resumed for a special two-day sitting on 12 September, positions had crystallised still further. The Opposition were pressing for a firm undertaking that force would not be used, except fully under the aegis of the United Nations. There then followed the long-drawn-out and, ultimately, futile attempts to find a peaceful solution: a Commonwealth delegation to Egypt on 3 September led by Sir Robert Menzies of Australia, who did everything he could; and, secondly, the transatlantic shuttle diplomacy of Selwyn Lloyd and the American Secretary of State, John Foster Dulles. On 4 September, Dulles proposed to our ambassador in Washington the establishment of a Suez Canal Users' Association. Eden was obliged to refer the matter to the Security Council of the United Nations, where it was approved. Tripartite negotiations began between Selwyn Lloyd, the French Foreign Minister Christian Pineau and their Egyptian counterpart, Mahmoud Fawzi. Agreement was soon reached on the 'six principles' for a settlement. These required free passage throughout the Canal, with its operation insulated from politics and the tolls being agreed between Egypt and the Canal users, a fair proportion of them being allocated for development purposes. The sovereignty of Egypt should be respected and unresolved disputes between Egypt and the Canal users should be settled by arbitration.

There followed an uneasy time in the negotiations, with a bitter and stupid quarrel about who was going to be responsible for providing pilots on the Canal, collecting tolls and managing it in the future. How sincere were the protagonists? Selwyn Lloyd certainly was and so, I believe, were the Egyptians. Indeed, soon after Selwyn Lloyd was recalled from the negotiations in New York to lead the secret talks with the French and Israelis, he told me just before a Cabinet meeting that, despite the remaining difficulties over who should manage the Canal, he believed he could have got a settlement at the United Nations. Eden, he told me, held a different view.

The French, however, remained bellicose and Eden, though beginning to worry about the danger of using force, was still looking for a way to do so. When the French offered him a plan, he grasped it. Dulles was as devious a character as I have ever met. It was clear to me that he was simply trying to drag out the proceedings so that it would be impossible for any effective action to be taken by Britain and France. The delay did give us time to get the invasion forces ready and sent out to Malta from where the assault on Alexandria was launched. However, as Dulles hoped, the delay also allowed international opposition to any form of military action to build up. Moreover, once we were locked into negotiations with the Egyptians which looked as if they might resolve the crisis, it became even harder to justify resorting to force. Later, after the invasion had taken place, the delay intensified suspicion that Britain and France had acted with duplicity, because the invasion was, so evidently, thoroughly planned.

While negotiations were going on, my task was to reassure the right of the party that it was necessary to continue with diplomatic action, but that a military solution was not excluded. At the same time, I had to reassure the left that the diplomatic effort was genuine and not just a holding operation while the military got ready. At the party conference in October, the debate on Suez was naturally at the centre of proceedings. I went up to Llandudno on the day before it began in order to gauge the mood of the rank and file. The Foreign Secretary was at the United Nations in New York and Lord Salisbury, the Lord President of the Council, had been taken ill, so Eden at first thought that he might reply to the debate himself. I judged that feelings were running very high indeed and that the Suez Group, a group of right-leaning backbenchers including Julian Amery, Fitzroy Maclean and Charles Waterhouse, would try some rabble-rousing. I advised the Prime Minister that he should not take that speech on under any circumstances and should wait until his keynote speech at the end of the week, when tempers might have calmed a little. Eden agreed and decided instead that Anthony Nutting, Minister of State at the Foreign Office, should make the speech. This was a good idea because, although Nutting did not have the standing of Lord Salisbury, he had become a highly popular speaker with the party.

Nutting travelled up to Llandudno from London as quickly as he could and I stayed up late to meet him at the hotel. I brought him up to date with the situation and told him that, when he answered the debate, he must tell the conference that he was reading Lord Salisbury's speech to them. I emphasised that this was essential to maintain the confidence of the right wing of the party. During the debate, the party seemed to be remarkably steady. There was no criticism of the Prime Minister, and much of what was said was constructive. Then, when the time came for the reply to the debate, Nutting made absolutely no mention of the fact that it was Lord Salisbury's speech he was delivering. He also toned down a couple of passages. But the speech went well, and did much to calm the party's nerves. The fact, however, that he had taken such a robust line at Llandudno made his resignation from the government a month later completely incomprehensible to most people both inside and outside the party, and left him open to the charge of hypocrisy. In fact, I knew all along that Nutting was profoundly unhappy with the direction of policy, but had felt at the time of the conference speech that we might still come back from the brink.

The Prime Minister's speech at the end of the conference was also well received. He reiterated the official line, stressing the government's desire to see the problem settled peacefully in the interests of the Canal users, while not excluding the use of force if all other means should fail. We all travelled back on the train together, which was stopped at Watford to enable Eden to be driven straight to Chequers. He left us heartened by the reception he had received, but it was obvious to those of us who were close to him that he was becoming more and more tired as the weeks of crisis passed. He had already had to spend one weekend in University College Hospital. We were all worried about his health and uncertain how long he would hold up.

Throughout these weeks I was able to observe Eden closely. In particular, I watched the animated way in which he worked on his papers. As he went over telegram after telegram from our ambassadors at the United Nations and in the major capitals of the world, one could only admire the skill and the speed with which he worked. Like all the best leaders in peace and war, he seemed able to visualise the situation many moves ahead. He was also able to make realistic assessments and imaginative proposals for dealing with them. The only exception I noticed was his readiness to accept the information coming in from the intelligence services in the Middle East. All too many of them were misleading enough taken at face value, but at times he seemed to read into them what he wanted. This was especially the case with regard to Nasser's personal position in Egypt and his relationship with other Middle Eastern countries. Eden was determined that Nasser and his regime should be brought down. The intelligence services often provided gossip and items of tittle-tattle which seemed to show that this was about to happen. But it never did and Nasser emerged more or less intact from the whole episode.

Secret discussions on the possibility of an invasion between the British, French and Israelis were carried out in Paris in the latter part of October. I was first told of these discussions after a meeting of the inner circle of Ministers and officials held at Chequers on 21 October. I was alarmed, but far from surprised, that a plan was being hatched to circumvent the negotiations in New York. Four days later, I went into the Cabinet Room as usual shortly before Cabinet was due to start, and I found the Prime Minister standing by his chair holding a piece of paper. He was bright-eyed and full of life. The tiredness seemed suddenly to have disappeared. 'We've got an agreement!' he exclaimed. 'Israel has agreed to invade Egypt. We shall then send in our own forces, backed up by the French, to separate the contestants and regain the Canal.' The Americans would not be told about the plan. He concluded, somewhat unnervingly, that 'this is the highest form of statesmanship'. The Sèvres Protocol, as it became known, had been signed the day before, in a suburb of Paris. Sir Patrick Dean had signed on behalf of the Foreign Secretary, Selwyn Lloyd, and Christian Pineau and David Ben-Gurion had signed, respectively, on behalf of France and Israel. Only Lloyd, Macmillan, Butler and myself were to know about it. I did my utmost to change Eden's mind, warning him that it was unlikely that people would believe him – and that, even if the Protocol remained a secret and people accepted the official reason for going in, the very act of doing so was likely to split the country. Eden did not dispute any of this advice, but simply reiterated that he could not let Nasser get away with it.

Before we could have a proper discussion, the door opened and the Cabinet began to file in. At the meeting which followed, Eden repeated what he had said to our conference about the need to use force only if necessary. Although several Ministers had doubts about military action, the only one who actually resigned was Walter Monckton, the Minister of Defence. He was replaced by Antony Head on 18 October and took a non-departmental post. On 30 October, the Prime Minister interrupted business in the House at 4.30 p.m. to make a statement announcing that Israel had attacked Egyptian territory and was moving towards the Canal. At the same time it had given an undertaking that it would not attack Jordan or other neighbouring countries whose independence we were concerned to maintain.

As provided for in the Sèvres Protocol, Britain and France had thereupon called on Egypt and Israel to cease hostilities and for each of them to withdraw ten miles from the Canal, under threat of invasion should they fail to comply. Eden's statement was at first received comparatively quietly by the House. Hugh Gaitskell confined himself to a couple of logistical questions but did not comment on the invasion which now seemed imminent. As the evening wore on, however, Members began to realise the full implication of the Prime Minister's statement and the debate became more fierce. By the time the debate finished just before ten o'clock, tempers had risen and accusations of illegality were being thrown across the House. There was a clear indication of what we were in for in the weeks to come when the Opposition forced a vote even though the debate had only been on the adjournment of the House. The situation then intensified when Egypt refused to withdraw from the Canal Zone and, on 31 October, Eden gave the order to bomb airfields in northern Egypt in tandem with the French. At the UN, Britain and France vetoed American and Soviet resolutions calling for a cease-fire. In the House of Commons, Hugh Gaitskell denounced the invasion as 'an act of disastrous folly whose tragic consequences we shall regret for years'. On the same day, the Anglo-French task force set sail from Malta.

As these debates proceeded, more and more questions were being asked and were remaining unanswered by an increasingly exposed, embarrassed and truculent government. In between the two front-bench wind-up speeches on Thursday 1 November, the drama moved on to another plane when the Conservative Member for the Wrekin, William Yates, interrupted on a point of order and said, 'I have come to the conclusion that Her Majesty's Government has been involved in an international conspiracy,' and the House had to be suspended amid considerable uproar. It was already becoming difficult for Ministers to justify a demand for Egypt to withdraw ten miles from the Canal Zone when it was plain that it was Israel which had advanced into Egyptian territory. The explanation prepared for not fully consulting the United States and the Commonwealth, that time had simply not allowed it, was not even offered, and would not have carried much conviction with those who were well aware of the capabilities of modern telecommunications. While the difficulties of producing a legal or moral justification for bombing Egyptian airfields were becoming increasingly obvious, Egypt still declined to withdraw its forces from the Canal. Matters came to a head in the House of Commons on Saturday 3 November. It was the first Saturday sitting since the 1940s, a measure of the seriousness of the situation.

Despite this, the great majority of the Conservative Party in the House of Commons was fully in support of the Prime Minister and his colleagues. As the conference had shown, Eden was still loved by his party. The Suez Group even appeared to be happy about the government's actions, although some were already expressing doubts about whether the government would see it through. Those on our own side who were against any military ventures had also formed themselves into a group and were meeting regularly at Sir Alec Spearman's home in Queen Anne's Gate. Their number varied between twenty and thirty, among them Bob Boothby and Nigel Nicolson. They were all fully co-operative throughout the crisis. Spearman came to see me before and after each of their meetings and, in return, Oliver Poole, the party Chairman, and I did all we could to smooth things over with their constituencies, all of which were hostile to the position they were taking, particularly after the ministerial resignations of Edward Boyle and Anthony Nutting.

Some may ask why, given my doubts about Suez, I did not resign as Chief Whip. There was one overriding reason. When you accept that position, you do so knowing that it demands service in all conditions. The Chief Whip is not called upon, indeed is not expected, to speak in the House of Commons or make publicly known his views on matters of government policy. He and his colleagues in the Whips' Office are expected to keep in the closest touch with the views and feelings of government backbenchers, to report them faithfully to the Prime Minister and his senior colleagues, and to ensure that the government's business is sustained by them in the House of Commons. It is also his responsibility to make the best possible arrangements with the Chief Whips of the opposition parties for the sensible management of business in the House. As this crisis developed, the feeling between the two sides of the House became so bitter that only the two Chief Whips were on speaking terms with each other. If that bond were ever to be broken, the parliamentary system would collapse.

The Chief Whip's relationship with the Prime Minister is a special and personal one. He owes his complete loyalty to the Prime Minister, who is entitled to count upon it. Any doubts or reservations should be expressed completely privately, one to one – which I did. For a government Chief Whip to resign as a consequence of disagreement on a matter of Cabinet policy is unknown, and would be tantamount to saying that he was not able, or was not willing, to persuade government backbenchers to support the government in the division lobbies. To my mind it is no exaggeration to say that the resignation of a government Chief Whip on a major issue of policy would be a mortal blow to confidence in the government. Certainly a Prime Minister could hardly survive it. For a Chief Whip to resign, particularly during a national crisis such as Suez, would be an act not only of utter disloyalty, but of wilful destruction.

I thought that the situation did not call for or justify an act of such devastating disloyalty to the Prime Minister as my resignation would have been. After all, though Conservative Members felt unhappy about the way in which policy had been made, and then changed, in the Suez affair, the party in the House had more or less held together, and relatively few of them were driven to resigning from office or to refusing to vote for the government in the division lobbies. But the party remained deeply unhappy and traumatised by these events, and uncertain of the future. A further consideration in my mind was that there might be a useful part for me, as Chief Whip, to play in rebuilding morale and self-confidence in the parliamentary party in the coming months. The crisis was bad enough already, and my task was to try and hold the party, and the government, together. If I could do that, I knew that the more sensible elements within it would be able to protect the party from complete disaster. So I just got on with doing my job.

My military experience came in useful during this period. The Whips were in continuous touch with all our Members, in order to judge their reactions to every move, statement and debate. We were piecing all these views together day and night, and then making sure that the Prime Minister and his senior colleagues were kept constantly informed of the position. We had to persuade the party that, whatever their individual views about government policy, our country was in fact at war and the lives of Her Majesty's forces were at stake. This was accepted almost without exception.

However, it was much harder to influence public opinion, which quickly made itself felt after the invasion. The Labour Opposition was consistently voting against us and, as I had warned Eden, the nation was being split down the middle. On Sunday 4 November, reports came in of a massive protest meeting being held in Trafalgar Square and around tea-time word was passed around that the demonstrators were marching down Whitehall. I went from my office in No. 12 Downing Street through the interconnecting series of corridors to the corner of the Cabinet Office building, where I could see out to Whitehall below. As the demonstrators advanced from Trafalgar Square down towards the Houses of Parliament, I could see a large and angry crowd, in which tempers were evidently running extremely high. Opposite Downing Street, near the Cenotaph, the marching stopped. As the crowd grew larger, the shouting grew louder. Some of the most militant demonstrators had clearly resolved to get into Downing Street. The police were equally determined to prevent them, and those on horseback charged the crowd when they began to break down the temporary barriers that had been erected to keep them out. It was a terrifying scene. Gradually the police got the situation under control and the crowd began to move towards Parliament Square, though many hung around late into the evening. It was a revelation of how passionately people felt about the whole Suez affair and how deeply divided the country had become. This was not a demonstration organised by a few left-wing extremists. It was supported by thousands of people who genuinely believed that what was happening was politically, militarily and morally wrong.

Eden was convinced that it would be a good thing if he made a direct appeal for national unity on television. I told the BBC that we considered it to be in no way a party political broadcast, but an address to the people at a time of national emergency. It was an historic occasion, the first time that a Prime Minister had used television to address the British people at a time of war. I watched it from No. 10 with William Clark, Eden's press secretary. The Prime Minister did well. His broadcast, though brief, was authoritative and it made a considerable impact, not only by heartening his natural supporters on the right, but also by persuading many doubters that the country was now at war.

Only a few minutes after the broadcast had ended, Herbert Bowden, the Labour Chief Whip, telephoned me to say that he was asking the BBC to grant Hugh Gaitskell a right of reply to the Prime Minister. I told him that this was an appeal to the nation at a time of great danger, not a party political matter. Bowden accepted that we were in the middle of a crisis, but reminded me that there was no consensus, either inside Parliament or in the country at large, that we should continue with our actions. Eden was furious when I told him. He had gone to extreme lengths to ensure there was nothing in his broadcast which in any way reflected on the Labour Party or its front bench, and sincerely believed that Gaitskell's reply might endanger the chances of success of Her Majesty's forces. I then telephoned Harman Grisewood, chief assistant to the BBC director-general, Sir Ian Jacob. Jacob was himself a military man, but took the view that this was a contentious issue, in which the Leader of the Opposition should be able to convey his views to the general public. I accepted that, under this pressure, the BBC had no justifiable alternative. In his broadcast, Gaitskell declared that the only thing that could 'save the honour and reputation of our country' was for Eden to resign. It was the first of a series of body blows which we were to receive.

On Monday we heard that the army was making progress after landing at Port Said. There were few casualties, and the news came through that the Egyptian Commander had surrendered. This was indeed the case, but later that evening he withdrew his undertaking and the war continued with the army making rapid progress towards its ultimate destination. The following morning, Tuesday, there was a Cabinet meeting at the Prime Minister's room in the House of Commons. Although the military news continued to be good, the rest was bad. There had been massive selling of sterling and, because neither the Americans nor anyone else were pre-pared to support it, the pound was on the point of collapse. Eden's relations with Eisenhower were now so bad that they were barely talking, and he had no influence with the American government as a whole. Harold Macmillan, however, maintained contact with his opposite number in Washington and it was clear from his discussions that the Americans would not lift a finger to help us with sterling unless we accepted the United Nations solution to the conflict. Torn between the potential collapse of our economy and the long-term implications of a humiliating withdrawal from Egypt, we were forced to accept the latter and dress up the operation as a successful attempt to internationalise the crisis.

During the break in that Cabinet meeting, Macmillan took me off into a corner and asked, 'What about it? Can you see any alternative? What is the party going to say?' I told him that, of course, the party would not like it one bit. Having embarked on this venture, they wanted us to see it through. But, in view of what he had said as Chancellor of the Exchequer, I could see no alternative. We had come full circle. Macmillan, who had supported the venture from the beginning and who had so strongly and consistently urged a full-blown military operation, was also the first to recognise that it could not be completed. The Cabinet agreed that we had no option but to surrender to the American ultimatum. In the light of the decision, Macmillan was sent off to Washington, to try to gain renewed support for sterling. Later that evening, the Prime Minister announced to the House of Commons that agreement had been reached over the use of United Nations forces and that military operations would cease at midnight. There were those in the party who argued privately that, if our forces had been given rapid instructions to ignore everything except reaching their destination, the government could have held off the political attacks just long enough for them to do so. The Cabinet was not convinced of this and the risks of attempting it appeared far too great. Virtually the entire parliamentary party was now in a sombre mood, depressed by a humiliating failure, but the Suez Group was completely disillusioned with the leadership of the party. The crisis culminated with a debate on a vote of no confidence in the government on 8 November.

That evening, I was sitting at the Chief Whip's table at the corner of the Dining Room when a message was brought in to me that some Members wished to see me outside. I found Captain Charles Waterhouse, the leader of the Suez Group, and Julian Amery, one of the strongest and most effective advocates of its policies. Waterhouse told me he could ensure that all the members of the group would vote with the government in the division that night, provided I would give an undertaking to bring about Eden's downfall as leader of the Conservative Party. I told him to go to hell and, without further discussion, went back to finish my dinner.

In the division later that evening, none of our MPs voted against the government and we had only six abstentions. One of these was Nigel Nicolson, who said he would support the government if I could assure him that there had been no secret plot to carry out the invasion. In my position, there was no way that I could deny or confirm this. I looked Nigel straight in the eyes and said nothing. He understood completely. At the end of the debate, after a reasonable result in the division lobby, there was a sense of relief that the worst of this dreadful episode was over. I received a number of letters thanking me for holding the party together during the crisis and for doing so with courtesy. Flattering as these remarks were, I was perfectly clear in my own mind that it was one thing to save the Conservative Party from the abyss, but it was quite another matter to convince the British people that we were still fit to govern.

Nine days later, on Saturday 17 November, Eden had to address a large meeting of Young Conservatives in the Royal Festival Hall in London. The meeting was chaired by Peter Walker, and the Prime Minister received a tumultuous welcome. He was obviously desperately tired and did not make a particularly impressive speech, but the Young Conservatives were keen to show their support for him. Afterwards, I went back to No. 10 with Anthony and his wife Clarissa for tea. While I was there, his doctor, Sir Horace Evans, took him for an examination. He then declared that Anthony must go and have a complete rest. After a brief discussion with Clarissa, Anthony settled on the West Indies as the best place for his recuperation. I had no wish for the Prime Minister's health to deteriorate any further, but I was alarmed at the idea that he should leave the country at this time. Unless a Prime Minister is in complete command of his government, as Harold Macmillan was during his tour of Africa in 1960, it is never wise for him or her to be away for too long. Moreover, in those days, most of the population had never been abroad, so leaving the country was no small matter.

Shortly after this discussion, Harold Macmillan came through from No. 11. When he heard the proposal, he was equally horrified and, while Anthony was talking to his doctor, he came over to me and said, 'Ted, you must stop this happening. It will be disastrous for him and for us. It will look as if he is making a quick getaway and leaving the mess for us to clear up.' Our protests were to no avail. Anthony, always the most dutiful and responsible of men, had no strength left to resist the powerful advice of his doctor, and Clarissa, quite naturally, was thinking of the best way to restore her husband's health.

Anthony left for Jamaica five days later and my task was to continue managing the party while he was away. I had to recognise that, however hard I tried to maintain the parliamentary party's confidence in him as a leader, it would become more difficult as the weeks went by. Furthermore, no one could foretell what his state of health would be when he returned. Almost immediately there was speculation about a successor and widespread lobbying on behalf of the two obvious candidates, Rab Butler and Harold Macmillan. I did all I could to maintain a balance between the two of them. At the last meeting of the 1922 Committee before the House rose for Christmas, someone had to give the party a general survey of the political position following Suez. It turned out to be the official start of the campaign for the leadership, although the forces at work behind it were not as malign as some have since supposed. Technically, Rab Butler had been left in control of the government, so it was natural that he should address the Committee. Nonetheless, I believed that if he alone appeared it would cause ill-feeling, so I arranged for Harold to speak after him. Butler made a balanced and worthy speech which was, sadly, uninspiring. Macmillan, on the other hand, turned in a magnificent performance. His speech was laced, as it usually was in private, with sparklingly apposite historical and philosophical allusions and was lightened with the witty, ironical humour of which he was a master.

When Anthony returned on 14 December, he looked bronzed and clearly better, but he was not still completely fit. Despite the *de facto* leadership battle that was already under way, I and many others continued to hope that his health would improve and he would become the fine Prime Minister we knew he could be. However, in the parliamentary debate on 20 December he misled the House. As I sat and watched him deny any 'foreknowledge' of Israel's invasion of Egypt, I felt like burying my head in my hands at the sight of this man I so much admired maintaining this fiction. Some time during the afternoon after the debate, I went along from my room in No. 12 to No. 10 to have a word with Freddie Bishop, the Prime Minister's principal private secretary, about the general outlook. As we were chatting, Sir Norman Brook, the Cabinet secretary, came through the door from the Cabinet Room, where he had been seeing the Prime Minister, looking like an old Samurai who had just been asked to fall on his sword. We paused, as Brook said, 'He's told me to destroy all the relevant documents. I must go and get it done.' With that, Sir Norman, loyal as always to his Prime Minister, went off to destroy the Sèvres Protocol and other documents which confirmed the collusion between Britain, France and Israel over Suez. Anthony Eden always denied that any such agreement had ever existed. Despite revelations soon afterwards by French and Israeli sources, he never changed his position.

At the time he was absolutely convinced that the prevention of a dictator getting his own way was in the interest of Britain, the Middle East and the world as a whole. He considered it essential to safeguard world peace and the vital trade routes of ourselves and our friends. The fact that we managed for so long after the Canal was closed with the alternative route around the Cape, and developed carriers of large tonnage for that purpose, proved how wrong that premise was, but it does not alter the genuine nature of his concern. Similarly, the fact that, once the Canal was opened, the Egyptians were able to run it so easily contradicted all the previous assertions that an international consortium was essential for operational purposes if traffic through the Canal was to survive. But that too was a genuine belief at the time. Eden also claimed that introducing international control, backed by international forces, into the Middle East would limit Nasser's power, and that this was a future safeguard against any further expansionist ideas from him. The fact that, later on, his expansionism led him into the Yemen and into treaties of union with Syria and Libya rather countered this claim.

What, then, did Suez achieve? Nasser's international prestige and apparent invulnerability never recovered. His country had been invaded, albeit partially and briefly, and it was clear that, despite the American opposition on this particular occasion, the West was willing and able to act in the Middle East if it felt that its interests were seriously under threat. However, perhaps the greatest legacy of Suez was that it forced many of the British establishment to accept that the sun was setting on the British Empire and that America was the new superpower. This in turn forced many who had hitherto been sceptical about European unity to realise that our future lay in our own continent and not in distant lands which our forefathers had coloured pink on the map. Even Eden, who had crucially kept our seat empty at Messina in 1955 (see p. 201), acknowledged this fact in one of the last memos he circulated as Prime Minister. On 28 December 1956, he wrote that 'the consequences of this examination may be to determine us to work more closely with Europe'. In my office at No. 12, I read these words with delight, mixed with sadness at all it had taken to bring about Anthony's change of heart on the subject.

I was in my office again on Wednesday 8 January 1957 when the Prime Minister sent for me to see him, in the Cabinet Room. He told me that, on his doctor's advice, he had decided to resign. This was not entirely surprising, but it was an event which I had desperately hoped would not occur. He was not in the least emotional about his decision. He showed fortitude, perhaps even an air of inevitability. He held a brief meeting at which he told his colleagues, and then went to Sandringham later that day to tell the Queen. Her Majesty decided to wait a day before announcing the Prime Minister's decision so that people would be assured that she had considered it sufficiently.

That evening and the next day were entirely taken up with consultations between myself, the Whips and our Members at their homes, about who should succeed Eden. As the meeting of the 1922 Committee had indicated, Macmillan's support among backbenchers was considerably greater than Butler's. Whereas the centre and left of the party would reluctantly accept Macmillan's leadership, because he had been quick to advocate withdrawal from the Canal, many on the right could never forgive Butler for being so fainthearted at the outset. In the meantime Lord Salisbury and Lord Kilmuir were interviewing each member of the Cabinet separately about their position. I knew that only Patrick Buchan-Hepburn, my predecessor as Chief Whip, was a firm supporter of Rab, in part because he too had always been doubtful about Suez and also because he profoundly distrusted Macmillan.

In the afternoon, the Queen's private secretary, Sir Michael Adeane, asked me to see him at his home in St James's Palace. I already knew both Michael and his wife, and he wanted to know my views before Salisbury and Kilmuir reported to him. I told him that, after being in the closest possible touch with the party over the previous few weeks, my judgement was that a substantial majority would prefer Harold to Rab. As for my personal view, I emphasised that, although I was a friend of both, I was sure that Harold would be the right appointment. Adeane concurred and said that the Queen would also be seeing Churchill, as a courtesy extended to a former Prime Minister. As I was leaving, Adeane added that she would be considering the situation very carefully, because she realised the crucial juncture at which the nation now stood. The next morning, Michael telephoned me to say that the Queen would be sending for Mr Macmillan. He suggested that I break the news to Rab personally. This was not a happy prospect, but I realised that I could probably fulfil the role of bearer of bad tidings better than anyone else. However big a shock, it was certainly better for him than being the recipient of an impersonal telephone call.

I knew that Rab was waiting in the Privy Council Chamber, a splendid room with high windows looking on to Horse Guards Parade. There I found him sitting at the table, deep in thought. Unusually for him, for he was a prodigious worker, he had no papers or folders in front of him. He was just patiently waiting for the news. As I entered, his face lit up with its familiar, charming smile. Every newspaper that morning, save one, had announced that he would be the new Prime Minister. All but one were wrong. I had a sad mission to carry out, but there was nothing I could do to soften the blow. 'I am sorry, Rab,' I said, 'it's Harold.' He looked utterly dumbfounded.

After a pause, I explained that the Queen had sent for Harold to go to the Palace after lunch. There was nothing Rab could say. I said again how sorry I was, adding that, perhaps, he would like a little quiet to himself before the announcement was made. Still he said nothing, and I left him, once again alone, in that large, grand room where so many matters of state had been decided over the centuries. I realised later that this had been a shock from which he never fully recovered and to which he never really adjusted his life or his personality. On many occasions in later years as we strolled around the grounds of his home in the country, or talked in his beautiful house in Smith Square with its glorious collection of Impressionists, he would suddenly ask me, 'Why do you really think that they did not want me to become leader of the party?' When a second opportunity for Rab arose on the resignation of Harold Macmillan six years later, he was still asking himself the unsolved question why it had not worked out for him last time around.

Harold Macmillan was summoned to the palace at 2.30 p.m. As I learned later, he and his wife Lady Dorothy lunched together beforehand in the dining room at No. 11, a small attic room at the top of the house. After a typically frugal lunch he got up and announced that he must leave as he had business to do. As he rose from the table, Lady Dorothy looked up and commented, 'Oh, you've got your tailcoat on. Where are you off to?' 'I have got to go to the Palace to see the Queen,' replied Macmillan and disappeared without further comment through the door. Lady Dorothy finished her lunch and then drove down to Birch Grove, their house in Sussex, to do some gardening.

On his return from the Palace, the new Prime Minister sent for me and told me that he must see Rab on his own before he did anything else. He knew that Butler would ask for the Foreign Office, but he was determined not to let him have it. I thought this was rather unfair. Rab would have been a useful Foreign Secretary at that point. Although his inscrutability would have contrasted with the directness of the Americans, his quiet charm could have won them over, and we desperately needed that after the bitterness of Suez. I did not see how keeping Selwyn Lloyd in the post could repair the 'special relationship'. Half an hour later, the Prime Minister summoned me once more to the Cabinet Room. He told me that, after some discussion, Rab had accepted the Home Office and would continue to be Leader of the House of Commons. This, I thought, would be a tremendous burden on him, but it would be a pleasure to continue working with him as Leader of the House. Moreover, the Home Office would give Butler plenty of scope for activity in the field of social policy which had always concerned him, and would enable him to maintain his reputation as a reforming Conservative.

The Prime Minister then set about constructing the rest of the government. He had already resolved to part company with old friends such as James Stuart, but there were no problems here because all agreed that the time had come to introduce some fresh blood. Macmillan was also determined to resolve the differing views which had emerged within the party by bringing representatives of both the right and the left into the government. Julian Amery, who happened to be his son-in-law as well as a prominent member of the Suez Group, became Under-Secretary for War. Edward Boyle, who had resigned over Suez, became Under-Secretary for Education. At around 8 p.m., after we had spent two hours poring over names, the Prime Minister said the time had come to have some food, as we might continue late into the night.

'I think we had better go to the Grill Room at the Savoy,' he said. I stared at him in amazement. 'Don't you realise,' I said, 'that you are now the Prime Minister and wherever you go in public tonight you will be besieged by the press, radio and television, as well as large crowds? In any case, haven't you seen what is happening now outside? All the cameras are there, and lighting has been fixed on the wall of the Foreign Office. The exit is surrounded with press and Downing Street is packed with people.' He insisted we had to have some food and then suggested the Turf Club off Piccadilly as a quieter, more private, alternative. I arranged for his car to be backed from the front of No. 10 to the door at No. 11. When we got to the hall, the door-keeper flung open the door. Macmillan took two paces across the pavement and disappeared into the car. I immediately followed but some lively pressman, realising what was happening, put out his foot and tripped me up. I fell into the car, half dragging myself and half being pushed by the doorman, and scrambled into the seat beside the Prime Minister. He told his driver to get away and up Whitehall as quickly as he could, then to the Turf Club, where we arrived without anyone having caught up with us.

We strolled into the bar of the club, sat down on two stools and ordered drinks. There was only one other man at the bar. He was reading the *Evening Standard* which carried the large headline 'Macmillan Prime Minister'. The man looked up, saw the Prime Minister and then asked, rather casually, 'Have you had any good shooting recently?' 'No,' answered the Prime Minister. 'What a pity,' the man observed. We ordered our dinner, finished our drinks and then got up to make our way to the dining room. As the Prime Minister was going out, the fellow looked up and said, 'Oh, by the way, congratulations.' After we had consumed oysters, steak, coffee and cognac, the manager of the Club approached our table, bowing every few steps, before stopping to say, 'Excuse me, sir, but I have arranged for you to leave by the back door in Shepherd Market.' Macmillan, controlling his mirth, said, 'How very kind, but I think it is perfectly all right for me to leave by the front door. I am not ashamed of being Prime Minister, you know.' His car was waiting at the front door and the press were now lined up on the steps, having tracked us down. A charming girl pushed herself forward, announced she was the night correspondent of the *Daily Express* and asked the Prime Minister what we had been discussing. 'Oh, just the future,' said Macmillan with a typically nonchalant wave of the hand. I rather wished he had said, 'Just form!' We returned to Downing Street to complete the task of forming a government. It was announced the next day, in time for the six o'clock news. The Macmillan era had begun.

For Anthony Eden's friends, there was still one more sad ordeal. After an immediate rest, he arranged to go on a cruise to New Zealand where his family had always had close associations, as part of a world tour to restore his health. On a dark, dank and gloomy day at the end of January, Oliver Poole and I drove down to the docks at Tilbury to say farewell. We went on board ship and along to Eden's cabin where we found him and Clarissa with Robert Carr, his parliamentary private secretary for the last five years. The cabin was stacked high with flowers from well-wishers. We stood around talking rather awkwardly. There was really nothing to say. We had talked it all out before. Finally, with the warning to disembark being sounded, we gave them both all our good wishes for a cruise in sunnier climes and a restoration to robust health, which we knew could never be complete.

On shore we watched the ship pull away and, with a final wave, turned our backs on that passage of history. We were all depressed that what had begun with such high hopes, less than two years before, of a new and younger Prime Minister, so much in tune with his people of the New Elizabethan Age, had come to an end so sadly. For Oliver Poole and myself, who had grown up with Eden's brand of Conservatism and who had believed that it was there that our future would lie, this was a poignant moment. We both went on to work with Freddie Bishop, the principal private secretary at No. 10, with the same faith and fervour as before, but we also kept in close and warm touch with Anthony Eden until the end of his life twenty years later. Although Anthony's later years were marked by physical pain and by torrents of virulent criticism of him, his interest in overseas affairs never waned. Nor did the desire of his many admirers at home and abroad to write to him and, whenever possible, to come and see him to discuss the pressing issues of the day.

Eden's successor, Harold Macmillan, had by far the most constructive mind I have encountered in a lifetime of politics. He took a fully informed view of both domestic and world affairs, and would put the tiniest local problem into a national context, and any national problem into its rightful position in his world strategy. Macmillan's historical knowledge enabled him to view everything in a realistic perspective, and to illuminate contemporary questions with both parallels and differences in comparison with the past. His mind was cultivated in many disciplines: literature, languages, philosophy and religion, as well as history. Working with him gave great pleasure as well as broadening one's whole life.

Harold loved Oxford and, above all, Balliol, where he always felt at home throughout his long life. He was awarded a first in his Moderations, but the Great War, during which he was wounded three times on active service, prevented him from completing his degree. He also distinguished himself during the 1930s, when, like Eden, he was a staunch opponent of appeasement, and then during the Second World War, when he was Churchill's Minister Resident at allied HQ in North Africa, working alongside Field Marshal Alexander and General Eisenhower. His friendship with Eisenhower stood him in good stead in later years. Harold had nothing but admiration for his fellow soldiers, but, like everyone who has actually seen action, he passionately hated war itself.

Harold Macmillan cared nothing for other people's backgrounds, and judged them by their intelligence and their character. His social policies were informed by his own generous spirit and unquenchable desire to help the underdog, and to ensure that everyone in this country had the opportunity of a decent life. His speeches as a maverick and compassionate backbencher in the 1930s gained support for his views when the Conservative Party came to reassess its policies and priorities in the wake of the massive general election defeat of 1945. Before 1945, he had been the Member of Parliament for Stockton, where the unemployment rate had been almost 30 per cent at the time he was first elected, back in 1924.

Macmillan was later fond of saying that, when he took office as Prime Minister in January 1957, he doubted whether his administration could last longer than six weeks. Certainly, the opinion polls at the time gave Labour a comfortable lead in double figures. Nevertheless, there was no justification for such doubts. In circumstances of this kind, the Conservative Party had always pulled itself together. With a fresh start and changes in high offices, the party showed itself able to forget the immediate past, to abandon some of the more extreme positions that had been taken up and to set about regaining its own self-confidence and that of the public. It increasingly emerged that, in fact, the Eden government had enjoyed more sympathy for its attempt to deal with the Suez Canal crisis than had hitherto appeared. Supporters recognised that the ultimate outcome was far from ideal, but little more could now be done about it. Those who had opposed the venture had seen it brought to an end and were just as anxious as its supporters to create a stable and peaceful situation in the Middle East.

Internationally, the situation changed immediately with the new government. The American attitude swung from one of opposition to Eden into one of co-operation with Macmillan. Washington realised that, if it wanted to save anything out of the wreckage of Suez, it could be done only through the new Prime Minister's administration. Macmillan, like Churchill half-American himself, skilfully made the most of this. He and Selwyn Lloyd met President Eisenhower at Bermuda in March 1957, where they reaffirmed the Security Council Resolution of October 1956 regarding the freedom of the Canal; the Queen and Prince Philip made a goodwill visit to the United States in October 1957; and, in the same month, Macmillan signed a 'Declaration of Common Purpose' with the USA. Fortunately, there was also little backbiting from the French and the Israelis. All these factors enabled Harold Macmillan's administration to cope with any threat to sterling or our trade. Far from collapsing after six weeks, this government lasted for nearly seven years.

Macmillan's constructive approach was seen most clearly in strategic matters, as he pursued detente between NATO and the Soviet bloc and became one of our first statesmen to recognise the importance of European unity in the post-colonial era. Yet he was neither aloof nor prone to high-mindedness. As Minister of Housing and Local Government, he had pressed on strenuously with the details of a radical housing programme and, as Chancellor of the Exchequer, had introduced the innovation of premium bonds. There were those who thought that in handling these affairs he showed an unnecessary degree of cynicism. For me it was a question of taking account of human nature as he had experienced it, and of making judgements which were both justifiable and politically effective. He was usually a shrewd judge both of individuals and of nations.

Harold's cultured background and his manifold interests, augmented by his life's work as a publisher, gave him something in common with almost everyone, and he was fond of describing himself as the grandson of a crofter, who had married into the Whig aristocracy. His natural affinity, however, was with the Latin civilisation of Europe and, in particular, with the French, of whose language he had a perfect command. He had worked closely with the Americans during the war and was particularly close to Presidents Eisenhower and Kennedy and always enjoyed an excellent rapport with the countries of the Commonwealth. His first tour of Asia and Australasia, followed by his tour of Africa culminating in the 'Wind of Change' speech, testify to that. Macmillan's one aversion was to Germany and the Germans. I suppose that this was understandable in the light of his experiences during the First World War, but it always seemed to me strangely inconsistent with his support for a united Europe, and the initiative he took in starting negotiations for our entry into the Community.

His feelings got the better of him on this subject at a dinner he once hosted, as Prime Minister, for the Duke of Edinburgh. Prince Philip had recently returned from an extensive voyage round the world in *Britannia* studying wildlife, and was very anxious to pass on some of his experiences to senior Ministers. Harold was far from enthusiastic about this project, for he had no great personal interest in wildlife. Nonetheless he invited a few Cabinet colleagues, including myself, to a small dinner for this purpose. Macmillan did not attempt to hide his boredom during the discussion. At times he even appeared to doze off. Then, however, the discussion got on to wider subjects and Germany was mentioned. Thereupon Macmillan opened his eyes and erupted, proclaiming with staccato emphasis, 'The Huns are always the same. When they are down they crawl under your feet, and when they are up they use their feet to stamp on your face.' The Duke looked astonished and the subject was hastily changed.

In his term as Prime Minister, Harold Macmillan was faced with a whole series of personnel crises. The first was the unexpected resignation of Lord Salisbury. It was true that he had been one of Anthony Eden's oldest and closest friends, having resigned with Eden back in the 1930s, when he was Under-Secretary at the Foreign Office. At the same time he had always been close to Macmillan, for family reasons and thanks to their similarity of outlook in foreign affairs. But he now found himself at loggerheads over the question of releasing Archbishop Makarios of Cyprus from his exile in the Seychelles. In Cabinet, it was difficult to discern exactly what was worrying him. In any case, nothing that was being discussed seemed to give sufficient cause for a resignation.

I was sent along by the Prime Minister to Salisbury's room in the House of Lords to try to ascertain what it was all about. Were he to resign, many people thought, his loss would be a body blow to the government. I was myself very anxious about the possible consequences. When I talked to him, however, it rapidly became evident that no single issue was forcing him into resignation. Salisbury had lost the energy and freshness which had previously been his hallmarks and he was simply fed up, wearily concluding our conversation by asking me to thank the Prime Minister for his concern, but emphasising that nothing could make him change his mind. I reported this to the Prime Minister, who accepted Salisbury's resignation. When the newspapers came out the next day, our fears were realised. The headlines were devastating. I remained deeply anxious, but the Prime Minister was unmoved. It was as though he wanted to prove to the world that the man who had been dubbed the 'kingmaker' for his own accession to the premiership was not indispensable. Fortunately we had the weekend to recover and the government survived this first severe challenge comparatively unscathed.

The second major dispute between the Prime Minister and some members of his government arose over the control of public expenditure. In the autumn of 1957, the Cabinet discussed the Chancellor of the Exchequer's proposals for expenditure in the forthcoming year in the usual way. The Chancellor, Peter Thorneycroft, supported by the two other Treasury Ministers, Enoch Powell and Nigel Birch, had agreed with Ministers a limitation on the expenditure of government departments, but there still remained a gap of £50 million between the aggregate spending that had been agreed and the Chancellor's demands on public expenditure control. Looking back on those events, it is interesting to see how the Cabinet's views changed in the process. The initial attitude of the Chancellor's Cabinet colleagues, as they expressed it almost unanimously to me after the first meeting, was broadly supportive of the Chancellor. There was a general feeling that this could surely be speedily resolved. After the second meeting, the view was that the situation was becoming more serious. I was asked to urge those dealing with the matter to find a compromise so that the Cabinet could get on with the rest of its work. After a third meeting, the fear was expressed that the Chancellor and the other Treasury Ministers had dug into their positions and it was going to be extremely difficult to move them. At the meeting in the New Year, it was realised that there was little time left to settle the problem amicably.

I was asked by a number of colleagues to tell the Prime Minister that he had to intervene personally to break this deadlock. He must make up his mind about what he wanted and then formally set it out, either in favour of his Chancellor, in which case he might lose some of the departmental Ministers, or against him, in which case there was a danger that the Chancellor would resign. What most concerned everyone was that a decision should be reached quickly. News of these divisions was beginning to leak, although the full extent of their seriousness was still not known publicly. Finally, the Prime Minister called a Cabinet meeting on the evening of Sunday 5 January 1958, at which he knew he had to settle the question one way or the other because he was due to leave on a tour of Asia and Australasia the following Tuesday morning.

At this Cabinet meeting, however, no progress was made in resolving the situation. It was quite apparent that the members of the Cabinet were becoming irritated and frustrated by the rigidity of the Chancellor's views. Finally, at 8.45 p.m., Macmillan adjourned the Cabinet for a break and I went up with him to his study. He asked me what I thought. I again emphasised that, ultimately, there was no hope of keeping the Chancellor except by meeting his demands in full – which the Prime Minister was not prepared to do. When we returned to the Cabinet, Macmillan told his colleagues that, much to his regret, he had not been able to resolve the differences that existed. He was, therefore, afraid that some might feel that it was not possible to remain as a member of the team. The Chancellor indicated that he agreed with this view and that his resignation would now take place. The Cabinet then broke up.

Outside the Cabinet Room, the atmosphere was one of almost unanimous relief that a decision, however damaging it might turn out to be, had at last been reached. Everyone now knew where they stood and could once again get on with their own work. The break had not come over a difference of economic philosophy between the Keynesians and the monetarists. No one at that time was thinking in such terms. But the influence of Nigel Birch and Enoch Powell over Thorneycroft certainly had a lot to do with it. The general attitude was that departmental Ministers had gone a long way to meet the demands of the Chancellor, but that he, for his part, had shown singularly little understanding of the problems they faced.

After the Cabinet dispersed, the Prime Minister again summoned me and told me that he proposed to appoint Derick Heathcoat Amory as Chancellor. The next morning, the resignations of Nigel Birch and Enoch Powell both arrived at No. 10. I noticed that Nigel Birch's letter of resignation had originally been dated four days earlier, indicating that the three Ministers had expected to resign after the usual Thursday morning Cabinet meeting. I felt then, and still do, that the whole episode was ultimately a political challenge to Macmillan's leadership. Heathcoat Amory was then called in and accepted office on the basis that the firm control of government expenditure exercised by his predecessor would be maintained. Having learned this I found him sitting alone in the Cabinet Room, munching his handkerchief as was his wont, while writing his statement. The Prime Minister accepted this, together with my nominations for the other two ministers, Jack Simon and Reggie Maudling, both of which were agreed by the new Chancellor. I said that I would arrange for the announcement to be made in time for the six o'clock news, and took the precaution of warning the Governor of the Bank of England of the announcement and its timing. He insisted that I hold it until Wall Street had closed and that it should not be put out until the late evening news on the BBC. Although I advised him that there was a serious danger of a leak from one of the Ministers who had resigned, he was adamant that nothing official should be said until after ten o'clock.

When I went up to the Prime Minister's study to tell him of this delay in the announcement, I found him sitting in his armchair with his feet up on a stool, reading in front of the fire. I then explained the new situation. 'Well,' he said, 'if that is what he wants, you had better get on with it, but please don't worry me any more. Can't you see that I'm trying to finish *Dombey and Son* before I go off on this tour tomorrow morning?' I left him with Dickens while I rang up the editors of the major newspapers to give them the news confidentially and warn them that it was embargoed until after Wall Street closed. With a single exception, they all accepted this. The only one who caused me anxiety was the editor of the *Daily Telegraph*, Colin Coote, who said that he already knew all about it. This made me think there could have been a damaging leak. I promptly rang up the deputy editor, Donald McLachlan, a close friend, who said he knew nothing whatever about the resignations or the new appointments. Nor, he added, did he believe that his editor did either. 'Don't worry at all,' he said. 'Whenever you tell him anything, he inevitably says he already knows it!'

At 8.30 the next morning, I drove with the Prime Minister out to Heathrow to see him off on his plane for the momentous tour on which he was embarking. Between us on the seat of the car was a pile of all the day's newspapers. As we drove along he picked them up one by one, skipped through them and then dropped them into my lap. The blazing headlines were on only one subject, the resignation of the three Treasury Ministers. In fairness to them, they may have held their peace until after the official announcement was made. I never knew. It was clear that Donald McLachlan had been right in saying that his editor had no previous knowledge of the resignations, for he had clearly not had time to write his usual scathing attack on the government. The leader was a moderate, balanced judgement written by Donald. At the airport we found Rab Butler and many other senior Ministers waiting for Harold. As we said goodbye, Macmillan turned to me and said, 'Now, look after the show. Rab will do all he can to help you.' With that, he put his 'little local difficulties' behind him and flew off for an absence of nearly six weeks. What a contrast with the mad dashes demanded of a Prime Minister today.

His visit did not receive much coverage, except for an incident right at the beginning. When the plane landed at Darwin, he failed to wake up in time to be received formally by the Australian official waiting for him. On Macmillan's return to Britain, I worked hard to build up his position as a Commonwealth statesman, but it was hard work convincing the television companies to arrange adequate coverage and the interviews that were arranged were not very satisfactory. It was after this that Oliver Poole, the Deputy Chairman of the party, and I decided that we would have to take steps to ensure that the Prime Minister's image was properly projected on to the small screen, whose influence on public opinion was now becoming very significant indeed.

At the end of Question Time one Thursday in 1957, Churchill beckoned to me to leave my corner seat above the gangway and sit beside him in his customary place. 'You are coming to us for the weekend,' he said. 'Could you come a little earlier than you usually do for lunch on Saturday, say about midday?' 'Of course,' I replied, not knowing the reason.

I arrived at Chartwell just before noon and found Churchill and Clemmie sitting on the terrace with Field Marshal Montgomery. After we had enjoyed a drink together, Clemmie said we must go in for lunch. 'We have not got much time,' she explained. 'We are going to the races where one of Winston's horses is running. The cars are already outside and we must be off.' After a brisk lunch, she and Winston got into the first car, Monty and I into the second. I assumed we were going to a local course, probably at Sevenoaks. In the car Monty complained bitterly about the forthcoming publication of diaries by Lord Alanbrooke, my regimental commanding officer, of which he had seen a draft script. He urged me to do everything possible, including involving the Churchills, to get them stopped. I gave him no encouragement to think that I could possibly do such a thing.

By this time the cars were slowing down and, to my surprise, I found we were at an airfield where a plane containing Christopher Soames was waiting for us. 'We are off to Newmarket,' Churchill declared. Over the Thames we flew on this glorious afternoon, and over the eastern counties to come down just outside the racecourse. A Rolls-Royce took us to the Jockey Club enclosure, where we were greeted by stewards and taken to our seats in time for the three o'clock race. 'I want to put some money on a horse,' said Monty. I could not offer him any tips, and told him to ask a Jockey Club dignitary, who named a horse for him. 'What do I do now?' asked Monty. I took him over to the single betting stall with a charming girl behind the grille. 'I want to put money on a horse,' said Monty. She looked at him as if thinking why on earth did you come here if you did not? 'How much?' she asked. 'Two shillings,' replied Monty firmly. 'Field Marshal,' I stammered, hoping that the girl would not hear, 'you must put on more than that.' 'Well, how much?' 'At least ten shillings,' I explained, 'preferably a pound.' We returned to our seats and watched as his horse won. 'Now where do I claim the money?' I took him back to the girl, who gave him his winnings. He was triumphant.

Winston's horse was running in the next race, the 3.30. We all formed up into a long procession and followed the great man down to the paddock where the horses were being paraded. All went well until Monty proclaimed in a loud voice, looking at one of the horses, 'It's steaming; they should take it away.' I quietened him down and we returned to our seats, stopping to put some money on Churchill's horse as we went. For us the race was a fiasco and Churchill's horse was not placed. 'I have lost my money,' complained Monty miserably.

Winston had a second horse in the last race, the 4.30. I went to the girl and put my money on his horse. Monty declared somewhat dyspeptically that he was not making the same mistake again. He had been given the names of three horses by one of the stewards who guaranteed that he was bound to win with a series of each-way bets. The race was exciting and Churchill's horse won. 'I have lost every penny I paid out,' said Monty bitterly. 'Churchill's horse was not expected to win but you made the money.' 'Yes, Field Marshal,' I replied with undisguised glee, 'it shows that loyalty always pays in the end.' We resumed our procession to congratulate those attending the horse. We boarded our cars and then the aircraft, recrossing the Thames and the Kentish towns.

By six o'clock we were back on the terrace at Chartwell enjoying a drink, as we had been six hours before. That evening Clemmie dealt the final blow to Monty. Sitting at one of the small tables opposite her, he intervened in a break in the conversation, beginning haughtily, 'When I was last in South Africa—' Then, unwisely, he paused. 'Yes,' said Clemmie, 'you behaved positively disgracefully.' We heard no more from him.

I went to Cornwall for a week's holiday at New Year 1959, to stay with Sir Alec Martin and his wife. At the end of it I had to address a meeting in Birmingham, so I drove to London in order to take the train up to the Midlands. Just outside Exeter, I encountered a heavy snow storm and, as I pressed on up the long hill, the road became completely blocked with other vehicles. I thought the only thing to do was to slide gently backwards, take the crossroad and drive along the coast, which was only slightly less awful. At 2 a.m. I found a pub in a small village and spent the night there in a freezingly cold room, leaving early the next morning. I had started to feel ill the previous night and felt worse by the time I reached my flat in London. On the train I obtained some whisky to keep me going for my speech. That only made me feel still worse. Back in London the next day, I phoned my HAC regimental doctor, who lived out in the country. He rang a wartime colleague from the Guards, Brian Warren, who came at once to my flat.

Brian Warren told me he thought I ought to go to hospital immediately, and went off to arrange it. Returning after lunch, he informed me that everything was prepared for me to go into the King Edward VII Hospital, where I could be admitted because of my military connections. I was whisked off at 3.30 p.m. and well looked after on arrival. Once I was in bed, the doctor came along and agreed with Brian that I had jaundice. Shortly afterwards, the matron appeared, a trim and imposing figure. 'It is so tiresome to have jaundice,' she remarked, with a degree of understatement. She then asked me if there was anything I especially needed. 'Only one thing,' I replied. 'Not to be woken up with breakfast at five o'clock in the morning.' She stiffened but promised, 'I'll see that doesn't happen.' The following day, Brian Warren said that he wanted me to see Sir Horace Evans, celebrated at the time as a kind of top people's general practitioner, and had arranged for him to come round the next morning. At that point the sister came along and said, 'I see, Sir Horace will be here? You must be very important if he's coming.' 'I don't know about that,' I said. 'Don't get too excited,' the sister then warned. 'He'll just feel your chest and say, "This is terrible. This really is a serious case" – and then he'll say, "We'll have to do something special. What can it be? I think the answer is regular doses of B12."'

At 11 a.m., the procession duly appeared and, sure enough, the celebrated doctor stuck to his usual script. 'This is rather a serious case,' he began. The sister stuck up one thumb behind his back. 'All the usual treatment,' he continued. She stuck up both thumbs. Finally, he proclaimed, 'B12 for him.' She clasped her hands together in delight as he turned and led his procession back out of the room.

I was allowed no alcohol once the diagnosis of jaundice was confirmed, and had a regime of orange squash, lemon, lime and currant juice. I was forced to endure this teetotal life for six months. At the end of that period I had recovered sufficiently to return to drinking champagne, ironically and appropriately the only form of alcohol I was allowed to imbibe in the early days.

When, on 8 September 1959, Macmillan called a general election for 8 October, our prospects looked better than anyone could have believed possible when Eden resigned. Heathcoat Amory's budget that April had succeeded in raising the economy from its post-Suez depths, by cutting income tax, purchase tax and the price of beer and by restoring investment allowances. Large gains in the municipal elections in May had returned us to our pre-Suez strength at local level. However, the result of the general election was by no means a foregone conclusion. The polls were erratic and many people on both sides thought that, despite all our efforts, Labour might just snatch victory away from us. Hugh Gaitskell had begun to modernise his party, in particular by trying to shed its commitment to nationalisation. The intellectual momentum for this came from Anthony Crosland, whose book *The Future of Socialism*, published in 1956, attempted to bring the Labour Party back to the centre in the same way that we had succeeding in doing through *One Nation*. Fortunately for us, the socialists' modernisation was in its embryonic stages at the time of the election. Still unable to accept that modern Conservatism could deliver full employment and widespread affluence, Labour had no convincing answer to the unequivocal evidence that the country had become better off since we had returned to power in 1951. They were also unable to exploit the Suez débâcle during the election campaign, not only because Macmillan had turned things around, but because it was widely thought to be unpatriotic to do so.

The 1959 general election went down in history as the first campaign in which television played a major part. Both Macmillan and I disliked the medium, worrying that it would destroy the traditional British political traditions of canvassing and public meetings in which voters were not simply passive recipients of what are now called 'soundbites', but had the opportunity to challenge their candidates face to face. We were also afraid that the 'media circus' which television was creating would be open to abuse by any charlatan who was capable of manipulating it properly. So it proved in the following decade.

Bexley was exactly the kind of seat the Labour Party had to win if they were to regain power, and Macmillan himself came to speak in my constituency during the campaign. He spoke warmly and in a way that went beyond the usual endorsement given to candidates on such occasions, saying that I represented 'everything that is best in the new progressive modern Tory Party . . . [he] is one of the creators of the new policies which are brought up to date with modern life. He stands for the new philosophy and modern thought in the party. You send him back, for he is a good man.'

Although no promises were made, I felt that, if we won the election and I held on to my seat, my exertions as Chief Whip in helping Macmillan to reunite the party would be rewarded by a senior ministerial post in the next government. In the meantime, hard work was required to ensure that my old opponent, Ashley Bramall, returning to the fray after an election off, did not snatch the seat back from me. There was no feeling of coasting as there had been for most of Eden's campaign four years earlier. In the end, however, the party's overall national record proved to be decisive. We won a third election in a row, our majority increased to a comfortable 100 seats and the Conservative vote increased by nearly half a million. I almost doubled my majority, which rose to 8,633.

That election showed clearly for the first time that class was no longer the deciding factor in British politics. Of course, the popularity of the national government in the 1930s demonstrated that people could abandon their party and social loyalties on occasion, but they had done so then because it was a time of crisis caused by the depression, just as they did during the war. Now here we were in peacetime, without a grave crisis of any kind, and with substantially more people voting according to which party could improve their standard of living. That is not to say that we had achieved a classless society, nor indeed that any degree of affluence could ever do so, but the election did signify what I believed to be a healthy change in our democracy, after which a person's class mattered less to them than their desire to get on in life and to contribute something to their community, in short, the ideals of *One Nation*.

Six days after the general election on 14 October 1959, Harold Macmillan reformed his government and appointed me Minister of Labour. He told me that he had promised the Board of Trade, which was what I really wanted, to Reggie Maudling, but then offered me my choice. The press said that the Ministry of Labour was the most important domestic appointment other than the Treasury, for upon it rested the fate of the government's economic policy for the next term. My friends seemed to think so too. Lord Chandos (as Oliver Lyttelton had become) wrote to say it was 'the hottest seat in Whitehall and I am sending you a piece of asbestos for your pants as a mark of my esteem'. He added, not inaccurately, that, 'the Trade Unions are much easier things to manage than the Conservative Party'. I asked Macmillan to leave me at the Ministry for the full five years of the Parliament. It was the minimum time I needed to reconstruct our industrial relations and play a full part in modernising our economy.

The attempt to find a progressive way forward in industrial relations, and to shake off the oppressive image we had acquired during the General Strike, had been a dominant theme within the mainstream of the party since the war. The Industrial Charter, drawn up by Rab Butler's policy group in 1947, emphasised the need for competitive industry if Britain was to recover from the war and continue to be a major world power. At the same time, it upheld the voluntary principle in industrial relations, maintaining that negotiations between unions and employers should be based upon a system of mutual trust, not compulsion by the state. *One Nation* had supported this policy, concluding that 'a strong and independent Trade Union movement is essential to the structure of a free society'. To us, the unions were an estate of the realm with whom co-operation was both desirable and necessary, if the nation was to remain united. In those days, hardly anyone wanted to damn the unions by bringing in tougher legislation.

It is true that the unions had become more militant since the war, in part because of some communist infiltration which had stirred up otherwise responsible unions such as the electrical workers. I quickly found, however, that the general secretary of the ETU, Frank Haxell, whose victory over John Byrne in the ballot of December 1959 was later overturned in the courts, was a tough negotiator. When he made an agreement he stuck to it and would tolerate no troubles about it from his members. The most militant of the union leaders was Frank Cousins of the TGWU, and it was with him that my predecessor as Minister of Labour, Iain Macleod, encountered the worst difficulties of his time at the Ministry. In autumn 1957, the TGWU made a claim for a substantial increase in the pay of London bus drivers. The London Transport Executive turned them down, and the dispute ran bitterly into 1958. Encouraged by the Prime Minister, Iain took a robust line with Cousins and the drivers. In an action which would have been unthinkable only ten or fifteen years later, the leadership of the TUC also intervened, encouraging Iain to bring Cousins down a peg or two, and warning Cousins himself that attempts to spread the strike would be inadvisable. It is amazing, in retrospect, to recall that a militant union could be rapped across its knuckles in such a way at that time.

Despite the more moderate attitude of the TUC leadership, and of its general secretary Vincent Tewson in particular, more frequent strikes had caused the unions to become steadily more unpopular. Only 38 per cent of the public thought that they were a 'good thing' by the time I became Minister, as compared with 59 per cent in 1954, shortly before Macleod took over. As a result, the right wing of the party was beginning to call for legislation to end the closed shop and the political levy, and to enforce secret balloting. I still believed, however, that most union leaders were ultimately responsible men who could be reasoned with, and that to treat them like criminals would do us no good in the long run. When I arrived at the Ministry, I found a letter of advice from Macleod waiting for me on my desk which confirmed my opinion. It said that 'we should make it quite clear that although we believe the best solution for the unions is to put their own house in order . . . we cannot stand aside if their enquiries are not pursued vigorously'. The letter concluded that 'with luck we ought to have a favourable climate now. The moderate element in the TUC should be in the ascendant and they may well be ready to co-operate with a Tory government now that the election is behind them.'

My first task at the despatch box, on 2 November 1959, was to deal with a battery of questions on national service, which was then coming to an end, and unemployment. Industrial relations were a major concern from the beginning, and I knew that dealing with the union leaders would not be a simple job. A fortnight later, I met them for the first time at the quarterly meeting of the National Joint Advisory Council, which comprised representatives of the employers, the TUC and the nationalised industries, under my chairmanship. I hit it off straight away with Vincent Tewson, and with his TUC colleague Vic Feather, who shared my passion for the arts, but Frank Cousins was clearly never going to see reason and would have to be watched closely.

Soon after I was appointed Minister of Labour, Walter Monckton, who had been at the Ministry throughout the Churchill government, advised me to cultivate the moderate union leaders by giving them meals individually as soon as possible. I rang William Carron, president of the Amalgamated Engineering Union, and offered him dinner. He accepted my invitation, adding that he would prefer a lunch. I suggested various restaurants, but he drew back from these, explaining that his presence at any of them with me might be reported to other leaders of the labour movement. Could we lunch instead at the Carlton Club, where it would be easier for him to remain incognito? He did not feel able to be seen in public with me. I agreed and our lunch there went on until 4 p.m. On a visit to Sweden some months later to talk to unions and employers, I was struck by how much the two sides socialised together. The atmosphere of co-operation, coupled with the high level of their social services, confirmed my belief that good industrial relations were both the product of, and essential to, a prosperous and fair society.

I had a good team at the Ministry: Sir Laurence Helsby, the permanent secretary; St John Wilson, the deputy secretary and chief industrial commissioner; Peter Thomas, the parliamentary secretary; and John Howard, my PPS. Throughout my time there, I made it clear that I did not believe workers were solely to blame for poor industrial relations. In a speech to the Conservative Labour Committee on 23 March 1960, I said that companies should encourage more participation by workers in management decisions so that workers 'feel that they are corporate members of an organisation and not just numbers on a pay sheet'. I also encouraged

Conservative trade unionists to take a more active role in their firms.

We brought in a good deal of legislation during what turned out to be my brief tenure at the Ministry of Labour. In co-operation with Reggie Maudling at the Board of Trade, we introduced a Local Employment Act, offering incentives to industry to locate themselves in areas of high unemployment. This did much to help the worse off, without impeding competition. Our Payment of Wages Act made it possible for workers to be paid by cheque, in the face of considerable opposition from trade unionists. They feared that, with cheques, it would be easier for working men's wives to find out the size of their husbands' weekly pay packets. The Dock Workers' Pension Bill marked the culmination of efforts since 1889 to decasualise dock labour and give those workers the degree of security that they deserved. We also introduced new Government Training Centres, which were intended to offer support to the unusually large numbers of school-leavers at that time. Throughout the introduction of all these measures, I stressed the need for workers to be more flexible as new technologies were introduced.

However, my main aim was to reassure the British worker that, if he put his back into making the nation more prosperous, a 'One Nation' Conservative government would treat him fairly and do its best to ensure that he was properly rewarded for his efforts. On 4 January 1960, I made my position clear in a letter to Conservative MPs. Rejecting right-wing calls for a Royal Commission on trade unions, I concluded that, although some trade union members were abusing their position, the TUC should be given a further chance to deal themselves with their undisciplined minority.

Within a month of that letter, my faith in the unions was put to the test. On 26 January 1960, the Cabinet agreed to offer Britain's railwaymen a pay rise of 4 per cent, in lieu of a then unknown rise due to be recommended by the Guillebaud Committee, which had been set up by the British Transport Commission (abolished by the Macmillan government in 1962) to halt the decline of Britain's railways. Three days later, the National Union of Railwaymen (NUR) gave notice of a strike on 15 February. My feeling was that we should not employ heavy-handed tactics, lest we alienate the moderates in the TUC, whose support we would need if the dispute was to be resolved to the satisfaction of all sides. The Cabinet agreed, and I maintained secret contact with Vincent Tewson, who talked to the railwaymen in an attempt to end the dispute. By 9 February it was clear that Tewson had failed to convince them, so I advised the Cabinet that we should prepare emergency measures to transport foodstuffs, to which they agreed. The following day, I told the House of Commons that, after the failure of the TUC intervention, I was inviting the rail unions and the British Transport Commission to the Ministry for direct talks in order, as I put it, 'to avert catastrophic action'. I was heartened to receive a telegram from Macmillan, who was then in Cape Town in the middle of his famous 'Wind of Change' tour of Africa. It read, 'I am thinking of you all the time. Do not hesitate to let me know if there is anything you want me to do.'

Two days later, on the morning of the talks, Friday 12 February, Rab Butler and I faced Manny Shinwell and Liberal leader Jo Grimond in the House of Commons. I assured them and our colleagues that we were devoting all our efforts to finding a solution to the dispute. I realised that a 4 per cent increase would not be enough. At the same time, I had no wish to settle at any cost, for fear of pushing up inflation. When I addressed the NUR representatives at the Department, emphasising the importance of having a negotiated settlement, I was slightly surprised that there was no real reaction from them. They made no new proposals of their own, and did not respond in any way to mine. They just went on asking for their 5 per cent.

I could see no credible alternative to awarding the 5 per cent, and asked for a special Cabinet meeting to get approval for that. At 4.30, the Cabinet met, chaired by Butler. Everyone in the Cabinet agreed except Derick Heathcoat Amory, the Chancellor of the Exchequer, who believed that acceding to the demands of the NUR would do lasting damage to the reputation of the government. I was a little surprised at Derry's stance. When he had taken over from Peter Thorneycroft, he had been widely seen as a reasonable man, who would not give Macmillan any 'little local difficulties', as his predecessor had. In my view his protest was an attempt to appear tough when it came to public spending. Despite his reservations, Butler and the rest of the Cabinet agreed with my proposal, on the grounds that, three weeks later, Guillebaud would probably recommend at least 8 per cent and that greater damage would be done to us then if the offer was not increased now.

I took the offer back to the negotiating table at the Ministry late that afternoon and, after some further bargaining over details, I was able to announce at 9.30 p.m. that the unions had accepted my offer. I had passed my first major test as a Cabinet Minister. Although I knew that there would be the inevitable protests from the right, the settlement pleased the majority of the public, the press and most of the party. I immediately sent a telegram to Macmillan in Cape Town, warning him that, 'although the Press reaction has been reasonable, there may be criticism from some sections of the party in the House'. Sure enough, Thorneycroft appeared on BBC Television's *Panorama* soon afterwards, to condemn what he said was another inflationary pay rise. When Guillebaud recommended pay increases for the railwaymen of between 8 and 20 per cent on 4 March, Heathcoat Amory again protested at the award we had made and proposed that the £50 million increase should be phased in over several months. I successfully argued that, given the higher Guillebaud conclusions, there would be harmful strikes if the increase was not paid immediately. Such was the general relief that the initial strike had been averted, to the satisfaction of both sides, that the Cabinet agreed and the voices of protest elsewhere were also silenced.

After settling with the NUR, I slept late on the Saturday morning. I was woken up by the telephone ringing, and on answering it I heard a voice declare, 'This is Clemmie Churchill. Do come and stay the weekend with us so that you can have a rest.' I told her that I would love to do so, but I had to go to my constituency on the Saturday afternoon. 'Very well,' she replied, 'then drive straight over to us as soon as you are free.' I accepted gladly and arrived there at about 5.30 p.m. To my astonishment, the front door was opened by Churchill himself who smiled and said, 'Well done, you have had a great success. Many, many congratulations on preventing that railway strike.' 'Yes,' I replied, 'but I am afraid that for some people in our party it has ruined my political reputation and all my future prospects.' 'You mustn't worry about that,' he said. 'I have had my reputation ruined countless times.' On entering the house I found that Aristotle Onassis and his wife Christina were also guests. Clemmie invited me to join her and Christina Onassis as they finished tea. Winston, Aristotle Onassis and Winston's private secretary, Anthony Montague Browne, were seated at another table playing poker.

After tea, Clemmie said, 'Now, Ted, you must join them in their game.' I declined as they were well into the contest, but went and sat alongside them. I thought that they would be playing for money, but to my relief I saw that they were using matchsticks. At seven o'clock Winston said, 'We must now go and change for dinner. Anthony, count up the matchsticks and we must then settle among ourselves – one pound for each of the small sticks, and five pounds for each of the large ones.' At this my heart beat violently. That night I stayed awake wondering how I should handle the situation on Sunday when I was invited to join them. Should I start and, when I had reached the maximum I could afford, beckon the butler, whom I would already have briefed, to tell me that I had an urgent telephone call and had to return to London? Or should I decline to join in the game altogether on the basis that I had never played it before, which certainly was not true? I remained undecided.

On Sunday I went downstairs to join Clemmie just after midday, and the two of us had a glass of sherry and exchanged gossip. We were soon joined by Aristotle and Christina Onassis. Winston came down shortly after one o'clock. After a splendid lunch we walked down to the lake, on the way stopping to feed the golden carp and then the black and white swans. We returned to the house where, at five o'clock, Winston pronounced that we would resume our poker. This time Christina also joined the party and it rapidly became clear that she and Aristotle had been having a furious row. The atmosphere persisted throughout the game at which they constantly tried to out-bid each other. I was still worried about how I should pay for all this, but, as it proved, unnecessarily so. Winston was too sleepy to play properly and the Onassis couple lost hand after hand. When seven o'clock came all three of them owed Anthony and me considerable sums of money. Onassis paid in cash. Churchill wrote out a cheque which I still possess.

The following week, I was able to celebrate the fiftieth anniversary of the establishment of the labour exchanges, which Churchill had set up when he was President of the Board of Trade in a Liberal government. They had first been managed by William Beveridge. The anniversary gave me an opportunity to demonstrate the achievements of a very important aspect of the political heritage of One Nation politics. Former Ministers of Labour, and Beveridge himself, attended the formal opening of the newest labour exchange, in the Edgware Road in London. Afterwards, luminaries from all walks of life attended a reception at Westminster including Princess Margaret, the actress Dame Sybil Thorndike and the couturier Norman Hartnell. The evening was a great success.

I followed up this work by submitting my first memorandum to the Cabinet. It called for a new approach to industrial relations and recommended that the Prime Minister should chair a meeting of the major employers and unions to discuss the way forward. This was not received as enthusiastically as I had hoped. During a lengthy discussion on 26 May 1960, the Cabinet decided that, unless the two sides formally agreed before such a conference that there would be some concrete outcome, for example employers linking pay awards to profit levels and unions agreeing to improve productivity levels, it might be a politically damaging anti-climax. Macmillan, however, agreed that the time was ripe for a fresh initiative because of the need to secure support from both sides of industry for the government's emerging European policy. As a result of his intervention, the Cabinet invited me to give further thought to my proposals and to submit a practical plan of action. Although the Cabinet reshuffle two months later deprived me of the chance to do so, the later establishment of the National Economic Development Council (NEDC or 'Neddy') certainly owed something to my original conception.

In the spring, I attended my first meeting of the International Labour

Organisation (ILO). This had been founded at the same time as the League of Nations, after the First World War, and was the oldest surviving international body. Consisting of Ministers, employers and employees, it gave me another opportunity of meeting not only our own trade unionists, but also those of the other member countries, together with their employers. In many ways it was the informal discussions outside the formal meetings which mattered most. I was impressed above all by the cordial tripartite relations which appeared to exist in other countries. The small dinner that I gave for our own people embodied the same atmosphere, but it was purely a social occasion, not a forum for discussing serious issues. The ILO had already carried through many important reforms for improving the conditions of employment and raising the standards of living for those working in its member countries. It is a pity that recent British governments have shown so little interest in it.

Another thing I was very keen on was improving the health of the working population, as I had discovered that around 300 million working days each year were being lost because of ill-health or injury. It was impossible for anyone to say how much was unavoidable and how much was merely the result of workers feeling the need for a break. We also had no way of establishing how much of this was paid for by employers, how much by insurance and how much of it went unremunerated. I suggested that we should create a support organisation specifically for the health of industrial workers in addition to the National Health Service. Some of the bigger firms already had something of this kind, and I found that the idea enjoyed widespread support among employers. The unions were also in favour, so I put a paper to the Cabinet. The Chancellor was adamantly opposed, however, and I got no support from the rest of the Cabinet. We could not go ahead with it.

After the Cabinet meeting before the 1960 summer recess, Derick Heathcoat Amory carried out his long-held intention of retiring as Chancellor. This gave Macmillan the opportunity of making several other Cabinet changes. The most important was moving Selwyn Lloyd from the Foreign Office, where he had been since December 1955, to the Treasury. In his place Macmillan put Lord Home, for whom he had very great respect. At the same time Duncan Sandys was named the new Commonwealth Secretary, Christopher Soames took over as Minister of Agriculture and Peter Thorneycroft returned to the government in the rather lowly post of Minister of Aviation. Sir Frank Lee had already moved from the Board of Trade to become joint permanent secretary of the Treasury at the beginning of the year. Pro-Europeans were now occupying all of the posts that would prove important in any negotiations on accession to the European Community.

Macmillan anticipated a stream of protest against having a Foreign Secretary sitting in the House of Lords, which had not been done since Lord Halifax occupied that position in the last Chamberlain Cabinet, and wanted another member of the Cabinet in the House of Commons to handle all Foreign Office matters. He asked me to leave the Ministry of Labour and take over the office of Lord Privy Seal at the Foreign Office for this purpose. I pointed out to him that he had promised that I would stay as Minister of Labour for the full five years of the Parliament, to reform the legislative basis of the trade unions and to bring about a firm and stable relationship between both sides of industry and the government. He soon talked me round, however, and I was in truth delighted to go to the Foreign Office, long my objective in political life, and looked forward immensely to working with Alec Home. This happy and fruitful partnership persisted, in one form or another, for nearly fifteen years.

If I had been given more time at the Ministry of Labour, would my premiership have been less blighted by industrial strife? I do not believe so. I was always in favour of co-operation and regular high-level meetings between government, unions and employers. This, of course, presupposes a responsible leadership of the trade union movement. It was only later in the 1960s that militants really came to dominate the TUC. When they caused unacceptable levels of industrial strife and serious damage to the economy, I immediately set the Conservative Research Department to work on legislation that would restore power to the moderates and codify a system across industry which eventually became the 1971 Industrial Relations Act. By July 1960, I had established excellent relations with most of the union leaders and, indeed, Vic Feather wrote to tell me that he was sorry to see me moving on because I had 'so quickly won the respect and confidence of the unions'. It was ironic to look back on this from a different perspective a decade later.

Chapter 8

'CRIS DE PERROQUET'

The First European Negotiations 1960–1963

The most significant challenge in my new job as Lord Privy Seal was to negotiate for Britain's accession to the European Community. The European Coal and Steel Community, established under the Treaty of Paris on 18 April 1951, was never an end in itself. Its primary purpose was political, to prevent France and Germany from ever fighting each other again and so to preserve peace in our own continent. Its instruments were economic, to control the materials required for the production of weaponry. As Robert Schuman had recognised, however, this was only an intermediate objective along the road to creating an 'ever-closer union' in Europe. On the continent of Europe support for the idea of European integration came from all sections of mainstream opinion, and it was always widely acknowledged, accepted and understood that these first glimmerings of economic union were the beginning of a process which would unite the free nations of Europe politically. The Belgian Foreign Minister, Paul-Henri Spaak, provided the impetus and leadership for the next major development with his memorandum to the governments of Western Europe containing a list of proposals for their Foreign Ministers to discuss at their meeting at Messina on 1 June 1955. In the months that followed, the British government had grievously underestimated the importance of the Messina Conference. It is now rightly recognised as a turning point in the development of the Community.

I first met Paul-Henri Spaak in 1961, during the preliminary talks before negotiations began for Britain's entry into the European Community. He had recently returned to the post of Belgian Foreign Minister, having been secretary-general of NATO between 1957 and 1961. He looked at the world as a whole, and regarded European unity as a prerequisite to lasting world peace. Everything else was of secondary importance, although he could on occasion be a stickler for his own country's interests. The final Spaak Report included a plan for removing obstacles in the market.

Although some of it was actually transferred directly into treaty form, the report's greatest success was in providing a basis for common understanding and agreement on the overall direction of future developments. The Treaty of Rome's objective of creating closer political union is explicit, and with good reason. Its preamble states plainly the determination of its signatories 'to lay the foundations of an ever closer union among the peoples of Europe'. Spaak once reminded me that even such high-flown undertakings could founder on the most humdrum of issues. The last issue to be resolved under the agreement at Messina before the Treaty of Rome could be signed was the question of tariffs upon bananas from the Belgian Congo, which was settled only at 4 a.m. on the last day.

Throughout the 1950s, there was never a true understanding in Britain of the depth of the commitment to unity among our continental neighbours. Few opinion formers in the UK believed that the Monnet vision of Europe was feasible. During the Messina discussions in 1955 the British first developed their argument that the Community ought to be a free-trade area, as opposed to a customs union. Meanwhile, the Six came together even more resolutely in their belief that the unity had to be deeper than that. There remains this confusion in the public mind in Britain today, although not in the rest of Europe, about the difference between a free-trade association and the Community. A free-trade area is one in which countries agree, where possible, to fix the tariffs between themselves, with a provision for quotas where required. There is no agreement among them about the level of their external tariffs with the rest of the world, and any goods can be excluded from a free-trade agreement. There is, however, an even more fundamental difference. The Community is political and in part supranational, whereas a free-trade area is not. It is this vast conceptual gap that explains why the British proposals in the 1950s were such a non-starter with the Six, and why the present-day Euro-sceptics are wrong to argue that the Community was initially a free-trade area and can therefore return to being so.

As the Six moved towards European unity, at Messina in 1955 and through the Treaty of Rome in 1957, the United Kingdom turned its attention towards developing the European Free Trade Area (EFTA). The Conservative government hoped that, by setting up EFTA, it would be possible to extend Britain's opportunities for trading, irrespective of the development of the Six. This suited politically neutral countries such as Switzerland and Austria.

Some of those involved in establishing EFTA also believed that they could put pressure on the European Community to change its structure, and tone down that ultimate objective of genuine political integration. Proponents of this view wanted to persuade the six founding members of the Community to join up with EFTA and form one large free-trade area. Those who were in touch with the European Community knew that there was never any possibility of this happening. In practice, EFTA had no influence whatsoever on any aspect of Community policies. It just made the Six wonder about what Britain's ultimate intentions might be, and made our own eventual entry that much harder to negotiate.

From 1960, I saw EFTA's workings for myself, after taking over from Reggie Maudling as the British Minister at the organisation. EFTA met several times a year in the different capitals of its members, and its procedure was always the same. All the representatives had to agree unanimously on any proposal put forward if there was to be action of any kind. All too often the other members agreed on what they wanted and then turned to me, arguing that Britain was the largest and richest member country, the largest of course, but actually not the richest proportionally, and should therefore cover a disproportionate share of the cost of any undertaking. This did not appeal to us in the least. However, it did give me the opportunity of getting to know these other countries and their Ministers and politicians, as well as experiencing their different forms of negotiation. It was also a chance of enjoying their capitals and sometimes bringing home characteristic pieces of glass or porcelain which I had spotted.

The decision of Harold Macmillan's government to apply for membership of the European Community represented an historic moment in post-war politics. It determined the direction not just of British policy, but also that of Europe and the Atlantic alliance. In many ways this momentous announcement, enthusiastically supported within Cabinet, Parliament and the United States, was of much greater significance than the actual fate of the British application. It signalled the end of a glorious era, that of the British Empire, and the beginning of a whole new chapter of British history. The 'three circles' concept, to which Anthony Eden devoted his speech at the Conservative Party conference at Margate in 1953, and which had been the mainstay of British foreign policy since the war, was no longer valid. Eden described Britain then as being at the centre of three circles: the United States, the Commonwealth and Europe. Theoretically, this gave Britain an all-powerful position in world affairs. In actual fact, even by that time this was no longer justifiable. The United States became increasingly engrossed in its non-violent contest with the other superpower. As more and more of the colonies became independent they pursued their own policies, particularly in trade and other economic affairs, and Britain was less able to influence them in their general policies. So far as Europe was concerned its rapid recovery from the wartime destruction it had suffered, and its growth and prosperity starting with the European Coal and Steel Community, followed by the European Economic Community and EURATOM, was carried out without British participation. But Eden's speech had made a big impact, especially on those who were already expressing doubts about him as a suitable successor to Churchill.

During the late 1950s, there had seemed to be little prospect of British entry into the Community, which was already enjoying considerable success. In the early months of 1960, however, Macmillan seriously began to consider the benefits that Britain might receive as a member. Well aware that the United Kingdom, shorn of its Empire and its old dependencies, could no longer enjoy its former role as a world superpower, Macmillan had concluded that we might continue to play an influential world role through wholehearted participation in Europe. It was also apparent to the British government that EFTA was a weak organisation and one, moreover, whose progress would always be inhibited by its weakest members. Harold Macmillan's shift was not easy. The Suez crisis had nearly torn the Conservative Party and the country apart, and we were all aware that a number of people still had to be convinced of the political and economic merits of joining the Six. This decision turned the Conservative Party at that time into an explicitly pro-European party. In June 1960 Macmillan sent a questionnaire to all government departments on the subject of joining the Six.

Macmillan charged Selwyn Lloyd, then Foreign Secretary, with the task of sorting out whether it was possible for Britain to join the Community. By July, Selwyn Lloyd had concluded that the Six had tightly closed the door to our entry. On 25 July, shortly before the House rose for the summer recess, Selwyn Lloyd announced that no further progress towards joining the Six could be made for the foreseeable future, although he made a point of emphasising that the government was keeping open the aspiration of negotiating with the Six some day. Macmillan, however, was growing seriously concerned about the dangers of the division remaining between Britain and Western Europe. This anxiety was expressed in his booklet *Britain, the Commonwealth and Europe*, published in 1962:

> It is true, of course, that political unity is the central aim of these European countries and we would naturally accept that goal ... As a member of the Community, Britain would have a strong voice in deciding the nature and timing of political unity. By remaining outside, we could be faced with a political solution in Europe which went counter to our interests, but which we could do nothing to influence.

When Alec Home was walking with me from No. 10 to the Foreign Office following my appointment as Lord Privy Seal, he said that we must now decide upon our priorities. 'Very well,' I replied, 'what are they?'

'The first one,' he said, 'is our holidays . . . I think that you should go on holiday now, and come back by 10 August, for reasons which you will understand.' I was well aware that grouse shooting which was what concerned him started on 12 August, so off I went on holiday to Venice with my fellow MPs Julian Amery and John Hare and their wives. We stayed in Alan Lennox-Boyd's superb third-floor apartment on the Giudecca, which gave us every opportunity of enjoying Venice. My few visits since then have never been for recreational purposes. The last was in October 1997, when I was presented there with the Pro Arte Medal of the Förderergemeinschaft der Europäischen Wirtschaft at the Palazza Labia.

As we were sunbathing one morning on the Lido, we noticed a rather inappropriately overdressed young man strolling up and down the sands, cameras slung round his neck and over his shoulder, and holding a telegram. He looked quite lost and, as he wandered near by, we enquired whether we could help. He handed us the telegram. 'Get photographs of Heath, Hare and friends on Lido at all costs,' it read; and it was signed, 'Editor, Daily Express'. We did our best to appear benevolent, and said, 'Yes, you must go over there.' The man understood little English, so I simply pointed to the far end of the row of tents and said again, 'There, there.' Smiling broadly, the photographer went off, preparing his cameras as he went. Meanwhile, we picked up our towels and disappeared to our boat, leaving the young man to send back to the editor of the *Daily Express* pictures of the former Transport Minister Ernest Marples and his wife. We did not entirely get away with that. In St Mark's Square two days later, the same young man approached us. This time he was better briefed and knew who we were. With our agreement he took a photograph of us earnestly studying the architecture of the Doge's Palace, not realising that he would still fail to satisfy the editor's desire for a lurid picture of social cavortings on the Lido.

One sunny day later in the holiday, we were lying on the beach when a messenger came along waving his arms and shouting 'Signor Ita, Signor Ita, Signor Ita.' We beckoned him over and he handed me a telegram from Macmillan. To everyone's surprise, Adenauer had suddenly proposed that Harold and Alec Home should go to Bonn to discuss our future membership of the Community. Adenauer had previously been ambivalent towards any British involvement in the process. His immediate post-war priority, the forging of an unbreakable Franco-German alliance, had now been realised, however, and his attitude towards British entry had softened substantially. The Prime Minister's telegram said that he and the Foreign Secretary had accepted this invitation on the understanding that they could return to London by 8 August, 'for reasons which you will fully understand'. It was decided after this meeting that we would explore through various diplomatic channels, by official and ministerial talks, whether a basis for negotiations could be found. A few days after I had received this information we were back on the Lido, and again along came the messenger. This time the Prime Minister's telegram said, 'The Italians have heard of our visit to Bonn and have invited the Foreign Secretary and myself to go to Rome on 16 August. We were unable to accept his invitation for reasons which you will fully understand. We would both therefore be grateful if you would go to Rome on 16 August to have discussions with the Italian Prime Minister.' So, within a week of returning home, I travelled back to Italy to meet Amintore Fanfani, the Prime Minister, and his colleagues – the beginning of a continuous round of such exploratory talks with the leaders of Western European nations, Commonwealth representatives and Ministers from the EFTA countries.

Soon after my arrival in Rome, I had a meeting with the whole Italian Cabinet, at which I explained the British situation and our views on possible negotiations. I did so, to the astonishment and the anxiety of my advisers, without a note. The Ministers listened most patiently. After I had finished, I could not help noticing that the Prime Minister, who was sitting opposite to me, was concentrating on the pencil in his hand and the paper in front of him. At the end of the meeting he presented me with a drawing of my head and shoulders, which I have had framed, and which now hangs in my home. The Italians made it plain from the beginning that they would warmly welcome British accession. They undertook to help in every possible way, an attitude they maintained throughout the subsequent negotiations. Emilio Colombo, the Italian Minister of Finance, who later took part in them, was a skilful operator and ever anxious to make progress, even though the Italian enthusiasm for compromise sometimes tested one's patience.

On the second night they provided a delightful dinner in my honour in the Villa Madama, an historic house on a hill overlooking Rome. It had been damaged by wartime bombing but partially repaired, so we were able to dine on the ground floor. The upper floors were being rebuilt through the generosity of American benefactors. As I strolled around the garden with the Prime Minister after dinner, we leaned on the balustrade and saw below us all the structures for the forthcoming Olympic Games. 'It is a very odd world,' he suddenly said to me, and I put on an enquiring look. 'You see that arch over there,' he continued, pointing to an obviously modern, splendid arch shining brightly in the moonlight. 'That was built by Mussolini. They are telling me I must pull that down because he was a bad man.' 'Well,' I said, 'it looks to be a very good arch.' 'Yes,' he replied, 'and you see that one in the distance?' 'What,' I said, 'the one which is falling down?' 'Yes,' he said, 'they tell me I have to spend a lot of money on restoring that. Yet that was built by Nero – who was a very, very, very bad man!' Later on I continued my stroll around the garden with Carlo Alberto Straneo, who was then in the Italian Foreign Office and, later, ambassador in Moscow. 'Now tell me,' I said, 'how I should proceed? I am very new to the diplomatic game, but you are very experienced. Please explain it to me.' 'It all depends on two things,' he said, 'first of all on suspicion; and, secondly, on caution. If you stick to those two you will never go wrong.' How right he proved to be.

My visit to Paris in October 1960, however, was predictably difficult. In dealing with the French politicians and administrators, I have always been struck by their unique and inbred combination of a highly technocratic view of politics with conspicuously Machiavellian instincts. It was immediately apparent that the French were very suspicious of British intentions. Some would say that, in the light of the previous ten years' history, they had every right to be. I realised at once that the French Foreign Minister, Maurice Couve de Murville, and those of his colleagues whom I met on that occasion, in particular Olivier Wormser, were men of stature. They were all immensely able, and well versed in the affairs of the Communities. Their arguments were backed up by a consistent and logical Cartesian philosophy. They earned my admiration and respect, and, subsequently, my friendship. At the same time, despite all their formidable qualifications, they were puzzled as to what the British were up to and what they should do about us. Everything in the Community had recently been running smoothly and successfully, and the Six were just about to embark on the creation of the Common Agricultural Policy. Then, suddenly, along came the British to complicate everything. The cloak-and-dagger atmosphere reminded me very much of the presumably apocryphal story of Talleyrand at the Congress of Vienna. Sitting at the conference table, he was approached suddenly by an aide, who whispered in his ear, 'The Russian ambassador has died.' 'Really,' said Talleyrand. 'What can his motive be?'

We knew from the beginning, of course, that the old Commonwealth – Canada, Australia and New Zealand – would, at the very least, not much like any move on our part to join the European Community. At worst, we were prepared for encountering tough opposition from them. This was perfectly natural in the light of all the family relationships between our countries. Moreover it was only fifteen years since the end of the Second World War, in which they had fought so valiantly on the side of Britain against Germany and Italy. It was more surprising, however, that parts of the Third World which were members of the Commonwealth, led particularly by Ghana, should object so vigorously throughout the 1960s. It was only after our successful negotiations in the early 1970s that they reconciled themselves to our full membership of the Community. By that time they could see how beneficial the Community was to the former colonial territories of the other European powers, through the association arrangements made under Part IV of the Treaty of Rome. Our discussions with the European Free Trade Area countries were much more straightforward, especially as the subject of accession could be openly discussed at every regular meeting. They concentrated on ensuring that they were kept fully informed at this early stage and that their own interests would be protected in any subsequent negotiations.

During the many discussions with my foreign counterparts I became increasingly heartened, already sensing that the Cabinet's pessimism of only a few months before had been misplaced. The official line, however, remained that the British government was only considering a change of approach in the British relationship with the Six, a point that I made to the Council of Ministers of the Western European Union (WEU) on 27 February 1961, in those days the most useful forum for exchanging views with the Six. I also took this opportunity to reassure them that 'The British government has no desire whatever to weaken the ties of the Six-Power Community or to dilute or impede the flow of this great European organisation towards greater forms of unity.'

I informed the House of Commons on 17 May 1961 that the government had now identified the four options that faced us. The first was to abandon any thought of a settlement between the Six and Britain. This was unacceptable. The second course was to try to make an economic arrangement between the EEC and EFTA, with each retaining its own identity, but it had soon became apparent that it was not possible to secure an arrangement between the two separate organisations. The third option was some newly negotiated form of association with the Community. The fourth was full membership.

Enquiries undertaken by the British embassies in the Six had shown that there was a very general wish for the UK to join the European Community. This was partly for the selfish reason that the addition of the UK would widen the economic base of the Community. The main argument, however, was political. Our political stability and democratic tradition would strengthen the Community and, secondly, Britain's worldwide outlook would help to prevent the Community from turning in on itself. Our diplomatic contacts had also discovered that closer association between ourselves and the Six, short of full membership, would not be acceptable to the member states of the European Community. Any such proposal simply encouraged the belief that Britain wanted all of the advantages of the developments in Europe, without undertaking any of the obligations. In any case, no association agreement would grant us the political influence that we sought. The choice, therefore, was between accepting the Treaty of Rome in its entirety, together with the domestic and international problems that would arise as a result, or maintaining the status quo and reconciling ourselves to being stuck in Western Europe's second division.

Despite the lack of enthusiasm among Commonwealth countries, it became clear that the Cabinet would shortly reach a collective decision to proceed with an application to negotiate with the Community. Macmillan therefore informed President Kennedy of this and sent Ministers to the major Commonwealth countries to explain everything fully to them and to stress the political advantages of our membership: Duncan Sandys had a particularly rough ride in Australia and New Zealand. I visited Cyprus and discovered that they were not in any way hostile to the principle of negotiations. The President, Archbishop Makarios, wanted to discuss a variety of topics at our meeting, and he had his own technique for handling questions. He would raise each point very bluntly and provocatively. After I had dealt with it, he would abandon his position without further comment and rapidly switch his argument to another topic.

For lunch on the Sunday I flew by helicopter to the British base on the south of the island. During an excellent meal with the Commander-in-Chief, I was put fully into the picture regarding Eastern Mediterranean affairs, and the part which the British forces in Cyprus played in monitoring the activities of the Soviet Union in the Cold War. Returning to the helicopter after lunch, the pilot asked whether, as we had some time in hand, I would like to fly around the island, an offer which I gladly accepted. After a short spell we came to the foot of the Troodos mountain range and he started to climb. It was not long before the helicopter began to judder and the higher we went the louder became the judderings, so much so that I became somewhat apprehensive. 'At the top there is a beautiful little historic chapel,' said the pilot. 'I am sure you would like to see that.' By this time I was really alarmed. 'Is this how you would bring Archbishop Makarios up here to take a service in the chapel?' I asked. 'Good heavens no,' he replied. 'The risk of bringing people up here in this thing is far too great.'

On the way back to Britain I stopped in Athens. Greece had just become associated with the Community, and I had discussions over supper with Konstantin Karamanlis and Evangelos Averoff-Tositfas, the Prime Minister and Foreign Minister. I asked them what they thought our chances of membership were. The Foreign Minister replied that the British should promise three things if we wanted to be successful. I naturally enquired what these three things were. 'The first one is that you should adopt the metric system,' he replied. I told him that this was certainly possible, as we had been considering doing this for over a century and it was time the British reached a conclusion. 'The second point', he continued, 'is that you should drive on the right-hand side of the road.' I thought this was more difficult, but if it proved to be essential then it might be arranged; after all, Sweden had managed this change without even forcing every vehicle to alter the side of its steering wheel. I was wondering what all this might be leading to when the Foreign Secretary set out his final requirement: 'The third thing you have to do, if you want to be successful, is to return the Elgin marbles to Greece.' 'That,' I replied, 'is not only difficult; it is quite impossible.' It was fortunate that Greece did not have a say in our membership of the Community!

It was after this sojourn that I made my first, unintended visit behind the Iron Curtain. Returning to Britain from Athens, I was booked on to a plane to Vienna, and the Foreign Office failed to realise that it was scheduled to stop over at Sofia *en route*. As soon as the airport authorities were alerted to my presence, the Bulgarian government acted swiftly. A table was generously spread with national dishes, a plentiful supply of wine was produced and senior officials were rushed out to the airport to welcome me. It seemed very agreeable to me, but it was anything but pleasant for my private secretary, whose main concern was to get a message back to the Foreign Office as quickly as possible to explain what had occurred: we could not risk them hearing the news of our 'diversion' from the press, in case they thought that we had all defected.

The Cabinet unanimously decided to go ahead with negotiations in late July 1961, and this decision was announced in Parliament on the 31st. Harold Macmillan explained that we had examined the choices facing the UK using political criteria and that we were striving for the closest possible unity within Europe:

> This is a political as well as an economic issue. Although the Treaty of Rome is concerned with economic matters it has an important political objective, namely to promote unity and stability in Europe . . . In this modern world the tendency towards larger groups of nations acting together in the common interest leads to greater unity and thus adds to our strength in the struggle for freedom.

This decision was backed on 3 August in the House of Commons. The Labour Party did not oppose the negotiations in principle, but said that they would reserve their position on membership until the final agreement was known. As expected, the arguments raised against us covered our obligations to the Commonwealth, domestic agriculture and questions of sovereignty. I dealt with the latter point in my speech of 3 August:

From the point of view of sovereignty ... it seems to me that it is a conception much more of pooling sovereignty with others who are occupied in the same joint enterprise. Surrender means the abandonment of sovereignty to others. Pooling seems to me to share sovereignty with other people for a common purpose and there seems to me to be a firm distinction between those two. It is a pooling of sovereignty over a strictly defined field, and that is laid down in the Treaty itself.

That definition has been widely publicised right from the beginning and remains my position today.

As soon as our application to enter into negotiations with the Community had been accepted, I went off to join the Seligmans on holiday at the small house they rented at St Jacut-de-la-Mer in Brittany. A few days later, on 18 August, I was strolling up the village high street after breakfast to get a copy of any English newspaper available, and picking one up saw the headline 'Heath to negotiate with "The Six"'. That was the first indication I had that the announcement of my appointment had been made in London. Apparently, there had been some discussion between Macmillan and the secretary of the Cabinet, Sir Norman Brook, as to whether, after only a year in the Cabinet, I was senior enough to be at the head of the negotiating team. But it became quite clear that to add this job on to the Foreign Secretary's existing work was not a tenable proposition. Having spent a year preparing the ground for it, meeting all those involved and working out the structure necessary to carry the project through, there was nothing that I wanted more than this.

After my return to London, I was faced with some hectic activity before meeting the leaders of the delegations from the Community countries in Paris. The first matter to resolve was that of appointing members to the British delegation. I told Norman Brook that each member should be fluent in at least three languages. Sir Pierson Dixon, the British ambassador to France, was appointed as the head of the official side of Britain's negotiating delegation. As his deputy we brought in from the Ministry of Agriculture Eric Roll, an Austrian-born diplomat who spoke seven languages and had the ability to lipread in both French and German, a skill which gave us the huge advantage of always knowing what our main counterparts were saying to each other. The appointment of Sir Pierson Dixon has since been criticised by those who believe that he should have been left full-time in Paris, to keep up his work in strengthening Anglo-French relations. In fact, his selection did not prevent him from maintaining his excellent working relationship with de Gaulle, and he coped admirably with his increased workload. The other valuable members of this team were Sir Roderick Barclay from the Foreign Office, Sir Herbert Andrew from the Board of Trade, Sir Harry Lintott from the Commonwealth Office, Sir William Gorell Barnes from the Colonial Office and Raymond Bell from the Treasury. Along with Dixon and Roll they were collectively known as the 'Flying Knights'.

The 'Flying Knights' were stationed, on average, three days a week in Brussels and spent the rest of their time in London. This meant that they were long enough in London every week to be able to keep their departments in line with the development of thinking in the delegation as a whole and with the flow of the negotiations. Each member of the delegation was, of course, conversant with the work of his own department; but I stressed the need to ensure, at all times, that they were acting not in its interests alone but in that of our country as a whole. There was one exception. The Ministry of Agriculture, at all official levels, from the most senior down, systematically opposed, to the bitter end, all pressures to alter the British agricultural system. Although the Minister, Christopher Soames, was personally in favour of British accession, and was later a very good Commissioner, his senior officials undermined him at every turn. It was they who insisted that, alone of all the departments principally concerned, their representative on the delegation should be not a deputy under-secretary (DUS), but an official, Arthur Propper, who resided permanently in Brussels and therefore carried no real weight in his department. The reason offered for this, that Eric Roll had formerly been a DUS at their Ministry, was specious.

The Brussels delegation would be shadowed by a London delegation, and it was made clear that any inter-departmental politics had to be resolved in Whitehall. The alternative was paralysis in Brussels. Members of the London delegation, including Freddie Bishop from the Ministry of Agriculture, Sir Evelyn Shuckburgh from the Foreign Office and the joint permanent secretary at the Treasury, Sir Frank Lee, would operate within their departments, so it was inevitable that they would 'remain native' to some degree, pursuing a departmental agenda. But they still had the responsibility of persuading their departments that what was coming out from the negotiations was the best that could be achieved, and had to be seen in the context of the whole package.

At the same time, the London delegation would have to keep the Brussels team informed of what the government and its advisers felt it was essential to achieve and, when necessary, of what concessions we simply could not afford to make. Inter-departmental rivalry is famously ingrained in Whitehall culture, but the team members all did well. Both delegations also had the task of keeping the outside bodies with whom we were concerned, namely the Commonwealth countries, the colonies and the other EFTA countries, fully informed through their high commissioners and ambassadors, both in London and in Brussels. This continuous exchange of views and information made enormous demands on both negotiating teams. As individuals and as a team, they earned the admiration both of the Six and of the outside countries involved. It is difficult to convey the feeling of camaraderie within the delegation during those days. In Whitehall terms it must have been unprecedented and I remain in close contact with most of the surviving members of the team to this day. We all have fond personal memories of this period.

Jean Monnet strongly and repeatedly advised me in those early days that we should sign the Treaties of Paris and Rome straight away. His argument was that we should accede immediately and, once inside, seek adjustments of the Community's institutions and policies to meet our own particular needs. This was a tempting proposal. It would have saved a great deal of time, and it would have enabled us to take part at once in the negotiations on the Common Agricultural Policy, which were then in their early stages. It would also have made it possible to block, under the then rules of the Community, those aspects of its development which we considered to be against our interests. With each delay to our entry, further developments which would directly affect us were taking place within the Six, while we watched impotently from outside.

Such a robust and direct approach, however, could not conceivably resolve the difficulties regarding our existing commitments to the Commonwealth and the European Free Trade Area. They would have been at once cut off from their relationships with the United Kingdom, and it was questionable whether existing agreements could be changed, or even broken, in this way. Even if there had been an understanding with the Community that these existing arrangements could continue for a temporary period, and it was very doubtful whether the Community could possibly accept such an arrangement, uncertainty would have been created both in the Commonwealth and among the EFTA countries about their eventual future. Our membership would also have begun on the wrong basis as we would have been forced to engage in battles with the others immediately after accession. This would have produced immense friction and hostility towards Britain. Even if we could have taken this course legally, we could not have taken it with honour. We had played straight so far, and were determined to continue doing so.

This moral case was strengthened by practical considerations, for nobody could have secured the agreement of Parliament to the simple course of signing the Treaties and then negotiating from inside the Community. The leadership of the Labour Party, unsure of how opinion would move, both among its members and in the country, contributed nothing of any value throughout the negotiations. Yet there were many members of both Houses and all parties who genuinely and understandably wished to see the outcome of the negotiations before finally committing themselves. Simply signing the Treaty of Rome would have suggested a lack of confidence in our negotiating position. We therefore had to reconcile ourselves to the prospect of long and arduous negotiations. The United Kingdom Parliament would then take the final decision.

It was agreed among the Six that I would deliver the British opening statement in Paris on 10 October 1961. The original plan was for the meeting to take place in the French Foreign Ministry, the Quai d'Orsay, in the morning, but early on we received a message asking us to delay until after lunch. No reason was given. On arrival in the afternoon, we walked through the series of halls leading to the chamber where my presentation would take place. All along the walls were little groups of people, vigorously exchanging views. It was evident that a row had taken place in the morning, probably the reason why we had not been required. I beckoned over Christopher Audland and John Robinson, two junior members of the negotiating team, and asked them to move around quietly and find out what had happened. Meanwhile, the rest of us walked slowly down to the meeting place. That was empty, but we took our seats at the round table in the places marked for us. I was quickly joined by the two juniors who reported that there had been one hell of a row about how the negotiations were to be handled, and that everyone was worried about what was going to happen next.

The meeting then assembled and Dr Ludwig Erhard, the German Finance Minister in the chair, welcomed me and invited me to address them. This I did slowly and clearly, at times with considerable emphasis:

> The British government and the British people have been through a searching debate during the last few years on the subject of their relations with Europe. The result of this debate has been our present application. It was a decision arrived at, not on any narrow or short-term grounds, but as a result of a thorough assessment over a considerable period of the needs of our own country, of Europe and of the free world as a whole. We recognise it as a great decision, a turning point in our history, and we take it in all seriousness. In saying that we wish to join the EEC, we mean that we desire to become full, whole-hearted and active members of the European Community in its widest sense and to go forward with you in the building of a new Europe.

The effect at this the first of our many meetings was quite remarkable. Even the keenest of French minds could find no weakness in this statement. The only comment, made privately, was that it was doubtful whether such a positive and forthright declaration could truly represent the British position. Erhard himself had already made it very plain, in a letter to Macmillan, that he would do everything possible to bring these negotiations to a successful conclusion, and he echoed those sentiments very movingly in his opening remarks in Paris. 'We welcome the British step,' he said. 'In the spirit of freedom, we are today defending the existence of the whole free world through the process of European integration . . . but to accomplish this is unthinkable without the participation of Great Britain, to which Europe owes so much in all areas of national and human life.'

At the end of my presentation, Erhard asked me three questions. Would I agree that the meetings of ministers should take place every month? I replied, 'Yes.' Would I agree to the next meeting being held in the following month, November? I replied, 'Yes.' Would I agree that in future the meetings should be held in Brussels? To this I also replied, 'Yes.' Everyone seemed to be most impressed with the brevity and clarity of my answers, indeed so much so that Paul-Henri Spaak announced loudly, 'You see, we get on a damn sight better with seven than we do with six!' The representatives of the Six had apparently spent the entire morning arguing over the same three issues. This disagreement had obviously prompted the ill-feeling that we detected upon our arrival that afternoon. Couve de Murville was not in the least amused by Spaak's comment.

Couve de Murville was French Foreign Minister for the ten years from 1958 to 1968, and made good use of his political longevity to establish a dominant position in the Quai d'Orsay. He had a brilliant mind and was a remarkable negotiator. For much of the time he was operating within the bounds set by President de Gaulle, but one never gained the impression that he was only his master's voice. He protected immediate French interests, of course, but his mission was something more than that, for what he was really concerned with was the historic role of France in Europe as he conceived it.

Couve had the typical attributes of a Frenchman of his background and calling: an instinctive caution, a shrewd grasp of the principles at stake in any matter and an intimate and intricate familiarity with the most minute details. He was adept at playing his hand, and kept his cards to himself. Hardly a meeting went by in Brussels without the two of us lunching or dining privately in the British or French embassy and occasionally in one of the city's restaurants. Having been tutor to Harold Nicolson's children in the 1930s, and having served with de Gaulle in London during the Second World War, he knew the British well. Above all, de Murville admired and envied the continuity of British life, in particular its parliamentary institutions, the result of their deep roots in our history. Couve was, however, cordially disliked by many of his Foreign Minister colleagues on account of his considerable aloofness. A typical illustration of this was the way in which, at meeting after meeting, while other Foreign Ministers, or representatives of the Commission, were speaking, he would sit at the negotiating table blatantly reading a newspaper, usually the *Financial Times*. His unsympathetic, chilly, ascetic, French Protestant manner made him definitely 'not one of the club'. Despite these attributes, Couve de Murville was always a dedicated public servant and a consummate professional, and both France and those of its Presidents under whom he served owe an enormous amount to him. I admired and respected him, even though I wished he would at times be more forthcoming.

The French ambassador in London, Jean Chauvel, kept in close contact with me at the Foreign Office throughout the negotiations, always making sure I was fully informed of the French position and never hesitating to seek a clarification of our proposals. The Foreign Office has no interpreters as such and a call is usually made on one of the junior members of the FCO for translation. Fortunately Chauvel spoke very good English. The problem was that he spoke very quickly. During one meeting, I watched as the assistant's pen remained poised in the air over his notebook, desperate to record the interview but quite unable to keep up with the ambassador's remarks. After a brief interval, I felt bound to intervene to help him. 'Excuse me, ambassador, but as my English is so poor, would you mind speaking a little more slowly?' He smiled, bowed his head, and we resumed at a slower pace.

The first negotiating session opened on 8 November 1961 and like every subsequent meeting, was followed by a long and searching press conference. Then, immediately upon my return to London, I made a statement in the House of Commons on what had transpired, followed by up to an hour of answering MPs' questions. I remember one friend in the Community telling me how astonished he was that I could carry on negotiations at all in such circumstances. I had earlier reached agreement with the Six that, in order to facilitate a free and frank discussion, my opening speech would not be published either by ourselves or by another member country. Any statements to the media would be of a general kind, to indicate what progress we were making. This inevitably promoted demands and suspicion in the House of Commons and provided the hostile elements with ample ammunition for attacking us. There was a general hankering to know what was going on, and the Community itself was an extraordinarily open organisation. As a general proposition this was to be welcomed, but in highly complex and wide-ranging negotiations, complete transparency makes it difficult for participants to be flexible and to compromise. A balance between openness and national interest has to be struck. The time for fully informed debate and definitive decisions would come when I had a full set of proposals to put to the House.

At the meetings that followed, we got down to the issues. The question of Britain moving on to the same external tariff as the Six meant that we had to reduce the great majority of our existing tariffs, for the Community was considerably less protectionist than Britain. British industry was only too anxious to take advantage of the markets provided by the members of the Community and was quite prepared to see us adopt a lower external tariff, even though it would mean more competition from outside countries, such as the United States and Japan. The problem with the tariffs and quotas arose among those already closely connected with us, in particular the Commonwealth and British colonial territories and, to a lesser extent, the remainder of the European Free Trade Area countries. The countries of the Indian sub-continent negotiated particularly hard for free and unlimited entry of tea, which was, of course, in competition with coffee, and in the end we got agreement to this.

Our colonial territories were not a problem from the point of view of the Community, because the former colonial territories of the Six already had a special arrangement under Part IV of the Treaty of Rome, for the entry of most of their raw materials and foodstuffs, in addition to their underdeveloped industrial goods. Our difficulty was that some of our most influential colonial and former colonial territories did not wish to take advantage of these special arrangements. That was not the fault of either the Community or the British. Eventually, they accepted the advantages which exist under the Lomé Agreement (formerly the Yaoundé Agreement).

It had always been my hope that, once the former colonial powers were united in one Community, both they and the existing colonies, especially in Africa, would follow suit and work harmoniously together. However, there is still no indication that the former British, French, Belgian, Italian and German territories are following the European example, or even learning each other's languages so as to establish a natural relationship. Perhaps with the passage of time these African countries will appreciate how much there is to be gained by working for closer unity themselves.

From the beginning, I was greatly concerned by the imminent discussions on the proposed Common Agricultural Policy (CAP). This was clearly going to be a matter of enormous importance to the United Kingdom, but it quickly emerged that the Community had agreed, largely under pressure from the French, to sort out the framework of the new agricultural policy before entering into serious discussions with us on the arrangements for our entry. The French did not wish the British to be at the table taking part in the formative decisions on the CAP, for fear that we might disrupt the very favourable arrangements they otherwise had every reason to expect from their partners. It is often forgotten in this country that in our absence the Community was formed on the basis that Germany would have other industrial markets at its disposal and that France would take advantage of future agricultural developments.

In the autumn of 1961, the Six had agreed to finalise the shape of the CAP by 1 January 1962. In fact, agreement was not reached in time and, as a result, the Council of Ministers, the decision-making body made up of ministerial representatives from the member states, 'stopped the clock', a device used when their negotiations had overrun. The Council went on with its discussions until final agreement was reached on 14 January 1962, when the clock was restarted. I made it clear throughout the negotiations that where possible we would bring the CAP fully into operation by the end of the transitional period for the existing Community, in other words by 31 December 1969. We knew we had to tackle the problems of changing over from our own system of support for agriculture to the newly completed CAP. The negotiations would largely be concerned with how we were to do so.

The structure of what was now proposed was based upon the consumer paying the market price for products. It was not always possible in advance to say what this price would be, for it depended upon the supply and demand in the market and, in turn, upon the cost of production of the farmer or food producer. In case the market, because of conditions of over-supply, undercut the farmer's reasonable costs of production, a level of prices was to be fixed below which they could not fall. Imported food stocks would not be allowed to undermine the domestic market. To prevent this happening, a levy had to be placed on these imports, and a minimum 'threshold' price for imports was fixed. This could be set according to the comparative price levels of imported and Community-produced foodstuffs. By contrast, British support for our agricultural sector was based upon deficiency payments, a system under which subsidies to the food producers were paid by the Treasury, wholly incompatible with what our future partners had now decided upon.

Whereas it was possible for us to tell the British public that by lowering the level of our industrial tariffs to that of the Community we were, on average, reducing the prices of most goods to the consumer, the reverse was the case with foodstuffs. Furthermore, although a fairly precise indication of the effect could be given in the case of the former, it was difficult to estimate what the impact on the British consumer was going to be should we move to the structure of the CAP. In any case, it would be spread over a number of years according to what was agreed about the transitional period. Naturally, we warned consumers of the estimated impact of these changes. In fact, the increase over the transitional period later proved to be far less than we had calculated, thanks to the increasing efficiency of European farmers, including the British.

Horticulture posed separate problems. These were largely due to the backward nature of much of British horticulture and, especially, to its lack of modern equipment. In this the Dutch and the Belgians had become pre-eminent, but parts of France were also well advanced. The differences in the cost of oil and other fuels between Britain and the Community were a frequent source of complaint for the British horticultural industry, but it was never able to make a convincing case against this alleged subsidy for producers on the mainland. The subject was discussed in the negotiations and it was conceded that any such subsidisation of the horticultural industry would be against the Community's rules. After President de Gaulle vetoed our entry in January 1963, I agreed with Christopher Soames that the British government would devote serious expertise and finance to our horticultural industry before any renewed negotiations, in order that we would not have to negotiate a long transitional period for our horticulturalists because they were not efficient enough to compete. In this we were successful and the path was much easier after 1970.

In this first negotiation the transitional period which our delegation was being told by my ministerial colleagues in London to demand was always unrealistic, at times farcically so. During this period, the Community itself started laying down standards for the benefit of consumers. It was Community law that first prevented retailers from putting the best products on top of the stall for the consumer to see, while serving out on the scales inferior products from underneath. This was a sensible and efficient course to follow, providing safeguards for the consumer and forcing the horticulturalist to improve the quality of his produce. At that time, the regulation applied only to tomatoes and pears.

We were told by the Ministry of Agriculture that it would be necessary to train fifty-two inspectors to look for spots on tomatoes and pears, and that we would need a transitional period of fifteen years for this to become possible. If fifteen years was not agreed I could move down to twelve years. If that was refused, I should break off all negotiations. I really could not believe that these were serious instructions. However, when I came to discuss this regulation with the Foreign Ministers of the Six, well after midnight, I explained our position. There was a stunned silence. Everyone lowered their heads and looked at the table in front of them. After a time, as none of the ministers had intervened, the Vice-President of the Commission, Dr Sicco Mansholt, raised his head and quietly said, 'I would like to tell Mr Heath this. Everyone sitting around this table has the greatest possible respect for the British. First, we respect them for all they did in the Second World War in standing alone against the forces of the dictators. Secondly, because they were instrumental in winning the war and restoring to us the freedom which we now enjoy. And thirdly, we respect them because of Churchill, who was a great British leader and the man above all who was responsible for saving Europe. We are all agreed about that.' To which the others murmured, 'Hear, hear.' 'But I must also add this,' he went on. 'While listening to Mr Heath explaining his government's present policy, I could not help wondering whether in 1940, at the blackest moments of the war, Mr Churchill would have demanded fifteen years in which to train fifty-two pear and tomato inspectors to achieve the victory of which he was the creator.' There was no answer to that. We could never use such stupid arguments again.

At the end of January 1962, we had been negotiating with the Community for just over three months. In a letter to Eric Roll on 21 January 1962, I expressed my suspicion that the French wanted to drag out this process for as long as possible. I gave three reasons for this view. The French expected that opposition would grow in the UK the longer the negotiations progressed; that our own desire to reach an agreement would weaken; and, finally, that something else would turn up to prevent the negotiations from being successfully concluded. The third of these reasons was to prove the most crucial. The French also suspected that our position was becoming progressively weaker economically, politically and militarily vis-à-vis both the Six and the US. In their view, the longer matters were drawn out, the greater the opportunity for securing better terms for the Community and themselves in particular.

At my suggestion, Emilio Colombo proposed the idea of a 'Vue d'ensemble' in the negotiations at the ministerial meeting of 11 May in Brussels. This was accepted by the Six. The British delegation had let it be known that we would do everything possible to bring the negotiations to a successful conclusion by late July, or early August, 1962, in accordance with the normal Community procedure of setting a deadline for such agreements. This would also correspond with the normal date for the British Parliament to rise for the summer recess, and with the Commission, which always took up to five weeks' break from the end of July. We were determined to remove all the uncertainty created by the negotiations, not only at home, but also in the Community, EFTA and the Commonwealth. As a result we decided to propose a Commonwealth conference in the early autumn of that year, at which we wanted to be able to put the whole package to the leaders of the Commonwealth countries and the representatives of the colonies. Our domestic political calendar also dictated that we should endeavour to have something concrete in place in good time for the party conference in early October. Unfortunately, this proved impossible to deliver.

The burden of the negotiations, on top of the developing work of the Community, proved to be too much for the machinery of the EEC. It became overloaded, operating more and more hesitantly. We were hindered by the structure of the negotiations: there was no permanent chairman and the Six had to agree a common position before negotiating with the UK. In retrospect, the original British negotiating position was far too inflexible – and as time progressed we placed far more attention on what was likely to be negotiable, bearing in mind Community doctrine and the individual interests of each member state. I warned colleagues at home that we were unlikely to resolve the outstanding issues adequately on the kind of timescale we had previously wanted. In the face of this, we decided that our priority must be to hold out for concessions from the Six, rather than for an early end to the negotiations, which would come about only if we conceded unsatisfactory terms.

So far as the Commonwealth Conference was concerned, Macmillan sent me to Ottawa in March 1962 to give the Canadian Prime Minister, John Diefenbaker, a full explanation of developments in the negotiations, and of the decision taken to convene a Prime Ministers' meeting in London later that year. I stayed with our high commissioner, Derick Heathcoat Amory, who had been persuaded by Macmillan to go to Canada after his resignation as Chancellor, and we were summoned to meet Diefenbaker in his parliamentary office at 8.30 a.m. We duly arrived on time and, having shaken hands with the Prime Minister, Heathcoat Amory, taking out of his mouth the handkerchief which he always chewed, remarked, 'Prime Minister, the Lord Privy Seal has come to report to you on the state of the negotiations with the European Community.' 'Oh, I can tell you all about that,' he said. 'It's in the latest British newspapers – have you seen them?' 'We have not.' 'Then I can tell you that they are very hostile to these negotiations. Let me tell you what they say.' Reaching across, he removed one from a rack and opened it at the leader column. 'I will read it to you,' he said, and began to read what turned out to be a glowing tribute to what I had been doing in Brussels. Having got well into this, he suddenly stopped and said, 'This is not the one I meant to read to you. I will find the other one later.'

At this moment, I thought it right to bring up the question of the Commonwealth Conference. I explained how Macmillan wanted to consult him, as the Prime Minister of the senior country in the Commonwealth, before inviting the others to London. 'Well,' said Diefenbaker, 'there are two possibilities. The first is July, and the second is September. Now there are complications about me being absent from here in July. On the first

Monday we have some local elections; on the second Monday there is a visit from the Queen Mother; and on the third Monday there is a jazz festival. I need to be here for all of those. That only leaves the last week. But the really important thing is the state of the harvest and that, of course, will depend upon the rainfall. If we are dry in July the crop will be bad, and we shall lose support. If the rainfall is strong we shall get good crops in September and our position will be sound. So what I have to do is to find out what the rainfall will be. This I have arranged to do by sending a water diviner out to the plains, and he will be able to tell by the twitching of his stick whether it will be rain in July or rain in September.' I was rendered speechless by this exposition of the basis of Canadian policy, and Derick Heathcoat Amory had to reply. 'We would be grateful if you could let us know as soon as possible because all of the other Commonwealth countries wish to know,' he said. 'Yes, of course, I will tell you as soon as I can,' responded the Prime Minister. 'I think it will probably be September. Thank you for coming.' With that valediction, we left him.

We did continue with the negotiations into the first week in August, but by then almost all of the participants were exhausted. At our final meeting before we adjourned, during the night of 4–5 August, the chairman from Luxembourg, Eugène Schaus, collapsed at 2.00 a.m., and was forced to leave the discussions. As the unfortunate chairman was carried away on a stretcher, our delegation's chief press officer Donald Maitland announced, in a clearly audible stage whisper, 'We're playing in injury time now.' After a short break, Colombo took the chair and the gruelling session continued. A little before 4 a.m., the French unexpectedly demanded that we should sign a paper on financing the CAP, committing us to an interpretation of the financial regulation favourable to the French. They wanted a new tariff arrangement on imports from outside the EEC which would maintain the price of domestic produce. This action was self-evidently dilatory in intent, and I refused to be bounced into a snap judgement on such a complex matter. I was supported in this by the Germans and the Dutch, who were as irritated as I was. The French redrafted the document twice, but this only hardened my resolve. This was no way to carry out such important negotiations, and I was having none of it. In response, Couve de Murville said that he would reserve his position regarding food imports from the British Commonwealth, a matter which I had understood to be fully resolved.

Shortly afterwards, Paul-Henri Spaak understandably retired from exhaustion, and Henri Fayat, the Belgian Deputy Foreign Minister, stood in. By 6.30 a.m., only the chairman and I appeared to be active. It was obviously fruitless, if not actually life-threatening, for the rest of us to try to continue. We clearly had no option but to adjourn until the autumn, by which time the British government would have had the necessary time to evaluate the progress up to that point. The Cabinet knew that we would have to go public with our ruminations and, on 20 September, Macmillan pre-empted any leaks with a television address to the nation. He repeated that there were political and economic reasons why Britain should join the Community and, although he expressed his satisfaction with the progress reached thus far, he also warned frankly of the difficulties that still remained, particularly with regard to our existing trading arrangements with the Commonwealth.

The following evening, Gaitskell replied to Harold Macmillan's broadcast. It was clear at once that he had now come off the fence. He warned of 'the end of a thousand years of history' and explained that, in his view, the political case for entry was the hope of 'building a bridge between the Commonwealth and Europe; and we cannot do that if we destroy the Commonwealth . . . the present terms do confront us with this choice . . . I don't think the British people . . . will in a moment of folly throw away the tremendous heritage of history.' Two weeks later, in his famous speech at the Labour Party conference in Brighton, Gaitskell repeated the same sentiments. This dismayed many of his allies, and his wife remarked to a neighbour that 'All the wrong people are cheering.' The hostility he expressed towards accession took even his closest advisers entirely by surprise, and George Brown, a strong supporter of entry, was forced to wind up that debate by skilfully supporting the same policy document without ruling out entry, having not being warned in advance of Gaitskell's outburst.

I think that Gaitskell was probably well intentioned, although considerations of party advantage clearly weighed in his mind. He was genuinely concerned about the effects on the Commonwealth, in particular on its less-developed countries, which looked to Britain for trade and succour, in both the economic and political spheres. Gaitskell seemed to fear that some sell-out was being planned by the Conservative government, as the only way of getting Britain into the Community. He should have realised, however, that, as chief negotiator, I would ensure that the interests of the Commonwealth were not betrayed.

As well as discussions in Europe and the Commonwealth we had, of course, to convince our own backbenchers throughout the negotiations that our policy was right, in the face of some hostile press coverage from Lord Beaverbrook's newspapers and the government's general unpopularity. The Conservative opposition consisted of a few individuals including Derek Walker-Smith and Robin Turton. The majority of the parliamentary party was always supportive, however, and an unofficial group was set up in 1962 to meet after the weekly 1922 Committee to decide their policy for the ensuing week on Europe. The members, including Julian Critchley, Nicholas Ridley, Jim Prior, Peter Tapsell and Christopher Chataway, were from the 1959 intake and carried considerable weight with their contemporaries. I was also sent a survey on 5 June 1962 by Dudley Smith, a Conservative backbencher, on the views of his colleagues on the European Community. This calculated that 189 backbenchers were in favour of Britain's entry and 77 were opposed. I was confident throughout that, in the event of an agreement which met Britain's interests and obligations, Parliament would support the terms on offer.

At the Commonwealth Conference in London, the negotiations were, inevitably, the main subject of discussion after the usual political and economic reviews. I was asked by Harold Macmillan, who presided over the conference as a whole, to present a full picture of the negotiations. We had kept the High Commissioners in London personally informed at regular intervals about all the proceedings, as well as discussing aspects of particular concern to individual countries with their own High Commissioners. We had also sent regular information to every government in the Commonwealth. All of them around the table were busy men however, and it was doubtful whether they had altogether assimilated the details of the negotiations, or been able to arrive at fully informed conclusions. I went over the whole framework of the negotiations and then filled in all the details in a speech which lasted an hour. Afterwards, I was flattered when Sir Robert Menzies, the long-serving Prime Minister of Australia, said that it was the best speech that he had heard at a Commonwealth conference. I was grateful for such a positive response, even though Menzies and his colleagues still had some doubts about what Europe meant for their future relationships with the UK.

In the discussion around the table, the members were able to voice their particular concerns. The Indians asked once again about the market for tea, and the Australians raised the need to maintain the exports of currants from the state of Victoria, which were largely grown by war veterans. The major emphasis at this stage, however, was political, for there was a general fear that the relationship between the old Commonwealth countries – Canada, Australia and New Zealand – and Britain would be irrevocably damaged if we joined the European Community. To this we had to answer that Britain's only credible choice for economic development was in the European Community, that this would undoubtedly increase our influence both politically and economically in the world and that such a development could, in turn, be of great benefit to the Commonwealth. There were many at home and in the Commonwealth who could accept, however wistfully, that a new era beckoned. Others undoubtedly wished us to demand conditions from the rest of Europe that our prospective partners could never grant. This would be tantamount to terminating the negotiations. So, as we prepared for them to reconvene, we were walking a fine line. I was certain all along that the Commonwealth would survive, and that future generations at home would curse us if we allowed nostalgia to blind us to the real needs of our nation.

Within the Community, meanwhile, it was becoming ever clearer that the attitude of the French President Charles de Gaulle to our application was crucial to our success. I had watched him with great care on television and at his press conferences and, of course, we had all seen the enormous impact he had made during his state visit to London in April 1960. Who could forget the memorable address he gave to both Houses of Parliament assembled in Westminster Hall? He delivered it superbly from memory. On each seat was a copy of the text of his speech in both English and French, which I followed as he spoke. He omitted only one single, short sentence. I commented on this afterwards to the French ambassador. 'Oh, but I told him to do that,' he replied, 'because I was afraid it would give offence.'

I first met the French President in person when Harold Macmillan invited me to dine at his home at Birch Grove when de Gaulle and his wife were his guests on a private visit on 24 November 1961, six weeks after we began the negotiations. We saw a different side of him from our previous experience: quietly spoken, reserved, almost shy, revealing him to be a man who bore the marks of the heavy burdens he carried and the decisions he had to take. After dinner, de Gaulle took me and Julian Amery to one side. Holding his spectacles in one hand and gently tapping them with the other, he enquired, referring to the negotiations for our entry into the European Community, 'What is all this about? Is it serious or is it just a game?' He was not trying to provoke us; he was still unsure about what the British were really up to. In my halting French, helped by Julian Amery, I endeavoured to explain to him that our intentions were genuine, why we had decided that our future lay with Europe, and that we wanted Britain to be strong and influential again. 'And the Empire and the Commonwealth?' he questioned. I stressed that our membership would mean that the French and British territories in Africa would be able to work together in the same system and under new, common arrangements, instead of being at loggerheads as so often in the past. As for the old Commonwealth, they would come to realise that it was in their interests to have a Britain that was economically strong in a larger Community.

I gained the very clear impression that he was puzzled about it all, not least because of his own idiosyncratic view of history, later to be set out at the press conference in 1963 which he gave to explain why he was vetoing Britain's entry into the Community. President de Gaulle may never have really wanted, or expected, the negotiations to succeed. He did realise, however, that, by agreeing to negotiate at all, he had implicitly accepted in principle that British entry was an eventual possibility. On the other hand, Sir Pierson Dixon, in a memorandum of May 1962 alerted us to the likelihood, in his opinion, of a veto by de Gaulle. Apart from the fact that this view was widely challenged, it could not, of itself, be a reason for breaking off the negotiations. Macmillan was rather more optimistic at that stage. I received a letter from him on 7 August which congratulated me 'on the wonderful way in which you have conducted this whole affair. I only hope that your efforts will meet ultimately with success. I cannot help feeling that they will do so.'

Both the French and British governments regarded the possession of nuclear weapons as an important measure of national power, and active participation in nuclear strategy was one of the governing aims of de Gaulle's foreign policy. This brought him into inevitable conflict with the US. Macmillan and de Gaulle met to discuss international issues at Rambouillet on 15 and 16 December 1962. This was directly before Macmillan was due to meet Kennedy at Nassau in the Bahamas to discuss the cancellation of Skybolt, an American missile which the British had on order. It would have enabled Britain to extend the life of its 'V' bomber force, in effect our entire independent nuclear deterrent at that time. Macmillan had no intention of causing a row about that, but he was adamant that the US was still morally obliged to give us access to an alternative system for delivering nuclear warheads. He informed de Gaulle at Rambouillet that he intended to ask Kennedy for Polaris missiles. Although de Gaulle perfectly well understood Britain's determination to maintain its independent nuclear deterrent, he repeated his view that Britain should relinquish its special ties with America once and for all. This was anathema to Macmillan, whose political position at home would have become almost untenable without a nuclear deterrent. As their talks progressed, de Gaulle began to describe how Britain was not yet suited to membership of the European Community. This could only mean one thing to Macmillan, a French veto against our entry, and a surprised Prime Minister answered that, if the French were truly opposed to British membership, then de Gaulle should have made their sentiments clear before we had all wasted so much time and effort on the negotiations.

At Nassau, President Kennedy assured Macmillan that legitimate technical and financial grounds had prompted the American decision to withdraw from the Skybolt project. In response, Macmillan formally requested Polaris. George Ball, the US Under-Secretary of State, urged Kennedy to reject our request, on the grounds that supplying the missiles would cause France to block Britain's accession and prolong division in Europe. In reply, Macmillan pledged that the UK would make its nuclear power available to NATO, thus adding to its strength, and in the end the US acceded to his request. At a meeting of Cabinet on the morning of Friday 21 December 1962, over which Butler presided, we discussed a long telegram from Macmillan explaining what he had resolved with Kennedy. It was clear that he wanted to go ahead. Julian Amery and I were both very unhappy with this situation, but we did not pursue our grievances, for we recognised that the news could be politically beneficial at home. We had the opportunity to replace our ageing deterrent with a proven successor, for which the Americans had borne all the costs of research and development. Four days later, the offer of Polaris missiles to the UK became public knowledge, and we announced that they would form an integral part of a multilateral NATO force.

A similar offer was made to France by the Americans, only without submarines. As they had not been present at the conference when the agreement was made, the French regarded it as a calculated slap in the face and de Gaulle told Sir Pierson Dixon, still our ambassador in Paris, on 21 December this was further proof that we would not break our ties to the Americans and turn to Europe. In retrospect, I can well imagine de Gaulle's feelings at being asked to accept the terms of an agreement negotiated in his absence by the British and American governments. With more sensitive handling, we might, at the very least, have denied him this particular excuse for behaving vindictively towards the British.

This episode highlighted the contradiction between the government's broader foreign policy and its objective of accession into Europe. For the latter, good relations were necessary with Germany and France. In so many other areas, however, the government, showing a lack of understanding of European attitudes and problems, was carrying out inconsistent policies in the political and defence fields. I had warned in a minute of 10 March 1962 that Britain's support for the American policy on the non-proliferation of nuclear weapons offended France and gave the impression that we were not sufficiently European in our outlook. The Six were interested not just in jointly increasing their prosperity, but also in strengthening their defence against the persistent threat from the Soviet Union and its satellites. They could judge our own attitude towards this only by the proposals we put forward. The French in particular had convinced themselves that Britain and the United States wanted to prevent them from developing their atomic and nuclear defence and all of the Six perceived a tendency on our part to negotiate away German interests in order to appease the Russians over Berlin. There was also an understandable and widespread suspicion about the precise nature of what was already termed our 'special relationship' with the US. It was no wonder that these negotiations, already sufficiently difficult and complicated, threatened to become almost unmanageable. I ended my minute with a warning that the British government could not be seen to go on pursuing such divergent policies at the same time.

The events at Rambouillet and Nassau sealed the fate of Britain's first bid to join the Community. In a private letter of 26 December 1962 Macmillan informed me that he had reached the same conclusion:

> . . . I only trust that nothing I have done at Rambouillet or Nassau has increased your difficulties. My impression of de Gaulle is that he is friendly to me personally, not unfriendly to Britain (always remembering the insults he conceives were put upon him by Churchill during the War), wants friendly relations with Britain, but does not want us now in the Community because he is in a mood of sulks about the future of Europe politically and would prefer to stay where he is with France dominating the Five. At the same time I am not sure that he wants this to be too public. The only thing that seemed to worry his advisers were the moments in the discussion where he gave away his hand too obviously and I pounced upon this.
>
> You know how great a confidence and faith my colleagues and I have had in you throughout, and the wonderful work that you have done is fully recognised throughout the country. Come what may, your position will stand very high.

While this drama was unfolding, Britain and the Six agreed to finish all negotiations in January 1963, over a three-week period. I met Dixon and Roll in Paris immediately after the holiday break, and we arranged an urgent, private and totally frank meeting with Couve de Murville to agree on how these three weeks should be handled.

On Friday 11 January 1963, our meeting with Couve took place over lunch at the British embassy. Pierson Dixon and Eric Roll from my team were present, and de Murville was accompanied by his deputy, Olivier Wormser. Over lunch we had an interesting conversation about French literature, but after the coffee I turned to the negotiations. I said that the major outstanding issue appeared to be the problem of agricultural finance. I told him that I wanted to settle this at the lunch and I had in my pocket all the authority I needed from the Chancellor of the Exchequer to resolve it once and for all, to the satisfaction of the French. Shaking his head, Couve protested vigorously that this was not at all what was required. He was perfectly satisfied with what had already been arranged. I then asked him twice whether there were any insuperable political obstacles to our entry, even if the negotiations were concluded completely satisfactorily. Twice he rejected this possibility and then said, 'No power on earth can now prevent these negotiations from being successful.' His companion showed his agreement. The meeting then broke up and our guests departed. Dixon and I reported on the meeting to the senior members of the embassy, who listened approvingly – apart from Michael Butler, who remarked rather icily, 'He did say *no power on earth* could prevent it, didn't he?'

George Ball had also flown into Paris to see if he could help in any way, and we had arranged to meet at his hotel at seven o'clock after he too had discussed the situation with Couve de Murville. I went up to his hotel room, where we exchanged our experiences. It then emerged that Couve had expressed the same sentiments to George Ball. We decided that there was really nothing more for us to work on that evening, so we cancelled our dinner. George Ball flew off to Bonn to stay with his ambassador there, and I returned to London feeling rather satisfied.

When the Brussels negotiations reopened on Monday 14 January, we were all very optimistic, and an official English translation of the Treaty was arranged. Couve de Murville, however, was not present and we were told he had to be present at de Gaulle's press conference. I suggested that we should continue as usual and that, when Couve arrived, he could take over the reins. I concluded the meeting in an upbeat mood, even stating: 'We all seem to be in complete agreement.'

Immediately afterwards we were told what de Gaulle had said at his press conference. He had claimed that the negotiations had shown that Britain could not accept and accommodate the ways of the Six, and criticised Britain's unwillingness to give up its 'special political and military relations' with the Americans. He had also warned that, in the event of British accession, 'the cohesion of all these numerous and very differing states would not last long and what would emerge in the end would be a colossal Atlantic Community, dependent on America and directed by America.' Henry Kissinger wrote two years later that 'if Britain overestimated its special ties with the US, de Gaulle took them at face value . . . Britain's special relationship with the US in the nuclear field could have two meanings: it was either a challenge to de Gaulle's contention that a united Europe required its own defence; or else it seemed designed to assure Britain a pre-eminent place in a united Europe . . . neither contingency was attractive to de Gaulle.' Another popular view was that after the legacy of centuries of rivalry and bitterness between the French and the English, the French government just could not resist thwarting Britain when it was on the edge of triumphant entry to the European family, poised to come in with a great fanfare.

We were all astonished, and everyone at home assumed that this was the end of the story, for the time being at least. We had all underestimated the extent to which de Gaulle would be prepared to pit his judgement and his policies against the rest. The obvious question, therefore, was whether we should stop there and then. On balance, we decided to proceed and finish the negotiations. Couve de Murville was not present but Edgar Pisani, the French Agriculture Minister, attended. He did not obstruct, but reserved the French position on each item. Adenauer was going to meet de Gaulle in the middle of the following week, and the two German Ministers present, Ludwig Erhard and Gerhard Schroeder, agreed that they would attempt to persuade Adenauer to convince the French President that he was wrong. So we soldiered on.

During the two days after de Gaulle's intervention, we began to break the deadlock over tariffs and agriculture. At the ministerial session in Brussels on 10–12 December it had been agreed that a 'fact-finding' committee of Ministers of Agriculture, the Mansholt Committee, would be established to examine all of the remaining problems on agriculture. The final text of the Committee's report was made available just before the ministerial meeting on 14 January. On the 15th, in light of the explanations which were given to us about the difficulties for the Community of a transitional period going beyond 1970, I stated that, so long as we could reach agreement on reasonable transitional arrangements, it might be possible for us to accept that the transitional period should end by that date. This statement was warmly welcomed by several of my colleagues as a major contribution towards agreement.

On Wednesday the 16th, however, Couve de Murville arrived at the hotel in Brussels and became very agitated when he found discussions still progressing. He joined us all for drinks before our customary dinner and at one point turned to Josef Luns and exploded: 'Oh, you Dutch, you have always been the lackeys of the English.' 'Yes,' replied Luns. 'Yes, I suppose you could say that, in the sense that you could talk of you French as always having been the raw material of their victories.'

Informal discussions about the situation took up much of the following morning. I saw Monnet, Hallstein (the Commission President) and then Spaak and Fayat together. Monnet did not believe that de Gaulle would withdraw the French delegation if the Five insisted on continuing the negotiations. Spaak, however, was more robust. He was deeply offended by the dictatorial manner of de Gaulle's press conference and thought that the Five should take a very robust line with Couve during a special meeting of the Six that afternoon. I emphasised to him that, if the negotiations were to break down or to be adjourned *sine die*, it should emerge clearly that it was the French alone who were responsible. In that event, relations with the French would inevitably be damaged; but those among the Five would not.

Later, on my way to keep an appointment with Schroeder, I was intercepted and asked to meet Spaak again most urgently. He had just completed talks with Couve de Murville at which he had gained the impression that, in the face of a common stand by the Five, the French were extremely reluctant to take responsibility for breaking up the conference. While Couve had not disguised the fact that de Gaulle wanted to bring the present negotiations to an immediate stop, he appeared to be unsure exactly how to achieve this objective. Against this background Spaak, Fayat, Luns and Colombo had come to the conclusion that it might be a positive move to establish a Committee of Seven, comprising the Six plus the Commission. This would take stock of the provisional agreements reached so far and perhaps make proposals on outstanding problems. Spaak wanted to be sure that I had no objection. He pointed out that their proposal would have the great advantage that matters would be discussed *à sept*. While I could well see the advantages of the plan, I reflected that it might be a waste of time if at the end the French imposed a veto. Spaak appreciated this but assured me that it would be implicit in the setting up of the committee that it was designed to lead to an ultimate solution which would be acceptable to all concerned.

I then went to see Schroeder. He confirmed that Adenauer was troubled by the line taken by de Gaulle at his press conference, coming as it did just before his visit to Paris. Schroeder himself felt that it was intolerable for Germany, which attached importance to its friendships with both France and Great Britain, to be placed in such an awkward position. He assured me that there was no question of the German delegation agreeing to any French proposal for an adjournment which would be equivalent to a break, although he shared my doubts whether the proposal for a committee *à sept* could succeed.

The Six met that afternoon for three and a half hours. When the meeting adjourned so that Couve might 'reflect' on what had been discussed, Fayat gave Christopher Soames and me an account of the discussion thus far. Couve had argued that there was no point in continuing the negotiations, as Britain was not at present fitted to accept the Treaty of Rome and its underlying principles. He mentioned the possibility of association as an alternative arrangement, an obvious red herring. The Five, as promised, spoke strongly against suspension of the negotiations. The President of the Commission, Walter Hallstein, had been allowed to sit in the meeting at Couve's suggestion, and pointed out that it was untrue to suggest that the possibility of finding technical solutions had been exhausted. His intervention was a blow to the French and greatly encouraged the Five.

However, the proposal for a committee *à sept* had undergone some modification. Couve would accept this only if it was clearly understood that it did not constitute a continuance of the negotiations. At that point the Six had adjourned. Fayat pressed me hard to accept some 'neutral' formula which would fluff the question of whether negotiations were continuing. My immediate reaction, however, was one of great scepticism. I wanted nothing to do with any procedure which might enable the French to obscure their complete responsibility for breaking off the negotiations. This was fully justified when, after the meeting had reconvened, Couve refused once again to accept any deal which suggested that the negotiations were progressing. The plan was shelved.

At 5 p.m., the meeting of the Six broke up and I was briefed once again by Fayat. It had been decided that, after the imminent meeting of Ministers of the Seven, he would, subject to our agreement, make a statement to the press, the text of which would be approved in advance by all concerned. It was the most that the Six could agree and I reluctantly gave my own approval to the text. It read:

> The French delegation has requested that the negotiations with Great Britain should be suspended. The Five other delegations of the EEC and the British delegation have opposed this. Discussion of this question will be continued in the course of the next session of the conference which has been set for January 28, 1963.

We then went straight into a meeting *à sept* which confirmed the statement. As we left at the end of our talks, the British contingent passed each delegation, with the single exception of the French. Each Minister rose to shake hands warmly with us. It was a moving moment. The negotiations were then adjourned for two weeks, and the Five and ourselves spent the next fortnight trying to persuade the French to relent, albeit in an increasingly forlorn fashion. Our only hope was that Adenauer would persuade de Gaulle that his decision would imperil the Franco-German relationship. This in turn depended on the German Chancellor's judgement of the strength of hostility in Germany, and within other member states, to de Gaulle's veto. Reaction among the Five was justifiably fierce and our ambassadors were instructed to seize 'any opportunity available of discreetly sustaining and stiffening the reaction of press and public opinion'. Attempts to get Adenauer to intercede on our behalf and encourage de Gaulle to back down ultimately proved to be in vain. Instead of putting pressure on de Gaulle to reverse the veto, Adenauer signed a Franco-German treaty during his stay in Paris from 20 to 23 January, providing for enhanced bilateral foreign policy and defence co-operation. I was not at all surprised. During the negotiations, he had maintained his basic priority of strengthening the Franco-German entente, and opted not to stand up to de Gaulle in our interests. There was some hope, however, when de Gaulle conceded that the Commission might be asked to examine all the issues surrounding enlargement in a written report.

I returned to Brussels on the evening of 27 January, fearing the worst. There was solid support for the principle of a report by the Commission, although differences remained on the period required for such a step. The next day I had meetings with Spaak and Fayat, who had agreed with the Italians that all issues examined by the Commission should be precisely defined in terms of the items still pending in the negotiation and that a short time should be allowed for the completion of the report. The Belgians thought not more than two weeks; the Italians were prepared to contemplate a month. Spaak suspected that the French would attempt to widen the scope of the mandate so as to argue for a longer delay, of approximately six months. He also announced that, if the French refused their plan, he would be prepared to ask the Five to proceed without them. Spaak believed that this would demonstrate not only that the Five wanted us in on political and economic grounds, but that practical arrangements to this end had been worked out.

The decisive attitude, however, remained that of the Germans. Later that day I dined with Erhard. He was obviously angry and did not mince his words. His personal view was that the Franco-German agreement in present circumstances was valueless and he clearly indicated that he did not want to see it ratified by the Bundestag. As regards the mandate to be given to the Commission, he took exactly the same line as Spaak, although he was just as pessimistic about the French response. Erhard also voiced his doubts on how the Community could proceed in the event of a breakdown. The Germans had made sacrifices throughout the course of the negotiations to the French, especially in agriculture and concerning the Overseas Development Fund, and he did not see how they could possibly be asked to continue making the sort of continuing concessions that would be required if the French continued to behave in such an autocratic fashion.

Subsequently, accompanied by Eric Roll, I called on Hallstein. The President of the Commission was greatly handicapped by a streaming cold but seemed on the whole to be more robust than we expected. He said that, so far as the mandate to the Commission was concerned, the formal and unanimous view of the Commission was that they could not lend themselves to providing a 'façade' and a 'burial service'. They would be prepared to accept a mandate, provided it included proposals for resolving the outstanding problems.

I was buoyed by his attitude and left to meet Schroeder, whose arrival had been delayed by fog. His talks with de Gaulle had left him with the impression that the French would do anything necessary to keep us out at this juncture. They wanted three or four years in order to build up their industry and agriculture, develop their atomic weapons and consolidate the Community and its institutions. Then the French might be prepared to reconsider. Schroeder kept on reverting to the question of the length of time that would be needed for the Commission to prepare a report. If the French were given a breathing space, the German government would be able to say that it had done its best to save French face. I continued to take the line that the fundamental question was whether the French were prepared genuinely to continue the negotiations or not. Even if they accepted that the Commission should produce compromise solutions, people were bound to ask whether, at the end of the exercise, the General would not again exercise a political veto. I also stressed that the paramount importance of the political arguments must not mean that the Commission simply put terms which did not give us a fair deal. Our conversation was brought to an end as Schroeder had an appointment to see Couve. I left with the impression that Schroeder was not likely to be bamboozled by the French, although I was despondent about the forthcoming meeting of the Six.

In the event, this meeting was delayed for nearly two hours as talks between Couve and Schroeder progressed without reaching a breakthrough. Afterwards the situation changed from hour to hour and my spirits rose and fell accordingly. Couve's behaviour roused the Five to new levels of anger, although I did not think that they would have the stomach for the idea of carrying things to the point of breaking up the Community, after all an outcome that none of us wanted. The lunch interval failed to produce an agreement and we were invited to a meeting that afternoon. Fayat, who had taken the chair for the meeting, announced that the Six had been unable to continue the negotiations and declared 'the seventeenth ministerial meeting concluded'. He then asked whether any delegations wished to comment. Spaak opened with eloquence and deep emotion, arguing that it was a day of defeat for Europe: 'If the Rome Treaty does not explode, the Community spirit has been gravely, perhaps mortally wounded.' He ended with an expression of his profound regret and a strong protest to Couve. He was followed by Luns and Schroeder, who indicated their own great disappointment. It was then the turn of Couve de Murville. In an extremely dry, matter-of-fact and short statement, he admitted that this was a grave crisis on a serious question. The French had not changed their minds and he summarised his argument with the statement: 'We want to make a European Europe!'

Directly after the Ministers and the President of the Commission had declared their regrets, I made my concluding speech. I spoke of the high hopes with which we had all set out on the negotiations and the sincerity and wholeheartedness with which we had approached them. I also emphasised that, in my opening statement in Paris, Britain had accepted the Treaty of Rome and the structure of the Community as it had developed since the Treaty had been signed. We accepted without qualification the objectives of the Treaty, including the elimination of internal tariffs, a common customs tariff, a common commercial policy and a common agricultural policy. After destroying Couve's points one by one, I said that the real reason for the veto was clear: President de Gaulle feared that the negotiations were about to succeed. The French explanation for the veto was simply an *ex post facto* rationalisation. It could not be reconciled either with the spirit of the Treaty or with what the French had said before the negotiations commenced. I ended with a promise to my colleagues and, indeed, to all the people of Europe. The last sentence has been often and widely repeated. My mandate was such that I did not consult the Prime Minister or the Cabinet before I made it:

> The end of the negotiations is a blow to the cause of the wider European unity for which we have been striving. We are a part of Europe, by geography, history, culture, tradition and civilization ... There have been times in the history of Europe when it has been only too plain how European we are; and there have been many millions of people who have been grateful for it. I say to my colleagues: they should have no fear. We in Britain are not going to turn our backs on the mainland of Europe or the countries of the Community.

Everyone was deeply depressed at the outcome, and worried about the future. After the meeting, I went round and thanked Ministers and officials from the Five and the Commission, who in turn expressed their regret and their appreciation of what I had said. Couve and Wormser, however, went to a corner and turned their backs on me. I was shocked by Couve's attitude. It seemed to me that, ever since our talk at the embassy in Paris, when he had said that 'no power on earth' could prevent the negotiations from succeeding, he had gone out of his way to avoid any sort of contact with me. This was presumably because he felt embarrassed about the contrast between what he had told me at that meeting and what the General had said at his press conference shortly afterwards, and, to his credit, Couve later admitted that the veto was 'une sorte de trahison' – a kind of betrayal. I am sure that he had no idea about the contents of the Monday press conference when he met me in the British embassy on the previous Friday. Eric Roll has also recorded how Olivier Wormser told him that 'You don't know how close to success you were'. Indeed, as we left our office late that Monday after de Gaulle's press conference, we saw Olivier Wormser, walking up and down the corridor. As the lights were all down, he failed to notice us. As we came along we heard him say: 'If only he'd told me about it beforehand I could have done it so much better.' This made it plain to us that he, too, had been kept in the dark about de Gaulle's intentions. I never had any personal quarrel with Couve de Murville, but the positions of our countries made it impossible for us to maintain our hitherto reasonably cordial personal relationship for some time.

We had built up an immense amount of goodwill among the Five and I was not willing to let it go to waste. Directly after the meeting on 29 January the Five and I had further private talks. There was some discussion of a proposal that the Community should be reformed with fresh treaties between the Five and the British enabling us to go on working together, but it rapidly became clear that this would not be a practical proposition and so we quietly and sadly dispersed.

In February 1963 it was calculated that during eighteen months of negotiations I had made twenty-seven visits to Brussels, eleven to Paris and twenty-seven to other countries, covering a total of 50,000 miles in all. It had all proved to be of no avail. I was touched when, as I entered the final press conference, members of the press stood and applauded appreciatively. The only unpleasant moment came when Jock Bruce-Gardyne, then a journalist from the *Statist* magazine and later a Conservative MP and Minister in Mrs Thatcher's administration, asked me sarcastically what I was going to make a mess of next. The chorus of boos that greeted this comment was a far better answer to his question than I could manage. I made a full statement to the House of Commons the next day and there, too, I found much warm appreciation of what we had done. The letters poured in, not only from those who had taken part in the negotiations, but from others all over the world. Perhaps the most moving came from the Indian ambassador to the Community, who wrote, 'When the British left India, many people wept. When you leave Europe tonight, many people will weep. You are the only people in the world of whom these things could be said.' It was a very emotional time for us all.

On 28 January 1963 Macmillan wrote in his diary: 'All our policies at home and abroad are in ruins. Our defence plans have been radically changed, from air to sea. European unity is no more; French domination of Europe is the new and alarming feature; our popularity as a Government is rapidly declining. We have lost everything, except our courage and determination.' A few weeks later he would add:

> However bitter our feelings might be, we must not allow ourselves to be misled into statements which would endanger the future. Meanwhile, I was particularly sorry for Heath. No one could have been a better

negotiator and ambassador – but French duplicity has defeated us all
. . . At home, there is the return of the old feeling 'the French always
betray you in the end'. There is *great* and *grievous* disappointment (among
the younger people especially) at the end of a fine vision.

It was essential that Britain should maintain its constructive engagement
with, and influence in, Europe despite de Gaulle's veto. I therefore resolved
to do all that I could to prevent a xenophobic reaction back home, as
inevitably there were recriminations to follow. Shortly after the veto, the
England rugby team were playing the French at Twickenham, where I
usually attended international games. This time, however, I rang up Wavell
Wakefield, an internationally famed rugby figure and a former MP who
was normally my host, and asked to be excused. He told me not to worry,
for the French ambassador, Baron Geoffroy de Courcel, a former *chef de
cabinet* to de Gaulle who had taken over as ambassador from Jean Chauvel
in March 1962, had refused his invitation. He finally managed to persuade
me, and on Saturday I climbed the stairs to a small committee room where
they always had a buffet lunch. Opening the door into the salon, I walked
straight into the French ambassador. We politely bowed to each other and
went on. Before the start of the game we were all astonished to see a
stream of banners being carried around the ground, the last an enormous
one carried by six young men on three strong sticks. Each banner was
urging the British to beat the French. It gave me particularly great pleasure
when we won that game by six points to five, significant figures in our
recent negotiations.

At dinner that night, I turned to the English captain, who was still at
Oxford, and congratulated him on a great victory. 'I got the team around
me before the game and told them that this was an all-important game.
Everyone knew what I meant and they produced the necessary,' he replied.
Later on, the president proposed a toast to 'The Queen'. Then, looking
at his menu, he saw that the next toast was 'President de Gaulle'. Dropping
his menu on the table, he announced to the assembled teams and their
supporters, 'The President of France.' He then turned to me and explained,
while the microphones were still turned on, 'I wasn't going to mention
that bastard's name.' Feelings were certainly running high. It was because
of this that Princess Margaret's visit to Paris, which was due to follow
almost immediately, was cancelled. Looking back I have come to the
conclusion that this was probably a mistake. We gained nothing diplomatically by allowing an important international visit by a very senior
member of the royal family to be overshadowed, and indeed destroyed,
by an entirely unrelated negotiation.

Later that spring, I was rewarded with the Charlemagne Prize by the city of Aachen for 'encouraging international understanding and co-operation in the European sphere'. This was an especially prestigious honour, for the only Briton to have received it before me was Churchill, in 1956. With the £450 prize, I bought myself a Steinway grand piano. This piano had originally been built in 1922, and Steinway's had recently renovated it. Like wines, pianos have good and bad years, so I asked Moura Lympany, the distinguished concert pianist and a dear friend, to help me choose one. We toured the piano stores of London together, she playing to demonstrate every aspect of each instrument's capabilities to me. This was the first time I had a piano of my own, and Moura and I whiled away many happy hours together playing it at my Albany flat. All subsequent prizes that I have received have gone to charitable causes. I also received a warm letter of congratulations from Winston Churchill himself, who wrote: 'Permit me . . . to congratulate you on winning the Charlemagne Prize. Certainly your efforts for the unity of Europe have been on the highest scale, and I cannot think of anyone who deserves it more.'

I received the prize in Aachen on Ascension Day 1963. The whole event reminded me of my time travelling through the city as a student. I had never imagined that one day I might return there to extol the virtues of European unity, in the wake of another temporary setback. On receipt of the prize I remarked that, although the negotiations had failed to produce British membership, they had succeeded from a much wider perspective: 'I believe that the Community now has a better understanding of itself and the importance of its relations with the outside world.'

There were three further achievements arising out of the 1961–3 negotiations. Immediately after the veto, I decided that the delegation should remain in being for the weeks necessary to write a narrative report and analysis of the negotiations. This document proved very important. It contains a full and completely frank account of the development of our negotiating position and the considerations, whether technical or tactical, or of a personal character, that had influenced the course of events. It kept memories of those concerned in Whitehall fresh and, in 1967, when Harold Wilson launched his abortive preparations for new negotiations, it was taken as the starting point of the entire briefing operation. The outcome of the 1970–1 negotiations was also very heavily based on the position reached eight years earlier in Brussels. An even greater achievement, however, was that the methodology for the enlargement negotiations established in 1961–3 is one that has been followed in every enlargement negotiation since then, and is likely to be followed in future.

Buoyed by the support of the Five, I was determined to maintain links with the French. As I was preparing for my holiday in the South of France in the summer of 1963, I recalled that Couve de Murville had his country home at Saint-Raphaël, not far from where I would be staying, and I asked Baron de Courcel, the French ambassador, whether it might not be possible for the two of us to meet. He came back with an invitation from Couve for me to go over there for the day. We spent the time before and after lunch sitting by the swimming pool talking, in between bathing, about the future. After that sunny day we resumed our usual relationship, which I have maintained ever since.

I also remained in contact with Jean Chauvel after he had left his position as French ambassador to Britain. We usually had a meal together on my visits to Paris. After one excellent dinner in a restaurant overlooking the Seine, we sat silently sipping our cognac. His head was bowed and he began muttering to himself: 'Such a pity! Oh such a pity! Such a pity that Macmillan went to sleep when de Gaulle was talking to him after lunch at Rambouillet. It all might have been so different.' This certainly put a new spin on events!

I next met de Gaulle at the Elysée in 1965, after I had been elected Leader of the Opposition. I wanted to make it absolutely clear that my position, and that of the Conservative Party, had in no way altered since we entered into the negotiations in 1961. Rumour had it that he had been irritated by a speech I had made at Hamburg two years before, one of three speeches in Europe explaining what had really happened in Brussels. Referring to the arguments used by him at his press conference in Paris at which he vetoed our entry into the European Community I described them as 'cris de perroquet', by which I meant repeated parrot cries about the English being a maritime nation, unsuited to join a continental community. Apparently, he thought I was making a reference to the shape of his nose. I sent an explanation to him at the Elysée. We had a long discussion in his magnificent study with only an interpreter in attendance. His presence was still amazing, his manner was friendly though formal, and he spoke very freely on the need for European unity.

Jean Monnet said to me on one occasion, 'If you want to understand what is in de Gaulle's mind you must realise that, on every count, he asks himself what the historians fifty years hence will think about him when they look back at what he did and said.' That may well have been an accurate insight into de Gaulle's mind, but I have to say that his foresight often let him down very badly, especially in foreign affairs. His relations with the United States were always strained and his attempt to detach Quebec from the Canadian Federation not only led to him abandoning a tour of Canada, it soured French–Canadian relations for many years. He never succeeded in exerting effective French influence in Latin America, nor in re-establishing France's position in South-East Asia. What he did achieve was to withdraw France from Algeria and, at the same time, to restore the self-confidence of the French people, while preparing the way for their future progress. De Gaulle also succeeded in the short term in excluding the British from Europe, but the negotiations spelt the end of his ambition of turning the Community into a group that was protectionist, introspective and detached from the Atlantic alliance.

At the end of our talk in 1965, de Gaulle told me, 'If you become Prime Minister, you will be the man who will lead Britain into the European Community.' We continued to keep in touch and, two days after he died, I received a copy of the last volume of his autobiography, which he had inscribed warmly. It must have been among the last things he signed.

Chapter 9

~~~~~

CLIMBING THE LADDER
Front-bench Duties 1960–1965

Although the negotiations with the Six occupied the lion's share of my time as Lord Privy Seal, the other responsibilities of the job were many and diverse. One of them was to be a Trustee of the British Museum. My secretary informed me that a general meeting of the Trustees was to be held on Saturday 13 May 1961 at 12.00 noon. The *Evening Standard* had got wind of this meeting and asked whether or not I was going to be there. I suspected that this was an attempt by the *Standard* to prove that I was neglecting my constitutional responsibilities in favour of Europe. I therefore decided that I would attend, tiresome as it was to be in London at midday on a Saturday.

My car dropped me at the entrance to the museum and I asked an attendant the way to the meeting. He had no idea. I wandered down a corridor and asked the next person on duty. He had no idea either, but pointed the way to the only room where he thought it could be held. Having reached that point, I found one other fellow sitting at a round table. It was 11.55 a.m. I mentioned to him that we looked a bit thin on the ground for a meeting at noon. 'Oh no,' he said, 'the Trustees are already meeting.' As he spoke the large doors were suddenly opened and another attendant let us in. Sitting around an enormous table laden with exhibits of every kind were a dozen trustees. In the chair was the Marquess of Cambridge, an elderly figure who beckoned me to the chair on his right-hand side.

The Marquess called on the Secretary to read the agenda. 'The minutes of the last meeting –' he began. 'They've been confirmed,' interrupted the Marquess. 'Go on.' 'The election of the Standing Committee for next year —' announced the Secretary. 'They have already been re-elected. Go on.' 'The estimates for 1961–2—' 'They've been settled,' interjected the Marquess. 'Now we can get down to business.' The whole procedure had taken just three minutes. The Marquess then turned to me and said,

'If you would like to stay for the rest of the Standing Committee meeting, please feel free to do so. After the meeting we will have a spot of lunch. Now, Item 176.' I was astonished.

The rest of the time I spent looking at the impressive crowd around the table. I then saw the long list of regrets for absence from the meeting on the table in front of the Marquess. Among the twenty-one distinguished absentees were the Archbishop of Canterbury, the Lord Chancellor, the Speaker, the Chancellor of the Exchequer, the Master of the Rolls and the Attorney-General. I wondered what difference it would have made if the Lord Privy Seal had been included in this list. Soon after 1.00 p.m., however, we went to lunch. As the museum dining room was being redecorated, we were taken outside the building and made to 'walk the plank' into a wooden hut where we were offered very thick ham sandwiches and rather cool coffee. Some time later Henry Brooke, who was the Treasury Minister responsible for the British Museum, enquired about my experience as Trustee. After I told him about it, in excruciating detail, he promised to reform the control and management of the institution. I never had the opportunity of going again.

In the 1960s, the Foreign Office was still organising regional meetings of its diplomatic staff, a process which has now been abandoned, in my view a loss to everyone concerned. In January 1961, I went to such a conference in Singapore, attended by our diplomats in Asia, from Korea round to Singapore and up to Afghanistan, including Japan, Indonesia, India and Pakistan, as well as all the others in between. The ten-day discussions were most stimulating. I stayed with the high commissioner, the Earl of Selkirk, who asked me to do him a favour. Lee Kuan Yew, who had recently become Prime Minister of Singapore on its independence, had so far avoided any social contact with him. Now he wanted to use my presence as an excuse for inviting the Prime Minister and his wife to dinner one night. I readily agreed. They both came, we sat down, only five to dinner, and everything went happily. Since then, I have met Harry Lee on many occasions and, although our political labels differ and his sympathies in our country extend towards the Labour Party, his socialism contains a very large measure of privatisation and individualism and, although extensive social services exist in Singapore, considerable personal effort is always necessary on the part of any individual to meet the requirements of the authorities.

Whenever I have visited Singapore, except for the 1971 Commonwealth Conference, Harry Lee has generously settled me in his personal guesthouse, and extended his hospitality to me. His dinners are marked by an invitation card and a menu with 'Smoking is not permitted' heavily printed at the top. Dining with the Lee family one time outside in his garden, I was alarmed when the butler came up to Sir Timothy Kitson, my parliamentary private secretary, and handed him a note. After reading it, Tim apologised to the Prime Minister and asked to be excused while he made a telephone call to London. He returned after some twenty minutes, but half an hour later the same thing happened. Again Tim came back without a word of explanation. When we got up after dinner, I quietly went up to him and said, 'Tim, what was all that about? Is something wrong? What is happening in London?' 'I didn't worry you because everything is perfectly all right,' he replied. 'I just had to have a smoke!'

On another occasion, Harry apologised for moving the family dinner to one of the finest hotels in Singapore, because his own home was being redecorated. I was met by a secretary who accompanied me in the lift. As we went up, he told me that he ought to warn me that the Prime Minister would probably want to discuss his 'population policy'. 'I shall be most interested,' I replied. Sure enough, after a lively dinner, Harry said, 'Now I want to explain to you my new population policy, which is most important for the future of the Island. I am using our taxation policy as an instrument for raising the intellectual standard of our people. If a man with first-class honours marries a girl with first-class honours, they will have children who will get first-class honours. To encourage this, they will pay a reduced rate of taxation. If a man or a woman marry, and only one of them has first-class honours, they will pay the normal rate of taxation. If two people without an honours degree marry, the children will not be clever and they will all pay a higher rate of tax. That will encourage them to perform better.' I remarked that I found this a completely novel approach, and I would be interested to see the results. Although I thought better of mentioning the fact, I was aware that both Harry and his wife possessed double first-class degrees, and his son and daughter first-class degrees too. On the way back in the lift, I confirmed to the secretary that the Prime Minister had expounded his new population policy to me. 'Princess Anne was here recently,' he said, 'and he did the same to her. She listened carefully. Then, after a short pause, she commented, "All I can say, Prime Minister, is that it doesn't work with horses!"'

One man who has always understood the intricacies of the oriental mind is Henry Kissinger. My first encounter with Henry took place at Chequers in August 1962. I was on holiday at home at Broadstairs when Macmillan asked me to go up to Chequers for lunch, some four hours' journey by car. I asked him whether there was any particular reason. He replied that Nelson and Happy Rockefeller were passing through London and had asked to talk to him. At Chequers, I found that Julian Amery had been invited as well. It turned out that Nelson Rockefeller was making a European tour before the next American presidential election, for which he hoped to be the Republican candidate. So he was meeting most of the heads of government and discussing international problems with them. 'I really want to meet Happy,' said the Prime Minister. 'You two can do the rest of the talking!'

We arrived at the front door in time to see a long, low, black Cadillac pull round the drive and stop in front of the house. A security man opened the car door and Rockefeller leaped out, shook the Prime Minister's hand most vigorously and then introduced himself to us. Meanwhile, Harold Macmillan was peering into the car in search of Happy Rockefeller. 'Where is your wife?' he demanded. 'Oh, she decided to go shopping in Bond Street,' replied Nelson, to the obvious dismay of the Prime Minister. At this point, a bespectacled, stocky man emerged from the other side of the Cadillac. 'But I have brought my adviser, Henry Kissinger, with me,' announced our guest. The Prime Minister was not impressed.

Over lunch, Rockefeller continually tried to bring the conversation round to Macmillan's own views and policies, but failed completely in the attempt, as the Prime Minister skilfully got him to give a detailed description of his European tour, including a blow-by-blow account of his talks with other heads of government. Towards the end of lunch, Harold Macmillan suggested to Nelson Rockefeller that he ought to write a book about his European tour and thereupon, in his capacity as a publisher, embarked upon a detailed account of how he ought to go about it. The Prime Minister was playing games, which he always did so very successfully. Julian Amery and Kissinger were meanwhile having an argument about the role of the superpowers, which got rougher and rougher. It was brought to an end by the Prime Minister finishing lunch and leading his guests to the front door. A rather crestfallen-looking Nelson Rockefeller got into his car as Henry Kissinger nipped round to the other side. 'And don't forget to write the book,' said Macmillan as he waved goodbye. Then he turned to me and remarked, 'After all, he ought to have known that I am Jack Kennedy's man.'

Nelson Rockefeller never became President, perhaps one of the best men who never occupied that position, but Henry Kissinger went on to become one of the most powerful Secretaries of State. His success was based on his remarkable ability to analyse an international situation according to principles which he believed history had shown to be sound, while being always prepared as a negotiator to make sensible compromises. This was backed up by a limitless capacity for hard work and an imperviousness to the strains of travel and long hours of negotiation. He also has, when on his own, a disarming way of handling people and a delightful, if somewhat unoriginal, sense of humour.

*   *   *

When I returned home from the negotiations in Brussels on 30 January 1963, it marked the beginning of one of the most frustrating periods of my career. I was not held responsible for the failure of the government's European policy. On the contrary. The press and most of my Cabinet colleagues praised my efforts over the previous two and a half years and at a Conservative Central Council meeting on 8 March 1963, when doubts were expressed about Macmillan's leadership, I was mentioned publicly for the first time as a possible successor to him. This was all very flattering, but the fact remained: we were still outside the Community.

In the wake of President de Gaulle's veto, I rather hoped that Macmillan might find me another job. Perhaps, after the events of the previous summer, the Prime Minister was reluctant to have another early reshuffle. The 'Night of the Long Knives', Friday 13 July 1962, had been as big a shock to me as it was to the outside world. I was heavily preoccupied with the European negotiations at the time and I had received no hint of what was in the air. Although I had told Martin Redmayne when he took over from me as Chief Whip that I would always be available if he wanted to contact me on any matter, he never did. Harold Macmillan intended his reshuffle of senior ministers to revitalise the party's position in the country as well as boosting his own personal standing. When he made his manifold changes, it came not only as a surprise to the party and the outside world, but it also created intense ill-feeling. David Kilmuir, the outgoing Lord Chancellor, was one of the most even-tempered and mild of men, but even he was infuriated and, like several others, never forgave Macmillan. It was perfectly sensible that I should remain as Lord Privy Seal to continue with the European negotiations and Reggie Maudling's appointment as Chancellor showed quite clearly that occupying that position was one ambition I was unlikely to fulfil before the next general election.

Macmillan's plans to boost the government's popularity were dealt another severe blow the following year, as the position of his Secretary of State for War, Jack Profumo came under fierce media scrutiny. I had always found Jack and his wife, Valerie Hobson, excellent company although I knew very little about his private life. It was alleged that Christine Keeler was involved in intimate relationships with both Profumo and the Naval Attaché at the Soviet Embassy, Captain Ivanov. When it became known to the Whips on the evening of 21 March 1963 that the Labour MP George Wigg was about to raise this matter in the House, Iain Macleod as Leader of the House and the Chief Whip decided that they must act at once. They called in the Attorney General for a meeting at the House late at night and sent for Profumo. He was already in bed asleep after taking sleeping pills. He went along to the meeting, obviously in a drowsy state, and accepted that, if Wigg raised the matter, he would make a statement denying the accusation. It was this denial which later led to him having to leave the House of Commons.

In my view, if Jack had acknowledged his relationship with Keeler to the House from the beginning, it could have been treated as a private matter for him to sort out. But the fact that Jack was in the War Department, and Keeler was also involved with Ivanov, inevitably raised questions about security. In his subsequent inquiry, Lord Denning found that there was in no way any breach of security by Profumo. Jack has since organised his life outside politics in a way which has been of enormous benefit to the community, a fact which was recognised by his CBE in 1975. Jack and Valerie have withstood together all the personal trials and the intense publicity from the media and I am glad to have them as my friends. Although Macmillan clearly found it difficult to handle a situation in which one of his colleagues had lied not only to himself but also to the House of Commons, I do not share the views of those who claim that it was this incident which was primarily responsible for undermining Macmillan's position as Prime Minister or losing us the general election some eighteen months later. The picture is more complicated than that.

In my view, Jack Profumo never represented any serious security risk, but others at that time certainly did. In July 1963, I announced to the House that Kim Philby was the 'Third Man' who had been passing secrets to the Russians for much of the 1950s, and who had helped the other two spies, Burgess and Maclean, escape to Moscow in 1951. The Philby disclosure followed a series of security scandals, including those involving George Blake and William Vassall. It seemed incredible to me that these men could have gone undetected for so long. The whole issue was a severe embarrassment, not least with the Americans, just as we were trying to convince them that we were still a serious power on which they could rely.

In June 1963, Macmillan chose Quintin Hailsham to go to Moscow to begin discussions with the Soviet Union and the USA on a treaty to ban the testing of nuclear weapons in the air and on land. At the beginning of August, I accompanied Alec Home to Moscow for the signing of the Treaty. The Soviet government, no doubt mindful of the opportunity for a public relations coup, certainly made us welcome. The conclusion of the Test Ban Treaty marked a tremendous breakthrough and the Kremlin was determined to make the most of it. No lapse of protocol or shortcoming in their hospitality would be allowed to distract the world's attention. We stayed at the British embassy, which overlooks the Kremlin, and was said to command the best view of its spires and golden domes. The talks between ourselves and the Russians on a range of issues, and the continual co-ordination of our policies with the American delegation led by Dean Rusk, involved us in long hours of arduous work. I particularly lamented having to spend one complete afternoon waiting for replies from London, while others from our delegation were shown the priceless treasures of the Tsars in the vaults of the Kremlin.

In the Pushkin Museum, however, I did manage to see a fantastic group of French Impressionist paintings, including some of the finest works by Monet, Cézanne and Gauguin. Though these works were well protected, they were displayed dismally badly. It seemed that, so incredible was the collection of masterpieces which the Soviet authorities possessed, they could not care less about how to select them, or how to set them out to their best effect. Once again, I regretted that it was the Russians and the Americans who, in the early years of the century, first recognized the importance of the Impressionists, bought them cheaply and took them back to their own countries.

Naturally, Red Square and Lenin's tomb were a 'must', and I enjoyed a gala night at the opera one evening. What interested me most of all, however, was how the people of Moscow lived their lives. As I wandered across Red Square, which seems so impressive when filled up with a parade, I was able to observe many individual Muscovites at close quarters. I found the absence of colour among the people, the grey uniformity of their garb, almost as depressing as the slow-moving queues in the shops I visited. They were evidently oppressed both by the communist system and by the manifest failure of the grossly inefficient Soviet economy to provide them with consumer goods. So many were still living at subsistence level, intellectually as well as socially and economically.

At one hotel, we soon learned that there was almost no limit to the time it could take between ordering a meal and seeing it produced; nor did the crumbs and coffee stains left by generations of previous diners make an attractive setting. Yet the atmosphere in our group was generally high-spirited, uninhibited even, and we enjoyed many parties and meals together. The badinage and leg-pulling were relentless. Once we had been presented with the customary vodka and caviar by Foreign Minister Andrei Gromyko, there was little else that any of us could find to purchase. On my shopping expedition, however, I did manage to buy several stereo records which were unobtainable at home. We enjoyed a trip up the river on a hydrofoil, a form of transport that the Russians used long before we took advantage of it here in Britain. A drive to the forests outside Moscow gave us a glimpse of the city dwellers relaxing along the river bank and under the trees.

On the last night of the conference, the Soviet leadership gave a party in the Great Hall of the Kremlin for members of all the delegations.

Towards the end, I noticed Khrushchev standing alone, except for his interpreter a couple of paces behind him, and I was struck by how tired and dejected the Soviet leader looked. I went over to him and expressed my hope that he would now get a holiday. 'Yes,' he replied, 'but I shall only get a week on the Black Sea, then I shall have to come back to Moscow for more work.' 'At any rate,' I commented, 'you can go away knowing that the signature of this Test Ban Treaty is a diplomatic triumph for you as well as for the rest of us.' 'It's all right for you,' he answered. 'I know that when Lord Home comes here and signs a treaty, that is that. Under your system it will be ratified. But what about the Americans? Who knows what they will do? Dean Rusk cannot do what Lord Home can do. He even has to be accompanied by a delegation of Senators and Congressmen of both parties watching what he's up to all the time. And what will they say when they get back? And how will Congress vote on this Treaty? I don't know. No one knows.' He looked even more dejected. 'It's very difficult to do business with a system which works like that,' he concluded. 'It's a very unstable system.' What an insight into how one superpower saw another. I tried to reassure him, unsuccessfully.

That week in Moscow, fruitful though it was from a political and diplomatic point of view, ended in cultural disappointment. I had always wanted to see Leningrad and the pictures in the Hermitage. When Madame Furtseva, the Soviet Minister of Culture, had been my guest in London a couple of years before, she had presented me with an album of reproductions of the major masterpieces there. Before leaving for the conference, we had asked for special clearance for our Royal Air Force plane to come down at Leningrad on the way home for a brief stopover; and we had been assured that this would be straightforward. Then, on the eve of our departure, we were informed that clearance would not, after all, be granted. No reason was given. I have since been to that remarkable city – now, of course, re-established as St Petersburg – and commend it to everyone, for its treasures, for its grace and style and for its sense of history, especially its museum of the Second World War.

In the unsettled world of the 1960s, the charismatic President John F. Kennedy appealed to the younger generation and represented a hope for the future much as Anthony Eden had for my generation in the 1930s and 1940s. He also captured the mood of the time with his concern for the less fortunate and those who were still being politically oppressed around the world. Thanks to the development of modern communications, his popularity rapidly became worldwide. He was a commanding and highly respected figure in the developing nations, as well as in the developed world. He had all the advantages of birth and wealth and family connections yet, at the same time, he had a natural affinity with those less privileged individuals who were looking to their leaders for a way out of the impasse of their daily lives.

Harold Macmillan invited me to lunch at his home at Birch Grove on Sunday 29 June 1963 when President Kennedy was on a private one-day visit as part of a trip around Europe. Just a few days earlier, Kennedy had struck a resounding note, not only throughout West Germany, but throughout the Western world, when he had stood on the platform overlooking the Berlin Wall and declared, ignorant of the fact that he was proclaiming himself to be a piece of confectionery, 'Ich bin ein Berliner.' I was among the many millions who were deeply moved by his commitment to freedom, and when I met him I asked him which of his speech writers had produced this line for him. 'No one,' he replied. 'I just felt like that. It came to me on the spur of the moment, as I stood on the Wall.' I asked him what he was going to say in Rome. 'Heaven knows,' he replied. 'I have got to work on that this afternoon as soon as we get on board the plane. I hope that something will come to me.'

After lunch we had a long discussion about the negotiations I had carried out for British accession to the European Community. In July of the previous year, Kennedy had written to Macmillan congratulating him upon 'the bold decision which Her Majesty's Government has taken with respect to the EEC . . . we are wholly with you, as you know, and I admire your courage in moving ahead'. At Birch Grove, he explained his position to me in greater detail. 'I want to see a tall, strong pillar on each side of the Atlantic which can be the basis of the Western alliance,' he declared. 'You have a tall, strong pillar,' I answered, 'but on this side we only have a rather short and wobbly pillar.' 'That,' he declared, 'is why I want to see Britain inside the Community and will do everything in my power to help bring that about.' In fact, he had already been as good as his word, acting discreetly behind the scenes and using George Ball, the Under-Secretary of State, to back me in my efforts.

On 22 November 1963, I was in Liverpool dining with shipowners and merchants of that city. When we came out into the street after dinner, there was the expected long line of cars waiting for us, but no drivers were to be seen. We looked up the road and saw them all together bunched by one of the cars, evidently listening to the radio. As we walked up to them to get their attention, my own driver turned round and sobbed at me, with tears streaming down his cheeks, 'He is dead, he is dead, he is dead.' 'But who?' we asked. 'Kennedy, he has been shot.' Such was the impact of his death on the man in the street. Kennedy may have been more admired outside his own country than he was within it, and nobody can ever say for sure whether he would have been re-elected as President.

For millions of people, however, he represented a spirit of optimism and hope without which their lives seemed less meaningful.

There was not much optimism among Conservatives back home in the autumn of 1963, either. Many of us were by now uncomfortably aware of a distinct feeling of torpor about our party, which had been in power for twelve years. Although the Liberal surge of 1962–3, which had enabled them to capture Orpington with a swing of over 25 per cent, now seemed to have abated, the Labour Party was recovering strongly. In February, after the premature death of Hugh Gaitskell at the age of fifty-six, Harold Wilson had been elected leader. The man who was to be my political sparring partner for the next twelve years was already starting to look a dangerous opponent. Although ostensibly to the left of his party (he had resigned with Bevan over the introduction of NHS charges by the ailing Labour government in 1951) he was clearly a pragmatist above all else. Unlike Gaitskell who, despite his personal warmth and obvious decency, had often given the impression of being a somewhat remote Hampstead intellectual, Wilson had the common touch. Everything from his homely Yorkshire accent to that damned pipe was designed to reassure the voter that the country would be safe in his hands. Moreover, he was clearly adept at using the media to promote this image.

The local elections in May 1963 had brought a terrible result for our party and Macmillan was becoming increasingly weary. As his handling of the Profumo problem had shown, he was also beginning to lose some of the deftness and panache with which he had previously governed. He was by no means as debilitated as Eden had become by January 1957, but he was certainly not the leader who had dazzled me when I was his Chief Whip in the late 1950s.

It was Harold Macmillan who, more than anyone else, had been my political mentor and my patron. Publicly, Harold was always portrayed as imperturbable. Whatever the public image, however, this was certainly not the case in private, for he was a highly sensitive man, and I saw him on many occasions gravely disturbed by individual incidents and seriously worried by the train of events. Harold could also be deeply moved by the warmth of a reception, and horribly hurt by the accidents of politics. He always loved stimulating conversation in the Smoking Room of the House of Commons, or in one of his favourite clubs, but was easily bored by the stupid, the ill-mannered and the self-centred. Communicating through the media did not come easily to him, and it was really only several years after he retired from office that he became completely relaxed in responding to interviewers of all kinds. It was, perhaps, for this reason that he did not have a general appeal to young people in the country, although he always tried hard to encourage young members of our party, especially in the House of Commons. Many of my generation spoke of innumerable kindnesses from him. Today, those who expect to be in office within a year or two of their election, and certainly within their first parliament, would do well to remember that Harold Macmillan was on the backbenches for sixteen years before being given an opportunity in government.

In his sixties, Harold laboured under the belief that he was probably going to die at any moment. Ten days after the European negotiations were suspended in 1963, he and I were due to pay a visit to Rome. This was intended to be a celebration of our entry into the European Community. Now that this was not the case Macmillan protested that it was quite impossible for him to go. I urged him to keep the engagement, because of the disappointment its cancellation would mean for the Italian government and its supporters. 'What is more,' I constantly emphasised, 'the Italians have been extremely supportive of us throughout the negotiations.' Finally he agreed to make the visit, although he was all too obviously unenthusiastic about it and showed no sign of enjoyment while we were there.

It had been arranged that the Prime Minister would go to the Vatican to meet the Pope, the ailing John XXIII, and I accompanied him there on the Saturday morning. 'I want him to appoint my man as the new Archbishop of Westminster,' he told me. This was to replace Cardinal William Godfrey, who had died a short time before. The Pope gave us a warm embrace and took us to the podium. Despite his illness, the Pope was extrovert and loquacious, speaking in perfect French, which admirably suited the Prime Minister. After the first ten minutes the Pope paused for breath, at which point Macmillan attempted to intervene, beginning 'Oui, c'est vrai, mais —' At that point the Pope resumed talking, continuing for another ten minutes. Macmillan then said, 'Oui, mais peut-être je peux dire —' The Pope again took no notice and launched into another ten-minute contribution, at the end of which his personal chaplain opened the double doors at the bottom of the chamber to admit the British Minister to the Vatican, by tradition a Protestant, together with our two private secretaries. The Pope led us down to greet them.

The Prime Minister's private secretary, Philip de Zulueta, was the scion of a prominent Roman Catholic family and crashed at this point on to both knees in front of the Pope, to kiss his hand. He was lightly brushed away. He was followed by my own private secretary, who was well known in the Foreign Office as an atheist. He was having nothing of this Roman theatricality, and merely held out his right hand and looked up at the ceiling. The Pope met this challenge by throwing his arms around his shoulders, and then led us all to the door saying charmingly, 'Au revoir.'

Outside, his Chief of Protocol Monsignor Cardinale, later to become papal nuncio to Belgium, Luxembourg and the European Community, told us that he had collected all the British students close by to greet us. 'But,' protested Macmillan, 'I want to see the Cardinal Secretary of State.' 'Of course,' said the Pope's chaplain, 'I will go and arrange that at once while you are talking to the students.' Shortly afterwards, he came to fetch us and we were taken to the Cardinal's room, where we found him sitting in a magnificent chair in all his robes, in contrast with the Pope who had been in simple white garb. The Cardinal began by profusely sympathising with the Prime Minister on the breakdown of the European negotiations, and urging him not to become disheartened but to persevere with this mission. The Prime Minister then expressed his sympathy with the loss of the Cardinal Archbishop of Westminster. The Cardinal echoed this appreciatively and said the Vatican would be replacing him in due course. This gave Macmillan his opportunity at last. 'I have a very good man for you to replace the late Cardinal,' he said.

'Prime Minister,' said the Cardinal, 'all our top men in your country are very good men.' That was as far as the Prime Minister got. On our way out, he asked to see Cardinal William Heard, a Balliol man who had been elevated to this high position three years earlier. 'I wanted to offer you all our congratulations,' said the Prime Minister on being taken to his room. 'No, no, it's nothing,' said the Cardinal. 'I have been dealing with all these would-be divorce cases for years, and now they have given me this.' 'We are all very proud of you,' said Macmillan as we rose to say goodbye. 'There is just one little thing you might do for me,' said the Cardinal as we were about to leave. 'I read in *The Times* that professional people at home are getting a considerable rise in salaries. Is there any way in which you can let me have a list of these as I would like to compare my own with theirs?' 'Of course,' said the Prime Minister, 'as soon as I get back home.' Well, I thought to myself, that's one aspect of the temporal side of life, but in a rather unexpected place.

On the Sunday morning, after a press conference, our ambassador said to the driver of the car, 'Take us back to the embassy.' 'No, no, no,' said Macmillan. 'I want to see Rome.' Greatly embarrassed, the ambassador instructed the driver to make this tour. 'And what is that?' asked Macmillan, somewhat implausibly for an erudite classicist. 'That is the Colosseum, Prime Minister,' said the ambassador. 'Yes,' said Macmillan, theatrically, 'I shall never see that again, and what is that?' 'That is Nero's statue,' answered the ambassador. 'Nor shall I see that again,' came the response. So it went on, and we toured the beautiful city of Rome with this pining and morbid refrain of 'I shall never see this, that or the other thing again' droning in our ears. At that time Harold Macmillan was sixty-eight years old. He did not die until almost twenty-four years later, at the age of ninety-two.

In his last years, Harold was still constructive in his writings, up to date with current affairs and revealing in his comments. His pertinacity and skill carried him through a long life in which troubles and triumphs were combined in equal measure. He was always supported by a deep faith which strengthened his resolve and established an inner peace which many others would do well to emulate. Personally, I have always particularly cherished my memories of working with Harold as his Chief Whip. He always trusted me, and my instincts, implicitly. If I had any above-average influence as Chief Whip, it was not because I was autocratic, but because I was more democratic than some of my predecessors had been. I acted on the principle that, the more you know about the people for whom you are speaking, and to whom you have to give the leader's instructions, and the more they know about you and what you are being asked to do, the better. After the tribulations of Suez, working for Macmillan, in an increasingly united and confident party and with a leader in total command from the start, was easier than it had been under Eden.

I was deeply saddened when Macmillan was forced by ill-health to resign on 8 October 1963, at the start of our party conference. My first thought upon hearing Alec Home deliver the resignation statement to the conference on 10 October was that Rab Butler would, once again, fail to make it to No. 10. I had already sensed that Macmillan wanted to keep Rab out, although he never said as much. He had come to regard Rab as an indecisive personality yet, however much the Prime Minister might have tried to orchestrate the outcome from his sickbed, it was ultimately the party's decision, and when Redmayne consulted the parliamentary party, both peers and MPs, they simply wouldn't have Butler. Too many on the right despised him for moving the party to the left. Others, like Macmillan, simply saw him as indecisive.

R. A. Butler will always remain an enigma to many. Not only was his personality puzzling to them, but the very complicated nature of his relationships with others also left them mystified. For my generation, helping to rebuild the Conservative Party after the Second World War, he was the architect of the fresh new policies with a philosophy that we were all able to support. These brought the party back into power and were the basis of our achievements for the next twenty-five years. Yet, at the Foreign Office in Neville Chamberlain's time, he had played an integral part in pursuing the policy of appeasement to which most of my contemporaries were bitterly opposed. His greatest personal achievement was the far-reaching Education Act of 1944, which he carried through in the wartime coalition government with the aid of his Labour deputy, Chuter

Ede, and which prepared the ground superbly for so much of the post-war settlement which was to follow. Butler was always regarded as the epitome of intellectual Conservatism, which perhaps explains why correspondents from papers of every view adored him, while the public as a whole regarded him as somewhat aloof.

His was, indeed, a complex personality. Of his intellectual ability there was no doubt whatever: his academic performance bore witness to that. His grasp of a brief was always firm, and his mastery of detail was also formidable. Yet on numerous occasions I detected a certain insecurity when he would ask me to resolve a question about a procedure or policy. He would say, 'That is what we are going to do, isn't it?', to which I might often say no, describing the alternative. His response would then be, 'Yes, yes, I know that is the case and that is what I was saying.' He was the master, still unequalled even in present times, of the coded message, especially to the press, indicating quite clearly his own views of people and events, yet never quite really committing himself to anything. Even those public utterances which, on occasions, seemed to be costly blunders were, in hindsight, usually very much to the point.

Was Butler truly creative in the world of ideas? I found that he was, above all else, an organiser of ideas rather than a judge of how far it was politically expedient to implement them. Yet in this, too, his judgement was normally sound. It was true that he found it difficult at times to make up his mind, particularly after the death of his first wife. When this was followed by his rejection as leader of the party, his own health suffered and he never fully recovered either his own confidence or his political standing. When Rab became Leader of the House of Commons in 1955, I worked with him closely for four years as Chief Whip. He never interfered with the organisation of business in the party, and reliably passed on to the Cabinet advice that I had given to him. His handling of Members of the House at the despatch box was impeccable. Never did he fail to be courteous and, occasionally, his whimsical sense of humour emerged. Perhaps the greatest tribute to him as both person and politician is that everyone who worked with him in any capacity loved him as a man, for all his whimsicalities, and supported him throughout all his difficulties.

I went up to Blackpool to speak to the party agents at the 1963 party conference. Iain Macleod was in the chair, as president of the agents, and he had just finished dinner when he was called out. When he came back he told me that Macmillan was ill and would not be able to speak at the conference, so we would have to decide with the Chairman of the party who should be invited to do so. I went back to London to discuss this matter with Alec Home. We talked about who should follow Macmillan, and I urged him to. He said he would give it serious consideration, but he was not sure. The other major possibility was Rab Butler, but I now felt that the time for him was past. Alternatively, we could opt for a younger person, such as Reggie Maudling. I did not think the party would accept Iain Macleod.

I returned to Blackpool where, on the Thursday night, Quintin Hailsham addressed the annual CPC Meeting. It was as this meeting that he announced his intention to disclaim both his viscountcy and his barony, in order to stand for the leadership. I went into a small dining room and had dinner, as I did not want to attract a lot of attention by sitting on the platform of the meeting. About 9.30 p.m. John Morrison, chairman of the 1922 Committee, came into the dining room and sat at my table. 'How's it all going?' I asked him. 'Absolutely quiet,' he replied. 'No demonstrations of any kind.' So we finished coffee and went along to the entrance hall of the hotel, which was packed with people. 'What is going on?' I asked somebody. 'Quintin's going to stand for leader,' I was told. Quintin Hogg came down the staircase with his wife, holding their new baby in his arms, and he was cheered by many of those present. This proved to be an unwise move because too many of the party thought it was a tasteless publicity stunt, which increased their animosity towards him, and resulted in Macmillan withdrawing his support from him.

The next morning, Rab summoned a meeting including myself, Maudling, Macleod and Alec Home, at which we had to decide upon a conference speaker. Alec was then president of the Union of Conservative Associations, so he was bound to be in the chair. As he could not be both speaker and chairman, Rab was asked to address them. This was giving him a tremendous opportunity, but there was no alternative. Alec read out Harold Macmillan's letter of resignation, which was solemnly received, and then Rab made his speech, which was monotonous and ineffective and did him no good whatever.

Meanwhile Harold Macmillan had gone into King Edward VII Hospital to have his prostate operation. He had taken the opportunity of discussing his successor individually with colleagues. The Queen went to see him in the hospital, and expressed her regret as he gave her formal notification of his resignation. After he left the hospital he started his recovery at the Ritz Hotel, where he was invited to a splendid apartment, and where I called on him as soon as possible. He recounted how, after the Queen's visit to the hospital, he felt absolutely exhausted, and asked the sister to draw the blinds and put out the lights so that he could go to sleep, which he did. Almost immediately he was suddenly woken by a noise in the room and called out in a startled voice, 'Who's that? What is this? Who are you?', whereupon a man emerged from under his bed. Again he demanded, 'Who are you? What are you doing?' 'I am the electrician from the Post Office,' was the reply. 'And I am taking away your secret scrambler telephone.' 'When I heard that,' he told me, 'I knew that I was dead!'

When we discussed the leadership contest, Macmillan informed me that he favoured Home and asked me to use all my old whipping skills to ensure that Alec became leader. I had supported Alec from the outset. He seemed to me to be the only candidate who was able to unite the party. As it turned out, most of the party thought so too, and neither I nor John Morrison, who was also a Home supporter, had to do much persuading. Those who saw Alec as simply Macmillan's 'stop Butler' candidate forget that simple fact. Soon after Home's candidature was announced, Enoch Powell and Iain Macleod tried to persuade Rab to refuse to serve under him. As Alec himself later acknowledged, this would have made it difficult for him to form a government. However, Rab was too decent a man to use what Powell later described as a 'loaded revolver' and risk splitting the party he had faithfully served for thirty years.

I was lobbied only on one occasion, when Freddy Erroll, at that time President of the Board of Trade, came to the Foreign Office and asked me not to support Alec. 'You see, we have had so many of these upper-class people leading the party that we do not want another one. We really must have a middle-class fellow this time, and you should support one of the others, not Alec.' I replied that, unhappily, I could not share his approach. I came from a working-class family myself, and it would be deceitful to claim to be one of those he was mustering from the middle class. He quietly left. Once the consultation process was complete, Alec Home became Britain's new Prime Minister on 19 October. He promptly disclaimed his earldom, and stood for election to the House of Commons in the constituency of Kinross and West Perthshire, as Sir Alec Douglas-Home.

Both Macleod and Powell refused to serve in the Home administration, and Macleod then followed this up by writing an article in the *Spectator* shortly after the contest, in which he attacked what he called the 'magic circle' which had engineered the succession behind closed doors. Although I was saddened by Iain's outburst, I was relieved that the contest itself was all over, for it had not shown the party in a good light. Public displays of acrimony, coupled with an apparent lack of democratic accountability, had done nothing to improve our image.

It was at this time that I moved out of the small flat in Petty France that I had inhabited since the early 1950s and into a spacious apartment at Albany, a prestigious but secluded block just off Piccadilly, with a remarkably modest rent. It was inhabited mostly by people from the arts world, such as the playwright Terence Rattigan and Kenneth Clark, the former director of the National Gallery. Two of my colleagues from the Brussels negotiations, Pierson Dixon and Eric Roll, also came to live there later. I had put my name down on the waiting list as soon as I was elected to Parliament in February 1950. It took thirteen years before a set came up, because of the death of Clifford Bax, brother of the composer Arnold. It was a relief to have a proper home of my own at last where I could entertain my friends and I immediately brought in the interior designer Jo Pattrick to advise me on its decoration and furnishing.

On becoming Prime Minister, Alec appointed me President of the Board of Trade. When I went there I asked for Regional Development to be added to Trade and Industry, and the Secretary of the Cabinet then produced the title of Secretary of State for Trade, Industry and Regional Development. I told him that I had no desire to be known as the TIRD, and he therefore had to reconstruct it into Industry, Trade and Regional Development. Now I had an opportunity to put my beliefs on domestic matters into practice. I knew that I would not have long to make an impact in this posting, for there would have to be an election within twelve months. The Department had not enjoyed a particularly dynamic reputation during the preceding years, and I felt that it badly needed pulling together. My team there included the highly respected permanent secretary Sir Richard Powell, both Lord Drumalbyn and Edward du Cann as Ministers of State, and David Price as parliamentary secretary. We all did an immense amount of work as a team in the eleven months we were together at the Ministry and we generally got on well. The exception was Edward du Cann, whose ingratiating manner immediately led me to distrust him, a distrust which proved to be well founded in years to come.

The first thing I did was to ask Richard Powell to call together the top 150 civil servants so that I could address them and tell them what I had in mind. He was somewhat startled, but went off to get it organised. I soon had an example of how the Department functioned. Getting down to the work on my desk, I asked my private secretary to send for the official handling one particular matter. Shortly afterwards the permanent secretary was announced, saying he had come to deal with the question I had raised. I explained that I did not want to bother him, but only to talk to the official concerned. 'No,' he replied, 'everything here which the Secretary of State wants is handled by the Permanent Secretary personally.' This was a complete contrast with the Foreign Office. There, one always dealt directly with the relevant departmental official. I believe that this accounted for the general spirit of partnership there, the lack of which led to the apparent absence of drive and unity in my new Department.

I explained to the gathering of officials what I wanted to achieve in a comparatively short space of time. First, I wanted to bring the separate groups in our economy into a much closer relationship. This was particularly the case with the banking and other financial institutions on the one hand and all the different participants in our industrial, agricultural, commercial and consumer sectors on the other. I recognised that it was also the responsibility of government departments to be fully informed about the activities of these groups and to contribute to their success wherever possible. I had been much impressed during the time spent on the European negotiations with the close economic co-operation existing in the member countries, particularly in Western Germany and the Benelux countries. This involved not government direction, but limited government support for the private sector where necessary. I was convinced that this approach was essential if we were going to compete successfully with firms in the United States, Japan and the European Community. It would also enable smaller firms to amalgamate and combine so that they could compete in external markets as well as at home. We should quickly make all this known to those who ought to be involved.

Secondly, I wanted to follow up Quintin Hailsham's report on regional development (see p. 264) with the organisation necessary to modernise those areas of our country which had failed to adapt themselves adequately to the demands of contemporary industrial life and, as a result, were suffering from heavy unemployment and a continually declining standard of living. This would require major structural change in departmental organisations as well as in the areas themselves. It would, however, be an exciting adventure, the successful results of which would be satisfying for all those who had taken part.

Thirdly, I wanted to see the various monopolistic factors in our economic life removed and to get greater freedom introduced into both our production and trade. Here I had particularly in mind the abolition of Resale Price Maintenance (RPM) over the whole field of business. I finished by emphasising to the gathering of officials the immense importance of broadening the Department's requirements in this way and by asking them to embark wholeheartedly on the vital policies I had spelt out to them.

It was the first of these three objectives which proved to be the most difficult to attain. Indeed, there appears still to be a long way to go before we can say it has been achieved. I sometimes feel that our powerful, almost overwhelming historical background is still the main obstacle to modernisation in this country. Britain was first in the Industrial Revolution, at a time when both family traditions and individual ambitions were almost exclusively directed towards the armed services, the Church and the professions, or to agriculture. Industry came as a late runner, attracting those who wanted to establish themselves financially or to contribute to their family fortune. In this many were successful, and in such cases their most able sons might well have followed them. After that, however, one of two things would often happen. The next son, the third generation, might want to re-establish himself in one of the older, socially superior careers, and would leave industry to do so. Alternatively, the drive and capability of the third generation declined and led either to its downfall or to its replacement by outsiders. In the 1960s, too few of the products of our best schools were being attracted into industry, and I hoped that a Conservative government might play its part in improving the standing of our industrial sectors. Such a revolution would, however, take generations to complete.

Resale Price Maintenance was the system whereby a manufacturer or wholesaler selling goods to a shopkeeper could compel him to sell them to customers at a fixed price. If the shopkeeper tried to sell to the public at a lower price than the one fixed, he could be prevented from doing so. In some cases he could even be taken to court. This was clearly absurd and archaic, punishing the ordinary consumer by keeping prices higher than they needed to be. At a time when the economy was steadily expanding and it was of paramount importance to contain inflation, it made no sense at all. RPM did not allow the consumer to make a choice according to price, convenience or service. Moreover, it was rapidly being made nonsensical by the new supermarkets that were beginning to spring up all over Britain and by the introduction of trading stamps as a form of hidden discount, all of which was immensely popular. In short, I strongly believed that RPM had to be abolished in order to increase choice and competition. At home, numerous independent surveys confirmed my view, as did the Consumer Council and the Monopolies Commission, which publicly called for abolition in December 1963.

Almost all the press, with the conspicuous exception of the *Daily Express*, believed that the abolition of RPM was necessary to the national interest. The Liberal Party was officially committed to its outright abolition with no safeguards of any kind. In 1955 Harold Wilson had said that RPM was 'a scandalous practice and it is artificially keeping the cost of living higher than it otherwise would be'. Nevertheless, although my party declared its undying allegiance to competition, I began to realise that the abolition of RPM was a highly controversial measure among some Conservatives both inside and outside Parliament – because it would, in the short term at least, hit some small shopkeepers, many of whom were part of the bedrock of our support in the country.

On 17 December 1963 I wrote to the Prime Minister formally proposing abolition. Alec replied, 'This is very difficult,' and asked for the views of the Chancellor and Chief Whip. Reginald Maudling answered on Christmas Eve. He said that 'The economic arguments for abolishing RPM are decisive. It would benefit the consumer and the dire consequences predicted for the small trader would not necessarily arise.' There were a number of people, however, who argued that, because the government was already unpopular, we could not afford to alienate our traditional supporters so close to the coming election. The party Chairman, Lord Blakenham, and the Chief Whip, Martin Redmayne, were particularly worried about the mood in the party on this question and therefore advocated a more cautious approach. Redmayne minuted the Prime Minister's Office to argue that 'we should concentrate on short-term politics and remember that small traders are natural Conservative voters'.

Early in the new year, I submitted a forceful memorandum to the Cabinet, which concluded by urging my colleagues to 'seize all the advantage we can from the fact that this will be seen as a bold and courageous step fully in accord with our theme of the modernisation of Britain'. On 14 January 1964, we discussed the measure at length in Cabinet. Everyone present was behind the measure in principle, but we split over the timing of its implementation. My view was that the best way for us to shed the image of a tired government that had been in power too long was to implement a policy that was popular and that would show us to be a dynamic, modernising force. Time was running against us. The government's indecision on this matter was attracting widespread criticism and the Labour MP John Stonehouse was due shortly to table a Private Member's Bill to abolish RPM. I argued with my opponents for nearly three hours, but I certainly did not steamroller them as has sometimes been claimed. I had no means of doing so. The force of the argument for reform, and the consistent support of the Prime Minister and most of the Cabinet, won through. Moreover, in an attempt to pacify the fainthearts, I agreed to a compromise suggested by Alec Douglas-Home which would allow manufacturers the right of judicial appeal to a Restrictive Practices Court for every item of merchandise. I also accepted that it might be necessary to make certain products, books and possibly pharmaceuticals, exceptions.

The reaction from some members of the party in the weeks that followed was a strong one. I announced the Bill to the House on 15 January 1964 to uproar. Two days later John Stonehouse's Private Member's Bill on the subject was rejected without a division, giving us a clear run. Shortly afterwards, I received the roughest ride of my career from the 1922 Committee. To my disappointment, John Morrison, who had become a close ally during my years as Chief Whip, was among those who opposed my actions. On 26 February, he minuted Alec Home asserting that 'unless a very different approach is adopted by Ted Heath, quite frankly, HMG will be more likely to fall than not'. Suez had been a trial for me, but on that occasion I had been seen by all sides to be working to keep the party together, for everybody's good. Where the abolition of RPM was concerned, I was accused of supporting a measure that threatened to split the party.

Most of the controversy about the Bill centred not on its merits, but on its political impact in the run-up to the general election. Critics were concerned primarily with sectional interests. Even vociferous opponents of the Bill, however, had great difficulty countering the argument that it was in the national interest. Furthermore, where it could be proved that abolishing RPM on specific items would be detrimental to the consumer, the Bill provided for RPM to be retained. It has since been claimed that I exacerbated the tensions within the Conservative Party by stubbornly refusing to accept amendments to the Bill. This is nonsense. Before the Bill was even drafted, I accepted that there should be a judicial procedure enabling exemptions to be granted. Other concessions were made in Cabinet. The Bill was already substantially modified before its second reading in Parliament. In retrospect, this may have been a mistake. Had these compromises not been made at this early stage, we could have made them during the parliamentary battle, giving us more room for manoeuvre.

The announcement on 18 February that Britain had a trade deficit of £120 million, the largest ever recorded, caused further tremors of doubt to run through the party, although it only strengthened my resolve to press on with a measure which would help to reverse Britain's economic decline. The second reading of the Resale Prices Bill took place on 10 March. I explained to the House that the object of the Bill was to promote more competition throughout the economy. To my intense satisfaction, it was passed by 287 votes to 20, Labour abstaining. However, the Conservative rebellion, with twenty voting against and a further twenty-five abstaining, was the largest since the vote which brought down Neville Chamberlain's government in 1940, and showed that the battle had not yet been won.

It was unfortunate that Martin Redmayne, himself a small businessman, was opposed to the policy. Instead of trying to sell a decision that had been collectively agreed by the Cabinet as I had done in my day as Chief Whip, he kept up the pressure on the Prime Minister by arguing for a number of important changes put forward by recalcitrant MPs. These were primarily that the onus of proof should be shifted from the manufacturer to the Board of Trade and also that a number of statutory exemptions should be made from the outset on books, tobacco and pharmaceuticals. Fortunately, the Cabinet rejected that latter idea, but on 23 March, the committee stage of the Bill began and, to my consternation, 179 amendments and eleven new clauses were proposed.

The Bill ran into trouble the very next day, in what became known as the 'Chemist's Amendment'. This would have removed any drug and surgical appliance from the general operation of the Bill. I strongly opposed this amendment. The Bill had always recognised and stressed the need for adequate exemption when this was in the public interest, but this was a matter for the Restrictive Practices Court (see p. 260). Parliament now had to decide whether to rebel against the structure of the Bill and make a statutory exemption, setting an undesirable precedent, or to continue with the Bill and allow the Restrictive Practices Court to decide the matter. My view was that the Court should look at trades in the new climate which the Bill would create. In this way equality of treatment would be ensured. The abolition of RPM was, in any case, a completely different matter from the question of health and safety. Whether RPM existed or not, the control of drugs and medicine would remain exactly the same.

In the event the vote on the amendment after a full day's debate was 203 votes to 204. We won by just one vote. When the result was announced, I was immediately heckled and shouts of 'Resign!' went up. I had absolutely no intention of resigning. I just recalled to the House Winston Churchill's remark to me on a previous occasion when we had a majority of three. 'In the House of Commons,' he always said, 'one is enough' (see p. 155). What we needed now was not to dwell on a single amendment, but to press on with the government's legitimate business. For the next three weeks, however, I was engaged in parliamentary guerrilla warfare with my own colleagues, while the Labour Party looked on.

Finally, my patience snapped. The rebels had tabled what was clearly a wrecking amendment which attempted to give wholesalers and retailers, as well as manufacturers, recourse to judicial appeal. This already cumbersome process, suggested by Alec Douglas-Home as a compromise, would have been made entirely unworkable by the amendment. Alec had recently written to me pledging his full support. 'You have had the most gruelling time,' he wrote,

> and I do hope that you manage to get a few days off . . . to refresh yourself for the final round . . . I think that your sympathetic handling of the Committee will enable us to hold our party together, but the folly of some is almost incurable and sets the nerves jangling of the less robust in a pre-election time . . . Let me know if you want my help, but I am sure that you and Martin [Redmayne] between you can work out what is necessary to carry the day . . . I am sure that we were right, but we under-estimated the reaction and the short-term damage which the sight of a party in disarray would do . . . But the thing to do is to plug on and your skill and fortitude will get us through . . . The FO was chicken food!

In the light of the Prime Minister's robust and unconditional offer of support, I now rang No. 10 and requested an early meeting with him. In the late afternoon of 15 April, with Tim Bligh, his principal private secretary, present, I told the Prime Minister that, throughout the whole course of the Bill, I had continually been assured that it would take just one more amendment and the party would be happy. However, at no stage had any concession been met by a positive response from the rebels. Alec suggested that I should talk to more of the rebels. I replied that I would talk to as many of them as I could, but I could not go on for ever giving way on points of principle. The government, I said, had to draw the line and make a stand. Although I did not threaten to do so, I was close to resigning at this point, and I believe Alec and the party recognised that. Fortunately the rebels were eventually mollified by ten carefully worded but ultimately minor amendments. On 16 July 1964, the Resale Prices Bill finally received royal assent.

The abolition of RPM was one of the most satisfying successes of my ministerial career. RPM had been denying the British people choice and costing them money. Looking back, the Act clearly benefited the consumer in exactly the ways I predicted it would. I argued that people would like to be offered the choice of lower prices with a simpler service, that the small shop would survive by providing a complement to the superstore and that the Restrictive Practices Court would maintain RPM where it was in the public interest. All these things are now notable features of the life of the modern consumer. Many of my parliamentary colleagues at that time were over-impressed with the arguments of vested interests and, therefore, initially underestimated the political value of what we were doing. In turn, I underestimated the need for thrashing this question out among ourselves at an early stage. If we had enjoyed the luxury of more time before the next general election, we could undoubtedly have placated almost all of the opposition to RPM abolition. With the passage of time, however, we have been vindicated and nobody would now seriously argue against this reform.

It was this single measure, through an Act consisting of only fourteen sections, which transformed, and is still transforming, both the wholesale and the retail organisations for meeting consumer demand. At the same time, it has given the consumer an infinitely wider choice than ever before, including innumerable products from all over the rest of the world. Enormous progress was rapidly achieved by those shops and stores, self-service and otherwise, which were far-sighted enough to see what a golden opportunity was being opened up to them. It was made profitable by the demands of the public, who were rapidly appreciating more and more from radio, television and the rest of the media what range of choices was becoming increasingly easily and cheaply available to them. Yet the small efficient business remains to serve them successfully on their doorstep. All this was brought about, at an ever faster rate, over little more than thirty years.

The notion that abolition of RPM was a forerunner of the kind of policies that gripped the Conservative Party in the 1980s is ridiculous. Those who maintain this line have consistently misunderstood and misrepresented my career, because they see all political action as being either collectivist or free market, socialist or neo-liberal. Conservatism is none of these things, being inherently concerned with people, and therefore pragmatic as opposed to dogmatic. Indeed, at the same time as the Resale Prices Bill was making its way through Parliament, I was devising and implementing the most comprehensive regional policy ever seen in Britain.

The decision to bring regional development entirely within the ambit of a major economic department, which I persuaded Alec Douglas-Home to do against the wishes of the Department of the Environment, was of immense significance. The long-term decline of employment levels in older, labour-intensive industries was bringing social and economic dislocation to the regions affected, and it was clearly in the interests of social harmony for the government to do something about this. Our regional development policy had three objectives: a more even spread of economic activity, the preservation of the characters of individual regions and an improved quality of life across the country. We sought to reduce inequalities between individuals and between regions, as a way of keeping our country united. Once regional development was firmly established under the Department of Trade and Industry, I was convinced that we would make real progress, because economic considerations would at last always have priority.

Starting in early 1963, we had begun developing a set of regional policies to deal with the varying problems of structural change which people were facing in different parts of the country. Quintin Hailsham had started by launching a study into the north-east in January 1963, leading to a White Paper in November of that year, and further reports were planned, on London and the south-east, north-west England, central Scotland and the west midlands if we carried on in government. We introduced government funding for the North-East Development Council, and I set up an Inter-Departmental Steering Group of senior officials from all the relevant departments, to ensure that all aspects of government activity were having the maximum positive effect.

For the north-east, I established an inter-departmental committee of senior civil servants in Newcastle-upon-Tyne. There they were equipped with all the latest technology, enabling them to communicate in conference at any time with their counterparts in Whitehall. They co-ordinated regional policy developments for the whole area with local officials and industrialists. This involved not only the establishment of new industrial sites, but also a comprehensive programme of building roads, docks and airports. We speedily got this programme into action and I frequently visited every part of the region myself. Public service investment was substantially increased as we promoted both the reconstruction of existing towns and the accelerated development of new towns. Although there was widespread publicity for all this and financial inducements for individual firms, we still found it difficult to persuade their chairmen and advisers of the advantages of going to the north-east. I became aware that the greatest deterrent was their impression of the way of life in that part of the country. Almost every discussion ended up with the declaration, 'Well, my wife and family don't like the idea of going up north.' This made me realise that we should widen our scope to include the amenities of life, good house building, recreational facilities and the arts, including particularly music, opera and the theatre. This we achieved in the end, but it took time. It was some twenty-five years before I was invited to the opening of the Opera House in Newcastle.

It was our policies inaugurated at this time, including those for Scotland, implemented by its Secretary of State, Michael Noble, which brought about the transformation of these areas. The development of the technical industries in Scotland, in particular, has brought about a complete change of attitude as the older industries – shipbuilding, coal and steel – have declined still further. Conservative governments since 1979 have argued that, however painful structural change may be, such matters are best left to the market. If we had followed that sterile approach, the steady drift to the south would have continued, and the north-east and Scotland would have become more and more derelict. Instead, we followed the positive approach I have described, and with it we achieved immense success.

In the spring of 1964 the senior members of the Cabinet met to decide on the date of the general election. The Chancellor, Reggie Maudling, pressed very hard for an immediate campaign as he thought that the econ-omic situation would deteriorate over the next few months. The rest of us present, however, preferred to sit tight. On 9 April Alec put an end to the speculation by letting it be known that he did not intend to ask the Queen to dissolve Parliament before the autumn. I am sure that this was the right decision. The transition from Macmillan to Douglas-Home had not been easy but we certainly made substantial progress that summer and, when Alec Douglas-Home announced a general election for 15 October, Labour were only a few points ahead of us. That election remains to this day a controversial one for the party. Our manifesto, *Prosperity with a*

Purpose, pledged to construct 400,000 homes per year, promised to review the role of the trade unions, and set out proposals for following up the abolition of RPM by ending other restrictive practices through monopolies and merger legislation. It did little, however, to lay to rest the socialist claim that, after thirteen years in power, we were tired and shorn of new ideas. I had been in touch with Nigel Lawson, then a Special Assistant to the Prime Minister, during 1963 and 1964 about possible ways of livening up our 'pitch' to the country, but, as he wrote to me in August 1964, the usual process of manifesto-drafting had already taken place, with colleagues all bidding to get commitments to their favourite schemes set out in print, 'and too many people are too committed to particular sections of the early draft' for a radical reworking to be possible at that stage. He was obviously right, and the final result was worthy, but unexciting.

The Labour manifesto, *The New Britain*, emphasised Wilson's pet theme of science and technology. Although no serious thought had really been given to the hard choices needed to modernise the country, it appealed to a nation which was beginning to feel invigorated by the cultural changes of the 1960s and wanted a quick fix. Alec Douglas-Home decided to play to his strength by concentrating on foreign affairs. On polling day, news came that Khrushchev had fallen from power, and that communist China had exploded an atomic bomb. This vindicated Alec's emphasis on the importance of an independent nuclear deterrent, but it came too late to influence the election.

From the start, Wilson seized the initiative with the media. If the 1959 election had been a traditional British affair fought out in front of the television cameras, then the 1964 election was the first in which all the media strategies of American presidential campaigns were used in Britain. Whereas Wilson was adept at the big setpiece speech at a large, televised rally, Alec came across as rather stiff and prim. In town centre 'walkabouts' he found it difficult to respond effectively to heckling, some of which was noticeably more aggressive than I had seen on any previous campaign. Alec's personal charm and integrity were overwhelmed by razzmatazz and loutish behaviour. There were moments when he had the better of Wilson. None was better than his riposte to Wilson's jibe about him being the 14th Earl of Home, when Alec memorably told Kenneth Harris that 'I suppose Mr Wilson, when you come to think of it, is the fourteenth Mr Wilson.'

In the end, it was a testimony to Alec and our policies that the election result was so close. The swing to Labour was only 3.5 per cent, producing a majority of four for them, the smallest majority gained by any party since the 1840s. It has been argued that, given the narrowness of our defeat, I was personally responsible because RPM had alienated some of our traditional voters. In fact, the Nuffield study of the 1964 general election concluded that 'resale price maintenance figured hardly at all at the election'. The abolition of RPM was one of the few modernising reforms which we had carried through in recent years and I believe that it made the election result closer than it would otherwise have been. If other departments had thrown off their stale approach in that last year by bringing forward up-to-date proposals, we could have won.

After our defeat, Alec appointed me to the post of Shadow Chancellor. Over the next nine months I harried Wilson and George Brown in Parliament and on television as the hollowness of their economic plans became ever more apparent. Together with my team, including Tony Barber, Peter Walker and Edward Boyle, I ensured that Labour's Finance Bill was given a baptism of fire. We even defeated the government in one vote, an achievement which greatly improved the spirit among our colleagues. At Alec Douglas-Home's request, I also initiated and co-ordinated the biggest policy review in the party since Rab Butler's in the late 1940s. There were over thirty groups working on subjects ranging from agriculture to immigration, each chaired by a front-bench spokesman but including a host of experts from every area of national life. This process would carry on up to and beyond 1970, making us better prepared than any British political party coming into office had ever been.

On 26 June 1965, Wilson categorically ruled out an election that year. That left the way open for a Tory leadership contest, if the parliamentary party wanted it. On 5 July the 1922 Committee executive split in two after a discussion of the subject. Eight days later, *The Times* published the proceedings of that discussion, reporting that there was strong support at that meeting for me to succeed Alec. On 18 July, William Rees-Mogg, in a *Sunday Times* leader, told his readers that this was 'the right moment to change'. The momentum was building up and, on 20 July, Alec decided to resign the leadership. The rumblings against Alec in the parliamentary party had been on the increase and, although no public denunciations of him were ever made, most of the party knew what was being said. Nevertheless, his typically unselfish announcement came as a surprise.

Alec sent for me that morning and, when I arrived at his London home, he told me of his decision. I was saddened by it, and told him so. He then mentioned that he had informed Reggie Maudling at a similar meeting an hour earlier. The chairman of the 1922 Committee, John Morrison, and the Chairman of the party, Edward du Cann, whom he had appointed to that position after the election, had also been told. Alec had arranged to address a meeting of the full 1922 Committee that evening. When he did so, the parliamentary party was shaken and, as so many of them had taken part in the murmurings against him, there was a widespread sense of guilt. The election of the new leader was to take place immediately. Alec Douglas-Home himself had very sensibly introduced a new electoral system for the parliamentary party to elect its leader by secret ballot, to quell any remaining discontent about the manner of election. This time, therefore, it was a clear-cut contest, held in public view, whose outcome could not be disputed.

In the previous weeks, many people had urged me to stand for the leadership if Alec were to step down, and I certainly felt that I could be an effective leader. Many colleagues gave me credit for what I had achieved in several posts during thirteen years of Conservative government: for my time as Chief Whip, during which I made few enemies – a fact that may well surprise those who live on press gossip – and for my conduct during the negotiations for our membership of the European Community. Latterly, my colleagues had been able to observe the work that I had done in developing future policy now that we were in opposition.

I do not doubt that, above all, I benefited from the way in which we had so thoroughly organised, with a team of over a dozen, our attack on the Labour government's 1965 Finance Bill. We forced them to sit in committee for a record number of days and, in the process, seriously damaged both the reputations of Labour's Treasury team and their Bill. Peter Walker, who had played a leading part in all this, had been quietly keeping in touch with those of our Members who thought the same way, so as to be able to bring them in on any leadership campaign if a change came. None of them did anything whatever to bring it about, but when it did come Peter was well-prepared. The two other candidates were Reggie Maudling and Enoch Powell.

None of us carried out a personal public campaign. It was all done by teams of supporters, and Peter Walker led a magnificent campaign on my behalf in the few short days available to us, checking and double-checking every pledge. The campaign was free from rancour, and was anything but a left versus right struggle. I recall Peter informing me with glee that Keith Joseph had persuaded Margaret Thatcher to support me. Peter and his team were, by the end, quite clear that I was going to win. I had no reason to disbelieve them and, as it turned out, they predicted the number of votes that I would receive in the first ballot, 150 to Reggie Maudling's 133, with absolute precision. Enoch Powell received 15 votes. I had not quite won outright under the rules, and Reggie was entitled to a second ballot if he wanted to contest one. After hearing the result, however, I felt confident that he would withdraw in my favour. I then returned with Peter to his flat in Gayfere Street, which had served as our campaign headquarters. There we sat talking about the future and waiting to hear, either from the party whips or from Reggie Maudling himself, whether or not I was now the leader of the Conservative Party. After an hour or so, Reggie telephoned and informed Peter that he was stepping aside. I had won.

It is sometimes suggested that I helped to engineer Alec Douglas-Home's path to No. 10 for entirely selfish reasons, because I knew that he would lose the election and prove to be only a stop-gap, enabling me to become leader. In fact, I sincerely believed in 1963 that Alec was the only candidate capable of uniting the party. After the fuss caused by Macleod had died down, that is exactly what he succeeded in doing. Of course it is true that, had a younger candidate from my own generation, such as Reggie Maudling, succeeded Macmillan in 1963, it would obviously have been impossible for me to become leader when I did. But politics is an unpredictable business, and it would have been madness for me to assume anything about the longer-term at that stage. Moreover, Alec was a highly perceptive and shrewd politician and, had I really been playing such a game, he would have seen straight through me and would never have given me the responsibilities that he did between November 1963 and July 1965, nor would he have agreed to be my shadow Foreign Secretary after I replaced him as leader.

I was naturally overjoyed to be elected. I now had the chance to stamp my brand of Conservatism on the party and, in time, to make a bid for the job that would enable me to change the course of British history.

Chapter 10

MOULDING THE PARTY
Leader of the Opposition 1965–1968

I decided not to hold any kind of celebration after my victory in the leadership election. The priority was for us all to start working together again as soon as possible. This was made easier because relations between Reggie Maudling and myself had remained perfectly cordial throughout the process, as they did for the remainder of our political careers. Neither of us had made speeches, nor had we criticised each other in any way. Our supporters had also refrained from personal attacks. Moreover, as the result had been comparatively close, there was no excuse for triumphalism among my supporters. I made a fairly short statement, paying tribute to Alec and Reggie and dedicating myself to getting the Conservative Party back into government, and into the service of the country, at the earliest possible opportunity.

On 2 August 1965, the day that I was formally confirmed as leader, we debated a motion of censure against the Labour government. May and June had featured a series of speeches by Harold Wilson and his Chancellor of the Exchequer, James Callaghan, denying any intention to devalue the pound. The currency dealers did not believe them, and pressure increased on the exchange markets. Callaghan chose the day of my election to announce severe cuts in public expenditure and new restrictions on currency transactions to counteract speculation against sterling. The polls registered a drop in Labour's support and we now seemed to be edging ahead. At the same time, more than half of the voters said that they approved of me as Conservative leader. It was obviously a good time to call the government to account.

The occasion was presented by the press as a personal duel between myself and Harold Wilson. It certainly suited the Prime Minister for the debate to be seen in this light, since it was his best chance of deflecting attention away from the serious situation in the country. At the top of his form, he would create the impression that anyone with the barefaced cheek to question the record of his government must be trying to score cheap political points. As Wilson had built his parliamentary reputation by doing just that while we were in office, it was irritating to find him taking such a self-righteous line as Prime Minister. But what could be done about it? One might think that the significance of such a setpiece exchange was not as serious then as it would be now that the Commons is televised. This is not really true, however, because the morale of the parliamentary party depended upon a good performance. In the 1960s the audience was made up entirely of MPs and reporters – the most savage critics in the world. I knew that I could not compete with Wilson at his own game, and therefore attempted to deal seriously with the great problems with which the United Kingdom had been faced ever since the Labour Party came to power.

My point-by-point attack on government policies led to continuous interruptions from the Labour benches, with jeers and sneers, and the atmosphere became very heated. In his reply, Wilson took advantage of this and proceeded with his customary form of attack, the sole purpose of which was to whip up all the factions in his party, so that their divisions were forgotten for the moment. He read from a carefully prepared script, word for word. It is true, of course, that it is difficult, and rather more dangerous, to do anything else as Prime Minister, because a slip or a badly worded sentence can have damaging international repercussions. However, the voting on the motion that evening – we were defeated by 303 votes to 290 – emphasised once again Wilson's precarious majority, and our MPs ended the session in a mood to enjoy their vacation.

I flew off to the South of France with my father and stepmother, to join up with Madron and Nancy-Joan Seligman for a holiday in a house they had rented near Villefranche. For several years I had spent my summer holiday in different places on the continent and the arrangements for this one had been made long in advance. Looking back on it, however, I doubt whether it was really wise, in the week following my election as leader, to allow the public to be presented with photographs of me taking a holiday abroad. We were besieged by members of the press, full of ideas for inveigling me into interviews in situations, such as boating outings, from which it was impossible to escape. Moreover, there was a difficulty in discussing policies, for I had not yet had an opportunity, as leader, of thrashing them out with my colleagues. I also had to deal with the mass of congratulatory letters. Having no secretary with me, I foolishly attempted to answer each one in my own hand, which left me more tired at the end of the holiday than at the beginning.

When I became a Member of Parliament and, later, a Minister, the number of weekends I could spend at home became fewer. After I became leader of the Conservative Party, I could have filled my diary several times over. Almost every weekend there was a function to attend, or a speech to be made in some part of the country. Nonetheless, I always tried to keep at least one day free every weekend, for some sort of recreation. I well knew how stale I would get without that. I had seen four Conservative Prime Ministers exhaust themselves.

By the summer of 1965, my doctor and good friend Brian Warren had begun to get rather firm about this. For a year or more after my hepatitis attack in January 1959 I had still felt the effects of it and, in order to avoid any recurrence, I was told that I must make serious efforts to limit my workload. This was more easily said than done, for almost immediately I became involved in handling the first negotiations for Britain's entry into the European Community, followed by my time at the Board of Trade. By 1965, I was almost fifty and, once again, I was being told, by one adviser and friend after another, that I could not drive myself on indefinitely at the pace of the previous twenty years. So, when I returned to Broadstairs in the early summer of that year, I was looking around for some appropriate means of being 'sensible'.

One pleasant sunny afternoon back in Broadstairs, I walked along the cliffs down on to the jetty and to the edge of the Channel, which was in one of its quieter moods. The tide was in and some boats were floating at their moorings, with water softly lapping around them. Others were in the process of being rigged. Dinghies on trailers were being wheeled across the sand to the water's edge and some hopefuls were already out in the bay, trying to make some use of the light breeze. I looked over this bustling scene, as I had done so many times before, and then went on with my stroll. Then I came across an unfamiliar fixture, a small kiosk with 'Viking Sailing School' written over its entrance. In front stood a stocky, sunburned, dark-haired man whom I had not met before. Seeing me look at his enrolment centre, he pointed to it and said, 'If you are interested in sailing, why not start here?'

As a boy I had always wanted to sail, but the opportunities then were nothing like as numerous as they are today. A sailing club had been established in Broadstairs before the Second World War and small boats had begun to appear in the harbour, but the majority of craft had been cabin cruisers or motor boats used for fishing. There were also two or three larger boats owned by local boatmen who used them to earn their living by taking visitors round the bays or out to the Goodwins in summer, in between fishing or collecting their lobster pots. The most famous of these was called the *Perseverance* and, whenever I found myself racing against Sir Max Aitken's boat of that name in later years, I still thought of her. After playing her part at Dunkirk, the Broadstairs *Perseverance* was released from her moorings one night after the war, was picked up by a passing freighter and sank after being towed too fast.

When I was a youngster, very few boys sailed dinghies; and, even if a group of young people had thought to club together to buy a boat, that too would have been beyond my means. I tried to satisfy my own longings, as so many others must have done for generations, by voraciously reading the sailing periodicals. Occasionally, when there were special numbers, I would buy them for myself, but usually I read them in the public library. When I returned home after the war, I helped to refound the local sailing club, but that was as far as I got. My real delight in the 1930s had been watching the big J-class boats when they came to the week-long Royal Temple Yacht Club Regatta at Ramsgate, an event which was included by most of the big boats in their programme round the coast before and after Cowes Week. They were a splendid sight, competing for the Ramsgate Gold Cup, the 'Town Cup'. I was fortunate, too, in spending several childhood holidays around the Solent, either on the mainland or on the Isle of Wight. I spent hours wandering round the outer harbour wall at Ramsgate and the inner basin, or looking at the moorings at Seaview and Bembridge, fascinated by the activity there.

Now I was suddenly being presented with the opportunity to get down to sailing seriously. Should I take it? I already had music as a recreation, in the various forms of concert-going, opera, piano-playing, conducting a carol concert once a year and listening to my records. But that was a spiritual experience. I had nothing else active, except swimming. I had decided to give up golf, because I found that, as my political career progressed, it became inevitable that people on the links would insist resolutely upon talking politics all the time, and this was not what I understood by recreation. Nor was I ever really competent at the game of golf. Indeed, living in an area surrounded by championship courses, I felt considerable embarrassment at my inability to master more than its basics. But why should I be any better at sailing? After all, I was then a year off becoming fifty. Yet Gordon Knight, the owner of the little kiosk, was very persuasive, and I settled with him on the spot. We began to talk boats and how to sail them.

'How much do you know about it already?' Mr Knight asked rather curiously as we settled down to discuss how we might proceed. I replied that I had done some small-boat sailing, but only in Brittany with the Seligmans, who had a cottage on the harbour wall at St Jacut-de-la-Mer. We had messed around in a small French dinghy called a 'Vaurien'. On one occasion we had managed to race to St Briac on a somewhat choppy Brittany sea, but I could not claim that we had finished towards the fore. Although I had both crewed and helmed in the early 1950s, I asked Gordon

Knight whether it might be better for him to start me off from scratch, assuming that I knew nothing. He readily agreed, so I arranged to get down to the boat at Broadstairs one day every weekend, and spent part of August sailing there.

Despite the distractions of the summer, I was able to sort out office arrangements and reflect on the first fruits of the policy review which I had begun at the beginning of the year. When I became leader, I appointed John MacGregor as my private secretary. He proved to be first class. He was not only hard working, but the ease with which he handled everyone was invaluable. From my point of view the fact that he was not only a Scot, but that his family still lived in Scotland, meant that he was able to keep me well briefed on Scotland's problems and the attitudes there to our policies. During my time as Leader of the Opposition and Prime Minister, I spent more time in Scotland than any of my predecessors or successors, except for the two who lived there, Ramsay MacDonald and Alec Douglas-Home. John married Jean Dungey, one of my secretaries, and this happy union supported John immensely as he moved right up through government after 1979, and into the Cabinet.

As my political secretary, I appointed Douglas Hurd. His father Anthony had been elected Conservative MP for Newbury in 1945 and was, for many years, a masterly chairman of the Agriculture Committee. Because of his handling of this controversial body, I persuaded Anthony Eden to put his name forward for a knighthood. When I told Anthony Hurd this, he was both surprised and delighted, and accepted with alacrity. I was therefore surprised when I was told the next afternoon in the House that he wished to see me urgently. When he came in to my room he was obviously acutely embarrassed. Apologetically he explained that he had broken the confidence, believing that he ought to inform the editor of *The Times*, for whom he wrote a weekly article on farming, because he had been sure that he would be equally pleased. The editor immediately said, 'You have two choices. Either you turn down this knighthood or you leave the paper. You can't have both.' 'I can't afford to leave the paper,' responded Hurd, 'so I'll have to refuse the honour. I'm sorry to have caused you so much trouble, and please give my apologies to Mr Eden.' The attitude of editors today is quite different. I was glad that, when Hurd retired, he was elevated to the House of Lords.

I first met Douglas when I was Lord Privy Seal at the Foreign Office at the beginning of the 1960s, and he was private secretary to the permanent under-secretary. He struck me then as being the perfect diplomat. Later he decided to leave the Foreign Service for politics and went into the Conservative Research Department, at that time an independent, well-

staffed office under Michael Fraser. From there I seized Douglas as a foreign
policy adviser in my work as leader of the party. He travelled widely with
me in that role, and then came with me to No. 10, where he handled all
parliamentary matters which had any party flavour to them. His advice in
this respect was sound, and the information he always had to hand on
foreign journeys was invaluable. Sometimes I did not agree with the views
he expressed, but I invariably found it helpful to debate policy with him.
Although he had to work unduly hard to gain recognition in the first
years of the Thatcher governments, Douglas made the most of the major
opportunities that came later. Diplomatically, he had to suffer many challenges especially on European policy, but he handled them successfully.
As an outsider no longer engaged in day-to-day struggles over these affairs,
I sometimes felt that he could have been more outspoken in his views and
resolute in his decisions, but Douglas survived the turmoil of the Major
government with his dignity, and his principles, intact.

The immediate priority for my team was to get our ideas ready for a
publication called *Putting Britain Right Ahead* in time for the 1965 party
conference, to be held at Brighton in October. This document set the tone
of party policy throughout my years as leader. It began with a statement of
principles, declaring that 'the State should serve the people, not dominate
them'. We promised that welfare benefits would be both more generous
and more selective. There would also be changes in the pensions system,
putting more emphasis on occupational pension schemes, into which
almost two-thirds of the adult male working population were already
paying funds. We argued that the existing Ministries of Health and of
Pensions and National Insurance should merge, to create a body more
capable of carrying out the detailed research necessary to run an efficient
welfare system. There were also radical plans for trade union reform, and
a restatement of our determination 'to take the first favourable opportunity'
to join the European Community.

Putting Britain Right Ahead would form the basis for our 1966 general
election manifesto, and provided the platform for a successful conference
in 1965. I made two speeches and stayed at the conference throughout.
This was a break with tradition. Before 1965 the leader descended on the
conference at the end to deliver his oration. I wanted to show that members
of the Shadow Cabinet and I were interested in all the views expressed
on the different resolutions at the conference. Even in these days of stage-
managed conferences, party leaders rarely have everything their own way,
and the 1965 meeting contained some lively debates which even today's
spin-doctors would have had to struggle to contain. Lord Salisbury made
a powerful speech on the growing crisis in Rhodesia which gained him
some support from the right wing of the party. This we had expected, but

the other troublesome contribution came from a front-bencher. *Putting Britain Right Ahead* included a clear commitment about keeping our forces East of Suez, given the current tensions which affected the area. Yet in his speech to the conference, Enoch Powell, our Defence spokesman, appeared to some commentators to have cast serious doubts on our continued presence in the East, while all his listeners in the hall were convinced that he had upheld party policy. Fortunately, Powell's speech did no damage at the time.

The success of the conference, and the good reception for *Putting Britain Right Ahead*, made it even more difficult to understand why, in the following January, Angus Maude, the Shadow spokesman on Colonial Affairs, chose to launch a fierce attack against developments within the party. Writing in the *Spectator*, Maude claimed that the electorate saw the Conservatives as 'a meaningless irrelevance', and blamed this on an alleged tendency for us 'to talk like technocrats'. This bore no relationship to the facts, or to what the public was thinking. We had been attacking Labour whenever they were vulnerable, and we had set out our principles clearly. Labour's position in the polls had recovered, but we were still only 4 per cent behind, which hardly showed us to be 'irrelevant'. I had known Maude for some time as an able man, a capable writer and a fellow member of the original One Nation Group. But political judgement had never been his strongest suit. He had adopted a hawkish approach during the Suez period; and, after our withdrawal, he had thrown up his seat and gone to edit the *Sydney Morning Herald*, without success. With a new election likely to happen at almost any moment, his public intervention was most unwelcome. There was no alternative but to move him to the backbenches, although this inevitably left him free to criticise at will.

Maude's brief period as Shadow spokesman on Colonial Affairs must have been a significant factor in his decision to speak out. The issue of Rhodesia was the most difficult problem of my first year. Indeed, it continued to dog us right up to the 1970 election and then throughout our period of government. The difficulty arose out of the break-up of the Central African Federation, a well-intentioned experiment in multi-racial government set up by Churchill's administration in 1953. In the early 1960s, we granted independence to two of the federated states, Nyasaland (later Malawi) and Northern Rhodesia (later Zambia). For the third territory, Southern Rhodesia, the Home government had set out five guiding principles for a peaceful transition to majority rule which needed to be satisfied by the whites-only Rhodesian government, led by the hardliner Ian Smith, who had toppled Winston Field in April 1964.

On 14 October 1964, the day before the British general election, Smith had announced that he was considering a unilateral declaration of independence (UDI), based on a constitution which guaranteed rule by the white minority. Before we left office, Duncan Sandys confirmed that this was unacceptable. The new Labour government took up negotiations with Smith, but to no avail. Harold Wilson made it clear in a broadcast on 30 October 1965 that he would not contemplate the use of armed intervention to stop UDI, but threatened sanctions instead, particularly on oil. The Rhodesians decided to call what they thought was Wilson's bluff, and went ahead with their announcement on 11 November.

As soon as UDI was proclaimed, our postbag confirmed the extent of public support for the white Rhodesians. Rhodesia was an unfortunate issue for us, perhaps the worst that could have cropped up during what was sure to be a short parliament. Some of our supporters had ties of blood with the white population. Others had an odd and misplaced sympathy for 'underdogs', even though the 270,000 whites held all the power and wealth in the country. Some were just bigots. A lesser number appeared to be outraged by Smith's conduct. The Conservative Party view emphasised persuasion, rather than bullying talk or the imposition of more extensive sanctions which would produce chaos in Rhodesia. We knew that this would result only in a more bloody-minded attitude among the whites and, given the help that they could expect from other nations, notably South Africa, we disagreed with Wilson's view that sanctions would bring a speedy end to the illegal regime in 'weeks rather than months', as he memorably, if implausibly, put it. We were desperately worried that the situation could escalate.

When Ian Smith visited London in October 1965, for talks with Harold Wilson, I invited him to join me for a drink to discuss the future. Alec Douglas-Home and Selwyn Lloyd were also present. I told Smith quite bluntly about our anxieties. We were not in any way opposed to the white population in Rhodesia, but we were convinced that the result of UDI could well be an internal conflict between the races in which other countries of the former federation and, possibly, South Africa would become involved. Ian Smith brushed all this aside. The reaction to UDI, both internally and externally, was just a nine-day wonder. It would be quickly forgotten by the international community and everything in Rhodesia would continue as usual, he believed. We were accurate in forecasting a continuing conflict, but, as the white-dominated Rhodesia survived for another fifteen years, Smith maintained that he had been right all along.

In a vote on oil sanctions on 21 December 1965, the different attitudes within our parliamentary party could not be contained. The Shadow Cabinet and the majority of backbenchers abstained in line with our stated opposition to 'punitive' measures, but fifty MPs voted against the government and thirty-one supported these new sanctions. The issue died down a little after Christmas, as both sides waited to see what effect, if any, sanctions might have. I sent Selwyn Lloyd to Rhodesia in February 1966 and, after a difficult visit, he returned to report the same message that others had previously given us: that, although the Wilson government's measures were having some effect, the Rhodesian economy could stand up against sanctions for years. The visible party disunity did not help us at the 1966 general election.

Britain would never go to war over Rhodesia, but in South-East Asia we were already involved in conflict. In one of the forgotten wars of modern times, which had begun while the Conservatives were in office and went on until June 1966, British forces were involved in the fight to defend the Malaysian Federation against Indonesia. It was a reminder of the need for a continued British presence in the area, the policy which Enoch Powell had questioned so obliquely at the party conference. In December 1965 and January 1966, I visited the area as part of an extensive two-week tour which also took in Turkey, India and the most threatening trouble-spot of the period, Vietnam. A vivid memory is of the enormous contrast between social conditions in the various countries: I saw some terrible poverty in India's capital Delhi; and thriving people and up-to-date facilities in Kuala Lumpur. I also stayed for a night in Brunei, which our troops were defending, and saw for myself the formidable difficulties of campaigning in the jungle areas.

The tour was also memorable for some hair-raising journeys. In Vietnam, our pilot had to keep the maximum altitude for as long as possible to avoid being shot down. My first stop, in Istanbul, began with a very rough landing, during which the plane's undercarriage hit some inconvenient object alongside the runway, followed by a delay of several hours while the damage was repaired. Our flight from Brunei to Singapore was particularly bumpy during a period when Tony Barber, who had come with me, was in the cockpit with Jim Prior, one of my parliamentary private secretaries, at the invitation of the pilot. When Jim rejoined me, he announced that Tony had actually taken over the controls of the plane. In the heat of the moment I forgot that he had been a pilot during the war, and could only think of what the British press would have made of the news that the Leader of the Opposition had been killed because one of his front-bench spokesmen had always wanted to play at being Biggles!

I met both political leaders and military commanders in South Vietnam, including the Prime Minister, Air Vice-Marshal Ky, and was impressed by the Americans' remarkable build-up of men and armaments in that unfortunate country. Although I was startled by the progress which the well-equipped and disciplined Viet Cong forces had made, my visit did not shake my conviction that the United States would win, albeit after a long struggle. This was something that hardly anyone doubted. At no time, however, did I think that we should become directly involved. We would take up our responsibilities to defend the free world against communism wherever we could genuinely help, but a comparison of the efforts we were able to make in Malaysia and the massive commitment of the Americans in Vietnam showed that any help we could give there would be irrelevant to the conflict. As events showed, it is highly unlikely that the outcome could have been affected by any amount of firepower. As I said in the House of Commons on my return, the war there was already 'extraordinarily cruel and brutal'.

I became convinced that the general election could not be too far away when an important work of construction was announced just before a by-election at Hull North in January 1966. The government decided that this would be an opportune moment to proclaim the building of a new bridge over the Humber. Naturally enough, the government increased its majority in Hull. Apparently, Harold Wilson had already decided before then that the general election would be called in the early spring, which, in his view, made this bribe entirely forgivable. On 28 February 1966, he called a general election for 31 March. By this time, Labour had pulled ahead of us again in the polls and, immediately after the announcement, James Callaghan painted a very reassuring picture of the economy in a pre-budget statement. His speech did not tally with our knowledge of the situation and during the election campaign it was difficult to work out from ministerial speeches whether Labour wished to argue that Britain was riding on the crest of a socialist wave, or still sinking because of the previous thirteen years of Conservative rule. The currency was a little more stable now, but only at the cost of increasing Britain's international debts by more than £360 million (almost £4,000 million today). In September 1965, in a blaze of publicity, George Brown had unveiled his 'National Plan' for the economy, complete with ambitious targets for growth. During the confidence debate in August 1965, I had pointed out that the government's squeeze on the economy put any ambitious schemes in serious jeopardy, but it was not until after the 1966 election that the full extent of the Plan's failure became apparent. Furthermore, some radical changes were now needed in the way we organised our industrial affairs.

For various historical reasons, British trade unions had corporately remained effectively outside the law of the land throughout this century. Company law, quite rightly, is generally reviewed about every ten years, yet trade union law had not been properly reconsidered for more than sixty years, making it virtually the only major sector of British life which had been immune from modernisation. Such trade union legislation as there was at that time had been introduced in an age when unemployment was rife, when victimisation of working people was a common and very real threat, and when trade unions were relatively weak organisations demanding, with justice, legal protection without which they would be unable to survive and carry out their legitimate functions.

Between 1951 and 1964, successive Conservative governments had always tried to take a constructive attitude towards the unions, for the general good of the country. My own period as Minister of Labour had left me only partially convinced of the merits of reform and, by setting up the National Economic Development Council (NEDC), which first met in March 1962, Harold Macmillan showed that Conservatives still hoped to encourage unions to behave responsibly. If they were introduced to the problems of economic policy making, it was argued, they would take wider interests into account in their pay bargaining. Once the unions began to exercise self-restraint again, there would be no need for any external pressures, and free collective bargaining could return. Before our long-term strategy could bring concrete results, we were beaten at the polls in 1964 and the unions knew that they could make hay with the new Labour government.

Although the mood of the country had not yet turned sufficiently for us to pick up many votes on this issue, I was convinced that I should get some plain speaking on to the record and, in Southampton on 5 March, I made what was probably my most important speech in the run-up to the 1966 election. This speech was governed throughout by the One Nation principles which have always sustained me in politics: that we need greater prosperity if we are to support those in need, and partnership, not confrontation, in our industries to create that prosperity. I spoke of 'irresponsibility, injustice and the unnecessary, self-destroying conflict in the field of industrial relations', and warned that 'unless we can put the commercial and industrial life of our country in order, the outlook in this competitive age is bleak'. I acknowledged that 'industrial peace and progress, goodwill and morale are first and foremost a job for industry itself', but restated my belief that 'government must give the lead', pledging that 'the next Conservative government will . . . introduce what is to Britain something entirely new – an industrial relations act which will sweep away the outdated features of the present law and provide a firm foundation for positive co-operation in the future'.

I also set out in that speech the new founding principles that we proposed for British industrial relations: a Code of Good Industrial Practice spelling out the rights and duties of management and workers; a requirement that any association of employers or employees would have to register in accordance with that Code in order to enjoy the privileges of such an organisation; a new system of Industrial Courts; a new right of appeal against arbitrary dismissal; an end to the closed shop; and a provision making agreements between trade unions, including nearly all national collective bargaining agreements, legally enforceable for the first time. Although we did not get an immediate opportunity to put these proposals into effect, subsequent events hardened my determination to enact such legislation as a matter of the utmost priority upon returning to office.

I knew that Labour would react with the taunt that we had caused all their economic troubles, but I never doubted that the public should be fully warned. My consistent theme was that this was a 'vote Labour, pay later' election. On my tours around the country I was generally well received, but the 1966 general election was still a difficult one for us. I always felt that it was going to be used by the electorate to redouble its harsh verdict on thirteen years of Conservative rule; it was an opportunity for them to confirm a trend. Despite some comfort from the opinion polls, therefore, we knew from the start that we had very little chance of winning, but I still enjoyed fighting the campaign. There was one mildly embarrassing gaffe, when I joked in Cardiff on 18 March that the Prime Minister was so keen on gimmickry that 'No doubt it will be only another month now before we read of Mr Wilson having tea at No. 10 Downing Street with a pregnant panda.' The papers interpreted my words as a clumsy slip – for, since the election was less than a month away, this particular stunt could only happen if Labour won the election. But it was only a momentary lapse. There were more light-hearted events, such as the time when, at the Liverpool Press Club, I was given the chance to use one of two fruit machines. I could see that one was called 'Lucky Devil'; unfortunately the alternative bore the name 'You Win in Any Position'. I knew that this was a God-given opportunity for the assembled cameramen, but strode up to 'You Win in Any Position' anyway. After pulling the handle, I found that I had won seven shillings. To my regret, it turned out that this was not an omen.

The campaign has often been written off as a very quiet one. At the time, an American correspondent was quoted as asking, 'Are all English elections dull like this?' My own campaign tour was certainly not without incident. I was generally joined on our chartered Dakota between engagements by members of the press. On one occasion, we were flying towards Aberdeen at 2,000 feet when one of the plane's emergency-exit windows suddenly blew out. The person sitting nearest the window was Cyril Aynsley, a reporter from the *Daily Express*, and the piece of paper he was holding blew out of his hand and through the gap. Instinctively, I grabbed his shoulders, before he too could be sucked out. He wrote in his paper the following day that 'Mr Edward Heath has a firm grip on things.' I subsequently discovered that we were at a sufficiently low altitude for the external and internal pressures to be very similar, so the risk to him had been minimal. We were then diverted to Glasgow Airport because of high winds and, on arrival, I commented, 'One of the press party tried to vanish out of the window, but we managed to hold on to him ... no matter how much he dislikes the election, he is not getting out that easily.' I can recall few other moments of great excitement or comparable derring-do during the campaign.

The result of the election was a Labour majority of ninety-six. In my constituency at Bexley, which I had managed to visit five times during the campaign, my vote rose, although the very inexperienced Liberal did badly and his vote went to the Labour candidate. As a consequence, my majority fell to 2,300. The result nationwide was disappointing, even though few of us had expected to win. I knew that our defeat would damage me personally as well as the party, even though many objective observers thought our campaign highly effective. At least when the next election came, Harold Wilson would be forced to fight on his own record, unable to claim that his ambitions had been thwarted by a tiny majority, or win support by denigrating the performance of the previous government. More important, we had the opportunity of developing further the thorough policy review which had been started in 1965. Writing to me shortly after the election, Anthony Eden expressed his view that 'Wilson's lead, based on the propaganda which he had directed for so long, could not be overtaken.' With the benefit of hindsight, I think he was right.

My immediate task, once the election was over, was to reform the Shadow Cabinet. This involved some tough decisions. It was important to have experienced spokesmen, but we also needed an injection of new blood. I was keen to reduce numbers, and I intended to combine this with inviting individual backbenchers to the despatch box for particular debates. Some of the old faces had become rather too well known to the public, and there would be plenty of time for new people to gain front-bench experience. At the same time I asked Central Office to review the candidates' list, to ensure a more fresh and effective party image.

The major changes involved Selwyn Lloyd, Reginald Manningham-Buller (latterly Lord Dilhorne), Duncan Sandys, John Boyd-Carpenter and Ernest Marples. The first two stood down voluntarily, having served the party well for more than two decades. The others were not so happy, even though Sandys had first become a junior minister in February 1943, and the other two had joined the Churchill government after the general election of October 1951. They were all able men, but none had done anything to make himself indispensable. I promised to help John Boyd-Carpenter become Speaker of the House of Commons. When the time came I tried to do so, but he was not popular enough to win cross-bench support and Labour's Horace King was elected instead.

The new people I brought in all fully justified my faith in them. Willie Whitelaw became Chief Whip, and others promoted to the Shadow Cabinet were Geoffrey Rippon, Peter Walker and Anthony Barber, who had been an excellent Treasury minister in the Macmillan government. They would prove to be among the most successful Ministers in the 1970–74 administration. Elsewhere, I gave Home Affairs to Quintin Hogg, replacing Peter Thorneycroft, who had lost his seat. To my great regret, Christopher Soames also departed for this reason, but others remained where they were. I decided to keep Enoch Powell at Defence, although he had made a speech at Falkirk five days before the general election, claiming that Britain was about to commit troops to Vietnam. We disowned his comments, but Harold Wilson still quoted them back at us during a big debate on Vietnam four months after the election, thus deflecting attention from his own failure to support America over the bombing of some oil installations.

Just before the reshuffle, Powell had caused more embarrassment with an all-out attack on sanctions against Rhodesia. I was abroad when he made this speech, but called him in for a discussion when I returned. When I first appointed him to Defence in 1965 he had worried me with his insular attitude. Knowing that, apart from his wartime experiences in India and the Middle East and a stint in Australian academe, he had hardly ever been abroad, I asked him if we could arrange a tour of Europe for him. He declined the offer, saying that it might influence his views. Would he like to go to America? 'No,' he replied, 'I have never been there and have no wish to go in the future.' But he readily agreed not to make any other statements outside his own area, without consulting the relevant spokesman.

The appointments I made in 1966 marked a particularly significant stage in the transition towards a modern party. Figures such as Rippon, Walker and Barber did not come from wealthy backgrounds. Some drew the conclusion that I was trying to create a front-bench team in my own image. This was an absurd caricature, not least because both Barber and Rippon had attracted notice under Harold Macmillan. Peter Walker, who was only thirty-four in 1966, would have won promotion under any sensible leader. I wanted to choose the best team I could. Possibly some of the criticisms came from people who did not like the party getting in touch with developments within society as a whole. It became quite nonsensical when Margaret Thatcher, whom I promoted to the Shadow Cabinet in 1967, was identified as a 'Heathman'.

The 1960s was a crucial decade for our country and, after a bright start, it ended up as a period of missed chances. Some older members of the Conservative Party like to trace all Britain's problems to the social reforms of those years but I generally supported Roy Jenkins' spell as Home Secretary, although I had some reservations about the pace of change. I do not believe that Roy's reforms caused Britain's lasting problems. Those lay in economic matters. As Opposition leader travelling abroad, I could see the new developments elsewhere for myself. This was a mixed blessing: I was much better informed, but increasingly impatient for a chance to do something about the situation at home.

At the end of May 1966, a couple of months after the election, I visited the United States for talks with President Lyndon Johnson and saw the American Defense Headquarters at Omaha. A few months later, I was to meet one of Johnson's senior colleagues back at home. During his visit to London in January 1967, Bobby Kennedy asked to see me. He came to my flat in Albany and sank, thoroughly relaxed, into the couch in my study where we talked for an hour. He asked about the British parliamentary and administrative systems, and then moved on to the relations between our two countries. He did not have the public presence to match that of his elder brother, the late President, but I could appreciate what a source of strength he must have been to JFK. His death the following year was undoubtedly an immense loss, not only to the Democratic Party, but to the United States as a whole.

Harold Wilson invited Alexei Kosygin, then Prime Minister of the Soviet Union, to pay a formal visit to Britain in February 1967. When this was announced I wrote to Wilson asking him to include some form of meeting between Kosygin and the Shadow Cabinet. Having, after some delay, received a reply from No. 10 that this was not possible, I then approached the Soviet ambassador directly. I suggested that, if nothing could be fitted in during the tour itself, we could arrange something at the end of the formal programme. As Kosygin was going to finish up in Scotland on the Saturday and travel back overnight to London, maybe we could entertain him to lunch on Sunday? The ambassador came back to say that this was perfectly acceptable. After discussions with colleagues I arranged to provide lunch for Kosygin and the Soviet ambassador at the Carlton Club – 'the home of Toryism' as I described it to them – at one o'clock. The reply was that Kosygin would like it at 2.00 p.m., as he already had a programme to carry out after arriving at Euston on the night train from Scotland. He wished to drive out to the Great North Road and have breakfast with lorry drivers in a café, in order to find out what sort of people they were. He then wanted to see Karl Marx's grave and, after that, to go into the City of London to spend part of the morning at the

Moscow Narodny Bank to meet their staff and talk about their business. After that he would come to lunch.

I entrusted Jim Prior with the organisation of the lunch. He decided that it should be a sumptuous affair, and we would take each course from a different part of the country. All was set for the arrival of our guests and I waited at the front door of the club in St James's for their car. Promptly at two o'clock a very large limousine drew up, followed by others carrying the ambassador and his private secretaries, all surrounded by a heavy police escort. Rather to my surprise there was a large crowd facing us from the other side of the road and held back by police. As Kosygin got out of the car, they started booing and waving a few banners. Kosygin immediately turned around and, facing them, waved with a smiling face. Turning to me he said proudly, 'This is the largest demonstration I have had during my visit.'

'That,' I replied, 'is because it's a Sunday.'

'Not at all,' he said, 'it's because your people are much better organisers of this sort of thing than Mr Wilson's.'

Going inside we mounted the great staircase to the splendid room where my colleagues were awaiting us and drinking sherry. I introduced them to him and to start the conversation going enquired how he had enjoyed his visit to the Moscow Narodny Bank, their largest branch in Europe. 'Not at all,' he replied, 'our Paris branch is much larger. Here in London we have 250 staff in the office, but in Paris there are over 800.' This struck me as a remarkably detailed piece of information for the Prime Minister of the Soviet Union to possess. We went into the grand dining room and took our places at a superb oval table in the centre of the room. Looking up at two great paintings on the wall opposite, he commented, 'Ah, the Czar and Czarina.'

'No,' I said, 'King George V and Queen Mary.'

'No,' he insisted, 'I recognise them. They are the Czar and Czarina.'

'Downstairs after lunch I will show you another painting, of the Czar and King George V standing together, each wearing the uniform of the other's country. You will then see how alike they were. But these two are King George V and Queen Mary,' I responded firmly but politely. We started lunch with oysters.

'How do you like your oysters?' he asked.

'With just a squeeze of lemon and a little red pepper,' I replied.

'That is how I like mine,' he commented, and we then began an animated conversation which lasted throughout lunch. Having finished the first course he said, 'That is the first time I have ever eaten oysters. I will tell my wife when I get home. She will be astonished.'

After the third course the Soviet ambassador was summoned outside.

He returned to say there was a message from Mr Wilson requesting Kosygin to go down to Chequers for a further talk before he finally left the country.

'But I have spent nearly a week talking to that man. Why have I got to go all that way over to Chequers for another conversation?'

'I think it's about Vietnam,' said the ambassador.

'But we have talked about Vietnam and got nowhere. Well, I suppose I shall have to go. But I am certainly not going to hurry. I am enjoying my lunch too much.' At 4.45 p.m. he murmured that he had to leave. He and Wilson got nowhere over Vietnam with the further talk at Chequers. Wilson's self-appointed role as peacemaker which was the main reason why he had invited Kosygin, was unsuccessful. But on the way out of the Club I did show Kosygin the painting of King George V and the Czar together in each other's uniforms and, if he still had his doubts on that point, he was too polite to say so.

In August 1968, I visited Australia for three weeks, and saw for myself the iron-ore mines at Mount Newman and Mount Tom Price, all equipped with the most up-to-date machinery for extracting the ore, and the 176 miles of railway which linked the mines to the port of Dampier. The Australians had made a deal to supply the Japanese, and every obstacle had been overcome, eventually the railway only taking a few months to build. People I met in the pubs of Port Hedland epitomised this spirit of enterprise. Many of them were Britons who had left their native country for what they knew were brighter opportunities for working hard with high earnings, without distraction, providing large funds with which they could then return home. I realised that there were important differences between Britain and this sparsely populated area, where the 'frontier spirit' seemed a natural partner of the landscape. Why could these positive attitudes not find an outlet at home? After all, much of the investment in Western Australia came from Britain. The situation at home could be transformed, provided that we could create the right mood.

Unfortunately, the Australian opinion of Britain was very different from my admiration for them. I discovered this at a Canberra National Press Club lunch, when I unveiled the Shadow Cabinet's plans for restoring a British presence in the Far East. The plan for a five-country pact in the area, consisting of ourselves, the Australians, New Zealand, Malaysia and Singapore, was coolly received in the local press. It assumed that Britain could no longer be trusted to carry out the responsibility of sending assistance if any of the other countries were to be attacked. As I pointed out, the idea behind the pact was based neither on pure altruism nor on a hankering for our lost imperial status. Britain had substantial economic interests in the area, and it made sense for us to play a part in protecting them. The four national leaders quickly agreed with the plan and, when we regained office in June 1970, Peter Carrington set off for the Far East to conclude the deal.

As well as a change in attitudes, however, I was now hardening further in my conviction that Britain also needed radical reform of its economic and industrial structures. With militancy in the trade union movement growing, strikers were increasingly inclined to abuse their relative freedom from statutory restraints, to the detriment of industry and of consumers. The balance of power was moving steadily towards the unions and away from management and from government, with its responsibility for holding the ring for the protection of ordinary people. The growing abuse of power by trade unionists was most damagingly manifested in the growth of wildcat strikes and secondary picketing. Even the most moderate and responsible union leaders all too often found themselves genuinely helpless in the face of shop-floor militancy.

After the 1966 election our Industrial Relations Group, chaired by Robert Carr, was charged with developing and refining our policy towards the unions and, in 1968, we published *A Fair Deal at Work* on the basis of their extensive consultations with industrialists. The conclusion was that 'our Trade Union Acts give positive encouragement to practices which society would never tolerate in any other sphere of human relationships'. The solutions to this problem had been foreshadowed in my Southampton speech two years earlier.

A Fair Deal at Work proposed that unions and employers' associations should become corporate legal bodies and register with a new Registrar of Trade Unions and Employers' Associations. They could then make binding legal contracts, and would be liable for acts committed by their members such as negligence, assault, trespass and threats of injury. These cases would be tried before National and Regional Industrial Courts which would refer to a Code of Practice, to judge the behaviour of employers and employees. Certain types of strikes, such as boycotts and 'sympathy strikes' by workers uninvolved in the original problem, would no longer be recognised as lawful disputes. Following the practice in America, the new National Court would be able to order a ninety-day 'cooling-off' period before any strike likely to affect the national interest, during which time a secret ballot on the employers' most recent offer would be held. The 'closed shop' would be outlawed but, although nobody could require anyone to be a member of a trade union, individual workers would have their right to trade union membership enshrined in law. Furthermore, if a majority of workers wanted union representation, then their organisation would have the legal right to be recognised by the employer. Workers would also have a statutory right of appeal against unfair dismissal. Our proposals were carefully balanced, giving unions a clear interest in registering themselves, even though that process would be voluntary. Since this left to the parties concerned the question of whether or not contracts would be binding, it would encourage a much more co-operative outlook on what were regrettably seen as the 'two sides' of industry.

The press response to *A Fair Deal at Work* was generally positive. The *Daily Telegraph* commented that, if the unions succeeded in thwarting our plans, 'Britain will become a laughable Luddite backwater.' The *Financial Times* welcomed the prospect of a proper debate on the unions, and noted that 'there can be no question of claiming that the new Conservative policy is in any way anti-union'. Even the *Guardian* approved of our moves to make the unions more accountable. The proposals were still not set in stone, but we had made a good start on refining our ideas, seizing the initiative on a crucial domestic question.

Just before the 1966 election, the Chancellor of the Exchequer, James Callaghan, had told the Commons that 'I do not foresee the need for severe increases in taxation.' As soon as his party was safely returned to office, however, he introduced a new selective employment tax, designed to yield £315 million (getting on for £3,400 million in today's values) in its first year of operation. The tax, generally believed to be the brainchild of Nicholas Kaldor, was as bizarre as it was severe: as employers in manufacturing would have their money refunded, it particularly discriminated against the growing services sector. Understandably, the new tax triggered a run on the pound which was further exacerbated by a seamen's strike. The slide in sterling continued despite a rise in the bank rate and, by mid-July 1966, the Labour Cabinet had rushed through a package of deflationary measures including a six-month freeze on wages and prices, cuts in government expenditure, an increase in postal charges and surtax, and a limit of £50 (£500 today) on money taken by travellers abroad. The Cabinet was now deeply split between those who wanted to devalue the pound and those, including Wilson himself, who were determined to protect its current rate of $2.80. That Cabinet contained a number of talented people, but in combination they made for a volatile mixture. The divisions were widely publicised, and the thought that George Brown, at the Department of Economic Affairs until 1966 and then at the Foreign Office until 1968, was toying with possible resignation on an almost daily basis was hardly calculated to bring confidence to the exchange markets.

Labour's problems brought us electoral benefits. In April 1967 we handsomely won control of the Greater London Council (the successor body to the old London County Council) for the first time. In May, we took control in several other major cities, ranging from Southampton to Newcastle. As 1967 wore on, we consolidated our lead in the opinion polls and it grew clear, both in the polls and out in the country, that confidence in Labour, especially in the economic sphere, was fading. We still had hard work to do in transferring this sense of disillusionment into solid support for our own policies, but the potential for a Conservative victory was developing strongly at this time. We were winning parliamentary by-elections too: Cambridge and then West Walthamstow (Clement Attlee's old seat – with a swing of over 18 per cent) in September; and Leicester South-West in November. The nation's lack of confidence in its government was shared by the money markets and, in early November, there was a new and more violent flight from sterling. On Saturday 18 November 1967, sterling was devalued from $2.80 to $2.40.

Throughout the crisis, I had opposed devaluation. It might have looked like an easy way out for a government in trouble, but it would not be so easy for the country. Prices would rise, and devaluation would have to be accompanied by stern deflationary measures which would cause lasting damage to the economy. The conventional wisdom is that the government should have devalued as soon as it came into office in 1964, but severe pressure on sterling did not really arise until international financiers had observed Labour in action. By the time of the 1967 sterling crisis, they had no confidence whatsoever in Labour's ability to manage the economy. If the government had devalued in 1964, I am sure that it would still have had to do so again before long. So the real answer was not devaluation, but sensible policies. These Labour had failed to deliver, and now the country had to pay the price.

I was furious when I heard of the devaluation, and even more so when, on the following evening, I watched, with Iain Macleod and other members of my team, Harold Wilson's televised broadcast. I particularly recall the uproar in my Albany apartment when we heard him say that 'From now on, the pound abroad is worth 14 per cent less in terms of other currencies . . . This does not mean that the pound here in Britain, in your pocket or purse or bank, has been devalued.' In his memoirs, Wilson accused us of distorting his message, defending this phrase on the ground that he wanted to avoid the reaction to Labour's devaluation in 1949, when many people rushed to their banks in a wave of panic thinking that the value of their savings had suddenly shrunk. The fact was that people's savings had shrunk in real terms.

The night after Harold Wilson's broadcast I went on television. It is incorrect to claim, as some have, that I demanded to follow directly after him. That is never done. In my broadcast, I expressed the feelings which had built up during the crisis. I noted that, on twenty occasions in thirty-seven months, the government had denied that it would devalue. Now it had broken faith with people at home, as well as with people abroad, who would no longer trust Britain's word. Ever since it came to office in 1964, talking loudly about the mess allegedly left behind by the Conservatives, Wilson's government had mismanaged the economy. I was angry about devaluation and the parliamentary exchanges that followed were unusually rancorous. I even received a lecture on economic matters from one Labour backbencher with pretensions to be a respected businessman – the Member for Buckingham, Robert Maxwell.

I warned that neither devaluation nor the £3 billion (more than £31 billion in today's terms) which the government had obtained from international bankers to prop up sterling would be enough to placate the exchange markets. My message was reinforced in January when, in order to shore up the pound even at its new reduced value, the government introduced more brutal spending cuts, including the withdrawal of all British forces in the Far East outside Hong Kong. It was this panic measure which I pledged to reverse during my visit to Australia later in 1968. We had already let down the countries which held sterling balances by cutting the value of their deposits by 14 per cent overnight. Now the government was proposing to compound the damage by withdrawing our protection from the same countries. No wonder Britain's international reputation suffered so badly during the late 1960s.

I chose my Shadow Cabinet as a team for government. In almost every case the team performed to my high expectations, with sound and positive working relationships. There were only two exceptions which, unfortunately, attracted a good deal of publicity. Edward du Cann had proved a disappointment as my number two at the Board of Trade in 1963–4. Yet, by the time I became leader, he had been promoted to party Chairman. Instead of shaking up the party machine after the 1964 defeat, his only significant changes were increases in salaries at Conservative Central Office. Before the 1966 election there was no time to remove him. The obvious course was to agree on his departure after a decent interval, but in the meantime too much rumour was spread about to make the parting seem natural. He eventually agreed to go in September 1967, and his letter to me at the time revealed the badly bruised ego of a man who would cause trouble in future if he could. To replace him I appointed Tony Barber, a far less controversial character. He proved to be a good choice, welcomed by the constituencies.

A much bigger problem was Enoch Powell. Despite his mixed performance as Minister of Health and a poor showing in the leadership election of 1965, Powell's tendency to regard himself as an all-seeing prophet increased rather than diminished. My long-standing view was that he was incurably eccentric, but I still hoped that he would honour his promise to stay clear of controversy. My hopes were misplaced. Powell kept on stirring up trouble, both on the public platform and inside the Shadow Cabinet. In October 1967, he made a speech demanding restrictions on the likely influx of Asians expelled from Kenya, a subject that was self-evidently way beyond the ambit of his brief. The Home government had agreed that, on Kenyan independence, the 167,000 Asian settlers in that country could retain their UK citizenship if they wanted to. Powell knew full well that party policy had not been changed.

In a speech at Ipswich on 29 September, I had set out our four-point plan for dealing with the problem, and pledged that 'the wellbeing of all members of the community, not the hot-headed demands of doctrinaire agitators . . . must govern our attitude to race relations'. Harsh rhetoric from prominent politicians, distasteful in itself, was bound to increase tensions. It also ran the risk of encouraging a sudden and unmanageable flurry of immigration, in anticipation of any new and draconian future measures which the government might choose to make in view of the very difficult situation in Kenya.

Powell became intoxicated by the favourable response to his stand from some extremists. He made further speeches on the subject, and revealed his true thinking when he told a journalist, in an interview not published until after his enforced departure had proved his remarks to be inaccurate, that 'I deliberately include at least one startling assertion in every speech in order to attract enough attention to give me a power base within the Conservative Party. Provided I keep this going, Ted Heath can never sack me from the Shadow Cabinet.' On 12 February 1968, Iain Macleod sent me a private note, saying, 'I am afraid I am getting very fed up with Enoch. This is about the fourth time that he has pre-empted a Shadow Cabinet decision and taken a line which is going to be extremely embarrassing . . . and I feel that there is a policy [on immigration] quite different from the one now being demanded by Powell and Sandys. I feel myself free to express it during the course of this week.' Iain accordingly became one of fifteen Conservative MPs to depart from the party line by voting against the second reading when the Commons rushed through a Commonwealth Immigrants Bill to deal with the Kenyan problem and we decided to support the government in its attempt to stagger the entry of refugees.

In April 1968, the Home Secretary, James Callaghan, introduced a Race Relations Bill in the wake of independent research which showed that widespread discrimination existed in the fields of employment, credit facilities and housing despite the passing of a Race Relations Act in 1965. However laudable the Bill's intentions might have been, I was uncomfortable with the way in which Labour was singling out racial discrimination for special action, when there were many other forms of discrimination, for example against disabled people, religious minorities or women, which deserved equal condemnation. We had initially opposed the 1965 Race Relations Bill because we were not convinced that it was wise to bring questions of discrimination into the arena of criminal law. The Labour government eventually agreed with our view, and created a new civil offence instead, though incitement to racial hatred quite rightly remained a criminal offence. During our discussions some colleagues, including Iain Macleod, said that, although they disliked certain aspects of the Race Relations Bill, they did not feel that they could vote against it. We agreed to set up a group to frame a 'reasoned amendment'. This sub-committee included Enoch Powell. The drafted amendment followed the sense of what I had said, acknowledging the need for a new law but opposing the second reading of the government Bill. Quintin Hogg asked Powell if he agreed with the wording. He stated perfectly clearly and explicitly that he did and, on 23 April 1968, he voted for it.

Ten days later Powell made his notorious, so-called 'Rivers of Blood' speech in Birmingham. The content of the speech was deplorable enough, coming from someone who boasted of his scholarship, but the fictitious statistics, and references to alleged letters from constituents who could not be traced afterwards, were deceitful and disgraceful. The tone was still worse. At a time when all responsible politicians were trying to deal with a regrettable and delicate situation, here was a front-bencher, a former member of the One Nation Group, setting citizens of his own country against each other. Certain passages showed that he regarded as a traitor anyone who wanted any kind of legislation to improve the situation of coloured people in Britain. This included not only those of his own colleagues with especially strong views, such as Iain Macleod, but the entire Shadow Cabinet, since no one had suggested that we should repeal the existing Race Relations Act. All of this was in stark contrast to the line he took as Minister of Health in Macmillan's government, on one occasion telling the Cabinet that we could afford to stand up to the nurses in a pay dispute, 'because I can bring in all the nurses we need from the West Indies'. I was in the Cabinet Room at the time, and I heard him say it.

The first I heard about Powell's speech was when the press started to telephone me at my father's home in Broadstairs, from tea-time onwards on the Saturday afternoon. I contacted Tony Barber, the Chairman of the party, but he too knew nothing. The accepted procedure with all public speeches was for the text to be sent to Central Office for reproduction and circulation, or to me personally for my information, but the convention had been ignored. Powell had waited until he got to Birmingham and then passed his speech to the agent there. There were reports of what Powell had said on some radio and television programmes, but for a full account we had to wait until Sunday morning. When I saw this the next day I was appalled, and immediately recognised the immense damage it must have done to race relations in Britain and to the attitude towards our party among a large section of the population. It was certainly in conflict with the principles of my other colleagues in the Shadow Cabinet. During Sunday I contacted them and arranged a meeting in my flat at Albany for Sunday evening.

Everyone present shared my view that Powell could no longer remain on the front bench. Had I not sacked him, the party would not have had a Shadow Cabinet left. Quintin Hogg, Peter Carrington and Iain Macleod were particularly fierce about it. At around nine o'clock, I asked Willie Whitelaw, the Chief Whip, to get Powell on the telephone so that I could inform him of our conclusion. Willie returned to say that Powell had no telephone in his constituency home at Wolverhampton, but he was trying to get the number of his agent. He finally obtained this, and told the agent to contact Powell and ask him to telephone me at once. To Willie the agent seemed far from happy about doing this, but he was firmly told to get on with it. A short time later, Powell himself telephoned me. I informed him that I considered his speech to be racist in tone and liable to exacerbate racial tensions. I was, therefore, dismissing him from the Opposition front bench, after discussions with the Shadow Cabinet. Powell accepted this without protest and rang off. We never spoke again.

The action I took, I am sure, was absolutely right and, although it caused friction between the party and extremists among the public, it saved our position with the majority of our people. Of course, Powell was perfectly entitled to his views. But he never had the honesty to own up publicly to the logical conclusion of every speech he made on the subject of immigration. The argument he consistently put forward must lead inexorably to the mass expulsion of all coloured people from the United Kingdom. He dabbled with suggestions of offering people incentives, such as paying their fares to go to their old homes, knowing full well that the comparison between their earnings in the United Kingdom and what they could get if they returned to their original countries would make this quite unacceptable to them. It is fraudulent to disguise the real intention that lay behind his campaign.

In the immediate aftermath of the sacking I received a quantity of mail, often from disturbed people who shared Powell's fantasy that the apocalypse would arrive if any more coloured people came to live in Britain. The vast majority of Britons, in complete contrast, showed their common sense. Perhaps I should have dismissed him earlier; he had certainly offered plenty of provocation. Having made appointments, however, my instinct is to stick by them as long as possible. After his sacking, knowing full well that he would never hold any office while I remained leader, Powell sought by any means he could contrive to bring me down. In the Shadow Cabinet, the atmosphere was significantly improved, and in Peter Carrington I had an admirable replacement as Shadow Defence Minister. Later in the year, I was told of a One Nation dinner at which Powell, under pressure from an incandescent Geoffrey Rippon, himself regarded as a right-winger at that time, admitted that he favoured compulsory repatriation of immigrants. He never had the courage to come out with that publicly. No serious commentator could fail to concede that Powell's views have been entirely discredited by events, and the hatred of racism among so many of our young people is a noble monument to his profound political failure.

Powell's campaign, however, was not the only form of nationalism with which we had to contend. At the first by-election of the 1966 parliament, less than four months after the general election, Labour lost the West Wales seat of Carmarthen to Gwynfor Evans of Plaid Cymru, with a swing of 18 per cent. In March 1967, they lost Glasgow Pollok to the Conservatives, even though our share of the vote fell by over 10 per cent, thanks to an extraordinary haemorrhaging of votes from Labour to the Scottish National Party (SNP). On the same day, Labour only narrowly managed to hold on to Rhondda West, one of their safest seats in Wales, in the face of an extraordinary swing to the nationalists of almost 30 per cent. With the single exception of a by-election gain for the Liberals in Birmingham, this scale of 'anti-system' voting was confined to Scotland and Wales, and appeared to indicate a sudden, but potentially overwhelming, tide of nationalistic sentiment. Along with several senior colleagues, I grew concerned that, unless some pressure valve for moderate nationalist aspirations could be created, extreme nationalism might take a grip in Scotland and Wales. This would inevitably led to the break-up of the United Kingdom.

Our party policy in March 1966 had been robustly opposed to the establishment of a Scottish assembly, a policy that I had inherited from a whole string of my predecessors. In *Putting Scotland Right Ahead*, our separate manifesto for Scotland, we had stated that 'We regard the Scottish Nationalist and Liberal arguments for home rule as a prescription for poverty ... Scotland is best served by a vigorous Secretary of State presenting our case in a national cabinet and supported at Westminster by a lively team of Scottish MPs ... to set up a Parliament in Edinburgh would mean a rapid decline into parochialism.' But, in the light of the evident shift in opinion since that election, it would have been politically suicidal to stick to our guns. So, in June 1967, I set up a Scottish Policy Group with a completely open brief to explore every possible remedy for the growing sense of alienation from the centres of power which seemed to be developing in Scotland and Wales. The suggestion for a Scottish Assembly would therefore come from the Scottish Conservative Party. In *Putting Britain Right Ahead* we had stressed our general commitment to a more regionally based style of government and we were not opposed in principle to further decentralisation. By May 1968 I could announce the outcome of the Group's deliberations at the Scottish party conference in Perth, in what immediately became known as the Declaration of Perth.

We had arrived at the view that the outbreaks of nationalist sentiment in Wales and Scotland, although concurrent, were quite different from one another in their root causes, and in the direction in which they might eventually lead. Welsh nationalism was more of a cultural phenomenon, whereas the SNP-inspired nationalism was all about independence from the United Kingdom. I was not willing to countenance the break-up of the Union, and said so in my conference speech. Most informed observers, I told the assembly, joined with the Conservative Party in rejecting the untenable notion 'that if Scotland were standing alone in the world, the present standard of living of the Scottish people could be maintained'. I also reminded my audience that it was the Conservative Party that had established the post of a Cabinet-ranking minister for Scotland. In consequence, 'decisions over a wide field of Scottish affairs – roads, electricity supply and many other matters – were taken in Edinburgh instead of Whitehall'. I now proposed that the Board of Trade in Scotland should have its powers extended and that there should be a new Scottish Forestry Commission and Fisheries Authority.

The Scottish Policy Group had proposed a Scottish parliament, and this had now been discussed and accepted in outline by the Shadow Cabinet. I therefore informed the conference that we were to look at the possibilities offered by a policy of devolution. The preferred option of myself and my parliamentary team would be a single-chamber, directly elected Scottish assembly, but I would now establish a new committee, with sufficiently broad terms of reference to allow it to come to its own conclusion. Proponents of every sensible argument would be given their head before any decisions were reached. I said:

> The right way to go about this is through a small Constitutional Committee . . . set up to examine proposals for the reorganisation of Scottish Government to meet the requirements I have set out. Such a Constitutional Committee should consist primarily of Scots, but in addition it should include representatives from outside Scotland because of the wide implications of such changes for the rest of the United Kingdom.

On 25 July Conservative Central Office announced the terms of reference, and the make-up, of the proposed committee. It was to include two former

Prime Ministers, Alec Douglas-Home and Sir Robert Menzies of Australia; a former Lord Chancellor, Viscount Dilhorne; ex-members of the Scottish Office; and a range of experienced and expert academics. The terms of reference set out four aims for an assembly: to 'keep the United Kingdom united'; to 'make an effective effort to improve the machinery of government as it affects the people of Scotland'; to 'allow the people of Scotland to play their part in making decisions on Scottish legislation in Scotland'; and to provide the Scots 'with an increased opportunity to propose and discuss United Kingdom policy as it affects Scotland'.

The Committee reported in early 1970. Among its recommendations was indeed the establishment of a directly-elected Scottish assembly, which would coordinate Scottish views, meet and question Scottish Office ministers, scrutinise government proposals at an early stage and debate matters of concern for Scotland. Most significantly, the second reading and committee stages of all exclusively Scottish bills would be taken by the assembly. We accepted this report as the basis of future party policy, becoming the first major party publicly to declare its support for a Scottish assembly. This was a fundamental change, but I felt then, as I feel now, that it was the right thing to do for the people of Scotland.

As we approached the halfway mark of the 1966 parliament, we had new initiatives prepared for dealing with industrial conflict and demands for devolution. I knew, of course, that we still had some way to go before we could match the presentational prowess of Harold Wilson and his team. With the right team of advisers and close colleagues, however, I was always confident that we could build upon the firm foundations of our One Nation Conservative principles, and flesh out an election-winning combination of policies in time to take on the Labour Party at the next general election, and win.

Chapter 11

'To Govern Is to Serve'

Return to Power 1969–70

The party difficulties of 1968 temporarily threatened to distract the public from our work in opposition. During 1969 the picture changed, as the Wilson government continued to disappoint public expectations. Labour spent most of that year wrestling with the trade unions, which were providing around 80 per cent of the party's finances. Harold Wilson had set up the Donovan Commission to look into the trade union problem back in February 1965. Royal commissions can be useful as a way of keeping narrow political considerations out of difficult decisions. Yet they can also be a handy weapon for leaders more concerned with party management than the welfare of the country. This was the light in which Wilson seemed to regard the Donovan Commission. Trade union reform was essential to the future of Britain, but, if the growing menace of strikes was to be addressed, Lord Donovan needed to be backed by a government with the will to restrain union power. This kind of impetus was unlikely to come from Wilson, who marked the establishment of Donovan with the passage of a Trade Disputes Act which gave new legal protection to workers who threatened to break their contracts.

When the Donovan Report appeared in the summer of 1968, its recommendations were toothless. Although 'wildcat' unofficial stoppages were by now easily the greatest problem that industry faced, Donovan decided that legal curbs would be inappropriate. Of the Commission's members, only the economist Andrew Shonfield dissented, appending a memorandum to the effect that, in an interdependent society, trade unions could not expect to remain untrammelled by the law. The only proposal of substance suggested the establishment of a Commission for Industrial Relations which would try to persuade the unions to reform themselves.

By this time Wilson had come to regret the limited brief he had given Lord Donovan. He had realised that he would not be re-elected unless he relaxed the statutory control of incomes which his government had exercised since 1966; but, as we had already understood, the only workable and sustainable alternative to this was structural union reform. Helped, no doubt, by polls showing a drop in public approval for the unions, Wilson now reached the same conclusion. His Employment Secretary, Barbara Castle, therefore cobbled together a White Paper which did not go nearly far enough, but at least went further than Donovan in the right direction. At the suggestion of her husband, Mrs Castle decided to call it *In Place of Strife*, recalling the title of the book *In Place of Fear*, written by Nye Bevan. Nothing could have been more foolish. The militants in the trade union movement were bound to be upset by the suggestion of firm action. Invoking Bevan was an additional provocation.

The White Paper, published on 17 January 1969, proposed a twenty-eight-day 'cooling off' period before unofficial strikes, and imposed strike ballots in certain circumstances. Although we suspected that Mrs Castle had helped herself to some parts of our own proposals in *Fair Deal at Work*, she had missed the most important of our ideas. Instead of an independent court, for example, it would be the Minister who would adjudicate on unofficial strikes. The White Paper also ruled out making collective agreements legally binding. It was obvious from the start that Labour's leaders were heading for some kind of confrontation with the unions, and if we had come out in support it would certainly have made their problems worse, while we might have won credit for our open-mindedness. Although Labour's policy was preferable to the prevailing anarchy, however, it fell so far short of our own plans that we could not support it in the House of Commons. In the debate of 3 March we abstained and the Commons backed the White Paper by 224 votes to 62.

We could hardly expect that Wilson would be foolhardy enough to stir up the unions for nothing, so we assumed that the legislation would be pushed through, even though 113 Labour MPs had either abstained or voted against it on 3 March. After all, Wilson had said in public that the survival of his government depended on improving industrial relations and then, in his 1969 budget speech, Roy Jenkins, who had replaced Callaghan as Chancellor after the devaluation of November 1967, announced the end of pay controls in an obvious bid to win union support for the Castle legislation. He also announced that 'some of the more important provisions' from the White Paper would shortly be brought forward in the form of an Industrial Relations Bill. This was presented quite explicitly by Jenkins as a major new weapon in the war against inflation, an example of the developing consensus that structural change was desperately needed in processes of pay bargaining.

Praising the growing 'establishment of links between increases in pay and increases in productivity', the Chancellor explained in his budget speech on 15 April that the proposed Bill would seek to 'reinforce this by bringing about more orderly arrangements in industrial relations generally . . . we need to facilitate the smooth working of the process of collective bargaining in industry and to help to prevent the occurrence of unnecessary and damaging disputes, of which we have seen all too much recently, and which are totally incompatible with our economic objectives'. Yet it soon transpired that Wilson's move had been born out of panic and, for once, he had failed to square his colleagues in advance. The Cabinet was divided from the start, and some of his opponents saw this as a chance to launch their own strike against him. The Home Secretary, James Callaghan, led the way by voting against the proposals at a meeting of Labour's national executive in March but, even after a furious Cabinet meeting in May, Wilson refused to take the risk of sacking him.

On 5 June, a TUC conference, aware that the movement had well-placed friends, rejected the government's proposals. This vote was backed up by threats of industrial action. For Wilson, this was now a question of short-term personal survival. Having angered half his party by talking tough, Wilson proceeded to earn the scorn of the other half by caving in less than a fortnight later and dropping the proposals. The TUC had come up with some token ideas of their own in May. At first Wilson had rejected these, but they were now warmly embraced in what was called a 'solemn and binding undertaking'. The mythical 'Solomon Binding' subsequently joined the pantheon of trade union heroes. As the elected government of the country had surrendered to its union bosses, however, no one believed that this paper promise meant anything. As I said in a speech at Croydon later in the year, Wilson had shown himself 'to be a man of straw – a pushover'.

On 20 June I made a televised broadcast on the subject, promising that a Conservative government would not ignore the widespread feeling that we desperately needed 'a thoroughgoing overhaul' of trade union law, as Labour had initially promised, and explained our own ideas. Wilson's capitulation brought new difficulties for us. Having humiliated Labour, some irresponsible trade unionists were sure to argue that they had even more reason to resist our plans to improve industrial relations should we come to power. But all the evidence showed an increasing public anxiety over the issue of strikes, and we knew that many union leaders were keen to restrain the hotheads on the shopfloors. We had to convince the voters that at least one political party was prepared to accept responsibility for restoring order in the workplace.

Understandably, the voters registered an angry protest against Wilson's backsliding. A Gallup poll in July 1969 gave us a lead of 20 per cent. Back in March, we had won Walthamstow East from Labour and, before the end of the year, we would deprive them of two more seats, at Swindon and Wellingborough. But the opinion polls were fluctuating and, by October, our average lead had been whittled down to below 3 per cent. The outlook improved for us after the 1969 party conference, held in Brighton. In some ways, it was an awkward conference: immigration caused some difficulties again, although a Powellite motion was soundly beaten, and I had to spend part of my own speech explaining our approach to capital punishment, after the conference had supported an amendment advocating its reintroduction. I stressed that there would be a free vote for Conservative MPs when capital punishment came up for review in the near future, and urged the government to produce statistics to enable MPs to make an informed decision. Harold Wilson tried to exploit our divisions on this matter of principle by rushing forward a vote on permanent abolition before the end of the year, instead of leaving it until July 1970 as the existing temporary legislation allowed. His tactic failed. I was one of many Conservatives who took their support for abolition into the lobbies, and the vote was carried by 343 votes to 185.

Our activists were stirred up by these issues, but I recognised that their passions mostly arose out of frustration with a government which had neither the skill nor the nerve to address more significant problems. I reassured the conference that 'there is no need to attack this government; you only need to be fair to it'. Immediately after Brighton an unofficial strike in the coalmines proved my point. Eventually nearly a million working days were lost as a result of this single dispute. Since the famous 'solemn and binding undertaking' there had also been trouble from Port Talbot steelworkers, Southampton dockers and London dustmen. In these circumstances we could not allow ourselves to be distracted by what most sensible observers considered to be important but secondary matters. The conference responded, and endorsed with enthusiasm our main strategy for reversing Britain's economic decline.

My interest in sailing had steadily progressed since 1965 into a strong commitment to ocean-racing and to the acquisition in 1969 of an ocean-racing yacht I named *Morning Cloud*. After winning a major race at Cowes during the summer of that year, the crew of *Morning Cloud* asked if we could compete in the major Sydney–Hobart yacht race in Australia that Christmas. We did so and, to our satisfaction, although ours was the smallest out of seventy-eight boats in the race, we won this most gruelling of challenges. The details of this victory I have recorded elsewhere. *Morning Cloud*'s victory chimed in neatly with media talk at this time that I was exhibiting a new self-confidence, but the truth was that sailing had always refreshed me. Admittedly, I felt a little extra satisfaction at the thought of Harold Wilson gnashing his teeth. Yachting rarely seems to enjoy press coverage in Britain, unless one of our sailors performs a striking feat of endurance. Even so, the Prime Minister was usually very anxious to be photographed with any successful British sportsman or entertainer. This was one occasion when he was unlikely to emerge 'spontaneously' out of the crowd to greet a winner.

At the beginning of February 1970, however, it was back to serious politics. The Shadow Cabinet met at Selsdon Park Hotel, near Croydon, to co-ordinate the results of our policy reviews and discuss an early draft of our manifesto. There had been a regrettable departure from our team in the autumn. Sir Edward Boyle, who had done so much to ensure the success of the policy groups, had agreed to take up the post of Vice-Chancellor of the University of Leeds, and announced his decision to leave politics at the coming election. I had always regarded Boyle as a candidate for one of the first offices of state, and during the 1960s I offered him a variety of senior posts, but his interest in education, which had given him Cabinet rank under Macmillan, only deepened. He held liberal views on virtually every subject, but he was especially committed to equality of opportunity. Unfortunately, this made him unpopular with vocal members of our right wing and, unlike those who are wholly addicted to politics, Boyle would not compromise an inch to buy a respite from criticism. I understood when he told me about the Leeds appointment, and reluctantly accepted that he should leave. He helped out during the election campaign, however, and I recommended him for a life peerage in 1970 when I became Prime Minister. We stayed in touch until his early death in 1981. After some reflection I decided to offer the Shadow Education post to Margaret Thatcher, who had dealt effectively with Fuel and Power and Transport since joining the Shadow Cabinet in 1967.

The fuss which the press made about the Selsdon Park meeting reflected its growing conviction that we were going to form the next government. It certainly was no reflection of the meeting itself, which was quite unspectacular. In fact, we conducted a good deal of business, arguing over the details of policies which were still evolving in the light of new thinking and changing events. Although we covered a lot of ground, however, I can think of no major new departure which emerged from Selsdon Park. We never even discussed law and order, the subject on which the press focused. The press arrived unexpectedly for a briefing on the Saturday lunchtime, and because we were only halfway through our discussions someone, I think it was Quintin Hogg, suggested that we should say we had talked about law and order, just to satisfy their curiosity. It certainly did that, because it was a headline story in virtually all the Sunday papers. We wanted the press to report our meeting, but we did not expect such a response to policy ideas which were already well known.

Harold Wilson made a savage attack on us, claiming that we had made a cynical move to the right. He came up with the name 'Selsdon Man', and tried to portray us all as right-wing extremists. We knew that it would cost us votes if that label stuck. In later years some members of my party have talked about Selsdon Park as if Wilson was right all along, and that it did signal a move away from traditional Conservative politics. Norman Tebbit has even written of 'the Selsdon declaration', which allegedly marked my conversion to 'the new liberal economics'. There was no such thing. He has rewritten history. Although I remember Margaret Thatcher talking a good deal about the interests of the middle class at Selsdon, she and Keith Joseph were united with us at that time in designing a manifesto which would attract support from all parts of the community. The complacent acceptance of mass unemployment, as an instrument for controlling inflation, was as repellent to them then as it still is to me today.

We worked hard on the manifesto at Selsdon, but although the outlines of our policies were well advanced we were still some distance from a final draft and discussions continued at meetings of the Leader's Consultative Committee. Eventually there would be seven drafts and the final version was not approved by the Shadow Cabinet until 20 May, two days after the election date was announced. Even so, our manifesto, *A Better Tomorrow*, was published before Labour had produced theirs and our *Campaign Guide*, ever the candidate's authoritative compendium of policies and facts, had appeared in April. This showed the benefits of a good team of back-room staff: Michael Fraser and Brendon Sewill deserve special credit for their outstanding work at that time, while we had, in Geoffrey Tucker, an imaginative adviser on publicity.

The title of our manifesto was an unexpected bonus from the Sydney−Hobart race. During my time in Australia I had the use of an official car. When we arrived at the quay in Sydney on Boxing Day I noticed that the people gathered to watch the start of the race all seemed in a mood to match the brilliant weather. I asked my driver why everyone seemed so happy. He explained, 'It's because we all know that tomorrow will be better than today.' I thought that this was exactly the kind of feeling we had to create in Britain, after a decade in which cynicism had become all too prevalent. I found on this visit, as on my previous one, that many of the Australians to whom I spoke seemed to regard Britain as a nation in its dotage, lulled into complacency by tales of its past greatness. Later in the year Labour would plan, but never properly sustain because the election intervened, a publicity campaign which tried to portray the Conservative front bench as 'Yesterday's Men'. In reality, it was the Wilson government which lacked any vision for the future.

The fact that Labour had performed so badly in government made the task before us no easier. Much had to change, so we had a duty to spell out our intentions in some detail. We knew that Wilson would fight with every weapon to hand and, as he had so few positive achievements to boast about, it was likely that our proposals would be subjected to constant attack. Iain Macleod, in particular, was convinced that it would be a dirty campaign. As a result, the final draft of the manifesto was written in a tone which, with hindsight, may have sounded more strident than we really intended. We probably tried too hard to underline the crucial differences between ourselves and Wilson, in terms both of policy and of approach. Whatever his original intentions on entering politics, Wilson had become obsessed with party management and Labour's image as a party of government. No doubt the national interest had its place in his calculations, but it rarely seemed to come first.

As we finalised the 1970 manifesto, we knew full well that Harold Macmillan's greatest fear, 'events', might go against us once we had taken over from Labour, but our principles would never be changed. There is always, in politics, a temptation to set out preferred policies for achieving goals as if these were goals in themselves. The foreword, for example, included the phrase 'once a decision is made, once a policy is established, the Prime Minister and his colleagues should have the courage to stick to it'. This was an allusion to *In Place of Strife*, and no one could ever accuse us of having acted as the Wilson government had done over union reform. But the words did leave a hostage to fortune.

Prices and incomes policy is the clearest example of this. In a perfect world, where wage bargaining is conducted responsibly and no producer wishes to exploit his customers, it would be easy to say that any such legislation is wrong in principle. The market never does work perfectly, however, and there are circumstances in which governments must consider stepping in on an interim basis. The Wilson government had waded in to control wages and prices before trying the obvious alternative of putting the parties to wage negotiations back on an equal basis, within the ambit of the law. They then abandoned restraint in advance of the 1970 election, in order to win credit for the temporary rise in the standard of living. We had worked hard on our proposals for industrial relations, and had the political will to implement them. In the early days we very much believed that we should never need a statutory policy to keep wages and prices under control. Our recourse to one was never intended to be indefinite.

In the manifesto, this pragmatic position appeared as a firm rejection of the 'philosophy of compulsory wage control', a form of words which could be hurled back at us by opponents who had no better alternative to offer when circumstances demanded government action to control inflation. Another phrase from the manifesto in equally vivid language was quoted less often in future years. We said that 'we are not prepared to tolerate the human waste and suffering that accompany persistent unemployment, dereliction and decline', a pledge which said a lot about the Conservative Party in those days.

Politicians need to be on constant guard against slips of the tongue which can help their opponents, but sometimes they can run into trouble even when they are careful to make their meaning clear. On the last day of the 1970 election campaign there was an incident of this kind. At our meeting before the press conference, over which I was to preside, my Central Office economic adviser, Brian Reading, produced a press release explaining our approach to prices. I asked Iain Macleod, the Shadow Chancellor, if it was all right. He confirmed that it was. I had no time to read it myself. To drive home the point that our plans to abolish existing taxes on consumption such as selective employment tax (SET) would slow the rate of inflation, Reading wrote that 'This would, at a stroke, reduce *the rise in* prices.' This was perfectly true. One hardly needs a first-class degree in economics to see that removing a tax on an item will directly reduce its market price, thereby increasing the purchasing power of people's wages and reducing inflationary pressures. At the time, the words made no impact at all. It took Jim Callaghan six weeks before he raised the matter in the House of Commons, distorting that phrase into a promise that, as soon as we were elected, the cost of goods in the shops would go down.

On the evening of 18 May, Harold Wilson appeared on the *Panorama* programme, having just returned from asking the Queen for a dissolution of Parliament. Viewers were, no doubt, intended to feel reassured by the idea that, after the election on 18 June, things would go on as before. This was probably Labour's best strategy, but even Wilson must have realised that 'business as usual' was an unappealing prospect. In fact, if nothing changed, Britain would soon be out of business completely. The agreement with the unions had brought predictable results. Between the fourth quarter of 1969 and the fourth quarter of 1970 average earnings jumped by 13 per cent, an unsustainable figure, far ahead of productivity growth. Over the year between the abandonment of *In Place of Strife* and the 1970 general election the number of strikes increased by 80 per cent.

Wilson believed that his preparations for a new election had left nothing to chance. Although Roy Jenkins had, very responsibly, rejected the temptation of an electioneering budget in April, just before the election a number of hand-outs to industry were announced, and the Social Services Secretary, Richard Crossman, increased several benefits. Wilson also timed the dissolution of Parliament to ensure that a controversial Bill to nationalise the ports would be dropped. Meanwhile, James Callaghan announced that new proposals from the Boundary Commission, which would have altered the population and political complexions of many parliamentary constituencies, would not be implemented before the election. It has been estimated that this cost us up to twenty seats. Holding the election during the holiday season was another clever ploy. Of those who would be out of the country and unable to participate, the clear majority were likely to be our supporters. Typically, Labour's planners also discussed the possible electoral impact of England's fortunes in the World Cup which was taking place during June. This event produced what was possibly the lowest point of the campaign, when Labour tried to suggest that the Tories were pleased when Brazil beat the England team 1–0 in the first round of the tournament.

Our campaign was carefully planned to get the positive message of our policies through to the electorate. Before Parliament was prorogued on 28 May, we held a rally for candidates in Church House, Westminster. The mood at the meeting was enthusiastic, and I felt that the party was well geared up for the coming fight. Once the campaign had begun in earnest on 1 June, there would be a morning press conference every day. Labour's conference was always held before ours, which, of course, gave Wilson the chance to set the day's agenda. I was consistently well briefed by a group chaired by Michael Fraser before I faced the press at 11 a.m. Then I would leave by plane for visits to marginal constituencies. In just over a fortnight I travelled many hundreds of miles, taking in most of Britain's major cities. It was a punishing schedule, made more so by the fact that the weather was consistently hot. I relished the battle, and enjoyed the kind of heckling which has disappeared from today's stage-managed elections. Wilson had rather less fun ducking the fourteen eggs which were thrown at him during the campaign. After he had been hit by these missiles on two days running, I was asked what I thought about it, and replied that, as his visits were kept secret until the last minute, the implications were very disturbing. It meant that 'there are men and women in this country walking around with eggs in their pockets on the off-chance of seeing the Prime Minister'.

Our main theme was always going to be the state of the economy. The problem which faced us was to point out Labour's mismanagement without talking down the country's prospects. I think we struck just about the right note, though some of our officials would have liked a more gloomy presentation. Our private polls told us that the message was getting through. At the start of the campaign, voters thought that Labour would be better than we were at dealing with an economic crisis, but by polling day we were nearly ten points ahead on that issue, despite the government's attempts to portray our restrained criticisms as scare tactics. On 15 June our arguments were backed up by the announcement of a £31 million trade deficit for May, contradicting Labour's claims to have solved the balance of payments problem. On polling day, we also learned that May's unemployment figure was the worst for thirty years, something which Iain Macleod had predicted in advance. Instead of fighting effectively for the under-privileged, Labour in office had only ensured that their numbers had increased. Three-quarters of a million children were now living in poverty, and 2 million people were either homeless or living in sub-standard accommodation. I was able to make extensive use of findings by the Child Poverty Action Group to illustrate the extent of Labour's failure. All of this made a mockery of Labour's question-begging and stilted manifesto title, *Now Britain's strong again – Let's make her great to live in.*

Despite my suspicion of public opinion polls, I am glad that we commissioned surveys of our own during the 1970 campaign. Apart from ORC, which worked for us, all of the pollsters recorded Labour leads. Indeed, as late as 12 June, another polling organisation put us more than ten points behind. After a packed and exciting public meeting in Manchester, I returned to my hotel glowing with confidence to find a large ring of the press gathered in the hall. 'Have you read the latest poll?' one of them enquired. 'No,' I answered eagerly, waiting for a triumphant reply. 'Well, you've dropped back to eleven points down,' he informed me. We had all been convinced that the tide was coming our way, and this was quite the nastiest moment of all. The bookmakers were no closer to the truth. At one point Labour were 20–1 on to win the election. We knew from our canvassing returns that this was a wholly misleading picture and, although we had lost some seats in the local elections of 1970, the detailed results had been encouraging to us. I dare say that even some senior members of the party panicked at times, but I always remained confident. I do not believe that there was a 'late swing' to the Conservatives, as many so-called experts have claimed in an attempt to explain away the inaccuracy of the polls.

On 17 June I returned to Bexley for the eve-of-poll meeting, where my father, stepmother, brother and sister-in-law all sat in the front row. On the following day, the anniversary both of Waterloo and of Wilson's climb-down over union reform, we based ourselves as usual in the King's Head for our buffet lunch, where I thanked those who had put in so much work for me during the campaign. They had faced an unusual handicap in this election. An eccentric Euro-sceptic had gone to the length of changing his name by putting Edward in front of it and Heath after it, so that he appeared on the polling card as 'EJRL Heath'. He contested the seat purely in order to confuse my supporters. Local Conservatives were

The triumphant football team at 86 HAC

Marching through Hyde Park in peacetime as CO of the 2nd Regiment HAC. I am to the left of the front rank

Above left Campaigning in Bexley, 1950. Edward Dines, the Chairman, can be seen behind me (centre)

Above right Bexley 1950. Reg Pye, the Agent, is immediately behind me

Left With the painter Augustus John and his wife

Below At No. 10 in 1958. From left to right are Sir Freddie Bishop, Harold Macmillan, John Wyndham (Lord Egremont), myself, Philip de Zulueta and Anthony Barber

Left Two of the greatest political influences on my life, Anthony Eden and Winston Churchill, return to No. 10 for President Eisenhower's visit, 1959

Below left Another great influence. With Harold Macmillan at Chelwood Gate, April 1959

Explaining the functions of the Government Chief Whip's Office to Nikita Khrushchev, General Secretary to the Communist Party of the Soviet Union, Moscow, 1963

Visiting the 'Wall of Infamy', Berlin 1963; with Sir Frank Roberts, the British Ambassador to West Germany

Looking in on Igor Stravinsky and
Pierre Monteux – 50th anniversary of
the 'Rite of Spring', with the London
Symphony Orchestra, Royal Albert Hall,
1963

Below Conducting carols in Broadstairs.
My father and stepmother are bottom
right

Bottom With Her Majesty the Queen
Mother. On the left of the photograph is
Sir Arthur Bliss; to my left hand are Sir
Robert Mayer and Sir Malcolm Sargent

'I've got a lovely bunch of coconuts'

With my god-daughter Siân Gibson-Watt

Working on Beethoven at Albany

With Lyndon Johnson, the President of the United States, who replaced Kennedy in such tragic circumstances

A cartoonist's view of how Harold Wilson might have reacted to my sailing successes

HEATH WINS BIG YACHT RACE

"HAROLD, YOU´RE CHEATING AGAIN ! "

Below Right foot forward. With Robert Allan, a war hero and later Anthony Eden's Parliamentary Private Secretary, and his family. His son Alex became John Major's Principal Private Secretary at No. 10

Talks with the German Chancellor, Willy Brandt, London, March 1970

'To Govern is to Serve': Outside No. 10 Downing Street, June 1970

The government front bench, June 1970. Left to right: Francis Pym, Alec Douglas-Home, Reggie Maudling, Edward Heath, Iain Macleod, Keith Joseph and Geoffrey Rippon. Tim Kitson and Walter Clegg are behind

With Her Majesty the Queen and the President and his wife at Chequers, October 1970. The Queen's first official visit to Chequers

Inspecting British troops in Germany, April 1971. Tim Kitson is behind me, in the raincoat

Relaxing with Prince Charles, Balmoral, September 1971

therefore forced to parade alongside the polling stations with placards, pointing out that there was an impostor on the ballot paper. Despite all this, people later told me that they had fallen for this stunt and the bogus Mr Heath won nearly 1,000 votes.

At lunchtime there was an unexpected visit from Peter Carrington. After congratulating me on the fight, he told me that, should we lose, I would be expected immediately to stand down. This advice was well-meant, but quite unnecessary. This election campaign had been a fair contest and I would have stood aside without any prompting if the result had gone against us. It did not. From the declaration of the first result, David Howell's victory at Guildford, I knew that my instincts had been a better guide to the result than the supposed science of the opinion pollsters. My own majority was greatly increased. Instead of being a marginal seat, which some had advised me to abandon for an easier berth, Bexley had given me a lead of over 8,000. Nationally we had 46.4 per cent of the vote, rather more than Labour in 1997. At no election since then has the party won so high a share and, although our overall majority in seats was fairly modest at thirty, we were ahead of Labour by forty-three. That was a satisfactory basis for carrying out our programme.

I drove back to London once the victory looked secure, feeling that curious mixture of light-headed elation and exhaustion which is familiar to most politicians. The first stop was at Conservative Central Office, where party workers and ordinary supporters had turned out to cheer the result. There was a different sort of greeting from a Labour voter who had given up a good night's sleep for the chance of registering a belated protest, and stubbed out his burning cigarette on my neck as I struggled through the crowd. In those days we felt it unnecessary to have a swarm of police around us all the time, and this was not the last incident of its kind. It could do nothing to dampen my feelings. After Smith Square, I went to my flat in the Albany, where I took telephone calls and, finally, went to sleep at around 5 a.m.

I was woken up at midday by my housekeeper with a cup of tea, as I had arranged. I asked her if anything had happened. 'Yes,' she replied, 'a man called Nixon keeps telephoning and demanding to speak to you. He's rung at least three times. I told him that you mustn't be woken up before midday, so he may telephone again any moment now.' Shortly afterwards, President Nixon did ring up again and congratulated me very warmly, predicting that, for the USA, we would be a great improvement on the previous government. Then he remarked that I should now be able to use the two months between the election and the inauguration of the new government to relax and decide about new appointments which would have to be made. I explained to him that our system was rather different from the American one. I would be going to the Palace to kiss hands on my own appointment that same evening, and should get all the necessary Ministers into post in time to start work early the following week. Nixon's comment on that was: 'God, what a system.' I have never known whether that meant that he envied our system or disapproved of it and preferred his own. My good relations with Nixon would continue throughout our period of government. Nixon understood what we were doing – and why we were doing it – better than most of his colleagues.

At about two o'clock, I left Albany to go down to Central Office again. The porter told me that there was a vast crowd waiting for me in Piccadilly. As soon as I appeared, the crowd surged across the road, stopping traffic and requiring a great deal of police activity to clear it away. Everyone looked remarkably pleased, cheerfully shouting congratulations and waving, without any sign of a hostile protester. Inside Central Office, I listened to Wilson's concession of defeat at about half-past three and imagined that he had gone immediately to the Palace. The Queen, however, was at Ascot, having no doubt been advised that anything she might need to do as a result of the election could wait until she was back in London. Wilson therefore had to delay his visit to the Palace until 6.30 p.m., and I was summoned at seven o'clock. The Queen's private secretary, Sir Michael Adeane, took me through the private quarters to the Queen's room. Her Majesty invited me to form a government, smiling in the most delightful way as she spoke. I thanked her and asked whether, before I left, I could beg a favour of her. I had already accepted her invitation to go to the party that night at Windsor to honour the seventieth birthdays of the Queen Mother, Lord Mountbatten and the Duke of Beaufort. Would she forgive me if I were to arrive a little late as I would need to have an immediate session with Willie Whitelaw, whom I would make Leader of the House of Commons, and the new Chief Whip, Francis Pym? She threw her head back and laughed, saying that all the family had been discussing whether or not I would still be able to come to the Windsor party. Everyone would understand if I was late after such a contest.

After kissing hands I was driven to No. 10, which I had known so well as Chief Whip and as a member of the Cabinet under two Prime Ministers. As I got out of the car I found that all the staff were lining both sides of the passage down to the Cabinet Room. We exchanged friendly greetings. I then got down to business with Willie Whitelaw and Francis Pym. At around eight o'clock, I suggested that we should break off for a light supper, and I pressed the bell for the principal private secretary, who was in the office alongside. I asked him to arrange supper for us. 'There's no food here,' he replied, 'and no staff, so it's impossible to get you anything to eat. Everyone left with Mr Wilson and there are no supplies here.' Then I suggested that he might go out and find some sandwiches which he could bring back for us. He disappeared. Some twenty minutes later he knocked on the door of the Cabinet Room, put his head through the half-opened door and shouted: 'Grub's up!' This sent Willie into paroxysms of fury. 'How can anyone behave like that?' he demanded. 'He must be sacked at once.'

I led a still shaking Willie to the next room, where there was a pile of sandwiches waiting for us, and some coffee. We tucked into that and got back to work. We settled all the members of the Cabinet, and Francis worked out how to arrange their appearances at No. 10. I resolved to get the full Cabinet announced by six o'clock on Saturday evening, and the rest of the government by the same time on Sunday. Then I changed into a white tie, and arrived at Windsor Castle at eleven. Of course I was tired, but the mood at the party was infectious, and many people came up to me to express their pleasure at the result. I paid my compliments again to The Queen, to the Queen Mother and to other members of the royal family. It was a happy ending to a memorable day.

A tremendous collection of congratulatory letters and telegrams began to arrive from friends outside politics as soon as victory was certain. 'Thank God you're in!' wrote the composer Sir William Walton. 'It was a beautiful performance worthy of a Toscanini.' Lenny and Felicia Bernstein sent 'warmest congratulations and affectionate wishes for success and peace', Samuel Beckett conveyed 'a million blessings and congratulations', the pianists Gina Bachauer and Clifford Curzon sent felicitations and would subsequently play for me at Chequers. The Italian conductor Carlo Maria Giulini 'thanked providence with all his heart for having placed the reins of government of this great country in the hands of a man whose concerns and political decisions will always be illuminated and enriched by the strength of his own rich spiritual and artistic experiences'. Sir Thomas Armstrong, the former principal of the Royal Academy of Music under whom I had sung in the Oxford Bach Choir (see p. 34–5), wished me 'all the strength and skill and courage that you will need to put your ideals into practice'. Joe Mercer despatched a telegram from Mexico, saying that 'being knocked out of world cup not so bad now – congratulations'. Anthony Eden sent warm good wishes, and Bob Boothby generously wrote that 'as one who has fought his way through nine election campaigns, I have never seen one conducted with such consummate skill as yours'. 'Don't abolish the House of Lords before 1974,' he added, 'I want to notch up my half century before I kick the bucket.'

At a meeting held near Cromer in Norfolk in early July, I said that our victory was only the beginning. I told that audience:

I have always had in my mind's eye a vision about the people of this country . . . We are a great people and a great nation. We are *one* nation.

One nation in which men and women of all creeds and all races can live together not in conflict but as neighbours. One nation in which the young know they will have their fair share of the opportunities and the elderly know they will have their fair share of the rewards. One nation in which all those who work in industry share the same aim, of creating new prosperity for themselves and for the community. One nation which is ready to make a major contribution in Europe on terms that are fair and just. One nation the world will choose to listen to once more because it hears us speak with one voice. Because it sees us ordering our affairs with fairness and good sense . . .

A nation worth listening to. A nation worth living in . . . That is what this government – your government – will achieve.

When I first entered Downing Street as Prime Minister, I said that 'to govern is to serve'. I knew that hard times lay ahead, but whatever might happen I would never give my country anything less than my best efforts. My hands were certainly not tied in allocating posts in the new government. I had made no promises of any position to anybody. With one or two exceptions, however, the positions were given to the people who had acted as Shadow spokesmen during the Opposition period. Iain Macleod, who had prepared economic and tax policies which would help us after entry into the European Community, was the obvious choice for Chancellor of the Exchequer. Although Iain was our 'biggest hitter', he told me that he had never expected me to offer him the position of Chancellor. I knew that he had suffered for many years from crippling neck pain, and thought that he would probably need to be moved from such a stressful post within a couple of years. Alec Douglas-Home became Foreign Secretary again, and I made Reggie Maudling Home Secretary, acknowledging that his talents and experience made him indispensable in one of the three most senior government posts. Maudling was the first of the new Ministers to see me, visiting Downing Street on the Friday evening. Quintin Hogg, who had shadowed Home Affairs, took a life peerage and returned to the House of Lords as Lord Hailsham of St Marylebone, seven years after renouncing his two inherited titles in 1963. He became Lord Chancellor, which gave him particular satisfaction as his father had also held that office. Peter Carrington was my choice for Defence Secretary, with Robin Balniel as his Minister of State.

After some thought, I decided to send Keith Joseph to Health and Social Security rather than give him any responsibility for industrial policy. Instead of Joseph I chose Geoffrey Rippon, a man whom I considered to have more reliable judgement, to head what was then the Ministry of Technology. Some thought that Rippon was too much on the right of the party, but he became one of the great successes in the government. I made Tony Barber, for whom I had a high regard, Chancellor of the Duchy of Lancaster with the vital task of negotiating with our prospective European partners. Although he had no experience as a junior minister, I felt sure that Jim Prior, who had been an excellent parliamentary private secretary to me, was ready for a senior post, and he did a fine job as Minister of Agriculture. I appointed Margaret Thatcher as Education Secretary, because she had shadowed it so effectively.

In making my Cabinet appointments and compiling the list of junior Ministers which came a few days later, I was anxious to cut down the size of the administration. There were eighteen Cabinet posts compared to twenty-one in the previous government. Overall I cut the previous total of eighty-eight Ministers to seventy-one. This was not an attempt to make economies, although the saving of seventeen ministerial salaries might have been seen as a useful symbolic gesture. The main reason for the change was the need for efficiency. Small groups are always the most effective for decision-making and, in a smaller Cabinet, there is more opportunity for everyone to make a contribution, should they wish to do so. Prime Ministers can buy support by offering unnecessary positions in government to potential trouble-makers, but to my mind this should not be the purpose of a modern Cabinet. The result of disunity is bad government and, although I regretted that there could not be places for all the able people in the parliamentary party, most of the better-publicised omissions were made for good and sufficient reasons.

I also kept my private office as small as possible, retaining Douglas Hurd as my political secretary and sharing Michael Wolff, an excellent speech-writer, with Willie Whitelaw. After a short time, Robert Armstrong came in from the Treasury as principal private secretary. I had very much wanted someone from one of the economic departments. In addition to his first-rate mind, his remarkable skill as a draftsman and his ability concisely to state an argument, Robert shared my love of music. He proved to be an unfailing source of good advice, and still is.

In my account of my time as Prime Minister, it has seemed best to describe in separate chapters how each of the main issues – for instance, the economy, industrial relations, Northern Ireland or Europe – developed and was dealt with over the period. This makes for a series of more coherent accounts, but it does not reflect the sheer pace and variety of a Prime Minister's life from day to day. There is a regular framework of fixtures, meetings of the Cabinet once and, in those times, often twice a week, meetings of the main Cabinet committees over which the Prime

Minister presides and Prime Minister's Questions in the House of Commons, in those days twice a week on Tuesday and Thursday afternoons. Each of these has to be carefully prepared, through reading papers and having informal preparatory discussions when necessary, sometimes several days in advance. There are other, often bilateral, meetings with colleagues, and it is immensely important to devote sufficient time to meeting back-bench Members of the party in the House of Commons, in their committees or in the Smoking Room or Dining Room.

A Prime Minister has not only to discuss and agree the main lines on which foreign and defence policy is to be conducted. He plays a considerable part in our international relations, attending regular meetings with the heads of state or Prime Ministers of other European Community countries and with the President of the United States. He also has to deal with the steady flow of Presidents, Prime Ministers and Foreign Ministers visiting or passing through London, and all expecting a meeting, or even a meal, with the Prime Minister. Then there are constituency duties and social functions, up and down the country, often involving a speech which has to be prepared. Time and space in the diary must be found for all of these.

So keeping the diary is itself a formidable task, requiring the almost undivided attention of one of the private secretaries. The whole delicate balancing act which this entails can be thrown out of gear by an unexpected event which calls for immediate attention. For example, during my time we had a series of terrorist incidents, wars or threats of conflict in some corner of the world where British obligations and interests were involved. Even the death of a head of state or of government overseas upsets the balance, because one has to drop all other business to go to a state funeral. For these occasions a large amount of briefing has speedily to be prepared, on the personalities who will also be attending and on the issues which they may want to raise in bilateral discussions in the margin of the ceremonies.

It is difficult to impose order upon events as they come crowding in to one's life and one's time. A Prime Minister has to be ready to switch his mind and his concentration at a moment's notice from one issue or event to another, picking up the thread immediately where he last left it. There are times when life can seem like a juggling act, made even more hazardous by the sudden appearance of unexpected additional hoops and balls. This act can be managed only with the support and vigilance of the staff of the Prime Minister's private office.

I was exceptionally well supported by my private office team. In the office itself, apart from Robert Armstrong, there were Peter Moon and then Tom Bridges on foreign and defence affairs; and Peter Gregson on the home and economic desk, followed by Christopher Roberts, who started on the Parliamentary Questions desk and was later succeeded by

Robin Butler. Later Alan Simcock was followed by Nick Stuart on the fourth desk. Towards the end of my time, Caroline Stephens, who later married future government Chief Whip Richard Ryder, came in to take charge of the diary.

The private secretaries were supported by a team of duty clerks, one or other of whom was on duty at all times of the day and night, and who kept pace with the movement and filing of the mass of paper that flowed into and out of No. 10. The press office was run with supreme skill by Donald Maitland and, in the last few months, by Robin Haydon. Both came from the Foreign Office, and I had got to know Donald well in the course of the first European negotiations in the 1960s. A small, lively, intelligent and articulate Scotsman, he won much respect from the lobby correspondents for the integrity of his dealings with them, and for his clear understanding of the line that should always separate the handling of governmental news from party political briefings.

On the political side, in addition to my political secretary Douglas Hurd, who was succeeded after the February 1974 general election by William Waldegrave, I was supported by Timothy Kitson, who was my parliamentary private secretary and became and has remained a close friend. The avoidance of friction between the civil service team and the political team was helped by the fact that Robert Armstrong and Douglas Hurd were old friends from their schooldays.

The subsequent careers of these individuals bear witness to the quality of the team I had working for me at 10 Downing Street. I had complete confidence in their intellectual abilities, their competence, their commitment, their loyalty and their discretion. No Prime Minister could ask for a better or more agreeable team to support him in No. 10. I am told that I do not always find it easy to express my appreciation of people to their faces. I am the more glad to be able to record now how grateful I was, and am, for all that they did, and were, for me during my time there. They were not just colleagues but friends, and to me, on my own as I was, a kind of extended family.

John Hewitt handled the Church appointments conscientiously and with understanding. Before each recommendation to the Queen on the appointment of bishops, deans and clergymen for livings in the gift of the Crown, he canvassed opinion in the church and the laity. At one time he was asked to provide a pro forma, which he then devised, on which those he consulted could indicate the specifications they wanted their new bishop to meet. After some months, I asked him how the pro forma was going and whether he found it useful. 'Well, yes,' he said, 'but the trouble is that the replies all tend to be rather similar. They ask for a man aged between forty and forty-eight, married, with four children, two boys and two girls, two over twenty and two under twenty, and either a man with a background in the ministry in urban areas who can get along with farmers, or someone with an experience of rural responsibilities who can get along with industrialists and city dwellers. The only time they differ is when they write either "The last one was a bit high, can we have someone lower?", or "The last one was a bit low, can we have someone higher?" ' No doubt this was why John Hewitt once said, at a time when there were five vacancies on the bench of bishops, that five months' hard work lay ahead.

There are many people who say that it is an anomalous and, in these days, anachronistic aspect of the relationship between Church and state in England that bishops should be appointed on the recommendation of the Prime Minister, who may not even be a member of the Church of England. As it operated in my day, and I was responsible for recommending no fewer than forty-five men to the Queen for appointment as diocesan and suffragan bishops, the Prime Minister's recommendations were made as a result of a selection process conducted with care and good sense. They were also often – I shall probably be excommunicated for saying this – better than they would have been had they been left entirely to the Church, with no involvement from No. 10.

I came into office with a firm conviction that we needed to change the structure of government, based upon the thorough examination we had carried out in opposition. This was a subject which engrossed me, to some people's surprise, because I was concerned that Ministers spent too much time on day-to-day matters, instead of on strategic thinking. In October we produced a White Paper, *The Reorganisation of Central Government*, which incorporated the conclusions we had reached after a further review conducted over our first four months in office. Two new departments, first Environment and, secondly, Trade and Industry, were set up that month in place of five existing ministries. This move was consistent with my desire to keep the Cabinet as small as possible, while including spokesmen for all the most important government functions.

A quick example will show how necessary this change was. In 1966 the Minister of Aviation, the Minister of Health, the Minister of Pensions and National Insurance, the Postmaster-General and the Minister of Public Building and Works were all outside the Cabinet. After our changes, all of these functions were represented in the Cabinet, yet the Cabinet was still small enough to conduct business. We designed the new departments to be big enough to help long-term planning, but not so unwieldy as to do more than bring inter-departmental tensions under a single umbrella. Peter Walker, the Minister of Housing and Local Government, was my choice for the new appointment of Secretary of State for the Environment. He was able to delegate much of the less significant work to junior ministers and officials, while overseeing the general picture.

I made two further reforms. The system of Programme Analysis Review (PAR) was developed to assess the make-up of each government department, to see whether the taxpayer was getting value for money. My experience in government had taught me that, whereas departments were aware of the need to meet fresh contingencies and to obtain the finance for them, they seldom reappraised the machinery and money which had been required to cope with earlier problems to see if they were still necessary. Everything was just allowed to rumble on. The PAR would work in tandem with the existing Public Expenditure Survey Committee (PESC), which allocated resources to the departments. Our purpose here was to bring some of the methods of business into those areas of government where they are appropriate. Later, following the advice of the Fulton Report on the civil service which had been published back in 1968, we established agencies such as the Defence Procurement Executive and the Property Services Agency. These ensured a more businesslike approach by government when it acted as a purchaser or as a landlord. Towards the end of the parliament, we also legislated for a Manpower Services Commission to co-ordinate the work of labour exchanges and training boards throughout the country.

The second, and probably the most important and effective, reform was the setting up of the Central Policy Review Staff (CPRS), or 'think-tank' as it became known. This consisted of a group of some twenty people, mostly young and selected from the universities, business and the civil service. It was allowed, even encouraged, if not to think the unthinkable, then at least to express the uncomfortable. It had three main functions. The first was to keep under review the country's economic performance, and to tell ministers how well or badly the government was doing in terms of its objectives. The second was to undertake studies in depth of major long-term issues which transcended departmental boundaries. The third function was to provide collective briefs for the Cabinet, or sometimes personal briefs for the Prime Minister, on specific issues being submitted to Cabinet or Cabinet committees for ministerial approval.

The outcome of its reviews of economic performance was presented to six-monthly meetings of Cabinet ministers which were normally held at Chequers, so that ministers could feel a little detached from their day-to-day departmental preoccupations. The CPRS did not attempt to gloss over unfavourable developments or to pull its punches on what needed to be done if the government was to stay, or to get back, on course. What we heard was not always welcome or popular, but the discipline of hearing it was very salutary. I made arrangements for these presentations to be repeated at separate meetings of middle-ranking and junior ministers in London, so that every member of the government was aware of the assessment and advice coming out of the CPRS.

Their other studies and briefs were no less valuable. They were no respecters of departmental persons or prejudices: they could be iconoclastic, and if the emperor had no clothes they said so. Their work was invariably thoroughly researched and well presented. I regard the CPRS as one of the best innovations of my years at No. 10. As a group which advised ministers collectively, it helped to maintain the cohesion of the government. The knowledge that departmental issues and proposals would be examined in depth, without fear or favour, by the CPRS helped to ensure that new proposals and ideas were better researched and presented by departments. The introduction of such an entity was, predictably, not universally popular within Whitehall. Although the Cabinet Secretary, Burke Trend, had supported the new body's establishment, he did so on the understanding that he would be able to influence its work. When he brought the first CPRS report to me, he informed me that it had required rewriting, which was incorporated in the copy which he presented to me. I asked to see the report in its original form and, having done so, asked him to circulate it. It was infinitely more effective. All in all, the CPRS provided a valuable reinforcement of the government's capacity for the analysis of policy at the centre.

At first I hoped that Kit McMahon, an economist at the Bank of England, would be its founding Director General. He preferred to stay on at the Bank, where he later became Deputy Governor. The man I then chose was the third Lord Rothschild. I wanted someone with a mind of his own, who would stand up not only to me and my colleagues but also to the mandarins in the civil service. He was a distinguished biologist, a Fellow of the Royal Society, who had enjoyed a career in military intelligence during the war, and later became a vice-director of scientific research at Shell. His independence of mind and judgement was reinforced by the fact that he was a wealthy man in his own right, not dependent for his living on his earnings as a public servant.

He proved to be an excellent choice, and it was a great loss to the country when he stepped down from his post just before the election of October 1974, when Britain needed his disinterested services, and the government of national unity which he wanted, more than ever. He certainly became something of a celebrity. The only problem which arose between us was in the autumn of 1973, when he made a speech about Britain's economic future, without consulting either me or his colleagues in the think-tank in advance. I rebuked him and any difficulty was all over in a few days.

No bureaucratic system is perfect and, of course, none can ensure success, but we made a quick start in improving what we found. My team of ministers and advisers settled into their roles easily, as in most cases they were well prepared during the opposition years. Indeed, it was said that some civil servants were taken aback by the extent of their preparations. There was one tricky moment at Education, where Margaret Thatcher became involved in a row with her permanent secretary, William Pile. Instead of explaining her views on the subject of comprehensive education to her senior officials, she simply marched in with a list of demands which she expected Pile to carry out without question. I had to resort to a meeting at Chequers with Margaret, William Pile and the head of the Home Civil Service, Sir William Armstrong, to sort out the problem.

Our first Cabinet meeting was held on Tuesday 23 June, at 11 a.m. After thanking them all for their part in our victory, I remarked that naturally there would not be any smoking during Cabinet meetings. I noticed Tony Barber and Geoffrey Rippon quietly putting out their cigarettes. Several months later, I found that Tony, by this time Chancellor of the Exchequer, always left the Cabinet at 11.45 on Thursdays 'to find out if there is any change in the bank rate', returning some ten minutes later. 'Surely,' I said to a private secretary on one occasion, 'his people must tell him that before he comes here?' 'Of course,' came the reply, 'but he doesn't go out for the bank rate. He goes out for a smoke!'

Before that first Cabinet, there had already been a separate meeting of Ministers to discuss the developing situation in Northern Ireland, and this subject also came up at the full Cabinet. Indeed, so important was it that I made Ireland a permanent item on the Cabinet agenda, following Parliamentary Business and Foreign Affairs. The main purpose of our inaugural meeting, however, was to settle the shape of our legislative programme, to be announced in the Queen's Speech on 2 July.

Once in office I went for the weekly audiences with the Queen, on Tuesday evenings at 6.30. I looked forward to these for a variety of reasons. It was always a relief to be able to discuss everything with someone, knowing full well that there was not the slightest danger of any information leaking. I could confide in Her Majesty absolutely, not only about political matters, but also about the personal affairs of those, both at home and abroad, with whom we were dealing. I had first met the Queen shortly after her Coronation, when she and Prince Philip had instituted a monthly luncheon party at Buckingham Palace. It was quite informal and, as the details of the guests were published, demonstrated very clearly to the public and the press that she was taking the opportunity of meeting people from every sphere of life, not only politicians and businessmen, but also those involved with charities and members of the sporting fraternity. As a Junior Whip, I was invited to one of the earliest of these lunches. There were eight of us at the round table in the dining room. After sherry, we sat down with the Queen. Princess Margaret sat opposite her, as Prince Philip was on a Commonwealth tour in Australasia.

The Queen was a very friendly hostess, talking to us all before lunch. After we sat down, Princess Margaret naturally turned to the guest to her right, the chairman of the Stock Exchange. Their conversation proceeded for the whole of the first two courses. She then turned to me. I had always been taught not to initiate a conversation with a member of the royal family. So while awaiting her opening gambit I just looked back, and remained silent. So did she. On the third occasion she turned to me, I lost my nerve and said to her: 'Have you been busy lately, Ma'am?' 'That,' she replied, 'is the sort of question Lord Mayors ask when I visit cities.' I felt shaken by this unexpected riposte and, after a pause, stumbled out, 'And what do you reply?' She said, 'Oh, in the first four months they're so green it's not worth talking to them. In the last four they are so tired they can't answer any question and in the middle four I am on holiday!' That summed it all up very well.

The Queen is undoubtedly one of the best-informed people in the world. A junior government Whip sits through Questions and the first part of debates in the House of Commons each day, and then writes a summary of the proceedings and an appreciation of what has happened which he then sends to the Palace for the Queen to read before dinner. Jack Weatherill, later Speaker, was a consummately witty writer of these messages. Her Majesty also receives immediate copies of all the important telegrams and overseas reports from the Foreign Office. In addition, members of the Commonwealth which have Governors send regular reports direct to her. She then has the results of her visits abroad, her personal discussions with overseas heads of state and their governments, together with her innumerable visits here in Britain. Despite the sheer volume of all this, her interest in the information provided by the Prime Minister never wavers.

The procedure I followed for the weekly audience became well established so far as No. 10 was concerned. On the morning of each audience, Robert Armstrong used to discuss with Sir Michael Adeane and later his successor, Sir Martin Charteris, possible subjects for the evening's meeting. For my first audience, on 30 June 1970, my office initially put forward three subjects: Northern Ireland, our approach to Europe and our planned legislative programme. I added, at the top of the list, the formation of the government, civil service matters and the place of businessmen in the work of government, so that the Queen would know what had been in my mind when I was making all my appointments. After all, two days later, she would be announcing our legislative programme in the House of Lords. I then added, at the end, the problems in Africa, including the proposed sale of arms to South Africa, having realised that this would be a difficult issue for the Commonwealth.

The Queen's Speech on 2 July restated the economic priorities on which we had campaigned. Our 'first concern' would be to control inflation, but our longer-term objective was 'full employment and an effective regional development policy'. We promised that improved incentives for hard work would be introduced, together with 'a framework of law within which improved industrial relations can develop'. Some of our pledges could be carried out immediately, for example granting local authorities the right to sell council houses. We also introduced a special pension for the over-eighties who had retired before paying National Insurance contributions, helping more than 100,000 people. Some ten years later, I received a personal letter from a lady saying that, for many years, she had been meaning to write and thank me for the pensioners' Christmas bonus, but she had been too busy. She had just had her ninety-fourth birthday, however, so she thought the time had come for her to send this letter.

We expected that the Industrial Relations Bill would take up a good deal of parliamentary time, so there were few other specific legislative commitments in the Speech. Even so, in the debate that followed Harold Wilson worked himself up to denounce our programme. In my reply, I concentrated on the foreign policy aspects of the Queen's Speech, reaffirming our commitment to a strong NATO and to the existing British positions in the Gulf and South-East Asia. One point which later caused trouble was my pledge to rebuild 'vital defence interests' in South Africa. This referred to the existing Simonstown agreement with the South Africans, to help them defend naval routes around the Cape, and I was restating the position we had taken up in opposition. However, as the furore in Britain over the South African rugby tour had illustrated, the anti-apartheid movement was now extremely active and this policy stirred up more controversy than anyone envisaged (see pp. 476–81).

As the state of the economy had played such a significant role in the election we anticipated that the most important debate would be on economic matters. On 7 July, Iain Macleod set out the government's position. I expected that this first speech would be a terrific blast, removing any doubts that he was the right man for the job. In the event, Iain's speech fell flat, the first sign that he was suffering from a new illness. In fact he was rushed to hospital for an abdominal operation that night. We all thought that the operation had been a success, for in less than a fortnight he felt able to return to Downing Street, although he was not yet fit enough to resume his full duties.

Late on the evening of 20 July, Iain's wife Eve rang me to say that her husband had died, from a heart attack. I felt numb and sick. I could not believe that something so terrible could have happened. Although I was asleep when Eve rang, I dressed quickly and went with Willie Whitelaw through the connecting corridors to No. 11, to visit her and offer what consolation I could. I was shattered by the news. Iain and I had been allies ever since we had entered Parliament and, although our outside interests were very different, we had always remained on close terms. On the following day, 21 July, I delivered a tribute in the House of Commons, then spoke on television about the country's loss. Three days later, I read the lesson at his funeral service, held near his family home in Yorkshire.

Iain Macleod's death deprived us of an excellent communicator, with a devoted following in the party. It also meant that I had to reshuffle the Cabinet only a month after the election. Anthony Barber had already begun negotiations with the Community, but I decided to move him to fill the vacancy at the Treasury. Reggie Maudling had done the job before, but his tenure had ended in controversy and this ruled him out. Tony was the only other realistic possibility. He was trained in tax law, which equipped him to carry through our intended reforms, and he had served in the Treasury previously. Having been party Chairman until after the election, he knew the importance of presentation, and he had been heavily involved in many aspects of policy formation. It was a wrench to move him, but at least I was able to find an excellent replacement for the European negotiations in the genial Geoffrey Rippon. Geoffrey's political experience showed a natural bent for these matters. On 12 December 1956, he had tabled an Early Day Motion, a written motion to which debating time is not allocated. This stated that the best interests of the UK and the Commonwealth lay in closer association between ourselves and Western Europe. As a barrister, he had developed the art of persuasion, so valuable in negotiations, and combined it with a degree of stamina which always sustained him for as long as he needed.

What proved to be an unfortunate consequence of the reshuffle was the promotion of John Davies, until recently director-general of the CBI, to the Cabinet, as Minister of Technology, after only a few weeks in Parliament. At this point I was keen to minimise the number of changes, and the choice of Davies, a backbencher, meant that no other minister had to be moved. I was also eager to emphasise our desire to modernise industry and wanted someone with extensive business experience to head what would soon become the Department of Trade and Industry through a merger of Technology with the Board of Trade. Furthermore, John had offered constructive comments on our industrial relations policy before winning his seat in the Commons. As things turned out, however, this was not an inspired appointment, although I had discussed it privately with those who had worked closely with him in his days both at Shell and at the CBI.

The tragedy of Iain Macleod's death and the difficult reshuffle were unexpected troubles. More predictable was a dock strike, which had been brewing for some time and was declared official on 15 July. With food supplies certain to be disrupted, we declared a state of emergency the following day, and Robert Carr, the Secretary of State for Employment, began discussions at once with the Transport and General Workers' Union, led by Jack Jones, which represented the dockers. On the 17th Lord Justice Pearson was asked to head an inquiry into the matter. When he reported less than a fortnight later, he recommended a rise of 7 per cent for the dockers, less than they demanded but more than the employers originally offered. In the circumstances, this seemed not unreasonable, so we decided to allow this increase, and the men went back to work. It was far from an ideal settlement, but we had yet to publish our proposed union legislation and this was not the time or the issue for a bruising struggle, as ordinary people, deprived of fresh produce, would suffer most.

Parliament was in recess during August. After a week in Cowes, I spent the rest of the month at Chequers, where the flow of official red boxes continued unabated. I went back to London twice for meetings during the month. August is generally a thin month for news, but it is also the proper time for politicians to cut down on their work in preparation for the coming parliamentary year. We had hardly got back into our routine of full-time work at the beginning of September when we were confronted with a major international incident. On 6 September, Arab terrorists attempted to hijack four airliners. Two were forced to fly to Jordan and a third landed at Cairo. The fourth attempt, on an Israeli plane, failed, and one of the guerrillas, from the Popular Front for the Liberation of Palestine, was shot and killed on board by the Israeli guards who are present on every El Al flight. Leila Khaled, the female partner of the dead terrorist, was captured. The pilot of the Israeli plane decided to land at Heathrow, the nearest major airport, rather than complete his journey to the US with a dead body on board. Leila Khaled was arrested at the airport. When they learned of the arrest, the terrorists on board the other planes threatened to blow them up, together with their passengers, unless she was released. The major question to resolve was Khaled's legal position. Should she, or even could she, be tried in the British courts? The decision fell to Peter

Rawlinson, the Attorney-General. After much deliberation, he concluded that no attempt should be made to try Khaled in a British court.

This decision was a controversial one and it was later alleged, in a scurrilous article in the *Daily Mail*, that the Attorney-General had been put under considerable political pressure. This was emphatically not the case. No efforts were made to influence his decision and he confirmed this both in a letter to *The Times* when the crisis had blown over and in his memoirs. In his view, prosecution in Britain could not have succeeded because it was unclear whether or not the attack had occurred under British jurisdiction, and he announced this at the end of September. In the meantime, we continued to hold Leila Khaled under an Aliens Order.

The plane which landed at Cairo was blown up on the day after it was hijacked, without casualties. On 9 September another aircraft, a British VC10, was hijacked and forced to land at Dawson's Field airfield in Jordan where the two remaining planes were also being held. The terrorists were now holding several hundred hostages of many nationalities including, it was thought, Germans, Swiss, Americans and Israelis. Sixty-five of those held were British. We were told that the hostages from Britain, Germany and Switzerland would be released in return for Khaled and six Palestinians held by the other countries. Those on the planes who were Jewish would be released only if the Israeli government agreed to return several hundred Palestinians who were imprisoned in Israel. From the start I took the line that Leila Khaled would continue to be held until all of the passengers, of whatever nationality, were released unharmed.

It was essential that the other governments involved agreed not to deal bilaterally with the hijackers since this would weaken the united front which we wanted to present. Through diplomacy we were able to secure these guarantees, and we were also able to persuade the Germans and the Swiss that the release of the hostages would be possible only if Leila Khaled herself was released. The Israelis were the main stumbling block, since they opposed any deal which would involve Khaled's freedom. When we told them that we had all been misinformed and that, in fact, there were no Jews at all on any of the planes, they no longer had grounds for objection. The Americans were very keen to prevent further loss of life and positively urged us to free Khaled.

On 12 September, all three aircraft were blown up, but only after the passengers had been removed and hidden in a secret location in Jordan, a country then suffering from a bloody civil war. Over the next two weeks, while we were involved in tense negotiations with the other governments, the position was further complicated by the decision of the Israelis to respond provocatively to the guerrillas by arresting hundreds of Palestinian Arabs, and by King Hussein's decision to send the Jordanian army against known guerrilla camps in his country. The Khaled crisis preoccupied us throughout September, dominating our Cabinet discussions. I kept in constant contact with Alec Douglas-Home as the situation unfolded. Alec and I were in the study of 10 Downing Street at three o'clock on the morning of Friday 25 September talking over our options when I recalled a meeting that I had recently had with President Nasser of Egypt and a possible way out of this impasse occurred to me.

I had first met Nasser back in 1954, and quickly established a rapport with him (see p. 164–5). I did not meet him again for fifteen years, as our contacts were much restricted by the events surrounding Suez. During my tour of the Middle East in 1969, we met at his home in Cairo and talked together for two and a half hours. He repeated the admiration for Britain which he had expressed when I first met him, and his regret that he had never visited our country. As I left, he said that, if ever I became Prime Minister, he would very much appreciate the opportunity to pay a visit and offered, in return, to help me in any way that he could.

Recalling this meeting, I suggested to Alec Douglas-Home that we should see if President Nasser could now help us to resolve the hostage crisis. We had absolutely nothing to lose by such an attempt, so I sent a message to Nasser, reminding him of his pledge and asking if he could lend us any assistance. On Saturday 26 September I received a reply from our ambassador in Cairo, to the effect that Nasser understood the issue and would see what he could do. Before the end of September, every one of the hostages had been released unharmed. They would have been freed sooner, but there was a delay because the situation in Jordan complicated the arrangements for their release. I should have been delighted to fulfil my side of the bargain and invite Nasser to Britain, but on 28 September, two days after I received his message, he died.

On 30 September, we deported Leila Khaled, and the Germans and Swiss released six other people at the same time. Our need to keep our tactics secret meant that it was difficult to explain our actions to the British public, who were in any case unused to incidents of this kind. The *Daily Telegraph* wrote a hostile leader, and Enoch Powell and Duncan Sandys were critical from the Conservative backbenches. Despite their protests the Leila Khaled incident had reminded us all that a government's first duty is to negotiate, even with terrorists, rather than immediately sending in the Marines, with guns blazing. In this case, the hostages emerged unhurt and only token concessions were offered in return.

On the weekend of 19–20 September, the situation in the Middle East curtailed the first of my annual visits to Balmoral Castle at the Queen's invitation. On future weekends at Balmoral, I would stay until the Monday morning and then go over to spend a day or two with the Queen's private secretary, Sir Michael Adeane and then Sir Martin Charteris, at his house at Craigowan. On this first occasion, however, I had to go straight to Dyce airport after Sunday lunch and fly down to Heathrow in a plane of the Queen's Flight, in order to deal with the increasingly critical situation in the Middle East. But despite the interruption, this was still a remarkable experience. I particularly recall a barbecue in informal clothes, at a secluded spot by a loch. While the Queen and Prince Philip produced the lunch, the rest of us sat on a bank happily chatting away on a lovely September day. Prince Charles was always interested in what I was doing, especially in any plans that I had to travel. He also liked to be brought up to date with how everyone was getting on with their outdoor recreations, in my case ocean racing. In the early evening, I accompanied the Queen in her Land-Rover over to the Queen Mother at Birkhall for a drink. The Queen Mother's hospitality is renowned and her guests were numerous.

On Saturday I had the customary private audience with the Queen. I was already beginning to think about the reintroduction, on a limited scale, of political honours, which had been discontinued by Harold Wilson. The Queen is the 'fountain of honour'. Though on these, as on most, matters she is bound to act on the advice of her Ministers, I thought that I should let her know in advance the way I was thinking. I made an announcement in the House of Commons on this subject in November 1970, although the New Year List of 1971 contained no political awards. Apparently, my sparing use of honours for political services later caused some grumbling among party members. I nominated only thirty-four new peers during my three and three-quarter years in office, whereas, in the five subsequent years of Labour government, Messrs Wilson and Callaghan managed to find 144 suitable candidates whom I had, unaccountably, overlooked.

As 1970 came to a close, I had been Prime Minister for a little over six months, and we had endured both our first serious industrial dispute and our first international crisis. In those turbulent times, I knew that worse was probably to come before things got better, but I remained convinced that our One Nation principles were what the country both wanted and needed, and I was determined to put Britain back on the road to success.

Chapter 12

Trying to Turn the Corner

Economic and Industrial Affairs 1970–1972

As we prepared ourselves for government during the late 1960s, we knew that the scale of the economic challenges we would face was increasing day by day. Between 1965 and 1969, economic growth in the United Kingdom was consistently and significantly behind that of our major European competitors, France, West Germany and Italy. We identified two main factors behind our relative decline. First of all, our industrial investment was inadequate, never reaching 20 per cent of gross domestic product, while our competitors were consistently devoting up to 25 per cent of GDP to capital formation. The cumulative effect was increasingly critical. Second, we also faced growing inflation, primarily wage inflation, which represented a real threat to our wellbeing.

The more immediate of these problems was inflation, and the inflationary culture we inherited could be overwhelmingly blamed on the outgoing Labour government. Between 1966 and 1969, they had operated a statutory wages policy which, with an election in sight, had been effectively abandoned. The unions, still so powerful, then let rip. In May 1969, the average wage settlement was 4.6 per cent. By December of that year it was 9.9 per cent and, by July 1970, it had reached 15.2 per cent. In such a situation, wages were inevitably growing far faster than productivity. By the end of 1970, wage earnings were rising by 14 per cent annually, and prices by 7 per cent. Meanwhile, underlying productivity per head was being increased by only 3 per cent. We still lived in a world of fixed exchange rates, with sterling an important reserve currency. As our inflation grew, the profitability of our companies was coming under serious pressure from growing wage demands. Export profitability was almost back down to the same pitiful level as before Wilson's devaluation. This threatened another sterling crisis, rising unemployment and economic stagnation.

Both devaluation and the Labour government's selective employment tax had produced an immediate inflationary effect, lowering the living standards of trade unionists, and putting the unions themselves under pressure to seek ever more inflationary pay deals. As a result, businesses put up their prices even more, in order to restore their margins. It seemed to be in no individual concern's interests to break this cycle. If anyone tried, they would expect to be hit with wildcat industrial action. In all other industrial countries freely negotiated collective agreements were binding on both sides. Under our common law they were not, so it was little wonder that wildcat strikes and walk-outs now accounted for 95 per cent of all strikes in Britain.

The Donovan Commission, reporting in 1968, identified this fragmentation of power and growing indiscipline as a major problem. 'It is imperative,' the Commission warned, 'that the number of unofficial and especially of unconstitutional strikes should be reduced and should be reduced speedily ... This is not only a serious, it is also an urgent problem.' The Commission also pointed to the main shortcoming in procedures which was causing this epidemic, namely 'the inadequacy of our collective bargaining system, and especially the lack of clear, speedy, comprehensive and effective procedures for the settlement of grievances and other disputes such as exist in other countries.' During the 1960s, the main locus of power within the trade unions had shifted away from the centre and towards the shopfloor, so that the trade union leaders could no longer be sure that nationally negotiated agreements would be respected locally. To make matters worse, the débâcle over *In Place of Strife* had destroyed any prospects of fruitful relations between the Wilson government and the unions, and made orderly negotiations within industry increasingly difficult. The trade unions were now in a position to threaten not only our economic and industrial well being, but also our political stability.

Our endeavours were not helped by the competition between the excessive number of trade unions that we had in the UK in those days, competing with each other for the same potential members and refusing to act according to any notion of national good. In 1967 there were more than 600 unions, including 262 with fewer than 500 members. Only two, the Engineers and the Transport Workers, had more than a million members each. Throughout the 1960s, the motives and incentives of our trade unions amounted to something very different from the national interest, as they competed to contrive and defend wage demands more excessive than their rivals could manage. This situation was destabilising industry after industry and represented a serious threat to the welfare of this country. Furthermore, inflation was most harmful to those least able to protect themselves.

As we had said in our 1970 manifesto:

Inflation is not only damaging to the economy . . . it is a major cause of social injustice, always hitting hardest at the weakest and poorest members of the community . . . the main causes of rising prices are Labour's damaging policies of high taxation and devaluation . . . the Labour government's own figures show that, last year, taxation and price increases more than cancelled any increase in incomes . . . so wages started chasing prices up in a desperate and understandable attempt to improve living standards.

The most familiar governmental counter-inflationary policy at that time was incomes policy. We knew that we should inevitably have to pursue a policy on pay in the public sector if we were to be able to create a properly balanced social market economy. Iain Macleod had made this plain in April 1969, saying that 'it is inconceivable to me that anybody can be an economic minister . . . and not have a sort of incomes policy.' However, we set out in our manifesto an ambitious longer-term solution for the private sector, pledging that 'Our theme is to replace Labour's restrictions with Conservative incentive . . . We want instead to get production up and encourage everyone to give of their best.' Our wish was to create a fair and free market, in which the balance of power between labour and employers would guarantee that common sense could prevail. We wanted to restore a healthy system of free collective bargaining, within which both sides of industry would behave responsibly and sensibly, in their own long-term interests and in the best interests of the country as a whole. It would have been irresponsible, however, to move swiftly to free collective bargaining without first introducing a new framework of labour law. The two reforms had to come in tandem.

The Conservative government of 1959–64 had realised that action would be needed to improve the legal framework within which unions operate. Industrial problems were already beginning to occur because of the inadequacy or obsolescence of our legislation. Labour then came in and did nothing about the problem. By the time of my Southampton speech in 1966 (see pp. 280–1), we had decided that a long-term and radical measure was urgently required, to replace 'collectivist laisser-faire'. In April 1968 we warned, in *Fair Deal at Work*, that 'it would be a nonsense to claim that a new framework of law will inspire a new atmosphere of responsible co-operation overnight', but something had to be done. Our answer was a comprehensive legal framework to restrict conflict, promote individual liberties and reform collective bargaining. Roy Jenkins had introduced the Labour government's abortive trade union Bill as a radical new tool in the long-term battle against inflation (see p. 298). We would do the same with our Bill on industrial relations.

As it turned out, the 1970 general election campaign was fought very largely upon the battlefield of economic policy and it became evident that the voters shared my conviction that there was an enormous job to do. Labour had frittered away vast amounts of money fighting doomed battles to sustain the level of the pound and propping up employment levels in industries which had neither strategic importance nor any realistic prospect of profitability. Meanwhile, they offered nothing during that campaign that addressed the most critical features of Britain's industrial decline. Whatever labour leaders may make out these days, socialists have never really understood the workings of a market economy.

Having examined the books after our election victory, we saw no reason to retract any of the criticisms we had made of Labour's mismanagement. Wage inflation was still pushing up prices in the shops and undermining our ability to compete in the international market-place. At the same time, unemployment was continuing to rise. Within three or four months, we knew that the balance of payments difficulties of Labour's last years had begun to ease, but we could not assume that the improvement would last. This mixture of price inflation and economic stagnation was the phenomenon which came to be known as 'stagflation'. To pull the country out of this trough would obviously require a major effort from us, but success would ultimately depend upon the British people. If the outlook did not improve fast, it was possible that the old industrial areas would fall into permanent decline. Government could not replace the private sector in this respect, but we had an obvious responsibility to encourage it into greater activity. We knew that, in our fiscal and monetary policies, we would have to bear in mind the possibility of a recession. But our priority was to get essential supply-side reforms on to the statute book: simplifying the tax system and introducing the kind of measures to improve industrial relations that we had been honing for the past five years.

My first meeting as Prime Minister with Vic Feather, general secretary of the TUC, took place on 1 September 1970. I was keen from the outset that he and I should resume the cordial and constructive relationship that we had enjoyed a decade earlier. Although I knew that Vic was close to Harold Wilson, I was determined that the TUC should never be able to accuse me of being aloof or hostile towards them. At this meeting, I set out straight away to establish that I still shared the stated objective of the TUC, namely increased investment, leading to improved productivity and, in turn, to higher real earnings. I told him that our aspiration was to re-establish genuinely free bargaining, uncorrupted by bullying tactics from either employers or unions. I also warned him that, unless he and his colleagues did something to moderate increases in labour costs, then we might have to do it for them.

At that very first meeting, Vic Feather agreed with me that we had to stop the economic cat chasing its own tail through wage inflation, and even indicated that the TUC might help with a policy of wage restraint. He did not believe that he and his colleagues could, at this stage at least, sign up to such an agreement publicly. The meeting was an amicable one but, although I had always liked Vic, I knew that he was not really in a position to deliver: the General Secretary of the TUC has no troops.

Vic Feather was a delightful man in many ways, but my dealings with him were often frustrating. Time and time again, he was obliged to be inflexible in the face of perfectly straightforward problems, because of the fundamental weaknesses of his own position. Vic himself was very civilised. He greatly valued the arts and was a gifted artist. As General Secretary of the TUC, he always got on well with the trade union leaders, and could always humour them when they got upset. Quite rightly, he prided himself on his understanding of their psychology. However, he must go down in history as a victim of circumstances, for the early 1970s could not easily accommodate such a reasonable and inherently decent man in the position of the General Secretary of the TUC.

At Blackpool on 10 October 1970, I set out in my speech to the party conference the challenges facing the country and explained our approach to them. First of all, we would put our own house in order, by looking at the whole of government expenditure and cutting costs wherever we identified waste. This would enable us to reduce the tax burden, allowing hard-working people to keep more of their earnings. We were motivated by a general desire 'to bring our fellow citizens to recognise that they must be responsible for the consequences of their actions'. This remark applied to everyone in Britain, but most especially to those workers who demanded unreasonable pay deals, and to the employers who gave in to their threats. In this speech I had some hard things to say, but my words did not exaggerate the scale of our problems. Despite the difficulties of the 1960s, there were still those whose memories of Britain's past greatness prompted them to imagine that our former status somehow guaranteed a bright future. It was my duty to dispel this illusion.

For John Davies, the recently appointed Minister of Technology, and about to become Secretary of State for Trade and Industry, the conference was crucial. He had never addressed a similar gathering as an MP, let alone as a senior Minister. John's speech struck a powerfully anti-interventionist note. He did not use the phrase 'lame ducks' at this point – that was reserved for a speech in the House of Commons the following month – but the message was very similar. Perhaps John was trying too hard to prove his credentials, and those of the government. Many knew him to be an instinctive interventionist and, in retrospect, he used excessively tough language in this speech, which contributed to a belief that our government had a policy of total non-intervention towards any company, regardless of the consequences. That was not so. Our purpose was more pragmatic than people were led to believe. What we wanted was to put a stop to the Labour policy of propping up ailing concerns indefinitely, covering their current running costs or writing off bottomless debts. We would only help them in a way which would enable them, step by step, to stand on their own two feet. This was an essential part of our strategy for changing Britain's industrial psychology.

When I made my Blackpool speech I was sure that we could deliver our promise to cut government spending, which had risen from 44 per cent of GDP when Wilson took office in 1964, to 50 per cent by 1969. No one relished the thought of cuts to important spending programmes, but there was clearly scope for savings. The Chief Secretary to the Treasury, Maurice Macmillan, handled our first round of public spending negotiations ably. We both knew perfectly well that, even though we were committed collectively to reducing public spending, each individual Minister could fight like a cornered cat to protect his or her own fiefdom. Fortunately, at this stage, most of the Cabinet did give their full co-operation to Maurice. On 27 October, Tony Barber was able to inform the House of Commons, in his mini-budget, that we had agreed to £330 million in cuts for 1971–72 (£2,900 million in 1998 prices). By 1974–75 the annual cuts in expenditure would have risen to £1,560 million (around £13,700 million in today's values). Labour, predictably, denounced our savings, but they had all been agreed upon after much discussion, in line with our pledge to concentrate spending where the proven need was greatest. We reduced subsidies for council housing, raised NHS prescription charges, withdrew free school milk from children aged between eight and eleven (Labour having already abolished it in secondary schools) and proposed admission fees for some museums and art galleries.

Margaret Thatcher was the only Minister to clash seriously with Maurice Macmillan when he suggested ways of trimming her departmental budget, and later found herself the target of unfair abuse for the cuts in school milk. Critics claimed that it was unnatural for a woman to take milk from babies, overlooking the fact that these were rather grown-up babies, and that Margaret had to make reductions somewhere in order to protect her ambitious plans for primary school building. The ugly slogan 'Mrs Thatcher, milk snatcher' was another reminder that our attempts to turn Britain around would be hampered at every stage by our political opponents and their friends in the media. The critics also ignored the new family income supplement, to help those in low-paid work, which Tony Barber also announced. Together with a system of exemptions for the least well-off, this reflected our determination that the poor should be adequately protected, by carefully targeted programmes.

The mini-budget also fulfilled our long-standing and essential plans for bringing government policies towards agriculture and industry into closer line with the policies within the European Community, in preparation for negotiating entry. The system of deficiency payments to farmers was replaced by import levies, which would give our agriculture equal protection at far less cost to the taxpayer, and Labour's Industrial Reorganisation Corporation, a dirigiste body which had done more harm than good, was wound up. The old system of grants to industry was scrapped and investment allowances were introduced instead, with special help for the development areas. We wanted these measures to be of special assistance to businesses faced with the need to re-equip with the most modern technology, an urgent requirement at a time of great change in productive processes. Business incentives would also be improved by a cut in corporation tax, down by 2.5 per cent to 42.5 per cent. Finally, Tony Barber announced a reduction in income tax by sixpence in the pound – 2.5 per cent – from April 1971. Labour immediately protested that we were trying to help the rich, but of course the cut put more cash in the pockets of everyone who paid the tax and it restored the rate, 38.75 per cent, which Labour had inherited in 1964. This was the first reduction in income tax for eleven years. It was high time that hard-working people received some respite, and we hoped that the incentive of keeping more of their money would spur them on to greater efforts.

Tony Barber was constantly barracked during his speech, with cries of 'Resign!' from the opposite benches. Labour thought that public expenditure was a good thing in itself and that the more the public sector absorbs of the national income, the happier everyone is. My own experiences in office, and my own deeply held political convictions, taught a different lesson. This first package from Tony Barber deliberately concentrated help upon those in the greatest need, minimising the pain for the poorest in society at a time when a national crisis demanded sacrifices. Naturally we hoped that these cuts would be the last, and the rest of our measures were designed to produce the general prosperity which alone could sustain more ambitious, long-term plans for social spending. Without that, the poor would suffer along with everyone else and, without some kind of revolution in industrial and fiscal policy, we could see no way of generating that essential prosperity. After this mini-budget, we felt that we had gone a long way towards fulfilling our part of the bargain made at the general election.

*　　*　　*

Tony Barber's fiscal measures represented a positive opening barrage in the war against inflation, but I knew that time was short. I therefore decided to summon a meeting of senior Ministers at Chequers, on Saturday 14 November, to discuss how we could break the circle of inflation, and asked the Treasury to prepare a top-secret assessment of the problem, its origins and how we might now get to grips with it, which could provide a basis for the discussion. The resulting document was a great disappointment, a product of the civil service at its worst. It just painted a dire picture, offering not the slightest hope of finding a way out. It warned that 'there is no single centre in government which is consistently concerned with this problem', and went on to conclude, blandly, that 'we assume that Ministers will . . . wish to consider what combination of policies (including if necessary modification of existing policy objectives in other fields) would be preferable'. I felt that this was a total cop-out, and asked for a far more down-to-earth analysis from my economic adviser Brian Reading, who had now moved to the Cabinet Office. He was scathing about the failure of the Treasury to provide any answers, and argued that their briefing was so platitudinous that there was not even the slightest need for it to be classified. He then set out the six broad options before us, as he saw them: living with inflation; demand deflation; a statutory prices and incomes freeze; reflation of demand through tax cuts; a showdown with unions and companies; or a package of direct action on prices combined with radical supply-side reforms.

There was at least one serious shortcoming to each approach. Our present problems had been caused by the breaking of a dam which had squeezed personal living standards for a time and then burst, argued Reading. This not only created inflation. It also, very rapidly, created the expectation of further inflation, and accelerating inflation at that. 'A successful policy to deal with inflation,' he warned, 'therefore needs both to reduce the inflationary pressure in the economy and to convince people that something which is likely to succeed is being done.' His paper concluded that we needed real structural change in the longer term, built upon the foundations of our new approach to industrial relations and, in the shorter term, a combination of detailed policies which would work quickly to begin the process of bringing the problem under control. In the light of this, I delayed the ministerial meeting by two days and had a lengthy private talk with Tony Barber instead.

A general view, which I broadly shared, was now emerging that at some point we would have to face down at least one strike in the public sector. Going on strike had become too easy an option for a number of reasons: strikers were taking up other work while on strike, they and their families were drawing benefit, and they were receiving, through the tax system, what almost amounted to strike incentives. Until we dealt with all of that, I told Tony, I did not see how we could possibly win in a straight confrontation with any union. The Industrial Relations Bill, possibly with later fine-tuning, would surely bring about sanity in the long term, but we had to deal with our immediate problems. A dispute in the electricity industry provided an opportunity for making the stand that we all sought, so long as we were absolutely sure about the practicalities of seeing off a complete shutdown by the electricity workers.

We were conscious, however, that a robust approach in the public sector, given the climate that we had inherited, could always be undermined by two crucial factors: the unreliable nature of public opinion, and capitulation in the private sector. For a few months, we talked seriously about introducing an 'inflation tax' – a tax surcharge on employers who caved in to blackmail and paid out excessively inflationary pay settlements. This idea had floated around for fifteen or so years, but it was always felt that it would be overly bureaucratic and that employers would find some way around it. The best approach seemed to be that we should invite the TUC and the CBI to No. 10, to discuss voluntary measures to curb inflation. 'It is impossible,' I told Tony Barber, 'that wage increases should continue at the present rate and, in a free society, it is the responsibility of the two sides of industry to act accordingly.' Even at that stage I was motivated more by hope than by expectation.

When the ministerial group met at No. 10 on the following Monday, 16 November, I set out the scene for colleagues. 'The balance of industrial power,' I said, 'has swung in favour of those who are prepared to press unwarranted pay claims by industrial action, even at the risk of damage to the national economy . . . the discipline earlier provided by fears of unemployment and of hardship for strikers and their families and, indeed, the threat of higher levels of unemployment . . . are no longer the deterrent they used to be.' We all agreed that we had to get wage inflation under reasonable control by the spring of 1971, and that the government should take steps to ensure that the Electricity Council should not settle its wage negotiations with an increase in excess of 12 per cent. It was also agreed that a series of measures had to be expedited to change both the industrial climate and the legal framework which was so obviously open to abuse.

As well as preparing ourselves for a confrontation in the public sector, we also had to make sure that our economic policies were supporting the war against inflation. Our options were limited. Because of our manifesto commitment to reduce direct taxation, any fiscal restraint had to involve increases in indirect taxation which, in turn, would inevitably increase prices and add to wage-push pressures. If we ruled out tax increases altogether, then we had to consider higher interest rates which, during a period of low profitability, would have led to increased bankruptcies and unemployment. Subsequent governments were readier to run that risk, but it seemed to us a dangerous and divisive path. It was against this background that, before the end of 1970, Tony Barber and Robert Carr were warning senior colleagues that, despite our reservations in principle, we could not indefinitely rule out any anti-inflationary tool if we continued to discount unemployment as a weapon for reducing wage inflation.

The first serious industrial dispute that we faced, the dock strike of July 1970, had been settled quickly and on reasonable terms, but we knew that more unrest could not be far off. Our Industrial Relations Bill was published in December 1970, as promised. As Robert Carr explained, 'This Bill is essentially about regulating the eternal tension between, on the one hand, the desire of the individual person for complete freedom of action and, on the other, the need of the community for a proper degree of order and discipline . . . Unfettered freedom destroys itself . . . Liberty cannot exist without order, or rights be long sustained without corresponding duties.'

The Industrial Relations Bill became the subject of fractious exchanges between government and unions for the rest of the parliament. We knew that the trade union leaders would insist upon Labour trying everything possible to obstruct its passage. We had offered them the opportunity of consultation about the contents of the Bill, but they had declined. Their line was always that, as they were opposed to the very principle of the Bill, there was no point in their taking part in discussions about its content. We were not willing to concede on the principle, however. This was the centrepiece of our long-term economic programme, and we had a clear mandate to introduce it. For five years I had tried to engage with the leaders of the trade union movement in substantive discussions about what we might do in government, and they had stubbornly refused to talk. Now, in the wake of our victory, the TUC Congress had produced a composite resolution opposing our Bill in principle, and reasserting the desire of the unions to stay outside the ambit of the law. We were going to have an almighty fight on our hands, but we had to build the foundations of modern, responsible trade unionism.

I decided that, because the successful passage of this Bill was so intrinsic to our whole programme, I should speak myself during the second-reading debate. When I opened the second day of that debate, on 15 December 1970, I put on the record the thinking behind this piece of legislation. Governments of both complexions had attempted to induce those involved in industry to reform matters voluntarily, but the situation had just deteriorated. Until the past few years, there had been a general acceptance that there was not much potential for improving industrial relations through the law, because 'there was the feeling that industrial relations were human relations'. It was now widely accepted, however, that behaviour was greatly influenced by the legal structure and, in recent years, 'the competitive pressures inherent in the existing system of collective bargaining and the consequences of industrial disputes . . . have pushed up money incomes beyond what both sides of the House recognise to be possible'. The intention behind this Bill was to 'bring order, stability and confidence to the system of free collective bargaining'. I went on to say that, while 'it is possible . . . to say that this Bill will not produce an immediate answer to this problem . . . it is a vital element in the longer-term strategy for dealing with it'.

This Bill was not, as some would have it, a device for attacking either trade unions or working people. In it we established a number of new, positive legal rights. The basic principles were in Clause 1: collective bargaining, freely and responsibly conducted; developing and maintaining orderly procedures in industry through the use of negotiation, conciliation or arbitration; the principle of free association of workers in independent trade unions; and the principle of freedom and security for workers, with protection from unfair practices. In Part II of the Bill, we set down in statute, for the first time, the right to join, or not to join, a trade union and to take part in trade union activities. In Part III, we dealt with questions of collective bargaining. Clause 32 of the Bill introduced into statute a presumption that any future collective agreements were intended by both parties to be legally enforceable. This clause was subsequently attacked by Lord Donovan, and the unions soon found a way of getting around it, rubber-stamping agreement after agreement with the phrase 'This Is Not a Legally Enforceable Agreement'.

As we prepared to take the legislation through Parliament, we knew that we had to lead by example, through holding out against unreasonable pay demands from public sector workers. If in our role as employers we could restore common sense to price setting and wage bargaining, then private business would be encouraged to follow suit. After our early decision to allow the Coal Board only half of the price increase they requested, we continued our watch for any signs of inflationary actions by the nationalised industries, through prices or wages, and we settled upon a guiding principle that the pay deal in each year should be worth 1 per cent less than inflation. We knew, of course, that there would always be special cases, and were advised early on, for example, that the miners had fallen behind other categories of worker during the Wilson years. We were prepared to be flexible, up to a point, about some pay increases in the public sector, but we recognised the pitfalls of allowing one group after another to promote itself as a 'special case'. Trade union leaders might well have found that the inflationary illusion of an improving standard of living kept their workers happy, but we knew that, unless we had a revolution in industry, prices would go on catching up with earnings. Eventually, they would outpace them, by which time it might be too late to do anything about this mad merry-go-round.

Not everyone shared our resolve. In November 1970, the local authorities, faced with a strike by dustmen and other workers, called in a team led by Sir Jack Scamp as independent arbitrators. The result was a settlement which would give the strikers 14 per cent, most of what they demanded. In their report, the arbitrators implied that inflation would not be cured by moderating pay deals. As I said on *Panorama*, the settlement was 'patently nonsensical'. The Scamp award was a serious setback which sent the wrong signals to other workers. We redoubled our efforts with those employers whom we could influence more directly.

Robert Carr had already met the heads of nationalised industries, in order to drive home the importance of restraint. He now called them back to repeat that message. He also, quite rightly, made a point of stressing that the final responsibility for each settlement lay within the relevant industry. On 7 December, four days after the Industrial Relations Bill was published, power-station workers began a work-to-rule. As in the case of the dockers, this forced us to call a state of emergency, and we had to establish a system in which electricity was cut off for certain periods every day. While this revealed the enormous power of this particular union to cause harm to the country, it also alienated the many ordinary people who were hit hardest during the dispute. The outcry was so violent that the work-to-rule was soon called off. On the same day, we set up a committee under Lord Wilberforce to examine the pay claim. Wilberforce gave the workers a rise of around 11 per cent, much closer to the offer originally made by the Electricity Council than to the 30 per cent demanded by the strikers. We had taken the precaution of announcing that Wilberforce was to include considerations of the national interest when he made his calculations, to prepare the ground in advance for an award to the power workers at the top end of our informal scale. When, in the event, this deal fell within the framework we had set for pay, it was one of our few strokes of good fortune during this period.

The damage which these disputes were causing to the country was made clear in March 1971, the month after Wilberforce made his ruling. Henry Ford, whom I had met once before, in Florida, came to see me, along with the subsequently much celebrated Lee Iacocca. Ford hinted strongly that he was considering pulling his firm out of Britain altogether, because of the deplorable state of our industrial relations. He was fairly worked up, and seemed to think that a government should be able to wave a magic wand and solve the internal problems of a big company such as his. Fords were by now enduring a strike of their own, which confirmed our fears that irresponsible pay settlements in the public sector could start a vicious circle elsewhere. Eventually the strikers were rewarded with a staggering 33 per cent rise, to be phased in over two years.

My meeting with Ford took place after another strike in the public sector which was settled on satisfactory terms. Post Office workers had come out in January 1971, demanding up to 20 per cent. We held out against them. Eventually, after another enquiry, they accepted a deal which was on the table at the start of the strike. While this was a notable victory for common sense, we were aware that it was only partial: although the postal workers could cause disruption, indeed misery, for those who really depended upon their services, in particular older people, they were not as militant as the dockers or the power workers. Indeed, some members resigned from their union during the dispute. Although the postal strike was the last major dispute of its kind for some time, the experience of our first year in office left us even more convinced than before of the need for reform. If bullying tactics by strong unions in some industries could hold the country to ransom, then workers in those sectors would go on improving their standards of living. Meanwhile, those who behaved more responsibly would be left behind, to suffer the full inflationary effects of others' wage increases. This was purely about the wholesale abuse of power, and nothing to do with natural justice.

Such considerations cut no ice with those militant trade unionists who, in other circumstances, liked to pose as the friends of the underprivileged. They maintained their unquestioning opposition to the principles of the Industrial Relations Bill, and various one-day stoppages to protest against it were held. But union intimidation would not deter us from our purpose. After some marathon parliamentary sessions, including a record eleven hours of continuous voting on one day during the report stage, the Bill was passed, receiving royal assent in August 1971. We knew that the country as a whole was behind us at the outset and I was convinced that, if I and my party held our nerve, the people of the United Kingdom would hold theirs. An opinion poll taken at the time the Bill was published showed around 70 per cent of people in favour of each of the main proposals in the Bill. In March 1971, in the face of intensive propaganda from the other side, more than half the population approved.

On 8 April 1971, I had one of my regular private meetings with Vic Feather, who had joined Harold Wilson in whipping up the crowds during a demonstration against our Bill in London on 12 January. He was, he said, convinced that the new legislation would not have any practical effect whatsoever upon the state of industrial relations in the UK. He claimed both to suspect that this was also our view and that, in the majority of firms, management itself recognised that there would be no benefit in seeking to invoke the provisions of the Bill. Feather's own great fear now was that some 'small-town solicitor' would try to make a name for himself by talking some unfortunate, lesser company into trying its luck in the courts. Lord Donovan had said something similar in Parliament a few days earlier.

Such talk convinced me that the unions were, albeit reluctantly, beginning to recognise that the rules of the game were changing. The TUC leadership had already defeated a resolution, put forward by the militants, which would have forced them to expel any union which registered under the Act, when it came into effect. The TUC would 'discourage' unions from registering, but would implement no draconian sanctions against those who did. Jack Jones had now indicated that even the Transport and General Workers' Union was considering registration. Regrettably, the TUC line subsequently hardened considerably. It was also at this meeting that Vic Feather, who was as concerned as we were about the spiral of rising wages and costs, first proposed that we should, perhaps, begin preparatory discussions about an incomes policy. At this stage, however, he was quite clear that he was only willing to discuss a 'voluntary approach' to breaking the vicious inflationary circle.

Feather explained to me wearily that, in his view, the likes of Jack Jones of the TGWU and Hugh Scanlon, president of the Engineers since 1968, really just wanted 'the kudos of militancy without really desiring to achieve the results for which they are fighting . . . they are in a way relieved when they find themselves out-voted by the moderates'. The damage that they were doing by this process, however, was solid enough. Hugh Scanlon had the clearest, firmest and in many ways most persuasive mind of all the trade union leaders I met. I seldom heard him produce an argument which could be lightly dismissed. Employers very seldom attempted to argue with him at all. Nor do I recall any occasion on which his own members were tempted to overthrow his policies or weaken his position. At the same time, he always made a point of working very closely indeed with his colleagues in putting forward a common front on all the matters we discussed affecting economic and industrial policy.

Despite the sound and fury from the unions, we remained confident that they would eventually comply with the terms of the Act. Anarchy was in no one's interest, and we knew that many of the leaders, not least Vic Feather himself, privately agreed with what we were trying to achieve. But, as Feather had warned me at our first meeting back in September, we could expect only vitriol from the union leaders in public, whatever they might feel moved to say in private. I could see the dilemma faced by the more moderate trade unionists, but so much was at stake that it was difficult to sympathise very deeply. It remained to be seen whether the union leadership could live up to its private convictions and save the movement from itself.

Our trade union policy was handicapped from the start by the legacy of Labour's failures, and we soon found that the same applied to our strategy for industrial regeneration. The business community hardly leaped into action the morning after our election victory. Although I had made it clear early on in my party conference speech in Blackpool, that the revolution we intended would take more than one term, we were dismayed by the dire level of morale that we found. Too many industrialists had accommodated themselves to low expectations. If they could always rely on the government to bail them out, they reasoned, then they had no need to think carefully before they acted. We soon discovered that this extended to some of the most prestigious companies in the United Kingdom.

It was as early as 10 July 1970 that we got our first clue to the gravity of the situation at Rolls-Royce. Lord Poole, a respected former party Chairman and now chairman of Lazards, told me privately at a dinner at No. 10 that the company was in serious trouble. In March 1968, Rolls-Royce had negotiated a £150 million contract to supply a new aero-engine, the RB211, for the new L-1011 Tri-Star aircraft to be manufactured by Lockheeds. This fixed-price deal was agreed with the backing of Tony Benn, the Minister of Aviation, on behalf of the then Labour government. At the time, the launching cost of the new engine was estimated at £65 million. The government promised to cover, after certain adjustments, 70 per cent of that cost, a commitment of slightly over £47 million.

It had soon transpired that Rolls-Royce had been rashly over-confident when estimating the time needed to develop the engine and, in its anxiety to secure the contract, had agreed to design modifications, the cost of which was not covered by the contract price. The company was in trouble with this contract from the start, as its research and development costs immediately began to escalate. Labour's Industrial Reorganisation Corporation had investigated the position at the end of 1969, and promised a further unsecured loan to the company of £20 million for general purposes, £10 million in 1970 and the same amount in 1971. The financial situation had continued to deteriorate fast, however, and was now little short of a crisis. Lord Poole was fearful that Rolls-Royce faced ruin unless the government could help it financially. Sir Denning Pearson, chairman of Rolls-Royce, warned Fred Corfield, at the Ministry of Aviation, about the position at around the same time.

This presented us with a major difficulty. A private company had brought trouble on itself by signing a contract based on an unrealistic assessment of the likely development costs. It would be a serious step to involve the government. On the other hand, a host of significant considerations had to be taken into account. First of all, if Rolls-Royce collapsed, there would be serious implications for our own defence capabilities, as well as for those other, allied countries whose air forces were equipped with Rolls-Royce engines. Secondly, we were conscious that the engine was a potential market leader in just the kind of high-technology field which we were keen to encourage. Thirdly, Rolls-Royce at that time employed around 80,000 people, many of them in areas of high unemployment, including parts of Scotland and Northern Ireland. Of these, some 20,000 were directly involved in the RB211 engine (and another 20,000 or so jobs outside the company itself also depended upon it). Moreover, the knock-on effect on Lockheed of allowing the new engine to be cancelled would badly sour relations with the Americans. Finally, Rolls-Royce was one of the most prestigious names in British industry, although the motor cars which had established the company's reputation accounted for only a small part of the overall business. In Cabinet, William Whitelaw pointed out that the collapse of Rolls-Royce would have the most serious implications for confidence, both in the City and internationally.

Taken together, these factors meant that we had no serious alternative to offering Rolls-Royce additional help. We were anxious that there should be some contribution from the private sector, and I took the chair in the Cabinet Room at No. 10 when talks were held on 28 October with representatives of the four financial institutions, the Midland Bank, Barclays Bank, Lazards and the Prudential Assurance Company, which had already invested in Rolls-Royce. The response of the private sector was worse than disappointing. Far from stepping forward with new offers of help, they demanded impossible guarantees before they would even undertake to find the money for which they were already committed. Having learned how grave the situation at Rolls-Royce had become, one of these bankers even went straight back to his office and cancelled the last instalment of the money that his firm had already promised. The best the banks could come up with was a further £18 million, but the net additional sum needed had been estimated at around £60 million. The Cabinet was understandably unhappy about all of this, but we agreed what had to be done. In the House of Commons on 11 November 1970, Fred Corfield announced that the government would contribute the rest of the necessary cash, £42 million, amounting to 70 per cent of what was required.

We rightly insisted that, in return for our financial help, Rolls-Royce should submit its accounts for independent assessment. On 22 January

1971, the chairman of Rolls-Royce and his deputy called on Corfield at their own request, and informed him that the government had previously been misinformed about the situation at the company. We were told that even the promised £60 million would not be enough to save Rolls-Royce, whose costs and liabilities were wholly beyond its resources. The total bill was now estimated at around £150 million. There was no chance that this kind of money could be raised privately or publicly so Rolls-Royce, having already instituted some high-level management changes and frozen dividends for shareholders, was forced to call in the receivers. The members of the board were most reluctant to take this action, and we were compelled to put pressure upon them. It was quite unthinkable that we should step in and save Rolls-Royce in its present form. That would have meant accepting the seemingly almost limitless liabilities of the company, but, equally, we had to be very cautious about contemplating a foreign takeover of a concern which was such an important defence contractor. The misinformation which had consistently been given to us clearly illustrated for me the lack of control which the chairman and the board had over the company's affairs. I did not believe that they had deliberately misled us. They were obviously ignorant of their own firm's real position.

If the contract with Lockheed was to go ahead, meanwhile, it would have to do so on an entirely new basis. In the absence from Washington of President Nixon, I spoke to Henry Kissinger by telephone on 1 February, informing him about the difficulties with which we were confronted. I then met the president and vice-president of Lockheeds at No. 10 on 3 February 1971, to discuss how we might proceed. They wanted to be helpful and constructive, but were clearly nervous about the commercial risks that they were facing as a consequence of the situation at Rolls-Royce. That afternoon, the Cabinet decided unanimously to take responsibility for the aero-engine, marine engine and industrial divisions of Rolls-Royce at a meeting which was attended, against all precedent, by the accountant Sir Henry Benson of Cooper Brothers, who had gone over the books for us. This was not done in the usual form of nationalisation. Rolls-Royce (1971) was deliberately set up as a streamlined going concern with the structure of a private company, which could be rapidly sold off again to private investors when conditions were right. I interrupted that meeting to telephone President Nixon himself, to see whether the two governments could co-operate, in the interests of both companies. I remember that we tried to use the secure 'hot line', but this kept breaking down so we had to finish the conversation on an open line.

After our discussion, President Nixon fully understood the gravity of the situation, which threatened Lockheeds' future almost as much as that of Rolls-Royce. He himself had recently faced a dilemma like ours, and had given help to the bankrupt Pennsylvania Central Railway. He agreed to help with the refinancing of the Lockheed contract. In the event, Congress granted a substantial loan to Lockheed to help it pay the increased price for the engine, and a satisfactory deal with Rolls-Royce was worked out over the summer, putting both companies back on to a viable basis. Richard Nixon could not have been more helpful.

The rescue of the RB211 required eight months of intensive effort on both sides of the Atlantic. I have no doubt that it was worth it. By the end of 1972, the position of Rolls-Royce had recovered more or less beyond recognition and it had become clear that the government's actions had avoided a massive wave of redundancies, safeguarded our vital defence and international interests and put the company on a secure long-term footing. Some parts of the firm were retained within the private sector and, just over a year after taking over, the Receiver announced that he would sell off Rolls-Royce Motors by means of a public flotation. This went ahead despite fierce Labour opposition and raised almost £40 million.

By the end of the decade and with the arrival of the new Conservative government, Rolls-Royce (1971) too was ready to be put on to the market. The fluctuation of sterling, however, delayed this and it was not until 1987 that it was completely privatised. Our actions established the successful future of Rolls-Royce with all it has meant for our defence and that of the free world, for civil air transport worldwide, for tens of thousands of jobs and for our balance of payments. If we had taken no action, and allowed Rolls-Royce to collapse and disappear, we would have been guilty of letting down our country. We took the necessary action in the proper way at the right time.

The Rolls-Royce decision was complicated by another problem which cropped up at the same time. In some respects, the story of the Mersey Docks and Harbour Board resembled that of Rolls-Royce. The company running the docks had got into difficulties because of serious misjudgements by the management and, once again, the previous Labour government was greatly at fault. In this case, the expectation of nationalisation had tempted the company to keep its fees for port users ridiculously low. It also suffered from dockers who were militant even by the standards of that notoriously truculent profession. At the end of November 1970 we refused to save the Board, a statutory body which could not go into liquidation, from the consequences of its own miscalculations and mismanagement. We were aware that Merseyside was an unemployment black-spot, however, and agreed that we would continue to provide public money for port improvements on condition that the company be reorganised under a new chairman, John Cuckney, with its capital written down by 30 per cent. Needless to say, the existing shareholders protested strongly, but in vain.

As in the case of Rolls-Royce, Ministers had been forced to consider whether we should allow our political reservations about state aid to out-weigh considerations of the unemployment effects which would result if we let such a concern go to the wall. We certainly accepted that some activities were best conducted under public ownership, but nationalisation had gone much too far, and we followed up the studies that we had carried out in opposition, to see whether we could now make progress in the field of privatisation. This resulted in the travel agents Thomas Cook and Lunn Poly being sold off, together with the state-run brewery and public houses in Carlisle. We were advised by employers' organisations that the programme should go no further at this stage. British capitalism was at such a low ebb that no one would have taken over the major concerns which, on paper at least, might one day look like attractive candidates for privatisation. In some instances, notably that of the steel industry, which ideologues on both left and right in those days regarded as a totem, we were dissuaded by the management from causing any further upheaval. It was agreed that a more extensive programme should wait until our second term. Everyone in the Cabinet saw the need for delay. Even the Thatcher government, ten years later, waited for a full parliament to elapse before privatising British Steel.

Meanwhile we still faced the growing problem of wage inflation. Despite Labour charges to the contrary, all senior Conservatives at that time firmly rejected any proposition that inflation should be brought under control by deliberately introducing policies which were intended to increase unemployment. We had, nonetheless, expected that the high and rising unemployment which we had inherited in 1970 would itself, in time, bring some reduction in the level of wage demands and settlements as the fear of joblessness began to figure in workers' calculations. Instead, inflation and unemployment continued to defy the textbooks by rising together. There was no simple answer to this combination, because the effects of demand management are impossible to predict in such a situation.

Our tax changes of October 1970, together with our supply-side improvements, seemed certain to improve the position in time, but none of us could be entirely happy to sit back and await results. Both the press and people in general shared our impatience when the Treasury forecast of 3 per cent growth during 1970 proved to be over-optimistic. In fact, the economy barely expanded at all in the second half of the year. By the time Tony Barber came to announce his first full budget at the end of March 1971, the predicament was getting more serious. Although there was no sign of an end to the upward trend in unemployment, which now exceeded 800,000, the unions were determined to go on in their self-defeating ways. Until our industrial relations reforms began to moderate union behaviour, and we saw an increase in people's propensity to save along with a greater inclination towards industrial investment, we could not be confident that injecting demand into the economy would help to create jobs. It seemed far more likely to swell the wallets of those who already had work.

Tony Barber therefore very sensibly concentrated his efforts on further improving incentives. He announced the halving of Labour's selective employment tax, another 2.5 per cent cut in corporation tax, the raising of some tax allowances and increases in pensions and other benefits. This package was worth more than £500 million (£4,000 million), but Tony's judgement was that this would only maintain levels of demand, not increase them. Even so, this was one of the major reforming budgets, and Tony had every reason to be proud of his achievement when he announced a greatly simplified tax structure. Many of these ideas had been thrashed out in opposition by Iain Macleod and Arthur Cockfield but, as a skilled tax lawyer, Tony Barber was in his element. Selective employment tax and purchase tax would be replaced by value added tax (VAT) as from April 1973. Income tax and surtax would also be merged. Under Labour the income of children had been included for tax purposes with that of their parents, and Tony rightly reversed this. Most of today's taxpayers will have no recollection of how delphic the system was before these reforms. We made it infinitely easier for individuals to work out their tax liabilities for themselves, and the budget was received with enthusiasm by our back-benchers. It was a major achievement for Tony Barber and for the government.

On 3 May 1971, I held a meeting of senior ministers in Downing Street, where we carried out one of our regular reviews of the economic situation. Despite the action we had already taken to reinvigorate the economy, my worries were now increasing. Especially in the field of industrial invest-ment, exhortation was having a minimal effect, and I was beginning to feel that some gentle reflation in good time might be essential to prevent the inevitable demands for panic measures that would otherwise come when it was too late. I also expressed my view that we had to use regional policy actively to prevent the level of unemployment in Scotland, Wales and the development areas of England from prompting people to demand a substantial general reflation, which would have spelled disaster for our anti-inflation policy. Tony Barber and Robert Carr were more optimistic. They were critical of Britain's financial institutions, but thought that they could detect signs of improvement in the quality of management. The mood of the meeting was fully behind their view, that we should continue to wait until the budget measures had been given time to work.

By mid-1971, there were a few encouraging signs in the battle against inflation, but they came almost entirely from the public sector, where our policy of toughness was producing results. Future progress now depended upon a comparable moderation of private sector settlements, not least because the public sector unions and employees would start to consider their relativities. We were convinced that the case for statutory controls remained to be proven, and briefly considered other measures to curb wage inflation in the private sector, including a reduction in the tariffs applied to its importing competitors. We had abolished Labour's Prices and Incomes Board shortly after taking over, in the belief that such controls could be effective only as a temporary last resort.

Although we preferred a voluntary approach to these questions, we could not sit around indefinitely waiting for the employers and unions to start being reasonable. I was encouraged when Vic Feather, in a meeting with me in April 1971, began to moot the idea of a new, voluntary incomes policy. He returned to this theme in June, by which time he seemed far more certain that 'there was widespread realisation among leaders of the trade unions that it is not possible to continue with the present rate of wage and price increases'. He told me that the TUC would now look for 'something on prices' from the CBI, the clear implication being that such an initiative on prices would prompt a more constructive approach to wage bargaining from the trade unions.

I had a private meeting with the leadership of the CBI that same day, and their message was very similar. They shared my growing fears about inflation and confirmed my personal view that, in their words, 'business in this country has still not taken full account of the effects of inflation on real profits and on provision for the maintenance of real assets'. Then they asked whether the government thought it would be a positive step forward 'if they could persuade the members of the CBI, or at any rate the great majority of them, to limit their price increases within 5 per cent for a period of twelve months, in return for a further stimulus to expansion by the government'. This marked a significant breakthrough. Although they were not sanguine about their chances of reaching an agreement on pay with the TUC, the CBI were actually thinking along lines parallel to Vic Feather's. Tony Barber seized the opportunity to reaffirm the government's view that any CBI move on containing prices should indeed precede, rather than follow, further fiscal demand stimuli. Nonetheless, he did tell me privately that there was scope for raising the rate of economic expansion to as much as 4 per cent without any serious risk of fuelling inflation, because of the under-utilisation of both capital and manpower.

By the summer of 1971, I detected that more of my colleagues were coming round to the view that, although the battle against inflation was still of paramount importance, direct action to boost the economy was now essential. There was no sudden increase in our anxiety about unemployment, for we had been worried about that from the start, but two new factors persuaded us that we could no longer afford to delay the introduction of a more expansionary economic policy. In June we had the first evidence that our attempts to keep down wage settlements were working. In the second half of 1970 they had been increasing at an annual rate of 8 per cent, but this had now fallen back to 5 per cent. This was still too high and, while Tony Barber and I were discussing ways of reducing the rate further, there was another welcome signal from the CBI. They now made a firm offer to restrict price increases to 5 per cent over the coming year, provided that the government stimulated the economy. This was the first stage of the prices and incomes policy and it was, let us never forget, an initiative taken by business itself. Whatever CBI members have said since about the actions of the 1970–4 government, we owed the basis of it all to them.

We considered the position carefully and concluded that, with price and wage inflation looking to have moderated and economic growth still showing all too few signs of life, a modest measure of reflation was certainly safe, and probably necessary. On 19 July Tony Barber unveiled a second mini-budget, which included a new real growth target of 4.5 per cent. The latest forecasts showed that this was a realistic goal, and there seemed little danger that reflation would put strain on the balance of payments: the National Institute of Economic and Social Research was predicting a £300 million surplus in 1971, and the Treasury forecast gave us a higher figure. In fact, we were now steadily repaying Labour's debts to overseas monetary authorities. On coming to office we had inherited an accumulated debt of almost £1,500 million (around £13,000 million in today's prices), and by this time less than a third of that was outstanding. In a particularly far-sighted act of liberalisation, Tony Barber removed restrictions on hire-purchase and reduced purchase tax by nearly 20 per cent, the first cut in the rate since 1963. The Environment Secretary, Peter Walker, also announced a £100 million package to invest in infrastructure, mainly in targeted development areas. Taken together, we judged that these decisions would promote the kind of sustainable economic growth that the country needed. When I addressed the 1922 Committee at the end of the month, my warm reception from 200 backbenchers confirmed my feeling that we had judged the situation correctly.

Some of the problems bequeathed to us by Labour seemed to be fading, but other consequences of that disastrous period refused to go away. Upper Clyde Shipbuilders, a consortium of five companies which had come together under pressure from Tony Benn, had been causing us trouble more or less from the start. Two of the yards were in financial difficulties and the Yarrow yard, a naval builder, should never have been forced into such a conglomerate. The obvious solution was to disentangle Yarrow from the rest of UCS. This was agreed and in February 1971, John Davies announced the creation of an independent Yarrow company, to be launched with the help of a substantial government loan. Unfortunately, the remainder of UCS became insolvent in June, and we had to call in a liquidator whose brief was to find ways of saving as many as possible of the 15,000 jobs which were at risk. We could not, however, contemplate an open-ended public subsidy of the yards. On 14 June, we rejected the fresh demand for cash and, instead, set up an Advisory Group under Lord Robens, a former member of the Donovan Commission, to see what could be salvaged when the consortium went into liquidation.

Benn's actions in government had seriously debilitated the country, and he soon proved that he was still capable of causing mischief on the Opposition benches. He had got hold of a paper written in 1969 by Nicholas Ridley, the Conservative MP for Cirencester and Tewkesbury, before the election, which proposed complete government withdrawal from UCS. Neither I nor my ministers had endorsed this tactless document, and it certainly did not represent party policy, but Benn decided to leak it to the *Guardian* at the moment calculated to do most damage.

At the end of July, John Davies reported the Group's conclusions to the House of Commons: that shipbuilding on the Upper Clyde could continue, with existing orders concentrated in two of the four yards. In response, Tony Benn irresponsibly encouraged the UCS workforce to embark on a 'work-in'. This was even more difficult than the Rolls-Royce business. The Upper Clyde was a notorious unemployment black-spot and helping the company would be fully compatible with my long-standing belief in regional policy. Our existing doubts about the viability of UCS had been confirmed by Lord Robens and, if shipbuilding really had no future in this area, then perhaps we should let the blow fall now and work instead on ways of softening it. After the appearance of the Ridley memorandum, however, no government could have acted on purely commercial considerations. If we went ahead with Lord Robens's recommendations, we would surely be accused of having carried out a long-laid secret plot, and the communist leaders of the work-in would have been hailed as heroes.

Some extreme right-wingers on our backbenches agreed with every word of the Ridley memorandum, but its leaking ensured that their preferred policy could not be carried out. Labour and the TUC were trying to undermine our industrial relations legislation with the absurd claim that we wanted class-confrontation, and the public could have been forgiven for thinking that the 'Ridley Report' proved the point. John Davies worked hard during the autumn of 1971 to save as much of UCS as he could, although we all continued to have grave doubts about putting more taxpayers' money into the yards. We negotiated with the unions, who predictably proved much more amenable behind closed doors than they were in front of the cameras and, in return for assurances from them and essential management changes, we decided to inject capital into the UCS yards; one of which would be sold to an American company, for building oil rigs.

John Davies talked us into letting him announce this rescue package during a debate on unemployment in February 1972. In hindsight, I think that we were wrong to agree with the idea. We were running the risk of implying that we had initiated a new, general policy of baling out companies as a panic reaction to the prospect of seeing the unemployment figure rise above 1 million in January. John had been unlucky rather than incompetent, but I decided that he would have to be moved from the DTI for a less exacting post when a suitable opportunity arose. The demands of the job were proving too much for him. He also lacked the skills of a seasoned parliamentary operator. As an immediate result of our experiences, we set up a small unit to produce early warnings of other companies which might be heading for the same kind of trouble as Rolls-Royce and UCS, and the CPRS was asked to produce some guidelines for action in any future cases.

On 3 November 1971 I held another economic strategy review meeting with senior ministers at 10 Downing Street. Having just secured parliamentary agreement to the principle of entry into the European Community, I felt that this was an appropriate time for a review of the economic situation. Europe presented us with both a challenge and an opportunity: if we entered the Community from a position of strength, then our prospects would be bright, but many of the structural weaknesses of the British economy were still very much in evidence. On the previous day, the Queen's Speech had included the pledge that an attack on unemployment would be our top priority. I led off the discussion at the Downing Street meeting by suggesting that we perhaps needed something domestically along the same lines as the Marshall Plan, which had so successfully reconstructed the European economy in the wake of the Second World War. The difficulties in the old industrial areas were bad enough, but no part of the United Kingdom would be immune from decline unless we could help to inspire a new dynamism. It was a sombre meeting, but we all had faith in our country and believed that the challenge could be met.

I then had a meeting with the TUC General Council at 10 Downing

Street on Wednesday 1 December 1971. This time I saw a very different Vic Feather from the man I felt I knew, but I could understand his predicament. He opened the meeting by talking tough about growth and the level of unemployment. I explained to the TUC that the government remained committed to full employment and wanted the country's economic resources to be used to the utmost. I also reminded them that, whatever they or their political allies might suggest, it was simply not true to claim that the government wished to use unemployment as an economic weapon against the ordinary working man. Time and time again we had proved that. For their part, the trade unions now had to recognise that there were serious structural problems in the British economy – labour practices, bargaining methods and a rising level of long-term unemployment – which they had to help us address if the country was to become competitive. At least Vic Feather scorned the old union canard that we could solve unemployment by reducing everyone's working hours. Some of his colleagues, no doubt, believed that allocating the work available in an economy is like slicing up a cake. At least that era seemed now to have been drawn to a close, but they were hardly a forward-looking lot.

In the run-up to Christmas 1971, Tony Barber released additional funds for projects to modernise our infrastructure, and more money was made available for Margaret Thatcher at Education and Keith Joseph at Social Services. Of course, the Cabinet was worried about the political and social implications of unemployment reaching 1 million, even though we all agreed that a limited short-term increase in unemployment at this stage should not be taken as an indication that our fundamental approach was wrong. It might also be added that, if the method of calculating the total applied in the 1980s had been in use in 1972, unemployment would have peaked at below 800,000. Many companies had run up their stocks, so we had always expected a time-lag between increased demand for goods and services and any subsequent increase in domestic production and employment. People out in the country, however, rarely look beyond headline figures such as unemployment, inflation and output, so our political and presentational difficulties remained. So did the harsh realities faced by those who were becoming unemployed, the human suffering behind the headlines. If we allowed long-term unemployment to build up on any sort of scale, we knew that we should be creating a pool of people who would probably never work again. Such a thought was abhorrent.

The union movement was, however, determined to go on portraying us as men of flint. The union leaders wanted their people back in Downing Street, and were willing to do anything to achieve that. It should always be remembered that, with the single exception of the European question, the Labour Party, trade union leaders and ordinary union members, particularly in the public sector, were completely united in opposing Conservative reforms in the early 1970s. They were united too in their desire for industrial and political power. In our first two years, we had achieved much of what we had set out to do, but we always knew that a confrontation with organised labour was never far away, whatever its cause.

From the outset, we had expected trouble from the miners. Employment in the coalmining industry had been falling steadily since the war, and I was already wondering in the early 1970s whether there had ever been another industry where efficiency and productivity improvements had been so marked. The sadness has been that most of the hard-working miners have achieved nothing more than to work themselves out of work. The Wilson government had presided over a rapid run-down and, when we came to office, we recognised that, in addition to feeling insecure in their jobs as the collieries closed down, the miners were aggrieved at having seen the real value of their pay fall in relation to that of other workers. Ever since the early years of this century, the miners had enjoyed staunch public support, especially when their case for better treatment was sound, and we understood that we would have to handle any confrontation with them very carefully. In fact, from the start, we too privately regarded theirs as a special case, on account of the worsening pay position which they had endured under Wilson.

Our serious troubles with the miners began in July 1971, when the conference of the National Union of Mineworkers (NUM) voted for an unrealistic 45 per cent pay demand and also changed the union's rules, lowering the majority needed to call industrial action from 66 per cent to 55 per cent. When the National Coal Board offered a wage increase of around 8 per cent, the miners began an overtime ban in November. On 9 January 1972, they called the first national strike in the industry for almost fifty years. Dealing with the miners was made more difficult by the fact that the union's executive was split between sensible moderates, led by the president, Joe Gormley – and hot-headed extremists such as the communist Mick McGahey. The difference between the opening offer from the National Coal Board (NCB) and the initial demand from the union was so great that there seemed to be no grounds for compromise. What we did not anticipate was the spasm of militancy from a union which had been relatively quiet for so long, and the tactics which it was willing to adopt. The use of 'flying pickets', organised by Arthur Scargill, took us unawares. They turned a serious situation into a truly grave one, and the miners' strike soon forced us into declaring a state of emergency.

We had built up coal stocks, but too great a proportion of the coal was at the pithead and not at power stations. I remember a Cabinet meeting on 10 February 1972 being interrupted by a message arriving for Reggie Maudling, the Home Secretary. He was told that pickets had forced the closure of the gates at the Saltley coke works in the West Midlands. The police had been faced with around 15,000 demonstrators who were convinced, wrongly as it happened, that the depot contained thousands of tons of coke. Up until that point, the police had dealt very effectively with flying pickets, stopping their trucks before they reached their intended destinations, and sending them packing. At Saltley, however, they were weak, and frightened of a scrap with the pickets. They did not consult anyone, least of all the Home Secretary, about their new, 'softly, softly' approach, and it was to prove disastrous. On the same day, the leaders of the NUM had unilaterally broken off negotiations with the Coal Board, rejecting its latest pay offer not only as a settlement, but as any sort of basis for negotiation. This dispute and, in particular, the role of the pickets, was the most vivid, direct and terrifying challenge to the rule of law that I could ever recall emerging from within our own country.

The ugly incident at Saltley was more important for its symbolism than for any actual damage caused by the closure of the coke works. We were facing civil disorder on a massive scale. A politically motivated minority were flouting the law of the land. Their purpose was a straightforward one, namely to bring down the elected government of the United Kingdom. The problem was not the law, as such. The kind of obstruction, intimidation, molestation and threatening behaviour that we had witnessed was self-evidently both illegal and unacceptable. This was a question of enforcement. Although there was general repugnance in the country at some of the miners' tactics, however, it was clear all along that the basic widespread sympathy for the miners and their case was undimmed. It was not until after the late 1970s, and the winter of discontent, that public opinion in this country really decided that enough was enough, and supported a Conservative government in facing down the intimidation of the union militants.

We did not have much time to play with as we grappled with this crisis, because extensive lay-offs were now beginning to take place in the nation's factories and production was bound to suffer, despite the ingenuity of so many of our companies in maintaining their output despite all of these problems. Confronted with the prospect of the country becoming ungovernable, or having to use the armed forces to restore order, which public opinion would never have tolerated, we decided to set up a powerful and independent inquiry into miners' wages. Lord Wilberforce was again put in charge of it. We also invited the miners to go back to work, on the basis of the Coal Board's latest offer, pending the outcome of the inquiry. This they rejected, demanding that the pay increase, which they in any case regarded as inadequate, should be backdated to 1 November. In fact, the NCB was willing to consider doing that, but the miners were just being bloody-minded by this stage.

In talks with Feather on 15 February, I learned that I could seek no solace from that quarter. He fully endorsed both the miners' case and their tactics, including the use of pickets to prevent the use of coal stocks at pitheads. He was, however, willing to influence the NUM to react as quickly as possible to the report of the Wilberforce Court of Inquiry once it was made available. He also reiterated his call for some kind of pay policy which extended beyond the public sector, a view which was by now also being put forward by some of my ministerial colleagues. I suggested to him that the TUC would surely be unwilling to co-operate with such a policy. His reply was, simply, that they had not been asked to do so. They had just been asked to accept decisions taken by the government. He said that the TUC would always be ready to co-operate, if they were properly consulted and agreed in advance about the basis for co-operation.

I took forward ideas about a pay policy with the CBI later that same day. They were deeply troubled by the continuing loss of production caused by the miners' strike. Quite understandably, the CBI told me that they had no interest in dwelling upon the precise nature of the arrangements being imposed during the emergency. 'It is more important,' they informed us, 'to ensure that, as soon as the pickets are taken off, some priority is given to industry, as against domestic consumers, to enable normal production to be resumed as soon as possible.' If we could do that, there were some grounds for optimism. Furthermore, their initiative on controlling prices had been reasonably successful, they explained, and they would decide within the next six weeks or so whether they ought to extend it. Sir John Partridge, the president of the CBI, then suggested that there might be scope, once the current CBI prices initiative had expired in July, 'for some form of tripartite arrangement involving the CBI, the TUC and the government'. Campbell Adamson, the CBI director-general, echoed this. Although the CBI's informal and private contacts with Vic Feather had produced virtually no return, he believed, as I did, that Feather might be attracted by a tripartite arrangement to look at wages and prices.

On 18 February, Wilberforce reported, and went far more towards the miners than we had expected. The deal he recommended was worth substantially more than 20 per cent. Yet, even after lengthy talks between the union and Robert Carr, there was still no agreement. I therefore invited the NUM leadership to Downing Street that evening. Gormley, visibly under pressure from his colleagues, again asked for extra money, but I was just not willing to authorise any more than the already substantial amount that Wilberforce was recommending. The talks went on into the early hours. Gormley himself was clearly uncomfortable about the tactics that his union had used, but lurking behind him were the real destroyers, McGahey and Scargill. In the end, Gormley came back into the Cabinet Room at around 2.30 a.m. and said to me that he didn't want to 'grind the government down'. Grudgingly, the union gave up their final demands for additional pay increases, in return for a series of long-coveted concessions on fringe benefits. Wilberforce's work on the power workers' dispute had been satisfactory, but on this occasion he had produced a judgement which merely invited the miners to ask for more. This was a grim day for the country and for the government.

In a broadcast to the nation on 27 February 1972, I therefore warned that there was no point in pretending that the miners had 'won'. In fact, I explained, 'everyone has lost . . . in the kind of country we live in there cannot be any "we" or "they" . . . there is only us – all of us'. I praised the general trend towards more moderate wage settlements in recent months and stressed once again the serious dangers that accelerating inflation would pose to our society. I also warned my audience about the use, or the threat, of violence during industrial disputes, which jeopardised 'our traditional British way of doing things . . . If one group is so determined to get its own way that it does not care what happens to the rest of us, then we are not living in the kind of world we thought we were, and we had better face up to it'. It was time for everyone of goodwill to accept that 'we have to find a more sensible way to settle our differences'.

In the wake of the miners' dispute, the time had come not only for some straight talking, but also for subtle diplomacy behind the scenes. Everybody now seemed to appreciate the root causes of our inflationary problems, and everybody claimed to be willing to make a serious effort to deal with them. Two days later, with my authority, Victor Rothschild, head of the CPRS, launched a low-key initiative to set up a series of informal meetings between the likes of Hugh Scanlon and the TUC's assistant general secretary Len Murray, on the one hand, and himself and Sir William Armstrong, the head of the home civil service, on the other. We had to find out for certain whether the two sides of industry were serious about curing our national disease.

Chapter 13

FANFARE FOR EUROPE

Britain Joins the Six 1963–1974

On the beautiful sunny morning of Thursday 20 May 1971, I walked from the British embassy in Paris to the Elysée Palace, for a meeting with President Georges Pompidou. I was accompanied by Christopher Soames, the British ambassador in Paris, Robert Armstrong, my principal private secretary, and Michael Palliser, minister at the embassy, who was to be my interpreter. We all felt keyed-up, knowing that everything depended on this meeting. In two full days of discussions, we were going to thrash out the major problems outstanding in the negotiations between our two countries. If we were successful, the other five members of the European Community would be prepared to accept the arrangement we had reached. If we failed, there was nothing further they could do to help Britain. The Five had already played their part. The Chancellor of Germany, the Italian Prime Minister and the leaders of the Benelux countries had indicated to the French government their desire to see a satisfactory resolution of the issue which had bedevilled the unity of Western Europe for nearly a quarter of a century. Another '*Non!*' from Paris would have brought the negotiations to a complete and, this time perhaps, final stop. That would have been a devastating setback for the British people.

It had been a long story, coinciding almost exactly with my parliamentary career. President de Gaulle's first veto in 1963 was certainly a blow for European unity, but it was not the final chapter. Nobody, however, could have predicted the dramatic course of events that would follow. This began with Labour's election victory in 1964 and the end of thirteen years of Conservative government. The arrival of Harold Wilson at No. 10 did not offer much hope that a second application for entry would be planned and, for the two years of that parliament, no progress was made. Everything possible should have been done to avoid differences between Britain and the Six, even though it was hard to foresee circumstances in which Britain might join the Community. The Conservatives' 1964 manifesto had stated correctly that 'entry into the EEC is not open to us in existing circumstances'. During a meeting of our Consultative Committee on Policy on 30 March, 1965, Reggie Maudling circulated a paper which declared:

> 'Our basic policy remains to secure entry into the European Common Market on acceptable terms. This clearly cannot be achieved for some time to come. In the meanwhile our political objective must be to show ourselves to be more progressive and positive than the Government in our attitude to European unity.'

The only certainty about the Labour Party in relation to Europe has always been that its position is uncertain. Clement Attlee was adamantly opposed to membership. His government missed what proved to be the historic opportunity of taking part in the negotiations in 1950 which led to the formation of the ECSC, and as late as the 1960s he told a newspaper that 'I'm not very keen on the Common Market. After all, we beat Germany and we beat Italy and we saved France and Belgium and Holland. I never see why we should go crawling to them.' His eventual successor, Hugh Gaitskell, was a very different figure. Gaitskell was firmly established on the right wing of the Labour Party and in the centre of the overall political spectrum. Most of his political friends and allies, such as Roy Jenkins and Tony Crosland, were strong supporters of British membership. Yet Gaitskell himself suffered from acute ambivalence on this question, perhaps as a result of his colonial background. During the 1961–3 negotiations, I spoke to Gaitskell in the lobby of the House of Commons and offered to keep him informed, on a Privy Counsellor basis, of what was developing and being proposed. He responded by telling me: 'Go and talk to George Brown.' I do not believe that he was opposed in principle to the notion that the United Kingdom should tie its destiny with Western Europe. He was never in any sense an enthusiast, however, and I believe that he allowed nostalgia about Britain's past to convince him that, thanks to our relationship with the US and above all through the Commonwealth, we could continue to play a decisive role on the world stage wholly independent of our neighbours. It is to be regretted that a combination of circumstances drove him to his anti-European outburst at the Labour Party conference in the autumn of 1962 (see p. 223).

British policy on Europe from 1964 fluctuated greatly with Harold Wilson's capricious nature and tactical initiatives. It seems he never held any strong views on Europe and, in the absence of any conviction, the issue for him was which policy would best serve to hold the Labour Party together, and enable it to continue in office. This was unforgivable for those who knew how much serious consideration these questions deserved and demanded, and one could never predict with any certainty when he might change his 'declared' views on Europe.

My election as leader of the Conservatives in August 1965 clearly bolstered the party's commitment to European unity. My views on the subject had been on the record since 1950, and I was convinced that we were the only party which could lead Britain into the Community. Our European message was reinforced in the first comprehensive policy document under my leadership, *Putting Britain Right Ahead*, while our 1966 manifesto committed a Conservative government to 'work energetically for entry into the European Common Market at the first favourable opportunity'. Labour's manifesto, *Time for Decision*, stated that Britain 'should be ready to enter the European Economic Community, provided essential British and Commonwealth interests are safeguarded'. Before the election, however, the Labour leadership combined feeble expressions of goodwill towards the Six with insistence on conditions which were directly contrary to the Treaty of Rome, especially with regard to agricultural levies. During the campaign, Wilson publicly asserted that joining the Community with the CAP as constituted would entail an unacceptable rise in the cost of living. In effect, he ruled out entry.

The issue that really ignited passions was Wilson's accusation, made in a speech at Bristol on 18 March 1966, that Harold Macmillan had failed to deal honestly with de Gaulle at Rambouillet in 1962. I was appalled by this slanderous denigration of a man I had served and long admired. Yet, despite the widespread condemnation of Wilson's remarks, no withdrawal was forthcoming. I issued a statement on 28 March which put paid to the credibility of his allegations:

> In the circumstances I feel that I must put on the record again the view of a French source which must have greater authority than the vague one quoted by Mr Wilson . . . President de Gaulle himself told me in November 1965 that he was quite satisfied that Mr Macmillan had given him the relevant facts about Skybolt and Polaris at Rambouillet . . . I deplore Mr Wilson's refusal to do the honourable thing and withdraw.

The other unsavoury incident of the campaign occurred after I had attacked Wilson for his negative attitude towards Europe, and towards President de Gaulle in particular. Wilson was obviously stung by this, and he accused me of wanting to roll over like a spaniel to the French. I found his comments poisonous, and said so. This exchange was unpleasant enough at the time. It was even more regrettable that a similar argument went on at the 1997 general election, only this time it was the Conservative Party which was claiming that Labour would act like a spaniel.

After his second election victory, Harold Wilson announced to the

House of Commons, on 10 November 1966, that his government would conduct a high-level study of the possibilities of British membership of the Community. The appointment of George Brown, a pro-European, as Foreign Secretary in August 1966 had been a decisive factor in this move. I immediately welcomed the announcement and, although I assured Wilson of my support, I could not resist one or two digs at him during the two-day parliamentary debate that followed. 'One can sum it up,' I suggested, 'by saying that what, five years ago, was about to be abject surrender has become at least a merchant adventure . . . How much sweeter the words would have been five years ago, but I am grateful for them now.' I also reminded the House that 'the Community is so much more than a market . . . the phrase "Common Market" underestimates and undervalues the Community, and, for this reason, tends to mislead those who have to deal with it.' I then returned to the issue of sovereignty:

> Those who say that the British people must realise what is involved in this are absolutely right. There is a pooling of sovereignty. Member countries of the Community have deliberately undertaken this to achieve their objectives, and, because they believe that the objectives are worth that degree of surrender of sovereignty, they have done it quite deliberately . . . When we surrender some sovereignty, we shall have a share in the sovereignty of the Community as a whole, and of other members of it. It is not just, as is sometimes thought, an abandonment of sovereignty to other countries; it is a sharing of other people's sovereignty as well as a pooling of our own.

There can be no doubt that the Labour Party had shifted towards Europe although, at this stage, they still had quite a long way to go before all their backbenchers could be convinced that this was the right approach. There were still many Labour Members who failed to grasp the compelling political arguments behind our accession, and anti-marketeers on the left now voiced on their fears that the Community was a capitalist conspiracy. Since the late 1980s we have heard, this time from the right, that the European Union is a socialist conspiracy. It is neither.

On 2 May 1967, Harold Wilson announced his intention to apply for membership, and the government produced a White Paper assessing the constitutional and legal implications. This gave me the perfect opportunity to tackle Wilson on his true attitude towards European unity. I asked the Prime Minister to confirm that he now accepted the Treaty of Rome and the Common Agricultural Policy. To my delight, he replied, 'Yes.' After the climax of a three-day parliamentary debate on the application, I led my party through the division lobbies in support of the government's decision. During my own speech on 9 May, I told Parliament that 'There can be no doubt that the logical conclusion in a complete market is to move over *de facto* or *de jure* to a common currency.'

At these two parliamentary debates, in 1966 and 1967, I had set out once again the Conservative Party's exact position on the Treaty of Rome as a whole. That was thirty years ago. So much for those who claim never to have heard of my policy on these matters.

My pledge of support caused some disquiet within the party. Brendon Sewill, director of the Conservative Research Department, sent a note warning me that, if negotiations were to break down, it would be very difficult for us to criticise it *post hoc*, so we risked handing Wilson 'another glorious failure'. While it was certainly true that party capital could be made by embarrassing the government, I firmly rejected the temptation to play party politics on this issue. I did so for two reasons. In the first place, Britain's relationship with Europe is of supreme importance to the British people. It affects not only our role in the world, but also the practical and everyday concerns of all. By this time, it was already clear that no effective strategy for enhancing investment or combating cross-border crime could exist at a purely national level. I also knew that, if we played the issue cynically for party advantage, we should, sooner or later, deservedly pay a high price.

Secondly, if Britain was to gain the maximum benefits from its membership, a constructive attitude towards Europe had to exist across a wide spectrum of opinion. Our colleagues in Europe have never been impressed by confused signals about our commitment to the process of union. If the Opposition plays party politics on this question, it can raise a serious doubt in the minds of our partners as to whether the UK will deliver on its obligations under the treaties, because the Opposition of today may be the government of tomorrow. This is not to say, of course, that debate should be stifled. Exactly the reverse. There must be free and proper debate and the diversity of opinions must be respected, but where there is a broad pro-European consensus in the House of Commons, as there has been since the 1960s, this should not be sacrificed on the altar of adversarial politics.

The application by Harold Wilson and the Labour government was an abject failure. My misgivings were realised when President de Gaulle formally vetoed it on 27 November 1967. On this occasion there was no real sense of surprise or anger. The fact that he felt able to veto Britain before formal negotiations had even started suggests that he did not consider Labour's decision to seek membership as serious or genuine, and their application certainly had little significance for the future of Europe. The most dramatic effect of this episode was to alienate UK public opinion against the Community. In June 1966, opinion polls had shown 66 per cent of the British population in favour of our accession. According to private research commissioned by Conservative Central Office before the 1970 general election, this figure had by then fallen to just 18 per cent. I knew that Labour would be unable to resist indefinitely the temptation to swim with such a tide. The setback which we had suffered made some people doubt whether we were on the right track to European unity. Public opinion in Britain would not tolerate a third failure.

In my judgement, the unity of Europe will in the end be achieved by European governments coming to regard the habit of working together as the natural state of affairs. While the bedrock of European union is the consent of the people, such a union is implemented and carried on day by day through the actions of governments, which take the decisions. There must therefore be confidence and partnership in these relations. There was no bond of confidence between the 1964–70 Labour government and its European counterparts. Not only did Wilson fail to exploit British influence, but he also managed to antagonise the Germans and the French in 1969 through 'l'affaire Soames'. On 4 February, Christopher Soames met President de Gaulle and they discussed the form of a future European political association. De Gaulle then proposed secret talks between Britain and France. His comments were only exploratory and not intended to be repeated elsewhere. The fear in London, however, was that if the British said nothing the French would spread the rumour that we were seriously considering some bilateral arrangement with them. This in turn would cast doubts on our enthusiasm for the Treaty of Rome and undermine confidence between the UK and our supporters in the European Community. Just over a week later, Wilson visited Germany and gave his own interpretation of this conversation to Chancellor Kurt Kiesinger – without informing the French in advance. To make matters worse, the Foreign Office then proceeded to announce the form of the discussions. As a consequence of this, the French did not attend the meeting of the WEU in London that month. It was, quite frankly, a mess which increased the opposition within the Quai d'Orsay to our membership.

Britain's influence in Europe was never lower than it was between 1964 and 1970, not least because Britain's relative economic position was deteriorating badly. Announcing the 1967 veto, de Gaulle stressed that, 'the Common Market is incompatible with Great Britain's economy as it stands [and] with the state of sterling, as once again highlighted by the devaluation'. In 1960, the UK had enjoyed a standard of living comparable to that enjoyed by the Six, but by 1970 they had all experienced faster rates of economic growth than the UK, and had significantly overtaken us. Moreover, British companies were becoming increasingly uncompetitive relative to their American, Japanese and European rivals, because of their failure to invest to the same extent in research and development and because they did not benefit from the economies of scale of a large market.

The European outlook changed dramatically after the resignation of President de Gaulle in April 1969. De Gaulle was a formidable President. Yet, though he could veto the British application, he could still not forge Europe entirely in his own image. What he could do, and perhaps should have done, was to demonstrate sufficient statecraft and leadership to show the way to a new Europe of the 'Nine', including the United Kingdom, Ireland and Denmark. He would then have gone down in history as a creative man of vision, responsible for the establishment of a European unity which might have endured for centuries to come. He rejected this glorious opportunity.

Although de Gaulle was not alone in his views on British membership of the European Community, his departure clearly improved our prospects. The presence of his successor, Georges Pompidou, at the Hague Summit on 1–2 December 1969 reflected this dramatic shift in French politics. This summit marked a relaunch of European integration after a period of stagnation since the crisis of July 1965 and the withdrawal of French representatives from the Council of Ministers, when de Gaulle had been angered by plans to extend the power of the Commission and the European Parliament over allocation of the Community budget. This crisis was remedied by the 'Luxembourg compromise' of January 1966, the French interpretation of which declared that any member state could block proposals under discussion which it believed affected its vital interests, until unanimity was reached. This compromise caused much confusion because it did not alter the fact that the Community, under the Treaty of Rome, carried on much of its work under qualified majority voting. At the Hague Summit, European leaders concluded an agreement on financing the CAP and on a plan to proceed towards economic and monetary union, as I had envisaged back in 1967. This was to be outlined one year later in the Werner Report. Heads of government of the Six also agreed to open negotiations with a view to our entry into the European Community.

Early in 1970, however, the Labour government published a quite irresponsible White Paper, which exaggerated the likely economic costs of membership and failed to provide any clear and detailed explanations of the assumptions on which so many of the calculations were based. Nor was there a clear view of the non-economic criteria by which any overall negotiated arrangement could be more generally judged, in terms of our interests and those of the Six. Wilson wanted to ensure that, if there was any party advantage to be drawn from the issue, then it would go his way. He hoped that I would lose support by striking a positive note in the face of a sceptical public. In a speech to the House on 25 February 1970, I answered this challenge:

> If the Prime Minister wants to fight the coming election on who should negotiate for Britain, let him come out now and fight it. Let Europe see which government has the support of the people of Britain. And if the negotiations are successful, then let there be in power a government who will pursue policies which are essential . . . for this country to take its rightful place in the wider Europe which many people have worked so long to create.

My speech received fairly extensive coverage in the leading French and German papers. *Le Figaro* commented that I had 'succeeded in raising the level of debate above the question of the price of butter . . . Indeed, we witnessed a real proclamation of faith from a man who believes fervently in the future of European unity both as "internationalist" and as "patriot".'

On 5 May 1970, I travelled to Europe for individual meetings with Chancellor Willy Brandt, who had succeeded Kiesinger the previous year, with Jacques Chaban-Delmas, the French Prime Minister and with President Pompidou. It was clear that no decision had been taken on the form of British entry into the Community, and that nothing of consequence would happen until after our general election. We did, however, discuss the movement towards greater foreign policy co-operation among the Six. The French government, in particular, was very keen on introducing a counterweight to growing German assertiveness in foreign policy. This was intensified by Willy Brandt's policy of *Ostpolitik*, whose ultimate consequence seemed likely to be a permanent rapprochement between the two German states. Brandt always felt that his task in reaching an accommodation with his neighbours in the East would be easier once there was a European Community enlarged to include Britain, and working towards a common European foreign policy. In May 1970, the Davignon Report recommended bi-annual meetings of European Foreign Ministers, chaired by the state presiding over the Council of Ministers. In November of that year, the Six instituted a procedure of regular contacts at both ministerial and official level.

During my Godkin Lectures at Harvard in 1968, I had argued that Europe was now alone in both enhancing its political stature and remaining open to British influence. The Commonwealth was fissiparous, and the United States was increasingly beset by internal problems and a crisis of confidence abroad. Michel Jobert, President Pompidou's secretary-general at the Elysée, later told me that he had read my Harvard lectures and had realised at once that the second lecture on defence, and in particular on the nuclear policy which would be followed by a Conservative government, was of immense importance to the French. He translated this lecture and showed it to President Pompidou, who, having read it, immediately said, 'We can work together with that man.'

On my visit to Paris in May 1970, I addressed the British Chamber of Commerce in Paris, at a time of growing speculation that Wilson would go to the country. I rehearsed the argument which was to be included in the manifesto, saying that the Community could not be enlarged without the 'full-hearted consent of the peoples and parliaments' of the nations involved. Article 237 of the Treaty of Rome (now Article O of the Treaty on European Union) stated that 'The conditions of admission and the adjustments to this Treaty necessitated thereby . . . shall be submitted for ratification by all the contracting States in accordance with their respective constitutional requirements.' Both Denmark and Ireland required a referendum before entry. In Britain, of course, the situation was different. The voice of the people would speak *through* their elected Parliament. I could not have meant anything else, as the referendum was a device unknown to our constitution, but I had not reckoned with the later ingenuity of the anti-European brigade. They chose to interpret my speech as if I shared their view that national sovereignty was something that could be exercised either by Parliament or directly by the public, as the mood took them.

The complication arose because there was already talk of a referendum on the issue, although I do not recall any mention of this in the meetings of the Shadow Cabinet. It was possible in the abstract to see a referendum as a convenient way out. The Community was unpopular for the moment because of the extensive negative propaganda from the Labour Party, and it was an easy way for politicians to avoid taking a definite position on a difficult but vital issue. Such abstract arguments never appealed to me. I have always believed that when public opinion is uncertain about something, as it was about Europe at the time, what is required is not an abdication of leadership, but more leadership.

Under the British system of parliamentary representation MPs are elected as representatives, not delegates, on the assumption that voters trust them to exercise their judgement. Members of Parliament are chosen by the nation to consider public issues, and to reach informed views on them. It was Edmund Burke who best explained representative democracy, when he told his electors in 1774: 'Your representative owes you, not his industry only, but his judgement; and he betrays, instead of serving you, if he sacrifices it to your opinion.' On 27 May 1970, I told the BBC Election Forum: 'We will report the whole time to the country through Parliament what is going on in the negotiations. At the end when they see what has been negotiated, Parliament can judge completely as to whether it is in the interests of the country to go into the Common Market or not.'

Perhaps I could have been more precise in my language when I talked of 'full-hearted consent', but I will always maintain that it was unfairly exploited. My most important consideration was to make the electorate understand the choices that we faced. Our 1970 manifesto set out the pros and cons of membership, pledging us to negotiations with the Six – 'no more, no less'. I could not give a pledge of British membership, as that would depend on Parliament approving the terms on offer. Our private polls showed that, although the idea of accession no longer enjoyed strong support in the UK, 67 per cent of people still believed, in February 1970, that the next government should, at least, negotiate with the Six to see what terms they could achieve. I knew that a Conservative government would enter talks with a positive attitude, but the Community had developed since 1963 and Britain had obviously played no part in the changes. The increase in Britain's international indebtedness and the underlying weakness of our balance of payments made more formidable the heavy short-term burden which the Community and CAP would inevitably impose. Britain's future would be dismal outside Europe, but there was no possibility that the government over which I presided would sign up to unreasonable terms. So the manifesto correctly stated our position. This was reinforced during a Shadow Cabinet meeting on Monday 23 February 1970, at which we all agreed to emphasise that we would join the European Community only if the terms were satisfactory.

On 23 June, shortly after our general election victory, I had a breakfast meeting with Christopher Soames at Albany. Negotiations for our membership of the Community were due to reopen shortly, and we discussed the likely attitude of the French in considerable detail. Christopher wanted to return to domestic politics as soon as possible, but he was much too important and valuable as our ambassador in Paris for a move back to London to be contemplated. I persuaded him that he was more use to his country in France. Without Christopher's skilful diplomacy and wise advice, particularly at the time of my visit to Paris in May 1971, I am sure that we would never have been so successful. He was indispensable

On 30 June Alec Douglas-Home and Tony Barber went to Brussels to arrange the timetable for the renewed negotiations which would begin in July. They were under no illusions about the scale of the task ahead. Some observers claimed that the French were now more likely to admit the UK, as the Six had reached an agreement on the Community budget in April 1970 and, under this system, the UK would inevitably be a large net contributor to the budget after accession. The Community was now endowed with its own formidable resources, consisting of all levies on agricultural products and duties on industrial goods imported into the EEC.

The French, however, were concerned that the UK would attempt to destroy what the Six had painstakingly achieved. Our task was to reassure the French and find terms for entry which were tolerable for the British economy and people in the short term and visibly beneficial in the long term. Before Christmas 1970, we had put forward proposals to deal with our transition to full acceptance of the Community's financial arrangements. We resolved that we should assume our obligations gradually, because too large a contribution at the beginning, before the dynamic benefits of membership had had time to come through, would have damaged both Britain and the Community as a whole. It would have jeopardised the smooth passage upon which the enlarged Community's successful progress in the first few years would depend.

Our position, therefore, was much the same as in 1961–3 and 1967. Once again, we had to convince a French President that Britain was sufficiently 'European' and would not exploit membership to disrupt or dilute the Community. This had been reaffirmed during my last trip to Paris in May 1970, when President Pompidou had expressed his concern about our tendency to remain too closely attached to the United States. He was unsure whether the UK would be prepared to defend European interests in the face of likely economic and political onslaughts from outside: 'Il faut être prêt à faire la guerre pour l'Europe.' This trust was never going to be easy to establish, in view of the traditional suspicions which permeated Anglo-French relations, the fractious state of relations throughout the 1960s and the volatile nature of public opinion in the UK at this time.

Our negotiations in 1970–1 were highly complicated and difficult at home and abroad. It was clear from the outset that there were still some officials in the Foreign Office who wanted to isolate the French by working with the Five against them. I had rejected this tactic as far back as 9 November 1968 during my speech to the European Parliamentary Congress at the Hague: 'We would be wrong to seek to isolate France by creating new institutions without her. Even if it were to succeed, which I doubt, such a policy would only repeat in different form the same errors from which we in Britain have suffered in these last five years. A Europe without France in the long run makes as little sense as a Europe without Britain.' In a letter of 21 April 1971, Soames was to describe this situation to Denis Greenhill, the permanent under-secretary at the Foreign Office: 'the French still do not expect any serious pressure from their partners. They believe that in the last resort the Germans will acquiesce in what they decide and that the Italians can be fixed. The Belgians they patronise, and the Dutch they admire but disregard. So it comes down to an Anglo-French understanding.' Christopher told me at the House of Commons on 1 March 1971 that, in his opinion, President Pompidou would want to settle matters in bilateral talks with the British Prime Minister. He did not think that the other members of the Community would necessarily be unhappy at such a development. I too felt sure that gaining the trust and support of all of the Six would lead to better terms for the British and raise public support for entry, because people would get a real sense of progress being made. So it was to prove. As progress in the negotiations had been slow, I instructed Christopher to explore the possibility of my meeting President Pompidou with his secretary-general, Michel Jobert.

I had first met Jobert in 1960 while I was on holiday in Spain. I was staying in a delightful village just east of Marbella, hardly known at that time to tourists. After this break, I had planned to stay with Madron and Nancy-Joan Seligman in Brittany. Before I left England, I had met the Seligmans at Glyndebourne. I was astonished to see that Madron had lost a great deal of weight, and I accused him of cheating, on the ground that we should have dieted together while in Brittany. The result of this breaking of solidarity was that I had to lose weight in Marbella!

My small, but most attractive, hotel was owned by a retired antique dealer, who had decorated it with his many treasures. There were only a dozen or so people staying at the hotel, whose dining room, some hundred yards up from the beach, faced the sea and had huge windows which could be hauled up, bringing in the fresh sea breeze. The tables were some way apart, and to my left were a couple with their young son. I did not pay them any heed until the third day. As the family passed by me, the father stopped and said, 'I do not know how you expect to deal with de Gaulle when you eat so little food!' and then walked on. He was Michel Jobert. After this encounter, we spent many hours on the beach in the intervals between bathing, discussing European politics and the part Britain would play in them. He always displayed a considerable understanding of, and sympathy for, our position.

A private meeting between Soames and Jobert took place in the Elysée on 6 March 1971, just five days after I had met Soames in the House. They discussed the possibility of a summit and Jobert confirmed that Pompidou was in favour of the idea. Jobert then advised Soames not to say anything about their plans to the French Foreign Minister, Maurice Schumann, because 'If the Quai got wind of it at this stage it would create many difficulties.' Both agreed that nothing should be said to anyone outside a very limited circle in the Foreign Office and Downing Street in London and the Elysée in Paris.

Of course an Anglo-French summit meeting was not guaranteed to be a success. Many of my colleagues, including our chief negotiator Geoffrey Rippon, were worried that a bilateral summit could have many undesirable consequences. Rippon felt that it would prove difficult, at that late stage, to avoid what would amount to a detailed negotiation of outstanding issues, thereby increasing the problems and the risk of something going wrong. During the 1961–3 negotiations, Macmillan's two summit meetings with de Gaulle had served only to complicate matters further. However, I decided that this was our best chance to conclude the negotiations satisfactorily. After all, I had discovered to my cost in 1963 that the barrier to a successful outcome was political, not technical, and could therefore be removed only by agreement at the highest level.

The next question to resolve was the timing of the summit. If it was staged too early, there might not be sufficient urgency to break any political deadlock. If it was held too late, the atmosphere of urgency could have become one of crisis, and we certainly did not want the summit to be viewed as a heavyweight contest between myself and the French President. Soames had a further meeting with Jobert at the Elysée on 27 March, and the French secretary-general told him that his President's own preference was for the meeting to be held at the end of May. As Soames got up to leave, Jobert made two points: first, that Pompidou was determined the meeting should succeed; and, secondly, that 'Too many leaves should not be removed from the artichoke before these talks.'

On the basis of this information, we decided that the Brussels ministerial meeting in May should be used only for the settlement of some of the minor questions, or for some 'loosening' of items. The gap between our negotiating positions, however, had to be narrowed before the summit could take place, so as to avoid any atmosphere of crisis. It was a very difficult balance to strike. On Saturday 8 May, shortly before the ministerial meeting, I announced that a summit would take place on 20 and 21 May between the French President and myself in Paris. The ambassadors of the Five were informed shortly before the announcement was made. Apparently, Pompidou did not even inform Maurice Schumann about our plans until the Saturday morning. His excuse was that Schumann was going to Moscow with a crowd of journalists in his aircraft and it was far too dangerous. I am sure that news on 8 May of the impending summit contributed to the substantial progress made on sugar, agriculture and on tariff quotas just three days later in Brussels.

My preliminary briefing sessions were held in the garden at Downing Street. I was determined to leave nothing to chance, and teams of experts were brought in to discuss every item that might be raised by Pompidou. Every possible care was taken over the preparations for the meeting. The negotiators in Brussels had explored the ground thoroughly and reached agreement over a large area of it. Robert Armstrong and Michel Jobert, his opposite number at the Elysée, then worked together to set out the various options open to us both and ensured that, so far as possible, we knew each other's thinking in advance. Inevitably, it was still going to be a tough negotiation – very big issues were at stake, nationally and internationally – but I was convinced that reasonable individuals could reach agreement. I flew to Paris on the afternoon of 19 May and was met at the airport by Jacques Chaban-Delmas, the French Prime Minister. The following morning, Christopher Soames and I began our walk to the Elysée Palace to meet the French President.

I first heard of Monsieur Pompidou at dinner in Geneva one evening in December 1960. I had been at a European Free Trade Area meeting all day, and had intended to fly that evening to Paris to stay with Sir Pierson Dixon, our ambassador there, to discuss with him the prospects of future negotiations with the Community. Unfortunately, the low cloud level prevented us from taking off, so I decided to catch the late-night sleeper from Geneva to Paris. My Swiss colleagues invited me to dinner in a private room at a small restaurant. During dinner, one of my neighbours, who I knew was always in close touch with the French, turned to me and said quietly, 'If you want to influence de Gaulle, then you must first of all persuade Monsieur Pompidou.' 'Monsieur Pompidou,' I exclaimed incredulously. 'Can there be such a person?' 'Indeed, yes,' he replied. 'He is with Rothschilds Bank in Paris and he is President de Gaulle's special envoy dealing with the Algerian problem. At this moment he is not far from us. He is along the lake at Evian in a secret meeting with Algerian representatives. You ought to get in touch with him when he is in Paris, and try to convince him that Britain should become a member of the Community. He has a lot of influence with de Gaulle.' I was much impressed.

The next morning, after breakfast at the Paris embassy, Pierson Dixon called a meeting of his senior staff in which they expressed their own views about our prospects. After listening patiently, I commented, 'Well, I think the answer to all of this is to get in touch with Monsieur Pompidou.' 'Yes, yes,' the gathering assented as one, 'of course.' Then there was a silence during which one of them enquired, 'But who is Monsieur Pompidou?' I was not sure whether to be delighted or alarmed that their ignorance was as great as mine had been. But I was now able to tell them all about him and even where, at that moment, he was to be found.

I first met Pompidou in 1962, by which time he had already become Prime Minister of France. For some two hours we talked about the European Community, and what would be required for Britain to get into it. He had a very clear idea of the Community he wanted to create, namely one which would provide a large, sound basis for great industrial firms, to enable them to hold their own against their rivals in the United States and Japan, in an ever more competitive world. He also wanted an agricultural base which would give farmers and farm workers the opportunity of enjoying the same sort of standard of living as their counterparts in the cities. Later, at Chequers, he told me (in French!), 'If you ever want to know what my policy is, don't bother to call me on the telephone. I do not speak English and your French is awful. Just remember that I am a peasant, and my policy will always be to support the peasants.'

At the end of our talk, I asked Pompidou, if he had one wish for the future of the Community, what it would be. He replied without pausing, 'A common company law, which would be based very largely on British company law because it is more flexible than the laws of most countries, which are still working to a Napoleonic Code.' 'Why do you want it?' I asked him. 'Because I do not want companies in our member countries just throwing out tiny suckers in other parts of the Community, I do not want companies in Paris with small subsidiaries in Frankfurt and Rome, or companies in London with offshoots in Brussels or Milan. I want full-sized European manufacturing companies and the only way to get that is to make sure that they all operate on the same basis throughout the Community. We must enable them to join up with other large European companies, and then hold their own in the world outside.' We still do not have common company law in the European Union.

My two-day meeting with President Pompidou in May 1971 was followed by two others in Paris, and by him spending two weekends with me at Chequers. On the first visit to Chequers, I went to meet his special plane at Northolt on the Saturday morning. Although it was the weekend, I wore a fairly plain and darkish grey suit. The passenger door opened, the steps were let down from the plane and the President appeared at the top. He took one look at me standing at the bottom and paused. He then came down wearing a beautifully cut check country suit, followed by Michel Jobert. At Chequers, once President Pompidou had been escorted to his suite, Michel said to me, 'Now I shall be in terrible trouble. You see, some weeks ago the President asked me what the English would be wearing on a Saturday morning in the country, and I described to him what I thought was an English country suit. You may have seen how he was taken aback when he saw you standing there this morning in a plain grey suit.' 'Don't worry,' I said, 'I am just going to change, and in a few minutes I shall be down waiting to greet him again wearing a real English country suit.' Fortunately, he did not change into a grey one!

At the lunch party he was in very good form, but he never knew the story behind the wine which he praised so highly. Earlier in the week, I had gone from the Cabinet Room into my private secretaries' office to find them gathered together in a private conference. I asked them what was going on. 'We are trying to decide what to do about the wines at

Chequers for Monsieur Pompidou's visit,' they said. 'Should we give him the best wine for lunch on his arrival on Saturday and then move down the scale to Sunday night, or should we give him the least good at the first meal and build up to a climax on the Sunday?' 'What have you decided?' I asked. 'We cannot reach a decision,' they said, 'but we know you have several bottles of Burgundy Musigny from 1916, your birth year, and we thought you might like to give him that.' I replied, 'If President Pompidou and I were just having lunch *à deux*, nothing would give me greater pleasure, but running down my entire, precious stock at a single lunch with officials really does not appeal to me.' We then all decided that Château Latour 1945 would ensure a successful visit. When he first sipped it, Pompidou looked across at me and asked, 'How do the British manage to have such wines? When you come as my guest to Paris, I shall not be able to offer you anything as good as this.'

When the guests had departed after a long lunch, I suggested to him that he would perhaps like a rest. 'No,' was his reply. 'Then would you like to have a meeting with your staff?' Again the answer was 'No.' He wanted to do whatever I normally did on a Saturday afternoon. 'Then we will go for a walk along the top of the Chilterns,' I replied. We drove to the top on that glorious afternoon, and then walked along the ridge. He was delighted with the informal and natural way in which everyone behaved, as they raised their hats and smiled their greetings. The only uncomfortable people were his security men who, not being prepared for country life, were still wearing their black jackets and striped trousers. So obvious were they that they abandoned any idea of strolling along with our party and resorted to hiding behind the foliage and hopping from tree to tree. At the high point of the walk, we enjoyed a splendid view covering five counties. As he looked at the trim, well-cropped fields stretching far into the distance I heard Pompidou murmur to himself, 'What a countryside. The English have it all already.'

President Pompidou was a delightful man, and I always found him to be charming, cultured, beautifully spoken and with a splendid sense of humour far removed from the caustic wit often associated with the French. He enjoyed good food, good wine and good company, and he greatly encouraged the arts. His wife, charming, elegant and totally *au fait* with contemporary music and painting, fully shared his interests. When Pompidou became President of France, together they transformed part of the Elysée into a contemporary home, and brought modern decor to that fine old building. He and I always got on well together, at both personal and political levels. There was no Franco-British love–hate relationship in his make-up. He admired the British enormously for our achievements, but he was always quite sure the French could do just as well, given the right leadership.

The guard at the gate of the Elysée on that crisp May morning in 1971 sprang to attention as we approached. It was symbolic to me that all this should be happening in Paris, the city to which I had first come as a boy, to which I had returned so often, and in which I had started the first European negotiations in the Quai d'Orsay ten years before. I was greeted by Jobert and the chief of protocol, Jacques Senard, and escorted to the President's office on the first floor, where Pompidou was waiting to receive me on the staircase. We carried on our discussions in the same room where I had talked to General de Gaulle in 1965. For two days there were just the two of us, each with an interpreter. Michael Palliser, bilingual in English and French, joined me from our embassy, and Pompidou had Prince Andronikov, a distinguished and multilingual former Russian nobleman who was a senior member of his diplomatic staff. The French Prime Minister joined us just for the closing session, at which we agreed our joint minute.

It is difficult to think of more attractive surroundings in which to carry on talks of this kind. The elegance of the Elysée inspires a spirit of reasonableness. Before lunch on the Thursday we were able to stroll in its delightful gardens and, for a few moments at the beginning, we talked to the President's friends and colleagues. In our first session of talks, Pompidou had stressed that what he felt was needed was an historic change in the British attitude. If Britain was really determined to make this change, France would welcome us into the Community. He regarded his own country and Britain as the only two European countries with what he termed a 'world vocation' and said quite explicitly that, if the political and intellectual prestige and authority of Britain were added to those of the Six, the Community would be greatly enriched. My task was to convince him that this was also what we wanted to see. I assured Pompidou that there could be no special partnership between Britain and the United States, even if Britain wanted it, because one was barely a quarter the size of the other. Through Europe, on the other hand, such a partnership was possible within a Community applying the same rules and working to shared principles. Our purpose was to see a strong Europe, which could speak with one voice after a full discussion of the world problems affecting it, and could then exert effective influence in different parts of the globe.

After further talks in the afternoon, the French Prime Minister and I went to the Arc de Triomphe, where I laid a wreath on the tomb of the French Unknown Soldier. On that Thursday evening a state dinner, with the candelabra gleaming in the light of the flickering candles on the long tables and a string orchestra playing English and French music, found everyone intrigued about what had been going on but reassured by the warmth and friendliness of the occasion. Christopher and Mary Soames were the hosts at lunch in the British embassy on Friday, to which the President and Madame Pompidou came, together with all living former French Prime Ministers and others prominent in public, industrial and artistic life. The British embassy is one of the loveliest houses in Paris, formerly home to the sister of Napoleon I, Pauline Borghese, subsequently bought by the Duke of Wellington, and now one of the treasures of the British diplomatic service.

Before we went to lunch on the Friday, President Pompidou took me to one side and said that we should resume, and aim to complete, our talks in the afternoon. I readily agreed, and we returned to the Elysée together for a further three hours' discussion. The press conference which had been summoned was accordingly delayed until the evening. President Pompidou said to me, 'I am glad that we are doing this, but I am afraid it may make things very difficult for you. I understand that you are due to go racing in the Channel tonight and now you will not be able to do so.' 'I have sent the crew a message,' I replied, 'to carry on the race without me.' 'That,' he said, 'could be very embarrassing. If they win the race this weekend without you, everyone will say that you are quite unnecessary. On the other hand, if they complete the race and lose you will go down in the championship.' In the event, *Morning Cloud* came second, which was probably the best compromise! Christopher Soames reminded me of why he was such a successful diplomat in a letter dated 26 May 1971: 'How clever of her to do well enough, I imagine, to keep in the running for the Admiral's Cup, yet still to show that she needs her skipper.'

On Friday evening, we held our conference for the press, radio and television in the Salle des Fêtes of the Elysée Palace, a lofty and beautifully decorated room which has seen many splendid occasions in the life of France. It was also the scene of de Gaulle's press conference in 1963 when he had so astonished the world by announcing the French veto. The chattering ceased as the President and I took our places in the gilt armchairs on the platform. The air of expectancy was intense, for nothing whatsoever was known about our talks. It was obvious from the looks on their faces that the majority of the media believed that there could only be one explanation for the extended meeting throughout the afternoon and on into the evening, that we had found it impossible to reach agreement. I had not even confided in Douglas Hurd or in Michael Wolff, my senior political adviser, to their evident annoyance. They, too, obviously shared the fear of failure. Those present did not have long to wait for the answer. I had managed to convince President Pompidou, during twelve hours of talks, that Britain was genuine in its desire to enter the European family. President Pompidou finished his statement by saying:

> Many people believed that Great Britain was not and did not wish to become European, and that Britain wanted to enter the Community only so as to destroy it or to divert it from its objectives. Many people also thought that France was ready to use every pretext to place in the end a fresh veto on Britain's entry. Well, ladies and gentlemen, you see before you tonight two men who are convinced of the contrary.

It was marvellous to see the looks of astonishment on the faces of so many of those present. The President and I looked across at each other with delight, for we had secured success and also triumphed over the media. For me personally, it was a wildly exciting moment. Just forty years after my first visit to Paris, I had been able to play a part in bringing about the unity of Europe. It was an historic occasion.

The negotiations were duly completed the following month in Luxembourg as the French negotiators, under orders from the Elysée, watered down their demands. I had informed Pompidou that the British government accepted without reserve the system of Community finance which had been adopted, adding that we were prepared to work out transitional arrangements based on a framework proposed by the French government. We considered that a gross contribution equivalent to about 6 per cent of the total Community budget in the first year of UK membership would provide a plausible settlement. This was double our ambitious opening gambit of 3 per cent for the first year, a figure never taken seriously by the Six. On 21 January 1971, Pompidou had been asked at a press conference about his opinion of our proposals on Community finance. He replied, 'One must admit that the British have three qualities among others: humour, tenacity and realism. I have the feeling that we are slightly in the humorous stage.' We likewise had regarded the often quoted figure of 21.5 per cent as unacceptable. Pompidou assured me, however, that the French delegation would not press for a starting figure which constituted a serious burden for the British balance of payments, taking into account the other costs of UK membership and our need to repay debt. But he still believed that a starting figure of 11.5 per cent was reasonable. He also accepted that a period of 'correctives' should be provided after the end of the five-year transitional period and before we took on the full obligations of the definitive Community system.

Under the agreement negotiated in June, a favourable compromise was reached. Britain was required to pay 8.64 per cent of the budget of the enlarged Community in the first year, rising to 18.92 per cent in the fifth year, a figure comparable to our proportion of the gross national product of the enlarged Community. After the first five years, a further period of two years was allowed during which the size of our contribution was to be limited. Both the Labour government's White Paper of 1970 and the CBI report on entry predicted that the dynamic effects on our economy from membership would more than outweigh the short-term budgetary costs. Our White Paper of July 1971, however, was rightly cautious about the longer term, stating that 'in the Government's view, neither our contribution to, nor our receipts from the Community budget in the 1980s are susceptible of valid estimations at this stage. And it is for this reason that the Community declared to us during the course of the negotiations that if unacceptable situations should arise "the very survival of the Community would demand that the institutions find equitable solutions".' In other words, the UK had a right to renegotiate its budgetary contribution if it was unfair. Both Harold Wilson and Margaret Thatcher understandably took advantage of this concession in subsequent years.

I always expected that the Community budget would develop in ways more beneficial to the UK. At the Paris Summit in October 1972, for example, the Community committed itself to establishing a regional and industrial policy. The UK would have been a large net recipient from these policies, but the Community's plans for an industrial policy were later shelved because of the unforeseen economic slump and the ensuing retreat from further integration. Regional policy, however, was constructed with great effort and difficulty in October 1972. This has developed and lasted over the years, though it has been of less benefit to the UK than it might have been, thanks to the Treasury's insistence that the money should be paid into the Exchequer rather than directly to the regions as is done in other Community countries, and that grants from the European Community regional funds must be in substitution for, not additional to, grants from the British government.

We also reached an acceptable agreement on New Zealand. The interests of all Commonwealth countries were treated as a major concern throughout the negotiations, although New Zealand was by far our largest problem. Its dependence on the British market, although declining, was great. In 1970 New Zealand exports to the UK (as a proportion of total exports) stood at 34.4 per cent. The comparable figures in Canada and Australia were 8.9 and 11.1 per cent respectively. Our aim had been to secure satisfactory arrangements for the continuing access of New Zealand exports of butter and cheese to the markets of the enlarged Community.

I placed great emphasis in my discussions with Pompidou on the need for an acceptable settlement for New Zealand. That this problem could present an insuperable obstacle in Parliament was reflected in the fact that even the most ardent Europeans felt strongly about it. I received a letter from Duncan Sandys that May saying that, although he had been with Winston Churchill in the Hague at the launching of the European Movement in 1948, he would not be able to vote for British entry unless New Zealand received a fair deal in the negotiations. Pompidou indicated that the French would try to be helpful over New Zealand, taking account of the moral, sentimental and political aspects of the problem as much as the economic difficulties.

The eventual settlement provided guaranteed access in the fifth year after our entry for 80 per cent of New Zealand butter quotas before entry, and for 20 per cent of existing trade for cheese. There was also scope for a review of the terms over butter during the third year of UK membership. The arrangement was accepted by the New Zealand government as adequately safeguarding their interests. We also obtained the approval of the members of the Commonwealth Sugar Agreement on the terms we achieved for their sugar exports. This was done at Chequers on a hot, sunny evening after I had invited the representatives of all the Commonwealth countries involved to spend the evening with me there. Before dinner they sat on the steps at the south front of the house, looking into the rose garden, and there I explained to them how successful Geoffrey Rippon's negotiation had been. They approved of the agreement and enjoyed their evening.

Sir Con O'Neill, leader of the British delegation to the negotiations, believed that no subject was more problematic than sterling. It was an issue on which Pompidou felt very strongly. He was concerned about the position of sterling as a reserve currency, for a basic principle of the Community, especially with the prospect of economic and monetary union, was the equality of status for the currencies of the member states. No currency should have advantages, whether technical or juridical, over the others. During the Paris Summit these problems were raised once again. We soon reached full agreement. I told President Pompidou that we would make every effort to reduce sterling balances in accordance with certain conditions which any proposal for reducing them would have to satisfy: notably, of course, the protection of the interests of the balance holders and the avoidance of unacceptable burdens on our balance of payments. At the same time, we would endeavour to maintain the rate of sterling.

It was up to the ministerial meeting in June to finalise agreement on sterling and a plan was hatched by Soames and Jobert to secure this. It was arranged that the UK delegation would make a statement about the place of sterling in the enlarged Community. This was prepared by Soames and Jobert and, on the evening of 4 June, it was agreed by President

Pompidou. Jobert assured Soames that the French Finance Minister, Giscard d'Estaing, would act, in his deliberations both within the Six and at the negotiating meeting with us, in response to Rippon's proposed statement. The French kept their side of the bargain and, when the Council of Ministers met on 7 June, Rippon made his statement. He told the Six that 'the British government were prepared to envisage an orderly and gradual run-down of official sterling balances after our accession,' adding, 'We shall be ready to discuss after our entry into the Communities what measures might be appropriate . . . in relation to sterling with those of the other currencies in the Community in the context of progress towards economic and monetary union in the enlarged Community.' After this declaration, there was a short adjournment and Giscard, to the disbelief of the other delegations and the Commission, announced that the French were happy with what had been said. This aroused great suspicion, however, that a secret deal had been struck at my summit with Pompidou. I explained our position fully to the House of Commons on 10 June 1971:

> We have said that as members of the enlarged Community we would play our full part in the progress towards economic and monetary union. That was confirmed in my talk with President Pompidou and in my statement to the House . . . But let me make it clear that we have given no undertakings as to how fast or by what means these developments could or should be brought about. These would be matters for discussion after our entry, when we should be a full member of the Community with all the rights of a member.

This quotation, alongside Rippon's statement to the Six on 7 June, was later used in our White Paper of July 1971, *The United Kingdom and the European Communities*.

The foundations of economic and monetary union were laid in the Treaty of Rome, and reaffirmed in the 1960s. The Werner Committee was asked in 1969 to work out how economic and monetary union might be achieved. The report set out a 'First Stage', to cover 1971–3, when the Six governments would co-operate very closely in their economic and monetary policies. It then went on to outline other radical changes which would be required if EMU was to be attained by 1980. At every stage progress would depend on intergovernmental agreement. Outside the Community we had to accept, subject to any transitional arrangements, whatever plans for closer co-ordination would be agreed by the Six for 1971–2. If Parliament accepted our terms, however, we would be involved as full members in deciding the acceptability of any further measures to be taken after 1 January 1973. Our view, endorsed by the previous government, was that we were in favour of closer monetary integration and would be prepared, as members of an enlarged Community, to move towards this laudable objective alongside our partners.

Prices were the overwhelming obstacle in people's minds to joining Europe. Our opponents at home claimed that domestic prices would rise dramatically after our accession, because of the Common Agricultural Policy. In fact, domestic prices, including food prices, were already rising considerably faster in the UK than within the Community before our entry. The counterbalancing argument to the increase in prices for the consumer has always been that subsidies to the food producers would no longer have to be paid by the Treasury. This would allow reductions in taxation, or make available for other purposes money formerly spent on subsidies. This certainly had its appeal both to the Treasury, which would be spared the annual argument with the National Farmers' Union about the amount of subsidy on each product, and to the taxpayer, who was only too anxious to get a reduction in personal taxation. The British system of supporting agriculture was to subsidise artificially low prices in the shops with taxpayers' money. This was increasingly difficult to defend and sustain and, in any case, was being gradually phased out. Tony Barber had announced in his mini-budget of 27 October 1970 that the system of 'deficiency payments' to farmers was to be gradually replaced by import levies and threshold prices (see p. 331).

The UK adopted the Community system of support in 1973, introducing threshold and intervention prices of our own for a transitional period. Our White Paper estimated that membership would increase food prices by about 2.5 per cent each year. As food accounts for about a quarter of total consumer expenditure, the net effect on the cost of living was estimated at a little over 0.5 per cent each year, much lower than the figure quoted in the Labour government's 1970 White Paper. After British accession, our exports of foodstuffs, including those within Europe, greatly increased. We even managed large exports of butter to France and the Netherlands, at a time of butter surpluses in the rest of the Community.

Our task after the negotiations were concluded was to obtain Parliament's approval to the terms we had achieved. The only area left outstanding was fisheries. It had proved impossible to reach an agreement in the time available and a solution was not reached until December 1971 (see p. 702). I had always insisted that, after the conclusion of the negotiations, the fullest information about our position, together with explanations of the implications, should be given to Parliament and the public. There was widespread support for the principle of negotiations. It was our responsibility now to publish their conclusions. Typically, Wilson adopted the line most likely to reap electoral rewards, supporting entry in principle, but attacking the terms we had achieved. Both George Thomson, Labour's defence spokesman, and George Brown, however, publicly backed the settlement. Roy Jenkins, then Shadow Chancellor, described the Conservative entry terms as being 'as good as those which those with any knowledge of the situation could realistically have hoped to get'. Wilson was pushed into his anti-European position by his Shadow Foreign Secretary, James Callaghan. In a speech at Southampton in May 1971, Jim positioned himself with the left of his party by saying, 'Non, merci beaucoup' to the supposed plan for French to become the official language of the European Community – and, by implication, to the Community itself. After this speech there was never any real doubt that the Labour Party was split on this question.

Having finally settled the negotiations, I was anxious that Parliament should reach a decision on them before it rose for the summer. However, Francis Pym, our Chief Whip, advised me that it would be best to leave a vote in the House of Commons on the principle of accession until after the recess. He did not want the government to appear to be rushing Members of Parliament, before they had the chance to listen to the views of their constituents or indeed to digest the material themselves. A vote before the summer would also place pro-European Labour MPs in a difficult position, since it would clash with their special party conference on 17 July, which was likely to be quarrelsome. Francis suggested that a 'take note' debate should be sought before the recess, to be followed by the final vote on principle in October. Others, including Harold Macmillan, Douglas Hurd and Roy Jenkins, sought an earlier vote. I accepted the advice of the Chief Whip and we allocated four full days for the first, 'take note', debate in July, after which the House rose for the summer. After the break we set aside a further six days in the House of Commons, making a total of ten days' debate in all on the principle of our membership of the European Community.

Our publicity campaign, which had begun in May, became very extensive over the summer, involving two White Papers, one for Parliament and a shorter edition for the public. Both the White Papers and the arrangements for debate were favourably received by Parliament. Harold Wilson, on 7 July, accepted that 'the arrangements proposed for the debate are generous and will be acceptable to hon. Members, both as regards the "take note" debate this month and the definitive debate in October'. The leader of the Liberal Party, Jeremy Thorpe, added that 'The House will be grateful for this very detailed White Paper.' The public information campaign on the outcome of the negotiations was the most comprehensive ever by a post-war government. It was eagerly received by the public and an incredible number of the publications were snapped up. Between July and October 1971, nearly 300 ministerial speeches were made, with

Ministers explaining the implications of the settlement for their particular departments. Geoffrey Rippon also continued to develop informal contacts with prominent pro-Europeans in the Labour Party. It was agreed that the Foreign Secretary and I would stand back from the detail and take an overall view in the context of Britain's role in the world. In an interview with ITN on 27 May 1971, I said:

> I believe the British people ... the housewife who is worried about food, the trade unionist who may be worried about competition from others in Europe ... are going to see the wider issues and those are the issues of peace, they are the issues of prosperity, they are the issues of the future of Europe, its own defence as well as its own prosperity, its relationship with the outside world ... they are going to see the whole of this as a very great enterprise ... and I believe that they will become convinced that this is where the future of modern Britain lies.

The Foreign Secretary, in a speech published by the Conservative Group for Europe in June 1971, added: 'On two counts I am in full agreement with the most vocal opponent of our entry into Europe. The first is that our application is a step of the utmost political significance, and the second is that there is a danger of its political importance being overlooked in the public debate on the economic issues.'

Our campaign focused on both the political and the economic issues, and Ministers emphasised the bipartisan support for entry into the Community. The emergence of a multi-party consensus on Europe was crucial in overcoming the doubts of the public, who were concerned about the practical consequences of entry, not about ideology or abstract notions of sovereignty. The fact that the overwhelming majority of top-rank, mainstream politicians supported entry on the terms we had negotiated eased their concerns. This was subsequently repeated in the 1975 Referendum (see p. 549).

There was then the question of the form of the vote. Before the 1970 general election Iain Macleod had seized on the idea of a free vote as a way of defusing what he had concluded would be a vote-loser for us. I was, however, instinctively in favour of a three-line whip for our own party. I was convinced that Wilson would do the same for the Labour Party. Furthermore, both Alec Douglas-Home and I felt that the authority of the government depended on our ability to get our business, including every aspect of European business, through the House of Commons with Conservative votes. My anxiety was that, if we had a free vote and it went wrong, all those in power in the six member countries would take the view that we had not made the necessary effort to carry the result of the negotiations through Parliament and that we had, therefore, not been negotiating in earnest. This would not only prevent our immediate entry, but would undermine future attempts for a long time to come.

Throughout the summer of 1971, Alec and I remained unconvinced about a free vote. On 18 August, I received a minute from the Chief Whip informing me that a free vote might yield the best result in Parliament, although it was 'too soon to judge'. By October, however, Francis was convinced that a free vote was necessary and he had persuaded the Leader of the House, Willie Whitelaw, that this was the best policy. I received a further minute from the Chief Whip on 5 October, just three weeks before the crucial division in the Commons. It contained his assessment of the situation among Conservative backbenchers. Francis estimated that there were twenty-six 'Hard-Line antis', six doubtful MPs who 'were likely to vote against' and thirteen uncertain MPs 'with a good chance' of remaining loyal. This left a total of 281 Conservative MPs in favour of entry. Over half of these MPs, including Margaret Thatcher and Nicholas Ridley, were members of the Conservative Group for Europe. Their support was solid. Pym predicted a figure of thirty-eight defectors, which meant that the division could not be won without some Labour votes and/or abstentions. His difficulty was that the Labour Party position was impossible to assess with any accuracy. Estimates on the number of their rebels had varied enormously and the risk was that only some twenty pro-Europeans would come into our lobby if Wilson imposed a three-line whip. The outcome of the vote was clearly at risk.

On 14 October 1971, during the Conservative Party conference at Brighton (at which there was a huge majority of 2,474 to 324 in favour of entry), I had a private meeting with Willie Whitelaw and Francis Pym in my room at the Metropole Hotel. I finally accepted their view that to have a free vote would be healthier for our party and its future. MPs could bring their own judgement and the views of their constituents to bear in deciding on an important constitutional issue. Over the summer Conservative constituencies had swung firmly behind our accession to the Community. A free vote would also encourage the pro-European members of the Labour Party to break away and vote with us. There was a substantial cross-party majority in favour of membership in the House of Commons, and it made perfect sense to take advantage of it.

The Labour Chief Whip, Bob Mellish, had originally reassured pro-European Labour MPs that a three-line whip against the principle of entry would be imposed upon them 'over his dead body'. Under pressure from his party's left wing however, he imposed precisely that. Labour pro-Europeans at first discussed the possibility of abstaining on the vote, or of voting for a 'reasoned amendment', which would support the principle of entry but reject the terms which we had negotiated. To their immense credit, individuals such as Roy Jenkins and David Owen knew all along that this was not a time for fun and games. It was a time for men and women of principle to stand up and be counted. David Owen subsequently wrote that 'in 1967, when Labour applied to join, [Labour] were bitterly unpopular and . . . the Tories did not choose to play party politics with the issue but voted in support of the application to the EEC on the basis that this was an issue that transcended party politics'. This record of Conservative consistency, combined with Francis Pym's wise instinct in relation to the vote, was enough to guarantee us a handsome victory.

On 28 October 1971 the House of Commons voted, by 356 to 244, in favour of the United Kingdom joining the European Community. It was my greatest success as Prime Minister. I had been conscious of a tremendous weight of responsibility as I stood at the despatch box. No Prime Minister in time of peace has ever asked the House to take such a positive and historic decision as I was asking it to do that night. The world was watching Britain to see whether Parliament would decide that Western Europe would move along the path to real unity. I closed the marathon six-day 'Great Debate' in the House of Commons by making my aspirations for Europe perfectly clear: 'I want Britain as a member of a Europe which is united politically, and which will enjoy lasting peace and the greater security which would ensue.' The overwhelming majority of Conservative members backed membership and the thirty-nine rebels on our side were substantially outnumbered by Roy Jenkins and sixty-eight of his pro-European colleagues in the Labour Party. Francis Pym's minute of 5 October had proved incredibly accurate. The House of Lords endorsed membership even more resoundingly, by 451 votes to 58, a majority of almost 400 votes. Britain's decision was welcomed across the globe. President Pompidou told me that the vote was a 'personal success for you and a success for Europe'. Willy Brandt announced: 'I am convinced that it is good for England itself and for Europe, firstly economically and then increasingly politically'. Messages of congratulations were also received from Commonwealth Prime Ministers and the President of the United States, Richard Nixon.

Great difficulties still lay ahead, for we had to get the necessary legislation through the House of Commons and there was no guarantee of further support from the Labour benches. Nonetheless, I felt both relief and elation. For the Parliament of the United Kingdom had decided, by heavy majorities, that the destiny of our country lay in Europe. I had spent the twenty-one years of my parliamentary career working towards this moment. I thought back further, to the battlefields of France, Belgium and Holland, to the rallies of Nuremberg and to Wendell Willkie's voice, crackling over a radio set at my command post in Normandy, in 1944, speaking to us of

'One World'. He was speaking of one world at war. Now we were creating one world at peace.

Harold Macmillan, who had done so much for Britain and Europe in the previous decade, lit a bonfire of celebration that night on the cliffs of Dover. There were, of course, many impromptu celebrations in and around London that evening, and the media were pressing me for comments and expressions of triumphalism, but I felt the need for a moment of reflection with my closest friends before getting involved in any of that. So we returned to my private sitting room at No. 10, and I played the First Prelude from Book I of Bach's 'Well-Tempered Clavier' on my clavichord. It was the right choice for that moment. Bach was an early master in the European musical heritage, in which the British share and to which they have contributed so much, and that particular piece of music, at once so serene, so ordered and so profound, sounding through that silent room in the still, small voice of the clavichord, brought us the peace of mind that we needed before plunging into the busy round of celebrations.

On 20 January 1972, two days before I was due to sign the Treaty of Accession, the Labour Party initiated a European debate on a motion preventing the signing of the Treaty until the official text had been published by Brussels and considered by the House. Their motion was deliberately calculated to embarrass the government, for constitutionally there could be no final and authentic text of the Treaty until it had been signed. The signature of the Treaty was an exercise of the royal prerogative and the correct course, therefore, was to lay the full text of the Treaty before Parliament immediately after signature. We tabled an amendment stating the correct position under international law and this was easily carried by 298 votes to 277.

On Saturday 22 January 1972 I arrived at Melsbroek airport outside Brussels for the signing of the Treaty of Accession to the European Communities. I was joined by Alec Douglas-Home, Geoffrey Rippon, Con O'Neill, Harold Macmillan, Christopher Soames, Jeremy Thorpe and Lord George-Brown. Harold Wilson decided to go to a football match instead. We arrived at the Palais d'Egmont for the start of the signature ceremony. Nobody, however, was prepared for what followed. A young foreign woman had gained admittance to the building by pretending to be an agency photographer and her credentials had been inadequately checked by the Belgian authorities. Having entered through the great door of the palace, I started to climb the marble stairs leading to the Assembly Hall. There were people lining the other side of the stairs to the left applauding. As I paused briefly to let Alec catch up with me, the woman, who had been standing among a group of photographers in the entrance hall, thrust herself through the spectators and hurled a pot of ink at my head and shoulders, which splashed all over my suit. I was shattered, people in the crowd screamed and the police rushed to grab the woman, who became hysterical. Officials, including Robert Armstrong, led me to the top of the staircase and off to a side room where they started scrubbing my head and face to remove the ink, and some of my aides rushed off to the hotel to fetch me another suit and shirt. In all it took an hour before we were ready to carry out the ceremony and the distinguished gathering had to sit and wait without knowing the cause of the delay. I only caught a glimpse of the woman concerned in this episode. I had never seen her before, and I had not a clue who she was. It emerged later, when she was tried in a court in Brussels, that she had been involved in some business transaction in Covent Garden which she believed I had been responsible for preventing, and she had chosen this time and place to vent her frustration. I was certainly not going to let this young woman, or Covent Garden's redevelopment for that matter, spoil such a celebration.

On entering the hall at last, I received a tremendous ovation. It was packed with so many of those who had played a part in founding and building the European Community. Most prominent among them were Paul-Henri Spaak, who had presided over the Messina Conference (see p. 201) and Jean Monnet, responsible for the original concept of the Community. Monnet was in particular a good friend of Britain and he had showed me great kindness as well as always proffering me wise advice. It gave me enormous pleasure that, more than twenty years after the European Steel and Coal Community, Monnet finally saw the enlargement of the Community to include the United Kingdom. Throughout this long period he never lost sight of his governing principle, that the purpose of the European Community was to increase the prosperity of the peoples of Europe, to provide an unchallengeable bastion for the defence of their freedom, and to create the means through which a European influence for good could once again be exercised in the world outside. The Europe of Jean Monnet is free and democratic, prosperous and peace-loving, unselfish in recognising and accepting its responsibilities to those less fortunate than its own people.

As I sat at the table, flanked by Alec Douglas-Home and Geoffrey Rippon, the thrill of signing the Treaties was intense. The British effort, both in war and in peace, of setting out to establish a peaceful Europe had come to fruition. This historic occasion was completed when the King and Queen of Belgium gave a ceremonial banquet at their palace. The following day, I returned to my favourite restaurant, Comme Chez Soi, for a lunch with members of my team. We were all well aware that we still had a hard job to finish over the coming months, for Parliament had yet to pass the Accession Bill into British law. At the beginning of March 1998, I returned to the Palais d'Egmont for the first time, for a dinner to celebrate the close relationship between London and Brussels. It was a setting laden with powerful memories.

The Labour Party and our own rebels were convinced that the Bill would involve over 1,000 clauses. Harold Wilson had put Michael Foot and Peter Shore, both anti-Europeans, in charge of wrecking the legislation and they were determined to spin it out in Parliament for as long as possible. The Bill was expertly drafted by Sir Geoffrey Howe, the Solicitor-General, and Sir John Fiennes, first parliamentary counsel, so as to balance our wish for tight legislation not open to attack with the need for a proper debate on the issues. There was no question of the Bill, which consisted of twelve clauses and four schedules, having been deliberately drafted so as to mislead or to curtail debate. While a short, tight Bill naturally offers less scope for filibustering and wrecking amendments than a longer one, brevity is clarity. As the Bill was so concise, its purpose and implications were as clear as they could have been, and this had the virtue of concentrating parliamentary debate around the really important issues. The Labour Party produced a censure motion on the drafting of the Bill on 6 March, but this was rejected by a majority of forty-seven and no Conservative voted against the government. Even Enoch Powell, by now a fervent anti-European, announced that he 'could not possibly support a statement . . . which attributes ill faith to the Government'. A Bill of 1,000 clauses was quite unnecessary and would have been almost impossible for anyone to understand.

The second reading of the Bill occurred over three days, from 15 to 17 February 1972. This vote was always going to be difficult as there was never any possibility of allowing a free vote on the legislation required to give effect to the European Communities Bill. Most of the Labour rebels who had voted with us in October were unwilling to offer their public support during the latter stages. Some of them argued that it was the job of the government to enact its own legislation. David Owen has described his decision to vote with the Labour leadership on the second reading as 'the worst vote I have ever cast in Parliament and the one of which I am most ashamed'. Roy Jenkins has described it as 'a day of misery'. The Liberal Party, however, remained resolute thanks to Jeremy Thorpe's decision to treat this as an important issue of conscience. Thorpe was a natural politician and a consummate leader of the Liberals, who certainly held his small party together. His Oxford Union experience stood him in good stead as a debater and, despite his party's limited strength, he could be a commanding speaker in the House of Commons.

Spirits in the Whips' Offices rose and fell as voting intentions became known in the days preceding the crucial vote on second reading. The motion was eventually agreed by 309 votes to 301. Fifteen Conservatives, including John Biffen, Neil Marten and Enoch Powell, voted with the Opposition. As the result was announced, the Labour Party backbenches erupted in furious uproar. I could see the look of relief on the faces of the pro-European Labour MPs who had been forced to vote against their consciences. There was pandemonium as a crowd of furious left-wingers had to be physically restrained by Bob Mellish from lifting Jeremy Thorpe, whom they blamed for the result, across the chamber. It was certainly a close shave but, as *The Times* commented on 18 February, 'It is the majority of 112 which represents the real view of the House of Commons on the merits of the question, and the majority of eight which represents a political scheme . . . Last October was a vote of judgement; last night was a party device. On party votes of this character, one is indeed enough.'

The committee stage was taken on the floor of the House, not upstairs in committee, to allow full discussion by MPs. This complicated situation was handled with outstanding skill and sensitivity by the entire Whips' Office including Hugh Rossi, Jack Weatherill, Michael Jopling and, later, Kenneth Clarke. They all knew that the parliamentary arithmetic was tight and that, as we now had a parliamentary majority of under thirty, we were taking a gamble if we relied solely on our own backbenchers. Matters were made worse when, at the end of March 1972, seven of the eight Ulster Unionist MPs informed us that we could no longer count upon their support. On the plus side, we had the strong and consistent support of five of the six Liberals and we knew we could rely on four 'old and bold' backbench Labour MPs to abstain on every aspect of the Bill: Freda Corbet, Carol Johnson, George Lawson and Christopher Mayhew, an old friend from my days at Oxford. Christopher was later to leave the Labour Party in 1974 for the Liberals, not least because of his views on Europe. The Whips were also aware of the growing unhappiness of other Labour pro-Europeans who were demanding a two-line whip on the committee stage so that they might pair, or abstain with honour.

At the government Whips' morning meetings, they would estimate how many of our MPs were likely to rebel in each division. If we were ever likely to be in any trouble, one of the Whips, usually Ken Clarke, would meet informally with John Roper, Labour MP for Farnworth and the unofficial Whip for his party's pro-Europeans, with whom he had the closest possible relations. Roper was a committed European who later joined the SDP in protest at the Labour Party's shift to the left and, in particular, its growing hostility towards the European Community. He always managed to deliver just enough Labour abstentions to prevent us from losing in committee. Many of his colleagues would now, no doubt, look back and judge his actions harshly. After all, as I had told the House on 17 February, this was ultimately a matter of confidence in Her Majesty's Government. John, however, is a man of principle who believed passionately in doing what he thought was right for his country. So were those of his colleagues who supported his efforts. The cynical ones were the Labour leaders who insisted on trying to force many of their supposed comrades against their better judgement, to oppose accession. Roper took the utmost care to prevent havoc and ill-feeling in the Labour Party. To achieve this, he organised a rota among pro-European Labour MPs to ensure that there were different groups of people absenting themselves from the House for crucial amendments. All of the planning and information was kept in what was known as his 'Red Book'.

The Bill was discussed at committee stage for ten days before a guillotine motion was introduced and for twelve days afterwards. After a second reading, amendments are not allowed if they contravene the principle of a Bill and, consequently, most of the amendments proposed by the Labour Party were ruled out of order, and not even discussed. The European Communities Bill was not ratifying the Treaty of Accession, but implementing the necessary changes in domestic legislation to give that Treaty effect. Amendments proposed to alter the Treaty were, therefore, justifiably ruled out of order. By 27 April, the Bill had spent almost ninety hours in committee without disposing of Clause 2, which dealt with the general implementation of the Treaties of Paris and Rome, and the priority of Community over domestic legislation, which had been accepted by the Labour government in its 1967 White Paper:

> The Community law having direct internal effect is designed to take precedence over the domestic law of the Member States. From this it follows that the legislation of the Parliament of the UK giving effect to that law would have to do so in such a way as to override existing national law so far as inconsistent with it . . . It would also follow that within the fields occupied by the Community law Parliament would have to refrain from passing fresh legislation inconsistent with that law as for the time being in force. This would not however involve any constitutional innovation. Many of our treaty obligations already impose such restraints – for example, the Charter of the United Nations, the European Convention on Human Rights and GATT . . . Moreover, Community law operates only in the fields covered by the Treaties.

To ensure proper consideration of all the clauses of the Bill in committee, we had to resort to the guillotine. The use of the guillotine in Parliament is always controversial as it limits the time available for discussion, so it is, generally, only used *in extremis*, usually to prevent Members of Parliament 'talking out' a Bill. The resolution was carried by 304 votes to 293, with thirteen Conservatives voting against the government. Many of our own MPs who were opposed to our membership of the European Community, including Hugh Fraser and Toby Jessel, did nonetheless accept the use of the guillotine and, on most procedural motions, we faced only token rebellions from backbenchers.

Teddy Taylor, at that time, was a shining example of those European rebels who respected loyalty to the party. On forming a government I invited him to become Parliamentary Under-Secretary of State for Scotland. He gladly accepted, but told me that if the government's European policy developed beyond what he found acceptable, he would have to resign. I accepted his resignation on 28 July 1971 with regret. But there was none of the bitterness that became so depressingly familiar in the Conservative Party in the 1990s. During the debate on the second reading, Taylor announced that he would not defy his party as he had done in October. He had accepted that Britain was to join the Community and, under these circumstances, he did not want to 'undermine our nation's standing and prospects, as well as the standing of the government at a critical time'. He also confirmed that there had been no attempt to put pressure on those who were irreconcilably opposed to membership. After it was all settled I asked him to rejoin the government, and he accepted my invitation. His behaviour then is in stark contrast to the disgraceful behaviour adopted by the Maastricht rebels in 1992.

The committee stage consumed 173 hours of debate and produced 88 divisions, with over 200 amendments being discussed. It is remarkable that this vital piece of legislation was passed without amendment, particularly since our majority fell to single figures on no fewer than sixteen occasions. The third reading of the Bill occurred over a single day on 13 July 1972, the motion being agreed by a vote of 301 votes to 284. Norman Lamont made an excellent maiden speech during this debate. He described himself as 'strongly pro-European' and went on to say, 'One is bound to ask whether the interests of the House as an institution and the interests of the British people are necessarily the same. The legitimacy of political institutions is based upon consent, but it is also based on effectiveness . . . it is no service to the British people to block the development of new institutions geared to the problems of our time, or to see as an affront to the House what should be an exercise in the principles of representative democracy.' On 14 July the Bill was brought out of the Commons and went to the House of Lords for a further nine days of debate.

In total, Parliament spent thirty-nine days discussing the European Communities Bill, beginning with the first reading on 25 January 1972 and ending with royal assent on 17 October that year. In addition, we had allowed ten days of debate on the principle of entry in 1971. This made for a total of forty-nine days of debate. It is both absurd and insulting for anyone to suggest that Members of Parliament did not know what they were doing when this legislation was being discussed. The corresponding time spent for the Single European Act in 1985–6, under Mrs Thatcher's government, was only twelve days – and it was the Single European Act, not the Treaty of Accession, which greatly curtailed the national veto.

While the legislation was slowly progressing through Westminster, Pompidou and Brandt, following a suggestion by Jean Monnet, agreed in Paris on 11 February 1972 to propose that a summit of the Six, plus the four applicants, should take place in October that year. There were a lot of convinced Europeans who strongly objected, protesting, 'What right have you heads of government to have a summit? You are not mentioned in any of the Treaties. As you don't exist, you cannot have a meeting.' Pompidou wisely ignored these protests. During 1971 the Community had been preoccupied with its enlargement and relations with the United States. The Community's own internal development had been less of a priority. It was hoped that this summit would define the road ahead and test British participation within the new Community. Pompidou, however, became increasingly concerned that a conference would prove to be a damp squib, an event destined merely to celebrate enlargement. He was a man who desired action not words. He therefore grew doubtful about whether there was enough substance to justify a summit. Some of his colleagues were at least as sceptical.

I assured President Pompidou, through the usual channels, that the British government saw the summit not as a public-relations exercise, but as an occasion at which real decisions could be taken. We believed, for example, that there could be substantial progress towards economic and monetary union. On 22 March 1971 the Six had resolved to move in stages towards EMU. Plans had been overtaken by the international monetary upheaval of 1971, however, and reaffirmation of this objective was of major importance. The sticking point for the French was that we had not yet returned to a system of fixed parities. Under the Smithsonian Agreement of 1971, European currencies could move bilaterally against each other by up to 4.5 per cent. If governments decided to change parities to meet the immediate needs of their economies, they could do so in consultation with their colleagues. Pompidou saw this as a matter of trust rather than anything else. When sterling was floated on 23 June 1972 (see p. 410), we assured everyone concerned that a fixed rate of exchange would be reimposed as soon as was practicable. The time and rate for fixing sterling, however, were a matter for the UK government to decide.

Our major objective at the summit was to strike a balance between the economic and monetary elements. We had accepted the Common Agricultural Policy and agreed that the Community should advance towards EMU. Our priority was the establishment of a common industrial and regional policy. Britain was a highly industrialised but, in certain respects, industrially ageing country. The Community had concentrated on the CAP as the main aspect of its regional policy, which was understandable when such a large part of the population of the original Six was occupied in agriculture. Only 3 per cent of the British population, however, was so engaged and British agriculture was already a highly capitalised and mechanised sector.

Our main structural problem lay in older industrial areas, many of which had not been rebuilt since the war. American loans had been used in the immediate post-war period to meet our urgent financial needs and not for capital investment as had been the case on the continent. Areas such as the Clyde, Merseyside and Tyneside needed restructuring. Other member states were also planning their own schemes on regional development to suit their own particular problems. Much time was spent in the Cabinet Office trying to devise a European policy which would help our budgetary imbalance by spending more in the UK than in other member states, differentiating between our difficulties of declining industry and high unemployment and the problems faced by other countries. By taking the lead in the development of a Community regional policy we could also demonstrate our avowed intention to play our full part in building up and strengthening the enlarged Community.

Regional policy too was crucial to the long-term success of economic and monetary union. This remains the case today. As globalisation continues apace, our capacity for dealing with national and regional problems by purely national measures will be ever-more limited, hence the greater need for action and burden-sharing by the Community. Our position was described perfectly in a pamphlet published by the Conservative Political Centre in 1971:

> The development of more effective regional aid policies is virtually guaranteed, in fact, by the decision by the Community in March 1971 to work towards transforming the Common Market into a fuller Economic and Monetary Union. This is the long-term objective which the British Government endorses, and indeed we shall share in directing this process from within the Community . . . Europe offers the opportunity; there is nothing remotely comparable outside.

The author of this pamphlet was a Mr (later Sir) George Gardiner.

Shortly before the summit, in September 1972, the Norwegians voted in a referendum against joining the European Community. I was saddened by Norway's decision, as I had wanted as many members of EFTA as possible in the Community. This was not because, as some claimed, we wanted to organise a combined veto against the original Six. We never imagined for one moment that others who joined the Community from EFTA were going to acquiesce with us all of the time. Our experience in EFTA had shown that these countries were as adept as any at fighting for their own interests. Britain had close connections with Norway, however, and I believed that it would have been in their interest to come into the Community at that time. But that was a decision for the Norwegians. All we could do was to say that we all regretted their decision, as we wanted to have the largest possible part of Western Europe operating together and becoming more and more united. Sadly, the Norwegians rejected a further opportunity to join the European Union in 1994.

Pompidou sent me his personal draft declaration for the conference on 17 October 1972. I have always admired the lucidity and clarity of French literature and I was greatly impressed too with the concept and the style of the French President's declaration, which expressed the hopes and aspirations of us all. To judge from the remarks of those who have listened to my few speeches in French, some doubt seems to exist whether I have benefited much from my appreciation of French literature. I can get by in French, which at times I have used in public on television and radio. But on the occasions when these performances have been rebroadcast in my own country, I have been greeted on my return with cries of 'How could you make those ghastly noises? What on earth did you mean?' I was always consoled by the warmth of support from my French friends who commented, 'Well done, you were certainly trying.'

My own opinion was that I could accept Pompidou's draft as it stood, but that we needed to add to it a list of the detailed questions which would be resolved at the conference. It was clear from our bilateral discussions with the Germans that their ideas on social policy in the Community would complement our own proposals on regional policy. We seized this opportunity for a deal by which German interest in a European social policy could be combined with our desire to see a full commitment to working out, and introducing, a regional policy. Sir Nicholas Henderson, our ambassador in Bonn, discussed this possibility with Brandt shortly before the summit, and the German Chancellor proved to be receptive. Both Brandt and I were determined to revive wide public support and enthusiasm for the development of the Community. We agreed that Germany and the UK would meet Pompidou's wish to underline progress towards monetary integration, provided that the French accepted our wish to give priority to regional and social problems.

The British delegation arrived in Paris on 18 October and we were met by the French Prime Minister, Pierre Messmer, and the Foreign Minister, Maurice Schumann. It was appropriate that Schumann was there to welcome me on to French soil. I had first met him on the beaches of Normandy on 6 July 1944, when he was a French liaison officer with a British commando unit and had the job of ascertaining whether our unit's guns had landed. I was the Adjutant of the regiment. But now, thirty years later, diplomacy and negotiation had replaced the horrors of war. I had two important meetings to prepare for our discussions. At 5.30 p.m. I went to the Elysée Palace to see President Pompidou. I asked for his support in establishing a regional development fund inside the Community to help finance and modernise those areas which had not yet caught up with the progress made elsewhere since the war. This I knew would be difficult, because the post-war development of France was evenly spread right across the country. He listened to what I had to say and then remarked that it was not a cause he wished to espouse, because France did not need help from such a fund. 'Moreover,' he added, 'you have sent me a map showing where the funds would go. I immediately turned my eyes to my own country and looked at my own home, Auvergne, only to find that it would not be getting a penny or a franc. So there is nothing in it for us.' I told him I would send him a fresh memorandum on the subject in the morning, together with a new improved map, which I was sure he would find more acceptable. I then discussed these issues with the German Chancellor at the Hôtel Bristol, Paris. He readily agreed to support our plans on regional policy, but regretted that he could not help me on international aid. Franz-Josef Strauss, one of the major figures in the German opposition, had claimed that the German government was throwing away money on foreign aid projects and, as an election was approaching, Brandt had to be very careful not to make any additional commitments in this area.

I was convinced that the Community required a common approach to the problems faced by the developing world. We agreed with the objective of increasing trade with the developing countries by 15 per cent, although we could not accept the figure of 0.7 per cent of GNP for official development aid which had been raised by other member states. In 1971 total UK aid flows, from both official aid and private investment, amounted to 1.14 per cent of GNP. Of this, however, official development aid had been only 0.41 per cent, planned to rise towards 0.43 per cent. To accept 0.7 per cent would have produced an enormous increase in total aid at an economically difficult time. I have long believed that private investment is of more use to the developing countries than public investment, and we therefore opposed the idea of a Community commitment to minimum aid levels. I favoured the gradual untying of debts. If we had turned some of our loans into grants and claimed no more interest, it would have provided the developing world with some breathing space, rescuing them from a spiral of deflationary economic policy and falling living standards. It is psychologically wrong to give aid with one hand and to take it away in repayments with the other. Too many democratic regimes have been overthrown because they could not get over their debt problems, Ghana being an example. In any case, if countries are forced to default on their debts, it is usually the Western banking systems which suffer.

The summit took place at the French Government Conference Centre, which for the previous four years had been the home of the Vietnam peace talks. The heads of state and their delegations sat at a long table in the principal conference hall, and President Pompidou took the chair. The Commission was relegated to the far end of the table as Pompidou wanted to demonstrate that its status was not the same as that of the heads of government. The proceedings of the conference began, as usual, with a series of speeches. Speaking immediately after President Pompidou and Barend William Biesheuvel, the Prime Minister of the Netherlands, I called for a clear timetable for economic and monetary union. I also dealt at some length with those issues to which we had attached great importance, and I concluded:

> I hope that this conference will enter into clear commitments on both
> . . . the Community's regional and industrial policies . . . Only thus shall
> we lay the foundations for the social progress and the higher standards
> of living which all our peoples seek. Indeed, why should we not set
> ourselves the aim of bringing together our aspirations, commitments
> and policies in the regional, industrial, agricultural and social fields into
> a comprehensive social programme for the Community? . . . But the
> political development of the Community must keep in step with its
> economic consolidation . . . That means working towards a common
> foreign policy.

The main decision of the Conference was the affirmation by the member states of their intention to transform their relations into a European Union by the end of the decade. I had argued that European Union was an admirable objective which could be achieved only by pragmatic steps. The European Union has always developed *sui generis*. Historically, there has never been anything like it in the world and other groups of countries that have found the need to create a regional body have not been able to emulate the European Union's success. When the European Union reaches the end of its development, it will remain *sui generis*. I believed, therefore, that there was little point in debating theoretical arguments about federalism. What we were concerned with was making a success of the European

Community, and the word 'Union' allowed us to do just that. In contrast, the words federalism and confederation have always caused no end of confusion. In Britain there is still little understanding of either term.

As widely expected, the enlarged Community reaffirmed its determination to progress towards economic and monetary union, and it was fully accepted that progress in economic co-operation would move in parallel with progress in monetary co-operation. On the monetary side, the meeting agreed on the need for mechanisms to defend the non-floating, but adjustable, parities between member countries' currencies. It was further decided that the Community would move to the second stage of EMU on 1 January 1974, with a view to its completion by the end of the 1970s. The nine governments also agreed to adopt a common attitude to working for international monetary reform.

The summit accepted that structural and regional imbalances, which could affect the realisation of EMU, would be tackled on a Community basis. A Regional Development Fund was arranged, to be financed from the Community's own resources, my major negotiating success. This was finally achieved at the Paris Summit of December 1974. The problems of industrial change and structural under-employment would now be recognised as a Community responsibility. By 1980, we planned to have completely abolished all internal trade restrictions, establishing a complete free market with a single currency. In the political sphere, it was resolved that the Foreign Ministers would produce a second report on methods of improving political co-operation. Without a common foreign policy and a common trading policy, Europe could not hope to stand up alongside the United States, the Soviet Union, China or Japan. It was the British government's intention, therefore, to work towards a common foreign policy, as I had indicated in a speech at Zurich on 17 September 1971, and, eventually, towards a common defence policy, in order to exert the Community's full influence in the world.

Although there was some disappointment in the Dutch, Belgian and Italian delegations about the relatively slow progress towards political unity, all nine governments had good reason to be satisfied. It was a particular success for President Pompidou and for the three acceding countries. We had defined all of our aims in advance of the summit and our only failure was in the context of aid policy to alleviate the indebtedness of the hardest-pressed countries. The German government had been unwilling to accept any new commitment on aid, and the French government could not agree to any waiving of debt service. The option for further discussions was, however, left open for a later date. Overall, the summit provided the impulse for the next stage of the Community's development. It is a tragedy that this did not come about. The reason is obvious: the oil crisis of 1973-4.

At the end of the discussions in Paris, it was suggested that we ought to meet again in October 1980 to celebrate the achievement of what was set out in the communiqué. Then a rather more cautious member from the Dutch delegation pointed out that 1980 was eight years away, and we might have to adjust course before then. So we resolved that we would meet in October 1976.

In actual fact the heads of government met only a year later, in Copenhagen on 14–15 December 1973, to discuss the oil crisis. It was the worst summit that I have ever experienced. The result was calamitous for almost everybody. It was wrecked when four Foreign Ministers from Algeria, Sudan, Tunisia and Abu Dhabi publicly announced their intention of descending uninvited upon the conference to discuss the war in the Middle East and the future of the Mediterranean area. They duly arrived in Copenhagen. We talked about how to handle this event for most of the first day and decided that our Foreign Ministers would meet them. The four ministers then arrived at 10.30 p.m. and kept the Community Foreign Ministers talking until nearly 3.00 a.m. Much of the following day was taken up in hearing a report of these talks, after which it was agreed that the issue of a full communiqué was inevitable. The officials then wrote down the views of their respective countries on every subject and pinned them together, so we were faced with approving this as a communiqué. But we did decide that we would henceforth assemble three times a year, in the form of the heads of government meeting. The European Council now meets twice a year and is a regular and accepted institution of the Community. On any practical assessment, however, the European Council is inadequate as a top governing body for fifteen member countries, with a total population of over 350 million. To take but one example, it is the custom of the British Cabinet, under the chairmanship of the Prime Minister, to gather at least once a week. When the European Council convenes, its two days have to include individual press conferences, as well as civic receptions and banquets given by the leading political figures in the Presidency, together with the task of securing agreement on the communiqué. To provide a satisfactory organisation for the provision of policy, and its implementation at the top, remains one of the most urgent tasks now facing the European Union.

After both the passage of the European Communities Act and the completion of the Paris Summit, we had to learn to live as members, not as applicants for membership. I sent a personal minute to all members of the Cabinet informing them of the need to familiarise themselves with the techniques which the Community had developed for doing its business. I stressed that each department had to define its objectives and work out how they could be met in the complex bargaining situations of the

Community. We were also responsible for preparing our representatives and our procedures to deal with these problems. A European Secretariat was established in the Cabinet Office and I insisted on putting officials from Whitehall home departments into the staff of UKREP Brussels, our permanent office there, whose main task is to represent the UK in day-to-day negotiations with European institutions. This was a very effective way of propagating a European outlook within departmental culture and these structures endure to this day. I was particularly determined that Britain should have two top-rate members of the Commission, and that one should come from each side of the House, to demonstrate the depth of cross-party support. I appointed Sir Christopher Soames and George Thomson as our first representatives in Brussels. Harold Wilson took no part in these appointments, but I ascertained that Thomson would agree to become a Commissioner. George asked me not to approach Wilson about this; he would rather inform him himself. On 6 January 1973, Soames was given the responsibility of External Relations and Thomson took charge of the development of Regional Policy. These two appointments were welcomed across the European Community and both men proved to be excellent Commissioners for Britain and Europe.

On 1 January 1973, Britain formally entered the European Community. I saw this as a wonderful new beginning and a tremendous opportunity for the British people. To emphasise both the celebratory and the cultural aspects of British membership, we set up 'Fanfare for Europe', a series of performances by distinguished artists in various disciplines, to take place at the beginning of 1973. On Wednesday 3 January, 'Fanfare' opened with a gala night at Covent Garden, attended by Her Majesty the Queen, the Duke of Edinburgh and many other members of the royal family. This contained a mixture of music, poetry and drama, drawing widely upon our shared European heritage. Distinguished actors such as Laurence Olivier, Max Adrian and Judi Dench shared the stage with leading luminaries from the world of music, including Tito Gobbi, Elisabeth Schwarzkopf, Geraint Evans and the young Kiri te Kanawa. Many great performances have graced that world-renowned stage, but few can have been more moving or more appropriate. Performers and audience then mingled afterwards for a splendid dinner at Lancaster House. This was all an appropriately high-spirited and good-natured introduction to Britain in Europe, and my heart was full of joy that night at the recognition which Her Majesty the Queen had given to our country's great achievement.

This was followed by a concert in the Royal Albert Hall the next evening. I had asked Herbert von Karajan, as a special personal favour, to bring the Berlin Philharmonic Orchestra to London for our celebrations. The maestro informed me that such an appearance would have to be sandwiched in between other, long-standing engagements, with the orchestra flying in during the afternoon, and out again the morning after the concert. 'But,' he said, 'I will do it for you.' As the Berliners came on to the platform, the great audience of young people standing in the well of the concert hall surged towards the stage. Many members of the orchestra were clearly nervous and withdrew further back. Thankfully, there were no injuries as the orchestra played Beethoven's Fourth and Fifth symphonies as well as I have ever heard them played and accordingly received a deafening, and very well-deserved, ovation from the Winter Promenaders. Even von Karajan seemed a little taken aback by their warmth and vehemence. I hosted a dinner in his honour at No. 10 afterwards, and we had a fascinating discussion about sailing, as well as music. I also learned that von Karajan had arrived feeling rather tired; when the musicians had assembled for an afternoon rehearsal, he told them to play a single, common chord of C so as to get their balance right and then sent them away for a rest. Perhaps other touring musicians should try the same approach. It certainly worked wonders on that occasion, for there was no hint of weariness in their performance that evening.

After the oil crisis of 1973–4 the Community lost its momentum and, worse, lost sight of the philosophy of Jean Monnet: that the Community exists to find common solutions to common problems. Each member state drifted back to seeking its own, unilateral solution to unemployment and inflation. So we all had to relearn painfully that there is no solution if we act on our own. It was not until the mid-1980s that the original philosophy of Community action was properly restored. Pompidou's early death, on 2 April 1974, was another sad day for Europe. If President Pompidou, Chancellor Brandt and myself, the three men who created the enlarged European Community, had remained in power (Brandt and I both lost office in 1974), we might have been able to implement the communiqué issued after the Paris Summit in October 1972, the first part of which President Pompidou had drafted in his own hand. I am convinced that, had that been achieved, Europe would have been a more successful, influential, prosperous – and happier – place than it is today.

Chapter 14

~~~~~~

TRIPARTISM ON TRIAL

Economic and Industrial Affairs 1972–1973

My colleagues and I were aware that the settlement of the miners' strike of 1971–2 might have set a damaging precedent. The majority of miners were decent and hard-working men, who took considerable risks in difficult working conditions, which is why public support for the miners had been so solid. A highly politically motivated minority in the ranks of the NUM, however, had been at the forefront of an organised attempt to bring down an elected government, and it was imperative to demonstrate to them and their colleagues that this was intolerable. On 9 March 1972, I therefore invited the TUC General Council in for candid and wide-ranging talks and, a week later, held similar discussions with the CBI. My chief press officer, Donald Maitland, was very concerned about how all of this would be received in the country. He was convinced that the TUC were quite incapable of seeing sense and that they would do no more than mount a staged protest against the Industrial Relations Act and our proposed Housing Finance Bill, requiring local authorities to charge economic rents (see p. 454).

Very wisely, Donald encouraged me to set out for the trade unionists the true nature of the long-term economic picture. They had to recognise that, if our country was serious about competing in the modern world, not only would inflation have to be curbed, but working patterns would have to become more flexible and they would have to understand that employment levels in traditional industries might be in long-term decline. We had to reduce unit costs and raise productivity in our existing industries, and create leisure facilities and encourage the development of the services sector. For the more antediluvian of the trade union leaders, this was no brave new world. It was a hideous prospect, within which their own power-bases might crumble to dust within a decade or two.

This viewpoint was echoed by Robert Armstrong, who pointed out that there were two main barriers to increasing employment in the service industries: 'the attitude which regards work in at any rate some service industries as menial or even degrading, and secondly the low level of wages in some of the industries . . . How these barriers could be overcome would be a useful field for discussion with the TUC.' He then went on with a prescient warning, that we should:

> think carefully before saying anything which indicated Government willingness to see a further general reduction in the working week . . . Whatever may have been the case a century or a generation ago, more recently reductions in the working week have been demanded mainly as a means of increasing overtime earnings. Reductions in standard hours have not been matched by reductions in actual hours worked. The danger, therefore, is that a reduction in standard hours neither improves production nor makes possible higher output, but simply increases costs.

This added to the pressure on profit margins and prices.

At the meeting with the TUC, I started off by explaining that I wanted to have something more than the usual, routine exchange of views. I then set out the government's objectives: sustained and steady economic expansion and falling unemployment, secure employment within the context of changing technology and a steady and general improvement in the standard of living. We now had the best opportunity since 1945 of achieving these objectives. There was no ideal or instant solution to our industrial relations problems, but I sought at this meeting a frank expression from everyone of ways in which we could bring about sustainable improvements in our economic and industrial climate.

The recent miners' strike had been costly, not only to the National Coal Board and to the miners themselves, but also to the country as a whole. It was only reasonable to ask whether there were not better ways of settling such matters. In a week's time, I planned to have a similar meeting with the CBI, and hoped that they and the TUC might talk with one another on the basis of common objectives. The initiative from the CBI on controlling prices in July 1971 had been effective and, from all the evidence, it appeared that it could go on being so. The government recognised that questions of prices and wages were inextricably linked with important issues of social policy, in which field the TUC had in the past year or so come forward with certain suggestions. I hoped too that they might welcome some of the government's proposals, for example on pensions and post-war credits, which we fully redeemed through the repayment of all outstanding sums to approximately 5 million beneficiaries.

There followed an exchange which, despite the predictable and by now pointless complaints about the Industrial Relations Act, seemed to indicate that the trade unionists, too, were looking for common ground. Somewhat implausibly, one or two of those present argued that our poor industrial relations should not be identified as one of the root causes of our productivity shortcomings. Tony Barber retorted, quite rightly, that the most important aspect of any modern industry was its degree of competitiveness, and that was the challenge that we all now faced. British export prices had risen by 24 per cent between the last quarter of 1969 and the last quarter of 1971, while the export prices of our major competitors had risen by only 15 per cent. The main root cause was the unsustainable level of pay settlements, which were still significantly ahead of productivity improvements. In an era of fixed exchange rates, this was the road to ruin.

I summed up the meeting by reminding everyone that the country now expected something of the TUC and of the government, as well as of industry. The British people were acutely and painfully aware of the stresses of inflation, and its consequences for pensioners and the lower-paid. They looked to the government, to the unions and to management to work out a solution. The trade unionists present indicated their assent. I then set out a range of other areas where tripartite co-operation could yield positive results: assessing employment trends and their implications for leisure, improving methods of conciliation in pay disputes; and the whole area of regional policy, to which we might return after Tony Barber's next budget. Perhaps the best starting point would be to prepare some agreed statistical basis for further discussion, so that in future we would avoid getting bogged down in disputes about conflicting figures. Jack Jones proposed that the NEDC might be the best forum for all of this, to which Tony Barber agreed.

The overwhelming view on Fleet Street and in the City at this time was that we needed an expansionary budget. Growth for 1971 had been a disappointing 1.7 per cent and, although the balance of payments was healthy, this was taken to be a sign of weak demand at home rather than an export boom. When I met Tony Barber on 10 January 1972 for our first talk about the forthcoming budget, I too was already convinced of the case for a generous package, but he remained relatively cautious. When we held another meeting in early March, we covered more or less the same ground. Like all our conversations, this one was perfectly constructive and good-natured, but I still had to overcome too great a degree of traditional Treasury caution on his part.

The 1972 budget, unveiled on 21 March, was warmly received, although, because of the introduction of direct rule in Northern Ireland three days later, it never enjoyed the positive publicity it deserved. Tony Barber revised the target for growth upwards to 10 per cent over the next two years. To increase demand, he raised tax allowances by about £1 billion, made further reductions in purchase tax and proposed to change estate duty into a more lenient inheritance tax. In a full year, the national tax bill would fall by £1.8 billion (£13.5 billion today). We also gave greater incentives to industry through increases in depreciation allowances. Having decided that our system of regional tax allowances for industry was not bringing results as quickly as we wanted, we reverted to a system of capital grants, similar to the one that Labour had used. There was no argument in Cabinet about the principle of this, although John Davies did put forward a proposal, ultimately defeated, that the awarding of grants should be heavily devolved, to the regional offices of the DTI.

In that budget, Tony Barber introduced what he quite rightly described as a package to 'provide the climate in which industry can have the confidence to re-equip and expand'. The overriding challenge was helping the whole country to catch up with our competitors, especially within Europe. With the possible exception of the south-east, Britain was still handicapped by its outdated industrial plant. Despite our measures to stimulate it, manufacturing investment had actually fallen in the last quarter of 1971. If a patient fails to respond to treatment, any doctor worth his salt will respond by administering a stronger medicine, so we had to provide a lead. Tony Barber announced the extension to the whole country of a 100 per cent allowance for the first year of industrial investment, for which business leaders had been asking over many years. At the same time, we maintained preferential treatment to the more depressed regions, in the form of grants in addition to the existing allowances, on which we could not rely to bring about the necessary changes quickly enough.

The regions requiring special help would now be divided into four categories: Special Development Areas; Development Areas; Intermediate Areas; and Derelict Land Clearance Areas. Finally, we set up a new agency within the DTI, the Industrial Development Executive, with powers to invest in particular companies, and with a new regional organisation which would co-operate with the local authorities. This organisation would work in tandem with an Industrial Development Advisory Board, which included some of Britain's most dynamic industrialists. The whole structure would be under the direct control of Ministers.

On the second day of the budget debate, John Davies (still Secretary of State for Trade and Industry) explained our position in more detail. His speech on 22 March was badly received. Opposition Members heckled, and our own supporters were noticeably silent. The contrast with the previous day, when Tony Barber had delivered his budget speech with his usual polish, could not have been more marked. To make matters worse, I had also lost confidence in the DTI's junior ministers. Nicholas Ridley, in particular, had proved thoroughly indiscreet. It would have been preferable to reshuffle this team in advance of the new legislation that was now required. Unfortunately, rumours had circulated at the 1971 party conference that I was about to do this so, on balance, I judged it better to delay. But, while John Davies and Tony Barber were fully involved at all times, the junior ministers were not told about our plans for industry until just before budget day. On past form, there was every reason to fear that Nicholas Ridley would have ensured that the press were at least as well informed about developments as I was.

By the end of the month, I had offered Nicholas Ridley a sideways move to Minister for the Arts. He was an enthusiastic amateur painter, so I thought that this might appeal to him. He turned it down. In his memoirs, Ridley was to claim that he had resigned from the government, constructing a myth of self-sacrifice which he hoped might excuse his later behaviour, when he grasped every opportunity to make trouble for us. In fact, I had made it clear to him that he was no longer wanted at the DTI. Frederick Corfield, who shared many of Ridley's views and had given his own unhelpful briefings to the press, also left the government, while Sir John Eden accepted a new position at Posts and Telecommunications. Tom Boardman succeeded him as Minister for Industry. Both performed perfectly well. Christopher Chataway was brought in to the new post of Minister for Industrial Development. This reshuffle gave me the chance to promote Michael Heseltine to the level of Minister of State, replacing Frederick Corfield at Aviation, and he soon earned a formidable reputation.

John Davies saw the Industry Bill through to royal assent. Progress was not always smooth. The usual handful of troublemakers got themselves on to the committee scrutinising the Bill, and the right-wing chairman of the 1922 Committee, Harry Legge-Bourke, exploited the prestige of his position by exaggerating backbench opposition to the Bill. We had to allow some concessions in committee which restricted the amount of money which could be disbursed without parliamentary consent, but the basic principles were left unchanged. Once the Bill had been passed, Peter Walker, who had amply demonstrated his exceptional abilities at Environment, became Secretary of State for Trade and Industry and John Davies became Chancellor of the Duchy of Lancaster, with special responsibilities for Europe.

Some tried to make out that the Industry Act was a 'socialist' measure, an abandonment of principle. This was unjustifiable. It was a sensible, pragmatic and practical response to a disappointing state of affairs. As John Davies put it, 'the government cannot stand aside when situations arise which industry and the financial institutions cannot meet alone'. Whereas some Labour Ministers had hoped that their programme of investment would lead to much greater state ownership, our help was to be limited to the present predicament. Once the industrial climate in Britain had been changed and our companies had acquired some positive momentum, then the government could gradually withdraw and leave it to the entrepreneurs. Even while the Act was in operation, it would be used in accordance with proper commercial principles. As we found later, those who choose the more dogmatic alternative, of sitting back and doing nothing while our industrial base falls into decline, have soon been forced to spend billions on subsidising unemployed people. There are more productive uses for taxpayers' money, uses which will reduce the bill in years to come and create greater social stability. This was the thinking behind our Industry Act.

The new powers were used to help a variety of industries, including high-tech companies such as the computer firm ICL. Companies in traditional industries, such as the Mersey Docks and Harbour Company, Govan Shipbuilders and Cammell Laird, were offered substantial grants to support much needed programmes of modernisation. In spite of the inflationary pressures which affected this work, we had every reason for satisfaction until the oil crisis of late 1973 knocked all the world's economies out of their stride. After that, even the most ambitious government could not look far beyond the immediate struggle for survival.

The Act was never, however, going to please those who believed that it was impossible to justify helping to finance industry. We were by no means the only government which responded positively to calls for faster growth at this time. As a consequence, the demand for raw materials shot up and global commodity prices rose sharply. Certainly, this experience points to the need for better co-ordination among governments through institutions such as the G7, which brings together the seven major industrialised nations, but it does not prove that our drive for expansion was a mistake. Without it, we would have emerged from the international depression with our industries in a far worse state. The propensity to invest may be totally rational in most theoretical economic models, but in practice life is less neat and tidy. If investment is simply failing to happen when it is most needed, then the pragmatist does what he can to help and stimulates it. Conservatism at its best is always empirical, not dogmatic.

The surge in world commodity prices in 1972 would have affected Britain whatever any government had done. Where we could hope to make some impact was on the domestic inflationary pressure caused by excessive wage increases. We still hoped that the Industrial Relations Act would fulfil our needs in the long-term, but were realistic enough to recognise that in the end we might, after all, have to adopt a statutory policy for the control of prices and incomes. In America, President Nixon had taken this option as early as August 1971, having also earlier rejected the possibility. Although the majority of the Cabinet, including myself, remained uncomfortable in principle with statutory measures, after the miners' strike they had to be considered. We had good reason to hope that both employers and unions would appreciate the need for restraint in order to avoid this eventuality, but we knew that the next public sector pay round would prove to be a bloody battleground.

By this time, my political advisers were beginning to consider how we should respond politically to the worst-case scenario, a complete breakdown in relations with the unions. They devised a strategy for holding a general election on the specific issue of 'The People against the Unions'. Such a campaign, it was argued, could be based upon three main strands of attack on the recent behaviour of the unions. First of all, they were trying to make the task of a democratically elected government impossible. Secondly, they were asserting sectional power at the expense of the community. Thirdly, they were guilty of driving up prices and unemployment. Douglas Hurd, my political secretary, also argued that policies to curb picketing and curtail payments of benefits to strikers' families should be devised. If such policies seemed reasonable and necessary to the vast majority in the country, then the unions would either have to accept them, in which case we would have made substantial progress, or would run the risk of being exposed as self-serving and looking totally destructive by rejecting them.

I circulated a memorandum to the Cabinet on 28 April, asking Ministers to give the issue of controlling prices top priority. At a ministerial meeting on 23 May, we discussed a paper which Reggie Maudling had submitted in response. He had always broadly sympathised with the idea of a statutory incomes policy, and now gave an eloquent exposition of the case for one. Everyone agreed that the existing situation could not be allowed to continue. The majority, however, took Tony Barber's point that even a statutory policy would inevitably demand a substantial degree of willing co-operation from the public, which was not yet in evidence. After the miners' strike, and with the unions making the most of their 'grievances' over the Industrial Relations Act, the climate might be discouraging for a voluntary solution, but equally there were grave dangers in imposing more legislation on the unions. Even at this stage, few of my colleagues believed that we had much chance of arriving at any worthwhile and sustainable settlement with the unions, but we all felt that we should at least make an attempt to negotiate a voluntary deal. Public opinion would be alienated if we seemed unreasonable. I was prepared to be flexible, but there was never any possibility that I would countenance an agreement which would damage the national interest, and we were well prepared for legislative action in case the talks broke down.

The continuing trouble over the Industrial Relations Act gave us grounds for considerable pessimism. By 1 March 1972, the legislation was fully implemented, and the National Industrial Relations Court (NIRC) went into operation. Regrettably, the TUC had hardened its opposition to the Act the previous autumn. This was a baffling strategy, because those bodies which refused to register would lose their privileges and would no longer be recognised as trade unions. They could also be liable for unlimited damages if found guilty of unfair industrial practices as defined in the Act. We had run up against the traditional obstinacy of the trade union movement. Even if they recognised that something was in their interests, as a matter of principle they would not fall into line with it if they felt that they were being coerced. We and our predecessors had turned to legislative action only because trade unionists were so clearly unable to behave responsibly without it. Men like Jack Jones were still very much caught up in the historic struggles of their movement, against what they perceived to be a hostile class movement in the form of both the Conservative Party and the judiciary. The militants among union leaders were quite happy to exercise their own form of coercion against their 'brothers', however, and around thirty unions were eventually expelled from the TUC for obeying the law. We began to realise that more sensible counsels might not prevail until the TUC had led us so far down the road to ruin that we faced unemployment on the scale of the 1930s. We really could not contemplate that, and had to keep searching for solutions.

To this end, we were examining ideas emerging from the TUC and the CBI for an independent conciliation and arbitration mechanism between workers and employers, which would be required to take the public interest into account. If employers persisted in caving in to inflationary wage demands financed through inflationary price increases, it seemed that the government would have to take the lead once again, whatever the short-term political risks. As the discussion on 23 May moved on, it was clear that the mood of the meeting was in favour of doing something for the low-paid, who were so often the forgotten losers in a trade union free-for-all. A £20 per week minimum wage was mooted as a way of developing further the principles embodied by Winston Churchill when he set up the wages councils, in 1909.

The next major challenge to industrial peace began in April 1972, when the three railway unions started a work-to-rule in pursuit of a pay claim which, although less than the deal finally offered to the miners, was still over 20 per cent. Maurice Macmillan, who had replaced Robert Carr at Employment, referred the railways case to the NIRC after initial attempts at arbitration had failed. On 19 April, he was granted a fourteen-day 'cooling off' period, during which the work-to-rule was suspended. On 13 May, the Court ordered the unions to conduct a ballot on strike action.

The Court of Appeal reaffirmed this the following day, and the unions concurred. Pending the result of the ballot, the industrial action was again suspended. Even though the result was a sizeable majority for continued action, this represented an important breakthrough. Eventually the dispute was settled on 12 June with a 13 per cent deal, 5 per cent ahead of the rate of inflation. On the day after the railways settlement, we had a Cabinet meeting to discuss the implications of the agreement. We were now faced by a level of wage settlements which, if it continued, was clearly going to have the most serious national consequences, both economic and social.

Tony Barber and Maurice Macmillan were convinced that we had to work away at keeping wage settlements as low as possible and that we had to do so 'with a resolution which will be obvious to the nation'. They identified the Wilberforce settlement in the coal industry as the beginning of our real troubles. In setting out their argument, Barber and Macmillan explicitly precluded four possible policies as being unrealistic at that time: a wages freeze and/or legislation to control wages and prices; tax penalties for excessive settlements; new legislation on picketing and secondary industrial action (because our problem was one of enforcement rather than inadequate statutes); and the publication of a target figure for settlements. They took as their assumptions that we would wish to continue with our attempt to persuade the CBI to renew their voluntary price-restraint policy; to maintain the dialogue with the employers and the unions; and to examine more effective ways of negotiating wage settlements within the nationalised industries. All of this seemed very reasonable.

So what was to be done? Tony Barber and Maurice Macmillan suggested five possible new policies. First of all, they suggested government blessing for the new and independent conciliation agency which was emerging from discussions between the CBI and the TUC. Secondly, they recommended the establishment of a completely new, independent fact-finding agency, largely for the convenience of any new conciliation agency. Thirdly, they suggested that we might pick up an idea that had already been mooted in NEDC: that we might offer to work out acceptable formulae for threshold settlements. Fourthly, we might offer to devise with the TUC a phased programme to improve both the absolute and the relative position of the lower paid, without automatic adjustment and maintenance of differentials. We agreed strongly with this in principle, and the political pitfalls for the TUC if they blocked such a proposal were self-evident. Fifthly, they argued for legislation to deal with supplementary benefit for strikers. The generous provisions at the time were generally felt to have contributed to the widespread enthusiasm for going on strike, by softening the blow of industrial action upon those who took part in it.

I could understand the thinking behind the proposal for change, but I felt that we would have to approach it most cautiously.

On 19 June, Reggie Maudling produced another thorough and logical paper for Cabinet on 'the economic problem'. The most serious difficulty we faced, he argued, was inflation, which was fuelled by the cost-push created when incomes grew ahead of productivity increases. Our policy of expanding demand was essential to growth and employment and, therefore, broadly non-inflationary, on which basis inflation resulted largely from wage settlements. Other countries had seen similar wage increases, but had justified them with rising productivity. We were a long way from matching them. Maudling blamed the excessive rate of wage increases on the power of the trade unions: 'In the public sector resistance to this power is limited by their ability to disrupt the economy and by the uncertain state of public opinion . . . In the private sector ability to resist is limited by the threat of ruin.' The government's freedom of action to a great extent depended upon continuing public support for our stance. If we could not count on that, then we could scarcely take a strong stand against the trade unions at this juncture. 'We cannot at present count on such support when it is needed,' he argued. 'While there is much suspicion of the trade unions and fear of their powers becoming excessive, there is no general conviction that our policies are so fair that they should command general acceptance.'

Maudling's conclusion was that 'we can only hold the spiral of cost inflation on the basis of some agreement with organised labour . . . The basis of any such agreement must be an acceptance of a norm, which in effect means what the economy can bear in the way of general incomes inflation . . . Within the generality of incomes increases there must be an acceptable system to . . . identify the special case and to ensure that special cases do not, by becoming the general average, defeat both the general policy and themselves.' Some of the more hardline members of the Cabinet thought that Maudling's paper amounted to appeasing the unions, but I thought it proper to air these opinions. Regrettably, Maudling decided to resign over the Poulson financial scandal within a month of presenting his thoughts when the Metropolitan Police, for which he was responsible as Home Secretary, began an investigation into the affairs of John Poulson, with whom Reggie had once had a business association.

In a case parallel to that of the railwaymen, the Industrial Relations Act was now being even more grievously undermined, this time by the very courts which were supposed to enforce it. On 29 March and 20 April, the NIRC had fined the Transport and General Workers' Union a total of £55,000 because of the actions of some of its members on Merseyside in 'blacking' container lorries during the course of a dock dispute. Although the Act had specified that unions were responsible for the actions of individual members, the TGWU appealed and, in June, the Court of Appeal, in a judgement by the Master of the Rolls, Lord Denning, overturned the verdict of the NIRC. That decision was entirely unjustifiable from every point of view. He decided that, because the TGWU was unregistered, it was the individuals concerned who were liable for their actions in the dispute. This was exactly what the union militants wanted. Even though they had been using their strength to bully and blackmail the nation, they could now pose as the underdogs.

The dock strike was also causing problems in London, where three TGWU members were illegally 'blacking' container trucks at the Chobham Farm terminal. Sir John Donaldson of the NIRC was forced by Denning's ruling to threaten them individually with prison if they continued this behaviour. This time, it was workers at the terminal, ironically also TGWU members, who had obtained the injunction against the pickets. For once, the TGWU behaved sensibly, applying to the Official Solicitor for an injunction against the arrest of the men. Lord Denning also presided over the Appeal Court which granted this request. This decision was conveyed to us during a Cabinet meeting. Everyone was astonished. No representative of the government had had anything whatever to do with the Official Solicitor, but our political problems were still immediately exacerbated because, although the Official Solicitor was quite independent of the government and had been prompted to this action by the union and with the full knowledge of Lord Denning, his title gave many people the impression that he had been acting under our orders. They therefore questioned why we should have intervened in this fashion.

The fiasco was not finished, however. The docks dispute continued and, on 21 July, five dockers, including two of the original men, were jailed for contempt of court. They could hardly believe their luck, for this provoked public demonstrations, some unpleasant scenes in the House of Commons and even threats of a general strike. I held another meeting with Vic Feather, whose response was depressingly familiar and predictable. He asked me, yet again, to suspend the operations of the Act. I made it clear to him that I would not give in to blackmail, although I was quite prepared to review the situation once the Act had been given a fair trial. I repeated this to Robin Day on *Panorama*.

The fact was that, since these men had defied a court injunction, they would have been liable for prosecution quite independently of the 1971 Industrial Relations Act. Nothing in the Act itself could lead to a prison sentence. Tony Benn launched a series of pompous attacks on the Act, and Vic Feather joined him in expressing some anarchic sentiments, declaring that 'We don't regard this National Industrial Relations Court and the Industrial Relations Act as really legitimately a law of the land . . . the Industrial Relations Act is a politically motivated Act.' These chilling and reckless sentiments, which were echoed by Barbara Castle, still evoke for me that impossible time, when even the more moderate trade unionists arrogantly regarded themselves as beyond the reach of the rule of law assuming that they could operate a pick-and-choose relationship with the laws of this country. All of this merely hardened my determination to stick with our Act and, if necessary, to develop it further.

On 26 July, the Law Lords overturned Lord Denning's decision and re-established the proper interpretation of the Act. With my blessing, the Transport Minister John Peyton had encouraged Jack Jones and Lord Aldington to set up a committee to look into the problem. The day after the so-called 'Pentonville Five' were released, that committee reported on its proposed settlement for the dispute. Harold Wilson himself described their recommendations as 'a first-class set of proposals, designed to remove the anxieties of the dock-working community'. Despite the fact that Jack Jones had represented them, however, the dockers turned down the new offer and we were forced to call another state of emergency. The deal which eventually went through was the least defensible of this entire period. By now it was clear that things could not go on as they were. Instead of relying on the Industrial Relations Act to create a sensible climate, we would have to intervene more directly and make a concerted effort to bring the two sides of industry together.

In some respects, the court cases resulting from the Industrial Relations Act were a vindication of the Act. The basic principle of bringing the unions into the ambit of our civil law was having an effect and, even in the case of the railwaymen, the procedure laid down had been followed correctly. Although we were unhappy with the outcome of the railway ballot, the whole point of the legislation had been to impose some kind of order on industrial disputes. This had evidently been achieved. The rail unions had also honoured the fourteen-day 'cooling off' period ordered by the NIRC, because they knew that the alternative was a heavy fine. On this occasion the union members had held to their demands and voted for further action, but then we had never taken it for granted that the 'cooling off' period would invariably and necessarily produce a more realistic approach from the unions. I was thoroughly exasperated by the whole affair. These disputes were entirely politically motivated, and had nothing to do with social justice. The unions were engaged in a concerted attempt to subvert the law of the land. I was appalled that a senior judge should have failed to recognise that. Lord Denning's decisions at this time did immeasurable harm not only to our legislation and our social structure but indeed to the whole economy. They received widespread publicity which it was impossible for government resources immediately to counter. Denning had long been recognised for his idiosyncratic views and, while some admired him for his enthusiasm for interpreting the law creatively, many differed from his judgements in these cases.

The 1971 Industrial Relations Act is still widely misunderstood. It was conceived not as a way of weakening trade unions, but as a means of legitimising them and bringing them within the remit of the law. It was also a development of the Charters of the 1940s (see pp. 128–9), establishing in law the principle that an individual worker should always be entitled to join, or not to join, a trade union. With it we introduced a Code of Industrial Relations Practice, emphasising that the primary responsibility for good industrial relations rests with management and laying out explicitly the objective of establishing industrial harmony. The Code did not have the force of law, but the fact that parts of it had, or had not, been observed, would be taken into account by the NIRC or industrial tribunals in dealing with individual cases.

In the Code, we encouraged employers to issue all employees with clear and precise contracts of employment, to simplify and streamline methods of payment and to improve communications with staff. We also pre-empted European Community social affairs legislation by fifteen years, stating that 'any establishment with more than 250 employees should have an elected consultative committee'. The Code provided guidance about collective bargaining, collective agreements and 'bargaining units', the status and functions of shop stewards, grievance procedures and disciplinary procedures. All of this strengthened the hand, not of the trade union as a corporate entity, but of the individual worker. Other important reforms were introduced in tandem with the main Act. The training budget was increased, the Manpower Services Commission was established and we reduced the training bureaucracy imposed upon smaller firms. We revolutionised the Job Centres and, by supporting a Private Member's Bill introduced by a backbench colleague, Kenneth Lewis, brought in the licensing of private employment agencies. The 1970–4 government also instituted the Employment Medical Advisory Service for industrial employees and, at the time of the February 1974 general election, we were on the verge of introducing comprehensive and unified legislation on safety at work.

I do not claim that we made no mistakes in these affairs. Perhaps we were mistaken to try to achieve the changes we sought to make through the Industrial Relations Act at one go, rather than by a more gradual series of measures over time, as proved successful in the 1980s. On the other hand, these judgements are easy to make with the benefit of hindsight, and there was a fundamental difference between what we set out to achieve, and the reforms of the 1980s. In the Industrial Relations Act, Robert Carr set out, in the spirit of One Nation, to reform the entire field of industrial relations. Our intention was not merely to bring trade unions into line. We had nothing against trade unions as such and, in the early 1970s, neither did the people of this country. What we wanted to change was the balance of power in industry, and the climate of confrontation which had begun to develop during the late 1960s. It was the disruptive acts of individual trade unionists which had had to be dealt with, requiring us to give new rights as well as responsibilities to the trade unions, as institutions.

These turbulent domestic events took place against the background of a changing global economy, and we knew from the start that sterling could come under tremendous foreign exchange pressure at any time. One of the worst aspects of Harold Wilson's legacy had been the devaluation of the pound in 1967. Confidence had continued to drain away along with our foreign currency reserves, and Wilson got the worst of both worlds when he was forced to deflate the economy, in order to avert further pressure on sterling. The pound had been allowed a degree of freedom in autumn 1971, when President Nixon suspended dollar convertibility and, as the Bretton Woods system which had governed currency values since the war began to collapse, there was heavy selling of sterling. We were by no means dogmatically attached to the principle of fixed exchange rates, but it was important, given the potential volatility in the markets, that we should give no apparent signals about either revaluing or refloating the pound. Events now forced our hand.

The daily foreign exchange market report for Friday 16 June 1972 showed a marked fall in the exchange rate, and expenditure of about $500 million by the authorities in support of the rate. The vulnerability of sterling was greatly enhanced by nervousness about the rate of inflation in Britain as compared with that in other countries, and we realised at once that we might have to act quickly to calm things. These doubts about inflation were reinforced by the Court of Appeal's reversal of the NIRC's rulings over Chobham Farm, which I have already described. On Monday 19 June, the outflow of funds continued, albeit at a somewhat lower rate. That afternoon Denis Healey, the Shadow Chancellor, speaking in the Finance Bill Committee, said that devaluation was inevitable before the end of the summer. This ill-judged remark contributed to a significant slide in gilt prices and to renewed nervousness in the exchange market on 20 June. The outflow that day was another $500 million.

On Wednesday 21 June I met Tony Barber and officials from the Treasury and the Bank of England. We discussed a proposal from Barber to increase the bank rate from 5 to 6 per cent. The Treasury Bill discount rate had already risen to 5.5 per cent on Friday 16 June, half a percentage point above the bank rate. A failure to increase the bank rate in response would indicate that we had already decided not to defend the exchange rate. The following day we did increase the bank rate to 6 per cent, but this provided only a short-lived respite. Tony Barber returned that day at 4.15 p.m. for another meeting, again accompanied by officials. We were by now running down our foreign currency reserves at an alarming rate, and he and his advisers saw no alternative to abandoning the existing parity. We then agreed that a temporary flotation would be preferable to a devaluation. This decision was cleared with the necessary Cabinet colleagues that evening, receiving their unanimous consent, and we announced the flotation at eight o'clock the following morning. For technical reasons the statutory instrument that was required to implement some of the exchange control consequentials also abolished the old sterling area, which had originally been established in the days of colonisation, truly marking the end of a long song. Tony Barber and I signed that instrument at about 11 p.m. on 21 June. As we had expected, the pound did lose some value (at that time it had been worth around 8.3 DM) but there was no dramatic collapse. We intended this to be a temporary move, but as it turned out the arrangement stayed in place until 1990. We had acted firmly and promptly. There had been no protracted denials beforehand, as there had been with the Labour government five years before.

Before taking these decisions with members of the Cabinet, I informed President Pompidou of France of the seriousness of sterling's position and what our intentions were. I did so because of the undertaking I had given him at our meeting in Paris in May 1971 which had led to the agreement on Britain's membership of the European Community. This was that we would do everything possible to maintain the value of sterling and would not use any form of devaluation to improve our competitive position in Europe. He replied that he fully recognised our difficulties and the action it was necessary to take. He would certainly not regard it as going back on the assurances I had given him.

This enforced decision had an obvious effect on the strategy for prices and incomes which we were developing. The reduction in the value of sterling helped our exporters, but it also added to our rising import bill. Even though this depreciation of the pound temporarily took the heat off business, giving our exporters a temporary boost to their competitiveness, it was more important than ever that unit costs in British industry should be brought under control. Having agreed on our approach with all the relevant Ministers, I had a private meeting with Vic Feather on Monday 26 June. Vic had told Hugh Scanlon and Jack Jones that he wanted to see me urgently in order to set up a meeting between the TUC General Council and myself, at which they could call upon me 'to put the Industrial Relations Act on ice'. In fact, he wanted a private word about the likelihood of his colleagues co-operating with a co-ordinated, voluntary attempt to bring down inflation. I asked him frankly whether, in a tripartite agreement, the trade union leaders could deliver. 'When it comes to it,' Feather replied, 'ninety-eight per cent of them can, but in the docks no one will ever deliver.'

On Tuesday 4 July, Vic Feather was back at No. 10, this time accompanied by the TUC General Council. As usual, he began with a setpiece attack on the Industrial Relations Act. He said that the TUC case for the repeal, suspension or freezing of the Act was rooted not in self-interest, but in the economic interests of the nation. The number of working days lost through strikes had risen sharply with the introduction of the Act, he said, and only the intervention of the Official Solicitor had saved the dockers' representatives at Chobham Farm from going to jail. If they had been imprisoned there would certainly have been wildcat strikes in other industries. He was concerned, he said, that the NIRC was operating independently and without accountability to government, yet was in a position to put the national economy at risk.

I was ready for this tirade and pointed out that it was quite absurd to make a final judgement on an Act which had been in operation for only a year. What was more, the TUC had refused to enter into proper consultations before the Act was passed, so it was rather hypocritical for them to criticise it now. If I ever became convinced that the Act was indeed a failure, I assured the TUC representatives, I should certainly seek to have it amended or repealed. Feather responded by saying that the TUC 'could not engage in useful dialogue on industrial relations while the Act was on the statute book'. Step by step, he then retreated from this position, but I was constantly aware of the pressure he was under whenever the General Council was arrayed behind him.

I warned the assembled trade union leaders that the country now expected the government and both sides of industry to settle wage disputes together in ways that did not feed inflation or damage the economy. The fear that Britain was going to succumb to rampant inflation had provoked the flight from sterling which, in turn, had led to the decision to float the pound. There were good reasons for this. Over the four years from June 1968 to June 1972, average earnings had risen by 50 per cent, representing 5 per cent per year ahead of inflation. Unless some sensible and voluntary arrangement could be put in place to prevent this turning into an irreversible wages spiral, I warned them, we would find ourselves faced with a stark choice between three disagreeable options. We could encourage the development of free collective bargaining, accompanied by demand deflation to curb wage inflation; we could introduce statutory intervention, to which the TUC, the CBI and the government were opposed; or we could face a period of further confrontation combined with continuing inflation. None of these was an attractive option.

I reminded the TUC too that we had already responded positively to most of their earlier proposals. We had stimulated faster economic growth and acted directly on price inflation, both through cutting taxation and by urging the CBI to continue their voluntary restrictions on prices. During 1971–2, we had written off £350 million of the British Steel Corporation's debt under the terms of the Iron and Steel Act 1972, and had supported nationalised industries by almost £200 million. In 1972–3 this latter figure would rise to over £350 million. We had improved social services and pensions, we had greatly extended regional policies and, most recently, we had been willing to adjust our policy towards sterling in order to maintain economic expansion.

Summing up, I expressed my hope that the government and the TUC would, in future, be able to avoid the misunderstandings which, in the past, had arisen on both sides. I was delighted that the TUC were already engaged with the CBI in discussion on arbitration and conciliation. So long as the wider national interest was safeguarded, I was prepared to leave these matters to them. However, there were a number of other pressing issues in which the government, the CBI and the TUC had a common interest. These included the problems of the lower-paid, methods of defining, justifying and limiting 'special cases' in pay negotiations, questions of competitiveness and, most pressingly, the moderation of wage increases. Employers and employees needed to discuss these in detail, and the government stood ready to play a positive role in establishing a sensible consensus.

I reported on this meeting to Cabinet two days later and my colleagues showed that they shared my own strong view that public opinion was the key. We all agreed that Ministers now had to intensify their efforts to impress upon the general public the full gravity of the damage caused by inflation, of which the increases in house prices and rents were notable examples, and, literally, 'close to home'. If we achieved this, the TUC would feel themselves under far greater pressure to agree to some voluntary system of wage negotiation which would take account of the national interest. This conclusion proved to be absolutely right.

I then formally invited the CBI and the TUC to join the government in a series of discussions about the objectives of economic management, and the methods by which those objectives would best be pursued. At the suggestion of Donald Maitland, we always held a joint ministerial–

TUC–CBI press conference at the end of each session of talks, in order that the public should know what was being done in their name. An on-the-record report of the meeting was circulated to the media by telex. On Tuesday 18 July, over three months of intensive negotiations began. I presided over all ten tripartite meetings, usually accompanied by Tony Barber, Robert Carr, Jim Prior and other Ministers directly concerned with the matter under discussion. Fifty-two hours of meetings were held in all, either at No. 10 or at Chequers. The CBI and the TUC each provided six members. The CBI decided that only the chairman of its delegation would speak for it. This was a pity, because it put the employers at a disadvantage compared with the TUC, each of whose members was free to speak. Although the employers had as much at stake in the talks as anyone, their negotiating team was clearly under-prepared and inexperienced because, as chairmen of companies, they were not used to taking part in wage negotiations face to face with trade unionists. When the CBI delegation failed to perform adequately, Ministers sometimes had to step in to help them with the presentation of their case. This was precisely what we had wanted to avoid. We had no intention of taking sides with employers against employees, in this or any other context. The trade union leaders, on the other hand, were all widely experienced, immensely knowledgeable in such matters and skilled in persuasively putting their side of an argument.

We quickly reached tripartite agreement on our basic objectives: a high rate of economic growth, an increase both in real incomes and in the relative position of the low-paid and pensioners, and a moderation in the rate of cost and price inflation. As the meetings continued through August and September there seemed to be a general consensus that we should pursue our shared objectives through a voluntary approach. The government was then asked to put forward its proposals for the way forward. We did so at the tripartite meeting at Chequers on Tuesday 26 September. That evening, I spoke at a press club dinner in London, recounting the discussions and decisions at Chequers, over a range of policies. Britain had suffered from a short-term approach for too long and, I assured the audience, we were now serious in the search for lasting solutions.

Our proposals included a number of measures which should have been very welcome both to the CBI and to the TUC. Through a mixture of exhortation, agreement and direct policy in the public sector, we would seek to contain price increases within the range of 4–5 per cent annually. Through a voluntary policy of limiting wage increases to a flat rate of £2 per week, rather than imposing a percentage pay norm, we would help to reduce inequalities of income. We also brought forward proposals to increase the needs allowance and to extend the payment of certain benefits from six months to one year, regardless of increases in pay or other changes in circumstances. I also announced that, for the first time, we would pay a Christmas bonus to pensioners. This was supported by everyone in the Cabinet except for Keith Joseph, who maintained that his Department could not administer it. He was unduly pessimistic.

Before the next tripartite meeting on Monday 16 October, Vic Feather came to see me privately to explain the TUC's latest position. They had taken issue with our arithmetic, and were suggesting a maximum figure of £3 per week for wage increases. He also warned me that he and his colleagues were likely to dig in their heels by demanding a one-sided deal, under which price rises would be controlled by law, while any agreement to curb wage increases would remain voluntary. The only effect of this would have been to cut even further into commercial profit margins, at a time when industry needed greater incentives to invest. At the Chequers meeting, the unions claimed that our 5 per cent annual growth target would only take up slack in the economy and have a limited impact on unemployment. In fact, our predicted GDP growth of 5.9 per cent turned out to be an underestimate. The true outturn figure for 1973 was 7.9 per cent, which came to be known as the 'Barber Boom'. Although the TUC leadership was more accommodating in these meetings than in their public statements, we remained deeply concerned.

Matters came to a head in a matter of weeks. On Thursday 26 October, we held the most rancorous and difficult tripartite meeting so far and it became clear that the trade union negotiators were determined to be unreasonable. We finally broke up at 3.45 a.m., without agreement. The CBI had accepted our package of proposals, but the TUC were pressing us for the fundamental change mooted by Vic Feather ten days earlier. They stubbornly argued that, while wage increases were naturally constrained by the process of two-sided bargaining, prices were unilaterally determined. This was economic nonsense but, as a result, although the trade unionists remained resolutely opposed to the introduction of any statutory incomes or pay policy, they were now convinced of the need for legislation to curb price increases. The CBI prices policy was due to expire at the end of the month and, over the weekend of 28–29 October, I talked to senior colleagues, about our increasingly limited options, in the face of the likely inflationary surge that we now faced.

On the Saturday, I held a meeting with Cabinet Ministers and senior officials at Chequers. We all recognised that, despite our best efforts, the tripartite talks had now reached an impasse, largely because of the truculence of certain left-wing trade union leaders. We therefore had to be prepared for the worst. Colleagues did not really believe it was practicable to fight on without statutory backing. Whether or not we considered that a statutory policy would provide a long-term answer, there would undoubtedly be public demand for it as soon as the talks broke down, presumably within days. Maurice Macmillan then put forward a plan to introduce emergency measures for controlling inflation, which would tide us over until a full-scale policy could be devised, passed by Parliament and implemented. The degree of urgency was obvious. The following day, we held another emergency meeting with a different group of senior Ministers, this time over lunch at Peter Carrington's house in Buckinghamshire. The consensus was the same as the previous day. If the tripartite talks broke down, then we would shortly have to announce a statutory policy, consisting of a standstill followed by a compulsory version of the proposals put to the TUC and the CBI the previous month.

We managed to drag the tripartite discussions out into the following week, but to no avail. There were fifteen more hours of talks at No. 10 on 30 October and 1 November, ending after midnight on both days. On Thursday 2 November, we reached a point at which the union representatives agreed with our proposals, but still said they could not announce it to the public as TUC policy. We then decided to press ahead unilaterally with what we thought had to be done, in the form of statutory measures. On 6 November, I announced the new policy in the House of Commons. Despite the breakdown of the talks, we acted on the pledges to improve benefits and also introduced the pensioners' Christmas bonus. If this had been uprated in line with inflation, it would now be worth around £75. With regard to prices and incomes, I explained in that statement, we had no option but to try the non-voluntary route. The policy would begin with a ninety-day freeze on prices, wages, rents and dividends. Food and imported goods were exempted owing to the special difficulties of policing their prices. In due course, a longer-term policy would be introduced. Our action was well received, both in the Commons and in the press. The party conference in October had shown that the rank and file appreciated our difficulties, echoing the feelings of the public as a whole. Across the world, political leaders were wrestling with similar problems in an increasingly interdependent global market, and we were all coming up with similar solutions.

As I told the House, we did not enter this minefield gladly. I frankly described the new policy as 'action which I regard as less satisfactory than a voluntary arrangement could have been'. I emphasised too that we had certainly not foreclosed upon the possibility of further tripartite discussions, if a basis for agreement could be established. At this time, however, there was no credible alternative to what we did. It was inevitable that some would argue we were going against both our manifesto and our basic political convictions. The economic and industrial policies of 1972 and

1973, however, represented not a departure from our underlying aims and objectives, but a set of sensible and measured responses to enable us to maintain the pursuit of those aims and objectives in a changing situation. They could well have had the results we intended, had we not been blown off course by the quadrupling of oil prices in the autumn of 1973 and by the irresponsible and wrecking demands and actions of some of the leaders of the NUM, actuated more by declared political motives than by concern for the interests of their members or of the country.

In January 1973, I announced Stage Two of the prices and incomes policy with a press conference at Lancaster House, although the initial freeze was to stay in place until April. It represented a considerable relaxation. The norm for pay increases during the period of its operation would be £1 per week, plus 4 per cent, and no annual increase should exceed £250. Of course, this meant that the lowest-paid workers were best protected, while the highest earners would be restricted most. No employer could award excessive pay increases and simply pass on the extra cost to the consumer through increased prices. Company dividends were also limited. We were absolutely determined to break the inflationary mentality, but without resort to the kind of monetary and fiscal stringency which would have sent unemployment rocketing. The system was policed by two new bodies, the Pay Board and the Price Commission. Geoffrey Howe, who had joined the Cabinet as Minister for Trade and Consumer Affairs in November 1972, watched over this for the government.

Between the announcement of the freeze and the beginning of Stage Two, we had hoped that the unions would re-enter negotiations, but such was the influence of the militants that they would not shift from their obstructive stance. I met the TUC General Council on 17 February 1973 and informed them that the policy would stay. In fact, Stage Two was a remarkable success, as even Harold Wilson had to admit in his memoirs. Although there was a short-lived strike by gas workers, and the unions at Fords kept up their dismal record of disruption, across the country as a whole the infection of militancy seemed to be subsiding. This time, the TUC were divided over the question of a so-called 'day of action', and the protest they called on May Day 1973 was a non-event. Just when we had begun to become pessimistic about our chances, it finally seemed that our perseverance would pay off for the country. We began to look forward to the lifting of these temporary restrictions, and to the restoration of economic activity at a higher level. Perhaps the febrile mentality of inflationary Britain had been broken, after all.

While we struggled to control prices and incomes, we also had to consider the shape of our next budget. In response to our measures, growth was picking up fast. Indeed, for the first half of 1973 the rate was more than double our declared target of 5 per cent per annum. Exports were rising, although the increase in commodity prices meant that we were again running a balance of payments deficit. There was some evidence of overheating, especially in the construction industry and in land speculation, but unemployment remained higher than we would have liked and there was still some unused capacity in certain sectors of the economy. On balance we decided to introduce a fairly neutral budget.

The most important element of the budget came when Tony Barber announced the details of the changeover to VAT. It would be set at 10 per cent, with food, books, newspapers and children's shoes and clothing excluded from its scope. During the changeover to VAT, there was no increase in the tax burden. We had substantially cut the rates of selective employment tax and purchase tax and, had Labour's rates still been in force, VAT would have been 15 per cent, not 10 per cent, which was the joint lowest rate in Europe. Tony has never been given the credit he deserves for this reform, which both simplified the tax system and prepared us for our entry into the European Community. The budget also gave increased help to pensioners and raised benefits for sick and unemployed people. It signalled our resolve to maintain the strategy for growth, although we had decided to rein back public expenditure as soon as we had conclusive evidence that our reflationary measures had provided sufficient momentum to the economy.

The evidence was not long in coming. April's export figures were the best ever, at almost £1 billion (£7 billion at today's prices) and, after a run of difficult months, Britain's balance of payments was back in credit. The unemployment figures for this month also brought good news. There were now fewer people out of work than there had been when we took office, a downward trend which continued until the end of the year, when the jobless rate reached 2.1 per cent. In Cabinet on Monday 14 May 1973, I led the economic discussion by suggesting that, in the light of these indicators, it was time to ease gently off the accelerator, by reducing public expenditure. When the meeting reconvened on Wednesday and Thursday, Tony Barber reported that agreement had been reached on most of our proposed retrenchments, although as usual spending Ministers were concerned that their own savings should be matched by other departments. Most ambitious departmental Ministers try to keep up their spending figures, but some take this ritual further than others. Margaret Thatcher put up a particularly stubborn fight to protect her greatly expanded Education budget in full, even though the government's overall spending plans for 1973–4 exceeded those for any previous year by £1 billion. Keith

Joseph also proved to be a stout defender of his enlarged budget at Social Security.

While we were negotiating a package of cuts the press were enjoying a financial scandal which threatened to make a mockery of all our attempts to create a national mood of restraint. The Lonrho company was undergoing a boardroom battle, during which it emerged that $100,000 had been lodged tax-free for the chairman in a Cayman Islands account. For workers who were being urged at the time to moderate their wage demands in the long-term interests of the country this was a considerable provocation. Moreover for us it posed a particular problem because the chairman was Duncan Sandys, a former Conservative minister, who was himself a man of the highest integrity. I felt straight away that the payment was indefensible, no matter how strong my loyalty to Duncan. I denounced it at the Scottish party conference on 12 May. When the matter came up again during parliamentary Questions on the day after our Cabinet meeting on public spending, I described the affair as showing 'the unpleasant and unacceptable face of capitalism', adding that 'one should not suggest that the whole of British industry consists of practices of this kind'.

No true friend of free enterprise could have said less and, as it turned out, those remarks guaranteed my place in the dictionary of quotations! At a time when the extreme left was making its presence increasingly felt within the Labour Party and the trade union movement, the Lonrho scandal presented socialists with a marvellous propaganda coup. To have defended such behaviour would have been a disgraceful own goal. In later years the remark was sometimes used to imply that I had mixed feelings about capitalism. Those who attacked me in that way were generally people who believed that the market could never be wrong. It was no surprise when their tolerance of the excesses of those who came to be called 'fat cats' helped to produce a landslide defeat for the Tory Party in 1997. It is perfectly sensible for Conservatives to praise the positive aspects of capitalism, but it is sheer stupidity to fall into the trap of reflexively defending its most obvious defects.

On 21 May, Tony Barber announced the spending cuts in the House. We estimated that, in addition to changes included in the budget, they would reduce public expenditure by a little over £300 million in the current year. This was a sensible pruning, not the swing of an axe. We had all lived through the era of stop–go, with unpredictable and unsteady economic growth, and had no intention of returning to it. Naturally, the success of our strategy would depend very largely upon a continuation of the new mood of realism among trade unionists. The results of Stages One and Two of the prices and incomes policy were clearly seen in the reduction of wage settlements. Over the twelve months starting in November 1972, the average increase in hourly rates was 11.6 per cent, compared with around 19 per cent in the previous twelve-month period. The pressure of rising import costs meant that there would have to be a further instalment of the policy but, if current trends continued, it was certain that the next stage would bring a further relaxation. It was also likely that it would be the last. In October we made another prudent cut in public spending, and announced the details of Stage Three.

Stage Three was more complicated than its predecessors, because various anomalies had become apparent over the previous year and we had to take account of the rise in world prices. To cope with this there would be special 'threshold' payments, which ensured that pay increases were triggered automatically if inflation rose by more than 7 per cent. We relaxed the terms of Stage Two, so that the norm was now either £2.25 or 7 per cent per week. The upper limit rose to £350 per year. There were other clauses allowing room for manoeuvre in special cases, especially for those who worked unsocial hours. These had been influenced by a private discussion I had with the miners' leader, Joe Gormley. Always there was that balance to be struck between, on the one hand, the flexibility and freedom which we naturally preferred and, on the other, the externally imposed discipline which both the employers and the unions had now shown was necessary in the broader interests of the nation.

A consultative document on Stage Three was published in the week of our 1973 party conference, which went extremely well. In my closing speech on 14 October, I listed our achievements: living standards rising twice as fast as they had during Labour's period in office; the massive increase in exports; extra help for those who needed it; unemployment down and falling further; and entry into the European Community from a position of strength. Of course there were some worrying developments of which we had to beware, but I remember feeling during that conference that we were now really winning through. As I put it, 'This year has shown for the first time in a long time what we as a nation are capable of doing . . . we are beginning to remember how to work together, as we do at all the great moments in our history.' This apparent revival in the national outlook was more important than the bare statistics, yet even they now seemed to show that we had successfully carried out the task for which we had been elected. If Stage Three had been given a fair chance, I am sure that the confidence we felt in the conference hall would have continued through a successful election campaign. I did not know it at the time, but some news we had received on 6 October, just over a week earlier, would soon darken our mood. For, on that day, war broke out again in the Middle East.

Chapter 15

THE BROKEN EMERALD
Northern Ireland 1970–1974

M y first experience of Ireland was extremely enjoyable. I travelled to Northern Ireland during the Whitsun Bank Holiday of 1960, to stay with Robin Chichester-Clark, a parliamentary colleague. We had a common interest in music, both attending Glyndebourne regularly, and he had been a member of the Whips' Officer under me. A Unionist MP, he would later act as my polling agent in the leadership election of 1965 and become the Conservative Party's chief spokesman on Northern Ireland in opposition. It was a glorious weekend and I much wanted to see Dublin, but this was not the simple proposition that I had imagined. The IRA had been waging a small-scale conflict since the late 1950s, and Robin warned that I would undoubtedly be recognised and in danger. At first he held out against anything concerned with the Republic but, on the Monday, agreed to drive me along the north-west coast into Donegal. We stopped behind a wall a short distance from the border where he told me to lie down in the back and covered me with a blanket. At the border post, the guard was busy arranging to buy a donkey from a passing farmer and wasn't in the least interested in us. After a vigorous exchange of views with Robin, the guard let us through. I was then uncovered and allowed to sit up and, as we drove to a seaside hotel for lunch, the contrast between north and south became apparent. The countryside was simpler and less cultivated, the houses smaller and more dated, the roads narrower and far less modern. The nearest village was largely occupied with people weaving in their own homes, and there I bought a beautiful piece of tweed very cheaply which provided me with a sports jacket that I still possess.

I returned to Northern Ireland in the early 1960s during the European negotiations to discuss their progress with the then Prime Minister, Lord Brookeborough. What made the most impact on me was the desire of the Northern Irish that the Republic should also become a full member of the

European Community, because they believed this would enable the south to catch up with Ulster in its economic development. This would stop goods being smuggled across the border, reduce the permanent friction between the two parts of Ireland and be a major step forward to resolving the age-old conflict. They expressed their regret when President de Gaulle vetoed our application. Despite the religious differences, there were important cross-border activities, in particular those relating to modern technology such as electricity, transport and water supply. By the time I became Prime Minister, the situation had badly deteriorated.

I was determined to find a lasting political settlement which would unite moderate opinion across the religious divide. I never underestimated the challenge. Gladstone and then Asquith had tried to grant Home Rule to the whole of Ireland, but most people in the north had wished to remain within the United Kingdom, with the support of many people on the mainland. That had prevented a sustainable settlement. After the First World War, Lloyd George and others, including Churchill, had therefore negotiated the partition of the country. The creation of Northern Ireland, through the Government of Ireland Act of 1920, in some respects satisfied the Unionists of the north, but could not fulfil the aspirations of the many nationalists in the six counties of Northern Ireland. Violent campaigns of the IRA had periodically erupted ever since.

Those who have never visited the province cannot appreciate the bitter, tribal loathing between the hardline elements in the two communities, springing from an atavism which most of Europe discarded long ago. This chasm in Northern Ireland inspired the Protestant majority to discriminate shamelessly against their fellow citizens for almost half a century. Denied adequate housing, jobs and social services, and poorly represented as a result of gerrymandering, the Catholic minority in the north had eventually formed a Civil Rights Association in 1968 and the Prime Minister of Northern Ireland, Terence O'Neill, had introduced a series of legislative reforms which met some of the campaigners' demands. Sadly, Protestant extremists who objected to the reforms had responded by violently attacking Civil Rights marches while, on the other side, extremists from the newly formed Provisional IRA had infiltrated the Civil Rights movement and begun to stir up the Catholics.

The 'Provos', as they soon became known, were the product of a split within the Republican movement in 1969. The old 'Official' IRA which had carried out previous campaigns in the 1950s and 1960s had begun to advocate a policy of peaceful resistance and a non-sectarian approach to the problem. The Provisionals, on the other hand, wanted a return to armed struggle. As the Catholic community came under attack, it was the Provisionals to whom they turned for their defence when civil disturbances arose. As the violence escalated in the spring of 1969, O'Neill had resigned as Prime Minister of Northern Ireland and Harold Wilson, with my support, sent in the British army in an attempt to restore order and to protect the Catholic community from militant Protestants. The soldiers were initially welcomed by Catholics. In some instances, however, the Provisionals rather than the army took up arms to protect besieged Catholics and the IRA soon began not only to defend Catholic enclaves, but also to stir up violence against Protestants and the British military presence. Jim Callaghan, the Labour Home Secretary responsible for Northern Ireland, allowed the warring factions to erect walls and barriers of every kind, particularly in Belfast and Londonderry. This would only entrench divisions and did nothing to quell the 'Troubles'. It was against this unpromising background that I set out as Prime Minister to secure an equitable, lasting peace for all the people of Ireland.

The Conservative Party was at that time still closely allied with the mainstream Unionists from Northern Ireland. I knew that they would prove to be uneasy allies. As it turned out, they split evenly between moderate reformers and hardline incorrigibles. Our manifesto dealt with the question of Northern Ireland in very general terms, committing us to 'provide financial assistance to the Northern Ireland Government so that all parts of Northern Ireland may enjoy the full benefits of United Kingdom prosperity' and reasserting that we would 'support the Northern Ireland Government in its programme of legislative and executive action to ensure equal opportunity for all citizens in that part of the United Kingdom'. We also pledged to 'provide the military and other aid necessary to support the Royal Ulster Constabulary (RUC) in keeping the peace and ensuring freedom under the law', and reaffirmed our support for the Ulster Defence Regiment (UDR). We therefore made it perfectly clear to the loyalist community that things would not be allowed to return to the way they had been, with widespread discrimination against the Catholic minority in the province. Terence O'Neill, however, warned me at the outset that the extremists and hardliners were gradually seizing control of the Unionist Party. Ian Paisley's supporters were making good use of the opportunities presented by mandatory reselection of Unionist Stormont candidates and, O'Neill warned me, 'a Paisleyite Parliament will be on the cards'. Of the Unionists elected to Westminster, only Stratton Mills had been courageous enough to attack Paisleyism during the campaign and, even though his majority had risen, the tide was largely against his moderate views.

There were two important foundations upon which we had to build. First, we were determined to do our utmost to protect people's lives and property. Security in the province needed to be increased and our intelligence operation had to be vastly improved. The Chiefs of Staff, however, were adamant that no amount of military force could bring lasting peace. Force could only contain the problem *pro tem*. We had to introduce measures which would isolate the men of violence, even within communities that had hitherto given them a helping hand. Only a political solution could achieve that. Second, the reform programme, even though it had greatly improved the lot of the nationalist minority, had failed to bridge the divide between the two communities. Violence was increasing every month and there was no sign of it abating. Full-scale civil war might erupt in the north and then the south might become involved.

We had to rely upon continuing social and political reform, backed up by ever improving intelligence measures, to keep the province governable. Perhaps, if equal rights had been given to the Catholics in Northern Ireland a generation earlier, they might have reconciled themselves to the Union and to majority rule, but by 1970 reform alone was unlikely to bring peace, particularly with Ian Paisley as a thorn in the flesh at Westminster. The reform process divided the Unionists at Westminster, and eventually brought about a split with the Conservative Party.

There were scant grounds for optimism, but the foundations for a peaceful settlement were there. After all, the whole of Ireland, north and south, was becoming more open and cosmopolitan all the time. Soon, I hoped, both the United Kingdom and the Republic of Ireland would be members of the European Community, a body whose very *raison d'être* was to bring former enemies together in co-operation and with mutual interests. I always felt that it should be possible to unite moderate people, the peaceful and decent majority in Northern Ireland, across the sectarian divide, even though such an arrangement would meet with stiff resistance from the extremists, whose power was being eroded. If I could get the people of the province to find the political courage, as well as the personal courage that they were already showing, then we might win through. I had come to the view years before that there was only one way of achieving any permanent solution for Northern Ireland: some form of power-sharing between the two communities. If the Protestant, loyalist majority was to continue holding all the levers of power at provincial level, then the grievances of the Catholics would remain as deeply held as ever. In order to give Catholics a real stake in society, it was not enough for them to be protected from discrimination. They also had to be given a positive role in governing the country in which they lived, at both local and national level. I also believed that the Republic of Ireland had to be brought into the relationship once more.

Wilson's 'Downing Street Declaration' of 1969 had stated that the affairs of the province were entirely a matter of domestic jurisdiction. Far from being 'the key to the future' as he claimed, this betrayed a singular lack of vision. It seemed to ignore the history of Ireland, as well as the realities of the present day, in which the south still laid claim to the north, a claim enshrined in its constitution, and in which a substantial minority in the north gave their allegiance to the Republic. It was no good just pretending that these aspirations did not exist and that Irish nationalism in Northern Ireland would either be contained or burn itself out. The strength of feeling in the Catholic community had to be addressed, and that meant finding some way of involving the government of the Republic directly in the affairs of the province. But reactivating an 'Irish Dimension' was not a solution in itself. A great deal of consultation had yet to take place and the final shape of any treaty would have to be thrashed out over a period, with compromises made on all sides. The Ministers concerned – Reggie Maudling, Alec Douglas-Home and Peter Carrington – all agreed that a tripartite approach, bringing together the governments of the United Kingdom, Northern Ireland and the Irish Republic, was essential if we were to convince moderate opinion in Northern Ireland that we were acting in good faith.

This approach could succeed only if moderate men of goodwill remained in power on all sides. The Irish Taoiseach, Jack Lynch, was a charming man, who was trying hard, in the face of much conservative opposition from within his own Fianna Fail party, to refashion Irish nationalism. He took a less belligerent approach to Unionists than most of his colleagues, always recognising that the people of Northern Ireland had different traditions which had to be respected. He and I were not always in agreement, but the likeliest replacement for him was a government led by the likes of Charles Haughey, who had recently been forced to resign as a Minister in the Irish government when he was accused of complicity in smuggling arms for militant nationalists into the Republic. Alec Douglas-Home told me that 'Mr Lynch is the best Irish Prime Minister we are likely to have.' I never came to doubt Alec's judgement. Until we could establish a productive working relationship with the Irish government, the political deadlock could not be broken, and he was our best hope.

It was also vital, of course, that the Unionists were reassured about our ultimate intentions. My first action, therefore, was to ask the Prime Minister of Northern Ireland to a meeting at Downing Street. O'Neill's successor, Major James Chichester-Clark, was another of the 'old guard' of Unionist leaders. He too was ultimately a moderate man and preferable to extremists such as Ian Paisley, who wanted to reverse the reform programme and foreclose on any form of dialogue with nationalists. The normal diplomatic lines of communication with Chichester-Clark were augmented by my contacts with his brother Robin, who had turned down a government post in June 1970, but did eventually accept the post of Minister of State for Employment. At our meeting on 17 July 1970, James Chichester-Clark asked me to send more troops to the province and impose a curfew on nationalist areas such as the Lower Falls Road in Belfast and the notorious Bogside in Londonderry, self-styled 'Free States' which were becoming no-go areas for the security services. We could not allow that to develop any further, and Chichester-Clark's position depended on a full restoration of order throughout the province.

If Unionists were to be turned away from the demagoguery of Ian Paisley and his fellow travellers, they needed moderate leaders to protect them effectively against IRA violence. Equally, the 'marching season', the most volatile time of the year in the province, was now almost upon us and I was anxious to ensure that the inevitable intensification of security should not provoke moderate nationalists. I therefore insisted that Chich-ester-Clark should ban sectarian parades until the end of January 1971. These measures worked. The police were reasonably well received when the curfews were imposed on 31 July 1970 and Jack Lynch gave us his public support, which I much appreciated. This was a promising start and, building on the sterling diplomatic efforts of our experienced ambassador in Dublin, Sir John Peck, we had established warm working relations with the Irish government by the end of 1970.

Unfortunately, the government of Northern Ireland became increasingly concerned about what Robin Chichester-Clark described as our policy of 'benevolent neutrality' towards the question of the Union. Although relations remained outwardly cordial, the Chichester-Clarks continually claimed that not enough was being done to strengthen the Union, nor to tighten security. There was a good deal of shuttle diplomacy in late 1970 and early 1971 by Reggie Maudling's Home Office officials to convince them otherwise. I even asked the Home Secretary himself to go to North-ern Ireland when talks were needed. Wilson had usually summoned North-ern Ireland's leaders to Downing Street, which gave the false impression that they were puppets of the Westminster government, which they were certainly not. Reggie had a brilliant brain and a complete grasp of the complexities, and did his best to reassure Chichester-Clark and his col-leagues that we respected their views and political sensitivities, but he was not at his most effective in dealing with people less intrinsically reasonable than himself. After his first visit to Northern Ireland he was always alleged to have said, 'What a bloody awful country!'

The tension between the British government and Stormont increased when the first British soldier was killed in the province in February 1971. Chichester-Clark was beginning to buckle in the face of pressure from the more militant loyalist elements at Stormont, and was still willing to argue for a military solution. He was not prepared to go further politically than implementing the existing reform programme. He even put pressure on Peter Carrington to place the 7,000 troops stationed in Northern Ireland under his own political control. The Unionists at Westminster threatened to withdraw their support if we refused this, the first in a series of attempts at putting me under pressure, but I was not willing to cede control over troops under any circumstances and asked Chichester-Clark over to Downing Street for talks, on 16 March 1971.

This meeting was to be our last. Chichester-Clark simply demanded massive army reinforcements, claiming that, unless he could demonstrate that he was taking a sufficiently robust line, there would be a Protestant backlash. There was, as Peter Carrington pointed out, no military justification for such reinforcements. What was really needed was better intelligence. Despite the presence of many Special Branch officers from Scotland Yard in the province, the necessary improvement was not yet forthcoming from the Royal Ulster Constabulary. Moreover, I bluntly told Chichester-Clark, if the communities in Northern Ireland were really bent on civil war, then it was absurd to believe that this could be prevented by sending in more troops, not least because the very presence of such troops would be taken as an act of deliberate provocation. The situation required an imaginative, long-term, political solution. We did give a little ground, however, to prevent Chichester-Clark losing too much face, agreeing to send him two further battalions of troops, consisting of 1,300 men. I concluded by telling the Prime Minister that the extremist Unionists at Stormont ought not to suppose that they could effect a fundamental change in British government policy by bringing down the Northern Ireland government.

Chichester-Clark did not leave the meeting a satisfied man, but I was still surprised when, three days afterwards, he telephoned to tell me that he intended to resign. Bemoaning the fact that Stormont was not a sovereign parliament with control over its own armed forces, he once again claimed that he had not enjoyed the support from us that he required. I tried to persuade him to stay, even sending Peter Carrington over to Northern Ireland the following day to reinforce what I had said, but he was adamant.

I had first met his successor, Brian Faulkner, in London in 1958, when he was my counterpart as Chief Whip in Stormont, and we had stayed in touch ever since. His predecessors had generally been chosen from the old Protestant squirearchy, but Brian was the son of a businessman, a brisk, hard-working and dynamic politician who realised that Northern Ireland had to modernise or it was doomed. He was mistrusted by many of his colleagues in the Unionist Party, however, and I knew that, if his government failed, then there would be no more sufficiently credible moderates capable of taking over. As Terence O'Neill warned me, in chilling terms, the more or less inevitable successor to Faulkner would be a hardline and right-wing government led by Ian Paisley. I could not allow this to happen and made it clear to Faulkner that, if significant progress was not made in the next year or so, we would have to introduce direct rule of the province. He did not like the prospect and later claimed he had been duped by us. This is not so. He was aware, from the day he took office, that his premiership was Stormont's last chance.

Faulkner made a promising start, forming a more broadly based administration than his predecessor's and bringing the predominantly Catholic Social Democratic and Labour Party (SDLP) on to Stormont's committees, but it did not improve the general situation as we had hoped. As the spring of 1971 turned into summer, the situation came to a dramatic head. On 9 July, the Opposition in the Stormont parliament walked out in protest at the presence of some hardline Unionists in Brian's Cabinet and the killing of two unarmed Catholic men in Derry. This walk-out, led by the moderate SDLP leader Gerry Fitt, deprived Stormont of any remaining legitimacy, for it could no longer claim to be representing all the people of Northern Ireland. Seeing a chance to exploit the situation, the IRA stepped up its vicious campaign of violence. By the middle of July, the rule of law was in serious jeopardy. The Queen received me at one of my regular audiences after she had been watching the coverage of riots in Belfast on the television and was obviously shaken by the ferocity of the events in a part of her Kingdom. In particular she was horrified by the film of women's contorted faces as they clung to the high wired fences protecting British troops. I could only reassure her that we were doing all we could. Whenever the Queen is accused of remoteness, or indifference towards the tribulations of her subjects, I think back to that moment.

As the violence intensified we were put under immense pressure from Faulkner to introduce internment. Internment, the indefinite detention of terrorist suspects without trial, has always been a controversial measure. Reggie Maudling, Peter Carrington, Alec Douglas-Home and I all considered it very carefully before putting it to the Cabinet as a serious proposal. It could completely alienate moderate Catholic opinion in both the north and the south of Ireland, and damage our relations with America and Europe, which was also of great concern to me. Internment contravened the European Convention on Human Rights (ECHR) and, although a notice of derogation, excusing the measure from the ECHR's ambit, had been lodged in Strasbourg in 1957 by Macmillan, it had been done at a time when we were uncommitted to European unity. By 1971 we were in the middle of delicate negotiations with the Six and I had no wish to upset our putative partners on the continent. Although the ECHR is quite separate from the European Community, it was largely inspired by the British and sets out the standards of behaviour and liberty which are acceptable to modern Western Europeans. Regrettably, however, the situation in Northern Ireland was now too grave for us to be swayed by such considerations. We had to draw the sting of the paramilitaries.

It has been alleged that internment without trial was forced upon us by Brian Faulkner. In fact, the Cabinet Committee on Northern Ireland had already discussed the possibility of introducing it on 15 March 1971, before Chichester-Clark's resignation. Chichester-Clark, for all his protests about our supposed inaction on the security front, had actually opposed its introduction. However, internment had remained very much under review thereafter and in the early summer we had approved the construction of a special building at Long Kesh, just outside Belfast, which could be used to house detainees should the measure become necessary.

Faulkner was certainly in favour of internment from the start. He was adamant that terrorism had to cease before he would discuss Northern Ireland's future with anybody. I had deep reservations, because I instinctively dislike interfering with the democratic rights of the individual upon which our society is based, however deplorable the acts of our suspects. I also feared, rightly as it turned out, that the authorities in the province would use internment disproportionately as a weapon against Republicans. On the other hand, violence had risen to such a level over the summer that no meaningful peace process could begin until it had at least been contained. However successful we were at persuading the SDLP to return to Stormont, Unionists would still feel that they were being held to ransom by terrorists who were intent on their destruction.

General Sir Harry Tuzo, commander-in-chief of our forces in Northern Ireland, expressed doubts about whether internment could be militarily effective in the long run, but he conceded that there were compelling reasons for it. The normal processes of investigation, detection and trial were becoming extremely difficult because of continuing IRA intimidation of crucial witnesses from the law-abiding Catholic community. Internment offered us a chance to bypass this wall of silence by swooping on terrorist suspects without warning. There was a precedent, which has often been forgotten. The IRA campaign of 1956–62 had been halted largely by internment, which had then been imposed on both sides of the border by the British and the Irish governments.

On 2 August, Reggie Maudling heard that a formal request for internment from the Northern Ireland government was now imminent, and the next day I asked the Cabinet for the authority to take whatever action might be required to halt the violence, should any crisis occur during the forthcoming recess. This I received unanimously. Two days later, Faulkner flew to London to discuss what he described as a 'grave security matter'. Present at the meeting were General Tuzo, the Chief Constable of the RUC Graham Shillington, Reggie Maudling, Alec Douglas-Home, Peter Carrington and the Chief of the General Staff, Sir Michael Carver. The meeting was a tense but decisive one. I announced our agreement to internment on the condition that Faulkner would ban parades for six months. He agreed, and the introduction of internment was set for 10 August. Shortly beforehand, we received news from military intelligence that the IRA had learned of our plans, so we decided to bring them forward by twenty-four hours. I was due to sail in the Fastnet race and decided to go ahead with it so as not to arouse suspicion. At dawn on 9 August, 3,000 troops throughout the province swooped on IRA suspects, arresting 337 men in total, around 75 per cent of those targeted. All of the first tranche were Catholics. Immediately on landing at Plymouth after the race I flew to London and took charge of the operation. The introduction of internment was followed by serious civil unrest, with twenty-one deaths in three days, but the security forces held their nerve.

The reaction in Ireland and throughout the world was swift. Returning to Downing Street after the race, I heard that rioting had broken out on the streets of Belfast and Londonderry, subsequently spreading to smaller towns which were normally relatively peaceful. Protests were also received from Jack Lynch and from John Hume, then a leading moderate nationalist at Stormont, and the action was condemned by some world leaders as undemocratic. In the next few days, this sentiment was whipped up by the propaganda machine of the IRA, which predictably presented internment as another example of British oppression of Northern Ireland's Catholic minority. Jack Lynch went so far as to call for the immediate abolition of Stormont.

We underestimated the condemnation that internment would arouse, as well as the effectiveness of the IRA's propaganda machine. The intelligence information of the RUC turned out to be hopelessly out of date, in spite of help from Special Branch. Many of those arrested had not been active members of the IRA for years, some since the 1920s. Many of the real IRA leaders had fled across into the Republic as soon as they got wind of what was happening. Had we been able to persuade Lynch to introduce internment simultaneously south of the border, as in the 1950s, we would have achieved far more. About half of the leaders of the IRA were apprehended, however, and this sent a plain message to the terrorists that any settlement would be reached on our terms, not on theirs. At a meeting of the Cabinet on Monday 16 August, I reiterated to my colleagues that, although internment might offend against many of our most deeply held principles, it had begun to look like the only means by which violence could be ended. It was not a substitute for political progress, but seemed to be a prerequisite for it. The policy was debated in the House of Commons for two days in September. The Opposition abstained, but the Unionist MPs supported the measure despite their reservations.

The Cabinet held its nerve despite the furore because, unknown to our critics, we were making strenuous efforts behind the scenes to come up with ideas for a lasting settlement. On 3 September, the Central Policy Review Staff submitted a useful report which outlined three main routes that we might take. These it summarized as partition, coalition and condominium. The first involved dividing the six counties into Protestant and Catholic areas, and allowing the Catholic areas to join the Republic if they so wished. The second was a power-sharing executive, which would guarantee Catholics a place in a Stormont Cabinet, probably including a Deputy Prime Minister. The third option envisaged a province governed jointly by Britain and Ireland, with its citizens having dual citizenship.

My immediate reaction was that further partition would be a disastrous mistake, because geography would make it crude and ineffective. However the line was drawn, large groups of people would end up on the wrong side of it, and we would be left with pockets of disaffected nationalists in predominantly Protestant areas. Power-sharing was essential, at least as an interim measure. As for a condominium, I doubted whether Unionists would agree to the Republic having an equal say in the affairs of the north. A more practical option, and one that would be perfectly compatible with power-sharing in the north, was to encourage Northern Ireland, whatever its precise constitutional status, to co-operate with its southern neighbour on a variety of economic, social and cultural projects. This would help to establish, and then reinforce, links between the two countries. This plan was actually a revival of the Council of All Ireland, originally an optional provision in the Government of Ireland Act of 1920, which first brought about partition. Neither side had taken this up then, and I was convinced that this had been a major factor in the subsequent lack of understanding between the two communities within Northern Ireland.

These options were complex and I knew they would all come to nothing if they were merely hammered out by Whitehall officials behind closed doors and then telexed backwards and forwards between the three capitals. The essential protagonists in any proposed settlement had to meet and establish a working relationship. I therefore invited Jack Lynch to Chequers for a meeting on 6–7 September 1971. In an attempt to maintain some distance from the proceedings, he rather curtly refused to stay at Chequers and arranged instead to stay at the Irish embassy in London.

The first day of this meeting was generally constructive but he seemed to be growing restless as the afternoon wore on. At ten to six he got up, followed by his private secretary, and said that they would come back at six o'clock and tell me whether or not he was prepared to go on with the meeting. I looked across at our ambassador. 'Prime Minister,' he began, 'you do know why he has stepped out?'

'I presumed it was for the usual reason, a call of nature.'

'Not at all,' he replied. 'The time has come when he wants a drink of his usual Paddy.'

'What on earth is that?' I asked him.

'It's his favourite whiskey,' was the reply. 'I brought over two bottles from Ireland in my overcoat pockets and gave them to the housekeeper when I arrived, so that we would be ready for this.'

I sent for the housekeeper, who declared that the bottles had looked so awful that she had put them away at once. I asked her to rush off and get one of them. When Lynch returned I told him, before he could say anything, that it was customary for us all to have a little refreshment at six o'clock. Perhaps he would like to join us in a little sherry, a gin or even a glass of Paddy? The Taoiseach looked as pleased as he was surprised, the discussion got going and went on until 7.30. He then went off for dinner at his embassy, saying he would return the following morning. By this time the Irish ambassador was in a frenzy because he had invited a lot of special guests, and Lynch was now so late.

On that Tuesday morning Lynch arrived promptly at half past ten. At eleven o'clock I told him that it was customary in our country to have elevenses. Perhaps he would like tea or coffee or even some more Paddy? 'Paddy!' he exclaimed, and the second bottle was duly produced. He departed after lunch a happier man.

One of the main purposes of these talks was to obtain Lynch's agreement to a tripartite meeting between himself, myself and Brian Faulkner. Although such meetings are the bread and butter of normal international relations, where Ireland was concerned such a proposal was no easy matter. This was to be the first between the three premiers in seventy years. Lynch had to be persuaded to recognise Faulkner as the Prime Minister of a separate territory, and he had to face down those in his Fianna Fail party who said that he should not meet with ministerial representatives of the British government while internment was still in operation. Faulkner, meanwhile, had the usual bigotry to contend with on his side. After some hesitation, however, both Lynch and Faulkner agreed to what we were proposing, realising that their shared island might face another civil war with all its attendant miseries unless they began talking in earnest.

Between 27–28 September, the two premiers met face to face at Chequers. This was one of the historic events of my premiership, and I expected it to be very tense indeed. In fact, this meeting just went to prove that the two peoples of Ireland have more in common than they usually care to admit. Warm greetings were exchanged and then they got talking about Trinity College in Dublin. From the beginning, I felt slightly peripheral to the exchanges between my two guests, and pretty soon I was left out of the conversation altogether as they talked about their island and current events. It delighted me to see Faulkner, the Master of Hounds and keen huntsman, and Lynch, a president of the Gaelic Athletic Association and a hurling champion in his youth, discovering that they were not so very different after all. Eventually I had to intervene and remind them, 'Look, we really must get down to some of our problems.'

We discussed Lynch's failure to deal with the IRA in the Republic, and Lynch then expressed his concern about internment and the future of the reform programme. Reassurances were exchanged all round. The long-term future of the island was not on the agenda, but the summit did bring about what we had set out to achieve. It got the two men, and the two parts of Ireland, talking to one another, establishing a foundation of mutual trust upon which a lasting settlement might one day be built. The provision of drinks before lunch, however, presented a delicate diplomatic problem. We had already established that Jack Lynch liked Paddy, but that came from the Republic, so it would hardly have been tactful to offer it to Brian Faulkner. So we put a bottle of Paddy at one end of the drinks table, a bottle of Bushmills – a distinguished Northern Ireland whiskey – at the other end, and a bottle of Scotch whisky in the middle. The subtlety of our diplomacy was matched by that of our guests. Both of them chose the Scotch.

In the months that followed we made further progress, with tripartite meetings held at all levels. In November 1971, I made it clear to hardline Unionists that they could not expect to have an absolute veto over any political progress. I warned them too that the people of mainland Britain would not have infinite stomach for the Troubles, particularly if they perceived the loyalist veto preventing serious progress towards a peaceful settlement. I also reassured them, however, that, so far as our government was concerned, the people of Northern Ireland would become citizens of the Republic of Ireland only if a majority of them voted for it in a referendum. On 15 November, I kept the momentum going at the Lord Mayor of London's annual banquet. I also used this speech to remind the more extreme Unionists that the British government had no intention of being held to ransom by their obduracy. I became the first British Prime Minister to declare that Britain has no selfish interest in Northern Ireland and that, should the people of Northern Ireland ever wish to join the Republic, they would be free to do so.

Realising that we were actually making progress where he had failed, Wilson then put forward new proposals. On 19 November 1971, during a visit to Ireland, he met the IRA leadership in Dublin and released a 'Twelve-Point Plan'. Its essence was that all parties should work actively towards the reunification of Ireland within a timescale of fifteen years. I had no objection to reunification in principle, but I have always firmly adhered to the view that this should take place only with the consent of a majority of the people of Northern Ireland. This is not the result of obduracy on the part of the British. The principle of self-determination is a basic axiom of democracy, and the consent of the people must be fundamental. Critics of this approach must realise that reunification will only ever occur through strengthened links between Northern Ireland and the Republic, and not through bullying the Unionists.

By the end of 1971, I was much more optimistic than I had been a year previously. Although a total of 174 people had been killed that year, the most since the Troubles began, proper dialogue was at last under way. Just before Christmas, I made my first official visit to Northern Ireland as Prime Minister. When I arrived with my team at Northolt airfield at 8.30 a.m. in order to fly to Belfast, I was greeted as usual by the commanding officer of the RAF station, but noticed that he looked rather puzzled. As I walked to the aircraft with him, I realised that he was counting the number of people. I asked him if there was any problem. 'Well,' he replied, 'we are still waiting for Geoffrey Johnson Smith [then an Under-Secretary of State for Defence].' 'Don't worry about him,' I said, 'I am Geoffrey Johnson Smith. His name was given to you to protect my identity.'

We boarded the plane which slowly taxied to the end of the runway, where it turned round and stopped. The pilot explained on the intercom that he had to stop because the officer in command was sending out a fresh steward to replace the original one, who had been taken ill. After a few moments the aircraft door was flung open, the steps lowered, and a young aircraftman, panting heavily, came on board to serve refreshments. Once we were under way, my security staff informed me that on arriving at Belfast I would find two people waiting with all the necessary equipment: a lightweight camouflage suit which I would have to put on over my existing clothes, together with an armoured bullet-proof waistcoat. There would also be an army medical officer with the necessary oxygen equipment and a supply of blood, which I would need if I was wounded. They hammered home that, if anything happened to anybody, we must never, never stop to assist in any way or sympathise. We must keep going at all costs. Such chilling instructions did little to reassure us all.

At Belfast, everything was as arranged, and it was obvious that nothing had leaked. I put on the special clothes and climbed into a helicopter, and we flew over to Londonderry, a place of enormous significance for nationalists and, at that time, the home of some questionable politicking on behalf of the Unionists. I was taken to the top of the city wall and hastened along there, being warned to look only fleetingly between the two turrets to Londonderry on the other side. I realised then how critical the situation was. Back on the ground on the east side, I met and talked to various groups from that bitterly divided city. I was then flown off to the south of Ulster where I was able to meet some of our troops, and on to Belfast, where I was driven in an armoured car through the city streets. I could see the damage which had already been inflicted and the enormous barbed-wire security fences which had been erected to protect the guards on duty. On the other side of this were screaming women, banging the pavement with bin lids. Talking to the troops, I found their morale was high, even though Christmas was so close and their thoughts must have been very much with their families at home. I was then flown to my plane and we set off back to London, with plenty to occupy our minds and our conversation.

On the plane, I discussed with my private secretary, Christopher Roberts, the letters of thanks I wanted to send to all those who had been involved in the day's operations. Among them I included the RAF steward who had been rushed on board at the end of the runway at Northolt. 'But surely you don't mean that?' exclaimed Christopher. 'Why not?' I asked. 'He was hauled out of bed when his colleague was suddenly taken ill and I think he deserves thanks for that.' 'But, Prime Minister,' he protested, 'you don't seem to realise what really happened. The situation when we arrived was that no arrangement had been made for a steward to be present on the plane. They had not been told, for security reasons, that it was you who were coming. They were expecting Geoffrey Johnson Smith. As he is only an Under-Secretary at the Ministry of Defence, he is not entitled to a steward. As soon as you went on board, the Air Marshal sent the RAF Lieutenant dashing into the hut to find one. That was why he had to rush to the end of the runway to get on board.' 'In that case,' I replied, 'the young aircraftman appears to me to be even more deserving of a letter of thanks, so we will send it.' Which we did.

Within weeks of the beginning of 1972, a tragic and unforeseeable event occurred, which nearly destroyed all our efforts. On 30 January 1972, or 'Bloody Sunday' as it became known, during an operation by the army to contain a march in Londonderry shots were fired and fourteen people in the march were killed. This provided the IRA's propagandists with an opportunity to publicise what they claimed had been a barbaric and premeditated act of cold-blooded murder by the army.

Lynch rang me on the evening of 30 January in a very emotional state. I reminded him that the march had been illegal, precisely because he had requested that all such marches should be banned, in order to reduce tension in the province. He then tried to claim that the situation had arisen because of the existence of Stormont. I responded bluntly that 'It arises as a result of the IRA trying to take over the country.' There the conversation effectively ended. This was hardly a time for small talk.

I decided at once that a full inquiry must be held, to establish exactly what had happened and to ensure continuing confidence in British justice. The next day, the Cabinet agreed and the Home Secretary announced in the House of Commons that an inquiry would be set up, to be headed by the Lord Chief Justice, Lord Widgery. Wilson maintained the cross-party consensus by not prejudging the outcome. Everything was done to ensure that all the available evidence was heard, and that there was no attempt to interfere in Lord Widgery's deliberations. When his report was published in April 1972, Lord Widgery concluded that, although the firing of some soldiers 'bordered on the reckless . . . there is no reason to suppose that the soldiers would have opened fire if they had not been fired upon first'. This was also accepted by the Opposition at Westminster. It will be important to discover whether Lord Widgery's conclusions are confirmed as a result of the new inquiry into 'Bloody Sunday' set up in 1998, twenty-six years after the event.

On 19 April 1972 I told the House, 'The Government deeply regret that there were any casualties, whatever the individual circumstances. Situations such as that which occurred in Londonderry can only be avoided by ending the law-breaking and violence . . . and by a return to legality, reconciliation and reason.' Although Thorpe and Callaghan echoed Lord Widgery's reservations about the wisdom of departing from a 'low-key' operation, they concurred with my summary.

My cordial relationship with President Nixon ensured that the US did not intervene, despite the pressure to which Nixon was subjected by his large Irish-American contingent, but Anglo-Irish relations were undoubtedly damaged. In the meantime, no amount of rational enquiry could contain the fury of extreme nationalist sentiment. The independent Catholic MP Bernadette Devlin left her seat in the House of Commons, leaped across the gangway to the front bench and physically attacked Reggie Maudling. As well as the usual predictable and deplorable rioting in the north, there were also disturbances in the south, culminating in an angry mob marching on the British embassy in Dublin and burning it to the ground on 2 February. Fortunately, Sir John Peck was in London at the time and was uninjured. The violence spread not only to the Republic but also, for the first time in a century, to the mainland when, three weeks later, an IRA bomb exploded at the army barracks at Aldershot, killing seven people. These events, all in the space of a month, profoundly shocked public opinion in both Britain and Ireland.

The atmosphere had now grown more poisoned than ever and I feared that we might, for the first time, be on the threshold of complete anarchy. Northern Ireland was enduring around 100 bombs a month and the death toll in the first two months of 1972 was forty-nine, with an additional 257 people injured. I therefore decided that we had to assume direct control of law and order forthwith. At first, the Cabinet was not united on the question of direct rule. Reggie Maudling was reluctant to introduce it, not because he stood to lose responsibility for the province – indeed, I think he was rather glad to be rid of it – but because he believed that Stormont served a useful purpose. Although he did agree to support direct rule, Reggie wanted it to be a temporary measure, designed to get the peace process moving but informed by the ultimate aim of putting a new, reformed version of Stormont in place within two years. We agreed to this and Stormont was prorogued, rather than abolished. Alec Douglas-Home was against the move entirely, doubting whether a settlement could evolve within that timescale and fearing that we would end up being stuck with governing the province permanently. He wrote to me on 13 March saying that, in his opinion, no sustainable framework for keeping Northern Ireland within the United Kingdom could ever be contrived. He concluded that we should start to push the people of Northern Ireland towards a united Ireland, rather than trying to tie them more closely into the United Kingdom. Lord Hailsham and Peter Carrington were also sceptical about the prospects for a peaceful re-establishment of Stormont, although they did not favour a unification with the Republic. I was resolved all along, however, that we should now devote all our energies towards working for a lasting, cross-community settlement – and only direct rule could offer us the breathing space necessary for building it. At the end of its discussion, the Cabinet agreed unanimously.

We needed to enlist Brian Faulkner's support to have any chance of winning over a majority of loyalists. I therefore invited him to Downing Street on 22 March to put to him what we were now proposing: to begin phasing out internment; to hold a first plebiscite in Northern Ireland on the border issue; and to assume direct control of security in the province. All other aspects of government would remain in the hands of Faulkner and his Cabinet. I also put it to him that it was now time for the Northern Ireland government to consider power-sharing with the Catholic minority. Faulkner refused to do so, on the ground that he could never accept anyone in his Cabinet who was actively seeking unification. Initially, he seemed to think that we were bluffing. When he realised that we were in earnest, however, he argued vehemently that the withdrawal of these essential powers would render any government impotent. I remained convinced that it was the only way to restore confidence in the rule of law and to regain the political initiative from the terrorists. After a full day of talks, I could not persuade him to come round to our position, and he said that he could not continue in office on such terms. I could well understand why Faulkner was upset, but he was unjustified in claiming that he was surprised by the introduction of direct rule. Nor was he politically sound in refusing to carry on the rest of the functions of government in Northern Ireland after we had taken over complete responsibility for security there.

The general reaction, when direct rule was announced on 24 March 1972, was overwhelmingly positive. So too was the reaction to the appointment of William Whitelaw as the first Secretary of State for Northern Ireland. I had known Willie for the greater part of my political life at the House of Commons and regarded him as one of the most skilful and dependable men in politics. I was only too aware of the enormous gap he would leave elsewhere, but his political experience and personal qualities, especially his skill in handling people, made him eminently suitable for the position. The new arrangements were warmly welcomed as a breakthrough by British and overseas opinion. Our clearly framed longer-term objective, a properly balanced, devolved Northern Ireland government, was widely recognised as the only practical course. We began to think that we had turned the corner and started to work in earnest on the terms of a possible political concordat between the elected representatives of the two communities in Northern Ireland, founded on the principles of constitutionally based power-sharing. The last two years had diverted a great deal of the government's energies into Northern Ireland, but for the first time since 1922 a solution to the problems of the province seemed potentially within our grasp. Nonetheless, we were still braced for things to get worse before they got better, and they did.

An array of staunch Unionists responded virulently to direct rule, and within days we faced a forty-eight-hour protest strike by 200,000 loyalist workers in the province. Addressing a huge rally at Stormont, Faulkner at that point appeared to rule out any co-operation with Willie Whitelaw and the all-party commission which was to advise him. After tempers had cooled, however, he decided to back what we were trying to do, and persuaded a majority of his party to work with us. I cannot imagine that this was an easy task, for one of Whitelaw's priorities had to be reassurance of the Catholic community, in order to separate the mainstream of Republican opinion from the terrorists who claimed to act in its name. The one mistake that we made at this time, in retrospect, was when we granted 'special category status' to paramilitary prisoners. In many people's eyes, this amounted to making them political prisoners and, although it would have been impossible for us to reverse this, Merlyn Rees was quite right to do so in 1976. Any organisation which kills, maims and bombs in a free and democratic society has no claim upon political legitimacy. These are not freedom fighters, and they deserve to be treated like the contemptible criminals they are.

The IRA then announced a cease-fire, to begin on 26 June, and Willie met the IRA face to face the following month. A lot of fuss was made subsequently about such meetings by those who seem to have little grasp of British history. In fact, British government representatives have been meeting terrorists in different parts of the world for years, endeavouring to put an end to terrorism and establish a peaceful regime. It was Lloyd George's meetings in 1921 with de Valera and the leader of the IRA, Michael Collins, which had made an independent Ireland possible, and it is unlikely, to choose just one other example, that the Mau Mau revolt in Kenya would have been settled had it not been for meetings with the rebel leaders. The Good Friday accord of 1998 underlines the same point.

The IRA group, which included Gerry Adams, were unprepared to compromise at the meeting with Willie Whitelaw. They demanded British withdrawal, a referendum on Northern Ireland to be held right across Ireland and an amnesty for all paramilitary prisoners, all within five years. When they were not granted these impossible concessions, they waited only two days before resuming their campaign of violence. They also leaked word of Willie's secret meeting with them, in consequence of which there was an outcry in the press and I had to talk him out of resigning. On Friday 21 July, less than a month after their 'cease-fire', the IRA let off twenty-two bombs in just over an hour in the centre of Belfast, killing eleven people and seriously injuring 130. I was glad then that I still had William Whitelaw to help deal with what could turn into a crisis. At least the IRA had now proved conclusively that they did not want peace.

At dawn on Monday 31 July 1972, the army and the RUC launched Operation Motorman. Its purpose was to put an end to the 'no-go' status of the Bogside and Creggan, which were now effectively being run by the Provisional IRA. We were taking a considerable risk. All of us involved in the decision to go ahead with the operation knew that the Provisionals were capable of organising fierce and bloody resistance to the forces of law and order. We had the RAF on standby and the navy offshore below the horizon, and the night of Sunday 30 July was one of the worst of my life. I stayed up at Chequers waiting for word of the operation. When Willie phoned me on the stroke of 6 a.m., I feared the worst. In fact, despite the deaths of two civilians, the operation was successful, and the rule of law was, so far as possible, restored to 'Free Derry'.

The murderous behaviour of the IRA was undoubtedly strengthening the will for political reform among the law-abiding people of Northern Ireland and greatly hardened our own determination to get the mainstream Republicans and Unionists to agree to power-sharing, in order to isolate the terrorists completely. We knew that any successful power-sharing would require us to bring together representatives of a clear majority from each community. Such a thing had never been achieved before, but it gradually became clear that Faulkner was, despite his initial anger about the imposition of direct rule, now willing to make a go of this. As soon as he came round, however, the moderate Republicans started to become troublesome. At the end of September 1972, we arranged for all-party talks in Darlington, County Durham. Only Faulkner's Unionists, the non-sectarian Alliance Party and the Northern Ireland Labour Party attended, but it was a start. At the very least, other political leaders in the province were beginning to realise that a degree of statesmanship and maturity was now being asked of them. Willie was particularly disappointed that the mainly Catholic SDLP boycotted these talks, for no lasting peace settlement could ever be built without their participation, but we both felt confident that they would, in time, come around.

Willie was also working at this time on possible alternatives to internment. Normal trial by jury could never be an option in terrorist cases in Northern Ireland, because we were still faced with the endemic problem of paramilitary intimidation of witnesses and jurists. We therefore introduced the 'Diplock' courts, as a compromise, in which suspected terrorists are tried before a judge alone. As so often in our dealings with Northern Ireland, we found ourselves forced to introduce draconian measures which we would never have contemplated in any normal situation. Everything we did during the latter part of 1972 and early 1973, not least this, was intended to bring the moderate parties together in a serious discussion of the broad peace proposals that we were making. In the face of militancy within their own communities, however, both loyalists and nationalists produced a seemingly endless list of reasons for not playing their part.

Following consultations with interested parties in the province, we produced a White Paper on 20 March 1973, containing proposals for a new assembly with a power-sharing executive. Several Unionist MPs and a tiny handful of Conservatives attacked this, but the support of the House of Commons was never in doubt. A plebiscite was held in Northern Ireland in the early spring of 1973, and 58 per cent of the population voted for maintaining the union with England, Scotland and Wales. The overwhelming majority of Catholics abstained rather than vote against maintaining the Union. I am sure that this robust endorsement of the existing constitutional arrangements by the voters, along with reassurances from myself and other Ministers, played a part in a victory for Faulkner's policy of co-operation at the Ulster Unionist Council (UUC) shortly afterwards. Faulkner's victory at the UUC seemed to have marked a turning point, and we were feeling much more hopeful when the government's Northern Ireland Assembly Bill was presented on 10 April 1973. We proposed a seventy-eight-member assembly, with each Westminster constituency in the province returning between five and eight elected representatives, according to its population. The Assemblymen were to be elected by the single transferable vote system, to ensure that the Assembly would reflect the state of public opinion in the province as accurately as possible, and that the viewpoints of smaller minorities would also be represented.

This Bill went speedily through Parliament with unopposed second and third readings. The first elections to the new Assembly were then held on 28 June, only fourteen weeks after publication of the White Paper. The results reminded us of how unstable the situation really was: Faulkner's people won twenty-two seats, the SDLP nineteen, hardline Unionists led by Paisley and William Craig eighteen, 'unpledged' Unionists ten, the Alliance eight and the Northern Ireland Labour Party one seat. The pro-Assembly parties had won two-thirds of the votes, and seats, but Faulkner had captured less than half the Unionist vote. The scenes when the Assembly first met, in July 1973, were frankly farcical, thanks to Paisley going on the rampage again. Meanwhile, at Westminster, the Unionists were being as difficult as possible about our Northern Ireland Constitution Bill, which was necessary to establish the full constitutional framework envisaged in our White Paper. They forced votes at every stage and spoke bitterly against what we were trying to do, but the overwhelming majority of MPs were firmly behind us and we pressed resolutely on.

As 1973 wore on, the security situation seemed to be improving, but I grew impatient with the failure of Northern Ireland's leaders to get their act together. Until the terms of power-sharing could be agreed, the new Assembly could not take on its powers and bring about the political breakthrough which most people in the province told me that they desperately wanted. On a visit to Northern Ireland at the end of August 1973, I warned the politicians of the province that we could not go on waiting for ever. Unless the new institutions were in operation by March 1974, I reminded them, the legislation establishing them would lapse and the opportunity for peace would slip away, perhaps for ever. I did not see the British people forgiving the Northern Irish if that happened, and I said so in a speech just before leaving the province at the end of that visit:

Every day's delay in setting up and working the new institutions can only mean more lives lost, more maimed and more wounded. I realise full well that we are asking much of the parties of the Assembly to work together in the interests of the whole community of Northern Ireland. But I must tell you quite frankly that, having taken the necessary steps to enable a resumption of the political life of Northern Ireland, the people of Britain will not understand any reluctance to take full advantage of it.

On 17 September 1973 I flew to Dublin for a meeting with the Prime Minister of the Irish Republic, Liam Cosgrave. Soon after his election in March that year he had come over to London with his Foreign Minister for a meeting with me and Willie Whitelaw at 10 Downing Street, to discuss the situation in Northern Ireland and our future intentions there. At that time he had obviously still been completely exhausted by his election campaign, but it was still useful to become acquainted with him. I was now going over to discuss our strategy for obtaining agreement on the future organisation of Northern Ireland and the relationship between north and south. Having flown by helicopter from Chequers to Northolt, I left the aerodrome at 8.30 a.m. On approaching Baldonnel airfield, we were escorted over the sea and coast by planes from the Irish Republic's air force, and after we had landed we found that the short drive to the officers' mess was heavily lined by troops, right up to the mess itself. There, after some refreshment, we started our talks in a room which had a photograph of Sir Roger Casement, who had been found guilty of high treason and executed during the First World War, prominently displayed over the mantelpiece.

I concentrated on explaining the work which Willie Whitelaw was doing with the parties in the north to secure a successful outcome to talks on establishing real power-sharing at Stormont. I emphasised in particular the importance of the Republic agreeing to delete Articles 2 and 3 of its Constitution. Article 2 declares that 'the national territory' of the Republic of Ireland 'consists of the whole island of Ireland, its islands and the territorial seas', and Article 3 refers to the 'reintegration of the national territory'. Both had always caused intense discomfort and displeasure among Unionists in the north. I stressed that their removal would make it infinitely easier for the parties in the north to accept all the other arrangements which we both wanted. He replied that he thought this was possible, in which case I hoped that we could put it in the communiqué. I was greatly encouraged by this and, when we lunched in the officers' mess with several of his Ministers, the atmosphere was extremely agreeable.

We resumed our talks in the afternoon. After that I had a meeting with the previous Prime Minister, Jack Lynch, and a further discussion on the communiqué with Cosgrave. It was then that he told me that it was not possible for him to include support for the withdrawal of Articles 2 and 3 because he had not succeeded in getting the agreement to this from his ministers. This was a bitter disappointment, but it became apparent that, however much Cosgrave wanted it, there was nothing further to be done about it at that meeting. Our meeting had, by now, substantially exceeded the time allotted to it, so we had a cold buffet supper, after which the RSM of the guards invited me to their mess for a drink with their NCOs while the necessary preparations were made for a press conference. I was thankful to get away from the negotiating atmosphere and relax in the bar. It certainly made the press conference which followed go with more of a swing. We finally arrived back at Northolt at 11.30 p.m., and the discussions in preparation for our talks with the Northern Irish party leaders were well worthwhile, as was later shown.

At last, Willie Whitelaw managed to get a group of political leaders from Northern Ireland together on 5 October. Even this had been touch and go, because everyone was so sensitive about the numbers and proportions allocated between parties. That day, six Unionists, six senior figures from the SDLP and three Alliance Party representatives met at Stormont. The problems encountered were a mixture of the symbolic and the practical – and the elusive breakthrough just would not manifest itself. It was all intensely frustrating. After six weeks, the talks seemed to be on the verge of collapse and Willie telephoned me on 21 November in a desperate state, to prepare me for the worst. The parties were sticking on two main points: the make-up of the proposed twelve-person executive, and the likely role of the Council of Ireland, whose creation we had made a condition of the devolved executive we were intending to establish.

Remarkably, Willie Whitelaw dragged the talks back from despair to triumph, and shifted the ground brilliantly in the discussions about the executive. The parties had produced irreconcilable demands for seats on the twelve-seat body, insisting upon an aggregate total of fourteen seats between them, the Unionists wanting seven out of twelve, the SDLP five and the Alliance two. There seemed to be no possible compromise. Then Willie changed the arithmetic. He proposed an eleven-strong core executive, to include six Unionists, four from the SDLP and a single Alliance nominee. In addition, there would be four non-voting members, of whom two would be SDLP, with one each for the Unionists and the Alliance. Faulkner would be the chief executive and Gerry Fitt of the SDLP his deputy. This was the breakthrough for which we had all been slaving, and was an enormous tribute to the patience of William Whitelaw and to the courage of Faulkner. The seal was set upon this at a conference held at the Sunningdale Civil Service College (which I had opened in 1970) on 6–9 December 1973. I refused to invite Ian Paisley to these tripartite talks between the Northern Ireland parties and the British and Irish governments, because I knew that his policy was to wreck them. However, on the first day of the negotiations, Thursday 6 December, he appeared at Sunningdale and demanded to be allowed to attend. I told him that in no circumstances would I countenance that.

In return for a major concession on the part of the new Fine Gael–Labour government from the Republic, an acceptance in principle that the south had no claim on the north, Faulkner and his people agreed in principle to the establishment of a Council of Ireland. With peace seemingly within his grasp, I could see that this ultimately appeared to him to be a worthwhile concession to the lore, rather than the law, of Ireland. It was on the question of cross-border police co-operation that the Unionists became completely obdurate. They would accept no role at all for the new Council, in what struck me as an obvious sphere within which co-operation really could bring massive benefits. They would not give an inch and so, reluctantly, I had to concede that the control of security in Northern Ireland would be returned wholesale to the new Assembly, as soon as peace was restored. I reflected again on an apposite letter that I had received shortly before from Lord Hailsham which read, 'This is to bring you all my good wishes for the success of your talks. However, this has now been going on for more than 400 years so do not be too depressed if you do not solve everything by the end of the weekend!'

On the Thursday evening of the talks, I suggested to the participants that we could all do with a change of scene, and they readily agreed. We laid on coaches and had everyone driven to Downing Street for dinner. For security reasons, we did not inform anyone where we were heading, and it was soon evident that No. 10 had never hosted such a gathering before. As was our custom, I had the Martin Neary Singers perform grace for my guests, but asked them to drop the usual madrigals after dinner and perform items more likely to satisfy our guests from Ireland. Once they started, there was no constraining those guests and soon the Ulstermen and their counterparts from the Republic were all singing Irish songs together. We could not prise them away until after eleven o'clock. At the end of the dinner, two of the SDLP representatives, Paddy Devlin and John Hume, came up to me and John said, 'We never expected to be inside No. 10 . . . The last time we came here, we were lying on the pavement opposite in a protest demonstration and no one so much as offered us a cup of tea . . . What's more, it rained all night so we packed it in first thing in the morning.' All the Irish went back to Sunningdale feeling a little warmer towards each other and, I hope, towards the British.

The following day, we returned to the serious business of negotiation but no conclusions were reached. On the Saturday, regrettably, I had to absent myself intermittently because the Sunningdale talks clashed with an official visit by the Italian Prime Minister, Mariano Rumor. At tea-time, I flew to Chequers by helicopter for intensive talks with him, followed by an official dinner in his honour, and then returned to Sunningdale by car for what I thought would be only the tail-end of the evening's negotiations. In fact, they continued well into the night. Shortly after 2 a.m., Cosgrave asked for a private word with me and arrived looking flustered and irritated. 'I've come to tell you that I'm going to bed,' he said. 'It's not because of you or the conference, but my people have become impossible. There's no point in staying up with them. I'll be there in the morning.' With that he left.

First thing the following morning, Faulkner informed me solemnly that he and his Unionist colleagues would have to return to Northern Ireland at once, because they had to attend church there. Agonisingly we had seemed to be close to a settlement at long last, but everything now seemed to be slipping through our fingers. I went to talk to the other loyalist representatives, who were tucking into a very hearty breakfast, to see if I could dissuade them from their proposed course. They told me that this was the first they had heard of it. If they needed to go to church, they could do so in England. I then drove back to Chequers, for a final meeting and photocall with Rumor. I must confess that I was a little distracted.

The tripartite meeting got back to business after lunch, and everything was agreed that day. First, that there was an Irish dimension to the Northern Ireland problem and that a Council of Ireland should be set up with seven Ministers from each side forming a council, and a sixty-member Consultative Assembly, elected half by the Dail and half by the Assembly. It would have a permanent secretariat, and studies would be set up to identify areas of common interest where the Council could take on executive authority. During the subsequent general election campaign, some Unionists argued that this gave those from the Republic the power to dictate policy to them, but as each Minister had a right of veto, this was completely false. Second, the Irish government agreed that there could be no change in the status of Northern Ireland until a majority of its people desired it. Third, that as a result of this agreement, direct rule should end on 1 January 1974. This historic accord was one of the proudest moments of my premiership. At 8.45 that evening we signed it, and at 9.00 we told the world of our success. This was the first time that such a consensus had ever been reached for the government of Ireland.

The new Assembly took power on 1 January 1974. A new spirit of co-operation had been engendered between the men of goodwill on both sides. The hardline Unionists, however, continued to reject both the concept of a Council of Ireland and any thought of conceding their political ascendancy to any form of power-sharing, and soon toppled Faulkner from the leadership of his party. Meanwhile in the Republic the recognition of the fact of partition by the Taoiseach, Liam Cosgrave, was immediately challenged in the courts and found to be unconstitutional. The claim on the north was enshrined in the Republic's constitution, and Cosgrave had not shown the courage and vision to deal with this by at once putting a constitutional change to a referendum. Until 1998, neither had any of his successors. Cosgrave's concession therefore had to be watered down, which gave explosive ammunition to the Unionist opponents of Sunningdale north of the border. At the general election on 28 February 1974, the pro-Sunningdale Unionists, including two sitting MPs, Stanley McMaster and Rafton Pounder, were totally wiped out by a concerted campaign against them by Paisley and like-minded loyalist hardliners. Ultimately it was the people of Northern Ireland themselves who threw away the best chance of peace in the blood-stained history of the six counties.

The eleven-strong executive continued in office, carrying out the responsibilities of government, until 28 May 1974. Then, a strike of petrol tanker drivers took only a week to have its effect. Although a comparatively small number of vehicles was involved, the economic activities of Northern Ireland ground rapidly to a halt, and attempts by the TUC to lead a back-to-work movement were rapidly doomed. Brian Faulkner and his senior colleagues went to see Harold Wilson on Friday 24 May to ask for his help in providing drivers from the armed forces, which he undertook to do. However, none was forthcoming on the Monday and, as a result, the executive lost confidence in the Westminster government. This was a brutal and unnecessary ending to the three-party coalition and another bitter personal blow. At the time, Dr Paisley was in the United States campaigning for funds, and he had nothing whatever to do with it.

Under Margaret Thatcher and John Major, there were various false starts in the process of trying to bring peace to Ireland. There was an abortive attempt, in the early to mid-1980s, to re-establish an assembly in Northern Ireland, but this once again became a vehicle for destructive protests rather than for positive policy-making on behalf of the people of the province. I supported both the Anglo-Irish Agreement of 1985 and the Joint Declaration of 1993. I welcomed too the Agreement reached on 10 April 1998, and I can only hope that it will fare better than the Sunningdale Agreement, which in so many ways it resembles.

Chapter 16

THE HOME FRONT

Domestic Policy and Domestic Life 1970–1974

The Conservative government of 1970–4 pursued a thoroughly considered and innovative agenda in a wide range of policy areas both at home and abroad. Our housing policy, our education policy, our policy on law and order, our reform of local government, our immigration policy, our taxation policies – all of these redefined the terms of debate and in most cases the conditions of life for a generation. Furthermore, everything we did was supported unanimously by the Cabinet that I chose. To achieve all this, and full membership of the European Community, in a term of office lasting only three and three-quarter years, was by any standards no mean achievement. The government's policy on law and order was to encourage responsible freedom. We were determined to be tough on all those who made a nuisance of themselves, but helpful and progressive with those who minded their own business and kept themselves to themselves. In the parlance of later years, we were 'tough and tender'. One of our immediate priorities was to deal with the appalling overcrowding that we inherited in the prisons, by substantially expanding the prisons-building programme. In the three years from 1970–1 to 1972–3, work was started on some 6,000 new prison places. In 1971 and 1972, a record 1,750 extra prison officers were recruited.

The centrepiece of our policy on law and order was the Criminal Justice Act 1972, which had a number of far-reaching consequences. We increased the maximum penalty for firearms offences to life imprisonment and gave the courts the power to order offenders to compensate their victims. Possibly the most important and radical reform, however, was the introduction of two new forms of non-custodial sentences. We piloted community service orders, and a system of day-training centres to provide social education linked with intensive probation supervision. This too reduced overcrowding in prisons, and kept many non-violent offenders out of the 'university of crime'. To support this system, we dramatically increased the number of probation officers as well as simplifying and increasing police pay. To build up public confidence in the police, Robert Carr, who succeeded Reggie Maudling as Home Secretary, also committed himself to introducing independent appointees into police complaints procedures, a commitment which we were unable to fulfil because of the February 1974 election result. The major planks of this important reform package are all still in place today.

Our reform of the criminal justice system in 1972 was complemented in the same year by a modernisation of local democracy. The nineteenth-century structure of local government we inherited was able to adjust to the introduction of the welfare state, which it helped to administer. It was not, however, able to survive the growth of car ownership and of suburbia, which were undermining the distinction between town and country and consigning the clear-cut division between county boroughs and rural areas to history. By creating geographical mobility, the motor car was, for many people, relegating the city to a mere transit base. Moreover, there were too many small authorities which found it difficult to provide services of sufficiently high quality at an affordable cost to the local ratepayer. We therefore decided that a radical overhaul of local government was required, with larger authorities providing strategic services and small, district auth-orities for personal services. This was a sensible compromise.

The Local Government Act of 1972 heralded the first major reorganis-ation of local government for over eighty years. The number of authorities in England was reduced from some 1,200 to about 400. We set up the county councils, to deal with strategic functions, and a little over 330 district authorities to handle issues such as planning, housing management and environmental health. The reforms generally operated according to the principle which is now known as 'subsidiarity', meaning that we set out to balance the need to provide services economically against the desire for control of services by a body as close, and as accountable, as possible to local people. Local government ombudsmen were also introduced, as part of our policy to improve accountability to the citizen.

A sound education system is the necessary foundation of any modern society and the successful reforms to our system have generally been Con-servative-inspired. When we came to power in 1970, we certainly had a job to do, for the education system had been a victim of socialism at its most dogmatic during the late 1960s. The Education Secretary throughout my premiership was Margaret Thatcher. I generally left her to get on with her job, just letting it be known that education must never be unfairly hit in the public expenditure round. Margaret needed little encouragement in defending her corner and enjoyed the freedom that this gave her, proving very proficient at spending taxpayers' money. In 1969–70, expenditure on education amounted to 6.1 per cent of GNP. Within only three years, she succeeded in increasing it to 6.6 per cent of a substantially higher GNP.

We inaugurated 'Education Priority Areas' to target those areas of the country where standards were lowest. In June 1971, we began a massive building programme for primary schools and in November of that year we increased the grant for places at direct-grant schools. We also established the Bullock Committee to improve reading standards and raised the school-leaving age from fifteen to sixteen, with effect from September 1972. I am particularly proud of this measure, which finally honoured a pledge made in Rab Butler's Education Act of 1944 and until 1970 neglected by post-war governments. In December 1973, we published a White Paper entitled *Education: A Framework for Expansion*, which set out a long-term plan of how we could achieve substantial growth over the next decade benefiting every sector of education. This promised to provide free nursery education for all who required it and to increase the number of school teachers by 150,000, allowing teacher–pupil ratios to drop from one teacher to every twenty-two pupils to one for every eighteen. Had we won the February 1974 election, all this would have been implemented.

In the field of higher education, there were some, such as Iain Macleod and Edward Boyle, who favoured the abolition of the Open University, whose establishment had been one of Wilson's few achievements. Macleod and Boyle were champions of equal opportunity, but they were doubtful whether the OU, which had not yet received its first students, would attract enough people. I also wondered whether it could achieve the standards of a normal university, but believed we should go ahead with it, feeling sure that it would appeal not only to those seeking to advance their careers, but also to those, such as housewives or retired people, who simply wanted to improve themselves. Mrs Thatcher was in favour of home-learning for sound reasons of economy and believed that, in an age of scarce resources, it offered a highly cost-effective way of expanding the tertiary education sector – OU students would not require grants to cover their living expenses. We stuck with the Open University, and helped to establish it as one of Britain's most cherished institutions. In 1997, I felt especially pleased when it presented me with an honorary doctorate.

The other major change that we brought to education was to end the Labour policy of ruthlessly applying pressure centrally to turn grammar schools into comprehensives, on purely ideological grounds. I had benefited enormously from my time at Chatham House Grammar School in Ramsgate, and I wanted to ensure that others could have a similar opportunity in future. We therefore immediately withdrew and replaced departmental circulars that the Labour government had issued in 1965 and 1966 which, although they had no force of law in themselves, had put immense pressure upon local education authorities to reorganise themselves on completely comprehensive lines. In effect, Labour had indicated that they would give approval to building projects only from Local Education Authorities (LEAs) which agreed to the socialist line on secondary reorganisation. As soon as this disgraceful situation was brought to an end, Margaret could give immediate approval to £3 million worth of building projects which had been frozen by Labour's socialist dogma. As we had promised in our manifesto, we left individual authorities free to decide for themselves what system they wanted, and we encouraged a policy of diversity. Labour had intended to bring forward legislation to enforce uniform non-selection on all authorities, but this had fallen with their election defeat.

Margaret Thatcher's replacement circular set out a gentle but firm presumption against unnecessary disruption or change. 'Where a particular pattern of education is working well and commands general support,' explained this document, 'the Secretary of State does not wish to cause further change without good reason.' Henceforth, each plan would be judged non-ideologically and on its individual merits, according to the needs of the locality. In practice, if an LEA wanted to end selection, then the onus was still on supporters of the threatened local grammar schools to put the contrary case – for, given the 1970 government's belief in the discretionary powers of local government, the Secretary of State would need to demonstrate good reasons for overruling any LEA. From the beginning, Margaret had a political problem with this. In many cases, the proposals to end selection were coming not from socialists, but from Conservative-led authorities. Mostly they wanted to economise by replacing boys' and girls' grammar schools, which generally had large catchment areas, with co-educational comprehensives. The tide was strong, but I do wish, in retrospect, that the many supporters of selection had all campaigned more vigorously before it was too late.

I was able, however, to make a stand in my own constituency of Bexley. Speaking at the Bexley Grammar School Speech Day shortly before the 1970 general election, I had repeated my view that good schools should not become a party political battleground: 'That is why we here in Bexley have been fighting the proposals to destroy the grammar schools and with them so much that is best in education, in exchange for some half-baked scheme of reorganisation.' In 1966 the then Labour Council had introduced a comprehensive plan for education over the whole borough. These proposals were withdrawn after the Council returned to a Conservative majority in 1968. Unfortunately, in the local elections on 13 May 1971 Bexley Council fell once again under Labour control. The Local Education Authority immediately submitted proposals for the organisation of secondary schools in the borough, closely related to those of 1966. One of the proposed changes involved the merger of Bexley Grammar School with Westwood Secondary Modern, provoking fury among parents and staff alike. On 21 July, in my capacity as Bexley's MP, I received a deputation of five teachers from Bexley Grammar School, protesting against the plans. They explained their objections to the proposals at length, and it was clear that their case was a powerful one. I assured them that I would use my influence with the Secretary of State for Education to block these proposals and told them, 'Don't worry too much.'

Although I had to maintain the boundary between my constituency duties and my job as Prime Minister, I was extremely concerned about what was now being planned by left-wing activists on Bexley Council. During an adjournment debate on 23 July, Dame Patricia Hornsby-Smith, the formidable MP for Chislehurst, spoke very forcefully and eloquently against the scheme:

> I defy any educationalist to prove that this mean partisan scheme provides better education and opportunities . . . for the children in my constituency. It can only reduce the . . . education which is successfully pursued . . . in first-class schools with devoted staff . . . These proposals are opposed by all the schools concerned [and] by hundreds of parents . . . I can say without fear of contradiction that the schools in my constituency are well above the average. I ask the Minister to ensure that in any new scheme this provision is not reduced, and that opportunities for children . . . are not and shall not be destroyed.

In her reply Margaret Thatcher assured Patricia Hornsby-Smith that she would take into account 'educational and practical matters of the kind which she has mentioned'. She could not, however, give any assurances at this stage on the merits of the proposals which were being formulated. Margaret also confirmed that I had taken a direct interest in the matter and had spoken to her about it, which I had done immediately after meeting the Bexley delegation. On 4 October, Bexley Local Education Authority submitted statutory proposals for reorganisation of secondary schools, under Section 13 of the 1944 Education Act (as amended). Five months later, on 20 March 1972, I received a letter from Margaret Thatcher's assistant private secretary, Frank Clark. Before making a final decision, Margaret was formally seeking my opinion. The LEA had included four sets of proposals to link secondary modern schools with existing grammar and technical high schools as comprehensive schools for 11–14 and 14–18 age groups, with the destruction of Bexley Grammar School as part of the scheme. I could not countenance such a measure and indicated accordingly. On 7 May, I learned that both Bexley Grammar and Westwood Secondary Modern had been saved, when Margaret

Short tacking in the second short race, Admiral's Cup 1971

Outside Chequers with Jack Lynch, Taoiseach of the Republic, and Brian Faulkner, Prime Minister of Northern Ireland, 27 September 1971

President Nixon shows the strain of office. Lord Martonmere, the Governor of Bermuda, prepares to take away his support

Leaving HMS *Glamorgan* with President Nixon and Tim Kitson, having dined rather well

Above The proudest moment of my life.
Signing the Treaty of Accession, Brussels,
24 January 1972

'Suit alors!' President Pompidou arrives at
Northolt, March 1972

Below With Brian Trubshaw after my first
flight in Concorde, May 1972

Playing the renaissance organ in Frederiksborg, Denmark in June 1972. Built in the 1610s, this is the oldest organ in the world to retain its original workings. In the background is the Danish Prime Minister at the time, Jens Krag

Back in Northern Ireland, November 1972. My expression says it all

Below With Leopold Stokowski at the Royal Albert Hall, February 1973

With Chairman Mao in Beijing in 1974. My historic first visit to China

Left With Dmitri Shostakovich and Victor Hochhauser outside No. 10. The composer signed this photo for me two days later

With Anthony Eden and Harold Macmillan at the Savoy Hotel, December 1973

Sailing at Burnham, 1974. Duncan Kay, one of my regular crew, is seen enjoying himself shouting at the freedeck. In the other photograph, (*opposite*) *Morning Cloud* is holding *Toujaine*, steered by Sir Maurice Laing

The Great Debate – Oxford, 3 June 1975. The motion was 'This House would say "yes" to Europe'. It did

Forty million
people died in two
European wars this
century.
    Better lose a
little national
sovereignty than
a son or daughter.

Vote Yes to keep
the peace.

Keep
Britain in Europe

PUBLISHED BY BRITAIN IN EUROPE, 149 OLD PARK LANE, LONDON W.1.

ANYTHING WORTH FIGHTING TWO WORLD WARS FOR MUST BE WORTH VOTING FOR.

As these advertisements demonstrate, the political objectives of the European Community were never concealed from the people of the United Kingdom. In 1975 (*above, left*) the 'Yes' campaign strongly urged voters to reflect upon questions of sovereignty, whilst the 'No' campaign largely concentrated upon the prices of foodstuffs. In 1984, the Conservative campaign for the European Parliament elections (*above, right*) explicitly drew attention to the considerable achievement, through the EC, of almost forty years of peace in Western Europe. The deplorable and notorious 'Diet of Brussels' campaign of only five years later (*below left*) was an object lesson in political inconsistency, as well as distortion. The results of this election were a huge setback for the party, and marked the beginning of the end for Mrs Thatcher

STAY AT HOME ON JUNE 15TH, AND YOU'LL LIVE ON A DIET OF BRUSSELS.

VOTE CONSERVATIVE ON JUNE 15TH.

Right The 'Yes' campaign comes to Bexley – Young Conservatives at Crook Log, Bexleyheath, Spring 1975

informed me that she had rejected the proposals as 'educationally unsound'.

All too few schools followed Bexley's example, and Margaret Thatcher felt able to reject only 326 out of the 3,612 proposals to end selection that were submitted to her. The proportion of secondary schoolchildren in comprehensives consequently rose from 32 to 62 per cent. I remain proud of the achievements of all of the schools in my constituency, including Bexley Grammar School. My links to that school remain strong to this day. In 1982 I was invited to open a Sixth Form Centre which had been built by their Parents' Association. Just one year later, however, boundary changes took Bexley Grammar into the neighbouring seat of Bexleyheath. The wheel was to turn full circle in 1997. After further boundary changes, Bexley Grammar School returned to my constituency of Old Bexley and Sidcup, this time, I hope, for good.

The minister in charge of social policy was Keith Joseph. Keith was one of the biggest spenders in my Cabinet and, at the time, seemed to regard generous and properly targeted public spending as a good thing. After I wrote to him congratulating him upon a very good speech at the 1971 party conference, he replied, 'It is you – and Tony [Barber] – who have made the social improvements possible . . . I shall do my best to see that they are widely understood.' There was not a trace of his later views in such sentiments, nor should there have been. We used the money to good effect, for example in granting pensions to the over-eighties. Over 100,000 people who had retired before national insurance contributions were introduced in 1948 had never had a state pension and this was clearly scandalous. We also introduced the Christmas bonus (see p. 414), special benefits for the chronically sick and their children, an annual increase in benefits for all pensioners, attendance allowances for severely disabled people and pensions for widows under fifty.

Since its foundation by Aneurin Bevan in 1948, the National Health Service has steadily become an object of immense national pride. It is the most popular part of the welfare state and is still admired around the world. It also faces ever growing demands from its users, because of the expensive medical advances which it is quite rightly expected to provide. These advances, alongside a rising standard of living and combined with extended longevity, place further strain on the service through sheer weight of numbers. By the 1960s, everyone, including the medical establishment and moderates in the Labour Party, recognised that a major reform of the NHS was required, to tackle spiralling costs, but few were brave enough to say so at the time. Wilson in particular could not afford to launch what the left would see as an attack on one of the pillars of British socialism.

In the autumn of 1968, Keith Joseph circulated a paper to the Shadow

Cabinet suggesting a possible solution, echoing Harold Macmillan a decade earlier. He wanted to find ways of encouraging people to take out private insurance for health requirements such as visits to their GPs, out-patient care and boarding charges after more than a few days in hospital. Tax concessions would be granted to those taking out such insurance. At first, I supported these ideas in principle, but the costings made it clear that the financial savings would not have warranted the probable political damage. Moreover, at the Selsdon Park summit Iain Macleod showed that it might also cause distress for many people, potentially doubling the cost of compulsory insurance for those on average wages. We therefore dropped the idea, and concentrated on reforms to create a different managerial culture within the health service to improve efficiency without harming patients. Bevan's original structure was still in place. This was a three-tier system of GPs, hospitals and local authorities, the last of which remained in charge of services such as district nurses, child welfare, ambulance services and vaccination programmes. This system did not promote good community medicine, for there was no clear chain of command, nor enough co-operation between the different elements.

We brought in management consultants to find a way of integrating the service. They came up with a plan to replace 700 hospital boards and local authority management committees with fourteen regional health authorities, ninety area health authorities and 200 district management teams, each with a Community Health Council (CHC) to watch over it. An essential part of this integration was to bring healthcare and the other social services closer together so that, for example, if a GP or hospital treating a patient for a physical illness discovered mental problems, they could more easily refer him or her to a psychiatric hospital.

Although a clearer chain of command was created, it had too many links, and insufficient emphasis was placed on the day-to-day management of hospitals. However, once the reforms took root in the late 1970s, they did have lasting benefits. For the first time, Britain had health authorities responsible for planning all types of health services, rather than just primary medical care. The CHCs provided an effective complaints procedure, and the presence of local authority members with a wide knowledge of the social services on the boards of the new health authorities helped to make the medical establishment more accountable. The old, autonomous hospital boards had contained too many well-meaning, but far from professional, local dignitaries.

I have never thought that institutional reforms were enough on their own to modernise our NHS. We realised that it would take several years for our policy to take effect and, in the short term, more money had to be found to fill major gaps in health provision which had existed since

1948. Keith Joseph was committed to providing that money so, between 1970 and 1973, the annual rate of growth in health spending, after inflation, was around 4 per cent. An essential part of Joseph's plans was to inject more money into what he called the 'Cinderella services' such as geriatric and psychiatric care which, lacking the easy popularity that invariably greeted such exciting innovations as the mass distribution of penicillin after the war, had frequently been neglected.

We massively expanded the social services, so that, when the new integrated healthcare began in April 1974, those on the medical side had enough professionals working in the community to support them. We also established the array of social workers who do valuable and frequently thankless work to ensure that the weakest and most unfortunate in our society are properly looked after. Finally, we made the contraceptive pill, that symbol of personal freedom in the 1960s, available to all on the NHS, free from prescription charges. In doing so, we defied many in our own party who believed that this was 'immorality at the taxpayer's expense'. I have never believed that it is a legitimate function of politicians to lecture citizens on the morality of how they conduct themselves in their private lives. I am proud of what we did for the health of our people. The Chief Medical Officer, Sir George Godber, concluded, 'In time of need for myself or my family I would now rather take my chance at random in the British National Health Service than in any other service I know.'

As well as improving targeting of resources in our social policies, we also considered ways of reducing the distortions to individual incentives that any benefits system inevitably creates. In particular, we examined a 'negative income tax'. This was a radical suggestion for dealing with the 'unemployment trap' – when unemployed social security claimants set out to earn a wage, possibly through part-time work, but lose so much benefit if they do so that it is just not in their financial interest to work – and also to deal with the 'poverty trap', when someone in work finds that it is not worth while putting in extra effort to earn more, for similar reasons. In both instances, individuals are, in effect, penalised for attempting to better themselves, and the number of those who are naturally likely to fall into this trap has been growing – that is, those with high in-work costs, in particular child-care costs, and comparatively low potential wages.

Historically, the tax system and the benefits system have operated according to quite different principles. The former ultimately exists to raise revenue, while the latter is supposed to address the needs of the individual citizen. Although the two systems should have an overriding, shared objective, to create prosperity and stability for individuals and families, they have all too often cut badly across one another, with disastrous results. A negative income tax would have required us to merge the tax and benefit systems, so that both operated according to the same principles and all entitlements would have been provided through the tax system. At first sight, it promised to remove the stigma that was attached to those who were still claiming social security and, in practical terms, to smooth the transition between debit and credit so as to preserve or increase the incentive to continue working and, ultimately, to get a better job.

I am sorry to say that, after further examination, we were forced to drop the idea because it was not as simple as it had at first appeared. For example, the system depended on a test of income rather than need, which meant that all kinds of regional variations, particularly where house prices were concerned, would have to be calculated. Furthermore, we took the view that everyone affected by such an innovation – the overwhelming majority of the population, in all probability – would have to be protected from financial losses above a certain, moderate level. This would, of course, be extremely expensive, which is why reform on such a scale has never been brought forward. It was both an intellectual and a practical disappointment that we could not press ahead with this. I hope that with further analysis and study it may prove possible to institute a simplified system.

We also set out to improve the targeting of resources in housing policy, by establishing the principle of 'To each according to need, from each according to ability to pay'. The Housing Finance Act 1972 established that local authorities should charge economic rents for homes, backed up by a national statutory system of rent rebates for council tenants, and rent allowances for those in privately rented homes. (Under Labour, 40 per cent of local authorities had given no rent rebates at all, regardless of how acute local needs were, and resources had been used inefficiently.) For those who could afford to pay them, rents were allowed to rise ahead of inflation, and the money raised was used towards financing a dramatic increase in the number of housing starts. In the first three years of the 1970 administration, there were almost 2 million starts or improvement grants awarded, as compared with fewer than 1.5 million in the last three years under Labour. In 1972, to take one example, over a quarter of a million better homes were provided in the public sector. We also pioneered policies on increased home ownership. In our first three years, about 1 million people became home owners for the first time, and we instituted the policy of encouraging local authorities to sell off some of their housing stock. It is all too often forgotten that this ground-breaking reform was introduced back in the early 1970s. For many families, this was the first opportunity ever to become owner occupiers. We also took measures to renew the stock and to prevent people from merely cashing in by quickly selling their properties on.

*   *   *

Another aspect of the 1970 administration of which I am particularly proud is our record on immigration, which had seemed in the early days to be the most intractable problem of all. When I came to power, race was already a major source of conflict in Britain. Labour's 1948 British Nationality Act had granted British citizenship to all people in Commonwealth countries past and present and it was this that facilitated immigration in the 1950s. The racial prejudice that these immigrants encountered culminated in the Notting Hill race riots of 1958. Continuing inter-racial friction eventually prompted Rab Butler to bring in the Commonwealth Immigration Act in 1962 to limit the numbers of non-white immigrants entering the country by means of an employment voucher scheme. Although discriminatory in practice, the principle behind it was to give white Britons time to adjust to the new arrivals and, thereby, to give existing immigrants and their descendants more of a chance to integrate.

A considerable number of our backbenchers opposed Rab's scheme from the best of motives – that is, to preserve the freedom of immigrants. Every party has its extremists, however, and the Conservative Party, with its right wing, is no exception. There were elements within our ranks who saw the 1962 Act not as an example of Tory pragmatism, but as the start of a programme through which coloured immigration could eventually be stopped altogether, and those who had already entered the country could be repatriated. This first became evident to the public during the 1964 general election campaign in which Labour's Shadow Foreign Secretary Patrick Gordon Walker was defeated at Smethwick by Peter Griffiths' racist campaign. Griffiths was a severe embarrassment to us and he was rightly shunned in Parliament when he arrived.

It was against a volatile background that as Prime Minister I set about trying to improve the situation. Immigration was a new challenge to the whole philosophy of One Nation which had been unforeseen in 1950 and we could not afford to shirk it. Between 1968 and 1970, my mailbag had contained many letters, largely from Conservative supporters, in support of Enoch Powell. They were frequently abusive, towards me as much as towards black people, but this only made me more resolute. There were certainly those in the party, even on the front bench, who wanted to harness racialist support. Some commentators have argued that I bowed to this pressure and that, as a result, Powell helped me to win the election of 1970 just as he helped Wilson to defeat me in 1974 on the question of Europe. I totally disagree.

It is true that we promised to limit immigration in our manifesto, but we did so as part of the balanced approach to the problem that I have already described. Powell did not advise his supporters to vote Conservative because he believed that we were a racist party, but because he assumed, as many people did, that we should lose the election and that, having supposedly demonstrated both his robustness and his loyalty to the party, he would then be in a position to challenge for its leadership. I could not have made it clearer to voters that there would be no Faustian pact with Powell and that racism would get no encouragement of any kind from the Conservative Party, so long as I was its leader. Any support we did get from the far right was because such people were blindly following Powell, instead of listening to us.

In the debate on the Queen's Speech on 2 July 1970, I told the House that the aim of our immigration policy was to ensure 'justice to all those who are already in this country, whatever their race, creed or colour may be, to set the public mind at rest on this issue so that there cannot be any further justification for existing passions and so that there can be absolutely no reason for apprehension on the part of immigrants who are already settled here'. The Immigration Bill that we published in February 1971 fulfilled that pledge. Employment vouchers would be replaced by work permits, which would not carry the right of permanent residence or the right of entry for dependants, powers to prevent illegal immigration would be strengthened and some financial assistance for voluntary repatriation would be offered. These measures effectively ended the unqualified rights of any Commonwealth citizen to settle in Britain which the Attlee government had established in 1948. As Reggie Maudling told the House during the second reading of the Bill on 8 May 1971, it gave the government greater long-term control over immigration, in place of the piecemeal measures enacted by the Macmillan and Wilson governments. The Bill received little opposition from the other parties and, after a few minor amendments, became law on the same day that we entered the European Community, 1 January 1973.

We hoped that all these measures might settle the immigration issue once and for all. We found, however, that the best-laid plans could not prevent crises occurring, and racism soon reared its ugly head again. On 4 August 1972, the President of Uganda, General Idi Amin, announced that he was going to expel all 57,000 Asians from his country and gave them a month to leave. Amin was an African dictator from central casting (see p. 483). Through a combination of corruption, intimidation and incompetence, he had pauperised a country that was rich in natural resources, in order to line his own pockets and those of his cronies. With many of his people beginning to get restless, he cast around for a scapegoat and chose the Asian community – one of the most hard-working and law-abiding groups in Uganda, who had been there for generations.

At first, we did our utmost, via diplomatic channels, to try to persuade Amin to change his mind, both through making representations to him and by encouraging other Commonwealth countries to put pressure on him. It soon became clear, however, that, like most dictators, the man could not be reasoned with. Uganda was still part of the Commonwealth and we therefore had a moral duty to accept these unfortunate people. Over the next few weeks, intense pressure was placed on us by the right wing to renege upon our political and moral obligations. This was led by Enoch Powell, and some sections of the media joined in the ugly chorus. I was determined that we would once again face up to our responsibilities, as we had with regard to refugees from Pakistan and Bangladesh. Alec Douglas-Home was in full agreement with me and, on 31 August, he made a special ministerial broadcast on television, announcing the setting up of a Ugandan Resettlement Board that would work with local authorities to help the Ugandan Asians to settle in this country. We also made extra funding available to local authorities.

In an attempt to ease some of the burden, we contacted fifty other countries, twelve of which, including the USA, Canada and Sweden, agreed to take some of the refugees. We did what any civilised nation would do, by taking the greater share of the emigrants, some 25,000 people. I have never regretted this, for the Ugandan Asians have brought a wealth of endeavour, enterprise and natural talent to these shores. I was also determined that Amin should not get away too lightly, so we suspended a £10 million loan to Uganda for good measure. Arnold Goodman wrote a particularly pleasant letter to me after this episode, sending his 'warmest congratulations and admiration on the Government's policy over the wretched Asians . . . I do not remember an episode of Governmental behaviour as being more clear-cut in relation to morality and principle and less self-seeking in terms of popular appeal.'

Predictably, our decision provoked opposition from some of the party, in particular the Monday Club, which began a 'Halt Immigration Now' campaign. The divisions among the Conservatives came to a head at the party conference in October 1972. It had taken the Cabinet only five minutes to agree unanimously to this policy, and I resolved from the start that we would not flinch from our responsibilities, at conference or any-where else. An apparently nondescript motion reiterating support for our manifesto policy on immigration was placed on the agenda in the name of Hackney South and Shoreditch Conservative Association. This was moved by the president of the Association, Enoch Powell. In his speech, Powell argued that, because we had no legal obligation to these people, they should not be accepted. It was clear from the platform that he was swaying many of the delegates. Fortunately the Federation of Conservative Students and the Young Conservatives, swung into action. Both organisa-tions were then under sensible leadership. David Hunt, the national chairman of the Young Conservatives and a future Cabinet minister, moved an amendment, explicitly congratulating the government on accepting the Ugandan Asians. Other future ministers, including Robert Atkins and Tony Baldry, supported him.

I knew, after David's excellent speech, that the hall was coming back our way, and the amendment was carried by 1,721 votes to 736. I followed this up in December by dissolving the West Middlesex branch of the Monday Club for endorsing the National Front candidate during the Uxbridge by-election that was then being fought. The battle was still not over, however. David Hunt was deselected as a parliamentary candidate in Plymouth as a consequence of his bravery. I telephoned him as soon as I heard, and offered every possible assistance in getting his political career on track again. I had always respected the integrity and ability of David and his YC colleagues, and his deselection made me furious.

The extremists also had some revenge on me a year later, when Parliament came to vote on the Immigration Rules designed to implement the 1971 Immigration Act and also to bring us into line with European Community agreements on the free movement of workers between member states of the Community. The new rules were particularly galling for the right because they made it easier for European nationals to come to Britain than it was for non-patrial whites from Commonwealth countries. The whole question brought together the two questions around which the right of the party have increasingly gathered, immigration and Europe, and the chamber was alive with accusations that we were betraying the Commonwealth. The rules also applied to non-patrial coloured people, but there were those in the party who were quite happy to see them excluded. By 'Commonwealth' the right usually means Australia, New Zealand and Canada, which Her Majesty has made clear is not her definition of the Commonwealth, nor has it ever been mine.

The rebels, however, were determined to vote against us. They were supported by the Beaverbrook press and managed to mobilise a number of MPs who were not staunch opponents of our immigration policy, but who had reservations about Europe. The result was that we were defeated by thirty-five votes, the largest defeat that my administration suffered. Wilson immediately sprang to his feet and asked me if I was going to resign. I replied simply and calmly, 'The House has rejected two statements made in accordance with Acts passed by the House . . . Statements to replace them will be laid in due course.' I left the chamber soon after, trying to hide my profound distaste at the actions, and motives, of some of my colleagues. After consultations had taken place, a number of minor amendments were made, such as the extension of the Commonwealth Citizens Working Holidaymaker Scheme, from six to twelve months. The only major amendment was that anyone with a UK-born grandparent would be exempted from the provisions of the new Act, although they would still be subject to entry clearance, and liability for deportation would remain, for example if they were convicted of a serious criminal offence. The new rules were passed on 21 February 1973.

The development of technology during those years provided two opportunities to combine diplomacy with scientific advancement. As soon as we took charge, we discovered that we had to decide about the future of the Anglo-French development of a supersonic passenger aircraft, Concorde, whose costs had spiralled out of control. After much discussion, with the supporting evidence of a well-researched paper from the Central Policy Review Staff, we approved further funding. So much had already been committed that, despite the Treasury's predictable complaints, the potential savings hardly justified cancellation. Furthermore, the French, with whom we were still conducting negotiations about our entry into Europe, publicly set great store by the success of the plane. In Toulouse, where French Concorde-related employment was concentrated, a new mayor was even elected in 1971 on a pro-Concorde ticket. His deputy mayor was the chief test pilot for the aircraft. I also heard at that time that President Pompidou's next sortie into the provinces was to be a visit to Toulouse, and he was to fly there by Concorde. I knew then that we could not afford to cancel. I also signed, with President Pompidou, the Treaty for the Channel Tunnel. Although our Bill to carry this forward and get the Tunnel built by 1980 was 'lost' at the dissolution of Parliament in February 1974, we provided the basis for the very successful tunnel which now links us with the rest of our continent.

My election as Prime Minister happened to coincide almost exactly with the expiry of the lease on my Albany flat. Sadly, the fact that for the foreseeable future I would not be living in Albany and would not have been allowed to sub-let my flat made it impossible for me to renew the lease. When I moved into No. 10, therefore, it was to become my home. Almost at once, I was told that much of the building was suffering from acute dry rot. Little appeared to have been done there since the major reconstruction and refurbishment in 1959–62, whose legacy was a mixed one. In the middle of the work, the builders had gone on strike, and a temporary roof was left on for several months. Inevitably, the rain got in and rot followed. Harold Wilson had not been willing to sanction the necessary remedial work, but I felt at once that we should now do this properly. Renovation work started with the State dining room and, as soon as that was finished, they found it necessary to do all the other State rooms, and the study, one by one. All of them were rotten, and the work lasted from summer 1970 into 1971. When the Cabinet Room was repainted, it was brightened by the installation of a new, lighter-coloured carpet and lighter curtains. The improvement of the study was particularly successful, and when it was completed I preferred to work there rather than in the Cabinet Room itself, even though, or perhaps because, the study was further away from the private office.

The panelled walls of the State dining room were stripped and coated with a paler varnish, and the lighting was improved. Relatively modern copies of portraits whose only merit was that their subjects had played distinguished parts in British history were replaced by eighteenth- and early-nineteenth-century original portraits by major British painters, including four wonderful Gainsboroughs. As well as improving the architectural condition of the State rooms and the study, we were also able to redecorate them in a different style, again with the object of making the rooms lighter and more welcoming. To adorn the renovated building, I borrowed treasures from friends, and displayed some of my own porcelain. We also took the opportunity to redo the entrance hall and main staircase, on which are displayed likenesses of past Prime Ministers. Once all the work was complete, I held a dinner party in celebration. Harold and Mary Wilson came and, although Mary took great interest in all of my innovations, she made it clear at once that, if Harold ever became Prime Minister again, she would get rid of the whole lot – and bring back her own decorations, including the copies of paintings and her celebrated enamel swans alongside the main fireplace.

I gained an unexpected opportunity to add to the artistic treasures of No. 10 when I agreed to speak at a Variety Club lunch on Monday 7 December 1971. I sat at the right hand of the organiser, a businessman and not a performer, whom I praised warmly in my speech. At the end of the dinner, he asked if he might introduce his uncle to me. 'Of course,' I replied. It turned out that his uncle had flown in specially from the USA that morning in order to be present and would fly back to the States that same evening. We exchanged a few pleasantries and parted. I thought no more of this until, a few days later, I received a charming letter from the old man. 'I greatly enjoyed meeting you,' it ran, 'and thought that, as I have a large collection of paintings, you might like to hang one at No. 10.' This was certainly of interest, especially as the redecoration of Downing Street was now completed. 'Perhaps you would like a Renoir? I have several and I would be very happy to select one for you.' I wrote back thanking him very much for his kind offer and informing him that I would get in touch again once I had discussed the matter with my advisers.

Shortly afterwards, I received a note from a private secretary. There were grave difficulties associated with accepting such an offer, I was informed. Hitherto all the paintings at No. 10 had been by British painters, and belonged to British benefactors. I would be publicly criticised if we accepted this Renoir, and where would it all end? I was having none of that and said so. Another note then appeared, informing me that there existed no precedent for arranging the necessary insurance for such a valuable painting if it were to be hung at No. 10. I asked officials to establish a precedent. Finally, I received the advice that, even if arrangements could be put in place for insuring the painting once it was safely ensconced in Downing Street, how on earth were we to arrange its safe transit from the USA? Who would pay for its flight, its insurance and its protection?

As I pondered this latest counter-stroke against the Renoir, Alan Simcock, one of my private secretaries, was taking a call from the authorities at Heathrow. 'We've got a package here for you,' he was informed. 'Are you going to collect it, or are you going to leave it here or are we to send it on?' They were told to send it on and, two hours later, a package was delivered to No. 10. When undone, it was found to contain a magnificent Renoir, along with an explanatory note from my American friend. 'I have paid for the painting's transit and all the necessary insurance,' he informed us, 'for the full duration of its loan to you.' The picture was hung, to brilliant effect, in the White Drawing Room. A year later its owner came to see it, liked its position and arranged to replace it with a second Renoir. When, the following year, he offered a third Renoir, I gently indicated that as a change I would much appreciate a painting by Gauguin, one of my favourite painters. 'Why, of course,' he replied. 'I have a number of them.' Unfortunately the 1974 general election deprived me of that pleasure.

I was reminded by all this of a similar exchange in my early months at No. 10, when I had asked the National Gallery whether we might borrow some of their portraits for the dining room. They sent their regrets, 'because these paintings are for the public to see'. I asked them how many members of the public they admitted to their vast storage cellars each year. They still did not loan us the paintings.

As well as making 10 Downing Street properly inhabitable, I also took full advantage of Chequers, the Prime Minister's country home, spending many weekends there working and entertaining. Chequers is a superb house, which was given to the nation in 1921 by Arthur Lee, formerly the Conservative and Unionist MP for Fareham and latterly Lord Lee of Fareham. Arthur Lee died in the late 1940s, but his widow lived into the late 1960s – and she always refused to countenance anyone making changes to the house. By the time I moved into Chequers, rather like No. 10 it was in need of substantial renovation. The house at Chequers was the responsibility of the Chequers Trust, not of the government, and the endowment of the Trust was not large enough to finance major refurbishments, but my friend Sir Harold (later Lord) Samuel kindly agreed to take this on.

His generosity enabled us to improve the house almost beyond recognition. In particular, the Great Hall, originally the open court but now roofed over, the parlours and all the upstairs suites were completely redecorated and refurnished. I made sure that the many assets of the building – its remarkable collections of porcelain and books and some beautiful pieces of furniture – were used to full advantage, and the many guests I entertained at Chequers came to share my love of the place. Another major improvement to the amenities at Chequers was the installation of a swimming pool, made possible by the generosity of Walter Annenberg, the United States ambassador to the Court of St James's. I, my guests and my successors have enjoyed making use of this magnificent gift, which we greatly valued.

I stayed at Chequers a great deal, retiring there most weekends, and hugely appreciating the peace and quiet that it provided. I sometimes held sessions in the summer with my sailing colleagues, and very often used it for concerts and other social occasions, always delighting, as I did, in taking visitors around the house and its grounds. On 6 March 1971, I hosted a dinner for Harold Macmillan at which he spoke splendidly about the challenges that we faced. 'The English people do not like power,' he said. 'They distrust power and fight it when it appears. It has always been so. They broke the power of the barons in the Middle Ages, they broke the power of the Crown under Charles I, then the landlords in the Reform Bill, then the press, then the middle class. Now it is the trade unions. It has all happened before, dear boy.' Harold was right, even if it took the people a few more years to appreciate how great the threat to their liberties from the unions really was.

I was also determined to use Chequers for musical performances. There was already a Steinway piano in the house, but Steinway's agreed that they would loan us one of their own pianos for any concerts or recitals that we gave there. Alas, the Khaled incident (see p. 321–3) ruined the first concert that I arranged to host there as Prime Minister. This was arranged for 9 September 1970, and I persuaded Isaac Stern, who had been a friend for many years, to bring his trio down to Chequers to play a programme of Beethoven before an audience of eminent guests in the Great Hall. When the day came, however, we were still in the middle of the crisis and so much needed to be done that Alec Douglas-Home and I were unable to attend the concert. I spoke to Isaac Stern on the telephone to apologise for my absence and to express the hope that he would be prepared to go ahead with the programme for the benefit of the other guests. Stern and his two companions, Eugene Istomin and Leonard Rose, were all extremely worried about the effect that the hijackings would have on the Middle East but, although they were extremely tense when the evening began, they performed superbly. A tape recording made for me that evening testifies to that. They concluded the concert with Beethoven's 'Archduke' Trio, which they knew to be my favourite, and I was bitterly disappointed that I was not able to be there.

The second musical evening at Chequers followed soon after, when I invited Yehudi Menuhin to bring some of the pupils from the Menuhin School on 29 November 1970, to show my guests how talented they were. The young players included such stars of the future as Melvyn Tan, Nigel Kennedy, Felix Schmidt and Colin Carr. As a surprise for our guests, Yehudi agreed that he and I should play Handel's Violin Sonata in D as a finale. We decided on the edition we would use, and all went well until we came near to the end of the last movement. He appeared to leave out three or four bars of the violin part, possibly because he was playing from memory, and had switched to a different edition from the one which we were playing. I had to scramble to catch up with him, but I am glad to say that, having started together, we also finished together, the most important criterion of musical success.

At one party shortly after becoming Prime Minister, I met a man who was introduced by the hostess as Mr Sam Spiegel. I had never met him before and, after we had shaken hands, I enquired politely: 'What do you do?' He replied indignantly by throwing the question straight back at me, 'What do I do?' A little taken aback by his vehemence, I said, 'Are you a businessman, or a professional man, or perhaps you've already retired?' 'But you must know that I'm a film producer?' he asked incredulously. 'I'm afraid not,' I confessed. 'What films have you produced?' 'Well,' Spiegel said, 'there was *African Queen* – you must have seen that?' 'I've certainly heard of it,' I said, 'but I've never seen it. Wasn't Paul Robeson in it?' 'I also produced *Lawrence of Arabia*,' he declared. I had heard of it but I had not seen that either. 'Then there was *The Bridge on the River Kwai*,' he informed me. 'Ah,' I said, 'I've heard Malcolm Arnold's music, but I've never seen the film.' I then added, somewhat untruthfully, 'The last film I saw was George Arliss in *Disraeli*.' 'But that,' he said, 'was in 1929.' 'No,' I replied firmly, 'I saw it in 1932 to be accurate.'

Sam Spiegel then thought for a moment and decided that something must be done about my ignorance of his genre. 'I'll make you an offer,' he began. 'I'll get my people to go through every film since then and pick out the major successes, so that you can be brought right up to date. All my staff will need to know is the size of the equipment in your private cinema and I'll have the films delivered to you at 10 Downing Street or Chequers.' I had to tell him, 'I'm afraid that I haven't got a private cinema.'

'What, you're Prime Minister and you haven't got a private cinema?' he asked me in astonishment. 'In Washington, the President has his own cinema, and surely the Queen must have a private cinema. Well, without a cinema there's nothing I can do about it.' Fortunately, however, he did not wash his hands of me entirely. I was later invited to stay with him at his villa in St Tropez, where he also kept his 500 tonne cruising yacht, *Malahne*. Our voyages along the Mediterranean and down the Corsican coast were glorious holidays. The revolving series of guests from stage and screen was a revelation. To my regret, he never showed a film either on board or at his villa. He did, however, invite me to watch the final take of his last film, *Betrayal*. I even realised many a child's dream, by sitting on the chair marked 'Producer'.

In September 1971 I received a letter from John Peyton, at the Department of the Environment, inviting me to a small gathering which he was setting up to celebrate William Walton's seventieth birthday, on 29 March the following year. Walton was, along with Benjamin Britten, one of Britain's indisputably world-class composers. He was one of the greatest living symphonists and much of his choral writing, most notably *Belshazzar's Feast*, had earned him enormous fame and respect. Since Walton was already a knight and had the Order of Merit, I decided that the best way of officially recognising and celebrating his birthday would be to 'hijack' John's party, and transfer it, on a larger scale, to 10 Downing Street. John and Mary Peyton generously fell in with this proposal. Invitations to this expanded event were, naturally, extended to those who had already been invited to the Peyton party, including Malcolm Arnold and his wife, my former Albany neighbours Lord and Lady (Kenneth) Clark and Lord and Lady Olivier.

Just before Christmas, I wrote to Her Majesty the Queen Mother, asking whether she would do us the honour of joining us. On New Year's Eve, Her Majesty wrote me a delightful reply from Sandringham, in her own hand, accepting the invitation and adding, 'I wonder if I shall be honoured with one of those warm embraces to which great conductors and composers seem prone! Somehow I don't think so – not this time!' We then pressed on with a complete guest list, which included Georg and Valerie Solti, Benjamin Britten and Peter Pears, the Menuhins, the great violist Lionel Tertis – then into his nineties – and his wife, and Sir Arthur Bliss, the Master of the Queen's Music. We began with a special grace composed for the occasion by Herbert Howells, to words written by my principal private secretary, Robert Armstrong. This was performed that evening by the Martin Neary Singers. It was sung again at every subsequent dinner which I gave at No. 10 and was later published by Novello as 'A Grace for 10 Downing Street'. For these purposes Robert Armstrong changed the final couplet – 'May William Walton happy be, In health and wealth and harmony' – to 'May those we welcome happy be, In pastime with good company', widening the piece's franchise somewhat.

Arthur Bliss and Paul Dehn, a good friend and past collaborator of Walton's, produced a special 'Ode for William Walton', and the Martin Neary Singers performed this superbly after dinner. They followed it with a performance of Walton's own *Song of Solomon*. Then, we sat around the horseshoe table as members of the London Sinfonietta, with Alvar Liddell narrating, performed ten movements from Walton's precocious work from the 1920s, *Façade*. After that, as midnight approached, we made our way into the pillared drawing room, where a surprise was awaiting my guests. I told them how, ten years earlier, I had heard Walton being asked in an interview whether there was any piece of music which he wished that he had composed himself. Without hesitation, he replied, 'Yes. Schubert's B Flat Trio.' So, with the Queen Mother sitting in a great chair and the Waltons on the sofa and the rest of us on the floor around them or perched wherever we could find a convenient spot, we listened to a performance of that work. It was played for us by the leader of the London Symphony Orchestra, John Georgiadis, and the first cello, Douglas Cummings, together with the English pianist John Lill. They had never before played together as a trio, but their performance that night was as co-ordinated as it was spontaneous. Finishing not long before 1 a.m., they provided a joyous ending to a memorable evening. A great occasion had been fashioned, in celebration of a great man.

At the beginning of 1971, the principal conductor of the London Symphony Orchestra, André Previn, asked me whether I would be willing to conduct a piece at the gala concert planned for the LSO that autumn. There can hardly be a musician anywhere who has not dreamed of conducting a celebrated symphony orchestra and I could not possibly refuse. After all, although I had rejected music as a profession, I had plenty of conducting experience, going right back to my teenage years, and I had always kept in touch with the world of music. I chose Edward Elgar's Overture 'Cockaigne' for my première performance, a bravura piece representing the London of Elgar's time. I was sure that the audience at such a special occasion would enjoy the piece, and set about familiarising myself with it – in particular its tricky opening and closing sections. In 1963, I had heard Leonard Bernstein and the New York Philharmonic play the work with breathtaking élan in the Festival Hall, and I hoped to be able to capture some of the brilliance that they had brought to it.

I was allocated an hour's rehearsal on the day before the concert and resolved to explain to the orchestra my conception of the piece, and what I wanted from them. Then we played the work – all seventeen minutes of it – fully through, before returning to a detailed analysis of any short-comings that I was able to identify. I was far too excited to be nervous, and went home feeling that we had done rather well, although I was aware that my conducting style must have seemed a little wooden. I had perhaps been rather overawed, facing a professional orchestra for the first time, but now felt sure that I had nothing to fear. The following morning's rehearsal was rather shorter than the length of the piece itself, and had to be squeezed in before a Cabinet meeting. In the afternoon, I had Prime Minister's Questions, then a Northern Ireland debate and some meetings back at No. 10. I left for the Royal Festival Hall about fifteen minutes before I was due to conduct, so I certainly did not have time to get nervous beforehand. André introduced me to the audience from the platform, adding that, in return for loaning me the LSO for fifteen minutes, he now expected to take over No. 10 for the same length of time. Then I was off. Rather to my own surprise, I remember quite a lot about the performance itself, in particular the later parts of 'Cockaigne', when I was really beginning to relax and enjoy myself. I well recall the sensation of power, the knowledge that this superb orchestra, this array of hugely talented musicians, would do anything I wanted. It is little wonder, I thought afterwards, that conductors have a reputation for becoming somewhat egotistical! The critics were extremely generous the following morning, and the recording of this concert, subsequently remastered for compact disc in 1996, sold all over the world for EMI.

The last musical evening I had at Chequers, on 27 October 1973, was disrupted by affairs in the Middle East, as the first had been. I had invited Isaac Stern to come again, this time with Pinchas Zukerman, to play a programme of violin duets. Because of the Yom Kippur War, Zukerman felt unable to come. Isaac came, however, and I asked the members of the Amadeus Quartet, whom I had invited as guests, to bring their instruments with them. They concluded the evening with a memorable performance of Haydn's String Quartet Opus 54 No. 2. In the first part, Isaac spoke very movingly about Pablo Casals, who had recently died, and put on a video of the very last piece he had played, at a concert in Israel. Isaac then began to play the Bach D minor Chaconne in his memory. After only a few bars the hairs on his bow broke, and he was obliged to go upstairs for another. He then started again and this time completed the performance without incident. The enforced interruption had increased the tension for Isaac as well as for the audience. The result was an unforgettable performance. After it was over, my private secretaries got hold of the broken hairs from the bow, had them preserved in a transparent plastic casing, and presented them to me as a reminder of the occasion.

As well as bringing my enthusiasm for music into No. 10 with me, I was also determined to carry on with my sailing, which I am still sure was the right thing to do. It did not distract me from my important duties – indeed it refreshed my body and spirit – and I thoroughly deplore the oft-expressed view that people in public life must allow their responsibilities totally to dominate their lives. That is good neither for the individuals concerned nor for the quality of governance. A year after I became Prime Minister, the second *Morning Cloud* was chosen for the Admiral's Cup team of three boats, and I was invited to become team captain, the only occasion on which a British Prime Minister has skippered a British team in an international sporting event. Harold Wilson demanded my presence in the House for an emergency debate on the first day of the Cup, but I made it down to Cowes in time after duly taking my place on the bench. During the long-distance Fastnet Race, our spinnaker boom was damaged and we were badly slowed down, but I cannot adequately describe in words our mounting excitement as we calculated that, despite everything, we had made it. We had won the Cup back for Britain. Receiving it was one of the most exciting moments of my life. It was a great triumph for Britain, and I was glad to have played my part.

Chapter 17

THE WORLD STAGE
Foreign Policy (Non-Europe) 1970–1974

As well as negotiating for our accession into the European Community, the government of 1970–4 had to deal with a rapidly changing international situation beyond our own continent. This was a period of increasing fluidity in relations between the five major power centres: the United States, the Soviet Union, China, Japan and Western Europe. It was also the era of detente and *Ostpolitik* and, in common with our allies, we wanted to achieve a reduction of tension in Europe through improved East–West relations, especially with Moscow. Perhaps the most radical development, however, was the emergence of the People's Republic of China, which dramatically altered the international balance of power. I was determined from the outset that we would be among the first to establish good relations with the Chinese, not least because of our substantial historical interests in the Far East and particularly in Hong Kong.

Throughout my time as Prime Minister, I was served loyally and supremely well by Alec Douglas-Home as Foreign Secretary. One story in particular illustrates Alec's characteristic modesty and charm. When de Gaulle died on 9 November 1970, a service – not strictly speaking his funeral, which was private, at Colombey-les-deux-Eglises – was held in Notre Dame in Paris, and heads of state and government from all over the world attended it. The day before the service Alec came in for a talk about some unrelated foreign policy issue. When we had completed that discussion, I said to him: 'Alec, we are going over to Paris tomorrow for the de Gaulle service. The Prince of Wales is coming, as are Anthony Eden, Harold Macmillan and Harold Wilson. Would you like to come too?' 'Oh, I don't think so, thank you,' he replied. 'With all those former Prime Ministers you won't need your Foreign Secretary.' 'But you are a former Prime Minister yourself, you know,' I reminded him. He laughed, almost giggled, as he said: 'Oh, so I am. I'd quite forgotten.'

When the Conservatives won the 1970 general election, one of the first, and most gratifying, messages of congratulation came from the great Russian cellist Mstislav Rostropovich – 'Slava' – who was staying at Aldeburgh in Suffolk. He sent a telegram, informing me that 'I am very happy that this country which I love so much has a musician as Prime Minister.' Unfortunately, this was not the view which the voters always took. Slava is not only the finest cellist of the second half of the century, following Casals in the first. He is also a revelatory conductor and a marvellous and courageous human being as a citizen of the world. At the time he wrote to me, his relations with the Soviet government were at a low ebb, as were those of the United Kingdom. It is very hard merely to like Slava after meeting him. He is so elemental that individuals across the globe have found it necessary to take him to their hearts. He has also been the friend of many of the century's greatest composers and performers, and has inspired a substantial number of masterpieces, well known and less well known. Without his virtuoso performing abilities, I doubt whether Shostakovich, Prokofiev, Britten, Schnittke and Lutosławski, to name but five geniuses, would have felt moved to write the works that they did for the cello repertoire. Slava was best known in this country for his work with Britten, and has long had many friends here. I was soon to learn, however, that even music could not be disentangled from politics in those Cold War days.

I had first met the Soviet Minister of Culture, the formidable Madame Furtseva, when I was Lord Privy Seal, back in the early 1960s, when she had accompanied the Bolshoi Ballet on the company's second visit to London. The British ambassador to Moscow, Sir Duncan Wilson, had met her on 15 June 1970, at the beginning of the week that saw me appointed as Prime Minister, to open negotiations on a series of 'Days of British Music', to take place in the Soviet Union the following spring. British musicians of the highest calibre had indicated that they were willing to take part, including Benjamin Britten, William Walton, Peter Pears, John Lill and the Allegri Quartet. The London Symphony Orchestra and André Previn were also available to play in Leningrad and Moscow, on their way to Japan. Britten wanted to conduct his own Cello Symphony and Piano Concerto, but only on condition that Slava and the Ukrainian pianist, Sviatoslav Richter, were the soloists.

The first performance of the Cello Symphony had taken place in Moscow seven years earlier, under Britten's own direction and with Slava as the soloist. Unfortunately, Rostropovich had embroiled himself in controversy at the end of 1969, by writing a letter to four national newspapers in which he condemned the attitude of the Soviet authorities towards Solzhenitsyn after the latter had been awarded the Nobel Peace prize. For a time, the Soviet authorities assumed that the letter was a fake, and all was well. Once Slava had willingly confessed to KGB agents who followed him to the Austrian town of Bregenz both that he had written the letter and that he would not retract a word of it, however, all hell broke loose. Although Slava made it to London in October 1970 to give the première of Witold Lutosławski's Cello Concerto and receive the Gold Medal of the Royal Philharmonic Society from Sir Arthur Bliss, he was banned by the authorities from performing outside the USSR for the first six months of 1971. His participation in the Days of British Music also came under threat. In the end, the tour did take place – and Britten, Rostropovich and Richter all played – but that was not the end of the story.

At the concert in Moscow on 20 April 1971, Madame Furtseva herself turned up, with the statutory enormous retinue and, during the perform-ance of the Cello Symphony, she proceeded to put on a conspicuous display of boredom, conversing with her staff in the row behind her and with her neighbour, apparently a lady spy from Goskonsert, the state concert agency. At the end of the performance, she left with a great flourish before the ovation had reached its climax, taking with her Vice-Minister Kozyrev and his wife. The authorities also made sure that invitations for Rostropovich and Richter to an official lunch with the British ambassador two days later never reached their destinations. Even in the world of the arts, the spiteful hand of the Communist Party was in evidence and this was all a reminder that the Cold War was also a war of attrition, pursued on every conceivable front.

In 1974, Rostropovich and his wife Galina Vishnevskaya left the Soviet Union, and he lost his Soviet citizenship in 1978. The concert he gave upon his return in 1990 was broadcast across the world, and represented both a victory for *glasnost* (openness) and a triumph of Slava's own courage. When pro-communist revolutionaries imprisoned Mikhail Gorbachev in his holiday cottage in the Crimea and tried to overthrow his government in August 1991, who else but Slava should appear on the barricades outside the Russian Parliament, alongside his friend Boris Yeltsin, once again fight-ing for the forces of freedom and democracy.

Although Slava always courageously stood up to the communist system, he also understood it very well indeed. Once when I was Prime Minister, he agreed to play at a special gala concert in London with Peter Pears and Benjamin Britten, at which Her Majesty the Queen Mother was to be the guest of honour. Two nights before the concert, I received a telegram at No. 10 from the great cellist. 'When I arrive at airport on Sunday for concert,' it read, 'passport not to be stamped.' It was signed 'Slava'. I could not understand what this meant, but told Robert Armstrong to do what he could with the authorities at Heathrow. 'It's all right,' he told me after a brief telephone conversation. 'They won't stamp the passport.' Slava duly arrived and, at the concert, all went supremely well. Then, at the reception afterwards, I took him to one side and asked him, 'What on earth was all that about?' 'Well,' he explained in his wonderfully idiosyncratic and inimitable English, 'I told in Paris Friday to return Moscow at once, so I send to Moscow a telegraph saying, "No, I must stay in Paris till Monday." So, tomorrow Paris, then I return Moscow.' 'But, Slava,' I protested, 'there will be a review of your concert in every newspaper in this country, and across Europe and in America. The Soviet authorities will see that you have been to London for this concert.' 'Yes,' he said, 'but for the Russians my passport not stamped – so I not here.'

Slava's all-too-evident fieriness is in complete contrast with the public image of another friend from the 1970s, Richard Nixon. To the world outside, Nixon may have appeared to be a rather cold man, entirely pre-occupied with politics and the maintenance of power. Yet underneath that stern and sometimes apparently mechanical personal reaction to people and friends, there was a pleasingly human side. I maintained warm relations with him throughout my premiership. One of the first messages of con-gratulation I received upon winning the 1970 general election came from him (see p. 307–8) and, shortly afterwards, I received a formal message, through the British ambassador in Washington, that the President would very much like me to come to the US for confidential talks at an early date. Given the volume of urgent domestic and European business facing us, I suggested that I should take up the invitation later in the year. Then Nixon discovered that he was able to stop over at Chequers on 3 October 1970 for a day of talks. To my immense delight, Her Majesty the Queen agreed to fly down from Scotland to lunch with us, the first occasion on which a reigning sovereign had been formally to Chequers.

Since we planned to have the US President and Her Majesty under the same roof, I suppose it was inevitable that tiresome security problems would ensue. A fortnight before the visit, American Secret Service men went round Chequers and the surrounding estate with the head of my own security staff. They were especially determined to investigate and secure the source of the house's water supply. With some delight, which they later claimed successfully to have disguised, my security men walked them up to the top of a nearby hill. One pointed out that the water probably came from a spring there. 'We must have someone posted here to guard it,' they said. Halfway down the hill, he indicated a large mound containing a tank. 'Yes, and we must have another man guarding this, too,' he announced. At the bottom of the hill, my head of security showed them the junction where the water supply came into the house. 'We must have another man protecting that,' he concluded at last. The logistical problems appeared to have become insurmountable and, in the discussions afterwards, they came to the conclusion that our water supply was so vulnerable that the only satisfactory solution was to fly in a special supply of water for the President. This could then be kept in a secure and cool place, in the kitchen at Chequers. This was duly done before the President arrived. Our talks were very useful, everyone seemed to enjoy the lunch and after tea he left to fly on to his next port of call. That evening one of our cooks shouted out to the chef, 'What are all these bottles of water doing here? Surely we can get rid of them?' Everybody had forgotten about the special measures taken to protect the President. He had drunk the same water as the rest of us and, thankfully, had survived.

President Nixon clearly wished to establish a close relationship with the new British government and emphasised that he hoped that each country would be able to discuss its policies with the other with complete freedom and frankness. My second official meeting as Prime Minister with him was at the White House, when I took him up on his invitation shortly before Christmas 1970. There was a festive air in Washington. It was a dull, coldish morning, but the welcome at the White House was warm-hearted and sincere. It was a happy blend of formality and informality: the formality of the guard of honour, the drill perfectly executed, and the playing of the national anthems; and the informality of the greetings from the welcoming crowd. The brief speeches contributed to this atmosphere, and the President and his wife took endless trouble to please their guests.

In my speech, I declared that I did not favour the suggestion of a 'special relationship' between our two countries. Such a relationship could be broken at a moment's notice by either partner. What was more, it could give offence to America's other allies, either in Europe or in Latin America. I believed in a natural relationship, the result of our common history and institutions, which nobody could take away from us.

This was fully accepted by President Nixon, who always got on well with the British and, indeed, with most Europeans. He firmly believed in the creation of a strong European Community as the basis for an effective NATO. He wanted the British to join the European Community, and certainly did everything possible, particularly behind the scenes, both to encourage us and to drum up support for us among the existing members of the Community. When on 22 January 1971 Nixon sent his 'warm personal regards', my advisers and I noticed with interest his statement that 'I look forward to continuing our dialogue and to further strengthening the *natural relationship* [my emphasis] between our countries and ourselves; and I hope you shall always feel yourself at home here in Washington.'

At the banquet on the night of my arrival in Washington, the food and wine were obviously chosen to please my tastes, and the American army choir sang carols. To my delight and surprise, my hosts had assembled a formidable gathering of my old friends, including Olin Stephens, the designer of *Morning Cloud*, and his brother. I had learned that the President would very much like to receive the six volumes of Winston Churchill's *The Second World War*, and I presented them privately to him. I had no inkling of what, if anything, was in store for me. After the toasts and the speeches at the banquet in the White House, Nixon announced that he wanted to make a small presentation. It proved to be a specially constructed half-model of my next *Morning Cloud* racing yacht based upon the designs of Olin Stephens, from which my own new boat was about to be constructed. No doubt Bus Mosbacher, Nixon's chief of protocol and skipper of the victorious *Defender* in the America's Cup, and a close friend of mine, had something to do with this. Later President Nixon presented me with a coloured portrait of himself at the wheel of a twelve-metre with Bus Mosbacher beside him, under which he had written the inscription, 'To His Excellency Prime Minister Edward Heath. In our line of work it's always good to have a second skill! Smooth sailing in your new boat. Richard Nixon'. At the reception later in the evening, the music was beautifully performed. As we passed the enormous Christmas tree in the hall, brightly lit with gifts crowding the floor around it, and said goodnight, it was difficult to see how such an occasion could have been better presented. Nixon went a long way to give pleasure to his friends. I stayed in Blair House, the official guest-house. No doubt Tony Blair particularly relished the opportunity of staying there.

The trip in December 1970 was an undoubted success. The *New York Daily News* declared that the visit 'marked the first time since the Eisenhower Administration that genuine personal friendliness has been enjoyed by the political leaders of the two nations. To accent any dispute between the two countries is to lose sight of this.' This continued throughout my premiership. President Nixon assured me that he would be careful not to embarrass the British government on the issues of Rhodesia and the supply of arms to South Africa. I was to follow the same policy during the war in the Middle East (see p. 501). So much for the claims by misinformed critics of recent times, including Ambassador Seitz.

One of the first formal meetings that I had as Prime Minister came when Burke Trend, the secretary of the Cabinet, discussed national security with me. With him were the head of MI5, responsible for internal security, the head of MI6, responsible for operating outside the country, and Sir Dick White, the first-ever Intelligence Coordinator in the Cabinet Office. I had first dealt directly with Dick White in 1961, when I was Lord Privy Seal at the Foreign Office and he was the Director General of the Secret Service, with regard to the case of George Blake. Almost a decade later, I was again much impressed by him. The head of MI5 was not so convincing. Having described his work, he told me that he had a particular point to make. His people had heard that a church organist was being sent from Poland to London to give a recital, to which I would be invited, in the hope that he could have an interview in order to obtain the latest political information from me. As I had never heard of the organist, nobody else was able to identify him and there was no evidence whatsoever of any such organ recital in London, this kind of nonsense hardly seemed to represent a fruitful way of occupying either my time or that of MI5. A more serious matter was their concern about Soviet espionage in Britain.

High-level political exchanges between Britain and Moscow had been lacking since the invasion of Czechoslovakia in 1968 and we had been far more reticent than other West European countries in renewing exchanges with the East. The UK was now conspicuously lagging behind our European partners in the 'bicycle race', a phrase coined by President Pompidou to indicate the way in which ministerial exchanges with the East were sometimes regarded. Meanwhile, the Soviets were hardly playing their part in reducing tension. Their spying activities were becoming as blatant as they were widespread, so I resolved to deal immediately with our security arrangements. For several years during Harold Wilson's administration, there had been allegations of contacts between members of the Labour Party and Moscow for no good purpose. Many of these accusations were totally unjustified, and Wilson and George Brown did make an effort to deal with any really dubious cases in their party membership. When I was informed in autumn 1970 that well over 100 of the 500 staff at the Soviet embassy were intelligence officers, however, I became convinced that firm and carefully prepared action now had to be taken. This clearly represented a real threat to our national security.

I immediately talked to Alec Douglas-Home about how the problem of Soviet espionage could be handled. Alec raised this matter with Gromyko when he visited London earlier that autumn. Gromyko's reply was terse and to the point. 'These figures you give cannot be true,' he said, 'because the Soviet Union has no spies.' On 3 December, Alec wrote to Gromyko, formally requesting that Soviet intelligence activity in the United Kingdom should be curbed. He received no reply. Intermittent expulsion of individual Soviet spies always led to retaliatory action by Moscow, but I became convinced that serious action was unavoidable, whatever the short-term consequences. I formed the view, supported by Alec Douglas-Home, that we should take a hard line and launch a full-scale crackdown without giving the Soviet authorities time to regroup.

The complement at the Soviets' London embassy was still twice the number of our staff in Moscow, and the Soviet Trade Delegation in Highgate, on which we applied no limit, was growing steadily. On 3 August 1971 I endorsed the Home–Maudling proposals for tough action in the autumn, despite concern that we might give the Soviets an excuse for destabilising the ongoing East–West negotiations about the future of Berlin, which were taking place at that time, and Alec Douglas-Home sent another robust letter to Gromyko the following day about Soviet espionage activities in the UK. As usual there was no direct response, but an uncompromising attack on me and our foreign policies appeared in *Pravda* at the end of the month, a development which proved that our message was getting through. Once the new Quadripartite Agreement on Berlin was signed in early September, I felt that it was time to act. This was confirmed when Alec Douglas-Home again spoke to Gromyko at the United Nations' September meeting after the expulsions had taken place, when this time Gromyko did admit that the Soviet Union had such agents, although claiming that they were no responsibility of his.

I chaired a ministerial meeting on 21 September 1971 at which the agreement of senior colleagues was obtained for the *démarche* on the spies, known as Operation FOOT. It was now planned for Friday 24 September. A total of 105 individuals was to be expelled. The Soviet embassy was then handed an *aide-mémoire* on the Friday setting out the names of those individuals. This document also explained the reasons for our actions, reinforcing the contents of Alec Douglas-Home's letters to Gromyko. We warned them that we would react quickly and decisively against any additional retaliatory actions on their part and suggested that we might do this through further curbing the numbers of their personnel, ending immunity for members of 'trade delegations', or tightening the limits on the movement of Soviet personnel in the UK. I told them that we had no intention of making this a high-profile operation and, provided they acted in the same way, there need be no international row. In order that we should not be accused of neglecting detente altogether, we expressed our hope that we might enjoy better relations in future on a sounder footing, less threatened by espionage.

A press conference was then held under the D Notice Procedure, which prohibited the media from publishing any of the information with which they were provided, a procedure which at that time was always fully observed. Having described in detail what was happening, we emphasised that in no circumstances were they to publish this information, unless the Soviet Union first made it public in Moscow or elsewhere. If that happened, they would be free to publish everything I had told them. In fact, Moscow exploded on receiving my message and the press immediately published everything that had been said. Alec Home and our permanent representative at the UN, Sir Colin Crowe, did a marvellous job in dealing with Gromyko, who was at the Soviet mission in New York at the time, although the Soviets were true to form, expelling 18 of our people from Moscow. The expulsion of 105 spies was the most important security action ever taken by any Western government. Moreover, it completely destroyed the large Soviet intelligence network which had previously been conducted from London.

Another case which the Secretary of the Cabinet subsequently brought to my notice was that of Sir Anthony Blunt. Blunt had confessed to being a Soviet agent in April 1964 and, as he was prepared to provide information about the intentions of his colleagues, no action was taken against him by the Attorney-General of the time and, in return for his confession and co-operation, he was granted immunity from prosecution. He was also allowed to keep his knighthood and to retain his position as Surveyor and, later, Adviser, for the Queen's Pictures. In February 1972, however, he appeared to be dying and the Secretary of the Cabinet rushed to give me the fullest possible information about him in case, after Blunt's death, his treachery became public knowledge from various sources. In fact, Blunt recovered and it was not until 1979 that he was exposed, four years before his death. Mrs Thatcher would later claim that she alone had been aware of the true situation and declared that, had she known earlier, she would have exposed him and deprived him of his knighthood and his living. We knew the true facts many years before. I remain of the view that the government of the day acted properly and in the national interest. It can be more productive to offer immunity, if that induces such individuals to make a confession and provide information helpful for counter-intelligence. That was also the consistent view of those responsible for our national security, and of Her Majesty's advisers on these matters.

Britain had other responsibilities too, away from superpower relations and Europe. The total population of the Commonwealth was about one-quarter of the population of the world and we always tried to ensure that their interests and views were respected. My own concept of the Commonwealth was expressed on 15 January 1971:

> To me it is a body of friends brought together by history, free to come and go as they wish, to contribute as much or as little as they can but always concerned, as all friends are, with one another's welfare. We should think carefully before allowing this friendship to be fragmented by misunderstandings. If this is not to happen we need to treat each other in the true manner of friends as we have in the past. We must

not seek to bind one another or deny others freedom of judgment and choice on matters each rightly reserves to himself.

During my trip to Balmoral in autumn 1970 (see p. 323), I discussed with the Queen and Prince Philip the question whether or not the Queen should go to Singapore for the forthcoming Commonwealth Conference in Singapore, which the Wilson government had arranged. This was to be the first occasion on which the Queen would be present at a full conference of Commonwealth countries outside London, apart from a limited and brief conference about Rhodesia held at Lagos, when Wilson was Prime Minister. For that event, the Queen had made an appearance on the royal yacht *Britannia*. I fully supported having these conferences in the capitals of Commonwealth countries, with London taking its turn in the rota and, for personal reasons, I was glad that this particular conference was to be held in Singapore.

I had developed close connections with Singapore over the previous ten years, since attending a Conference of British Ambassadors in Asian countries there in January 1961. By this time, I regarded Lee Kuan Yew, the Prime Minister of Singapore, as a friend, although he certainly has different views from my own on a number of matters, both political and economic. It also seemed to me to be appropriate that the Queen should give audiences at such a conference to each of her Prime Ministers in turn, as well as entertaining them all together at a banquet, normally on the royal yacht. They would all cherish such an opportunity.

It was obvious, however, that there were going to be major differences of opinion at Singapore between Britain and many of the other Commonwealth countries over the question of selling arms to South Africa. The 1955 Simonstown Agreement provided for co-operation between Britain and South Africa in the defence of the sea routes around the Cape of Good Hope, but in December 1967 the Labour government had announced that Britain would not supply arms to South Africa. It was highly unlikely that the South Africans would have been able to maintain the agreement unless the British government was prepared to resume some sales of maritime equipment. Labour's policy also had wider strategic consequences in view of the Soviet threat in the Indian Ocean. This area was of major importance to Britain and no Conservative government could have seriously considered reneging on the Simonstown Agreement at that time. We needed the assistance of the South African navy and had a legal obligation to complete the equipment of their frigates. During the last three years of the Wilson administration the South African government had taken no precipitate action, in the hope that there would be a change after the election. If we had continued with Wilson's policy, however, the South African government might well have retaliated by refusing to co-operate under the Simonstown Agreement, denying us the security arrangements that we sought.

The position of the Conservative government was that we were prepared to supply to South Africa arms which could be used for its external defence, but not those which could be used internally against the civil population. This formula was not perfect, of course, and we immediately became embroiled in controversy over which grouping helicopters should be placed into, especially as Britain was willing and able to supply them. Labour predictably claimed that even the selling of naval equipment to South Africa gave symbolic support to a discredited regime, but the same argument could then have been applied to all other trading with that country, which the previous government had actively encouraged. This undoubtedly caused friction within the Commonwealth. African Commonwealth countries were convinced that change in South Africa could come about only by imposing full economic sanctions and, if necessary, by force. They believed that this should be precipitated by cutting off the South Africans completely from the outside world. Presidents Kaunda of Zambia and Nyerere of Tanzania regarded themselves as at war with South Africa, and saw the military option as a short-cut towards majority rule. Our disagreement was not over the moral issue of apartheid, nor over the principle of 'one man, one vote'. It turned on how best to deal with the South African government. A racial war would only bring suffering and misery throughout a large part of the continent, especially to those who were most directly affected by apartheid policies. Commonwealth African leaders certainly accepted the sincerity of my personal opposition to apartheid, but they were largely indifferent to our wider strategic considerations.

The second main problem for Britain at the Commonwealth Conference was Rhodesia. The black African countries would not be satisfied with any constitutional solution except on the basis of majority rule within an agreed timescale of ten to fifteen years. Immediately after our general election victory, Alec Douglas-Home began trying to see if it was possible to get a settlement of the Rhodesian problem which would satisfy both the black and the white communities. The core of any sustainable settlement, of course, had to be progress towards majority rule. Alec asked the Rhodesian regime whether it would be willing to negotiate on the basis of a settlement which provided for the operation of a common electoral roll. If the regime accepted that principle, Alec thought that it would be possible to reach agreement. Smith, however, wanted to negotiate on the basis of the 1969 constitution, which provided for parallel rolls and looked no further than parity between blacks and whites. He would also negotiate only on the basis of recognised independence for Rhodesia. To this Alec rightly replied that no country in the world regarded Rhodesia as independent and the achievement of internationally recognised independence would depend upon an Act of Parliament at Westminster. Alec's original judgement was that the odds were against reaching a satisfactory agreement with the Smith regime.

After sterling preparatory work by Lord Goodman, however, Alec went over to Rhodesia in November 1971 and signed a provisional agreement with Ian Smith. Alec was convinced that this was the last chance for a reasoned settlement. When he was in Salisbury he had learned that Smith had been sitting on numerous Bills which, if passed, would have had the effect of putting Rhodesia firmly in the South African camp. As a result of the settlement these were suspended. Under the agreement, a number of important changes would have been introduced into the Rhodesian constitution, including a Higher African Roll, a strengthened Declaration of Rights to be enforceable in the courts and an effective mechanism preventing retrogressive amendment to the constitution. The possibility would have been created for the Africans to achieve majority representation in the Rhodesian legislature, rather than parity of representation, which was the most for which the existing constitution provided.

The most crucial principle, on which successive British governments had believed any settlement must be based, was that 'any proposed basis for independence was acceptable to the Rhodesian people as a whole'. Alec had spent many days before meeting Smith seeking the opinions of a spectrum of Rhodesians, black and white, to the suggestions he was making. The extreme African nationalists, such as Joshua Nkomo, had told him that Britain had a duty to use force against the Smith regime and that for this reason they could not support a negotiated settlement. But the moderate Africans appeared receptive to, if not enthusiastic about, Alec's proposals. We therefore established an independent commission, under the chairmanship of Lord Pearce, a former Lord of Appeal and latterly independent chairman of the Press Council, to assess attitudes towards the settlement. Members of the Pearce Commission spent two months from January 1972 working together in both Rhodesia and London, and it soon became apparent that black opinion was strongly hostile to the terms of the proposed settlement. On 23 May 1972 the Commission concluded:

> We are satisfied on our evidence that the proposals are acceptable to the great majority of Europeans. We are equally satisfied, after considering all our evidence including that on intimidation, that the majority of Africans rejected the proposals. In our opinion the people of Rhodesia as a whole do not regard the proposals as acceptable as a basis for independence.

Neither Alec nor I could hide our disappointment at the report's conclusions and I felt extremely sorry that all his valiant efforts had been in vain. Our only option was to maintain the status quo and sustain sanctions. A lasting solution was not reached until 1979.

The fear of my senior colleagues and myself before the Singapore Conference of 1971, which I expressed in person to Her Majesty, was that, if these issues did ignite during the conference, and it seemed very likely that they would, then the Queen might well become involved against her will in controversy. Indeed, some African countries were already threatening to leave the Commonwealth over the question of South Africa and Rhodesia. In that instance, the ensuing publicity would be deeply embarrassing for her and for all of us. I was uncomfortably aware that a royal visit to other countries in that area had been proposed for a long time, alongside Her Majesty's appearance at the conference, and that her visits to Thailand and Malaysia, arrangements for which also predated the election of June 1970, would have to be postponed if she did not go to Singapore.

The Queen rightly pointed out that, if the conference had been in London, she would certainly have had to be there, and the situation would have been no less explosive. Therefore, the possibility of it being explosive in Singapore did not seem to her to be a conclusive reason for not going. The main consideration seemed to be whether her presence would, in fact, be of use to the Commonwealth. I could well understand her point. However, in my experience, Commonwealth conferences held in London have a completely different atmosphere from those elsewhere, due very largely to the impact of London itself as a great capital city, and to the atmosphere of the buildings in which all the meetings are held. Moreover, the Queen's permanent residence in Buckingham Palace, or close by at Windsor Castle, makes everyone most reluctant to be the cause of any embarrassment to her, however small.

On balance, I thought it was right to formalise my views into written advice and I sent a letter to Her Majesty on 15 October 1970 advising her against going, on the grounds that 'the risks of criticism and embarrassment in these circumstances would not be confined to Your Majesty's Ministers but might extend to Your Majesty . . . I am bound therefore to advise against your going, although I do so with considerable personal regret.' On 20 October, Michael Adeane, the Queen's private secretary, wrote back, informing me that 'Her Majesty's object in being present would be to assist the interests of the Commonwealth; as it seems probable that her presence on this occasion might well lead to controversy and embarrassment, she agrees that it would be better to stay away.'

The conference did indeed turn out to be unruly, despite excellent chairmanship from Harry Lee. The leaders of the three major African countries were determined to force their own will on British policy. I believe that this was due not only to the conflict over our policy towards South Africa. It was also an attempt to bully Britain out of carrying through the European policy on which we had embarked. Nor did these larger countries hesitate to lord it over the smaller members of the Commonwealth. They did so to such an extent that the President of Malawi, making his speech towards the end of the conference, bitterly condemned his colleagues and, with a wave of his stick and a flurry of feathers, departed the hall, and the conference, for good. My colleagues and I were proven right in the advice that we had given to the Queen. Those who have since claimed that I was keeping her away from the Singapore Conference because of my supposed dislike of the Commonwealth, and a wish to concentrate on our European policy, could not be more wrong. Nor has anyone ever been able to present a credible argument justifying the presence of Her Majesty at a time of such conflict. In their audiences with her, the Prime Ministers would have been put into impossible positions, finding themselves unable to express their true views, or to take sides in the disagreement. I have always been glad that we saved the Queen from such political and personal unpleasantnesses. Nonetheless, some good came out of the conference, in particular a Declaration of Principles and Values, including a section on the 'dangerous sickness' of racial prejudice. This Declaration represented something of a landmark, and was not superseded until the Harare Declaration of 1991.

During the conference, I entertained the Prime Ministers of Australia, New Zealand, Malaysia and Singapore to dinner on board HMS *Intrepid* in the harbour. Peter Carrington had successfully negotiated the new Five Power Defence Agreement (ANZUK) with their countries and, as a consequence, the withdrawal of our naval and military forces from Singapore was shortly to begin. It was very moving when a Royal Marine band beat the retreat on the flight deck after dinner, with floodlights playing on the red ensign and on the bandsmen as they marched to and fro in their topees, with other ships of the Royal Navy all around the harbour in the darkness fully dressed and lit. I do not think that anyone there can have listened dry-eyed to the Last Post, as we all reflected on the fact that, within a few weeks, those ships would have sailed out of Singapore for the last time, and the whole chapter of the British presence there would be ended.

There was a sequel to this dinner. When we got back to London, the Ministry of Defence sent us a bill which could not have been larger if we had all been dining at one of the most expensive restaurants in London or Paris. I gave instructions for this bill to be queried. It turned out that, in their keenness to make sure that the occasion went well, the officers and crew of HMS *Intrepid* had had a dress rehearsal, with the same dinner given to the same number of people (all officers and crew of the ship) and the same wines. The bill for this dress rehearsal was then added to the bill for the dinner itself. It took a good deal of patient and tough negotiation with the Ministry of Defence to sort this matter out to my satisfaction.

The situation in the Middle East required even more skilful negotiation. The Labour government of 1966–70 had given the undertaking to withdraw from the Gulf, and there was no way in which that decision could be reversed. I had made a tour of the Gulf in 1968, as Leader of the Opposition, and endeavoured to persuade the Shah of Iran and other rulers in the region that a Conservative government should be able to reverse the policy. They all responded in the same terms. They were very sorry, but all of their plans for the future were now based upon the assumption that Britain would be withdrawing. Moreover, the US administration of President Johnson was in favour of the Labour policy. They were telling the Gulf rulers, including the Shah, that they should now take care of themselves. This explained the great build-up in the Shah's forces at the time. We tried to develop a new relationship with the Gulf states, culminating in the treaties of friendship with the Union of the Trucial states (six territories, namely Abu Dhabi, Dubai, Sharjah, Ajman, Umm al Qaiwan and Fujairah), as well as with Bahrain and Qatar, on 14 December 1971. Relations between Britain and the two major players in the region, Iran and Saudi Arabia, developed enormously as a result.

At the end of the argumentative, rather unpleasant and tiring penultimate day in Singapore, our delegation moved towards the great door of the hall only to find that it was being blocked by the television crew who were interviewing the President of Uganda, Milton Obote. We therefore moved back a step or two to let him finish. We heard him saying, 'Yes, Heath is finished, absolutely finished, we have written him off. We have got our own way and he is a failure,' upon which complimentary note he waved to the television crew and left. We then went up to have lunch and returned for the afternoon session. That evening at Lee Kuan Yew's farewell dinner we sat around our tables and I noticed an empty seat at our own. Harry Lee told me that Dr Obote had departed, and I thought no more of the matter.

On the evening of the day after I had returned from Singapore I was in the sitting room in the flat at No. 10, reading the papers in my box and listening to some music, when Robert Armstrong came in. He said that he knew that I had suffered a disagreeable time at Singapore, not least at the hands of Dr Obote. At least, unlike Dr Obote, he said, I had got safely back home and was still Prime Minister. I asked him what he was going on about. He informed me that there had been a successful coup in Uganda, and Obote had been overthrown. I indicated that I was not wholly displeased to hear it, and asked who had taken his place, and what we knew about him. 'A Colonel Amin,' Robert Armstrong said. 'The Foreign Office don't seem to know anything about him, but I have spoken to an officer in the Ministry of Defence who served in the King's African Rifles. He says that he knows Amin, and he was the best sergeant he ever had.'

Two or three months later we got a message saying that Idi Amin proposed to pay a visit to the United Kingdom and would greatly value talks with myself and members of the government. He would also like to be received by the Queen. We made all the necessary arrangements and, when he arrived at No. 10 for dinner on 12 July 1971, he and his colleagues presented an impressive, smart, uniformed appearance. We talked during dinner and, afterwards, he said he would like to discuss Uganda's problems with the Foreign Secretary, so I asked Alec Douglas-Home to take him into the White Drawing Room after coffee, to see what he had to say. The rest of us carried on and, just before eleven o'clock, I noticed Amin's aide-de-camp going down to where the President and Alec Douglas-Home were talking, to point out that the time had come to leave. I saw Amin down to the front door and, promptly at eleven o'clock, he left the house. The rest of our guests followed and then, in our usual way, Alec and I went upstairs to relax and waited for Robert Armstrong to bring the whisky. When it arrived Alec said, 'You know, that Idi Amin is mad.' 'Good heavens,' I said. 'What makes you say that?' 'Well, he told me that he wished to discuss the question of the relationship between the People's Republic of China and Uganda, so I asked him what the problem was. He asserted that Uganda was about to be invaded by the Chinese navy and he wanted our military support to repel the invasion. I did not get into any details about how the Chinese were going to invade Uganda, pointing out that, since we had given up our colonial position in Africa, we no longer provided forces for the protection of individual countries, although of course we would like to be kept informed of Chinese intentions and how they were going to carry out the invasion. With that he left.'

Later that year, when President Tito of Yugoslavia was on his way back from a trip to North America, I invited him to stop over in the United Kingdom. He accepted, and came with his wife to Chequers for a dinner. The following day, after our talks, he had lunch with Her Majesty the Queen at Buckingham Palace. I had first met him in 1953, when he accepted an invitation from Eden to come to London, and he had not been back since. That was quite a controversial occasion because of Tito's communist background, but great emphasis was laid on the fact that Yugoslavia had remained independent of the Soviet empire, thanks to the fact that Tito had come to power by his own feat of arms – many of them supplied by Britain. He was certainly an impressive character, and I could well understand how he inspired such fierce loyalty.

At Chequers in November 1971, we discussed the international situation, particularly with regard to Soviet policy and its effect on Yugoslavia. I told him that he looked in good health and was still obviously strong, but what was likely to happen as the years passed? He replied that we had nothing to fear. He had bound the constituent parts of Yugoslavia so tightly together that they would never break apart. 'You look doubtful,' he said. 'But remember, alongside our mountain border we have Soviet territory and we are never going to let the Soviets into Yugoslavia.' That was reassuring. Of course, he could not foresee the collapse of the Soviet empire and the extent to which it would free the various parts of his country from the bonds which tied them together. The following year, 1972, Tito was to celebrate his eightieth birthday. At first, the Yugoslavs indicated that they regarded this as a Yugoslav, not an international, celebration, so the diplomatic community in Belgrade agreed that no gifts would be given. Then the Germans broke ranks, sending eighty bottles of wine, rather a futile gesture since Tito had given it up years before. This opened the floodgates. The Swiss sent a platinum watch, the Australians, I think, sent a painting – and the Belgians sent a shotgun! I had found at Chequers that Tito would only drink Scotch whisky, and of that stimulant he would only drink Chivas Regal. So we sent him two cases of this and, thereafter, I sent him a further case each year on his birthday, which helped us to maintain good relations until his death in 1980.

When it came to my turn to entertain President Nixon for discussions at Christmas 1971, I invited him to Bermuda, which neither of us had visited before. We both stayed at Government House and, for our final session, the complete delegation sat round the table which had previously been used by Churchill and Eisenhower and, later, by Macmillan and Kennedy. The Governor, Lord Martonmere, told me slightly apologetically that he hoped I would not mind having the second-best suite of guest rooms. I insisted that he was quite right to give the President the best, and he need not concern himself any further. He persisted, however, and said that he had an even deeper apology to make. My bathroom was not absolutely immaculate. Once we got to my suite, he pointed to the ceiling, which had obviously been hastily patched up. 'I am afraid that happened,' he explained pleadingly, 'when the President's security men insisted on going all over the attic. Unfortunately, one of them put both feet down too heavily and came straight through the ceiling and into the bath.' In the light of events since then I have wondered whether the Secret Serviceman's sole interest was in checking the attic, or whether the CIA had really wished to establish some covert means of recording what I sang in my bath.

I entertained the President and his colleagues to dinner on board HMS *Glamorgan*. Bermuda was delighted to have a ship of this size docked in its own harbour, along with her accompanying frigates. I am not sure that the navy was quite so pleased. It was only afterwards that I learned that *Glamorgan* had been in Mombasa preparing to spend Christmas there when she had suddenly been instructed to sail under sealed orders. Their final instructions brought them to Bermuda. Meanwhile many wives and girl-friends were on chartered aircraft flying to Mombasa hoping to spend Christmas with their loved ones. It must have been a bitter disappointment all round but, needless to say, the reception and banquet provided by the navy outshone anything else that could possibly have been arranged. After our return home, I suggested to Peter Carrington that the Ministry of Defence should compensate the families for what had proved to be pointless journeys. He explained that he could do nothing to help. 'The services are there to carry out orders,' he said. 'What their families do is their affair.' Unfortunately, there was nothing more to be said.

The President and I focused our discussions on the profound changes in world politics. He had visits planned for both Beijing and Moscow. I fully approved of these developments, particularly the need to open up relations with the People's Republic of China. To achieve this, Nixon had to overcome the opposition of a powerful lobby on behalf of Taiwan, the 'rogue province', particularly on the West Coast of America and within Congress. It may well have been because of his associations with California that Nixon foresaw the growing importance of the Pacific Basin and realised that it was going to become necessary to influence Beijing politically, and do business with the largest country in the world. The Chinese leadership also respected him, in particular because of his robustness towards the Russians.

We also discussed the tensions that had escalated on the Indian sub-continent, culminating in full-scale war between India and Pakistan in December 1971. The trouble had started in March after the Pakistani army had acted to quell disorder in what was then the Province of East Pakistan. As a result, an estimated 10 million people left the province for the Indian state of West Bengal, creating enormous problems for the Indian govern-ment. Britain contributed £14 million of relief aid to India, the second largest donation after that of the United States. Given the links between Britain and the sub-continent, it was inevitable that strong feelings were aroused in this country. There was never any question, however, of outside interference in the internal affairs of an independent Commonwealth country. The US took rather a different view. In August 1971, the Soviet–

Indian Friendship Treaty had been signed and the Americans were concerned that the Soviet Union was stirring up trouble in the region. Our assessment was that the Indian government had taken advantage of Soviet interests to conclude a treaty of convenience with the USSR, in response to the developing links between Pakistan and China. After hostilities commenced between India and Pakistan, there was a real danger of the two superpowers being dragged into the conflict. This was defused when the Pakistan army in the east surrendered to joint Indian–Bangladeshi forces within only two weeks.

At one point in our discussion during the morning in Bermuda, Nixon said to Kissinger, 'Well, Henry, we had our differences of opinion over the Indo-Pakistan War. Will you explain to Ted why we pursued the policy we did? He may then like to comment on it.'

'Yes,' began Henry. 'In that war, Pakistan was supported by China, and India by the Soviet Union. Pakistan was weaker than India, and China weaker than the Soviet Union. You had the two weaker countries lined up against the two stronger ones. We supported the two weaker nations so as to restore the balance and prevent them being overwhelmed, which would have been against our own interests. That, if I may say so,' added Kissinger, 'has been British policy throughout the ages.'

'What do you think about that, Ted?' asked Nixon.

'Henry,' I replied, 'is of course historically correct, with one exception. We never supported the weaker partners if we thought that all three of us would lose. That is what would have happened in this last Indo-Pakistan War.'

'Well,' concluded Nixon, 'that's that.'

On 29 February 1972, Alec Douglas-Home circulated a memorandum on British policy towards the Soviet Union and Central and Eastern Europe. He reported that there were now strong commercial and political reasons for adopting a more positive policy towards the East than had been possible in the past. Our exports to the communist bloc compared unfavourably with those of our main European competitors, and the Department of Trade and Industry certainly believed that the political coolness between London and Moscow since the Soviet invasion of Czechoslovakia in 1968 markedly contributed to poor British exports to the Soviet Union in subsequent years. Alec was never fooled by Soviet propaganda but he did accept that there might be political disadvantages in our holding aloof from bilateral contacts with Eastern Europe. We were handicapped in the 'bicycle race' for several reasons. The UK lacked the superpower status of the US and the perceived independence of the French. Meanwhile, Willy Brandt in Germany was busy pursuing his policy of *Ostpolitik*. Alec warned in his memorandum that 'In the absence of a comprehensive and positive policy of contacts, our relations tend to be overshadowed by negative events which capture the headlines . . . we need in 1972–3 to play an active and conspicuous part in East–West relations, in order to be in a position to influence the preparations for the Conference on Security and Co-operation in Europe, the Conference itself and the developments which could follow.'

Our ambassador in Moscow, Sir John Killick, had resumed normal contacts with the Soviet Foreign Ministry as soon as the furore over the Soviet spies had ended, but the atmosphere at the London end remained lukewarm for a year or so, after which the Soviets appointed a new ambassador. He asked to see me directly after his arrival. He exuded friendliness and presented a twelve-page memorandum of goodwill from his superiors. He then did the same thing twice more in quick succession, after which I had to insist that he should present such documents to the Foreign Secretary. In July 1972, we received a further sign that the freeze in relations was over. Victor Hochhauser, the impresario, heard from Moscow that Dmitri Shostakovich, the distinguished composer, wanted to visit Britain after receiving an honorary degree in music at Trinity College in Dublin. Shostakovich had also expressed an interest in meeting the press while he was here. Benjamin Britten invited him to stay, and Britten and Hochhauser arranged an interview with a reliable music critic. I received him as a guest of honour at No. 10 on 11 July.

I had discussed East–West relations and the proposed Conference on Security and Co-operation in Europe (CSCE) during talks with President Pompidou at Chequers in March 1972. The holding of such a conference was a Soviet initiative of some twenty years' standing and European governments and the US administration were originally rather suspicious of the Soviets' motives. We all knew that such a conference could result in strengthened Soviet hegemony over Eastern Europe, through the recognition of post-war divisions, while exposing divisions within the Western alliance. Other trends exacerbated these fears. Soviet armed forces had continued to increase and had reached parity with those of the United States, which in turn was showing signs of weakening resolution, stemming in part from the Vietnam War. The Nixon administration seemed likely to honour its obligations to Europe, but the trend of US opinion in the years ahead was less certain.

In October 1972, Peter Carrington had a meeting with his US opposite number, Melvin Laird, who suggested that the US might only maintain forces in Europe at present levels if European governments contributed a greater share of the economic burden. Peter, quite rightly, did not respond to this proposition, although he was extremely concerned by the deterioration in confidence between the US and Europe in the defence field.

'The root of this,' he wrote in a minute of 29 November 1972, 'was the impression of the European members of NATO that the Americans are now viewing the international scene increasingly in terms of their super-power relationship with the USSR, and that they may be prepared to subordinate the interests of their European allies.' A combination of increased Soviet military strength, diminished Western vigilance and reduced American commitment could lay Western Europe wide open to Soviet political domination. My feeling was that the security of Europe would depend on both the maintenance of the US commitment and increased co-operation between Western European governments over the question of European defence.

I had suggested in the late 1960s that an Anglo-French strategic nuclear deterrent should be formed and held in trust for the European members of NATO. Pompidou told me then that there was no point in pursuing the idea, as we were in opposition and he felt the Labour government was not fundamentally interested in the defence of Europe. Our election victory in 1970 provided an opportunity to bring France nearer to NATO once again, if not right back into the organisation. There were already signs that French defence policy was becoming more open, more flexible and less aggressively independent, and it seemed conceivable that we might be able to approach the idea of Anglo-French nuclear co-operation gradually and by successive steps of discussion and exploration. I discussed this possibility with President Nixon at Camp David, the presidential country retreat, on 18 December 1970. Nixon, much to the consternation of Kissinger, commented, 'You should feel that you have a great deal of running room on this . . . if exploratory discussions were to show that the concept of Anglo-French nuclear collaboration could be used for this purpose, then it would have American support.' After the meeting Kissinger spoke to Burke Trend privately in order to emphasise the risks which the President would be taking with American public opinion if he appeared to be lending his authority to any project of this kind. Such co-operation was therefore always a long-term prospect and unlikely to come about in the immediate future.

We did all agree, however, that if there was to be a CSCE it was essential that the Western European powers be firmly lined up together, in their resolve to maintain their genuine security. Proper co-ordination was needed if we were to examine seriously the question of mutual and balanced force reductions (MBFR). One of the conditions for the opening of the preparatory talks for a Security Conference was that there should be parallel talks on force reductions in Central Europe. That was agreed by the Russians in September 1972. Pompidou concurred with my views. He told me that when he had visited the Soviet Union he had been struck not only by the Soviets' strength but by the emphatic way in which they drew attention to it. Pompidou was also impressed that the countries which had pestered France to accept the Security Conference – such as Rumania, Yugoslavia and even, to some extent, Poland – were seeking some protection against Soviet domination and some assurance against being treated in the same brutal way as Czechoslovakia.

The West slowly moved towards a more constructive attitude as we approached the European security conference. Detente made such a conference inevitable and, through the Davignon machinery for European Political Co-operation (see p. 361), which we joined fully in February 1972, we worked with our European partners for a common approach. Negotiations commenced on 22 November 1972 in Helsinki and six months later the agenda for a conference was agreed. The agenda, in fact, represented a diplomatic triumph for the West, as it was widened to include security and economic and technical co-operation between the two blocs. Alec Douglas-Home had a large part to play in the subsequent negotiations, which ran in Helsinki during 3–7 July 1973. They were preceded, on 2 July, by a reception and dinner which I gave at No. 10 to celebrate Alec's 70th birthday. The dinner was attended by (among others) the French Foreign Minister, Michel Jobert, and the US Secretary of State, William Rogers. Dean Rusk, who had been Secretary of State in the Kennedy and Johnson administrations, was unable to attend. Instead he sent a letter, which I read out at dinner, praising Alec's 'personal integrity, his intellectual honesty, his eloquent and forceful advocacy of the attitudes of Her Majesty's Government, his simplicity and modesty of manner with high and low, his urbanity in crisis and good humour in disagreement'. There could not have been a more appropriate tribute. It was left to the Labour government, however, to finish the negotiations and sign the Helsinki Accords in 1975. The thirty-five signatories endorsed the post-war frontiers in Europe, pledged to respect human rights and allowed for economic, social and scientific co-operation between East and West. Agreement on MBFR proved more elusive. The reduction of military forces in Poland, Czechoslovakia, the Benelux countries and the two Germanies was laudable in theory, but became quite impossible to achieve in practice. Talks between the Warsaw Pact and NATO started in 1973, but a breakthrough was only reached in 1989, when the twenty-three nations of NATO and the Warsaw Pact met in Vienna to cut their non-nuclear weapons forces.

Both CSCE and MBFR were very difficult negotiations, of vast complexity and involving a host of players on the Western side. We achieved our objectives in both sets of negotiations, but most people would now agree that the CSCE turned out to be the more advantageous, as it brought communist recognition of certain principles of behaviour and human rights which had much to do with the unravelling of communist control of Eastern and Central Europe in the years which followed. This was a tremendous diplomatic achievement, probably the most significant since the drafting of the UN Charter in San Francisco in 1945.

Despite the rather inauspicious beginning, diplomatic relations between Britain and the Soviet Union improved tremendously from 1972, culminating in a visit to Moscow by Alec Douglas-Home from 2 to 5 December 1973. After his talks with Andrei Gromyko, a communiqué was issued noting the improvement in relations between the two countries which had 'underlined the importance of continuing and expanding political contacts and consultations at various levels with a view to giving them a regular character'. I gladly accepted an invitation to visit the USSR, although domestic events in 1974 made this impossible. The Conservative government's approach to detente and the Soviet Union was both firm and constructive, which even Moscow itself acknowledged.

In the event, the only country that came close to declaring war on the United Kingdom while I was Prime Minister was Iceland. Iceland was a fringe member of NATO, albeit with strategic importance, which felt aggrieved at the treatment that it was receiving from the Western world. It also had a recently elected, stridently left-wing government, and we in Britain were the focus for its discontents. We had been involved in a fishing dispute, a so-called 'cod war', with Iceland in the early 1960s, when Alec Douglas-Home had settled matters amicably, but the issue was now getting up a head of steam again. By the early 1970s, the well-established international twelve-mile limit was proving inadequate for Iceland's economic needs, and it was facing a serious problem of stock depletion. When the Icelanders unilaterally extended their intended fishing limits to fifty miles, I knew at once that their action was unacceptable. We would have lost out either from a bilateral agreement to this or from a general extension of fishing limits to fifty miles. In April 1972, together with West Germany, we referred this dispute to the International Court. The Court issued an interim order four months later which called upon Iceland not to enforce its new regulations for a fifty-mile limit, as well as instructing British vessels to limit their catch to 170,000 tonnes per annum.

Despite our adherence to the agreement, Iceland extended its limit on 1 September 1972 and began harassing British trawlers. As a sailor myself, I was certainly not prepared to see seamen victimised in this way. On 12 May 1973, with the full agreement of the British deep-water fishing industry, I ordered the Royal Navy to protect our trawlers in their traditional fishing grounds in the high seas. During discussions with the Icelandic

Prime Minister at No. 10 on 15 and 16 October 1973 an agreement of sorts was reached. This would last two years and was without prejudice to the legal rights of either government in relation to the substantive dispute. The main provision was for reductions in the number of British trawlers fishing in the disputed area and restrictions on the area in which they would operate. The area restrictions provided, broadly, that one-sixth of the disputed area was closed to British trawlers at any one time, although a substantial British trawler fleet was able to operate freely, without fear of harassment, in the major part of the disputed area. This was immediately welcomed by the British fishing industry. The 'cease-fire' proved to be only temporary and the 'cod war' was to return three years later.

In these circumstances we had to look for a broader opportunity for our major fishing fleet. I asked Joe Godber, our Minister of Agriculture, to organise a reconnaissance group to explore the seas west of Latin America to find out what opportunities existed there. We saw no point in investigating the position in the seas off the west or south-west African coast because we knew these were being exploited continuously by the Russian and South African fleets. It was already said that the sea off Namibia, not yet independent, and particularly the area of Walvis Bay, had already been so exploited that the fish stocks there were almost exhausted.

The report which came back from the reconnaissance group emphasised that there were excellent offshore supplies in the area they had covered, and these existed outside the international fishing limits as they were then drawn. These grounds were certainly some distance from home, but they were closer than some of the waters covered by the fleets of other offshore fishing countries. Big boats would certainly be required, but some of these existed in our Icelandic fleet, and building new ones would give our shipyards a fresh boost. The only disadvantage, the members of the group confided to some of us, was that the fish, although they were perfectly nutritious, came from a great depth and were sometimes hideous to look at. This, however, could be dealt with once they were landed on board, where they could be trimmed before being frozen. All this information was duly passed on to the fishing companies, but it emerged that, although garnering fish from the very deep sea did offer some commercial opportunities, stocks were extremely limited and such fishing seemed unlikely to prove sustainable.

On my second visit to the White House as Prime Minister, in February 1973, I again enjoyed the luxury of staying at Blair House, which had then been completely refurbished. I used a room named in honour of President Eisenhower, containing many of his former possessions. Along with the Cabinet secretary, the number two from the Foreign Office and my private secretary, I flew with the President and his staff by helicopter to Camp David. On the way, we came down and paid a visit to Mamie Eisenhower, the President's widow, at her home. As we approached Camp David, I could see the extent to which it was protected by high fencing, patrolled by guards and lit by searchlights. I could not help comparing this with the arrangements at Chequers. There the grounds were surrounded by a hedge, with a public footpath running across the garden of the house, which had a low wall around it.

The atmosphere once we were safely inside Camp David, however, was completely informal. The log cabin I used, with bedroom and sitting room, bathroom and every other amenity, was extremely comfortable and very attractive, as was the main cabin in which we held our talks and dined that evening. It was relaxing, and conducive to a real exchange of views with just half a dozen people being able to sit around and let their minds roam over world problems: President Nixon and myself, the British Foreign Secretary and the US Secretary of State, and our two ambassadors.

Richard Nixon deserves enormous credit for his foresight in opening up relations between the United States and the People's Republic of China and, above all, for facing reality in South-East Asia and removing American forces from Vietnam. In the Middle East, his administration worked untiringly to establish a secure position for Israel and a peaceful relationship with the Arab world. Theirs was an even-handed approach until the outbreak of the Yom Kippur War in 1973, when the US administration felt itself obliged to support Israel. However, Nixon never changed his view that in the long term the Israelis and the Arabs would have to live together on an equal footing.

In every respect, US foreign policy was driven forward by Henry Kissinger, a most effective operator whose diplomatic activities were carried out with complete loyalty to the President. The West as a whole, as well as his own country, owes an immense debt to him. I have never, however, understood Kissinger's failure to appreciate how Europeans react to matters affecting their own continent. He was born in Germany, so one might think that his would be a European personality with a highly developed American veneer. This is far from being the case. Indeed, so determined is he to be American that I have, on occasions, heard him refuse to speak German in interviews on German soil. It was this lack of sensitivity which led to his mistaken creation of the 'Year of Europe', which made a sudden emergence into international phraseology in 1973.

Although I had always told Henry that I thought it would be a splendid idea for the United States to show its support for the development of the European Community jointly with all the Europeans, we first heard about his idea for a Year of Europe indirectly. He discussed it first with the French, giving them strict instructions that it was to be kept secret for the time being from all the others concerned. To their great credit, the French informed their closest European partners, thus returning the compliment of 'l'affaire Soames' (see p. 359). Neither we nor the French were amused by this intervention, nor were our other European colleagues as they got to hear about it. When I next saw Henry, I enquired whether he really thought it was the responsibility of the Americans to organise a Year of Europe. For Henry Kissinger to announce a Year of Europe without consulting any of us was rather like my standing between the lions in Trafalgar Square and announcing that we were embarking on a year to save America!

What a tragedy it is that Watergate should have wiped Richard Nixon's achievements from the public mind, and will probably go on unbalancing the judgement of historians as well. Of course, it will always be impossible to dissociate Nixon totally from the unhappy events that led to his downfall, but it would be quite wrong for posterity to judge him purely by the Watergate Affair. There was so much more to him than that. Mao Tse-tung asked me, 'What is all this Nixon nonsense about?' 'What do you mean by "Nixon nonsense"?' I enquired. 'Well, they say he bugged his opponents, don't they? But we all bug our opponents, don't we, and everybody knows it? So what is all this fuss about?'

My next visit to a President at the White House was to Gerald Ford in September 1974. It was two days after he had announced the pardon for President Nixon. He had obviously passed through a period of intense anguish over his decision but, having made it, he was calm and quietly resolved to see it through. How much had changed since I last sat in the Oval Office. How strange the sequence of events seemed. It had never occurred to me for a moment that my conversations with the former President were being taped. In fact I do not know if they were. Furthermore, there were never any outbursts of indignation, or explosions of expletives, on these occasions. As for all the other characters in the Watergate drama, to my knowledge they never appeared during my visits. Their names meant nothing to me. What did matter were the various agreements on foreign policy I reached with the President during our talks, which were of vital importance for both our countries, and for Europe and the Western alliance. On my second visit to China in 1975, Mao Tse-tung asked me whether, if it came to any real test with the Russians, President Ford would take firm action. I replied that I was sure he would. 'Not at all,' commented Mao Tse-tung. 'Nixon would have done, we always knew where we were with him, but not Ford.'

Although at this time I had never visited the People's Republic of China,

I was deeply interested in it as a country, in its people, in their artistic treasures and in their future political development. I also regarded China as a potential market of major significance for the British, if we had the skill and the drive to take advantage of it. China had recently emerged from the Cultural Revolution, a period of very hardline communism, and by 1970 its leaders were showing very clear signs that they had broken completely from the USSR and were interested in pursuing an entirely independent foreign policy. Furthermore, they no longer regarded isolationism as an essential prerequisite for the creation of socialism. China was still an overwhelmingly rural country, and needed trade in order to develop itself economically.

We had not had full diplomatic relations with the Chinese People's Republic since the Revolution of 1949, led by Mao Tse-tung, ousted Chiang Kai-shek and brought his nationalist regime to an end. I learned later, when visiting the official museum in its new building in Taiwan, that as Chiang Kai-shek and his remaining forces were being driven out of the country, they took with them several train loads of historic treasures from Beijing. These were sufficient to put on three complete displays each year for fifteen years without duplicating anything. Since the Revolution, the British had only maintained a counsellor at the head of their diplomatic office in Beijing. From the beginning of the 1960s we had supplied them with aircraft, first of all the Viscount and then the Trident, totalling in all some thirty-nine planes. We had also sold them Spey engines. This seemed to me to be the beginning of what could be a major trading operation. The primary stumbling block to establishing diplomatic relations was the position of Taiwan, which in its chequered history had been part of China and then part of the Japanese Empire and, after Japan's defeat in the Second World War, an independent entity in the view of a number of members of the United Nations. I saw no reason why, so far as we were concerned, this situation should continue, and I was quite prepared to accept a realistic solution which afforded recognition to the People's Republic.

It was with this attitude of mind that Alec Douglas-Home approached the Chinese, who indicated their willingness to negotiate on the issue, and he began the necessary talks with the Beijing government. These appeared to be moving satisfactorily, but were suddenly halted by the Chinese without any explanation. It then emerged, when secret visits of Henry Kissinger to Beijing became known to us, that the Americans were carrying on diplomatic negotiations similar to ours. We had kept the American State Department fully informed about everything we were doing, but Henry Kissinger told me many years later that he, personally, had never seen our telegrams and had not known what was going on. On the first occasion when I had a meeting with Chairman Mao he asked me what I thought about Henry Kissinger. I told him that, in my view, President Nixon laid down the main objectives of American foreign policy, and Henry Kissinger was very skilful in operating it and usually in carrying it through to completion. 'I do not think that at all,' said Chairman Mao, 'I think Henry Kissinger is just a funny little man. He is shuddering all over with nerves every time he comes to see me.' On the other hand, Mao had immense respect for Richard Nixon. '*There* is a man who knows what he stands for, as well as what he wants, and has the strength of mind to get it,' was his verdict.

After this, we were able to complete our negotiations. We acknowledged the Chinese position that Taiwan was part of the mainland of China, after which we established an ambassador and full staff in Beijing, leaving in Taiwan a commercial representative. This process was completed in 1972, after which Alec Douglas-Home paid an official visit to Beijing, as the planned forerunner of myself as Prime Minister. He received a tremendous welcome in the Chinese capital, and when he climbed the stairs in the great Hall of the People to a grand dinner in his honour, he was deeply moved when the symphony orchestra at the top burst into a hearty rendering of the 'Eton Boating Song'. I had already, in September 1972, become the first British Prime Minister to visit Japan, and it now seemed likely that I could set a similar precedent with the People's Republic of China. President Nixon had visited China shortly before Alec Douglas-Home and, during 1973, we began to plan my own visit. I was scheduled to go in the middle of January 1974 but, because of Britain's industrial relations problems, it was only after I ceased to be Prime Minister that I was able to go to see Chairman Mao in Beijing in May 1974 and visit many of the other great Chinese cities (see pp. 634–7).

Ottawa, the capital of Canada, the senior member of the Commonwealth outside Britain, was chosen for the Commonwealth Heads of Government Meeting (CHOGM) in 1973. The heads of all the Commonwealth countries were invited by Burke Trend, a long-respected organiser of these conferences, to tell him which dates would be possible for them to attend. All requirements were taken into account by Burke, except those of his own Prime Minister. When he announced that the conference would be in the first two weeks of August, I was at once prevented from racing *Morning Cloud* in the Admiral's Cup that summer. It was just possible, if the conference finished on time, that I might get back for the Fastnet Race, but no doubt I would be suffering from jet-lag.

After the problems and tensions of the Singapore CHOGM in 1971, the Ottawa meeting, ably chaired throughout by the Canadian Prime Minister Pierre Trudeau, was altogether a more relaxed affair, although still not without its excitements. We arrived in our suite at the Château Laurier after our flight from London to find a message from the Queen's private secretary, asking if he could come round at once. When he arrived, he told us that he had received a telephone call from President Amin, who had not been invited to attend the meeting. Amin wished him to tell the Queen that he would be very happy to come and join his Commonwealth brothers and sisters at Ottawa, but he had no aircraft which could make the long flight from Kampala to Ottawa. Would Her Majesty therefore instruct her government to send out a Boeing 747 aircraft to convey him and his party to Ottawa, and would she also provide a band of Scottish pipers, to pipe him into and out of the aircraft? After consulting Alec Douglas-Home, I decided that this would be an unconscionably extravagant waste of public money, and I tendered advice to Her Majesty accordingly. I added, however, that we should have no objection if any other member of the Commonwealth were to furnish the President with what he desired! A few years later, after I had resigned as leader of the Conservative Party, I received an invitation from Idi Amin, to fly to Uganda 'with my band'. He had heard that I had been 'demoted to the obscure rank of music bandmaster', and offered to provide me and my band with the wherewithal for flying to his country – and as much as I needed in the way of goats, chickens and agricultural produce. Amin was finally overthrown in 1980 to be replaced by my even older friend and admirer Milton Obote (see p. 482) and, since then, has lived quietly in Saudi Arabia.

Once the conference got under way, Trudeau was anxious to avoid the stiff approach of Prime-Ministerial speech-making, reading out from formal and very often lengthy scripts, and to move over into an informal and open system of contributions, in which members would be able to interrupt speakers as they went along. It would be up to the chairman to control these interventions. Overall he was successful in bringing this about, and the whole conference acquired an atmosphere which, though businesslike, was generally free from stress. I was particularly pleased that this conference confirmed that our membership of the European Community had in no way undermined the Commonwealth as an association of independent countries, nor Britain's role in it. This was subsequently confirmed in the 1975 Referendum when all Commonwealth countries supported a 'yes' vote. The final communiqué of the Ottawa Conference noted that:

> When unanimous agreement was not possible, mutual understanding of conflicting viewpoints was achieved. It was agreed that in this regard the meeting established a useful precedent for future Commonwealth consultations. The Commonwealth has been greatly strengthened by the events and Heads of Government were heartened by this.

There was another significant development, with the election of Gough Whitlam as the first Labor Prime Minister in Australia since 1949. Whitlam was determined to make a contribution as early as possible in every debate. His favourite opening was always, 'Well, now we have got rid of the Liberals after a generation of their appalling government, we are going to do so and so.' This caused growing irritation among his colleagues, until the spell was broken by Lee Kuan Yew, who decided to test him on one specific aspect of Australian policy. Whitlam had claimed that his country was now going to abolish its policy of prohibiting non-whites from settling. In future, supposedly, it would be completely opened up, and all others would be warmly welcomed. At this point, Harry Lee interrupted to ask him how many immigrants would be accepted in the coming year. Whitlam turned round to his Cabinet Secretary, who turned to the official behind him, who also turned round. So it went on, right down the line to the most junior official present. The Prime Minister was finally authorised to say, 'A total of five thousand.' 'And what sort of people will they be?' asked Harry Lee. Gough Whitlam turned round to the Secretary of his Cabinet, and we watched as the Australian delegation went through the same process again. 'They will be professional individuals, of help to the community as a whole,' was the delphic reply. 'I can tell you what has happened in my own country,' said Harry Lee. 'Your people came to inform us about the change in policy and told me that we could send a hundred and twenty people from Singapore to Australia in the coming year. They would all have to be either qualified doctors or dentists. Shall I tell you why you want them? Because the people you've got won't work at weekends. You want me to cover the cost of training doctors and dentists so that they can then come to Australia to do the weekend work, which your people refuse to do. That is all your new policy means.' In the wake of that, Prime Minister Gough Whitlam looked rather cowed. Happily for me, Trudeau was then extremely helpful in bringing the business of the conference to a close in good time for me to take part in that year's Fastnet Race.

The rapid development of several Commonwealth countries has given them much greater influence in their own areas, as well as in international organisations. This does not necessarily mean that they all act together. There is, moreover, an unwillingness among many Commonwealth members to become involved in the affairs of countries in other regions, allied with a deep hostility to intervention in their own affairs from outside. Although some of its member nations are certainly open to criticism for their record on human rights, the Commonwealth is still a remarkable and, with all of its diversity, worthwhile enterprise.

*   *   *

The dealings with Uganda and Idi Amin notwithstanding, perhaps the most curious foreign policy episode of my time as Prime Minister involved the island of Malta and its extraordinary Prime Minister, Dom Mintoff. During the Second World War, Malta had been a courageous and staunch ally of the British and, when we came to power in 1970, the island still served as a useful naval base for us. Although our presence there was of immense significance to the Maltese economy, the islanders had, by 1970, convinced themselves that we were taking advantage of them. Soon after coming to power we offered Malta, on Peter Carrington's advice, a greatly improved financial package, worth over £5 million per annum. We hoped that the Prime Minister, Borg Olivier, would be re-elected on the back of this, and that we should, thereafter, hear no more of the matter. The plan fell to pieces when Dom Mintoff was narrowly elected in June 1971, with a mandate of sorts to try and extract far more money from us. Although he demanded a vastly increased offer, of £18 million annually, to be agreed within a month, we actually ended up negotiating with him into the early months of 1972. It was clear from the outset that Mintoff did not know what he really wanted, to get the British out and assert Malta's independence, or to extract more money from us. The hand he had to play was, in fact, woefully weak.

In September 1971, I suggested that Mintoff should visit England, so that he and I could discuss these matters in person at Chequers. At first, Mintoff claimed to misinterpret a phrase in a message to him from Peter Carrington, and refused to come. Mintoff's government had introduced sanctions against British military personnel on the island, and he had convinced himself that we were now insisting that these should be removed, as a precondition to my meeting him. He eventually confirmed, twenty-four hours before his arrival, that he would come after all. I am sure that there was a large element of self-importance and *amour propre* to all of this. I was briefed to be very robust with Mintoff, in the knowledge that Peter Carrington would already have told him his fortune. I knew also that a little flattery would go a long way with such a man. His visit provided an opportunity to test my diplomatic skills in the domestic, as well as international, sphere.

On the evening of his arrival, I let Mintoff do the talking, until he retired to bed, exhausted. He was concerned about the state of the Maltese economy, he told us, and believed that British accession to the European Community would greatly reduce our interest in his island. He therefore needed to secure Malta's economic future on a new, sound footing, which is why he wanted so much money from us. Then, on the following morning, I set out our position: that we wished to maintain good relations between NATO and Malta, and that we would do everything possible to find a mutually agreeable conclusion to our difficulties.

Once Peter Carrington had left after lunch, I sprang a surprise on Mintoff. It was common knowledge that he and his English-born wife were separated, and she now spent much of her time in England with her distinguished family. I invited her also to Chequers and arranged for her to be shown into the White Parlour when she arrived. I then took Mintoff by the arm and led him along to the White Parlour, saying that I was sure that there would be somebody there whom he would be very glad to see. I ushered him in. He was obviously astonished to find his wife there. They had tea and, when the time came to leave, they left together. Afterwards Mintoff flew off to Bonn for talks with Brandt. In the end, everything was settled satisfactorily – between Malta and NATO, if not ultimately between Mr and Mrs Mintoff.

Chapter 18

TOUGH GOING

1974–1975

I first discussed oil with Chancellor Willy Brandt of West Germany as early as April 1971. Although OPEC (the Organisation of Petroleum Exporting Countries) had just agreed at Tehran to guarantee existing prices for five years, we were both growing concerned that the West could face blackmail if a major crisis arose in the Middle East, where signs of instability were already apparent. There were certain steps we could take to guard against this, including the rapid development of new sources of oil in Alaska and the North Sea, more extensive and efficient exploitation of coal reserves and research into alternative forms of power, such as nuclear energy. We had made advances on all these fronts by October 1973, but oil from the Middle East still accounted for around 50 per cent of our energy needs. Until North Sea oil began to flow we would remain vulnerable, and we could not expect to become a net exporter of oil until 1980. This predicament was a major reason for our decision to invest heavily in our coal industry during 1972–3.

Brandt was on a visit to Britain when we heard about the outbreak of war between Israel and Egypt on 6 October 1973. We briefly assessed the crisis at Chequers, but it was still too early to tell just how bad the impact would be. During our talks we had looked at the prospects for European economic and monetary union, and he had responded positively to my suggestion that the EEC's Regional Fund should be a powerful engine for economic regeneration. Clearly these plans were endangered by the situation in the Middle East, but we could not foresee that the effects would still be felt a quarter of a century later.

Our immediate priority was to try to contain the conflict, although I thought it unlikely that the Soviet Union would become involved. The greatest threat of escalation came in late October when, having detected Soviet troop movements, the US put its troops stationed in Europe, including those in Britain, on red alert. It did so without informing us or any of the other European governments. In common with all our European partners except the Netherlands we refused permission for the United States to fly out equipment from our bases. With Cyprus unavailable to them, the US equipped Israel from the Azores. On 16 October, Alec Douglas-Home announced that we would not supply weapons to either side in the conflict. This was a genuinely even-handed approach because, unlike during the previous Middle East conflict of 1967, when most of our arms exports to the area went to Israel, in 1973 we had been providing arms to the Arabs and the Israelis in very similar quantities.

The Arab producers had long realised that oil was going to be their most effective weapon in the fight for a settlement in the Middle East. Since 1972 the rising cost of commodities on world markets had not escaped the notice of the Arab leaders, who were keen to develop their economies. OPEC had already introduced two relatively small price increases earlier in 1973 when, after a meeting in Kuwait on 16 October, they decided that oil supplies would be cut by 5 per cent each month until Israel withdrew from all of the territories it had occupied since 1967, including East Jerusalem, and the Palestinian people were given the right of self-determination. A complete embargo was imposed on the USA and the Netherlands, which were regarded as Israel's best friends in the West. The consuming nations would also have to pay more for what they got, whether they were 'friendly' or 'hostile'. Whereas a barrel of crude oil had cost around $2.40 at the beginning of the year, it would now cost more than $5. In the following month OPEC went further, threatening an additional 25 per cent cut in supplies.

In a rapidly changing situation we had to strike a careful diplomatic balance. We had to ensure our own economic survival without, if possible, alienating any of our friends in the world. I set out to work for a united European response, and the UK took the lead in promoting a joint EEC statement, issued on 6 November, which called for Israel to relinquish the occupied territories and respect the rights of Palestinians. This was based on the relevant United Nations Resolution (242), passed after the previous war of 1967. The matter was skilfully handled for us by Alec Douglas-Home. In recognition of our determination to stick to the UN line we were treated, along with France, as a 'friendly' nation by Saudi Arabia, the main oil producer. If the Saudis and others insisted on classifying nations in this way, we had to try to make sure that as many as possible of our own friends were put in the same category as us.

The minor tensions which arose between us and some of our partners were unavoidable. As President Pompidou said when he came to Chequers on 16 November, if we had intervened tactlessly with the oil-producing states on behalf of any less favoured Community country, 'any such action was more likely to result in [us] being attacked by the Arabs and treated by them in the same way as other countries than in agreement by the Arabs to restore the position [before the outbreak of the war]'. Quiet diplomacy was the most effective way to serve everyone's interests, and European countries were generally well advised to observe strict neutrality under the UN declaration.

Our position was improved by Sheikh Zayed bin Sultan al Nahayan, the ruler of Abu Dhabi, whom I had known well since the mid-1960s. He came to England and asked to see me, and we met at Chequers. He assured me that, because of our friendship, his country would continue to supply Britain with all the oil we needed. I expressed my deepest thanks, but I also pointed out to him that some of our friends in the European Community, especially the Dutch, were in difficulties and I would now feel obliged to supply them, but without any publicity. That, he said, was entirely a matter for me. Once the oil from Abu Dhabi reached us, he would be perfectly happy for us to decide what happened to it. I thanked him again. That was the basis on which we worked. The details of the operation never leaked.

The fighting in the Middle East lasted for only three weeks, ending in the cease-fire of 24 October, but it was still going on when I addressed the Conservative conference in Blackpool. The oil crisis was a tremendous test for the Community, but the very possibility of a united position on the Middle East situation revealed how far we had come. Even so, we could not avoid the economic impact of the price increases. The Copenhagen Summit in December was disrupted and prolonged by the arrival of OPEC Foreign Ministers. The oil crisis was also the main reason why, to my great regret, our proposal to establish a £1,250 million European Regional Fund was not accepted. The German government suggested only £250 million. In his memoirs, Brandt admitted that those present could not have taken him seriously. He had never committed himself to a precise figure in private, but I knew that he wanted a much larger budget for the fund. By the time this issue was settled, we were both out of office.

Our other diplomatic problem at this time concerned the oil companies. It was one thing for our friends in the Middle East to try to protect us from the worst effects of the shortages, but quite another to rely on major companies such as Shell and BP to deliver the oil to our shores. A significant proportion of the oil carried in British-registered vessels was intended to go to third countries, but the oil producers found it difficult to take account of this factor when deciding how much oil to give to us. The price of petrol in Britain was far lower than in other European countries. When we ran a comparison early in the New Year we found that a gallon of 4-star cost the equivalent of 71p in France, but only 42p (over £2.90 in today's values) here. Naturally the oil companies were anxious not to let down customers in other countries, but their apparent altruism was not unconnected with their knowledge that they could make higher profits elsewhere. With further concessions for North Sea exploration about to come up for consideration, we could have bullied the companies. I preferred a more reasonable approach. When I invited the chairmen of Shell and BP to Chequers as my guests, however, I was met with a complete refusal to co-operate. I was deeply shamed by the obstinate and unyielding reluctance of these magnates to take any action whatever to help our own country in its time of danger.

The oil crisis was a highly unwelcome disruption to our foreign policy, but for domestic affairs too it could not have come at a worse time. In July the NUM had decided to put in a pay claim which would have meant increases of up to 50 per cent for some workers. On 10 October, four days after war broke out in the Middle East, the National Coal Board (NCB) offered the NUM an average rise of around 13 per cent, more than 4 per cent of which was a special concession for 'unsocial hours'. This we had deliberately built into Stage Three of our counter-inflation policy. The idea had emerged from a meeting that I had with the NUM president Joe Gormley in the garden of No. 10 on 16 July, at which he had made it very clear that he wanted no rerun of the previous year's bitter strike.

The miners had been offered a very generous deal, but I was dismayed that the Coal Board had made its maximum offer so early in the negotiations. It was a major blunder by the chairman, and only encouraged the NUM to hold out for more. While the oil-producing countries were jumping at an opportunity to help their own economies, at the same time as exerting pressure for a settlement of the Palestinian question, militants within the NUM gradually realised that the oil crisis was a chance to win a massive wage settlement and damage the government in the process. The NCB offer was rejected. The miners' representatives came in for talks with me at No. 10 on 23 October, and Joe Gormley told me that he would take a vote directly after lunch. He assured me it was going to be all right. He came alone to my study after their meeting had resumed, looking pale and drawn, to tell me he had been defeated. 'I only got four votes,' he exclaimed in both sorrow and anger. The union then started an overtime ban on 12 November. The NUM could not be permitted to break through the terms of Stage Three. We had already acknowledged their special status with the 'unsocial hours' clause and knew that, as the mining industry was unusually dependent on overtime work to keep pits in safe working order, production would fall very quickly with the overtime ban. The following day, we introduced a state of emergency.

After the strike of 1972 we had carefully built up coal stocks in the expectation that there might be another dispute. We also put around £1 billion of public money into the coal industry, to reverse the decline which had marked the Labour years. The situation in the Middle East meant that we had to conserve our oil, and in those days the only other significant fuel at power stations was coal. The strong economic growth during 1973 also meant that the demand for fuel had been higher than usual. The commodity which was in the shortest supply in that period was time. We had to make decisions on the spot. At one point Alec Douglas-Home suggested that we should stop publishing our regular up-dates on our stocks of oil because, when people saw that we still had more than fifty days' worth of supplies, they might wonder why we were imposing restrictions. In fact, reserves for seven weeks were considered to be the absolute minimum, and we were fast approaching that. The Opposition encouraged people to think that we were trying to exaggerate the crisis in order to discredit the miners, but early drafts of several ministerial statements at this time were actually toned down to avoid the impression that we were blaming what a later government decided to brand the 'enemy within'.

An example of the troubles we encountered was our decision to prepare for a possible introduction of petrol rationing. Peter Walker, the Trade and Industry Secretary, rightly pointed out that these arrangements had to be hurried, because Christmas was approaching and the postal services were certain to be disrupted at that time. Any idea that rationing might be introduced before the public had been sent the necessary coupons was unthinkable. After much discussion we decided to authorise the printing and circulation of the coupons, a measure which we certainly would have delayed for longer at a different time of year. We were attacked from both sides, by those who thought we were scaremongering and by those who felt that we should have gone ahead with rationing immediately.

I could understand Alec Douglas-Home's reasoning when he suggested that we might limit the flow of statistics to the public, especially as information about the quantity of fuel landed in Britain gave a misleading impression. Even though we had just announced an extra £900 million to improve the railways, the train-drivers' union ASLEF then launched an overtime ban of their own on 12 December because of a dispute over how the new money should be shared out, thus further handicapping the distribution of oil products. There was even some small-scale industrial action in refineries. We had a duty to keep the public properly informed and, above all, we had a responsibility to protect car-owners and industry from a complete run-down of stocks. The actions we took included the introduction of a speed limit of 50 miles per hour and, although there was a certain amount of panic buying of petrol, especially in the south-east, the public acted responsibly. For the first time, people in this country began to make serious efforts in peacetime to curtail their energy consumption. I had already been considering the creation of a Department of Energy, separate from the Department of Trade and Industry, because the question of fuel resources would clearly be crucial to Britain over the coming years. This was opposed by Peter Walker, but after a damaging delay he agreed and I went ahead. In January 1974, I appointed Peter Carrington to head the new Department. Perhaps I should have insisted on this changeover earlier.

In the meantime the situation in the coalfields was still deadlocked. On 21 November the NUM executive rejected an improved offer from the Coal Board. Joe Gormley was outvoted when he suggested that there should be a ballot of NUM members on the new terms. It was obvious from the outset that more was at stake for the militant miners' leaders than the glory of prising an irresponsible pay increase out of the democratically elected government. Even the moderates in the union movement, including the new general secretary of the TUC, Len Murray, wanted to do away with the Industrial Relations Act, although no one ever offered a suggestion of what should take its place. Murray and Gormley, however, were not really in full control. The people making the running were the firebrands of the left. Mick McGahey, the long-standing communist member of the NUM executive, made this abundantly clear in a further meeting which was held on 28 November. When I asked him what he really wanted, he proclaimed that he wanted to bring down the government. During the election campaign, even the Labour Party had to disown McGahey when he demanded that any troops which might be called out to deal with a national emergency should support the miners.

In this threatening situation I decided to bring Willie Whitelaw back from Northern Ireland to replace Maurice Macmillan as Secretary of State for Employment. I had not lost faith in Macmillan, who had been a capable minister both at the Treasury and at Employment. Whitelaw, however, had proved his negotiating abilities amid all the tensions and difficulties of Ulster. I needed Willie to be close at hand for the task of dealing with a major national crisis. He took up his new office on 2 December. Francis Pym, the Chief Whip, moved to Northern Ireland and Humphrey Atkins replaced him.

The worldwide rise in commodity prices before the oil shock had already meant that the outlook for the 1973 balance of payments was depressing. After the events of October, it was clear that emergency action would have to be taken. On 12 December we held a Cabinet meeting which

Tony Barber opened by saying that we were facing the gravest economic crisis since the Second World War. The Treasury was forecasting a balance of payments deficit of £3 billion for 1974, even though our exports had risen by 12 per cent over the year to October 1973. Our advisers thought that, in place of an economic growth rate of 3.5 per cent, still very satisfactory, there would be a contraction of 4.5 per cent over the next year. This would bring output back to the level of December 1972. As a percentage of GDP, public expenditure would rise to 51.7 per cent if nothing was done. In these circumstances, it was necessary to cut demand in the British economy. Tony Barber thought the cuts for 1974–5 should be £1,500 million – about £9 billion today. The Cabinet responded to the crisis in the usual constructive spirit.

Discussions continued the following day, when I announced in the House of Commons the introduction in the new year of a three-day working week to conserve fuel. In the meantime, industry would receive only five days' electricity every week and television would close down at 10.30 p.m. Essential services, of course, were fully protected. We knew from the start that we had to avoid the confusion which arose during the miners' dispute of 1972, when industry had kept going at its regular rate until unpredictable cuts in supply were imposed. With coal deliveries to the power stations down by over one third and the power workers now imposing an overtime ban of their own, we had to bring order to the situation. By announcing the restrictions well in advance, we ensured that industry would have time to plan. As I told the nation on television on the evening of 13 December, 'At times like these there is deep in all of us an instinct which tells us we must abandon disputes among ourselves.' I find that nowadays people are astonished to learn that production fell by less than 2 per cent during the three-day week. This showed how much better industrial performance could, and should, have been at normal times.

On the evening of Sunday 16 December I talked over the necessary economic measures with Tony Barber. The package which he announced in the House on the following day was difficult for us all, because it represented a postponement of our ambitious long-term economic plans. It was hardly a consolation to us that others across the world were in the same position. In the end we had agreed that public spending had to come down by £1,200 million. Cuts on this scale were bound to hurt everyone to some extent, but, since the well-off were best able to cope during the present crisis, a surcharge of 10 per cent was levied on those liable to surtax. We also announced restrictions on credit and hire-purchase transactions, and capital gains tax on major land development deals was introduced. This move had been under consideration for some time, and Peter Carrington had pressed tirelessly for it. It was quite unacceptable that so many of the nation's resources were being channelled into land speculation instead of into the more productive investment which we had constantly encouraged. Although we ensured that the package did nothing to affect take-home pay or private industry directly, there was sure to be a knock-on effect. We had to accept that for us, as for other developed nations, there would be a temporary pause in the economic growth that we all sought. The important thing was to take swift action to ensure that the setback was not prolonged.

On 18 December, I opened a debate on the economic situation in the House of Commons. Having noted that 'Nothing that is happening now . . . in any way decreases the imperative need for this country to expand its industrial capacity and thus to be able to sustain economic growth,' I said that 'As a nation, we have real prospects and opportunities ahead of us, thanks to the availability of energy supplies which will shortly be within our control, but we shall not be in a position to take those opportunities if we seek to tackle our immediate problems either by feebly giving way to inflation or, in anything but the short term, abandoning plans for economic expansion.' I informed the House that we could have decreased demand to the equivalent amount by adding 7p to all rates of income tax. Instead, we had combined prudent management with a strong element of social justice.

While we were taking the necessary precautions at home, our diplomatic efforts were stepped up. It was vital that we kept looking to the future despite the immediate problems before us, and I believe that we were assessing the long-term prospects at an earlier stage than other nations. Our main problem was to convince our friends in the Middle East that their actions had done more than give Western governments a major headache. However happy some of the OPEC countries might have been with their additional profits, their banking systems could not possibly cope with the revenues flooding into them. The increased prices already announced were certain to cause a slowdown in Western economies and on developing countries such as India, which were dependent on imported fuel. Unless the Arab states invested their new-found wealth sensibly, the consequences for the world financial system would be grim. Accordingly, when the Governor of the Bank of England flew to Saudi Arabia on a long-arranged visit in November, we briefed him for discussions with King Faisal and his ministers about the possibility of constructive co-operation between our countries. In December, Toby Aldington flew out to reinforce the message. The Saudis knew that their oil would not last for ever and, unless they used part of their new wealth to build up their infrastructure, they would eventually have to answer to their people for the misuse of their resources. Similar discussions took place between Peter Walker and

Iranian ministers. I rang the Iranian Prime Minister myself to help negotiate a deal to exchange high-technology British products for oil.

We were spurred on in these bilateral talks by the knowledge that, although they were produced by an emergency, their effects in terms of better economic relations could be lasting. While the talks were designed to ensure that, if all else failed, British industry would benefit as much as possible from the new state of affairs, I believe that our diplomacy forced the majority of Arab states to recognise the new realities which their actions had brought about. Although an OPEC meeting in late December 1973 resulted in a further price increase to over $11 per barrel, a quadruple rise over the year, we also began to hear more conciliatory noises from the Arab states, and our efforts were rewarded by a promise that more would be done to ensure that our supplies quickly returned to normal. By the time we left office, this had been achieved, but it had become clear much earlier that the energy problem which had developed at home was a greater threat to our survival as a nation.

The coal dispute had been going from bad to worse. The majority of the NUM executive had priorities which no democrat could tolerate and, at one point, it was even suggested that, since we were having to pay the oil producers the price they demanded, we ought to treat the miners in the same way. Already we had been forced to announce a three-day week, and millions of workers would be laid off or work short-time as a result. If there really had been solidarity among the workers, as the left-wing slogans proclaimed, our problems might have been overcome. Instead it was every man for himself and the devil take the hindmost within the union movement. This was the unacceptable face of trade unionism. Willie Whitelaw was exploring a possible deal connected to payments for time spent by miners 'waiting and bathing'. After Harold Wilson had been privately notified of these secret talks by Joe Gormley, he asked me about the initiative at Prime Minister's Questions. This undermined any atmosphere of trust, and made further negotiations on the point impossible. Gormley was outraged, and never forgave Wilson for this breach of confidence.

In the tense and tragic situation which was developing, everyone had their own idea of how to proceed. We were getting messages from supporters on the backbenches and from voters urging us to fight the miners without a thought of compromise. To me that was just as bad as the attitude shown by McGahey on the other side. If people were talking of 'confrontation', it suggested that the nation was already hopelessly riven. Others were getting ready for a general election to resolve the issue. A draft Conservative manifesto was prepared by the middle of December, and rumours of an imminent general election began to appear in the newspapers. Although we were ahead in the polls, we had lost a by-election at Berwick to the Liberals on 8 November and other results that day had seen our support fall substantially, so the risks of an early election were all too self-evident. It had to be a last resort. It might act as a pressure-valve for the country, but equally it could raise the temperature even further, and it was not immediately obvious how a general election could resolve an industrial dispute. The rumours about an early election damaged our party badly. They raised expectations and, when no contest was called, some people concluded that we were frightened of facing the country. In fact, until the end of January, I and several senior colleagues were simply not convinced that an election was necessary.

I had a dinner at around the turn of the year with the Whips, to discuss the mood of the parliamentary party about a possible dissolution and general election campaign. I think that my PPS Tim Kitson expected them to back up his belief that the time was right for going to the country. In the event, they split exactly evenly, more or less along north–south lines. Kenneth Clarke, then a Junior Whip, was against an early election and Walter Clegg, the normally quiet and self-contained MP for North Fylde, spoke with unusual eloquence against the proposal. I know that Tim was very upset and annoyed about all of this, and my own misgivings about a dissolution deepened. I was increasingly conscious, however, that we were more or less in a corner and were likely to be accused of running scared if we did not go to the country within the next few weeks. Furthermore, the other options were not attractive. Sitting out a long coal strike would have been immensely damaging to our economy and industry, and settling the dispute on the NUM's terms would have been wholly unacceptable.

We kept up our normal contacts with both the CBI and the TUC throughout the crisis. At a meeting of the National Economic Development Council chaired by Tony Barber on 9 January, the day that Parliament reassembled one week earlier than usual, Sidney Greene, leader of the National Union of Railwaymen, without any notice, made a remarkable offer. He suggested that the TUC should pledge that, if the miners' settlement broke the terms of Stage Three, other unions would not attempt to exploit this. Tony Barber was immediately suspicious. He had been given no indication that such an offer was going to be made and thought that, whatever their personal views, the union leaders could no longer be regarded as the true voice of their movement. He therefore left the meeting in order to contact me, telephoning from a public kiosk so that our conversation should not be overheard. I agreed with his assessment, and Tony returned to the meeting to say that we could not accept the suggestion there and then, but wished to hold further discussions.

At the time there was some controversy about this meeting. We subsequently found ourselves accused of turning down a perfectly sincere offer, supposedly because we had already decided to hold an election and, if the miners' dispute had suddenly been settled, the whole point of the election would have been taken away. That proposition is irrational. Many people within my party wanted an election, including several of the ministers closest to me, because they saw no other chance of escaping the troubles which beset the country, but no decision whatsoever had been taken at that time about a general election.

The following day I met the union leaders in Downing Street, having received a copy of the offer in writing from Len Murray. I pressed the delegation on what I considered to be the crucial point. In his letter, Murray wrote that 'If the Government are prepared to give an assurance that they will make possible a settlement between the miners and the National Coal Board, other unions will not use this as an argument in negotiations on their own settlements.' The difficulty with this was that, instead of citing the NUM precedent to break Stage Three, other unions could easily think up different reasons to back up unacceptable pay claims. The TUC had already hinted that the power workers were another 'special case'. At the meeting on 10 January, Jack Jones suggested that no other workers were special cases in the same sense as the miners, but of course what the power workers did share with the miners was the ability to bring the country to a standstill. The TUC delegation could not give me the assurance that I needed. It was a very dispiriting meeting. Further discussions held on 14 January lasted for more than five hours, but produced little progress.

There was still one possible way out of the crisis. For some months the Pay Board had been preparing a report on 'relativities'. With the usual process of free collective bargaining between unions and employers in abeyance, anomalous situations could arise between groups of workers which would require special machinery. The Pay Board's report appeared on 24 January, and William Whitelaw welcomed it in the House of Commons. The miners' claimed that, over the years, their pay had fallen relative to other groups of workers, which the settlement of 1972 had demonstrably not rectified, as people were still leaving their industry. We always accepted that the miners had a special case and the relativities procedure offered, on paper at least, a way of awarding them a better deal without breaking Stage Three, although the Pay Board had specifically ruled out using it in a crisis. For this procedure to work, however, we needed union co-operation. They feared that any such co-operation would enable their militant critics to claim that they had caved in completely to a Conservative government. It was a difficult situation which required careful and steady negotiation, but time did not allow for that.

On 24 January the NUM decided to hold a ballot on an all-out strike, the wording of which avoided the main issue and instead asked union members whether they supported the line taken by the executive. The vote was held a week later and, when the result was announced on 4 February, there was an overwhelming majority for a strike, more than 80 per cent of those voting wanting a complete stoppage. The strike was due to begin on 9 February. We met another TUC delegation that afternoon, but the NUM now refused even to talk about the relativities report, so there was no further room for manoeuvre. There was now only one possible course of action, to ask Her Majesty the Queen for a dissolution of Parliament. That evening I broadcast to the nation, asking the British people to raise 'the true and familiar voice of Britain – the voice of moderation and courage'. During January 1974, we had two political Cabinet meetings, formal gatherings of members of the Cabinet without officials in attendance. At the first, both Willie Whitelaw and Francis Pym spoke out against an early election. At the second, there was not a single voice raised in dissent.

My formal request for a dissolution of Parliament was submitted to the Queen on board the royal yacht, in a telegram on 6 February. She had to interrupt a tour of Australia in order to be back in Britain on the day of the election. A week later, I wrote to Her Majesty, setting out in some detail our reasons for going to the country after less than four years.

Although the pressures, both official and political, during those early weeks of 1974 were incredibly intense, and there were certainly times when my friends told me that I looked tired, I remained sound in mind and limb throughout and, despite everything, actually felt very healthy and robust. I was spurred on by the fact that the Executive of the NUM was no longer motivated by industrial considerations. It was now dominated by those who wished to bring down the Government, as a stage in a process that was ultimately intended to undermine the entire structure and way of life of British society. It was clear from the outset that, although the election campaign would be comparatively short, it was bound to be sharp and strident despite my own intention of making it as non-divisive as possible. Just as I had thought that it would not be right to call an election immediately after the turn of the year, regardless of the pressures to do so, by the beginning of February I was convinced that we had no credible alternative. An election had become politically necessary, indeed virtually inevitable. I believed that the Conservative Party and the Government occupied the right ground from which to appeal to the electorate for support. I was fortified in this not only by the unanimous agreement of my Cabinet colleagues, but also by the enthusiasm of virtually all our supporters in Parliament. As *The Economist* said at the time, we were fighting on an issue on which it would have been good to win, but on which it would be no less good to go out, if that proved to be the country's mood. I believed that that was not the country's mood. It would have been so much better for the people of this country if we could have been spared the Labour governments of 1974–79.

In January 1974, I had a chat with Vic Feather about how things might be after the next election. I recall saying to Vic that 'your people are always complaining about some aspect of the Industrial Relations Act, but when I give you the opportunity to raise it in discussion you never utter a word'. 'Look, Ted,' he said, 'if you win the next election we will discuss it all with you, and it will be there for ever. But if you lose the next election the whole thing will be wiped out in the first week.' If we had won the election in February 1974, we would have reviewed the Industrial Relations Act and, where justified, would have made amendments, some of which we certainly wanted ourselves. But that was not to be, and the next generation of Tory leaders would give up on the unions altogether, casting them into outer darkness. Even after the frustrations of the past three and three-quarter years, I was not willing to lose faith entirely in the inherent common sense of the British people.

The Nuffield Study of the February 1974 general election says that 'Mr Heath performed well. He was much more relaxed and amusing than in 1970: he spoke eloquently, without notes, and displayed great versatility and grasp of detail.' It was good of the authors to say so. It was claimed at the time that I was suffering from ill-health during the campaign. This was not the case. I did need to recuperate from a thyroid complaint in 1980, but had no problems at all with it during 1974.

I always regarded the election as nothing better than a grim necessity. Once in a fight, however unwelcome, I was always ready to meet the challenge. On this occasion, in contrast to the circumstances of 1970, most people expected us to win. The campaign began quite well for us. Enoch Powell suddenly abandoned his seat as a Conservative MP. He did not even have the decency to warn the officers of his association or his agent in advance of his decision to abandon them.

As during the 1970 campaign, we held our 11 a.m. press conferences in London, and I was briefed in advance by a team including Peter Carrington, Michael Fraser and Michael Wolff. Our manifesto, *Firm Action for a Fair Britain*, appeared on 10 February. It explained our record of implementing the policy proposals we had advanced during the 1970 campaign. It also contained an honest and clear exposition of the scale of the problems that the United Kingdom was facing:

The world has changed dramatically since we last sought the support of the electorate. In the last two years there has been a dramatic rise in the world price of almost all the essential raw materials and foods which we have to import from overseas. Many of these prices have doubled in the past year alone, making it impossible to stem the rise in the cost of living. Now on top of these increases comes the huge increase in oil prices, which in turn will affect the cost of almost everything that we produce or buy in the country . . . let no one suppose that as a nation we can deal with the immediate problem without hardship and sacrifice . . . What we must continue to ensure is that any sacrifices are shared equitably and that hardship does not fall on those least able to bear it.

We also included in the manifesto the reform we had been discussing to the social security system, to stop strikers and their families being automatically subsidised by the taxpayer. For many years, Conservative supporters had demanded changes to this arrangement and, given our efforts to ensure a fair pay policy, we could not resist these demands any longer. As we said, 'it is only right that the unions themselves . . . should accept the primary responsibility for the welfare of the families of men who choose to go on strike'. This was firm action. It was not 'union bashing', but an attempt to stop trade unionists bashing their more responsible fellow citizens by exploiting what could be regarded as a free licence to strike.

Our entire election campaign was thrown off course a week before polling day, when the Pay Board announced that it had discovered an apparent discrepancy between the evidence of the NCB and that of the NUM. The Pay Board considered it necessary to resolve this for the purposes of its report on the dispute. On Tuesday 19 February, senior officials of the Board held a public session during which its chairman, Sir Frank Figgures, said that the Board's members would prepare an explanatory note of the situation as they saw it. They would then invite comments on their views from both the NCB and the NUM. I suppose that we should have expected real trouble, but I had no reason to believe that anything serious would ensue. However, though statistical in nature and neutral in tone, the note could arguably be cited as evidence that miners' average earnings had been consistently overestimated, because such things as holiday money were being counted as part of their remuneration, while other industries excluded them. When they were published on the Thursday, the Pay Board's figures appeared to indicate that the miners were around £3 per week worse off than previously thought, a substantial amount in those days. It was alleged in the following day's newspapers that, whereas everyone had understood that the miners were earning rather more than the national average for manufacturing workers, in reality they were earning about 8 per cent less. We subsequently discovered that there were sound, well-established reasons for this apparent anomaly. Other items which the miners did get as part of their package, including concessionary coal, had not been taken into account.

When they had been given the briefing note, industrial correspondents requested a non-attributable briefing on its contents which was then given by a senior spokesman for the Pay Board. According to Frank Figgures subsequently, that spokesman 'neither gave, nor expressed agreement with, any interpretation of the statistics . . . he confined himself to technical questions and drew attention to the difficulty of making valid comparisons . . . he did not suggest that a mistake had been made or that anyone was to blame'. That may well have been true, but the media were soon overflowing with misleading interpretations of the new data and, for the two following days, the newspapers made hay with the explanatory memorandum. It appeared to show, wrongly as it turned out, that the miners were worse off than even the NUM had thought. The press had a field day, suggesting that the government had made a calculating bungle with regard to the main issue upon which the election was being fought. Harold Wilson claimed that an arithmetical error had thrust the country needlessly into a national pit strike, the resultant industrial disruption and what he termed a 'farcical general election'.

I put the onus firmly back on to the NUM. It was up to them to calculate the basis for their pay claims, and they had been doing so in the same way for many years. If they wished to calculate the value of the miners' remuneration package differently, and then defend the new basis, that was up to them. I was furious that the Pay Board, in part through a non-attributable briefing, should pronounce on such a sensitive issue in the middle of the general election campaign. It made a grievous contribution to the loss of nerve in the country. In practical, political terms, it was actually now up to us to demonstrate, during the last few, hectic days of the campaign, that this was no more than a red herring. Wilson, with all of his rhetoric, had the easier task. Our argument was a complicated one requiring patient explanation. We had no effective answer in kind to Wilson's slogans.

At a press conference at Conservative Central Office, I denied, under fire from Wilson's proxies, that 'a ghastly mistake has been made . . . when a statistical basis of earning has been accepted by the coal board, the miners and Wilberforce, I am certainly not going to say that a ghastly mistake has been made . . . I am certainly not willing to prejudge the conclusions of the Pay Board.' Under pressure, I added that 'all negotiations . . . for two decades have always been on the October earnings inquiry . . . it is not a question of somebody making an arithmetical mistake . . . the responsibility for putting forward a pay claim always rests with the union'. That evening, Harold Wilson went on the offensive, with all guns blazing. He accused us of deliberately using industrial unrest for election purposes, and said that we should have taken direct charge of the miners' pay dispute. He aligned himself lock, stock and barrel with the miners and he was echoed by Jeremy Thorpe. Back at Central Office, we all knew that the campaign was slipping away from us. It was not enough to be right. In order to maintain momentum, it was essential to have a simple and easily digested message. The Pay Board had given our opponents the chance to blow the ground from under us with specious arguments that would not stand up to a moment's scrutiny.

There is a most curious coda to this story. At the beginning of May, I was interviewed by Peter Jay on *Weekend World*. He asked me about the Pay Board's intervention in the election campaign, and I said that 'there was absolutely no justification for the briefing in the form which took place'. Frank Figgures took exception to that, and wrote me a strong letter, claiming, to my astonishment, that 'to the best of my knowledge the briefing of the press which you describe did not take place and despite the enquiries which I have made . . . I can find no clear evidence that it did'. This was extraordinary, for Figgures had written to George Gardiner about the briefing only a few weeks before. In my response, I challenged him to 'justify the wisdom of allowing a senior official to give a non-attributable briefing to correspondents in the middle of an Election campaign on an issue which was being examined daily in public by the Board'. Figgures defended his spokesman, but at least had the good grace to concede that he did 'regret that I [Figgures] did not deal with the matter in open session on the Thursday afternoon'.

I felt that this represented a concession that the Pay Board had behaved, if not improperly, then foolishly. This, in turn, appeared to vindicate my expressed view that the off-the-record briefing was impossible to justify. I did not wish to protract the exchange of correspondence without good cause, but I wrote again to Frank Figgures, reminding him that 'the one clear fact is that immediately following this briefing stories alleging muddle and a sensational slip over the calculation of miners' pay were written . . . since the NUM, the NCB, the Pay Board (on the record) or the eventual Relativities Report made no such suggestion, there is little room for any conclusion other than that this impression was left with journalists as a result of the unattributable briefing'. Our final exchange of letters was fairly brusque. Frank Figgures never accepted that the unattributable briefing by a senior official of the Pay Board adversely influenced the media or the election campaign, and I never accepted that such a briefing, at such a time and on such an issue, could be justified. What cannot be denied, however, is the publicity fillip that this story handed to the Labour Party, at a crucial point in the campaign.

On 23 February, Enoch Powell made a speech criticising the policy of accession to Europe, a policy which he had once advocated. Two days later, he let it be known that he had already cast a postal vote, for the Labour Party and its full-blooded socialist policies. This champion of the right showed that he would sacrifice all his principles for a remote chance that Labour might take Britain out of Europe. On this point all Labour had done was to promise 'renegotiation' of the terms, which was always likely to be a meaningless charade. On the same day, the trade figures for January were released, a little late because of the effects of the three-day week. The deficit of £383 million was the largest ever recorded, to go along with equally bad retail price figures released ten days earlier. These statistics were only to be expected. Considering the massive increase in oil prices, it could all have been much worse. In an opinion poll only 20 per cent blamed the government. Even so, the figures were undoubtedly set-backs during the election campaign. They were quickly wiped from the headlines by a remark from the director-general of the CBI, Campbell Adamson, at a conference unrelated to the election. Two days before the poll, Campbell Adamson chose to proclaim his newly minted views on our Industrial Relations Act, telling his audience that he hoped the next government would not simply amend it, but repeal legislation which in his view had proved counter-productive. It was claimed that he was unaware that he was being recorded at the time, but there was a micro-phone on his table and he must have known that his remarks would be reported. It was incredible enough that he felt the way he did.

The Industrial Relations Act had been introduced to correct the balance of power in the workforce, which had swung too far in favour of union militants on the shopfloor. It gave employers an opportunity to create an enterprising climate free from the threat of irresponsible strike action. As Lord Donovan had warned they might, however, the employers had proved unequal to the challenge which we set for them. In most cases, they had chosen not to use the legislation. Now their most prominent representative had decided to denounce the law, two days before the most important general election since 1945. If Campbell Adamson had wanted Labour to win, he could not have worked more effectively on their behalf. I had to spend much of the day fending off questions on this subject rather than discussing our positive agenda for the future. Against this background, the personal appeal which I made to the electorate in the party political broadcast that night became nigh on impossible to get right.

On the eve of polling day, I went to my constituency and spoke at two meetings there, finishing as was customary at the Freemantle Hall in Bexley Village. Inevitably, given my itinerary, my arrival there was badly delayed, but I was delighted with the roar of approval from the assembled media representatives as I walked into the Hall, a little over half an hour late. I subsequently discovered that my aide Richard Simmonds, who had been charged with being the warm-up act, had reached the climax of his own performance perfectly on schedule, expecting me to arrive at any moment, at which point someone had shoved a note under his nose, informing him that I would be thirty minutes late. Fortunately, he had a copy of the manifesto with him and, point by point, talked his audience through it. As he reached the end of the document, with his sense of panic rising, I had walked through the door. The press were filled with both admiration and, knowing that Richard's material was about to be exhausted, relief!

My mood as the counting began was hopeful, but not confident. The campaign had been short, and the electorate had had no time to put the bad news of the last few days into its proper context. We were particularly worried about the Liberal vote. The party had been as high as 30 per cent in the opinion polls of September 1973 and, of course, we could not count on help from the Ulster Unionists in a close election because we had established power-sharing in Northern Ireland. When the early results came in, we knew straight away that the support of minor parties could be needed. In my own seat I now had a majority close to 10,000, but that was little reason for cheer. As I was driven back to Downing Street after the announcement of my result, I still could not be sure whether I would be Prime Minister the next day. I was certain, however, that we could no longer hope to be returned with the sort of lead we had enjoyed in 1970.

The last results were not in until the Saturday. We had won more votes than Labour, but had fallen short of their tally of seats, mainly because the Liberals' 19 per cent of the vote had taken support from us. The final score was Labour 301, Conservatives 297 and Liberals 14. In addition, there were nine Nationalist MPs from the mainland, twelve Ulster MPs and two Independents who were formerly Labour. Oddly for an indecisive election, the turnout was high. Although the result was a bitter disappointment, the government of the country had to be carried on regardless of what I felt and, on the basis of the results, I had a clear constitutional duty to see if I was best placed to carry on that responsibility. Labour had fought the election on the most extreme platform of any party since the war, which had been more or less ignored thanks to the inevitable media focus on the miners' strike. I could not leave office without trying everything within my power to form a moderate alternative government.

The general election of February 1974 produced the worst possible result for the country, a hung Parliament. The press had portrayed the contest as a trial of strength between the elected government and an extra-parliamentary force. Once people began to talk about the question 'Who governs Britain?' an indecisive outcome was bound to be a threat to democracy, no matter which party actually formed the next administration. The Conservative campaign had been conducted on the assumption that a Labour government of any kind would be a disaster, but we had special reason to fear the consequences if Labour was to form a weak minority government in the prevailing circumstances. Before all the results were in, we held a Cabinet meeting which confirmed my decision to see whether we could form an arrangement with other parties.

I tried to contact the Liberal leader Jeremy Thorpe, who was in the west country celebrating his party's improved showing. On the Saturday afternoon, when all the votes had been counted, he turned up at Downing Street for talks. He agreed that his party was much closer to the Conservatives than to Labour on the major issues of the day: like us, the Liberals favoured a prices and incomes policy, and they supported a constructive approach to Europe. I asked Thorpe to consider three possible arrangements if we stayed in office. First, a loose arrangement within which the Liberals could pick and choose which governmental measures they supported; secondly, full consultation on the contents of a government programme to be announced in a Queen's Speech, which the Liberals would then support; or, thirdly, a coalition, in which Thorpe would be offered an unspecified Cabinet seat. I told him that the third arrangement would be my preferred option, to ensure stability. Thorpe expressed a strong preference for the post of Home Secretary, but I made no such offer to him. Before the meeting took place I had been warned by the Secretary of the Cabinet that there were matters in Thorpe's private life, as yet undisclosed to the public, which might make this a highly unsuitable position for him to hold. Thorpe also raised the subject of proportional representation. I replied that I would have to consult my colleagues before committing the party to electoral reform. He promised to hold discussions with his own senior colleagues, although the full Liberal parliamentary party would not be meeting until the morning of Monday 4 March.

After my meeting with Thorpe I held consultations with members of the Cabinet, with particular reference to proportional representation. The overwhelming feeling was that the most we could offer the Liberals would be a Speaker's Conference, established by the Speaker at the request of the government, to consider electoral reform, followed by a free vote in the House of Commons. We would not, however, put pressure on the conference to decide one way or the other. I explained our position to Thorpe at a second meeting, on the Sunday evening. Although he was very keen to enter a coalition, as were many of his colleagues, he wanted firmer pledges on proportional representation, which we were not ready to offer to him. In addition to his desire for the Home Office, he wanted me to step down as Prime Minister. I discussed this with senior members of the Cabinet, all of whom refused to contemplate such a deal.

Ironically, of course, a deal with the Liberals would have presented no problem at all if the February 1974 general election had been held under a system of proportional representation. Together, with over 57 per cent of the vote, we would have held a clear majority of the seats. The gulf in February between the size of the Liberal vote and the number of MPs it secured certainly represented a powerful argument for reform, and the pledge of a Speaker's Conference was retained in our manifesto for the October 1974 election. At the same time, the overall state of the parties meant that we could not have made large concessions to the Liberals without upsetting many of our supporters.

The full Cabinet met on the Monday morning, before the Liberals held their own formal discussions, and after our meeting a letter to Thorpe was drafted, setting out our position. It was agreed that I should delay submitting the resignation of the government until the Liberals responded to the letter, but as this process was likely to be nothing more than a formality I took the opportunity of thanking my Cabinet colleagues for the support they had given me over the three and three-quarter years that we had been in government together. Lord Hailsham spoke in similar terms on behalf of the Cabinet. We met again very briefly in the afternoon, once we had heard from Thorpe. In his statement announcing the end of negotiations, Thorpe had called for a 'Government of National Unity' – an impossible idea at the time, because Harold Wilson had already ruled out Labour participation in such an arrangement and Thorpe had snubbed us.

It was our duty to negotiate with the Liberals, even if this gave ill-disposed people an opportunity to claim that we were trying to hang on to office. Mrs Thatcher, for example, wrote in her memoirs that the 'horse-trading was making us look ridiculous'. The alternative, however, was to give up without a fight, and to hand power straight over to a left-wing Labour Party which had less support in the country than we did. She certainly did not advocate that at the time. If we were to make any attempt to form a government, what she chooses to call 'horse-trading' had to be prolonged. Even with Liberal support we could not have commanded a majority in the House of Commons. I examined the possibility of gaining support from seven of the more moderate Ulster Unionists who were indeed anxious to keep out Labour, but they had all been elected on a platform of opposition to the Sunningdale Agreement, and I was not willing to jeopardize peace in the province. I do not really believe that the Unionists would have voted down a Conservative government in a vote of confidence, but their support would have been unstable at best, and I was not willing to be blackmailed by anyone.

I left Downing Street on the Monday evening to submit the government's resignation to the Queen. After our talk I went down to my official car. As my security officer closed the door, he said, 'Goodbye, sir.' 'Where on earth are you going?' I asked. 'Sir, you are no longer Prime Minister, and therefore no longer entitled to special protection,' he replied. That brought home to me the reality of the sudden change. I had been far too busy in the run-up to the election to make contingency plans for my own future, so I was temporarily without a home. I tried to get the lease back on my Albany flat, but a French couple had taken it up and were not enthusiastic about making way for me. So much for European unity! Timothy Kitson, who had remained solid in his support throughout, stepped in with the offer of his flat near Vauxhall Bridge while new arrangements were made. My piano and other larger possessions were put into storage before I moved in mid-July into a terraced house in Wilton Street, Belgravia, leased from the Grosvenor Estate.

I made few changes to the front bench after the election. I had been glad to fight the campaign with such a strong team, and I had no cause at the time to doubt anyone's loyalty. Tony Barber had long expressed a desire to leave politics, and he reaffirmed this decision after the election. Unlike some ministers in less exposed positions, he had received heavy, largely undeserved, criticism. I was sad to see him go. Alec Douglas-Home stayed on to shadow Foreign Affairs. His conduct in office had enhanced his high reputation. Robert Carr moved from Home Affairs, where he was replaced by Jim Prior, to shadow the Treasury, and Willie Whitelaw remained at the crucial post of Employment. Then, in a summer reshuffle, Whitelaw became party Chairman, and Prior took his place.

Keith Joseph apparently expected to be promoted to Treasury spokesman, but the arguments against that were overwhelming. At a time when we were sure to be pressing for tough government measures, it would have been absurd to entrust the Shadow Chancellorship to one of the biggest spenders of our period in government. With his favoured position occupied by Robert Carr, Joseph asked for a non-specific role in which he could concentrate on studying the reasons for Britain's long-term relative economic decline. I thought that potentially this would be valuable, so I agreed. This was a mistake. In June 1974, the senior treasurer of the party asked to see me urgently. He said that donations to the party had been falling. On enquiry, he had found that Joseph was approaching our traditional donors, saying that he did so with my full authority, asking for their contributions to go to him for his research. I was furious and challenged him about this, telling him to stop at once.

At this time, Joseph also began attacking the established party line on economic policy. He had resumed an old friendship with a person called Alfred Sherman, a former communist, and undergone what he liked to term a 'conversion' as a result. They spuriously argued that this country had enjoyed a free-market golden age in the nineteenth century, and that we should now turn the clock back by deregulating and allowing the worst excesses of capitalism to reassert themselves. I agreed to let Keith Joseph put these arguments to a special meeting of the Shadow Cabinet. He and the monetarist economists he brought with him, Alan Walters and James Ball, failed to cut any ice with the great majority of his colleagues, although we did them the courtesy of listening.

Then, during the summer of 1974, Joseph developed a method of attacking previous Conservative governments, while excusing himself. We, along with our post-war predecessors, had allegedly made the 'mistake' of trying to do something about Britain's economic decline and to mitigate unemployment. Joseph himself had supposedly been too busy with his own department's affairs, spending taxpayers' money, to notice what was happening. On the other hand he was always present when Cabinet discussed our overall strategy, as was Mrs Thatcher, who also kept quiet at this time. Joseph went on to set up the Centre for Policy Studies with her support, as rivals to our Conservative Research Department which had been serving the party for nearly fifty years.

If anything, our task was more difficult than it had been after the inconclusive election of 1964. Harold Wilson's reputation for tactical skill was well deserved and, although it was becoming apparent that he was no longer quite the consummate politician he had been, this was the kind of situation which he relished. He calculated that he could count on several months in office, because the opposition parties would hesitate before voting him down even though they had the strength to do so. If Wilson lost a vote of confidence, we were sure that he would ask the Queen for a new election and that, if she agreed to one, Labour would gain more seats. There is, as Shakespeare wrote, 'a tide in the affairs of men, Which, taken at the flood, leads on to fortune'. Every election since the war which has been held on the back of another has reaffirmed the earlier tide with greater power, as in 1951 and 1966.

In the aftermath of our defeat, however predictable it might have been, the inevitable rumours concerning my position as leader of the party began to surface. I could not afford to be distracted by them. Labour did not have a majority and a second election could be called at any time. When a government has been in office for only a short time, it is natural for the public to give it the benefit of the doubt, as I had found to my cost in 1966, after just one year as leader of the Conservative Party. A leader needs at least two years to establish some sort of authority, both within the party and in the eyes of the electorate, so it would have been quite wrong for me to desert the Conservative Party at this crucial stage. After our defeat the following October, when the parliamentary situation was scarcely more stable, I reached a similar conclusion. Mindful of what happened to me in 1966, I thought that this would be a thankless inheritance to pass on to any successor.

In 1974, Wilson knew that he could run a second successful campaign by saying that his government had never been given a chance. People understandably resent having their lives disrupted by elections, and tend to look unfavourably on parties which cause such contests to take place. So, ironically for us, the worst thing that could happen in the first few months of this parliament would be to defeat the government in a vote which the Prime Minister could claim was a matter of confidence. The Conservative historian Robert Blake reminded me that, in the event of Wilson seeking another dissolution after losing a vote of confidence on the Loyal Address, the Queen's constitutional duty would be to see whether a government of some kind could be formed from the existing parliament. We should not, therefore, wholly discount the possibility that she might refuse a new election in such circumstances. Everyone in the Shadow Cabinet agreed that taking on Wilson in a vote of confidence would, at best, be a calculated risk. Nonetheless, as I said in the debate on the new government's Queen's Speech, we certainly had a duty to oppose where we disagreed on a matter of principle. Having bought off the miners, the government said that it would scrap our controls on prices and incomes as well as the Industrial Relations Act. Whatever the dangers of winning a confidence vote on this issue, we had to make a stand against the abandonment of policies which we had just recommended to the country in an election campaign and, on prices and incomes, the Liberals agreed with us. In the end the government announced that it would not, after all, completely dismantle our mechanisms for curbing inflationary pressures in industry, so the affair blew over and Labour managed to win the vote on the Loyal Address.

Between March and October 1974 the Labour government acted as we had expected. Denis Healey, the new Chancellor, reversed our income tax cuts in the first of two 1974 budgets. The basic rate was increased from 30 to 33 per cent, and Value Added Tax was extended to sweets, soft drinks and ice cream. Corporation tax and stamp duty were significantly increased. Overall, the tax burden was increased by over £2,000 million per year in this budget, about £12,000 million in today's values. Significant price increases were announced for the products of nationalised industries, including coal and steel. Postal charges also rose considerably. In Healey's second budget, delivered in July, the rate of VAT was lowered from 10 to 8 per cent, but the government poured in subsidies to keep other prices down, notably that of milk.

Given the instability of the parliamentary situation, I believe that we did as well as could be expected in opposition. We won both arguments and parliamentary votes, substantially improving various pieces of legislation and defeating the government more than twenty times on the floor of the House. Notably, we thwarted an attempt by Labour to award the unions tax concessions which they had forfeited by failing to register under the Industrial Relations Act and saved the Code of Industrial Relations Practice. Morale was not particularly high on the backbenches after the defeat in February, and anxiety about when Wilson might call an election further dampened spirits. Ironically, having been more than 10 per cent behind in the Gallup polls for April and May, we narrowed the gap to less than 5 per cent by September.

As soon as the February election was over we had started work on the policies which would feature in our next manifesto. Four policy groups were established – on industrial relations, incomes policy, housing and devolution. With an election likely to be called at any time, we needed to concentrate our efforts. It was agreed that we should not try to reintroduce the Industrial Relations Act, although in our manifesto we stressed that the legislation had been right at the time. In pursuit of our traditional aim of wider home ownership, we proposed that council-house occupiers of more than three years' standing would have the right to buy their homes, at discount prices. This policy was implemented by a later Conservative government, but without our additional suggestion that a proportion of any capital gain on a quick resale of the house be returned to the council by the buyer. Our proposals would have contributed far less to the kind of unstable housing boom which we witnessed in the 1980s. We also promised to abolish the rates, replacing them with a system related to the ability to pay, and to keep mortgage interest rates lower than 9.5 per cent. Peter Walker was responsible for much of the creative thinking in these areas. Our Environment spokesman, Mrs Thatcher, strongly advocated these policies during the election campaign, so few would have guessed that, originally, she had opposed them just as strongly within the Shadow Cabinet. Indeed, I had to hold a private meeting with Mrs Thatcher and William Whitelaw in order to talk her round to supporting these ideas. She had opposed the sale of council houses on the basis that it would offend Tory voters in privately-owned residences nearby. How different the story would become in the 1980s.

The policies on which we fought the second general election of 1974 were based on the Conservative principles which I had followed throughout my political life. On 9 May I had an opportunity to outline these principles once again in the Iain Macleod Memorial Lecture. I told my audience of London Young Conservatives that 'anybody who acts in disregard of the requirements of fairness and reason ... damages the only bond which today holds us together in society'. Having outlined the achievements of the 1970–4 government, I warned against acting as if we had a 'monopoly of virtue – the people of Britain have always had an effective way of dealing with humbug of that kind'. Politicians of goodwill should set aside their differences in the face of the dogmatists on each side of the debate. As I put it, 'We do not believe that some nineteenth-century system of economics – be it doctrinal Marxism or be it laisser-faire liberalism – we do not believe that these have defined all the rules of morality, all the canons of behaviour, or all the goals of people's lives.' This speech, of course, was delivered before Keith Joseph announced his conversion to the dogma of laisser-faire which I had specifically denounced. The lecture was a restatement of the One Nation approach which both Iain Macleod and I had helped to establish. In my conclusion, I referred back to another foundation-stone of post-war Conservatism – the Charters published by the party from 1947 onwards, which had helped to convince voters that our party was dedicated to the welfare of the whole community. I advocated a 'Charter for the People' to make all of our citizens feel that they had a stake in society. It embodied a 'national philosophy'.

The industrial relations problems of recent years had been deliberately stoked up by extremists whose philosophy was built upon class conflict, and they had left our nation grievously divided. As a consequence, I felt that we had to restate our One Nation credentials in a far more positive way. In short, I came around to Jeremy Thorpe's view, that such a crisis required a government of national unity. When our election manifesto was finalised in August, it included a promise to 'consult and confer with the leaders of other parties and with the leaders of the great interests in the nation, in order to secure for the government's policies the consent and support of all men and women of good will. We will invite people from outside the ranks of our party to join with us in overcoming Britain's problems. The nation's crisis should transcend party differences.' This was a difficult concept to put across, as cynics were bound to say that it was forced out of us by the expectation of defeat. It would have held good, however, whether we had formed a minority government or won a landslide victory. We could never be precise about the details because we could not know in advance who would respond to the call. I have every reason to think that such an arrangement would have been a success. In the following year I was to experience at first hand the benefits of cross-party co-operation when I fought for a 'yes' vote in the European referendum. Our manifesto was prematurely leaked, in early September, while I was visiting President Ford who had just replaced Nixon in the White House. On balance this was probably a disguised favour to us, because the manifesto was extremely well written, by Ian Gilmour, whom I had put in charge of the Research Department, and Christopher Patten, and the leak meant that it was more widely discussed than these documents usually are.

I particularly wanted people to reflect upon the importance of Europe during this campaign, and the risks that would be posed to our membership by a Labour government under Wilson. Our manifesto therefore reminded people of the reasons why we had joined:

> Membership of the EEC brings us great economic advantages, but the European Community is not a matter of accountancy. There are two basic ideas behind the formation of the Common Market; first, that having nearly destroyed themselves by two great European civil wars, the European nations should make a similar war impossible in future; and, secondly, that only through unity could the western European nations recover control over their destiny – a control which they had lost after two wars, the division of Europe and the rise of the United States and the Soviet Union.

We also set out the thinking behind our policy towards wage inflation, restating our opposition to the brutal deflationary policies which were now being advocated by the monetarists, both within our own party and beyond it:

> We must . . . work out with the trade unions and the employers a fair and effective policy for prices and incomes . . . if after all our efforts we fail to get a comprehensive voluntary policy we shall need to support the voluntary restraint that *is* achieved with the back-up of the law . . . It would be irresponsible and dishonest totally to rule this out . . . In the absence of an effective prices and incomes policy and Government would have to take harsher financial and economic measures than would otherwise be necessary.

We lost the election which Harold Wilson called for 10 October after the shortest parliament for almost a century. Labour won 319 seats, and we were forty-two behind on 277. For the first week we deliberately ran a quiet campaign, knowing that the electorate would have a low tolerance for politics so soon after the last election. Later we tried a new campaign idea, holding 'talk-ins' with small groups to get away from the impression that political leaders were remote from the voters. I also stepped up my attacks on Labour, which was marketing an extreme election platform almost identical to that of February. Wherever I went, the reception was enthusiastic and, as ever, I enjoyed campaigning. But, as in 1966, I sensed that this would be a 'vote Labour, pay later' election. The government was trying to disguise the true nature of the crisis from the people, and had prepared its ground before the election by releasing White Papers on all the subjects which could possibly generate enthusiasm. We knew that its promises on subjects such as pensions would have to be broken once reality returned, but I always thought it likely that, also just like 1966, the voters would be tempted to give Labour another term of office.

During the campaign, we attempted to use new methods of influencing the public, in particular by the informality of our meetings up and down the country. On a number of occasions I spoke to large gatherings from the platform, sitting on a chair answering questions on any of the points raised. It seemed to satisfy the audience, although the media were not very happy about it. They preferred a more intense degree of stage management, with an advance copy of every speech for their convenience. We also played on major national themes, rather than concentrating on attacking the government and its individual members. I was in Bexley for the count, where my own majority fell slightly – to just over 7,500. Of course the national outcome was a disappointment, but I was well prepared for it. Although Labour had been widely expected to win a large majority, in the event its overall majority was only three, so our performance had been far better than in 1966, when we had been faced with very similar circumstances.

The October election came in the wake of a personal tragedy, the loss of my third *Morning Cloud* in September. We had done particularly well during the second half of Cowes Week and, following that, at Ramsgate where we won the 'Round the Goodwins' Race. On Saturday 31 August I left the boat after another enjoyable, albeit less successful, week at Burnham-on-Crouch, flying from Southend to Antwerp for the thirtieth-anniversary celebrations of my regiment's entry into the city. Meanwhile, the boat had been taken over by the movement crew, which sailed the boat between races. Just before it set off for Cowes, it was joined by my godson Christopher Chadd, who had never been on *Morning Cloud* but had sailed on other boats. When he had asked if he could sail with the crew to broaden his sailing experience I had told him that he could, provided that the skipper, Donald Blewett, gave his permission, which he did. There was a warning of bad weather when they began the journey, but the boat was well adapted for rough conditions and they set off in light winds. As they crossed the Thames estuary the wind strengthened considerably and they could have put in at Ramsgate or Dover. The wind then slackened to Force 6 so they decided to continue.

Past Beachy Head the wind increased again, to a Force 9 gale. The boat, as expected, was handling well, and the wind, blowing south-south-west, was helpful at that point. At about 11 p.m. on Monday 2 September *Morning Cloud* was still moving comfortably off Shoreham, only a few miles from calmer waters, when a freak wave knocked the boat over. There was a certain amount of damage, but the boat righted itself. Two of the crew had gone overboard. One was retrieved, but the other, Nigel Cumming, could not be found, even when the boat turned around to search for him. A broken life-line was discovered, still attached to the port rail. After starting the boat's engine, Donald Blewett tried to set off distress flares, but the first two failed to work and the third was quickly blown downwards into the sea, so he rightly decided not to fire any more for the time being.

With the weather now worsening, the crew continued to search for Nigel Cumming. Then it was hit by a second wave and, once again, overturned. Christopher Chadd had been wearing a life jacket but not a safety harness. He was swept off the deck as he moved towards the cockpit, and was lost. The boat was now leaking seriously, and Blewett rightly concluded that none of them would survive unless the five of them crammed into the four-man life raft, a six-man raft having been swept away. He and another crew member were, by now, badly injured. After eight hours in the raft, during which all the remaining crew suffered badly from the still very rough water, they were washed ashore near Brighton. I was at home in Wilton Street on the Tuesday morning when the police rang me with the news that the two men were missing, with little chance of having survived in those rough seas. I immediately drove down to visit the crew in hospital, and telephoned George Chadd with the dreadful news. The shattered shell of the boat was soon recovered, and the bodies of the two lost men were washed ashore some days later. In the same storm, the original *Morning Cloud* was smashed against rocks, having been torn from her moorings off Jersey.

At the inquest, the coroner reached a verdict of death by misadventure. There were obvious lessons for the sailing community, but no fault whatsoever could be attached to the crew who had no reason to suspect that the boat would founder in the conditions which they had anticipated. In fact, a smaller racing vessel had got through about an hour before *Morning Cloud*. Additional safety precautions were clearly necessary in future. In particular, life-lines needed to be strengthened, and the cockpit redesigned to reduce the danger of waterlogging. To the extent that important lessons were learned, the tragic deaths of Christopher Chadd and Nigel Cumming were not entirely in vain. The sinking and tragic loss of life were a great personal blow to me for many reasons, but it had no effect on my conduct in the October campaign. Whatever private feelings a politician has, he is a public figure who, in the pursuit of his chosen profession, must try to put aside even the deepest personal grief.

I spent the day after the October election in low spirits at home in Wilton Street, tired, and disappointed that we had come so close once again. With Labour having gained overall majority, my own position as leader was going to come increasingly under scrutiny. I had been leader for nearly ten years and it was only natural that, over such a period, there would be a number of malcontents on the backbenches. Many felt bitter at their lack of progress under my leadership – it is impossible to include everybody in a Shadow Cabinet or government. In addition, some MPs would genuinely think that it was time for a change. I received a great deal of advice that day from friends and colleagues. Tim Kitson advised me to step down, and both Jim Prior and Kenneth Baker warned that I should resign to avoid getting hurt. Toby Aldington and Francis Pym, however, both advised me to tough it out. Lord Thorneycroft also urged me to stay on as 'Most of the things you have predicted will, alas, come true and at that moment the Conservative Party will be very much weaker unless you are still at its head.' I sent a letter to the chairman of the 1922 Committee, Edward du Cann, on 17 October which stated that I looked forward to meeting, if invited, the 1922 Committee to hear and discuss the views of our parliamentary colleagues about the best way forward for us in opposition. However, before this could take place, elections had to be concluded for the officers and members of the executive committee.

Back in my office as Leader of the Opposition the week after polling day, William Waldegrave, who had followed Douglas Hurd as my political private secretary, came in to bring me up to date on the strength of feeling against me in the parliamentary party. He reported that Edward du Cann had called a secret meeting of the pre-election executive of the 1922 Committee on the previous Monday morning. This was held not in the House of Commons or in Conservative Central Office, nor in any other building of the party organisation, but at du Cann's house in Lord North Street. They were meeting to discuss how to get rid of me, which was why they needed such secrecy. Shortly afterwards, du Cann told me that the executive committee had decided that I should resign. I pointed out to him that the new House of Commons had not yet met and there had been no opportunity for a discussion within the party. What was more, I added, the group he had got together secretly at his house represented no one except themselves. The committee had to be elected afresh with each parliamentary session. In the case of a new parliament this was particularly important. The executive of the old 1922 Committee then met again, at the offices in the City of London of du Cann's merchant bank, Keyser Ullman, to consider their tactics. William Waldegrave made sure that this secret meeting was leaked to all the media as widely as possible.

It was natural that the party should be in low spirits during the debate on the Queen's Speech and it was obviously tepid towards myself. But, so long as we were seen to be an effective Opposition, the party would unite and gather strength. The government had an overall majority of only three, and it had few ideas on how to deal with the deteriorating economic situation. As the main Opposition party, we had a clear task, but speculation about my own position played into the hands of Harold Wilson, diverting attention away from the failings of his government.

After the retirement of Tony Barber and Alec Douglas-Home in the autumn, it was necessary to reshuffle the Shadow Cabinet. This was duly completed on 7 November. I appointed Mrs Thatcher to the Treasury team, to assist Robert Carr as Shadow Chancellor. I trusted Robert's political philosophy and judgement completely, but I also knew from experience that he had not found the transition back to opposition terribly easy. I hoped that appointing Margaret Thatcher as his number two would alleviate this problem, and disarm the right. Her appointment to the Treasury gave her the opportunity she needed to make runs in the House of Commons. She took full advantage of this, which undoubtedly improved her support in the subsequent leadership contest. Kenneth Baker and Willie Whitelaw both suggested that I should appoint as the new Shadow Leader of the House John Peyton, Minister of Transport from 1970 to 1974. He accepted. Edward du Cann, however, refused to join my team, undermining my attempt to unify the party. This was exacerbated when some of those Members who had been secretly plotting to remove me as leader were re-elected to the Executive of the 1922 Committee on 3 November. This intolerable situation could not continue for much longer.

The question had also been raised, both by my supporters and by my opponents within the party, of the suitability of the machinery for the election of the leader of the Conservative Party. Under the existing rules, I did not have to submit myself for re-election at any time. George Gardiner, who had been elected Conservative MP for Reigate in February 1974, advocated a ballot to 'restore some stability to a dangerously unstable party situation'. In a letter of 27 October, Gardiner stressed that he was not advocating an election out of any criticism of my leadership, rather because 'It is natural that after an election defeat many of our colleagues should talk vaguely about a change of leadership. But concentrate their minds on the real choice in a ballot, and I am convinced your leadership would be endorsed by a convincing majority.' Imagine my surprise when I discovered shortly afterwards that George Gardiner was a member of Mrs Thatcher's campaign team who also used the apparatus of Central Office to help her campaign. In the face of such behaviour, it was no surprise that my team overestimated my backbench support.

After careful reflection, I decided that it was probably in the interests of the Conservative Party to rethink its rules on the election of its leader. Although the Whips still thought that I should be unchallenged, I knew that a revision of the rules might provide an opportunity for enemies to demand a ballot or stage a revolt. Nonetheless, on 14 November, I informed the 1922 Committee that I would discuss arrangements for the review of the procedure for electing the leader of the party. I assured the packed meeting that I considered myself a servant of the party, although I gave no indication of resignation. On Wednesday 20th, I announced that a special panel, under Alec Home, by then Lord Home of the Hirsel, would be established to examine this question. Other members of the committee included Edward du Cann, Willie Whitelaw and Humphrey Atkins. The die had now been cast and the weekend media were full of speculation.

I was not, therefore, totally surprised when Mrs Thatcher asked to see me on Monday 25 November, to inform me that she wished to challenge for the leadership. Just four days earlier, Keith Joseph had told her that he would not be putting his own name forward. She insisted that she wanted to let me know before she announced the decision publicly. This was strange, for the whole of the weekend press had clearly foreshadowed what was going to happen, effectively making the declaration for her. But I thanked her. The other candidate was to be Hugh Fraser, who had been a member of previous governments, and with whom I had been close since our Oxford days. He was never a serious contestant, and he was quite unable to explain his decision to stand.

Alec Home came to see me to report privately on the conclusions of his panel, before they were published on 17 December. The Committee proposed that there should be a regular, annual leadership election with the victor requiring an overall majority, with a margin of at least 15 per cent of those entitled to vote. In 1965, I had needed only an overall majority of 15 per cent of those actually voting in the first ballot. An outright win was now far more difficult to attain. Furthermore, if a second ballot was almost inevitably going to be required, then candidates who had not entered the previous round could join the race. MPs who did not actually want Mrs Thatcher to win would now be more likely to vote for her, in the expectation that their own preferred candidate would come forward in the next round. I had great misgivings about these changes, not least because they undoubtedly weakened the position of the elected leader of the party. These worries were shared by many backbench MPs. Winston Churchill, grandson of our war-leader and then an MP, wrote a very strong letter against the new procedure, arguing that it was likely to have disastrous consequences for the future standing of the party.

The developments which followed were entirely unprecedented. Hitherto the appointment of a leader of the Conservative Party and, in my own case, the election of a leader, had been unaccompanied by any public campaigning, and the candidates themselves had taken no part in the discussions which went on. Now, however, I found that not only was there intense lobbying in the House of Commons, but the media, especially radio and television, were being prompted by the other candidates the whole time. I had already hosted a party for new Members on 5 November and, seeing all the activities of the other two candidates in the campaign, Kenneth Baker, one of my parliamentary private secretaries, arranged three lunches at Buck's Club for undecided MPs, and Nick Scott, Kenneth Baker and Tony Berry each gave a dinner for backbench MPs. These certainly proved to be helpful and built on two small lunches I had already hosted at Wilton Street for MPs with marginal seats, meetings which had been set up primarily to obtain their ideas on how we could do better in industrial areas.

On 15 January 1975, Airey Neave, MP for Abingdon since 1953, took over the management of Mrs Thatcher's campaign. She was not his first choice but he had failed in his attempts to persuade Edward du Cann to stand against me. It has since been written, and passed from author to author, that Airey Neave was motivated by spite towards myself. According to this rumour, Airey wanted revenge for an alleged spiteful comment that I had made to him about his health while I was Chief Whip. I have never been asked about this and, in fact, there are absolutely no grounds for claiming that I was unsympathetic towards him. As a junior minister he informed me that his health had broken down and that his doctor had told him he should resign. I expressed my sympathy, told him that he must recover his good health, and stressed that he should come to see me as soon as his doctor felt he could accept another appointment. As his health improved Airey took up various business interests, but never indicated that he wanted to come back into government. During the election campaign, in autumn 1974, he visited me at home, bringing with him the chairman of one of our major companies who wanted help in dealing with a government department. I listened carefully and said I would immediately take it up with the minister concerned. There is absolutely no justification for these false stories about my telling Neave that he was 'finished'. I would never behave in that way towards a colleague.

There was, however, one occasion, just before Christmas 1974, when

Airey Neave told me that he believed the time had come for me to resign. He informed me that he was in a position to guarantee that I would be given a top job in the Shadow Cabinet or in any Conservative government which should follow it. I thanked him, but replied that I was not proposing to resign and, in any case, would not be prepared to accept covert deals of this kind from him or anybody else. Neave was a shrewd tactician. I am convinced that I would have won the first ballot if he had not taken charge of the Thatcher campaign. On polling day and, indeed, during the whole campaign, he told colleagues that he was not expecting Mrs Thatcher to win in the first round, but hoped specific individuals would vote for her in order to prevent my majority from becoming too great. I was told afterwards of the Conservative Members who fell for this cunning manoeuvre.

Shortly after my meeting with Airey Neave, my house at Wilton Street was bombed by the IRA. It was a narrow escape. I had been delayed on my return from my annual carol concert at Broadstairs and missed the attack by some five minutes. A two-pound bomb was thrown from a car towards the house and caused substantial damage to my property although, thankfully, my housekeeper was in her basement room and escaped unhurt. The following day, I insisted on honouring a long-arranged trip to Ulster. I was certainly not going to be intimidated by a cowardly attack from the IRA which, as with all their attacks on the British mainland, did them nothing but harm. The Queen sent both her sympathy and congratulations after the attack. Her sympathy was for the damage to my home, while her congratulations were for my 'escape'.

Airey Neave also wrote, on 27 December, that 'Diana and I were distressed to hear of the damage to your house and your narrow shave. I hope it will not take too long to put things in order. I am grateful to you for seeing me the other day and listening to my point of view. Best wishes for the New Year.' This letter has special significance, of course, because of Airey Neave's tragic death on 30 March 1979. He had not been as lucky as I was. A bomb was planted under his car by Irish Republican terrorists and exploded as he left the House of Commons car park. Neave was a courageous man who had first achieved fame by escaping from Colditz. He had been murdered by contemptible cowards. When I heard the terrible news, I thought at once of his wife and children, and my mind went back to his own letter of sympathy. The most robust response of all to the bomb attack on my home came from Julian Amery, who commented, 'The bastards! Almost makes me sorry we voted against the rope.'

When the House returned after Christmas, our Chief Whip Humphrey Atkins told me that, according to soundings by the Whips, I would be re-elected as leader of the party. I was sure they were honest in their assessment of the situation when, on 23 January 1975, I announced my intention of standing again for the leadership on the terms set out by the Home panel. I remained deeply unhappy about the new procedure for electing a leader. Wider considerations, however, had to take priority. The serious situation facing the country meant that any further delay was unacceptable. Nominations for the leadership were closed on 30 January, and the date of the ballot was set for 4 February. On 31 January, I spoke at a dinner of the Leeds Chamber of Commerce, and began with words which turned out to be rather prophetic: 'I have found myself in the last twelve months spending much more time than I should have liked in voicing warnings on Britain's situation . . . It is not a role I relish. I have never fancied myself in the garb of a latter-day Jeremiah; and I am well aware that Cassandra in the legend came to an unhappy end.'

Despite the downbeat nature of these remarks, the consultation exercise undertaken by the 1922 executive committee had proved that I had over-whelming support among representatives of Conservative peers, the National Union, covering England and Wales, and the Scottish Conserva-tive and Unionist Association. I was later shocked to hear that the 1922 executive did not officially release these findings in a written report, nor relate the conclusions to a full meeting of the 1922 Committee, of which all Conservative MPs in opposition are members, apart from the Leader and Chief Whip. As *The Times* commented on 8 February, individual Members were left to ask the 1922 executive what they understood the consultations to show: 'leaving aside the fact that the 1922 Executive has throughout had a large anti-Heath majority, who were not therefore the most impartial of witnesses, this was plainly an inadequate way of reporting the consultations to those with the electoral power'.

However, I was still assured by a variety of sources that I would win the leadership contest on the first ballot. On 3 February, the day before the election, the *Daily Express* published a Harris poll which showed that 70 per cent of Conservative voters wanted me to remain as leader, and Alec Home announced his own support for me. Woodrow Wyatt, a former Labour MP who later moved to the right, sent his best wishes for a resounding triumph, and assured me that I was 'doing fine'. I also received good wishes from my friends in music and the world of sailing. Indeed, the constant support and encouragement from my friends outside West-minster was always inspiring. The great Welsh baritone Sir Geraint Evans, who had performed at Fanfare for Europe at Covent Garden in January 1973, sent a particularly warm letter of support, as did Sir Maurice Laing. He had owned *Clarion of Wight*, the vessel on which I had sailed in my first ever ocean race.

On 3 February the *Daily Telegraph* published an article that I had written for their 'My Kind of Tory Party' series. I was careful to congratulate the party for displaying a fundamental Conservative principle, that open discussion within a party or a nation need not be the same thing as factionalism, also acknowledging that the party had been worried over many aspects concerning the future leadership at a time when 'the attack on socialist measures and administrative incompetence of the present Labour Government demands all our time and energy'. The historic role of the Conservative Party, I wrote, was to use its political and diplomatic skills to create a fresh balance between different elements within the state at those times when, for one reason or another, their imbalance threatens to disrupt the orderly development of society. I went on:

> This role means that at various times we have found ourselves espousing the cause of different limbs of the body politic against the overweening claims of others, in order to restore harmony to the whole . . . Our underlying beliefs about the nature of the individual citizen and his paramountcy within the state do not change; the practical politics of preserving an open and healthy society in which the individual has the freedom to exercise his creative ability – and in this way to provide the necessary power for society to regenerate itself – change constantly.

On 4 February, I sat in my room as Leader of the Opposition awaiting the result. It was brought by Sir Timothy Kitson, who was my teller at the count. Tim rushed in saying, 'I am sorry, Ted, but it's all up.' He was followed by Hugh Fraser, a rival candidate, who said, as tears started to stream down his cheeks, 'I am terribly sorry – I never wanted this to happen.' Others gradually gathered around. We had all got it so badly wrong. Mrs Thatcher, against all expectations, had won the first ballot, with 130 votes to my 119. Hugh Fraser had received only sixteen votes. We were all stunned. Reggie Maudling, normally so calm and assured, was overheard to remark, 'The party's taken leave of its senses. This is a black day.' I issued a statement to announce that I would not take part in another contest, and would relinquish the leadership at once:

> As a result of the first ballot today for the leadership of the Conservative Party, I have decided not to stand in the Second Ballot. It has been a great privilege to serve my party as its leader, and my country as its Prime Minister. I would like to thank all those at Westminster and in the country who through the years, in hard times as well as in good, have given me their support and friendship.

Mrs Thatcher's campaign team immediately went off to a champagne party to celebrate. I arranged for Robert Carr to handle the Opposition front bench of the party until the election of a new leader was confirmed. Robert was an obvious choice, as he was highly respected and had assured me that he did not want to be a candidate for the leadership. This appointment enabled the party to fulfil its obligations as Her Majesty's Opposition, and it prevented Wilson from exploiting the situation still further.

There was, understandably, tremendous speculation in the newspapers about my political future. The media coverage was, on the whole, sympathetic about the shabby way in which I had been treated. *The Times* leader stated, 'There must be great sympathy for him in this situation. He has served his party and his country honourably and with great energy and determination. His work in Europe has been his greatest achievement . . . He has many of the qualities of a great man and has deserved the gratitude of his country. He has also behaved with complete dignity in the painful months since last October.' In view of all the press speculation over my future, however, I felt obliged to issue a second statement on 5 February:

> I intend to remain in the House of Commons to look after the interests of my constituents. I have no intention of going to the House of Lords or of taking up a European appointment. After the process for the election for the Leader of the Conservative Party, I intend to take a rest. Thereafter, freed from the routine daily labours of both Opposition and Government which I have sustained for nearly ten years, I shall do all I can to serve the interests of my country and my Party by concentrating on the great issues facing Britain at home and overseas.

Harold Wilson made a generous tribute on 6 February. He told the House of Commons that I had always been concerned to serve the best interests of the House and its Members, adding: 'There, and in other ways, I can recall many acts of individual consideration and kindness going far beyond the normal exchanges and activities of parliamentary life in our democracy.' I immediately sent a handwritten note of thanks to him at Downing Street. Letters displaying a mixture of anger and sadness poured in from a variety of sources, including Harold Macmillan, Roy Jenkins, Yehudi Menuhin, Chris Patten and Malcolm Rifkind. Losing the leadership was a terrible blow but my friends all rallied round. One letter, warmly addressed to 'Ted' and signed 'Jimmy' went as follows: 'What a tragic day for you, for Britain, for Europe and for us all. I am, of course, entirely at your disposal if I can be of any use.' James Goldsmith was later to show his appreciation by campaigning vigorously for a 'yes' vote in the 1975 Referendum, as chairman of the Britain in Europe Food Committee. He was subsequently elected as a French MEP but spent much of his time in Mexico, before his death in 1997. By that time he had convinced himself that his strongly pro-European stance during the 1970s and 1980s had all been a terrible self-deception.

I was shocked to discover from letters received from Conservative activists that many were threatening to leave the party in protest at the events since the October election. These were reaching damaging proportions and I knew that I had to act for the good of the party. I sent a standard reply to each letter in an attempt to restore a semblance of morale: 'I am immensely grateful for your support and loyalty and understand your feelings. But I must beg you to continue to support the Conservative Party at this critical time in our country's fortunes; otherwise there is a danger that all I have tried to do will be swept away by a long period of Labour rule.'

As Mrs Thatcher did not receive the required number of votes on the first poll to win outright, a subsequent ballot was necessary. On the second vote the candidates were Margaret Thatcher, Willie Whitelaw, Geoffrey Howe, Jim Prior and John Peyton. I did not publicly express a preference for any of the candidates or involve myself in the campaign as, in my position as the outgoing leader of the party, I felt it would have been quite wrong to do so. I am sure that this was the right thing to do in the circumstances. John Major took a similar decision in 1997. I did, however, exercise my right to vote. After careful reflection, I opted for Willie Whitelaw as the next leader of the Conservative Party. Willie had many excellent qualities and I am sure he would have proved to be a fine leader. I considered him to be a loyal colleague and a close friend. What is more, I was sure that I could serve under him, as Alec Douglas-Home had done under me. But Mrs Thatcher, having won the previous poll, was in too strong a position and was duly declared the winner with 146 votes against Willie's 79. I issued a statement of congratulation.

The next day Tim Kitson was approached by Mrs Thatcher's PPS, who asked whether the leader could come to see me at my home at Wilton Street. It was suggested to Tim that she was going to offer me a job in the Shadow Cabinet. I received this message and, after careful consideration, I instructed Tim to take a message back saying that I had decided that I did not wish to join the Shadow Cabinet for the time being. I was therefore somewhat surprised when Mrs Thatcher arrived at Wilton Street at 10.30 the following morning. I have heard some extraordinary accounts of what went on at that meeting. This is an answer to all those spurious descriptions that have been produced of our discussion. To begin with, it was not held in the drawing room as some sources have suggested. This was not physically possible because it had been bombed by the IRA six weeks earlier and was no longer usable. She was received by Sir Timothy Kitson, who showed her down the passage to my small study at the back of the house. Mrs Thatcher was obviously and understandably flustered, but I congratulated her again on her victory in the second ballot. After these preliminaries, she said there was one point on which she would value my advice. How should she handle the press, particularly at the weekly press conference held in the lobby of the House of Commons, each Thursday? This press conference was used mainly to find out the attitude of the Opposition on the parliamentary business for the coming week. I told her that handling the press was an individual matter. We all had our own ways of dealing with them, and I suggested that she should develop her existing techniques. She thanked me, rose and said goodbye. It took only a few minutes.

At the front door, where Tim Kitson was waiting to let her out, Mrs Thatcher asked to stay for a while longer, lest the press outside should conclude that the meeting had been a disaster. Tim took her upstairs as he was concerned that, if he took her to the downstairs dining room, they would be seen by the large number of press photographers who were waiting outside. Ten minutes later, he said goodbye to her as well. At no time during the meeting did she invite me to become a member of the Shadow Cabinet or to play any part on her front bench. This is confirmed by Tim Kitson who, standing in the hall, heard every word that passed between us, through the open door of my study. When this suggestion first appeared in the press, I was told that the hand of Humphrey Atkins, the Chief Whip, was behind it. We assumed that he must have been acting upon a misunderstanding of something Mrs Thatcher had said to him. I took no action then to correct the record, because I had no wish to embarrass the Chief Whip at a difficult time.

On 18 February, Mrs Thatcher announced the composition of her new Shadow Cabinet. I was shocked to learn that she had dropped Robert Carr, Paul Channon, Nicholas Scott and Peter Thomas from the front bench, although I was glad to see that Reggie Maudling had returned as Shadow Foreign Secretary. Peter Walker and Geoffrey Rippon had both refused to join the Shadow Cabinet. Keith Joseph was given a roving research brief, far beyond the specific tasks I had allocated to him. This completely undermined the official apparatus of the Conservative Research Department, which became more and more drawn into the propaganda work of the rest of Central Office, and has never recovered its proper status since then. On that same day, I left to go on a month's holiday to the south of Spain, where I had stayed on so many occasions over the previous fifteen years. Tim Kitson arranged for me to have the use of a friend's villa on the coast north of Marbella, together with the staff who looked after it. I felt both disillusioned towards the party and apprehensive about the future of our country. The economy was faltering and Britain's future in the European Community was unpredictable. All of my hard work and achievements were threatened, and I had to work out in my own mind what role I could establish for myself in the years ahead.

Chapter 19

~~~~~

A FRESH LEASE OF LIFE

1975–1979

T he purpose of my month's holiday in Spain was twofold. First, I
wanted to have a complete break from the ten years I had spent
as Leader of the Opposition and Prime Minister. Secondly, I felt I
should give my successor the opportunity of establishing herself opposite
the Prime Minister without having me near by as an apparent Banquo at
the feast. My holiday was enlivened by visits from friends who flew down,
including Tim Kitson and his wife; Geoffrey Tucker, with all the latest
news; Michael Wolff, whom I had left as the senior official at Central
Office; and several Spanish friends from the sailing world against whom I
had previously raced at Cowes. The only jarring note was the news brought
to me of the changes already being made by the new leader in the party
organisation. Michael Wolff had been abruptly sacked and Willie Whitelaw
had been replaced as Chairman of the party by Peter Thorneycroft, whom
we had thought to have given up activities of this kind. Furthermore, he
had sent a personal note to me only a few months before, in which he
wrote that 'it would be a grave mistake for the Conservative Party to
change its leadership'. However, I became fully refreshed and strengthened
as the holiday progressed, ready to play my full part again in the House
of Commons on my return.

When I announced my resignation as party leader, on 4 February 1975,
I indicated that afterwards I wanted to concentrate on addressing the major
issues facing this country. On 17 March, the date of my return to the UK
from Spain, I had an immediate opportunity to put these words into
practice. An issue had to be resolved that was to affect every man and
woman in the United Kingdom and the future of Europe. It was also the
question to which I had devoted so much of my political life: British
membership of the European Community. Although the 1975 Referendum
was an exciting episode in British history, it need never have taken place.
It had absolutely nothing to do with public opinion. The British people

were saddled with this unwelcome constitutional innovation, simply because Harold Wilson thought that his acceptance of a referendum on the European issue was the best way to paper over the deep division in the Labour Party.

The Labour Party was hopelessly divided even before the summer of 1971, when the negotiations for our entry into the European Community had been successfully concluded. The whole spectrum of opinion was represented on its benches, from staunch devotees of Europe such as Roy Jenkins, Harold Lever and David Owen to the cluster of vocal anti-Europeans, including Michael Foot and Peter Shore, who were opposed to entry on any terms. It was this group who really pushed for a referendum, in their mistaken belief that the British people shared their insular mentality, but it was the substantial group of pragmatic Europeans, including Harold Wilson and James Callaghan, who were running the show and gave the Referendum the go-ahead.

The Labour leaders and their close supporters had now begun to believe their own rhetoric against the terms we had secured. In a desperate attempt to prevent a deepening split, they settled on a twin-track formula designed to appeal to all. Thus, after February 1974, when the British government should have been wholeheartedly committed to the continuous task of developing the Community from a position of strength and influence, the Labour Cabinet instead took up the time and patience of our partners with a process of so-called 'renegotiation', culminating in a referendum campaign which reopened the issue of principle settled in Parliament by a large majority in October 1971.

Both Harold Wilson and I had ruled out a referendum prior to the 1970 general election. Enoch Powell had also argued against the idea, in a speech at Tamworth on 15 June 1970, principally because 'it is inconsistent with the responsibility of government to Parliament and to the electorate'. He was correct in this. On 27 May 1970, during the BBC's *Election Forum*, I said that Parliament could be relied upon to make the final decision on accession. Harold Wilson agreed with this view and replied very strongly when asked whether he would ever change his mind:

> The answer to that is 'No'. I have given my answer many times, and I don't change it because polls go either up or down. Heavens, when the polls have been 28 points against me it hasn't made any difference to going on with policies I knew to be unpopular . . . The answer is I shall not change my attitude on that.

Tony Benn was the prime architect of the European Referendum. He had previously supported the Labour government in 1967 when it made its unsuccessful attempt to join the European Community. During the

1970–4 parliament, however, he first introduced a Referendum Bill in the House of Commons, and then steamrollered his colleagues into accepting a referendum as official party policy. On 15 March 1972, the Shadow Cabinet discussed his proposal and he was defeated by eight votes to four. Then, on the following day, President Pompidou announced his decision to call a referendum in France on the question of the enlargement of the Community.

The French referendum was an internal matter for President Pompidou and the French government and should not have made any difference to our own ratification of the Treaty. It is not for the British to cast aspersions on the referendum procedures in other countries, nor should we mimic them inappropriately. Other countries have different constitutional arrangements. Article 11 of the French constitution provides that the President may submit to a referendum any draft law which 'provides for authorisation to ratify a treaty that . . . would affect the functioning of the institutions'. There was no reason why our confidence in our own procedure should have been upset by the practice of other countries.

On 22 March 1972 Benn, buoyed by President Pompidou's decision, took the issue back to the Labour Party's national executive. This time he was backed by thirteen votes to eleven and the issue returned to the Shadow Cabinet on 29 March. By now Harold Wilson had sensed which way the wind was blowing within his party and voted in favour of a referendum. His intervention was decisive and the vote was carried by eight votes to six. This led to a mass of departures from the Labour front bench, the most significant being Roy Jenkins' resignation as deputy leader on 10 April 1972. I sympathised with him. He had been provoked time and time again by Harold Wilson's unwillingness to stand up to the likes of Benn, Shore and Foot. I was well aware that resignation was never an easy decision, but it was obvious, even for an outsider looking in, that his position was becoming untenable.

On 18 April 1972, during the committee stage of the European Communities Bill, Michael Foot and Peter Shore moved an amendment to delay the coming into force of the Bill until there had been an affirmative resolution of each House of Parliament, following a general election. The call for a general election on this issue was totally unjustifiable, so long as entry remained the official policy of all the three parties. Tony Benn, however, had his eye on the amendment tabled by the Conservative rebel Neil Marten to the European Communities Bill which aimed to delay the coming into force of the Bill until there had been an affirmative resolution of each House of Parliament, preceded by a 'consultative advisory referendum'. Labour leadership issued a two-line whip in support of this amendment. On 18 April, it was defeated by forty-nine votes after sixty-three

Labour MPs defied their leader once again and abstained. Despite this defeat, the Labour Party was still committed to a referendum on British membership of the European Community.

The Labour Party's draft policy statement *Labour's Programme for Britain*, published in July 1972, revealed their plans for 'renegotiation' of the terms that we had achieved. Later that year, at the Labour Party conference, it became official party policy. The policy of renegotiation was a sham. It would not placate those who were irrevocably opposed to membership, and Dr Sicco Mansholt, the President of the European Commission, told me on 8 October 1972 at Chequers that it was quite unrealistic of the Labour Party to expect our European partners to renegotiate the terms of entry, although once Britain was in the Community, it could of course suggest changes in the way the Community worked. Mansholt had also explained this fact to Harold Wilson. The Community, as part of its ongoing development, is always prepared to change its policies and institutions as new circumstances arise, but this could have been achieved without Labour's threats and dangerous posturing. After our accession on 1 January 1973, I tried to strike the right balance between modifying existing Community policy in order to accommodate the particular national interests of Britain, and helping to formulate and develop new common policies which would be of mutual advantage to us all. I told the 1973 Conservative Party conference:

> Of course we are not satisfied with the European Community as it stands today. I do not know anyone in the Community who believes that it has reached its final form, or indeed its perfect form . . . Should there be changes in the Common Agricultural Policy? Certainly. And it is precisely because we are now members of the Community that it has been agreed that plans for change should be set in hand . . . Should there be changes in the way the Community spends its money and in its control over it? Most certainly. And it is precisely because we are now members of the Community that we have already reached agreement on the setting up of the Regional Development Fund from which Scotland, Wales and the regions of England will benefit.

James Callaghan, as the new Foreign Secretary after the February 1974 general election, listed the seven points on which the Labour government needed to be satisfied. These included Britain's contribution to the Community budget, the operation of the Common Agricultural Policy (CAP), policy towards the developing world and the retention of national powers in regional, industrial and fiscal policy. All of these areas had been prime concerns of the 1970–4 government.

It was Joe Godber, when Conservative Minister of Agriculture, who started the Community rethinking on many aspects of the Common Agricultural Policy. On 21 November 1973, he listed the six points by which we set particular store. These included the need to reduce surpluses and costs of the CAP as well as a simplification of the price-support mechanisms. Richard Wood, as Minister for Overseas Development, pressed our partners to take fuller account of the interests of a wider range of developing countries which had not been able to benefit from the full munificence of the Community's trade and aid policies. It was John Davies who, in the summer of 1973, had safeguarded our national interests in the fields of regional and industrial policy and, at the same time, carried to an advanced stage the negotiations on the Community Regional Development policy, proposed by me at the Paris Summit of October 1972, and agreed upon there. The government that I led was always careful to insist that if, for any reason, the burden of Britain's net payments into the Community budget became manifestly unfair, it might feel obliged in the last resort to use its veto in the Council of Ministers. In January 1974, I personally discussed with West German Chancellor Helmut Schmidt the rearrangement of the budgetary provisions of the Treaty of Accession. The referendum was politically and constitutionally otiose.

I oppose national referenda for reasons of principle. Euro-sceptics claim to be the guardians of British democracy, but then say that the House of Commons cannot legitimately speak for the people on issues of major importance, such as Europe. What sort of argument is this? If Parliament cannot be trusted to take decisions on vital issues, then surely it cannot be trusted to take decisions at all. In Great Britain, our political system is built upon centuries of precedent and tradition on these matters. How would we be able to decide which policy issues should be determined by a democratic vote in the House of Commons and which would require direct public consultation through a referendum? The 1970–4 government had initiated a referendum in Northern Ireland, but only because we had closed its own parliament at Stormont, so there was no other way of learning the opinion of the people of Northern Ireland. The United Kingdom, on the other hand, had a fully effective parliamentary system for debating and deciding crucial national issues.

Harold Wilson confirmed in the House of Commons on 23 January 1975, some time after Labour had been returned to power, that a referendum on Europe would be held. Six days later, during a speech to the Conservative Group for Europe, I announced that the Conservatives would vote against the government's Referendum Bill on second reading, but would then, if we lost that vote, concentrate on trying to improve it in detail. On 20 February 1975 the Labour Cabinet decided on the details of its European White Paper. Although I had resigned the Conservative leadership earlier that month, our policy remained the same. The responsibility of attacking the Bill fell to Mrs Thatcher on 11 March 1975. In a most impressive speech she attacked the use of referenda on constitutional grounds, warning that

> There is no power under which the British constitution can come into rivalry with the legislative sovereignty of Parliament . . . To subject laws retrospectively to a popular vote suggests a serious breach of this principle. To subject laws prospectively before the final assent of the popular vote suggests we are using a different rule to validate laws. To have several referenda would create a new rule. We should be saying that some proposals require popular ratification and others do not. Without a written constitution one might ask: which proposals and what kinds of measures? . . . Presumably the answer would be: in cases of constitutional change.
>
> But it is hard to define such a change in the British tradition because so much depends on convention and precedent. A referendum may, however, become acceptable if given a proper constitutional foundation – that is to say, if the conditions under which it could be used were defined. But that would mean, like many other democratic countries, going as far as a written constitution or at least part of the way. The implications for parliamentary sovereignty are profound.

In the subsequent vote, however, the House of Commons ignored our constitutional objections. I was kept fully informed of this debate in Spain and, on my return to the UK, I knew that I had to ease the air of uncertainty surrounding my role in the forthcoming campaign. On 19 March I issued a statement through Conservative Central Office, in which I made perfectly clear my intention of playing a full part in the campaign, both within my own party and within the all-party organisation 'Britain in Europe'.

Between 7 and 9 April, the House of Commons debated the government's White Paper on the 'renegotiation', on which final agreement had been settled a month earlier during a meeting of the European Council in Dublin. Helmut Schmidt has since revealed that he offered Harold Wilson a deal during talks at Chequers, seeking the Prime Minister's assurance that he would campaign for a 'yes' vote in the Referendum in return for a few concessions on the 'renegotiation'. Wilson, eager for some sort of breakthrough and weary of the whole business, signed up to what Helmut was suggesting.

The two improvements from the 'renegotiation' were, first, a new corrective mechanism containing provision for a refund to any member state whose contribution to the Community budget went significantly beyond what was fair in relation to its share of Community gross national product; and, second, greater flexibility within the operation of the Common Agricultural Policy. Both Harold Wilson and James Callaghan were now convinced that British membership of the European Community was essential, and Wilson had to abide by his deal with the German Chancellor. The Labour Cabinet, however, remained split. The anti-Europeans wanted a fundamental renegotiation and there was no way that the agreement reached could be sold as such. On 7 April 1975 Harold Wilson was forced to inform the House of Commons that, in the 'unique circumstances' of the Referendum, ministers were free to advocate different views in the country, but this freedom did not 'extend to parliamentary proceedings and official business'. It was an astonishing breach of collective Cabinet responsibility.

Two days later, on 9 April, I made my first speech since returning to the backbenches. While I applauded the improvements that had been made in Europe, I stressed once again that these could have been achieved through the normal development of the Community. I also objected to the specious way in which the Prime Minister, in his speech, implied that the issue at stake in the Referendum was his government's so-called 'renegotiation' – no more, no less. Fortunately, his argument cut no ice in the country. I suppose he was trying to get as many of his own waverers as possible on to the 'pro' side. From the point of view of the country, however, this was never the great issue. I went on:

> For that we have to go back to the primary purpose of the European Community when it was founded. It was founded for a political purpose, not a party purpose, not even a federal purpose, as some would argue ... the political purpose was to absorb the new Germany into the structure of the European family, and economic means were adopted for that very political purpose ... From the time of my speech to the House on 17 May 1961, I said that the first purpose of the negotiations was political, for the reasons which I have explained. Today, the issue is still a great political issue. That is the reason for my regret that the Prime Minister placed the whole of his emphasis on a difference in arrangements and completely avoided any mention of what I believe to be the supreme issue here.

The motion to approve the White Paper on 'renegotiation' was passed by a majority of 226 – although, of the 315 Labour MPs who voted, 145 (including thirty-eight Ministers) voted against, and only 138 voted in favour. According to *The Times* the next day, I had 'rescued the Commons from the doldrums'.

*　　　*　　　*

The Conservative 'Yes' campaign was launched by Mrs Thatcher on 16 April at St Ermin's Hotel. I had received a letter from Douglas Hurd while I was holidaying in Spain asking whether I would take the chair at this dinner. I readily agreed, as I felt that my presence might help to stiffen her commitment to Europe. I knew that it would prove a difficult situation for us both as it was the first time that we had appeared on the same platform since the leadership election, but it turned out to be an excellent meeting and she did go some way towards alleviating my fears about Mrs Thatcher's attitude towards European unity. We both agreed that the first task of the Conservatives was to demolish some of the myths spread by the anti-Europeans. I described my own favourite scare story, that British girls in Brussels felt so threatened by the virility of European men that they were having to take instruction in ju-jitsu! Mrs Thatcher made some kind comments about my own role in ensuring Britain's place in Europe at this event, adding, 'It is naturally with some temerity that the pupil speaks before the master, because you know more about it than the rest of us.' She quoted Disraeli, Churchill and Macmillan to demonstrate that the Conservatives were the pro-European party, adding:

> It is a fact that there has been peace in Europe for the past quarter of a century, and for that alone I am grateful – grateful that my children have not been embroiled in a European conflict as was their father and as were children of the two previous generations. We should not take that peace which has been secured too much for granted, for it has been secured by the conscious and concerted effort of nations to work together . . . It is a myth that the Community is simply a bureaucracy with no concern for the individual. The entire staff of the Commission is about 7,000 – smaller than that of the Scottish Office. It is a myth that our membership will suffocate national tradition and culture. Are the Germans any less German for being in the Community, or the French any less French? Of course they are not.

However, I was disappointed at her subsequent modicum of campaigning up and down the country.

Despite my misgivings about the reasons for holding the Referendum, I immensely enjoyed touring the country campaigning for a 'yes' vote. The Referendum date was set for 5 June and the question put forward asked: 'Do you think that the United Kingdom should stay in the European Community (The Common Market)?' I was always confident that we would win the argument. The 'Yes' campaign was tremendously well organised and had people from the three main parties including Roy Jenkins, Shirley Williams, Jeremy Thorpe, Willie Whitelaw and Reggie Maudling, who all put in an enormous amount of hard work. Looking back, the cross-party co-operation was quite remarkable for the post-war years. Our European policy was treated as a non-partisan national issue.

My main priority was to state quite clearly the true nature of the question that the British people had to resolve in the coming referendum. There were both political and economic strands to the debate over whether we should stay in Europe and they needed to be disentangled and analysed separately. I was sure that the arguments in favour were overwhelming on both fronts. The question was also about our honour and integrity as a nation, and whether we should unilaterally tear up the Treaty that had been signed and ratified with the authority of Parliament. Some of the anti-marketeers naively believed that, if we were to tear up one treaty with our partners in the Community, then those same European countries would sign a new agreement with us based on a new free-trade-area arrangement.

During my nationwide tour, I constantly urged all British citizens to 'think big' on 5 June. The country was not voting in a parish or district election, but on Britain's role in the world. The anti-Europeans were engaged in a carefully concerted campaign to downgrade the issues involved, and they systematically trivialised the issues at stake. They did this because they knew that they could not win the debate on the fundamental issues of peace and security. Speaking in Central Hall, Westminster on 2 June, I produced some well-deserved lampooning for the anti-Europeans. 'The anti-marketeers' campaign,' I said,

> is . . . pitched . . . on nothing more than bread and butter issues, which though important, are only part of the far wider debate about Britain's place in the world . . . Is the future of a great nation like Britain – a nation that has . . . twice this century . . . fought in Europe and in the process bled itself white in the cause of liberty and democracy for the peoples of Europe – really to hinge on nothing more than the price of sliced bread?

As the UK had by the time of the campaign been a member of the Community for over two years, it was easy to answer the claims, peddled by the anti-marketeers, that membership would rapidly bring us to our knees economically. The opening statement of the official anti-market booklet alleged, baldly and without qualifications, that membership had been a bad bargain for the British people. Yet, on 5 May 1975, a Labour Treasury minister, speaking on behalf of the entire Labour government, announced that, in the 1974–5 financial year, Britain had benefited financially from membership to the tune of £35 million (over £200 million in 1998 prices). That, of course, was looking at the balance sheet in only the narrowest financial sense. It did not include the wider advantages, the political security and the economic opportunities that membership today still brings. Britain's trade deficit had deteriorated since 1973, but that had nothing to do with the Community. Our position relative to the US and the Commonwealth was the problem. When the period of two and a quarter years after becoming a member of the Community was compared with the same period before we joined, our exports to the other eight member states had increased by 78 per cent, to the rest of Europe by 55 per cent and to North America by 43 per cent. This was *before* all tariff barriers had been removed, and clearly demonstrated the trading advantages we had so speedily gained from our membership of the Community.

The highlights of my campaign were the meeting at Trafalgar Square on 4 May, one of several successful rallies, and the live television debate at the Oxford Union on 4 June. Huge numbers of young people attended these events, all enthusiastic about the opportunities in Europe. This is still very much the case today, but young people in 1975 were already the true internationalists. The irony was that those on the far left, who talked most loudly about international brotherhood, were the most frightened about the big wide world. As I said at the rally in Trafalgar Square, for people like Peter Shore international brotherhood finished at Margate. This speech ended with the young crowd yelling 'Yes!' in answer to all the questions that I posed to them concerning Britain and Europe. It was an exhilarating experience and I departed overflowing with optimism.

At the televised debate at the Oxford Union on the motion 'That this House would say "Yes" to Europe', I was supported by Jeremy Thorpe and opposed by Barbara Castle and Peter Shore. I suspect that Barbara and Peter later regretted participating in this debate. Jeremy and I were ex-presidents of the Union and we felt both relaxed and confident. It was clear from the outset that the overwhelming majority of those present wanted a 'Yes' vote. One pro-European supporter caught the eye both in the chamber and on television by turning up bedecked in a hooped shirt, black beret and string of onions. His name was Alistair Burt, and he later served as an excellent Minister for the Disabled in John Major's administration.

My main theme during this debate was reflection upon the tragedies in the first half of this century, the result of nation states ruthlessly pursuing their own national interests. The lessons of 1914 and 1939 proved conclusively that, however much we might try to avoid it, Britain could not escape the consequences of events in Europe. Inside the European Community we could influence the development of our continent and so increase the effective sovereignty of Britain. By pulling out, we would have diminished the true influence of our sovereignty, becoming weaker and less able to defend our interests.

The response of the public who tuned in to watch that debate was most stimulating. It had obviously attracted some celebrated viewers, as I received congratulatory letters from Kenneth Williams, the star of the *Carry On* films, and the comedian Dave Allen. I was particularly thrilled to receive many supportive letters from pensioners who, like myself, had experienced the agonies of war. They knew just how important this Referendum was to their children and grandchildren. As one eighty-six-year-old lady movingly wrote: 'You answered all the queries of the opposite side with very great clarity and conviction, going back to before the First World War and after. We were so glad you mentioned this, as so many ignore it and want to forget it, but you made it so clear . . . what we suffered is the prime reason we should keep in the Common Market.' It angers me that, in more recent years, the natural patriotism of older people in particular is being exploited by those who are conducting a political vendetta against the European Union and against myself.

On 5 June, Britain voted by a huge majority (67.2 per cent to 32.8 per cent) to stay in the European Community. The result showed conclusively that the British people – in each of the four constituent countries, in every region (apart from the Shetland Islands and the Western Isles), in every class, in every age group – wholeheartedly backed the decision taken in 1971 by the Conservative government, over which I presided, to join the Community. It temporarily silenced the voices of all those who had refused to accept the decision of Parliament as final. Our historic decision, with all the preparations which had led up to it over fifteen years, was firmly and finally acclaimed.

I could not help reflecting on a more personal note. Having spoken, worked, negotiated and campaigned for Europe over the preceding twenty-five years, there is nothing that has given me greater satisfaction than seeing the British people endorse the cause to which I had devoted myself for so long. What is more, they had endorsed it by a massive majority, not grudgingly but enthusiastically. If there is a moral in this it is that you must never give up a cause in which you strongly believe both intellectually and emotionally. After the depressing time that had gone before, I also enjoyed plenty of favourable press coverage in recognition of the part I had played in the campaign. On 9 June 1975 Harold Wilson, Margaret Thatcher and Jeremy Thorpe all paid tribute to my own contribution to a 'Yes' vote. What was important was that the British people had, when given the opportunity, given their full-hearted consent to Britain in Europe.

Immediately after the Referendum, my friends urged me to take things a little easier, and that was certainly my intention. In actual fact, 1975 was a very hard year. The leadership contest, the Referendum campaign and my series of major speeches, at home and abroad, were all proof of that. On the other hand, I was once again enjoying life to the full. In particular I relished my new-found freedom. As I was no longer presiding over the Shadow Cabinet, I was not tied to one specific area of activity. In addition, having been freed from day-to-day responsibilities, I could speak freely on all the questions confronting Britain.

My immediate political aim was clear: to see the Conservative Party returned to office as soon as possible. The country faced immensely complex problems which presented agonising conflicts and dilemmas. If these were to be tackled successfully, clear thinking was required about the means of survival for the free-enterprise system in Britain. This was the theme of my speech to the Young Conservatives in Folkestone on 16 November. I called for a constructive national debate on what was needed to save Britain from decline. Earlier that month I had attended the Conservative Party conference at Blackpool. I did not speak then, for I knew from my own experience that it is important for a new leader to establish his or her own authority at a conference, but I was moved by the reception I received from the party's rank and file when I first entered the conference hall.

The second attempt by the IRA to destroy me was troublesome, but not successful in causing any damage. On Saturday 8 November 1975, after a lunchtime meeting with President Sadat of Egypt, himself later to be murdered by terrorists, I was due to go down to Lymington on the Hampshire coast as the guest of honour at a celebration dinner at the Royal Yacht Club. My programme was delayed, however, because I had been given information about a piece to appear in the *Sunday Times* the next day about Slater Walker and their management of various investment accounts, including mine. As it was completely false, I hurriedly called a meeting of legal advisers at my home in Wilton Street to discuss a possible injunction. The most prominent among them was the former Attorney-General, Peter Rawlinson. The discussion on this took some time, and finished with Peter Rawlinson arranging for a judge to hear our request (which was refused) at his home. By this time it was well after six o'clock.

I decided that I would still go ahead with the dinner, and telephoned a message through to the Commodore to start the meal as arranged, promising that I would arrive in time to make my speech. I then changed into a dinner jacket and came down to my car, which was parked in front of my house. I slammed the car door, started the engine, put my foot down hard on the accelerator, shot out to the end of the road, turned left and made my way as speedily as possible to Lymington. After an exuberant dinner, I drove back and arrived at the opposite end of my street just after 2.00 a.m. to find white tape stretched across it, and the road junction blocked by police cars, all flashing their blue lights. My heart sank as the memory of the first IRA bomb immediately came back to me.

A senior police officer rushed to the door of my car and said, 'Thank God you are all right. We thought that some of them might have gone down to Lymington in an attempt to get you there.' He added that the bomb outside my house had been defused, and they would very much like me to meet the two members of the Bomb Squad who had done this, so that I could thank them for it. The whole story then emerged.

A bomb had originally been tied to the undercarriage of my car, but when I had shot off so suddenly earlier in the evening the string broke, leaving the bomb behind. Shortly afterwards, a boy, out for the evening with his girlfriend, had seen this open space and parked his own car, a mini, in it. They went off to enjoy themselves and returned shortly after midnight. The girl, carrying out the instructions so frequently broadcast at that time, lay down on the pavement to look under the car and saw there, for the first time, the bomb. She jumped up screaming, and the two of them dashed off in search of the police and, fortunately, found an officer near Victoria station. He immediately telephoned for the Bomb Squad, who rapidly appeared. Unusually, the press informants apparently did not learn of the telephone call and, for some time, the Squad was left in peace.

At this point in the policeman's explanation, two men from the Bomb Squad appeared, and the senior one, a quietly heroic man by the name of Geoff Biddle, said, 'We have been lucky. This is a new type of bomb, which we have not handled before, and we just managed to defuse it in time. Let me show you the bomb.' I went over to his van with him and he produced a large block for me to examine. Then, turning it over, he said, 'I will show you the points where it is different from others.' By this time I was a little anxious and, no doubt, showing it. 'Perhaps Mr Heath has now seen enough,' said the younger man, 'and he would like to go to his home.' I thanked the two saviours of Wilton Street again, and retreated to a safe distance. I was told later that Major Biddle's only personal comment on the incident, after lying in the gutter and working by torch-light on this fearsome device, was that it had been rather cold, because 'The wind was blowing up my trousers.'

Because the alert was still not over, I was not allowed to go into my own house, so I drove around to the end of the road to join my evacuated neighbours, in the then headquarters of the Coal Board, Hobart House. There I found a most extraordinary situation. Field Marshal Sir Gerald Templer, from the house opposite mine, a former Commander-in-Chief in Malaya, was fast asleep alongside his wife in opposite corners of a couch. Both were wearing very thin night clothes, and he had very short trousers. Hiding behind a pillar on the left-hand side were the boy and the girl, concealing themselves as much as they could, since they clearly did not wish to be recognised. At the far end, some children were playing around with a bat and ball. In the middle, there was Lord Trevelyan, a very senior retired diplomat and a former High Commissioner in Saudi Arabia, wearing pyjamas and a thick woollen dressing gown, striding up and down with his hands behind his back. 'This would never have been allowed to happen in my day,' he repeatedly muttered. At the far end, my distinguished next-door neighbour had an elderly nightwatchman cowering in front of her as she said to him in her commanding voice, 'Now, come along, my man, we all want some tea. You must have a tea urn somewhere. Bring it along, and let me make them all tea.'

Gradually, I pieced together the events of the night. Apparently, when the police arrived and saw the bomb, they knocked on all the doors in the street and asked the occupiers to go to the rear of their houses. However, many of them possessed only one room, running from front to back. Nearing 1.00 a.m., the two members of the Bomb Squad were afraid that they would not be able to defuse the bomb in time. The police then went down the street asking everybody to leave their houses entirely and go round the corner to Hobart House. This they did, in their night clothes, except for a very elderly lady in the last house who opened a window and said, 'Go to hell! I am staying here,' and slammed the window in their faces. Because the bomb disposal experts had to check for a second device, we were all made to stay at the Coal Board until 4.30 a.m. when, slowly and rather raggedly, we returned to our homes for the rest of the night. I had an early start the next morning. I was due at the Cenotaph to honour those servicemen, many of them from Ireland, who had given their lives in the fight for freedom.

By the time of the 1976 party conference at Brighton, Mrs Thatcher had been leader for eighteen months, and the first real Conservative statement of policy under her leadership, *The Right Approach*, had recently been published. I therefore decided to address the conference. At the beginning of the week, I received a *cri de coeur* from Douglas Hurd, warning that my speech would be interpreted politically rather than on its merits and urging me to praise the work of Geoffrey Howe in sorting out party differences on monetary and incomes policy. 'I think you have quite enjoyed being a volcano on the edge of the plain, watching the tribesmen scurry about when you erupt,' he wrote, 'but I wonder if that period shouldn't come to a close!' As it turned out, this was a little melodramatic.

The Right Approach had been drafted by Chris Patten, Angus Maude, Keith Joseph, Geoffrey Howe and Jim Prior and represented a compromise acceptable to us all. It was essentially a continuation of the mainstream policies of the Conservative Party over many years, and I was quite happy to inform the conference that I did not find myself in major disagreement with any of it. I also took this opportunity to reiterate the grave economic problems that were facing the nation under the Labour government. The external value of the pound had fallen by one-third since we left office in February 1974 and by one-fifth in the last six months alone. As a trading nation, depending almost entirely on imports for our supply of raw materials, this had severe implications. It also meant that Britain's standard of living was being eroded. I had no doubt that the prime consideration for any government in such a situation was to maintain the external value of the pound. This required hard choices and unpleasant measures. It was not enough to say that the problem could be solved by cutting out waste and pruning extravagance. The nation had to accept that a large number of people were going to see their aspirations thwarted in the short term to provide for that necessary reduction in the budget deficit. All that a government could realistically hope to achieve when faced with problems on this scale was to help and protect those who were most affected and no longer able to help themselves. As I told the conference:

The Conservative Party is well equipped to deal with these problems. We have an honourable record. We have never failed to explain the situation . . . The Conservative Party is in a strong position because we have never flinched from taking difficult decisions that are in the national interest. I have complete confidence that they will be taken by Margaret Thatcher and her colleagues on the platform.

My speech was warmly welcomed both by the party delegates, relieved at my show of unity, and the leadership, but it was to be the last time that I was to receive such a welcoming reception. Soon after *The Right Approach* was published, it became apparent that Mrs Thatcher was determined to move sharply away from mainstream Conservative economic policy – and, indeed, from her own *Right Approach to the Economy*, which was published before the 1977 party conference.

I went from the 1976 party conference back to our home in Broadstairs where, on Sunday 11 October, my father celebrated his eighty-eighth birthday. We had a large family gathering, with many local friends, and he was in good form. Only a couple of days later, however, he was taken ill at home and, after two days in bed, he died on 15 October. I stayed with him each day during his illness, as my stepmother was understandably distraught. His funeral was held in our old parish church at St Peter's, and his ashes were buried alongside those of my mother in Charing. He had always supported me unquestioningly, his only criticism coming after our defeat at the February 1974 election, when he remarked, 'You were always far too honest.' He left it at that.

I always tried to protect him from the press and any other interference, but on his eightieth birthday I had failed lamentably. I drove down to Broadstairs for the celebrations but arrived too late to stop the press forming up in front of the house and congratulating him. They were very polite until one of them remarked, 'Mr Heath, looking back now on your eighty years is there anything which you deeply regret in your life?' 'Yes,' replied my father immediately. 'How interesting,' his questioner said, 'can you tell us what it is?' 'Yes,' answered my father, 'what I regret most in my life is that the permissive society did not begin fifty years earlier!'

I was once again grateful for the kind words expressed by my friends and colleagues at my loss, not least Alec Home, John Junor, Christopher Soames, Jack Lynch, Liam Cosgrave, Alastair Burnet and George Thomas. Perhaps the most moving letter was sent by Lord Hailsham:

> I feel I must write a word of sincere condolence to you on the death of your respected father. It is a blow which falls on all of us sooner or later if we live out life's normal span but, whenever it falls, it is always grievous and life is never somehow the same again. I lost my own father in 1950 when I was almost 45, and I could not be sorry for him because he had longed for release for 14 years from a humiliating and crippling illness . . . but . . . I think of him in love and respect, and I still miss his presence terribly.
>
> Your own father must have been immensely proud to see his talented son rise to become a great national, and even international, figure. The thought that you brought him this great happiness must surely be a consolation to you now. But nothing blunts the pain of parting. It is the price which, in this world, we pay for love.

*

Leaving the Conservative Party front bench gave me more time to pursue my enthusiasms outside the world of politics. Shortly before Christmas 1975 my first book, *Sailing*, was published. After my resignation in February 1975, first Sir Charles Forte, then majority shareholder of the publishing house Sidgwick & Jackson, and then Lord Longford, the company's Chairman, had asked whether I would consider writing an illustrated book on sailing. I had always wanted to tell the story of *Morning Cloud*, not just because I thought it was a good story in itself but because I knew from my postbag that many other people found it interesting as well. This would be an autobiographical book, describing my experiences in dinghies, and then in ocean racing, including my time as captain for three years of the British Ocean Racing team, and two years as captain of the British Admiral's

Cup team. I dictated the book over the summer of 1975 and chose the photographs from my private collection. It was published on 27 November and serialised in the *Sunday Times*.

The launch day was immensely enjoyable but incredibly tiring. It started early in the morning with an interview for BBC2's *The Book Programme*; this was followed by an endless round of interviews and photo-opportunities. Even *Private Eye* endorsed the book in its own inimitable style: 'Here at last, the publishing event of the year – you can forget The Cruel Sea – Moby Dick – Captain Pugwash – it's all here.' During the day I was joined by Shirley Conran, who was busy publicising her book *Superwoman*. That evening, I turned to Stephen du Sautoy, the sales and publicity director of Sidgwick & Jackson, and remarked: 'Authors are a funny bunch, aren't they?' He put me firmly in my place by reminding me, 'You've just joined their ranks.' I was delighted with the reviews of *Sailing*. The *Guardian*'s, by William Golding, author of the classic *Lord of the Flies*, was the lead article of their six-page Christmas books feature. It was especially agreeable to read this, as the *Guardian* had been the only paper to deride our victory in the Sydney–Hobart Race in Australia six years before, and I was flattered by what Golding wrote:

> All this he describes in prose of remarkable clarity and simplicity. It is a professional job. The book itself is a triumphantly lavish display. It is of the best available materials and profusely illustrated. Some of the photographs it contains are going to be famous. Mr Heath has enjoyed his racing and I have enjoyed reading about it. Indeed, I beg him to concentrate his great talents on getting us back the America's Cup and to leave politics in the Eighteenth Century manner to be his hobby.

It is a truism that personal friends can turn out to be your sternest critics. It was therefore a delight to obtain the approval of Douglas Bader, the wartime hero, and Herbert von Karajan, the great musician and a keen sailor himself. I had sent him a copy after he had been taken ill. He wrote later that he had:

> lived with it for three months. It was first sent by a friend to the hospital in Zurich, where I was on the lowest point of my illness and arriving here in Salzburg, I found it as a gift from your hand. Most certainly you have achieved your intention, conveying the joy of sailing to your readers and the result is a beautiful blend of knowledge about the art of sailing and the emotional side of it.

I never expected that *Sailing* would become such a best-seller. In the first year it sold over 90,000 copies in the UK alone, as I embarked on an extensive book tour round the UK and then the world. As well as signing sessions in Singapore, Bermuda, New York, Brussels, Copenhagen and Hong Kong, I also recorded twelve separate seven-minute programmes of readings from the book which were then transmitted on the majority of commercial radio stations. By far the most enjoyable experience of this episode was my UK tour. It was marvellous to meet so many people and I have countless fond memories of these encounters.

On 1 December 1975, I travelled to Scotland for the day. I seriously wondered whether anybody would venture out in the terrible climatic conditions, with freezing rain, snow and slush underfoot in the Glasgow streets. After three interviews with the media, we arrived at John Smith's, the book-sellers, to find that there was already a very long queue, though the signing session was not scheduled to start for half an hour. By the time we started, the queue had wound three times round the inside of the shop and was already down the street, turning the corner into the next road. It quickly became apparent that we were not going to have enough copies to satisfy the demand. By one o'clock, we had run out of the book, which meant that we had sold 530 over the counter, on top of the 470 reservations for all those people who were unable to be present in person at lunchtime. There were still 300–400 people standing outside in the Glasgow snow, for whom signed copies were later provided. It was unfortunate that we could not supply all the customers immediately, but afterwards I was told that the event had broken the book-selling record of Alistair Cooke. His record – for the book *America* – stood at 750 copies. I had nearly doubled this number, selling 1,400.

The finale for the year, except for a nostalgic trip to Broadstairs, was a signing session at Lillywhites in Piccadilly. It was the first time that they had ever done a signing and they imported models of both *Morning Cloud 1* and *Morning Cloud 4* to their sailing department. Halfway through the proceedings, Lord Longford arrived to make a celebratory speech to the assembled company, after which he presented me with a leather-bound copy of *Sailing*. He also announced that there were now 100,000 copies in circulation. *Sailing* became the best-seller that Christmas in the *Sunday Times*, *Evening Standard* and *Newsagent and Bookshop* charts. It was a marvellous, and totally unexpected, end to the year.

During the thirty-seventh signing session, in Harvey Nichols, Knightsbridge on 16 March 1976, I was called away to receive a message on the phone from Tim Kitson. He told me that Harold Wilson had resigned. Soon afterwards the store was overwhelmed by journalists and television cameras seeking my reaction to the news. I was very surprised that my old rival had chosen that moment to make such a sudden exit from the political stage. The country was enduring high inflation, great unemployment and debt burdens and the last thing the country needed was the uncertainty of the election of a new leader. It was far too early then to assess Wilson's place in history, so I restricted myself to complimenting him on his skill in showing 'an infinite capacity to adjust to the circumstances of the moment and a remarkable ability to persuade everyone that he was really on their side'.

Twenty years later it is possible to make a balanced assessment of Harold Wilson's contribution to our political life, particularly in his first period as Prime Minister. There was then no doubt about his skill as a professional politician. Although he won the 1964 general election with a majority of only four, his personality appealed to a considerable section of the electorate, and he certainly developed a manner which carried the viewer, the listener and the reader with him. After the 1966 election, however, he never hesitated to reverse his position when he found his own forces lining up against him. Barbara Castle's attempt at trade union reform was a major example of this (see p. 298). He also had little lasting success in foreign affairs, and became far less effective after the elections of 1974, when he had not really expected to win again. He was already tired and no longer possessed that freshness and energy which had previously served him so well. Nevertheless it came as a surprise when he resigned on his sixtieth birthday. It may be that he himself already realised the impact which his illness, later to prove fatal, was having upon him. Jim Callaghan later told me that he thought that Wilson had realised soon after 1974 that he was past it. 'That,' I said, 'rather backs up what Roy Jenkins said to me recently, namely that Wilson was ten years older than he had publicly admitted and, when he resigned, he was really seventy and not sixty.' 'Yes, that is very interesting,' commented Jim, 'and I suppose that, when all those well-known photographs were taken of him outside No. 10 when he claimed to be eleven, he was really twenty-one!' Harold Wilson's lasting achievements are difficult to discern, except for the fact that he held the Labour Party together for nearly fifteen years, whereas under his successors it collapsed, thereby helping to sustain eighteen years of Conservative government. Harold was, above all else, a great political survivor, a fine politician if, perhaps, never truly a statesman.

The suggestion for my next book came during my book-signing sessions in 1975. After a rather tiring morning, a bookseller asked me whether I was ever going to write a book on music. If I produced something which was an introduction to the subject, designed to banish diffidence and encourage enthusiasm, as I had tried to do in *Sailing*, he told me, he was convinced it would be a success. After some lengthy and positive discussions with Edward Greenfield, the distinguished *Guardian* critic, I decided to go ahead. Music had given me so much joy, and I determined to pass on something of that to others.

Music: A Joy for Life was duly launched with a concert in the Great Room of Grosvenor House on 22 November 1976, at which I conducted the London Symphony Orchestra, with Clifford Curzon and Anneliese Rothenberger as soloists. It had already sold 42,000 copies in advance orders, and the total rose to 60,000 by the end of the year. I repeated the same process as in the previous year, touring the country signing copies. Many of my most cherished musical highlights, however, occurred after the book was published. In 1996, therefore, I began work on a heavily revised version of *Music*, which was published in 1997.

Two further books were completed for the following year, *Travels: People and Places in my Life* and *Carols: The Joy of Christmas*. Travel was an obvious choice for my third book as it had been a part of my life for almost as long as music. Even from a young age I liked to talk to people, find out what they thought at first hand, and form my own judgements. This has, I believe, stood me in good stead in both my personal and professional life. Through *Travels* I wanted to encourage other people to be as naturally inquisitive as myself. In my journeys round the world, as a politician, as a tourist and, in Europe, as a member of the armed forces pressing towards Germany in the last world war, I have heard many carols from many lands, but I have always regarded Christmas as a time to be at home, a time for family and for friends, a time for relaxing with them and my sixteen godchildren.

Carols contains my own collection of favourite Christmas songs, including some from the Town Carol Concerts, arranged so that they can be sung in unison with piano arrangements. Sidgwick & Jackson organised another promotional tour for these books. From 5 to 10 December I visited twelve cities, travelling in a specially commissioned British Rail train. At each of these major city stations, I signed copies of all four books that had been published over just three years. After this marathon, it came to be said that I had signed so many that the most valuable copies were the unsigned ones. I was pleased with the response to both *Travels* and *Carols*.

During this period I received a letter from a gentleman in the south of England. He wrote: 'I understand that you have written three best-sellers.' (He was wrong – it was four.) He went on, 'I find this positively disgraceful. People only buy and read your books because once upon a time you were Prime Minister. On the other hand, I am an extremely distinguished author. I have produced the manuscripts of two books. The first is a translation of early-thirteenth-century financial accounts from a French château. The second is a collection of love letters by unknown British people in the nineteenth century. I have shown both manuscripts to a large number of publishers, who have all refused to print them. Will you kindly advise me what to do in these circumstances?' My very efficient secretary had written a note across the top of the letter: 'Propose you reply to this gentleman suggesting that he first of all become Prime Minister.'

I had never intended that my first engagement with the London Symphony Orchestra, in the Royal Festival Hall on 25 November 1971 (see p. 465), should lead to any form of 'second career', but I was soon conducting the LSO again, opening its seventieth-birthday gala concert on Sunday 9 June 1974, with Richard Wagner's 'Meistersinger' Overture. This was a singular privilege, for this piece had been the first item the orchestra had ever played, under Hans Richter precisely seventy years earlier. In April 1975, I conducted outside the United Kingdom for the first time, travelling with the LSO and their conductor, André Previn, for a pair of concerts in Cologne and Bonn. We had a punishing schedule, and I ended this three-day trip with far greater sympathy than before for professional musicians. While I was in Bonn, I was interviewed by a magazine correspondent who asked me about my role as an amateur conductor, my relationship with the audience and the criteria by which I expected to be judged. I responded:

> I expect them [the critics] to react naturally. There is a tendency for them to be more critical than usual because they think 'he is not there for his musical merit alone, there is more to it than that', so they go behind the scenes to try to pick up bits of gossip. Normally they would not ask the members of the orchestra about the conductor, but they do it quite readily in my case ... I expect the critics to use their normal criteria: did the orchestra follow me, what was the quality of the performance, did I achieve something satisfying and fulfilling both with the orchestra and with the work?

I started conducting as a teenager, and from the mid-1930s until the present day have done so regularly, with the inevitable exception of the war years. I think that all musicians, especially those who have direct experience of conducting, yearn to conduct a symphony orchestra. I would not pretend to challenge the supremacy of the professionals, but I always enjoy creating something for myself. Everyone has their own ideas about how works should be interpreted, and we all listen to others' performances with a highly critical ear, often with score in hand, and do not always agree with every aspect of each performance we hear. This is why I enjoy the opportunity of giving my own interpretation. A similar motivation brought me into politics. I have never found it easy to be an armchair critic in relation to matters which really concern me, and both public life and music fall into that category: participation becomes a necessity, not a luxury. I have been very fortunate that my position in public life has given me the opportunity to work with so many leading musicians. Directing an orchestra is one of my most satisfying activities. The production of music nourishes both the mind and the soul and, although playing an organ gives one a greater range of sound and movement than other instruments, an orchestra gives by far the biggest excitement of all.

After my performances with the LSO, other invitations followed. I was invited by Eugene Ormandy to be the guest conductor of the Philadelphia Orchestra in a gala 1976 concert on Wednesday 22 September, and I conducted Elgar's 'Cockaigne' Overture, the piece with which I had made my debut with the LSO five years earlier. Georg Solti then invited me to conduct a benefit concert with the Chicago Symphony Orchestra just six days later. This time, I was able to select and conduct an entire programme of around seventy minutes in a special Musicians' Pension Fund concert. I did Wagner's 'Meistersinger' Overture, Elgar's 'Enigma' Variations and Beethoven's Symphony No. 8, a particular favourite of mine. Two years later, I took part in a summer concert with the Cleveland Orchestra. I conducted the Brahms 'Academic Festival' Overture and then, with Lorin Maazel leading the orchestra, narrated Aaron Copland's *Lincoln Portrait*. The Copland is a stirring piece, and it was a great honour to give a performance of it in one of the Northern states which had rallied behind Lincoln over a century earlier. Lincoln's words still ring true across the decades: 'Fellow citizens, we cannot escape history . . . the dogmas of the quiet past are inadequate to the stormy present . . .'

As well as conducting in the USA, I have now performed in Portugal, Germany, China, Turkey, Japan, Israel, Hungary and Russia. In 1978, I was able at last to take up Herbert von Karajan's long-standing invitation to conduct the Berlin Philharmonic, in a charity concert in Paris. Once again, I chose the 'Cockaigne' Overture. The leader of the orchestra admitted to me at the reception afterwards that it had been very hard work for them to learn this piece, which they had never played before. I was deeply impressed by their technical proficiency. What a bracing and uplifting experience it is to conduct such a superb orchestra.

In 1974, I first became involved in the bold initiative of Lionel and Joy Bryer to establish a new European Community Youth Orchestra, and accepted their invitation to become its first president. On 14 June that year, less than eighteen months after our accession to the European Community, Baroness Elles, a British member of the European Parliament, put forward an all-party proposal for the formation of such an orchestra, consisting of instrumentalists drawn from all member states. Elaine Kellett-Bowman, another British Conservative, secured the multi-partisan approval of the European Parliament for this idea.

I had long felt the need for the Community to extend its activities beyond political and commercial affairs. This is possible with music because it is a single common language. Likewise with the ballet, although we have not yet succeeded in bringing this about. The theatre is impossible because one cannot secure performers who speak all the necessary languages. Other arts such as painting, sculpture and architecture are individual pursuits without any communal aspects. The orchestra, however, through emphasising our shared European heritage by bringing people together in a positive atmosphere, can only be beneficial. In the words of the original proposal it would 'create in each of the European Community countries men and women in all walks of life who can experience in their idealistic and formative years the profound co-operation and creative period of other members of the Community'. Claudio Abbado agreed to become the first music director of the orchestra and I was asked to be their guest conductor.

The orchestra's first tour took place in the summer of 1978, after a ten-day rehearsal period. The Germans were at first reluctant to take part because they were afraid it would damage their existing national arrangements but they eventually joined us. The British had the most comprehensive coverage of orchestral instruments. James Judd, the young assistant director, and a fellow musician took part in the auditions to ensure that the same standards were maintained in each country. The first tour included all the capitals except Copenhagen and Dublin, with Milan added because of Abbado's connection with that city. The nine Prime Ministers of the member states had all become honorary patrons. I then wrote to each of the royal families and to the presidents who were head of state, inviting them personally to attend the concert in their capital.

Everyone, including the media, agreed that the tour was an outstanding success. But it was not without its 'little local difficulties'. Claudio Abbado objected to starting each concert with the national anthem and the European anthem, namely the choral theme from Beethoven's 9th Symphony. I insisted on them. He then told me to go off and conduct them myself. At the rehearsals for the first concert in Amsterdam I was confronted with the Dutch anthem, of which there were only faint echoes ringing in my ears from the Sunday evening broadcasts of all the allies' anthems during the war over thirty years earlier. After we had run through it, the Dutch leader of the orchestra said, 'Too fast.' A Dutch cellist then said, 'Too slow.' I said, 'I will stay where we are.' At this point a tall lean gentleman standing below me tugged at my trouser leg and asked me to play it through twice at the beginning of the concert. I felt like telling him that we had enough difficulty in trying to play it once, instead of which I politely enquired, 'Why twice?' 'Her Majesty the Queen of the Netherlands would be in her private rooms at the top of the balcony,' he explained, 'and to walk from there down the steps and along to the middle row for her seat takes exactly two national anthems.'

At the concert it all worked beautifully, but to my horror the crowd burst into loud and prolonged applause after their national anthem. The instructions to the orchestra were that there would be no applause between the Dutch and European anthems, but with all the commotion it was impossible to go straight on. When we started the European anthem there was the noise of 3,200 seats clattering, as everyone sat down. I learned afterwards that the Queen had turned at that point to the chairman of the orchestra, who was sitting next to her, and enquired, 'What is this? I thought they were going to play the "Meistersinger" Overture.' 'This,' he replied, 'is the European anthem.' 'Well then, if it is an anthem ought we not to be standing up for it?' she asked. 'I am sure that would be appreciated,' he commented. Halfway through the anthem there was then the noise of 3,200 seats being pushed back as everyone followed the Queen's example and stood up again.

In Paris on 31 March 1978 I was told at the rehearsal that we could not play the 'Marseillaise', because President Giscard d'Estaing could not be present as he was slightly unwell. Furthermore, he had not yet appointed a new government after the national assembly elections so there was no one else in a public position in whose honour the anthem could be played. I asked the messenger at once to go back to the Elysée to ask for the President's authority for me to play the French national anthem. The messenger returned saying that I could do so, because he had now decided to reappoint Raymond Barre as Prime Minister just before the concert. That evening we played the 'Marseillaise' with great verve, but at the end there was prolonged booing. Then, at the first chords of the European anthem, cheering broke out. In the interval I asked Barre whether I had taken the 'Marseillaise' too fast. 'Not at all,' he replied with a smile. 'They booed because they did not like me and the new government. They cheered Beethoven because they like you and Europe.' Three years later François Mitterand's Socialists swept into power.

In Rome I persuaded William Walton and his wife to come to the concert. Afterwards I asked what he had thought of the performance of Mahler's 6th Symphony. He sniffed two or three times and then said, 'That fellow does go on a bit doesn't he?' I have since learned from his wife that it was only a few weeks previously that he had first heard any of Mahler's symphonies. One well-wisher had sent them to him on LPs. 'Would you prefer the orchestra to play a Haydn or Mozart symphony?' I asked. 'No, no, not at all,' he explained. 'It would be far too difficult for an orchestra of this kind to do justice to them.' In the summer tour later that year, the orchestra was scheduled to visit Dublin. For security reasons I had not planned to go with them but Lorin Maazel, the scheduled conductor for that concert, twisted his ankle getting off the plane in Vienna. So I decided to go over to play a part after all. We made no announcement of my intention and, to reduce the risks, we postponed the rehearsal without giving the orchestra any reason, leaving only a short break between that and the concert, which took place in the Hall of the National Library on what happened to be the eve of the seventh anniversary of the introduction of internment in Ulster. The audience was completely startled when I appeared on the podium and gasped audibly with astonishment. As was by now customary, I began the programme with their national anthem before the European one. I suspected that this was the first – and surely the last – occasion on which a former British Prime Minister has conducted this particular work.

The time soon came when I felt that the presidency of the orchestra should not be the prerogative of one Britisher, and we arranged for it to circulate after I had resigned. The orchestra has continued to be an outstanding feature of the European Union, one which makes its mark on all those who participate in it, ensuring for each of them a more satisfying artistic life in later years.

Both music and sailing continued to provide me with much needed relaxation away from Westminster throughout the late 1970s. As the Labour government under Wilson and then James Callaghan struggled on from 1974 to 1979, however, I was to experience increasing difficulties with the policies which were being put forward by my successor. As the parliament developed, *The Right Approach* became more and more redundant. It was obviously only a matter of time before Mrs Thatcher and I would experience our first policy clash. It was to come soon after the 1976 party conference over the issue of devolution.

After we had taken the initiative to establish a committee on the question of Scotland in 1968 (see p. 295), Harold Wilson belatedly set up a Royal Commission on the Constitution in April 1969 to examine the relations between central, regional and local government, and to judge whether any changes were desirable. Our manifesto in 1970 promised that the contents of the Douglas-Home committee's report, including the Scottish Convention, would 'form a basis for the proposals we will place before Parliament, taking account of the impending re-organisation of local government'. The continuing deliberations of the Royal Commission, however, prevented us from introducing such legislation immediately upon taking office. Although we had not set up the Royal Commission, we thought it best to hold back on any comprehensive legislation until after it had concluded. This was the view both of Lord Crowther, chairman of the Commission, and, following his death in 1972, of his successor Lord Kilbrandon. We promised to give the report our full consideration after it was published.

When this substantial report was published on 31 October 1973, it had taken four years to complete. It rejected both separatism and federalism, and set out instead radical proposals for devolution. Although the members of the Commission did not unanimously endorse its recommendations, this document ensured that these important questions were properly considered and discussed. In May 1974, after a rigorous and lively debate within the party and in the country, we reiterated our commitment to devolution. If we had been re-elected in October 1974 we would have honoured our manifesto commitment to set up a single-chamber Scottish assembly to work in conjunction with Parliament. The members of this assembly would initially be drawn from elected councillors on the new local authorities, although we did not rule out direct elections in the future. The assembly was to be a forum for Scottish opinion, to enable any purely Scottish legislation to be handled in Scotland and to allow further administrative devolution wherever possible. I had seen for myself the lack of understanding and imagination in the treatment of Scotland by central government. When, in 1964, I took the EFTA conference to Edinburgh, it was the first time that city had hosted an international political conference. This neglect did not arise from any malice, but from an adherence to routine and a lack of vision.

For Wales, we promised in October 1974 to increase the powers and the functions of the Secretary of State for Wales and proposed a new select committee of Welsh MPs. This was planned to meet in Cardiff as well as at Westminster. We were particularly keen to ensure that Wales' share of the UK budget was spent in accordance with decisions taken in Wales. These proposals did not go quite so far as our plans for Scotland but I was aware that, once Scotland had its own assembly, there would be pressure from the Welsh for their own as well.

I was no longer leader of the Conservative Party when Harold Wilson announced his proposals in November 1975 to establish directly elected assemblies in Scotland and Wales. The House of Commons debated the Labour government's White Paper on devolution, *Our Changing Democracy*, over four days from 13 to 19 January 1976. Speaking on the last day, I warned the House that I believed the Union to be in great danger. Looking back, I do not think that I was being unduly alarmist. Successive governments had been unable to produce a constitution of any kind in Northern Ireland acceptable to both communities, with the exception of the power-sharing coalition under the Sunningdale Agreement. We had also seen a steady and continuing growth of nationalism in Scotland, as well as problems in Wales. Having considered the history of the matter, and through my dealings with Scotland, Wales and Northern Ireland during a frontbench career of almost twenty years, I did not feel that this could be treated as a passing whim. I also recognised that Scottish views on devolution had advanced since the Declaration of Perth in 1968. It was now necessary for the form of devolution to provide wider opportunities and responsibilities in Scotland than was originally suggested by the Douglas-Home Committee in 1970.

At this stage, the Conservative Party leadership restricted themselves to attacking the Labour government's proposals, while supposedly supporting devolution in principle. Indeed, Mrs Thatcher had pledged herself, quite rightly, to direct elections. I shared the general misgivings concerning the government's White Paper, and my speech in the House on 19 January 1976 was highly critical of their proposals. The Bill had a number of failings, especially in the inadequate financial arrangements for Scotland. The real problem, however, was that, in certain aspects, it felt like an English Bill. The White Paper seemed to say implicitly, 'You can run things your way, so long as it is our way.' I believed that, for example, instead of having a Secretary of State in a position constantly to intervene, certain powers should be completely devolved. The House of Commons could always change matters by Act of Parliament if it so desired. Although the Wilson government, in its second White Paper, heeded many of the points made in that debate and tried to find more acceptable solutions to the objections raised, it did not achieve a broad measure of agreement about the legislation which was to come. I was not, however, convinced by the so-called 'West Lothian Question', named after the constituency of Tam Dalyell, the Member of Parliament who has raised it most assiduously over the years. Why, it is asked, should Scottish MPs be entitled to sit at Westminster and vote on English matters once Scottish devolution is in place, while English MPs would not be able to participate on those equivalent matters which had been transferred to a Scottish Assembly? My own view was that dealing with this problem should be perfectly straightforward. The Speaker of the House of Commons could be given the power to certify that any item in this category was purely 'English' in scope, thereby preventing Scottish Members from voting on it. I was sure that the majority of Scots could happily live with this arrangement at Westminster if they were offered proper devolution.

On 14 September 1976, speaking in Aberdeenshire, I called for a referendum on whether the Scottish people wanted to remain part of the UK, as soon as the Bill was passed, as there was no institution which could speak for Scotland and its people. Our accession to Europe needed no referendum because it was concerned with the entry of the whole of the United Kingdom, and the Westminster Parliament could speak for the entire country. The Labour government later accepted referenda on devolution, largely as a consequence of its vanishing majority in Parliament.

Unfortunately, on 2 December 1976, shortly before the Bill's second reading, the Shadow Cabinet decided to oppose Labour's Bill on a three-line whip. This precipitated the resignations of Alick Buchanan-Smith, the Shadow Scottish Secretary, and Malcolm Rifkind, Opposition front-bench spokesman on Scottish Affairs. This put me into a difficult position. There was nothing in the government's Bill which could not be dealt with by amendments in committee, and there was no reason, therefore, why the Conservative Party should have voted against it at its second reading in December 1976, unless they were determined to reject devolution completely in principle. The leadership had now decided that devolution should not be given a chance and, step by step, the Party's commitment was reversed. I have never believed that devolution conflicts with Conservative principles. It is the basis of them. As a party, we believe in freedom. What is the point of making ringing declarations about freedom if we are not prepared to give Scotland and Wales the greater freedom of governing their own domestic affairs? That sort of democratic decentralisation is the very basis of the doctrine of freedom. We should give responsibility to people at the same time as we give them freedom. It was unthinkable that those of us who had for so long believed in this principle should be expected to vote against it. That was especially so in the case of those MPs who, as I did, believed that devolution for Scotland was the only way of maintaining the Union. During this debate I regretted the position that I had been forced into:

> I do not think that in these circumstances anybody would expect me to vote against the Government's Bill. People know my history. I may be inflexible and very obstinate. On the other hand, it may be that I sustain my beliefs . . . I believe that the best way of maintaining this Union is to have devolution. I wish that I were not faced with the particular problem that faces me, especially since I was the leader of my Party for ten years and Prime Minister for nearly four years . . . I cannot go against my record of the last ten years. I cannot go against the beliefs I honestly and sincerely hold and which, I believe, are in the interests of the people of Scotland and of the whole of the United Kingdom. I regret that I cannot vote against this Bill tonight.

Twenty-seven Conservatives joined me in abstaining that night and five Conservative MPs, including Alick Buchanan-Smith and Malcolm Rifkind, voted with the Labour government, which won this vote with a majority of forty-five. This proved to be a pyrrhic victory. A month later, handi-capped by their precarious overall majority, the government was defeated in a motion allowing the use of the guillotine in committee. Its devolution proposals were now in ruins.

On 15 April 1977, in a speech to Conservatives in Glasgow, I renewed my call for Scottish devolution. In November that year, separate bills were introduced for Scotland and Wales, providing for devolved assemblies, subject to the agreement of the respective peoples in a referendum. Once again, the issue was badly bungled by the Labour government, because of amendments forced upon it at committee stage by one of its recalcitrant back-benchers, George Cunningham, a Scot who represented a London constitu-ency and later joined the SDP. The Act specified that, in the event of a 'yes' vote from fewer than 40 per cent of those entitled to vote, the referendum result would be void. This was quite unnecessary and self-defeating, as was proved on 1 March 1979 when the proportion of the electorate voting 'yes' in Scotland was only 32.5 per cent. As widely predicted, the Welsh people voted overwhelmingly against Labour's plans for devolution.

I have long been appalled by the total lack of intellectual backing for the arguments put forward by the opponents of devolution. The British were themselves responsible for devolution in Canada, Australia, South Africa, Central Africa, the West Indies and, in our own continent, Germany. Each of these had had its own problems over decades, but no greater than we have had under our centralised system. The major argument put forward against devolution is that it will 'inevitably lead to the break-up of the United Kingdom'. There is no evidence for this, either in the Commonwealth or in post-war Germany. Without devolution, in fact, individual parts might well have decided that the only answer to their problems was to go their own way, in a full secession. Decades of delay in Scottish devolution have now allowed nationalist sentiments to take a firm grip.

I continued to support the principle of devolution throughout the 1980s and 1990s and it is with much regret, and some anger, that I have seen the destruction of the Conservative Party in Wales and Scotland over this period. This came to a head at the 1997 general election when the Conservative Party, devastatingly, had no MPs returned in either Scotland or Wales. The fiasco of the poll tax (p. 587) still particularly haunts the Conservative Party in Scotland, and will do for a long time to come. We have paid a severe penalty for ignoring the political aspirations of the people of Scotland and Wales. Assembly elections in both countries give us a chance of putting ourselves back on the map, but we shall succeed only if we can convince people that we have a serious and positive contri-bution to make in their own decentralised areas.

*   *   *

An early general election became increasingly likely after the Liberal leader David Steel, on 25 May 1978, announced the demise of the Lib–Lab pact at the end of the 1977–8 parliamentary session. The Lib–Lab agreement had been reached in March 1977 after Mrs Thatcher had tabled a no-confidence motion, following the government's refusal to grant a vote in the Commons on its public expenditure plans. David Steel announced that he would agree to support Labour on a negotiated basis, and the government duly secured a majority of twenty-four in the vote on 23 March 1977. The Lib–Lab pact was a grave mistake for the Liberals. Apart from a few minor concessions, all they achieved was to entrench the Labour government in office for a few more years and to associate themselves with a discredited administration. I had offered the Liberals a place in government in 1974 but they had chosen not to take it. Their subsequent actions in 1977–8 showed that, at that time, they wanted the benefit of government, but not the responsibility, and they were punished for this in the 1979 general election.

The ending of the pact certainly increased the temperature at Westminster. During a Penistone by-election meeting on 5 July 1978, I stressed once again that the change of leadership made no difference to my determination to install a Conservative government once again in office, and I wished Mrs Thatcher every success. However, I warned the party against moving further to the right:

> The British people are moderate and fair-minded. After the last four and a half years they want to see a government that reflects this attitude and cares about their future. This is the tradition of the Conservative governments in which I have served under Churchill, Eden, Macmillan and Home. It was the purpose of the government over which I presided and in which Mrs Thatcher and many of those now on the Opposition front bench were ministers. I want to see the British people again represented in this way.

In fact James Callaghan surprised the pundits by announcing on 7 September 1978 that an election was to be postponed until the following spring. Looking back at my speeches from the beginning of 1978, it is clear that I expected Callaghan to go to the country early. What is more, Callaghan made a personal appeal to the leaders of the trade unions in the week before his party conference asking for all the funds necessary to fight an election. They felt betrayed by his reversal a week later, and were infuriated by it. This undoubtedly contributed to the bitterness in the Winter of Discontent which led to Callaghan's downfall. In the interests of good government, a shorter delay would have been better, for ministers had clearly lost their way and, from his own point of view, Callaghan made a mistake by not calling an election that autumn. Opinion polls were showing, by November 1978, that Labour actually had a higher approval rating than we Conservatives had.

During his thirty years as a minister of the Crown, Jim Callaghan demonstrated a balanced attitude both to people and to their problems. I seldom saw him lose his temper with his own supporters, although this did not prevent him from being personally abusive to me and my colleagues, especially during our disagreements over industrial relations. As Home Secretary in 1969, it became apparent that he had lost his confidence when the Labour Party's proposals for the reform of the House of Lords, which had been supported by a large majority in the Lords itself, came before the Commons. As a result, the Bill was abandoned. It is difficult to point to any major feats of Callaghan's government, but since its defeat Jim's contribution in both Houses has been constructive and dignified.

In 1978, the Labour government set a guideline for pay rises of 5 per cent, which I thought was both reasonable and acceptable to the British people. James Prior, the Conservative spokesman on Employment, had also indicated his support both for the 5 per cent figure and for the principle of an incomes policy. In this he was reiterating the line adopted in *The Right Approach*, which stated that 'Restraint in pay bargaining . . . serves to curb the alternative of unemployment, to secure the growth of profits as the basis for future jobs, to control the size of the pay and salary element in public spending and to diminish inflationary expectations.' Shortly before the conference, however, Mrs Thatcher blamed the 5 per cent figure for the Ford strike and implicitly called for a return to free collective bargaining.

Mindful of the forthcoming general election, I was careful not to stoke the flames of a potentially damaging row. Of course, the Labour policy might well end in disaster but in my speech at the party conference, I said that all Conservatives should grieve for our country if the government's pay policy had indeed broken down. I also praised Jim Prior, who had earlier said that the Conservatives would never undermine the government's pay policy in the same way that Labour had undermined ours in 1972–4. My speech was politely received by the party faithful. Geoffrey Howe then ended the conference debate with an explicit attack upon the principles underlying the government's approach. His speech was interpreted as an attack on what I had said. He has since claimed that his speech was not, in fact, an endorsement of free collective bargaining, but it was clear that the Party was now opposed to an incomes policy and Conference was buzzing with talk of a serious rift between myself and the Shadow Cabinet.

In such circumstances, it was pointless to continue with any charade. In an interview with *News at Ten*, I acknowledged that my views contradicted those of Mrs Thatcher and warned of the danger that free collective bargaining at that time could lead to massive inflation. I was heavily criticised within the party for this, and the accusation was made that my comments were motivated by 'sour grapes'. The fact that I was sticking to *The Right Approach to the Economy*, which stated that both an incomes policy and a monetary policy had a part to play in handling the economy, cut no ice with my critics. On 12 October, Keith Joseph bitterly attacked any form of incomes policy and suggested that the commitment to an incomes policy in *The Right Approach to the Economy* was intended to apply only to the public sector, wherein Treasury cash limits enforced their own discipline. Despite the ferocity of the attacks upon me from the right wing of the party, I could at least point out that I had never tried to stifle discussion at the conference as leader. In the great debates on Europe, for example, we were always generous to the minority opposing membership. I still believe that I was right to remind Conference, and the country, about the lessons of the previous twenty years.

For my generation within the Conservative Party, it was not heresy to be in favour of an incomes policy. It had been Macmillan, as Prime Minister, and Peter Thorneycroft, as Chancellor of the Exchequer, who, in 1957, set up the Council on Prices, Productivity and Incomes. Indeed, in setting it up, Thorneycroft had said, 'There is clearly no simple act of policy which is a remedy for inflation. If there had been, it would have been discovered a very long time ago.' Furthermore, it was a Conservative government in 1962 which had further entrenched the principle of an incomes policy and set up the National Incomes Commission.

In the late 1970s, I did not want the Conservative Party to repeat my own mistake of 1965–70, when we had come to oppose a statutory pay policy on principle, even though we should have known that circumstances might one day force us into implementing one. Time and time again, from the 1950s until the 1970s, negotiators faced with the consequences of inflation and unemployment in the absence of an incomes policy did make inflationary settlements. Unfortunately, it takes a long time for those concerned to see the folly of their ways. Meanwhile, everybody suffers. No responsible government could stand by, allowing inflation to soar and unemployment to rise, in the hope that eventually, at some unspecified time in the future, the unions would see the error of their ways. That is not government. It is abdication of government.

Under the Labour government since 1974, the British people had lived through hard times. They had witnessed an unprecedented wages explosion, suffered the worst inflation in living memory and seen our country brought to the brink of bankruptcy. The last thing that they needed was to go through all of that again. To have unleashed, at that time, a new wages explosion would have been an act of madness. I did not believe, for one minute, that Labour's pay policy was the best one could ever hope for, but it was the best that we could hope for under that Labour government. For that reason, I thought that we should give it a chance, and do absolutely nothing to undermine it.

Although they could see the shortcomings of Labour's pay policy very clearly, members of my party had to realise that dismantling an incomes policy would not have removed all of our problems. Government can remove a pay norm and then negotiators will press for more than the company or the country can afford. Government can try to opt out of pay bargaining in the nationalised industries, but negotiators will still bargain in the firm belief that the government could not, in the final analysis, allow the public utilities to go bust. It is possible to impose cash limits in the public sector and lay off workers, but the unions in response could still bring coal, electricity, railways or sewerage to a standstill in protest against the lay-offs. None of these problems was created by an incomes policy. Back in the 1970s, they were palpably part and parcel of our industrial life.

Reliance on sound monetary and fiscal policies, important though they are, was not enough, but I did not want the debate over incomes policy to acquire the characteristics of a religious war. We were not having to choose between competing catechisms. We were concerned with the practical questions of running the economy and choosing the 'least worst' of the options before us. On 10 November 1978, the *Daily Express* published a poll which showed that my views had widespread support in the country. When asked who would make the best Conservative Prime Minister, I received 55 per cent support, to Mrs Thatcher's 33 per cent. The poll also suggested that, if I was still leader, the Conservative lead over Labour would jump from 3 per cent to 14 per cent. With a general election approaching, however, my only concern was to see the return of a Conservative government and, on 13 November, I publicly stated that I would never challenge Mrs Thatcher for the leadership.

The moment when I knew that there was no serious likelihood of my ever serving in a government headed by Mrs Thatcher came when I was flying back to Geneva for a meeting of the Brandt Commission on Development Issues (see p. 607–8) on Sunday 25 February 1979 with Katharine Graham, publisher of the *Washington Post*. She passed a copy of the *Observer* to me, and drew my attention to an interview with Mrs Thatcher. She was quoted as saying, 'There are two ways of making a Cabinet. One way is to have in it people who represent all the different viewpoints within the party. The other way is to have in it only the people who want to go in the direction in which every instinct tells me we have to go – clearly, steadily, firmly, with resolution . . . As Prime Minister, I couldn't waste time having any internal arguments . . . It must be a conviction Government.' This made it quite plain that I would not be invited to serve in her Cabinet. Nonetheless, I continued to tour the country working hard for the return of a Conservative government.

It was a gift for the Conservative Party to have to fight a general election after the Winter of Discontent. This unrest, the intensity of which shocked all politicians, was a revolt by millions of people against stagnation and a backlash against our national decline. The British people had been frustrated by the seemingly endless failures of the last five years, thwarted by the apparent lack of opportunities available to them. Looking at other countries in the Western world they could see that they were enjoying a fuller, more creative life, while we were falling further and further behind. The Winter of Discontent generated examples of man's inhumanity to man which most of us never believed possible in a civil society. They were rightly condemned. The fact that they could occur was chillingly indicative of the callousness which had crept into industrial disputes.

The Labour government had been elected after doing its utmost to undermine the Industrial Relations Act of 1971 and to impede those who were fighting the battle against inflation until early 1974. In that campaign Labour promised the unions an end to many of the existing restraints, both legal and financial, and one of its first actions in government was to wipe out the Industrial Relations Act. The consequences were seen in the most damaging breakdown in industrial relations Britain had ever known. The union leaders accepted the Labour Party's undertakings in good faith and used them as the basis of their relationship with the shopfloor. It was not, therefore, surprising that the Labour government's relationship with the unions, and any remaining authority of the union establishment among their own members and shop stewards, disintegrated over this period. At the end of the Callaghan government, the British people were ready, in a way they had not been in 1974, to stand behind a Conservative government as it again took action to deal with this problem.

Following defeat in a confidence vote in the House of Commons, largely on the issue of devolution, Callaghan finally set the election date for 3 May 1979. I threw myself into the campaign by embarking on a tour of the country that was handled by Conservative Central Office. My tour started with a visit to marginal seats in Scotland, followed by trips across the country from Cornwall to Yorkshire and from Wales to East Anglia. I spent most of my time discussing foreign policy and attacking the disastrous economic record of the Labour government. The latter was not difficult. Callaghan's attempt to limit pay increases overall to 5 per cent had now led to the worst outbreak of industrial unrest since the end of the Second

World War. Over a million more workers were involved than had been active in the winter of 1974. Five years earlier, in February 1974, James Callaghan had incited the Welsh miners to strike against the Conservative government and the pay policy which Parliament had then approved. As his own government fell, he was generously paid back in his own coin. The pay policy had failed, not because it was wrong in principle, but because the Labour government had lacked the necessary resolve to enforce it, or to introduce the legal means necessary to make the unions more responsible and accountable.

The industrial situation was extremely bleak under that Labour government, as the figures testify. During the period 1970–4, growth in British productivity, particularly in the manufacturing sector, compared favourably with what our major rivals were achieving. Between 1974 and 1979, however, the position was reversed. According to some methods of calculation, industrial productivity in the UK actually fell during the Wilson and Callaghan years. Since other countries had managed to cope so much better than we had, the world recession could not take all the blame for our ills.

As I predicted, the Conservative Party won the 1979 election and Britain elected its first woman Prime Minister. Although the Conservative Party had a bigger majority in the House of Commons than in 1970, the share of the popular vote was lower. There was no justification, therefore, for the claim that the country had swung decisively to the right. The Labour Party emerged as the biggest loser in the House of Commons, with fewer seats than at any time since 1959. My own majority in Old Bexley nearly doubled to 13,456, a pleasing result and a tribute to my local team, as I had spent most of the campaign elsewhere, visiting marginal seats.

I had done all I could to help Mrs Thatcher secure a working majority in the House of Commons. Our disagreement over incomes policy had subsided in the run-up to the election. The Conservative manifesto had been scrupulously vague, simply stating that a Conservative government would frame its monetary and other policies in order that it should be able to come to some conclusions on the likely scope of pay increases. At my adoption meeting at Bexley on 9 April, before the campaign, I had said that Britain needed a government which was capable of bringing the nation together to face our problems and the challenges ahead: 'It is the Conservative Party, the party committed to the ideal of One Nation, that can give Britain this lead.' When asked, I also indicated that I would accept an appointment in Mrs Thatcher's government, if I was offered one. If anyone was going to issue a rebuff, it was not going to be me.

Chapter 20

THE DOGMA THAT BARKED ON THE RIGHT

Domestic Politics 1979–1997

I campaigned hard in the 1979 general election campaign, right across the country. Once it was clear that the election was won, I wrote a personal note of congratulation to the new Prime Minister, and then went off to spend the weekend with Charles and Sara Morrison at their home in Wiltshire. On Saturday morning, after a telephone warning, a handwritten note from Mrs Thatcher was delivered by a motorcycle despatch rider. 'After the usual consultations,' she wrote, 'I shall be seeing several people tomorrow . . . I have thought long and deeply about the post of Foreign Secretary and have decided to offer it to Peter Carrington who – as I am sure you will agree – will do the job superbly.' I was not in the least surprised, and informed a number of journalists that I intended to stay on as a backbench Member of Parliament. This was widely reported by all the media, national and worldwide.

Ten days later, Mrs Thatcher wrote to me once again, to inform me that 'Peter Jay [Jim Callaghan's son-in-law and our ambassador to the USA at that time] is likely soon to want to leave our Washington Embassy . . . Before making any move whatsoever I should like to know whether you have any interest yourself in being our Ambassador there.' This was a clear indication that she wanted me out of the way. Winston Churchill had dealt with Lord Halifax in a similar way in 1940. I replied by return:

Dear Margaret, Thank you for your letter of today's date . . . I announced publicly last week that I am remaining in the House of Commons, where I intend to continue to play a major part in its affairs . . . I am sure that you will have no difficulty in finding a suitable replacement for Peter Jay, if he wishes to leave Washington.

I then set about thinking how I might most effectively campaign for the things in which I continued to believe. I was not a member of the government, but the prospect of spending the remainder of my parliamentary career serving my constituents and, if needed, offering advice to sympathetic ministers on the basis of my experiences was entirely agreeable.

During the election campaign Mrs Thatcher had, for the most part, kept quiet about her monetarist economic views. Voters had punished Labour for their mismanagement, but a significant part of their unpopularity had arisen because the Chancellor of the Exchequer, Denis Healey, had followed monetarist policies under pressure from the International Monetary Fund. I was convinced that a further, more severe dose of monetarism from a Conservative government would bring misery to many Britons, and deep unpopularity for the party. Common sense suggested that a more judicious mix of economic policy should be used to tackle our problems. In Mrs Thatcher's first Cabinet, there were several people who could be relied upon to offer this advice if necessary.

Any hopes for moderation proved to be unfounded. The economic ministries were filled with firm believers in monetarism and, unlike the practice during my period in Downing Street, major decisions on the economy were kept away from the full Cabinet, leaving the moderate majority impotent. Before the end of 1979 the government had dismantled price controls, almost doubled VAT, raised interest rates and abolished exchange controls. The inevitable effects were increased inflation and a soaring exchange rate, a double blow from which many exporters, including some in my own constituency, never recovered. The government was right to argue that inflation needed to be tackled urgently, and tough policies would evidently be needed, but I disagreed with the chosen measures and deplored their results. The policies were indeed tough, but seemed certain to make our difficulties worse, not better.

Those in charge of our economic policy were simply implementing the theories which they had learned from their right-wing advisers, at a time when more constructive policies would have had a real chance of succeeding. The government never seemed to understand the true nature of the problem, which was not only the level of inflation. For a start, the volatility of inflation in the UK was now as much of a problem as its level. In May 1977, the rate was 17 per cent; in 1978, it was 7.7 per cent; in 1979, 10 per cent; in 1980, 21.9 per cent; and in 1981, it was back at 11.4 per cent. More importantly, in the early 1980s it was high (and fluctuating) exchange and interest rates – the direct consequence of government policy – which were destroying so many jobs and companies.

To make matters worse, the world would soon be heading into the era of Ronald Reagan's devastating deficit financing, with the Americans exporting high interest rates and, with them, recession. This caused particularly severe problems for the developing world. I had always paid attention to developments in the wider world economy, and my experience as a member of the Brandt Commission was reinforcing my concerns for the future. In June 1980 I spoke in the House of Commons on the problems of Third World debt, but I found the government unresponsive despite my attempts to alert it to the growing threat to financial markets unless the governments of the developed world worked out a new policy for expansion. After one intervention during my speech I jokingly admitted that I had reached the stage when I would welcome support no matter where it came from. This was only just a year into the new government.

I believe that politicians must be guided by experience, not by theories. Throughout my political life the Conservative Party had rightly criticised socialists for their attachment to doctrinal, impractical ideas. The purpose of politics is to bring benefit to one's country, not to experiment with academic theories. Monetarism, the idea that inflation is a purely monetary phenomenon, the product of nothing more than an increase in the money supply, is perhaps the most deceptively simplistic of all economic theories. As such, it was always likely to be especially attractive to those whose understanding of economics was limited.

My realisation that the economic policy of this Conservative government was going to be dictated by monetarism meant that, before long, I would be forced to speak out on a more systematic basis. The situation deteriorated badly when Mrs Thatcher made her well-known speech at the 1980 party conference including the line 'The lady's not for turning.' To me this seemed to add a personal edge to our disagreements. The Prime Minister knew as well as anyone that it was an absurd caricature to describe the limited policy changes which had to be introduced between 1970 and 1974 as 'U-turns'. Indeed, in her speech she herself dismissed 'U-turn' as a 'media catchphrase'. She should not have allowed media obsessions to infiltrate, or dictate, such an important statement. The obvious subtext of her words, and of others from her admirers, was that the government of 1970–4 had changed tack because it had been weak. The irony of it was that, far from succeeding with its stated course of controlling the money supply and public expenditure, the new government comfortably missed all of its targets.

The main reason for the government's failure was that monetarism is self-defeating. The unemployment created by the crude application of tight monetary policy after 1979 meant that public spending could not be brought down. Benefits had to be paid for, and many people who could have been paying taxes were forced instead to look to the state for help. Similarly, companies which would have been paying corporation tax went bankrupt. Like Napoleon's execution of the Duc d'Enghien, the government's policy was worse than a crime; it was a terrible mistake. Apart from anything else, the decimation of manufacturing industry, which lost over one-sixth of its capacity between the second quarter of 1979 and the first quarter of 1981, meant that, when recovery eventually came, there was sure to be a balance of payments crisis. Consumers with money in their pockets would have no choice but to purchase imported goods. In time, I believe that some of the ministers who trumpeted the brilliance of the government's so-called 'Medium-Term Financial Strategy' came to realise this too. Others always regarded the implementation of right-wing policies as a crusade, from which there could be 'No Turning Back'. It was a dismal change from the pragmatic Conservatism of the past.

After Mrs Thatcher had made it plain that she was 'not for turning' in October 1980, I intervened during the debate on the Queen's Speech on 27 November to remind the House that my generation had come into politics to prevent unemployment. The Prime Minister then decided that the best way of dealing with the country's problems was, in a radio interview the following day, to attack the record of the 1970–4 government, in which she had served. Mrs Thatcher's strategy was now perfectly clear. The Conservatives were well behind Labour in the polls, despite that party's lurch to the left, and there had been several surveys which asked people to say whether I should be a better leader than Mrs Thatcher. I had not the slightest intention of challenging the leader's position, and made no attempt to co-operate with colleagues who were well-known opponents of monetarism, but the spotlight was very much on.

No matter how hard I tried to keep the debate over policy away from questions of personality, the media would try to undermine my views by presenting it all as a clash between myself and my successor. I was not prepared to stay silent with my country and party in difficulties, and therefore spoke out forthrightly. The formation of the Social Democratic Party (SDP) in the spring of 1981 made it even more important to urge the government to change course. Although it was born out of the Labour Party, the SDP seemed for a time to be a natural home for discontented Conservative voters and, at one point, hit 50 per cent in the opinion polls. The SDP never for one moment appealed to me personally, although some of my younger colleagues felt differently. Senior moderates such as Peter Walker did sterling work in keeping all but one of them on board. Several later enjoyed successful careers in government.

I argued from the outset that those of us who still believed in traditional Conservative principles and policies should stay within the party. If One Nation Conservatives had abandoned ship in serious numbers, we could have faced a very damaging, perhaps even fatal, defeat at the next general election, branded as the champions of only a narrow section of the population. I thought the SDP was unlikely to sustain its popularity, and the most likely outcome, if a sizeable number of Conservatives joined it, was that Conservative support would be siphoned away and Labour, now very left-wing and rather dangerous, might have a renewed chance of getting into government.

There had been some early measures after 1979 of which I warmly approved – the first cuts in income tax, for example, and Jim Prior's early moves to curb union militancy. Sometimes I supported the government through hope rather than conviction, as in the case of the 1981 budget, which further reduced demand during the depths of the worst recession since the 1930s, but which at least recognised the seriousness of the problems which the country was being forced to endure. At the time of that budget, I was recuperating in Torquay from a thyroid complaint which required a month's rest but which has caused me no trouble since. Against doctor's orders, however, I made a point of going to London to vote for the government, having detected in the Chancellor's speech some signs that he was moving away from crude monetarism. The Prime Minister wrote me a short note thanking me for my support.

Just before the 1981 party conference, however, I spoke to the Federation of Conservative Students, outlining alternative Conservative policies which could help Britain to recover. In particular, I argued that the government should move towards exchange rate stability by joining the European Monetary System (EMS). This would prevent the kind of volatility which had driven so many exporters out of business, and greater co-operation at the European level was urgently needed to counteract wrong-headed US policy. I repeated my message in the conference hall. My speech was quite well received, although there was some of the heckling which I had fully expected. I began by asking delegates not to applaud too loudly, in case they irritated their neighbours.

With the United States enduring a similar recession to ours, inspired by the same monetarist theories, I was convinced that we needed a serious change of thinking. I was reminded of the sufferings during the slump of the 1930s. No one who had grown up at that time could fail to draw the parallel. Since those days we had developed our welfare state, so the plight of unemployed people was less desperate in material terms, but generations brought up in the era of full employment could not be expected simply to cash their dole cheques and sing the praises of the new orthodoxy which made them dependent on the taxpayer. When the inner-city riots broke out in the summer of 1981 I was not surprised. The growing division between the prosperous south and the depressed north was also reminiscent of the 1930s, an experience that had led responsible politicians to implement the first regional policies, which the government of the early 1980s sneeringly rejected as 'corporatism'.

We Conservatives had taunted Labour at the 1979 election with the slogan 'Labour isn't working', yet our own policies had now driven unemployment relentlessly from 1 million to over 2.3 million by autumn 1981 (it would remain at around 3 million throughout the mid-1980s). Some regions were hit especially hard. In the mid-1970s, for example, the west midlands had been second only to the south-east in its gross domestic product per head. In the early 1980s, following the collapse of its manufacturing base, it became the poorest region in England. There were also signs that recession was developing into depression. Companies had run down their stocks and reduced their workforces and now, in the face of punitively high interest rates, they were beginning to reduce their working capital. British industry was disinvesting.

After the 1981 party conference, I visited Croydon to help our candidate in a parliamentary by-election there. The voters, however, were looking to punish the government, and the seat fell to the SDP–Liberal Alliance. In the fight of his life, Roy Jenkins, having left the European Commission, followed this up with his victory for the SDP at Glasgow, Hillhead, which he won from the Conservatives at a by-election in March 1982, even though the Conservative Party had recovered slightly from our third-placed position in the late 1981 opinion polls. Then, while I was in Beijing on 2 April, Argentinian troops invaded the Falkland Islands. I immediately returned to London.

At that time, the vast majority of people knew little, or nothing, of the islands. The government too was less informed than it should have been. Before the invasion it had given a number of misleading signals to Argentina, the most misguided being the Ministry of Defence's decision to withdraw HMS *Endurance*, the Royal Navy vessel which regularly visited the Falklands. *Endurance* conveyed the small contingent of Marines to and from the islands and was regarded in the area as the symbol of Britain's commitment to the islanders.

Successive British governments had negotiated with Argentina to seek out some mutually acceptable arrangement over the islands, so long as we did not concede on the fundamental question of sovereignty. It was clear to me when I was Prime Minister that the only way of keeping the islands defensible was by maintaining a cordial and constructive atmosphere in our dealings with the Argentinian government. In 1972, Alec Douglas-Home reached agreement with Argentina on a variety of arrangements to suit the islanders. The new airfield in the Falklands was built jointly. Argentina was to provide air transport to the islands, while we would retain charge of sea transport. Private education and health care was provided in Buenos Aires for the islanders, who had always appeared open to such arrangements. Their position, so far away from the natural British sphere of influence, had always made them vulnerable. We were completely successful in improving their standards of living by co-operation with the Argentinians, and making clear our intention to stay put. In 1980, when I had spoken in a debate on the government's Defence White Paper, I had assumed that the situation in the Falklands was still secure.

The British government rightly resolved to uphold the rights of the Falkland islanders, and to end the illegal occupation of the islands. The Americans were persuaded to support the British cause, despite their involvement with the Organisation of American States, as were our European partners and the Commonwealth. The day after the invasion, UN Security Council Resolution 502 was passed, demanding an immediate cessation of hostilities, a complete Argentinian withdrawal and a diplomatic solution, with the two governments negotiating a long-term agreement over the islands. Meanwhile, since British territory had been violated, international law recognised our right to use force. In this, we had to reassure the international community about our motives. Primarily, we were resisting aggression. Other countries in Latin America generally supported the Argentinian claim over the Falklands in principle. Our best chance of winning them round, or at least keeping them neutral, was by emphasising our own benign purpose. On 4 April, two days after the Argentinian invasion, the Foreign Secretary, Peter Carrington, resigned, along with two of his ministerial colleagues. This was afterwards described as honourable. It is doubtful, however, whether it was necessary. If there was a failure of responsibility, it was a failure of collective responsibility. Francis Pym then took charge at the Foreign Office.

I argued that we had to do our best to provide a way out for those who, through malice and an error of judgement, had launched this invasion. We were in conflict with General Galtieri and his junta not because of their internal policies but because they were a menace to British interests. In 1982, I therefore supported the government's policy of firm negotiation, with the task force standing by as a back-up to diplomacy, if required. As it turned out we were obliged to have recourse to arms, and the British armed services acquitted themselves most effectively. Now that the Falklands have returned to peaceful existence and Argentina is a democracy, we should resume our search for a long-term arrangement for the area.

Afterwards the government set up an inquiry into the whole affair under the chairmanship of Lord Franks. Mrs Thatcher announced to the House of Commons that papers from previous administrations, where relevant, would be available to the committee. I was concerned that this represented a serious break with precedent, because Ministers in one administration have never had the right to see papers from a previous one. Before any announcement was made, previous Prime Ministers should have been consulted, not as a mere matter of courtesy, but because a question of constitutional propriety was at stake. I raised this point strongly at Prime Minister's Questions. Mrs Thatcher subsequently wrote to me and confirmed that the government accepted my view. I commented to the House of Commons, 'I find myself in a very difficult position in what I have to say next. I find, in the terms of reference and in the letter . . . the Prime Minister kindly sent me, that the government are now in agreement with what I proposed. I also find myself the recipient of compliments from the Leader of the Opposition. It is difficult, at short notice, to assess which is the more damaging to me!'

The 'Falklands factor' greatly enhanced the ratings of the Conservative Party and burst the SDP bubble, but this did nothing to lift the British economy out of the doldrums. High US interest rates were now pulling in vast amounts of cash from countries in Europe and the Far East. The US administration, with Paul Volcker as chairman of the Federal Reserve Board, had also tried out the 'new economics', but this had generated economic decline in 1980, weak growth in 1981 and another downturn in 1982. Then, the Americans just let rip. The federal budget deficit rose from 1.1 per cent of GNP in 1979 to 5.6 per cent in 1983. By mid-1984, the US would be running a budget deficit of US$200,000 million, and a trade deficit of US$130,000 million. All of this was being met by massive inflows of capital from Europe and Japan. In consequence, we were being seriously denuded of the capital that we needed to finance new plant and machinery, and create jobs. The Americans were borrowing, in effect, three times as much as we were. Their savings ratio, however, was around 6 or 7 per cent, as compared with 11 or 12 per cent in the United Kingdom. They were living on borrowed time and borrowed money. Yet, ironically, we were still being told that we should become more like the US, and Reagan was being acclaimed as a superb President.

In the budget of March 1982, Geoffrey Howe confirmed that the government had learned a brutal lesson in the limits of monetarism. As a consequence of that budget, the government introduced some special inducements to industry, subsidies and even price controls in the public sector. I was able to congratulate Geoffrey Howe on his actions, if not on his rhetoric, which continued to praise monetarism after it had been effectively buried. But the country had already paid a grim price for the experiment of the early 1980s, and the pain was far from over. As economic recovery in the United States finally started to feed through into a modest recovery in Europe, I began to fear that the government had no idea of what to do when the inevitable upturn came. This was our opportunity to look at some radical ideas on encouraging investment, on negative income tax and on back-to-work programmes. The recovery was clearly fragile, and we now faced the gradual run-down of our North Sea oil revenues. This was no time for *laisser faire*

The orthodoxy of British monetarism was now discredited, even by its own standards. As I pointed out in the 1982 budget debate, during the first three years of that administration, £M1 ('narrow money' – coins and notes in circulation and other very liquid assets) had increased by 29 per cent, while £M3 ('broad money', over which government has much more limited control) had increased by 62 per cent. The government had fallen consistently short of achieving its own much vaunted monetary targets. In the four years following the setting out of the Medium-Term Financial Strategy in 1980, increases in the public sector borrowing requirement (PSBR) exceeded the government's target in every single year. The increase in £M3 was also above the top end of its target range, sometimes dramatically so. It is not surprising that the PSBR came under pressure. With the rise in unemployment and deprivation, government transfer payments had risen to 17.7 per cent of GDP, as compared with 12.5 per cent in 1973.

Nonetheless, the contribution of the 'Falklands Factor' and the effect of the SDP on Labour support ensured the return of the Conservative Government by a massive majority at the election in June 1983. Indeed, the main achievement of the SDP and its Alliance with the Liberal Party was to siphon off votes from Labour at the general elections of 1983 and 1987. Despite winning over 20 per cent of the vote at both elections, the Alliance won only twenty-three and twenty-two seats respectively, but it so weakened Labour, even in its historic heartlands, that the Conservative Party, with under 45 per cent of the vote, won majorities of 144 and 101 in those polls. Labour paid the price for its strident left-wing agenda, but it also became clear, after 1987 in particular, that Francis Pym had been right to warn that government by too large a majority can become dangerously remote from the people.

As we went into the mid-1980s, the economy began to grow, but the rate of unemployment remained stubbornly high and people first began to speak of a 'jobs-free recovery'. At the beginning of 1985, despite several years of renewed economic growth, unemployment in some regions was still stuck at around 20 per cent. In some areas in the north-east, a third of the male population was unemployed. When I visited Consett, the hometown of my private secretary at the time, Peter Batey, I was appalled to see for myself the effects of 60 per cent youth unemployment. In the country as a whole unemployment was also still rising. The official figure in excess of 3 million disguised the true situation, which was far worse, the method of calculating the total having been changed in 1982. Nigel Lawson, Geoffrey Howe's successor as Chancellor, at that time described policies of state intervention and regional policy as 'voodoo witchcraft'. I reminded the House of Commons on 15 January 1985 that, as President of the Board of Trade in 1963–4, I had been responsible for implementing some rather successful voodoo, in the form of a policy for the north-east which Quintin Hailsham had designed to help the region overcome the rapid loss of 120,000 jobs in its traditional heavy manufacturing sector. We drove unemployment down to below 5 per cent.

Every Conservative used to believe in full employment as a laudable objective. Changes in the international economy, as well as our own problems with competitiveness, make it far more difficult to achieve than it was in the 1950s, but unemployed people deserve more than a weekly hand-out to keep them quiescent. The right wing, who talk about 'scroungers', think that only money matters, when it is obvious that most of those on benefits also want a purpose in life. They should at least have the option of performing useful community work. Both John Major and Michael Heseltine indicated, during the 1992–7 parliament, that they supported 'Workfare', the provision of socially desirable activities for those without jobs. I hope that, if a stated commitment to full employment is no longer regarded as viable or credible, then something along these lines will be seriously considered. In an economic debate at the end of 1986, I was wryly amused when the government boasted that unemployment was now falling 'faster than it had done for 13 years'. I suppose that I should have taken this reference to 1973 as a backhanded compliment, but I was more concerned at the complacent attitude of ministers when unemployment was still scandalously high.

As unemployment began to fall at last in the mid-1980s, the shortcomings of the British labour market were brutally exposed. Employers in the south began to expand at great speed in response to the 'Lawson Boom', and found that they could not find the skilled staff that they needed. Meanwhile, the employment situation in several of the regions remained as bleak as ever. In the wake of every cyclical economic downturn since 1945, the pattern had been the same: the south-east had come out of recession first, and the waves of recovery had rippled out to the west and north. In the 1980s, the north–south divide moved further south than ever and in the early 1990s, the line vanished altogether, and the south-east suffered as badly, if not worse than, the rest of the country in the wake of a difficult recession. The Conservative Party ultimately paid a high price for that.

In March 1985, I was invited by Channel Four to present an alternative budget, in advance of Nigel Lawson's real one. We combined clips of me talking with members of the public, interviews with business people and some of the bizarre sentiments expressed by Professor Brian Griffiths, one of the Conservative Government's monetarist gurus. Then we moved on to my own proposals. The 1984 budget had been presented as a 'Budget for Jobs', and the previewing of its successor was very similar. I was convinced that more of the same simply would not do. We had seen a cruel decline in production within the tradeable sector of the economy, especially in manufacturing. Our balance of payments position was very vulnerable, and any expansionary measures would have to be targeted in areas which would suck in the lowest level of imports. The people I consulted from academia and the City, as was my usual habit at budget time, agreed. The government did not take the same view, and its indiscriminate tax cuts were always bound to lead to trouble.

In my alternative budget, I proposed a carefully targeted programme of expanded public investment, putting up public borrowing by £5 billion, with £1.5 billion extra for the Department of Trade and Industry, to invest in rebuilding seriously under-capitalised industries such as steel and shipbuilding. After all, we were not being undercut by competition from low-wage and low-skill countries. We were being left in the wake of countries such as Sweden and Germany. Reflecting on the already considerable successes of the Welsh and Scottish Development Agencies, under a government which really had no place for them in its philosophy, I suggested that a Northern Development Agency be set up.

I also warned that, as the economy began to grow again, we faced, thanks to years of neglect, a serious shortage of skilled labour. I proposed that an extra £1.5 billion should be allocated to the Department of Employment, for expanded training and community programmes. However, it was not only our 'human capital' which needed urgent additional investment. The CBI had recently warned that 'Britain is dropping to bits', and it was painfully apparent that the state of our roads, bridges and railways was becoming both a national embarrassment and a serious impediment to industry and individual citizen alike. I emphasised this by going to the spot where a Black Country link road to the M6, years in the building, still ended in the middle of a field. I proposed an extra £2 billion for the development of infrastructure, a drop in the ocean perhaps, but at least a move in the right direction.

In 1985, the old monetarism was truly dead. Its core argument, that inflation could be curbed only by tight monetary policy and cuts in public spending, was discredited, and the grievous effects of a high-exchange-rate, high-interest-rate policy were there for all to see. Meanwhile, the government's free-market housing policy was largely responsible for growing labour-mobility problems. The stock of decent and affordable rented housing, particularly for young people and those on low incomes, was allowed to fall. Meanwhile, the scale of the council-housing sell-off, and the gradual erosion of the privately rented sector, made it far more difficult for people to 'get on their bikes', unless they could afford to buy a home. The council properties sold off during the 1980s were never adequately replaced, mainly because the government forced councils to set off their receipts for these sales against their debts, when they should have been allowed to reinvest income from the sales either in new building or in improving their remaining stock. This was done not for sound political reasons, but because the Treasury refused to redefine its method of calculating the PSBR.

I had similar misgivings about the government's privatisation programme, which began in a piecemeal fashion during the 1979 parliament. A reduction in the size of the state-owned sector was welcome. Instead of using so much of the receipts to fund tax cuts, however, it would have been more prudent to invest in the country's deteriorating infrastructure. Apart from fostering a frothy mood of 'casino capitalism', the developing policy had three specific drawbacks. First of all, consideration of possible privatisations, like the selling of council houses, was bedevilled by the intransigence of the Treasury. In many cases, utilities were privatised purely because they required massive capital investment, and the Treasury had decided that this must not be allowed to take place within the public sector, again for fear of adding to the PSBR.

Secondly, rather oddly for an administration which talked of the market as some sort of deity which must never be affronted, the government paid insufficient attention to market conditions when it conducted its sales. It also missed the public mood, by showing complete indifference to the ultimate destination of the concerns which were sold off. I campaigned hard against the proposed sale of British Leyland trucks and Land-Rover to the American company General Motors, and received numerous letters and widespread support. On that occasion, the government backed down.

Thirdly, and most seriously of all, privatisation was extended to cover utilities and other natural monopolies which had always been exclusive operations of the state. Electricity, water and even parts of the prison system all became candidates for transfer into private hands. As I never accepted the notion that the private sector is inevitably more efficient than the public, I was able to foresee the nightmarish problems of regulation which would always bedevil these initiatives, leaving their long-term viability open to serious doubt. The 1970-4 government never implemented a full-scale programme of privatisation, because only three and three-quarter years in power did not permit it, not least because any lasting settlement of the public–private debate would have to be planned and introduced gradually over many years if it was to be sound. The profiteering behaviour of privatised utilities was a major factor in public disenchantment with the Conservative Party. I remain convinced that the caution of the 1970–4 government was entirely sensible.

Radicalism was also taken too far in the field of trade union reform. The government which I led introduced measures to reform the entire field of industrial relations. Mrs Thatcher's administration more or less confined itself to dealing with the trade unions. No doubt the government was helped in its policy by the mass unemployment of the early 1980s. More significantly it could count upon staunch support from the public at large, thanks to the deep unpopularity which the unions had earned during the Winter of Discontent. In trade union matters, there should be a proper balance between workers and employers. By the late 1970s, things had gone too far away from the employers. The balance of power in industrial relations has now shifted away, not just from trade unions as institutions, but from individual workers as well. As a consequence, many employers have come to think of workers as temporary factors of production, rather than integral members of their concerns, or as individuals with families and mortgages.

I supported the government during the miners' strike of 1984–5 although, as in the early 1970s, the situation was a tragic one for those who believe in One Nation. The government was able to face down the miners on this occasion, partly because demand for coal was one-third less than it had been in 1973–4, partly because the miners were split and the breakaway Union of Democratic Mineworkers did not follow the NUM in striking and enabled coal production to be maintained in the Derbyshire and Nottinghamshire coalfields, and partly because adequate stockpiles of coal had been built up to see the country through a lengthy trial of strength. The government had also learned from the bitter battles of Saltley that coal stocks were all very well, but they were needed at the power stations, not just at the pithead, to protect the country from the blackmail of secondary action. In direct contravention of the law of the land, the NUM also refused to ballot its members. There was an unpleasant atmosphere of triumphalism on the Conservative benches at this time, but I could only reflect that the leaders and members of the NUM had to a great extent brought their fate upon themselves. I was never, however, one of those who wanted 'revenge' for 1973–4, a fact which trade union leaders privately recognised.

In the middle of the course of that strike, any divisions within the party were transcended by the bomb in October 1984 at the Grand Hotel, Brighton, which was occupied by so many senior figures. I had returned home the evening before the explosion but, as soon as I heard news of it,

I returned at once to the conference to show sympathy with those who had been killed or injured, and solidarity with the principles of freedom and democracy which were being challenged by such callous acts. The emotion in the hall that morning was intense, and it was to the credit of everyone involved that the business of the conference proceeded as it did. I was glad to have played quite literally a 'walk-on' part in that, joining members of the Cabinet as they went on to the platform for the highly charged final session of the conference.

In the wake of Mrs Thatcher's 1987 general election victory, another controversial policy emerged to threaten the future of the Conservative Party. Ministers had long since declared war against local government, flying in the face of traditional Conservatism, which has always prized local autonomy. In 1984, I had voted against a three-line whip on a Bill implementing 'rate-capping', the curtailment of local councils' discretion over raising money. On the basis of a few lurid tales about financial waste, the government took the extreme view that no local authority was competent to decide on the level of funding it required. This was a strange decision coming from a government which, in other contexts, railed against central bureaucracy. I also spoke out against the spiteful abolition of the Greater London Council, carried through to prevent it competing with the Whitehall government. This left London as the only significant world capital without a strategic authority. After the 1987 election, the government then introduced the community charge, the 'poll tax'. Ministers had decided that this flat-rate charge would bring home to everyone the cost of local government. The logical conclusion of that, in theory at least, was that everyone would then vote for the party which offered the cheapest services, even in areas where high expenditure was unavoidable to maintain anything like civilised life.

This new system was flawed in a number of ways. Because of earlier rate-capping measures, the proportion of council revenues raised locally would only be 25 per cent. This created a problem of 'leverage'. In order to raise its total income by 25 per cent, for example, a local authority would have to double its poll tax. Furthermore, the link between local government and business was cut by the imposition of a uniform business rate. I forcefully attacked it. 'That is not a radical proposal,' I warned on 2 July 1987, 'it is a reactionary, regressive proposal for the tax not to be related to people's ability to pay.' In the debate on the Local Government Finance Bill on 17 December 1987, I pressed even harder in an exchange with Nicholas Ridley, the Environment Secretary. 'The poll tax is unfair and unworkable,' I said. 'It does not increase accountability and it will be immensely damaging to the Conservative Party ... This measure will always be held against us.' I even had Adam Smith, the government's eighteenth-century guru, on my side. In *The Wealth of Nations*, Smith had written that 'The subjects of every state ought to contribute towards the support of the government, as nearly as possible . . . in proportion to the revenue which they respectively enjoy under the protection of the state.'

Successive governments since the 1960s had looked at various ways of replacing domestic rates, as a means of levying a local contribution towards the expenditure of local government. In October 1974, the Conservative Party was committed to rates reform, and to a new system which would be 'more broadly based and related to people's ability to pay'. Over the years, I have become more convinced that some system of local income tax would be the most progressive and practical way of achieving this. In the wake of the poll tax, councils only have to raise rather less than 20 per cent of their total spending for themselves, the rest coming from central government, so the levels would not be punitive. Furthermore, the whole Inland Revenue system is now fully computerised, so the two systems, national and local, could easily be run in tandem.

While the poll tax was stealing the headlines, and drawing most of the opposition's fire, an Education Reform Bill was piloted, far too hastily, through the House of Commons by my former parliamentary private secretary, Kenneth Baker. We were taken into a second-reading debate only seven working days after the Bill was published, and a single day was allowed for that entire debate – four hours of parliamentary time after the preliminaries had been taken, when seventy MPs had indicated that they wished to speak. This was as much a result of Labour ineffectiveness as of Conservative arrogance. In that debate, I expressed my fears about the new system of testing and the 'opting out' provisions which, it should be noted, came to very little in the end, but which carried a clear threat of creating a two-tier education system. It was, as I told the Commons, a 'confidence-trick'. Once again, the highly publicised madness of a few Labour-run local authorities had given an increasingly authoritarian government an excuse for ill-conceived and radical measures, setting the scene for dismantling the national education system, and further eroding the autonomy of elected local government.

Through this gigantic piece of legislation, Kenneth Baker arrogated to himself far more power than any previous Education Secretary, or even perhaps any previous Minister, had enjoyed. Another area of general consensus was broken. The record was very similar on the National Health Service. When the government's 'internal market' reforms in this area came up for discussion in their turn, I attacked them too. They have enjoyed some successes, no doubt, but I have encountered little evidence myself to indicate that the health service has generally become more comprehensive, or more responsive, as a consequence of the internal market reforms. The bureaucracy seems to have been vastly increased. I have an excellent hospital, Queen Mary's, on the Sidcup edge of my constituency. It has certainly not suffered as a result of the reforms, but there is no doubt whatever that it needs increased and reliable funding, rather than changes to its management structure.

There is, of course, a series of links between questions of economic progress, social policy and social cohesion. In the face of the challenge of the 1980s, with long-term unemployment on a prodigious scale, I became convinced that we needed something akin to Roosevelt's New Deal in 1930s America. Otherwise, we risked losing a whole generation of youngsters who would simply acclimatise themselves to unemployment, low expectations and, probably, a life of petty crime, encouraged by the growing incidence of illegal drugs. Far too many young people were throwing away their entire futures by turning to these, and then moving ineluctably on to criminal activities to finance their habits. Meanwhile, many older people were forced to come to terms with the fact that they would never work again. In the early 1980s, this was happening to manual workers and, in the early 1990s, it caught up with the white-collar worker. Whenever I drew the obvious parallels with the 1930s, I grew more and more weary of condescending people who had no personal recollections of that terrible time, or who were cushioned from the effects of economic slumps both in the 1930s and in the 1980s. Over a decade later, I do not retract a word of what I said.

Ministers and Conservative Party officials stuck throughout the 1980s to the view that there was no connection between high unemployment and rising crime. It is plain to see that there is an inherent connection, a cycle of despair. Endemic criminality causes further unemployment, just as surely as unemployment leads people to crime. Even in these secular times, the devil still finds work for idle hands to do. In 1979–81, the Conservative Party did not pay a high political price for these policies, because the recession at that time did not hit our own areas of support particularly heavily and the left, of course, was divided. The recession of 1989–92, however, left a legacy of bitterness and insecurity which still haunts us.

One area in which there is still most certainly a positive role for government to play is in the field of employment training. Back in the days before the Second World War, there was far greater stability in each individual's working life. The expectation then was that vocational training would be almost entirely undertaken by large concerns. Many of the trained individuals would later find their way into smaller companies, who could not afford to train workers. This was something that the big firms always understood and accepted. That system has now all but vanished. The requirements of companies are quite different, and ever changing. In most cases, companies now seem to have concluded that it is just not worth getting involved in much training activity.

In many parts of the service sector in particular, the strategy now seems to be not improving the base of skilled workers and, accordingly, productivity and profitability, but paying low wages to itinerant workers, who acquire the minimum level of skills and develop no loyalty whatsoever either to their employer or to their trade. This is a form of exploitation. If the private sector is not going to deal with the emergence of such a low-skill, low-loyalty and low-productivity sector, then government should. The Training and Enterprise Councils, set up in the early 1990s, have enjoyed some successes, but I am convinced that ultimately all of this must be taken in hand within the mainstream education system. We need to ensure that youngsters are given true training for life.

I am still not sure about the government's real intentions in the fateful budget of 1988. It was clear from the outset that stimulating consumer demand at that juncture would feed inflation and put pressure on our balance of payments. Cutting the standard rate of income tax from 27 to 25 pence in the pound, and the top rate from 60 to 40, was evidently going to stimulate consumer demand. With skill shortages and domestic supply bottlenecks, this was, in turn, self-evidently going to reignite inflation. There were other warning signs too. Between 1979 and 1988, domestic debt had doubled as a proportion of GDP, and there was no sign that people were inclined to reduce it. In fact, people were saving less as well as borrowing more. In 1980 individuals were saving almost 15 per cent of their incomes, a ratio which fell steadily throughout the 1980s until, by the end of 1987, it was heading down towards 5 per cent. This was very much in keeping with the short-term, consumerist spirit of the age and resulted in a desperate shortage of capital for our industries. Combined with the fact that British industry was by now largely operating at, or close to, its capacity, this meant that cuts in personal taxation would inevitably feed inflation and cause a trade deficit. City experts warned at the time that even dramatically increased levels of capital investment – and there was, in any case, no sign of them – could not raise the productive capacity of our industries quickly enough to satisfy the rampant consumer demand that a loose fiscal policy would unleash.

When I made these points in the 1988 budget debate, Nigel Lawson, as Hansard put it, 'indicated dissent'. Even more strongly than before, I argued that it was essential to take sterling into the Exchange Rate Mechanism (ERM) of the European Monetary System (EMS), in order to maintain economic stability. As I said in that debate, however, it was vital to get the value of sterling down to something credible and sustainable first. I was convinced that this budget was profoundly flawed, but I ended my speech with the hope that 'the risks inherent in the budget . . . will prove to have been taken rightly, that we shall not find inflation increasing, that we shall not find a great consumer boom, and that we shall find our industry and skilled labour force rapidly expanding'. My fears, however, were justified. The problem was a straightforward one. Because the Chancellor supposedly rejected the use of demand management, and regarded the exchange rate as a matter for the markets to resolve, he was left with only one tool in his battle against inflation: the level of interest rates.

The combination of a loose fiscal policy and a rapidly tightening monetary policy was always bound to end in tears. As I put it in the debate on the Queen's Speech in November 1988, 'In golfing terms, the Chancellor could be described as a one-club man, and the club is interest rates . . . But, if one wishes to take on Sandy Lyle and the rest of the world, one needs a complete bag of clubs.' Towards the end of 1988, interest rates were beginning to reach levels which profoundly threatened UK industrial development, and the Chancellor was engaged in a damaging public dispute with the Prime Minister, having come round to supporting UK membership of the EMS.

A few months later, the use of inflated interest rates was beginning to curb underlying inflation, but it was also, as I had feared, choking off the economic recovery. Most notoriously, it was creating the phenomenon of widespread 'negative equity'. For all too many people, the early 1980s dream of home ownership was becoming a ghastly nightmare. Until the late 1980s, nobody had even heard of negative equity. When they purchase shares or buy into pension funds, individuals are warned that 'the price of shares can fall as well as rise', but no such warning has ever been attached to homes. In the late 1980s, however, the cold reality of high interest rates and falling property prices brought misery to many thousands of families across the land.

By the time of the 1989 budget debate, the golf metaphor was becoming ever more appropriate, and I described Nigel Lawson as 'my favourite one-club golfer . . . on the last occasion, he made a splendid drive from the tee', but I warned that 'he now finds himself in a bunker, and he is discovering how difficult it is to get out of a bunker with the wooden club with which he drove off'. The government was, by this time, running a considerable current surplus in its accounts which, in the light of the inflationary pressures that its own policies had created, it was using to pay off the national debt. It was right to be wary about adding extra consumer demand to the economy, of course – it had done enough damage with that the previous year – but I knew, from my trips around the country, that a huge amount of infrastructure investment was desperately needed. Several of our major motorways were in need of large-scale building work, and our railways were in a state of disrepair. Funding such activities would have done no significant damage to the balance of payments, but would have created jobs and enhanced the quality of life for our people. My pleas fell on deaf ears. Interest rates stayed at their pernicious mid-teens level, the poison of negative equity continued to spread across the country and we experienced a recession which, for once, also hit our own supporters in the home counties.

It still seems distasteful that, when so many critical challenges were facing the government, it should have expended its energies on introducing a measure as pointless and pernicious as the War Crimes Bill. Attlee, as Prime Minister, supported by Churchill, as Leader of the Opposition, had proposed in 1948 that the time had come for the British to finish looking in our country for those allegedly connected with war crimes. This was subsequently confirmed by Parliament. The search continued in those countries in Europe which had been directly affected by such crimes, and each national government was accountable for the trials of those considered responsible. Many of them reached the conclusion, after some years, that they too had completed their task. In 1989, under Mrs Thatcher's Government, a Bill was introduced to establish such trials afresh in Britain. This was the result of lobbying, largely on the Labour side of the House of Commons but supported by a considerable number of Conservatives, instigated by the Simon Wiesenthal Center, a Jewish-American organisation based in California. This had contrived to bring about trials in many parts of the world outside Europe, and the United Kingdom was almost the last land to which they turned.

I strongly opposed this Bill in the House of Commons, not leasst because there were so many faults in the procedure put before the House. We were jettisoning without the slightest justification the bipartisan agreement reached almost forty years earlier. We were also introducing legislation against a known, named list of individuals, all of them now aged. Those listed had been accepted when they sought refuge in our country. Indeed, some of them had been brought to Britain in order to give information to our own officials about what had happened in their places of abode during the war, particularly in the Baltic countries. All had lived respectably after their arrival here. Every one was now being asked to deal with events which took place over forty-five years earlier. Many were in poor health. As the witnesses required were also likely to be frail, and unable to travel to London for a court case, the system was invented of giving evidence before television cameras in their own towns, often many thousands of miles away. How could any witness be certain after such an interval that the person in the dock was really the evil-doer they were condemning?

This process took several years to inaugurate and cost millions of pounds. In fact, although a handful of men were alleged to be culpable, no one was ever condemned in a court of law. Only one prosecution, that of Joseph Serafinowicz, was brought under the Act. That ran on for several years, inevitably reaching no conclusion. It would have been a hard heart indeed that could feel no pity for the wretched and confused old man who, after living peacefully in Banstead, Surrey for forty years, was now forced to endure an ineffective and miscalculated show trial, as well as for his family. The whole episode was the consequence of a government whose members had no personal experience of the Second World War. An emotional, irrational outburst led to a legal and political disaster, and a humiliation of our parliamentary system.

In the end, however, it was a combination of the poll tax and her growing hostility to Europe which brought the premiership of Mrs Thatcher to such an unhappy end. Ironically, by the time she left office she had already authorised Chris Patten to look at ways, however radical, of limiting the political damage of the tax. But it was too little, too late. In November 1989, Mrs Thatcher was challenged as leader for the first time, by Sir Anthony Meyer. Sixty MPs either voted for Meyer, or withheld their support from her. At the time, this result was brushed aside by her supporters, but it was undoubtedly a serious blow.

Mrs Thatcher's leadership was challenged again a year later. During those twelve months, she appeared increasingly out of touch and detached, even from her Cabinet colleagues, as her style became increasingly autocratic. By that time even those who agreed with Mrs Thatcher's policies must have harboured serious doubts about her leadership style. She had reached the point where her own sentiments, fed to the press by her close advisers, were being reported back to her as if they represented the independent views of most British people. Her fall from power became inevitable when Geoffrey Howe, whom she had unceremoniously dismissed as Foreign Secretary, made a statement in the House of Commons on the reasons for his subsequent resignation from the office of Lord President of the Council and Leader of the House, to which she had effectively demoted him. This statement, surprising in its strength coming from so mild a man, exposed the extent to which Mrs Thatcher had forfeited the sympathies and loyalty of many of her colleagues and former colleagues. Many backbenchers feared for their chances of re-election if she remained as Leader of the party at the time of the next general election. For everyone's sake, including her own, I wish that she had handed over power voluntarily soon after winning her third general election. The method of her removal enabled her supporters to set up a myth of heroism betrayed which, I believe, is a major reason for our party's unsettled state so long after her fall.

In the second round of the 1990 leadership election, the choice was between three able and moderate men, and I was pleased that the new Prime Minister seemed anxious to free himself from background, or back-seat, influences. When he was Chancellor of the Exchequer, John Major had consulted me about the 1989 budget, a symptom of open-mindedness which I had not encountered from the government front bench for many years. He was not a man to broadcast his views, but it was clear that his sympathies in social policy lay with progressive Conservatism, rather than the hardline ideas which now had so many unappealing representatives on the backbenches. In most cases, John Major's misfortunes were legacies from the previous regime. He was bequeathed the poll tax, a deep recession and a party split on the question of Europe. At least Michael Heseltine dealt with the first, the new council tax signalling a resounding defeat for those who thought that a duke should pay no more than a dustman.

I became Father of the House of Commons after the general election of 1992, as the Member with the longest continuous service. The only procedural responsibility is to take the chair in the place of the Senior Clerk of the House in order to preside over the election of a new Speaker when required. On this occasion Jack Weatherill had retired, and five candidates, some from each side of the House, put themselves forward. This provided certain complications in the customary procedure, which I discussed at some length with the Clerks. Faced with a contested election, I had to decide which of the candidates should be proposed first. Then I had to resolve the order in which the others should be taken. An alphabetical procedure was the only possibility. The remaining difficulty was how all five candidates could be given an opportunity of bidding for a vote. It was decided that the House would divide as soon as the first two contestants had spoken. The victor would then be challenged by the next candidate, and so on. This would continue until all had enjoyed their chance.

I called Betty Boothroyd from the Labour benches first, as she was alphabetically the leading contender. She was followed by Peter Brooke, the former Conservative Cabinet Minister. The House then divided, and Betty Boothroyd won 372 votes to Peter's 238. Recognising that Miss Boothroyd's position was unassailable, the other candidates announced their withdrawal from the contest. I was immensely relieved, and Betty Boothroyd made a brief well-balanced speech of thanks. I then evacuated my seat and went to stand at the bar of the House while she was dragged in the usual way to the Speaker's Chair, where she made a further acknowledgement of the honour conferred upon her. What could have been a controversial and embarrassing process had passed off successfully.

Madam Speaker took office at a turbulent point in our nation's public life. Her enduring and well-deserved status as a much loved icon is in sharp contrast with the contempt in which most public figures are held these days. I think that the principles of public service have been eroded, but reckless campaigning by the media and rival parties has given a quite false impression that the House of Commons is full of knaves and fools. This led to the creation of the Nolan Committee on Standards in Public Life in 1995, a move which implied that the House of Commons itself accepted the view that Members of Parliament were no longer able, or entitled, to take care of their own standards of behaviour. For my genera-tion, this was an extraordinary and deplorable development, which can only serve to deter people of the highest quality from coming into public life, by legitimising unacceptable levels of intrusion into their private affairs. As I said in a debate in the House on 18 May 1995:

> When I entered the House forty-five years ago, in 1950, we recognised every Member of Parliament – man or woman – as a person of integrity. That was the attitude, and it was fully accepted. We have now reached a stage at which every man and woman in the House is an object of suspicion. Why has that come about? I do not consider it healthy or satisfactory . . . in those days, chairmen of major companies were Members of Parliament, as were trade union leaders . . . we now have an entirely different situation, which I think is regrettable.

In recent years, I have been involved with various organisations. None of them relates to my being a Member of Parliament. I should keep them all up if I left the House. What they do achieve is to broaden my knowledge and interests, and make me a better-informed contributor to debates in the House. The spirit of this age, which seizes on the misbehaviour of a small minority to damn everyone in public life, seems to be in favour of driving MPs away from any form of outside interests. I fail to see how that can be in the best interests of democracy. The Nolan Committee represents an unprecedented abrogation of responsibility by Members of Parliament. In effect, they have told the world that they can no longer be trusted. If that is how they feel, then they should step down and let others take their places. So long as the House of Commons enjoys some public standing, there will be no shortage of people to replace them.

'Sleaze' certainly played a role in the Conservative Party's defeat at the 1997 general election. The intrusion of the press into the private lives of public figures is nothing new, but by launching his ill-advised 'Back to Basics' slogan, John Major only succeeded in turning this distasteful preoccupation into a frenzied witch-hunt. In the great majority of cases, the behaviour uncovered by the media inquisition could have had no effect at all on the performance of ministers. The press had the feeling that the party had been in office too long, however, and towards the end of the period nothing the party leadership did could disrupt the mood of disillusionment. One can only hope that we study the record of those years with care, and absorb the right lessons.

Some people talked before the 1997 election as if the problem of standards in public life affected only the Conservative Party. In fact, it is a general problem. Politicians are now far less respected than at any time during my career. I can understand why Labour made so much of 'sleaze' during the last parliament, but they did nothing to help us all address seriously an issue which should be non-partisan. Corrosive cynicism about the country's leaders encourages lax conduct throughout society and, unless the current mood is reversed, our quality of life and social fabric will suffer permanent damage.

As Father of the House, I do indeed take this question seriously. I believe that I have inherited responsibility to attend debates which affect the public's view of Parliament, and put my experience at the disposal of the House. I have favoured live television broadcasts from the House of Commons ever since it became a serious possibility and I spoke strongly in favour of it when the matter was debated in November 1985. We already had television coverage of the House of Lords, and I was convinced that we could no longer rely upon the media to report our debates and decisions accurately and fairly.

The argument against televising our proceedings was that MPs would play to the cameras all the time. In fact, exactly the opposite has happened. In any case, the spectators in the public gallery can see and hear all the proceedings, so why should not the rest of the world do so too, now that the necessary technology is available? Moreover, the absence of cameras had never deterred unruly behaviour in the past. Bernadette Devlin would have assaulted Reggie Maudling on the front bench with or without a live audience. It is only right that the public should see, as well as hear and read about, their elected representatives. If conduct has either deteriorated or improved since television was admitted, that is the fault of the MPs, not of the cameras. Although television does show meetings of select committees, as I suggested it should back in the early 1980s, it tends to concentrate on the more sensational aspects of parliamentary life. Unfortunately, Prime Minister's Question Time has been improved neither by television nor by Tony Blair's post-election changes to it. To concentrate Questions into one half-hour slot each Wednesday, rather than allocating two fifteen-minute slots each week, can only serve to ensure that the

Prime Minister is tired by the end, with his temper frayed by the inevitable, co-ordinated interrogation from the Opposition. While the Prime Minister must be accountable to Members, and must be seen by the public to be held to account, we must improve the quality both of the questions and of the answers.

It would be regrettable if the considerable achievements of the Conservative government elected in 1992 were all to be forgotten because of the problems of party management which beset John Major. Most important, the Major government's economic policies after our withdrawal from the ERM mark out Kenneth Clarke as one of the most successful post-war Chancellors. It was thanks to Kenneth's deliberate and steady policy of keeping interest rates at a moderate level that a Conservative government was able to create the longest post-war period of sustained and non-inflationary growth. The problem we faced as a party was that the traditional link between economic wellbeing and support for the governing party was broken on 'Black Wednesday', when sterling made its costly exit from the ERM (see p. 711).

Kenneth Clarke's predecessor, Norman Lamont, once felt able to state that unemployment was 'a price well worth paying' for bringing down the inflation which the previous government had caused. This was not the view of John Major, but unfortunately he felt unable to get rid of Lamont until almost a year after Black Wednesday. This was the kind of delay which earned him a reputation for indecisiveness. The situation that had occurred, with a Prime Minister and Chancellor at daggers drawn, must never be allowed to persist. Tony Barber and I always had a wholly frank relationship, settling any disagreements entirely in private. Outside our private counsels, we were totally loyal to one another. Subsequent Prime Ministers – Thatcher with Lawson, Major with Lamont, Blair with Brown – have allowed questions to arise about who is in charge of economic strategy and what that strategy might be. That has a woeful effect on confidence in the House of Commons, in the City of London and in the international arena. Rightly or wrongly, John remained convinced that his decent brand of Conservatism was not shared by the vast majority of his MPs, and that his survival in office therefore depended upon a generally cautious approach to politics, with the occasional scrap of red meat being thrown to the right-wing whipper-snappers on the backbenches. By the time he spoke out for One Nation policies during the 1997 general election campaign, most people were bound to wonder why he had left it so late to set out his views so boldly, and probably concluded that he was only reacting to Tony Blair's initiatives.

Kenneth Clarke and John Major were, however, quite right to ignore the calls in 1996–7 for cynical pre-election tax cuts. People would have treated them with contempt. Clarke was fiscally responsible until the end, and the subsequent Labour government accepted his gift-wrapped legacy with open arms. Furthermore, it quickly recognised that the British economy was strong enough and sufficiently well balanced to look seriously at entry into the single currency.

I regard the 1980s as an aberration, when a combination of economic and political circumstances, a divided centre-left, vast regional disparities in unemployment and changing working patterns seriously but temporarily unbalanced the political equation. The 1990s marked a return to more traditional attitudes. One very clear message of Tony Blair's election is that people are, once again, concerned with ideas of justice and security. I have argued throughout my career that industry should be founded upon co-operation and that the alternative, in a 'conveyor-belt' society, is that citizens will channel their energies into disruptive behaviour. I do not feel that we have yet established true 'popular capitalism', and governments still do not do enough to moderate the often harsh effects of change upon individuals and families.

In 1975, I was invited to address a conference in Rome on the 'Future of Capitalism'. At that time, it was not at all clear that capitalism even had a future. Communism still seemed to represent a serious threat to our way of life. The US had been humiliated in Vietnam, the USSR was still an expansionist and, in some fields, technologically advanced superpower – and our own political and industrial affairs back in the UK were in an anarchic state. My own major concern was that private enterprise could hardly be said to enjoy the positive and enthusiastic backing of the majority of British people. They seemed, at best, profoundly indifferent to it. Yet it was private enterprise that, 'like an industrial Charles Atlas', as I put it, was providing 90 per cent of our exports, supporting the government, the social services and the loss-making nationalised industries, and providing a livelihood for the majority of families.

For most of my life, too many advocates of private enterprise have fallen into the trap of making their case with the same stridency adopted by socialists. This comes across as a defence of the ruthless and highly acquisitive values of early capitalism, when the prosperity of the few truly did depend upon the poverty of the many. Such a concept is hardly likely to have popular appeal to a mature electorate. I argued in 1975, and would still argue today, that the task facing modern free enterprise is, therefore, to convince the majority of the people in democratic countries that it is capable of providing economic justice for all. The more extreme advocates of the free market would again do well to heed the actual words of Adam Smith, whose name graces our leading free-market 'think-tank'. He observed, in 1776, that 'people of the same trade seldom meet together, even for merriment and diversion, but the conversation ends in a conspiracy against the public, or in some contrivance to raise prices'. There is nothing to be gained from a doctrinaire attachment to the unleashing of unchecked free-market forces.

As I said in 1975, 'Most people do not believe that they should be thrown out of a job simply because of somebody else's failure . . . for better or for worse, most people do want a sense of security . . . they want to be sure that, in the event of accident or sickness, or come old age, they will be reasonably looked after.' Ten years later, I found myself making a similar point, this time during a period in which the free marketeers were very much on the front foot, and the 'yuppie' had become a familiar, if unpopular, icon of the age. 'The responsibility of business,' I reminded an audience in London, 'is the creation of wealth by enterprise . . . its rights are the creation of conditions in which enterprise can flourish.' The Conservative Party in the 1980s lost sight of the balance between rights and responsibilities.

The Conservative Party, until a generation ago, was the party of public service. Disraeli wrote that 'power has only one duty – to secure the social welfare of the PEOPLE'. He described the mission of the Conservative Party in very simple terms. In 1867 he said in Edinburgh that:

> In a progressive country change is constant; and the question is not whether you should resist change which is inevitable, but whether that change should be carried out in deference to the manners, the customs, the laws and the traditions of a people, or whether it should be carried out in deference to abstract principles and arbitrary and general doctrines.

In his emphasis upon the two great strands of Conservative thought, the need to manage change and the need to improve the lot of all the people, Disraeli was echoing Edmund Burke. Leading Tories have always recognised that the party succeeds only when it goes with the grain of the people. The recent advocates of a far more radical agenda have always come unstuck when they have taken a policy too far, on privatisation, trade union legislation or the community charge.

Conservatives never used to regard the free market as an end in itself. Certainly, it underpins our political freedoms and the legitimate aspirations of millions of citizens, but it also provides the resources necessary for providing public services of the highest possible standard. The message on the doorsteps in 1997 was quite clear. The British are a moderate and fair-minded people, who need to be convinced that Conservatives care about public service, with the highest standards. Conservatism is about the shared values and experiences which bind a society together, about retaining what is good in a country and gradually amending that which is in need of reform. A peremptory neo-liberal attachment to the free market and individualism spreads insecurity and fear like wildfire. It has allowed our main political opponents, whose old principles and beliefs have been shown to be bankrupt, to masquerade in our clothes and mouth our slogans. If the most successful political party in the democratic world vacates its traditional ground, it must expect its opponents to occupy it pretty quickly, presumably unable to believe their good fortune.

Thanks very largely to divisions on the left, the Conservative Party survived in power through four successive elections. The party's victory in 1992 was very much John Major's victory, but he had to contend with an impossible legacy, of a profoundly divided parliamentary party, unpopular policies and a deeply tarnished national image. Now that the centre-left is united again, and so determined to carry on governing, it is only if we return to, and reclaim, our political roots that we shall ever regain the trust of the people.

Chapter 21

NORTH–SOUTH AND EAST–WEST
International Affairs 1975–

For as long as I can remember, I have been fascinated by other countries, by their traditions, their peoples and their policies. I have always loved travelling, finding out for myself at first hand what is going on. My lifetime has been spent in a rapidly changing world moving at a pace never experienced before. In this, Britain has probably been subject to wider developments than any other major power. In the 1930s, the older territories, Canada, Australia, New Zealand and South Africa, became the independent Commonwealth countries, with Rhodesia sharing many of their advantages including attendance at Commonwealth conferences. After the Second World War, under heavy pressure from the United States, India, Pakistan and Ceylon became independent republics within the Commonwealth. These were followed in the 1950s and 1960s by countries in the colonial Empire. I have already related how Anthony Eden, at the Conservative Party conference in 1953, described Britain's position as being at the centre of all three power groupings, the United States, the Commonwealth and Europe. This was an imaginative and morale-raising prediction, but events were already moving in other directions.

The opportunity Anthony Eden was seeking was to be found in British membership of NATO where, because of our military forces, we were able to exert influence, although always in the knowledge that the United States played the leading part in that organisation. The major problem facing Britain throughout this period has been to adapt our attitudes, our resources and our policies to this new situation. The problem still remains. This is demonstrated in a widespread desire to maintain military forces sufficient to support action on our own, rather than concentrating on a system closely interlinked with neighbouring countries. We should have learned from Suez, from the Falklands and from the Gulf War how severely limited our own national power has become.

I have always taken an active interest in the development of the decolonised countries as the old European empires have contracted and vanished. My direct association with these issues stretches back to 1964, when I represented the government in Geneva at the first United Nations Conference on Trade and Development (UNCTAD). For the first time, seventy-five of the developing countries confronted the industrialised nations face to face with their needs. In my submission to the conference, I said that we must expand world trade in order to speed up sustainable economic development, and almost every speaker echoed this view. Speaking on Monday 6 April 1964 I added:

> Together we face the intolerable problem of poverty in the world . . . We are determined to find ways in which trade and growth can help to end it . . . This conference is the greatest collective effort that mankind has yet made for this purpose. It must be made to succeed. What is required for this is firmness of will and generosity of spirit . . . The United Kingdom is firmly committed to the objectives of the conference.

I also set out a ten-point plan calling for, amongst other developments, a moratorium on trade barriers, an end to quantitative restrictions affecting the trade of developing countries, a variety of tariff reductions, the stabilisation of commodity prices and supplementary financial assistance. Over twelve weeks, speaker after speaker drew attention to the trade problems of the developing countries. They depended heavily upon exports of primary products and were desperate to import capital equipment. Worse, their trade was rising then at under half the rate of trade among the developed countries. They needed to expand and diversify their exports, to enlarge their markets in the developed countries, to stabilise commodity prices and to increase their trade among themselves.

Having addressed the full conference at its opening session, I also took a leading part in bringing it to a successful conclusion. In this I had a close ally in George Ball, the American Under-Secretary of State, who later became a close friend even though our views sometimes markedly differed. On this occasion he tired of the constant haggling which went on and gradually dropped out of the arguments. At the end, the whole conference appeared to be deadlocked. The cause seemed to be the Algerian delegation. The chairman then adjourned the meeting and asked the appropriate leaders to join him in a private room. It was there that I recognised another participant.

On the evening before the conference had begun, I had attended a party given by the British delegation in a lovely villa alongside the lake. Moving around our delegation I joined a couple talking, one of whom I did not recognise. I introduced myself and said, 'I don't think we have met before. Which department of the Office are you in?' He smiled and replied in perfect English, indeed in what many would describe as an Oxford accent, 'No, we have not met before. I am from the Algerian Foreign Office.' I was astonished. In his light-grey pinstriped suit he looked so English. In fact, it turned out, he had been to Oxford.

Back in the private meeting some time later, I could see that this man was advising the Algerian Minister and telling him what to do. I was sitting next to the chairman and, as we were making no progress, I asked him whether we could have a short break so that I could deal with the cause of the trouble. He granted my request, and I immediately went up to the Algerian and asked him for a private word. I told him that I just wanted to make the position of the developed countries absolutely clear. We could offer one more concession to him and his friends, but no more. He must then accept the whole arrangement we had negotiated. If he refused, I would make sure that he and his Algerian colleagues were personally blamed in both the developed and the developing countries for the complete breakdown of all the negotiations. He pondered that, and then said he would agree. I thanked him, and added, 'We are both Oxford men and, as such, we both keep our word.' He nodded. The chairman reconvened the meeting, and I told him the result of our conversation. We then went back to the full conference and everything was settled.

The first UNCTAD was certainly valuable as a forum for airing old problems and, from time to time, new solutions. No one, however, could realistically have expected such a conference to solve, in twelve weeks, all the economic, geopolitical and climatic problems of the developing countries. I was particularly pleased that the first UNCTAD reaffirmed the principle that 'developed countries should not expect reciprocity from developing countries in negotiations for the reduction or removal of barriers to trade'. It also affirmed that developed countries should 'do their best to provide at least 1 per cent of their national income in aid and other capital flows to the less developed countries'. We further agreed that the United Nations should now establish continuing institutions to consider development questions. Most importantly, we had found a new way of bringing countries together to deal with difficult problems involving trade and aid and acknowledged the developing world's wider responsibilities.

As the conference closed, I celebrated its successes, saying 'how great a privilege it has been to take part in this conference, to share its hopes and fears, its disappointments and its successes . . . If we who leave this conference pass on to a wider public in our countries the impressions we have formed and the lessons we have gained here, if we turn them to practical effect, we can help to create a growing prosperity from which all our peoples will benefit – and we shall have made no small contribution to the future peace of the world.' All the states involved in the UNCTAD agreed to the elimination or reduction of tariff barriers against imports of manufactured goods from developing countries. This was a considerable step forward at the time, and the general approval for liberalisation of trade was an important part of the background for the Kennedy Round of the General Agreement on Tariffs and Trade (GATT), which was also taking place in 1964. At UNCTAD we were able to win over many colleagues from other countries to our call for a 50 per cent linear cut in tariffs.

Fourteen independent members of the Commonwealth were at that time classified as developing, which gave Britain a special position at UNCTAD. Around 620 million people, more than half the population of the developing countries represented there, were within the Common-wealth, and enjoyed the benefits of a special trading relationship with us. They were already well established as important trading partners of the United Kingdom. They also appreciated that trade was the only sustainable way to development. After I became leader of the Conservative Party in 1965, our 1966 manifesto pledged that we would 'strengthen and expand existing Commonwealth links', 'encourage voluntary service overseas' and 'help Commonwealth development by technical and other assistance'. In a keynote speech to the Royal Commonwealth Society in 1968, I reiterated the policy that I had helped to establish in 1964:

> I have no doubt that we have been right to emphasise the aid that we in this country can give towards exorcising some of the evils of poverty in the under-developed world. But our idealism has been matched by self-interest. We declared it to be so at the world conference in Geneva.
>
> There is nothing wrong with this. On the contrary, I believe that genuine aid to the under-developed countries on a long-term and regular basis can only be effective if we in this country and those who receive British aid recognise our mutual interests. Britain when giving aid can expect to receive opportunities for her exports and fair treatment for her investments.

By the time of the 1970 general election, our concerns about the structural economic weaknesses that we might inherit from Harold Wilson forced us to offer rather less in this area than we might have wished. I knew that it would be quite wrong to stir up in our manifesto the sort of excessive expectations that would then turn out not to be deliverable. Nonetheless, we retained a strong commitment to overseas aid:

> Britain must play a proper part in dealing with world poverty. We will ensure that Britain helps the developing countries: by working for the expansion of international trade; by encouraging private investment

overseas; by providing capital aid and technical assistance to supplement their own efforts. We have accepted the UNCTAD target for aid to developing countries, and will increase the British programme as national prosperity returns.

*   *   *

In the years that followed, the United Nations and individual nations all worked hard to spread prosperity and to reduce the population explosion which threatened to create a catastrophe in the Third World. There was, however, a need for a new strategy to deal comprehensively and multilaterally with these problems. In the spring of 1977, Robert McNamara, the president of the World Bank, publicly proposed to set up an independent commission on development issues, at that time normally described as the North–South problem. This was never particularly accurate, because so many developing countries in Asia were in the northern hemisphere, while some of their southerly neighbours, such as Australasia and South Africa, were already substantially developed economically.

Bob McNamara is an energetic, widely travelled and experienced statesman, highly respected, in particular because of his achievements as Secretary for Defense in Washington, at which he had been able to draw upon his previous chairmanship of the Ford Motor Company. No one doubted the reality of his personal commitment to the welfare of the peoples of the developing world, and I knew of his passionate belief that aid programmes should be founded upon arrangements into which everyone had entered freely and willingly. He maintained that the developing countries should be invited to play a full and active part in refining the development efforts of the industrialised world. He wanted a full examination of the problems and solutions to take place on a worldwide basis, both to provide a better guide for the World Bank and to bring home to governments and public opinion throughout the world the need for urgent action. He appointed Willy Brandt, the former Chancellor of Western Germany, as chairman of the new group, leaving him to decide the detailed terms of reference and the membership, after consultation with world leaders. It has always been known as the 'Brandt Commission'.

I found Willy Brandt one of the most perplexing personalities with whom I have had to deal. I first met him when I visited West Berlin in 1965, as leader of the Conservative Party, while he was still mayor. I was impressed with the way in which Berlin was being run, and with its recovery from its wartime destruction. It had been modernised, its industries had been rebuilt and its inhabitants were now prospering, despite difficulties which arose over its status from time to time. There was no evidence that being surrounded by the East German Republic created any feeling of claustrophobia among its people. When Brandt later became

Foreign Minister of West Germany it seemed an ideal position for him, given his political experience of dealing on the spot with the occupying powers. He speedily improved relations with the outside world, as well as playing a major role inside the European Community.

As Chancellor of the Federal Republic, Brandt gave me full support in the British negotiations to become a member of the European Community, carrying his government and party with him. The fact that I was a Conservative Prime Minister dealing with a socialist Chancellor created no problems. He always offered wise advice on dealing with the French, and knew exactly how far he himself could go in urging Britain's case upon them without becoming counter-productive. After the three new members had signed the Treaty enlarging the Community, he also played a constructive role at the Paris Summit in October 1972. As his English improved rapidly, we came to have no need of interpreters, and very often would talk alone or with just a simple record taken by either side. A more disturbing habit of Brandt's, however, was his lapsing into silences which, as the years passed, grew longer and longer. He would remain absolutely still, and lost wherever his thoughts had taken him. Should I interrupt to get the conversation moving again, I would ask myself, thereby possibly breaking into some important line of thought, or wait patiently until he broke his own silence? I usually opted for the latter course.

Brandt's charm and ease of manner and his courtesy, combined with his openness of approach, nonetheless enabled him to exert considerable influence in international affairs. He was, in some respects, the least Germanic of men, perhaps because of his long and close association with the Scandinavian countries. Although Brandt was informal and humorous in private and, in public, very much a man of the world, he consistently maintained a moral attitude towards the problems of East–West relations and the difficulties of the developing world. His resignation as Chancellor was a great loss to West Germany and to Europe, precipitated by the unmasking of his secretary as an East German spy.

Brandt decided on a commission of eighteen members, and wisely allocated ten to the developing countries, thus avoiding the customary complaints that their views were not taken sufficiently into account. Prominent among them were Sonny Ramphal, secretary-general of the Commonwealth, whose home country was Guyana, but who was based in London, where he had the opportunity of being in permanent touch with both developed and developing countries of the Commonwealth; the Kuwaiti Finance Minister Abdlatif Al-Hamad; Rodrigo Botero Montoya, a highly placed academic from Colombia, based at Harvard; Amir Jamal from Tanzania; Layachi Yaker from the Algerian government; Antoine Kipsa Dakouré from Upper Volta; and Lakshmi Kant Jha from India. Among those from the developed countries were Olof Palme, Prime Minister of Sweden; Joe Morris, a leading trade unionist from Canada; Kay Graham, the owner of the *Washington Post* and other publications; Pete Peterson, a very successful American financier; Haruki Mori from Japan; and myself.

When we first met, I had some anxiety about the balance of the Commission, knowing that some from the developed world, such as Olof Palme, might well always take the side of the developing countries. This proved not to be a serious problem, however, as Al-Hamad, Montoya and Sonny Ramphal very often supported the views of the spokesmen for the developed countries. None of the Commissioners was acting under any government's instructions. The expenses involved were largely covered by the Dutch government, together with one or two other contributions. Mrs Thatcher's government contributed nothing.

Our objective was set out as the 'identification of politically feasible courses of action which are in the mutual interest and can command the support of rich and poor countries alike'. The recommendations were to be for measures which would, within a period of about ten years, enhance the development process in the less privileged parts of the world and contribute to a more equitable world order. At our first meeting, at Schloss Gymnich, outside Bonn, early in December 1977, we decided that our best approach to these problems would be to hold regular meetings in different parts of the world, so that we could see and hear for ourselves what was happening.

Our second meeting was held at Bamako, the capital of Mali, in May 1978, in conditions of stifling heat. On enquiring about a choice of hotels, our staff were told that there was only one hotel in the capital. We were taken from the airport to the hotel in cars with some air conditioning, which fortunately also existed in the hotel. We were kept indoors for our meetings until we had to return to the plane some three days later. As we could see from our cars, the conditions there were appalling, the roads were in a terrible state and people's living conditions were dreadful. There could not have been a better place to bring home to us the problems we faced trying to find solutions to the ordeals of the world's poorest people, and noted the existence of Timbuktu in the upper part of the state. This was followed by meetings in Delhi, Kuala Lumpur in Malaysia, Vienna and Tarrytown, New York State.

In February 1979 we met in Switzerland for four days. We were getting near to the end of the eighteen-month period we had set ourselves for the report, but there was little sign of any conclusion. Kay Graham and I were frustrated by getting nowhere. She asked me what we could do. I proposed that on the next day, Saturday, we should quietly slip away at tea-time to the airport and fly to Paris. The British ambassador invited us to stay the night at the embassy, adding that at the Opera House they were putting on the first full performance of Cerha's completion of Alban Berg's *Lulu*. Until then, the family had permitted only the first two acts to be performed, in their belief that to perform the whole work in a version completed by another composer would only harm Berg's reputation. That night at the opera turned out to be a truly magnificent occasion. I have never since seen a performance of that opera to compare with it. Although President Giscard could not be present, because he was unwell, every other dignitary in politics, business, music and the arts was present. It was just unfortunate that the Austrian ambassador, who gave the dinner party after the performance, at 1.30 a.m., failed to recognise the owner of the *Washington Post* — or her need for a seat at a table. We returned to the conference on Sunday refreshed and with renewed optimism about our task.

By this stage, all of us on the Commission were growing very concerned about Brandt's chairmanship. We had spent getting on for two years debating the problems faced by developing countries, and trying to find solutions to them. Brandt appeared quite incapable of guiding the discussion along the specific paths set out in the agenda, or of keeping contributions to a reasonable length. Rather than trying to bring all of this to some kind of conclusion, he could not resist the temptation constantly to bring new and powerful personalities into the picture, regardless of the balance of the Commission as a whole. His absorption in press conferences, and publicity of every kind, may have brought the Commission greater prominence, but did nothing to put our limited time to effective use. Members began to feel that the Commission might ultimately come to be seen as an exercise in publicity, rather than of substance.

In fact, at no time did Willy Brandt bring the Commission to the point of reaching a decision on any topic. Nor did he realise that, by heading the secretariat with two equally powerful but intellectually opposed personalities, he had prevented it from carrying out its necessary role in support of the Commission. After eighteen months of hard work which had ranged both geographically and intellectually all over the world, and millions of words, the Commission had reached not a single conclusion. How had he managed to chair the Cabinet meetings in Bonn? Were Ministers allowed free rein to carry through their policies regardless of other considerations? Was it left to the Minister of Finance, Helmut Schmidt, to keep the whole system of government under control? Was this the explanation of the constant series of leaks from Bonn, which had kept us so well informed about the attitudes of members of the West German Cabinet? Yet, for all that, we should all acknowledge that Willy Brandt did place firmly on the political map his determination both to ensure peace between East and West and to reduce poverty in developing countries. For both of these achievements he will be warmly remembered, however perplexing he may remain as a personality.

As we came into what really had to be the final straight for the project, all of us on the Commission realised that something had to be done about this situation, lest all our labours on a matter of such import should go to waste. It had been planned that the Commission would complete its discussions and approve a full report at its four-day meeting in Brussels in October 1979. Many of us felt, however, that it was most unlikely that this would prove possible, in part because some of the problems had not been sufficiently thrashed out and, even more importantly, because of the differences of view that persisted among its members. Finding solutions was not helped by the conflicts which we detected between the two principal members of the staff, the Swede Göran Ohlin, who had been appointed as the official executive secretary, and the Yugoslav Dragoslav Avramović, whom Willy Brandt had insisted on appointing to an equal position, as director of the secretariat, to handle the economic aspects of our work.

When we got down to settling everything, the gaps became more and more obvious and members began to despair about how we were going to cope. This had an adverse effect on Brandt himself. On the third day of the meeting he collapsed entirely with what was described as 'a heavy cold'. He was taken to his room in the hotel and took no further part in the proceedings. The rest of us were left to sort things out. It was agreed that Sonny Ramphal and I, one from the developing and one from the developed world, would ensure that the rest of the work was completed so that the whole report could be presented at a further meeting to be held in England in mid-December. We chose to hold it at Leeds Castle in Kent, a historic building with a calming atmosphere, set in one of the most beautiful spots in England. The Commission was, of course, independent of any government and, knowing that Mrs Thatcher's new government would be unwilling to cover the cost of this meeting because of her indifference to what we were trying to achieve, I asked the Dutch to finance the meeting, which they swiftly did. The work on the report proceeded satisfactorily and, on the Friday night, we all assembled for dinner at the Castle.

We were then confronted with the news that Willy Brandt himself would not be able to join us until, probably, tea-time on the Saturday, as he felt it essential that he should attend the funeral of a very old SPD colleague from the German parliament. After having a word about this, Sonny and I agreed that we should start the weekend's programme on Saturday morning, that I should take the chair and that he would be close at hand to give support. After dinner, I described the situation to the Commission and told them how I proposed to handle it when we started the next morning. There were to be seventeen chapters in the report and the time available, two days, would allow only three-quarters of an hour to be devoted to each. This would still enable questions to be asked and amendments to be proposed, but it also meant that interruptions and comments had to be brief. If the discussion on a chapter was not completed within the time limit specified, the rest of it would have to go in without being discussed. If we did well, it might be possible to devote a little more time to the final chapter, 'A Programme of Priorities'.

On Saturday morning this scheme worked well and, in fact, each chapter was finished in less than the three-quarters of an hour allotted. By lunchtime, we had already approved the first five chapters, and felt immensely pleased with ourselves. After lunch, Willy Brandt's private secretary told me that he was going to Gatwick Airport to meet the former Chancellor's plane. He added that he had now discovered that Gatwick was quite a long way away, and the journey would take a considerable time. Moreover, he was not absolutely sure of the way and it would be especially difficult returning to the castle in the dark. What was more, Brandt's plane might very well be late. The point he wished to make, he explained with a certain emphasis, was that he might well not be able to get Brandt to us until after dinner. He hoped that I would not be too upset. From the look in his eyes, I knew very well what he meant. We then kept up our pace in the afternoon and, towards the end of dinner, Willy Brandt arrived, obviously tired out. Having missed 'so much of the book', he told us, he did not feel in a position to take over the next day, and would like us to carry on as we had been doing. He would sit and listen. This was agreed. Early on the Sunday evening we had completed *North–South: A Programme for Survival*, as it came to be called. It was rapidly prepared for printing and then publication.

The report proved to be the clearest analysis of the problems of the North and South, together with the most constructive and detailed series of proposals for dealing with them, that has ever been published. It was acclaimed throughout the world, and its emphasis on sustainable development, rather than temporary famine relief, considered radical at the time, has become the accepted wisdom of development economics. Reading it today, two decades later, brings home how right we were, only emphasising in turn how much remains to be done. The last proposal in the final chapter was that an international conference of heads of government should be held, at which they could agree upon how to implement our recommendations. No support for this was given by President Reagan or Mrs Thatcher, although both attended the conference, which was held at Can-

One of the last photographs
of my father with me, 1976

Below Rehearsing Mozart
with Clifford Curzon, 1976

Below 'The Great Book-
Signing Tour' – Second
Leg, 1976

One of my earlier meetings with Deng Xiaoping in Beijing. Unusually, he agreed to sign this photograph

10 DOWNING STREET

THE PRIME MINISTER

Friday evening

Dear Ted,

Thankyou for your kind note — it was good of you to write.

After the usual consultations I shall be seeing several people to-morrow.

I have thought long and deeply about the post of Foreign Secretary and have decided to offer it to Peter Carrington who, — as I am sure you will agree, — will do the job superbly.

Yours ever

Margaret Thatcher

'Thou unnecessary letter!' – but more of a dis-appointment than a real disappointment …

Campaigning with my lifelong friend
Madron Seligman in Chichester, 1979

Recuperating in Torquay, 1981

At home in Wilton Street

Harold Macmillan's 90th birthday party at Wilton Street, with Alec Home

'You've never had wine so good'

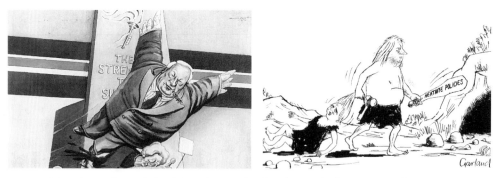

Two views of my relationship with Mrs Thatcher during the latter stages of her premiership. I couldn't possibly comment

With Fidel Castro in Havana, September 1984

A reunion of all the
remaining Prime Ministers
with Her Majesty the
Queen, December 1985

Right Visiting one of the
pandas at London Zoo,
mid-1980s

Meeting Saddam Hussein
in Baghdad, negotiating
for the release of British
hostages, 1990

'I'm back!' Eightieth birthday celebrations at No. 10, July 1996

Below Slava Rostropovich seems
pleased to see me back at No. 10

Bottom With the Majors, Sara
Morrison and the Priors. Robin
Butler, then Secretary of the
Cabinet, is lurking in the trades-
men's entrance!

With Yasser Arafat, the Palestinian leader, at Wilton Street, 1997

With Zhu Rongji, Premier of the People's Republic of China, in London, 1998

With Alastair Stewart, the broadcaster, and the Mayor of Bexley after my 1997 carol concert

With Joe Cooper, the musician and broadcaster, at Arundells

In my garden. The spire of Salisbury Cathedral is visible in the background

On the doorstep of Arundells, my home in The Close at Salisbury

cun in Mexico. It has gone down in history that President Reagan took the opportunity there of lecturing Dr Julius Nyerere, the former President of Tanzania, on how he should conduct his affairs. Reagan objected to receiving a request for financial support, saying his philosophy was that everybody should become self-supporting. 'In other words,' he explained, 'I will help you buy the fishing rod, but after that the rest lies with you. You must fish in your own pond to support yourselves.' 'That is fine,' replied Nyerere, 'but what happens if you haven't got a pond with any fish?' America and Britain could not prevent a constructive approach, however, although Mrs Thatcher and members of her government refused to take notice of debates on the report in the House of Commons.

When the Brandt Commission produced its report, many British Members of Parliament began to call for a proper debate on the proposals. From the government of the day there was a deafening silence. Eventually, the Conservative MP for Cambridge, Robert Rhodes James, succeeded in getting a debate on a Friday morning, 28 March 1980. Fridays are tradition-ally quiet days, when issues of marginal interest can be discussed in the chamber by those Members with a specialist interest in them, while the majority of their colleagues return to their constituencies. All of us in the House that day felt that the subject of North–South deserved greater prominence than this, but although the attendance was small we still had a good discussion. I sat and listened to the entire proceedings, without making a speech myself, because all my views were embodied in the report.

Robert Rhodes James opened the debate, and a series of impressive speeches followed, all of which showed that these questions were of greater concern to my colleagues than most people realised. One notable and excellent contribution came from Alastair Goodlad, then the recently elected Conservative Member for Northwich but, latterly, government Chief Whip and then a Conservative spokesman on international develop-ment. He said, 'For many years it has been an accepted orthodoxy in politics in Britain that the better-off have a duty as well as an interest to help the less well-off . . . the coincidence of morality and self-interest has been a British tradition for many years. The present symptoms of imbalance between world population and its resources and productivity are appalling.' This was the true voice of the One Nation Conservative Party, and it was echoed by a broad cross-section of the House. Julian Ridsdale, then the Conservative MP for Harwich, summed up the position very fairly when he skilfully put the view that international co-operation should transcend normal differences of political philosophy: 'Whether we are free traders or protectionists, the important issue is to recognise that this problem must be met through co-ordination by governments.'

Although the Thatcher government took a very cool view of the Commission's report, it was clear from the outset that many of my Conservative colleagues felt as strongly about North–South as I did. So did many people out in the country, as a huge demonstration at Westminster in May 1981 testified. They recognised this to be a question of how we could help to foster a sustainable world order for the future. We all waited for a sign from the government that we were, as a nation, to start taking our responsibilities towards the developing world more seriously. We waited in vain. At last, these questions were debated again in the House of Commons something over a year later, on another Friday, 24 July 1981.

This time, a Cabinet minister was deputed to quell the troops, the Lord Privy Seal Ian Gilmour. He spoke with genuine feeling to a House which, like a year before, made up for comparative paucity of numbers with a tremendous intensity of feeling. 'It is utterly wrong that hundreds of millions of people should live their lives in poverty, hunger and disease,' Ian told the House.

> If only for reasons of humanity and justice, we must take part in the fight against poverty and assist those in the Third World to achieve a better life . . . as Brandt says, this is not only a moral imperative, it is also a matter of mutual economic interest. This, too, is a view that we share. We should all benefit if we could work out better international economic arrangements and remove obstacles to development.

Having sat listening to almost two full days of debate, I now felt that I should contribute my thoughts. 'The real, outstanding purpose of the recommendations of the Brandt Commission was to deal not only with the problems of poverty, hunger, disease, mortality, justice and fairness in the world,' I explained, 'but to recreate world prosperity so that we should all be able to gain, and so that the differences between us would be decreased and the North would be able to help the South as well as helping itself.' It was Stanley Clinton Davis, later to become a European Commissioner, who wound up this debate on behalf of the Labour Opposition. Even though the Conservative administration could manage nothing more than a limited response to the report, he made it clear that the Labour Opposition was willing to call for something more ambitious. 'Those of us who have read the Brandt Report unanimously join in the tribute to [Edward Heath] for his dedication, together with that of his colleagues on the report, in making a unique and remarkable contribution to international thinking,' he said. 'It is an inspiring example.'

As it turned out, the Brandt Commission was to meet again in Kuwait, and produce a second report in 1983. In this we looked at the increased problems now being faced by the developing world, in the light of the general economic downturn at that time. Although the first report was warmly received, little positive action was taken and the same old problems persisted. Indeed, they were increasingly exacerbated during the 1980s by the economic policies of the Reagan administration. As 'Reaganomics' required a vast influx of foreign capital into the American money markets, interest rates started to climb. Each 1 per cent rise in US interest rates during the early 1980s added US$3–4 billion to the debt-service costs of the Third World. Although the political debate may have gone quiet, this is a matter which will, inevitably, continue to haunt the developed world for many years to come.

The publicity and interest surrounding the Brandt Report even aroused the interest of Fidel Castro. In 1980, he invited me, through his ambassador in London, to visit Cuba and I travelled to Havana in January 1981. John Ure, the British ambassador, was in the UK, but the hospitality provided by the Cuban government in a villa on the outskirts of the city was both simple and satisfying. The villa's immense but well-kept garden and swimming pool provided ample opportunity for relaxation. Castro had arranged for us to have a meeting at 5.00 p.m. on Thursday 15 January. We then received a message informing us that he had been tied up in a committee and would let us know when he was free. We heard nothing, however, and my Cuban minder suggested that we might go to the ballet and wait for Castro's call there. No call came and, after the show had finished, we returned to the villa for a nightcap. Around midnight, we heard the noise of hooting horns and the screaming of brakes as a convoy pulled up in front of the villa. When the staff dashed to the door and flung it open, in rushed a weary-looking Castro. He threw himself down on to the couch at the opposite end from me. 'Oh my God, these committees are awful,' he began. 'They never stop arguing but then there is no point in telling you. You know all of this. As it is after midnight, there is no point in us doing any business. Let us have a drink and talk. Tell me all you know about Churchill. I have read every one of his books because I am fascinated by him and what he did. You worked with him and knew him well. Tell me all about him.'

Around 2.00 a.m., after I had told him all I could, Castro decided to leave and we arranged a further meeting for 5.00 p.m. the following afternoon, in his office. He was again completely relaxed and we talked about those things that concerned him most in Cuba's development. He was proud of their educational achievements and arranged for me to visit some of their schools. They had also improved their housing, some of which I saw for myself during my stay. Castro, however, boasted of the improvement of the health of the Cubans, emphasising that their longevity was the greatest of all countries south of the US. The Cuban medical research into the causes and treatment of cancer, he told me, was one of the five top systems of the world and these five countries, with one exception, all exchanged their results with each other. The exception was between the US and Cuba. Castro's doctors had to rely on obtaining the results of the United States research through one of the other countries.

At 7.00 p.m. I apologised to Castro as I was to be the co-host at a party at the British embassy. 'Why was I not invited?' asked Castro. 'But you were,' I insisted. 'We understood that you could not come. The invitation is of course still open.' 'Then I will come for just five minutes. I must go and change my uniform,' Castro replied. I left for the embassy where I found a large gathering of diplomats and business figures. I mentioned our possible unexpected guest to Michael Perceval, the British consul, who was acting as host, but did not tell anyone else in case he never arrived. I had just shaken hands with all of the guests when there was a by now familiar screeching of brakes and hooting of horns. Castro certainly knew how to make an entrance. With one hand on his hip, he threw the other in the air and shouted, 'Welcome, welcome, welcome!' We then began a joint tour of the guests, who were both astonished and excited at seeing him. When we got to the first corner of the room, there stood a tall, thin fellow, who had been introduced to me as 'the special Swiss representative'. I immediately knew what that meant. He was an American observer. Although he pushed himself as far back against the wall as he could on recognising Castro, nothing could hide his embarrassment. Castro stopped, looked at him, grinned broadly and said, 'I've heard all about you.' It took him fifty minutes to meet everybody and, having stayed three-quarters of an hour longer than he had intended, he left waving and shouting 'Goodbye, goodbye, goodbye to you all!'

After a pleasant day on the coast, my host suggested that we should go over to the new hotel which had been completed to watch a cabaret. The room was packed but, unfortunately, the cabaret proved to be excessively long and incredibly boring. It set out the history of the Afro-Caribbean people, from their earliest beginnings on the African content through their movement westwards to present-day Cuba. The next day I visited Fidel Castro's elder brother Ramon, who was responsible for all agricultural affairs. His house was well placed on a hillside with a refreshing view of the forest before it. Over lunch I told him how much I had enjoyed the visit, but mentioned how dreary the cabaret had been. 'Could they not possibly hot it up a bit?' I asked. 'Well, I'm glad you've told me about it and I'll see what I can do,' he replied. 'With all those visitors,' I added, 'it would also be useful to have a casino. The gambling would keep them occupied and bring in much money.' Ramon Castro looked appalled at the suggestion. 'Never, never, never,' he said firmly. 'We saw the disastrous results of gambling on our people before the revolution. They were reck-lessly exploited and bankrupted and we will never allow it to happen again. It's the same with prostitution. People can have as much sex as they like, whenever they like, wherever they like and with whomever they like – but it must all be for free.'

When I visited Cuba again in September 1984, Castro and I returned to the subject of world development, discussing both the original Brandt Report and the second report which our Commission had produced. He then presented me with a copy of a Cuban report expressing his own views after he had digested both of our documents. This he inscribed for me, 'To our esteemed friend Heath, who so often honours us with his visits to Cuba, and helps us so much with his worldwide experience.' This had an unusual consequence some years later, when I received a letter from a lawyer friend in Chicago who was also a book collector. He enclosed a catalogue of a bookseller in Los Angeles in which he had highlighted a page. On opening it, I found a large printed square containing an advertise-ment for an exceptional pamphlet, written by Fidel Castro and personally dedicated to Edward Heath. It was priced $3,000. Underneath the square was an advertisement for a volume of Churchill's memoirs, priced at $2,000.

I realised that my volume must have been stolen. I telephoned the bookshop and asked if I could buy the book. The shopkeeper replied that he had already sold it, but would I like anything else? I then revealed who I was and enlisted his help in getting back my stolen book. He was horrified, assuring me that his shop had bought it from a dealer in New York in good faith and promising that he would now try to retrieve it. He tele-phoned later to say that he had contacted the purchaser, a Hollywood film director. He had confessed that he had given the book to his wife, who had donated it to a charity sale in Canada. He would contact them. By now I had little hope of the book ever being returned to its rightful owner. The next call, however, brought the good news that the film director had bought back the book and he would come to London to present it to me personally. I readily agreed. Unfortunately, he was then sent to Africa to complete a film, and was forced to abandon his plan. The book was returned to me by special delivery. It is now back on my shelf in Salisbury, where I check it frequently, to make sure it is still there.

Since the end of the Second World War, successive British governments of both parties have supported and contributed to the development of the nuclear deterrent. In the early 1980s, however, there was increasing disquiet in all Western countries concerning the morality and practicality of this potentially devastating, crude yet effective device. This provides some kind of explanation for the Labour Party's disastrous decision to support a policy of unilateral disarmament at the 1983 general election. The Conservative Party and the SDP were quite right to demonstrate clearly and firmly that they still stood solidly behind our nuclear deterrent. The renewal of the British deterrent was a sign of the resolve not just of Britain, but of Western Europe more widely, to bolster its own defences against the growing Soviet threat to its security. Speaking during a debate on the Defence White Paper in July 1981, I gave my strong support to the Trident nuclear missile programme, but urged Western nations to make greater efforts to secure multilateral arms-control agreements with the USSR.

All warfare is horrifying. With the development of technology, more and more innocent people have become victims, as we saw in the 1939–45 conflict when many of our cities were substantially destroyed by pre-nuclear bombing. This makes it impossible to limit the concept of a just war, one whose *purpose* is justified, to one in which only conventional weapons are used. In fact, it is precisely the dreadful characteristics of nuclear warfare which impose caution on a would-be aggressor in a potentially catastrophic situation. The nuclear deterrent prevented the two superpowers and their allies from waging war against each other, but this also increased the possibility of conflict between non-nuclear countries without the risk of outside interference, as in the Middle East. It also allowed a superpower to overrun a small country, Afghanistan, because the United States could do little without using nuclear weapons. These were the limitations in the 1980s on the exercise of power.

The solution to the wave of questioning that swept across Europe and the United States lay in convincing our people that a genuine and determined attempt was being made to control and reduce the number of nuclear weapons held both by the Atlantic alliance and by the Soviet bloc. In the 1960s and 1970s everyone could see that was happening. The first Test Ban Treaty (see p. 246) was followed by a Non-Proliferation Treaty of 1968 and, in 1972, the first Strategic Arms Limitation Treaty (SALT) was signed. It is only when both superpowers are prepared to negotiate multilaterally towards parity that a general reduction can be achieved. In the early 1980s the public saw no such efforts being made nor results produced. The anxieties in Europe about the deployment of Cruise and Pershing II missiles in 1983 were prompted by doubts whether there had been a genuine attempt at negotiation. It was part of the 'twin-track' agreement within NATO that Cruise missiles must be deployed in Europe in order to restore some balance in the face of Soviet SS-20s, and enable disarmament discussions to be pursued from a position of strength. Co-operation and negotiation with the USSR were portrayed by President Reagan in his early years as a favour to the Kremlin, but even his administration came to realise that this process was of mutual interest to East and West. SALT II, which was signed by Carter and Brezhnev in 1979, would have placed important limits on the Soviet Union's strategic nuclear systems, and it made it easier for the US to channel its resources into those practical areas of military spending where they were most needed. This is why the suspension of that treaty before its ratification by the US Senate was so damaging.

The opportunities for stumbling into East–West conflict in the early 1980s were so great that there should have been no choice for Washington and Moscow but to develop to the full their direct communication and mutual understanding. Yet the proposals shouted from the White House and the Kremlin, and occasionally from the UK, amounted to little more than exercises in propaganda. This was fruitless and self-defeating, a fact well understood by Mikhail Gorbachev by the time he became General Secretary of the Soviet Communist Party in 1985. The tone of East–West relations improved only after the successful summit between Reagan and Gorbachev in Reykjavik in 1986.

The process of detente in the 1970s not only began to break down divisions in Europe between East and West, but also accentuated those areas in which our interests and those of the United States could diverge. In particular, the European countries acutely felt the need for continuing bilateral contacts and negotiations with the Soviet Union, whatever the prevailing temperature of US-Soviet relations. This was a consequence of geography and history. In the United States, there was an increasingly impatient feeling that Europe should either shut up, or put up more for its own defence. This growing concern went to the heart of the US–European strategic relationship. For when the US nuclear guarantee was first extended to Europe to compensate it for its conventional inferiority, the balance of terror in Europe involved no danger to the US itself. The advent of the intercontinental ballistic missile changed the position completely. It has therefore been a consistent aim of American defence policy from the early 1960s to persuade Europe to invest enough in conventional defence to sustain the doctrine of flexible response. That would require sufficient conventional force to hold any attack for long enough to negotiate its de-escalation if it was accidental, or, in the event of an intentional attack on Europe, long enough for the West to signal its determination to defend itself using whatever means proved necessary, giving the aggressor a chance to back down. If the Western European nations had established more coordinated defence arrangements in the 1980s, it would have enabled us to speak to the United States on equal terms, contribute more to the formulation of Western defence policy and, at the same time, inspire greater public support.

The policies pursued by President Reagan, and so enthusiastically supported by Mrs Thatcher, tended to intensify problems in the Atlantic alliance. The persistently high interest rates of the Federal Reserve Board and the expanding budget deficits pursued in Washington deflated the world economy, throwing millions out of work, and provoked a desperate race by governments to subsidise exports in order to cling to what they could of the world's dwindling markets. The reaction of the US government to the resulting turbulence of currencies was only to reaffirm that counter-balancing intervention to stabilise the markets would not be pursued. This abrogation of responsibility turned the world's monetary system into a giant casino, from which only the speculators could benefit. The Reagan administration consciously downgraded the most fundamental principle of alliance: the need to work for unity in both strategy development and policy implementation. President Reagan's unilateral decision to impede the work of European companies engaged in constructing the proposed pipeline between Siberia and West Germany in 1981–2 was just one example of this breaking down. The united opposition of the Europeans, who saw some advantage in diversifying their sources of energy supply, and disliked the strong arm of US law being used to control the commercial decisions of the licensees of the Westinghouse company in Europe, fortunately obliged the US to change its policy.

It is vital to recognise that Britain's rulers cannot ride two horses at the same time, as I found out during the first European negotiations in 1961–3. We cannot behave like an adjunct of the United States and simultaneously carry out our responsibilities as a member of the European Union. If we are to influence the United States we must do so as one Community, through an agreed policy thrashed out between all the member states. Until we accept these facts and behave accordingly we shall always be regarded with suspicion by our European partners.

There was a welcome recognition of this fact by President Bush, who showed clearly that he intended to give no preference to the United Kingdom in his dealings with Europe. Even the so-called 'special relationship' under President Reagan did not prevent him from invading a Commonwealth country, Grenada, without consulting the British. The 'special relationship' merely provided an excuse for the UK to kowtow to the United States, as we saw during the Westland crisis, the withdrawal from UNESCO in 1985 and the bombing of Tripoli and Benghazi on 14 and 15 April 1986.

I could not support the decision by Mrs Thatcher to allow the Americans to use F111s stationed in England as part of the attack on Libya, in response to terrorist attacks. Article 51 of the United Nations Charter was never intended to be an approval of pre-emptive action and, although international arrangements for dealing with terrorism need constant re-evaluation, that was an inadequate justification for citing Article 51 in this case. In 1956 there was only one international lawyer who believed that Article 51 was the right way to deal with Nasser. We had to face a similar question during the Yom Kippur War in 1973. We were asked by President Nixon for the use of bases, including those the British operated in Cyprus. As we did not want to take sides in the conflict, we refused. This decision was based on a realistic assessment of British interests and was respected by the Americans as such. During the Commons debate about the raids on Libya, on 16 April 1986, I told the House:

> I cannot come to the conclusion that this action by the United States will destroy terrorism, nor do I believe that bombing cities is the right way to attempt to destroy terrorism . . . It has never been suggested that we should bomb IRA camps on the west coast of Ireland. The real point is how we overcome terrorism by the use of our intelligence system, and our forces of law and order. It is that upon which we should concentrate . . . We should also deal with the basic problem that is the cause of terrorism in so many countries – the conflict between Israel and the Arab world.

*

Three months later, I was to disagree with the Conservative government over another potentially embarrassing foreign policy issue, the question of sanctions to South Africa. I first went to South Africa as part of the British delegation to the Commonwealth Parliamentary Association Conference in 1954. Although the South Africans failed in their attempt to break up the CPA delegations into the whites and the non-whites, the discrimination between white South Africans, the coloureds and the blacks was all too apparent. It was impossible for us to take a black African into our hotel in Johannesburg or Cape Town and at the receptions, luncheons and dinners given for us, only whites were present. We were invited to the formal opening of a gold mine by Sir Ernest Oppenheimer, but we had no chance to talk to the African workers there. It was an interesting performance during which we watched the gold smelting and the cooling of the blocks, and then saw the gold oblongs, whose bases were slightly wider than their tops, resting cold on the table. After an explanation of the process, Sir Ernest announced that it was the tradition in South Africa that if anyone could lift a block in one hand he would be allowed to keep it. This had never happened. The British delegation was sitting on the lowest level of seats of the rising tiers of the stand, which had been especially erected for the purpose. I was surprised when Bernard Braine, the MP for Castle Point, got up and walked across to the gold bars, but I was truly astonished when he picked one up with his right hand and began to move back to his seat, amid much merriment. The staff rushed after him in order to regain his prize. Apparently, he had noticed that one bar was not lying absolutely flat on the table, and he got his thumb under it to lift it. Unfortunately for him it was then found that the tradition of making the recipient a free gift no longer existed, and a rather disappointed MP returned to his seat.

In Natal, where those of English stock were predominant, the atmosphere seemed somewhat less tense. There was even talk, among the whites there, of pulling out of the Union and creating an independent country. Although nothing came of such talk, it was evidence of how unhappy those of British stock felt about developments in South Africa since the Nationalist Party government of 1948 had taken over.

As we were driven from event to event, we could see the contrast between the luxury of the hotels and of the homes of the whites compared with the dinginess and poverty of the black areas. It was the divisions on the beaches at Durban, between different colours, which made the greatest impact upon me. For one brought up free to rove wherever I wished along beaches, it was horrifying to find racial groups herded into their own enclosures. What natural beauties we saw, though. I shall never forget standing atop Table Mountain for the first time, taking in that unrivalled view of the bay, nor visiting Rhodes' House, where we could grasp how that remarkable man attained his vision of a united Africa. We also spent a day in Kruger National Park. I believe that none of us had ever before witnessed such a magnificent variety of wildlife, at such close quarters. What a contrast that made with the hard utilitarian buildings of Pretoria and Johannesburg, and a political system which seemed so alien, so unnatural. How sad it was that the people of such a remarkable land should be divided by such an outdated constitution.

But how to deal with it? It was difficult to find many politicians who were prepared to discuss the obvious problems. Harry Oppenheimer, an Opposition MP and the diamond magnate son of Sir Ernest, was clear that the politicians would have the utmost difficulty in taking any positive initiative: the answer lay with the business community. South African firms should not be allowed to compete by using labour at subsistence rates of pay. They would have to draw more and more skilled workers from the black community, with pay nearer to that of the whites. Coloureds and blacks would then need to be trained in junior management, and they would then expect comparable pay and the realistic prospect of promotion.

At that stage, any South African government would recognise that industry and commerce could not sustain a high rate of wealth creation unless political barriers between the races were broken down and discrimination was truly wiped out. Even those residents descended from the original settlers would come to realise that only a more liberal system could conceivably maintain them in their customary standard of living. This view did not seem to be fanciful. Without the more extreme measures taken by successive South African governments, which solidified the differences between the races, it might have been possible to reach a peaceful solution far earlier. I have myself often seen the businessmen far ahead of the politicians in making contentious changes, as for example when Britain changed over to the metric system. In political terms, that was a tricky operation, but the business community had got there long before us because they had realised that their products had to compete throughout the world, which was based almost entirely on that system.

In the 1980s both Mrs Thatcher and Ronald Reagan would publicly concede only with the greatest reluctance that any action against the South African regime could be taken. In fact, behind the scenes, both administrations were actively and rightly supporting attempts to end apartheid. At the 1985 Commonwealth Heads of Government Meeting at Nassau, it was agreed that a Commonwealth Eminent Persons Group (EPG) would be appointed for a peacemaking mission to South Africa. I was particularly pleased that the British representative was my former Chancellor Tony Barber. While the EPG was in South Africa, however, the internal situation deteriorated rapidly and its members concluded that there was no possibility of negotiations for the abolition of apartheid. In these circumstances, I felt that the application of full sanctions was necessary. I have never been an instinctive supporter of sanctions, but I have never thought them 'immoral': in some cases they can be fully justified. We lived through fifteen years of Rhodesian sanctions and we all saw the disunity that was caused in some parts of the Conservative Party over the matter. Sanctions did take a long time to have an effect, and they were often violated, but they induced Ian Smith to negotiate with Alec Douglas-Home, when Alec was Foreign Secretary (see p. 478–80).

South Africa had been an enormously tricky issue during the 1970–4 Conservative government (see p. 477–8), but circumstances had changed since those early days. I then thought that Simonstown was important in world strategy and East–West relations. In 1975 the Labour government had allowed that agreement to expire and, by 1986, I too felt that South Africa was no longer of great importance in any possible East–West arms clash. Indeed, the situation had become quite ironic. Every time it was claimed that South Africa was a bulwark against communism, the South African government's policies on apartheid were reinforced. This, in turn, had the effect of encouraging the black population over the whole of Africa to move towards a communist outlook. Until this self-defeating argument had been wiped from our minds, I felt that we would be unable to make any progress with negotiations.

The black majority in South Africa has now found the high quality of leadership that it has long deserved. The statesmanship of Nelson Mandela and Frederik de Klerk enabled the majority of white South Africans to conquer their long-held fear of a universal franchise, by killing off the old canard that the only alternative to apartheid was a black-dominated communist state. For the old hardliners, change of any kind still represented submission to Marxism and to the Soviet Union, with all the associated evils. The National Party finally realised that, so long as the South African government maintained the fundamental principles of apartheid, it was fanning the flames of communist developments, not only inside its own territory but among groups of activitists in the surrounding countries. This contradiction was always a time-bomb at the heart of apartheid. There is no doubt now, as I found for myself during a visit to South Africa in 1993, that the relationship between the different coloured races has gained a humanity it had previously lacked. My anxiety is that progress may be much slower than the black citizens expected, which will lead to the growth of damaging pressures in society as a whole.

Another system whose internal contradictions would inevitably cause it to collapse was to be found in the Soviet Union itself. I always thought that the essential weaknesses of the Soviet economy would sooner or later undermine its political institutions. Like many people, however, I was surprised by the speed at which this happened. By the time communism finally broke up, everyone could see that Soviet industry was so outdated and inefficient that it could not produce adequate goods for domestic consumption, still less anything worth exporting. This was a long-standing problem nonetheless, which I recall discussing with Khrushchev on one occasion in the early 1960s. 'You must make the British people buy Russian goods,' he told me.

'I cannot make them buy anything,' I explained. 'I can't even make them buy British goods. If you want to sell Russian goods, you must persuade people that these goods are what they want.'

'Well,' he said, 'you could help.'

'I will do what I can, in the interests of trade and diplomacy, but what do you suggest they should buy?' I asked him.

'They should buy Russian watches,' he proclaimed.

'Oh really,' I replied, somewhat taken aback. 'Why watches?'

'They're better than Swiss watches and better than Japanese watches,' he said, 'and they're cheaper than Swiss and Japanese watches.' Perhaps seeing some doubts in my expression, he added firmly, 'And they go faster than Swiss and Japanese watches.'

By the 1980s, the Soviet agricultural sector was also so incompetent that the USSR could not even feed its own people. As I put it in 1984, 'In order to keep their people alive, they have to import from the United States, allegedly their greatest enemy, 25 million tonnes of grain every year ... they have to sell to the Europeans, allegedly their second greatest enemy, sufficient natural gas to get the currency to pay the United States ... What sort of superpower is this?' If the Soviet leadership ever lost the will to use force and oppression in order to maintain the political status quo, it was hard to see how the USSR could be held together.

I was never optimistic about the likelihood of Russia and the other Soviet republics being steered steadily and quickly towards democracy and the rule of law. Any relaxation of the mechanisms of state control in such countries was always bound to unleash historically chaotic and revolutionary traditions, especially within Russia itself. This is quite different from China, where collectivism and stability are so much more traditional and managed change is proving to be such a successful option, based of course upon solid economic foundations. When Mikhail Gorbachev took over, I suspect that he himself did not know whether his ambition was to save communism or to dismantle it. What was clear from the outset was that the old order was coming to an abrupt end.

The positive aspects of his policies are obvious. The old nations of Central Europe have re-established themselves, and are working towards democratic institutions in place of the old oppression. The Baltic states, although still feeling the after-effects of the Soviet settlement and immigration policies, are normalising themselves. The old East–West tension has gone but, rather like India after the British left, Russia is going through a period of lawlessness. When a discredited regime is swept away at a stroke, it requires great courage and an enormous effort of will to re-establish a just rule of law. People need time to become accustomed to their new rights and, perhaps even more important, to their new responsibilities as citizens of a participative, free-market democracy. Openness and accountability, *glasnost*, has proved to be a lot easier to introduce than a policy of restructuring the whole Soviet economic and political system, *perestroika*. To open something up takes a day or a week, to build a free and responsible society takes a generation.

I went to Moscow in March 1994 to take a look at the progress being made under President Yeltsin in the transition from a highly centralised communist economy to a market economy. The British government was assisting in this through its 'Know-How Fund', which provided help for some of the reorganisation. Arthur Andersen, the worldwide firm of

accountants and consultants, of whose advisory board I have been a member
for some twenty years, was invited to reorganise and transform the baking
industry in Moscow. Over 600 bread retail managers had completed Andersen Consulting's training programmes and we visited two bakeries which
were both owned by women. The businesses had become quite attractive
and their variety of products had considerably expanded. At one, the
proprietor, Natalya Pelenetsina, was about to build a new bakery at the
back of the shop. This was, at least, encouraging.

During my discussions with British businessmen in Moscow, however,
it was clear that the immediate future was bleak. The task ahead was both
gigantic and daunting. It took the British government eleven years to
abandon our formal control system imposed during the war. Spain took
ten years to get over Franco. The comparison between Russia and East
Germany, made by some Western commentators, was also not a valid one.
East Germany had only 16.25 million citizens compared to the 148 million
of Russia, and the East Germans were absorbed by the third largest economy
in the world. Russia had nobody else to pick up the bill and was starting
from a lower base. Its businessmen had no concept of the free market and
no experience of democracy to draw upon. They also had little confidence
in their politicians and there was not much evidence of the will needed
to reform the economic and political systems. Yegor Gaidar, one of Russia's
leading reformers, told me that public opinion was also strongly divided
over reform, and he described two main threats to Russian democracy, the
communists and the nationalists. Gaidar feared that the Russian people
would be tempted by a lethal cocktail of collectivist sentiment. The task
facing President Yeltsin was therefore immense.

In 1994, Yeltsin himself and his Foreign and Defence Secretaries had
dined with me in London shortly before I had left Britain, and I met some
other departmental ministers during my stay in Moscow. It was Gorbachev,
however, whom I particularly wished to meet. I arranged this in a suite
at a hotel as I thought he might be embarrassed at coming to the British
embassy. Our discussion centred largely on Russia's economic problems.
After we had finished, I escorted Gorbachev down to the hotel hall where
we were joined by the manager. As we walked across the lobby, I noticed
that everybody present turned their backs on Gorbachev as he moved over
to the front entrance and into his car. I recalled the remark of the Russian
Foreign Minister in London, 'Gorbachev is the most loved man outside
Russia but inside he is the most hated.' This was reflected in the 1996
Russian presidential election at which he received only 0.5 per cent of the
total vote.

After Gorbachev had left the hotel, I went back to the lobby and had
a chat with the manager. I asked him for his view on the mafia about

whom everyone seemed to be talking. Organised crime was blossoming in Moscow and was even affecting Western-owned businesses. There was often an 8 per cent tax on all goods, imposed by the mafia, although it is often forgotten in the West that the Russian mafia is a collection of different gangs rather than a united single body. I was careful not to insult the manager. 'Of course,' I empathised, 'in a magnificent new hotel, you will have no dealings with the mafia but no doubt you hear from others who get involved.' The manager exploded. 'If I didn't pay the mafia,' he said, 'this hotel would be in ruins!'

The atmosphere in Moscow had obviously changed with the end of communism. People were moving about very freely. It was still light as I returned to the guest-house just after midnight. I watched as youths were racing madly over the bridge across the river on their bikes, shouting and laughing. This would never have been allowed under the old regime. There is, however, a strong feeling of betrayal in Russia today. Many expected instant rewards as the old communist command structures crumbled. Andrei Kokoshin, then Russian Deputy Defence Minister, told me in 1994 that Russia had the feelings of a country that had lost much without being defeated on the battlefield. Western leaders would be wise to acknowledge these emotions in their dealings with the Russian government. The Russian people do not like comparisons with Germany, Italy and Japan after the Second World War, nor references to the regeneration programmes those countries needed then. They do not want to be treated in a condescending manner. The Russians are still a proud people and resent any implication that they have been defeated, but the teachings of the old communist system have left their citizens ill prepared for the disorder and uncertainties of today. It is no wonder the Russians are turning against the West.

The break-up of the USSR affected the whole of Europe. In one case, it contributed to a tragic sequence of events. The federation which became Yugoslavia was born in July 1917, a year after me. It was a by-product of the First World War, which began in the Balkans and resulted in the end of Austro-Hungarian power in the western Balkans, and the final collapse of the Ottoman Empire. Rivalry between the Habsburg Empire and Serbia for control of Bosnia–Herzegovina had been one of the major causes of the Great War. After that war, Serbia took the former Habsburg states of Slovenia, Croatia and Bosnia–Herzegovina under its wing. For many Serbs, the existence of this combined state was a realisation of a long-cherished dream to create a 'Greater Serbia', but there was not much love lost between the different ethnic and religious groups in this diverse new land. An estimated 1,700,000 Yugoslav citizens died during the Second World

War, over a tenth of the pre-war population, and it is widely believed that rather more than half of these died at the hands of fellow Yugoslavs.

In the early 1990s, with Tito dead and communism collapsing across Europe, it was entirely predictable that nationalism would resurface in the component parts of Yugoslavia, despite Tito's own optimism about his legacy (see p. 484). Even after almost seventy-five years of the federal state's existence, few people thought of themselves as Yugoslavs, first and foremost. Without the unifying effect of Tito and his unchallenged communist apparatus, first Slovenia and then Croatia broke away from Yugoslavia. Since Slovenia borders both Italy and Austria, the European Community naturally took a close interest in these developments. It was, however, a great mistake, in my view, for the European Community to make a series of German-inspired direct interventions in 1991–2, encouraging the complete dismantling of the federal state. The member states of the Community had no common policy for dealing with the break-up of Yugoslavia. Germany, in recognising Croatia and Slovenia so precipitately, clearly acted in a non-*communautaire* manner. The Germans have always been politically close to Croatia, and it was the Croatian government which pressed them to adopt this position. This was perceived by Serbs in both Serbia and Bosnia as a provocative act.

Soon, British troops were involved in policing parts of the former Yugoslavia, as part of the United Nations Protection Force (UNPROFOR). Along with many of my colleagues, I was concerned that we were being drawn into a brutal conflict, without any form of considered withdrawal strategy. The fact that United Nations troops were in the area was resented by many of the locals and, for some reason, the British government was unwilling to exclude explicitly any possibility of military intervention beyond the UN-mandated peacekeeping activities. The presence of a sizeable contingent from our Royal Navy in the Adriatic was hardly calculated to reassure anyone. In 1993, as the appalling 'ethnic cleansing' was reaching its peak, both the government and the Labour Party began to toy with the idea of UN-sanctioned air strikes against the Bosnian Serbs. As I warned at the time, this required us to drop the neutrality which is essential for peacekeepers, and would surely have required us to withdraw our land forces, so as to protect them from the risk of attack.

There were many Members of Parliament throughout this period who continued to advocate direct intervention against the Bosnian Serbs. Many of them, I am sure, failed to realise that greatly increased direct intervention would ultimately have required us to go to war. The government, thanks to the good sense of both John Major and Douglas Hurd, always stuck to its view that the outside world could never impose a solution on the former Yugoslavia by force, and recognised that we could achieve an enormous amount so long as we limited our activities to the field of peacekeeping and policing.

Unfortunately, once air attacks on the Bosnian Serbs had become the overriding objective of the many people afflicted with what I call the 'something must be done' syndrome, they were soon judged to have a UN mandate and, in 1995, air attacks were indeed launched. The Serb reaction was swift, and threatened to turn an already substantial crisis into a Balkan Vietnam. Crucially, the international community held its nerve when 300 UN soldiers were taken hostage by the Bosnian Serbs in response to UN-legitimised air attacks on them. If we had attempted to rescue them by force, we could have found ourselves wholly, and probably irrevocably, embroiled in the conflict.

One obvious conclusion after the Yugoslavian débâcle was that the arrangements within the European Community were hopelessly inadequate for dealing with such a crisis just outside the 'city gates'. It is essential that the European Union should develop machinery for doing so. The unclear, often destabilising policies of the Western powers during this business added to the confusion and the dreadful human misery caused by a bitter and unnecessarily protracted civil war. Time and time again, we take far too long to get our act together. Then we fail to take into account the realities on the ground. The proposal, agreed at Amsterdam in 1997, that the Common Foreign and Security Policy should be administered by a secretary-general is a step forward. We should never have allowed ourselves to be rushed into a precipitate recognition of the breakaway states, and we should have realised that nobody thanks an outside agent for making an apparently one-sided intervention in a civil war. Once again, the Americans had their fingers burned when trying to tell everyone else how to conduct their affairs.

The clash between different cultures and values has also generated the prolonged dispute over Salman Rushdie and the *fatwa*, or sentence of death, passed on him by the Iranian Moslem hierarchy in February 1989. When I visited Iran in September 1995, some but not all of the leaders I met mentioned the controversy over Rushdie and his book *The Satanic Verses*. As a result of that book, its author continues to live in hiding and diplomatic and trading relations between our country and Iran have never been restored. After the death of Ayatollah Khomeini, the Iranian government gave a series of assurances that it would not send agents to kill Rushdie, but it emphasised that it could not speak for the Moslem hierarchy. Moreover, outside Iran the offence caused by the book has been so considerable that the risk to his life from Moslem extremists is still thought to be significant. We lost both political capital and a great deal of potential trade through this episode. On my visit I saw our European partners developing strong trading links with the Iranians, while we sat on the sidelines. They have said privately, all along, that this is really a British matter. Unfortunately, British influence, which has historically been very strong in the region, has also suffered a grievous blow.

When I spoke with Iran's leaders about the *fatwa*, I was chillingly reminded of the differences between the Moslem world and the West. We simply cannot afford to judge a Shi'ite government by our own accustomed standards. I tried to explain that people in Britain who observe one of their fellow citizens living in fear because he has been condemned to death have doubts about Iran's intentions. The Iranians made it clear that they regarded the British government's defence of Rushie as a pretext for bad relations. The only possible key to unlock the situation came from the deputy chairman of the Iranian parliament's Foreign Relations Committee, who suggested that Salman Rushdie was in danger not just because of the *fatwa*, but because of what he had written. He might be able to extricate himself if he were to interpret his book differently and if Iranian intellectuals could be convinced of the validity of the new analysis.

The position is that writers should have the freedom to write whatever they choose. At the same time, they must recognise that if they break the law or cause offence, they may suffer unpleasant consequences. Under British law if a written statement is judged to be libellous in a court of law the author can be required to pay damages. There are still national penalties for treachery of the most drastic kind. Salman Rushdie must have known of the offence his book would give to Moslems and that the hierarchy would feel bound to take action. It is not justifiable for the whole of the British people to pay the price of lost diplomatic relations, reduced trade and a lower standard of living to protect him. This chapter must be closed by him in the near future. He could give an apology quite simply, and say that he did not mean to insult the Moslem faith. That alone might be enough to settle matters, but he has never offered that apology. The new Iranian government, furthermore, is the first since the overthrow of the Shah to introduce any degree of liberalisation.

After my last trip to Iran, I felt that I understood the leadership there rather better, but felt no need to depart from my analysis of a year earlier, when I reflected that 'Now we have a situation in which the death decree was laid down by the head of the religion. He is the only person who can remove it, and he is dead. That must test the ingenuity of the Foreign Office a little!'

Chapter 22

THE DRAGON AWAKES

China 1974–1997

When I finally made it to China in spring 1974, two months after the February election, what I saw as our aircraft taxied off the runway and across the tarmac in Beijing was beyond my wildest imaginings. We came to a halt in the middle of a vast square containing thousands of young people waving flags, playing music and dancing to celebrate our arrival. I had never thought that such a reception in my honour was possible. To judge from the looks on their faces, neither had the rest of the passengers. At the foot of the steps I was met by Deng Xiaoping, then recently rehabilitated, accompanied by a Deputy Foreign Minister. After we had exchanged greetings, Deng led the way round the square so that I could see the splendour of the welcome close to. After completing our circuit, we got into the official cars and drove off, feeling somewhat drained, to our guest-house.

Driving from the airport I got my first glimpse of rural China, with people still busy working on the land. Then we came to the broad streets of Beijing itself, with innumerable cyclists on each side and a continuous stream of pedestrians on the pavements, some of them obviously returning home from work, others taking the air in the early evening. Passing through a gate into a private tree-covered park, the car pulled up in front of our guest-house, which had previously been occupied by President Nixon. Our host bade us farewell saying that, after such a long journey, we would undoubtedly like to rest, before we started on our programme the following day. That was certainly true.

The next day consisted of visits to see the treasures of Beijing, old and new. I was slightly surprised when my study of contemporary Chinese paintings was interrupted by the deputy protocol officer, who asked me to return at once to the guest-house. I told him that I was very interested in these exhibits, and in no hurry to go back. He replied that he was sorry, but he must ask me to return to the guest-house. In that case, I said, I really ought to explain to the press and television crews why I was behaving in such an apparently eccentric fashion. 'That is unnecessary,' he replied. 'We shall just leave the exhibition at once.'

I got no explanation until I arrived back at the guest-house, where the chief protocol officer introduced himself and said that he had an invitation from Chairman Mao Tse-tung for me to visit him at once. Was there anything that I needed to know before we left? As it was just after midday, I felt like asking whether the Chairman's invitation was to lunch, but I thought better of that and instead said that I should like to take Her Majesty's ambassador, Sir John Addis, with me to join the discussion. I also wanted to take my staff, in order that they should be introduced to Mao Tse-tung and pay their respects to him. They would not, of course, be present at the talks. The chief protocol officer had to telephone for authority for these arrangements, but came back to say that everything was agreed.

We set off in the official cars, soon coming to the outside wall of Zhongnan Hai, the party leaders' inner sanctum in the Forbidden City, where a gate opened for us. Inside, the roads were tree-lined. In the distance we could see a lake, and the atmosphere was one of quiet withdrawal from the hurly-burly of life in the city outside. We drew up in front of a pleasant-looking but modest villa. There on the steps to greet us I recognised Prime Minister Chou En-lai on the right facing me and, on the left, a young man introduced to me as Wang Hongwen, then the third most powerful man in the Communist Party in China. Two years later he was discredited and removed from power as one of the 'Gang of Four', radical adherents of the Cultural Revolution who tried to seize political control of the People's Republic of China after Mao's death.

Chou En-lai took me inside the house and along a short corridor to a door, through which I was ushered into Mao Tse-tung's study. Mao, who was then eighty years old, rose from his chair unaided to greet me and warmly placed both his hands on mine, his two women interpreters standing beside him. The ambassador, who had not met Mao before, was greeted as a friend of China. Then I introduced each of my staff to shake hands with the Chairman. All went well until I came to my press secretary and, introducing him by name only, said, 'Mr Maurice Trowbridge.' Mao Tse-tung shook Maurice's hand and then held on to it, looking – in a slightly menacing fashion, I thought – straight at him. There was rather an ominous silence and then he said, 'You are a very dangerous man.'

My press secretary was understandably rather taken aback and, searching round for something to say, finally stammered, 'Do I look it?' 'No,' said Chairman Mao, 'but that makes you even more dangerous.' I recalled that two days before we were due to leave for Beijing, my private secretary had told me that everything was arranged except that the visa for my press secretary had not arrived. I told him to remind the Chinese embassy about it, but meanwhile sent for Maurice to ask him whether he had written anything in the press or expressed any views which might have caused the Chinese to think him undesirable. He was quite adamant that, until he started to prepare for this journey, he had known nothing about China. He had never written a word about it, nor had he commented in any way upon either the country or its regime. The whole affair was unexplained and remains so today, although I suspect that the Chinese had come to the view that Maurice was some form of propagandist for capitalism and its values. The incident in Mao's study had another remarkable aspect. In introducing Maurice Trowbridge I used only his name, not commenting that he was my press secretary, yet Mao Tse-tung recognised his name and function at once. He was certainly well briefed.

After Mao had welcomed me, I thanked him for the reception I had received at the airport. 'Yes,' he said. 'I saw it on television myself.' Then, looking at Chou En-lai on the other side of me, he said, 'But why wasn't he given a military guard of honour?' There was a pause, 'Tell me, why not a full guard of honour?' Another pause followed, while Chou En-lai cleared his throat. 'Well, why not?' insisted Mao Tse-tung.

'Ah, Chairman Mao, we thought' – another pause – 'we thought' – another pause – 'it might upset Mr Wilson.'

'Upset Mr Wilson!' exclaimed Mao Tse-tung, flicking his thumb against his finger. 'Upset Mr Wilson! When he leaves Beijing, Mr Heath will have a full guard of honour.'

With this introduction, we went on to discuss international affairs. Mao was in excellent form throughout our meeting, which lasted for more than an hour and a half. It was clear that there was a special relationship between himself and the Prime Minister, Chou En-lai: a relationship founded not only on similarity of age but also on experiences shared during the Long March and the Civil War from 1934 to 1949. I saw nothing of the subservient deference which Chou is now alleged to have shown towards Chairman Mao.

Mao began our talk by testing me, saying almost casually, 'I suppose this European policy of yours is to make yourselves strong enough to get the Russians to turn to the east and attack China?'

'No,' I said, 'that is not its objective.'

'But', he went on, 'that's what your Mr Chamberlain tried to do before the war.'

At this point, Chou En-lai intervened and, leaning forward, said, 'Chairman Mao Tse-tung, Mr Heath was opposed to Mr Chamberlain and his policy before the war. He was a supporter of Mr Eden.'

'Ah yes, ah yes,' said Mao Tse-tung. 'I know, but I just wanted to make sure.'

Turning to the substance of our discussions, Mao Tse-tung then asked me, 'What is it that you want from this visit?'

I replied, 'Three things. First, I want the shooting across the border, from the mainland into Hong Kong, to stop, and for our citizens who are being held along the border on various charges to be released.'

'I agree,' he answered, 'the shooting will now stop and I will arrange for those who are being held to be released. And what is next?' he enquired.

'I want the hand-over of Hong Kong to the mainland when the Treaty expires in 1997 to be smooth and peaceful, in the interests of both our countries.'

'That is what I also want,' he said. Turning to Chou En-lai, he added, 'You and I will no longer be here when that takes place, but Mr Heath will be. And so will Wang Hongwen,' he added, pointing to the much younger man sitting at the far end of the horseshoe ring. 'How old is he, by the way?' asked Chairman Mao. Rather hesitantly, Chou En-lai replied, 'I think he is thirty-eight.' At this point, Wang pulled himself up to his full height and said, rather proudly, 'Chairman Mao, I will have you know that I am now thirty-nine.'

'Exactly,' said Mao, 'you and Mr Heath will still be here to see the smooth hand-over of Hong Kong.' That hand-over has now taken place, albeit with a few tricky moments on the way, and Wang is dead.

'And the third thing?' asked Mao.

'I want to see the trade between our two countries increase steadily from year to year.'

'That, too, is what I want to see,' said Mao. 'We must work together for that.'

From the outset of the discussion, I was aware that Chinese hostility to Moscow was as bitter as ever. Mao and his colleagues regarded themselves as the legitimate heirs and protectors of true Marxist–Leninist doctrine, from which the Russians had deviated. I therefore expressed my surprise at seeing Stalin's portrait alongside those of Marx, Engels and Lenin in the Great Square of the People. I could understand the first three, but why Stalin? 'Because', said Mao Tse-tung, 'he was the last of the true Soviet Marxists.'

'But', I added, 'he was a terrible man with the blood of millions of people on his hands.'

'Yes,' said Mao Tse-tung with a wave, 'there have been a number of people in the world like that, but he is there because he was a Marxist.'

The doctrinal difference between Mao and the USSR was reinforced by an intense emotional feeling that, at a critical time in the history of the

Chinese People's Republic, in 1960, the Russians had let them down badly by cutting off their supplies of defence equipment and all technical aid and assistance. 'You have a phrase for it,' said Mao, clenching his fists and pulling them towards his chest.

'You mean pulling the rug from under you,' I said.

'Yes,' he said forcefully, 'they pulled the rug from under us. Never again will we trust anyone, not even our friends. We will work with you, but we will never become so dependent on anyone again that they can pull the rug from under us.' He went on to describe the treachery of Lin Biao who, as the Chinese Minister of Defence, had allowed his ambition to get the better of him. He had died in an air crash three years earlier, apparently as he attempted to flee to the Soviet Union in the face of Mao's wrath against his purges. 'Here he was among us, but now we know that all the time he was under the control of the Russians. That is what they will always try to do, to control us from inside.' Not for the first time during the interview, a slight chill ran down my spine.

I had looked forward to visiting the Great Wall and, on a lovely Sunday morning, we set out to see it. As we got further away from Beijing, the traffic became lighter, the countryside ceased to be flat and after a couple of hours' drive we were in the foothills. When we reached the Great Wall it was even more impressive than the many photographs, embroideries and paintings I had seen of it. Hills rose up steeply from both sides of the road we were on and the wall mounted each hill, riding over the top like a boat on a wave. As we climbed the wall, the view became more and more exhilarating. It was such a beautifully clear day that, once we were high enough, we were able to see almost across to the mountains of Mongolia and, looking back, we could see the wall snaking for mile after mile over the undulating hills.

After a considerable climb, we paused for a rest at the first guard post. At this point the Deputy Foreign Minister suggested that we might now like to go back down the wall for some refreshment. As I knew he had been unwell, this was understandable. On the other hand, I wanted to get as far along the wall as I could. Looking out through the doorway, I saw that Tim Kitson had already started to climb the next part of the wall, closely followed by Sally, his wife, and Douglas Hurd. I explained to the Deputy Foreign Minister that, as they had already gone ahead, there would be great loss of face for me if I returned to London without having done the same, adding that I would quite understand if he wished to go back down to the restaurant at the roadside. He did so.

I then set off for the next guard post, which involved some steep climbing on a turn in the wall. Having reached this, we got an even better view. After a suitable pause, the General who was now the senior official still accompanying us suggested that we should return for our refreshment. Fortunately, Tim, Sally and Douglas were already halfway to the top guard post. I explained again that I could not possibly afford to descend before they did, and set off for the highest point, which involved a further series of very steep steps. It was worth it. At the top, the view was absolutely magnificent. We could also see how derelict the wall had become before the Chinese government had started restoring it.

We began the slow climb down, in many ways more tiring on the leg muscles than the ascent. 'Now,' I said to the guide, 'you must tell us how far up each of your other visitors managed to get. How far did President Pompidou go?' He pointed to a spot halfway up to the first guide post.

'Ah, but he was ill,' I said. 'Who got to the first post?'

'President Nixon got there,' he said.

'And who got to the second post?' I asked.

'Mr Tanaka, the Japanese Prime Minister, got there,' he said.

'And who has got to the top?'

'Only you and your friends,' he replied.

At this point, Douglas Hurd handed me a sheet of paper. 'You might like to see this,' he said, 'in case any of the press ask you for a comment now that you have climbed the wall. It's what President Nixon said when he got down.' I looked at the note, filled with expectation that I should read something suitably rhetorical and presidential upon it. 'I think you would have to conclude that this is a great wall,' it ran, 'and has had to be built by a great people.' I immediately knew that there was no point in trying to match such peerless wordsmithery.

Two banquets were held in the Great Hall of the People in Beijing during my visit. The first was given by the Chinese government, with Deng Xiaoping as host. After the second, which I hosted, my guests graciously showed us over the whole building. Each province has its own hall decorated in its own style with its own products, timber, carpets and wall decorations. The main hall has 10,000 seats, each with its own interpretation system, and remains the largest of its kind I have seen anywhere in the world. As I stood on the colossal stage and looked at the giant auditorium, I could well imagine how an orator would feel with a captive audience there in front of him.

As our cars brought us on to the tarmac at Beijing airport for our flight to the ancient city of Xian, our next destination, we saw that, as for our arrival, there was a large crowd of children and bands waiting for us. In addition, alongside the aircraft was a full military guard of honour of all three services, all exactly the same height, their white blancoed belts gleaming in the sun, their boots perfectly polished. I walked down the line, inspected them and congratulated the commander. The press were mystified that the farewell had been so much more grandiose than the welcome. I did not explain it to them. I could hardly say that Mao Tse-tung overruled his advisers, because he did not care a jot about giving offence to Mr Wilson.

After our brief stopover in Xian, the historical capital of China, we went on to Shanghai. The permanent industrial exhibition there displayed the areas in which indigenous Chinese industry was still backward; and other areas in which it was advanced, for example some medical and electronic developments. Many of the consumer goods on display were surprisingly attractive. The coloured fabrics, which I was told were being produced in immense quantities, were quite delightful. Having seen no one on the streets or in the shops wearing them, I wondered why so much was being manufactured. Apparently, even then, these goods were being made overwhelmingly for export, though they were in fact just beginning to be worn by the Chinese themselves, mainly in their homes.

A film on continuous view at the exhibition showed an operation under acupuncture. Some of the party found it difficult to face, but there was no doubt about its fascination. At seven o'clock the next morning my own doctor, Sir Brian Warren, went to the main hospital in Shanghai to watch such an operation being carried out in person, on a woman suffering from a disease of the thyroid gland. It was a difficult operation, lasting some four hours. She was conscious throughout and, when it was completed, got off the operating table, shook hands with those who had taken part and was introduced to Brian. Through his interpreter, Brian recollected how President Nixon's personal physician had told him that, after their operations, patients in China always expressed their thanks to Chairman Mao for having made the miracle possible. The woman then walked down the corridor to her bed. When Brian and I discussed this with him, our host claimed that acupuncture anaesthesia was successful in about 80 per cent of cases, a figure treated with some scepticism nowadays. For the remaining 20 per cent, Western methods of anaesthesia were used. No precise explanation could be given for why acupuncture worked. They were using the experience of centuries and had only just begun making a fresh effort to see if the results could be evaluated in scientific terms.

While the operation was taking place, I was taken round a system of underground tunnels, living rooms, dining rooms, offices and control centres, all of which run beneath the city. In Beijing I had been introduced to the bold injunction, 'Dig tunnels deep, store grain everywhere, resist hegemony.' The general system of underground tunnels linked factory to factory, and their construction was the responsibility of groups of factory workers. In addition I saw a large and apparently unused tunnel under the river, ready for public occupation if any emergency made an evacuation of the city imperative. Fresh grain was always stored in these underground systems, in preparation for any outside attack which might come. This was how the Chinese planned to defeat the 'hegemony' of either of the superpowers, the Soviet Union or the United States of America, though I doubt whether they had Washington in mind.

A plan to spend a day in a commune outside Shanghai came to nothing because of the weather. Instead I suggested a trip down the river on a launch so that I could see the waterfront, the shipping and the mighty Yangtze ahead, which was marked by a change in the colour of the water, from a darkish grey to a startling yellow ochre, and hundreds of huge junks in full sail. I had especially asked to visit southern China, which I expected to be quite different from anything else I had seen. We flew to Kunming, near the Burmese border, and I was immediately reminded of Kenya. The town is situated at an altitude of 6,000 feet, flanked to the west by a large range of mountains and to the east by lake Dian. It was hot as we drove through the crowd-lined streets on our way to the guest-house, but in the cool of the evening we sat on the balcony, sipping our whisky, looking at the rosebeds and watching the changing light on the mountains as night suddenly fell. It was just like being back at Government House in Nairobi.

The next day a drive of sixty miles or so took us south-east towards the border with North Vietnam. We passed acres of rice and vegetables growing in the fertile soil and saw the immense amount of manual labour which was used in the paddyfields, as well as primitive buffalo-pulled ploughs. At the end of our drive we came to the extraordinary 'Stone Forest'. Along the hills for mile after mile were giant stone figures, standing like stalagmites, creating the impression of a petrified forest. Before lunch we were able to wander round the stones and waterfalls, curious natural phenomena, so very remote and, at that time, rarely visited. I explained to my hosts that they were losing a large addition to their balance of payments by failing to attract more visitors. A successful tourist organisation would make a fortune out of it for them. They were not impressed by this and, leaving one of the most remarkable sights I have seen anywhere, we returned to Kumming for an evening concert. On the return journey, we passed a railway. 'That,' they said, 'goes to North Vietnam.' I asked if this was the railway which carried the Russian supplies down to the Vietnamese.

'Yes, of course,' they said. 'There is no other.'

I was a little confused by this. 'I have tried to understand Chinese policy towards the Soviet Union,' I ventured, 'but I find it difficult to reconcile your enmity towards Moscow with your allowing them to use this railway to transport military supplies across China and into Vietnam. How can you explain this?' I asked.

'It is very straightforward,' they said. 'After the North Vietnamese have taken over the whole of Vietnam, no outside country is going to be able to control it. Surely it makes sense to let the Russians pour millions of roubles' worth of equipment into Vietnam when it isn't going to do them any good in the end? That is why we let them use our railway.' We have much to learn from such a sophisticated approach to geopolitics.

The following evening's concert of music and song was remarkable for one particular incident which came to light in the aeroplane during the flight to Canton, the last stop on our visit to China. Some of the press correspondents asked me whether I had seen the notices outside the theatre before I went in. I replied that I had not particularly studied them, because they looked much the same as notices anywhere else. They were very important, they said, because they were political. On them was the name of the vice-chairman of the Provincial Committee who had accompanied me to the Stone Forest, printed upside-down with a red line running through it. That meant that he was under severe criticism and the heaviest punishment was being demanded. What astonished the press was that such posters should have been put up while I was visiting Kunming. I was the first foreign visitor to have been there for many years and it was perhaps because they were not accustomed to receiving visitors from overseas that they carried on as usual. In the aircraft, my Chinese hosts explained that this was their usual method of criticising those responsible for running their affairs. The posters detailed the alleged faults and misdemeanours of the vice-chairman. The argument would now go on in public. If the criticism became any greater, then he would have to explain and defend himself to the Provincial Committee as well as to the public. 'Every country has to have some way of doing this,' they said. 'You have a different system. You do it in your Parliament or local council. Here we do it by posters, then in the committee.'

Outside Canton, I was finally able to visit a commune. I drove some thirty or forty miles out to one that contained over 50,000 people. It was much larger both in area and in population than the word 'commune' might suggest, and it was almost entirely agricultural. The only subsidiary activity of any kind was the drying and packaging of some of the fruits from the intensive farming which we saw. Although the housing in one of the villages was extremely primitive, the people there had experienced no famine for more than a decade, and they had a small clinic where they could get herbal medicines and be treated for less serious illnesses, as well as a school at the centre of the commune where the children could go regularly.

*   *   *

When we were preparing for the visit to China, we enquired what sort of presentation I should make to Beijing. We received the reply that they would greatly appreciate receiving a pair of Père David deer for Beijing zoo. These deer had been indigenous to China but had gradually become extinct there. They were hoping to find a means of reinstating them. In Britain Père David deer are to be found only at Woburn Abbey, north of London, and they agreed to let us have some deer to send to Beijing. These arrived successfully and were warmly welcomed by the zoo. Unfortunately, because of the February 1974 general election, I could not be there to greet them.

I decided that I should make some other presentation to Mao personally when I saw him. One of his particular interests was Darwin, and William Waldegrave was able to find a special volume of his writings. Mao was delighted with it. I was naturally interested in what he, in return, would invite me to bring home, but nothing happened in Beijing, and we set off empty-handed on our tour of China. On our farewell night, the Deputy Foreign Minister, who had been accompanying us all the time, organised a splendid dinner and party, after which we all stayed up late discussing the tour. We finished at about 2.00 a.m., still without any sign of a presentation. My host knew that London Zoo very badly wanted to have a pair of pandas, but no mention had been made of this throughout my visit. Was it, I wondered, because such a gift was not possible? Or was it expected that the guest should raise the question? I decided that I could not return home without at least mentioning it.

So, as we prepared to break up, I told my host once again how glad I was that we were all agreed the tour had been a success. Only one thing was required to cement the friendship between the Chinese and British people. Our own government had already made its gesture, which had been warmly welcomed. If the Chinese government felt able to make a similar presentation of pandas to London Zoo, everyone would be delighted. At this the Deputy Foreign Minister's eyes lit up. Of course, he would immediately telephone Beijing, he said, but as it was already late he suggested that I go to bed. He would then wake me up at seven o'clock with the reply.

He was as good as his word and, at seven on the dot and beaming broadly, he said that the reply had come from Beijing. The Chinese Government would be delighted to make such a presentation from the Chinese to the British people. I, too, was extremely pleased. The suggestion was that London Zoo should send its staff out to Beijing so that they could be comprehensively trained in the habits and care of pandas. After this, the pandas would be sent to London and the Chinese staff would accompany the British staff and remain in London until the pandas were fully settled. He hoped this would give great pleasure to the British people who would be able to see them.

I did wonder how all this had been so satisfactorily arranged between 2.00 a.m. and 7.00 a.m. Could it all have been arranged in advance, and were they only waiting for me to mention the subject? However it came about, the scheme worked perfectly. During their time at the Zoo, the pandas attracted tens of thousands of people. The only sadness was that, although they occasionally went forth, they never multiplied. The female, Ching Ching, died in 1985, and the Zoo then loaned her mate, Chia Chia, to Mexico City Zoo, where he bred successfully. After Ching Ching's death, a replacement by the name of Ming Ming was sent from Beijing, but then the rules were strengthened against any more exports of pandas from China and, after Ming Ming flew back home in October 1994, we had none left at the Zoo.

In the meantime, the Chinese had carried out a major scheme for the protection of pandas, because of the decline in the numbers of those living in the wild, the Giant Panda Research Base at Chengdu. During my visit to China in April 1995, I asked for this protected area to be included in my tour. On arrival there, we received a very warm welcome. There was a splendid headquarters and the whole area was superbly well organised. I was taken first to the full-grown pandas, then brought back close to the headquarters where the cubs were situated. Some of these were placed in our arms and were delightful to hold. Over refreshments back at head-quarters I commented how sad it was that pandas could no longer leave China. 'Oh,' said the director, 'all that is out of date and they can now be sent to any part of the world.'

I pricked up my ears. 'In that case,' I said, 'I would like to take some more pandas to England.'

'Of course you can,' he said. 'Just say how many you want and how long you want to keep them for. Each one costs $1 million per year, and you can keep them for up to ten years. So if you want them permanently, you can have them for $10 million each.'

'But,' I expostulated, 'two pandas were presented to me by Chairman Mao himself. I would like that to be repeated.'

'I am afraid that is all over,' he replied. 'You see, in China we now live in a free-market economy!' This was the unacceptable face of market socialism.

At the end of that first visit to China, we boarded a superb modern train at the station in Canton, and two hours later we were at the bridge leading across to Hong Kong. When I returned to Beijing eighteen months later, I was again able to see Chairman Mao, but by now he had obviously aged.

He had to be lifted to stand to greet me, which he did just as warmly as before. He was accompanied only by Deng Xiaoping, and I took the new British ambassador, Sir Edward Youde, with me. The call to see Mao had come just as suddenly as on the previous occasion. At the beginning of my talk with him the previous day, Deng had two messages for me. The first was from Chou En-lai. Although he had set aside a day to talk to me, his doctors now said that it was necessary for him to have medical treatment over that period and he would not be able to see me. I expressed my regret and asked Deng to give him my good wishes for a rapid improvement in his health. 'As you appreciate,' Deng Xiaoping went on, 'Chairman Mao Tse-tung is now of advancing years and it has not been possible to make arrangements for you to see him.' Afterwards, the ambassador told me how sorry he was that I was not going to see either of the leading figures. I, however, discerned a difference between the clear and non-negotiable message that Chou En-lai was unable to talk to me and the statement that 'no arrangements had been made' for Mao to see me.

My long talk with Deng Xiaoping continued over lunch, covering the whole field of international affairs and matters of common interest to our two countries. At my meetings eighteen months earlier the main issues had been handled by Mao Tse-tung and Chou En-lai. Deng had only just become a vice-premier. I had noticed that, in our discussion then, he had quite often referred points to others on his side of the table. On this occasion, he was in complete command. He was already carrying much of the load of the ailing Chairman and Prime Minister and he had everything at his fingertips. I enjoyed our discussions, and found Deng Xiaoping to be open and straightforward in putting his arguments. He always seemed receptive to what I told him, prepared to give a direct answer to a direct question, and also loved to spice our discussions with humour. Deng obviously kept his long-term objectives clearly in mind and had thought deeply about how to achieve them. His stamina was remarkable, and his staying power was proven time and time again. Soon afterwards, he was punished for his qualities when he was briefly removed from his official positions by those who later became the 'Gang of Four', but he was soon restored to power, and China was put back on to a more sensible path.

The following morning, a Sunday and a national holiday, we went off to see the Summer Palace. The lovely grounds were full of people strolling around with their children. After going over the Palace itself, we went down the steep flights of steps to the lake, which is a miniature of the lake of Kunming. We were strolling along towards the marble ship built out from the shore for the Dowager Empress to take afternoon tea when running towards us came my host. 'I have a personal message for you,' he said and, taking me to one side, whispered, 'You are invited to see Chairman Mao Tse-tung at once, and to bring the ambassador with you if you wish. I have ordered the car to come round to the ship and we will go straight from there.'

'I wondered why you'd put a suit on this morning,' the ambassador said in the car. 'You must have known something.'

In his conversation, Mao Tse-tung still had a strong grasp of international issues. Only once did I feel that he was living in the past, when it became plain that he was thinking of the next war, which he believed was bound to come, in terms of the last. I thanked him for all I had seen of China after our last meeting.

'Yes,' he said, 'but you didn't go up to the north-east. You must come again and go there to see our mines and our industry.' He sounded weary. 'Ah, there is so much to be done and progress is so slow,' he went on. 'Don't let them kid you,' he added, 'we have had a little progress, but there is still such a long way to go.' Mao Tse-tung had about him the same qualities that I had seen in Churchill, Adenauer and Tito. Particularly towards the end of their lives, they each had the ability to go to the heart of the matter, to sort out the great issues from the small, to see their policies through to the end. How separate they were as personalities, how incompatible were their philosophies, and how different their political techniques. Yet they had this in common: they were giants of their age who, by their character, dominated events.

The transformation in the People's Republic of China since the mid-1970s has been absolutely astonishing. Much of the credit for that belongs to Deng Xiaoping, who died in 1997. Until he finally consolidated his power in the late 1970s, he was repeatedly vilified and attacked by hardline elements in the Chinese Communist Party. He showed great courage in both surviving internal exile and sticking to his belief that only liberal economic reform could maintain the stability of his country. I remember a fascinating talk with Deng during a visit in 1977, my first after the death of Mao, when the 'Gang of Four', including Mao's widow, had finally been dealt with and he could breathe easily for the first time. He told me in great detail about how he had been plotted against, removed from office, sent into exile and humiliated by his enemies. 'But,' he said, 'I endured it all and' – with a sweep of his hand, he gestured at the trappings of power around him – 'here I am!' 'Ah,' I responded with a wry smile. 'The Vice-Premier gives us all cause for hope!' Thanks to the reforms begun by Deng and carried on by his successors, China today is by no stretch of the imagination a traditionally communist country. The people enjoy far greater freedoms in the economic sphere, and political change is in the air. They are also exposed to far more Western culture.

This was particularly brought home to me in 1987. I had arranged to go to China in the spring of that year, taking in Shanghai, Hong Kong and Beijing. In advance of my trip I received two invitations to conduct, first at a trio of concerts in Shanghai. Then, from what has now become the China Philharmonic Orchestra, came a proposal that I should conduct them in the Great Hall of the People in Beijing, to raise funds for the China Welfare Fund for the Handicapped, whose chairman is Deng Xiaoping's son, Deng Pufang, who was crippled when he was thrown out of a window by Red Guards during the Cultural Revolution. I accepted both, but when I arrived in Shanghai, and they asked if I would do a fourth concert, I drew the line at four concerts in three days.

The public performances were due on a Thursday, Friday and Saturday, so we started rehearsing at the beginning of the week. The hall was old and not very satisfactory, but the Shanghai Orchestra is the oldest and most experienced in the People's Republic of China, having been established in the 1930s, and they generally acquitted themselves well. After an hour and a half of the first rehearsal, I stopped and said, 'Now is the time for a break.' Everything I had said up to this point had been interpreted by the first viola, who spoke perfect English. But at this point he looked at me and said he was puzzled, so I asked him why. 'I don't understand what you mean by "It is time for a break," ' he replied. 'Well,' I responded, 'we are halfway through the rehearsal, and now it is the time when we will all have a rest.' He still looked puzzled but passed on my clarification to the orchestra. He then returned and said that the orchestra didn't understand why this was necessary. 'Ah,' I explained. 'My union, the conductors' union, says that I must have a rest halfway through the rehearsal, so I shall now go back to my room where I shall have some orange juice and some rest. So, kindly tell the orchestra that they can now do whatever they like, so long as they are back within a quarter of an hour.' Then I made my way off the platform, aware of the baffled expressions around me.

On the second day, halfway through the rehearsal, I addressed the first viola again and said, 'Kindly tell the orchestra that my union says that I must now have a break.' This time, he was ready for me. He passed on my message, and I noticed that, this time, there seemed to be a little amusement, rather than bafflement, rippling through the orchestral ranks. 'If only it were that simple,' he began. 'The players' union says that this is a matter for collective discussion, to be settled upon by agreement.' I was dumbfounded. 'The musicians' union?' I asked my interpreter. 'You didn't have one yesterday.' 'No,' he replied with a grin, 'but, after you told us about your union, we met before the rehearsal this morning and formed the musicians' union. So the question of having a break is now a matter for collective agreement!'

The concerts were a great success, and the one in Beijing was televised nationwide. A former private secretary of mine, Peter Batey, was by now working in Beijing, and made all the arrangements. We succeeded in raising a substantial amount of money which went towards the building of a special facility for deaf children.

When we established full diplomatic relations with the People's Republic of China in 1972, we did so for three reasons. Our first objective was to take account of China's strategic position in the balance of world power. I was influenced by my earlier days when we saw the Soviet Union ostracised by the Western world, which unwittingly drove it into Hitler's hands. The second objective was the pursuit of Britain's own economic interests. The third, uniquely British, objective was to ensure the best possible future for Hong Kong. We wished to avoid any repetition of the civil disturbances that had occurred in the 1960s, and to make the best possible arrangements for when the Treaty expired in 1997.

The safe and peaceful return of Hong Kong to China in 1997 was an historic and moving event. As well as marking the end of empire for the British, it also showed how far China itself has now developed since the dark days of the Cultural Revolution and purges. It must be remembered, of course, that Britain was committed under international law to return the greater part of Hong Kong to China, so this was always a question of how, not if. Hong Kong became British as a result of treaties imposed on the Chinese in the nineteenth century. Under the Second Convention of Peking, signed in 1898, China granted Britain a ninety-nine-year lease for 92 per cent of Hong Kong's present-day territory. These treaties aroused the same anger among the Chinese that Versailles did among Germans after the First World War.

The victory of the communists in the Chinese Civil War meant that Hong Kong was deemed vital to the Western cause. We were always aware, however, that the colony was not militarily defensible. The years of detente in the 1970s helped create a new, informal Anglo-Chinese understanding, based on mutual self-interest, and I was delighted to play my part in establishing that. In effect, China agreed not to challenge Britain's authority in Hong Kong and, in return, we would take no action in Hong Kong which would jeopardise China's interests. During the early 1970s, sustained by the stable political climate at the time, Hong Kong had the highest overall rate of economic growth in the world. While Hong Kong was a British Dependent Territory, it had considerable autonomy, particularly in its own domestic affairs and in international trading relations.

When the new Conservative government under Mrs Thatcher took over after the General Election of 1979, it was soon persuaded by the then Governor of Hong Kong to raise formally the question of the colony's future, twenty years still had to pass before the treaty expired. Although, the undertaking given to me by Chairman Mao about a peaceful hand-over still held good, this new initiative immediately made the Chinese extremely suspicious about British intentions. These suspicions substantially intensified after Mrs Thatcher suggested that the UK administration in Hong Kong might be extended for another fifty years once China had re-established its sovereignty over the Colony in 1997. Deng Xiaoping flatly refused any such proposal and said that discussions about the new arrangement for Hong Kong must be finished within two years. He raised this robustly with me at our meeting in Beijing in 1983. We started with a general discussion about the international situation, but then he turned to Hong Kong. I noticed that at this point his colleagues, far from relaxing against the backs of their chairs, immediately sat bolt upright and concentrated on listening to him. This gave me a cue that something significant was about to be propounded. 'I said that we had two years for this negotiation with the British,' he began. 'A year has already passed and we have got nowhere at all. When you get home, go and tell Mrs Thatcher that there is only one more year left for us to settle these affairs. If she has not done so with me before another year is up, I shall settle it entirely on my own.' Everyone looked duly impressed. A senior minister, however, leant forward and said, 'Chairman Deng Xiaoping, may I inform you that Mr Heath cannot do this because he is not on speaking terms with Mrs Thatcher'.

'I know all that,' said Deng Xiaoping. 'Everybody in the world knows all that. But when they leave here, the Embassy will send a message containing what I have said to the Foreign Office, and the Foreign Secretary will send it across to Mrs Thatcher. That is how it all works. It has all got to be done in the next year.' In fact, both sides adhered to the timetable.

It was entirely predictable that China would become more insistent with the British over Hong Kong during the 1980s. China was in a strong geopolitical position, having dramatically improved its relations with both the US and the USSR, at a time of deteriorating East–West relations, or the 'Second Cold War'. Furthermore, the ending of the British lease in 1997 provided a ready-made deadline and a justification for China pressing the issue of Hong Kong. In April 1982 Deng Xiaoping had told me that China envisaged Hong Kong as a Special Administrative Region of China, with certain defined elements of autonomy, but no administrative links with Britain. Although my critics have claimed otherwise, I consistently campaigned for greater democracy in Hong Kong. I just felt that direct elections should have been introduced earlier, as a genuine measure of democratisation in which we really believed, not as a last-minute act of defiance by a Governor with no cards to play. On 16 May 1984, for example, I argued in the House of Commons that 'it is desirable that, when the agreement has been reached between the two governments, they should begin to work out a timetable for democratic arrangements in Hong Kong'. Later that year, I was calling for 'proper, working representative government [in Hong Kong] by the time the hand-over takes place . . . With only twelve years to develop representative government, the question of rushing or not rushing does not arise . . . Post-colonial history shows that we have always suffered when we have seemed to be dragging our feet.'

On 19 December 1984, the British and Chinese governments reached a firm agreement on the future of Hong Kong. The Joint Declaration proclaimed that Hong Kong would be 'restored' to the People's Republic of China with effect from 1 July 1997 and that China would therefore 'resume the exercise of sovereignty' from that date. The Hong Kong Special Administrative Region would be allowed to retain its capitalist economy and existing freedoms, and its basic lifestyle would remain unchanged. I argued at the time that the first stage of democratisation should be completed by 1989, to give the process time to bed down properly. The British government, however, did not organise early direct elections, although more representative elections to the legislative council were phased in. After the unforeseeable horrors of Tiananmen Square in June 1989, the situation changed again, but I still do not see how the position in Hong Kong could be improved by saying that we would unilaterally extend democratisation, not out of principle but as a kind of afterthought and intellectual reproof against Beijing. Speaking in the House on 19 April 1990, I said that 'the government's obligation is to do their utmost to ensure that Hong Kong retains its stability and prosperity until the time comes to hand it over in 1997 . . . to restore confidence to Hong Kong, we must establish a relationship between London and Peking'. I was encouraged when, nine months after Tiananmen Square, the British and Chinese governments at last agreed a joint timetable for elections in Hong Kong.

Unfortunately, the British chose not to adhere to the arrangement so far as the 1995 election was concerned. For obvious reasons, we had no right to organise elections in Hong Kong for any term of office that extended beyond 30 June 1997, but Governor Patten then did precisely that. This led to China's decision to abolish the Legislative Council upon the hand-over, and to replace it with an unelected body for the short term. This transitional body would be replaced within twelve months by a chamber elected by a combination of proportional representation and the use of electoral colleges. I am confident that the great majority of people in Hong Kong want to make a success of the new arrangements. They regard China as their homeland and want to take advantage of all the trading opportunities there for them. In my discussions with those in the great mainland cities of China I find that they are not jealous of Hong Kong's success, but want to share in it. It is essential that trust is created between the mainland Chinese, the people of Hong Kong and the international community.

It was for these reasons that I decided to attend the swearing-in ceremony for the new Chinese administration for Hong Kong on 1 July 1997, including the legislature, despite the decision of the Labour government, and its ministerial representatives in Hong Kong, to boycott it. Of course I would have preferred direct elections to be held immediately after the transfer of sovereignty, but we allowed our people to engage in pointless political gestures, so we cannot be too self-righteous when we receive something similar in return. In 1997, we had to respect China's pledge to hold free elections in Hong Kong in future, and encourage them to implement this and other commitments. In my experience, this can be achieved only by establishing good diplomatic relations. This, in turn, requires personal contact between representatives from both countries. The appointment of C. H. Tung, a successful magnate and an extremely urbane graduate of Liverpool University, as the first Chief Executive of the Special Administrative Region could hardly have been better judged to reassure international opinion about Chinese intentions. The basis of one country with two systems is entirely new, and was created specifically to address Hong Kong's needs. I believe that it can work successfully. The Labour government's boycott of the Hong Kong wearing-in ceremony was, in my view, a misjudgement. It was also ignored by virtually every visiting dignitary, and by senior British officials. They recognised that, at best, staying away from this celebration was a futile gesture. At worst, it could only have irritated the Chinese government and lessened our subsequent influence over them.

The international community must play a positive role in encouraging Chinese stability and, of course, we have our own interests to protect. A peaceful and stable China is less of a threat, both to its immediate neighbours and to other leading players in the international system. The thought of a country the size of China lapsing into instability or anarchy is too appalling to imagine. Many of our firms are now taking advantage of the spectacular trading opportunities which exist with China. In 1996 our trade with China was worth US$4.6 billion. This contrasted unfavourably with the equivalent figures for some of our major competitors: Sino-German trade, for example, totalled US$19.1 billion for that year. In recent years, the Chinese economy has seen consistent growth of 10 per cent. The economic difficulties experienced in 1997 elsewhere in the Far East, which provides the main market for Chinese goods, must have a negative effect, and I know that the Chinese government is also sensitive to the first serious signs of price inflation, which began to emerge in the mid-1990s.

At the time of the Tiananmen Square massacre, I expressed my horror in the House of Commons at the use of troops, which caused so many unnecessary deaths, and I have been consistent in this view. During the earlier stages of the demonstrations, those responsible had handled the protesters without casualties. Simultaneous demonstrations in Shanghai were dissipated entirely peacefully. I know that many Chinese leaders afterwards deplored the death toll and resolved that measures should be taken to prevent such a terrible incident ever being repeated. But we shall get nowhere if relations with China are always to be conducted with the tragedy of Tiananmen Square alone at the forefront of our minds. Of course, it was right to deplore and condemn the brutal suppression which occurred in June 1989, but, in general, we in the West must learn to be rather more cautious about judging the political arrangements in other parts of the world by our own subjective standards. When Alec Douglas-Home returned from China in 1972, the aspect of life there that he most forcibly emphasised in his report to me was the hugely successful process of communising that had evidently taken place in the People's Republic. Happily, although subordination of the individual to the larger unit remains a far more culturally ingrained way of life in the East, this particular experiment in social engineering has now been superseded.

On one of my early visits to China, I said to Deng Xiaoping, 'I do congratulate you on what you have achieved. Economically, you now almost have a market economy, but what about the political situation?'

'When it is a matter of dealing with over one billion people,' he said, 'what political system would you recommend?' I couldn't answer, because the Foreign Office hadn't told me what to say! So, playing for time, I asked him instead which direction his thinking was taking.

He replied, 'I know what we don't want. Take the United States. They have a President, alongside a Congress containing both the Senate and the House of Representatives. The President delivers his State of the Union address in January, and Congress then shoots it down. In turn, Congress passes laws which then go to the President, and he repudiates them and vetoes them. I don't want that sort of system for the whole of China – of course not.' I rather wished that I had not broached the subject. 'Or take India,' continued Deng. 'You gave India democracy, and what has happened there? Some of their states have gone communist, so Delhi has taken them over. Now, that's not democracy, is it? And that's not the sort of system I want.'

This was all rather disarming. I later learned that, a month afterwards, he discussed the same question with the Japanese Prime Minister and gave the same examples, but added another one. 'Now take the British,' he said, 'look at their system. They had Ted Heath as Prime Minister, an absolutely first-rate Prime Minister, and they got rid of him. That's not what I want!' This was a very flattering diversion, but there was a serious point behind it. In considering the People's Republic of China, with its vast population of 1.25 billion people and consistent increase in production of between 10 and 12.5 per cent per year, we have to realise that the world has a very considerable number of religious doctrines, faiths, attitudes and historical backgrounds. That is why we should not judge every other country and culture by our own familiar standards, and why we cannot impose our will on others. Our friends in America particularly need to bear that in mind.

In this country, it took us more than 100 years to develop our present democratic system, with a small population, compared with those 1.25 billion Chinese, of whom the overwhelming majority are peasants working on the land. It is widely recognised throughout China that to produce a democratic organisation is a mammoth task if it is to be successful and lasting, and nobody in China wishes to tread the same path as the former Soviet Union, where the rule of law has virtually disintegrated in the wake of rapid political collapse. The prospects for democracy depend overwhelmingly on stability and a successful economic transformation. It is in all our interests for the People's Republic of China to make that transition successfully.

Three months after attending the hand-over of Hong Kong to the People's Republic of China on 30 June 1997, I paid my twenty-second visit to the Chinese mainland starting, as always, in Beijing. In the course of these visits I have covered almost the whole of the country, including Tibet, and every major city in it. I have watched the transformation of this country in its agriculture, its industry, in the size of its population, the immense growth of its cities and the standard of living of its people. This has been brought about by the change in structure of the economy from the earliest design of a Communist state to that of a market economy in which there is still a considerable degree of public ownership. The beneficial results of all this are undeniable. They deserve our praise.

At the discussion I had with President Jiang Zemin in 1995, he proclaimed that I had now survived three generations of Chinese leaders. 'You had long talks with Chairman Mao,' he said, 'a large number with Chairman Deng, and now you are having one with me. You are the only political figure who has been able to do this.' From it all I have learned to understand the country and its people, and I am glad to say that its leaders have learned to trust me, because I will tell them clearly and frankly what I believe to be true about our relationship with them. This relationship can be beneficial to both our countries and our peoples, and I hope very much that the new generation of British political leaders will choose to pursue a similarly constructive dialogue with their opposite numbers in Beijing. It is inevitable that commentators in the West will continue to find much to criticise in the Chinese government's conduct, but there is every reason to suppose that the People's Republic of China will remain a formidable bastion of stability and an economic powerhouse which we would be fools either to ignore or to alienate.

Chapter 23

MISSIONS OF MERCY

Iraq and the Gulf 1990–1997

After my first tour of the Gulf in January 1961, following the Foreign Office Conference in Singapore, I made regular visits to the Arab countries during the rest of that decade. The one country which I could not visit was Iraq. In the wake of its revolution in July 1958, a psychological barrier grew up which prevented outsiders from contacting the country's rulers. Saddam Hussein became President in 1979 and first established himself in the public mind during the war against Iran, in which he was supported by the United States, Britain and other Western countries. After eight years he was finally able to claim at least a partial victory.

On 2 August 1990, Saddam's forces attacked and conquered the small independent state of Kuwait. The Iraqi Revolutionary Command Council announced:

> God has seen fit to plague the world with the tyrant of Kuwait and his lackeys, the enemies of the morals and principles which God decreed should prevail on earth, they who betrayed and violated the tenets of nationalism and the rules of good neighbourliness . . . now God has aided the freedom fighters to destroy the treacherous regime in Kuwait that had erred by complying with Zionist and foreign plots and stratagems . . . they have been overthrown by young men who put their faith in God, and who were guided by Him.

The Ruler of Kuwait and his family had already fled into Saudi Arabia and escaped unharmed, but his country was grievously wounded. In the process of the Iraqi invasion, immense damage was done to Kuwait and it has been estimated that between 1,000 and 1,100 Kuwaiti lives were lost as a consequence of the invasion, and many more Kuwaitis were imprisoned or tortured. The US and Britain announced an immediate freeze on Kuwaiti assets, and the US also froze Iraqi assets and suspended purchases of Iraqi oil. The United Nations Security Council adopted Resolution

(UNSCR) 660, condemning the invasion, requiring an immediate with-drawal of Iraqi forces from Kuwait and, although this was often disregarded later on by the world community, also requiring Iraq and Kuwait to resolve their differences once and for all. By a clear majority, the Arab League condemned Iraq's aggression, and even countries such as Libya and Syria joined in the criticism. On 6 August, UNSCR 661 imposed sanctions on Iraq, which were, very largely, still in effect eight years on. Within a week of the invasion of Kuwait, George Bush had despatched US troops to Saudi Arabia. On 10 August, Saddam Hussein called for the Arab world to unite in a jihad against the West. An Emergency Arab Summit in Cairo responded by passing, by fifteen votes to three, a resolution calling upon Iraq to withdraw immediately from Kuwait.

Saddam Hussein's next step was to take under his own control a sizeable number of foreign citizens within Kuwait and Iraq, who were then moved to strategic points in his country, in the hope that this would deter United Nations forces from attacking them. Over one thousand British expatriates were caught up in this scheme, which came to be known as the 'human shield'. Some of these prisoners were in poor health after spending much of their lives in Iraq, which intensified international revulsion at this tactic.

It was subsequently alleged that the American ambassador to Iraq, April Glaspie, had told Saddam Hussein before the invasion that the Americans would have no objection if he embodied Kuwait in his own country. In my discussions with him, however, Saddam Hussein never mentioned this. What is not open to question is that this invasion was foreseeable. The immense wealth of Kuwait, with vast reserves of oil available for only 2.2 million people, had long caused intense jealousy throughout the poorer countries of the area. Moreover, Saddam Hussein had recently enjoyed the support of other Arab states in Iraq's war against Iran, which had only just ended, and he might have concluded that they would fall in behind him once again in any subsequent adventure.

This all immediately put me in mind of three historical parallels during my political career: the Suez crisis of 1956, the Kuwait crisis of 1961 and the Cuban missile crisis of 1962. The British had signed a treaty with Kuwait in 1899, in which the Ruler of Kuwait, in return for British protection, undertook not to alienate any of his territory without prior British agreement. In 1914, the United Kingdom recognised Kuwait as an independent government under UK protection. By the early 1960s, the Gulf countries were seeking greater independence from the West. When I visited the area in January 1961 as Lord Privy Seal, I agreed on behalf of the British government to the request of the Ruler of Kuwait, Sheikh Abdullah as-Salim-as-Sabah, for full independence, including control over foreign and defence policy. The Kuwaitis were already enjoying *de facto* independence on all other matters and had all the aspects of any highly developed country, a major road system, a full-scale general hospital, schools and shopping centres. I did, however, inform the new government of Kuwait, privately, that if it ever faced any threat from an external aggressor, it could still come to us for help. In June, it became all too clear to us that such a threat did indeed exist, and it came from Iraq.

The Iraqi leader, General Kassem, announced on 25 June 1961, in a broadcast on Baghdad Radio, that Iraq had never recognised the 1899 Agreement, for it had been 'imposed by imperialists'. He cited an Ottoman agreement from 1871, and declared, on the basis of that, that Kuwait was 'an integral part of Iraq'. We offered to help repulse this, and the Kuwaitis accepted immediately. Speaking in the House of Commons on 28 June, in response to a question from Denis Healey, I reminded MPs that this was not a case of Western imperialism, for most of the Arab world now recognised Kuwait. Indeed, Kuwait's independence had even been recognised by the Iraqis, when they had voted for its admission, as an independent country, to the International Labour Organisation only a fortnight earlier. I also affirmed that, in close consultation with the US government, we were prepared to carry out our obligations.

Our attitude was strengthened by strong support for Kuwait across the Arab world. From 1 July, we began to line the borders of Kuwait with our forces, including 600 Royal Marines, a Dragoon Guards tank squadron and substantial air support. The Iraqi troops which were already on the road to Basra, thirty miles from the border with Kuwait, thought better of their escapade, halted and then withdrew. Within a week, we had 6,000 men in Kuwait, and they were soon supplemented by Saudi forces. We had recognised all along that our presence could not be a long-term solution to Kuwait's difficulties, and quickly agreed with the Kuwaiti government that it should arrange for forces provided by the Arab League to patrol the Iraq–Kuwait border to prevent further incursions. It accepted this advice and, after Kuwait had been admitted to the Arab League on 20 July, signed a joint defence agreement with the League on 12 August. Thenceforth, Arab League forces would defend Kuwait against any outside attack. The first such troops arrived on 9 September, and British forces began to withdraw on the 19th. Within a month, the last of our soldiers had departed, and Arab League troops then remained in Kuwait for almost eighteen months.

From the outset my view in 1990 was that diplomatic, as well as military, solutions should be investigated. My statements on the Gulf crisis were interpreted by right-wing critics as being akin to the appeasement of Hitler in the late 1930s. This was a spurious allegation. My intentions were threefold: to ensure that every diplomatic route to a settlement was fully explored before a military adventure was contemplated; to put the 1990 crisis into its proper cultural and historical perspective; and to do my best to ensure that whatever arrangement was made at the end of the crisis was a sustainable one, and overwhelmingly acceptable to the Arab world. I put this view forcibly in a television interview with Brian Walden, the former Labour MP, on 16 September 1990:

> We've got to try to find a way through diplomatic means of getting a solution to the problems, which have, after all, bedevilled the Gulf for a long time . . . this is a United Nations operation, and the United Nations . . . obviously doesn't want to have a major war . . . they want to get a permanent settlement, and . . . I think it's got to be done by the Arab countries.

There was simply no comparison between Saddam Hussein before the Gulf War and Hitler. First of all, Saddam Hussein had neither Hitler's industrial power nor his military capability. Secondly, the entire international community was united against him and could act decisively against him, so we were negotiating from a position of strength. Above all, negotiation is not appeasement. Appeasement involves a sacrifice of a moral principle in order to avert aggression. Negotiation requires some change of the status quo in order to make progress, without giving up any basic point of principle. This is the very stuff of diplomacy and, throughout history, negotiation has been the only peaceful way of resolving serious differences between nations. The practical problem was that Saddam had entered into his foreign entanglement without any strategy for withdrawing from it. The Arab world was quite clear that such a strategy had to be found for him. What is more, those, such as myself, who have served during a war rarely share the relish for armed confrontation displayed by those who have seen less of the horror of war for themselves.

The *Walden* interview prompted one particularly offensive attack on me, from the right-wing historian Norman Stone, then a professor at Oxford University. He quite unjustly accused me of siding with Saddam Hussein, and wrote that 'the role of Edward Heath in British politics was malign . . . he espoused power-worship, all concrete blocks and paper money'. I responded quickly and vigorously, pointing out that:

> Professor Stone's remarks are misplaced and ill-informed . . . he fails to understand the reasoning behind my statement over the Gulf . . . I was shocked by the extent to which he distorts some facts and ignores others . . . most of all, it was the tone of his remarks which showed an

aggressiveness and a lack of objectivity which is scarcely tolerable in a politician and is, surely, intolerable in a Professor of History . . . many parents of Oxford students must be both horrified and disgusted that the higher education of our children should rest in the hands of such a man.

As my view, that we should work to avert a war, became more widely known, I began to receive letters from relatives of those imprisoned in Iraq demanding that action should be taken by the government to secure their release. There was extensive public support for these families' requests that diplomatic efforts should be intensified, and I fed this into the normal government channels. I heard nothing for the first few weeks, but towards the end of September the government finally began to respond to the calls for somebody to go to Baghdad to organise the release of those prisoners whose health was known to be especially fragile. Their medical problems included virtually every complaint from asthma and heart problems to severe arthritis and acute haemorrhoids.

On Friday 28 September, William Waldegrave, then the Minister of State at the Foreign Office, telephoned me to say that the Foreign Office had agreed to such a mission and had three possible candidates in mind. Would I be prepared to go if asked? 'Of course,' I replied. I learned afterwards that the other two had been Jim Callaghan and David Owen. William called back later in the day to say that it had been decided I should go and that the government would make all the necessary arrangements for my visit, including security, and would cover its cost. I at once informed the detainees' relatives who had written to me that I would indeed be carrying out the mission for which they had asked and told my staff to make the necessary preparations.

Douglas Hurd, the Foreign Secretary, then went off to join Mrs Thatcher in New York for a United Nations meeting. When he told the Prime Minister what had been arranged, she was apparently furious and, according to those present, 'exploded'. Two days later, on the Monday, I received another telephone call from William Waldegrave, saying that the government's position had entirely changed and it no longer wished anyone to carry out this operation. Of course, he added, the government was unable to stop me if I wanted to continue my mission, but it would not be responsible for the arrangements, provide security nor cover the cost. I informed him that I had already told the relatives that I had started discussions with the Iraqi ambassador about the arrangements and that I could not cancel the visit without some tenable explanation. To say that Douglas Hurd had given in to Mrs Thatcher's anger would be no justification in the eyes of relatives extremely concerned about their loved ones.

Baghdad proposed that I should arrive there on the following Saturday, 13 October, to which I agreed. Meanwhile, the Conservative Party conference had begun at Bournemouth and I drove over to it each day from Salisbury. It was essential to make a public announcement before the news was leaked. I decided to do this at the party conference where all the political press were assembled. The head of my private office arranged matters with the press office of Conservative Central Office, and I spoke to the media at 4.15 p.m. on Thursday 11 October, on the balcony of the Conference Centre itself, explaining why I was going to carry out this personal mission. Most of the media appeared at my conference, leaving Tom King, the Secretary of State for Defence, to make his wind-up speech in the hall with hardly any press to report it. I then returned to my home in Salisbury, where I was due to give a long-prearranged dinner for some members of the press, as is my custom during party conferences. They were all very excited by the prospect. It later transpired that, on BBC *Question Time* that same evening, Michael Heseltine had been highly critical of my proposed trip, making remarks which were unusual for him, but not untypical of views subsequently expressed by the party leadership.

Just after the journalists left my home, a call came through from Baghdad, asking me to postpone my trip by a week. This was, of course, acclaimed by my critics as a deliberate personal insult to me from Saddam Hussein. In fact, the Iraqi Foreign Minister, Tariq Aziz, had been summoned to an Arab conference in Morocco, and the Iraqi government preferred him to be present for my visit. I too wanted Tariq Aziz to be present. As Foreign Minister, he was acknowledged to be very influential and, as a Christian, would be able to present a view other than the Moslem one. Moreover, he spoke excellent English and was an immensely experienced diplomat, thanks to his time both as Iraqi ambassador in Washington and as the Iraqi permanent representative at the United Nations. I accepted the postponement.

As a consequence of my proposed trip, I had to endure some choice newspaper headings, including 'Heath: Appease Saddam' in the *Daily Express*; 'Traitor Ted!' from the *Sun*; 'Fury at Ted the Traitor' in the *Daily Star*; and a personal favourite of mine, 'Heath, isolated and wrong, a clear essay in ineptitude', an especially generous-spirited sentiment from the *Sunday Times*. All of this attention was through no fault of my staff or myself. Nor was our press conference timed so as to strike a counter-blow to the conference or to Mrs Thatcher, although that was how it was described by some of the right-wing press, in their usual fashion. The *Observer* came closest to reporting what had really occurred, under the front-page headline 'PM "hits roof" at Hurd over Heath trip to Iraq'. The article went on to reveal that the Foreign Office had been responsible for instigating the trip, and reported that, even after the Prime Minister's outburst, 'Mr Hurd, true to his word, expressed quiet support for the visit.' But the attitude of Foreign Office contacts towards me had chilled.

All of this at least showed that my project was a major news story, and the general public were totally unmoved by these hostile editorial attitudes. That same month, a Gallup poll showed that 85 per cent agreed that I was right to go to Baghdad to secure the release of the British hostages. It was gratifying to know that we had the support of the public in helping our fellow citizens out of this critical position, into which they had been placed through no fault of their own. The week's delay to my journey led to a flood of correspondence, almost all of which was entirely in favour of the proposed meeting and gave me the opportunity to refine the arrangements, greatly helped by my friend from Iraq, Sabih Shukri.

On Friday 19 October, accompanied by the head of my private office, Robert Vaudry, and my personal doctor, Jeffrey Easton, I flew by Royal Jordanian Airlines to Amman. The plane also contained a large number of press representatives. My party was met by the British ambassador in Jordan, Anthony Reeve, and went on to stay the night in the palace of King Hussein of Jordan. I had dinner with the King, his brother, their wives, the Jordanian Prime Minister and a few others. We had an animated discussion about how the situation in the Middle East seemed to be developing, but nobody could suggest any way out of the impasse.

The next day we flew by Iraqi Air to Baghdad, on a flight which was heavily delayed because of the controls imposed upon the airline. Only two planes per day were allowed into Baghdad. All around were the signs of a nation well used to conflict: armed men, gun emplacements and an enormous memorial to the Iraqis' own Unknown Soldier. I was met at the airport by the British ambassador, Harold 'Hooky' Walker, whom I already knew well, together with Iraqi representatives, and was then driven in a high-speed cavalcade to the Al Rasheed Hotel. We had a brief opportunity that day to visit Mansur Elmelia, which was serving as a kind of transit camp for foreign nationals found in Kuwait, who were then moved secretly to strategic installations. After a few hours at the hotel, we were taken to 'better accommodation', a very pleasant modern guest-house. The journalists who went out with us remained in the hotel, and, by all accounts, rather enjoyed themselves in a Moslem country whose alcohol laws are still rather relaxed. After unpacking, I went to the Foreign Ministry for a meeting with Tariq Aziz at which we discussed the reasons for the dispute.

The Foreign Minister began with a heavy rhetorical barrage, describing the United States as the most evil power in the history of mankind and alleging that the Kuwaitis had been trying to ruin Iraq's economy. He then outlined his President's role in the Arab League, and it was clear that deeply troubling parallels with the Suez crisis were already emerging. Saddam Hussein, like Nasser before him, was exploiting the widespread jealousy among poorer Arabs towards the small and disproportionately rich oil-producing states. He was presenting himself as their figurehead in a holy war against the West, Israel and those in the Arab world who had, despite their professed Moslem religious beliefs, gradually accommodated themselves to Western values. This was an explosive mixture of class war and religious rhetoric, all too redolent of what we had heard from Nasser decades before.

I responded to all of this by reminding him that UN Resolution 660, deploring Iraq's infraction, had been strongly supported and was being upheld. One of his colleagues retorted that, in the eyes of the Iraqis, the conflict was one of Thatcher and Bush against the Arab world and Iraq, and that Kuwait was breaking the OPEC agreements on the scale of its oil production. The figures he gave for this were later proven to be correct. I reiterated my own view that Kuwait was certainly not alone in breaching such agreements. In any case, this was no justification for going to war. I returned to the guest-house, where we were joined by Tariq Aziz and two officials, one of whom was the President's interpreter. He had gained a first-class degree at Birmingham University, spoke immaculate English and later asked us to pass on his best wishes to the Shakespeare Institute at Birmingham. The conversation at dinner was intelligent and well informed: the Iraqis were right up to date with world affairs, frequently referring to articles in the latest *Sunday Times* and other British publications. When we switched on the television, we found channels in three languages – English, French and Arabic.

The next day I had breakfast with Jeffrey Easton, my doctor, and recall treading on what felt like a microphone under the table. I can imagine a member of the Iraqi security services nursing a headache for the rest of the day. We then started on a tour which began at the British embassy, where I met the few remaining staff. Apparently, as soon as I left the guest-house, the chief of protocol and my minders put their feet up on the settee and began to relax. Outside we were greeted with a rally denouncing British policy towards the Gulf, and Mrs Thatcher in particular. In the compound small tents were rigged, accommodating those who worked for Bechtel, an American company which had apparently panicked when the invasion of Kuwait began, rushing its non-American workers to the British embassy. As there was no room there for them in the building, they had sought refuge in the garden. The ambassador was worried about what would happen when winter came and my doctor immediately sensed that, for all their protestations, some of these people were already seriously ill. They were trying to escape being noticed, but he resolved to return to the embassy and to deal privately with them. We then went on to the hotel, where some of the people detained as human shields had been placed. These included a number of people on our list, and in particular Tony Wilbraham and his wife from Blackpool. Next, we went to a Western-style hospital, which was owned by Aer Lingus and staffed with British and Irish nurses. The British obviously wanted to get back home, but I was told that this would not be permissible unless they could be replaced with further Irish nurses. Fortunately this was later carried out. That evening we attended a tense but moving evensong at St George's Church with the ambassador.

My meeting with Saddam Hussein had been arranged for the next morning, and I was to go alone. Robert Vaudry told me some time afterwards that, as they watched me leave in the ambassador's bullet-proof car, the assembled British wondered whether they would ever see me alive again. I was driven directly to the President's palace. There was no great display, just a servant to take me along to a waiting room. I was then led almost immediately into the President's private study. Dressed in uniform and accompanied by Tariq Aziz, he greeted me quietly at the door and led me to my seat. There were only two interpreters present, along with one photographer and a television cameraman, both of whom withdrew after we had sat down. There was no fuss, and it was clear that we would get down to business at once.

President Saddam Hussein welcomed me and then began to give me the history of Iraq and its relations with its neighbours, pointing out that, although Iraq was a modern state in its present form, it was in fact one of the oldest civilised areas in the Middle East. I mentioned that the porcelain from Iraq which I had seen in Western museums was older than that from Iran, which was apparently new to him. We finally moved on to the subject of the recent war between Iraq and Iran, and he pointed out that, until recently, the Western powers had supported him and his country against revolutionary Iran. He emphasised the threat of Kuwait's oil policies to his country and stated that a discussion about these problems had been arranged recently by the Egyptian President with Jordanian and Kuwaiti leaders, in the hope of obviating any conflict.

This Egypt-inspired meeting had not reached any conclusions, and a second meeting had then been arranged in Saudi Arabia. Saddam Hussein had given an undertaking that nothing irregular would occur until a further attempt to resolve the problem had been made there. However, when he had learned that the Kuwaitis had decided not to attend the meeting in Jeddah on 1 August and, as a result, had failed to proceed with the discussions, he had felt that Iraq had no alternative but to invade Kuwait. It later emerged that the Kuwaitis had boycotted this meeting on 1 August because they had misunderstood a message from the Egyptian President and thought that Saddam Hussein had ruled out Iraqi aggression against Kuwait indefinitely. By the time I went to Iraq, the Western media had grown accustomed to portraying Saddam Hussein as a madman. Whatever he may be, he is certainly not a lunatic. As I told the *Independent* in December 1990, 'he is not mad in the least . . . he's a very astute person, a clever person . . . he made a misjudgement about Kuwait, and I am sure that he recognises now that it was a misjudgement'.

I told Saddam Hussein I believed that, unless he withdrew, international military action was inevitable. This would be immensely damaging to Iraq as well as to him personally. He should order his troops out of Kuwait, and then request the Arab League to place their combined forces along the borders between Iraq and other Arab countries, as had been organised by the British in 1961. That would mean that any external aggression against him would have to confront the Arab League as well as Iraq. It would also get his troops out of Kuwait. Saddam Hussein neither agreed nor disagreed.

After nearly two hours, I was given the opportunity of raising the question of the British citizens. I began by informing Saddam that his detention of the hostages, to whom the Iraqis referred as 'guestages', was doing him far more harm than good, and that I had brought with me a list of thirty-three individuals who were ill and, in some cases, close to death. I wished to track them down and take them back home with me. This, he said, could certainly be done. There were also two Moslems from the north of England trapped in Baghdad, and they too wanted to return home. 'Of course,' he said. I also wished to plead for two other special cases. One was Alex Duncan, a student from my own college at Oxford. The Master of Balliol had been to see me before I left home to say that the term had already started and Alex had not appeared, which had made him understandably concerned. I understood that he also had his younger brother Rory with him, and he was overdue back at school. 'Take them with you,' said Saddam Hussein.

I then went on to say that there were some seventy-odd British building workers in Baghdad whom I understood to be in the process of building a new palace for the President, which was due to be finished in three weeks' time. Once their task had been completed, I would like them to return. Turning to Tariq Aziz, Saddam Hussein said, 'I do not understand this. I have no new palace being built.' 'I think he is referring to the guest-house,' said Aziz, 'but as they are not British workers they are a quite separate case. They are Irish.' 'In fact they are from Northern Ireland,' I replied, 'and that is part of the United Kingdom.' 'I understand,' said

Saddam Hussein, 'and they can return as soon as they have finished their work here.' All these arrangements were carried through. Our meeting ended, after three hours, much as it had begun, in a quiet, low-key fashion.

After all this, I returned directly to the embassy for lunch, feeling quite exhausted. We ate a hearty and reviving meal, though Dr Easton seemed alarmed when I asked him to taste my food before I would risk eating it myself! We then set about identifying and locating the individuals on the list supplied by London. In Baghdad the names had been transliterated into Arabic, and when they were returned to us they had been crudely transliterated back into English, rendering many of them incomprehensible. The greatest problems arose when there were several people with the same British surname. All this required patient detective work by both sides late into the night. The most difficult cases of all proved to be those of Alex Duncan and his younger brother, for they were believed to be in Kuwait but the embassy had no idea exactly where they were. Other methods having failed, I asked the BBC World Service to make a specific announcement inviting them to go to a named hotel in Kuwait, where we would arrange for a car to bring them up to us in Baghdad. We soon got the reply from the hotel that they had indeed presented themselves, and were now waiting for the car to arrive. It later emerged that they had been hiding with their father Bruce since the Iraqi invasion of Kuwait. Their case was still fated to end in tragedy. They were being driven through the night to Baghdad when their car crashed into another at one of the main crossroads *en route*. Alex was killed, and his brother was badly injured. The drivers of both cars were also killed, which makes it seem very improbable, as was suggested by some British, that this could have been deliberately arranged by the Iraqis. The younger brother was immediately rushed back to hospital in Kuwait and I received a message from Saddam Hussein informing me that, as soon as the boy was fit to travel, he would be flown back to England.

Within a day or so, we had identified all those on our list and they were gathered together from all over Iraq into our hotel in Baghdad. Robert Vaudry was hardly ever off the telephone, trying to arrange a plane to take us back home. Richard Branson came to the rescue, by providing a Boeing 747 to fly us all back to Gatwick. I had already accepted an offer from him to pay the air fares for the party to come to Baghdad, and the offer of a Virgin Airlines Boeing 747 solved our remaining transport problems.

Our return still proved to be far from straightforward. Richard Branson sent me a message from London to say that he had thought that he had received all the necessary papers and permits, but he had now been told that he required United Nations approval before the plane could take off. Under UN Resolution 670, no plane could fly in or out of Baghdad without the permission of the UN Sanctions Committee. Richard had so far found no way of resolving this so could I intervene? Inevitably, we learned this at a time when New York would be in the small hours of the morning, and the members of this committee would be fast asleep. I then got a message through directly to the secretary-general of the United Nations asking him to intervene personally to grant this permission, which he speedily did. However, the delay meant that the plane arrived in the dark, and we could not leave until nearly midnight.

When the plane arrived, Richard Branson himself was on board and the lower deck of the plane had been divided up into three sections, each of which contained a fully equipped medical centre, staffed with nurses and doctors. A splendid lady by the name of Dr Jenny Sykes, from Mondiale Assistance, was in charge of this fearsomely effective provision. The plane layout was arranged so as to ensure that everyone returning from a period of detention would be seated in, or within reach of, one of the medical facilities. The rest of us went on to the upper deck where we were also able to accommodate some of the press. Once the plane had taken off the celebrations began. Supplies of champagne had been put on board by Richard Branson, large amounts were consumed and toast after toast was drunk. We were ultimately responsible for getting home over a hundred British citizens. The trip had been a risk worth taking.

The only difficulty we encountered occurred when the Iraqi authorities decided that the papers of one of the journalists in our party, Adrian Lithgow of the *Mail on Sunday*, were not in order. After the rest of us had embarked, Robert Vaudry was still trying to convince the armed Iraqi guards to let him travel, and even Mr Lithgow's normally urbane and self-assured attitude was wearing rather thin. He had not intended to offer himself as a replacement hostage, after all. In the end, Robert bravely dragged him on board, despite the opposition of a group of men with rifles. I am sure that Adrian enjoyed his champagne more than most.

As we drew near to Gatwick, both the excitement and the tension began to increase. We landed some time after four in the morning to find the families of all our patients waiting in a state of intense excitement to greet the freed passengers, some of whom had to be carried off the plane. One was still suffering acutely from a heart problem, and was rushed off to an intensive-care ward. I had the opportunity of saying just a few brief words of thanks to everybody concerned in the operation. I recall trying to persuade Richard Branson to accept our gratitude, but he insisted on remaining out of sight. Then in the background, hiding away, I spotted Mark Lennox-Boyd, the most junior Under-Secretary of State at the

Foreign Office, who had been sent down to the airport to represent the government. I heard later that no Foreign Office Minister had been prepared to come, in the light of the criticisms made against us, and Mark had needed to be ordered to do so by his superiors. I then quietly slipped away from this emotional atmosphere to a small private plane which I had hired and flew to Berlin, where I was billed to give a lecture at a conference on European economic affairs. The overwhelming view seemed to be that our five-day operation had proved well worth while.

In the wake of our trip, Jeffrey Easton, together with Dr Stuart Turner from the Middlesex School of Medicine, set about studying the effects of the entire episode upon those who had returned from the Gulf with us. They also undertook a broader examination of the effects of the conflict on others who had been directly involved. In their conclusions, they recommended the establishment of a Traumatic Stress Unit here in the United Kingdom. I took up these proposals directly with the Prime Minister, John Major. In October 1991, the government accordingly came forward with a proposal to establish a Post-Traumatic Stress Disorder Unit at the Maudsley Hospital in London. The two doctors warned me immediately that, although this was a welcome step forward, it would take time to set up such a department from scratch at the Maudsley. What was being proposed failed to provide an adequate response to the pressing psychological needs of the affected individuals, some of whom were deeply traumatised. They would be better treated, at least until the Maudsley Unit was properly up and running, at the Middlesex Hospital, which was already a well-established centre of excellence in this field.

I wrote to John Major again on 28 October, informing him that this was the considered view of my team. This point was accepted, and as a result I was able to announce on Thursday 14 November that the government had agreed to make extra transitional funds available to the Middlesex, in the form of a special 'national contract', made directly between the Department of Health and the Local Health Authority. This enabled the Middlesex to continue treating former Gulf hostages, as well as to take on more patients, while the Maudsley unit was being established. This very rapid positive response was in complete contrast to the hostility of the previous government, and was an example of the Major administration at its best, compassionate and responsive to the needs of its citizens, even if a degree of external stimulus was sometimes required to prod it into action.

In December 1993, I paid a further visit to Baghdad for discussions with President Saddam Hussein, about three British citizens who had been awarded heavy prison sentences for offences allegedly committed in Iraq. They had all made appeals but these had been rejected. Michael Wainwright, aged forty-two, had been sentenced on 18 August 1992 to ten years' imprisonment. He was arrested in Mosul, northern Iraq, in April 1992 while travelling overland on his bicycle to Australia (though he was never able to explain to me how he proposed to cycle across from Singapore to Darwin!). He claimed that he had been given a visa to enter Iraq from Turkey, but the Iraqis declared that it was not valid. Paul Ride, aged thirty-three, was a senior chef for a catering firm in Kuwait, who had also been tried for spying on 18 August 1992, and had been sentenced to seven years' imprisonment. He claimed that he was following signs to the UN observer mission camp in Kuwait, when he was arrested at an Iraqi checkpoint on the way. Simon Dunn, aged twenty-three, whose parents lived in Dubai, had been arrested in May 1993 at another Iraqi checkpoint, together with a German national, Kai Sondermann. They claimed to have been unaware that they had strayed over the border between Iraq and Kuwait, but were still sentenced to eight years each in jail.

The British government had requested eight other countries to intervene on its behalf, but they had not been successful. In addition, the United Nations secretary-general, Dr Boutros Boutros-Ghali, had several times pressed for the release of the men. The reply had always been that the prisoners would not be liberated unless the United Kingdom freed Iraqi assets, which had been frozen upon the invasion of Kuwait and, at the time of writing, remain substantially impounded. UN Resolution 778 forbade any government to make a bilateral deal with Iraq in an instance such as this and, in any case, the British government was still following the Americans in taking a very hard line against Iraq. However, three Swedish prisoners had been released on 22 September after the King of Sweden had sent a personal letter to Saddam Hussein, a Moroccan had been freed on 30 September and an American on 15 November.

I had received a letter from Simon Dunn's parents, asking me to intervene on behalf of the three men, and a similar call came from a non-political group by the name of Prisoners Abroad. I told them that, if I was asked to go again to Baghdad, I would certainly do so. To my surprise, the government agreed on this occasion that I should go – albeit, as before, without any official presence accompanying me. Simon Dunn and Paul Ride had been allowed to give a press conference in Baghdad on 30 September, and a week later sent a joint letter to their families, in which they suggested that a high-level delegation of three, led by myself, should visit Baghdad to negotiate for their release. They soon claimed to have received indications, in the wake of their television appearance, that their release was now a formality, so long as diplomatic protocol was observed, and a suitable group came to collect them.

President Saddam Hussein agreed to another visit by myself, and my office once again made the necessary arrangements. I travelled by Royal Jordanian Airways to Amman, taking with me both Jeffrey Easton and Nicholas Edgar, the new head of my private office. A government helicopter flew us to the Iraqi border, where three of Saddam Hussein's Chevrolets were waiting to collect us. There followed a drive of some 350 miles down to Baghdad, on a splendid motorway. I was astonished at how well it was built, and the excellent condition in which it was maintained. This impression of recovery was reinforced when we drove around Baghdad, where the only remaining war damage we could find was to one bridge over the river. Everything else had been rebuilt. It seemed that, although the Iraqis had, in the past, relied upon foreign firms to carry out most of their structural needs, sanctions had forced them to develop their own construction sector, with considerable success.

On arrival in Baghdad, we had dinner with Tariq Aziz and his staff. In a wide-ranging discussion, they complained bitterly that, each time they had complied with United Nations resolutions, the goal posts had then been moved, so as to keep the Iraqi government in the wrong. In particular, Tariq Aziz strongly disagreed with the proposal to put the Iraqi assets frozen abroad into a central account to be administered by the United Nations, not least because the first money given up in this way had been eaten up by the United Nations' administration costs. He claimed that Iraq was distributing its food supplies correctly, and that its rationing and distribution systems had been praised by the UN observers. What the Iraqis most needed, apart from medicines, were spare parts for water-purifying plants, electricity generators and sewerage plants. Iraq was much criticised at the time for its policy towards the Marsh Arabs, and Aziz claimed that northern and central Iraq had actually benefited from the drainage of part of the marshes, as had the Marsh Arabs themselves. Over a million Marsh Arabs had been living happily in Baghdad since the 1950s, enjoying the normal facilities of the capital. He also reminded me that the Iraqi government regarded the Marshes, above all, as the base for rebels supporting Iran, and that any country would want to crack down on rebels of this kind. Aziz accepted the recent resolution partially relaxing the oil embargo, but no one had told them that the Iraqis would have to wait six months before it could be effective. This delay was a result of American pressure, again with British support. The undertone was that if the Americans and British were going to alter the guidelines whenever Iraq agreed to a resolution, then the Iraqis would sooner or later come to the conclusion that there was no point in signing up to any of them.

The Americans have never forgiven themselves for not getting rid of Saddam Hussein in the Gulf War. In the years since then he has been sustained by his formidable political skills, the brutal methods he has used to reinforce his position, and, like Nasser, to some extent by the will of his people. The British, French and Israelis sought to destroy Nasser at Suez, but he remained President of Egypt, with the overwhelming support of his people, until his death fifteen years or so later. One of the repeated lessons of history is that even the most questionable regime can sustain itself if it can rally the people behind its cause, and no cause is more compelling to the Arab masses than loathing of the West in general, and the United States in particular.

The next morning I was taken to see Saddam Hussein and, this time, he was in civilian clothes. There was a complete absence of press and photographers. 'You can take these three men back to England with you,' he began. 'They have been rightly treated as criminals because we believed that they had deliberately come into Iraq to cause damage, but I now recognise that this is not the case. I will send them round to your guest-house at nine o'clock in the morning. You cannot withstand that long car drive again. Tomorrow I will provide you with my own helicopter to fly you up to the border. It will easily take the three prisoners, as well as you and your staff.'

We then spent the rest of our two-hour meeting discussing the general international situation. 'You and Herr Brandt', he added, 'were the only people who ever told me the truth. Now Brandt is dead and you are the only one remaining.' He wanted to know about American policy and how it was likely to develop, and about what would now happen to Russia, following the collapse of the communist regime in the USSR. He was evidently fascinated by economic and political developments in the Far East, in particular the industrial strides being made in China, as well as those in South-East Asia. Knowing of my regular travels in that part of the world, he pressed me very hard on how I saw matters developing. He was also intrigued by European affairs. He remained calm and agreeable throughout, until the last moments of our talk, when he erupted in the same way Tariq Aziz had the night before, denouncing the United Nations and accusing it of being totally dominated by the Americans and the British, who had constantly failed to acknowledge both the Iraqi compliance with their demands and the favourable reports of the various international moni-toring committees sent to Baghdad.

Meanwhile Dr Easton had been having discussions with doctors, medical administrators and advisers in the city. They revealed a dreadful state of affairs. We put this information to the World Health Organisation upon our return home, and they confirmed the figures and the opinions which we had passed on to them. The evidence showed a substantial increase in the incidence of several illnesses which had been more or less vanquished in the developed industrial world, including cholera, typhoid, rabies, whooping cough, diphtheria and measles. To these were added 50,000 new cases of malaria in the northern provinces. The WHO claimed the Iraquis needed enough money to buy 200 tonnes of insecticide to control malaria, but their funds would not stretch to even 10 tonnes. Health was also being adversely affected by the contaminated water supplies, and 75 per cent of the water tested in Iraq by the WHO had shown serious bacterial contamination. In Basra, a low-lying city with a high water table, sewage was ankle-deep in places because of the lack of structural repairs to the decrepit sanitation system. These facts were seldom allowed to percolate through to the people of the West. I did not believe that this could really be the intended result of Western foreign policy.

My doctor's own investigations showed that the embargo was leading directly to acute shortages of anaesthetics, antibiotics, insulin, cardiac drugs and immunisations, together with a lack of equipment including gloves, syringes and ambulance tyres. There were also problems over the control of stocks. In addition, we were told that there had been a significant increase in the number of low-birth-weight babies since the Gulf War. Mortality under the age of five was said to be up fivefold. In normal times, drug imports into Iraq were £350 million per annum, for a population of 20 million. The target of the Red Cross, which was providing relief, was to invest £750,000. The medical needs could be met only by the release of Iraqi assets abroad, or by the lifting of the oil embargo, both of which could be internationally supervised, but neither of which was forthcoming.

When the three men arrived from prison after breakfast the following morning, I had a quiet talk with them about what had happened. They described the first fortnight of their detention as very rough-going while they were cross-examined, but afterwards the situation had, apparently, improved. They had been put in a hut on their own with a radio on which they could listen to the BBC World Service. Here they were able to cook their meals, and enjoyed as much exercise as they liked in the garden outside. However, I at once sensed a difficult atmosphere among them, and it soon became evident that a bitter feud had developed between the two older men. They had little in common and sharing incarceration had turned them into sworn enemies.

I asked them not to discuss their time in Iraq with anyone on the journey back to the United Kingdom and not to make any statements to anyone from the media, or any other organisation. This they accepted. We were then driven to Saddam Hussein's helicopter. At the border we changed over to the smaller, slower, civilian machine provided by the King of Jordan. I had also told the men that their families had been informed of what was happening and would probably be at the airport at Amman to greet them. I wanted them, first of all, to meet their relatives in a separate room, before we went to the larger hall where the media and the photographers would be.

As we landed I could see that a massive number of people in the waiting crowd were jostling each other precisely outside the rooms at which we were aiming. We had the utmost difficulty in penetrating this crowd to get the men into contact with their families. Their happy reunions were marred only by one of the wives walking across the room waving a piece of notepaper and proclaiming that she was being paid £30,000 by a newspaper for an account of what had been happening to her husband. Meanwhile, the main crowd of press and officials had moved into the hall where I explained in a few words what had happened, and answered some questions. As agreed, the men declined to make any comment. Simon Dunn's parents had arrived from Dubai, and took him back there with them. The rest of us got on the plane for London. The operation had been completed. On this occasion, in contrast to the autumn of 1990, I was delighted to receive personal letters of thanks from both the Prime Minister of the day, John Major, who generously described my trip as 'courageous – and right', and from the Foreign Secretary, Douglas Hurd.

The after-effects of Saddam's invasion of Kuwait are still being felt. Over 600 Kuwaitis taken prisoner by the Iraqis have never been accounted for, and the people of Iraq continue to endure hardships as a result of UN-imposed sanctions. Hundreds of families still grieve for loved ones and survivors still suffer from the physical and psychological scars of the Gulf War. The mystery of 'Gulf War Syndrome' among our troops has never been cleared up satisfactorily, but many lives here in the West seem to have been blighted by it.

The ordinary people of Iraq continue to suffer, too. The so-called 'oil for food' agreement, UNSCR 986, was adopted in April 1995. In the words of the document confirming this Resolution, the Security Council was 'concerned by the serious nutritional and health situation of the Iraqi population, and by the risk of a further deterioration in this situation', and it was 'convinced also of the need for equitable distribution of humanitarian relief to all segments of the Iraqi population'. UNSCR 986 was finally implemented on 10 December 1996, allowing Iraq to export some oil to finance purchases of food and other humanitarian supplies. The first shipment of food was received by Iraq in March 1997 and the first shipment of medicine arrived in May of that year. On 4 June the UN Security Council voted to renew the 'oil for food' agreement for another six months. The US ambassador to the UN, Bill Richardson, clearly stated that Washington supported renewing the Resolution, despite being 'not entirely satisfied with the implementation so far by the Iraqis'. Richardson also said that 'the main objective here is the humanitarian needs of the Iraqi people . . . The Iraqi government doesn't seem to be concerned with that, they seem to be concerned with playing political games.' Consequently, UNSCR 1111, 'a temporary measure to continue to provide for the humanitarian needs of the Iraqi people until the fulfilment by Iraq of the relevant Security Council resolutions', was adopted.

On 12 September 1997, the UN Security Council adopted yet another Resolution, UNSCR 1129, which extended for one month a 5 September deadline, by which Iraq was supposed to have exported $1 billion worth of oil. By the time of the deadline, Iraq had exported only about $600 million worth. Bill Richardson said that, by limiting its sales in this fashion, Baghdad had 'made a callous decision to put at risk the wellbeing of its people in order to seek to score propaganda points . . . The Iraqi government, by refusing to sell oil, is using the Iraqi people as a pawn to pursue political ends at odds with those of the international community.' This shadow-boxing between the Americans and the Iraqi government looks set to run and run for a long time yet.

Personally, I have never been comfortable with the idea that any one group of countries should seek to isolate others economically or politically in order to try and change their way of doing things. The best hope of encouraging positive progress lies in widening contacts of all kinds and then influencing those in power in the direction of peaceful change. If this fails, as proved to be the case in South Africa by the 1980s, the use of sanctions may well be a regrettable necessity. It is important to remember, though, that the true victims of sanctions are rarely the political class. Sanctions generally punish the weak, the sick, the elderly, the poor and the vulnerable. In Iraq, I have seen the consequences with my own eyes, and it is scarcely to be on the side of 'appeasement' to be moved by the plight of decent, humble people who are forced to cling to life and dignity by a thread, because of the arrogance and obduracy of politicians whom they can never hope to influence, either at home or abroad.

This was changed by the intervention of the secretary-general of the United Nations, Kofi Annan, in February 1998. In the previous November the Security Council, at its meeting in New York, had passed another Resolution, despite the misgivings of France, Russia and China, which condemned 'the continued violations by Iraq of its obligations under the relevant resolutions' and expressed 'the firm intention to take further measures as may be required . . .' Hearing that Tariq Aziz, the Iraqi Deputy Prime Minister, was in New York, I telephoned him and asked for an explanation of what was going on. He told me that the Security Council would not allow him to make a statement to it explaining Iraq's position. This, I thought, was intolerable. I then telephoned the secretary-general, who rang me back giving me a summary of the position, although he was quite unable to provide a justification for the Council's refusal to hear a declaration from Iraq. I urged him to do everything possible to remedy this. I was immensely glad, therefore, when he decided to pay a visit himself to Baghdad, despite the doubts of the American Secretary of State. There he succeeded, through Tariq Aziz, in formulating an agreement with Saddam Hussein, which was then implemented. I looked on this as a possible means of stabilising the situation and freeing the people of Iraq from the damaging impact on their health, and their future, as a result of nearly ten years of sanctions.

In November 1992, I was present at Buckingham Palace for the dinner which was being given by the Queen for the heads of government and their Foreign Secretaries who were attending a meeting of the Seven. Both President Bush and his Secretary of State, James Baker, were present. I was chatting to a group of guests when my instinct, which has often stood me in good stead, made me turn around. I found the Queen looking at me while she was talking to Baker. 'We were just talking about Saddam Hussein and the Gulf War,' she explained, 'and of course you went over to see Saddam Hussein, didn't you?'

'Yes, Ma'am,' I replied, 'I secured the release of over a hundred British who were being kept in Iraq.'

'Yes, but you also talked to him, didn't you, about the war?'

'Yes, Ma'am,' I said. 'I told him that, in his own interest, he should withdraw from Kuwait, failing which he would precipitate a major war with the United States and other Western powers which would drive him out of Kuwait and greatly damage Iraq.' Turning to Baker, I added, 'That is what you should have done. You should have gone to Baghdad for talks with him and brought home to him exactly what would happen.'

'Certainly not,' said Baker. 'I invited him to Washington several times, but he never came.'

'That is not the right way to have gone about it,' I said. 'You are the major power. You can afford to go to him to make him realise the immense danger that he was in and get him out of Kuwait as quickly as possible. That is what I did. I was absolutely blunt with him,' I went on, 'and I told him the situation. But nobody else went and told him this.'

At this point, the Queen intervened again, saying to me, 'But he couldn't get to Baghdad, like you could.'

'Why not, Ma'am? I went to Baghdad,' I said.

'I know you could,' responded the Queen, 'but you're expendable now.'

'Ugh,' spat out Baker, by this time all too obviously infuriated, and strode off to the other end of the room.

The next occasion when I was presented to the Queen was at a reception given by a visiting head of state. I bowed and shook hands. 'You see, Ma'am,' I said to Her Majesty before moving on to Prince Philip, 'I am still expendable!'

Chapter 24

BEYOND WESTMINSTER

1979—1997

I was appointed once again as captain of the British Admiral's Cup ocean racing team in 1979. This time I was sailing the fifth *Morning Cloud*. On the evening of Sunday 5 August 1979, I read the lesson at a special service held in Holy Trinity Church, Cowes, for the sailors taking part in Cowes Week. My text invoked the maritime equivalent of hellfire and brimestone, 'And there arose a great storm of wind, and the waves beat into the ship so that it was now full.' Little did I imagine that many of us would experience this horror for ourselves only ten days later.

The Fastnet Race was first sailed in 1925 and, thereafter, every second year. Until the 28th Race, it was remarkably free from damage to boats and loss of life. That all changed in August 1979. Of the 316 boats that crossed the starting line at Cowes to sail round the Fastnet Rock lighthouse off southern Ireland, only 128 finished the race at Plymouth. One hundred and thirty-six crew members had to be rescued, and fifteen lives were lost. It was not until two days into the race that we learned, from the evening weather forecast, that the wind would go beyond gale force later that night 13–14 August. In the small hours of 14 August, *Morning Cloud* was to encounter gusts of Force 11, well over 60 knots of wind. Very few of the 3,000 crewmen in the Irish Channel that night had ever experienced anything like it before and all kinds of inadequacies were exposed, in the design of many of the boats and in their emergency equipment and charts.

As captain of the team, I had tried to ensure that every crew had done everything possible to prepare for the race, not only in their equipment and their knowledge of the course, but also through a detailed preparatory study of the weather conditions which were developing. When we left the starting line, conditions were reasonable with a fair wind, but around the Needles it began to blow. We knew from the forecast that, as we approached the Rock, we were likely to face still heavier pressures, all from the north-west. This proved to be the case. It became impossible for us on *Morning Cloud* to keep up any sort of spinnaker and we had speedily to reduce our sail area. We rounded the Fastnet Rock successfully and, as we began to head for home, it seemed as though the wind was easing slightly, so what happened then was unexpected. A second gale came up from the south-west, and of this we had had no warning. The clash of the two winds produced cross-seas of immense force and soaring height. With our navigator I decided that we should head to the west of the Scillys as a turning point, rather than directly at them. We both felt acutely our responsibility for the safety of everyone on board.

On that fateful night, we had two helmsmen and two crewmen on deck, all harnessed to the boat. By 4 a.m., the sea was a raging inferno. Huge waves topped with long, rising rollers were crashing into us and, suddenly, one of them hit *Morning Cloud* astern, picking her right up. One helmsman was thrown against the wheel, which buckled, and then bounced on to a stanchion, which also bent with the force of the impact. The other helmsman crashed against the compass, which promptly shot off into the foaming sea. We took resounding blows from both sea and wind and were knocked on to our side. I was down below with the navigator at the time, working out how best to reach Plymouth, and we were hurled on to the starboard side of the boat. My right leg was badly injured. The navigator was to some extent cushioned on top of me. The boat then righted itself after what seemed an age, but was really only a few seconds.

Although we were all badly shaken, once we got the lights back on we quickly established that no permanent or grievous damage had been done. The crew were superb and, without any fear of being swept overboard, they immediately set about getting the boat moving again, a task made supremely difficult by the damage done to the large steering wheel. Owen Parker, the number two of the crew, was on the wheel and, with immense strength, handled it manfully. I gave the order that we should ease up so as to avoid any further knock-downs, which could prove even more damaging. This enabled us to get completely sorted out, but because of my leg I found it physically difficult to get right up on deck myself. No doubt we could have made it home more quickly, if I had given orders to tighten sails earlier. After the wind had dropped somewhat, it was a smooth run into port but with little chance of making up lost time.

As the sea began to calm later that afternoon, we were intrigued to hear dramatic radio reports about how *Morning Cloud* was in difficulties. It was said that we had lost our rudder and were being towed into both Cork and Falmouth, apparently at the same time. I knew that it was only thanks to a strong boat and a tough crew that I had survived seas which had robbed others of their lives. On arrival at Plymouth we found a mass of deeply anxious relatives and a large gathering of the press, radio and television. We also learned that the first boat home belonged to the American media owner, Ted Turner, who had sailed many times at Cowes and in the Fastnet Races. His sixty-one-foot boat *Tenacious* was too large for the American Admirals' Cup team. While he was tying the boat up, the press and the rest of the media rushed around to get his reaction to the events at sea. 'What did you do in the storm?' they asked. 'What was it like?' 'Storm?' he replied. 'I didn't notice any storm.' This remark caused much bitterness among the seafaring community, and it was many years before he raced again on the Solent.

Apparently the reports which had been put out on radio, television and the press had vividly described the scenes offshore, and had also announced an immense loss of boats and of life with them. It had been reported in the United States, and repeated at home, that *Morning Cloud*, my crew and I had all perished together. We were able to give them more accurate information. I told the waiting press that 'It was the worst experience I have ever had . . . we were fighting massive seas . . . it was very frightening – the sort of thing you would never want to experience again.' Then I was rushed off to the naval hospital for treatment. The blow to my leg troubled me seriously for some time afterwards, and the marks on it remain to this day.

As the full story emerged, we learned of children orphaned and of many acts of tremendous heroism. Some helicopter rescue crews spent as much as eight hours in the air, and the Falmouth lifeboat *Elizabeth Ann* was at sea for over forty-three hours. The memorial service held in Plymouth a few days later was the most moving aspect of the sea I ever experienced, as together we sang:

> Eternal Father, strong to save . . .
> O hear us when we cry to Thee
> For those in peril on the sea.

Our hearts bled for our colleagues who had crewed with us or sailed against us. At the same time, we were thankful that, despite everything, we had still survived. The report into the 1979 Fastnet Race was a sobering read. It raised questions about the construction of boats, the robustness of safety harnesses and the quality of life rafts, and suggested that emergency engines might be made mandatory. It also questioned whether it was wise to have over 300 vessels involved in such a race, and whether it was practicable for even the best-manned vessels to monitor outside radio channels for possible storm warnings on a regular basis. All of us who took part knew that lives might have been saved by more accurate, and more timely, information about the gathering storm. I was clear in my own mind, however, that these events should not spell the end of my boats and my own sailing career. Fortunately, my crew agreed with me.

The following year, 1980, *Morning Cloud* headed the Class I division in the Cowes–Dinard–St Malo race in July, and we continued to pick up trophies, including the Queen's Cup, the Beverley Cooper Challenge Cup and the Harold Edwards Cup. We had another good year in 1982, performing well in the Morgan Cup Race in June and again heading the Class I category in the Cowes–Dinard–St Malo Race at the beginning of July. We achieved a similar result in the Royal Thames Yacht Club Regatta later that month. I sailed until 1986, by which time I was seventy, and that year I took part in Cowes Week for the last time. Shortly afterwards, I sold the fifth *Morning Cloud*. Together with my marvellous crews, I had won two of the most coveted trophies in sailing, the Sydney–Hobart Race and the Admiral's Cup, with the British team. I never had any doubt that my sailing was beneficial, both for my physical health and for my sanity. I would not have missed it for the world. This was not the view of a lady who wrote to me asking if I did not realise that I was elected and paid to work twenty-four hours a day, seven days a week, fifty-two weeks a year, not to waste my time sailing. I replied that those MPs who did that drove themselves into the ground, which made their constituents suffer in turn. She allowed me to continue sailing.

My earliest experience of conducting in public came from conducting a mixed-voice choir in the Thanet and Folkestone competitive musical festivals. We were successful in both. I was aged fifteen. At Oxford I organised and conducted a mixed choir and orchestra to perform in the Balliol Concerts. At the same time I created the town carol concerts at Broadstairs where I conducted them for forty years, with the exception of the war years, until they pulled down the only hall where we could hold them. Some enthusiasts wanted to maintain the tradition and move the concerts into a local church, but the other organisers shared my own view that, by having it in a particular church, we would run the risk of alienating people from other faiths by giving the impression of supporting only one specific aspect of the Christian faith. Various musically minded people in my constituency had heard about the Broadstairs concerts and prevailed upon me to transfer the tradition to Bexley. I agreed, on the understanding that all the proceeds would go to charity, as they always had done at Broadstairs, and that it be open to everybody. In the early 1980s we moved to a newly built hall at Crook Log in Bexleyheath accommodating 1,500 people, and we have been going strong ever since. Over the years we have managed to build up a well-trained choir and a substantial orchestra from those at the top of local schools and their predecessors returning home for Christmas. We have also had a string of celebrities come down to make the appeal including, in recent years, Viscount Tonypandy (the former George Thomas), Frank Muir, Terry Waite, Bob Holness, Sir Robin Day, Sebastian Coe and Alastair Stewart.

I have also continued my association with the EC Youth Orchestra. After the huge success of the orchestra's opening tours in 1978, I redoubled my efforts to get Herbert von Karajan on board (see p. 560). When I contacted him again, even though I could demonstrate that the ECYO was properly up and running, he would still not agree to conduct them: 'But you may bring them to Salzburg to play, and I will hear for myself what they can do.' We already planned to tour again in the summer of 1979, and the orchestra were delighted with this opportunity to play at one of Europe's most prestigious festivals. The orchestra also appeared live on television for the first time during that tour, and were watched by an estimated 16 million people in a broadcast on the German ZDF channel. Herbert von Karajan was as good as his word and, having heard the ECYO play at the 1979 Salzburg Festival, he said that I could bring them back in 1980 and, this time, he would conduct them himself. When this was all agreed and arranged, I sent him the programme that we were playing at the other concerts. He rejected it all. He conducted Beethoven's Violin Concerto with Anne-Sophie Mutter and then Mozart's 'Jupiter' Symphony. The orchestra could not believe their good fortune.

On 22 July 1980, the third ECYO assembled for rehearsal, in the same magnificent resort as the previous year, Courchevel in the Haute Savoie. Typically, Karajan arrived by helicopter, flying down the slope of the mountain. Both he and his young protégée on the violin were phenomenal during that first rehearsal. At the final rehearsal in Salzburg, after he had done his two pieces, von Karajan asked me to hold the orchestra there until after the audience had left, as there were one or two more things he wanted to do. First of all, he asked the leader of the second violins to leave his seat for a moment. He then sat down in his place and explained, 'When I come on to the platform, you stand. We will now rehearse that.' So he gave the chair back to the violinist. Then he said, 'I am in. Stand. No, no, no. You mustn't behave like droopy, half-dead people. I said "Stand" and that is what we will now rehearse again.' He repeated this three times before they got it right. Finally he said, 'When we are finished, it is the audience's job to applaud. You don't applaud yourselves, and you don't applaud me. It is the job of the audience to do that, do you understand?' At the public performance that night in Salzburg, all went well. The musicians stood up on cue at the beginning of each half, looking very smart and alert. Then, as von Karajan came on for his fifth ovation after the Mozart, a young cellist began stamping his feet as he went past, just as Claudio Abbado encouraged them to do. As Herbert von Karajan got level with him, his elbow shot right into this player's ribs. He stopped stamping his feet.

On the 1980 tour, I was again a guest conductor, this time leading the orchestra in the overture to Mozart's opera *The Magic Flute*. After a performance in the Abbey of Fontevrault on 16 August, a critic in *France-Soir* wrote a bilious review, accusing me of 'massacring Mozart'. Gian Carlo Menotti, however, the renowned Italian-American composer, particularly of opera, congratulated me personally on a 'truly Mozartian performance of the overture', and the audience seemed to enjoy themselves. Three evenings later in Lucerne, the orchestra gave its first performance outside the European Community, which we introduced with both the Swiss and European anthems. Introducing the orchestra and the programme, I described what a successful effort at integration the orchestra represented, 'in which the Germans have begun to understand the Dutch, the Irish the Italians. It is also said, although not confirmed, that the English are beginning to understand the French'.

Since those early days, I have watched as the orchestra has gone from strength to strength. Nowadays, young people from fifteen different lands are taking part, and the musical standards are higher than ever. Most of the major musicians now clamour to perform with the orchestra, including such fine conductors as Colin Davis and Bernard Haitink. No allowance whatsoever has to be made for the youth of the players, and the orchestra's performances at the London Proms are now well established as a regular highlight of the season. Their recordings, particularly of works by Mahler and Bruckner, are a permanent testament to the power of music to unite people in a powerful tribute *an die Freude*.

My brother John remarried on 13 December 1958. I was present again, and his second union, with Muriel, provided him with over two decades of happiness. John had been unwell for some time, however, when he was taken into the Brompton Hospital in London on 28 May 1979 for an open-heart operation, which took place on 14 June. I visited him and he seemed to make a full recovery, returning home in July. Then, on 8 October 1982, Muriel telephoned to tell me that he had collapsed at home and been rushed to hospital, apparently suffering again from an affliction of his chest. The following day, Muriel told me that he had died on admission. John had been the only close member of our family remaining for me, the only one who had experienced and known the whole story. His loss was devastating. He could never be replaced.

Harold Macmillan celebrated his ninetieth birthday on 10 February 1984. The previous autumn, I had told him that, as one of his oldest and most loyal supporters, I would like to celebrate it with a party at my home. It could be either a drinks party for forty or a dinner party for eight, the maximum number I could seat around my oval table.

'Oh, dear boy, I don't want a large drinks party,' he responded. 'Let's just have dinner together.'

'Very well,' I replied, 'but whom would you like me to invite? Do you want to meet the up-and-coming generation, or your old friends?'

'Just the old cronies,' replied Macmillan. 'Let's relax and enjoy ourselves.'

The dinner was arranged for Tuesday 25 February 1984 and a group of highly distinguished former colleagues, all peers, accepted my invitation – Aldington, Barber, Hailsham, Harlech, Home and Soames. Macmillan always liked simple, straightforward food, and often wanted it cold. On this occasion he said he would be happy with smoked salmon, roast lamb and vegetables, followed by a dessert. There was then the question of wine, which he much enjoyed and about which he knew a great deal. I went down to the small wine cellar in my home and, among some bottles with which I had been presented and never touched, I found a magnum of Château Margaux 1884. I checked the year and found that it was good, but knew that this would be a risky operation if it had not stood the test of time. So I rang up Sir Charles Forte at Grosvenor House and asked his advice. 'What time is the dinner?' he asked. I told him eight o'clock. 'I will have my top man down at your place at six o'clock,' he said. 'He will open it up for you, check everything is all right, pour it into the decanter and leave it ready to drink at half-past eight. Give him the chance to taste it.' I expressed my gratitude.

At exactly six o'clock, the chief wine waiter from the Café Royal arrived. I took him down to the cellar where he stripped off his jacket, donned his white coat, opened his bag, put his tools on the table and asked for the bottle. 'This should be very good,' he ventured, holding it up to the light. He gently opened it, and poured it into the decanters. He then tipped a little into a glass, sniffed it and said, 'Perfect.' Then, bearing in mind what I had been told, I asked him, 'Ought you not to drink a little to make sure?' 'Why yes, of course,' he said, and this confirmed his enthusiasm. 'I am slightly worried,' I told him, 'because the guests coming to dinner are healthy drinkers. They will get through two bottles of Chablis with the smoked salmon and I am afraid they will run out of this with the lamb.'

'All right then,' he replied, 'let's give them a bottle of something to start the lamb with and then you can bring the real stuff out for him. What have you got?' I showed him a bottle of Château Lafite 1953. 'This is splendid also,' he said and, having treated that bottle in the same way, he decanted it and said how satisfied he was with it. Finally, moving the decanters up to the kitchen, he bade me farewell.

My colleagues arrived together on time and went upstairs to the drawing room. I waited at the front door for Macmillan, and saw that television and press cameramen and journalists were all bunched up together on the pavement, although we had given the dinner no publicity. He stepped slowly out of his car wearing a magnificent black cape over his dinner jacket. He moved straight up towards me and I greeted him. 'You must turn around and be photographed,' I said, knowing full well that this was precisely what he wanted. He did so, and smiled brightly at them. I had asked them not to throw questions at him, but one interviewer could not help asking him, 'What title are you going to take now that you have been created a peer?'

'I can't tell you that. I don't know,' replied Macmillan. 'I don't even know on which side of the Lords I am going to sit,' he concluded, provoking both a gasp and a laugh. At this point, I thought that I had better get him upstairs, where I sat him down with a large glass of champagne. We were all so pleased to have him there. Having settled in, he looked at Quintin Hailsham, who was still the Lord Chancellor in Mrs Thatcher's Government, and said brusquely, 'She's going to sack you.'

Quintin stiffened and looked horrified.

'I said she's going to sack you,' repeated Harold.

'No, she is not,' replied Quintin firmly.

'How do you know?' asked Macmillan.

'Because I am making sure I'm strong enough to stop her,' said Quintin. We cheered.

Dinner went well, and after we had drunk the bottle of Lafite, Macmillan commented, 'That was very good.'

'I must apologise,' I said. 'It is the only bottle I had, but I have some other claret here that we can finish off with.' I then poured out the aged Margaux.

Harold picked it up. 'But this is superb,' he said. 'I cannot remember when I last had anything as good as this.'

'It ought to be good,' I replied, 'it's ten years older than you are. So let's drink your health and enjoy it.' It was an unforgettable evening.

It was not until 1985 that I first moved into a house of my own that I could call home. I had long been looking for a house outside London for weekends and the holidays when the House of Commons is not sitting. Originally I had thought of buying one in my own family town of Broadstairs, but when my brother died, my ties with the Kent coast more or less died with him. The next obvious choice was on the Isle of Wight, the centre of so much English yacht racing. 'We shall never come to lunch on a Sunday if we have to cross the water to the Isle of Wight in any sort of weather!' said my friends, but even this did not discourage me. I assured them that I would have a launch to take them across, and it would be an experience for them. It was only when I went to stay on the island for four or five days to recover from the 1983 General Election that I realised what it is like when we sailors are not there on a Saturday and Sunday: it can be as dead as a dodo.

I then started to search along the south coast opposite the Isle of Wight, but I learned that the number of suitable houses within twenty or thirty miles of the sea was few, and they were very difficult to obtain. Furthermore, our beaches and sands had not really become popular for residential purposes until the late Victorian and early Edwardian eras, and the architecture of that period has no interest for me. Then Robert Key, the Member of Parliament for Salisbury and my parliamentary private secretary at the time, telephoned to tell me that a charming house had become available in his constituency, because its occupant had died at the age of ninety-four, and that I ought to go down and see it the next day. When I first saw Arundells, in the Cathedral Close at Salisbury, it was love at first sight.

Arundells is primarily a thirteenth-century house built during the construction of the Cathedral and having its origin as a medieval canonry. As a home for a canon of the Cathedral, it was probably first used by Henry of Blunston, Archdeacon of Dorset, who died in 1316. The resident canon was deprived of the house in 1562 for practising magic. After that the house was leased by the Chapter to secular tenants. The house name is derived from the Arundel family, who were the tenants from 1752 to 1803. In the early nineteenth century it housed, successively, two small schools, and considerable Victorian additions were made. The house was returned to the Cathedral in 1921 for another canon who died there in 1964, at the age of ninety-eight. In the first half of the twentieth century there was a period of decay. After the canon's death, demolition was considered, but the house was renovated in its entirety after the lease was purchased by Mr and Mrs Robert Hawkings. As well as reorganising and modernising the interior, they removed all the Victorian accretions, leaving the house consisting primarily of thirteenth- and seventeenth-century structures. This meant the removal of the Victorian ballroom, leaving a spacious terrace on the secluded back of the house. The Hawkings lived in the house until 1974, when the lease was taken up by Mrs Margaret Booth-Jones, my immediate predecessor.

Arundells is one of the few houses in the Close which is well set back from the narrow road surrounding most of the lawns. The very sight of the balanced Queen Anne stone front as I first looked through the railings of the wrought-iron gates set my heart beating faster. Standing on the steps up to the front door I found that I had an ideal view of the Cathedral, looking at it from a north-westerly angle. The main windows in the front bedrooms take full advantage of this. Salisbury Cathedral is considered by many to be the loveliest in Europe, and its spire the most elegant. Commemorated by Constable in his paintings, the spire was also the highest in Europe until Ulm's was built. The Cathedral has two great virtues. It remains as it was built during the thirteenth and fourteenth centuries, without appendages or other disfigurements, and it is set in a spacious close of well-mown lawns which enable one to see the entire structure to full advantage from a decent perspective, without interruption from other edifices. Around the lawns are residential buildings constructed with a variety of styles in different ages, but all deferring to the grandeur of the Cathedral itself.

When I demonstrated the commanding view of the Cathedral to Roy and Jennifer Jenkins, Roy said, 'Ted, it must be one of the ten finest views in Britain.' I could not help responding, 'Oh really. Which do you think are the other nine?' Looking out from the back of the house there is a splendid vista of trees and shrubs with a lawn extending down to the River Avon, which is joined there by its tributary, the Nadder, and then flows on into the English Channel. Beyond the river lie the water meadows where cows may safely graze, and on which nothing may ever be built. Each summer the swans show a friendly interest as they proudly swim upstream followed by cygnets, and ducks walk down the lawn followed by crowds of ducklings.

On my first visit it was evident that the house would need to be completely refurbished from top to bottom. It was more than twenty years since the reconstruction and redecoration of 1964. Moreover, my insurance company insisted that the house be completely rewired electrically and a new heating installation be fitted. After much thought and discussion it was decided that, on economic grounds, oil heating was preferable. The first step was to engage a new interior designer. Jo Pattrick, who had been responsible for the interior decoration of my apartment in Albany and my Georgian house in Wilton Street in London, had now retired. She introduced me to Derek Frost and Associates, whom she knew professionally. I told Derek that I wanted light, life and colour throughout the house. 'You should go away and come back with proposals for everything in the house,' I told him. 'If I dislike anything, I will tell you, and there is no point in arguing. I know what I want. If you argue you are only wasting your time and my money, and I do not propose to do either.'

What we have attempted to do throughout is to construct a contemporary interior inside a pre-eminently thirteenth-century and Queen Anne

building. The major construction work was to install a pair of doors opening from the hall into the dining room. Hitherto, the entry into the dining
room had come from a small door in the kitchen. As, on the whole, I
prefer my guests to see their food only after it has been prepared, new
large doors directly into the dining room were essential. This, however,
caused a problem. We had to secure the approval of the Historic Buildings
Commission, responsible for listing historic houses, and of all the planning
authorities in the area. After public notification of the proposals, we had
to wait for two months to see if anyone objected. They did not, but time
was lost. It was, therefore, slightly irritating to be sent a typescript of the
history of Arundells by the Historic Buildings Commission shortly after
permission had been given in which the original plans of the house attached
showed that the new entrance that we intended to create had, in any case,
been part of the seventeenth-century dining room.

Everywhere the colourings are light, both on the walls and in the fabrics
for the curtains, cushions and coverings. In the leg of the L-shaped hall
we have built a display cabinet for the models of my five *Morning Cloud*
ocean racing boats, and the walls are hung with paintings of them. My
books are provided for with cases in the library, and in my study upstairs.
This study looks over the whole length of the garden and gives one an
even better view of the varying shades and colourings of the trees and
shrubs going down to the river. The house also gives me the opportunity
of hanging the oils and water colours, prints and maps which I have been
collecting over the past forty years.

I had never been able to do justice to my pictures in my previous
homes. Now they can be hung to best effect. At the back of the house, I
have a cartoon gallery, featuring caricatures of politicians (including me)
by most of the post-war cartoonists. As one might expect, many of them
are not particularly flattering, but I like them and they seem to make a
good impression on visitors. In my hallway, I am now able to hang paintings
and drawings by Augustus John, Sickert and Sargent, along with what I
believe to be the only painting by Winston Churchill that he signed twice.
This is a fine landscape of the South of France, between Aix and Arles,
painted in 1947. When he gave it to me in 1958, he promised to sign it
for me. He had forgotten he had already signed it – one signature is almost
imperceptible against a dark background – and signed it again. It has pride
of place in my hallway, along with an earlier Churchill, painted in 1925
on the Duke of Westminster's estate.

Over the years, I have collected a huge amount of memorabilia of every
kind, and I am now able to display much of it appropriately. In my dining
room, I have a montage including everything from a T'ang horse in perfect
condition to a glass goblet given to me by the Trustees of Chequers, a

china dish which once belonged to Disraeli and a glass orchid, presented to me by the Harvard Business School Club of Atlanta. In the drawing room, I have set up my electrostatic speakers and displayed photographs of many of the world figures I have met over the years. I also have a framed original working sketch of the concluding bars of the first act of Richard Strauss's opera *Der Rosenkavalier*. Strauss autographed this and gave it to Mrs Asquith, the wife of the Liberal Prime Minister, in 1910, and it was presented to me when I was Prime Minister. I also have an original letter, given to me by the Strauss family, from Richard Strauss to his wife Pauline, describing a meeting with Asquith in June 1914.

The house is full of flowers, mainly taken from the garden at the back, a long, winding stretch of lawn, of around two acres. It includes a dell with a pond, a rose garden and a vegetable plot. My guests and I never eat vegetables from anywhere else. I also have an orchid house, with plants from all over the world. A particularly virile orchid was sent by Fidel Castro, and lives in a tree trunk strapped to a steel bench. There are two gardeners, myself and Stuart Craven. He is the practical, working one and I am the innovative, creative supervisor! This garden is the habitat of Pharaoh, an Egyptian goose which has adopted us. Apart from a few weeks each year, when he flies off to other climes, this creature definitely runs the show among the fauna of Arundells. At first, he used to hide behind a wall at the far end of the garden, but now he thinks nothing of wandering up to, or even into, the house and honking noisily at the inhabitants. He is thoroughly domesticated, and a tremendous favourite of visitors. A year or two ago, just after he had settled in, he went on the rampage in a local car park, ripping the rubber from the windscreen wipers of several cars. He was photographed, but made good his escape before the forces of the law could apprehend him. Fortunately, nobody at that stage knew where he lived and his malefaction went unpunished. He is rather more celebrated now, and it would not be so easy for him a second time.

Whenever I am in the country I entertain at Arundells, giving a lunch party each Sunday – and Pharaoh can generally be relied upon to amuse my guests. The other things that catch people's imagination are the pictures (notably my two Churchills), my sailing models, the Chinese wallpaper and Fidel Castro's cigars. At these parties, we usually have from eight to twelve people. I try to include a wide range of guests – leading figures from the arts, sport, diplomatic circles, politics and the Church, as well as many old friends and neighbours. My visitors' book features a variety of people from Princess Margaret, Dame Maggie Smith and Kay Graham to Sting, Steve Redgrave, Sir Alec Guinness and the Archbishop of Canterbury – and two of the 'Pythons', John Cleese and Michael Palin. Most guests remark on the quiet and village-like atmosphere of the Close, maintained despite our proximity to the centre of Salisbury. It was, of course, this very peace that attracted me to Salisbury in the first place.

One of the other great pleasures for me in recent years has been celebrating birthdays and anniversaries in style, which gives me the opportunity to bring together friends, old and not so old, and catch up with what they have been doing. I celebrated my seventieth birthday on 9 July 1986 with a dinner at Leeds Castle hosted by Toby and Araminta Aldington, at which the Trio Zingara, whose excellent cellist, Felix Schmidt, had played for me at Chequers in 1970 when he was a pupil at the Menuhin School, performed for us. The following evening, my former private secretaries, with my former and present constituency and parliamentary staff and Bexley supporters, held a special dinner for me at Chiswick House, at which another string quartet played. In 1990, a lunch was held at the Savoy to celebrate my fortieth anniversary as Member of Parliament for Bexley. Alec Home was the main speaker, and several hundred friends and parliamentary colleagues attended, including the Prime Minister, Mrs Thatcher. My main seventy-fifth birthday party, eighteen months later, was held aboard a fine boat called the *Silver Barracuda*, with 220 guests dining and enjoying a splendid performance from the Ronnie Scott Quintet as we sailed gently up and down the Thames. The following evening, we were back at Leeds Castle, again with the Trio Zingara.

It was also with the Trio Zingara that I made a studio recording of classical music. At the suggestion of my friend Sabih Shukri, a generous patron of the arts, I went into the studio – or, rather, into All Saints' Church, Tooting Graveney – for Pickwick Records in October 1988 to record works by Beethoven and Boccherini. Beethoven's Triple Concerto, for Piano, Violin and Cello, is one of the least known jewels in the classical repertoire. Yet its vigorous outer movements and its profound second movement are all bursting with melodic invention. The work also reveals Beethoven at his most creative, as he weaves together orchestral texture with the tones of a trio of solo instruments for which few notable concerto compositions have been produced. For this recording, the Trio combined with the English Chamber Orchestra. I was determined from the start that we should come as close as possible to re-creating the sense and feel of a live performance, and we all did our best to use long takes, with a minimum of editing. It is a source of pride to me that this recording is still available, and receives three stars in the prestigious *Penguin Guide*. Felix Schmidt plays a concerto by Boccherini as a substantial addition to the CD. Making a commercial recording requires both technical discipline and substantial subsidy, and I shall always be grateful for this opportunity.

At the end of March 1989, I sent a CD of this performance to Herbert von Karajan, who was then rehearsing for what turned out to be his last Easter Festival at Salzburg. He wrote back to me almost at once, saying that he was 'delighted with your gift and enjoyed to play it ... it is satisfying to know that you are still in wonderful form and I wish you good luck'. I was struck at once by how his signature had deteriorated. By the summer of that year, the maestro was dead, and Georg Solti took over his performance of Verdi's *Un Ballo in Maschera* at Salzburg at short notice. The Salzburg Easter Festival has survived the death of von Karajan, its creator and inspiration, but it has never been quite the same again.

I believe that almost every music lover I know has a desire, either open or covert, to appear on the Radio 4 programme *Desert Island Discs*. Although I always thought that narrowing down one's musical preferences to a mere eight choices was a rather daunting task, I must admit that I myself occasionally wondered during the 1970s and 1980s why I had not been invited to take part in this show. When Olivia Seligman, Madron's only daughter, was appointed to produce it in the late 1980s, I was delighted when she immediately invited me to make the 1988 Christmas broadcast. She was then told by the BBC that this was forbidden, because I had already appeared on the programme. I immediately told her that this was quite untrue, but not to bother about it, even though I had certainly had plenty of time to select my discs.

When she heard about this, Sue Lawley, who was in charge of the programme, took Olivia at once to see the archives at the BBC. The Keeper turned to the volumes of *Desert Island Discs* programmes and, going through the performers, finally came to 'H'. Chanting to himself, 'Ha, He,' he finally said, 'Yes, here it is, "Heath, Ted – band leader" ... He has been on before.' He was, apparently, unaware of my namesake's pre-eminence in the world of jazz, and the contrast with my own far less celebrated musical position. Sue was then allowed to put me on for Christmas 1988.

I suppose that everyone's choice of records for this show is always a snapshot, and many people would make radically different choices at various stages of their life. However, I really had reflected on the criteria for selecting my eight discs, and all of them had a special significance for me, rooted in my own life and experiences. From the start, I knew that my top choice would have to be from Beethoven's only opera, *Fidelio*, in particular the 'Prisoners' Chorus'. Its message of human devotion and freedom is timeless and overwhelming.

I went on to select my own recordings of Elgar's 'Cockaigne' Overture, with the LSO, and of Mendelssohn's glorious setting of 'Hark! The Herald Angels Sing' with the Geoffrey Mitchell Choir and the ECO; the *Sea*

Symphony of Vaughan Williams, in which I sang at Oxford; Schubert's B Flat Piano Trio, which the LSO principals had performed at Downing Street for William Walton's birthday; the gorgeous final trio from Strauss' *Der Rosenkavalier*, which I first heard at Glyndebourne; and part of Dvořák's 'New World' Symphony, which I had performed in China the previous year. I also chose 'If I Were a Rich Man', from *Fiddler on the Roof*. This has always vividly portrayed for me the sadness of the dispossessed, and I still find Topol's famous performance of that song very moving.

Sue Lawley is also very proficient at moving the conversation beyond the realms of music and, on this occasion, she opened the programme a little provocatively, describing me as 'a man who has tasted triumph and endured isolation . . . greatly admired abroad, but treated with a certain caution at home . . . his good taste and wide interests have allowed him to enjoy many things: politics, music and a love of the sea'. This interview took place at the height of the controversy over the poll tax, and a year or so before Anthony Meyer challenged Mrs Thatcher for the Conservative leadership. In consequence, Miss Lawley pressed me on the future of the Conservative Party, which was deeply unpopular. I reminded her that the current leadership:

> always describe themselves as radical, some would even say revolutionary . . . well, this isn't the language of Conservatism or Toryism, because Toryism has always believed in development . . . radicalism is something for liberals, who are prepared to overturn everything in their way, whereas we've always believed in keeping as much as possible of what we value and developing the rest so that we improve it . . . Toryism will come back to its rightful philosophy. I've got no doubt about that at all.

*

Not long after I left No. 10, Harold Wilson wrote to ask whether it would be agreeable to me for him to recommend me for appointment as a Companion of Honour. I much appreciated his thoughtfulness, but replied to the effect that, grateful as I was, I should prefer him not to put my name forward: I did not think it appropriate in the wake of the election result. At this time there were also rumours that I might be offered the Garter. No such offer was made, nor would I have thought it appropriate so long as I was actively, and sometimes controversially, involved in the current political scene. In 1992, I was 75 and more the 'elder statesman', so when, after the general election of that year, Her Majesty the Queen did me the great honour of appointing me a Knight of the Garter, I accepted with gratitude and pleasure. Quintin Hailsham sent me a letter immediately in his own elegant hand, expressing his delight and adding:

you have deserved well of your country and, in this field, the Garter is the highest honour of its kind . . . I also should like to take the opportunity to thank you from the bottom of my heart for all your kindness, generosity and unfailing consideration and courtesy towards myself, which I do not think I have ever before found the occasion to express . . . Loyalty and friendship between colleagues are two jewels in the crown of our political tradition.

Although I had joined the coalition opposed to him at his first parliamentary election, back in 1938, Quintin and I always remained on the best of terms, and I was very touched by his good wishes.

Another old opponent, Jim Callaghan, wrote a letter about how agreeable it is to be a Knight of the Garter – 'no responsibilities, a seat in the Royal Chapel, and an enjoyable lunch' – and I also received congratulations from Clarissa Avon, Anthony Eden's widow, and my old friend from Broadstairs days, Margaret Raven, now living in Harare. One of the other particularly warm letters that I received came from the Conservative back-bencher Sir Nicholas Fairbairn. 'Your much deserved knighthood', he wrote, 'gave me the greatest pleasure, because it so obviously gave you the greatest pleasure.' He signed off with 'warmest and admiring good wishes, Nicky'. I responded cordially, thanking him for his good wishes and telling him to keep in touch. Less than two weeks later, I was astonished to read a letter in the *Sunday Telegraph* from Sir Nicholas, denouncing 'the beknighted Mr Heath, to whom chivalry is unknown . . . since the Order and its motto arose out of an incident in which a man of little rank despised a lady of great standing, what could be more fitting?' I never worked out quite what to make of this, but I suppose that I should cherish a rare example of someone being pleasant about me in private but rude about me in public.

Roy Jenkins sent a warm note, saying that 'Your Garter has, in my experience, given more general pleasure than any other honour I can recall, and not least to: Yours ever, Roy'. I appreciated this enormously. Only a few years before, Roy had defeated me in the only contest in which we ever competed directly, that for the Chancellorship of Oxford University. Harold Macmillan had become Chancellor in 1959, when he was Prime Minister, and remained active and extremely popular in that post until he died. Up to the very end, he was still presiding over major official functions and greatly enjoying his contacts with the colleges, especially when dining at Balliol, his old college.

I would have liked to succeed him but I thought it was quite improper to announce my candidacy for the post, let alone organise a campaign, until after his memorial service in the Oxford University Church of St Mary's on

7 February 1987. In this I was completely mistaken. To my surprise I found after the service that Roy Jenkins was not only standing, but his supporters had already organised a widespread campaign in his favour and he was by this time backed by a sizeable and high-powered number of dons and university members. What was more, the hitherto unknown situation had arisen of an active member of the University, the Provost of the Queen's College, Lord Blake, also putting his name forward – because, it was supposed, he was an ardent supporter of Mrs Thatcher. It was generally assumed that Harold Wilson would also be a candidate. In the event he decided not to stand, no doubt because of his health.

I knew at once that Roy was liable to take away Balliol votes from me, although I learned afterwards that I had received the majority from our old college. Furthermore, Robert Blake, as a Conservative, would undoubtedly take away ill-disposed Conservative votes. Although John Wakeham controversially endorsed me as the 'official' Conservative candidate, Blake made it impossible for me to win. The result was that, despite the highly effective campaign run for me by Ashley Raeburn, Roy Jenkins became Chancellor, a post which he occupies with great distinction both in his duties at home and in his visits abroad. This has in no way interfered with our friendship. He himself wrote immediately after the contest, 'I am very sorry that my election involved your losing . . . I hope it will not affect our relationship . . . It will certainly not affect my admiration and affection for you.'

Roy will probably be remembered above all else. as a foremost politician who time and time again risked his career and reputation on an all-important point of principle. He will remain known as a passionate supporter of Europe, later becoming President of the European Commission and then a powerful orator in the House of Lords. In the Commons, when we were carrying through our first negotiations in the early 1960s, he strongly and bravely supported our efforts to obtain full membership. He and others like him must have been under the impression that their influence over the leadership would prevail, and I am sure that it came as one of the greatest shocks of Roy's political life when Gaitskell so violently dissociated himself from this view in his speech at the Labour Party conference of 1962. It did not alter Roy Jenkins' views or his behaviour, but it made his relationship with a considerable section of his party more difficult. He was the leading light among the sixty-nine Labour MPs who supported us in the exciting vote in the House of Commons which secured our membership of the European Community, and his role in establishing and then leading the SDP ensured that the Labour Party, at last, came back to its senses.

*   *   *

In recent years, my artistic interests have taken me to Tokyo every autumn, for the ceremonies linked with the Praemium Imperiale arts prizes. The Praemium Imperiale was founded by the Japan Arts Association to take over where the Nobel Prizes leave off. The Nobel Prizes deal overwhelmingly with the sciences, the only two exceptions being the Peace Prize and the Prize for Literature, and the Praemium Imperiale seeks to extend the same principles further into the realms of artistic attainment by recognising and rewarding major international contributions to the arts.

I am one of six international advisers to the committee which each year selects a winner in five areas and awards each winner a prize of $100,000. The categories are music; architecture; film and theatre; painting; and sculpture. In the first ten years of the prize, many distinguished international figures have been honoured, including Leonard Bernstein, Mstislav Rostropovich, David Hockney, Sir John Gielgud and the Chilean painter Matta. It also falls to me to organise the celebrations to mark the announcements of the winners in London every fifth year. This I have now done on two occasions. The first, in the summer of 1990, was a fairly low-key affair, as the award was not so well known. In June 1995, however, my private office, headed at that time by Nicholas Edgar, was set the task of organising three days of lavish celebrations for our visitors at the most prestigious London venues.

The celebrations began on the evening of Wednesday 14 June, with a welcoming banquet at the Tower of London for my fellow international advisers at the time: Dr Helmut Schmidt, the former Chancellor of West Germany; Professor Amintore Fanfani, the former Italian Prime Minister; David Rockefeller Jr; and Yasuhiro Nakasone, the former Japanese Prime Minister. Our sixth adviser, Jacques Chirac, had just been elected President of France, which unfortunately prevented him from joining us (since then his involvement with the awards has, sadly, been limited to a purely honorary role). After a private showing of the new display of the Crown Jewels and other royal treasures, we enjoyed a relaxing dinner in the Officers' Mess of the Royal Regiment of Fusiliers. The evening culminated in the chilly evening air with the Ceremony of the Keys. This interesting, if archaic, ceremony has been perpetuated every night without fail since the thirteenth century. After confirming that the lock to the Tower of London is secured, the sentry on duty turns over the key to his replacement. This solemn ceremony is not normally open to the public, nor are photographs permitted, a ruling which proved almost too much for our Japanese visitors from the Praemium Imperiale secretariat to resist.

The announcements of the winners were made the following morning at a press conference in the Banqueting Hall on Whitehall. This hall, the only portion of the White Hall Palace built by Henry VIII that was not destroyed by fire in 1698, was selected for this event because of its splendid painting on the ceiling by Peter Paul Rubens. Over 100 members of the British and foreign press attended the conference to hear the names of the winners, and three of the recipients – Matta, the distinguished Italian architect Renzo Piano and Andrew Lloyd Webber – were present for the occasion. News of the awards was taken up in the press worldwide. The Queen hosted a reception at Buckingham Palace for the recipients of the 7th Praemium Imperiale on the evening following the announcement of the awards. Her Majesty was joined by the Duke of Edinburgh, Princess Margaret and several other members of the royal family. Along with the winners, the reception was attended by several past laureates as well as many other eminent figures of British art and culture.

The climax of the celebrations, however, appropriately came on the final day, Friday 16 June. After a pre-luncheon reception at 10 Downing Street hosted by Norma Major, the Prime Minister himself being abroad, and following an afternoon break, the party moved downstream for the grand finale, a commemorative concert and banquet at the Royal Naval College in Greenwich in the presence of Princess Alexandra and her husband. The guests travelled down the Thames by boat, generously accompanied by champagne, and we were joined for this occasion by Crown Prince Hassan of Jordan, Norma Major, the Archbishop of Canterbury and over 400 other leading figures from the international political, business and arts worlds. I conducted the English Chamber Orchestra in a concert, opening with Beethoven's 8th Symphony, followed by Delius' 'Walk to the Paradise Garden', one of my favourite orchestral pieces. I then succeeded in persuading a former laureate, Mstislav Rostropovich, to perform as the 'cello soloist in Tchaikovsky's 'Variations on a Rococo Theme'. After a magnificent dinner in the Painted Hall, we all moved outside to watch the band of the Royal Marines Beating the Retreat. It was a spectacular end to a memorable evening.

As my eightieth birthday, due on 9 July 1996, approached, my private office began to prepare a remarkable set of celebrations. The head of my office at the time, Michael McManus, is a great lover of classical music, so it was foreseeable that a strong musical element would be included. In the event, I conducted no fewer than five symphony concerts in celebration. The first was in the Sheldonian Theatre in Oxford, the scene of so many of my happiest musical memories; the second in the German Rhineland; the third in Salisbury Cathedral; the fourth before an audience of 10,000 at an outdoor concert at Kenwood in north London; and the fifth was a studio recording for BBC Radio 2, with the BBC Concert Orchestra. Denis Healey was the ever acerbic commentator.

There were also several parties. The day of my birthday itself began with an appearance on the *Today* programme, followed by Channel Four's *Big Breakfast*. I was interviewed outside my home in Salisbury by the formidable Vanessa Feltz, and presented with a Thomas the Tank Engine birthday cake. They also brought a string orchestra from a local girls' school, South Wiltshire Grammar, to serenade me with 'Happy Birthday'. In recent years, I have tended to avoid the zanier end of broadcasting, but this was an amusing and agreeable interlude. Later in the day, I had a special 'family lunch', attended by my closest friends from over the years, including my brother's widow Muriel. I then listened to Prime Minister's Questions in the House of Commons and went on to a ceremony in Madam Speaker's House, at which I was presented with a grand silver platter, towards which MPs from every party in the House had contributed. In the early evening, I entertained members of my staff, past and present, to drinks at home in London. Then I attended a state banquet held at Buckingham Palace, held in honour of President Mandela. All in all, it was quite a day.

On 18 July, there was a dinner for seventy people at 10 Downing Street. This was hosted by John and Norma Major, and the Queen and the Duke of Edinburgh were the guests of honour. Most of the surviving members of my Cabinets from 1970–4 were invited, along with other old friends, and the widows of old friends. Giscard d'Estaing, former President of France, was there, as was Madame Pompidou, widow of the man who was so crucial in getting Britain into Europe. From the musical world, we had Yehudi and Diana Menuhin, Mstislav Rostropovich, Moura Lympany, Ivo Pogorelich and Susana Walton, widow of Sir William. The Martin Neary Singers returned to No. 10 for the occasion, and sang the special Grace for the building which Robert Armstrong and Herbert Howells had written during my premiership (see p. 464–5). At the end of the dinner, they performed madrigals and part-songs, which were both beautiful and entertaining. The Queen has only been to No. 10 on a handful of occasions, and it was a great privilege for all of us to have her there. She stayed until after 11.00 p.m. and, on the way out, confided that she could not recall enjoying herself so much in ages.

The following evening, we had a dinner for over 430 people at the Savoy. Despite a strike on the railways, everyone made it, apart from my old friend Julian Amery. We had a place prepared for him at the top table, but learned on the evening that he was too frail to attend. This caused me great sadness, and he died shortly afterwards. Norma Major sat at my right hand and Mary Wilson, the widow of my old adversary, sat at my left hand. It was an impressive and moving sight as the largest room in the Savoy was packed with colleagues, old friends, godchildren, former members of my staff and a large selection of individuals from every walk of life. Six speeches were made by friends and colleagues: Denis Healey and Roy Jenkins from Balliol days; Sir Robin Day; David Hunt, who so courageously defeated Enoch Powell at the 1972 party conference; Kenneth Clarke; and Michael Heseltine.

Kenneth Clarke, then still Chancellor of the Exchequer, made a particularly amusing speech. I regard Ken as the most formidable politician of his generation and it is to the discredit of the Conservative parliamentary party that it did not have the courage to make him its leader when it had the chance. He was on particularly good form that night at the Savoy, and began by saying, 'I met Geoffrey Rippon on the way in and he teased me and encouraged me in his usual way. He said, "If you are down to pay a tribute to Ted Heath that will be the last nail in your political coffin!" I said, "It may not be the last but it will be one of the better ones!" ' He went on in a typically complimentary vein: 'Ted is stubborn . . . Ted is difficult . . . He has been stubborn and difficult for a very long time . . . But he now speaks to me because I don't work for the boss that followed!'

A similarly tongue-in-cheek tribute came from the Deputy Prime Minister, Michael Heseltine. 'I still remember how, when I was a junior minister in his government,' he recounted, 'I first experienced that piercing wit, when Ted would pass me in the division lobbies of the Commons and say, "I think the speech you made last night was even worse than the one you made the night before." ' I am always glad when someone discerns my humour. But Michael went on to make a serious point, too:

> I voted through the Commons in the long nights and the tensions of the 1970s to support Ted as he took us into Europe, the most controversial decision of the second half of the twentieth century, the biggest, the most dramatic – and, history will prove, the most important and the most correct. I have seen and watched the vilification which has been poured on Ted for that decision; and that is perhaps the nature of politics – you do not get immediate acclaim, you do not get universal acceptance.
>
> The idea that Ted, who had fought with such distinction for the causes which he believed, who served our country with such courage and bravery in the Second World War, would sell out British interests is a travesty of the truth . . . It was a total determination that Britain should excel that drove Ted into Europe.

My old friend Slava Rostropovich, who had also been at Downing Street the evening before, handed over a special tape from Abbey Road to be played to this gathering. He instructed a nonplussed Jim Naughtie, who hosted the evening with great style, to introduce J. S. Bach's newly discovered Seventh Suite for Solo Cello. In fact, to the delight of everyone present, the tape turned out to be of Slava, playing and singing 'Happy Birthday, Dear Ted'. To celebrate the occasion, EMI released a special CD, which included a remastered version of my live 'Cockaigne' recording from 1971. During that week, the press carried a predictable mixture of hostile and less hostile appraisals of my life and times. Happily the more malicious and politically-motivated of these were put into their proper perspective both by the warm good wishes of so many friends, and by the formidable number of felicitations that I received from the general public.

Chapter 25

EVER CLOSER UNION

Britain and Europe 1975–1997

T he overwhelming support given by the British people to continued membership of the European Community at the Referendum in June 1975 was certainly personally satisfying. I had promised my European counterparts back in 1963 that Britain would 'never again turn our backs on Europe', and I was thrilled by this popular endorsement just twelve years later. This result provided the British government with an opportunity to show its full commitment to European unity. This was the wish of not just the British people. Our friends across Western Europe, the United States and the Commonwealth had all wanted Britain to remain in the European Community. They now wanted us to make a positive contribution to its development. These hopes were expressed in a letter from ex-Chancellor Willy Brandt on 6 June:

> You will see [the Referendum result] as a confirmation of all that you have been working for over so many years against great opposition. And you know that I have always considered it a mistake to prolong the decision on British membership. I hope that Britain will now be able to make its full constructive contribution to the Community.

The Labour government's response was deeply disappointing. I would have liked to see a recognition that we were full and equal partners, able to contribute to the development of the Community. No longer should it have been a question of them and us. The simple question of membership may have ended in June 1975, but the uncertain attitude of mind evident in that period persisted within the Labour Party.

By the late 1970s, the Community was stagnating. Worldwide economic problems had checked its growth and undermined its cohesion and self-confidence. The Nine were ill-prepared: enlargement had just been completed, and the habit of working together was not yet firmly established. Unfortunately, this gave Labour Ministers the opportunity to unite their party by being ambivalent towards Europe. The Community has survived, developed and made progress only when people have had sufficient self-confidence to think in terms of seeking common solutions to common problems.

The main difficulty was that neither Harold Wilson nor James Callaghan was a committed European. Their agnostic position was understandable in the narrow confines of Labour Party politics. After the Referendum, the Cabinet remained paralysed over European policy, because the minority who opposed British membership had not really accepted the verdict of the people. They never have done. Under Labour's stewardship the opportunities in Europe were not taken, and our negotiating capital was dissipated on irrelevancies. British interests were prostituted to the personal ambition of certain ministers. It was no wonder that our partners were frustrated with Britain, as the British people were with their government.

On 6 January 1977, Roy Jenkins took over from François-Xavier Ortoli as President of the European Commission. Finding under Jim Callaghan's leadership of the Labour Party that any positive relationship with Europe had again been abandoned, Roy willingly quit domestic politics and accepted the position in Brussels, where his conduct proved both firm and decisive. He was much respected by the leaders of other countries, and the Community's lack of progress was certainly no fault of his presidency. His greatest achievement was the relaunching of monetary union in 1977. For nearly thirty years after the Second World War the standard of living of the Western world had improved enormously. That was achieved on the basis of arrangements for a stable currency which abruptly ended in August 1971 when the US abandoned Bretton Woods, throwing currencies into disarray. The German Chancellor, Willy Brandt, and I discussed at Bonn in March 1973 a proposal for the pooling of the reserves of all the member countries of the Community. We aimed to fight the speculators, but his Cabinet would not support our proposal and the idea was shelved. Perhaps we were too ambitious in wanting to pool all the reserves, but if we had achieved all of our aims the economic story of the 1970s and 1980s might have been very different.

The European Monetary System (EMS) was an essential step towards the development of a more ordered and stable monetary system. In July 1978, for the first time since the oil crisis in the autumn of 1973 dislocated the world's economies, the heads of government of the European Community accepted a major proposal for dealing with the problems of inflation, unemployment and economic stagnation. The plan was put to the European Council in Bremen through a joint initiative of Helmut Schmidt, the German Chancellor, and President Giscard d'Estaing of France. But that is not the whole story.

During a visit to Egypt in December 1977, I had gone up the Nile to Luxor to see the famous illuminations at night. I then went on to Aswan where, to my surprise, I found that Helmut Schmidt was staying at my hotel. We each had an interview scheduled with the Egyptian President, Muhammad Anwar al-Sadat, but agreed that after lunch we would meet to discuss the European economic situation. During our talks, I urged upon Helmut the need for what became the EMS. Our discussion went on until his wife came in after four hours and advised him to put on his formal attire for the official dinner which he was due to attend. I had no wish to damage marital relations between the Schmidts and left immediately, unsure whether I had succeeded in persuading him about both the need and the benefits of moving towards monetary integration. It emerged later in Bremen that he was a strong supporter of such a system. He was, however, both politically and economically astute. Instead of pushing it forward as a major German proposal, he arranged with Giscard d'Estaing for the French to take it over as their initiative, which Giscard did successfully. This avoided any accusation of German hegemony and permitted a smooth transition to the new system for those member countries which wished to take advantage of it. These did not include Britain.

Although not committed to the EMS, the British Labour and Conservative parties were wholly committed to the policy priorities which membership of the EMS demanded, in particular to low inflation and the rejection of currency depreciation as a means of improving Britain's international competitiveness. Full membership would also have reinforced the confidence of investors and money markets in the British economy. That was why it did not make any sense for Britain to have one foot in and one foot out of the EMS, by participating in the co-ordination of economic policies but remaining out of any mechanisms which accompanied it. Moreover, non-participation in the Exchange Rate Mechanism at the heart of the EMS inevitably meant that Britain would not play a full role in shaping the evolution towards monetary union and a single currency. Once again, despite all the experience of the past, Britain excluded itself from the mainstream of European developments.

The return of a Conservative administration under Mrs Thatcher in 1979 renewed the possibility that Britain would have a government determined to make a success of our membership of the European Community. At that time the Conservative Party remained strongly pro-European. In April 1976 I had been nominated for the office of president of the Conservative Group for Europe and I suggested to Jim Spicer, the director, that Mrs Thatcher's name be put forward as patron of this group. I received a letter from her on 27 May 1976. 'I am most grateful to you for suggesting me,' she wrote, 'and I accept with pleasure.' The Conservative Party was then, in principle, in favour of British membership of the ERM, but on some undefined timescale. The reality, however, as later events illustrated, was that Mrs Thatcher had absolutely no intention that Britain should become a full member of the EMS.

On 7 June 1979, one month after the general election, Britain experienced its first direct elections to the European Parliament (EP). Since the creation of the European Assembly in 1958, its members had consisted of delegates from each member state but, after we joined the Community in 1973, it was clear that this placed excessively heavy burdens on parliamentarians, who were combining their European obligations with domestic responsibilities at home. The creation of a directly elected parliament had long been an aim of the Community. The evolvement of democratic discussion about proposals and parliamentary checks on policy were essential if European policy was to develop effectively, while preventing an excessive growth of executive power. Direct elections would enable our voters to feel that they were playing a personal part in the creation and running of their own Community. As the UK now had some first-hand experience of Europe, the time had come for the British government to start taking a positive stance on this issue. After all, we had the best-established parliamentary traditions. Moreover, it was what our fellow members expected of us and one of the reasons why they had always wanted us in the Community. James Callaghan as Prime Minister, however, postponed the legislation until June 1977 and Britain failed to meet the target date of May–June 1978 for the European elections. They were therefore delayed across Europe until June 1979.

I was dismayed by the lack of effort in campaigning by all three main political parties in the 1979 European elections. Mrs Thatcher and most of her Ministers each made a single speech. Perhaps politicians were weary after the general election, but there was no excuse for the lethargic nature of the campaign. These direct elections were one of Europe's crowning achievements after centuries of warfare. How many would have thought, as they landed on the beaches of Normandy in 1944, that just thirty-five years later, former friend and foe alike would be electing members together to a parliament they could share? The *Conservative Campaign Guide* summarised the importance of these elections very well:

> Perhaps the most important, although often forgotten, result of the gradual movement towards European unity since 1945 has been to make war between the western European states almost unthinkable ... the United Kingdom and the other Member States of the Community are

... pooling their national sovereignty in certain agreed areas in order to secure a wider and more effective common sovereignty.

My only reservation was the suitability of the 'first past the post' (FPTP) system for these elections. European constituencies are so much larger than their domestic equivalents and the link between member and constituent, so important at Westminster, is more or less lost as a result. Most people in this country still do not even know who their MEP is. I would have preferred a system of proportional representation which combined single-member constituencies with a national or regional list of party candidates. This procedure would also be closer to the systems adopted by other countries, with the exception of the Irish Republic. In 1950, under the Treaty of Paris, the Common Assembly – the precursor of the EP – was charged with drafting a scheme for its own elections by direct universal suffrage, with a uniform procedure in all member states. No one could seriously believe that the rest of the Community would adopt the system of FPTP for its eventual uniform arrangement.

Two-thirds of Europe's 200 million electors voted on 7 June 1979. They recognised the importance of the Community to their prosperity, their jobs and their security. The turnout in the United Kingdom, however, was a pathetic 32 per cent, the lowest figure in the European Community. There was some solace in the fact that the Conservatives won sixty of the eighty-one seats and my old friend Madron Seligman was elected for West Sussex. I had campaigned vigorously for the establishment of a strong Conservative presence in the chamber, visiting thirty-nine constituencies during the campaign. My personal highlight was a trip to Chichester on 2 June to support Madron. His majority of 95,484 far surpassed even my general election result in Old Bexley and Sidcup! He wrote that my speech 'certainly did the trick, because Chichester put in the highest turnout of all my seven constituencies, much against all predictions!' He went on: 'I thought it was a wonderful occasion, coming as it did after a whole suc-cession of red-letter days we have experienced together. It would have been perfect if both our parents could have been there. But no doubt they were together, enjoying it from some vantage point above. Ah! well! Now, on to the next challenge.'

Since that election, the powers of the EP have steadily increased. Those who decry the Union and refer to its 'democratic deficit' not only refuse to acknowledge the EP's present powers but are invariably reluctant to take further measures to strengthen it. The increase in competence in the European Union to which the member states have agreed in the Single European Act, and the Maastricht and Amsterdam treaties, needs to be matched by an increase in the power of the European Parliament, so that new EU responsibilities can be made democratically accountable. The 1997 Amsterdam Treaty extended and simplified the co-decision procedure, introduced by the Maastricht Treaty, of the EP with the Council of Ministers. This was a step in the right direction. The British government now supports a regional-list system of PR for elections to the EP. This will allocate seats proportionally according to voters' preferences, within each of eleven regions. This too will be a major improvement.

Deepening public cynicism towards the Community during the 1970s and early 1980s produced a hardening of national partisanship in Community decision-making. This gravely threatened its unity and its political credibility in the wider world. The disproportionate size of Britain's net contribution to the Community budget was a case in point. The 1970–4 Conservative government recognised that countries with a much larger agricultural industry than ours would gain proportionally more from the budget. Because we joined late, the structure of the Community's income and expenditure policies at the time of our entry was inevitably not designed to suit us, as we were not involved when they were designed. We got the best deal we could – and, during the five-year transitional period, our contributions to the budget never rose to the limits that we had anticipated before entry. As a full member, however, our net contribution to the Community had become out of balance with our relative wealth by any method of calculation, largely because our relative wealth had declined so much under the 1974–9 Labour government.

The CAP had also come to consume a far greater proportion of the budget than anyone had envisaged during the accession negotiations. The Commission had predicted in 1970 that the share of agricultural spending would fall to 40 per cent of the total budget. Instead, by 1979, it stood at 70 per cent. The first few years of Mrs Thatcher's premiership were marked by her avowed battle to 'get our money back'. As there was a major inequity by the start of the 1980s, she was quite right to deal with this. This illustrated, once again, how the 1974–9 Labour government, for all its rhetoric, had achieved nothing for Britain. Its so-called renegotiation in 1974–5 was completely fruitless. It wasted two years and Britain did not receive one penny out of the 'corrective mechanism' negotiated by James Callaghan. Mrs Thatcher was able to tackle this because of the acceptance that I had gained for Britain in 1971 that questions of budget contributions 'could always be reopened in future if any member state found itself in an inequitable position' (see p. 373). The differences between certain member states on the nature of the British budgetary problem, however, were far too great for us to expect an immediate solution after the Conservative Party took office in 1979.

What Mrs Thatcher failed to realise was that Britain could never achieve a budget solution on the basis that what we put in we must exactly get out. No other member could agree to that doctrine, because one cannot organise any community, even in a village or a club, on this basis. Subsequent threats, such as illegally withholding funds from the Community, were equally unwise. The satisfactory temporary deal negotiated by Peter Carrington and Ian Gilmour in 1980 ended in 1983 and, if serious progress was not made in reaching a permanent solution, Mrs Thatcher threatened to withhold our contribution to that year's budget. This was presumably a bluff. Britain's legal obligations, however, should never be treated as negotiating weapons. I discussed this with many of my parliamentary colleagues and found that they were as horrified as I was. On 21 March 1984, after the Prime Minister had pointedly ignored my worries in the House of Commons, I expressed to her my anxieties in writing:

> I could not support, indeed I would strongly oppose, any act of illegality by HM Government affecting the European Community just as I have always opposed illegality at home. Moreover, as the Chief Whip will confirm, this is also the position of many senior members of the Party in the House of Commons as well as that of many backbenchers who did not make their voice heard this afternoon.

Three months later, at the Fontainebleau Summit on 25–26 June, a long-term agreement was finally reached. Under its terms Britain was guaranteed an annual rebate of 66 per cent on its contributions, in return for allowing an increase in the permitted size of the budget. The agreement concluded that 'any Member State sustaining a budgetary burden which is excessive in relation to its relative prosperity may benefit from a correction at the appropriate time'. Greece joined the Community in 1981 and was followed by Spain and Portugal five years later. If these countries were eventually to suffer such a budgetary inequity, their new democracies would have been denied the support which membership was supposed to provide. It was a fair and just agreement and Mrs Thatcher is to be congratulated on negotiating it, and even Germany has now sought to invoke it. For our European contribution, we enjoy unrestricted access to one of the wealthiest markets in the world and we have the opportunity to influence policy across the whole of Western Europe, both internally and with regard to world trade. It is an investment in peace and prosperity.

Mrs Thatcher's government in the early 1980s also saw the establishment of the Common Fisheries Policy (CFP). This has lately been the source of much anger and I have been constantly attacked in the press for this policy by ignorant and biased contributors. I was in no way responsible for the precise arrangements that were agreed in 1983. The allegation that I somehow 'betrayed' the fishermen of this country in the early 1970s is absurd and insulting. I was born by a fishing port. On my way to school, I would watch the fishermen coming into port, and I would stop to talk to them. The service that they perform, in peace and war, demands gratitude from their fellow countrymen. Those of us who know and respect the sea always respect those who use it in their daily business. I have spent fifteen years of my life ocean racing and we knew that in times of danger we could owe our lives to fishermen. I have always maintained good relations with them. As Prime Minister, I acted to defend British fishermen after live ammunition had been fired against them by Icelandic gunboats in May 1973 (see p. 490–1).

As a result of the 1964 European Fisheries Convention, the UK, like other countries, exercised sovereignty over water within twelve miles of its coast. Of these twelve miles, the first six were reserved entirely for British fishermen. Between six and twelve miles, certain other countries had fishing rights, provided that fish stocks were sufficient. Beyond twelve miles, waters were open to fishing by boats of any country. This agreement, negotiated by a Conservative government, undoubtedly contributed to the improvement in the fortunes of Britain's inshore fishermen.

The fishing industry did rather well during the years 1970–4. Despite pressure on fish stocks and increased rivalry between fishermen, British fishermen caught almost exactly the same tonnage of fish when I left office as they had done when I assumed office in 1970. The total annual catch by British vessels then was 963,000 tonnes; in 1971 it was 964,000 tonnes; in 1972 it was 942,000 tonnes; in 1973 it was 998,000 tonnes; and in 1974 it was 954,000 tonnes. In 1972, inshore vessels, under eighty feet, caught 314,750 tonnes of white fish valued at £32.5 million compared with 298,000 tonnes valued at £24.6 million in 1971 – a rise in catch value of almost one-third, substantially ahead of inflation.

Article 38 of the Treaty of Rome, and the inclusion of fish in its Annex II, provides the legal basis for the Community's Common Fisheries Policy. By 1968 the first steps had been taken after the Commission submitted its formal proposals on fishing. Impetus for a final resolution came when the Six agreed, after the Hague Summit of 1969, on the principle of enlarging the Community. The Six now had to thrash out a common negotiating position on a variety of highly complex, technical and emotive issues.

Fisheries were clearly going to be very important in the accession negotiations, at a time when there was a worldwide move towards increased fishing limits. This was particularly the case for Britain and Norway. Norway had established its own twelve-mile fishery limit in 1961 and had not signed the 1964 Fisheries Convention. In December 1969, the Six agreed to adopt basic regulations before 30 April 1970. In the event, the Community missed this deadline and a settlement was reached two months later, just after negotiations had opened between the applicant countries and the Six. These were outline decisions only, but included a reference to access 'up to the beaches' – an unhelpful start to the negotiations. On 20 October the Six agreed two regulations relating to the principle of equal access, and the common organisation of the market in fish products. The common structural policy was set up to ensure common access for European fishermen to national waters, not to usurp the sovereignty of member states over those waters. The preamble of the relevant regulation makes it clear that the Community 'must have equal access to and use of fishing grounds in maritime waters coming under the sovereignty or within the jurisdiction of Member States'. From the early 1960s, the French government had been interested in a common fisheries policy to prevent cheap fish imports into France. This had nothing to do with British accession. Indeed the French first proposed a common fisheries policy in March 1963, only two months after they had vetoed British membership of the Community.

The leader of the UK delegation, Sir Con O'Neill, was a fisherman and I, of course, was a keen sailor. We were both therefore determined to ensure an agreement that would suit the interests of British fishermen. This was no easy task. In the early 1970s, the majority of British distant-water fishermen favoured the principle of equal access. In 1973 less than a fifth of the potential catch within 200 miles of the UK coast was being caught by British fishermen, as they had never used these waters to any great extent. The bulk of the British fishing fleet was making lucrative earnings close to Iceland, and they feared that advocating exclusivity in our own waters would merely encourage the Icelandic government to extend its own exclusive fishing rights at our expense. Distant-water fishermen also wanted to recover lost fishing rights in Norwegian and Faroese waters. Their position was well summarised by the director-general of the British Trawlers' Federation in 1971:

> It would seem that inshore fishermen on this issue can hardly look for the support of distant-water fishermen because the latter seek – within the bounds of equity and properly observed conservation measures designed to preserve maximum sustainable yield – the utmost freedom of access to waters everywhere . . . distant-water fishermen find Article 2 perfectly acceptable.

Inshore fishermen, however, were deeply hostile to the principle of equal access. Our problem during the negotiations was to reconcile these different interests.

During my talks with President Pompidou on 20 and 21 May 1971, I expressed Britain's objections to what the Six had agreed the previous October. On 12 July, Geoffrey Rippon put forward proposals based on the principles of the 1964 European Fisheries Convention. The Six were at first unenthusiastic. Our plans involved substantial derogations from what had already been negotiated, and, Rippon rightly refused to be bounced into a settlement which entailed unacceptable terms for British inshore fishermen. Delay was inevitable. When the Commons voted in October 1971 to join the European Community, the fishing agreement had not been concluded, but the Minister of Agriculture, Jim Prior, made it quite clear that the government would agree only to a deal which preserved our existing inshore fishing rights. Our White Paper stated that 'the arrangements governing access to coastal fisheries will have to be reconsidered in the perspective of enlargement.' Despite these assurances Patrick Wolrige-Gordon, the Conservative MP for Aberdeenshire East and an acknowledged expert on fisheries, abstained in the vote specifically because of the uncertainties on this issue.

In the early hours of Sunday 12 December we finally reached an agreement which broadly maintained the status quo, through a ten-year derogation which was subsequently renewed and is still in force today. British fishermen did not lose any access to home waters. Article 100 of the Treaty of Accession reads:

> the Member States of the Community are authorised, until 31 December 1982, to restrict fishing in waters under their sovereignty or jurisdiction, situated within a limit of six nautical miles, calculated from the base lines of the coastal Member States, to vessels which fish traditionally in those waters.

There was no change at all in the protection afforded in areas from which approximately 95 per cent by value of the total inshore catch was taken (the Orkneys and Shetlands, the north and east coasts of Scotland, north-east England from the River Coquet to Flamborough Head, Devon and Cornwall including the Isles of Scilly). We retained full jurisdiction over the whole of our coastal waters to twelve miles outside these coastlines. Exclusive fishing rights within six miles remained unaffected. Within the six-to-twelve-mile zone the UK undertook to continue to admit foreign fishermen who had traditionally fished there, obtaining in turn reciprocal rights and the assurance that no member state increasing limits beyond twelve miles would be able to discriminate against the fishing vessels of another member state. The UK retained its jurisdiction over the water and the right to regulate the size of nets and the method of trawl.

The next day the fisheries agreement was presented to the Commons.

Patrick Wolrige-Gordon described the arrangements for the initial period as 'perfectly acceptable' and voted with the government. The majority of fishermen – including, crucially, the Scottish inshore fishermen – also accepted the deal. Although the Labour Party continued to attack the government on the outcome of the negotiations, even they did not mention the terms of our fishing agreement in their renegotiation of 1974–5. Fishing has become controversial only because of four developments since 1974: the extension of national fishing limits to 200 miles, the accession of Spain to the European Community, the necessity of conserving fish stocks and the sale of fishing licences by British fishermen to Spanish interests.

The CFP was agreed by Mrs Thatcher's administration on 25 January 1983. This divided fish within the Community 200-mile limit into agreed quotas. What is particularly important is that it respected the existing agreement concerning the first twelve miles and traditional fishing patterns. Nothing was changed there. Contrary to popular belief, Britain did well out of the allocation of fishing quotas, and received more than would have been expected on the basis of past British catches. Our overall share of the catch nearly doubled, with Britain receiving 47 per cent of North Sea cod, 52 per cent of West Scotland cod and 81 per cent of West Scotland haddock. The terms obtained by the then government were accepted by the British Fishing Federation, the National Federation of Fishermen's Organisations and the Scottish Fishermen's Federation.

It is certainly deplorable that quota-hopping, where foreign fishermen take over British quotas, is taking place. The European Court of Justice should not have applied a non-discrimination ruling to a system of national quotas in 1991, for a quota must by definition discriminate. As a friend of the fishermen, I fully support the campaign to end quota-hopping and I share the government's commitment to defend the British quota vigorously. At the same time we must be realistic. In 1996 there were on the UK register 160 vessels which were foreign-owned or had a significant foreign interest in them. This represented approximately 20 per cent of the UK's offshore fleet. Of these 160 vessels, 110 were Spanish. This is the result of British fishermen themselves selling their boats and licences in the 1980s, either directly to foreign interests, in particular Spanish, or to British intermediaries. There are few Spanish fishermen buying up British quotas today. Those 160 boats on the UK register became foreign-owned between 1980 and 1989, and the number has remained relatively static ever since. The British owners of boats are solely responsible for that.

There is without question an overwhelming case for some form of Europe-wide policy on fishing. The setting of quotas in the CFP is influenced by political pressure and, therefore, still allows too much fishing and there is a general responsibility among all member states of the European

Union to deal with this problem. Fishing grounds controlled by a single country do not make for better conservation. Fish move around a great deal, and stocks have been severely reduced over recent years by over-fishing. We have taken too many fish, and those left have been unable to breed fast enough to make up the shortfall. It is therefore in everyone's interest for the industry to reduce its fishing if we are to have a fishing industry worth speaking of in the years ahead. In 1973, the number of active British fishing boats was 6,569. In 1995, we had 10,297 registered fishing boats. It is obvious that there is surplus capacity in the industry. We should work within the EU to deal with this problem and that of the effective enforcement of existing rules and procedures. This will make the remaining fleet more competitive and bring funds into the industry which can be used for the financing of new or refurbished vessels.

The 1983 general election was one of the most important post-war British elections. The choice for the British people was clear. The Labour Party conference in October 1980 had voted for a future Labour government to withdraw from Europe. The anti-Europeans inside the Labour Party knew how difficult it would be to foist their brand of left-wing socialism on the British people if we remained part of a Community based on the principles of free enterprise and the mixed economy. This reckless decision fractured the Labour Party, as almost thirty of its MPs deserted it. Roy Jenkins, Shirley Williams, David Owen and Bill Rodgers, all of whom had voted with the Conservative government over Europe in October 1971, formed the pro-European Social Democratic Party. The long-threatened split on Europe in the Labour Party had arrived.

The Conservative leadership should learn the lessons of the 1983 campaign. Labour pledged in their manifesto to 'extricate ourselves from the Treaty of Rome and other Community treaties which place political burdens on Britain'. The Conservative manifesto, in contrast, proudly stated that 'the creation of the European Community has been vital in cementing lasting peace in Europe and ending centuries of hostility'. We won by a majority of 144 seats and the SDP–Liberal Alliance received almost as many votes as Labour. There is no future for any mainstream political party which is avowedly Euro-sceptic.

The summits of Community leaders in the early 1980s were too often used to turn understandable household quarrels into major confrontations and unholy battles of will between national leaders. Britain bore a heavy share of the responsibility for debasing the real purpose of these summits, which should take major initiatives to deal with urgent European and world problems. Mrs Thatcher's intransigence certainly cost the UK dear in terms of potential allies in the European Community. I attended a meeting of prominent pro-European politicians at the Château Stuyvenberg in March 1984, at which Leo Tindemans, Helmut Schmidt and Emilio Colombo were present. We were discussing the possibility of reviving the Monnet Committee, which had performed such important work in the 1960s and early 1970s. Our aim was to set out a coherent medium-term programme, showing how the Community should develop in order to meet the new challenges of the 1980s. I recall Helmut Schmidt expressing his disappointment at the attitude of the British thus far in Europe. In his view no British Prime Minister since 1974 had been genuinely committed to the Community, and the differences between Wilson, Callaghan and Thatcher were simply of style. 'At root,' he concluded, 'Mrs Thatcher only wanted her money back.'

However, the Conservative Party remained strongly pro-European and our positive manifesto for the 1984 European elections was rewarded when we received forty-five seats to Labour's thirty-two. Our campaign focused on both the political benefits of peace and security and removing obstacles to trade within the Community. Mrs Thatcher's foreword for the Conservative European manifesto, with which I fully agreed, declared:

> Britain joined the European Community with a vision. We saw opportunities for trade and greater prosperity. But we also saw . . . the promise of peace and security . . . For the first time in history, the very idea of an armed conflict between the countries of Western Europe has become unthinkable . . . Membership of the Community has had its problems . . . We have been right to fight for improvements to the Common Agricultural Policy and for a fairer system of finance. We want these things so that we can put behind us the endless haggling over money and begin to develop the full potential of the Community. These coming European elections are part of our commitment to peace with freedom and justice . . . We do not want to see our accomplishments and our future damaged by those who seek only to destroy what has already been achieved.

The economic objective of the European Community was the creation of an open, vigorous free market among the member states. The customs union brought about the first step in the creation of a truly unified market by abolishing tariffs between member states. Without a single market, British and other Community firms would have found themselves increasingly unable to compete in world markets. Industry in the United States already enjoyed the advantages of a continental-scale single market, and the Japanese home market was twice the size of the home market of any individual European country. In 1985, after the appointment of Jacques Delors as President of the Commission, the EC regained its momentum.

Delors proposed the most significant change to the Community since its birth. This was the creation of a truly single market, based on the free movement of goods, people, services and capital, across a frontier-free Europe. Much of the credit for achieving this must go to the British Commissioner Arthur Cockfield, who was later abruptly sacked by Mrs Thatcher. In December 1985, European heads of government came together to sign the Single European Act (SEA). This created a market of over 370 million consumers, one and a quarter times the size of the US market and two and a half times the size of the Japanese market. In signing this Treaty, the twelve heads of state or government, including Mrs Thatcher, endorsed a commitment 'to transform relations as a whole among their states into a European Union' and to 'the objective of the progressive realization of Economic and Monetary Union', echoing the Paris communiqué that I had signed in 1972.

The second major feature of the SEA was the introduction of a new voting system, under Article 100A, into the Council of Ministers. Mrs Thatcher agreed to an extension of qualified majority voting (QMV), in order to quicken the process of decision-making which was so necessary to create the single European market by 1992. She was quite right to do so. The increased use of majority voting inevitably meant that individual countries could not get everything they would have liked on every subject, but encouraged member states to overcome narrow, sectional differences to work for a solution that benefits everyone. On 16 May 1989, Mrs Thatcher acknowledged the necessity of extending majority voting when she told Parliament, 'We wished to have many of the directives under majority voting because things which we wanted were being stopped by others using a single vote.'

After the 1987 general election, Margaret Thatcher reopened the question of whether Britain was committed to the European enterprise. The Foreign Office, capably led by Geoffrey Howe, continued the good work begun by Lord Carrington and Francis Pym earlier in the decade, but Geoffrey's constructive views earned the scorn of the Prime Minister. I never expected that any British Prime Minister could make a speech as hostile and ill-informed as the one Mrs Thatcher delivered in Bruges in 1988. This led to the disastrous 'diet of Brussels' propaganda campaign by the Conservative Party in the 1989 European elections, the resignation of Geoffrey Howe in November 1990, Mrs Thatcher's own resignation as Prime Minister that same month and the difficulties which plagued John Major after the 1992 general election.

At home, Bruges shattered the unity of the Conservative Party on Europe and indirectly led to the establishment of the Referendum Party before the 1997 general election. It became apparent that Mrs Thatcher wanted to convert the Community into nothing more than a market, a trading centre lacking the other facilities and institutions of a common enterprise. The Conservative government's 1971 White Paper had explicitly said that 'The Six have firmly and repeatedly made it clear that they reject the concept that European unity should be limited to the formation of a free trade area,' and the SEA went far beyond creating a single market. Margaret Thatcher was a member of the 1970–4 Cabinet which accepted the Treaty of Rome in full and it was she who helped negotiate the SEA. The enabling legislation for the SEA was then passed through the House of Commons with huge majorities, including a majority of 159 on its second reading in April 1986. The British Parliament, therefore, endorsed the use of qualified majority voting over a wide area of Community life.

The bitter and public that followed dispute between Mrs Thatcher and myself on the goals and aims of the European Community after Bruges was unavoidable. I once again came under heavy attack from the right wing of the party and their supporters in the press, but I have few regrets. It is important to remember that several of the most loyal members of her Cabinet from the early 1980s, including Nigel Lawson and Geoffrey Howe, were also dismayed by Mrs Thatcher's growing aversion to Europe. They could not speak out, however, and nobody else appeared to be strong enough to stand up to her increasingly emotional public behaviour. Meanwhile, as the process of change had begun in the Labour Party, marked by a shift back in favour of British membership of the European Community, they could concentrate their fire on the painful and embarrassing split between the Prime Minister and her Foreign Secretary. In addition, speeches from representatives of the European Commission and other European leaders were routinely distorted by the press and party Eurosceptics to support Mrs Thatcher's argument that Brussels was unnecessarily interfering in our own affairs. In the eyes of the public, I was the man most associated with Europe and I could not stand back and watch history, and my own record, being grossly misrepresented.

Mrs Thatcher's most famous comment in Bruges was that 'We have not successfully rolled back the frontiers of the state in Britain only to see them reimposed at a European level with a European superstate exercising a new dominance from Brussels.' In fact European integration is not about creating a 'superstate', but about enabling the peoples of Europe to stand more closely together in a very big and tough world, big and tough both politically and economically. The Treaty of Rome was not, to use Mrs Thatcher's words at Bruges, 'a charter for economic liberty'. The aim was, and remains, ever closer political union. There is nothing sinister in the means for bringing this about being partially economic.

Neither was there any truth in the claim, echoed by the Referendum Party in 1997, that the United Kingdom was being governed unaccountably 'from Brussels'. The European Commission has no final authority over the British or any other people. Its role is to submit proposals, in draft, for new legislation on the basis of the Treaty of Rome (as amended). All decision-making is undertaken by the Council of Ministers, on which the British are fully represented. The Council may decide to accept a Commission proposal, to reject it or to send it back to the Commission to be amended, taking account of the views expressed by Ministers. Even on decisions made by majority voting the positions of individual states matter a great deal. Although QMV is now the rule in the Community, every effort is still made, as it was while the so-called Luxembourg Compromise of 1966 was in force, to achieve a consensus, even where this is not strictly required. Moreover, the voting weights within the Council have been very carefully negotiated to ensure that no member state and no group of states with similar interests can dictate to the rest. It is neurotic paranoia to suppose that we British always end up on the losing side. The UK was outvoted in the Council of Ministers on only fourteen occasions in 1996–7. Germany, in contrast, was outvoted twenty-two times during this period. It is only when agreement has been reached on any proposal that it is possible for the Commission to issue the regulations necessary to implement it. As one of the prime purposes of the Community's institutions is to ensure that everyone is treated fairly, the regulations are very largely issued to ensure that the same standards are maintained by all. For every single regulation issued by the Commission, fifteen different ones can be abolished in the member countries. This is a reduction in bureaucracy and 'red tape', not an increase in it.

The philosophy behind the single market regulations is flexible in application, with the emphasis on mutual recognition rather than harmonisation. A flurry of scare stories about European regulations has certainly fuelled public prejudice in Britain against Europe and, even though these have rarely contained a shred of truth, our own government has not been immune from capitalising upon them for political purposes. It is true that we impose excessive, and excessively complicated, regulations on our industries. The overwhelming majority of these regulations, however, are not 'European'; they come from within member states and are approved by their Ministers. Both the UK and Germany have been criticised for 'gold-plating' European directives, adding unnecessarily to their complexity and to the costs which they impose on industries when introducing them domestically. Most of these directives are about very basic standards, and it is up to national governments to look for the often great degree of flexibility explicitly contained within them.

There is only one form of regulation which the Commission has power under the Treaties to issue itself, and that is narrowly defined and severely limited under Article 145 of the Treaty of Rome. This Article grants the Commission powers for implementing the rules upon which the Council has decided. If Ministers feel that regulations issued by the Commission do not reflect their collective views then, of course, the Commission can be challenged in the European Court of Justice. We generally comply with European law not because we are *forced* to, but because we accept that in the overall scheme of things we benefit from the existence, and uniform enforcement, of a framework of European law. The most obvious example is the laws governing the operation of the single market. A vast single market needs policing, according to a single set of rules. This is the job of the European Commission and the European Court of Justice. European laws can be enforced in member states only by the member states themselves.

British Conservatives base their entire approach to politics on the rule of law, and rightly so. Without it, life would quickly descend into anarchy and chaos. In the single market, the European Court of Justice obliges member states to follow the path of legality. Britain has always been seen as a country which plays by the rules, and we have had a commendable record in implementing European legislation. We should view the judgements from the Court of Justice as a way of upholding the rule of law. If any country does not agree with the law it can always attempt to change it through the Council of Ministers. In 1996, only one of the ninety-two referrals to the Court (under Article 169) applied to the UK. Those who call for a repatriation of powers must recognise that this would render it far more difficult, if not impossible, to bring wrongdoers to account, whoever they are. Outside the European Union, we would be unable to use the Commission and the Court of Justice to act against monopolies and state aids distorting markets across Europe.

The scale of bureaucracy continues to be wildly exaggerated. There are approximately four European Commission officials for every 100,000 citizens in the European Union. In contrast there are 3,220 national civil servants for every 100,000 European citizens. In 1988 the bureaucracy in Brussels, responsible for 322 million Europeans, was smaller than the Scottish Office bureaucracy in Edinburgh, which was responsible for 5.5 million people. Mrs Thatcher had made this very point herself during the Referendum campaign of 1975 (see p. 546). The comments about Brussels bureaucrats are in part malicious, because in addition to being officials a high proportion of them are foreigners and, therefore, so far as the newspapers are concerned, soft targets. Often the condemnation of able, hard-working, devoted men and women springs from an inferiority complex and from resentment that the officials maintain standards that the politicians and journalists themselves cannot match. Members of the Conservative Government in the 1980s should be the last to complain about the European Commission. No other British government in peacetime has systematically arrogated powers to the centre in the way they did.

At the 1988 Conservative Party conference I decided to answer the Bruges speech. It was similar, in many ways, to the stand I had taken at the 1981 party conference over economic policy. I reminded the conference that our party and its leaders had always been in the forefront of the move towards European unity, and I paid tribute to the role of Geoffrey Howe in moving the Community forward towards the single market. I ended my speech as follows: 'As far back as 1940, our leaders had the vision to see a Europe which was going to be united. We have maintained that vision in our party and amongst our leaders. That is where the future lies for us and for Britain. If we carry ahead that vision we shall be successful.'

The helpful response from Geoffrey Howe at the end of the debate was in complete contrast to the boos and hisses from some sections of the Hall during my speech. Many of the delegates were eager for more of the 'Brussels-bashing' that had become so depressingly repetitive during the debate, and which would hit new heights of offensiveness during Michael Portillo's 'Who Dares Wins' speech at the 1995 party conference. I was followed to the rostrum in 1988 by Jonathan Aitken, the MP for my own birthplace. It had originally been planned that he would speak before me in the debate. By a deliberate manoeuvre of the party officials, however, he was called after I was. Aitken attacked me in strong personal terms, and described me as the 'unacceptable face of Conservatism'. I never thought that my hometown would elect a non-Conservative as its representative in Parliament, which it did in the 1997 general election. Aitken's one political achievement and testament is the presence now in the House of Commons of a Labour Member of Parliament for Thanet.

The contents of the Bruges Speech also came as a bombshell to other countries in the European Community. Indeed, such was its impact that one European Foreign Minister said to me, 'You British have gone back to where you were before 1950.' On Monday 29 May 1989, therefore, I went to Brussels intending to 'wipe away the stain on its [the European Community's] principles and beliefs left behind last September by what is now known as the Bruges Speech by the British Prime Minister'. In doing so I was breaking the convention, which I had always hitherto observed, that you should never criticise your country's leaders from abroad, a convention which was subsequently repeatedly broken by Mrs Thatcher herself during John Major's premiership. The situation had become critical, however, and there was a dangerous amount of ill-feeling being generated between Britain and the rest of the European Community. This was not the fault of the British people, who had heard nothing but negative propaganda about our European partners for many years. The blame lay at the hands of some members of the British government and some of the British press.

In that speech, I repeated the arguments that I had raised during the party conference the previous year and scotched the idea that the Community was socialist, let alone Marxist. This suggestion had gained currency after Jacques Delors had addressed the TUC conference on 8 September 1988 and was later intensified by the Community Charter of Fundamental Social Rights in 1989. It was, of course, false. Opinion polls show that business representatives are among those groups most likely to favour membership of the European Union. The anti-European policy of Labour in 1980–3 was spearheaded by left-wing trade unions, and Jacques Delors deserves full credit for moving the British trade unions towards supporting the European Community with his speech at their conference.

After my Brussels speech, I expressed my fear that the British Prime Minister wanted to see the break-up of the Community. My comments received a predictably hostile reaction from the media at home and I was even attacked by Douglas Hurd and Kenneth Baker, both of whom had once worked closely with me. I defended my comments by saying: 'We have reached the stage where there is no point in going on talking in coded terms. Ex-Ministers have been doing that for ten years. One has to speak out because the situation is so serious.' I have always believed that I should air publicly any substantial disagreements with my successors, rather than stirring up trouble for them in private. I prefer this method to off-the-record briefings and coded criticism.

When Mrs Thatcher authorised entry into the Exchange Rate Mechanism of the European Monetary System in 1990, she was falling into line with what was understood to be the view of virtually every other member of the Cabinet at that time. But they were so keen to prove that the pound was strong and buoyant that it went in at palpably too high a level, which proved to be both deflationary and, ultimately, unsustainable. If we had entered the ERM in 1985, it would have been at an exchange rate from which we would have benefited greatly. We could have avoided the inflation of the late 1980s and might have been able to resist further attacks on sterling. As it was, during our two years in the ERM both our interest rates and the rate of inflation decreased substantially. What drove us out of the ERM in September 1992 was the sheer scale of 'hot money' speculation in international financial markets, particularly encouraged in this case by the well-founded belief that the Conservative government was unsure of its attitude to the European Union. Whereas the Bundesbank supported the French, we went down the drain because we were seen to be so anti-European.

This served as a warning to those who believe in the long-term sustainability of 'fixed peg' systems, such as the ERM. Our experience on 'Black Wednesday' should have hardened our determination to get into a single currency in Europe, as early and as enthusiastically as possible – at the right rate. So long as the ERM remained a multi-currency system, and no matter how tight the bands were, it could never have been rigid enough. That is because the investors who were selling currencies and betting against the system know that, once the pressure on any particular currency mounted beyond a certain point, governments would have to devalue, or withdraw from the ERM. This illustrates the distinction between monetary convergence and monetary union, and highlights the latter's superiority.

The Euro can be as strong as the dollar, and will present a strong buttress against speculation. It will also put an end to so-called 'competitive devaluation' within Europe. If we are in economic trouble in future, we shall just have to take serious action to deal with it by improving our productivity. With a single currency, no individual country will be able to cheat by allowing, or encouraging, its currency to depreciate, thereby making its exports more competitive. Our industries will have to do what their continental rivals do – invest, innovate and research on a larger scale. Only then will we have a true single market. No single market has ever survived with competing currencies.

Undeniably, the German government's decision to finance Germany's unification by increasing borrowing, rather than raising taxes, exerted a huge strain on the ERM. It deepened the recession in non-German countries by forcing up their interest rates. West Germany, however, deserves the highest praise for accepting responsibility for 16 million people in the East who had been under Soviet domination for forty years. I warmly and unreservedly welcomed the unification of Germany in October 1990. One could only admire the speed and effectiveness with which the Germans acted. Speaking on the occasion of the fortieth anniversary of the Federal Republic of Germany in Frankfurt on 9 May 1989, I had said, 'While the Berlin Wall remains erect as a symbol of the current ideological divide, we cannot expect to see a solution of all East–West problems. If *perestroika* is for real then let them tear down the wall. One day we will see a united Europe, sooner than many think.' To my astonishment, the Wall came down that same year.

It was understandable that the idea of a united Germany struck fear into the hearts of many European countries. There still remained a residue of anxiety that, despite the passage of time, the new Germany might behave like its forebears and become militarily aggressive again or at least seek to exert political and economic power over its neighbours. This fear was intensified after the remarkable break-up of the Soviet Union in 1991. I was appalled by the rabid, bigoted, xenophobic attacks on Germany within the UK during this momentous period. Support for German unity had been a consistent feature of British foreign policy since the late 1940s. By abandoning it, Mrs Thatcher undermined at a stroke the trust which a whole generation of German politicians had reposed in us. West Germany had acted as a model member of the European Community and a united Germany had no designs on 'taking over Europe'.

Under Adenauer's leadership, the West Germans rebuilt their cities and their political institutions and became a bastion of freedom. Under the leadership of Ludwig Erhard, they pioneered the social-market economy and became the economic powerhouse of Europe. Under Willy Brandt and Helmut Schmidt, they played a broker's role at the heart of Europe, ensuring peace between the power blocs of the day. Under Helmut Kohl, they succeeded in assimilating the people of Eastern Germany. This was despite the economic chaos and the daunting environmental challenges which came together with the collapse of the communist regime in that country. The only mistake in retrospect was that the rate of exchange at which the West German government converted East German Marks into West German Marks was excessively generous. If they had followed the Bundesbank's original advice of a ratio of 3:1, then there would not have been so many problems. Nevertheless the Germans will overcome any teething troubles. Germany has, at last, conquered its dark side and joined the free world for good. The answer to people's fears of an aggressively expansionist Germany or an economically dominant one still lies in binding the Federal Republic of Germany more and more tightly into the European Union. This remains the stated wish of the federal government and of the German people. It means that Germany will be bound not only by any external undertakings it might give, but also by the institutional bonds of being a member of the Union.

Looked at from this perspective, the events of the late 1980s and early 1990s made further European integration more, not less, desirable. Gone are the days when the nations of Europe were completely encapsulated in the cauldron of the Cold War. In its place was a rapidly emerging multi-power world in which Europe, as one of these powers, has a profoundly important role to play. The case for a Common Foreign and Security Policy became unanswerable, and the problems in the Gulf and Yugoslavia demonstrated that the Community countries had no serious means of co-ordinating their response on vital security issues. Meanwhile, the strength of the German economy resulted in the Bundesbank effectively being able to govern monetary policy for the whole of Europe. The Deutschmark is already a dominant European currency. Economic and monetary union will not make Germany any less powerful, nor should it, but it will prevent German power being asserted independently of the wishes of the other members of a single currency. This is why EMU has the support of almost all European leaders, whatever their political hue. It would serve three essential European interests: anchoring Germany firmly in Western Europe; enabling all member states to exercise real influence over European monetary policy; and ending the currency instability that has impaired pan-European trade and investment.

When John Major became Prime Minister, relations with Germany swiftly improved. In Bonn on 11 March 1991 he said: 'My aims for Britain in the Community can be very clearly stated. I want us to be where we belong – at the very heart of Europe, working with our partners in building the future. This is the challenge we take up with enthusiasm.' His greatest success in Europe came during the Maastricht negotiations in December 1991. The Maastricht Treaty updated and supplemented the Treaty of Rome, creating the European Union. This is based on the existing European Community, flanked by two inter-governmental pillars, a Common Foreign and Security Policy (CFSP) and Justice and Home Affairs (JHA). The Maastricht Treaty also established the procedure for EMU, and the principle of subsidiarity which meant that power would not be vested in the Community if it could be better exercised at national or local level. John Major and Douglas Hurd deserve the warmest praise for their contribution to the final agreement and all three major political parties adopted pro-Maastricht manifestos during the 1992 general election. Conservative MEPs also ended their 'glorious isolation' within the European Parliament and joined the European People's Party group of Conservatives and Christian Democrats on 1 May 1992.

As his premiership went on, however, John Major was lured into a policy of trying constantly to appease the Euro-sceptics. This resulted in his moving further and further away from what he had said in Bonn. It led to incidents which were quite humiliating for the UK, for example the disputes over voting weights in the Council of Ministers and over the choice of President of the Commission after Jacques Delors. The British often boast of having the finest democracy in the world. How can such a system, in which all three major political parties fought the 1992 general election in favour of Maastricht, have taken such an interminable time to reach a conclusion on the Maastricht Bill? Was it really necessary to allow the large majorities in both Houses of Parliament in favour of the Treaty to be constantly thwarted by a small group of vocal Euro-sceptics, who managed to exact more undertakings from Ministers which further weakened John Major's position? Having been a member of the Conservative Party for over fifty years, I cannot recall any similar episode. The Maastricht rebels were quite entitled to hold views different from those of the government. Naturally, divisions over policy had arisen before, for example during the battles over India in the 1930s and throughout the Suez crisis in 1956. The treacherous antics of the Maastricht rebels, however, were quite unprecedented and their spoiling tactics extended even to a widespread refusal to support a Conservative government on business motions, something which had not occurred on anything like that scale during the long debates on the ratification of the Treaty of Accession in 1972.

The Major government did not handle the Maastricht Bill well. After receiving massive support at second reading, the government should immediately have pressed ahead in the Commons to finish the process. Instead it delayed. After the negative result of the Danish referendum on Maastricht in June 1992 it promised, in response to a sizeable backbench revolt, not to complete the UK procedure in the House of Commons until the Danish referendum result was reversed. This was absolutely unnecessary and constitutional nonsense. The Danish referendum was their affair, not ours. All this decision achieved was to create a deep suspicion within the EU that the British were ganging up with the Danes to break up the Community. This poisonous atmosphere continued in the run-up to the 1997 general election.

Since 1950 I have experienced many unpleasant incidents in British politics. However, all these paled into insignificance beside the negative, personal and deliberately mendacious nature of the Referendum Party's 1997 general election campaign. By the private financial contribution of one man, the late Sir James Goldsmith, the Referendum Party had £25 million to spend on their billboard posters and all of the misleading material which was placed through the public's letterboxes. The Referendum Party decided to target me as their prime enemy, and I was the victim of constant smears and lies. They may have thought it was in their interests to personalise their attacks on me, although in fact they were really denigrating many leading figures of the Conservative Party, including Churchill, Macmillan, Home, Thatcher and Major. Why then did the Conservative Party make the suicidal decision not to stand up to the Referendum Party's lies and smears? I do not recall one Cabinet Minister, with the notable exception of Kenneth Clarke, taking the argument to the Referendum Party. Presumably they were running ahead of provoking the right wing of the party, who had held John Major to ransom ever since the 1992 general election.

This was kamikaze politics. Although I had my own policy differences with John Major, he had my support at all times. He deserved so much better from his colleagues.

My views on Europe go back to when I was a young man travelling through Germany in 1937. They have remained steadfast ever since. I do not doubt the sincerity of those who oppose further integration, nor that they are motivated by a genuine belief that they are fighting for Britain. But so am I. The nationalistic card blinds some people to the motivation behind the European treaties, and the goal of an ever-closer union to which we have constantly committed ourselves. I have no objection to people changing their minds on Europe. That is their right in a free country. Nonetheless those politicians who now hide behind the charge that I wilfully deceived the people of this country should know better. There was no conspiracy. I have been debating Britain's role in the world and the question of sovereignty since the 1950s. Looking back on my political career, perhaps at times it would have suited me to have been more wily. My mother and father, however, instilled in me at a young age the importance of honesty and sincerity. I have an honest disagreement with those who oppose European integration, and I always have done. I just wish that they all took a similarly mature view, rather than resorting to foul-mouthed accusations and historical distortions. I believe that I have demonstrated in this book that it is not I who would rewrite the history of our relationship with Europe.

One of the Referendum Party's advertisements during the election campaign referred to one-half of a statement in the 1971 White Paper: 'There is no question of any erosion of essential national sovereignty.' Their advertisement presented this as a complete sentence, followed by a full stop. It was not. There was a semi-colon. They deliberately and misleadingly omitted the second, explanatory half of the sentence which clarifies the practical nature of the concept being presented: 'what is proposed is a sharing and an enlargement of individual national sovereignties in the general interest'. Furthermore, and this is no mere sophistry, the word 'essential' is very important. It refers, for example, to our powers of self-government, our right to safeguard national interests and to keep sole control of our armed forces. I have used the phrase 'pooling sovereignty' since the early 1960s. A campaign pamphlet produced and widely proliferated by Conservative Central Office in 1971, entitled *Europe and You*, spelt out the nature of sovereignty in the modern world:

> Stripped of its emotional overtones, sovereignty is the freedom to act independently of others – something rarely possible for individual countries in the modern world.

Britain does not have complete freedom of action now. So many decisions are governed by outside influences, to say nothing of the views of friends and allies. And we already have many international obligations.

If Britain joins, certain important decisions will become a joint responsibility instead of just a British one. But as an equal partner we would have an equal say in influencing those decisions . . . For this reason it is misleading to talk of Britain 'surrendering' sovereignty. As others would influence our future, we should influence theirs . . . membership would mean that Britain and her partners would exercise sovereignty in a new and larger dimension.

The Referendum Party also gave a false impression from an exchange of letters that I had with the ardently pro-European Lord Chancellor, Lord Kilmuir, back in December 1960. Right at the beginning of David Kilmuir's letter to me he writes, 'At the end of the day, the issue whether or not to join the European Economic Community must be decided on broad political grounds and if it appears from what follows in this letter that I find the constitutional objections serious that does not mean that I consider them conclusive.' He emphasises at the end of his letter that 'although these constitutional considerations must be given their full weight when we come to balance the arguments on either side, I do not for one moment wish to convey the impression that they must necessarily tip the scale'. Why then did the Referendum Party omit his balanced judgement?

Kilmuir's letter was sent on 14 December 1960, when the British government was considering an application to join the Community. The Cabinet did not make a final decision until July 1961 and Parliament was informed of this decision on 31 July. During the debate that followed, I dealt with the whole question of sovereignty (see p. 210). I made the same points during Labour's flirtation with Europe of 1966–7 (see pp. 357–8) in the 'Great Debate' of October 1971, I said:

It is right that there should have been so much discussion of sovereignty. I would put it very simply. If sovereignty exists to be used and to be of value, it must be effective. We have to make a judgement whether this is the most advantageous way of using our country's sovereignty. Sovereignty belongs to all of us, and to make that judgement we must look at the way the Community has actually worked during the last twelve years. In joining we are making a commitment which involves our sovereignty, but we are also gaining an opportunity. We are making a commitment to the Community as it exists tonight, if the House so decides. We are gaining an opportunity to influence its decisions in the future.

We hear much these days about threats to British sovereignty, but sovereignty is not an absolute good in itself. Its value is defined by the use we make of it. Sovereignty for a nation means the right to decide for itself how best to preserve and foster the peace, freedom and prosperity of its people. There are times when that purpose may be best served by sharing sovereignty between historic nation states. The British shared an important element of sovereignty when we joined NATO because we thought, quite rightly as it turned out, that to do so was in the best interests of preserving national peace and freedom. We shared sovereignty in economic and monetary affairs when we joined the International Monetary Fund and the World Bank, because we thought that our national prosperity would be best served by our adherence to the global financial system which they created. We shared sovereignty again in joining the European Community and, under Mrs Thatcher's leadership, on a gigantic scale in signing up for the single market and the Single European Act. Any international co-operation or alliance involves some sharing of national sovereignties. It is surely self-defeating, in the modern world, to reject all such arrangements. History warns us that it is only if nation states are prepared to share sovereignty in international institutions that they will be able to avoid the destructive conflicts which have resulted from attempts to assert national sovereignty without regard to the rights and needs of others. International institutions can sublimate the destructive old rivalries which were the seedcorn of wars. Today's co-operation has a powerful synergy. A united, peaceful and prosperous Europe is demonstrably more than the sum of its historically fissiparous parts.

Furthermore, it is only through international institutions, in which sovereignty is pooled, that we shall be able collectively to manage the many international problems which human progress brings in its wake: environmental change; trade liberalisation; economic and social dislocation; and criminal activity. We surely cannot hope to deal with these problems by ourselves. In the modern world, so many of the problems and challenges that we face have no respect for national boundaries. It is perverse for politicians to ignore such a development. The nation states of Europe, including Britain, need the European Union to perform tasks that none of them can perform on their own. The Union could, in fact, be described as an attempt by its member states to regain collectively part of the sovereignty that each has individually had to yield to market forces.

The Referendum Party also used an answer that I gave to Peter Sissons on BBC Television on 1 November 1990. They said that this proves that I always had in mind a 'United States of Europe' with a single currency. It proves no such thing. The question was 'Single currency? United States of Europe? Was all that in your mind when you took Britain in?' I answered the first part of the question, concerning a single currency, by replying, 'Of course. Yes.' EMU has been an aim of the Community for many years, a fact which no-one has concealed. Then I went on to answer the second half of the question about a 'United States of Europe'. I said: 'There is no point using the general term "United States of Europe" because when Churchill first proposed this . . . he said we shall be a kind of United States of Europe. We shan't be exactly the same as the United States because we are going to form our own unity.' The common values between the US and the EU are a love of liberty, a belief in democracy and a sense of responsibility to the wider world outside.

I was often asked why I did not sue Sir James Goldsmith for defamation of character. My answer is simple. I could not afford a court case against a multi-billionaire. There would have been nothing that Goldsmith would have liked more than a high-profile court case against a former Prime Minister and I was determined not to give him the publicity that he, and the Referendum Party, craved. Moreover, the letters of support that I received from the public reassured me that they were not going to be taken in by this expatriate demagogue and his assorted cronies. I was particularly grateful for the support of Teddy Taylor, the only member of the 1970–4 Conservative government to resign over the decision to join the European Community. In a letter to the *Daily Telegraph* on 21 January 1997, Taylor reminded its readers that I 'made it abundantly clear that membership would lead to further Euro-integration' and 'didn't hide the consequences'. Vernon Bogdanor, the respected Professor of Government at Oxford, and John Campbell, who had a biography of me published in 1991, were also tremendously helpful in answering these ridiculous charges. From the left, Margaret Beckett, who voted against membership in the 1975 Referendum, told BBC Television during the 1997 election campaign that 'one thing I would say to you . . . and I think others will confirm this, everything that's being said now, by people say in the Referendum Party, about how all of this was unforeseen, about how none of this was mentioned, I am afraid it's not so. It was all spelt out, it was all discussed and aired. People may or may not have decided to take this seriously, but it was all on the table twenty-two years ago and now we have made our decision.'

There was therefore absolutely no justification for the allegations made by the Referendum Party during the 1997 general election. I was astonished to hear the name of their candidate in Old Bexley and Sidcup, who turned out to be my former economic adviser at Conservative Central Office and later at the Cabinet Office, Brian Reading. He wrote to me on 30 December 1996 to explain his decision.

You may wonder why I am standing against you . . . You were bound to be opposed by a Referendum Party candidate. It therefore seemed desirable that it should be one who holds you in great respect – which I do . . . your views on Europe are forthright and openly expressed. I disagree with them and will argue against them. In this way it may be possible for the issues to be debated without fudge or rancour.

I was rather perplexed by this ingenuous-sounding letter. As the Referendum Party's campaign appeared to be wholly based on the accusation that I had misled people, or, even worse, lied, it seemed rather odd for their candidate to say that my 'views on Europe are forthright and openly expressed'. Then, in a public meeting at Chislehurst and Sidcup Grammar School on 28 April 1997, Reading disappointed his tiny throng of supporters by admitting, 'I did not like our advertisement accusing him of lying . . . Heath did not lie.' As Brian Reading knew full well, the Referendum Party's national campaign was an abuse of wealth, privilege and our liberal political institutions. It was unforgivable to distribute unprovable charges in this way. It was a very dangerous precedent, and I am glad that the good sense of the British people enabled them to judge the issues for themselves. And what was their judgement? Referendum Party candidates lost their deposits in virtually every constituency in which they fielded a candidate, including those of Brian Reading and, in Putney, Goldsmith himself.

I was well aware that the 1997 general election campaign would be my toughest campaign since 1966. This had nothing to do with the Referendum Party or Europe. Boundary changes had not been kind to me. My electorate was increased by 18,619 and my pleasure at welcoming back Welling and the many old friends there from past campaigns was marred by the fact that this had become a mainly Liberal and Labour area. The unpopularity of the Conservative Party, in sharp contrast to the new and invigorated Labour Party, made the task even tougher. My election agent, Howard Ruse, warned in a letter of 28 November 1996:

You are, of course, aware that there has been a continuing decline in membership since 1989 . . . Younger, traditionally Conservative supporters have mostly had a very difficult period over the last 6 or 7 years . . . having had to face, in worse cases, redundancy, negative equity, failing businesses or even bankruptcy. Those who are in work or are running their own businesses are gaining confidence in the future but have not yet forgotten the past. Small businessmen . . . who have tended to provide our most active support, are putting in very long working hours and have very little spare time available; a problem I know only too well myself!

Shortly before the election a Council by-election was held in the previously safe Sidcup East ward of my constituency, after the death of Councillor Peggy Flint, a long-standing public servant who had been on the Bexley parliamentary selection committee which chose me in 1947. Our candidate was Peggy's husband William, a former mayor of the borough. He won by just thirty-eight votes and, if this result had been repeated across the whole constituency in the general election, my record of thirteen consecutive victories since 1950 would have come to an abrupt end.

I was fortunate that I could, once again, count on a number of people who performed heroically during the election campaign. As well as Howard Ruse, I had an experienced campaign secretary in Barry Fowler and my private office was represented by Michael McManus Anthony Staddon and Jay Dossetter. Our campaign was also helped by many of my former private secretaries, including Douglas Hurd, Peter Batey and Wilf Weeks, and other colourful characters such as Derek Brierley and Jeffery Speed, my former agent. Together we toured the whole of the constituency and, in the early hours of Friday morning, our efforts were rewarded. As Conservative seats across the south-east of England and London fell like dominoes, I was returned with a majority of 3,569. In the context of the evening, this seemed like a triumph, for the Conservative Party experienced a shocking defeat in the 1997 general election. I had warned the party that many of our policies, in particular on devolution, the minimum wage and Europe, were completely remote from the views of the country. Even so I was devastated by the result on 1 May.

The decision to campaign on an increasingly Euro-sceptic ticket was a huge and costly mistake, which served to highlight the Conservative government's own internal divisions while overshadowing those issues about which the voters were really concerned. Unfortunately, Central Office ignored these issues in favour of negative and, at times, deliberately falsified attacks on Brussels and Germany. Crude tactics will never win elections in this country and I am sure that a more dignified and positive campaign would have proved more popular with the voters in 1997.

With his ill-motivated gloating over the weekend of 3–4 May 1997, Sir James Goldsmith made it perfectly plain that the Referendum Party had succeeded in its true objective, namely losing seats for moderate pro-European Tories. In fact, even this dispiriting and malevolent claim to infamy was bogus. Goldsmith wasted his money. The Referendum Party's votes cost almost £25 each. The respected Nuffield study of the 1997 general election suggests that the Referendum Party cost the Conservative

Party only one seat net in 1997, as there were up to three seats where it may well have helped to avoid a Conservative defeat. So why are there so many senior Conservative figures willing to give the Referendum Party credit for a futile campaign which was designed solely to impose Euro-sceptical 'ethnic cleansing' on the Conservative Party? All Goldsmith succeeded in achieving was a massive pro-European majority in the House of Commons. The Nuffield study itself concludes: 'Insofar as the objective of Sir James Goldsmith's campaign was to inflict losses on the Conservatives, it must largely be deemed to have been a failure.'

A cynical myth perpetuated by Euro-sceptics since the election is that almost all of the Referendum Party's voters were ex-Conservatives and to win the next general election the party needs to adopt a clearer Euro-sceptical message. There is no empirical evidence for this. Peter Kellner, one of our best-informed psephologists, analysed the results of 1 May and, writing in the *Observer* on 18 May 1997, reported that the results showed that 'Had this year's turnout matched 1992's level, and had the Referendum Party not existed, Labour would still have won its biggest victory, and the Tories would still have won their smallest share of the vote since 1832.' According to Kellner's figures, 3.2 million people who voted Conservative in 1992 switched to a different party in 1997: 1.4 million to Labour; 1.2 million to the Liberal Democrats; 400,000 to the Referendum Party; and 200,000 to nationalist and other minority parties. The Referendum Party received 811,827 votes. Fewer than half of them came from people who had voted Conservative in 1992. In contrast the Conservative Party lost 2.6 million voters to the Labour Party and the Liberal Democrats. These facts speak for themselves.

The Conservative Party must return to sound mainstream policies if we are going to win back those floating voters. We will not achieve this by becoming rabidly anti-European. Euro-sceptical parties are committing demographic suicide. Support for EU membership among those under the age of thirty-five is twice as high as among those over that age. This is an additional problem for the Conservative Party as the average age of our members is approaching sixty-five. The Conservative Party's strategy of attracting right-wing extreme Euro-sceptics was given a trial run in the unnecessary by-election in Winchester. Gerry Malone, the Conservative candidate, is himself a moderate and sensible man. His by-election tactic, of publicly welcoming back on board senior Referendum Party supporters within the constituency, however, backfired spectacularly. No doubt Malone won back a few dozen wandering Euro-sceptics, but a herd of moderates leaped into the arms of the Liberal Democrats, turning their majority of 2 into 21,556. The national lessons of such a result must be self-evident.

Let the Conservative Party make no mistake about it. The case for a European Union, and for British membership of it, is as strong today as it was in 1950 and in 1975. NATO and the European Union have, in the last half-century, been dazzlingly successful in providing a political and institutional framework which has prevented the resurgence of Franco-German rivalry, and accordingly minimised the risk of a further outbreak of war. That risk has now become so remote that it seems unimaginable that things could be otherwise. But we should not conclude that we now no longer need the European Union, because the threat is somehow past. It is not scaremongering to warn that, if the European Union were to atrophy, Franco-German rivalries could still revive. A unified Germany, with its 80 million people and its fundamentally strong and successful economy, can be contained within the European Union, and can contribute to the greater cohesion and prosperity of Europe as a whole. Without the European Union, a unified Germany could all too easily become a threat to the prosperity and cohesion of its neighbours.

Nor does the collapse of the communist regime in Russia and of the old Soviet Union lessen the need for the European Union in the global context. Today's world situation is not like those of 1914 or 1939. In those days, if Europe sneezed, the world caught a cold. What happened within the individual countries of Europe was central to the world situation, and events in other parts of the world seemed, to the Europeans, to be peripheral. For the foreseeable future, the associations and the rivalries that are going to matter are not those between the nations of Europe but those between far larger political and industrial power blocs: North America, the European Union, Russia, Japan and China.

What I fear people do not fully appreciate is how much the world has changed since the end of the last world war. For over forty years, we seemed to be living in a world of two superpowers – the United States of America and the USSR. Any other country which stepped out of line could expect to be fallen upon by one or the other. It was a balance of terror, but the balance was there for all to see, and enabled people to know where they stood. Now the picture is far more complicated, for we have one of those – the US – still a superpower, but suddenly far more dominant. The former USSR remains a military superpower, but is politically unstable. Then we have China, with 1.25 billion people. Japan is also worthy of superpower status. Alongside these, there is the European Union, with over 350 million citizens. In this situation, political union, which was already on the agenda in the two-superpower world of the early 1960s, is becoming imperative. The supposed 'option' of going it alone politically while retaining all economic advantages is simply not one which other countries are going to make available. Our partners have chosen their course, and we have signed up alongside them, so they are extremely unlikely to make fundamental changes in order to accommodate us.

My commitment to the union of the peoples and nations of Europe springs directly from my One Nation principles. So does my belief in the great benefit for Europe, as well as for Britain, of our being a full, and full-hearted, member of the European Union. I have not wavered. In 1945 we were looking back on four wars within a century and a half, three of which were world wars in the sense that they were fought beyond, as well as within, the boundaries of Europe itself, and all of which had roots in the rivalry between France and Germany for hegemony in Europe. In three of those four wars, Britain had been a participant. In 1945 all of Europe, including Britain, was painfully aware of the loss of life, the physical damage and the economic cost inflicted by the wars on the victors as well as on the vanquished. My own outlook was deeply coloured by my first-hand experience of the conflict itself, which served only to confirm and strengthen views which I had already formed.

Geographically, historically and culturally, Britain is a European country. Our history has been defined primarily by our relations with the countries of continental Europe. British culture is a part of European culture, whether in art, music, drama or literature. We share with our European neighbours Shakespeare ('unserer Shakespeare' as they say in Germany) and Britten, Beethoven and Goethe, Rousseau and Renoir, Cervantes and Velasquez, Dante and Verdi. Even the development of the British Empire, though it turned our attention and energies to some extent outside Europe, was in large measure a product of the expansion of European rivalries into a global setting. In widening our influence, we were seeking to establish, in the face of challenges from other European powers, a British position in world trade routes and in sources of food products and other raw materials.

Now that the British Empire, great and often noble venture though it was, is indeed 'one with Nineveh and Tyre', our future lies clearly and inescapably where our roots are, in Europe, and in membership of the European Union. The case for British membership was not clearly recognised by the British establishment in the 1950s, and we missed the opportunity to be a founder member of the European Community, and to benefit, as our European neighbours did, from its growing prosperity in the early years. But it continued to be the profound belief of men like Jean Monnet and Robert Schuman that the European Community would not realise its full potential without Britain as a member.

By the 1960s, the decline in British economic power at home and political influence abroad, particularly in the wake of the Suez crisis, was so marked and self-evident that even the most stubborn League of Empire loyalists knew that the clock could not be turned back. It had also become clear to most senior politicians that neither a satellite relationship to the United States nor our relationship with the sovereign countries of the Commonwealth would be satisfactory as a foundation for Britain's international political and economic policies. More and more politicians accordingly came to the view that Britain's future, like so much of its history, lay in Europe – and that we needed to become part of the European Community, or risk becoming marginal in the development of world economic, monetary and trade relations. Some came to support European integration for political and pragmatic reasons, Harold Macmillan and, later, Reggie Maudling being cases in point. Others, such as Roy Jenkins and myself, were more attracted culturally to such unity. But the general movement was firmly in the direction of Europe.

A further point was much in my own mind through successive rounds of negotiations for British membership of the European Community. So long as the war-torn economies of continental Europe were still labouring away in the early stages of economic and industrial recovery, British industry found it relatively easy, deceptively easy perhaps, to maintain a healthy share of world trade. As the continental economies recovered, modernising their industries in the process, British industry found the going harder. It was clear to me that the challenge and stimulus of being part of a single European market and competing, in Europe and beyond it, with industry and commerce from the countries that were already members of the European Community, would provide a significant reinforcement of Conservative policies to promote industrial regeneration, efficiency and productivity in the United Kingdom. So it has proved.

Twenty years later than I would have liked, it fell to me as Prime Minister to complete successful negotiations for British entry. Thereafter, we spent ten years negotiating within the Community to improve the terms of our membership; and we were then late joining the European Exchange Rate Mechanism, eventually taking the pound in at a rate which was unsustainable. We played our part, though perhaps dutifully rather than enthusiastically, in the creation of the single market and the adoption of the Single European Act. At Maastricht we insisted upon the right to opt out from the final stage of EMU and the single currency, as well as from the social chapter. Since the mid-1970s, we have earned a reputation as reluctant, backward-looking and foot-dragging Europeans. It is scarcely surprising, therefore, that we have not been able to exercise the influence that we should have been able to exert if our partners had perceived us to be at the heart of Europe, and fully committed to its ideals. Jean Monnet always thought that the British would join Europe when we saw that it was successful. We failed in 1950, 1958 and in the EMS. In each case, the British began by saying that the project was utopian, that it would never come to fruition. Then we said that we would see how it worked before we joined. This approach is short-sighted and extremely damaging to the national interest. It puts us in the position of joining a club when the rules have already been agreed without our participation.

I do hope that the British government will not repeat past mistakes in decisions concerning economic and monetary union. Whether to join the final phase of EMU will be a very important choice for us. It must be made on the basis not of Euro-phobic prejudice, nor of romantic illusions based on past glories, but of a careful and thorough analysis of where the balance of national advantage lies. I have no doubt that the balance of advantage will be in favour of our joining and, for the sake of our ability to provide the leadership at the heart of Europe, I hope that our decision to join will be taken sooner rather than later. To rule out membership of EMU indefinitely, or even for a long period of ten years, is just absurd. If a week is a long time in politics, ten years must be like an eternity.

I foresee for the European Union a process of gradual but steady evolution towards greater integration. There is much to do. The institutions and procedures of the Union must be developed, to accommodate the views and aspirations of a larger number of members. A more even distribution and balance of powers must also be devised, based on the principle of subsidiarity, as between the institutions of the European Union, national governments and regional and local government. We in the United Kingdom are particularly centralised, and need to get on with putting our own house in order, by developing local and regional democracy.

I do not doubt that we can continue to have a close relationship with the United States and the Commonwealth, based on common interests and on ties of kinship, language and a shared history. But the US nowadays values its relationship with us as a member of the European Union, and would have far less interest in us if we were outside it. Our membership of the Commonwealth is still important to us, but it cannot be the main bedrock for our pursuit of our fundamental national interests. We should stop hankering after an imperial past which will not return, and make the most of our membership of the European Union, in which our best hopes for peace and prosperity lie. The sooner the Conservative Party comes to its senses on this question, the better for the country.

CODA

The time has now come to reflect on a long and busy life. I inevitably look back on it all with personal reflections on the successes which have meant most to me, and on the failures and the disappointments. Temperamentally, I believe that, in meeting with Triumph and Disaster, one must try to treat those two impostors just the same. I can certainly claim to have been consistent in my main beliefs. These were forged against the background of events at home and abroad during my formative years, and heavily coloured by the views of those whom I respected at that time, but they are in my view no less valid and relevant today.

Along with most of my contemporaries who played their part in defeating the dictators, I built my politics upon a profound commitment to liberty. Having seen the chaos in Germany and elsewhere in Europe after the war, I was always convinced that true and sustainable liberty must be, as Edmund Burke said, 'a liberty connected with order . . . that not only exists along with order and virtue . . . which cannot exist at all without them'.

Anyone who embarks upon an active political career must realise that it is a roller-coaster of a life, full of ups and downs, twists and turns and uncertainties. Mine has been no exception. I have much to be thankful for, first and foremost my upbringing, and the education made possible for me by my parents' loving support and sacrifices. Then there was my time at Oxford, invaluable for the friends I made there and the opportunities it gave me to cut my political teeth. My wartime and post-war experiences were also integral to the development of my political thinking, establishing the conviction in my mind that it was a duty of European statesmen so to manage the affairs of Europe that such things never happened again. I must also be grateful to my constituents for sending me to Westminster as their representative in the general election of 1950 and in every subsequent general election up to and including 1997. My first duty is to the people of Old Bexley and Sidcup, and I represent them with pride.

I have explained earlier in this volume why I joined the Conservative Party and I have never wavered in that commitment. I concluded as a young man that it is the Conservative Party which can most be trusted to govern in the best interests of the people of Britain. It was this conviction which brought me into Parliament in 1950, and inspired me to become one of the newly elected MPs who founded the One Nation Group, and to help write the pamphlet of the same title, setting out the likely problems of the post-war world, and how the policies and traditions of the Conservative Party could deal with them.

My colleagues and I were looking to create a new, post-war settlement which would bind our nation together and establish the kind of society for which we all fought. We quoted Churchill's credo of 1947: 'the scheme of society for which we stand is the establishment and maintenance of a basic minimum standard of life and labour below which a man or woman of good will, however old and weak, will not be allowed to fall'. We were determined that such a situation must not be allowed to persist. The values contained within that work – a restatement of the beliefs which have sustained the Conservative Party for generations – can, and should, still provide guidance today.

'One Nation' does not imply a monolithic and uniform society, and no Conservative should ever attack the very idea of society. What this title does imply is a society in which diverse interests flourish in their own spheres, but are mediated in a unity which embraces and reconciles sectional diversities and differences to bring about a society with a sense of national purpose. 'One Nation' also implies a certain set of presumptions about human behaviour. We based everything upon the assumption that it is natural for individuals within a family to co-operate with one another, for families within a neighbourhood to co-operate and for localities to co-operate within a wider body politic. I would take this a stage further, in the realm of international affairs. It is not only sensible for nations to work together for the common good. It is essential, and consistent with the freedom of individual citizens.

I think I can claim to have done the party some service since the early days of 'One Nation'. At the time of Suez and its aftermath, as Chief Whip, I was able to help hold the parliamentary party together and to support Harold Macmillan in restoring its morale to the point where we were able to win the 1959 general election with a three-figure majority. I am proud to have been elected as the leader of the Conservative Party in 1965 and to have served as such for ten years, three and three-quarters of them as Prime Minister.

It is an extraordinary experience to come from Buckingham Palace, having been appointed Prime Minister and First Lord of the Treasury, and to enter 10 Downing Street – officially the residence of the First Lord of the Treasury, as the brass plate on the front door makes plain – for the first time as Prime Minister. It is difficult to describe the complex of thoughts and feelings that crowd in at such a moment. Some pride and some elation, to be sure: to be Prime Minister is, after all, the pinnacle of a political career and it is a great achievement to attain it. I certainly looked back over the long road by which I had come to reach Downing Street; and I wished that my mother could have lived to share the happiness of that moment, and the fulfilment of her dreams and ambitions for me, as did my father and brother and the other members of my family.

I was profoundly conscious of the plans with which I was coming into the job that lay ahead, and of the hopes and prayers of those who had helped to achieve the electoral victory that brought me there. Elation at such a time is bound to be tempered by a sense of awesome responsibility. It must be impossible not to be mindful of all those others who have gone through that door in similar circumstances, of all that has happened in that house, and of the opportunities and challenges that lie ahead, those unforeseen as well as those predicted and planned for. It was also a moment of political theatre, with the pressmen and photographers crowding round and the people who like to assemble on the spot and see for themselves when momentous events are taking place. I was conscious of the need to find the right words to say as I stood on the doorstep. That is a moment to be sure of one's lines.

I also felt, as others have no doubt felt in their turn, the need not to lose time in getting down to work. Within a few minutes of arriving at No. 10, I was joined by a few of my most senior colleagues and we started at once on the process of deciding upon the appointments in the new administration.

We came into office in 1970 with the aim of building a vigorous and growing economy, with a high level of employment and a low rate of inflation. In pursuit of these aims, we adopted policies to reform company taxation and trade union law, with a view to restoring the spirit of enterprise in British industry. We wanted to encourage industry to become more dynamic, productive and competitive; to remove the constraints of excessive and unnecessary bureaucratic regulation of industry; to encourage and reward self-reliance and business acumen in industrial management; to concentrate government support for industry in regions and industries where it was most needed; and to reverse the failure of the Labour government, to bring about responsible attitudes to industrial relations and to curb abuses of trade union power. We also sought to negotiate fair terms for British entry into the European Community, and worked towards detente between East and West.

We moved fast to introduce measures to put these policies into effect, but such policies take time to work through in a complex economy. By the end of 1971, it was clear that they were not likely to do so sufficiently quickly to prevent a rise in unemployment to levels which we believed would be unacceptable, in terms of economic consequences and in terms of deprivation and despair in the homes and families of those affected. So we sought in 1972, by means of the budget of that year and of the Industry Act, to increase output, to raise the level of industrial investment, and so to halt and reverse the rise in unemployment. These measures were all exploded by the dramatic oil price increases of 1973, but let us not forget that, when we left office in 1974, unemployment was down to 580,000. What a contrast that makes with the eighties and nineties.

Inevitably, these reflationary measures intensified upward pressure on prices and incomes, and thus threatened our aims on inflation. So I tried, through a long series of meetings with leaders of industry and the trade unions, to develop a counter-inflation policy whose purpose and reason-ableness would commend it to responsible opinion on both sides of indus-try, and within the main political parties. We always knew that it was going to be difficult, particularly after the Wilberforce settlement in the coal industry, to secure voluntary agreement to a satisfactory policy. But it was right to try to do so; and the attempt went far towards establishing public understanding of the need for such a policy. Thus it helped to establish broad public acceptance for the statutory policies which we were obliged to introduce.

After two full discussions on a possible general election, the whole Cabinet supported the proposal to hold it in February 1974. I accept final responsibility for that decision. Although it was taken with some reluctance, there seemed to me and my colleagues to be an important issue on which it was right to go to the country. The result of the election was very close, giving no party an overall majority of seats in the House of Commons. We had a larger number of votes than any other party, and might well have won a small overall majority in seats, but for the unforeseen diversions by the Pay Board and by Sir Campbell Adamson. But events did not work out like that.

It has been argued that we might have done better to make a settlement with the NUM on the best terms available, accepting at face value the TUC's assurances that other unions would not seek to cite a settlement with the NUM as a reason for demanding, and going on strike to achieve, increases inconsistent with the incomes policy. An election could then have been postponed until, say, October 1974. If the assurances given by the TUC had, as we feared, not been honoured by other unions in the meantime, the government's position in a later election might have been much stronger. It is impossible to say now how that might have been. I can only repeat that, at the time, it seemed to me and my colleagues that a settlement with the miners in flagrant breach of the counter-inflation policy would in all probability have fatally undermined it. Although I believed that the TUC's assurances were sincere, it seemed to be very doubtful whether they would have been able to deliver on them. One could not be confident that the assurances would stand the strain.

I still regret the outcome of that election, followed as it inevitably was by another election within a few months which gave the Labour government a small majority. I regret it, not so much because of my own loss of office, but because an election victory with an overall majority would have vindicated our policies and strengthened our hand in pursuing them. I believe that we should then have been able to curb the behaviour of militant trade unionists without having to incur the severe penalties, in terms of lost output and employment, which resulted from the measures to which my Conservative successor later resorted. As it was, the years of Labour government from 1974 to 1979 were very damaging to the country in a number of respects at home and abroad.

By 1979 the industrial situation had become even more serious than in 1970, and the bulk of public opinion clearly recognised that the trade unions' abuse of power had become a threat to democracy. The Conservative government under Mrs Thatcher fought hard and, in the end, successfully to rein in the political ambitions of the unions. This was the right thing to do. But I do not regret having tried, and tried very hard, when restraint in the growth of prices and incomes was necessary, to bring the unions to accept, and co-operate, in a voluntary system of wage restraint and so to avoid the need for statutory measures or economic deflation. I do not believe that policies which allow unemployment to rise to levels of 3 million or more, and which in effect marginalise the trades unions, are likely to promote long-term economic, social or political stability. They certainly do not hold out much prospect of uniting the nation.

Ceasing to be Prime Minister, at any rate when that cessation is involuntary, is as melancholy a business as becoming Prime Minister is joyful. In my case it came after weeks of economic and industrial crisis, after an election which was inconclusive, and after a weekend of ultimately fruitless discussion with the Liberals. I was very depressed, and I felt acutely aware that what had begun in such high hopes was ending in disappointment. Before I left for the Palace to tender my resignation, the whole of the staff at No. 10 were assembled so that I could say a few words of thanks and farewell. I felt, and I know that many of them felt, that we had all been part of an extended family during those years, experiencing some remarkable highs and lows together. It was a moving occasion.

It was also a personal disappointment to me when I was defeated in the election for the party leadership in 1975, the more so because I was out of sympathy with the monetarist, neo-liberal doctrines to which my successor was beginning to become attached and which I could not believe to be in the long-term interests of the party or of the country. Whatever my hopes, I realised that, after ten years and two election defeats, the parliamentary party might well decide that it was time for a change of leadership. That did nothing, however, to reduce my sense of disappointment. I campaigned vigorously for the party during the 1979 general election, but when we won I knew from Mrs Thatcher's past declarations that no place would be found for me in her first Cabinet. This at least left me free to express views which did not accord strictly with government policy, when I thought it right to do so.

The matter of Europe has been a recurring theme in my political life, as I have striven to give expression and effect to my convictions. If I had to choose the three points of my life at which I have felt the most profound sense of satisfaction, the first would have to be the successful outcome of my meeting with President Pompidou in May 1971, which effectively consigned de Gaulle's veto to the dustbin of history. The second would be the moment on 28 October 1971, when the tellers in the House of Commons announced that the motion to approve the accession of the UK to the European Community had been passed with a majority of 112. The third would be 22 January 1972 when I signed the Treaty of Accession in the Palais d'Egmont in Brussels.

It had been a bitter blow to us all when President de Gaulle's veto brought the first round of negotiations for British membership of the European Community to a sudden halt in 1963. Subsequent history would have been different and, I believe, better had we been able to join the Community in 1963 rather than in 1973. But I did not feel in any way personally responsible for the failure. Indeed, the fact that de Gaulle considered himself obliged to terminate the negotiations as with an Olympian thunderbolt was, ironically, a tribute to the fact that the negotiating process had come so close to a successful outcome.

My share in that process stood me in good stead. As the leader of the British negotiating team, I mastered the dossiers on every detailed negotiating issue, from New Zealand butter to Caribbean sugar, so it was not for nothing that at this time I won from the editors of *Private Eye* the mocking sobriquet 'Grocer Heath' or, more simply, 'The Grocer'. The knowledge of the issues that I gained then proved to be useful to me at the time of the 1970–1 negotiations. I also came to know, often as friends, the principal participants from the Community countries. They and their contacts likewise proved to be valuable when we reopened negotiations in 1970. My conduct of the 1961–3 negotiations was recognised in the parliamentary party to have been competent and businesslike, an assessment which no doubt strengthened support for my candidature for leader of the party in 1965, as I believe did the management of our opposition to the Labour government's Finance Bill earlier that year, when I was the Shadow Chancellor of the Exchequer.

I have written separately about sailing, and its importance for me as a stimulating contrast – I can hardly say relaxation from – the pressures of political life. I was never a mere 'hobby' sailor. My interest was in serious ocean racing, and I took with corresponding seriousness every aspect of it, from the design of successive *Morning Clouds* to the preparation for racing and the management of each and every race. I was fortunate enough to assemble a fine crew, and we made a hard-working team on board. There were times of unalloyed triumph: the winning of the Sydney–Hobart race at the end of 1969 and, when I was captain of the British team, Britain's victory in the Admiral's Cup in 1971. There is nothing to match the excitement of an ocean race, and the elation of winning it.

But there were also times of adversity. No one who competed in the 1979 Fastnet Race will forget the experience of the storms that disrupted that race, sank so many boats, and cost the lives of fifteen crew members. I certainly shall not forget what it was like to be on the open sea in *Morning Cloud* during that race. When we eventually got back, I was rung up by a friend who had been worried when for forty-eight hours there was no news of where or how we were. I am told that, when I was asked how I had felt, I replied that I had been 'shit-scared'. These words do seem a little more spicy than my usual vernacular. However, if I did use them I did so advisedly. They were no more than the exact truth.

I have also written about music as a joy for life, and I need not say a great deal more about it here. If I had not taken up politics as a career, I might very well have become a professional musician. It was a real choice at the time. As it is, I have perhaps had the best of both worlds. I had the excitement and the fulfilment of a political career, while being able to turn to music for refreshment and spiritual sustenance all my life, either playing or conducting or just listening. I have also been lucky enough to enjoy the friendship of many of the finest musicians of our time.

The performance of Elgar's 'Cockaigne' Overture with the London Symphony Orchestra on 25 November 1971 marked the first time that I had conducted a fully professional orchestra, and since then I have conducted the LSO, and many other orchestras, all over the world. It is a great privilege, as well as a rare pleasure, for a part-time musician to conduct a top-class professional orchestra in one of the masterpieces of the repertory. Each individual in the orchestra is a gifted musician and a skilled player on his or her chosen instrument, and each player is required to play to the top of his or her ability. In the end, however, the contribution of each individual player must harmonise and fit in with the contribution of all the other players to make a coherent and satisfying performance by the orchestra as a whole. It is by this that their standing will be judged. It is a paradigm for collective responsibility. The conductor's function in a performance is to direct and inspire his musicians to respond to his concept of what will so often be recognised as a masterpiece of the repertoire.

The years since the end of the Second World War have been marked not only, or even mainly, by radically improved means of transportation, but also by the universal growth of the immediate intercommunication of information. Nothing happens anywhere in the world today without the rest of the world immediately hearing about it on radio and, almost equally quickly, seeing it on television. One would have thought that this would have greatly increased mutual understanding among the peoples of the world. In all too many cases, however, it has failed to do so, with the consequent strife which we have seen widely spread in Africa, as well as in the Pacific Rim, the former Soviet republics and the Balkans. There is, perhaps, nothing especially original in a politician making a plea for greater international and intercultural understanding. I do sincerely hope, however, that I have been able to play my part in making people in the United Kingdom more open-minded and outward-looking in our new, European era and that this process will continue.

The conduct of our international affairs is now all too often marked by our leaders publicly lecturing other countries and other peoples about how they should behave and organise themselves politically. This loses friends and makes enemies. Balanced co-operation, respecting the traditions and opinions of others, as well as understanding their difficulties, must be our governing principle. We need to reassess in particular our relations with the countries of the Middle East and Far East. Ultimately, we help no-one by throwing away goodwill or breaking relationships between nations. I have learned through long experience that it is essential to obtain the trust of others to gain influence. It takes time and patience. Others also need to be convinced that, by trusting you, they obtain more satisfactory out-comes for themselves. That is the nature of diplomacy.

Today, the young have both the means and the incentive to leave home much earlier than when I was a youth. In most respects this development is beneficial, both in broadening their experience and in encouraging them to travel more widely in making their careers. It is therefore foolish to slow it down by allowing young people to receive wages more appropriate to slave labour than to a modern industrialised economy. A system of minimum wages is essential for a properly balanced society. In Britain, we had industrial wages councils through every form of party and coalition government, from the time Churchill introduced them in 1909 until John Major's government abolished them in 1993. The argument that such arrangements adversely affect competitiveness cannot be sustained. Our economy was extremely successful during a significant part of that time, and the United States, that powerhouse of capitalism, still has minimum wage legislation. Set at a realistic level, a minimum wage forces the employer to improve his own efficiency rather than exploiting his employees. What I also want for the young is for them to take every opportunity to see more of the world for themselves. I hope that they will enjoy not only the cultural diversity of the developing world, but that they should also explore closer to home, getting to know the rest of Europe, upon which their economic future will depend.

It is true that the family unit can provide the soundest foundation for a stable and satisfying life. To achieve this, it needs the understanding and co-operation of all its members. These, however, are not qualities which can be imposed by any outside body. It has become fashionable, in the face of so many difficulties in our society today, for some to demand that a way of life should be somehow imposed by governments and politicians, either through financial incentives or by the use of legislation. This is a complete fallacy. If politicians can set an example in this field, so much the better, but whenever they go beyond legitimate exhortation in this realm, they court disaster.

That is what has happened in these last few years, and is part of the explanation why the standing of politicians today is lower than at any time in my memory. Let politicians stick to putting forward policies, backed by solid arguments, showing that they are for the benefit of our country as a whole. Let us bear in mind, moreover, that our people today are not bound by one set of beliefs, the Christian faith in its various forms, but are widely supported by different religious values, particularly within immigrant communities, or by none. Different religions and cultures display a variety of attitudes to family life, as well as to political questions. A politician has a responsibility to all his constituents, whatever their origin and guiding principles may be.

I have written about the support of my own family. After revisiting the Municipal Gallery in Dublin, in which he surveyed the portraits of many of his friends, Yeats famously wrote, '*Think where man's glory most begins and ends, And say my glory was I had such friends*'. I can but echo that sentiment. Let me, then, end with a few words about my friends. No man, I think, could sustain a long, active and varied life without the boundless dedication of personal friends. I certainly could not have done so. There are some commentators on public life who claim that I have none. I am glad to say that they are wrong. I have, and always have had, many friends in all walks of life, but I have taken infinite care to ensure that I did not embarrass them by getting them involved in politics. As a result, they have never been pestered by the press or the other media, and many are completely unknown to them. I have enjoyed throughout my life the unwavering support and loyalty of these personal friends, some mentioned in this book and others not, and some now dead. Without them I could never have achieved whatever I have achieved. I have greatly valued their friendship, and I have tried as best I could to reciprocate their loyalty, their support and their affection. Let the last words of this book express my profound thanks to them for all that they have done for me, and all that they have meant to me, throughout the course of my life.

List of Abbreviations

AA	anti-aircraft
ACAS	Advisory, Conciliation and Arbitration Service
ASLEF	Associated Society of Locomotive Engineers and Firemen
BAOR	British Army of the Rhine
BOAC	British Overseas Airways Corporation
CAP	Common Agricultural Policy
CBE	Commander of the Order of the British Empire
CBI	Confederation of British Industry
CFP	Common Fisheries Policy
CH	Companion of Honour
CHC	Community Health Council
CHOGM	Commonwealth Heads of Government Meeting
CIA	Central Intelligence Agency
CO	Commanding Officer
CPA	Commonwealth Parliamentary Association
CPC	Conservative Political Centre
CPRS	Central Policy Review Staff
CRD	Conservative Research Department
CSCE	Conference on Security and Co-operation in Europe
DM	Deutschmark
DTI	Department of Trade and Industry
EC	European Community
ECHR	European Convention on Human Rights
ECO	English Chamber Orchestra
ECSC	European Coal and Steel Community
ECYO	European Community Youth Orchestra
EEC	European Economic Community
EFTA	European Free Trade Area
EMS	European Monetary System
EMU	Economic and Monetary Union
EP	European Parliament
EPC	European Political Co-operation
EPG	Eminent Persons Group
ERM	Exchange Rate Mechanism
ETU	Electrical Trades Union
FA	Football Association

FC	Football Club
FPTP	first past the post
G7	Group of Seven
GATT	General Agreement on Tariffs and Trade
GDP	gross domestic product
GNP	gross national product
GPO	General Post Office
HAA	heavy anti-aircraft
HAC	Honourable Artillery Company
HMG	Her Majesty's Government
ILO	International Labour Organisation
IMF	International Monetary Fund
IRA	Irish Republican Army
JCR	Junior Common Room
KBE	Knight Commander of the Order of the British Empire
LCC	London County Council
LEA	Local Education Authority
LSO	London Symphony Orchestra
MBFR	Mutual and Balanced Force Reduction
MEP	Member of the European Parliament
MI5	Security Service
MI6	Secret Intelligence Service
MO	Medical Officer
NATO	North Atlantic Treaty Organisation
NCB	National Coal Board
NCO	Non-Commissioned Officer
NEDC	National Economic Development Council
NHS	National Health Service
NIRC	National Industrial Relations Court
NUM	National Union of Mineworkers
NUR	National Union of Railwaymen
OCTU	Officer Cadet Training Unit
OPEC	Organisation of Petroleum Exporting Countries
OU	Open University
OUCA	Oxford University Conservative Association
PAR	Programme Analysis Review
PESC	Public Expenditure Survey Committee
PPS	parliamentary private secretary
PSBR	Public Sector Borrowing Requirement
PT	physical training
QMV	qualified majority voting
RA	Royal Artillery

RPM	Resale Price Maintenance
RSM	Regimental Sergeant-Major
RUC	Royal Ulster Constabulary
SALT	Strategic Arms Limitation Treaty
SDLP	Social and Democratic Labour Party
SDP	Social Democratic Party
SEA	Single European Act
SET	selective employment tax
SNP	Scottish National Party
SS	Schutzstaffel (Nazi elite corps)
TA	Territorial Army
TGWU	Transport and General Workers' Union
TUC	Trades Union Congress
UCS	Upper Clyde Shipbuilders
UDI	Unilateral Declaration of Independence
UDR	Ulster Defence Regiment
UKREP	United Kingdom Permanent Representation to the European Union
UMCA	Universities' Mission to Central Africa
UNCTAD	UN Conference on Trade and Development
UNESCO	UN Educational, Scientific and Cultural Organisation
UNPROFOR	UN Protection Force
UNSCR	UN Security Council Resolution
USSR	Union of Soviet Socialist Republics
UUC	Ulster Unionist Council
VAT	value added tax
VE Day	Victory in Europe Day
VJ Day	Victory over Japan Day
WAAF	Women's Auxiliary Air Force
WEA	Workers' Educational Association
WEU	Western European Union
WHO	World Health Organisation
YC	Young Conservatives
YMCA	Young Men's Christian Association

Index

Aachen, 238
Abbado, Claudio, 561, 675
Abu Dhabi, 502
Abyssinia: Italy invades, 49
Acland, Richard, 72
Adams, Gerry, 438
Adamson, Sir Campbell, 352, 516, 730
Adamson, Jennie, 117
Addis, Sir John, 630
Adeane, Sir Michael, 178, 308, 318, 324, 480
Adenauer, Konrad: and European union,
    142–3, 148; and British application to join
    EC, 205, 230–2; signs treaty with France
    (1963), 232; qualities, 641; and German
    revival, 713
Admiral's Cup (yacht race), 467, 495, 671–3,
    733
Adrian, Max, 394
Afghanistan, 616
agriculture see Common Agricultural Policy
Aitken, Jonathan, 710
Aitken, Sir Max, 272
Al-Hamad, Abdlatif, 606–7
Alanbrooke, Field Marshal Alan Brooke, 1st
    Viscount, 114, 156, 188
Albany, Piccadilly: EH occupies apartment in,
    256–7, 307–8; EH's lease expires, 459, 520
Aldershot, 436
Aldington, Araminta, Lady, 683
Aldington, Toby Low, 1st Baron, 108, 407,
    528, 677, 683
Alexander, Field Marshal Harold, 1st Earl, 154,
    182
Alexandra, Princess, 689
Algeria, 602–3
Allegri Quartet, 469
Allen, Dave, 549
Allen, Sir Hugh, 34–5, 68
Allen, Maurice, 32
Alliance Party (Northern Ireland), 439–40, 442
Alport, Cuthbert (later Baron; 'Cub'), 140
Amadeus Quartet, 466
Amery, Julian (later Baron): at Oxford, 46, 51;
    as MP, 51; and Suez crisis, 165, 168, 175; in
    Macmillan government, 180; holiday in
    Venice with EH, 205; meets de Gaulle, 225;
    and disagreement with France over nuclear
    strategy, 227; at Chequers with Macmillan,
    243–4; condemns IRA attack on EH's house,
    532; illness and death, 690
Amery, Leopold Stennett, 46, 64–5
Ames, Leslie, 15

Amin, Idi, 456–7, 483, 496, 498
Amsterdam, 561–2
Amsterdam Treaty (1997), 697–8
Andersen, Arthur (accountancy firm), 623–4
Anderson (chairman of Oxford University
    Conservatives), 39
Andrew, Sir Herbert, 212
Andronikov, Prince, 370
Anglo-Irish Agreement (1985), 445
Annan, Kofi, 668–9
Anne, Princess Royal, 243
Annenberg, Walter, 462
Antwerp, 97–9
ANZUK (Five Power Defence Agreement),
    481
Arab League: condemns Iraqi aggression, 651;
    and 1961 Kuwait crisis, 652; Saddam and,
    657, 659
Arabs: conflict with Israel, 321–2, 419, 466,
    492, 500, 502, 619; and oil supply, 501–2,
    507–8; hostility to West, 665
Ardennes offensive (1944–5), 100
Argentina: in Falklands War, 579–80
Armstrong, Robert (later Baron): as EH's
    principal private secretary, 21, 311–13; and
    EH's weekly audiences with Queen, 318; and
    Britain's renewed application to join EC,
    354, 366; and attack on EH in Brussels, 382;
    and employment in service industries, 396;
    writes grace, 464, 690; and Rostropovich's
    visit, 470; on Obote's replacement by Amin,
    482–3
Armstrong, Sir Thomas, 21, 309
Armstrong, Sir William, 317, 353
Arnhem, 99–100
Arnold, Malcolm, 464
Arsenal Football Club, 10
Arundells (house), Salisbury, 679–83
Ashford, Kent, 116–17
ASLEF (rail drivers' union), 504
Asquith, Herbert Henry, 1st Earl of Oxford and
    Asquith, 421
Asquith, Margot, Countess of Oxford and
    Asquith, 682
Astor, Nancy, Viscountess, 33, 49, 64
Aswan Dam, 165
Atkins, Humphrey (later Baron Colnbrook),
    505, 530, 532, 537
Atkins, Robert, 458
Attlee, Clement (later 1st Earl): as Party leader,
    29; EH meets in wartime, 101; leads 1945
    government, 114, 123, 125, 127–8; and

social services, 130–1; calls 1950 election, 134; in Commons, 139; and European affairs, 148; calls 1951 election, 152; opposes entry into EC, 355; and Commonwealth immigrants, 456; and war criminals, 591

Audland, Christopher, 214

Australia: EH visits, 286, 290, 302; ANZUK defence agreement, 481; immigration policy, 497

Austria: EH visits, 42; Hitler annexes, 50–1, 55

Averoff-Tositfas, Evangelos, 209

Aveton Giffard, Devon, 1

Avon, 1st Earl of see Eden, Anthony

Avon, Countess of see Eden, Clarissa

Avramović, Dragoslav, 609

Aynsley, Cyril, 281

Aziz, Tariq, 655–6, 658–9, 664–5, 668–9

Bachauer, Gina, 309

Bader, Douglas, 555

Baghdad see Iraq

Bahrain, 482

Bailey, Cyril, 35, 37

Baker, James, 669

Baker, Kenneth (later Baron), 528–9, 531, 588, 711

Baker-White, John, 43

balance of payments: in credit (1972–3), 417; deficit (1974), 516; and monetarism, 577

Baldry, Tony, 458

Baldwin, Stanley (later 1st Earl), 32, 40, 44

Balfour, Arthur James (later 1st Earl), 83

Balfour, Captain H.H., 17

Ball, George, 226, 229, 249, 602

Ball, James, 521

Balliol College, Oxford: EH attends, 21–2, 23–40, 46–71; EH's organ scholarship at, 26–7, 37; EH's presidency of JCR, 31, 38, 47; Choral Society, 36; Music Society, 36; chapel renovation, 37; fund-raising dinner for unemployed, 66; Macmillan and, 182, 686; music at, 674

Balliol Players, 37

Balmoral: EH visits, 323–4, 477

Balniel, Robin, 310

Bamako, Mali, 607

Bank of England: nationalised (1946), 127

Barber, Anthony (later Baron): in Opposition, 267; on flight to Singapore, 278; in EH's Shadow Cabinet, 283; as Party Chairman, 290; and Powell's 'Rivers of Blood' speech, 292; as Chancellor of Duchy of Lancaster, 311; smoking, 317; as Chancellor of Exchequer, 320, 332, 343, 349, 400; public spending cuts, 330–2; anti-inflation measures, 332–4, 343–6; and negotiations for EC membership, 363; and agricultural subsidies, 376; on industrial competitiveness, 398; opposes statutory incomes policy, 402; and control of wage settlements, 404; and

pressure on sterling, 409–10; increases bank rate, 410; in TUC-CBI discussions, 413; and GDP growth, 414; budgets: (1972), 398–9; (1973), 417–18; and VAT, 417; and social services, 451; on 1973–4 economic crisis, 505–6, 509; rejects Sidney Greene's proposal, 509; leaves politics, 520, 529; relations with EH, 597; in Eminent Persons Group to South Africa, 621; at Macmillan's 90th birthday dinner, 677

Barbirolli, Sir John, 74

Barclay, Sir Roderick, 212

Barnes, Sir William Gorell, 212

Barre, Raymond, 562

Barrow, Colonel, 89

Bartlett, Vernon, 65

Batey, Peter, 582, 643, 721

Bath Abbey, 37

Battle of Britain (1940), 87

Battle of the Bulge (1945), 100

Bavin, A. Robert W., 25, 46

Bax, Sir Arnold, 87

Bax, Clifford, 257

Beaufort, Henry FitzRoy Somerset, 10th Duke of, 308

Beaverbrook, William Maxwell Aitken, 1st Baron, 108, 149, 223

Beckett, Margaret, 719

Beckett, Samuel, 309

Beevor, Humphry, 121, 123–4

Beijing, 629–31, 634, 638, 642–3, 648; see also China; Tiananmen Square

Belfast, 422, 425, 429, 433–4, 438

Belgium: EH's war service in, 97–9

Bell, Raymond, 212

Ben-Gurion, David, 169

Beneš, Edvard, 82–3

Benn, Tony, 339, 346–7, 406, 540–1

Bennett, Jim, 5

Benson, Sir Henry, 341

Berg, Alban: Lulu, 608

Berlin: Airlift (1948), 114; Kennedy in, 249; Brandt and, 606; EH lectures in, 662; Wall demolished, 712

Berlin Philharmonic Orchestra, 394–5, 560

Bermuda, 484–6

Bernstein, Felicia, 309

Bernstein, Leonard, 309, 465, 688

Berry, Anthony, 531

Better Tomorrow, A (Conservative Party manifesto), 302

Bevan, Aneurin: in Commons, 140; resigns, 151, 250; and National Health Service, 451; In Place of Fear, 298

Beveridge, William, 1st Baron, 198

Bevin, Ernest, 29, 139, 151–2

Bexley Grammar School, 449–51

Bexley, Kent: EH selected as parliamentary candidate, 118–22, 123, 125; party organisation and reform, 122, 132–4; EH

Bexley, Kent – cont.
retains in 1959 election, 191; EH's majority reduced in 1966 election, 282; and 1970 election, 306–7; Labour council (1971), 449–50; schools policy, 450–1; EH holds in October 1974 election, 526; EH increases majority in 1979 election, 573; Referendum Party candidate in (1997), 719–20
Bexleyheath: carol concerts in, 674
Bexleyheath Observer, 119
Bidault, Georges, 143
Biddle, Major Geoffrey, 551
Biesheuvel, Barend William, 391
Biffen, John, 384
Birch, Nigel, 185–6
Birchington, Kent, 15
Bird (Oxford Union steward), 62
Bird, James, 7
Bird, William, 7
Bishop, Sir Frederick, 177, 182, 212
Black Dyke Mills Band, 38
'Black Wednesday' (1992), 597
Blair, Tony: election victory (1997), 109; in Washington, 473; and Prime Minister's Question Time, 596; relations with Gordon Brown, 597; popular appeal, 598
Blake, George, 246, 474
Blake, Robert, Baron, 522, 687
Blakenham, John Hugh Hare, 1st Viscount, 260
Blanesburgh of Alloa, Robert Younger, Baron, 37
Blewett, Donald, 526–7
Bligh, Sir Edward, 118
Bligh, Tim, 46, 118, 263
Bliss, Sir Arthur, 464–5, 470
'Bloody Sunday' (Londonderry, 30 January 1972), 434–5
Blunt, Anthony, 476
Boardman, Tom, 400
Bogdanor, Vernon, 719
Bonham Carter, Mark (later Baron), 81
Bonham Carter, Lady Violet (later Baroness Asquith), 141
Book Programme, The (BBC), 555
Booth-Jones, Margaret, 679
Boothby, Robert (later Baron), 171, 309
Boothroyd, Betty: elected Speaker, 594–5
Bosnia, 625–7
Botswana, 150
Boundary Commission, 305
Bourne, Captain Robert, 58
Boutros-Ghali, Boutros, 663
Bowden, Herbert, 173
Boyd-Carpenter, John, 142, 282–3
Boyle, Edward, Baron: and 1955 budget, 161; resigns over Suez, 171; in Macmillan's 1957 government, 180; in Opposition, 267; leaves politics, 301; favours abolition of Open University, 448
Bracken, Brendan (later Viscount), 149

Brackenbury, Rev. B.V.F., 62
Braine, Bernard, 619
Bramall, Ashley: at Oxford, 48; parliamentary career, 118; political debates with EH, 126; EH defeats in 1950 election, 137; and EH's mother's death, 153; contests Bexley in 1959 election, 192
Brandt Commission on Development Issues, 571, 576, 605–10; Reports, 611–13, 615
Brandt, Willy: EH meets, 361; *Ostpolitik*, 361, 486; welcomes British membership of EC, 380, 395, 606, 693; and 1972 EC summit, 387, 390; Mintoff visits, 499; and oil prices, 500; and proposed European Regional Fund, 502; relations with EH, 605–6; as West German Chancellor, 606, 608–9; Saddam praises, 665; favours monetary union, 694; and German revival, 713
Branson, Richard, 660–1
Bretton Woods agreement, 694
Brezhnev, Leonid, 617
Briand, Aristide, 84
Bridges, Edward (later 1st Baron), 84
Bridges, Thomas (later 2nd Baron), 84, 312
Brierley, Derek, 721
Brightman, Miss (of Broadstairs), 11
Brighton: Grand Hotel bombed, 586–7
Britain in Europe (organisation), 544
British Fishing Federation, 703
British Museum: EH's Trusteeship of, 241–2
British Nationality Act (1948), 455
British Steel Corporation, 412; privatisation, 343
British Trawlers' Federation, 701
Britten, Benjamin, Baron, 464, 469–70, 487
Broadstairs, Kent: Heath family in, 1, 6–8, 10; carol parties and concerts, 11–12, 162, 674; EH holidays in from Oxford, 36, 57; EH revisits, 114, 553
Broadstairs Literary and Debating Society, 17
Bromley-Davenport, Colonel Walter, 151
Brook, Sir Norman (later Baron Normanbrook), 177, 211
Brooke, Henry (later Baron), 242
Brooke, Peter, 594
Brookeborough, Basil Stanlake Brooke, 1st Viscount, 420
Brown, George (later Baron George-Brown): supports British entry into EC, 223, 355, 357, 377; EH opposes on economic policy, 267; 'National Plan' for economy, 279; resignation threats, 288; as Foreign Secretary, 357; at signing of Treaty of Accession to EC, 381; and Labour contacts with USSR, 474
Brown, Gordon, 597
Brown Shipley (merchant bank), 124–5, 152–3
Browne, Anthony Montague, 197
Bruce-Gardyne, John (Jock), 236
Bruges: Thatcher's 1988 speech in, 706–7, 710
Brunei, 278

Brussels, 381–3; EH's 1989 speech in, 710–11;
   see also European Community
Brussels Treaty (1948), 160
Bryer, Lionel and Joy, 560
Buchan-Hepburn, Patrick, 151, 153, 158, 161,
   178
Buchanan-Smith, Alick Laidlaw, 566
Bulganin, Nikolai, 164
Bulgaria, 210
Bundesbank, 712–14
Burgess, Guy, 246
Burke, Edmund, 362, 599, 727
Burnet, Alastair, 554
Burt, Alistair, 548
Bush, George, 618, 651, 657, 669
Butler, Mr and Mrs (Crayford neighbours), 5
Butler, Michael, 229
Butler, Richard Austen (later Baron): as
   Conservative policy maker, 109, 115, 127–8,
   192, 253, 267; on Industrial Charter, 129;
   Party hostility to, 131; and social services
   reform, 131; as Chancellor of Exchequer,
   153, 158, 160–1; takes over during Eden's
   illness, 160; death of first wife, 161, 254;
   made Lord Privy Seal, 162; and Suez crisis,
   169, 178; loses 1957 leadership to Macmillan,
   176, 178–9; as Home Secretary under
   Macmillan, 180; and Macmillan's departure
   on 1958 tour, 188; and 1960 rail strike, 196;
   character, 253–4; Education Act (1944), 253,
   448; fails to succeed Macmillan as leader,
   253, 255–6; and Commonwealth
   Immigration Act (1962), 455
Butler, Robin, 313
Butler, Sydney (Mrs RAB): death, 161, 254
Byrne, John, 193

Caen, 96
Callaghan, James (later Baron): as Chancellor of
   Exchequer, 270, 279, 288; introduces Race
   Relations Bill, 291; as Home Secretary, 298;
   and Conservative prices policy, 304; and
   Boundary Commission proposals, 305; and
   award of honours, 324; opposes EC
   membership, 377, 540; and Northern Ireland
   divisions, 422; and 'Bloody Sunday', 435; and
   changes to EC, 542; attitude to British
   membership of EC, 545, 694, 705; on
   Wilson's resignation and age, 557; delays
   election until 1979, 568–9, 572; qualities and
   character, 569; and industrial relations,
   572–3; proposed for mission to Baghdad,
   654; as Knight of Garter, 686; and elections
   to European Parliament (1979), 696; and
   British budgetary contributions to EC, 698
Cambridge, George Francis Hugh Cambridge,
   2nd Marquess of, 241
Camp David, 492
Campbell, John, 719

Canada: and British application for EC
   membership, 221
Cancun, Mexico, 611
Canton, 637
capital punishment, 300
capitalism, 598
Cardinale, Monsignor, 252
Carey, George, Archbishop of Canterbury, 689
Carl XVI Gustaf, King of Sweden, 663
Carmichael, Duncan, 43, 109, 111
Carr, Colin, 463
Carr, Robert (later Baron): in Commons,
   139–40; and Eden, 181; and industrial
   relations, 287, 334, 336, 409; and dock strike
   (1970), 321; anti-inflation measures, 334, 344;
   and miners' settlement, 352; leaves
   Employment Ministry, 403; in TUC-CBI
   discussions, 413; as Home Secretary, 447; as
   Shadow Chancellor, 520, 529; leads
   Opposition during 1975 leadership election,
   534; Thatcher drops from Shadow Cabinet,
   537
Carrington, Peter Carington, 6th Baron: and
   Far East defence pact, 287; and Powell's race
   speech, 293; as Shadow Defence Minister,
   294; and 1970 election, 307; as Defence
   Secretary, 310; and anti-inflation measures,
   415; and Northern Ireland, 424, 426–7, 436;
   negotiates ANZUK defence agreement, 481;
   and HMS Glamorgan movements, 485; and
   US forces in Europe, 487; offer to Malta,
   498–9; heads Department of Energy, 505;
   restrictions on land development, 506; and
   1974 election, 512; as Foreign Secretary
   under Thatcher, 574; resigns over Falklands,
   580; negotiates budgetary contributions to
   EC, 699; pro-Europeanism, 706
Carron, William, 194
Carter, Jimmy, 617
Cartland, John, 121
Carver, Field Marshal Sir Michael (later Baron),
   429
Casals, Pablo, 466, 469
Casement, Sir Roger, 441
Castle, Barbara (later Baroness), 298, 548, 557
Castro, Fidel, 613–15, 682
Castro, Ramon, 614
Central African Federation, 276
Central Policy Review Staff (CPRS; 'think
   tank'): set up, 315–16; and industrial
   companies, 348; and unions, 353; and
   Northern Ireland, 430; and Concorde
   aircraft, 459
Centre for Policy Studies, 521
Chaban-Delmas, Jacques, 361, 367
Chadd, Christopher, 89, 526–7
Chadd, Major George, 88–9, 527
Chamberlain, Neville: pre-war activities, 44–5,
   49–50, 52, 55; and Munich Agreement,
   57–8, 60–1, 83; and 1938 Oxford

Chamberlain, Neville – *cont.*
by-election, 60–1; EH condemns, 61; resigns (1940), 64, 83; declares war on Germany, 72–3, 105; Butler and, 253; Mao on, 631
Chandos, Oliver Lyttelton, 1st Viscount, 124, 139, 153, 192
Channel Tunnel: treaty signed, 459
Channon, Paul, 537
Chapman, A.P.F., 15
Charles, Prince of Wales, 324, 468
Charteris, Sir Martin (*later* Baron), 318, 324
Chataway, Christopher, 224, 400
Chatham House Grammar School, Ramsgate, 2, 7, 9, 12–18, 448
Chauvel, Jean, 216, 237, 239
Chequers: Pompidou visits, 368–9, 501; TUC-CBI discussions at, 413–14; Jack Lynch and Faulkner at, 430–2; Mariano Rumor at, 444; refurbished and improved, 461–2; entertaining and concerts at, 462–3, 466; Nixon visits, 471–2; Queen lunches at, 471; Tito visits, 483–4; protection at, 492; Mintoff at, 498–9; Sheikh Zayed at, 502
Cherwell, Frederick Lindemann, Viscount, 38, 64, 154
Chiang Kai-shek, 494
Chicago, 78–9
Chicago Symphony Orchestra, 560
Chichester-Clark, James (*later* Baron Moyola), 424–6, 428
Chichester-Clark, Sir Robin, 420, 424–5
Child Poverty Action Group, 306
China, People's Republic of: UK relations with, 468, 494–5; Amin's fear of, 483; Nixon visits, 485, 492, 629, 634–5; relations with Pakistan, 486; EH visits, 493–4, 579, 629–42, 648; hostility to Russia, 632–3; presents pandas to EH, 638–9; reforms under Deng, 641–2, 647–8; EH conducts in, 642–3; British diplomatic relations with, 643; and Hong Kong transfer of power, 643–7; trade with, 646–7; as superpower, 723
Chirac, Jacques, 688
Chou En-lai, 630–2, 640
Christadelphian Church, 5
Church of England: appointment of bishops, 313–14
Church Times, 121–4
Churchill, Clementine, Lady, 146, 188–9, 197
Churchill, Randolph, 38, 60
Churchill, Sir Winston: EH admires, 29; visits Oxford (1936), 38–9; invites Oxford students to lunch, 50–1; warns of German threat, 58; declines EH's invitation to speak at Oxford Union, 64; premiership (1940), 64, 83; proposes union with France (1940), 84; dines with EH as Chief Whip, 100; gives paintings to EH, 100, 146, 681–2; defeat in 1945 election, 108–9; hostility to socialism, 108; on Rotherham, 110–11; on 'iron curtain',

114; post-war policies, 128; addresses parliamentary candidates (1949), 130; in 1950 election campaign, 136; in Commons, 139; addresses 1922 Committee, 141–2; supports post-war united Europe, 145–8; Zurich speech (1946), 146–7; on EH's appointment as Whip, 151; sorrow at Bevin's decline, 151–2; 1951 premiership, 153, 155; attacked in 1951 election campaign, 153; summoned from Savoy to Commons, 154–5; on Commons majority of one, 155, 262; rebukes EH for pronunciation, 155; EH invites to HAC dinner, 156–7; EH's relations with, 157–8, 188, 197–8; suffers stroke, 158; hearing aid, 159; relinquishes premiership, 159; and succession to Eden, 178; EH accompanies to Newmarket, 188–9; poker playing, 197–8; awarded Charlemagne Prize, 238; and minimum wage, 403; and partition of Ireland, 421; appoints Halifax to Washington embassy, 574; and war criminals, 592; Castro's interest in, 613; qualities, 641; and Referendum Party campaign, 715; political principles, 728; introduces wages councils, 735; *The Second World War*, 473
Churchill, Winston, Jr., 531
Civil Aviation, Ministry of, 111–14, 116, 120
Clarion of Wight (yacht), 533
Clark, Elizabeth, Lady, 464
Clark, Frank, 450
Clark, Kenneth, Baron, 256, 464
Clark, William, 173
Clarke, Frank, 117
Clarke, Kenneth: and EC Bill, 384; opposes 1974 election call, 509; as Chancellor of Exchequer, 597–8; at EH's 80th birthday celebration, 691; criticises Referendum Party, 715
Cleese, John, 682
Clegg, Walter, 509
Cleveland, Ohio, 79
Cleveland Symphony Orchestra, 21, 560
coalmining: industrial decline and strike (1971–2), 350–3, 396, 503–4, 506; pay claim and dispute (1973), 503–6, 508–10, 513–14; 1984–5 strike, 586
Cockburn, Claud, 39
Cockfield, Arthur (*later* Baron), 344, 706
Coe, Sebastian, 675
Cohen, Harriet, 87
Cole, G.D.H., 33
Cole, George James, Baron, 110
Collins, Michael, 438
Colnbrook, Baron *see* Atkins, Humphrey
Colombo, Emilio, 206, 220, 222, 231, 705
Comet (aircraft), 113
Common Agricultural Policy (CAP), 207, 213, 217–18, 356, 376, 388, 542–3, 545, 698, 705
Common Fisheries Policy (CFP), 699–700, 703

Common Foreign and Security Policy (Europe; CFSP), 714

Commons, House of: life in, 139–40; votes in favour of accession to EC, 377–80, 732; EC Bill passed (1972), 383–5; and European referendum, 543–4; election of Speaker, 594; Members' standards and integrity, 595; live TV broadcasts from, 596; debate on North-South issue, 611–12; 80th birthday presentation to EH, 690

Commonwealth: and British membership of European Community, 203, 207–10, 212–13, 217, 220–5, 361, 373, 496, 726; EH's interest in, 476–7; hostility to arms for South Africa, 477–8, 480; and Rhodesia, 478, 480; developing countries in, 604; *see also* immigration policy

Commonwealth Eminent Persons Group (EPG), 621

Commonwealth Heads of Government Meetings: (London, 1962), 224; (Singapore, 1971), 242, 477, 480–1, 495; (Ottawa, 1973), 495–6; (Nassau, 1985), 621

Commonwealth Immigrants Bill (1968), 291

Commonwealth Immigration Act (1962), 455

Commonwealth Parliamentary Association: 1954 Conference, 619

Commonwealth Sugar Agreement, 374

community charge *see* poll tax

Community Health Councils (CHCs), 452

Concorde (aircraft), 459

Confederation of British Industry (CBI): and Conservative anti-inflation measures, 333, 345; and pay and prices policy, 345, 352, 397, 404, 412; discussions with EH and TUC on economy, 396–7, 403–4, 412–15; and industrial relations, 403, 516; and 1973–4 economic crisis, 509; pessimism on state of country, 584

Conference on Security and Co-operation in Europe (CSCE; Helsinki), 487–9, 489

Coningsby Club, London, 115

Conran, Shirley, 555

Conservative Group for Europe, 379, 543, 695

Conservative Party: EH joins, 29, 728; pre-war weakness, 45; 1945 election defeat, 108–9; Research Department (CRD), 115–16, 128, 521, 537; reorganised under Woolton, 122; post-war problems and policies, 126–31, 192–3; Industrial Policy Committee, 128; Political Centre (CPC), 128, 388; Central Council, 130; 1951 election victory and government, 153–4; 1955 election victory and government, 161; and Suez crisis, 171, 175, 183; 1959 election victory, 192; and industrial relations, 193–5, 198, 200, 280–1, 287–8, 299, 303, 327–39, 344, 353, 396–8, 405–16, 508–11, 524, 730; attitude to European Community, 204, 223–4, 356, 358, 380, 695, 704–5, 706–7, 712, 716–17,

726, 730; decline (1963), 250; 1963 leadership contest, 254–6; loses 1964 election, 265–6; EH heads policy review, 267, 274; EH elected leader (1965), 268–70; 1966 election defeat, 275, 281–2; and Rhodesia crisis, 277–8; local government and by-election gains (1967–69), 288–9, 299–300; Scottish Policy Group, 294–5; Selsdon Park Hotel meeting (1970), 301–2; 1970 election victory, 302–3, 305–10, 729; incomes and prices policy, 303–4, 327, 345–6, 352, 398, 401, 404–5, 410, 413–19, 513, 569–70, 735; 1997 election defeat, 418, 595–6, 721–2; and Northern Ireland Unionists, 422; domestic programme (1970–74), 446–67; and Commonwealth immigration, 455–8; and 1973–4 economic crisis, 508–9, 730; February 1974 election campaign and defeat, 512–18; post-war Charters, 524; October 1974 election defeat, 525; leadership contest (1974–5), 530–6; leadership election procedures revised, 530–1; and referendum on EC membership, 546; and Scottish and Welsh nationalism, 565–6; loses Scottish and Welsh MPs, 567; 1979 election campaign and victory, 572–3; monetarist policy under Thatcher, 575–7, 584; 1983 election victory, 582, 704; 1987 election victory, 582, 587; and full employment ideal, 583; privatisation programme, 585–6; acts against local government, 587; introduces poll tax, 587–8; 'sleaze' in, 595; 1992 election victory, 597; and free market, 598–9; ideology and mission, 599–600; supports nuclear deterrent, 616; campaign guide for European Parliament elections (1979), 696; in European Parliament, 714; and Referendum Party campaign (1997), 715–16; *see also* 1922 Committee

Conservative Party Conferences: Llandudno (1948), 129; Olympia, London (1949), 129, 131; Margate (1953), 158, 203–4, 601; Llandudno (1956), 168; Blackpool (1963), 254–5; Brighton (1965), 275–6, 278; Brighton (1969), 300; Blackpool (1970), 329–30, 339; Brighton (1971), 379; Blackpool (1972), 415, 457–8, 691; Blackpool (1973), 419, 502, 542; Blackpool (1975), 550; Brighton (1976), 552–3; Brighton (1978), 569; Blackpool (1981), 579; Brighton (1984), 586–7; Brighton (1988), 710; Bournemouth (1990), 655

contraceptive pill, 453

Cooke, Alistair: *America*, 556

Cooper, Joseph, 20–1, 88

Coote, Colin, 187

Copenhagen: 1973 EC summit, 393, 502

Corbet, Freda, 384

Corfe Castle, Dorset, 37

Corfield, (Sir) Frederick, 339–41, 400

Cosgrave, Liam, 441–2, 444–5, 554
Council of Ireland, 442–5
Council on Prices, Productivity and Incomes, 570
Courcel, Baron Geoffroy de, 237, 239
Cousins, Frank, 193–4
Couve de Murville, Maurice: qualities, 207; and British application to join EC, 215–16, 222, 228–32, 234–6; relations with EH, 235–6, 238–9
Craig, William, 440
Craven, Stuart, 682
Crayford, Kent, 1, 5–6
Creasey (Broadstairs pork butcher), 8
Criminal Justice Act (1972), 446–7
Cripps, Sir Stafford: debating tour of America, 72; devalues sterling, 125–6; in Commons, 140; opposes Schuman Plan, 144–5; retires, 151
Critchley, (Sir) Julian, 223
Croatia, 626
Crosland, Anthony: at Oxford, 47; supports entry into EC, 355; *The Future of Socialism*, 191
Crossman, Richard: and 1938 Oxford by-election, 59; social service benefits, 304
Crowe, Sir Colin, 476
Crowther, Geoffrey, Baron, 564
Cuba: EH visits, 613–15; missile crisis (1962), 651
Cuckney, (Sir) John, 342
Cumming, Nigel, 527
Cummings, Douglas, 465
Cundell, Edric, 92
Cunningham, George, 567
Curzon, (Sir) Clifford, 92, 309, 558
Cyprus, 209
Czechoslovakia, 55, 57, 64, 83; Soviet invasion of (1968), 474, 486

Daily Express, 259, 533, 571
Daily Mirror, 153
Daily Telegraph, 187, 534, 719
Dakouré, Antoine Kipsa, 606
Dalton, Hugh, 47–8, 64, 127
Dalyell, Tam, 565
Danzig (Gdansk): EH visits, 68–70
Darlington, 439
Dartford consituency, 126–7
Dartmouth College, New Hampshire, 78
Davies, Ivor, 59
Davies, John, 320–1, 329–30, 347–8, 399–400, 543
Davignon Report (1970), 361, 489
Davis, Sir Colin, 676
Davis, Stanley Clinton, 612
Day, Sir Robin, 406, 675, 691
Dean, Sir Patrick, 169
Deedes, William, Baron, 117
Defender (yacht), 473

de Havilland, Geoffrey, 113
Dehn, Paul, 465
de Klerk, Frederik, 622
De La Warr, Herbrand Brassey Sackville, 9th Earl, 81
Delmer, Sefton, 142
Delors, Jacques, 705–6, 711, 714
Dench, (Dame) Judi, 394
Deng Pufang, 642, 647
Deng Xiaoping, 629, 634, 640–1, 644
Denman, Teddy and Pempy, 18
Denmark: referendum on Maastricht Treaty, 715
Denning, Alfred, Baron, 246, 406–8
Desert Island Discs (radio programme), 684
de Valera, Eamon, 438
devaluation see sterling
developing countries see Third World
Devlin, Bernadette (*later* McAliskey), 435, 596
Devlin, Patrick, Baron, 443
Dickens, Charles, 6
Diefenbaker, John, 221
Dilhorne, Reginald Manningham-Buller, 1st Viscount, 282, 296
Dines, Edward, 119
Disraeli, Benjamin, 129, 599
Dixon, Sir Pierson, 211–12, 226–8, 257, 367
dock strikes: (1970), 321, 334; (1972), 406–7, 411
Dodds, Norman, 127
Donaldson, Sir John (*later* Baron), 406
Donovan Commission, 1965–68 (on trade unions), 297, 326, 347
Donovan, Terence, Baron, 335, 338, 516
Dossetter, Jay, 721
Douglas-Home, Sir Alec (*later* Baron Home of the Hirsel): as Chamberlain's PPS, 58; as Foreign Secretary in EH's Cabinet, 83–4, 204–5, 310, 378, 468, 536; Macmillan appoints as Foreign Secretary, 199–200; and British application for EC membership, 205–6, 363; and Moscow Test Ban Treaty, 248; succeeds Macmillan as leader, 253, 255–6, 269; and abolition of Resale Price Maintenance, 259–60, 262–3; relations with EH, 262–3, 269; calls 1964 election, 265–6; as leader of Opposition, 267; resignation and succession to as Party leadership, 267–8; as Shadow Foreign Secretary under EH, 269, 520; in Scotland, 274; meets Ian Smith, 277, 621; and Scottish constitutional question, 296, 563; and Leila Khaled crisis, 323, 462; and parliamentary debate and vote on EC accession, 378–9; at signing of Treaty of Accession to EC, 381–2; and Northern Ireland, 424, 427, 429, 436; and Ugandan Asian immigrants, 457; character and qualities, 468; and Soviet espionage, 474–5; attempts Rhodesia settlement, 478–80; meets Amin, 483; memo on USSR and Eastern

bloc, 486; and Helsinki Accords, 489; seventieth birthday, 489; and improving relations with USSR, 490; and recognition of China, 494–5; and Amin's requests for Ottawa Conference attendance, 496; declares neutrality in Arab-Israeli war (1973), 501; and coal crisis (1973), 504; retires, 519; heads panel to consider leadership election procedures, 530, 533; sympathy at EH's father's death, 554; agreement on Falklands (1972), 579; reports on China, 647; at Macmillan's 90th birthday dinner, 677; speaks at EH's 40th anniversary as MP, 683; and Referendum Party campaign, 715

Downing Street: music at, 443, 464–5; no.10 renovated, 459–61

'Downing Street Declaration', 1969 (on Northern Ireland), 423

Drumalbyn, Niall Macpherson, 1st Baron, 257

du Cann, Edward: at Board of Trade, 257, 267, 290; resigns as Party Chairman, 290; and EH's position as Party leader, 528–30; refuses post under EH, 529

Dublin: British embassy burned, 435; EH visits, 441–2; European Council meeting (1975), 544; European Youth Orchestra plays in, 563; Yeats in, 735

Duke, Colonel Augustus Cecil Hare, 27–8, 66

Dulles, John Foster, 167

Duncan, Alex and Rory, 659–60

Duncan, Bruce, 660

Duncan-Sandys, Baron see Sandys, Duncan

Dunkirk evacuation (1940), 85

Dunn, Simon, 663, 667

du Sautoy, Stephen, 555

Düsseldorf, 40

Easton, Dr Jeffrey, 656–7, 660, 662, 664, 665–6

Easton, Marian: marriage and divorce with John Heath, 120

Eccles, David, 1st Viscount, 110

Economist, The, 512

Ede, James Chuter, 253–4

Eden, Anthony (*later* 1st Earl of Avon): and new Conservatism, 29; and Chamberlain, 44, 83; resigns (1938), 49–50, 83; visits Oxford, 50; and Spanish Civil War, 55; in post-war opposition, 108–9; and post-war domestic policy, 128; in Commons, 139; on Schuman Plan, 144–5; as Foreign Secretary (1951), 153; ill-health, 157–8, 169, 175–6; invited to HAC dinner, 157; resents Churchill's retaining premiership, 158; parliamentary performances, 159; premiership, 159–60, 161–2; calls 1955 election, 160–1; interest in art, 160; EH's relations with, 163, 172, 181–2, 253; entertains Bulganin and Khrushchev, 164; and Suez crisis, 166–73, 177; addresses nation on TV, 173; holidays in

Jamaica, 175–6; and Messina conference, 178; resigns premiership, 178; world tour, 181; in retirement, 192; 'three circles' foreign policy, 203–4, 601; appeal, 248; on 1966 election result, 282; congratulates EH on 1970 election victory, 309; invites Tito, 483; Chou En-lai on, 631

Eden, Clarissa, Lady (*née* Churchill; *later* Countess of Avon), 175–6, 181, 686

Eden, Sir John, 400

Edgar, Nicholas, 664, 688

Edinburgh: EFTA Conference (1964), 564

Education: a Framework for Expansion (White Paper), 448

Education Act (1944), 253, 448

education reform (1970–74), 447–51

Education Reform Bill (1988), 588

Edward VIII, King (*later* Duke of Windsor): abdication, 39–40

Egypt: EH visits, 164–5, 323, 695; and Suez crisis, 164–71, 174, 177; and Iraqis, 658

Eisenhower, Dwight D., 182–4

Eisenhower, Mamie, 492

Election Forum (BBC programme), 540

elections see General Elections

Electricity Council, 333, 336

Elizabeth II, Queen: coronation, 156; and Eden's resignation, 178; and Macmillan's appointment as premier, 178–9; visits USA (1957), 183; and Macmillan's resignation, 255; and EH's 1970 election victory, 308–9; EH's weekly audiences with, 317–19, 324; EH visits at Balmoral, 323–4; and award of political honours, 324; attends 'Fanfare for Europe' performance, 394; and troubles in Northern Ireland, 427; lunches at Chequers, 471; and Singapore Commonwealth Conference (1971), 477, 480–1; dissolves Parliament (1974), 511; expresses sympathy on bombing of EH's house, 532; describes EH as 'expendable' on visit to Iraq, 669–70; reception for Praemium Imperiale recipients, 689; at 10 Downing Street for EH's 80th birthday celebration, 690

Elizabeth, Queen Mother, 308–9, 324, 464, 470

Elles, Diana Louie, Baroness, 560

Ellis, Arthur, 109

Employment Medical Advisory Service, 408

employment training, 589–90

EMU (Economic and Monetary Union) see *under* European Community

Endurance, HMS, 579

Energy, Department of: formed, 505

English Chamber Orchestra, 683

Epstein, Sir Jacob, 19

Erhard, Ludwig, 214–15, 230, 233, 713

Erroll, Frederick, 256

EURATOM, 148, 204

Euro (currency), 712

Europe and You (Conservative pamphlet), 716
European Coal and Steel Community, 143–4, 147–8, 201, 204–5, 355
European Commission: Jenkins's Presidency, 694; Delors' Presidency, 705–6, 714
European Communities Bill and Act (1972), 382–7, 541
European Community (*later* European Union): British entry vetoed by de Gaulle, 57, 219, 225–6, 228–30, 239–40, 245, 732; and Schuman Plan, 142–5; Churchill's views on, 146–7; early British suspicion of, 148, 202; economic performance, 148, 359; EH negotiates unsuccessfully for British entry (1961–3), 201, 203–4, 206–23, 228–35, 249, 366; principles and ideals, 202–3; and Commonwealth, 203, 207–10, 212–13, 217, 220–5, 361, 373, 496, 726; Labour Party view of, 210, 213–14, 355–60, 362, 377–9, 516, 525, 545, 547, 693–4, 704, 707; and national sovereignty, 210–11, 716–18; and colonies, 217; horticultural considerations, 218–19; and defence, 227, 229; Wilson seeks entry (1967), 238, 357; and Barber's budget, 331; British entry application renewed and accepted (1971), 348, 351, 357, 363–7, 370–7, 687, 717, 732–3; popular opinion of, 358–9, 363, 723; and 'Luxembourg compromise' (1966), 360; foreign policy co-operation, 361; British referendum on membership (1975), 362–3, 378, 539–49, 693, 709; British budgetary contributions, 372–3, 543, 698; concessions to New Zealand, 373–4; economic and monetary union (EMU), 375, 387–8, 391–2, 500, 694, 714, 718–19, 725–6; and fear of price rises, 376; fisheries policy, 376–7, 699–704; Commons debate and vote on accession, 377–80, 732; Treaty of (British) Accession signed (1972), 381–2, 385, 543, 702, 715; Commons Bill on (1972), 383–6; precedence of law over national law, 385; and Single European Act, 387, 697, 706–7, 718, 725; Norway rejects membership, 388–9; and regional policy, 388, 390, 392, 500, 542–3; aid to developing world, 390–1; federalism and political union, 391–2, 707–8, 718–19; organisation and procedures, 393–4; Britain formally enters (1973), 394; Irish membership, 420–1, 423; and Convention on Human Rights, 427–8; free movement of labour, 458; and Israeli occupied territories, 501; EH defends during second 1974 election campaign, 525; British proposals to modify, 542–5; effects on British trade, 547–8; musical and cultural activities, 561, 563; and single market, 705–6, 708–9, 718; Council of Ministers, 706, 708–9, 714; voting procedures, 706, 708; powers and regulations, 708–9; bureaucracy, 709–10; Charter of

Fundamental Human Rights (1989), 711; Conservative group in, 714; sceptics and, 714–15; EH's commitment to membership of, 722–6, 732; *see also* Common Agricultural Policy; European Summits
European Community Youth Orchestra, 560–3, 675–6
European Convention on Human Rights (ECHR), 427
European Council, 393, 544
European Court of Justice, 703, 709
European Fisheries Convention (1964), 700
European Free Trade Area (EFTA), 202–4, 208, 213, 217, 220, 389; Edinburgh Conference (1964), 564
European Monetary System (EMS), 578, 590, 694–6, 711
European Parliament (EP): elections, 696–8, 705; powers, 697
European People's Party group of Conservatives and Christian Democrats, 714
European Summits: The Hague (1969), 360, 700; Paris (1972), 387, 390–1, 543, 606; Copenhagen (1973), 393, 502; Paris (1974), 392; Fontainebleau (1984), 699
European Union, Treaty of, 362
Evans, Sir Geraint, 394, 533
Evans, Gwynfor, 294
Evans, Sir Horace, 175, 190
Evening Standard, 241
Exchange Rate Mechanism (ERM), 590, 597, 695–6, 711–12, 725
exports *see* balance of payments

Fair Deal at Work, A (Conservative Party document), 287–8, 298, 327
Fairbairn, Sir Nicholas, 686
Fairweather, Pamela, 18
Fairweather, Wallace, 18
Faisal, King of Saudi Arabia, 507
Falklands War (1982), 579–81, 601
Fanfani, Amintore, 206, 688
'Fanfare for Europe', 394
Farmer, John, 36
Farnon, Robert, 38
fascism, 32, 54–5
Fastnet Race, 467, 495, 497; 1979 storm and damage, 671–4, 733
Faulkner, Brian (*later* Baron), 426–8, 431–2, 436–7, 439–40, 442–5
Fawzi, Mahmoud, 167
Fayat, Henri, 222, 230–2, 233–4
Feather, Vic, 194, 200, 328–9, 337–8, 345, 352, 406, 410–11, 415, 512
Federation of Conservative Students, 578
Federation of University Conservative Associations, 39–40, 52
Feltz, Vanessa, 690
Fianna Fail, 424, 431
Fiennes, Sir John, 383

Figaro, Le (newspaper), 361
Figgures, Sir Frank, 513–15
Fine Gael, 443
Firm Action for a Fair Britain (Conservative manifesto, 1974), 512
fisheries: EC policy on, 376–7, 699–74
fishing industry, 490–1
Fitt, Gerry (*later* Baron), 427, 442
Fleming, Peter, 65
Flint, Councillor Peggy, 721
Flint, William, 721
Fontainebleau: EC summit (1984), 699
Foot, Michael: debating tour of America, 72; opposes EC membership, 383, 540
Ford, Gerald, 493, 525
Ford, Henry, 336–7
Forrest, Joe, 115
Fort, Richard, 140
Forte, Sir Charles (*later* Baron), 554, 677
Fowler, Barry, 721
France: EH's 1939 visit to, 71; Churchill proposes union with (1940), 84–5; EH's wartime service in, 95–8; and proposed European union, 142–4, 147; and Coal and Steel Community, 143; EH holidays in, 149, 238–9, 271, 464; and Suez crisis, 167, 169–70, 177, 665; obstructs British application for EC membership, 220, 222, 228–37, 239–40; nuclear strategy and weaponry, 226–7; treaty with Germany (1963), 232–3; defeated by England in 1963 rugby match, 237; and Britain's renewed attempts to enter EC (1971), 354, 363–4, 370–2, 374–5; and 'Soames affair', 359, 493; and co-development of Concorde, 459; defence policy, 488; EH proposes joint nuclear deterrent with, 488; referendum on enlarging EC, 541; and fisheries policy, 701; rivalry with Germany, 723–4; *see also* Paris
France-Soir, 676
Franco, General Francisco, 52–7, 68
Franks, Oliver Shewell Franks, Baron, 580
Fraser, (Sir) Hugh Charles Patrick Joseph: at Oxford, 24, 46, 51, 61, 64; as MP, 51; elected president of Oxford Union, 65; war service, 72–3; and Conservative 1970 campaign, 302, 305; opposes membership of EC, 386; in 1974 leadership election, 530, 534
Fraser, Michael: friendship with EH, 91, 115; in Conservative Research Department, 115–16, 275; and 1974 election, 512
free market, 598–600
Freeman, John, 151
Freeman, 'Tich' (cricketer), 15
Fritsche, Hans, 105
Frost, Derek and Associates, 680
Fulton, John Scott (*later* Baron), 32
Furtseva, Ekaterina A., 248, 469–70
Fyfe, Alan, 48

G7 (group of industrialised nations), 401
Gaidar, Yegor, 624
Gaitskell, Hugh: appointed Chancellor, 151; and Suez crisis, 166, 170, 173; and 1959 election, 191; ambivalence over British entry into EC, 223, 355; death, 250
Galbraith, Vivian, 31–2
Galtieri, General Leopoldo, 580
Gandhi, Mohandas Karamchand (Mahatma), 27
Gardiner, Sir George, 388, 515, 529–30
gas pipeline (Siberia-West Germany), 618
Gaulle, Charles de: vetoes British entry into EC (1963), 57, 219, 225–6, 228, 229–37, 239–40, 245, 354, 421, 732; Churchill's proposal for union with France, 84; and European union, 148; relations with Dixon, 211; and Couve de Murville, 215; questions EH on British intentions in EC, 225; relations with Macmillan, 225, 239, 356, 366; nuclear strategy and weaponry, 226–7; Macmillan on, 228; EH meets, 239–40, 370; sends signed autobiography to EH, 240; vetoes Labour's application for EC membership (1967), 358–9; and 'Soames affair', 359; resigns, 360; death and memorial service, 468
General Agreement on Tariffs and Trade (GATT), 604
General Elections: (1945), 102, 108; (1950), 134–8; (1951), 152–3; (1955), 160–1; (1959), 191, 728; (1964), 265–7; (1966), 275, 279, 281–2; (1970), 302–10, 328, 604; (1974; February), 313, 511–18, 730–1; (1974; October), 525–6, 731; (1979), 568, 572–4, 732; (1983), 582, 704; (1987), 582, 587; (1992), 597, 600; (1997), 418, 595–6, 715–22
Geneva, 367, 571, 602–4
George V, King, 34
George VI, King, 40, 154
Georgiadis, John, 465
Georgic (ship), 80
Germany: EH visits (1937), 40–4, 716; annexes Austria, 50–1; supports Franco, 55; EH travels in (1939), 69–71; invades and occupies Poland, 71–3; 1940 offensive, 83–4; Allies advance into, 100–1; EH with occupying forces in, 101–7; EH conducts in, 559; recognises Slovenia and Croatia, 626; and European directives, 708; reunification, 712–13; in European Union, 723; *see also* West Germany
Gielgud, Sir John, 688
Giles, Frank, 61
Gilmour, (Sir) Ian, 525, 612, 699
Giscard d'Estaing, Valéry, 375, 562, 608, 690, 694–5
Giulini, Carlo Maria, 309
Gladstone, William Ewart, 421
Glamorgan, HMS, 485
Glasgow, 556

Glaspie, April, 651
Gobbi, Tito, 394
Godber, Sir George, 453
Godber, Joseph, 491, 543
Godfrey, Cardinal William, Archbishop of
    Westminster, 251–2
Godkin Lectures see Harvard University
Goebbels, Josef, 44, 65, 104
Golding, William, 555
Goldsmith, Sir James, 535, 715, 719, 721–2
Goodlad, Alastair, 611
Goodman, Arnold, Baron, 457, 479
Goodram, 'Tufty' (schoolteacher), 16
Gorbachev, Mikhail, 470, 617, 623–4
Gordon Walker, Patrick (later Baron): and
    Seretse Khama, 24, 150; in 1938 Oxford by-
    election, 59; defeated in 1964 election, 455
Göring, Hermann, 44, 83, 104
Gormley, Joe, 350, 352–3, 419, 503, 505, 508
Government of Ireland Act (1920), 421, 430
Graham, Kathleen (Kay), 571, 607–8, 682
grammar schools, 448–9
Gray's Inn: EH wins scholarship to, 67–8, 109
Greater London Council, 288; abolished, 587
Greece: and British application to EC, 209–10;
    joins EC, 699
Greene, Sidney, 509
Greenhill, Denis (later Baron), 364
Gregson, Sir Peter, 312
Grenada (Caribbean), 618
Griffiths, Brian, 584
Griffiths, Peter, 455
Grimond, Jo (later Baron), 196
Grisewood, Harman, 174
Gromyko, Andrei, 247, 474–6, 490
Guardian (newspaper), 347, 555, 557
Guillebaud Committee, 195–7
Guinness, Sir Alec, 682
Gulf: British withdrawal from, 482; EH visits,
    650; EH proposes diplomatic solution in
    (1990), 652–3
Gulf War (1991), 601, 664, 713
'Gulf War Syndrome', 667
Guthrie, Sir Giles, 110, 124

Hague, The: European Congress (1948), 122,
    147; EC summit (1969), 360, 700; European
    Parliamentary Congress (1968), 364
Hailsham, Quintin McGarel Hogg, Baron: wins
    1938 Oxford by-election, 59–61; supports
    Seretse Khama, 150; in Moscow for test ban
    treaty, 246; in leadership contest at 1963
    Blackpool conference, 255; and regional
    development, 258, 264, 583; in EH's Shadow
    Cabinet, 283; and Race Relations Bill,
    292–3; and Selsdon Park Hotel meeting,
    301; resumes peerage and becomes Lord
    Chancellor, 310; and Northern Ireland
    problem, 436, 443; and Conservative 1974
    election defeat, 519; condolences at EH's

father's death, 554; at Macmillan's 90th
    birthday dinner, 677–8; congratulates EH on
    award of Garter, 685–6
Haitink, Bernard, 676
Halifax, Edward Frederick Lindley Wood, 1st
    Earl of, 59, 83, 200, 574
Hallstein, Walter, 230–1, 233
Hankey, Robert, 70
Hanover, 101–2
Harare Declaration (1991), 481
Harding, Kathleen, 11–12
Hare, John, 205
Harlech, William David Ormsby Gore, 5th
    Baron, 677
Harrington, Major William, 96
Harris, Kenneth, 266
Harris, William, 37
Hart, Miss M.E., 137
Hartnell, (Sir) Norman, 198
Harvard University: EH delivers Godkin
    Lectures (1968), 361
Harvey, Ian, 130
Hassan, Crown Prince of Jordan, 689
Haughey, Charles, 424
Hawkings, Mr and Mrs Robert, 679
Haxell, Frank, 193
Haydon, Robin, 313
Head, Antony, 108, 170
Healey, Denis (later Baron): at Balliol, 47;
    predicts devaluation (1972), 409; as
    Chancellor of Exchequer, 522–3, 575; and
    1961 Kuwait crisis, 652; and EH's 80th
    birthday celebrations, 689, 691
Heard, Cardinal William, 252
Heath, Edith Anne (née Pantony; EH's mother):
    background, 2; character, 3–4; domestic life,
    8; in Broadstairs house, 9–10; and EH's
    Oxford education, 23, 26; illness and death,
    152–3; and EH's achievements, 729
Heath, Sir Edward:
    Education: early schooling, 6–7; attends
        Chatham House Grammar School, 9,
        12–18; School Certificate and
        matriculation, 13; studies economics at
        WEA, 15; school prefect and honours, 18;
        at Oxford (Balliol College), 21–2, 23–40,
        46–71; student loan from Kent Education
        Committee, 25; wins Balliol organ
        scholarship, 26–7, 37; as president of
        Junior Common Room, 31, 38, 47;
        reading, 32–3; elected secretary and
        librarian of Oxford Union, 48–9; contests
        presidency of Oxford Union, 51–2;
        presidency of Oxford Union, 61–6;
        named 'Isis Idol', 63; Gray's Inn
        scholarship, 67–8, 109; degree, 68, 96;
        effect of, 727
    Health: reaction to army vaccination, 86;
        appendectomy, 92–4; puts on weight, 107;
        jaundice, 190, 272; fatigue, 272; thyroid

complaint, 512, 578; injures leg in 1979 Fastnet race, 672–3

Honours: Knight of the Garter, 121, 685–6; Charlemagne Prize, 237–8; Open University honorary doctorate, 448

Interests: gardening, 5; motorcycling, 7; owns dog, 10, 36; sports, 10, 15, 35, 273; amateur dramatics, 15–16; debating, 16–17, 29, 34, 39, 47–8, 76–7; arts, 18–19, 70, 247, 681, 688; punting, 35; reading, 94, 114; theatre-going, 113–14; as Trustee of British Museum, 241–2; sailing, 272–4, 300–1, 429, 466–7, 497, 526, 533, 563, 671–4, 733

Military service: called up, 81–2, 86–7; serves in Royal Artillery, 88–94; with occupying forces in Germany, 101–7; commands firing squad, 103; leaves army, 107; commands peacetime HAC territorial regiment, 114–15, 117, 155; as Master Gunner within Tower of London, 156

Musical interests: learns piano, 7–8; choral singing, 9, 34–5, 68; Broadstairs carol parties, 11–12, 162; visits to opera, 14, 420, 608; with school orchestra, 15; wins school piano prize, 16; organ playing, 20, 27, 37; conducting, 36, 38, 465–6, 558–63, 642–3, 674–6, 689, 733–4; composing, 37; concert-going, 42, 47, 74, 92; EH considers professional career, 67–8, 733; in army, 88; wartime, 88–9, 92; buys Steinway piano, 238; as recreation, 273, 733; plays clavichord, 381; attends Glyndebourne, 420; concerts at Downing Steet, 443, 464; concerts at Chequers, 462–3, 466; as President of European Community Youth Orchestra, 560, 563; recordings, 683, 692; *Desert Island Discs* choice, 684–5

Personal life: ancestry, 1; birth, 1; upbringing, 4, 5–6; confirmed, 9; life in Broadstairs, 11; attachment to Kathleen Raven, 12–13; religious beliefs, 33–4, 66, 121; considers post-war business career, 109–10; lives in London, 111–14; works in Civil Aviation, 111–14; resigns from civil service, 120; works at *Church Times*, 121–4; banking work, 124–5, 152–3; motoring, 131–2; and mother's death, 153; Albany apartment, 256–7, 307–8, 459; social and official commitments, 271–2; attacked with ink in Brussels, 382; spoken French, 389; improves 10 Downing Street, 459–61; Renoir paintings loaned to, 460–1; Wilton Street home, 520, 527–8; Wilton Street house bombed by IRA, 532; second IRA attempt on, 550–2; Salisbury house, 655, 679–83; entertains Macmillan, 676–8; possessions, 681–2; lunch parties in Salisbury, 682; birthdays and

anniversaries celebrated, 683, 689–91; advises on Praemium Imperiale arts prizes, 688–9; friendships, 735–6

Politics: schoolboy activities, 16–18; principles and ideals, 28, 524–5, 598–600, 685, 727, 734–6; student activities, 28–30, 33, 38–9, 49–51; economic reading, 33; meets Nazis in Nuremberg (1937), 43–4; first elected to Parliament (1950), 51, 138–9, 727; selected as candidate for Bexley, 116–22, 125–7, 134–6; early Europeanism, 122–3, 178; speechmaking, 122–3; maiden speech supporting Schuman Plan, 144–5, 147; defies Whips over Seretse Khama, 150; as parliamentary Whip, 150–1, 154, 161–2; in 1951 election campaign, 153; appointed Lord Commissioner of the Treaury, 153–4; in 1955 election, 160–1; as Chief Whip, 163, 171–2, 175, 192, 253; and Suez crisis, 169, 171–2, 174–5; retains Bexley in 1959 election, 191–2; dealings with trade unions, 192–3, 195, 200, 730; as Minister of Labour (1959), 192–200, 280; and threatened rail strike (1960), 195–7; as Lord Privy Seal at Foreign Office, 200, 201, 241–2; negotiates for British entry into EC (1961–3), 201, 203–4, 206–22, 228–36, 238, 249; speaks at 1962 Commonwealth Conference, 224; statements on failure of EC negotiations, 235–6; as President of Board of Trade, 257–64; heads Party policy review, 267, 274; as Shadow Chancellor after 1964 election defeat, 267, 733; elected Party leader, 268–70; as leader of Opposition, 270–1, 520; duels with Wilson, 271; campaigns in 1966 election, 281–2; reforms Shadow Cabinet (1966), 282–3, 290; broadcast on 1967 sterling crisis, 289–90; takes up premiership and forms first government, 310–11, 729; on Prime Minister's role and duties, 312–13, 729; secretariat, 312–13; government and departmental reforms, 314–16; renews negotiations for entry to EC (1970–1), 354, 361–8, 370–2, 377, 717, 732–3; Godkin Lectures (Harvard, 1968), 361; and Commons vote in favour of EC accession, 380; at signing of Treaty of Accession to EC, 381–2; talks with TUC and CBI on economy, 396–7; and economic crisis (1973–4), 505–7, 730–1; calls February 1974 election, 509–12, 730; resigns premiership (1974), 520, 731; 1974 speech on Conservative principles, 524–5; denounces laisser-faire dogma, 524; leadership challenged (1974), 528–33, 732; loses leadership to Thatcher, 534–8, 732; opposes referendum on EC membership,

Heath, Sir Edward *—cont.*
  Politics – *cont.*
    545; campaigns for 'yes' vote in EC
    referendum, 546–9; speech at 1976 Party
    conference, 552–3; policy clashes with
    Thatcher, 563, 568–9, 573, 707, 710–11;
    supports Scottish devolution, 566–7;
    popular support for, 571; campaigns in
    1979 election, 572–4, 732; declines
    Thatcher's offer of Washington embassy,
    574; retires to back benches (1979), 574,
    732; opposes Thatcher's monetarist policy,
    575; presents alternative 1985 budget, 584;
    opposes War Crimes Bill, 592; as Father of
    the House, 594, 596; on capitalism and
    free market, 598–600; advocates trade to
    developing countries, 602; serves on
    Brandt Commission, 607–10; mission to
    Iraq (1990), 652–62; campaigns in 1979
    European Parliament election, 697;
    speeches defending EC (1988–9), 710–11;
    attacked by Referendum Party (1997),
    715–20; campaigns in 1997 election,
    720–1; commitment to European Union,
    722–6, 732; achievements, 727–34
  Travels: Aachen, 238; Australia, 286, 290,
    302; Bermuda, 484–6; China, 493–4, 579,
    629–42, 648; Cuba, 613–15; Cyprus and
    Greece, 209; Danzig and Poland, 68–71;
    Egypt, 164–5, 323, 695; Europe (wartime
    service), 95–107; France, 149, 238–9, 271,
    464; Geneva, 368, 571, 602–3; Germany
    and Austria, 40–4, 68–71, 142, 238, 605,
    716; Gulf tour, 482, 650; Hong Kong, 639,
    642; Iran, 627–8; Iraq, 654–65; Ireland,
    420, 441–2; Japan, 495, 688; Mali, 607;
    Middle East tour, 323; Moscow and
    St Petersburg, 246–8, 623–5; Northern
    Ireland, 433; Ottawa, 221, 495–6; Paris,
    14, 239, 354, 362, 368, 370, 390, 607–8;
    Rome, 206, 251–2; Singapore, 242, 477,
    480–2, 650; South Africa, 619–20, 622;
    South-East Asia, 278; Spain, 52–7, 365,
    537, 539, 544; Sweden, 194; USA and
    Canada, 72–80, 152, 158, 284, 471, 488,
    491–3, 525; Venice, 205
  Writings: on education and class, 81–2;
    Carols: The Joy of Christmas, 558; *Music: A
    Joy for Life*, 92, 558; *Sailing*, 554–7; *Travels:
    People and Places in my Life*, 558
Heath, George (EH's great-grandfather), 1
Heath, John (EH's brother; 'Bubbles'): birth, 4;
  relations with EH, 4–5, 36, 93; career, 5,
  107–8; musical interests, 8; war service, 80;
  in Dunkirk evacuation, 85; meets EH on
  return from war, 107; first marriage and
  divorce, 120; remarries (Muriel), 676; death,
  676
Heath, Julia Louisa (*née* Hobday; EH's
  grandmother), 2–3

Heath, Muriel (John's second wife), 676, 690
Heath, Richard (RH's grandfather), 2–3
Heath, William George (EH's father): lives and
  works in Crayford, 1, 5–6; character and
  interests, 3; in Broadstairs, 6, 10–11; takes
  over building firm, 21; and EH's Oxford
  education, 23, 26; council election defeat, 67;
  works with City of London Corporation in
  war, 85; revives building firm after war, 107;
  and EH's dissatisfaction at *Church Times*, 123;
  and wife's death, 153; birthdays, 553–4;
  death, 553–4
Heathcoat Amory, Derick: as Chancellor of
  Exchequer, 186, 191; and rail settlement
  (1960), 196–7; retires as Chancellor, 199; as
  High Commissioner in Canada, 221–2
Heathrow airport (London), 113
Helsby, Sir Laurence, 194
Helsinki Accords *see* Conference on Security
  and Co-operation in Europe
Hely-Hutchinson, Victor, 37
Henderson, Sir Nicholas, 389
Henry of Blunston, Archdeacon of Dorset, 679
Heseltine, Michael, 400, 583, 691
Hess, Dame Myra, 92
Hess, Rudolf, 104
Heuseman, M. (mayor of Antwerp), 98
Hewitt, John, 313–14
Hicks, John, 33
Hilton, Roger, 24
Himmler, Heinrich, 44
Hitler, Adolf: rise to power, 32, 41; as war
  threat, 39, 64; at Nuremberg rallies, 43, 104;
  annexes Austria, 51; Chamberlain meets,
  57–8; invades Czechoslovakia, 57–8, 64; and
  Danzig, 69
Hobbs, Jim, 18
Hobson, Valerie (Mrs John Profumo), 245–6
Hochhauser, Victor, 487
Hockney, David, 688
Hogg, Quintin *see* Hailsham, Baron
Holland: EH's wartime service in, 99
Holness, Bob, 675
Holt, Martin, 132–3
Home, 14th Earl of (*later* Baron Home of the
  Hirsel) *see* Douglas-Home, Sir Alec
Hong Kong, 632, 439, 642–7
Honourable Artillery Company (HAC), 102,
  114–15, 117, 155–7
honours lists: EH reintroduces political honours,
  324
Hood, Rev. George, 25, 46
Hope, Lord John, 108
Hornsby-Smith, Dame Patricia, 127, 138, 450
Horrocks, General Sir Brian, 99
Housing Finance Act (1972), 396
housing policy, 454, 523, 584–5
Howard, John, 194
Howe, Sir Geoffrey: drafts EC Bill, 383;
  supervises pay and prices, 416; in 1975

leadership contest, 536; on monetary and incomes policy, 552; at 1978 Party conference, 569; as Chancellor of Exchequer, 581–2; denounces Thatcher in Commons, 593; resigns, 706; supports EC commitment, 706, 710; and Thatcher's hostility to EC, 707

Howell, David, 307

Howells, Herbert, 464, 690

Humber Bridge, 279

Hume, John, 429, 443

Hunt, David, 457–8, 691

Hunt, Kenneth, 144

Hurd, Anthony (later Baron), 274

Hurd, Douglas, Baron: career, 111, 274–5; as EH's political secretary, 274–5, 311, 313, 528; and EH's discussions with Pompidou, 371; and parliamentary approval of EC membership, 377; and control of trade unions, 402; and referendum on EC membership, 546; and EH's speech at 1976 Party conference, 552; and former Yugoslavia, 626; in China with EH, 633–4; and EH's missions to Baghdad, 654–6, 667; attacks EH for criticising Thatcher on EC, 711; commitment to Europe, 714; campaigns for EH in 1997 election, 721

Hussein, King of Jordan, 322, 656

Iain Macleod Memorial Lecture, 524

Ibarruri, Dolores ('La Pasionaria'), 55

IBM (company), 79–80

Iceland: fishing disputes with UK, 490–1, 700

Immigration Act (1971), 456, 458

immigration policy, 455–9

income tax: reduced under Barber, 331

incomes policy: Conservative reform and control of, 327, 345–6, 352, 398, 401, 404–5, 410, 413–16, 418–19, 513, 569, 735; under Labour, 327, 522, 569–71; and average earnings, 411; EH's views on, 571

Independent (newspaper), 659

India: war with Pakistan (1971), 485; Soviet Friendship Pact (1971), 486

Indonesia: conflict with Malaysia, 278

Industrial Charter (1947), 128–9, 192

Industrial Development Advisory Board, 399

Industrial Relations Act (and Bill) (1971), 200, 319, 333–9, 396–7, 401–2, 405–9, 411, 505, 512, 516, 523, 572

Industrial Reorganisation Corporation, 331, 339

Industry Act (1972), 400–1, 730

inflation: Conservative measures against, 325–9, 332–5, 343–6, 401, 405, 414–16, 570; rises with sterling devaluation, 409, 411; increase under Labour government, 572; volatility, 575; and monetarism, 584; and tax cuts, 590; and interest rates, 591

In Place of Strife (White Paper), 298, 303–4, 326

Inskip, Sir Thomas, 50

interest rates, 591–2, 613, 618

International Labour Organisation (ILO), 198–9, 652

International Monetary Fund (IMF), 346, 575, 718

Intrepid, HMS, 481

Iran: relations with UK, 482; oil supplies, 508; EH visits, 627–8; fatwa against Rushdie, 627; war with Iraq, 651, 658

Iraq: assets frozen, 650, 663–4; invades Kuwait, 650–1, 654, 658–9, 667; United Nations resolutions on, 650–1, 657, 661, 667–8; British detainees and hostages in, 651, 654, 657–63, 665–6; war with Iran, 651, 658; and 1961 Kuwait crisis, 652; EH's 1990 mission to, 654–62; EH revisits (1993), 662–5; health and conditions in, 665–7, 669

Ireland, Republic of: EH visits, 420; membership of EC, 420–1, 423; and partition, 421; and reform in Northern Ireland, 423, 425, 430, 444; proposed reunification with North, 433, 436; and IRA violence, 436; territorial claims in Constitution, 441–2, 445; UN restrictions modified, 667–8; see also Northern Ireland

Irish Republican Army (IRA): campaigns, 420–1, 425, 427–8, 438; internments, 429; in Republic of Ireland, 432; violence on British mainland, 435–6; declares cease-fire (1972), 438; bombs EH's Wilton Street house, 532; second attempt on EH, 550–2; see also Provisional IRA

Iron and Steel Act (1972), 412

Irving, Robert, 87

Irwin, Jack, 79

Isis (Oxford magazine), 34–5, 63

Israel: and Suez crisis, 167, 169–70, 177, 665; and Arab terrorists, 321–2; and Yom Kippur War (1973), 419, 466, 492, 500, 502, 619; occupied territories, 501

Istomin, Eugene, 462

Italy: invades Abyssinia, 49; supports British entry into EC, 206, 251

Ivanov, Captain Evgeny, 245–6

Jacob, General Sir Ian, 174

Jamal, Amir, 606

Japan: EH visits, 495, 688; strength, 723

Jay, Peter, 515, 574

Jenkins, Arthur, 47, 101

Jenkins, Dame Jennifer, 680

Jenkins, Roy (later Baron): at Balliol, 47; in Oxford Union debate, 58; as Home Secretary, 284; as Chancellor of Exchequer, 298–9, 304; and 1970 election, 304; and inflation, 327; supports membership of EC, 355, 377, 540, 546, 687, 725; and Commons votes on EC membership, 380, 383; and EH's loss of Party leadership, 535; resigns as Labour deputy leader, 541; on Wilson's true age, 557; wins Hillhead by-election (1982),

Jenkins, Roy – *cont.*
    579; on EH's Salisbury house, 680;
    congratulates EH on award of Garter, 686;
    elected Chancellor of Oxford University,
    686–7; reputation and achievements, 687; at
    EH's 80th birthday celebration, 691;
    Presidency of European Commission, 694;
    forms Social Democratic Party, 704
Jessel, Toby, 386
Jha, Lakshmi Kant, 606
Jiang Zemin, 648
Job, C., 137–8
Job Centres: established, 408
Jobert, Michel, 361, 365–6, 368, 370, 374, 489
Jodl, General Alfried, 104
John XXIII, Pope, 251
John, Augustus, 19
Johnson, Carol, 384
Johnson, Lyndon B., 37, 284, 482
Johnson Smith, Geoffrey, 433–4
Joint Declaration (Northern Ireland, 1993), 445
Jones, Aubrey, 162
Jones, Jack: in Spanish Civil War, 53; and 1970
    dock strike, 321; and 1971 Industrial
    Relations Act, 338, 403, 407; in TUC
    discussions on economy with EH, 398, 410;
    in economic crisis (1974), 510
Jopling, Michael, 384
Jordan: hijacked aircraft blown up, 322–3
Joseph, Keith (*later* Baron): and EH's leadership
    bid, 268; at Selsdon Park Hotel meeting, 302;
    as Health and Social Security Secretary, 310,
    349, 414, 451; departmental budget, 418;
    National Health Service reforms, 451–3; in
    post-1974 Opposition, 520–1; sets up Centre
    for Policy Studies, 521; laisser-faire beliefs,
    524; non-candidature in 1974 leadership
    election, 530; serves under Thatcher, 537
Jowett, Benjamin, 26, 36
Juan Carlos, King of Spain, 57
Judd, James, 561
Juliana, Queen of the Netherlands, 563
Junor, John, 554
Justice and Home Affairs (Europe; JHA), 714

Kaiser, Philip, 49
Kaldor, Nicholas (*later* Baron), 288
Karajan, Herbert von, 42, 394–5, 555, 560,
    675, 684
Karamanlis, Konstantin, 209
Kassem, General Abdul Karim, 652
Kaunda, Kenneth, 478
Keble College, Oxford: organ scholarship,
    20–1
Keeler, Christine, 245–6
Keitel, Field Marshal Wilhelm, 104
Kellett-Bowman, Elaine, 560
Kellner, Peter, 722
Kennedy, John F.: relations with Macmillan,
    184, 226, 244, 249; and British application to

join EC, 209, 249; and Nassau agreement
    (1962), 226–7; popularity, 248–9;
    assassinated, 249; in Berlin, 249
Kennedy, Nigel, 463
Kennedy, Robert, 284
Kennedy, Rev. Studdert ('Woodbine Willy'), 9
Kent County Cricket Club, 15
Kenya: Asian immigrants from, 291
Kerruish, Jerry, 58, 61
Key, Robert, 679
Keynes, John Maynard, Baron, *General Theory
    of Employment, Interest and Money*, 33
Khaled, Leila, 321–3, 462
Khomeini, Ayatollah, 627
Khrushchev, Nikita S., 164, 248, 266, 622
Kiesinger, Kurt, 359, 361
Kilbrandon, Charles James Dalrymple Shaw,
    Baron, 564
Killick, Sir John, 487
Kilmuir, David Maxwell Fyfe, Earl of, 105, 127,
    178, 245, 717
King, Horace, 283
King, Thomas Jeremy (Tom), 655
Kingsgate, Kent, 7, 18, 107
King's Head, The, Bexley village, 119, 136, 306
Kisch, Royalton, 25
Kissinger, Henry: on Britain's relations with
    USA, 229; EH meets, 243–4; and Rolls-
    Royce collapse, 341; in Indo-Pakistan war,
    486; and proposed Anglo-French nuclear
    deterrent, 488; policy on Europe, 492–3;
    negotiates in China, 494–5
Kitson, Sally, Lady, 633–4
Kitson, Sir Timothy, 243, 313, 509, 520, 528,
    534, 536–7, 539, 556, 633–4
Knight, Gordon, 273–4
Kohl, Helmut, 713
Kokoshin, Andrei, 625
Kosygin, Alexei, 284–6
Kozyrev, Vice-Minister (USSR), 470
Krupa, Gene, 79
Kunming, 636–7, 640
Kuwait: invaded by Iraq, 650–1, 658–9, 667;
    1961 crisis, 651–2; Iraqis condemn, 657–8
Ky, Air Vice-Marshal Nguyen-cao-, 278

labour exchanges: 50th anniversary celebrations,
    198
Labour, Ministry of: EH as Minister, 193–200,
    280
Labour Party: EH rejects appeal as student,
    28–9; 1930s decline, 32; Dalton speaks for at
    Oxford Union, 47–8; nationalisation
    programme, 47–8, 127; 1945 government,
    108–9; austerity plans, 125; devalues sterling,
    125–6, 289; 1950 election success, 138–9;
    decline (1951), 151; and Suez crisis, 172–4;
    and 1959 election, 191; views on British
    membership of EC, 210, 213–14, 355–60,
    362, 377–9, 516, 525, 545, 547, 693–4, 704,

707; 1964 election victory, 265–6; and Rhodesia crisis, 277; 1966 election victory, 279, 281–2; economic policy, 288; and race relations, 291–2; and trade union legislation, 297–8, 304; 1970 election campaign and defeat, 304–7; and industrial relations, 331, 339, 572–3; obstructs Treaty of Accession to EC, 381; opposes EC Bill, 383–5; education policy, 448–9; housing policy, 454; contacts with USSR, 474; opposes arms supply to South Africa, 477–8; 1974 election campaigns and victories, 516–17, 521, 525–6, 731; government (1974–9), 522–3; holds referendum on EC membership, 540–2; and Scottish devolution, 565–7; Liberal pact ends, 568; incomes policy, 569–71; 1979 election defeat, 573; industrial productivity declines under, 573; supports unilateral disarmament, 615–16; and expiry of Simonstown agreement, 621; boycotts Hong Kong hand-over ceremony, 646; and EC fishing agreement, 703; Conference (1980), 704; 1997 election victory, 722

Labour's Programme for Britain (1972), 542
Laing, Sir Maurice, 533
Laird, Melvin, 487
Lamont, Norman: maiden speech on EC membership, 386; as Chancellor of Exchequer, 597
Lang, Cosmo, Archbishop of Canterbury, 37
Lansbury, George, 29
Laski, Harold, 33
Laughton, Charles, 65
law and order: Conservative programme on (1972), 446
Lawley, Sue, 684–5
Lawrence, Sir Geoffrey (Lord Justice), 104
Lawson, George, 384
Lawson, Nigel (*later* Baron): and 1964 election, 266; as Chancellor of Exchequer, 583, 590–1, 597; and Thatcher's hostility to EC, 707
Lee, Arthur, Viscount Lee of Fareham, 461
Lee, Sir Frank, 199, 212
Lee Kuan Yew (Harry Lee), 242–3, 477, 480, 482, 497
Leeds Castle, Kent, 609, 683
Legge-Bourke, Henry, 400
Leningrad *see* St Petersburg
Lennox-Boyd, Alan (*later* 1st Viscount Boyd), 205
Lennox-Boyd, Mark, 661–2
Lever, Harold, 540
Lewis, Kenneth, 408
Liberal Democrats: in 1997 election, 722
Liberal Party: by-election successes, 250; supports abolition of Resale Price Maintenance, 259; and vote on EC Bill, 383, 384; in 1974 election, 517; EH approaches for coalition (1974), 518–19, 568, 731; ends

pact with Labour, 568; alliance with SDP, 582
Libya: bombed (1986), 618–19
Liddell, Alvar, 465
Lill, John, 465, 469
Lin Pao, 633
Lindemann, Frederick *see* Cherwell, Viscount
Lindsay, Alexander Dunlop, 1st Baron: and Workers' Educational Association, 15; as Master of Balliol, 27, 30–1, 66; Socialist beliefs, 30–1, 34; and renovation of Balliol chapel, 37; contests 1938 Oxford by-election, 59–61; heads Oxford recruiting board, 81; and EH's post-war career, 109
Lintott, Sir Henry, 212
Lithgow, Adrian, 661
Liverpool: bombed in war, 90
Lloyd George, David, 1st Earl, 83, 421, 438
Lloyd, Selwyn (*later* Baron Selwyn-Lloyd): as Foreign Secretary, 162, 180, 199; and Suez crisis, 167, 169; meets Eisenhower in Bermuda, 183; moves to Treasury, 199; and British application for EC membership, 204; and Rhodesia crisis, 277–8; stands down from Shadow Cabinet (1966), 282
Lloyd Webber, Andrew, Baron, 689
local government: Thatcher government acts against, 587–8
Local Government Act (1972), 447
Local Government Finance Bill (1987), 587
Locke, Grace, 8
Lockheed (aircraft company), 339–42
Lomé Agreement (*formerly* Yaoundé Agreement), 217
London Symphony Orchestra: EH conducts, 465, 558–60, 733; plays in Russia, 469
London University, 20
Londonderry, 422, 429, 434–5, 438–9
Long Kesh prison (Northern Ireland), 428
Longden, Gilbert, 140
Longford, Francis Aungier Pakenham, 7th Earl of, 59, 554, 556
Lonhro company, 418
Lords, House of: votes in favour of EC accession, 380; debates EC Bill (1972), 386; Labour's proposed reforms of, 569; TV coverage of, 596
Lothian, Philip Henry Kerr, 11th Marquess of, 75–6
Low, Toby *see* Aldington, 1st Baron
Luns, Josef, 230–1, 234
Lush, Ernest, 7
Lutosławski, Witold, 469–70
Luxembourg Compromise (1966), 708
Luxor, Egypt, 695
Lymington, 550–1
Lympany, Dame Moura, 238, 690
Lynch, Jack, 424, 425, 429–32, 435, 442, 554
Lyons family, 40
Lyttelton, Oliver *see* Chandos, 1st Viscount

Maastricht Treaty (1992), 386, 697–8, 714–15, 725

Maazel, Lorin, 563

MacDonald, James Ramsay, 274

MacDowell, Edward, 47

McGahey, Mick, 350, 353, 505, 508

MacGregor, Jean (née Dungey), 274

MacGregor, John, 274

Mackeson, Brigadier Harry, 150

McLachlan, Donald, 187

Maclean, Donald, 246

Maclean, Sir Fitzroy, 168

Macleod, Eve, 320

Macleod, Iain: in Conservative Research Department, 116; on social services reform, 130; enters Commons (1950), 139; in One Nation Group, 140–1; and trade unions, 193–4; and Profumo affair, 245; at Blackpool Conference (1963), 254–5; opposes Home's succession as leader, 256, 269; and 1967 sterling crisis, 289; and Enoch Powell, 291, 293; and race relations, 291–3; and 1970 election campaign, 303–4, 306; and price control, 304; as Chancellor of Exchequer, 310, 319; illness and death, 319–21; advocates incomes policy, 327; and tax reform, 344; favours free vote on EC membership, 378; advocates abolition of Open University, 448; opposes compulsory private health insurance, 452; Memorial Lecture (1974), 524

McMahon, (Sir) Christopher William (Kit), 316

McManus, Michael, 690, 721

McMaster, Stanley, 445

Macmillan, Lady Dorothy, 179

Macmillan, Harold (later 1st Earl of Stockton): and pre-war new Conservatism, 29; manner, 44, 50; EH meets, 50; supports Lindsay in 1938 by-election, 59–60; dines with EH as Chief Whip, 100; ambiguity, 130; praises EH's speech on Schuman Plan, 145; EH campaigns for (1955), 161; as Chancellor of Exchequer, 162; EH's relations with, 163, 253, 280–1; and Suez crisis, 169, 174, 728; succeeds Eden as premier, 176, 178–81; tour of South Africa (1960), 176, 184, 196; forms 1957 government, 180; qualities, 182–4; 250–1, 253; policies and administration, 183–4; relations with USA, 183; relations with Kennedy, 184, 226, 244, 249; and Salisbury's resignation, 184–5; Asia-Australasia tour (1958), 185, 187–8; and dispute over public expenditure, 185–7; calls 1959 election, 191; reforms government (1959), 192, 728; and threatened rail strike (1960), 196; government shuffle (1960), 199–200; applies for EC membership, 203–6, 209–10, 215, 223, 226, 356, 366; and Diefenbaker, 221; presides at 1962 Commonwealth Conference, 224; relations

with de Gaulle, 225, 239; disagreement with de Gaulle over relations with USA, 226; and Nassau agreement on US-British nuclear strategy, 226–7; praises EH's negotiations for EC entry, 226, 228; on failure of British entry into EC, 228, 236; invites EH to meet Rockefellers at Chequers, 243–4; Cabinet reshuffle, 1962 ('Night of the Long Knives'), 245; criticised as leader, 245; and Profumo affair, 245–6, 250; fatigue and pessimism, 250–2; meets Pope John XXIII in Rome, 251–2; death, 253; resignation (1963) and succession, 253–6; prostate operation, 255; and trade unions, 280; and parliamentary approval for EC membership, 377; celebrates parliamentary vote for EC accession, 381; at signing of Treaty of Accession to EC, 381; and European Convention on Human Rights, 427; and National Health Service, 452; and immigration policy, 456; dines with EH at Chequers, 462; at de Gaulle's memorial service, 468; and EH's loss of Party leadership, 535; and incomes policy, 570; 90th birthday dinner, 676–8; peerage, 678; as Chancellor of Oxford University, 686; and Referendum Party campaign, 715; converted to pro-Europeanism, 725; Britain, the Commonwealth and Europe, 204; The Middle Way, 33, 50

Macmillan, Maurice (later Viscount), 330, 403–4, 415, 505

McNamara, Robert, 605

McNamee, Daniel, 78–9

Maitland, Donald, 222, 313, 396, 412

Major, John: and Northern Ireland problem, 445; in 1997 leadership election, 536; belief in Workfare, 583; succeeds Thatcher, 594, 706; 'Back to Basics' slogan, 595; premiership, 596–7; 1992 election victory, 597, 600; and former Yugoslavia, 626; supports Traumatic Stress Disorder Unit, 662; on EH's 1993 mission to Iraq, 667; celebrates EH's 80th birthday, 690; criticised by Thatcher, 711; improves relations with Germany, 714; policy on Europe, 714–15; and Referendum party, 715; abolishes wages councils, 735

Major, Norma, 689–90

Makarios, Archbishop, 184, 209

Malahne (yacht), 464

Malawi (formerly Nyasaland), 276

Malaysia: conflict with Indonesia, 278–9

Malcolm, George, 26, 36

Mali, 607

Malone, Gerry, 722

Malta, 498–9

Mandela, Nelson, 622, 690

Mann, Anthony, 69

Mann, Thomas: Buddenbrooks, 94

Manpower Services Commission, 408

Mansholt, Sicco, 219, 542; Committee, 230
Mao Tse-tung, 493, 494–5, 630–3, 635, 638–41, 644
Margaret, Princess, 166, 198, 237, 318, 682, 689
Margesson, David, 51, 83
Marples, Ernest (later Baron), 205, 282
Marten, Neil, 384, 541
Martin Neary Singers, 443, 464, 690
Martin, Sir Alec, 18–19, 189
Martonmere, John Roland Robinson, 1st Baron, 484
Marylebone Cricket Club (MCC), 15
Masaryk, Jan, 83
Masefield, Sir Peter, 112–13, 120–1
Matta, Roberto, 688–9
Matthews, W.R., Dean of St Paul's, 63
Maude, Angus (later Baron), 139–40, 276, 552
Maudling, Reginald: enters Commons, 139; as Treasury minister, 187; at Board of Trade, 192; and EFTA, 203; as Chancellor of Exchequer, 245; considered as successor to Macmillan, 255; and abolition of Resale Price Maintenance, 259; and 1964 election, 265; in leadership contest after Home's resignation, 267–9; relations with EH, 270; as Home Secretary, 310; and Macleod's death, 320; and miners' actions, 351; on hopes of entry into EC, 355; advocates incomes policy, 402, 405; on problem of inflation, 405; resigns, 405, 447; and Northern Ireland, 424–5, 427–8, 436; attacked by Bernadette Devlin in Commons, 435, 596; and immigration control, 456; and Soviet espionage, 475; on Thatcher's election to leadership, 534; in Thatcher's Shadow Cabinet, 537; supports EC membership, 546, 725
Maudsley Hospital, London, 662
Maxse, Marjorie, 116, 132–3
Maxwell Fyfe, David see Kilmuir, Earl of
Maxwell, Robert, 290
Mayhew, Christopher, Baron, 58, 72, 384
Mellish, Robert (later Baron), 379, 384
Menotti, Gian Carlo, 676
Menuhin, Diana, Lady, 690
Menuhin, Yehudi, Baron, 463–4, 535, 690
Menzies, Sir Robert, 224, 296
Mercer, Joe, 309
Mersey Docks and Harbour Board, 342
Messina Conference (1955), 178, 201, 382
Messmer, Pierre, 390
Meyer, Sir Anthony, 593, 685
MI5, 473–4
MI6, 473
Middle East: Arab-Israeli war (1973), 419, 466, 500–2, 619; oil production, 500, 507
Middlesex Hospital, 662
Mills, Stratton, 422
Minney, Rubeigh James, 160–1
Mintoff, Dom, 498–9
Mintoff, Moyra, 499

missiles (ballistic), 616–17
Mitterand, François, 562
Molotov, Vyacheslav M.: pact with Ribbentrop (1939), 71
Monckton, Walter (later Viscount), 170, 194
Monday Club: opposes immigration policy, 457–8
monetarism, 575–7, 581–2, 584
Monnet, Jean: and Churchill's proposal for union with France, 84, 143; and European union, 142–3, 148, 202, 724; and British application for EC membership, 213, 230, 725; on de Gaulle, 239; judgment, 239; at signing of Treaty of Accession to EC (1972), 382; and 1972 EC summit, 387; European vision, 395; Committee, 705
Montgomery, Field Marshal Bernard Law, 1st Viscount, 99, 102, 188–9
Montoya, Rodrigo Botero, 606–7
Moon, Peter, 312
Mori, Haruki, 607
Morning Cloud (yachts): in Seine Bay Race (1971), 10; sunk, 89, 526–7; EH acquires, 300, 733; in Channel race, 371; in Admiral's Cup team, 467, 495, 671; Nixon presents half-model to EH, 473; EH writes on, 554, 556; in 1979 Fastnet race, 671–3, 733; wins trophies, 674, 733; painting and models of, 681
Morris, Charles, 32, 68
Morris, Joe, 607
Morrison, Charles and Sara, 574
Morrison, Herbert (later Baron), 140, 152
Morrison, John, 255–6, 260, 267
Mosbacher, Bus, 473
Moscow, 246–8, 623–5
Mosley, Sir Oswald, 32
motor industry, 585
Motorman, Operation (Northern Ireland, 1972), 438
Mountbatten, Admiral of the Fleet Louis, 1st Earl, 165–6, 308
Moyola, Baron see Chichester-Clark, James
Muir, Frank, 675
Mulholland, A.G., 119, 131–4
Munich, 40–1
Munich agreement (1938), 57–61, 64
Murray, Len, 353, 505, 510
Mussolini, Benito, 32, 49
Mutter, Anne-Sophie, 675
mutual and balanced force reduction (MBFR), 488, 489

Nakasone, Yasuhiro, 688
Nassau: agreement (1962), 226–8; Commonwealth Heads of Government Meeting (1985), 621
Nasser, Gamal Abdel, 164–5, 169, 177, 323, 619, 657, 665

National Coal Board, 350–2, 503, 505, 510–11, 513, 515

National Economic Development Council (NEDC; 'Neddy'): established, 198, 280; and economic statistical base, 398; and wage settlements, 404; and 1974 economic crisis, 509

National Federation of Fishermen's Organisations, 703

National Gallery (London), 461

National Government (1931), 32

National Health Service: reforms, 451–3, 588

National Incomes Commission, 570

National Industrial Relations Court (NIRC), 403, 405–9, 411

National Institute of Economic and Social Research, 346

National Union of Mineworkers (NUM), 350–1, 503, 505, 509, 511, 513–15, 586, 730

National Union of Railwaymen (NUR), 195–7

nationalisation: EH condemns, 127; Labour Party extends, 148; and Conservative privatisation policy, 342–3; Conservative support for industries, 412

nationalism (Scottish and Welsh), 294–6, 564–5

NATO (North Atlantic Treaty Organisation): and British nuclear strategy, 183, 226–7; Nixon's faith in, 472; and US rivalry with USSR, 488; and European security, 489; Malta and, 499; British membership and influence, 601; US dominance, 601; amd Cruise missiles, 616; and sovereignty, 718

Naughtie, James, 691

Nazism, 40–4

Neave, Airey, 531–2

'negative equity', 591–2

Negrín, Juan, 54–5

Netherlands: and Israel, 501; finances Brandt Commission, 607, 609

Neurath, Constantin von, 105

New Britain, The (Labour Party 1964 election manifesto), 266

Newcastle on Tyne, 94, 264–5

New Deal (USA), 33, 589

New York, 74–5, 78, 152

New York Daily News, 473

New Zealand: and EC, 373–4; ANZUK defence agreement, 481

News at Ten (TV programme), 569

Nicolson, Sir Harold, 25, 215

Nicolson, Nigel, 25, 171, 175

Nijmegen, 99–100

1922 Committee: EH attends, 141–2, 346; and succession to Eden, 176, 178; and entry into EC, 223; and Home's resignation and succession, 267; and EH's position as Party leader, 528–30, 533

Nixon, Richard M.: EH entertains in Washington, 76; congratulates EH on 1970 election victory, 307–8; and Rolls-Royce collapse, 341–2; congratulates EH on vote in favour of EC accession, 380, 472; and prices and incomes control, 401; suspends dollar convertibility, 409; and Northern Ireland, 435; relations with EH, 471–3, 493; visits Chequers, 471–2; EH meets in Bermuda, 484–6; relations with China, 485, 492; maintains US forces in Europe, 487; and EH's proposal for Anglo-French nuclear deterrent, 488; EH meets at Camp David (1973), 492; and Watergate affair, 493; and foreign policy, 495; Mao's opinion of, 495; replaced as President by Ford, 525; requests British bases, 619; in China, 629, 634–5

Nkomo, Joshua, 479

Noakes, Philip, 48

Noble, Michael, 265

Nolan Committee on Standards in Public Life, 595

Non-Proliferation Treaty (1968), 616

Norman, H.C., 9, 30

Norman, Montague, Baron, 124

Normandy: D-Day invasion (1944), 95

North Atlantic Treaty Organisation see NATO

North Sea oil, 500, 503, 582

North-East Development Council, 264

North-South: A Programme for Survival (Brandt Commission report), 610

North-South problem, 605, 610–12

Northern Development Agency: EH proposes, 584

Northern Ireland: attitude to Irish Republic, 420–1; and partition, 421; sectarianism and violence in, 421–3, 430, 435–6; British troops in, 422, 425–6, 428; security in, 422–3, 440, 443; Conservative reforms and actions in, 423, 425–7, 430–2, 439–40, 442, 445; Irish nationalism (republicanism) in, 424; intelligence services in, 426, 429; Stormont parliament, 426–7, 436; internment in, 428–30, 438–9; EH visits as PM, 433–4, 440; proposed reunification with Republic, 433, 436; direct rule introduced (1972), 436–7; 'Diplock courts', 439; plebiscite (1973) favours maintaining union, 439, 543; Assembly established, 440–1, 443–4; and Sunningdale agreement, 444–5; 1998 Agreement, 445; petrol tanker drivers' strike, 445; constitutional difficulties, 564

Northern Ireland Assembly Bill (1973), 440

Northern Ireland Constitution Bill (1973), 440

Northern Ireland Labour Party, 439–40

Norway: votes against EC membership, 388–9; fishing limits, 700

Notting Hill race riots (1958), 455

nuclear deterrence, 488, 615–17

Nuffield Study on 1974 election, 512

Nuremberg: Nazi rallies, 42–3, 69; International War Crimes Tribunal, 103–5

Nutting, Sir Anthony, 168, 171

Nyerere, Julius, 478, 611

Obote, Milton, 482, 496
Observer (newspaper), 571
Ohlin, Göran, 609
oil crisis (1973), 416, 500–3, 505, 507–8
Olivier, Borg, 498
Olivier, Joan, Lady (Joan Plowright), 464
Olivier, Laurence, Baron, 394, 464
Onassis, Aristotle, 197–8
Onassis, Christina, 197–8
One Nation, 191, 193, 728
One Nation Group (Conservative), 33, 131,
    140–1, 150, 198, 276, 294, 296, 524, 728
O'Neill, Sir Con, 374, 381, 701
O'Neill, Terence, Baron, 421–2
Open University, 448
Oppenheimer, Sir Ernest, 619
Oppenheimer, Harry, 620
Organisation of American States, 580
Organisation of Petroleum Exporting Countries
    (OPEC), 500–2, 507–8
Ormandy, Eugene, 560
Ortoli, François-Xavier, 694
Ostpolitik, 361, 468, 486
Ottawa: EC visits (1962), 221; Commonwealth
    Heads of Government Meeting (1973),
    495–6
Our Changing Democracy (White Paper), 564
Overton, William, 16
Owen, David (later Baron): and vote on EC
    membership, 380, 540; votes against EC Bill,
    383; proposed for mission to Baghdad, 654;
    forms Social Democratic Party, 704
Oxford (City): 1938 by-election, 58–61
Oxford Bach Choir, 34–5, 68, 309
Oxford Union Debating Society: 'King and
    Country' debate (1933), 16, 38, 62; EH joins,
    29–30; EH speaks at, 34, 39, 47–8, 51, 61;
    EH elected secretary and librarian, 48–9;
    EH's contests presidency of, 51–2; and war
    threat, 58, 61, 83; EH's presidency, 61–6;
    management and membership reforms, 62–3;
    Beneš speaks at, 82–3; TV debate on
    European membership, 548
Oxford University: EH at, 21–2, 23–45, 727;
    EH's degree at, 68, 96; EH visits in wartime,
    88; Chancellorship, 686–7; see also Balliol
    College
Oxford University Conservative Association,
    29, 38–40, 49–50, 59

Paisley, Ian: extremism, 422–5, 427, 445; and
    Northern Ireland Assembly, 440; refused
    admission to Sunningdale meeting, 443; fund
    raising in USA, 445
Pakistan, 485–6
Palin, Michael, 682
Palliser, (Sir) Michael, 354, 370
Palme, Olof, 607
pandas: given to EH by China, 638–9
Panorama (TV programme), 304, 336, 406

Pantony family, 2
Pantony, Bill (EH's uncle), 2
Pantony, Edward (EH's uncle), 2, 535
Pantony, Gladys (Bill's wife), 2–3, 6
Papen, Franz von, 105
Paris: EC summits: (1972), 373–4, 390–3, 395,
    543, 606; (1974), 392; EH visits, 14, 239,
    353, 362, 368, 370, 607–8; EH conducts in,
    562
Paris, Treaty of (1950), 697
Parker, John, 64
Parker, Owen, 672
Pasionaria, La see Ibarruri, Dolores
Patten, Christopher, 525, 535, 552, 593,
    645
Pattrick, Jo, 257, 680
Paulus, Field Marshal Friedrich, 105
pay see incomes policy
Pay Board, 416; and 1973–4 coal dispute, 510,
    513–15, 730
Pearce, Edward, Baron, 479
Pearce, Sandy, 90
Pears, Sir Peter, 464, 469–70
Pearson, Colin Hargreaves Pearson, Baron
    (Lord Justice Pearson), 321
Pearson, Sir Denning, 339
Peck, Sir John, 425, 435
Pelenetsina, Natalya, 624
pensions: Christmas bonuses, 414–15, 451;
    increases, 417
'Pentonville Five', 407
Perceval, Michael, 614
Perth, Declaration of (1968), 295, 565
Pétain, Marshal Philippe, 85
Peterson, Pete, 607
petrol rationing, 504
Peyton, John, 407, 464, 529, 536
Peyton, Mary, 464
Philadelphia Orchestra, 560
Philby, Kim, 246
Philip, Prince, Duke of Edinburgh: visits USA,
    183; and Macmillan, 184; EH meets, 317,
    324, 670; attends 'Fanfare for Europe'
    performance, 394; and Singapore
    Commonwealth Conference (1971), 477; at
    Praemium Imperiale celebration, 689
Piano, Renzo, 689
Pile, William, 317
Pineau, Christian, 167, 169
Pisani, Edgar, 230
Pittsburgh, 75–6
Plaid Cymru (party), 294
Pleven, René, 84
Pogorelich, Ivo, 690
Poland, 70–3
Polaris missiles, 226–7
police reform, 447
poll tax (community charge), 567, 587–8,
    593–4
Pollitt, Harry, 64

Pompidou, Claude (*née* Cahour), 690
Pompidou, Georges: discusses and agrees British
    membership of EC with EH, 354, 361–2,
    364–8, 370–2, 374–5, 732; at Hague
    summit (1969), 360; influence with de
    Gaulle, 367; at Chequers, 368–9, 501;
    relations with EH, 369; welcomes British
    vote on accession to EC, 380; and 1972 EC
    summit, 387, 389–92, 395; death, 395; and
    pressure on sterling, 410; co-signs Channel
    Tunnel Treaty, 459; and relations with
    Eastern Europe, 474, 487; defence strategy,
    488–9; and oil supplies, 501; referendum on
    enlarging EC, 541; in China, 634; and EC
    fisheries policy, 702
Ponsonby, Colonel Sir Charles Edward, 117
Poole, Oliver, 1st Baron, 171, 181–2, 188, 339
Popular Front for the Liberation of Palestine,
    321
Port Said, 174
Portillo, Michael, 710
Portugal: joins EC, 699
Poulson, John: scandal, 405
Pounder, Rafton, 445
Powell, J. Enoch: in Conservative Research
    Department, 116; in Commons (1950),
    139–40; in public expenditure dispute,
    185–6; and Butler's service under Home,
    256; in 1965 leadership contest, 268; foreign
    policy speech at 1965 Party conference, 276,
    278; attacks Rhodesia sanctions, 283; in EH's
    Shadow Cabinet, 283; provocative views,
    290–1; and race relations and immigration,
    291–4, 300, 455–6, 457; EH dismisses from
    Shadow Cabinet, 293–4; criticises Leila
    Khaled release, 323; votes against EC Bill,
    383–4; abandons Conservative seat, 512;
    speech opposing accession to Europe, 516;
    votes Labour, 516; opposes referendum on
    EC membership, 540; Hunt defeats at 1972
    Party conference, 691
Powell, Sir Richard, 99, 257
Praemium Imperiale arts prizes (Japan), 688–9
Pravda (newspaper), 475
Previn, André, 465, 469, 559
Price Commission, 416
Price, David, 257
prices: and inflation, 326, 328, 345–6, 397; and
    membership of EC, 376; control of, 401–2,
    404, 410, 413–14, 416, 418; and pressure on
    sterling, 410; Labour policy on, 522–3
Prices and Incomes Board: abolished, 345
Prior, James (*later* Baron): and British entry into
    EC, 224; on flight to Singapore, 278; and
    Kosygin's visit, 285; as Minister of
    Agriculture, 311; in TUC-CBI discussions,
    413; Shadow posts in Opposition, 520;
    advises EH to resign leadership, 528; in 1975
    leadership contest, 536; co-writes *The Right
    Approach*, 552; supports incomes policy, 569;

    curbs union militancy, 578; and EC fisheries
        policy, 702
prison reform, 446
Prisoners Abroad (organisation), 663
Private Eye (magazine), 555, 732
privatisation, 585–6
Profumo, John, 245–6, 250
Programme Analysis Review (PAR), 315
Propper, Arthur, 212
Prosperity with a Purpose (1964 Conservative
    election manifesto), 265–6
Provisional IRA ('Provos'), 421, 438; *see also*
    Irish Republican Army
Public Expenditure Survey Committee (PESC),
    315
public sector borrowing requirement (PSBR),
    582, 585
purchase tax, 417
Putting Britain Right Ahead (Conservative Party
    publication), 275, 295, 356
Putting Scotland Right Ahead (Conservative Party
    manifesto), 294
Pye, Reginald: as Bexley Conservative agent,
    134; and 1950 election success, 138
Pym, Francis (*later* Baron): as Chief Whip, 308;
    and parliamentary debate and vote on
    accession to EC, 377, 379–80; as Northern
    Ireland Secretary, 505; opposes early 1974
    election, 511; advises EH to retain leadership,
    528; succeeds Carrington as Foreign
    Secretary, 580; warns of effects of over-large
    majority, 582; pro-Europeanism, 706

Qatar, 482
Quebec: de Gaulle and, 239

Race Relations Bill (1968), 291–3
Raeburn, Ashley, 46, 86, 111, 686
railways: industrial dispute (1973), 504
Ramphal, (Sir) Shridath Surendranath ('Sonny'),
    606–7, 609
Ramsgate, Kent, 1
Rattigan, Sir Terence, 256
Raven, Dr Hugh, 12, 36
Raven, Kathleen (Kay), 12–13
Raven, Margaret, 12, 686
Raven, Dr Martin, 12, 36
Rawlinson, Peter, Baron, 321–2, 550
Reading, Brian, 304, 332, 719–20
Reagan, Ronald: deficit financing, 575, 581,
    613, 618; attends Cancum conference,
    610–11; dealings with USSR, 616–18;
    defence strategy, 617–18; and South Africa,
    621
Redgrave, Steve, 682
Redmayne, Martin, 164, 245, 253, 260–2
Rees, Merlyn (*later* Baron Merlyn-Rees), 438
Rees-Mogg, William (*later* Baron), 267
Reeve, (Sir) Anthony, 656

Referendum Party, 706, 708, 715–22

regional development, 258, 264–5, 399, 579, 583

Renoir, Auguste: paintings loaned to Downing Street, 460–1

Reorganisation of Central Government, The (Conservative White Paper), 314

Resale Price Maintenance Bill (and Act, 1964), 258–64, 266–7

Restrictive Practices Court, 262–3

Reykjavik: Reagan-Gorbachev summit (1986), 617

Reynaud, Paul, 85

Rhodes James, Sir Robert, 611

Rhodesia (*later* Zimbabwe), 275–8, 283, 477, 478–80, 621

Ribbentrop, Joachim von, 71, 104

Richard atte Hethe, King, 1

Richardson, Bill, 667–8

Richter, Hans, 559

Richter, Sviatoslav, 469–70

Ride, Paul, 663

Ridley, Nicholas (*later* Baron): and British entry into EC, 224, 379; memo on Upper Clyde Shipbuilders, 347–8; at Department of Trade and Industry, 399–400; and poll tax, 587; in North-South debate, 611

Ridley, Roy, 27

Rifkind, Malcolm, 535, 566

Right Approach, The (Conservative document), 552–3, 563, 569

Right Approach to the Economy, The (Conservative document), 553, 570

Right Road for Britain, The (Conservative document), 131

riots (1981), 578

Rippon, Geoffrey (*later* Baron): in EH's Shadow Cabinet, 283; and Powell's racial views, 294; as Minister of Technology, 310–11; smoking, 317; negotiates for British entry into EC, 320, 365, 374–5, 378; at signing of Treaty of Accession to EC, 381–2; declines post in Thatcher Shadow Cabinet, 537; at EH's 80th birthday celebration, 691; and European fisheries policy, 702

Robens, Alfred, Baron, 347

Roberts, Christopher, 312, 434

Robinson, John, 214

Rochester and Chatham constituency, 117

Rockefeller, David, Jr, 688

Rockefeller, Nelson and Happy, 243–4

Rodgers, Sir John, 117, 140, 149

Rodgers, William (Bill), 704

Rogers, William, 489

Roll, Eric (*later* Baron), 211–12, 220, 228, 233, 235, 238, 257

Rolls-Royce (company): collapse and nationalisation, 339–42

Rome: EH visits, 206, 251–2; conference on the 'Future of Capitalism' (1975), 598

Rome, Treaty of (1957), 202, 208–9, 213–14, 217, 234–5, 357–9, 362, 375, 700, 709

Roosevelt, Franklin Delano, 33, 589

Roper, John, 384–5

Rose, Leonard, 462

Rosenberg, Alfred, 105

Rossi, Hugh, 384

Rostow, Walt, 37

Rostropovich, Mstislav ('Slava'), 469–71, 688–92

Rothenberger, Anneliese, 558

Rothschild, Nathaniel Mayer Victor, 3rd Baron, 316, 353

Royal Artillery: EH serves in, 81–2, 86–90

Royal Commission on the Constitution (1969–73), 563–4

Royal Commonwealth Society, 604

Royal Temple Yacht Club, 18

Royal Ulster Constabulary (RUC), 422, 426, 429, 438

Rumor, Mariano, 444

Ruse, Howard, 720–1

Rushdie, Salman, 627–8

Rusk, Dean, 247–8, 489

Russia (and USSR): and 1963 Test Ban Treaty, 246–7; 'Days of British Music' series in, 469–70; espionage in Britain, 474–6, 487; Tito resists, 484; Indian Friendship Pact (1971), 485–6; Douglas-Home's memo on, 486; improved relations with UK, 487, 490; and Western Europe defence strategy, 488–9; and Arab-Israeli war (1973), 500; and nuclear deterrence, 616–17; Soviet collapse and reform, 622–5, 713; organised crime in, 624–5; relations with China, 632–3; supplies to Vietnam, 636–7; as superpower, 723

Ryder, Caroline (*née* Stephens), 312

Ryder, Richard, 313

Sabah, Sheikh Abdullah as-Salim as-, Ruler of Kuwait, 651

Sackville-West, Vita (Lady Nicolson), 25

Sadat, Muhammad Anwar al-, 550, 695

Saddam Hussein, 650–1, 653, 655, 657–60, 662–6, 669

Said, Nuri es-, 165

St Catharine's College, Cambridge, 20

St Lawrence College, Ramsgate, 14, 24

St Peter's-in-Thanet, Kent, 1, 6–7

St Petersburg (Leningrad), 248

Salisbury, Robert Cecil, 5th Marquess of: and Suez crisis, 168; and 1957 leadership question, 178; resigns, 184–5; speech at 1965 Party conference, 275

Salisbury, Wiltshire: EH's home in, 655, 679–83

Saltley coke works, West Midlands, 351

Salzburg, 42; Festival, 675, 684

Samuel, Sir Harold (*later* Baron), 462

Sandys, Duncan (*later* Baron Duncan-Sandys): returns to Commons (1950), 140; and Churchill's Zurich speech, 146; as Commonwealth Secretary, 199; in Australia and New Zealand, 209; and Rhodesia crisis, 277; leaves Shadow Cabinet (1966), 282; on immigration policy, 291; criticises Leila Khaled release, 323; and British entry into EC, 374; as chairman of Lonrho, 418

Sargent, Sir Malcolm, 68

Saudi Arabia, 482, 501, 507

Scamp, Sir Jack, 336

Scanlon, Hugh, 338, 353, 410

Scargill, Arthur, 350, 353

Schacht, Hjalmar, 104

Schaus, Eugène, 222

Schirach, Baldur von, 105

Schmidt, Felix, 463, 683

Schmidt, Helmut: and British EC budget provisions, 543; offers Wilson deal on EC referendum, 544; and Brandt's indecision, 608; as adviser to Praemium Imperiale prizes, 688; advocates EMS, 694–5; EH meets in Egypt, 695; at Château Stuyvenberg meeting (1984), 705; and German revival, 713

Schroeder, Gerhard, 230–1, 233–4

Schuman, Robert: European Plan, 142–5, 201, 724

Schumann, Maurice, 365–6, 390

Schwarzkopf, Elisabeth, 394

Scotland: industrial development, 265; EH's interest in, 274; nationalism in, 294–6, 565; constitutional position and devolution, 563–7

Scott, (Sir) Nicholas, 531, 537

Scottish Fishermen's Federation, 703

Scottish National Party (SNP), 294

security services, 473–4

Seitz, Raymond, 473

selective employment tax (SET), 288, 304, 344, 417

Seligman, Madron: friendship with EH, 46–7, 68–9, 70–1, 73; as Oxford Union president, 82; EH holidays with in France, 211, 271, 273, 365; sailing with EH, 273; elected to European Parliament (1979), 697

Seligman, Nancy-Joan (*née* Marks), 271, 365

Seligman, Olivia, 684

Selkirk, George Nigel Douglas-Hamilton, 10th Earl of, 242

Selsdon Park Hotel meeting (1970), 301–2, 452

Selwyn-Lloyd, Baron *see* Lloyd, Selwyn

Senard, Jacques, 370

Serafinowicz, Joseph, 593

Serbia and Serbs, 625–7

Seretse Khama, 24, 150

Sevenoaks constituency, 117

Sèvres Protocol (1956), 169–70, 177

Sewill, Brendon, 302, 358

Seyss-Inquart, Arthur, 105

Shackleton, Edward, 152

Shah of Iran (Mohammed Reza Pahlavi), 482, 628

Shanghai, 642

Shaw, George Bernard, 33, 63

Shebbeare (president of Oxford Union), 39

Sheppard, Canon Dick (*later* Dean of Canterbury), 9

Sherman, (Sir) Alfred, 521

Shillington, (Sir) Graham, 429

Shinwell, Emmanuel (*later* Baron), 126, 152, 166, 196

Shonfield, (Sir) Andrew, 297

Shore, Peter, 383, 540, 548

Shostakovich, Dmitri, 487

Shuckburgh, Sir Evelyn, 212

Shukri, Sabih, 656, 683

Sickert, Walter, 19

Sidgwick & Jackson (publishers), 554–5, 558

Silver Barracuda (yacht), 683

Simcock, Alan, 313, 461

Simmonds, Richard, 517

Simon, Sir Jocelyn (Jack), 187

Simon, Sir John, 30, 49, 51

Simon Wiesenthal Center, 592

Simonstown (South Africa), 319, 477–8, 621

Simpson, Wallis (*later* Duchess of Windsor), 39

Singapore, 242–3, 650; Commonwealth Heads of Government Meeting (1971), 242, 477, 480–2; Britain leaves, 481

Single European Act (1985–6), 387, 697, 706–7, 718, 725

Sissons, Peter, 718

Slater Walker (company), 550

Slovenia, 626

Smith, Adam, 27, 598; *The Wealth of Nations*, 587–8

Smith, Dudley, 224

Smith, Ian, 276–7, 478–9, 621

Smith, Dame Maggie, 682

Smithsonian Agreement (1971), 387

Snowdons (Builders, Kingsgate), 7

Soames, Christopher (*later* Baron): and Churchill's racegoing, 188; as Minister of Agriculture, 199; supports and negotiates for British entry into EC, 212, 231, 364–7; and British horticulture, 219; loses seat in 1966 election, 283; meets de Gaulle on European political association ('*L'affaire Soames*'), 359, 493; Ambassadorship in Paris, 363, 371; on *Morning Cloud*, 371; and position of sterling in EC, 374; at signing of Treaty of Accession to EC, 381; as EC Commissioner, 394; sympathy at EH's father's death, 554; at Macmillan's 90th birthday dinner, 677

Soames, Mary, Lady, 371

Social and Democratic Labour Party (SDLP; Northern Ireland), 427–8, 439–40, 442

Social Democratic Party (SDP): formed (1981), 577–8, 687, 704; decline, 581; alliance with

Liberals, 582; supports nuclear deterrence, 616

social services: reforms, 451−3

Solti, Sir Georg, 147, 464, 560, 684

Solti, Valerie, Lady, 464

Solzhenitsyn, Alexander, 469

Sondermann, Kai, 663

South Africa: and Rhodesia crisis, 277; defence agreements with, 319, 477−8; arms supply to, 477−8, 481; Commonwealth hostility to, 477−8, 481; conditions in, 619−22; EH visits, 619−20, 622; sanctions question, 619, 621, 668; Eminent Persons Group in, 621

Soviet Trade Delegation, Highgate, 475

Soviet Union see Russia

Spaak, Paul-Henri: proposals for European co-operation, 201−2; and British application for EC membership, 215, 222, 230−1, 233−4; at signing of Treaty of Accession to EC (1972), 382

Spain: EH visits, 52−6, 365, 537, 539, 544; joins EC, 699; and fisheries policy, 703

Spanish Civil War, 39, 49, 52−6

Spearman, Sir Alec, 171

Spectator (journal), 81

Speed, Jeffery, 721

Spender, (Sir) Stephen, 64

Spicer, James, 695

Spiegel, Sam, 463−4

Staddon, Anthony, 721

Stalin, Josef V., 632

Stanley, Oliver, 139

state of emergency (1973), 504

Steel, (Sir) David, 568

Stent, George, 52

Stephens, Olin, 473

sterling: devalued: (1949), 125−6; (1967), 289−90, 325, 359, 409; and British membership of EC, 374; floated (1972), 387, 410; under pressure (1972), 409−11; external value declines, 553; fluctuations under Thatcher, 575, 578, 591; leaves Exchange Rate Mechanism, 597, 711−12

Stern, Isaac, 462, 466

Steward, William, 127, 138

Stewart, Alastair, 675

Sting (musician), 682

Stockton, 1st Earl of see Macmillan, Harold

Stokes, John, 39

Stone, Norman, 653

Stonehouse, John, 260

Straneo, Carlo Alberto (Italian ambassador to Moscow), 207

Strategic Arms Limitation Treaty: 1st (SALT I, 1972), 616; 2nd (SALT II, 1979), 617

Strauss, Franz-Josef, 390

Strauss, Pauline, 682

Strauss, Richard, 682

Street, Peter, 73−4, 76

Streicher, Julius, 104

strikes see under trade unions

Stuart, James, 180

Stuart, Nick, 313

Studholme, Henry, 150

Stuyvenberg, Château, 705

Sudetenland, 57

Suenson-Taylor (of Dumpton Gap), 26

Suez crisis (1956), 164−76, 183, 601, 651, 657, 665, 728

Sumner, Humphrey, 31−2; Russia and the Balkans, 32

Sunday Express, 61−2

Sunday Times, 550, 555

Sunningdale conference and agreement (1973), 441, 443−5, 519, 564

Sutton, Surrey, 85, 101

Swanley, Kent, 118

Sweden, 194

Swindin, George, 10

Swinton, Philip Cunliffe-Lister, 1st Earl, 150

Sydney-Hobart yacht race (1969), 300, 302, 733

Sykes, Dr Jenny, 661

Symonds, Richard, 52

Taiwan, 485, 494−5

Tan, Melvyn, 463

Taplin, Frank, 79

Tapsell, Peter, 224

Tasker, Rev. Derek, 52

Tatham, Alfred, 20

Tawney, R.H., 33

taxation: reforms under Barber, 344; and social services, 453−4; under 1974 Labour government, 522−3; under Thatcher, 590

Taylor, Teddy, 386, 719

Taylor (primary school headmaster), 7

Tebbit, Norman (later Baron), 302

Te Kanawa, (Dame) Kiri, 394

Temple, Frederick, Bishop of Malmesbury, 25, 46, 121

Temple, William, Archbishop of Canterbury (earlier of York), 25, 33, 37, 46

Templer, Field Marshal Sir Gerald, 551

Tenacious (yacht), 673

Territorial Army, 155−6; see also Honourable Artillery Company

terrorism: Arab, 321−3; international, 619

Tertis, Lionel, 464

Test Ban Treaty (1963), 246, 248, 616

Tewson, Vincent, 193−5

Thanet: bombed in war, 85

Thatcher, Margaret, Baroness (née Roberts): EH meets, 126−7; stands in 1950 General Election, 136, 138; sends condolences on EH's mother's death, 153; supports EH's leadership bid, 268; in EH's Shadow Cabinets, 283, 301, 521, 523, 529; at Selsdon Park Hotel meeting, 302; as Education Secretary under EH, 311, 349, 447−51; disagreement with Pile, 317; and cut in

Thatcher, Margaret, Baroness – *cont.*
school milk, 330; and British budgetary
contribution to EC, 373; in Conservative
Group for Europe, 379; and Single European
Act (1985–6), 387, 706, 718; Education
budget, 417, 447–8; and Northern Ireland
problem, 445; and EH's proposed 1974 deal
with Liberals, 519; in post-1974 Opposition,
521, 523; wins Party leadership contest
(1974–5), 530–2, 534, 536; visits EH in
Wilton Street, 536–7; forms Shadow
Cabinet, 537; attacks referenda, 544; leads
'Yes' campaign in European referendum
(1975), 546, 549, 709; economic policy and
monetarism, 553, 575–6; policy
disagreements with EH, 563, 568–9, 573,
707, 710–11; on Scottish and Welsh
nationalism, 565; and Lib-Lab pact, 568;
favours free collective bargaining, 569; EH
beats in popularity poll, 571; on forming
Cabinet, 571–2; first premiership (1979),
573, 695; excludes EH from government
post, 574, 732; offers Washington embassy to
EH, 574; on 'U-turns', 576–7; and Falklands
War inquiry, 580–1; acts against unions, 586,
731; 1987 election victory, 587; leadership
challenged, 593–4, 685; relations with
Lawson, 597; and Brandt Commission
meeting at Leeds Castle, 609; attends Cancun
conference, 610–11; defence strategy, 618;
and South Africa, 621; and Hong Kong,
643–4; anger at EH's mission to Baghdad,
654–6; Iraqi view of, 657; attends EH's 40th
anniversary as MP, 683; as patron of
Conservative Group for Europe, 695; and
election campaign for European Parliament,
696, 705; reservations on membership of
EMS, 696; claims refunds from EC, 698–9;
intransigence at EC meetings, 704; Bruges
speech (1988) on Europe, 706–7, 710;
authorises entry into ERM, 711; German
reunification, 713; and place among
Conservative pro-Europeans, 715
Third World: debts, 576; trade and aid to,
602–5; Brandt Commission and, 606–12
This is the Road (Conservative 1950 manifesto),
131
Thomas, George *see* Tonypandy, Viscount
Thomas, Peter, 194, 537
Thomson, George, 376, 394
Thomson, Roy, 1st Baron, 149
Thorndike, Dame Sybil, 198
Thorneycroft, Peter, Baron, 185–6, 196, 199,
283, 528, 539, 570
Thornton Bobby, Messrs (piano manufacturer),
8
Thorpe, Jeremy: and 1971 White Paper on EC
entry, 377; at signing of Treaty of Accession,
381; as Liberal leader, 383; and 'Bloody
Sunday' inquiry, 435; supports miners' claims,

515; and proposed Liberal deal with
Conservatives, 518–19, 524; supports EC
membership, 546, 548–9
three-day week (1973–4), 506, 508
Tiananmen Square, Beijing, 645, 647
Tickner, A.C. ('Tick'), 67
Time for Decision (Labour Party manifesto,
1966), 356
Times, The: and Anthony Hurd, 274; and vote
on EC Bill, 384; and EH's leadership contest,
533, 535; on EH's speech on renegotiating
EC arrangements, 545
Tindemans, Leo, 705
Tito, Josip, 483–4, 626, 641
Tokyo, 688
Tonypandy, George Thomas, Viscount, 554,
675
Topol, Chaim, 685
Toscanini, Arturo, 42, 47
Toulouse, 459
Tovey, Sir Donald, 26
Tower of London: EH appointed Master
Gunner, 156
Toynbee, Philip, 99
Trade, Board of (Department of Trade and
Industry): EH heads, 257–64
trade unions: EH's dealings with, 192–3, 195,
200, 280; and law, 279–81, 287, 407; control
of, 287–8, 298; Donovan Commission on
(1965–68), 297; Labour Party problems with,
297–9, 304; strikes and industrial action, 300,
321, 326, 332–3, 336–7, 403–4, 504; wage
settlements and demands, 325–9, 333,
336–7, 343, 346, 398, 403, 405, 414;
numbers and membership, 326; oppose
1970–71 Industrial Relations Bill, 334–9,
572; hostility to Conservative government,
349–51, 402–3; Conservative attitude to,
409; and reducing inflation, 411; as threat,
462; and economic crisis (1973–4), 508–10;
free collective bargaining, 510; and payments
to strikers, 513; Prior curbs militants, 578;
reforms under Thatcher, 586, 731
Trades Union Congress: in Margate (1935),
28–9; delegation to Ruhr (1945), 143;
dealings with unions, 193, 195; militants in,
200; and union legislation, 299; EH's
relations with, 328; and anti-inflation
measures, 333; and 1970–1 Industrial
Relations Bill, 334, 338, 403, 411; and
incomes and prices policy, 345, 352, 411–12,
414, 416; and unemployment, 348–9;
discussions with EH and CBI on economy,
396–8, 403–4, 411–16; expels unions, 403;
and wage settlements, 404; 'day of action'
(1973), 416; and 1973–4 economic crisis,
509–11, 730–1; Conference (1988), 711
Training and Enterprise Councils, 590
Transport Denationalisation Bill (1953), 157
Transport and General Workers Union, 406

Trend, Burke (*later* Baron), 316, 473, 488, 495
Trevelyan, Humphrey, Baron, 552
Trident nuclear missile programme, 616
Trinity College, Oxford, 27−8
Trio Zingara, 683
Trowbridge, Maurice, 630−1
Trudeau, Pierre, 495−6
Tucker, Geoffrey, 539
Tung, C.H., 646
Turner, Dr Stuart, 662
Turner, Ted, 673
Turton, Robin, 223
Tuzo, General Sir Harry, 428−9

Uganda: Asian immigrants from, 456−8, 498;
    Amin's coup in, 483
Ulster *see* Northern Ireland
Ulster Defence Regiment (UDR), 422
Ulster Unionist Council (UUC), 440
unemployment: rises under Labour (1969−70),
    306; and anti-inflation measures, 343, 346,
    597; Conservative attempts to reduce, 348−9,
    577; rates (1972−3), 417; rates under
    Thatcher, 579, 582−3, 589, 731; and
    training, 589−90
UNESCO, 618
Union of Democratic Mineworkers, 586
Union of the Trucial States, 482
Unionist Party (Northern Ireland): and EC Bill,
    384; and Troubles, 422, 424, 426, 430, 432;
    opposes direct rule in Northern Ireland, 437;
    at Darlington meeting (1972), 439; and
    representation at Stormont, 442; at
    Sunningdale meeting, 443; rejects power-
    sharing, 445; in 1974 election, 517, 519−20
*United Kingdom and the European Communities,
    The* (White Paper), 375
United Nations: and Suez crisis, 174; and
    Falklands War, 580; and developing
    countries, 603, 605; Resolution condemning
    Iraqi invasion of Kuwait, 650−1, 657, 661;
    Saddam denounces, 665; relieves embargoes
    on Iraq, 667−8
United Nations Conference on Trade and
    Development (UNCTAD), First (Geneva,
    1964), 602−5
United Nations Protection Force
    (UNPROFOR, former Yugoslavia), 626−7
United States of America: New Deal, 33, 589;
    EH's 1939 debating tour in, 72−80; attitude
    to World War II, 73, 75−6; global
    dominance, 148, 177, 723; EH revisits, 152,
    158, 284, 472−3, 488; and Suez crisis,
    170−1, 174, 177; relations with Macmillan,
    183; and European Community, 203, 229,
    361, 364, 370, 492−3, 618; conflict with de
    Gaulle over nuclear strategy, 226; cooperates
    with Britain on nuclear strategy, 226−7, 229;
    signs 1963 Test Ban Treaty, 247−8, 616; in
    Vietnam, 279, 487, 598; and Northern

Ireland problem, 435; and Indo-Pakistan war
    (1971), 485−6; forces in Europe, 487−8;
    negotiations with China, 494; supports Israel
    in 1973 war, 500−1; EH conducts in, 560;
    deficit financing and high interest rates,
    575−6, 581, 613, 618; recession in, 578;
    supports Britain in Falklands War, 580;
    dominance in NATO, 601; defence strategy,
    616−17; bombs Libya (1986), 618−19;
    British relations with, 618, 726; and former
    Yugoslavia, 627; freezes Iraqi assets, 650; and
    Gulf War, 664; Arab hostility to, 665; and
    European federalism, 718−19
United States (ship), 73−4
Upper Clyde Shipbuilders, 346−8
Ure, (Sir) John, 613
USSR *see* Russia
Uxbridge by-election (1972), 458

Value Added Tax (VAT), 344, 417, 575
Variety Club of Great Britain, 460
Vassall, William, 246
Vaudry, Robert, 656, 658, 660−1
Vaughan-Morgan, Emily (*née* Cross), 74
Vaughan-Morgan, John, 74
Vaughan Williams, Ralph, 35, 92
Vayo, Alvarez del, 54−6
Venice, 205
Verney, Stephen Edmund, Bishop of Repton,
    46
Vietnam: EH visits, 278; US war in, 279, 487,
    598; British and, 283; Kosygin discusses with
    Wilson, 286; Chinese and, 636−7
Vishnevskaya, Galina, 470
Volcker, Paul, 581

wage demands *see* incomes policy; trade unions
Wainwright, Michael, 662−3
Waite, Terry, 675
Wakefield, Wavell, 237
Waldegrave, William: as EH's political
    secretary, 313, 528−9; and EH's gift to Mao,
    638; and EH's mission to Baghdad, 654
Walden, Brian, 653
Wales: nationalism in, 294−5, 565;
    constitutional proposals, 564−5, 567
Walker, Ernest, 26, 36−7
Walker, (Sir) Harold ('Hookey'), 656
Walker, Peter (*later* Baron): chairs Young
    Conservatives meeting (1956), 175; in
    Opposition, 267−8, 523; supports EH's
    leadership bid, 268; in EH's Shadow Cabinet,
    283; as Environment Secretary, 314−15, 346;
    at Department of Trade and Industry, 400;
    and oil crisis (1973−4), 504, 507; and new
    Department of Energy, 505; declines post in
    Thatcher Shadow Cabinet, 537; prevents
    Conservative migration to SDP, 577
Walker-Smith, Derek, 142, 223
Wallace, David, 27

Walters, Alan, 521
Walton, (Sir) Raymond, 39
Walton, Susana, Lady, 562, 690
Walton, Sir William, 309, 464–5, 469, 562, 685
Wang Hongwen, 630, 632
War Crimes Bill (1989), 592–3
Warren (Broadstairs butcher), 8
Warren, Sir Brian, 190, 635
Warrington, Lancashire, 88–9
Warsaw: EH visits (1939), 70
Warsaw Pact: and European security, 489
Washington, DC: EH in, 76, 472–3, 491–3, 525
Watergate affair, 493
Waterhouse, Captain Charles, 168, 175
Watson, Tom, 79–80
Watson, Trevor, 67, 109
Weatherill, Bernard (later Baron; 'Jack'), 318, 384, 594
Weekend World (TV programme), 515
Weeks, Wilf, 721
Weigall, Fitzroy, 17, 42
Weigall, Rev. Tony, 42
Werner Committee (1969), 375
West Germany: EH visits, 142, 605; and European unity, 142–4, 147; post-war revival, 142–4; trade unions in, 143; treaty with France (1963), 232; and British application to join EC, 233; and EC social policy, 389; and Iceland fishing dispute, 490; gas pipeline with Siberia, 618; and reunification, 712–13; see also Germany
'West Lothian Question', 565
Western European Union (WEU), 160, 208, 359
Westland crisis, 618
Westwood Secondary Modern School, Bexley, 450
Weygand, General Maxime, 85
White, Sir Dick, 473
Whitehead, Messrs Harold and Staff (consultants), 62
Whitelaw, William, Viscount: on military service, 115; as Chief Whip (1966), 283; and Powell's dismissal from Shadow Cabinet, 293; as leader of Commons, 308; anger at Cabinet Room secretary, 309; and Michael Wolff, 311; and Macleod's death, 320; and Rolls-Royce crisis, 340; and Commons debate and vote on accession to EC, 378; as Northern Ireland Secretary, 437–9, 441–2; meets Cosgrave, 441; as Employment Secretary, 505, 508; on coalminers' pay claim, 510; opposes early 1974 election, 511; as Party Chairman in Opposition, 520; and Mrs Thatcher in Opposition, 523; recommends Peyton, 529; and leadership election procedures, 530; stands against Thatcher in 1975 leadership election, 536; replaced by

Thorneycroft as Party Chairman, 539; supports EC membership, 546
Whitlam, Gough, 497
Wickens, Stephen, 3
Widgery, John Passmore Widgery, Baron (Lord Chief Justice), 435
Wigg, George (later Baron), 245–6
Wight, Isle of, 678–9
Wilberforce, Richard, Baron, 336, 351–2, 404, 514, 730
Wilbraham, Tony, 658
Wilde, Stephen, 96
Williams, Captain (Regimental Medical Officer), 88
Williams, Kenneth, 549
Williams, Shirley (later Baroness), 546, 704
Willkie, Wendell, 380
Wilsher (schoolmaster), 16
Wilson, Sir Duncan, 469
Wilson, Harold (later Baron): and soccer, 10; as President of Board of Trade, 125, 127; resigns (1951), 151; seeks British entry into EC, 238, 357–9; succeeds Gaitskell as leader of Labour Party, 250; opposes Resale Price Maintenance, 259; wins 1964 election, 266; EH opposes in Commons, 267, 270–1; and devaluation, 270, 289, 325, 409; and Rhodesia crisis, 277; calls 1966 election, 279; 1966 election victory, 282; and Vietnam war, 283; invites Kosygin to Britain, 284–6; popularity and status, 296; and trade unions, 297–9, 326; and capital punishment, 300; 1970 election campaign and defeat, 302–5, 308, 362, 604; attacks Selsdon Park Hotel meeting, 302; prices and incomes policy, 303; denounces EH's government policy, 319; and award of honours, 324; opposes Industrial Relations Bill, 337; and coalminers, 350; attitude to membership of EC, 354–7, 360–1, 376–7, 378, 525, 694, 705; accuses Macmillan of dishonesty with de Gaulle, 356; and Soames affair, 359; and British budgetary contribution to EC, 373; absent from signing of Treaty of Accession to EC, 381; and EC Bill, 383; and George Thomson's appointment as EC Commissioner, 394; and enquiry into Industrial Relations Act, 407; and Conservative prices and wages policy, 416; sends in army to Northern Ireland, 422; 'Downing Street Declaration' (Northern Ireland), 423; and negotiations over Northern Ireland, 425, 433; and 'Bloody Sunday', 435; and Northern Ireland petrol tanker drivers' strike, 445; establishes Open University, 448; and immigration policy, 456; in Downing Street, 460; and EH's sailing commitment, 467; at de Gaulle's memorial service, 468; and contacts with USSR, 474; and miners' dispute (1973–4), 508, 514–15; in February 1974 election campaign, 515; refuses 1974

coalition government, 519; 1974 premiership, 521–2; calls October 1974 election, 525; and threat to EH's Party leadership, 529, 535; tribute to EH on losing Party leadership, 535; holds referendum on British membership of EC, 540, 542–4, 549; deal with Schmidt over referendum, 544; converted to British membership of EC, 545; resigns, 556–7; achievements and record, 557; sets up Royal Commission on Constitution, 563; proposals for Scottish and Welsh assemblies, 564–5; and EH's visit to China, 631, 635; offers Honour to EH, 685; and Chancellorship of Oxford University, 686

Wilson, Sir John, 194
Wilson, Mary, Lady, 460, 690
Wilton Street: EH's house in, 520, 527–8, 532, 536
Winchester by-election (1997), 722
Winckler, Professor and Mrs, 41–2, 70, 108
Windsor Castle, 308–9
'Winter of Discontent' (1978–9), 568, 572
Winterton, Edward Turnour, 6th Earl, 51
Wolff, Michael, 311, 371, 512, 539
Wolrige-Gordon, Patrick, 702–3
Wood, Alan, 52
Wood, Richard, 543
Woodage, Leslie, 16
Woolf, Dr E. Alec, 13
Woolley, Frank, 15

Woolton, Frederick Marquis, 1st Earl of, 109, 122, 128–9
Workers' Educational Association (WEA), 15
Workfare, 583
World Bank, 605, 718
World Health Organisation: and conditions in Iraq, 665–6
Wormser, Olivier, 207, 228, 235
Wyatt, Woodrow (later Baron), 533

Yaker, Layachi, 606
Yates, William, 170
Yeats, William Butler, 735
Yeltsin, Boris: and Rostropovich, 470; EH meets, 623–4; and Russian reform, 624
Yom Kippur War (1973), 419, 466, 492, 500, 502, 619
Youde, Sir Edward, 640–1
Young Conservatives: in Bexley, 126, 132, 135, 138; and immigration policy, 457–8; EH addresses, 524, 550
Yugoslavia, 483–4, 625–7, 713

Zambia (formerly Northern Rhodesia), 276
Zayed bin Sultan al Nahayan, ruler of Abu Dhabi, 502
Zhongnan, Hai, 630
Zimbabwe see Rhodesia
Zingara, Trio see Trio Zingara
Zukerman, Pinchas, 466
Zulueta, Sir Philip Francis, 251